MUSEUM OF BROADCAST COMMUNICATIONS

ENCYCLOPEDIA OF
TELEVISION

MUSEUM OF BROADCAST COMMUNICATIONS

ENCYCLOPEDIA OF
TELEVISION

VOLUME 1
A–F

Editor
HORACE NEWCOMB

Photo Editor
CARY O'DELL

Commissioning Editor
NOELLE WATSON

FITZROY DEARBORN PUBLISHERS
CHICAGO AND LONDON

Copyright © 1997 by
FITZROY DEARBORN PUBLISHERS

For information, write to:
FITZROY DEARBORN PUBLISHERS
70 East Walton Street
Chicago, Illinois 60611
U.S.A.
or
11 Rathbone Place
London W1P 1DE
England

Library of Congress Cataloging-in-Publication Data

Encyclopedia of Television / editor, Horace Newcomb;
    p. cm.
  Includes bibliographical references and index.
  Contents: v. 1. entries A–F

British Library Cataloguing in Publication Data

Encyclopedia of Television
I. Newcomb, Horace, 1942

ISBN 1-884964-24-9
Set ISBN 1-884964-26-5

First published in the U.S.A. and U.K. 1997
Typeset by Acme Art, Inc.
Printed by Braun-Brumfield, Inc.

Cover photographs: *The Avengers, 60 Minutes, The Howdy Doody Show, All in the Family, Perry Mason, Doctor Who, The Flintstones, Soul Train* (courtesy of Don Cornelius).
Covers designed by Peter Aristedes, Chicago Advertising and Design

CONTENTS

PREFACE

The Museum of Broadcast Communications (MBC) is proud to present the *Encyclopedia of Television*. Since the founding of the MBC in 1987, one of our primary concerns has been the role of the Museum in the field of media education. We are convinced that all forms of mass communication—first broadcast and now cable, satellite, and computerized interactivity —have been central to both public and private life throughout the world. An educated citizenry is essential to the best use of these media.

Our commitment in this arena has led the MBC to sponsor a wide variety of programs. We have invited broadcasters and critics, media professionals, and historians to our discussions, lectures, and seminars. These programs are open to the public, and those who have attended often take part in lively discussions, demonstrating a vast concern for the role of mass media in our society. Topics such as the representation of women in television programming, the images of blacks and Hispanics in programs and commercials, or the impact of television on presidential politics have drawn special interest and have shown that the users of mass media—the audiences—are deeply involved with such matters. Moreover, these public programs have made it clear that audience members are good critics of what they see on television screens.

The MBC's collection of artifacts related to the history of radio and television enables these same viewers and others to see "behind the scenes" of many of their favorite programs, to be more aware of the technologies of broadcasting and of the history of those technologies. Our facilities allow MBC visitors to produce their own "newscast" or to sit in the audience of a live radio broadcast, thus helping to make mass media less mysterious and more immediate.

At the center of all these activities is the MBC Radio and Television Archive in our A.C. Nielsen Jr. Research Center, a collection comprising thousands of hours of programming, commercials, newscasts, and special events. These materials are available to anyone who wishes to listen to, or view the past of, broadcast communication. They are readily accessible by computer catalogue and easily used in private listening or viewing facilities. It was the presence and the constant expansion and use of the Archive that led to the idea of the *Encyclopedia of Television*.

For too long television—one of the most crucial aspects of contemporary life—has been neglected by scholars, considered too common, too trivial to merit serious attention. And even though a growing body of study devoted to television has begun to take the medium far more seriously, students, scholars, teachers, critics, historians, and others committed to understanding more about this complex topic have been hampered by a lack of adequate research tools. Collections of programming at the MBC and other facilities have begun to remedy one part of that problem, making their holdings available for scholarly research as well as for public use. The *Encyclopedia of Television*, a joint venture between the MBC and Fitzroy Dearborn Publishers, was commissioned as a logical step in making even more material available to all those groups. The MBC undertook to set up the editorial team and to make the resources of the Museum available to them; Fitzroy Dearborn undertook to prepare the manuscript for publication and to publish it throughout the world.

To prepare the *Encyclopedia* the MBC chose Dr. Horace Newcomb, Heyne Professor of Communication at the University of Texas at Austin as curator and editor. Professor Newcomb, one of the first scholars to examine the content and history of television, then assembled an advisory committee and with their assistance reduced the vast array of possible "television topics" to around 1,000. An early decision was made to focus the majority of the work on major English-speaking, television producing countries, and for that reason the bulk of the material presented here deals with television programs, people, and topics drawn from the United States, Britain, Canada, and Australia. Concerns for the international scope and influence of television led to the inclusion of entries discussing the history and current status of television in a number of other countries.

The *Encyclopedia* has been three years in the making, and more than 300 authors from around the world have contributed to this work. They write from different perspectives and ask different questions. But their entries are thoughtful descriptions and analyses. Some deal with the significance of television programs and events. Some focus on the actions and roles of individuals who have contributed in important ways to the medium. Still others explore topics and issues that have been central to the actual practices of television.

All of us who have participated in the design of this work recognize that it could be still larger—much larger—but practical considerations are always present in such projects. This first edition of the *Encyclopedia*, then, is selective, but it is, we believe, the most useful, the most thorough work of its kind. Our aim is for this collection to be the reference work of first record, the beginning point for anyone interested in exploring and understanding the significance of television in our time. The editor, the authors, and the staff of the MBC and Fitzroy Dearborn also recognize, however, that television continues to change even while we try to provide this guide. So the *Encyclopedia of Television* can also be used to look forward, to examine new developments in the medium.

The Museum of Broadcast Communications also looks forward. The *Encyclopedia of Television* has now become our "map" for future exhibitions and public programs. With a stronger knowledge of television's past our aim is for those projects to continue our role as an important participant in media education. We will continue to assist scholars and teachers, students and critics—all citizens—to know more about this medium and therefore, to understand and use it well as part of their personal and social experience.

The Museum of Broadcast Communications is most grateful for the continuing assistance and enthusiastic support of the Robert R. McCormick Tribune Foundation in this project. We are also grateful to Fitzroy Dearborn Publishers where professional experience and expertise in the specialized area of reference book publications has been crucial to the success of this project. Special mention must be made of Noelle Watson, the Fitzroy Dearborn commissioning editor who took the *Encyclopedia* through the arduous process of final editing to publication. Cary O'Dell, director of the MBC Archives, also deserves special recognition for his passion and professionalism. Cary loves television and his dogged research and photo acquisition was vital to the *Encyclopedia's* success. His research was done while continuing to expand our collections and directing his staff to meet our public mission. I also wish to thank personally the entire staff of the Museum for their assistance in the preparation of the *Encyclopedia of Television.* Their constant efforts, often in the midst of many other activities, have made it a richer, more complex and valuable work.

—Bruce DuMont, Founder and President
Museum of Broadcast Communications
Chicago Cultural Center

ACKNOWLEDGMENTS

A great many people have contributed mightily to the creation of the *Encyclopedia of Television*. First, I am deeply grateful to Bruce DuMont , Founder and President of the Museum of Broadcast Communications, for his confidence in my ability to guide such a project. Bruce DuMont's vision for the book was central to its creation and his support for the project has been unwavering. The *Encyclopedia* would not exist without that support, or without the Museum of Broadcast Communications. Assisting in the preparation of such a significant work is a rare opportunity, an experience for which I will remain forever appreciative.

Equal thanks must go to George Walsh and Noelle Watson of Fitzroy Dearborn Publishers. Their guidance and instruction was detailed, concise, and effective. With their help I have learned much about the making of encyclopedias and without that help—and most especially their patience—this work would still be in process, groping toward completion.

For the outstanding photographs that enrich the entries in the *Encyclopedia of Television* I am completely indebted to the tireless efforts of Cary O'Dell, Archives Director of the Museum of Broadcast Communications, who secured every one of them. His administrative skills, institutional and industrial contacts, and knowledge of television history have added immensely to the project. Moreover, his keen eye for the interesting and unusual, the truly illustrative as opposed to the conventional, will enlighten readers and researchers for years to come.

I also wish to thank my colleagues at the University of Texas at Austin who permitted me a two-year leave of absence in order to prepare the *Encyclopedia*. I am most especially grateful to John D.H. Downing, Chair of the Department of Radio-Television-Film, and to Ellen A. Wartella, Dean of the College of Communication, for their support of this arrangement and their encouragement of this project.

A large group of individuals have assisted with basic research and preparation of supporting materials for the entries in the *Encyclopedia*. I list them here in alphabetical order and rank all efforts, large and small, of equal significance, for each contribution is major in its own way:

Adam Beechen, Steven Blackburn, Sue Brower, Kathryn Burger, Paula Feldstein, Thomas Field, Rodney Gibbs, Lisa Lewis, Sue Murray, Kate Newcomb, and Annette Petrusso in Austin. For international information I would have been lost without the assistance of Martin Allor, Monica Guddat, and Manon Lamontagne in Canada, Chris Keating and Albert Moran in Australia, and David Pickering in England.

Cary O'Dell also wishes to express his appreciation to those individuals who provided special assistance in the collection of photographs:

Holly Mensing, at the Public Broadcasting Service; Helicia Glucksman, at the Canadian Broadcasting Corporation; Doris Kelly, at *Broadcasting and Cable* magazine; Bobbi Mitchell at the British Broadcasting Corporation; Mandy Rowsan at the British Film Institute; Ann Wilkins, at the Wisconsin Center for Film and Theater Research; Geoff Harris, at the Australian Broadcasting Corporation; Katrina Ray, at Grundy Television Australia.

It could—but must not—go without saying that the *Encyclopedia of Television* would not exist without the contributions of its more than 300 authors. In many cases I have made special requests on short deadline. In other cases I have depended on authors who secured the services of their colleagues. In every instance I have relied on those who knew more about their specific topics than did I. I have made new friends and established new collegial relationships around the world and count myself fortunate to be part of a community of scholars so committed to so important a subject.

Finally, I wish to express my deepest and continuing gratitude to Sara Newcomb. She has contributed enormously to this project, offering her administrative assistance, her own interest in and knowledge of television, her ongoing encouragement, her gentle patience, her sound advice, and her unfailing sense of proper perspective in the face of what seemed at times an endless project that consumed space of many sorts within our household. The *Encyclopedia of Television* is, in this regard, one of our finest collaborations.

—Horace Newcomb
Austin, Texas
September 1996

INTRODUCTION

The second half of the 20th century may well come to be known as the television era. In the years following World War II various individuals, groups, institutions, and governments in the developed nations financed and built the infrastructure of the television industry—the broadcasting technologies, industrial organizations, financial support systems, and policy environment—that led to the presence of television in the everyday life of citizens. Those same individuals, groups, institutions, and governments drew upon earlier forms of expression, information, and instruction to create broadcasting schedules that expanded to fill every hour of the day with televised "content." In pubs, classrooms, and, most significantly, in homes, citizens took the new medium into their lives and routines, their lessons and sermons, their dreams and fears.

In many ways television was merely an extension of other forms of communication and art—the stage, the movie screen, the newspaper, the lecture hall, and most significantly in many cases, the radio broadcast. Yet, in other ways it was a new thing, presenting forms of common language where there had been dialect, shared experience where there had been difference, routinized patterns of address where there had been surprise. It brought connection where there had been isolation, newness where there had been repetition, alternatives where there had been only the accepted—and acceptable—expectations for a future. This medium has shattered prior notions of political behavior and of politics, remodeled minute patterns of daily behavior, shifted relations within and among families, transformed fundamental notions of play and sport, and mutated entire industrial structures. By the final years of the century television was insinuated into every country and any search for community, village, tribal group—even individual—unfamiliar, at least in some rudimentary way, with the medium might have proved futile. Yet by that time even the term "television" was approaching obsolescence. What had seemed so monolithic, so pervasive and powerful, so established, was in a process of massive reconfiguration, its core characteristics intact, but rapidly changing, its broad outlines blurred.

Satellites, videocassette recorders, cable systems, and computers had all but obviated any necessity for the locally familiar transmitting tower, the antenna, even conventional forms of tuners and receivers. Regularized program schedules had given way in most cases to an array of choices, even in regions where official agencies still attempted to control access to televised content. Moreover, the shifts in technology, with consequent alterations in economic underpinnings, and the power alignments accompanying them, showed up new failures—shortcomings, really—in policies and legal arrangements designed to monitor and rationalize the systems of broadcasting commonly thought of as "television."

What these changes, these newer technologies, made clear, however, was that the single term had never encompassed, described, or explained anything like the complexities it obscured. "Television" has never been a thing, neither a set of technologies, a pattern of economic support, a cluster of policies, a collection of programs and stories, nor a system of information. It is and has been, of course, all these things and many more, but it is in the complex interrelationships within and among categories that the medium has achieved its primary significance.

During a brief half-century television has been a site, perhaps the principle site, on and over which social forces struggled for various forms of ascendance—for profit, for cultural dominance, for personal expression, for the control of intellectual, spiritual, emotional, and political power. Television, then, is perhaps best described as an intersection, a switchboard of sorts, through which has passed every major issue, every cultural shift, every event deemed—by someone at some switcher (mechanical or conceptual) at some level—significant. And each of these issues, shifts, and events has been necessarily altered by moving into and through the television matrix. The struggle to control that alteration, to dominate the patterns of expression, the amount and nature of information, the styles and levels of learning, even the form and model of moral and ethical tone, has been a central struggle in these times.

Significantly, though perhaps predictably, these matters have become clearer as the "age of television" ends, gives way to a different set of technologies, forms, meanings, arrangements, policies, and patterns. What is most evident at this juncture is that all those who thought themselves to have finally arrived at "the definition" of "television" were in fact operating from specific stages, perceiving in particular ways, organizing their thoughts, strategies, policies, and institutional arrangements in sometimes well-considered, but constantly—inevitably—skewed and limited fashion.

Nowhere are these limited approaches more visible than in the broad questions related to the problem of "national" television systems. The bulk of details—topics, programs, individuals—presented in this collection, for example, come from four countries, the United States, Britain, Canada, and Australia—major countries in the "English-speaking" world. A huge range of difference emerges in this most general description. Certainly it is likely that most television users in the United States assume that "television" is organized throughout the world as it is in their own national context. Yet every careful student of the history of the medium recognizes that until the last quarter of the 20th century, the U.S. model of television has been the anomaly. Far more countries organized their television systems along lines of state-supported, public service patterns than as commercial, advertising supported systems in which audiences—made available to advertisers—are the true unit of exchange.

But such a qualification, based on comparison of basic policies, masks as much as it explains. Canada and Australia, for example, along with many other countries, have built television systems drawing on elements of both models and have shaped them according to special concerns for matters of language, geography, and relations to other regional powers. Moreover, in recent years the cases of Britain, Canada, and Australia have become more and more "mixed" as technologies have increased distribution channels, which have led to increased and varied forms of "competition" for state as well as private funds, and as individuals and transnational corporations have sought to consolidate power in order to control media industries. And as other essays presented here, focused on other national television systems, make even more evident, there is no predictable pattern, no systematic, rational explanation that can account for the range of national variation in the organization of "television." In point of fact, the ability to transmit television signals across national borders has made the very concept of "national" systems of broadcasting problematic, not only for students of television, but for policy makers, production industries, cultural guardians, and audiences.

Still, the primary focus of the collection is on these four major English-speaking countries, each with highly-developed television systems. Advisers from each country helped shape a list comprised of significant individuals, programs, and topics related to television. The individuals may be actors and performers, producers, directors, or writers, policy makers, broadcasting executives, or media moguls. But they may also be commentators who discuss television from outside these professional arenas, or critics and historians who have sought to construct explanations and descriptions with which others might better understand the medium. The programs presented here are, in most cases, familiar at least to audiences within national contexts, and in some cases to audiences throughout the world. Some are important because they are critically acclaimed. Some, perhaps critically scorned, are significant because huge audiences affirmed and enjoyed them, bestowed upon them "cult" status. Still others are included because they contributed to greater understanding of a particular social problem or became test cases involving the rights of producers and broadcasters and the concerns of regulators and legislators. Topical entries deal with the widest range of subjects. Some explain particular technical aspects of television. Others deal with institutions, agencies, or organizations. Still others focus on continuing "problem" areas related to the experience of television such as the special questions surrounding "children and television," "violence and television," or "history and television." Entries dealing with numerous countries other than the four major English-speaking nations have been added to the collection in order to demonstrate the increasingly international character of television.

And while the latest changes in conceptions of "television" illustrated in this collection may seem particularly dramatic, they should not obscure the fact that change and conflict have been at the core of any understanding, organization, or use of the medium since its invention, development, and application. The shifts in technological, institutional, organizational, financial, and policy arrangements have been constant, always ebbing and flowing as economic, political, and cultural power have been used to varying advantages in struggles among individuals, groups, and institutions. Many of the contests have been for the right to claim "television" as a prized object, a means of concentrating and displaying particular ideologies, theories, explanations, moralities, and policies. The only constant has been the perception that control and use of this medium are essential aspects of contemporary social and cultural life.

Add to this mix the participation of artists and craftspersons who wish to use "television" as a means of presenting their work to audiences. Or consider the positions of those audiences, once thought to be simple (perhaps simple-minded), passive, uniform in response—but now recognized as varied, complex, critical and analytical at times, active interpreters comparing what they take from the medium with what they experience in other realms and arenas of their lives. Both artists and audiences have learned from the history of a medium with which many have spent most of their lives. Both groups can make comparisons, cite precedents and predecessors, and call upon members of their communities for discussion. Even "last night's favorite show," then (or last night's game or speech or announcement or even commercial advertisement), can become the topic of conversation, subject to formal and informal critique, dissection, celebration.

How then should one study such a complex arrangement of such distinct but interrelated phenomena? How is sense to be made of systems in constant flux? How is an encyclopedia to be organized? Put another way, what knowledge about "television" is most worth having? The *Encyclopedia of Television* does not pretend to final answers for these questions. It offers no definition of its own for "television." Instead, it offers a multitude of beginning points from which to trace the intersections, conflicts, struggles, and convergences that can be applied, used as partial explanations for particular events, policies, developments, even for the existence of particular television "shows." To perhaps predict a future development of the project, and certainly to rely on the increasingly common term that has been central in the planning this collection of entries, the *Encyclopedia of Television* is best used "interactively." Connections are pervasive. Cross-references are crucial. Multiple explanations are essential. Comparisons are to be expected. Contradictions are inevitable. In every case the connections, cross-references, explanations, comparisons, and contradictions should be sought out and used to understand any particular item presented here.

No attempt to "organize knowledge" related to television, however, can escape or avoid the kinds of interrelated issues—the struggles surrounding the medium—outlined above. This is made most clear by the fact that individuals, programs, and topics related to television in the United States form the single largest sub-category in the collection. This fact reflects an industrial reality—the

U.S. industry is the largest, richest, and most industrially powerful television enterprise in the world.

Recognition of size, however, provides no explanation. It too easily obscures the fact that the U.S. television industry is also the *dominant* television industry in the world, and that dominance is fought for and won on various fronts—economic, cultural, technological, political. It is true that the U.S. industry has achieved international success. It is true that U.S. television programs have been accepted and in some cases become popular throughout the world. It is the case that U.S. models of industrial organization, technological application, and narrative strategies have often been adopted in other regions.

But it is also the case that in the aftermath of World War II, the United States was the only major industrialized nation where previously developed media industries remained intact. It is also the case that the U.S. film industry had long maintained organized international distribution systems throughout the world. And, significantly, the United States is the largest single-language market in the world served by a fully developed television industry, a fact that makes possible the recovery of production and distribution expenses in the domestic arena. And this fact in turn makes it possible for U.S. production and distribution companies to sell U.S. television programs in every other country at a price far below the costs incurred in producing indigenous materials. In short, the U.S. advantage has, in many cases, slowed the development of television systems in other countries, other regions, often blocking or retarding the fullest possible production of indigenous forms of expression, instruction, and information.

None of these observations should be taken to mean that the U.S. individuals, programs, and topics present in this encyclopedia are somehow undeserving of inclusion. All are significant to the full understanding of the medium. What must be recognized, however, is that there are always multiple, interacting, sometimes contradictory conditions determining matters of "significance."

U.S. dominance in the realm of television has clearly affected the organization of this encyclopedia in ways that extend beyond the numbers of subjects. One sub-category of topical entries, for example, approaches the history of television programs as the history of genres: the Situation Comedy, the Detective Program, the Police Program, and so on. These entries, however, focus on U.S. versions of these genres. Canadian, Australian, and British examples are discussed in overview entries combining discussions of all programming in the television history of those countries. The same approach holds for other topical entries. The large entry on "Children and Television" is focused on issues, policies, and studies in the United States, but the topic may be discussed as a sub-category in other "national" essays. For countries other than the four organizing nations, all subjects, including the history of the medium, the policies governing it, the financial arrangements supporting it, the programs, issues, and controversies encountered, are dealt with in single entries.

Still, in spite of what might be thought of as unbalanced organizational factors, national, regional, and systemic differences are highly visible in the entries presented here. They are most prominent in formal analyses of economic and regulatory policy and in explicit discussion of how various national systems have dealt with international flows of television content. But they are also evident even in the presentation of data.

Each program discussed in the *Encyclopedia of Television* is accompanied by information considered necessary for a complete description. The cast of players and the roles they play, the producers of the program, the distribution service on which the program appeared, and the schedule of delivery are all listed as supplementary data. For the U.S. programs most of the data related to the schedule shows that they were broadcast by one of three major networks, that they appeared in either 30-minute or 60-minute units programmed at specific times on specific days, during certain periods of the year. In the vast majority of cases these programs run for a number of years and then disappear from the schedule.

For programs produced and programmed in Britain, however, other patterns apply. There is less sense of a television "season" that begins at one point in the year and ends at another. Clusters of episodes—called series—of a particular program may be produced at varying times throughout the years. Even more commonly, these clusters of episodes may be produced in one year, disappear from the schedule for a year or for several years, then reappear.

Such differences in programming strategy are reflected in the supporting data provided with essays discussing these programs. But the differences indicate far more extensive relationships to other aspects of television than merely two different industrial strategies. The regularized programming schedule in the United States is fundamentally linked to the advertising industry which encourages regularized viewing, predictable viewing, familiar viewing that will bring audiences into a similar familiar relationship with commercials. Similarly, corporate decisions linking certain types of programs, even specific programs, to certain periods in the schedule, are indicative of assumptions about appropriate content, appropriate behavior, the organization of the domestic sphere, the gendered organization of labor, child-rearing practices and a host of other social and cultural categories. Moreover, these decisions are designed not merely in acknowledgment of these categories, but also as a means of regulating and enforcing them.

The British pattern makes similar assumptions, enforces similar categories of behavior and attitude. The difference in programming strategy does, of course, demonstrate certain parallel social distinctions. The fact that programs can be off the air, then return months or years later, suggests an assumption that the relation of audiences to programs is less a matter of routinized behavior than of an affinity for characters and narratives.

But even these possible differences are complicated by U.S. audience attention to favorite programs in reruns, and even more to the rise of nostalgia channels and various forms of "re-framing" television programs with irony (in the case of Nick at Nite and TV Land), or with specifically religious sentiment (in the case of the Family Channel). And as new technologies such as the videocassette recorder and the remote control device have altered patterns of regularized viewing, as the proliferation of distribution channels via satellite and cable have created more viewing choices, programmers, producers, and policy makers in every country, and every cultural context, have been forced to re-examine their assumptions about the role of television in daily life, in cultural experience, in social context.

These alterations are acknowledged throughout the *Encyclopedia of Television*. While it is true that this medium has always been in a constant state of transformation, the changes currently in process are among the most significant in its history. The very term may become less and less useful as a description, a name, for a set of interrelated communication phenomena now replacing what we have known as "television." Consequently, this encyclopedia does not look exclusively to the past, to the history that has led to the current situation. While a significant portion of the entries are historical in focus, while most of the programs discussed here are no longer in production, many of those same entries draw conclusions and suggest implications for what may yet occur. Others are specifically forward looking. And almost all recognize process, change, and interrelatedness as fundamental components of their subjects. Future editions and versions of the *Encyclopedia of Television* will undoubtedly revise some of the predictions and implications offered here. But at the same time they will risk their own best analysis of "television" as it is formed at the time of their writing. Short of massive disaster, there is no way to look at this medium and say "this is what it was; this is what it is." "Television" has been and is always becoming.

—Horace Newcomb
Austin, Texas
September 1996

ADVISORY BOARD

CONTRIBUTORS

Sean Cubitt
Paul Cullum
Stuart O. Cunningham
Ann Curthoys
Michael Curtin

Daniel Dayan
Kathryn C. D'Alessandro
Pamala S. Deane
Roger de la Garde
Mary Desjardins
George Dessart
Robert Dickinson
John Docker
Thomas Doherty
David F. Donnelly
Kevin Dowler
John D.H. Downing
Phillip Drummond
J.A. Dunn
Nannetta Durnell

Ross A. Eaman
Gary R. Edgerton
Greg Elmer
Susan Emmanuel
Michael Epstein
Robert Erler
Anna Everett
Robert Everett

Irving Fang
Norman Felsenthal
Robert Ferguson
Dick Fiddy
Robert G. Finney
Frederick J. Fletcher
James E. Fletcher
Terry Flew
Nicola Foster
Jeanette Fox
Eric Freedman
Katherine Fry

Ursula Ganz-Blaetller
Ronald Garay
Paula Gardner
Frances K. Gateward
Susan R. Gibberman
Mark Gibson
William O. Gilsdorf
Ivy Glennon
Kevin Glynn
Peter Goddard
Donald G. Godfrey
Douglas Gomery
Hannah Gourgey
August Grant

Sean Griffin
Alison Griffiths
Lynne Schafer Gross
David Gunzerath

Jerry Hagins
Daniel C. Hallin
Geoffrey Hammill
Susan Hamovitch
Keith C. Hampson
Denis Harp
Cheryl Harris
Roderick P. Hart
John Hartley
Amir Hassanpour
Mark Hawkins-Dady
James Hay
Richard Haynes
Michele Hilmes
Hal Himmelstein
Olaf Hoerschelmann
Junhao Hong
Stewart M. Hoover
Ed Hugetz
Donald Humphreys
Darnell M. Hunt

Elizabeth Jacka
Matt Jackson
Jason J. Jacobs
Sharon Jarvis
Henry Jenkins
Ros Jennings
Clifford A. Jones
Jeffrey P. Jones
Judith Jones
Garth Jowett
Guy Jowett

Lynda Lee Kaid
Nixon K. Kariithi
Michael B. Kassel
Janice Kaye
Mary C. Kearney
Phillip O. Keirstead
C.A. Kellner
Douglas Kellner
Brendan Kenny
Vance Kepley Jr.
Lahn S. Kim
Won-Yong Kim
Howard M. Kleiman
Robert Kubey
J. Jerome Lackamp
Christina Lane
Manon Lamontagne
Antonio C. Lapastina
Jim Leach

Stephen Lee
Nina C. Leibman
Debra A. Lemieux
Robert Lemieux
Lisa Anne Lewis
Tamar Liebes
Lucy A. Liggett
Val E. Limburg
Sonia Livingstone
Pamela Logan
Guy E. Lometti
Amy W. Loomis
Lynn T. Lovdal
Moya Luckett
Catharine Lumby

Ted Magder
Sarita Malik
Brent Malin
Chris Mann
David Marc
P. David Marshall
William Martin
Tom Mascaro
Michael Mashon
Kimberly B. Massey
Richard Maxwell
Sharon R. Mazzarella
Matthew P. McAllister
Anna McCarthy
Tom McCourt
Mark R. McDermott
Alan McKee
Lori Melton McKinnon
Susan McLeland
Peter McLuskie
Bishetta D. Merritt
Fritz J. Messere
Cynthia Meyers
Mary Jane Miller
Toby Miller
Bob Millington
Jason Mittell
Margaret Montgomerie
Nickianne Moody
Albert Moran
James Moran
Jennifer Moreland
Anne Morey
Michael Morgan
David Morley
Margaret Morse
Megan Mullen
Graham Murdock
Matthew Murray
Sue Murray

Diane M. Negra

Horace Newcomb
Poul Erik Nielsen
Joan Nicks
Dawn Michelle Nill
Gayle Noyes

Cary O'Dell
Peter B. Orlick
David Oswell

Lindsy E. Pack
Lisa Parks
Chris Paterson
Tony Pearson
Lance Pettitt
David Pickering
Joanna Ploeger-Tsoulos
Gayle M. Pohl
Rodolfo B. Popelnik
Vincent Porter
Julie Prince

Andrew Quicke
Marc Raboy
Jimmie L. Reeves
Jane Revell
Jef Richards
William Richter
Jeremy Ridgman
Karen E. Riggs
Trudy Ring
Madelyn Ritrosky-Winslow
America Rodriguez
Aviva Rosenstein
Karen Ross
Lorna Roth
Eric Rothenbuhler
Steve Runyon
Paul Rutherford

Michael Saenz
Eric Schaefer
Thomas Schatz
James Schwoch
Christine Scodari
Jeffrey Sconce
Beth Seaton
Peter B. Seel
Mitchell E. Shapiro
Marla L. Shelton
Jeff Shires
Robbie Shumate
Jane Sillars
Ismo Silvo
Ron Simon
Nikhil Sinha
Jeannette Sloniowski
B. R. Smith

Paul A. Soukup
Colin Sparks
Lynn Spigel
Mike Sragow
Janet Staiger
Christopher H. Sterling
Joel Sternberg
Nicola Strange
Joseph Straubhaar
Daniel G. Streible
Sharon Strover
Joan Stuller-Giglione

Zoe Tan
Gisele Tchoungui
John C. Tedesco
David J. Tetzlaff
Robert J. Thompson
David Thorburn
Bernard M. Timberg
Paul J. Torre
Raul D. Tovares
Mary Triece
Liza Treviño
Soti Triantafillou
John Tulloch
Marian Tulloch
J.C. Turner

Joseph Turow

Tise Vahimagi
Leah R. Vande Berg

Clayland H. Waite
Cynthia W. Walker
James R. Walker
Kay Walsh
Charles Warner
Mary Ann Watson
James Wehmeyer
Tinky "Dakota" Weisblat
Mimi White
D. Joel Wiggins
Derek Wilding
Karin Gwinn Wilkins
Carol Traynor Williams
Mark Williams
Suzanne Hurst Williams
Pamela Wilson
Brian Winston
Richard Worringham

Rita Zajacz
Sharon Zechowski
Nabeel Zuberi

ALPHABETICAL LIST OF ENTRIES

Volume 1

Volume 2

Volume 3

A

ABBENSETTS, MICHAEL

British Writer

Michael Abbensetts is considered by many to be the best black playwright to emerge from his generation. He has been presented with many awards for his lifetime achievements in television drama writing and, in 1979, received an award for an "Outstanding Contribution To Literature" by a black writer resident in England. His work emerged alongside, and as part of, the larger development of black British television drama.

Abbensetts was born in Guyana in 1938. He began his writing career with short stories, but decided to turn to playwriting after seeing a performance of John Osborne's *Look Back in Anger*. He was further inspired when he came to England and visited the Royal Court Theatre, Britain's premier theatre of new writing, where he became resident dramatist in 1974. *Sweet Talk*, Abbensett's first play, was performed there in 1973.

In the same year, *The Museum Attendant*, his first television play, was broadcast on BBC2. Directed by Stephen Frears, the drama was, Abbensetts says, based on his own early experiences as a security guard at the Tower of London. After these two early successes Abbensetts, unlike most black writers in Britain at the time, was being offered more and more work. He wrote *Black Christmas*, which was broadcast on the BBC in 1977 and featured Carmen Munroe and Norman Beaton. Like *The Museum Attendant*, *Black Christmas* was based on actual experience and was shot on location for television.

During the 1970s and 1980s, a number of Abbensetts' plays were produced for the London theater. *Alterations* appeared in 1978, followed by *Samba* (1980), *In the Mood* (1981), *Outlaw* (1983) and *Eldorado* (1983). *Inner City Blues, Crime and Passion, Roadrunner*, and *Fallen Angel* were produced for television.

Abbensetts' success led to participation in British television's first black soap opera, *Empire Road* (1978–79), for which he wrote two series. Horace Ove was brought in to direct the second series, establishing a production unit with a black director, black writer and black actors. The television series was unique in that it was the first soap opera to be conceived and written by a black writer for a black cast, but also because it was specifically about the British-Caribbean experience. Set in Handsworth, Birmingham, it featured Norman Beaton as Everton Bennett and Corinne Skinner-Carter as his long-suffering screen wife. Although *Empire Road* was a landmark programme on British television, it managed to survive only two series before it was axed. The late Norman Beaton said of the programme, "It is perhaps the best TV series I have been in."

Norman Beaton continued to star in many of Abbensett's television productions including *Easy Money* (1981) and *Big George Is Dead* and *Little Napoleons* (1994/Channel 4). *Little Napoleons* is a four-part comic-drama depicting the rivalry between two solicitors, played by Saeed Jaffrey and Norman Beaton, who become Labour councillors. The work focuses on a number of themes including the price of power, the relationship between West Indian and Asian communities in Britain and the internal workings of political institutions.

Much of Abbensetts' drama has focused on issues of race and power, but he has always been reluctant to be seen as restricted to issue-based drama. His dialogue is concerned

Michael Abbensetts
Photo courtesy of Michael Abbensetts

with the development and growth of character and he is fundamentally aware of the methods and contexts for his actors. Abbensetts has always actively involved himself in the production process and his dramatic works have provided outstanding roles for established black actors in Britain— Carmen Munroe, Rudolph Walker and Norman Beaton— giving them the chance to play interesting and realistic roles as well as creating stories about the everyday experiences of black people. Abbensetts' work thrived at a time when there was very little drama on television which represented the lives of Black British people and his television plays have created new perspectives for all his viewers.

—Sarita Malik

MICHAEL ABBENSETTS. Born in British Guiana (now Guyana), 8 June 1938; took British citizenship, 1974. Attended Queen's College, Guyana, 1952–56; Stanstead College, Quebec, Canada; Sir George Williams University, Montreal, 1960–61. Security attendant, Tower of London, 1963–67; staff member, Sir John Soane Museum, London, 1968–71; resident playwright, Royal Court Theatre, London, 1974; visiting professor of drama, Carnegie Mellon University, Pittsburgh, Pennsylvania, U.S.A., 1981. Recipient: George Devine Award, 1973; Arts Council bursary, 1977; Afro-Caribbean Award, 1979. Address: Heinemann Educational Books Ltd, Halley Court, Jordan Hill, Oxford OX2 8EJ, England.

TELEVISION SERIES

1978–79	*Empire Road*
1994	*Little Napoleons*

TELEVISION PLAYS

1973	*The Museum Attendant*
1975	*Inner City Blues*
1976	*Crime and Passion*
1977	*Black Christmas*
1977	*Roadrunner*
1982	*Easy Money*
1987	*Big George Is Dead*

RADIO

Home Again, 1975; *The Sunny Side of the Street,* 1977; *Brothers of the Sword,* 1978; *The Fast Lane,* 1980; *The Dark Horse,* 1981; *Summer Passions,* 1985.

STAGE

Sweet Talk, 1973; *Alterations,* 1978; *Samba,* 1980; *In the Mood,* 1981; *The Dark Horse,* 1981; *Outlaw,* 1983; *El Dorado,* 1984; *Living Together,* 1988.

PUBLICATIONS

Sweet Talk (play). London: Eyre Methuen, 1976.
Samba (play). London: Eyre Methuen, 1980.
Empire Road (novel). London: Panther, 1979.
Living Together (play). Oxford: Heinemann, 1988.

FURTHER READING

Leavy, Suzan. "Abbensetts an Example." *Television Today* (London), 19 May 1994.
Walters, Margaret. "Taking Race for Granted." *New Society* (London), 16 November 1978.

ABSOLUTELY FABULOUS

British Situation Comedy

The half-hour BBC sitcom with a large and growing cult following, *Absolutely Fabulous,* debuted in 1992 with six episodes. Six additional episodes appeared in 1994, and a final six in 1995. The American cable channel Comedy Central began running the series in 1994.

Ab Fab, as fans call it, is about idle-rich Edina Monsoon (Jennifer Saunders), a 40-year-old spoiled brat who owns her own PR business but works at it only rarely (and incompetently). Stuck in the self-indulgences of the 1960s, but showing no sign of that decade's political awareness, Edina refuses to grow up. Her principal talent is making a spectacle of herself. This she achieves by dressing gaudily, speaking loudly and rudely, and lurching frantically from one exaggerated crisis to the next. All the while, she overindulges—in smoking, drinking, drugs, shopping, and fads (Buddhism, colonic irrigation, various unsuccessful attempts at slimming down). She lives extravagantly off the alimony provided by two ex-husbands.

Edina's best friend, Patsy Stone (Joanna Lumley), is equally a caricature. Employed as fashion director of a trendy magazine, she almost never works (she has the job because she slept with the publisher). She is even more of a substance abuser than Edina, and trashier in appearance with an absurdly tall, blond hairdo, and far too much lipstick. Most disturbingly, Patsy is overly dependent upon Edina for money, transportation, and especially companionship.

Patsy often behaves like an unruly daughter, thereby displacing Edina's real daughter Saffron (Julia Sawalha), of whom Patsy is extremely jealous. Edina humors Patsy's excesses and seems parental only by virtue of her money and domineering personality. The real "mother" of the house is Saffron, a young adult who, in being almost irritatingly virtuous, is both a moral counterweight to the evil Patsy and a comic foil for the two childlike adults.

Thus Saffron represents conscience and serves a function similar to that of Meathead in *All in the Family,* except that in *Ab Fab* the generational conflict is not one of conservative vs. liberal so much as bad vs. good liberalism. Neither Saffron nor Edina is conservative. Although Saffron is somewhat nerdy in the manner of Alex Keaton in *Family Ties*, she lacks his predatory materialism and serves as a reassuring model of youth. While Patsy and Edina illustrate a pathological mutation of 1960s youth culture, Saffron provides hope that liberalism (or at least youth) is redeemable.

Ab Fab's focus on generational issues also plays out in Edina's disrespect for her mother (June Whitfield). The relationship between the four main characters, all women, is all the more interesting because of the absence of men. Edina's father puts in only one appearance in the series—as a corpse, and only Saffron cares that he has died. Similarly, Edina's son is never seen in the first twelve episodes and is only mentioned a few times. It is not that men are bad—rather, they are irrelevant.

This allows *Ab Fab* to have a feminist flavor even as it portrays women in mostly unflattering terms. Edina and Patsy are certainly not intended as role models, and in presenting them as buffoonish and often despicable, series creator-writer Saunders ridicules not only bourgeois notions of motherhood and family life, but also media images of women's liberation. For example, Edina and Patsy, although "working women," actually depend upon the largesse of men to maintain their station in life. Edina's business and Patsy's job are a joke. This cynical vision of professionalism may seem regressive, but at the same time it is a refreshing critique of advertising and fashion, two industries invariably depicted by TV as—absolutely fabulous.

Ab Fab developed from a sketch on the *French and Saunders* show and is a fine example of the flowering of alternative comedy, the post-*Monty Python* movement that also produced *The Young Ones*. Rejecting what has been referred to as the "erudite middle-class approach" of the *Python* generation, the new British comics of the 1980s approached their material with a rude, working-class, rock-and-roll sensibility. *Ab Fab*, while focusing on the concerns of middle age, nonetheless has a youthful energy and eschews sentimentality. Flashbacks and dream sequences contribute to this energy and give the show a mildly anarchic structure. A smash hit in Britain, *Ab Fab* has won two International Emmy awards and has given the somewhat obscure Comedy Central cable channel a significant publicity boost.

—Gary Burns

CAST

Edina Monsoon . . . . Jennifer Saunders
Patsy Stone . . . . Joanna Lumley
Saffron Monsoon . . . . Julia Sawalha
June Monsoon (Mother) . . . . June Whitfield
Bubble . . . . Jane Horrocks

Absolutely Fabulous
Photo courtesy of BBC

PRODUCER   Jon Plowman

PROGRAMMING HISTORY

• BBC

November 1992–December 1992	Six Episodes
January 1994–March 1994	Six Episodes
March 1995–May 1995	Six Episodes

FURTHER READING

"An Absolutely Fabulous Finale." *The New Yorker*, 20 March 1995.

Kroll, Gerry. "The Women." *The Advocate* (San Mateo, California), 16 April 1996.

Lyall, Sarah. "Absolutely Catching, Bad Habits and All." *The New York Times*, 13 July 1995.

O'Connor, John. "Absolutely Fabulous." *The New York Times*, 12 June 1995.

Saunders, Jennifer. *Absolutely Fabulous*. London: BBC Books, 1993.

———. *Absolutely Fabulous 2*. London: BBC Books, 1994.

See also Lumley, Joanna; Saunders, Jennifer

A.C.NIELSEN COMPANY

U.S. Media Market Research Firm

Under the banner of Nielsen Media Research, the A. C. Nielsen Company measures and compiles statistics on television audiences. It sells this data in various formats to advertisers, advertising agencies, program syndicators, television networks, local stations, and cable program and system operators. Nielsen Marketing Research is the larger part of the company, providing a variety of standard market analysis reports and engaging in other market research. By some reports only 10% of Nielsen's total business relates to the television audience, though they are very well known to the general public for that work. This is due, of course, to the ubiquitous reporting and discussion of program and network ratings produced by Nielsen.

The company was started in 1923 by A. C. Nielsen, an engineer, and bought by Dun and Bradstreet in 1984 for $1.3 billion. They first became involved in audience studies in the 1930s as an extension of Nielsen's studies tracking retail food and drug purchase. In 1936 Nielsen bought the Audimeter from its designers, Robert Elder and Louis F. Woodruff, two Massachusetts Institute of Technology professors. The Audimeter (and a previous design for a similar device patented in 1929 by Claude E. Robinson, then sold to RCA, who never developed it), was intended to automatically record two aspects of radio listening which would be of interest to programmers and advertisers. The device recorded which frequencies a radio set was tuned to when it was on and the length of time the set was on. This technique had an obvious problem—it could not assure who, if anyone, was listening to the radio. But compared to the use of telephone surveys and diaries used by competing ratings companies, it had important advantages as well. The other ratings methods depended to a much greater degree on audience members' active cooperation, memories, honesty, and availability.

After a period of redesign and a four-year pilot study, the Nielsen Audimeter was introduced commercially in 1942 with an 800-home sample in the Eastern United States. The number of Audimeters and the sample size and coverage were expanded after World War II, eventually, by 1949, to represent 97% of U.S. radio homes. The Cooperative Analysis of Broadcasting had ceased providing ratings in 1946; in 1950 the A. C. Nielsen Company bought Hooper's national radio and television ratings services and thus became the single national radio rating service. This allowed the company to increase rates and the new capital was used to increase sample size. As the television industry grew, Nielsen's attention to television grew with it; they left the radio field in 1964.

In 1973 Nielsen began using the Storage Instantaneous Audimeter, a new and more sophisticated design for the same purposes as the original (surely not the only modification over the years; this one was much publicized). Set in a closet, designed with battery backup for power outages, and hooked to a dedicated telephone line for daily data reports to a central office, the device kept track of turn-on, turn-off, and channel-setting for every television in a household, including battery operated and portable units (through radio transmitter).

While the Audimeter, widely known as the Nielsen black box, was their most famous device, it was used only for household television ratings. For ratings by people and demographic descriptions of the audience, Nielsen required supplementary studies of audience composition based on a separate sample using the diary technique. This separate sample was smaller and there was concern in the industry that the people who cooperated with the diaries were not representative of people in general.

In the 1970s Nielsen experimented with Peoplemeters, a system for measuring the viewing of individuals without diaries, but brought no new services to market. In 1983 AGB Research of Great Britain proposed a commercial Peoplemeter service in the United States similar to the system they were using in other countries. This proposal attracted funding from a group of networks, advertising agencies, and others for an evaluation study in Boston. In 1985, in response to this competitive threat, Nielsen initiated their own Peoplemeter sample, as a supplement to their existing samples. Reports became available beginning in January 1986. The system depends on a box sitting atop the television set that keeps track, in the usual way, of what channel is tuned in. But the meter is also programmed with demographic descriptions of individual viewers in the household and their visitors. Viewers are asked to push a button indicating when they begin or end viewing the television, even if the set is left on when they leave. The data then indicate which (if any) viewers are present as well as set tuning. (There have also been experiments with passive meters that use infra-red sensing rather than requiring viewers to cooperate by pressing buttons; but so far these devices have not been sufficiently reliable.)

Because the Peoplemeters produced different numbers than diaries, they generated controversy in the industry. Ratings points are the reference for negotiations in the purchase of advertising time, in deciding which programs are syndicated, and other issues vital to the television industry. Thus, when different measurement techniques produce different ratings, normal business negotiations become complicated and less predictable. For this reason many participants in the television business actually prefer one company to have a monopoly on the ratings business, even it if does allow them to charge higher rates for their services. Even if this service provides inaccurate numbers, those numbers become agreed upon currency for purposes of negotiation. Eventually the most recent controversies were settled and Nielsen's Peoplemeter system now dominates the production of national television ratings.

The Audimeter was originally conceived as a means to the testing of advertising effectiveness. To at least some

A Nielsen "Peoplemeter"
Photos courtesy of A.C. Nielsen Company

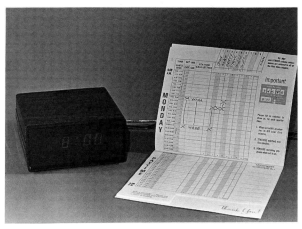

A Nielsen viewing diary
Photos courtesy of A.C. Nielsen Company

extent Nielsen's own interest in broadcast audiences was originally motivated by his marketing and advertising clients. But the ratings have grown to be an end in themselves, a product sold to parties interested in the composition of audiences for broadcasting.

Among the ratings reports provided by Nielsen were, until 1964, the Nielsen Radio Index (NRI) for network radio audiences. Currently the company provides the Nielsen Television Index (NTI) for network television audiences, the Station Index (NSI) for local stations and Designated Market Areas (DMA's), the Syndication Service (NSS) for the audiences of syndicated television shows, and the Homevideo Index (NHI) for the audiences of cable networks, superstations, and homevideo. They periodically produce reports on special topics as well, such as video-cassette recorder useage, viewership of sports programming, or television viewing in presidential election years.

—Eric Rothenbuhler

FURTHER READING

Beeville, Hugh Malcolm. *Audience Ratings: Radio, Television, and Cable.* Hillsdale, New Jersey: Erlbaum, 1985; revised edition, 1988.

Buzzard, Karen. *Electronic Media Ratings.* Boston, Massachusetts: Focal, 1992.

Dominick, Joseph R., and James E. Fletcher. *Broadcasting Research Methods.* Boston, Massachusetts: Allyn and Bacon, 1985.

Clift, Charles III, and Archie Greer, editors. *Broadcast Programming: The Current Perspective.* Washington, D.C.: University Press of America, 1981.

Webster, James G., and Lawrence W. Lichty. *Ratings Analysis: Theory and Practice.* Hillsdale, New Jersey: Erlbaum, 1991.

What TV Ratings Really Mean, How They are Obtained, Why They are Needed. New York: Nielsen Media Research, 1993.

ACADEMY OF TELEVISION ARTS AND SCIENCES

The Academy of Television Arts and Sciences (ATAS) is known primarily for bestowing Emmys, the top awards for television. These are peer awards, selected by vote of members of the academy—the people who work in the television industry. In addition to presenting this most public face of the television industry in an annual award ceremony, the academy also engages in a number of other educational and public functions.

The academy was founded in 1946 in Los Angeles by Syd Cassyd, a trade journal writer who recognized the need for a television organization similar to the Academy of Motion Picture Arts and Sciences. Cassyd and a group of associates held several exploratory meetings, then decided they needed a major television industry figure to support

the project. They succeeded in interesting ventriloquist Edgar Bergen, who became the academy's first president in 1947.

One of the earliest activities of the new academy was to establish a creative identity (and a degree of publicity and prestige) for the developing television industry by presenting awards—the Emmys—in recognition for outstanding work in the medium. Originally, the awards were to be called "Ikes," an abbreviation for the television iconoscope tube. Because "Ike" was so closely associated with Dwight D. Eisenhower, however, the group decided on "Emmy," a feminine form of "Immy," nickname for the television camera image orthicon tube. A contest was held for the design of the statuette and the winner was Louis McManus, an

The Emmy Award
Photo courtesy of Academy of Television Arts and Sciences

engineer, who used his wife as the model for the winged woman holding up the symbol of the electron.

In the first year of the award Emmys were presented in only five categories. And because television did not yet have a coast-to-coast hookup, they were given only to Los Angeles programs and personalities. Shirley Dinsdale (and her puppet Judy Splinters) was the Most Outstanding Television Personality and *Pantomime Quiz* the Most Popular Television Program. By the second year any show *seen* in Los Angeles could receive an award and New York-based personalities such as Milton Berle and Ed Wynn were winners.

At this point there was more backstage intrigue in the academy than on-stage. In 1950, Ed Sullivan, host of *Toast of the Town*, produced in New York, initiated a rival TV awards program, but these lasted only until 1953. No awards were presented in 1954 (the only year there have been no Emmys), because the Los Angeles group had decided the show had become too expensive. By 1955, however, the television networks were interested and the Emmys were broadcast nationally for the first time. Sullivan, realizing the Hollywood-based Emmys were a success, became upset and called together New York's television leaders. They demanded and were granted a New York chapter of the academy. They then asked for another academy, with equal "founding chapters" in both New York and Hollywood. Thus, in 1957 a newly-formed and newly-named National Academy of Television Arts and Sciences (NATAS) was created with Sullivan as the first president.

The animosity between the East and West coasts continued. In the early years, New York had the upper hand because the networks were based there and much early live dramatic programming, as well as news and documentaries, emanated from the east-coast city. From 1955 to 1971, the Emmys were simulcast with cameras cutting between New York and Los Angeles, often creating technical blunders that left screens blank for several minutes.

By 1971, however, Hollywood was firmly established as the predominant site for television program production. New York was no longer producing the live drama, and, although the east coast city was still the seat of news and documentaries, the audiences tuned in to the Emmys to see Hollywood stars. In addition, the Emmys were growing in number and the telecast in length, so in 1973 and 1974 the news and documentary categories were removed from the regular show (now produced totally in Hollywood) and given their own telecast. Ratings were low, however, and the show was dropped.

During this period, other cities such as Atlanta, Chicago, and Cincinnati organized academy chapters. Hollywood producers resented the fact that academy members, scattered throughout the country, all had equal votes in determining the Emmy awards. From their beginning, the Emmys were conceived as peer awards, and the powerful Hollywood community hardly considered a camera person in Cincinnati to be a peer. New York, however, sided with the smaller chapters.

In 1976, the Hollywood chapter of NATAS decided to split from that organization. A year of lawsuits followed but the end result was two academies—the National Academy of Television Arts and Sciences (NATAS) comprised of New York and outlying cities and the Hollywood-based Academy of Television Arts and Sciences (ATAS). NATAS would bestow daytime, sports, news, and documentary Emmys and ATAS would oversee prime-time awards, using its Hollywood member base as voters.

The two academies remain separate, although from time to time they hold talks regarding reunification, and ATAS has indeed helped NATAS produce the Daytime Emmy Awards. When those prizes first aired nationally in 1991, they achieved higher ratings than the primetime awards. During this period, ATAS was having its own problems with the primetime show. For many years the telecast rotated sequentially among ABC, CBS, and NBC. When the upstart FOX network went on the air, it offered the academy more money for the telecasts than the other networks had been paying, and from 1987 to 1992 the Emmys were shown exclusively on the new network. Ratings plummeted, largely because FOX programming did not appear on local stations throughout the entire country. Eventually the academy returned to the "wheel" concept with FOX as one of the participants.

ATAS's membership is based on peer groups—writers, art directors, performers, sound editors, production executives, etc. Each peer group establishes its own requirement for membership, usually defined in terms of the number of shows or number of hours of television the person has to his or her credit. The Board of Governors is composed of two members from each peer group.

Voting for primetime Emmys is also conducted on the peer group basis so that only members of the music peer group vote for awards involving music, directors vote for directing awards, etc. Some "Best Program" awards can be voted on by much of the membership. Individuals may nominate themselves for awards and producers may nominate individuals or programs. All nominated material is then judged by panels of peers who come together to watch all the nominations in a particular category. Their votes are tabulated and the winners are announced, either during the on-air telecast or at a luncheon ceremony. In general, the awards that the public is most likely to find interesting (performers, outstanding shows, directors) are presented during the prime time telecast.

While the Emmy Awards are the most visible of its projects, the academy undertakes many other activities including.

- sponsoring a paid student internship program through which outstanding students from around the country spend eight weeks working with Hollywood professionals.
- conducting a contest for student TV productions with the winners receiving cash sums.

- inducting outstanding industry professionals into a Hall of Fame.
- holding an annual Faculty Seminar in which college teachers come to Hollywood and are introduced to people and ideas related to TV programming.
- hosting luncheons and meetings at which people from within and without the industry share ideas and information.
- participating, with UCLA, in overseeing a television archives.
- publishing *Emmy*, a magazine devoted to articles about the TV industry.

In 1991 the Academy of Television Arts and Sciences moved into new headquarters containing office and library space as well as a state of the art theater in which to screen television materials and hold large meetings.

—Lynne Schafer Gross

FURTHER READING

Michael, Paul, and James Robert Parish. *The Emmy Awards: A Pictorial History.* New York: Crown, 1970.

O'Neil, Thomas. *The Emmys: Star Wars, Showdowns, and the Supreme Test of TV's Best.* New York: Penguin, 1992.

See also National Academy of Television Arts and Sciences

ACTION ADVENTURE SHOWS

In 1961 Newton Minow, the newly-appointed chief of the United States Federal Communications Commission, told a stunned audience of broadcasters that television had become "a vast wasteland." He asked them to watch their own television stations where they would find "a procession of game shows, violence, audience participation shows, formula comedies about totally unbelievable families, blood and thunder, mayhem, violence, sadism, murder, western badmen, western good men, private eyes, gangsters, more violence, and cartoons." Outside of his complaints about quizzes and comedies, much of Minow's anger was directed against the sudden dominance of a new style of drama called action-adventure in the primetime offerings of all three networks.

Action-adventure is a style and a quantity that has characterized shows drawn from the genres of crime stories (both police and detective), westerns and science fiction, spy thrillers, war drama, and simple adventure. The style offers viewers a spectacle: lots of jolts, conflict, movement, jeopardy, and thrill. Its importance has waxed and waned over the years, in part because it has been the target of severe public criticisms about the "pornography of violence" on American television. John Fiske has borrowed the terms

"carnival" and "carnivalesque" from the cultural critic Mikhail Bakhtin to highlight the physical excesses, the emphasis on the body, the grotesqueries and the immoralities, the offensiveness which characterize examples of action-adventure. A show that boasts a great deal of action-adventure is less thoughtful and less complicated than its compatriots: the quantity of action-adventure, for example, was usually low in such hits as the later *Gunsmoke* (1960s) or *The Rockford Files* (1970s). It is the lack of "action" (the moving body) and the significance of "thinking" (the reasoning mind) that sets apart *Columbo* (1971–), the story of a brilliant police lieutenant, from other crime dramas, indeed which makes it more of a mystery. Action-adventure can be traced back to crime shows (notably *Dragnet*) and kids westerns (*The Lone Ranger*) on television in the early 1950s, to film noir and the cowboy movies, and to all sorts of pulp fiction. But its growth in American television, the growth to which Minow seemed to be responding, was a response to the needs of ABC. This third-ranked network sought to improve its finances and stature by scheduling telefilms with more punch than previous efforts. An alliance with Warner Brothers brought to television such adult westerns as *Cheyenne* (1955–63) and *Maverick* (1957–62) as well as glamorous detective programs like *77 Sunset Strip* (1958–64) and *Hawaiian Eye* (1959–63). The most violent of the shows, *The Untouchables* (1959–63), came from Desilu where the initial work was supervised by Quinn Martin, who would later produce *The Fugitive, The FBI,* and *The Streets of San Francisco,* though none so full of gun play. *The Untouchables,* a police drama about Eliot Ness, the Capone gang, and Chicago in the Prohibition Years, was stuffed with bullets, blood, and death, a style which won the attention of younger viewers and provoked much criticism, even in Congress.

ABC's rivals responded with their own brand of mayhem: in the 1958–59 and 1959–60 Nielsen rankings, the three top programs were all westerns (CBS' *Gunsmoke,* NBC's *Wagon Train,* and CBS' *Have Gun, Will Travel*) and thirteen of the top twenty-five programs were westerns or detective dramas. Such a glut led to burnout, and the wave of westerns receded, eventually disappearing from TV in the next decade. Even so the networks did experiment with new kinds of action-adventure: war dramas (notably ABC's *Combat*), the cult hit *Star Trek* (1966–69), and spy stories like *I Spy.*

Never again would action-adventure dominate the schedule as it had in the years around 1960. But the popularity of action-adventure did revive, especially in the early 1970s when crime shows became all the rage. The Nielsen rankings of 1974–75 had nine in the top twenty-five, although only CBS' *Hawaii Five-O* was in the top ten. Some of the most graphic violence appeared on this series (1968–80) in which a stern Steve McGarrett led a highly competent team of detectives against local crime and international intrigue. Paramount TV produced for CBS what was considered the most violent detective show, *Mannix* (1967–75), about a private eye who loved to brawl. The true exemplar of this kind of excess, though, was ABC's briefly popular *S.W.A.T.* (1975–76), produced by Aaron Spelling and Leonard Goldberg, which brought heavy weapons to bear on the problem of urban crime. ABC eventually ordered the quantity of violence reduced on another, more successful Spelling-Goldberg creation, *Starsky and Hutch* (1975–79) which featured two buddies who tackled crime with zest and wit, California-style. All of which provoked a new public outcry plus demands that the networks both reduce violence and banish what was left to the hours after 9:00 P.M. Nearly all of the violent crime-fighters had left the air by 1980.

Producers had turned from the excess of violence to seek other ways of stimulating the audience. First off the mark was Universal TV: it created ABC's *The Six Million Dollar Man* (1974–78), about the cyborg, Colonel Steve Austin, who could perform incredible feats of strength and speed. Realism gave way to fantasy here. Its success spawned imitators like *The Bionic Woman, Wonder Woman, Spiderman,* and *The Incredible Hulk,* all of which downplayed violence for displays of muscles and gimmicks. (In its defense *The Incredible Hulk* was also reminiscent of *The Fugitive,* complete with the anthology-like approach to emotional, psychological, and social problems.) Stephen Cannell, a veteran of action-adventure who had been involved in *Adam 12,*

Baretta, and *The Rockford Files,* finally spoofed the superhero genre with *The Greatest American Hero* (1981–83) for ABC. Special effects were even more central to the expensive science-fiction thriller, *Battlestar Galactica* (1978–80) which followed the travails of a huge space fortress and its fleet of beaten-up spacecraft as they struggled toward Earth under constant attack from the Cylons. It was not only reminiscent of the movie *Star Wars* but of many a western as well (read Indians for Cylons), except that the warfare was somehow sterile and bloodless.

Spelling-Goldberg substituted sexual titillation, and blatant sexism, to make *Charlie's Angels* (1976–81) a smash hit for ABC. The "Angels" were three very attractive female detectives, ordered on missions by an unseen male; they rushed around, often in peril, sometimes in abbreviated clothing, all to please the voyeur. The show was a sudden, raging hit that propelled one angel, Farrah Fawcett-Majors, to celebrity status. In 1980 an otherwise ordinary private-eye show, *Magnum, P.I.,* turned the tables by starring a male "hunk," Tom Selleck.

In CBS' *The Dukes of Hazzard* (1979–85), a Warner Brothers product, realism lost out to comedy: two fun-loving cousins sped all over Hazzard County in their Dodge Charger, outwitting the sheriff, doing good, but above all winning chases and surviving crashes. A few years later, Cannell produced *The A-Team* (1983–87) for NBC which registered in the top ten Nielsens three years in a row. The story of four unjustly persecuted Vietnam veterans featured lots of firepower, scenes of massive destruction, but very little blood or death. Its African-American star, the physically impressive Mr. T., who played B.A. Baracus, became a youth hero. But the show itself was almost as much a parody as had been *The Greatest American Hero,* except now the target was this whole style of action-adventure.

The 1980s saw a revival of crime drama. Cannell himself created *Hunter* (1984–91) for NBC, a police drama about a rebellious and tough cop, reminiscent of Clint Eastwood's "Dirty Harry" role in the movies. Barbara Corday and Barbara Avedon shaped the first successful female "buddy" show, CBS' *Cagney and Lacey* (1982–88), about two female cops fighting crime and managing life in the big city. That show was saved by its fans in 1983 who wrote in protesting its cancellation. But aside from the novelty of using women as the stars, the show added little to the style of action-adventure. Much the same could be said of ABC's imaginative version of the detective drama, *Moonlighting* (1985–89), in which action-adventure usually played second-fiddle to romance, comedy, or even fantasy. Still it launched the career of Bruce Willis who would become one of the great stars of action-adventure in the movies. More novel was the police documentary *COPS* that FOX began to air in 1989: the camera followed real police as they tracked down ordinary criminals, offering viewers a spectacle of sleaze and decay in the unsavory parts of America.

There were two experiments with the drama of crime on NBC during the 1980s. The most interesting was Mi-

Tarzan

Wonder Woman

MacGyver

Sea Hunt

chael Mann's product, *Miami Vice* (1984–89). In part it represented a return to convention: a buddy show with two policemen, albeit one white and the other black, plus lots of speed and doses of violence. Indeed the taste for glamour even evoked the memory of *77 Sunset Strip*. But Mann, another veteran of action-adventure (he had written for *Starsky and Hutch* as well as the anthology *Police Story* in the 1970s), made *Vice* unusual by appropriating the look and feel of MTV's videos. He gave the show special colors, "an impressionist way of working with vibrating pastels" (see Winship), dressed his stars in hip clothes, presented them in both glamorous and tawdry surroundings, and featured rock music backgrounds. In short *Miami Vice* offered viewers an extravaganza of sights and sounds. Such effort cost money, up to $1.5 million per episode, which made *Vice* one of the most expensive series of the period. Although a cult favorite, it only broke into the top twenty-five Nielsens once, in 1985-86. Perhaps that is why *Vice* had no real successors.

This was not true of the other experiment, MTM Enterprises' *Hill Street Blues* (1981–87), although that program challenged the conventions of action-adventure. The two creators, Steven Bochco and Michael Kozoll, drew upon the techniques of both comedy and soap opera to fashion a different kind of police story, a serialized version of the everyday life of the men and women in a particular precinct. The result won much critical acclaim, not the least because *Hill Street* boasted excellent scripts and well-drawn characters. The transformed police drama proved a model for some hits of the mid-1990s such as NBC's *Homicide* and ABC's *NYPD Blue*, another Bochco product. This last program became notorious for its use of both nudity and violence, sufficient to spark protests from the religious right—even before it aired. Still, the most imaginative addition to the list of action-adventure shows lately has been a hybrid of the horror and the police drama offered by FOX, *The X-Files* (1993–). The occult had rarely won much of an audience on mainstream TV, even though movies had demonstrated its potential as an audience grabber many times over. But the inquiring male-female duo, the motif of a hidden government conspiracy, and the focus on visible evil seemed to give *The X-Files* a special appeal to the so-called "Generation X," viewers in their late teens and their twenties.

If comedy surpassed the appeal of action-adventure after the late sixties, that style nonetheless remained a staple of American television, popular abroad as well as at home. The action telefilms pioneered the expansion of American programming overseas in the late 1950s and early 1960s. Producers in other countries developed their own varieties, of course. English Canadians fashioned some mild versions for children, notably *The Littlest Hobo* (akin to *Lassie*) and *Beachcombers*, both of which have been seen around the world. According to Tom O'Regan, the success of *The Untouchables* on Australian TV inspired the creation of the local hit *Homicide* that launched homegrown drama in the 1960s. Francis Wheen has explained that Japanese television

at the end of the 1970s replaced Hollywood police stories with samurai dramas, both historical and modern, which were full of murder, revenge, and executions. Over the years the British have designed a modest collection of action shows, such as the three spy thrillers fashioned for Patrick McGoohan in the 1960s, *Danger Man, Secret Agent,* and *The Prisoner,* as well as such police dramas as the grim *Z Cars* or *The Sweeney*. Still, in the end, the masters of action-adventure, on television and in the movies, have remained the Hollywood community of writers and producers.

Action-adventure shows have never represented what critics consider the best in television drama. Epithets such as "mindless," "unrealistic," "demeaning," "intolerant," or "immoral" have often been thrown at this brand of entertainment. These shows have been the source of much of the violence, sometimes sex as well, which has distressed a large number of viewers. Action-adventure cannot claim the same sort of defenders who have lauded soap operas and sitcoms as sources of worthwhile entertainment. Perhaps that is because these shows are obviously escapist, their moral tales trite, so lacking in the redeeming qualities of tolerance or female empowerment or studied ambiguity which appeal to critics. When a police drama has won praise, as in the case *Hill Street Blues*, it was despite of any lingering evidence of a taste for action.

Even so, action-adventure fulfills a special cultural role in North America. The significance of the style lies in the way it deals with the properties and the problems of masculinity. Action-adventure has brought men to their television sets more often than any other form of programming, excepting sport. It amounts to a special stage where they can see their fears and hopes embodied. Overwhelmingly, the stars of action adventure drama have been male, and until very recently the few female stars have remained exotics, or objects, (consider Angie Dickinson's role in *Police Woman*, 1974–78) in this masculine world. Viewers have been offered a range of masculine types: leaders (McGarrett), the he-man (Baracus), the sex symbol (Crockett, *Miami Vice*), the loner (Paladin, *Have Gun, Will Travel*), the rebel (Mannix), the anxious male (Mulder, *The X-Files*), and on and on. Whatever the role, these characters find satisfaction through acts of command and aggression. Typically action-adventure offers a resolution, achieves a closure, in which the male star triumphs over his environment and his enemies. The heroes exercise power over villains, bureaucracy, machines, even friends and helpers, and normally they relish that exercise. In the end the power manifests itself through the expression of the body rather than the mind, a body freed of personal, social, and sometimes, in the superhero mode, of natural restraints. Strike first, think later—that would be a good motto for action-adventure.

This is why the appeal of action-adventure is rooted in excess, particularly visual excess whether fights and killings, explosions and crashes, chases, horrifying images, or awesome displays. Perhaps that is a demonstration of the continuing authority of masculinity in a North America where the gendered definitions of maleness have come under increasing scrutiny and criticism. More important it constitutes a continuing source of pleasure to viewers of both sexes and all ages who share a taste for the traditions of heterosexual masculinity and its generalized form, the Macho.

—Paul Rutherford

FURTHER READING

Alley, Robert. "Television Drama." In, Horace Newcomb, editor. *Television: The Critical View.* New York: Oxford, 1976; second edition, 1979.

Bakhtin, Mikhail. *Rabelais and His World.* Cambridge, Massachusetts: MIT, 1968.

Barnouw, Erik. *Tube of Plenty: The Evolution of American Television.* New York: Oxford, 1975.

Brooks, Tim, and Earle Marsh. *The Complete Directory to Prime Time Network Shows 1946–Present.* New York: Ballentine, 1979; fifth edition, 1995.

Castleman, Harry, and Walter J. Podrazik. *Watching TV: Four Decades of American Television.* New York: McGraw-Hill, 1982.

Fiske, John. *Television Culture.* London: Methuen, 1987.

Giles, Dennis. "A Structural Analysis of the Police Story." In, Kaminsky, Stuart M., with Jeffrey H. Mahan. *American Television Genres.* Chicago: Nelson-Hall, 1985.

Gitlin, Todd. *Inside Prime Time.* New York: Pantheon Books, 1985.

———. "Car Commercials and Miami Vice: 'We Build Excitement.'" In, Gitlin, Todd, editor. *Watching Television.* New York: Pantheon Books, 1986.

Marc, David. *Demographic Vistas: Television in American Culture.* Philadelphia: University of Pennsylvania Press, 1984.

Miller, Mary Jane. *Turn Up The Contrast: CBC Television Drama Since 1952.* Vancouver: University of British Columbia Press/CBC Enterprises, 1987.

O'Regan, Tom. *Australian Television Culture.* St. Leonards: Allen and Unwin, 1993.

Rose, Brian G., editor. *TV Genres: A Handbook and Reference Guide.* Westport, Connecticut: Greenwood, 1985.

Sparks, Richard. *Television and the Drama of Crime: Moral Tales and the Place of Crime in Public Life.* Buckingham, England: Open University Press, 1992.

Wheen, Francis. *Television: A History.* London: Century Publishing, 1985.

Winship, Michael. *Television.* New York: Random House, 1988.

See also Detective Programs; Police Programs; Westerns

ACTION FOR CHILDREN'S TELEVISION

U.S. Citizens' Activist Group

A "grass-roots" activist group, Action for Children's Television (A.C.T.) was founded by Peggy Charren and a group of "housewives and mothers" in her home in Newton, Massachusetts in 1968. The members of A.C.T. were initially concerned with the lack of quality television programming offered to children. In 1970 A.C.T. petitioned the Federal Communications Commission (FCC) asking that television stations be required to provide more programming for the child viewer. In that year the organization also received its first funding from the John and Mary R. Markle Foundation. A.C.T. later received funding from the Ford and Carnegie foundations as well, grants which allowed the group to expand from volunteers to between 12 and 15 staff members at the height of its activity.

A.C.T. was not generally viewed as a "radical right-wing group" advocating censorship. According to Charren, "too many people who worry about children's media want to do it in. A.C.T. was violently opposed to censorship." Partially due to this attitude, the group was able to gain support from members of the public and from many politicians.

A.C.T. also became concerned with issues of advertising within children's programming. Of particular concern was their finding that one-third of all commercials aimed at

Peggy Charren
Photo courtesy of Peggy Charren

children were for vitamins. Partially due to their efforts, the FCC enacted rules pertaining to program length commercials, host selling, and the placement of separation devices between commercials and children's programming.

A.C.T. was responsible for many cases brought before the courts in regard to the FCC and its policies concerning children's television. These cases include a major case in media law, Action for Children's Television, et al. v. Federal Communications Commission and the United States of America (821. F. 2d 741. D.C. Cir. 1987).

One of the major successes of A.C.T. was the passage of the Children's Television Act of 1990. Shortly after the passage of this act, Charren announced the closing of Action for Children's Television, suggesting that it was now up to individual citizens' groups to police the airwaves. In recent years Charren, a strong supporter of the First Amendment, has fought against FCC regulations limiting "safe harbor" hours.

—William Richter

FURTHER READING

Alperowicz, C., and R. Krock. *Rocking the Boat: Celebrating 15 Years of Action for Children's Television.* Newtonville, Massachusetts: Action for Children's Television, 1983.

Cole, B. G., and M. Oettinger. *Reluctant Regulators: The FCC and the Broadcast Audience.* Reading, Massachusetts: Addison-Wesley, 1978.

Duncan, Roger Dean. "Rhetoric of the Kidvid Movement: Ideology, Strategies, and Tactics." *Central States Speech Journal* (West Lafayette, Indiana), Summer 1976.

See also Activist Television; Children and Television

ACTIVIST TELEVISION

Artists and activists outlined their plan to decentralize television so that the medium could be made by as well as for the people, in the pages of *Radical Software* and in the alternative movement's 1971 manifesto, *Guerrilla Television*, written by Michael Shamberg and Raindance Corporation. These "alternative media guerrillas" were determined to use video to create an alternative to what they deemed the aesthetically bankrupt and commercially corrupt broadcast medium.

Earlier in the 1960s, various versions of "the underground"—alternative political movements, cultural revolutionaries, artists—began to search for new ways of reaching their audience. Cable television and the videocassette seemed to offer an answer. The movement was assisted, perhaps inadvertently, by federal rules mandating local origination programming and public access channels for most cable systems. These channels provided a forum for broadcasting community-driven production. The newly developed videocassette allowed independent media producers to create an informal distribution system in which they could "bicycle" their tapes—carrying them by hand or delivering them by mail—to other outlets throughout the country, or even the world.

These new forms of exhibition and distribution were accompanied by the development of a portable consumer-grade taping system. In 1965 the Sony Corporation decided to launch its first major effort at marketing consumer video equipment in the United States. The first machines were quite cumbersome, but in 1968 Sony introduced the first truly portable video rig—the half-inch, reel-to-reel CV Porta-Pak. Prior to this, videotape equipment was cumbersome, stationary, complex, and expensive, even though it had been used commercially since 1956. With the new international standard for half-inch videotape, tapes made with one manufacturer's portable video equipment could be played back on competing manufacturer's equipment. In the hands of media activists these technological innovations were used to realize radical changes in program form and content.

Underground video groups appeared throughout the United States, but New York City served as the hub of the 1960s underground scene. Prominent early groups included the Videofreex, People's Video Theater, Global Village, and Raindance Corporation. Self-described as "an innovative group concerned with the uses of video," Videofreex was the most production-oriented of the video groups and developed a high expertise with television hardware. In 1973 the Videofreex published a user-friendly guide to use, repair and maintain equipment entitled *The Spaghetti City Video Manual.* The People's Video Theater made significant breakthroughs in community media; members used live and taped

Paper Tiger Television
Photo courtesy of Paper Tiger

Paper Tiger Television
Photo courtesy of Paper Tiger

Paper Tiger Television
Photo courtesy of Paper Tiger

feedback of embattled community groups to create mini-documentaries that "spoke back to the news." The Global Village was perhaps the most commercial of the original groups, and initiated the first closed-circuit video theater to showcase their work. Raindance Corporation functioned as the counter-culture's research and development arm; Shamberg described it as an "analogue to the Rand Corporation—a think tank that would use videotape instead of print." Raindance chronicled the movement by publishing *Radical Software*, underground video's chief information source and networking tool.

Top Value Television (TVTV), one of the earliest *ad hoc* group of video makers, assembled in 1972 to cover political conventions for cable TV. Equipped with porta-paks, TVTV produced hour-long documentary tapes of the Democratic and Republican national conventions, providing national viewers with an alternative vision of the American political process and the media that cover it. *Four More Years* (1972), a tape covering the Republican National Convention, was produced with a crew of 19, and featured footage of delegate caucuses, Young Republican rallies, cocktail parties, antiwar demonstrations, and interviews with the press from the convention floor. TVTV's success with its first two documentaries for cable television attracted the interest of public television and it became the first group commissioned to produce work for national broadcast on public TV. In 1974, shortly after TVTV introduced national audiences to guerrilla TV, the first all-color portable video documentary was produced by the Downtown Community Television Center (DCTV) and aired on PBS.

In 1981, the Paper Tiger Television Collective formed—a changing group of people that came together to produce cable programming for the public access channel in New York City. Drawing upon the traditions of radical video, Paper Tiger Television invented its own home-grown studio aesthetic using rather modest resources to make rev-

olutionary television. Many of Paper Tiger's half-hour programs are live studio "events," faintly reminiscent of 1960s video "happenings." The show's hosts are articulate critics of mainstream American media who examine the corporate ownership, hidden agendas, and information biases of the communications industry via the media in all forms.

In 1986, Paper Tiger organized Deep Dish TV, the country's first alternative satellite network, to distribute its public access series to participating cable systems and public television stations around the country. The successful syndication of this anthology of community-made programs on issues such as labor, housing, the farming crisis, and racism promised a new era for alternative documentary production.

With a similar agenda, the 90's Channel first began "shattering the limits of conventional TV" in 1989 as a PBS television show, and has since established an "independent cable network" carrying blocks of activist programming on leased access over a number of cable systems owned by Telecommunications, Inc. (TCI), while also bicycling its programs to public access channels and universities around the country. The 90's Channel programming (now known as Free Speech TV) is a compilation of activist, community-based and experimental media produced by independent film and video makers.

Activist media are oriented towards action, not contemplation—towards the present, not tradition. Politically integrated opposition against mainstream broadcast television by marginalized groups has considered the form, content, and regulatory structures of the medium. As a mode of activism, television may be used as a occasion for media analysis and intervention, as a pathway for the exchange of information, as well as a vehicle for securing representation for those groups otherwise marginalized from the media. The ultimate goal of committed alternative video groups, however, is to secure universal access to the tools of production and the channels for distribution and exhibition. For these reasons, community-based programming has not simply followed the lead of network television, but rather served as a forum for envisioning the future of the medium.

—Eric Freedman

FURTHER READING

Fabaer, Mindy, editor. *A Tool, a Weapon, a Witness: The New Video News Crews.* Chicago: Randolph Street Gallery, 1990.

Goldberg, Kim. *The Barefoot Channel.* Vancouver: North Star, 1990.

Hall, Doug, and Sally Jo Fifer, editors. *Illuminating Video: An Essential Guide to Video Art.* New York: Aperture Foundation, 1990.

Kahn, Douglas, and Diane Neumaier, editors. *Cultures in Contention.* Seattle: Real Comet Press, 1985.

Roar! The Paper Tiger Television Guide to Media Activism. New York: The Paper Tiger Television Collective, 1991.

Shamberg, Michael, and Raindance Corporation. *Guerrilla Television.* New York: Holt, Rinehart and Winston, 1971.

Videofreex. *The Spaghetti City Video Manual: A Guide to Use, Repair and Maintenance.* New York: Praeger, 1973.

ADAPTATIONS

Adaptations have become a mainstay of commercial television, and have been since programming began in the 1940s. All manner of pre-existing, written properties have been turned into adapted teleplays—short stories, novels, plays, poems, even comic books have been altered for presentation on television. They appear in formats ranging from half-hour shows, as in some episodes of *The Twilight Zone*, to 30-hour epic miniseries, as in 1988's *War and Remembrance*.

Adaptations are attractive to producers for a variety of reasons. In many cases, audiences for such fare are "presold," having purchased or read the original text, or having heard of the work through word-of-mouth. Sources for adapted works may come from public domain materials drawn from classical literary sources, or, more frequently from hotly-pursued novels from best-selling writers. Authors like Judith Krantz, John Jakes, Alex Haley, and Stephen King have solid book sales and loyal audiences; adaptations of their works generate good ratings and audience share. Synergy between book publishers and networks may also be a factor in the purchasing or optioning of works for adaptation—a successful miniseries can prolong the life of a book currently in print, and may resurrect older books which are out-of-print or no longer readily available in the mass market. When *War and Remembrance* was adapted in 1988, not only were its sales improved, but an unexpected million copies of the first book in the series, *The Winds of War*, were ordered.

Another reason for television's reliance on adaptations, especially in the form of miniseries, is the lack of good scripts, along with television's voracious need for sponsor-attractive, time-slot filling product. Few miniseries are produced from wholly original concepts; experts estimate that 75 to 90% of all miniseries use novels for source material. Novels have overcome basic, yet essential dilemmas in constructing narratives: they have well-defined characters, interwoven subplots filled with ideas and events which can be rearranged, highlighted, or deleted by scriptwriters, and enough story for at least two hours of product. A producer holding something complete and tangible, in the form of a pre-written story, can feel more confident when searching for financing; in turn, sponsors and networks are more likely to commit money and resources to a finished property, even one that is not yet a bestseller. Consequently, producers option many books which are never produced, in the belief that some of these unknown and untried works may become popular.

What producers see as a "sure thing," however, professional screenwriters often view as a challenge. Adaptation is far more than slavishly reproducing a previously constructed story in a different format—the requirements of the two forms are significantly different. From the perspective of screenwriters, novels take characters and subplots and let them career willy-nilly into unstructured chaos. Screenwriters rearrange and augment material to stress the visual and storytelling requirements of the television medium. They purge the script of unnecessary characters, or combine the traits and experiences of several characters into one. They try to structure the script so it moves from crisis to crisis, keeping in mind the constraints imposed by the presence of commercial breaks. They find opportunities to make the internal world of thoughts and feelings more external, through dialogue and action. The process of adaptation requires a level of creativity which may be equal to that expended in the writing of the source material, as writers hone and pare and expand and modify concepts from one medium to the other.

Because novels frequently include dozens of characters interacting over vast periods of time, screenwriters often find the miniseries format essential in marshaling the scope and flavor of the original text. PBS, considered the "godfather" of the miniseries, introduced America to the concept of long-form sagas with its imports of British productions and presented the aegis of *Masterpiece Theatre, Mystery,* and *Great Performances.* The audience for upscale adaptations of *The Forsyte Saga, Brideshead Revisited,* and *The First Churchills* was small, but the form was successful enough to encourage the adaptation of more popular, less highbrow novels such as Irwin Shaw's *Rich Man, Poor Man* (ABC, televised 1976-1977). It was the phenomenal success of Alex Haley's *Roots,* a 12-hour adaptation broadcast over eight consecutive evenings in 1977, however, which cemented this

Little Lord Fauntleroy
Photo courtesy of Rosemont Productions, Ltd.

form of adaptation and established it as a staple of television production.

Most genres of television have had their adaptations: children's programming (Showtime's 1982–1987 *Faerie Tale Theater*, NBC's 1996 *Gulliver's Travels*); the western (CBS' 1989 *Lonesome Dove*); historical romance (NBC's 1980 *Shogun*; ABC's 1985–86 *North and South*); science fiction (episodes of CBS' 1959–1964 *The Twilight Zone*) are a few of the seemingly endless number of outstanding adaptations produced for television. The adaptation continues to be popular, lucrative, and entertaining; as long as the form holds an audience, this narrative form will remain an essential element in broadcasting.

—Kathryn C. D'Alessandro

FURTHER READING

Brady, Ben. *Principles of Adaptation for Film and Television.* Austin: University of Texas Press.

Bulman, J.C., and H.R. Coursen, editors. *Shakespeare on Television: An Anthology of Essays and Reviews.* Hanover, New Hampshire: University Press of New England, 1988.

Davies, Anthony, and Stanley Wells, editors. *Shakespeare and the Moving Image: The Plays on Film and Television.* Cambridge: Cambridge University Press.

Edgar, David. *Ah! Mischief: The Writer and Television.* London: Faber and Faber, 1982.

Giddings, Robert, Keith Selby, and Chris Wensley. *Screening the Novel: The Theory and Practice of Literary Dramatization.* New York: St. Martin's, 1990.

Leonard, William T. *Theatre: Stage to Screen to Television.* Metuchen, New Jersey: Scarecrow, 1981.

Marill, Alvin H. *More Theatre: Stage to Screen to Television.* Metuchen, New Jersey: Scarecrow, 1993.

Willis, Susan. *The BBC Shakespeare Plays: Making the Televised Canon.* Chapel Hill: University of North Carolina Press, 1991.

See also *Brideshead Revisited; Forsyte Saga; I, Claudius; Jewel in the Crown; Miss Marple; Poldark; Rich Man, Poor Man; Road to Avonlea; Roots; Rumpole of the Bailey; Sherlock Holmes; Thorn Birds; Tinker, Tailor, Soldier, Spy; Women of Brewster Place*

ADVANCED TELEVISION SYSTEMS COMMITTEE

The Advanced Television Systems Committee (ATSC) was formed in 1982 by representatives of the Joint Committee on Inter-Society Coordination (JCIC). The purpose of the ATSC is to facilitate and develop voluntary technical standards for an advanced television system to replace the aging American NTSC television standard. The ATSC is also charged with making recommendations to the Unites States Department of State to assist the U.S. in developing positions on various standards issues that are raised in front of the International Radio Consultative Committee (CCIR). Advanced Television Systems Committee membership consists of 53 organizations including representatives from the National Association of Broadcasters, the National Cable Television Association, the Institute of Electrical and Electronics Engineers, the Electronic Industries Association and the Society of Motion Picture and Television Engineers.

The ATSC is involved in various efforts to improve the quality of the television picture and audio signal. In 1993, the Advanced Television Systems Committee recommended adoption of a ghost-canceling reference signal which is expected to dramatically improve the quality of television reception suffering from multipath interference in large metropolitan areas. ATSC has been actively involved in advocating adoption of a unified production and transmission standard for high definition television (HDTV). In 1981, Japan's NHK broadcasting organization demonstrated a working HDTV system called MUSE, which produced startling clear, rich color images of exceptional resolution. The MUSE system utilized analog technology that was incompatible with the American NTSC color television standard. The MUSE system also required substantially larger spectrum allocations than current NTSC signals. The ATSC accepted the recommendations of the Society of Motion Picture and Television Engineers (SMPTE) by calling for the American and world-wide acceptance of Japan's 1,125/60 standard for high definition television production. In 1986, the CCIR refused to accept the standard, claiming that adoption would be detrimental to the interest of many of its members and participants. Renewed recommendations by the ATSC in 1988 for adoption of the 1,125/60 Japanese standard met with opposition from U.S. network broadcasts because the system requirements were not easily convertible for NTSC usage.

In 1987, the Federal Communications Commission (FCC) invited proponents of HDTV to propose a system that would provide terrestrial high definition television to the United States. By 1990, several American entrants proposed all digital transmission systems that proved preferable to the analog MUSE system. Perhaps the biggest advantage

Courtesy of ATSC

of these digital systems was the potential for scaling HDTV signals into a 6 MHz bandwidth allowing transmission by terrestrial broadcasters. Later various proponents of digital systems merged their proposals into a compromise hybrid digital system. The ATSC reevaluated its recommendation and is now working with various FCC committees, including the Advisory Committee on Advanced Television Services, to promote an all digital television standard.

—Fritz J. Messere

FURTHER READING

"HDTV Production: The Future is Almost Now." *Broadcasting* Washington, D.C: Broadcast Publications, 17 October 1988.

Head, Sidney W., Christopher H. Sterling, and Lemuel B. Schofield. *Broadcasting in America, 7th edition.* Boston: Houghton Mifflin, 1994.

"High Definition in High Gear in '88." *Broadcasting* (Washington, D.C.), 4 January 1988.

Rice, John F., editor. *HDTV.* New York: Union Square Press, 1990.

Rosenthal, Edmond. "Broadcasters Find it Easy to Get Rid of Their Ghosts." *Electronic Media* (Chicago), 5 April 1993.

Schreiber, William F. "HDTV Technology: Advanced Television Systems and Public Policy Options." *Telecommunications* (Norwood, Massachusett), November 1987.

"Step by Step to HDTV Standard." *Broadcasting* (Washington, D.C.), 1 February 1988.

"Tres Grand Alliance: World Standard?" *Broadcasting and Cable* (Washington, D.C.), 21 June 1993.

U. S. House of Representatives, Committee on Energy and Commerce, *Public Policy Implications of Advanced Television Systems.* 101 Congress, First Session. Washington, D.C.: U.S. Government Printing Office.

See also High-Definition Television; Standards and Practices

THE ADVENTURES OF OZZIE AND HARRIET

U.S. Domestic Comedy

The Adventures of Ozzie and Harriet was one of the most enduring family-based situation comedies in American television. Ozzie and Harriet Nelson and their sons David and Ricky (ages 16 and 13 respectively at the time of the program's debut) portrayed fictional versions of themselves on the program. The Nelsons embodied wholesome, "normal" American existence so conscientiously (if blandly) that their name epitomized upright, happy family life for decades.

Ozzie and Harriet started out on radio, a medium to which bandleader Ozzie Nelson and his singer/actress wife Harriet Hilliard had gravitated in the late 1930s, hoping to spend more time together than their conflicting careers would permit. In 1941 they found a permanent spot providing music for Red Skelton's program, a position that foundered when Skelton was drafted in 1944. In that year, the energetic Ozzie Nelson proposed a show of his own to network CBS and sponsor International Silver—a show in which the Nelsons would play themselves. Early in its run, the radio Adventures of Ozzie and Harriet jettisoned music for situation comedy. Ozzie Nelson himself directed and co-wrote all the episodes, as he would most of the video shows.

The Nelsons signed a long-term contract with ABC in 1949 that gave that network the option to move their program to television. The struggling network needed proven talent that was not about to defect to the more established—and wealthier—CBS or NBC.

The television program premiered in 1952. Like its radio predecessor, it focused on the Nelson family at home, chronicling the growing pains of the boys and their parents and dealing with mundane issues like hobbies, rivalries, schoolwork, club membership, and girlfriends. Eventually the on-screen David and Ricky (although never the off-screen David and Ricky) graduated from college and became lawyers. When the real David and Rick got married, to June Blair and Kristin Harmon respectively, their wives joined the cast of Ozzie and Harriet on television as well as in real life.

Ozzie and Harriet lasted 14 years on American television, remaining on the air until 1966. Although never in the top ten of rated programs, it did well throughout its run, appealing to the family viewing base targeted by ABC. The program picked up additional fans in April 1957, when Rick sang Fats Domino's "I'm Walkin'" on an episode titled "Ricky the Drummer."

As soon as the Nelsons realized how popular their singing son was going to be, the televisual Rick was given every opportunity to croon over the airwaves by his father/director/manager. Sometimes his songs fitted into the narrative of an episode. Sometimes they were just tacked onto the end— early music videos of Rick Nelson in performance.

Despite this emphasis on Rick's vocal performances, and despite the legion of young fans the program picked up because of its teenage emphasis, the character of Ozzie dominated the program. The genial, bumbling Ozzie was the narrative linchpin of Ozzie and Harriet, attempting to steer his young sons into the proper paths (usually rather ineffectually) and attempting to assert his ego in a household in which he was often ill at ease.

That ego, and that household, were held together by wise homemaker Harriet. Although she may have seemed something of a cipher to many viewers, clad in the elegant dresses that defined the housewife on 1950s television, Harriet represented the voice of reason on Ozzie and Harriet, rescuing Ozzie—and occasionally David and Rick—from the consequences of over-impulsive behavior.

Ironically, in view of the weakness of paterfamilias Ozzie's character, the program was viewed, during its lengthy run as now, as an idealized portrait of the American nuclear family of the postwar years. The Nelsons eventually shifted their program into color and into the 1960s. Nevertheless, in spirit, and in the popular imagination, they remained black-and-white denizens of the 1950s.

—Tinky "Dakota" Weisblat

CAST

Ozzie Nelson . . . . Himself
Harriet Nelson . . . . Herself
David Nelson . . . . Himself
Eric Ricky Nelson . . . . Himself
Thorny Thornberry (1952–59) . . . . Don DeFore

Adventures of Ozzie and Harriet

Darby (1955–61) . . . . Parley Baer
Joe Randolph (1956–66) . . . . Lyle Talbot
Clara Randolph (1956–66) . . . . . . Mary Jane Croft
Doc Williams (1954–65) . . . . Frank Cady
Wally (1957–66) . . . . Skip Jones
Butch Barton (1958–60) . . . . Gordon Jones
June (Mrs. David) Nelson (1961–66) . . . . . . June Blair
Kris (Mrs. Rick) Nelson (1964–66) . . . Kristin Harmon
Fred (1958–64) . . . . James Stacy
Mr. Kelley (1960–62) . . . . Joe Flynn
Connie Edwards (1960–66) . . . . . Constance Harper
Jack (1961–66) . . . . Jack Wagner
Ginger (1962–65) . . . . Charlene Salerno
Dean Hopkins (1964–66) . . . . Ivan Bonar
Greg (1965–66) . . . . Greg Dawson
Sean (1965–66) . . . . Sean Morgan

PRODUCERS   Ozzie Nelson, Robert Angus, Bill Lewis, Leo Penn

PROGRAMMING HISTORY   435 Episodes
• ABC

October 1952–June 1956	Friday 8:00-8:30
October 1956–September 1958	Wednesday 9:00-9:30
September 1958–September 1961	Wednesday 8:30-9:00
September 1961–September 1963	Thursday 7:30-8:00
September 1963–January 1966	Wednesday 7:30-8:00
January 1966–September 1966	Saturday 7:30-8:00

FURTHER READING

Barringer, Felicity. "Dialogue that Lingers: 'Hi, Mom.' 'Hi, Pop,' 'Hi, David,' 'Hi, Rick.'" *The New York Times*, 9 October 1994.

Holmes, John R. "The Wizardry of Ozzie: Breaking Character in Early Television." *Journal of Popular Culture* (Bowling Green, Ohio), Fall 1989.

Weisblat, Tinky. "Dakota." *Will the Real George and Gracie and Ozzie and Harriet and Desi and Lucy Please Stand Up?: The Functions of Popular Biography in 1950s Television* (Doctoral dissertation, University of Texas at Austin, 1991).

See also Comedy, Domestic Settings; Nelson, Ozzie and Harriet

ADVERTISING

During ABC's broadcast of Super Bowl XXIX in 1995 advertisers were willing to pay roughly $1 million to secure 30 seconds of airtime. Pepsi-Cola purchased four game slots, three of them a minute long, to launch its "NOTHING ELSE IS A PEPSI" campaign. The $8 million investment was deemed justifiable because Pepsi executives expected the Superbowl to fulfill its projections: to attract the largest television audience of the entire year. The example is merely one indication of advertising's central role in the story of television.

In the beginning the numbers were hardly extraordinary. In 1941, for example, Bulova Watches spent $9 to buy time on the first advertising spot offered by NBC's fledgling New York station. Soon, however, success stories such as the case of Hazel Bishop cosmetics, whose jump into TV produced a sales explosion, convinced advertisers that it was worthile to pay much more to reach the expanding TV audience. Ad revenue fueled the television boom in the United States during the 1950s, and by 1960 TV had become the chief medium of national advertising, earning $1.5 billion as a result. Rating agencies, notably A.C. Nielsen Company, played a crucial role by measuring the audience size and estimating the audience composition of particular shows. Advertising shaped both programming and the schedule to maximize hits, at that time, largely sports and entertainment offerings. Indeed, ad agencies controlled the actual production of many shows, securing writers, technical personnel, and talent, and overseeing scripts and production design. It was not until the quiz scandals at the end of the decade led the networks to take control of their programming that the advertising agencies focused their work primarily on brokering air time and producing commercial spots.

The success of commercial television as a medium linked to the selling of products provoked an outcry. Vance Packard's 1957 exposé, *The Hidden Persuaders*, identified television as one of the chief villains in the effort to manipulate the American consumer. In 1961 the new FCC chair Newton Minow told a stunned audience of broadcast executives that television was "a vast wasteland," funded by a seemingly endless supply of commercials.

Initially few countries followed the American example of supporting their new broadcast media with a commercial, advertiser supported financial base. Britain, Canada, and much of western Europe organized television as public service systems. Program development and production, as well as the technical aspects of broadcasting, were funded in part by taxes. But the expenses of television broadcasting were so high and the private demand for commercial airtime so great that some services accommodated advertising: the Canadian Broadcasting Corporation used ad revenues to finance indigenous programming. Both Japan and Australia launched separate commercial and public services in 1953. A year later ad agencies, now fully international in scope and influence (notably the American-based J. Walter Thompson agency) played a part in convincing the British government to end the BBC monopoly and allow a new channel, a commercial service to be placed on the air.

Kellogg's Tony the Tiger
Photos courtesy of Leo Burnett

Kellogg's Tony the Tiger
Photos courtesy of Leo Burnett

Maytag's Lonely Repairman
Photos courtesy of Leo Burnett

Maytag's Lonely Repairman
Photos courtesy of Leo Burnett

Pillsbury's Jolly Green Giant
Photos courtesy of Leo Burnett

Pillsbury's Jolly Green Giant
Photos courtesy of Leo Burnett

Even so, television commercials, the visible artifacts of advertising in their familiar 30 or 60—and later their 15—second versions, long retained the imprint of their American birth. Canadian advertisers hired American talent in New York. Young and Rubicam, an American agency, created *Ice Mountain* for Gibbs toothpaste, the first British television commercial ever aired (September 1955).

The prevalent strategy of American advertising in the 1950s was the 60-second hard sell: hit the viewer with bits of information, explain how the product was unique, repeat this argument to drive home the message. The earnest enthusiasm might please the advertisers but it disturbed its victims. If American viewers were largely satisfied with their television fare, according to a 1960 survey, they were upset by the frequency, the timing, the loudness, and the style of commercials. Still, few were ready to pay for noncommercial television through their taxes or a license fee on the television receivers that sat in their living rooms.

Television advertising grew more sophisticated and extravagant during the 1960s. The advent of color TV accentuated the visual dimension of advertising. The increasing cost of air time fostered a move toward 30-second commercials which relied on metaphor even more than logic. Just as important was the "Creative Revolution" which swept over Madison Avenue, led by newcomers and new agencies who experimented with the soft sell. Their emblem was the funny and imaginative Volkswagen cam-

paign that was widely credited with making the "Beetle" an American icon. In fact commercials were more important to Marlboro: sales doubled in the late 1960s, reaching 51.4 billion units, launching the brand on a trajectory that would make it the American leader. One by-product of the "revolution" was the appearance of spots which pleased viewers: the bouncy tune and happy images of Coca-Cola's famous *Hilltop* (1971) may not have taught the world to sing, but it led enthusiastic viewers to phone television stations requesting more showings of the ad.

After the mid-1960s, television advertising also became a significant tool of public power. The free public service announcement (PSA) won favor as a way of convincing people to donate moneys, to stop smoking or drinking and driving, to fight drugs.

Political advertising was transformed by *Daisy*, a miniature horror movie which used visuals to link Republican candidate Barry Goldwater to a nuclear holocaust. Shown only once (on CBS, 7 September 1964), the outcry it provoked amply demonstrated how the political spot could be an emotional bomb. By 1988 half of the $92.1 million expended by George Bush and Michael Dukakis went to advertising, mostly on television. Even if these sums were much smaller than Coca-Cola or Procter and Gamble might spend in any given year, political advertising now challenged the news as the chief source of election discourse, evidenced by the attention paid to the "Willie

Horton" attack ads which smeared Dukakis in 1988. By Campaign '94, not only had total ad spending approached $1 billion but negative advertising had exploded in what *Advertising Age* (November 14, 1994) called "the season of sleaze." Meanwhile the partial repeal of the Fairness Doctrine in 1987 had opened the airwaves to advocacy advertising. In 1993 the Health Insurance Association of America managed to catalyze public suspicion of the Clinton Health Initiative with its "Harry and Louise" spots, which eventually contributed to the defeat of health reform.

Americans have remained the masters of political and advocacy advertising. Not so in other realms, however. The inventiveness declined in part because the "Creative Revolution" waned in the 1970s. American advertisers came to favor once more the hard sell. Another reason lay in the victory of private over public television in country after country, thereby creating new channels for advertising. In the Third World, ad revenues were crucial to the expansion of television, though a fear of excessive commercialism justified Indonesia's ban on television ads in 1981. First in Italy (mid-1970s), then in France (mid-1980s), and soon everywhere, the airwaves of western Europe were opened to private television. Following the collapse of the Soviet empire, ads swiftly appeared in eastern Europe and Russia—the Marlboro cowboy, banned from American screens after 1970, could be found riding proudly on Russian television in the summer of 1993. The spread of satellite TV in Europe after 1990 offered even more time for marketing.

The British were the first to break free from American tutelage. There, ad-makers refined the ironic sell—one of the first major successes was the ongoing Heineken "Refreshes" campaign launched in 1974 —-which became a key marketing strategy in Europe and America during the late 1980s. Also in the 1970s, the British government sponsored social ads to shape public behavior, an initiative that was pursued in Canada as well, where the state often proved the largest single advertiser. British ad-makers soon developed the shock-style of social advertising which used brutal images of misery, death, and horror to jolt people out of their complacency. This too became commonplace in the late 1980s and early 1990s, during the global war against AIDS, drugs, drinking and driving, racism, hunger, and other ills.

Worldwide, the best of television commercials had become works of art that reflected the tastes, the fears, and the hopes of their communities. The sums of money spent on making commercials were enormous: it was estimated that the ads for Pepsi-Cola's "New Generation" campaign of the mid-1980s cost about $20,000 a second to produce, far more than regular TV programming. European ad-makers usually eschewed the American passion for the hard sell and comparative advertising. Many ads acquired a kind of national signature: bizarre imagery (France), a humorous emphasis (Britain), gentleness (Canada), sensuality (Brazil and France), exposé (Germany), or beauty (Japan). Run-of-the-mill advertising might still irritate. But in the 1980s television networks offered up collections of old and new ads, movie houses showed the world's best (the Cannes award winners), newspapers and magazines reviewed ads and advertising trends. There was some truth to the claim by Marshall McLuhan—cited once again by *Time* in 1990—that advertising was "the greatest art form of the twentieth century."

It would, of course, be an exaggeration to apply that label to every form of television advertising. Consider the infomercial. American ad-makers pioneered this form during the late 1980s. Typically the infomercial is a sponsored message, 30 minutes long, which masquerades as a regular program, often as a talk or interview show complete with commercial inserts. The form has been used to hype hair restorers, diet plans, memory expanders, real estate techniques, living aids, gym equipment, and so on. The earnest enthusiasm of the infomercial harks back to the ad style of the 1950s, while the element of direct response (the insistence on phoning now to purchase the brand) looks forward to the future of interactive television. The infomercial proved so successful by the mid-1990s that it had spread into Britain and western Europe. In the United States and Canada major national marketers such as Ford or Philips were experimenting with this long-form advertising. It was estimated that infomercials were generating around a billion dollars worth of ad business a year.

That figure nevertheless remains modest by comparison with the scale of conventional television advertising. Altogether, television attracted over $34 billion of the total $150 billion of U.S. advertising volume in 1994, which put the medium roughly on a par with newspapers. Indeed TV beat out all other media in Japan, Germany, Britain, France, Italy, Brazil, and Spain. Only in South Korea and Canada were newspapers ahead, and in Canada that was because advertisers could reach so many customers via American television.

Yet such success was little comfort to an industry worried by the future of pay or subscriber-based television. The record of television advertising as a marketing tool is not spectacular: people avoid, discount, or disdain most commercials they see. The enormous clutter of ads on television has made recent campaigns much less memorable than ten or twenty years ago, or so surveys suggest. In 1994 Edwin Artzt, then chair of Procter and Gamble, the largest single TV advertiser in the United States (spending $1,051.2 million in 1993), frightened listeners at the American Association of Advertising Agencies with his warning that ad-supported television could soon disappear.

Many people would find that welcome, though they would be less impressed with Artzt's proposed remedy, a return to the days of sponsor-controlled programming. The laments of a Packard or a Minow have been echoed by an assortment of critics around the world who have blamed advertising for vulgarizing TV, degrading politics, and emphasizing materialism. Indeed, television advertising is often viewed as the most potent agent of a gospel of consumption. A central tenet of that gospel preaches that satisfaction is for sale. "What advertising has done is to seep out beyond its proper sphere," asserted Mark Crispin Miller in a NBC documentary *Sex, Buys, and Advertising* (aired July 31, 1990), "and to kind of take over the culture."

Ultimately such claims rest upon a presumption of the awesome cultural power of advertising. Advertising has conditioned the character of television programming, sometimes even inspired a program: Coca-Cola's *Mean Joe Greene* (1979) was the model for a later NBC movie. Ad slogans have entered the common language: "Where's the beef?" (Wendy's) found a place in the 1984 presidential campaign. Ad critters, notably Kellogg's Tony the Tiger, have become kids' favorites. Ad stars have become famous: the appearance of Nick Kamen in a Levi's 501 ad in Britain in the mid-1980s made him a symbol of male sensuality.

Such examples demonstrate that commercials are another source of popular culture, a vast collection of meanings and pleasures created by the public to understand and enrich their ordinary experience. The appropriation, creation, and manipulation of these meanings and pleaures by those who assume that they help to sell products continues to be a source of intense cultural and social scrutiny and debate. All the while, the variety of effects of TV advertising on our lives remain contested and unproven.

—Paul Rutherford

FURTHER READING:

Arlen, Michael. *Thirty Seconds.* Markham, Ontario: Penguin, 1981.

Barnouw, Eric. *The Sponsor: Notes on a Modern Potentate.* New York: Oxford, 1978.

Berkman, Dave. "TV Advertising: The Beginnings." *Television Quarterly* (New York), Summer 1990.

Brown, Les. *Television; The Business Behind the Box.* New York: Harcourt, Brace, Jovanovich, 1971.

Clark, Eric. *The Want Makers.* London: Hodder and Stoughton, 1988.

Cook, Guy. *The Discourse of Advertising.* New York: Routledge, 1992.

Davidson, Martin. *The Consumerist Manifesto: Advertising in Postmodern Times.* London: Comedia, 1992.

Diamant, Lincoln. *Television's Classic Commercials: The Golden Years 1948-58.* New York: Hastings House, 1971.

Diamond, Edwin, and Stephen Bates. *The Spot: The Rise of Political Advertising On Television.* Third Edition Cambridge, Massachusetts: MIT Press, 1992.

Dunnett, Peter. *The World Television Industry: An Economic Analysis.* London: Routledge, 1990.

Henry, Brian, editor. *British Television Advertising: The First 30 Years.* London: Century Benham, 1986.

Kurtz, Bruce. *Spots: The Popular Art of American Television Commercials.* New York: Arts Communication, 1977.

Jhally, Sut. *The Codes of Advertising: Fetishism and the Political Economy of Meaning in the Consumer Society.* London: Frances Pinter, 1987.

Mattelart, Armand. *Advertising International: The Privatisation of Public Space.* London: Routledge, 1991.

Miller, Mark Crispin. *Boxed In: The Culture of TV.* Evanston, Illinois: Northwestern University Press, 1988.

Pope, Daniel. *The Making of Modern Advertising.* New York: Basic Books, 1983.

Rutherford, Paul. *The New Icons? The Art of Television Advertising.* Toronto: University of Toronto Press, 1994.

Schudson, Michael. *Advertising, the Uneasy Persuasion: Its Dubious Impact on American Society.* New York: Basic Books, 1984.

Sinclair, John. *Images Incorporated: Advertising as Industry and Ideology.* London: Croom Helm, 1987.

Steiner, Gary. *The People Look at Television: A Study of Audience Attitudes.* New York: Knopf, 1963.

Wilson, H.H. *Pressure Group: The Campaign for Commercial Television.* London: Secker and Warburg, 1961.

See also Advertising, Company Voice; Advertising Agency; Cost-Per-Thousand; Demographics; Magid Associates; Market; Narrowcasting; Pay Cable; Pay Television; Pay-Per-View Cable; Ratings; Share; Sponsor; Zapping

ADVERTISING, COMPANY VOICE

Company voice advertising typically presents its sponsors as good corporate citizens, forward-thinking providers of products, jobs and services, and as active supporters of causes such as environmentalism. Historically a staple of magazines, radio and sponsored motion pictures, company voice advertising helped shape sponsorships of dramatic anthology, spectacular, news and documentary programs. After 1970, the practice helped shape Public Broadcasting Service program underwriting.

Alternately known as "public relations," "institutional" or "advocacy advertising," company voice advertising seeks a favorable political climate for the expansion of its sponsors' commercial activities and interests. One of the earliest campaigns of its kind dating to 1908, for example, promoted the "universal service" of the AT and T Bell System telephone monopoly. By the late 1920s public-minded "progress" had become the highly advertised hallmark of General Electric (GE), General Motors and other center firms. The practice picked up political significance during the New Deal and later during World War II, when all manner of advertising promoted business's patriotic sacrifice and struggle on the production front.

After the war, business leaders remained suspicious of centralized government, confiscatory taxation, politically powerful labor, and what many believed to be the public's outmoded fear of big business. In bringing postwar public and employee relations to television, business invested in programs whose objectives ranged from economic education to outright entertainment. Factory processes and free enterprise rhetoric appeared regularly. The National Association of Manufacturers, for example, launched *Industry on Parade,* a syndicated telefilm series that toured the nation's industrial centers. Initially produced by the NBC News film unit, the series ran from 1951 to 1958. Business and trade groups worked television into training and employee relations. Drexel Institute of Technology's *University of the Air,* for example, took advantage of marginal television time in the Philadelphia area for noon-hour panel discussions of labor-management issues. Designed for in-plant reception by audiences of supervisory trainees and managers, the scenes attracted spouses in the home viewing audience, who, one publicist proudly noted, had become the new fans of industrial human relations.

Entering television for the first time, major corporations predicated their public and employee relations activities upon the experience of entertainment. General Electric and DuPont, both active in economic education, favored the editorial control of dramatic anthology programs. The company voice specialists of the *General Electric Theater* ruled out the sponsorship of panel discussions such as *Meet the Press* and *Youth Wants to Know,* because the format posed the threat of comment inimical to business. DuPont continued its investment in tightly controlled drama with the transfer of radio's *Cavalcade of America* to television in 1952. DuPont specialists justified their television investment with projected declining costs per-thousand, that by 1954 would equal radio's peak year of 1948. Further delineating the audience for company voice messages, specialists anticipated the maturity of a generation with no first hand knowledge of the Depression—or as GE's Chester H. Lang put it, "no adult exposure to the violent anti-business propaganda of the 'depression' years. The opinions the young people form now, as they grow up," Lang explained, "will determine the climate in which we will operate in the decades of their maturity." "Television offers us the most effective medium ever created by man for the communication of ideas and attitudes." DuPont's F. Lyman Dewey suggested that his company's investment in television affirmed its executives' appreciation of the fact that there was no longer a question of "*shall we as DuPont representatives use these powerful tools of communication*—but shall we use them well."

Recoiling from television's expense and unproved effect, other company voice advertisers hesitantly incorporated the new medium into their plans. More than a few invested in alternating-week sponsorships that further divided commercial breaks between product sales and company voice messages. U.S. Steel predicated its television plans in part upon a tax code that allowed deductions for product sales and company voice advertising as a business expense. Its first telecast Christmas night 1952 presented Dickens' *A Christmas Carol.* The *U.S. Steel Hour* later apportioned commercial breaks between company voice messages read by "Voice of U.S. Steel" announcer George Hicks, and industry-wide product sales promotions acted out by U.S. Steel's "family team" Mary Kay and Johnny.

Spectacular programs built around light entertainment, sports and special events presented sponsors as adjuncts of national life and culture. General Motors, reminiscent of its massive investments in wartime institutional advertising, entered television in the 1952/53 season with a weekly schedule of *NCAA Football,* followed by the Eisenhower Inauguration and the Coronation of Elizabeth II. Ford Motor Company and the electrical industry each invested in light entertainment. The success of the *Ford 50th Anniversary Show* simultaneously telecast on NBC and CBS led to similarly conceived "horizontal saturation" for the 1954 television season. *Light's Diamond Jubilee,* for example, a two-hour spectacular celebrating the 75th anniversary of Thomas Edison's invention of the electric light, appeared on four networks. The David O. Selznick production featured a filmed talk by President Eisenhower, narration by Joseph Cotten and sketches and musical numbers with Walter Brennan, Kim Novak, Helen Hayes, Lauren Bacall, David Niven, Judith Anderson and Eddie Fisher.

By the mid-1950s nearly every major American corporation had entered television to build audiences for company voice advertising. The Aluminum Company of America sponsored Edward R. Murrow's *See It Now* to boost its name recognition with the public and with manufacturers using aluminum. Reynolds Aluminum sponsored *Mr. Peepers,* while the Aluminum Company of Canada with others sponsored *Omnibus.* Underwritten by the Ford Foundation as a demonstration of "television at its best," the Sunday afternoon series presented diverse entertainments hosted by Alistair Cooke. Not averse to commercial sponsorship, *Omnibus* anticipated the "making possible" program environment of the Public Broadcasting Service.

While politically active corporations embraced the prestigious possibilities of drama, light entertainment and special events, by 1960 many had become willing sponsors of science, news and documentary programs. The promotion of scientific and technological competence took on special urgency after the Soviet launch of the Sputnik spacecraft in 1958. The corporate-cool television presence of the Bell System exemplified the trend. In 1956 Bell entered television with half-hour dramas entitled *Telephone Time.* 110 episodes ran until 1958 dramatizing the success stories of "little people." In 1959 Bell returned to the air with four musical specials that evolved into the *Bell Telephone Hour.* Light orchestral music, musical numbers and ballet sequences accompanied "Of time and space" company voice messages. Bell also developed preemptive documentary programs on weather, genetics, circulation of the blood and cosmic rays, and the *Threshold* series treating the American space program. Bell also purchased related CBS documentaries such as

"Why Man in Space?" Adopting a similar strategy, Texaco, Gulf and Westinghouse each televised network news and special events laden with scientific and technological news value. Texaco became an early sponsor of NBC's *Huntley-Brinkley Report.* The "unassuming authenticity and easy informality" of co-anchors Chet Huntley and David Brinkley were thought to complement Texaco's "dependability" message. Gulf raised its institutional profile with "instant specials" featuring NBC correspondent Frank McGee, who covered the events of the 1960 presidential campaign and the U.S. space program. Documentary films such as "The Tunnel" rounded out the schedule. *Westinghouse Presents* featured documentary specials "Our Man in Vienna" with David Brinkley, "The Land" with Chet Huntley and "The Wacky World of Jerry Lewis." Company voice messages promoted Westinghouse's "scientific achievements, dedication and sincere interest in people," qualities thought to mitigate the negative public relations impact of 641 civil damage suits stemming from charges of price-fixing.

The multinational aspirations of Xerox Corporation sought complementary qualities of excellence. Not unlike the program strategies pursued by steel, automotive and electrical producers, Xerox embarked upon an aggressive public relations campaign by purchasing programs that "get talked about": *Huntley-Brinkley Reports* treating the Kremlin, Communism, Jimmy Hoffa, Cuba and Korea, the making of the president, 1960 and 1964, and a series of 90-minute specials dramatizing the work of United Nations social agencies. Broadcast without commercial interruption on NBC and ABC, the U.N. series targeted the international community identified as key to the expansion of the office copier market. A model of corporate underwriting, Xerox's U.N. dramas won critical acclaim that helped justify the series' $4 million expense to stockholders who questioned its value. The series' most celebrated program, "Carol for Another Christmas," featured a Rod Serling script that revisited the horrors of Hiroshima, the millions unavailable to Western abundance, and the bleakest of futures prefigured by the hydrogen bomb. Xerox later sponsored *Civilisation* with Kenneth Clark. Thirteen one-hour programs presented "leading social issues and advanced art forms" reviewing "1600 years of Western man's great art and ideas. . . man at his finest on television at its finest."

While company voice advertisers of the early 1950s anticipated the maturity of a television generation with no direct knowledge of the Depression, the company voice advertisers of the early 1960s bemoaned that generation's expectation that business extend its interests beyond the balance sheet to include social goals in the areas of minority employment, consumer protection and environmentalism. Public opinion pollster Louis Harris described the public image of U.S. business as "bight, but flawed." Specialists set out to narrow the distance between corporate claim and performance said to be as great as the so-called generation gap. Not only had society become more impersonal and complex, they argued, but increasingly polarized and problematic. Hoping to erase lingering doubts about advertising's impact and effect, specialists sharpened claims for advocacy advertising as "the one remaining tool with which business can apply counter pressure in an adversary society."

John E. O'Toole, the thoughtful president of the Madison Avenue agency Foote, Cone and Belding, suggested that business leaders learn to emulate the "adversary culture" of intellectual and academic pursuits, political activists and consumer groups "who seek basic changes in the system." O'Toole noted that while each "culture" had necessary and legitimate functions, the adversary culture dominated the media. In complex times, O'Toole argued, business should make certain that its unique claims of social leadership rose above the dissident clutter.

Led by the oil industry, the 1970s witnessed significant investment in company voice television. Reeling from the public relations fallout of rising energy prices, American-based petroleum producers became a presence on the Public Broadcasting Service. Mobil's *Masterpiece Theatre* with one-time *Omnibus* host Alistair Cooke debuted in January 1971. As historian Laurence Jarvik notes, Mobil soon displaced the Ford Foundation as the single largest contributor to public television, raising its initial program grant of $390,000 to $12 million by 1990. *Masterpiece Theatre, Mystery!* and *Upstairs, Downstairs* provided cultural cover for a heavy schedule of combative advocacy ads published in the op-ed sections of *The New York Times* and the *Washington Post.* In the late 1970s the ad campaign came to television: elaborately costumed "A Fable for Now" spots featuring mimes Shields and Yarnell, the Pilobolus Dance Theatre, the Louis Falco Dance Company, the Richard Morris Dance Theatre and members of the American Ballet Theatre enlivened Mobil's anti-regulatory rhetoric in parables of scarcity and abundance drawn from the animal kingdom. "Mobil Information Center" spots aired locally before network newscasts employed an anchorman-correspondent simulation to tout "the freedom of the press," along with the pro-growth logic of offshore drilling, nuclear power plant construction, deregulation of natural gas and the restriction of environmental regulation.

While sympathetic critics wondered if Mobil could have carried out its advocacy campaign without the expense of television drama, others suggested that big oil's enthusiastic underwriting of public television had turned PBS into the "Petroleum Broadcasting Service." PBS president Lawrence K. Grossman urged perspective on the funding issue. In 1977 Grossman explained that though oil company funding had increased tenfold since the early 1970s, oil company moneys represented less than 3% of system income. "What conclusion," asked Grossman, "do we in public television draw from these numbers? Not that oil companies should contribute *less* but rather that corporations of all other types should be asked to contribute more!"

By 1983 corporate support for PBS had flattened out at $38 million for the two previous years, presaging a decade of declining Federal appropriations that left PBS ever more dependent upon the market for support. In 1981 network officials won congressional approval for an

18-month experiment in "enhanced underwriting." Two-minute credits at the beginning and conclusion of programs telecast by nine PBS affiliates allowed mention of brand names, slogans and institutional messages beyond previously restricted verbal mentions and static displays of logos. The discussion of corporate mascots, animated logos, product demonstrations and superlatives to tap a new class of advertising revenue alarmed established underwriters. In an effort to conserve PBS' uncluttered institutional character, national program underwriters Mobil, the Chubb Group of Insurance Companies, Chevron, AT and T, Exxon, Ford, General Electric, IBM, GTE, J.C. Penny, Morgan Guaranty Trust, Owens-Corning and others formed the Corporations in Support of Public Television (CSPT). The CSPT promoted the concept of "quality demographics" among potential corporate underwriters who desired to advertise "excellence," social cause identification and the occasional product.

AT and T, for example, had recently provided $9 million for expanded one-hour coverage of the *MacNeil/Lehrer Report* (later *News Hour*). Emphasizing performance and communication, specialists expected the buy to enhance AT and T's image as an information provider after of its breakup into regional "Baby Bells" by the U.S. Justice Department.

Reviewing their company voice accounts, specialists themselves perhaps wondered just what effect their long-term advertising campaigns had bought. Increasingly business found itself the subject of critical television news stories treating the environment, the OPEC oil shock, inflation and recession. Corporate critics charged that public television had become a prime example of what Alan Wolfe described as "logo America," in which "the only price a company will charge for its public service activities is the right to display its logo." Near the opposite end of the political spectrum, critic David Horowitz described PBS' broadcast schedule as a "monotonous diet of left-wing politics," though it would have been hard to find such programs equaling the possibilities, much less access, available to the company voice advertiser. Mobil, for example, financed an hour-long PBS documentary program criticizing the anti-business thrust of prime time network television drama. Hosted by writer Benjamin Stein, *Hollywood's Favorite Heavy: Businessmen on Prime Time TV* used clips from *Dallas, Dynasty* and *Falcon Crest* to contend that television had destroyed youth's outlook upon business and business ethics. A peculiar assumption, wrote critic Jay Rosen in *Channels* magazine, since television itself was a business, and advertisements had made consumption "the nearest thing to religion for most Americans." Mobil, however, had decided that it could not countenance Blake Carrington, J.R. Ewing and other stereotypes of rapacious businessman in prime time. Interestingly, General Electric declined to join Mobil as a *Hollywood's Favorite Heavy* underwriter, preferring instead to stick with its "We Bring Good Things to Life" spot campaign. Having rethought its aversion to panel discussions, GE aired its "Good

Things" campaign on ABC's *This Week with David Brinkley* and *The McLaughlin Group*. The latter appeared commercially on NBC's five owned and operated stations, and publicly on a 230 station PBS network.

As the century draws to a close and funding for all forms of television continues to be squeezed by new outlets and new technologies such as computer access to the Internet, corporations continue to seek new connections to media. The trend that began with the origins of mass media shows no sign of abating.

—William L. Bird Jr.

FURTHER READING

"Answer for a Giant." *Television Age* (New York), 25 December 1961.

Barnet, Sylvan M., Jr. "A Global Look at Advocacy." *Public Relations Journal* (New York), November 1975.

Barnouw, Erik. *The Sponsor: Notes on a Modern Potentate.* New York: Oxford University Press, 1978.

Brown, Les. *Television: The Business Behind the Box.* New York: Harcourt Brace Jovanovich, 1971.

"Business Thinks TV Distorts its Image." *Business Week* (New York), 18 October 1982.

Chew, Fiona. "The Advertising Value of *Making Possible* a Public Television Program." *Journal of Advertising Research* (New York), November-December 1992.

"8 Advertisers Examine Their Radio and TV Problems." *Sponsor* (New York), 20 April 1953.

Fones-Wolf, Elizabeth. *Selling Free Enterprise: The Business Assault on Labor and Liberalism, 1945–1960.* Urbana, Illinois: University of Illinois Press, 1994.

Gladstone, Brooke, and Steve Behrens. "And That's Why I Underwrite PTV (Just Between Us Corporations)." *Current* (Washington, D.C.), 12 July 1983.

Griese, Noel L. "AT and T: 1908 Origins of the Nation's Oldest Continuous Institutional Advertising Campaign." *Journal of Advertising* (Provo, Utah), 1977.

Harrison, S.L. "Prime Time Pabulum. How Politicos and Corporate Influence Keep Public TV Harmless." *Washington Monthly* (Washington, D.C.), January 1986.

Horowitz, David. "The Politics of Public Television." *Commentary* (New York), December 1991.

"How AT and T May Help Bankroll PBS News." *Business Week* (New York), 16 August 1982.

Howlet, Robert Michael, and Rebecca Raglon. "Constructing the Environmental Spectacle: Green Advertisements and the Greening of the Corporate Image, 1910–1990." *Environmental History Review* (Newark, New Jersey), Winter 1992.

"Instant News." *Television Age* (New York), 5 August 1963.

Marchand, Roland. "The Fitful Career of Advocacy Advertising: Political Protection, Client Cultivation, and Corporate Morale." *California Management Review* (Berkeley, California), Winter 1987.

Mareth, Paul. "Public Visions: Private Voices." *Sight and Sound* (London), Winter 1976–77.

Murphy, M. J. "TV: Newest Way to Get Your Story into the Home." *Factory Management and Maintenance* (New York), May 1952.

Nader, Ralph. "Challenging the Corporate Ad." *Advertising Age* (New York), 24 January 1983.

Northart, Leo J. "Editor's Notebook." *Public Relations Journal* (New York), November 1975.

O'Toole, John E. "Advocacy Advertising Shows the Flag." *Public Relations Journal* (New York), November 1975.

Rosen, Jay. "Chatter from the Right." *The Progressive* (Madison, Wisconsin), March 1988.

———. "Giving Them the Business." *Channels* (New York), February 1987.

Schudson, Michael. *Advertising the Uneasy Persuasion: Its Dubious Impact on American Society.* New York: Basic, 1984.

Schutnann, David W., Jan M. Hathcote, and Susan West. "Corporate Advertising in America: A Review of Published Studies on Use, Measurement, and Effectiveness." *Journal of Advertising* (Provo, Utah), September 1991.

Shayon, Robert Lewis. "They Sang Along with Mitch." *Saturday Review* (New York), 30 May 1964.

———. "Warm Scrooge, Cold Grudge." *Saturday Review* (New York), 16 January 1965.

"TV's Quiet Marketer." *Television Age* (New York), 30 April 1962.

"What Americans Really Think of Business" and "The Disenchanted Campus." *Newsweek* (New York), 2 May 1966.

Wolfe, Alan. "The Rise of Logo America." *The Nation* (New York), 26 May 1984.

Yore, J.J. "Enhanced Underwriting: A Corporate Perspective." *Current* (Washington, D.C.), 11 March 1986.

See also Advertising; *Alcoa Hour*

ADVERTISING AGENCY

In the early years of U.S. broadcasting it did not take long for advertising agencies to embrace new media. Fortunately for advertisers, the ability to reach a mass audience with radio intersected with an expansion of the American economy in the 1920s. The techniques of mass production championed by Henry Ford, the rise of Taylorism, and an increase in disposable income in the years following World War I sustained an ideology of consumption that advertising both reflected and nurtured. NBC President Merlin H. Aylesworth proclaimed that radio was "an open gateway to national markets, to millions of consumers, and to thousands upon thousands of retailers."

The vision of eager consumers gathered around this remarkable appliance was irresistible to potential sponsors. The expansion of commercial broadcasting came with such astonishing speed that by 1931 radio was an enormous industry, accounting for $36 million in time sales on the networks alone. Larger agencies such as N.W. Ayer, BBDO, and J. Walter Thompson set up broadcasting departments and actively encouraged clients to pursue the medium.

The emergence of radio as an economic force was reflected in a crucial change regarding program development at the agency level. Through the 1920s most commercial programming originated with networks or local stations, with the agency serving as broker, casting about for clients willing to purchase the rights to a broadcaster-produced show. By the early 1930s, however, the agencies had reversed the equation—they were developing shows in-house for clients, then purchasing air time from the broadcasters. The key function for the agency thus became to analyze a client's particular needs and design an entire program around it, an enormously complex and financially risky undertaking, yet one in which Madison Avenue was entirely successful. By the end of the 1930s, agencies produced more than 80% of all network commercial programming.

With the advent of commercial television in 1946, there was considerable sentiment within the networks that program creation and execution would best be left in their hands, although the personnel demands and expense of video production made it impossible for any network to produce all its programming in-house. Thus, as in radio, agencies assumed a major role in the evolution of the television schedule. There was not, however, a wholesale rush of sponsors begging to enter the medium, and the networks were compelled to offer time slots at bargain rates to attract customers. Companies such as Thompson, and Young and Rubicam, had already developed some television expertise, but the vast majority of agencies found themselves at the bottom of a very steep learning curve. Still, Madison Avenue produced some of the most enduring programs of the "golden age" of television, including *Texaco Star Theater*, *Kraft Television Theatre*, and *The Goldbergs*.

As more stations began operation—particularly after 1952—the cost of purchasing air time on the networks and local stations increased dramatically, as did production budgets. Most agencies accepted as an economic fact that they could no longer afford to create and produce their own shows as they had in radio, and the recognition on Madison Avenue that complete control of television production was unprofitable to the agencies themselves contributed to the evolution in programming hegemony away from the agencies to the networks. Thus, agencies never assumed the kind of production control in television they enjoyed in radio; they could never put into play the same economies of scale as the networks and independent producers. The 15% commission that served as the source of agency revenue simply was not enough to cover the ever-increasing expenses associated with television production. Many agencies subsequently shifted their emphasis to the production of commercial spots, while others moved aggressively into syndication, forming partnerships with Hollywood producers to create filmed series that could be sold to a variety of sponsors.

As costs rose during the 1950s, the gap between agency income and expenses narrowed considerably, forcing a reconsideration of organizational structure, leading to the emergence of what was termed the "all-media strategy," which remains the dominant paradigm. Most agencies had relied on specialists in a strict division of labor such that a client's advertising might be divided up between three or four different departments. The all-media approach rejected this diffusion of responsibility, placing a single person or team in charge of a client's overall needs. By eliminating specialists and fostering cooperation between divisions, agencies could streamline personnel, coordinate functions, improve efficiency and thereby reduce overhead.

Advertising agencies had an agenda distinct from that of their clients. Although publicly they represented the clients' interests, many Madison Avenue executives also promoted network control of programming in the trade press. Because of their concerns over the increasing costs and complexities of program production, and their frustration with mediating disputes between advertisers and networks, many hoped television would not continue the radio model of sponsor ownership of time slots. Concerned that the expense of television programming far outstripped that of radio production, agency executives sought ways to develop television as a mass advertising medium while also seeking to avoid draining agency revenues with television program costs. In this sense, the evolution of the all-media strategy is illustrative of how the economic pressures brought to bear on agencies during the 1950s changed the way Madison Avenue approached programming, from an advertising vehicle to one (albeit primary) component of a marketing plan.

Today, the advertising agency is primarily responsible for the production of commercial spots as well as the purchasing of air time on behalf of clients. The situation has become murkier in recent years, however, as some large companies (Coca-Cola, for example) have begun producing much of their own advertising in-house, bypassing Madison Avenue. Further, the networks now frequently approach potential advertisers directly rather than going through the client's agency. In an era when even large shops such as Chiat/Day are acquired by enormous multinational holding companies, the role of the agency is now focused more on using powers of persuasion in many different media than merely in creating a single great advertisement.

—Michael Mashon

FURTHER READING

Agnew, Clark M., and Neil O'Brien. *Television Advertising.* New York: McGraw-Hill, 1958.

Hilmes, Michele. *Hollywood and Broadcasting: From Radio to Cable.* Urbana: University of Illinois Press, 1991.

Lears, T. Jackson. *Fables of Abundance: A Cultural History of Advertising in America.* New York: Basic Books, 1994.

McAllister, Matthew P. *The Commercialization of American Culture: New Advertising, Control, and Democracy.* Thousand Oaks, California: Sage Publications, 1996.

McMahan, Harry W. *The Television Commercial: How to Create and Produce Effective TV Advertising.* New York: Hastings House, 1954.

Settel, Irving, and Norman Glenn. *Television Advertising and Production Handbook.* New York: Thomas Y. Cromwell, 1953.

See also Advertising

ADVOCACY GROUPS

Advocacy groups—also called public interest groups, citizen groups, consumer activist groups, and media reform groups—have existed in the United States since the 1930s as consumer checks on a broadcast industry where decisions quite often have been based not on public interest standards but rather on economic incentives and regulatory mandates. Advocacy groups have carved a niche for themselves in the broadcast industry's policy-making apparatus by first defining key public interest issues and then by advocating ways by which broadcasters may address these issues.

Advocacy group characteristics have varied widely. Some have operated nationally with or without local chapters, and some have operated only locally. Some have remained active for many years, whereas the life span of others has been brief. Some advocacy groups have been well-financed, often receiving substantial foundation funding, while others have operated with little financial support. Practically all advocacy groups have relied on newsletter subscriptions, video purchases, and lectures as means of raising money. Finally, some advocacy groups have devoted exclusive attention to the broadcast industry, whereas other groups with a more varied menu of concerns have developed subsidiary units to deal with broadcast-related issues.

The total number of advocacy groups, past or present, is difficult to determine, given their ephemeral nature. However, a 1980 publication listed some 60 national and 140 local advocacy groups. Some of the more prominent groups have included the National Association for Better Broadcasting, the

National Citizens Committee for Broadcasting, Action for Children's Television, Accuracy in Media, the National Black Media Coalition, and the Coalition for Better Television. Besides these, the Office of Communication of the United Church of Christ has been a particularly effective advocacy group as have the Media Task Force of the National Organization for Women and the National Parent Teachers Association. Assisting these groups in legal, regulatory, and legislative matters have been pro bono public interest law firms such as the Citizens Communication Center.

Early advocacy groups such as the Radio Council on Children's Programming and the Women's National Radio Committee, both formed in the 1930s, were concerned with program content. Group members monitored radio programs, reported their opinions on acceptable and unacceptable content in newsletters, and gave awards to radio stations and networks airing exceptional programs. That practice and mode of consumer/broadcaster interaction continued until the 1960s when the broadcast industry became caught-up in a sweeping consumers' movement. During the latter part of the 1960s, advocacy groups, led most effectively by the United Church of Christ, began challenging television station license renewals through a legal instrument called a "petition to deny." Such petitions were aimed at denying license renewal for television stations whose programming or employment practices were considered discriminatory. Advocacy groups also were successful in forcing broadcasters to accede to programming and minority employment demands contained in "citizen agreements." When such unprecedented public access into the regulatory and station decision-making process won approval of both the federal courts and the Federal Communications Commission (FCC), advocacy groups blossomed.

The most common targets of advocacy groups during the 1970s continued to be minority programming and employment practices. However, violent program content, children's programming, and general public access to the airwaves also took on significance. Advocacy group tactics during this period included the petitions to deny and citizens agreements noted above as well as participation in FCC rule making and congressional hearings, actual or threatened program sponsor boycotts, and publicity. Advocacy group achievements during the 1970s usually came in small doses, but major successes included the improvement in broadcast station employment opportunities for women and minorities, greater public participation in the broadcast regulatory process, improvement in children's programming, and the banishment of cigarette advertising from the airwaves.

The nature of advocacy groups began to change during the 1980s. A more conservative political agenda derailed the consumers' movement that had bolstered the more liberal-minded advocacy groups of the 1970s. Moreover, public interest law firms and foundations that had funded many of the more prominent advocacy groups during the 1970s began either disappearing or turning their attention elsewhere. Changes in the broadcast industry itself—

deregulation, the rise of cable television, and changing station/network ownership patterns—also reversed many of the early advocacy group achievements and left the leadership as well as membership of many of the groups in disarray.

Advocacy groups did not disappear; rather their issue emphasis took a decidedly conservative turn. Groups such as Accuracy in Media and the Coalition for Better Television gained momentum in the 1980s with a large constituency, substantial funding, and a focus on ridding the airwaves of programs that either were biased in news reporting or contained an excess of sex and violence. Extensive mailing lists also helped these groups to quickly galvanize public support for their causes.

Advocacy groups promoting a liberal agenda and with sights set on molding public opinion on a more tightly focused set of special interests than in the past also began appearing in the 1990s. These interests included gun control, AIDS awareness and prevention, abortion rights, world hunger, and the environment. Led by Amnesty International, the Environmental Media Association, and Center for Population Options, these advocacy groups succeeded to some extent by convincing a number of television network producers to insert messages in prime-time entertainment programs that addressed the advocacy groups' concerns.

The role of advocacy groups through the years has engendered a mixture of praise and criticism. While the objectives, methods and zealotry of some groups have met with scorn, the efforts of others have been viewed as beneficial for, at the very least, making the broadcast industry sensitive to public needs and concerns.

—Ronald Garay

FURTHER READING

Bittner, John R. *Law and Regulation of Electronic Media.* Englewood Cliffs, New Jersey: Prentice Hall, 1982; 2nd edition, 1994.

Branscomb, Anne W., and Maria Savage. *Broadcast Reform at the Crossroads.* Cambridge, Massachusetts: Kalba Bowen Associates, 1987.

Brown, Les. "Is the Public Interested in the Public Interest?" *Television Quarterly* (New York), Fall 1979.

Cole, Barry, and Mal Oettinger. *Reluctant Regulators.* Reading, Massachusetts: Addison-Wesley Company, 1978.

Friedman, Mel. "Will TV Networks Yield to New Pressure Groups?" *Television/Radio Age* (New York), 4 May 1981.

Garay, Ronald. "Access: Evolution of the Citizen Agreement." *Journal of Broadcasting* (Washington, D.C.), Winter 1978.

Guimary, Donald L. *Citizens' Groups and Broadcasting.* New York: Praeger, 1975.

Hodges, Ann. "Pressure Group Crusade Seen as Top Problem by Networks, Producers." *Houston Chronicle,* 19 May 1981.

Krasnow, Erwin, Laurence D. Longley, and Herbert A. Terry. *The Politics of Broadcast Regulation.* New York: St. Martin's, 1978; 3rd edition, 1982.

Leddy, Craig. "Probing a Pressure Group." *Electronic Media* (Chicago), 26 April 1984.

Mahler, Richard. "How the Crusades Became Prime for TV." *Los Angeles Times,* 14 April 1991.

Montgomery, Kathryn C. *Target: Prime Time: Advocacy Groups and the Struggle over Entertainment Television.* New York and Oxford: Oxford University Press, 1989.

National Citizens Committee for Broadcasting. *Citizens Media Directory, 1980 Update.* Washington, D.C.: National Citizens Committee for Broadcasting, 1980.

Rowe, Chip. "Watchdog Watch." *American Journalism Review* (College Park, Maryland), April 1993.

Shapiro, Andrew O. *Media Access.* Boston: Little, Brown, 1976.

Smith, F. Leslie, Milan D. Meeske, and John W. Wright, III. *Electronic Media and Government.* White Plains, New York: Longman, 1995.

See also Action for Children's Television; Experimental Video; Public Access Television

AILES, ROGER

U.S. Media Consultant/Producer/Executive

Roger Eugene Ailes is one of television's most versatile, outspoken, and successful producers and consultants. He has been described as "the amusingly ferocious Republican media genius" and a "pit-bull Republican media strategist turned television tycoon." He has had a variety of careers, including producer of television shows, Shakespearean plays, and Off-Broadway, and president of the cable television channels CNBC and America's Talking.

Ailes' career in television began in Cleveland, Ohio, where he was a producer and director for KYW-TV, for a then-locally produced talk-variety show, *The Mike Douglas Show.* He later became executive producer for *The Mike Douglas Show,* which syndicated nationally. He received two Emmy Awards for *The Mike Douglas Show* (1967, 1968). It was in this position, in 1967, that he had a spirited discussion about television in politics with one of the show's guests, Richard Nixon, who took the view that television was a gimmick. Later, Nixon called on Ailes to serve as his executive producer of TV. Nixon's election victory was only Ailes' first venture into presidential television.

Ailes founded Ailes Communications, Inc., in New York in 1969, and consulted for various businesses and politicians, including WCBS-TV in New York. He also tried his hand in theater production with the Broadway musical *Mother Earth* (1972) and the off-Broadway hit play *Hot-L Baltimore* (1973-76), for which Ailes received 4 Obie Awards. He was executive producer for a television special *The Last Frontier* in 1974. He produced and directed a television special, *Fellini: Wizards, Clowns and Honest Liars,* for which he received an Emmy Award nomination in 1977.

Ailes carried out political consulting for many candidates during the 1970s and 1980s, but returned to presidential campaigning as a consultant to Ronald Reagan in 1984. He is widely credited with having coached Ronald Reagan to victory in the second presidential debate with Walter Mondale after Reagan had disappointed his partisans with a lackluster effort in the first debate. In 1984, Ailes won an Emmy Award as executive producer and director of a television special, *Television and the Presidency.* In 1988, Ailes wrote a book with Jon Kraushar, *You Are the Message: Secrets of the Master Communicators,* in which he discusses some of his philosophies and strategies for successful performance in the public media eye.

Ailes also won acclaim for his work in the 1988 presidential election, in which he helped guide George Bush to a come-from-behind victory over Michael Dukakis. He did not work on the losing 1992 Bush campaign against Bill Clinton. In 1991, Ailes convinced a syndicator to bring Rush Limbaugh from radio to television and became executive producer of the late-night show. He announced his withdrawal from political consulting in 1992.

In 1993, Ailes became president of NBC's cable channel CNBC and began planning another NBC cable channel, America's Talking. The new channel debuted on 4 July 1994. Ailes also hosts his own nightly show, *Straight Forward.* Since Ailes took over at CNBC, ratings have increased 50% and profits have tripled.

—Lynda Lee Kaid

Roger Ailes
Photo courtesy of CNBC

ROGER (EUGENE) AILES. Born in Warren, Ohio, U.S.A., 15 May 1940. Graduated from Ohio University, Athens, Ohio, B.A. 1962. Began television career as property assistant, *The Mike Douglas Show*, KYW-TV, Cleveland, Ohio, 1962; producer, 1965; executive producer, 1967–68; media adviser to Richard M. Nixon Presidential Campaign, 1968; founder Ailes Communication, a media production and consulting firm, 1969; producer, Broadway plays, *Mother Earth*, 1972, *The Hot L Baltimore*, 1973–76; producer, various television specials, 1974–82; media consultant, Ronald Reagan Presidential Campaign, 1984; George W. Bush Presidential Campaign, 1988; various senatorial and congressional campaigns; president, CNBC, cable television network, 1993–96; president and program host, America's Talking, and all-talk cable television network, 1994–96; chair and chief executive officer of FOX News and the FOX News Channel, from January 1996. Honorary Doctorate, Ohio University. Recipient: Obie Award, Best Off-Broadway Show, 1973; Emmy Award, 1984.

TELEVISION

1991   *An All-Star Tribute to Our Troops* (producer)

PUBLICATIONS

"Attorney Style: Charisma in a Court Counts." *The National Law Journal* (New York), 21 July 1986.
You Are the Message. Garden City, New York: Doubleday, 1987.
"The Importance of Being Likeable." *Reader's Digest* (Pleasantville, New York), May 1988.

"Sam and Diane: Give 'em Time." *Advertising Age* (New York), 21 August 1989.
"How to Make a Good Impression." *Reader's Digest* (Pleasantville, New York), September 1989.
"A Few Kind Words for Presenter Tip O'Neill." *Advertising Age* (New York), 8 January 1990.
"They Told the Truth...Occasionally." *Adweek's Marketing Week* (New York), 29 January 1990.
"How to Make an Audience Love You." *Working Woman* (New York), November 1990.
"Campaign Strategy." *Time* (New York), 11 May 1992.
"Lighten Up! Stuffed Shirts Have Short Careers." *Newsweek* (New York), 18 May 1992.

FURTHER READING

Barnes, Fred. "Pulling the Strings." *The New Republic* (Washington, D.C.), 22 February 1988.
Devlin, Patrick L. "Contrasts in Presidential Campaign Commercials of 1988." *American Behavioral Scientist* (Princeton, New Jersey), March-April 1989.
Hass, Nancy. "Roger Ailes: Embracing the Enemy." *New York Times Magazine* (New York), 8 January 1995.
Miller, Stuart. "Roger Ailes Hits TV with a Rush." *Variety* (Los Angeles, California), 21 June 1991.
Oneal, Michael. "Roger Ailes Fixed CNBC, But Now Ted Turner Looms." *Business Week* (New York), 3 July 1995.
Wolinsky, Leo C. "Refereeing the TV Campaign." *Washington Journalism Review* (Washington, D.C.), January-February 1991.

THE ALCOA HOUR

U.S. Anthology Drama

The *Alcoa Hour* was a 60-minute live anthology drama which replaced *The Philco Television Playhouse* and began alternating broadcasts with *The Goodyear Theatre* in the fall of 1955. (For a few months *Philco, Alcoa,* and *Goodyear* shared a three-way alternation of the Sunday evening 9:00 to 10:00 P.M. slot on NBC. Philco withdrew sponsorship in early 1956.) The program was sponsored by the Aluminum Corporation of America and was produced by Herbert Brodkin, formerly of ABC-TV. Among the program's directors, many of whom went on to distinguished careers in television and film, were Dan Petrie, Robert Mulligan, Sidney Lumet, and Ralph Nelson. Coming near the end of the "golden age" of live television anthology drama, *The Alcoa Hour* had a relatively short run of just under two years, but this was despite generally high quality programs and mostly favorable reviews.

The first broadcast of *The Alcoa Hour* was on 16 October 1955. An original teleplay by Joseph Schull entitled "The Black Wings," the production starred Wendell Corey and Ann Todd and was directed by Norman Felton. Both *Variety*

and *The New York Times* praised the high quality of acting and the attractive sets but criticized the script. *Times* reviewer J.P. Shanley went so far as to say that the story was "melodramatic hogwash." Schull's narrative dealt with a German physician (Corey) who had been a Luftwaffe pilot during World War II. He secretly endows a clinic for the treatment of victims of a bombing raid he led over England, then falls in love with an English girl (Todd) who was crippled by the bombing. In spite of the script's weaknesses, the program was deemed a success because of the excellent performances and fine directing, and critics felt that *The Alcoa Hour* would become a worthy successor to the famous *Philco Television Playhouse*.

During its two years, *The Alcoa Hour* broadcast a wide variety of dramas, including the sixth consecutive Christmas season airing of Gian Carlo Menotti's television opera *Amahl and the Night Visitors* on 25 December 1955. During the Christmas season of 1956, *The Alcoa Hour* broadcast a musical version of Charles Dickens' *A Christmas Carol* entitled "The Stingiest Man in Town." The adaptation featured

Basil Rathbone in a singing role, crooner Vic Damone, songwriter Johnny Desmond, opera singer Patrice Munsel, and the Four Lads, a popular singing group.

Typical programs were "Thunder in Washington" (27 November 1955), and "Mrs. Gilling and the Skyscraper" (9 June 1957). "Thunder in Washington" was an original script by David Davidson, directed by Robert Mulligan. The broadcast featured Melvyn Douglas and Ed Begley in a story about a competent business executive, Charles Turner, who answers a call from the president of the United States to introduce efficiency into numerous sprawling governmental agencies. Turner's efforts at reform offend almost everyone and he finds himself defending his actions before a House Appropriations Committee. The program ends with Turner vowing to continue his crusade to clean up Washington and the committee chair promising to stop him. *New York Times* reviewer Jack Gould praised the broadcast by saying that it was "a play of uncommon timeliness, power, and controversy. With one more scene, it could have been a genuine *tour de force* of contemporary political drama." Actor Luis van Rooten, hired to play the part of the president of the United States, spent hours studying the voice and mannerisms of then President Dwight D. Eisenhower to make sure his performance was authentic, even though the president was to be seen only in a head and shoulders shot from behind.

"Mrs. Gilling and the Skyscraper" was a very different sort of play. An original script by Sumner Locke Elliot, it was a vehicle for distinguished actress Helen Hayes who played the part of an elderly lady who tries to save her apartment from the owners of her building who intend to demolish it to make way for a skyscraper. The script was noted for how it dealt with the generational clashes between the old lady and new tenants in her building. Confrontations between the old and new were becoming increasingly common during the 1950s as large stretches of turn-of-the-century dwellings were leveled to make way for modern buildings. The plight of Mrs. Gillings was a familiar one for many older Americans and their families.

Perhaps the most noteworthy *Alcoa Hour* was the broadcast of 19 February 1956 entitled "Tragedy in a Temporary Town." The script by Reginald Rose told the story of a vigilante group formed after a girl is assaulted at a construction camp. According to Jack Gould, "Mr. Rose's final scene—the mob descending on an innocent Puerto Rican victim—did make the viewer's flesh creep. And the raw vigor of the hero's denunciation of the mob—the man's language had uncommon pungency—was extraordinarily vivid video drama." Directed by Sidney Lumet and staring Lloyd Bridges as the man who opposed the mob, "Tragedy in a Temporary Town" won a Robert E. Sherwood Television Award and a citation from the Anti Defamation League of B'nai B'rith as the best dramatic program of the year dealing with intergroup relations.

The 1956–57 season saw the networks shifting away from live broadcasts and turning more to the use of film.

Faced with this change and competition from a new crop of popular programs, *The Alcoa Hour* went off the air after its 22 September 1957 broadcast of "Night" starring Franchot Tone, Jason Robards, Jr., and E. G. Marshall. As of 30 September 1957, both *The Alcoa Hour* and its companion program *The Goodyear Theatre* became thirty-minute filmed programs and were moved to Monday nights at 9:30 P.M. Other Alcoa shows followed in the late 1950s and early 1960s: *Alcoa Premiere*, *Alcoa Presents*, and *Alcoa Theatre.*

—Henry B. Aldridge

PROGRAMMING HISTORY

• NBC

October 1955–September 1957   Sunday 9:00-10:00

FURTHER READING

Hawes, William. *The American Television Drama: The Experimental Years.* University, Alabama: University of Alabama Press, 1986.

Kindem, Gorham, editor. *The Live Television Generation of Hollywood Film Directors: Interviews with Seven Directors.* Jefferson, North Carolina: McFarland, 1994.

MacDonald, J. Fred. *One Nation Under Television: The Rise and Decline of Network TV.* New York: Pantheon, 1990.

Skutch, Ira. *Ira Skutch: I Remember Television: A Memoir.* Metuchen, New Jersey: Scarecrow Press, 1989.

John Newland, host of Alcoa Presents
Photo courtesy of Worldvision Enterprises, Inc.

Stemple, Tom. *Storytellers to the Nation: A History of American Television Writing.* New York: Continuum, 1992.

Sturcken, Frank. *Live Television: The Golden Age of 1946-1958 in New York.* Jefferson, North Carolina: McFarland, 1990.

Wicking, Christopher, and Tise Vahimagi. *The American Vein: Directors and Directions in Television.* New York: Dutton, 1979.

Wilk, Max. *The Golden Age of Television: Notes from the Survivors.* New York: Dell, 1977.

ALDA, ALAN

U.S. Actor

Alan Alda is a television and film star best known for his work in the long-running CBS television series *M*A*S*H.* He has been well honored for that role, having garnered twenty-eight Emmy nominations, two Writers Guild Awards, three Directors Guild Awards, six Golden Globes from the Hollywood Foreign Press Association, and seven People's Choice Awards. Alda is the only person to have been honored by the Television Academy as top performer, writer and director.

The son of actor Robert Alda, he traveled with his father on the vaudeville circuit, and began performing in summer stock theater as a teenager. During his junior year at Fordham University, Alda studied in Europe where he performed on the stage in Rome and on television in Amsterdam with his father. After college he acted at the Cleveland Playhouse on a Ford Foundation grant. Upon returning to New York, Alda worked on Broadway, off-Broadway and on television. He later acquired improvisational training with Second City and Compass in Hyannis Port, and that background in political and social satire led to his work as a regular on television's *That Was the Week That Was.*

Alda found fame on *M*A*S*H,* where his depiction of sensitive surgeon Hawkeye Pierce won him five Emmy Awards. Set in the Korean War of the 1950s, and broadcast in part during the Vietnam War in the 1970s, *M*A*S*H* won acclaim for its broad and irreverent humor, its ability to effectively combine drama with comedy, and its overall liberal humanist stance. In adapting the show from the 1970 Robert Altman film, producer and director Gene Reynolds and writer Larry Gelbart used distinctive telefilm aesthetics and a complex narrative structure that set the show apart from the proscenium style series that dominated television in the 1960s. The show's influence was broad—traceable perhaps most directly in the large number of multi-character "dramedies" (such as *Hill Street Blues* and *St. Elsewhere)* in the 1980s whose narratives also centered around a tightly knit workplace group who became like family to one another.

Alda, who also wrote and directed many episodes of the show, has become indelibly associated with *M*A*S*H,* which continues to be watched as one of the most successful comedies in syndication. His "sensitive male" persona, derived in large part from his characterization on *M*A*S*H,* has lingered into the 1990s and continues to be sustained by public awareness of his efforts on behalf of women's rights.

An ardent feminist, Alda campaigned extensively for ten years for the passage of the Equal Rights Amendment, and in 1976, was appointed by President Ford to serve on the National Commission for the Observance of International Women's Year. Alda's status as a feminist led a writer in *The Boston Globe* to dub him "the quintessential Honorary Woman: a feminist icon." Despite such associations, Alda's most acclaimed recent performance was his portrayal of a conniving producer in the 1989 Woody Allen film *Crimes and Misdemeanors.* Alda won the D.W. Griffith Award, the New York Film Critics Award, and was nominated for a BAFTA award as Best Supporting Actor for his work in the film. Perhaps Alda seeks to alter, or at least add other dimensions to his "character type" following this success. He has more recently continued this exploration of a "darker side" with his portrayal of a driven corporate executive in the HBO original production, *White Mile.* The more familiar, inquisitive, humorous Alda is currently host of the series

Alan Alda
Photo courtesy of Alan Alda

Scientific American Frontiers on the U.S. Public Broadcasting Service, since 1993.

—Diane M. Negra

ALAN ALDA. Born in New York City, U.S.A., 28 January 1936. Graduated from Fordham University, Bronx, New York, 1956; studied acting at the Cleveland Playhouse, Ohio, 1956–59. Married: Arlene Weiss, 1957; children: Eve, Elizabeth, and Beatrice. Appeared in off-Broadway productions and television guest roles through 1960s; worked with improvisational groups, Second City, Chicago, Illinois, and Compass, Hyannis Port, Massachusetts; appeared in movies, 1960s and 1970s; began role as "Hawkeye" Pierce in the television series *M*A*S*H*, 1972, also wrote and directed episodes of the series; actor, writer, and director of films, since 1983. Presidential appointee, National Commission for the Observance of International Women's Year, 1976; co-chair, National Equal Rights Amendment Countdown Campaign, 1982. Trustee: Museum of Television and Radio, 1985; Rockefeller Foundation, 1989. Member: American Federation of Television and Radio Artists; Directors Guild of America; Writers Guild of America; Actors Equity Association. Recipient: five Emmy Awards; five Golden Globe Awards; Humanitas Award for Writing; D.W. Griffith Award; New York Film Critics Award; seven People's Choice Awards.

TELEVISION SERIES

1964–65	*That Was the Week That Was*
1972–83	*M*A*S*H*

MADE-FOR-TELEVISION MOVIES

1972	*Playmates*
1972	*The Glass House*
1973	*Isn't It Shocking?*
1974	*6 Rms Riv Vu*
1977	*Kill Me If You Can*
1984	*The Four Seasons*
1993	*And the Band Played On*
1994	*White Mile*

FILMS

Gone Are the Days, 1963; *Paper Lion*, 1968; *Jenny*, 1969; *The Extraordinary Seaman*, 1969; *The Moonshine War*, 1970; *Catch-22*, 1970; *The Mephisto Waltz*, 1971; *To Kill a Clown*, 1972; *Same Time, Next Year*, 1978; *California Suite*, 1978; *The Seduction of Joe Tynan* (also writer), 1979; *The Four Seasons* (also director and writer), 1981; *Sweet Liberty* (also director and writer), 1986; *A New Life* (also director and writer), 1988; *Crimes and Misdemeanors*, 1989; *Betsy's Wedding* (also director and writer), 1990; *Whispers in the Dark*, 1992; *Manhattan Murder Mystery*, 1993; *Canadian Bacon*, 1994; *Flirting With Disaster*, 1995.

FURTHER READING

Alda, Arlene, with commentary by Alan Alda. *The Last Days of M*A*S*H: Photographs and Notes.* Verona, New Jersey: Unicorn, 1983.

Bennetts, Leslie. "Alda Stars in *M*A*S*H* Seminar." *The New York Times,* 18 October 1986.

Clauss, Jed. *M*A*S*H, The First Five Years, 1973-77: A Show by Show Arrangement.* Mattituck, New York: Aeonian, 1977.

Kalter, Suzy. *The Complete Book of M*A*S*H.* New York: H.N. Abrams, 1984.

Kolbert, Elizabeth. "Hawkeye Turns Mean, Sensitively." *The New York Times,* 19 May 1994.

O'Connor, John J. "Hawkeye and Company in a *M*A*S*H* Salute." *The New York Times,* 25 November 1991.

Reiss, David S. *M*A*S*H: The Exclusive, Inside Story of TV's Most Popular Show.* Indianapolis, Indiana: Bobbs-Merrill, 1983.

Schatz, Thomas. "*St. Elsewhere* and the Evolution of the Ensemble Series." In, Newcomb, Horace, editor. *Television the Critical View.* New York: Oxford, 1976; 4th edition, 1987.

Straut, Raymond. *Alan Alda: A Biography.* New York: St. Martin's, 1983.

See also *M*A*S*H*

ALL CHANNEL LEGISLATION

U.S. Communications Policy Legislation

In July 1962 President John F. Kennedy signed into law legislation that required all television receiving sets shipped across state lines be able to adequately receive all UHF as well as VHF frequencies. The goal of this law was to put UHF channels (channels 14 through 83) on a more equal technological footing with the VHF channels (2 through 13). Until this time, virtually all sets manufactured in or imported into the United States were equipped to receive the VHF channels only. Viewers interested in watching UHF channels were required to purchase a cumbersome UHF converter and attach it to their sets. These converters, which resembled metal bow ties and sat atop the receiver, did not allow viewers to "click in" the desired channel. The tuning dial operated fluidly, like a radio tuning knob, and viewers had to literally "tune in" the desired channel. With the commercial networks occupying the VHF channels and viewers disadvantaged in receiving the UHF frequencies, the UHF channels (primarily independent commercial and educational or non-commercial stations) were in danger of extinction. The immediate goal, then, of all-channel legislation was the preservation of these channels. The longer-term goal was the encouragement of diversity (or the creation of "a multitude of tongues") which was a guiding force behind much Federal Communications Commission (FCC) rule-making at the time.

Therefore, on 12 September 1962, the commission proposed that any set manufactured in or imported into the United States after 30 April 1964 be all-channel equipped. The proposal became an official FCC order on 21 Novem-ber 1962. Later amendments to FCC rules and regulations specified performance standards for the UHF circuit in the new receivers relating to sound and picture quality.

—Kimberly B. Massey

FURTHER READING

Barnouw, Erik. *A History of Broadcasting in the United States, Volume III: The Image Empire.* New York: Oxford University Press, 1970.

ALL IN THE FAMILY

U.S. Situation Comedy

For five years, *All in the Family*, which aired on CBS from 1971 to 1983 (in its last four seasons under the title *Archie Bunker's Place*), was the top-rated show on American television, and the winner of four consecutive Emmy Awards as Outstanding Comedy Series. *All in the Family* was not only one of the most successful sitcoms in history, it was also one of the most important and influential series ever to air, for it ushered in a new era in American television character-ized by programs that did not shy away from addressing controversial or socially relevant subject matters.

All in the Family's storylines centered on the domestic concerns of the Bunker household in Queens, New York. Family patriarch and breadwinner Archie Bunker (Carroll O'Connor) was a bigoted loading dock worker disturbed by the changes occurring in the American society he once knew. To Archie, gains by the "Spades," "Spics," or "Hebes" of America (as he referred to Blacks, Hispanics, and Jews, respectively), came at his expense and that of other lower-middle-class whites. Countering Archie's harsh demeanor was his sweet but flighty "dingbat" wife, Edith. Played by Jean Stapleton, Edith usually endured Archie's tirades in a manner meant to avoid confrontation. But that was hardly the case with Archie's live-in son-in-law Mike Stivic (Rob Reiner), a liberal college student who was married to the Bunkers' daughter, Gloria (Sally Struthers). The confrontations between Archie and Mike ("Meat-head") served as the basis for much of *All in the Family*'s comedy. As surely as Archie could be counted upon to be politically conservative and socially misguided, Mike was equally liberal and sensitive to the concerns of minorities and the oppressed, and, because both characters were ex-tremely vocal in their viewpoints, heated conflict between the two was assured.

Producers Norman Lear and Alan (Bud) Yorkin brought *All in the Family* into being by obtaining the U.S. rights to the hit British comedy series, *Till Death Us Do Part*, which aired on the BBC in the mid-1960s and featured the character of bigoted dock worker Alf Garnett. Lear developed two pilots based on the concept for ABC, with O'Connor (Mickey Rooney had been Lear's first choice to play Archie) and Stapleton in the lead roles. But when ABC turned down the series, then known as *Those Were the Days*, it appeared that it would never get off the ground. Luckily for Lear and Yorkin, CBS President Rob-ert D. Wood was in the market for new shows that would appeal to the more affluent, urban audience the network's entrenched lineup of top-rated but aging series failed to attract. As a result, CBS jettisoned highly rated programs like *The Red Skelton Show* and *Green Acres* in an effort to improve the demographic profile of its audiences, and *All in the Family* seemed a perfect, though risky, vehicle to put in their place. CBS therefore made a 13-episode commit-ment to air the series beginning in January 1971, as a midseason replacement.

The network had good reason to be wary of reaction to its new show. *All in the Family* seemed to revel in breaking prime time's previously unbreakable taboos. Archie's fre-quent diatribes laced with degrading racial and ethnic epi-thets, Mike and Gloria's obviously active sex life, the sounds of Archie's belching and of flushing toilets—all broke with sitcom convention. They also and made people sit up and take notice of the new CBS series. In fact, its unconvention-ality caused *All in the Family*'s pilot episode to consistently rate below average in research tests conducted by both ABC and CBS. Nevertheless, CBS went ahead and debuted the show on 12 January 1971, though with relatively little fanfare or network promotion.

Viewer response to *All in the Family* was at first tepid. CBS' switchboards were prepared for an avalanche of calls in response to the show's initial airing, but this onslaught never materialized, in part because of the poor 15% audi-ence share garnered by the first episode, which put it a distant third in its time period behind movies on NBC and ABC. But while the show continued to languish in the Nielsen ratings in its first few months, TV critics began to take notice. Despite the negative reviews of a small number of critics, such as *Life*'s John Leonard ("a wretched pro-gram"), the critical response was generally positive. Com-bined with strong word-of-mouth among viewers these evaluations helped the show's audience to slowly grow. The May 1971 Emmy Awards helped to cap *All in the Family*'s climb. The midseason replacement was featured

All in the Family

in the opening skit of the Emmy telecast, and earned awards in three categories, including Outstanding Comedy Series. *All in the Family* shortly thereafter became the top-rated show in prime time, and held onto that position for each of the following five seasons.

The program was able to keep an especially sharp edge over its first half dozen years thanks to the evolving character development of the series' primary cast members and the infusion of strong supporting characters. Both the Bunkers' African American next-door neighbors, the Jeffersons, and Edith's visiting cousin, Maude Findlay, eventually went on to star in successful spin-off series of their own. *All in the Family* also benefited from an occasional one-shot guest appearance, the most memorable of which featured entertainer Sammy Davis, Jr.

All in the Family's impact went beyond the world of television. The show became the focus of a heated national debate on whether the use of comedy was an appropriate means by which to combat prejudice and social inequality. In addition, the character of Archie Bunker became nothing

short of an American icon. While *Till Death Us Do Part*'s Alf Garnett was generally unlikable, producer Lear chose to soften the character for American TV, patterning him in many ways after his own father. As a result, Carroll O'Connor's characterization of Archie contained notable sympathetic qualities, allowing many viewers to see Archie in a favorable light despite his obvious foibles.

By the late 1970s, however, it was becoming clear that the show had lost much of its earlier spark. Major cast changes occurred in 1978, when Struthers and Reiner left the series, and again in 1980, when Stapleton departed. (The fact that this contractual arrangement was written into the show as Edith's death allowed Lear and company to show once again what had made this series truly memorable.) Archie quit his job in 1977 to buy and run a neighborhood tavern, and the series was retitled *Archie Bunker's Place* in 1979 to reflect the changed nature of the program. By that point, however, though still highly rated, the show no longer stood out as unique, and had become what seemed to many a rather conventional sitcom.

All in the Family's lasting impact on American television is difficult to overestimate. It helped to usher in a new generation of comedic programs that abandoned the light domestic plotlines of television's early years in favor of topical themes with important social significance. In this sense, its influence on prime time programming continues to be felt decades later.

—David Gunzerath

CAST

Archie Bunker	Carroll O'Connor
Edith Bunker (1971–80)	Jean Stapleton
Gloria Bunker Stivic (1971–78)	Sally Struthers
Mike Stivic (Meathead) (1971–78)	Rob Reiner
Lionel Jefferson (1971–75)	Mike Evans
Louise Jefferson (1971–75)	Isabel Sanford
Henry Jefferson (1971–73)	Mel Stewart
George Jefferson (1973–75)	Sherman Hemsley
Irene Lorenzo (1973–75)	Betty Garrett
Frank Lorenzo (1973–74)	Vincent Gardenia
Bert Munson (1972–77)	Billy Halop
Tommy Kelsey (1972–73)	Brendon Dillon
Tommy Kelsey (1973–77)	Bob Hastings
Justin Quigley (1973–76)	Burt Mustin
Barney Hefner (1973–83)	Allan Melvin
Jo Nelson (1973–75)	Ruth McDevitt
Stretch Cunningham (1974)	James Cromwell
Teresa Betancourt (1976–77)	Liz Torres
Stephanie Mills (1978–83)	Danielle Brisebois
Harry Snowden (1977–83)	Jason Wingreen
Hank Pivnik (1977–81)	Danny Dayton
Murray Klein (1979–81)	Martin Balsam
Mr. Van Ranseleer (1978–83)	Bill Quinn
Veronica Rooney (1979–82)	Anne Meara
Jose (1979–83)	Abraham Alvarez
Linda (1980–81)	Heidi Hagman
Raoul (1980–83)	Joe Rosario
Ellen Canby (1980–82)	Barbara Meek
Polly Swanson (1980–81)	Janet MacLachlan
Ed Swanson (1980–81)	Mel Bryant
Billie Bunker (1981–83)	Denise Miller
Gary Rabinowitz (1981–83)	Barry Gordon
Bruce (1982–83)	Bob Okazaki
Marsha (1982–83)	Jessica Nelson

PRODUCERS   Norman Lear, Woody Kling, Hal Kanter, Mort Lachman, Don Nicholl, Lou Derman, Brigit Jensen Drake, John Rich, Milt Josefberg, Michael Ross, Bernie West, Bill Danoff

PROGRAMMING HISTORY   204 Episodes

• CBS

January 1971-July 1971	Tuesday 9:30-10:00
September 1971-September 1975	Saturday 8:00-8:30
September 1975-September 1976	Monday 9:00-9:30
September 1976-October 1976	Wednesday 9:00-9:30
November 1976-September 1977	Saturday 9:00-9:30
October 1977-October 1978	Sunday 9:00-9:30
October 1978-March 1983	Sunday 8:00-8:30
Mar 1983-May 1983	Monday 8:00-8:30
May 1983	Sunday 8:00-8:30
June 1983	Monday 9:30-10:00
June 1983-Septembery 1983	Wednesday 8:00-8:30
June 1991	Sunday 8:30-9:00
June 1991-July 1991	Sunday 8:00-8:30
September 1991	Friday 8:30-9:00

FURTHER READING

Arlen, Michael. *The View from Highway 1.* New York: Farrar, Straus and Giroux, 1976.

Barnouw, Erik. *Tube of Plenty: The Evolution of American Television.* New York: Oxford University Press, 1990.

Bedell, Sally. *Up the Tube: Prime-Time TV and the Silverman Years.* New York: Viking, 1981.

Brooks, Tim, and Earle Marsh. *The Complete Directory to Prime Time Network TV Shows, 1946-Present.* 4th ed. New York: Ballantine, 1988.

"CBS Sked Shake; Shift *All in Family* to Lead Sat." *Variety* (Los Angeles), 18 August 1971.

"CBS-TV's Bigot that BBC Begat Figures to Salt Up Second Season." *Variety* (Los Angeles), 22 July 1970.

"Family Fun." *Newsweek* (New York), 15 March 1971.

Ferretti, Fred. "Are Racism and Bigotry Funny?" *New York Times,* 12 January 1971.

Gent, George. "*All in the Family* Takes First Place in Nielsen Ratings." *New York Times,* 25 May 1971.

Gitlin, Todd. *Inside Prime Time.* New York: Pantheon, 1985.

Hano, Arnold. "Can Archie Bunker Give Bigotry a Bad Name?" *New York Times Magazine,* 12 March 1972.

Kasindorf, Martin. "Archie and Maude and Fred and Norman and Alan." *New York Times Magazine,* 24 June 1973.

Leonard, John. "Bigotry as a Dirty Joke." *Life* (New York), 19 March 1971.

Metz, Robert. *CBS: Reflections in a Bloodshot Eye.* Chicago: Playboy, 1975.

O'Neil, Thomas. *The Emmys.* New York: Penguin, 1992.

Shayon, Robert Lewis. "Archie's Other Side." *Saturday Review* (New York), 8 January 1972.

———. "Love that Hate." *Saturday Review* (New York), 27 March 1971.

Waldron, Vince. *Classic Sitcoms.* New York: Macmillan, 1987.

Wander, Philip. "Counters in the Social Drama: Some Notes on All in the Family." In, Newcomb, Hotrace, editor. *Television: The Critical View.* New York: Oxford University Press, 1976.

See also Comedy, Domestic Settings; Lear, Norman; O'Connor, Carroll

ALLEN, DEBBIE
U.S. Actor/Director/Producer/Choreographer

Debbie Allen began her show business career on Broadway in the 1970s. Her debut in the chorus of *Purlie* and her performance in *A Raisin in the Sun* were noted by stage critics, and in a 1979 production of *West Side Story* her performance as Anita earned her a Tony Award nomination and a Drama Desk Award. Allen later returned to Broadway as a star, and garnered her second Tony nomination, with a 1986–87 performance in *Sweet Charity*. In 1988, she choreographed *Carrie,* a newly composed American musical, with the Royal Shakespeare Company.

Allen's stage presence and choreography quickly moved her from the Broadway stage to the larger venue of television. Through the 1970s she made guest appearances on popular programs such as *Good Times, The Love Boat* and *The Jim Stafford Show.* Her roles in the miniseries *Roots: The Next Generation* and the special *Ben Vereen—His Roots* allowed her to work with some of the most prominent African-American performers in show business and to demonstrate her dramatic and comedic acting range. She also appeared in the short-lived 1977 NBC series *3 Girls 3.* Her latest television role was in the NBC situation comedy, *In the House.* In this series, which first aired in April 1995, Allen played a newly divorced mother of two who shares her house with a former football star, played by rap artist L.L. Cool J.

In the early 1980s, a portrayal of a dance instructor, Lydia Grant, on the hit series *Fame* brought Debbie Allen to international prominence. Although the NBC show was canceled after one season, the program went on to first-run syndication for four more years. Its popularity in Britain prompted a special cast tour there and spurred a "Fame-mania" fan phenomena.

Allen's success as a dancer and actor allowed her to move behind the camera to direct and produce. While still a cast member of *Fame* she became the first African-American woman hired by a television network as a director in prime time. In 1989, after directing episodes of *Fame,* she co-wrote, produced, directed, choreographed and starred in *The Debbie Allen Special* for ABC. She received two Emmy nominations, for direction and choreography, of this variety show.

In 1988, Allen solidified her reputation as a television director and producer by turning a flawed television series, *A Different World,* into a long-running popular program. Under her leadership the program addressed political issues such as apartheid, date rape, the war in the Persian Gulf, economic discrimination, and the 1992 Los Angeles riot. The highest rated episode focused on sexual maturity and AIDS and guest starred Whoopi Goldberg, who was nominated for an Emmy award. Allen was awarded the first Responsibility in Television award from the Los Angeles Film Teachers Association for consistently representing important social issues on *A Different World.*

In 1989, Allen made her debut as a director of made-for-television movies with a remake of the 1960 film, *Pollyanna.* The telefilm, titled *Polly,* starred two players from *The Cosby Show,* Phylicia Rashad and Keshia Knight Pullman. Set in 1955, *Polly* is a musical tale of an orphan who brings happiness to a tyrannical aunt and a small Alabama town. The film was produced by Disney and NBC. Television critics hailed the display of Allen's keen sense of innovative camera work, stemming from her ability to choreograph. The film is also notable for its all-black cast and for succeeding in a genre, the musical film, rarely popular on television. Allen followed *Polly* with a sequel which aired in November 1990.

In the 1990–91 season, Allen directed the pilot and debut episode of *Fresh Prince of Bel-Air,* a series which had high ratings on NBC. That same season, she directed a highly rated episode of *Quantum Leap* in which she co-starred. In October 1991, Allen received her star on the Hollywood Walk of Fame for her achievements in television.

In 1992, Allen directed *Stompin' at the Savoy* for the CBS network. This program included a cast of prominent African-American performers: Lynn Whitfield, Vanessa Williams, Jasmine Guy, Vanessa Bell Calloway and Mario Van Peebles.

Complementing Allen's versatility as a television actor is a repertoire of critically acclaimed film roles. In 1986 she played Richard Pryor's feisty wife in his semi-autobiograph-

Debbie Allen

ical film *Jo Jo Dancer, Your Life Is Calling*, and she co-starred with Howard E. Rollins and James Cagney in Milos Foreman's *Ragtime* in 1981. Allen's debut as a feature film director will be the upcoming film *Out of Sync* starring L.L. Cool J, Victoria Dillard, and Yaphet Kotto.

Allen is one of the few African-American women working as a director and producer in television and film. Her success in TV and film production has not deterred her from her love of dance and she continues to dazzle television viewers with her choreography. In 1982, she choreographed the dance numbers for the Academy Awards and for the past consecutive five years, her unique style of choreography has been featured on the worldwide broadcast of the award ceremony. For over twenty years, Allen's contributions to television, on the three major networks and in syndicated programming, have highlighted the maturity of a performer and artistic producer with an impressive spectrum of talents in the performing arts.

—Marla L. Shelton

DEBBIE ALLEN. Born in Houston, Texas, U.S.A., 16 January 1950. Educated at Howard University, Washington, D.C., BFA (with honors) 1971; studied with Ballet Nacional and Ballet Folklorico (Mexico); Houston Ballet Foundation, Houston, Texas; New York School of Ballet. Married: 1) Wim Wilford (divorced); 2) Norm Nixon; children: Vivian Nicole and Norm, Jr. Began career as dancer with George Faison Universal Dance Experience; AMAS Repertory Theatre; taught dance, Duke Ellington School of Performing Arts; actor in television, from 1973; actor/producer/director/coreographer of various television shows, miniseries, and specials. Recipient: three Emmy Awards; one Golden Globe Award; Ford Foundation Grant; Black Filmmakers Hall of Fame Clarence Muse Youth Award, 1978; Drama Desk Award, 1979; Out Critics Circle Award, 1980.

TELEVISION SERIES

1977	*3 Girls 3*
1982	*Fame*
1987	*Bronx Zoo* (director)
1987–93	*A Different World* (producer, director)
1990–96	*Fresh Prince of Bel-Air* (director)
1990	*Quantum Leap* (also director)
1995	*In the House* (also director)

TELEVISION MINISERIES

1979	*Roots: The Next Generation*
1984	*Celebrity*

MADE-FOR-TELEVISION MOVIES

1977	*The Greatest Thing That Almost Happened*
1980	*Ebony, Ivory and Jade*
1983	*Women of San Quentin*
1989	*Polly* (director and choreographer)
1990	*Polly—Comin' Home!*
1992	*Stompin' at the Savoy*

TELEVISION SPECIALS

1982, 1991-95	*The Academy Awards* (choreographer)
1983	*The Kids from Fame*
1989	*The Debbie Allen Special* (co-writer, producer, director, choreographer)
1992	*Stompin' at the Savoy* (director)

FILMS

The Fish that Saved Pittsburgh, 1979; *Ragtime* , 1981; *Jo Jo Dancer, Your Life Is Calling*, 1986; *Mona Must Die*, 1994; *Blank Check*, 1994; *Forget Paris* (choreographer), 1995; *Out-of-Sync* (director), 1996.

STAGE

Purlie, 1971; *Ti-Jean and His Brothers,*1972; *Raisin in the Sun*, 1973; *Ain't Misbehavin'*, 1978; *The Illusion and Holiday*, 1979; *West Side Story*, 1979; *Louis*, 1981; *The Song is Kern!*, 1981; *Parade of Stars at the Palace*, 1983; *Sweet Charity*, 1986; *Carrie*, 1988.

FURTHER READING

"Doing It All—Her Way! Versatility Reaps Multiple Successes for this Exciting Entertainer." *Ebony* (New York), November 1989.

Dunning, Jennifer. "Debbie Allen Chips Away At the Glass Ceiling." *The New York Times*, 29 March 1992.

Randolph, Laura B. "Debbie Allen on Power, Pain, Passion and Prime Time." *Ebony* (New York), March 1991.

Stark, John. "It's a Different World for Dancer and Choreographer Debbie Allen: She's Moved to Prime-Time Directing." *People* (New York), 14 November 1988.

ALLEN, FRED

U.S. Comedian

Fred Allen hated television. Allen was a radio comedian for nearly two decades who, as early as 1936, had a weekly radio audience of about 20 million. When he visited *The Jack Benny Show* to continue their long running comedy feud, they had the largest audience in the history of radio, only to be later outdone by President Franklin Roosevelt during a *Fireside Chat*. The writer Herman Wouk said that Allen was the best comic writer in radio. His humor was literate, urbane, intelligent, and contemporary. Allen came to radio from vaudeville where he performed as a juggler. He was primarily self-educated and was extraordinarily well read.

Allen began his network radio career in 1932 after working vaudeville and Broadway with such comedy icons as Al Jolson, Ed Wynn, George Jessel, and Jack Benny. This was a time when the United States was in a deep economic depression, and radio in its infancy. In his autobiography *Treadmill to Oblivion*, Allen wrote that he thought radio should provide complete stories, series of episodes, and comedy situations instead of monotonous unrelated jokes then popular on vaudeville. With this idea in hand, he began his first radio program on NBC called *The Linit Bath Club Review* (named after the sponsor).

Allen's world of radio was highly competitive and commercial, just as TV would be many years later. He wrote most of the material for his weekly shows himself, usually working 12-hour days, 6 days a week. Most comedians, like Bob Hope, had an office filled with writers, but Allen used only a few assistants in writing his comedy. And some of these assistants went on to have successful careers in literature and comedy, such as Herman Wouk, author of *The Caine Mutiny* and *The Winds of War*, and Nat Hiken, who created Phil Silver's *The Phil Silvers Show* for TV. Allen's program was imbued with literate, verbal slapstick. He had ethnic comedy routines in *Allen's Alley*, appearances by celebrities such as Alfred Hitchcock, musical numbers with talent from the likes of Richard Rodgers and Oscar Hammerstein, and social commentaries on every conceivable subject, especially criticisms of the advertising and radio industry. His radio producer, Sylvester "Pat" Weaver (later to become head of NBC-TV programming), observed that Allen's humor was so popular that three out of four homes in the country were listening to Allen at the zenith of his popularity. In writing his comedy scripts, Allen compiled a personal library of over 4,000 books of humor, and read 9 newspapers (plus magazines) daily. According to the scholar Alan Havig, Allen's style of comedy had more in common with literary giants like Robert Benchley and James Thurber than with media comedians like Jack Benny and Bob Hope.

In the 1946–47 season Allen was ranked the number one show on network radio. World War II was over, Americans were beginning a new era of consumerism. And a very few consumers had recently purchased a new entertainment device called television. When Fred Allen was asked what he thought of television, he said he didn't like furniture that talked. He also said television was called a medium because "nothing on it is ever well done." Allen dismissed TV as permitting "people who haven't anything to do to watch people who can't do anything." But, after nearly two decades on radio, he fell in the ratings from number 1 to number 38 in just a few months. Such a sudden loss of audience was due to a new ABC radio give-away show called *Name That Tune*, starring Bert Parks, as well as a general decline in listeners for all of radio. Listeners of radio were rapidly becoming viewers of TV. And where the audience went, so went the advertisers. In a few short years the bottom fell out of radio. Fred Allen quickly, but not quietly, left radio in 1949.

Fred Allen

Allen was first to leave radio, but Bob Hope, Jack Benny, George Burns and Gracie Allen soon followed. They all went to star in their own TV shows. All but Fred Allen. He made a few attempts at TV, but nothing more. He first appeared on the *Colgate Comedy Theater*, where he attempted to bring to TV his *Allen's Alley* from radio. For example, the characters of the Alley were performed with puppets. Such attempts seldom successfully made the transition to the new medium. On the quiz show *Judge for Yourself* (1953–54), he was supposed to carry on witty ad-libbed conversations with guests. But as Havig states, Allen's "ad libbing was lost in the confusion of a half hour filled with too many people and too much activity". In short, Allen's humor needed more time and more language than TV allowed. He then was on a short-lived *Fred Allen's Sketchbook* (1954), and finally a became a panelist on *What's My Line?* in 1955 until his death in 1956.

Fred Allen's contributions to TV has taken two forms. First, he became one of the true critics of TV. He has remained, many decades after his death, the intellectual conscience of TV. His barbs at network TV censorship still hit at the heart of contemporary media (Allen: "Heck...is a place invented by [NBC]. NBC does not recognize hell or [CBS]"). Second, his comedy style has become part of the institution of TV comedy. His *Allen's Alley* created the character Titus Moody who turned up on TV as the Pepperidge Farm cookie man. His Senator Claghorn, also of the Alley, was transfigured into Warner Brothers TV cartoon character Foghorn Leghorn the rooster. And later, the "Senator" appeared on the Kentucky Fried Chicken TV commercial. A variety of TV comedians have done direct take-offs of Allen's performances. For example, Red Skelton's "Gussler's Gin" routine and Johnny Carson's "Mighty Carson Art Players" can be traced back to Fred Allen. And Allen's "People You Didn't Expect to Meet" is an idea that has worked for David Letterman. And of course, radio's Garrison Keeler's "Lake Wobegan" is a throw-back to Allen's style of comedy.

Allen wrote in *Treadmill to Oblivion,* "Ability, merit and talent were not requirements of writers and actors working in the industry. Audiences had to be attracted, for advertising purposes, at any cost and by any artifice. Standards were gradually lowered. A medium that demands entertainment eighteen hours a day, seven days every week, has to exhaust the conscientious craftsman and performer." He was talking about radio, but his remarks could apply just as well to television many decades later.

—Clayland H. Waite

FRED ALLEN (Fred St. James, Fred James, Freddie James). Born John Florence Sullivan in Cambridge, Massachussetts, U.S.A., 31 May 1894. Married: Portland Hoffa, 1928. Served in Army, World War I. Began performing on stage as an amateur teenage juggler, eventually adding patter and turning pro with the billing of the "World's Worst Juggler"; for ten years as humorist toured the vaudeville circuit, including 14 months in Australia, Tasmania, New Zealand and Honolulu, 1914–15; dropped juggling, settled on the professional name of "Fred Allen," and moved up from vaudeville to Broadway revues, early 1920s; worked on radio, notably *Allen's Alley* and *Texaco Star Theatre,* from 1932; a panel regular on the television quiz show *What's My Line?,* 1955–56. Died in New York City, 17 March 1956.

TELEVISION SERIES

1953	*Fred Allen's Sketchbook*
1953–54	*Judge For Yourself*
1955–56	*What's My Line?*

FILMS

Some film shorts, 1920s; *Thanks a Million,* 1935; *Sally, Irene and Mary,* 1938; *Love Thy Neighbor,* 1940; *It's in the Bag,* 1945; *We're Not Married,* 1952; *Full House,* 1953.

RADIO

The Linit Bath Club Review, 1932; *Allen's Alley,* 1932–49 ; *The Salad Bowl Revue,* 1933; *Town Hall Tonight,* 1934 ; *Texaco Star Theatre,* 1940–41.

PUBLICATIONS

Treadmill to Oblivion. Boston: Little Brown, 1954.
Much Ado about Me. Boston: Little Brown, 1956.
Fred Allen's Letters, edited by Joe McCarthy. Garden City, New York: Doubleday, 1965.

FURTHER READING

Havig, A. *Fred Allen's Radio Comedy.* Philadelphia: Temple University Press, 1990.
Taylor, R. *Fred Allen: His Life and Wit.* New York: International Polygonics, 1989.

ALLEN, GRACIE

U.S. Comedienne

Gracie Allen transferred her popular fictional persona from vaudeville, film, and radio, to American television in the 1950s. Allen had performed with her husband and partner, George Burns, for nearly 30 years when the pair debuted in *The George Burns and Gracie Allen Show* on CBS in October 1950. They had enjoyed particular success in radio, popularizing their audio program with a series of stunts that involved Allen in fictitious man hunts, art exhibits, and even a candidacy for the presidency of the United States. The transfer of their program to the small screen both extended their career (the couple were becoming too expensive for radio) and helped to legitimate the new medium.

The Burns and Allen act, a classic vaudeville routine involving a "Dumb Dora" and a "straight man," proved infinitely malleable. Initially a flirtation act, by the time it was transferred to television, it was housed in a standard situation-comedy frame: Burns and Allen played themselves, a celebrity couple, enduring various matrimonial mix-ups.

The impetus to comedy within the program was the character portrayed by Allen. Her humor was almost entirely linguistic. Often an entire episode hinged on her confusion of antecedents in a sentence, as when the couple's announcer (who also took part in the program's narrative) informed her that Burns had worked with another performer until he (meaning the other performer) had married, moved to San Diego, and had two sons—at which point she concluded that her husband was a bigamist.

The onscreen Gracie's reinterpretations of the televisional world proved extremely disruptive to people and events around her, although the disruptions were generally playful rather than serious, and were quickly settled (usually by her husband, the straight man) at the end of each episode. Allen's character thus challenged the rational order of things without ever actually threatening it.

The character's success on the program, and popularity with the viewing public, depended in large part on her total unawareness of the comic effects of her "zaniness." The onscreen Gracie was a sweet soul who on the surface embodied many of the feminine norms of the day—domesticity, reliance on her man, gentleness—even as she took symbolic pot shots at the gender order by subverting her husband's logical, masculine world.

The program, and Allen's character, were always framed by audience knowledge about the "real" George Burns and Gracie Allen. Audience members were aware, partly from well orchestrated publicity for the show and partly from observation, that only a talented and intelligent actress could manage to seem as dumb as Allen did onscreen.

The offscreen Burns and Allen were sometimes also invoked explicitly within episodes, when characters reminded the fictional George that he was financially dependent upon his co-star/spouse, who had always been the greater star of the two.

The strongest link between on- and offscreen Burns and Allen, however, was the marital bond both pairs shared—and the affection they displayed as actors and as people. Burns' first autobiography, *I Love Her, That's Why!*, placed the couple's relationship at the center of his life, reflecting its centrality to the program in which the two starred.

Burns and Allen went off the air upon Allen's retirement in 1958. Burns tried for a number of years to sustain programs and acts of his own, but it took him almost a decade to emerge as a performer in his own right. Much of his stage act for the rest of his life featured numerous jokes and stories about his wife, perpetuating the memory of her comedic energy even for those who had never seen her perform.

—Tinky "Dakota" Weisblat

GRACIE ALLEN. Born in San Francisco, California, U.S.A., 26 July 1895. Attended Star of the Sea Convent School. Married: George Burns, 1926; children: Sandra Jean and Ronald John. Joined sister Bessie in vaudeville act, Chicago, Illinois, 1909; played vaudeville as "single" act, from 1911; teamed with George Burns, 1922; toured Orpheum vaudeville circuit; toured United States and Europe in the Keith theater circuit, from 1926; played BBC radio for twenty weeks, 1926; first United States radio appearance, with Burns, on *The Rudy Vallee Show*, 1930; premiered as star of *The Adventures of Gracie* on CBS radio, 15 February 1932; starred, with Burns, in *The Burns and Allen Show* on NBC radio, 1945–50; performed in movies, 1930s; starred, with Burns, in *The George Burns and Gracie Allen Show*, CBS television, 1950–58; retired from show business in 1958. Died in Los Angeles, California, 27 August 1964.

TELEVISION SERIES

1950–58   *The George Burns and Gracie Allen Show*

FILMS

100% Service, 1931; *The Antique Shop*, 1931; *Fit to Be Tied*, 1931; *Once Over, Light*, 1931; *Pulling a Bone*, 1931; *Oh, My Operation*, 1932; *The Big Broadcast*, 1932; *International*

Gracie Allen
Photo courtesy of George Burns

House, 1933; *We're Not Dressing*, 1934; *Six of a Kind*, 1934; *Many Happy Returns*, 1934; *The Big Broadcast of 1936*, 1935; *College Holiday*, 1936; *The Big Broadcast of 1937*, 1936; *A Damsel in Distress*, 1937; *College Swing*, 1938; *Honolulu*, 1939; *Gracie Allen Murder Case*, 1939; *Mr. and Mrs. North*, 1941; *Two Girls and a Sailor*, 1944.

PUBLICATION

"Inside Me," as told to Jane Kesner Morris. *Woman's Home Companion*, March 1953.

FURTHER READING

Blythe, Cheryl, and Susan Sackett. *Say Goodnight Gracie! The Story of Burns and Allen*. New York: Dutton, 1986.

Burns, George. *Gracie: A Love Story*. New York: Putnam, 1988.

Burns, George, with Cynthia Hobart. *I Love Her, That's Why! An Autobiography*. New York: Simon and Schuster, 1955.

"....Burns and Allen..." *Newsweek* (New York), 24 June 1957.

"How Gracie Gets That Way." *TV Guide* (Radnor, Pennsylvania), 8 October 1955.

Hubbard, Kim. "George Burns Writes a Final Loving Tribute to Gracie Allen..." *People Weekly* (New York), 31 October 1988.

See also Comedy, Domestic Settings; Burns, George; *George Burns and Gracie Allen Show*

ALLEN, STEVE

U.S. Comedian/Host/Composer/Writer

Steve Allen has appropriately been termed television's renaissance man. He has hosted numerous television programs, appeared in several motion pictures, written more than forty books, and composed several thousand songs. He once won a $1,000 bet that he couldn't compose fifty songs a day for a week.

Allen began his career as a radio announcer in 1942. In 1946 he joined the Mutual Broadcasting System as a comedian and two years later signed with CBS as a late-night disc jockey on KNX in Hollywood. He first gained national attention when his program was booked as a thirteen-week substitute for *Our Miss Brooks* during the summer of 1950. This led to his first television program, *The Steve Allen Show* which debuted on Christmas Day 1950 on CBS. The show was later moved to Thursday nights where it alternated with the popular *Amos 'n' Andy*.

In 1954 Allen began hosting a daily late-night show on NBC, *The Tonight Show*. During the next three years, he introduced many television innovations continued by his successors. Most of these involved his audience. Using a hand microphone, he went into the audience to talk with individuals; he answered questions submitted by the audience; members of the audience would attempt to "stump the band" by requesting songs the band couldn't play. Allen involved his announcer Gene Rayburn in nightly chit chat and he spoke with the band leaders, Skitch Henderson and Bobby Byrne. These techniques epitomized Allen's belief that "people will laugh at things that happen before their eyes much more readily than they will at incidents they're merely told about."

In 1956 Allen became a part-time host on *Tonight* because he was appearing in a new version of *The Steve Allen Show*. Still on NBC, he was now programmed on Sunday nights—opposite *The Ed Sullivan Show* on CBS. Thus began one of the most famous ratings wars in television history. Steve Allen and Ed Sullivan were perhaps as distinct from one another as two men could be. Allen was a witty, innovative performer, willing to try virtually anything. Sullivan was a stiff master of ceremonies who compelled his guests to conform to rigid standards of decorum. Although Allen occasionally received higher ratings, Sullivan eventually won the war and after the 1960 season NBC moved *The Steve Allen Show* to Mondays. A year later Allen took the show into syndication and continued for three more years. From 1964 to 1967 he hosted the highly successful game show *I've Got a Secret* on CBS.

Steve Allen's most innovative television offering was *Meeting of Minds*. The format was an hour-long dramatized discussion of social issues. Allen would act as the moderator accompanied by his "guests" in this imaginative exercise, historical characters such as Galileo, Attila the Hun, Charles Darwin, Aristotle, Hegel or Dostoevski. The idea for this program came in 1960, following Allen's reading of Morti-

mer Adler's *The Syntopicon*. Rejected by the major networks, the series was accepted by the Public Broadcasting Service in 1977 and ran until 1981.

Through his long career as an entertainer Allen also developed a reputation as a social activist. He considered running for Congress as a Democrat from California; he actively opposed capital punishment; he openly supported the controversial comedian Lenny Bruce. He wrote about the plight of migrant farm workers in *The Ground is Our Table* (1966) and what he considered the collapse of ethics in America in *Ripoff* (1979). Allen still occasionally appears on television but spends most of his time operating Meadowlane Music and Rosemeadow Publishing, located in Van Nuys, California.

—Lindsay E. Pack

STEPHEN (VALENTINE PATRICK WILLIAM) ALLEN. Born in New York City, U.S.A., 26 December 1921. Attended Drake University, 1941; Arizona State Teacher's College, 1942. Married: 1) Dorothy Goodman, 1943 (divorced, 1952); children: Stephen, Brian, and David; 2) Jayne Meadows, 1954; child: William Christopher. Worked as radio announcer at stations KOY, Phoenix, 1942; KFAC and KMTR, Los Angeles, 1944; entertainer-comedian, Mutual Network, 1946–47; entertainer-comedian and disc jockey, CBS television, 1948–50; created and hosted *The Tonight Show*, NBC television, 1954–56; created and hosted *Meeting of Minds*, Public Broadcasting Service, 1977–81; continued television guest appearances,

Steve Allen
Photo courtesy of Steve Allen

1970s–90s; composed more than 5,700 songs, several musicals; author of 46 books; vocalist, pianist, over 40 albums/CDs. Recipient: Grammy Award, 1964; Emmy Award, 1981; named to Academy of Television Arts and Sciences Hall of Fame, 1986.

TELEVISION SERIES

1950–52	*The Steve Allen Show*
1950–52	*Songs for Sale*
1953–55	*Talent Patrol*
1954–56	*The Tonight Show*
1956-61	*The Steve Allen Show*
1964–67	*I've Got a Secret*
1967	*The Steve Allen Comedy Hour*
1977–81	*Meeting of Minds*
1980–81	*The Steve Allen Comedy Hour*
1985–86	*The Start of Something Big* (host)

TELEVISION MINISERIES

1976	*Rich Man, Poor Man*

MADE-FOR-TELEVISION MOVIES

1972	*Now You See It, Now You Don't*
1979	*Stone*
1979	*The Gossip Columnist*
1984	*The Ratings Game*
1985	*Alice in Wonderland*
1996	*James Dean: A Portrait*

TELEVISION SPECIALS

1954	*Fanfare*
1954	*The Follies of Suzy*
1954	*Sunday in Town* (co-host)
1955	*Good Times* (host)
1957	*The Timex All-Star Jazz Show I* (host)
1966	*The Hollywood Deb Stars of 1966* (co-host)
1976	*The Good Old Days of Radio* (host)
1981	*I've Had it Up to Here* (host)
1982	*Boop Oop a Doop* (narrator)
1983–86	*Life's Most Embarrassing Moments* (host)
1984	*Stooge Snapshots*

FILMS

Down Memory Lane, 1949; *The Benny Goodman Story*, 1955; *College Confidential*, 1960; *Warning Shot*, 1967; *Where Were You When the Lights Went Out?*, 1968; *The Funny Farm*, 1982; *Amazon Women on the Moon*, 1987; *Great Balls of Fire!*, 1989; *The Player*, 1992; *Casino*, 1995.

PUBLICATIONS (selection)

The Funny Men. New York: Simon and Schuster, 1956.
Mark it and Strike it: An Autobiography. New York: Holt, 1960.
Dialogues in Americanism, with William F. Buckley; Robert Maynard Hutchins; Brent L. Bozell; and James MacGregor Burns. Chicago: H. Regnery, 1964.
The Ground is Our Table. Garden City, New York: Doubleday, 1966.
Bigger than a Breadbox. Garden City, New York: Doubleday, 1967.
Ripoff, with Roslyn Bernstein and Donald H. Dunn. Secaucus, New Jersey: L. Stuart, 1979.
How To Be Funny: Discovering the Comic You, with Jane Wollman. New York: McGraw-Hill, 1987.
The Passionate Non-smokers Bill of Rights: The First Guide to Enacting Non-smoking Legislation, with Bill Adler, Jr. New York: Morrow, 1989.
Hi-ho, Steverino!: My Adventures in the Wonderful Wacky World of TV. Fort Lee, New Jersey: Barricade Books, 1992.
Make 'em Laugh. Buffalo, New York: Prometheus, 1993.
More Steve Allen on the Bible, Religion and Morality. Buffalo, New York: Prometheus, 1993.

FURTHER READING

Carter, Bill. "Steve Allen: The Father of All Talk Show Hosts." *The New York Times*, 14 April 1994.
Gould, Jack. "TV Comedians on Serious Side." *The New York Times*, 3 February 1960.
"Steve Allen's Nonsense is Pure Gold on NBC Radio." *Television-Radio Age* (New York), 7 March 1988.

See also *Steve Allen Show;* Talks Shows; *Tonight Show*

ALLISON, FRAN

U.S. Television Personality

Fran Allison is perhaps best known for playing the warm-hearted human foil to the Kuklapolitan Players, a troupe of puppets familiar to almost every viewer in the early days of U.S. television. Allison appeared with the puppets on the children's program *Kukla, Fran and Ollie*, which aired regularly from 1948 to 1957, and in subsequent reunions in the late 1960s and mid-1970s.

Born in Iowa, Allison began working as a songstress on local Waterloo, Iowa, radio programs and eventually moved to Chicago in 1937, where she was hired as a staff singer and personality on NBC-Radio. Audiences became familiar with her from numerous radio appearances, first as a singer on such programs as *Smile Parade*, and *Uncle Ezra's Radio Station* (also known as *Station EZRA*), and later on *The Breakfast Club* as the gossipy spinster Aunt Fanny—who loved to dish gossip about such fictitious townsfolk as Bert Beerbower, Orphie Hackett and Ott Ort—based on a character she first created for a local Iowa radio program. Allison appeared on both the radio and television versions of *Don McNeill's The Breakfast Club* for more than 25 years. The Aunt Fanny character was briefly spun off on her own 30-minute radio program in 1939, *Sunday Dinner at Aunt Fanny's*. But it was on *Kukla, Fran and Ollie* that Allison became the "First Lady of Chicago Broadcasting."

While her husband, Archie Levington, was serving in the army, Allison worked on bond-selling tours, during which she met and became good friends with puppeteer Burr Tillstrom. When the time came to choose an appropriate sidekick for his new television series, Tillstrom wanted to work with "a pretty girl, someone who preferably could sing," someone who could improvise along with Tillstrom and with the show's informal structure. According to Tillstrom, when he and Allison met four days later, she was so enthusiastic about the show and working with her friend that she never asked how much the job paid. With only a handshake, they went on the air live for the first time that very afternoon.

Shortly before his death in 1985, Tillstrom tried to capture the nature of the unique relationship that Allison had with his puppets: "She laughed, she sympathized, loved them, sang songs to them. She became their big sister, favorite teacher, babysitter, girlfriend, mother." More than just the "girl who talks to Burr [Tillstrom]'s puppets," Allison treated each character as an individual personality, considered each her friend, and, by expressing genuine warmth and affection for them, made the audience feel the same way. She once remarked that she believed in them so implicitly that it would take a few days to become accustomed to a new version of one of the puppets.

It was through Allison that the Kuklapolitans came to life as individual personalities with life histories. Each show was entirely improvised. The only prior planning was a basic storyline. Characters discussed their backgrounds, where they attended school, and their relatives. Allison was the first to mention Ollie's mother Olivia and niece Dolores, and Tillstrom added them to their growing number of Kuklapolitans. In addition to prompting the characters to talk about themselves, Allison herself invented some of the characters' histories, such as announcing that Buelah Witch's alma mater was Witch Normal.

Allison's radio and television work continued after the initial run of *Kukla, Fran and Ollie*. In the late-1950s, Allison hosted *The Fran Allison Show*, a panel discussion program on local Chicago television, telecast in color and considered, at that time, "the most ambitious show in Chicago's decade of television." She also continued to appear on television musical specials over the years, including *Many Moons* (1954), *Pinocchio* (with Mickey Rooney in 1957), *Damn Yankees* (1967) and *Miss Pickerell* (1972). Allison was reunited with Burr Tillstrom and the Kuklapolitans for the series' return in 1969 on Public Broadcasting and as the hosts of the *CBS Children's Film Festival* on Saturday afternoons from 1971 to 1979. In the 1980s, Allison hosted a local Los Angeles (KHJ-TV) program, *Prime Time*, a show for senior citizens.

Fran Allison

Allison was nominated once for an Emmy Award as "Most Outstanding Kinescope Personality" in 1949, but lost to Milton Berle. In 1988, she was inducted into Miami Children's Hospital's Ambassador David M. Walters International Pediatrics Hall of Fame, which honors men and women of medicine and laypersons who have made a significant contribution to the health and happiness of children everywhere.

—Susan R. Gibberman

FRAN ALLISON. Born in La Porte City, Iowa, U.S.A. Attended Coe College, Cedar Rapids, Iowa. Married: Archie Levington. Began career as radio singer, Waterloo, Iowa; staff singer, various shows on NBC Radio, Chicago, from 1937; star of radio show, *Sunday Dinner at Aunt Fanny's*, 1939; regular guest, *Don McNeill's Breakfast Club*, radio and television program, through 1940s and 1950s; joined Burr Tillstrom, puppeteer, with *Kukla, Fran and Ollie* television program, Chicago, 1947; host, with Tillstrom's puppets, *Children's Film Festival*, PBS, 1971–79; in local radio and television from 1970s. Died in Sherman Oaks, California, 13 June 1989.

TELEVISION (selection)
1948–52, 1954–57
  19 61–62, 1969–71
  19 76–76   *Kukla, Fran, and Ollie* (host)
1950–51   *Don McNeill's TV Club*

TELEVISION SPECIALS
1954   *Many Moons*
1957   *Pinocchio*
1967   *Damn Yankees*
1972   *Miss Pickerell*

FURTHER READING
Anderson, Susan Heller. "Fran Allison, 81, the Human Side of 'Kukla, Fran and Ollie' Show, Dies." *The New York Times,* 14 June 1989.
Fay, B. "Allison in Wonderland." *Colliers* (New York), 4 March 1950.

"Fran Allison." *Variety* (Los Angeles), 21 June 1989.
Hughes, C. "Kukla and Ollie's Real-Life Heroine." *Coronet* (Chicago), October 1951.
Kogan, Rick. "Fran Allison, of 'Kukla, Fran and Ollie.'" *Chicago Tribune*, 14 June 1987.
Long, J. "Dragon's Girlfriend." *American Magazine*, March 1950.
"Triple Life of Fran Allison." *McCall's* (New York), March 1953.

See also Chicago School of Television; Children and Television; *Kukla, Fran, and Ollie*; Tillstrom, Burr

ALLOCATION

U.S. Broadcast Policy

The Federal Communications Commission's (FCC) methods of allocating broadcasting frequencies in the United States have long been a subject of debate and controversy. The key issues have been: first, whether television should be controlled by the few strongest networks; second, whether the FCC is responsible for setting aside frequencies for non-commercial or educational broadcasters, even though the media operate within a privately held system; and third, whether spectrum allocations should change when new technologies, requiring use of the airwaves, are introduced. The Communication Act of 1934 provides for a way to maintain federal control over all channels of interstate and foreign radio transmission, and to provide for the use of such channels, but not their ownership.

The act outlines a four-step process for allocating frequencies. An entity that applies for a construction permit (the right to build a broadcast station) must seek a specific channel, antenna location, coverage area, times of operation and power level of preference. If that applicant is selected for an allocation, the FCC then issues the construction permit. When the station is built, the owners must prove their transmitter and antenna can perform to FCC standards. The aspirant can then apply for a station license. Usually, applicants must also prove U.S. citizenship, good character free of criminal records, sufficient financial resources and proof of expert technical abilities.

When a few experimenters first put voice over wireless telegraphy at the turn of the century, there was no immediate need for a system of allocation. Many "broadcasters" were amateurs working with low-power systems. Even so, other uses were apparent and growth of radio use was rapid. It was interrupted, however, by World War I, when the government chose to take over all domestic frequencies to insure control of airwave communication. After the war, when the British government chose to retain political power of its broadcast frequencies and form a public broadcasting system, the U.S. government instead decided to rely upon the entrepreneurial spirit and allow private profit from broad-

casting. The technology and the industry were regulated under the provisions of the Radio Act of 1912 which placed control in the U.S. Department of Commerce, then administered by Secretary Herbert Hoover.

The Second National Radio Conference, 20 March 1923, addressed problems associated with increasing the number of signals on the broadcast spectrum. The Conference recommendations included the equitable distribution of frequencies to local areas and discussed wavelengths, power, time of operation and apparatus. More importantly, the Conference suggested three concepts that have not changed with time and technology. The first recognized that broadcasting usually covers a limited area and sanctioned local community involvement in the licensing process. The second concept acknowledged the limited amount of frequency space in the electromagnetic spectrum and supported the assignment of one consistent wavelength to broadcasters. The third concept proposed that once a broadcasting organization was assigned a certain frequency, it should not have to move that placement due to new regulation.

These recommendations died in the U.S. House Committee on the Merchant Marine and Fisheries and in Senate committee. No action was taken. Commerce Secretary Hoover believed government control had no place in American broadcasting; those using the airwaves should join together and regulate themselves.

Congress reflected the conflicting views. Though litigation against the government rendered the Radio Act of 1912 virtually inoperable, 50 separate bills failed in Congress before the federal legislature passed the Radio Act of 1927. Cases such as *Hoover v. Intercity Radio* (1923) held that the government could not refuse a license to an interested party, but could designate a frequency and police interferences. In the next major case, *United States vs. Zenith Radio Corporation* (1926), a federal judge ruled the Commerce Department had no jurisdiction to regulate radio. Other rulings by the U.S. Attorney General completely nullified Department of Commerce control.

Yet more radio broadcasters wanted frequencies and with 716 radio stations on the air, national regulation was more and more necessary. With the Radio Act of 1927, the federal government decided to retain ownership of the airwaves but allow private interests to hold continuing licenses. The licenses were renewable after three years, depending on the holder's ability to serve the "public interest, convenience, and necessity."

Networks had grown substantially after 1926. Religious, educational, cultural, civil liberties and labor organizations also sought a voice amidst the privately held, commercially supported licensees. Yet the 1927 Act did not successfully regulate the system. It was replaced seven years later by the Communications Act of 1934.

The two acts had many similarities and neither altered the allocations already in place for the burgeoning broadcast networks CBS and NBC. Among existing non-profit broadcasters, many educational institutions were still forced to share frequencies and in the end most educators dropped their partial licenses and chose to be silent. Yet the lobbying efforts of Paulist Priest John B. Harney made Congress realize the airwaves could be used for social good by non-profit interests and the 1934 Act included a provision to study such allocations. Still, the conflict was not resolved until 1945 when 20 FM channels between 88 and 92 MHz were reserved for non-commercial and educational broadcasting. These frequencies represented 20 percent of the broadcast band.

Among the commercial networks, each had considerable power over its affiliate stations until an FCC ruling limited the degree of contractual control over affiliate operations. But practical authority over the dependent affiliates persisted since networks supplied most programming.

By 1938 NBC and CBS commanded the great majority of licensed wattage through owned stations or affiliates. In 1941 the FCC's Report on Chain Broadcasting was accepted by the Supreme Court in *NBC v. U.S.* (1943). The ruling led to a separation of NBC into two radio networks, one of which was later sold and became ABC. Four way network competition began in the radio marketplace among Mutual, the fledgling ABC, and the dominators, CBS and NBC.

As of 1941, six television stations had been approved and two were in operation; CBS and RCA stepped in early to receive construction permits and licenses. The major networks were joined by receiver maker Allen B. DuMont and each ventured into television as network programmers in the 1940s. The three networks divided the week, each programming two or three nights without competition.

The FCC settled the placement of the radio bandwidth in 1945, but allocation problems did not end. Television's impending maturity created more spectrum confusion. As it had done with radio, the government had issued experimental and early frequency allocations for television on the VHF and UHF spectrums. Large broadcasting corporations obtained early signal assignments both to monopolize the new medium and to sell a new product, television receivers.

The problem with television allocations was the limited amount of bandwidth compared to radio signal space. The

FCC had planned eighteen channels, each six megacycles wide between 50 and 294 megacycles. In the VHF spectrum space, only 13 channels existed which could support television signals. Cities 150 miles apart could share a channel; towns 75 miles apart could have consecutively placed station signals. When the commission considered rules in September of 1945, it was decided that 140 metropolitan districts would be allocated VHF broadcasting channels.

The Television Broadcast Association supported shorter distances between localities using the same spectrum space for signal transmission. ABC and CBS believed the future of television existed in the more generous UHF spectrum space. Several network leaders argued either to transfer all television delivery to the more capacious UHF or to allow existing stations to slowly move to UHF. Instead, the FCC approved a VHF delivery plan in November 1945. 500 stations would be allocated to the 140 communities, with no allocations planned for channel 1. The FCC plan did not move any previously granted station frequencies. It did, however, allow shorter distances between eastern U.S. station assignments. New York City was given seven channels; smaller towns were allocated limited coverage and lower powered television signals.

By 1948, the FCC realized the November 1945 plan would not work and advocated moving all television to UHF. By then fifteen stations were on the air. While a final plan could be developed, the FCC added some VHF signal restrictions and completely eliminated use of channel one. Also that year, the FCC again held further allocation hearings. The resulting ruling increased the number of stations but questioned the use of UHF for television delivery. The new plan now placed 900 stations in more than 500 communities, still utilizing only the VHF band. Confusion, conflict, and controversy continued and on 29 September 1948 the FCC halted further allocation of station licenses. Only 108 stations were on the air. This action became known as the Freeze of 1948.

Construction of the stations previously approved, but not built, continued and more VHF stations did begin broadcasting between 1948 and the end of the freeze in April 1952. Many television industry interests still supported UHF utilization, but manufacturers had not yet developed transmission equipment for UHF. Television sets were not being built to receive the higher signals. Potential problems with UHF included signal strength and interference. Nevertheless, the FCC decided to begin UHF television without additional testing.

With regard to station allocations, the FCC's Sixth Report and Order was a most salient document. There the Commission decided to maintain placement of the existing VHF stations, though a few were ordered to change bandwidth within the VHF spectrum. The new plan created 2,053 allotments in 1,291 communities.

The FCC aggressively assigned UHF stations to smaller towns and left VHF for large cities. The number of stations per community depended upon population. For example, a community with 250,000 to one million people received four to six stations. Except for Los Angeles and New York which secured seven stations in the VHF spectrum, the FCC allocated no more than four VHF stations per locality. Spacing of the same channel between communities depended on such factors as geographical location, population density, and tropospheric interference. Cities at least 170 miles apart could have received allotment of the same channel.

The FCC made a historically significant ruling when it chose to enter UHF broadcasting without materially altering existing allocations. Since many sets had no UHF equipment, the stations with VHF station assignments had the upper hand over new UHF stations. It would be years before any large population could receive UHF. More importantly, the decision created a situation of the early bird catching the worm. The companies with the first granted allocations, namely NBC and CBS, also had the best signal positions. The FCC chose to maintain network dominance of television and essentially gave the large networks control over the future of the new medium. For most viewers, it was easier to tune to the broadcasting giants than to new networks or independent stations.

Allocation of non-commercial stations was another important provision of the Sixth Report and Order. FCC Commissioner Frieda Hennock, a New York attorney, argued for spectrum space for educational television. She established her place in broadcasting history when the FCC decided to make 252 non-commercial assignments, including 68 VHF and 174 UHF stations. This was one tenth of all stations assigned. Any community with one or two VHF stations in operation won a VHF educational television frequency. The first non-commercial station reached the airwaves in 1954.

Television station allocations moved slowly until the middle 1970s. ABC, operating largely on UHF stations, jockeyed for positioning against the stronger networks, CBS and NBC. In 1975, in a period of government deregulation, the FCC liberalized both frequency allocations and methods of television delivery. The large fees required for satellite receiving stations had diminished, enhancing the possibilities for both satellite and cable delivery of television to homes and businesses.

The FCC again began an aggressive period of television station allocations between 1975 and 1988, primarily assigning UHF spectrum licenses. During this period, more than 300 stations began telecasting. In 1975, 513 VHF and 198 UHF stations were on the air. By 1988, 543 VHF and 501 UHF stations broadcasted shows. The advent of cable somewhat leveled the competitive lead of lower-numbered VHF stations; the reception of each station was equal when provided through the wire and many homes now subscribed to cable systems. The added popularity of remote controlled, hundred-plus channel, cable-ready receivers made any signal a finger-press away.

Deregulation also created still more television signal competition, all governed through FCC allocations. Low power television, or short range signals serving communities within cities and smaller towns in rural areas, grew as additional licenses were granted in the 1980s. Though these stations were originally expected to handle either home shopping or community access programs, many low power stations became competitive with other television stations by becoming cable carriers.

Because the major networks already held affiliate contracts in most markets, these new UHF and LPTV stations were largely independently owned. The existence of more and more unaffiliated stations opened a door for the creation of new television networks and new program providers. In 1985, the FOX Broadcasting Network was created as a fourth network by linking a number of the new, largely independent stations. Specialty networks, such as the Spanish-language Univision and Telemundo networks, and broadcast-cable hybrid networks such as Home Shopping Network and Trinity Broadcast Network (religious) developed in the late 1980s. In 1994, Paramount and Warner Brothers Studios entered the arena with networks of broadcast stations airing new programming. The shows presented on these alternative networks have most often been outside the scope of the large networks. Some have challenged traditional network notions of "taste" or programming standards and have presented new types of shows. Others have focused on a selected audience such as Spanish-speakers or home shoppers.

In 1994, FOX Broadcasting Company became concerned with the signal power, and resulting audience reach, of its affiliates. The network made a series of contract changes, in essence trading several of its UHF outlets for stronger VHF stations. In those deals, many independent broadcasters were pushed aside for stations owned by broadcast groups such as New World Entertainment. The end result was an increase in VHF placements for FOX shows without resort to issues or problems related to allocation.

The future of station allocation is unclear. In the early 1990s, when High Definition Television (HDTV) was expected to overtake U.S. television, skeptics pointed to the history of U.S. television allocations. HDTV could have required more extensive bandwidth, and therefore, the reordering of spectrum allocations. But in the past, except for the shifting of some VHF stations required by the Sixth Report and Order, the FCC has not changed a previously granted allocation no matter how compelling or leveling the reason. The dominance of the major networks has always been preserved. The channel positions have never changed materially, and audiences have remained comfortable with familiar placements. It is unlikely that the FCC will dabble with allocations in the future. Yet, as viewers grow increasingly dependent on cable as their television provider, the role of station placement may decrease in importance. Future station assignments and changes will hardly affect either cable channel placement or the social routines of the television viewer.

—Joan Stuller-giglione

FURTHER READING

Barrows, Roscoe L., with others. "Development of Television: FCC Allocations and Standards." In, Lichty, Lawrence W., and Malachi C. Topping, editors. *American Broadcasting: A Sourcebook of Radio and Television.* New York: Hastings House, 1975.

Brown, James A. "Struggle Against Commercialism: The 1934 'Harney Lobby' For Nonprofit Frequency Allocations." *Journal of Broadcasting and Electronic Media* (Washington, D.C.), 1984.

Head, Sydney W., and Christopher H. Sterling. *Broadcasting in America.* Sixth edition, Boston, Massachusetts: Houghton Mifflin, 1990.

Krasnow, Erwin G. "Public Airwave Ownership Was Always a Myth." *Legal Times* (Washington, D.C.) 6 August 1984.

Lichty, Lawrence W. "The Impact of FRC and FCC Commissioners' Background on the Regulation of Broadcasting." In, Lichty, Lawrence W. and Malachi C. Topping, editors. *American Broadcasting: A Sourcebook of Radio and Television.* New York: Hastings House, 1975.

Mayes, Thorn. "History of the American Marconi Company." In, Lichty, Lawrence W. and Malachi C. Topping, editors. *American Broadcasting: A Sourcebook of Radio and Television.* New York: Hastings House, 1975.

Obuchowski, Janice. "The Unfinished Task of Spectrum Policy Reform." (Special Issue on the Sixtieth Anniversary of the Communications Act of 1934). *Federal Communications Law Journal* (Los Angeles, California), December 1994.

Pepper, Robert. "The Pre-Freeze Television Stations." In, Lichty, Lawrence W. and Malachi C. Topping, editors. *American Broadcasting: A Sourcebook of Radio and Television.* New York: Hastings House, 1975.

Rivkin, Steven R. "FCC to Electrics: Move, Use, or Lose!" *Public Utilities Fortnightly* (Arlington, Virginia), 1 May 1992.

Sterling, Christopher H. "WTMJ-FM: A Case Study in the Development of FM Broadcasting." In, Lichty, Lawrence W., and Malachi C. Topping, editors. *American Broadcasting: A Sourcebook of Radio and Television.* New York: Hastings House, 1975.

Sterling, Christopher H., and John M. Kittross. *Stay Tuned: A Concise History of American Broadcasting.* Belmont, California: Wadsworth, 1990.

Stern, Robert H. "Television in the Thirties." In, Lichty, Lawrence W., and Malachi C. Topping, editors. *American Broadcasting: A Sourcebook of Radio and Television.* New York: Hastings House, 1975.

Turow, Joseph. *Media Systems in Society: Understanding Industries, Strategies, and Power.* White Plains, New York: Longman, 1992.

See also Educational Television; Federal Communications Commission; "Freeze" of 1948; Hennock, Frieda B.; United States: Networks; United States: Communication Act of 1934

ALMOND, PAUL

Canadian Producer/Director

Paul Almond is the producer and director of more than 100 television dramas in Toronto, London, and Los Angeles between 1954 and 1967. Almond has produced and directed dramas for such Canadian Broadcasting Corporation (CBC) shows as *Folio, The Unforeseen,* and *Wojeck.*

Among his many accomplishments in "live" or "live to tape" television are the early experimental religious drama *The Hill,* which used simple wooden platforms, a cyclorama and improvisation; Arthur Hailey's realistic early drama about the threats of nuclear technology, *Seeds of Power;* the fascinating, televisual adaptation of Dylan Thomas' radio piece *Under Milk Wood,* which alternated between stylized shots of elements of the set with realistic shots of the actors; Harold Pinter's controversial *Birthday Party; A Close Prisoner,* the self-reflexive and chilling satire by Clive Exton; and television versions of Christopher Fry's *Sleep of Prisoners, Venus Observed,* and *A Phoenix too Frequent,* and Jean Anouilh's *Antigone.* He also produced and directed a chilling adaptation of *Crime and Punishment,* called *The Murderer;* the dark, anti-war comedy *The Neutron and the Olive* and his creative partner, designer Rudy Dorn's drama about World War II from the point

Paul Almond

of view of a German soldier, *The Broken Sky*. Other successful adaptations included *Macbeth*, with Sean Connery and Zoe Caldwell, using only a flight of steps and a huge throne, and *Julius Caesar*, using one 12-foot decorative column. At the time of these "experimental" productions Dorn and Almond shared a theory that the "only real thing was the emotion expressed on the face of a really good actor".

Almond directed for the most successful series in CBC television history, *Wojeck*, including the prescient episode on drug abuse ("All Aboard for Candyland"), at a time when such subjects were rarely seen on television.

Two of his 1960s dramas were censored by the CBC: Anouilh's *Point of Departure*, which showed two unmarried people in bed together, and *Shadow of a Pale Horse*, a vivid anti-war drama which depicted, according to the broadcaster, a too explicit hanging in one scene. In instances such as these, when the CBC management threatened to cancel a programme (which became easier when tape came into use), the corporation, under pressure from its creative staff, sometimes compromised by scheduling the drama at 11:30 P.M. when it was hoped that everyone likely to complain was in bed. In the case of Michael Tait's *Fellowship* the CBC canceled the show altogether, but relented and broadcast it at a later date. In a rare return to television in 1978 Almond directed the award-winning docudrama *Every Person Is Guilty*, on the anthology *For the Record*.

Television critics and colleagues said of Paul Almond that he was "the mystic", "the romantic", "the man with an eye for symbolic levels of meaning", an "actor's director". Camera-man and well-known television writer Grahame Woods said, "he's very responsive and creates a lot of energy. He had a passion for what he was doing and it's infectious." The actor and director David Gardner characterised Almond's work as "moody... The camera moved a great deal. He was a very volatile director. But once you got to know Paul it was terrific."

Paul Almond himself has said that in some ways he preferred live television to any other form, because it had not only an excitement but a flow of action. In his view, live television allowed both the camera-man and the director more freedom to respond to the performance itself and literally "call the shots" in unforeseen patterns and rhythms. Early television did not require three people to run a camera. Almond was one of the most influential of the generation of producers and directors in the 1950s and 1960s who were discovering what could be done with the huge, clumsy and unreliable cameras of live television. He and his co-conspirators took "live-to-tape" drama, which was supposed to be taped with minimum interruption because it was very difficult to edit into territory which demanded many pauses for change of scene, costume, or special effects. From those early experiments and the eventual discovery of cleaner easier ways to edit tape came true electronic drama.

With limited CBC experience of filmed TV drama, Almond adapted to film so well that his first full-length feature film *Isabel* in 1968 (shown on the CBC in 1969) was a critical success and was followed by such films as *The Act of the Heart, Final Assignment,* and *Captive Hearts*. He is still producing and directing feature films.

—Mary Jane Miller

PAUL ALMOND. Born in Montreal, Quebec, Canada, 1931. Attended Bishop's College School, Lennoxville, Quebec; McGill University, Montreal, B.A.; Balliol College Oxford, M.A.. Married: Geneviève Bujold, 1967. Director for a Shakespearean repertory company, England; returned to join the CBC in Toronto, 1954; directed or produced various drama, action, comedy and horror series and specials for TV until 1967; independent producer since 1967. Recipient: Bronze Prize, Houston Film Festival, 1981.

TELEVISION (selection)
1955–67	*Folio*
1958–60	*The Unforeseen*
1959–67	*Festival*
1960–61	*R.C.M.P.*
1960–61	*First Person* (producer)
1961–64	*Playdate*
1963–66	*The Forest Rangers*
1966	*Wojeck* (director)

MADE-FOR-TELEVISION MOVIES (selection)
1956	*The Queen of Spades* (producer)
1957	*Who Destroyed the Earth*
1963	*The Rose Tattoo* (producer)
1967	*La Roulotte aux Poupées* (director)
1979	*Every Person Is Guilty*

FILM (selection)
Isabel, 1968; *The Act of the Heart*, 1969; *Journey*, 1971; *Final Assignment*, 1979; *Ups and Downs*, 1981; *Kiss Me Better*, 1981; *Eye of the Falcon*, 1985; *Captive Hearts*, 1987; *The Dance Goes On*, 1991; *Freedom Had a Price* (narrator), 1994.

FURTHER READING
Arsenault, Andre G. "On Location: Paul Almond's Fate of a Hunter." *Cinema Canada* (Montreal), February 1987.
"Director Almond Misses Prep Bandwagon." *Calgary* (Canada), *Herald*, 11 December 1983.
Drainie, Bronwyn. *Living the Part: John Drainie and the Dilemma of Canadian Stardom.* Toronto: Macmillan, 1988.
Rutherford, Paul. *When Television Was Young: Prime Time Canada 1952-1967.* Toronto, Canada, and Buffalo, New York: University of Toronto Press, 1990.

See also Canadian Programming in English; *Wojeck*

AMEN

U.S. Situation Comedy

From 1986 to 1991, *Amen* aired on NBC. Set around a Philadelphia parish, this was the first hit situation-comedy to focus upon religion, an African-American church in particular, depicting, as a Jet magazine article put it, "the political as well as humorous side of [this] centuries-old institution." Emphasizing the relationship between the church's virtuous minister, played by Clifton Davis, and its shrewd, quick witted deacon, played by Sherman Hemsley, this comedy highlighted the continuous conflicts between these contrasting principals. By centralizing these characters' comedic struggles, Amen proved a successful parody, satirizing as well as exploring the everyday workings of their church, from service to choir to congregation. Produced by Carson Productions, Amen gained top-ratings throughout much of its prime-time life.

Focusing primarily on the apparently endless conflict between Deacon Ernest Frye and the Reverend Reuben Gregory, *Amen* was able to capitalize on the humorous dissimilarities separating these perpetually arguing characters. Frye, played expertly by Hemsley, was not unlike George Jefferson, Hemsley's arrogant, determined character for eleven seasons on *The Jeffersons*. The deacon was stubborn, aggressive and extremely vocal. He had taken over the church from his father, the founder of the First Community Church of Philadelphia, and resisted giving up his control and decision making power, especially to Reverend Gregory. Ironically, however, Deacon Frye's melodramatic antics usually lost more control then they gained, leaving a situation Reverend Gregory was often forced to resolve, and opening Frye to the sarcastic ridicule of the congregation.

Gregory, on the other hand, was a kind-hearted, ethical pastor with the church's best interests at heart. Mild-mannered in action and even-toned in voice, Reverend Gregory was a distinct contrast to the boisterous, authoritarian Deacon Frye. Played by Davis (star of the 1974 series *That's My Mama*), who was an established real-life minister, Reverend Reuben Gregory slowly and patiently established an influence over the church, the deacon, of course, fighting him throughout. A rational voice amid the deacon's fiery outbursts, Reverend Gregory helped to temper Frye's melodramatic excitement, aiding in the resolution of the program's various episodes.

Thelma Frye, the deacon's adult, socially awkward daughter, also played an important role in many episodes of *Amen*. Thelma, a romantically distraught thirty-year-old who still lived with her "Daddy," provided a constant source of humor, her own childlike naiveté a comical contrast to the clever, often scheming Deacon Frye. Later episodes focused on the developing romantic relationship, and eventual marriage between Thelma and the Reverend Gregory, a marriage which signaled Thelma's coming into adulthood as well as lessened the distance between the reverend and Deacon Frye. Additional characters included

Rolly Forbes, the church's spunky elder church board member and sisters Casietta and Amelia Hetebrink, all adult church members who frequently made humorous and sarcastic contributions to the show, most often at the expense of Deacon Frye.

Throughout its five years, *Amen* offered a light-hearted look at an African-American church, playfully satirizing its day to day activities. Focusing humorously on this everyday conflict between Reverend Gregory and Deacon Frye, as well as these other familiar characters, *Amen* proved a satiric, yet human, portrait of ordinary church life and people.

—Brent Malin

CAST

Deacon Ernest Frye	Sherman Hemsley
Reverend Reuben Gregory	Clifton Davis
Thelma Frye	Anna Maria Horsford
Casietta Hetebrink (1986–90) . . .	Barbara Montgomery
Amelia Hetebrink	Roz Ryan
Rolly Forbes	Jester Hairston
Lorenzo Hollingsworth (1986–87)	Franklyn Seales
Leola Forbes (1987–89)	Rosetta LeNoire
Inga (1988–90)	Elsa Raven
Chris (1988–90)	Tony T. Johnson
Clarence (1990–91)	Bumper Robinson

Amen

Photo courtesy of Carson Productions

PRODUCERS Ed Weinberger, Michael Leeson, Marcia Govons, Reuben Cannon, Kim Johnston, Arthur Julian, Lloyd David, James Stein, Robert Illes

PROGRAMMING HISTORY   110 Episodes

• NBC

September 1986–April 1987	Saturday 9:30-10:00
June 1987–September 1988	Saturday 9:30-10:00
October 1988–July 1989	Saturday 8:30-9:00
August 1989	Saturday 8:00-8:30
September 1989–July 1990	Saturday 8:30-9:00
August 1990	Saturday 8:00-8:30
December 1990–July 1991	Saturday 8:00-8:30

FURTHER READING

Collier, Aldore. "Update: Jester Harrison." *Ebony* (Chicago), March 1988.

Dates, Jannette, and William Barlow, editors. *Split Images: African Americans in the Mass Media.* Washington, D.C.: Howard University Press, 1990.

MacDonald, J. Fred. *Blacks and White TV: Afro-Americans in Television since 1948.* Chicago: Nelson-Hall, 1983.

Stoddard, Maynard Good. "'Amen's' Clifton Davis: A Reverend for Real." *Saturday Evening Post* (Indianapolis, Indiana), July-August 1990.

See also Hemsley, Sherman; *Jeffersons*

AMERICAN BANDSTAND

U.S. Music Program

Like the soap opera, *American Bandstand* represents the transference of a successful radio format to burgeoning arena of American television. Unlike the soap opera, however, the radio broadcast format of playing recorded music developed as popular entertainers from radio migrated to the newer medium of television. Initially located in the margins of broadcast schedules, the format of a live disk jockey spinning records targeted toward and embraced by teenagers soon evolved into the economic salvation of many radio stations. For one thing, the programs were relatively inexpensive to produce. In addition, the increased spending power of American teenagers in the 1950s attracted advertisers and companies marketing products specifically targeting that social group. Not the least of these were the recording companies who supplied the records without cost to stations, often including economic incentives to disk jockeys to play their products. In effect, the recorded music was a commercial for itself. Given the convergence of these factors, the teen record party became entrenched as a radio format during the 1950s and throughout the 1960s, eventually developing into Top Forty Radio.

For these same reasons, this format became highly lucrative for local television stations to produce as well. While the three networks provided the majority of prime-time programming and some early afternoon soap operas, local television stations had to fill marginal broadcast periods themselves. Since the primary audience for television viewing in the late afternoons included teenagers just out of school for the day, the teen record party apparently made sense to station managers as a way to generate advertising revenue during that broadcast period. As a result, a number of teen dance party programs found their way into television schedules during the early 1950s.

Bandstand, one of these, appeared on WFIL-TV in Philadelphia during September 1952. Hosted by Bob Horn, a popular local disk jockey, the show was presented "live" and included teenagers dancing to the records that were played. As the success of the televised *Bandstand* grew, Dick Clark took over the disk jockey duties of the radio program while Bob Horn was broadcasting in front of the cameras. In 1956, Horn was arrested for driving under the influence of alcohol, in the middle of an anti-

Dick Clark
Photo courtesy of Dick Clark Productions, Inc.

drunk driving campaign by WFIL. Soon thereafter, Dick Clark replaced him as the host of the televised program. Clark's clean-cut boy-next-door image seemed to offset any unsavory fallout from Horn's arrest, because the show increased in its popularity. By the fall of 1957, Clark, who had been shepherding kinescopes of the show to New York, convinced the programmers at ABC to include the show in its network lineup.

Adapting the name of the program to its new stature (and the network identity), *American Bandstand* first aired on the ABC network on Monday, 5 August 1957, becoming one of a handful of local origination programs to broadcast nationally. Initially, the program ran Monday through Friday from 3:00 to 4:30 P.M., EST. Almost immediately, the show became a hit for the struggling network. In retrospect, *American Bandstand* fit in nicely with the programming strategy that evolved at ABC during the 1950s. As the third television network, ABC could not afford the high-priced radio celebrity talent or live dramatic programming that generated the predominantly adult viewership of NBC and CBS. Therefore, ABC counterprogrammed its scheduled with shows that appealed to a younger audience. Along with programs such as *The Mickey Mouse Club*, ABC used *American Bandstand* to build a loyal audience base in the 1950s that would catapult the network to the top of the prime-time ratings in the mid-1970s.

From a cultural and social standpoint, the impact of *American Bandstand* should not be underrated. Even if the show diffused some of the more raucous elements of rock 'n' roll music, it helped to solidify the growing youth culture which centered around this phenomenon. But the show was important in another way as well. Once Clark took over the helm of *Bandstand* in 1956, he insisted on racially integrating the show, since much of the music was performed by black recording artists. When the show moved to the network schedule, it maintained its racially mixed image, thus providing American television broadcasting with its most visible ongoing image of ethnic diversity until the 1970s.

In 1964, Clark moved the production of *American Bandstand* to California, cutting broadcasts to once a week. In part, the move was made to facilitate Clark's expansion into other program production. Additionally, it became easier to tap into the American recording industry, the center of which had shifted to Los Angeles by that time. The show's popularity with teenagers continued until the late 1960s.

At that point, white, middle-class American youth culture moved away from the rock 'n' roll dance music that had become the staple of *American Bandstand*, opting instead for the drug-influenced psychedelia of the Vietnam War era. As a response to the specialized tastes of perceived diverse target audiences, radio formats began to fragment at this time, segregating popular music into distinct categories. While *American Bandstand* attempted to integrate many of these styles into its format throughout the 1970s,

the show relied heavily on disco, the emerging alternative to psychedelic art rock. Though often denigrated at the time because of disco's emergence in working class and ethnic communities, the musical style was the logical focus for the show, given its historic reliance on presenting teenagers dancing. Consequently, *American Bandstand* became even more ethnically mixed at a time when the predominant face of the aging youth culture in the United States acquired a social pallor.

The foundation of *American Bandstand's* success rested with its ability to adapt to shifting musical trends while maintaining the basic format developed in the 1950s. As a result, Dick Clark helmed the longest running broadcast program aimed at mainstream youth to air on American network broadcast television. After thirty years of broadcasting, ABC finally dropped the show from its network schedule in 1987. In its later years, *American Bandstand* was often preempted by various sporting events. Given the commercial profits generated from sports presentations, apparently it was only a matter of time before the network replaced the dance party entirely. Additionally, the rise of MTV and other music video channels in the 1980s also helped to seal *American Bandstand's* fate. The show began to look like an anachronism when compared to the slick production values of expensively produced music videos. Nevertheless, the music video channels owe a debt of gratitude to *American Bandstand*, the network prototype that shaped the format which they have exploited so well.

—Rodney A. Buxton

HOST

Dick Clark (1956–1989),
David Hirsch (1989)

PRODUCER   Dick Clark

PROGRAMMING HISTORY

• ABC

5 August–5 September 1957

• SYNDICATED

1957–1963 Daily, Various Local Non-Prime Time Hours
1963–1969

Saturday, Various Local Non-Prime Time Hours

• USA Cable

8 April–7 October 1989   Saturday, Non-Prime Time

FURTHER READING

Clark, Dick, and Richard Robinson. *Rock, Roll and Remember.* New York: Popular Library, 1976.
Shore, Michael, with Dick Clark. *The History of American Bandstand.* New York: Ballantine, 1985.

See also Clark, Dick; Music on Television

AMERICAN BROADCASTING COMPANY

U.S. Network

The American Broadcasting Company, more commonly referred to as ABC, has been a forerunner in the evolution of television network history. Although often recognized as the third-place network in ratings, behind CBS and NBC, ABC has several times been a "first," with bold decisions and changes that often served as catalysts to its competitors.

The following headline from the *Los Angeles Times* describes ABC's most memorable "first": "Merger of Top TV Network and Media Giant with Premier Movie Producer to Create One-Of-A-Kind Global Powerhouse." This notice referred to the Walt Disney Company's surprising purchase of Capital Cities/ABC for $19 billion in cash and stock in August 1995. While the merger is recognized by media executives and Wall Street investors as a landmark in network television, historians tell of ABC's beginnings more than four decades ago as much less dramatic.

ABC grew out of a Federal Communications Commission (FCC) "monopoly" probe. The 1938–41 radio-network investigation resulted in a highly publicized and controversial report which included specific proposals for reform. The FCC reported cited several problems with CBS and NBC, the two then-existing radio networks. The first problem cited was that NBC owned two networks, NBC-Blue and NBC-Red. The report proposed "divorcement," and on 12 October 1943, ABC was born, the offspring of the separation of NBC. As a result of the FCC report RCA sold the Blue Network Company, Inc., for $8,000,000. The buyer was the American Broadcasting System, Inc., owned by Edward J. Noble, who had made his fortune with Lifesavers candy.

By the mid-1940s, it was clear that the struggle for power in the broadcasting arena was now a three-network battle involving ABC, CBS and NBC. All had substantial radio earnings, but television technology developments loomed before them, threatening to change the face of the radio landscape forever.

By 1948, the FCC had issued approximately a hundred television-station licenses. By 1952, with sponsorship declining, death seemed imminent for network radio. The years between 1948 and 1955 for network television were a period of industry transition comparable to the mid-1920s for network radio. The FCC needed to develop a comprehensive plan for allocating TV frequencies and until it was completed the transition from radio would be incomplete.

As networks focused on the transition into television, a battle to takeover ABC, the weak sister of the Big Three, ensued. Noble's network was overextended and nearly bankrupt. And in 1951, Leonard Goldenson and United Paramount Theaters bought ABC for $25 million. Goldenson had begun his career at Paramount Pictures in 1933 as a 27-year-old Harvard Law School graduate. Eventually, however, he gave up law and became chief executive of United

Courtesy of ABC

Paramount Theaters and after spending the first half of his career at Paramount, he gambled his way to the top of ABC.

A new era in American broadcasting, another "first", began with that merger. With the help of the television industry the silver screen entered the home. In 1954, Walt and Roy Disney approached Goldenson with the idea of building a new theme park in California. The brothers needed financing and they offered to supply Goldenson with new programming. He lent them $15 million in return for 35% of Disneyland. ABC also agreed to pay $35 million in license fees over seven years for a new Walt Disney TV series. *Disneyland*, which premiered in the fall of 1954 was the network's first Nielsen Top Ten Hit. A year later in the fall of 1955, ABC had another successful "first." *Cheyenne*, the first prime-time series produced by a major studio, Warner Brothers, aired on ABC the show and also became a network hit.

Still, it took nearly another decade for ABC to be Number One in the Nielsen ratings. But in 1964, ABC won the ratings race in the fifty largest U.S. markets with such successful series as *Peyton Place*, *Bewitched*, *The Addams Family*, *McHale's Navy*, *Combat*, and *My Three Sons*. But this success was short-lived and lasted a few weeks. Seven years later during the 1970–71 season, ABC had its first Number One show in all of television with *Marcus Welby, M.D.*

Even with this success, however, there were still many problems with ABC's programming that season, starting and ending with *All in the Family*. After financing the development of two pilot shows of *All in the Family*, Goldenson decided, in what has been hailed as the worst programming decision of his career, to turn down the Norman Lear show. He was worried that this new brand of realistic comedy would offend conservative affiliates.

All in the Family went to CBS—replacing *The Beverly Hillbillies* as American's leading comedy. To make matters worse, CBS' chief programmer, Fred Silverman, developed such spinoffs as *Maude* and *The Jefferson* for the network.

The effects on ABC's ratings were disastrous. *Welby* dropped from first to thirteenth place in one year.

ABC wooed Fred Silverman away from CBS in the mid-1970s. Six months after Silverman's arrival at ABC, two events took ABC to first place in the ratings: Roone Arledge's Winter Olympics in Innsbruck and a mini-series, a twelve-hour TV adaptation of Irwin Shaw's *Rich Man, Poor Man*. It was network TV's first big miniseries.

At the end of the 1975–76 season, ABC's Silverman scheduled a new show, *Charlie's Angels*. On the edge of a new programming wave in which sex would replace violence as the preferred "quick fix" for American television audiences, *Charlie's Angels* and other similarly cast ABC series came to be known as the "jiggle" shows. CBS and NBC executives labeled them "tits and ass" programming. These shows were Silverman's specialty and the cornerstone of a new entertainment creed.

The new programming resulted in a flood of advertising demand and surging Nielsen ratings for ABC. ABC's profits in 1975 totaled more than $29 million; in 1976, they were $83 million; and in 1977, $165. Not all the successes fell into the more exploitative categories, however. ABC aired another miniseries in 1977. A twelve-hour adaptation of Alex Haley's *Roots* attracted 130 million viewers, scored the largest Nielsen ratings in broadcast history, solidified the role of the miniseries in network programming, opened a national discussion of the history of American race relations, and garnered high praise for the network.

But the bulk of ABC programming was still highly conventional. During the 1977–78 season, ABC's successful lineup included *The Six Million Dollar Man*, *The ABC Sunday Night Movie*, NFL games, *Happy Days*, *Laverne and Shirley*, *Three's Company*, *Soap*, *Eight Is Enough*, *Charlie's Angels*, *Baretta*, *Welcome Back, Kotter*, *Barney Miller*, *The Love Boat*, and *Operation Petticoat*. The network had twelve programs in the Nielsen Top Twenty.

Taxi, *Mork and Mindy*, and *Happy Days* headlined ABC's 1978–79 season of fourteen Top Twenty shows including the best five shows of the season. ABC made history again. It was the first time that a TV network had broken the billion-dollar revenue mark. But it was the last year of ABC's success streak. That year, Fred Silverman left the programming empire he had built at ABC and took over NBC. For the first time since 1975, ABC finished second in the November sweeps.

A year later, ABC was a "first" again. This time, as the first network to hire a woman as its evening anchor, bringing the network an avalanche of publicity. ABC hired Barbara Walters from NBC with a contract worth $1 million in 1976. Hired to co-anchor the *ABC Evening News* with Harry Reasoner, Walters, then forty-six, was the most celebrated woman in television news. The Reasoner and Walters merger was not successful, however, and Walters went on to her highly acclaimed series of interview programs and a regular spot on the ABC news magazine, *20/20*.

The mid-to-late 1970s also saw the era of satellite television developing strength with such newcomers to the television industry as cable networks HBO, CNN and WTBS. Taking advantage of this trend in the early 1980s, ABC purchased ESPN, a cable sports network, with hopes that it would give the network a window on pay-per-view sports and help it bid for big sporting events.

Innovative programming in the early 1980s was not in prime-time series but made-for-TV movie programming, daytime shows, long-form miniseries and news. The most lucrative part of the ABC schedule in 1981 was daytime television which generated almost three-fourths of its profit. ABC, unlike CBS and NBC, owned most of its soap operas so the high daytime ratings of shows such as *General Hospital*, *All My Children*, and *Ryan's Hope* could be converted directly into profit. But the profits were matched by the network's burden of high expenses and sagging ratings. Once again ABC found itself lagging its competitors at NBC and CBS.

In 1986, Capital Cities Communication engineered the first television network takeover since Leonard Goldenson's merger of United Paramount Theaters and ABC. The $3.5 billion merger signaled the start of the purchase of all major networks in 1980s, but the resulting Capital Cities/ABC Inc. became what was widely considered by investors as one of the best run of media companies. Capital Cities cut costs dramatically while continuing to invest in news and entertainment programming. ABC rebounded to become Number One in the ratings.

A decade later, ABC was in the forefront of network financial news once more setting the way for a flurry of media corporate buyouts that would make network history. In 1995 Walt Disney Company acquired Capital Cities/ABC for $19 billion, the second-highest price ever paid for a U.S. Company in U.S. history. The biggest media merger in history, touted as one of the best-kept secrets in the industry, "sparked a flurry of buying activity in other entertainment stocks," said the *Los Angeles Times*. Shortly after the Disney/Capital Cities/ABC merger, Westinghouse merged with CBS and Time Warner with Ted Turner's cable network empire including CNN, TBS, TNT, and Turner Classic Movies.

The future of Disney/Capital Cities/ABC will be closely watched by media observers and critics. In many ways, the conglomerate suggests a model for a new era in media industries, an era in which global communication and economic strategies may override national and local concerns.

—Gayle Noyes

FURTHER READING

Goldenson, Leonard, H. *Beating the Odds: The Untold Story Behind the Rise of ABC: The Stars, Struggles, and Egos That Transformed Network Television by the Man Who Made It Happen*. New York: Scribner's, 1991.

Quinlan, Sterling. *Inside ABC: American Broadcasting Company's Rise to Power*. New York: Hastings House, 1979.

Sugar, Bert Randolph. *"The Thrill of Victory": The Inside Story of ABC Sports*. New York: Hawthorn, 1978.

Williams, Huntington. *Beyond Control: ABC and the Fate of the Networks*. New York: Athenaeum, 1989.

AMERICAN MOVIE CLASSICS

U.S. Cable Network

During the final sixth of the 20th century the television cable channel American Movie Classics (AMC), quietly became one of the fastest growing television networks in the United States. Half owned by Cablevision Systems and mammoth TeleCommunications, Inc., AMC is one of the great success stories in the emergence of cable TV in the United States. Film fans loved AMC for showing classic, uncut, uncolorized Hollywood films of the 1930s, 1940s, and 1950s, with no interruptions for advertisements.

Over-the-air television had already served as the principle second run showcase for Hollywood films from the mid-1950s into the 1970s. But the number of over-the-air TV stations in any one market limited the possible showcases for classic Hollywood films. Film buffs in major markets did have independent television stations which frequently counter-programmed with Hollywood movies, but they hated the ways in which stations sanitized the presentations of theatrical films, cut them to fit them into prescribed time slots, and interrupted moving moments with blaring advertisements. With the emergence of cable television in the 1980s, AMC offered a niche for these fans, who sometimes referred to the channel as the "Metropolitan Museum of classic movies." Indeed, AMC created a "repertory" cinema easily operated by a remote control.

AMC began in October 1984 as a pay service, but switched onto cable's "basic tier" in 1987 when it had grown to seven million subscribers in one thousand systems across the United States. This growth curve continued and by the end of 1989 AMC had doubled its subscriber base. Two years later it could count 39 million subscribers.

No cable service in the United States ever received more favorable reviews. Critics raved at AMC's around-the-clock presentation of Hollywood favorites and undiscovered gems, a stark relief from the sensory overload of MTV. AMC bragged about its sedate pseudo-PBS pacing.

AMC also has created first run documentaries that focus on some part of the movie business, such as a corporate profile of Republic Studios, a compilation history entitled "Stars and Stripes: Hollywood and World War II," and a history of boxing movies labeled "Knockout: Hollywood's Love Affair with Boxing." AMC regularly features interviews by Richard Brown, professor at the New School of Social Research, as part of its on-going series "Reflections on the Silver Screen," and also cablecasts Ralph Edwards' *This Is Your Life* episodes from the 1950s.

American Movie Classics regularly fills slots between films with old 20th-Century-Fox Movietone Newsreels. Fans can once again watch as a bored John Barrymore puts his profile into the cement in front of Grauman's Chinese Theatre or Shirley Temple accepts her special Oscar, then asks her mother if it is time to go home. In short here is the perfect nostalgia mix for anyone who lived through (or wished they had) the "simpler" time of the 1930s and 1940s.

AMC unabashedly promotes its nostalgic escape. Consider a typical stunt. The room, painted black and white (the purity of American Movie Classics), is filled with the sounds of Gordy Kilgore's big band playing Glenn Miller's "In the Mood" as more than two hundred couples spin, remembering a better time. The celebration of the fiftieth anniversary of Pearl Harbor? No, this was a late 1980s marketing device by American Movie Classics and the local cable system (owned by Time Warner), in Wichita Falls, Texas, a moment designed to launch AMC in that market.

By June 1988 American Movie Classics was successful enough to begin a colorful magazine. An old time classic star graces the cover of each issue; the first featured Katharine Hepburn, later came James Stewart, Marilyn Monroe, Gregory Peck, John Wayne, and Henry Fonda. Inside the cover comes a short, picture laden piece about a classic movie palace. Then comes a table of contents filled with articles about the stars of the Golden Age of Hollywood (keyed to American Movie Classic showings). The core of the magazine is the listings of that month's American Movie Classics offerings, highlighting festivals constructed around stars, series (such as Charlie Chan) and themes ("Super Sleuths," for example).

But there are limitations to the successes and benefits of AMC. Unless a new preservation print has been made (as was the case with the silent 1927 classic *Wings*), American Movie Classics runs television prints. These versions of the films are often incomplete, having been edited during the 1950s and 1960s to eliminate possibly offensive languages and images. Often TV prints have been cut to run a standard 88 minutes, timed to fit into two hour slots, with advertisements. American Movie Classics runs these incomplete prints, deciding not to spend the necessary moneys to create a complete version.

Fans rarely complain about the TV prints, however, and cable operators herald American Movie Classics as what is

Courtesy of American Movie Classics

best about cable television. The channel has replaced the repertory cinemas which used to dot America's largest cities and college towns and serves as a fine example of specialized niche programming in cable TV of the 1990s.

—Douglas Gomery

FURTHER READING

Alexander, Ron. "AMC, Where the Movie Never Ends." *New York Times*, 17 November 1991.

Brown, Rich. "Cablevision Pays $170 Million for AMC." *Broadcasting and Cable* (Washington, D.C.), 20 September 1993.

Dempsey, John. "Profitable AMC Turns 10; Sets for Some Classic Competition." *Variety* (Los Angeles), 26 September 1994.

Moshavi, Sharon D. "AMC Buys Universal Packaging." *Broadcasting* (Washington, D.C.), 20 May 1991.

See also Cable Networks; Movies on Television

AMERICAN WOMEN IN RADIO AND TELEVISION

American Women in Radio and Television (AWRT) is a nonprofit organization headquartered in Washington, D.C. Originally conceived as the women's division of the National Association of Broadcasters, AWRT became an independent entity in 1950. At its first convention, AWRT had 282 women members. Today, the group maintains more than 2,300 men and women members, largely employed by television and radio stations nationwide.

Although people of both genders can join and serve as officers, the organization's mission is to advance the impact of women's careers in broadcasting and related fields. The group furthers community service, member employment and education. The organization also has a definite social consciousness. AWRT produces an award-winning series of public service announcements which have focused upon preventing sexual harassment in the workplace. Its agenda has also included, as an issue for study, a concern for indecency in broadcast content.

The organization serves many functions for its members. Its nearly 50 local chapters provide a place for social and professional networking. Some chapters are an important force in their local broadcast communities; others are merely meeting places for people in similar professions. Local activities vary, but often include "Soaring Spirits" benefits to help children's hospitals, scholarship fundraising for area college students, awards for local media professionals, educational seminars, career development and job listing dispersal. Local chapter members also mentor meetings of the affiliated College Students in Broadcasting, a club composed of dues paying students organized at university campus chapters.

On the national level, the organization provides many services. The main office is helmed by full-time employees and directed by both nationally elected officers and an advisory board. Within the organization, the most essential activity is an annual convention held each spring. Convention activities have included lobbying in Washington, recreation in Phoenix and education in Florida. The organization also houses the AWRT Foundation, which is designed to help fund research, publication, institutes, lectures and the general advancement of the electronic media and allied fields. The Washington office sponsors AWRT's annual Star

Courtesy of American Women in Radio and Television, Inc.

Awards which recognize media professionals or companies facilitating women's issues and concerns, and the Silver Satellite and the Achievement Awards commend success or advancements in electronic media fields.

The chapters differ greatly from each other. For example, the Austin, Texas chapter's monthly luncheon serves as the primary local meeting place for executives and managers in cable, broadcasting and advertising. Its activities include speakers with the latest news on industry developments, a preview night for each network's new fall programs in September, a Soaring Spirits 5K run, sponsorship of student scholarships and the definitive Austin media Christmas party.

In contrast, the Southern California chapter has a large sampling of television producers, on-air talent, network executives, educators, screenwriters and actresses in its ranks. Its main annual fundraising event is the Genii Awards luncheon, which honors an outstanding broadcast executive and a performer. Past winners have included producers Marian Rees and Linda Bloodworth Thomason and actresses Tyne Daly and Candace Bergen. Other activities include a "Meeting of the Minds" seminar updating the legal and technical knowledge in communication operations, a "Boot Camp" night where teams wearing military gear attempt to rearrange network programming schedules to maximize competition, and the more typical mixers and guest speakers. The chapter gives more than five scholarships annually, each awarded to a College Students in Broadcasting member.

Though different in membership, clout and structure, each local chapter uses the services of the national office to disseminate industry knowledge and job information. American Women in Radio and Television helps keep its members up to date in a rapidly changing industrial setting.

—Joan Stuller-Giglione

FURTHER READING

American Women in Radio and Television, Inc. *AWRT 1992 Resource Directory*. Washington, D.C.: AWRT, 1992.

"AWRT Prepares for the 21st Century." *Broadcasting* (Washington, D.C.), 6 May 1985.
"Patricia Niekamp: Raising the Visibility of AWRT." *Broadcasting* (Washington, D.C.), 14 May 1990.
Rathbun, Elizabeth. "AWRT Looks Ahead to Take Place on Superhighway." *Broadcasting and Cable* (Washington, D.C.), 30 May 1994.
Sheridan, Patrick J. "AWRT Panel Addresses Indecency Issue." *Broadcasting* (Washington, D.C.), 28 May 1990.

AMERICANIZATION

During a nightly newscast of *CBC (Canadian Broadcasting Corporation) Prime Time News*, the anchorman, in the last news item before the public affairs portion of the program, presented words to this effect: How would you like to have a house that would cost next to nothing to build and to maintain, no electrical, and no heating bills? Viewers were then shown four young Inuit adults building an igloo. They were born in the Arctic region, said the spokeswoman of the group, but had not learned the ancestral skills of carving (literally) a human shelter out of this harsh environment (-35 Celsius at night). It was a broad hint that the spin on this story would be "Young Aboriginals in search of their past." The real twist, however, was that their instructors, a middle-aged man and woman, were Caucasian and that the man was born in Detroit. The American had studied something which sounded like environmental architecture and was teaching this particular technique to the young Inuits.

When asked if they were embarrassed by this arrangement, the spokeswoman answered, "No. If he teaches us what we need to know then that's all right." When asked if he found the situation a bit strange, the Detroit born man also answered in the negative, "I was born in Detroit but I do not know how to build a car." In fact it was one of the Inuit hunters who had taught him how to repair his snowmobile. So why shouldn't he teach young Inuits to build igloos? In the last scene the igloo builders lay out their seal rugs and light a small fire using seal oil, enabling the heat to ice the inside walls, thus insulating the dwelling from the outside cold and creating warmth within. A final shot shows the lighted igloos against the black night sky.

Many things can be read into this short narrative. First, the typical, white, Canadian anchorman, by referring to concerns of Southern Canadians (low building and maintenance costs, no taxes, clear air and quiet neighborhoods), trivializes a technology which, over thousands of years, has allowed populations to survive and create specific societies and cultures in this particular environment. Secondly, we are made aware of the benefits of international trade: an Inuit teaches a Detroit born American how to repair a motor vehicle and, in return learns how to build an igloo. Thirdly, we are led to understand that what the students expect from the teacher is basic working skills.

The temptation to build a case denouncing cultural imperialism, bemoaning the alienation of aboriginal cultures and the shredding of their social fabric, is strong here. On the basis of this one example, however, the argument would at best be flawed, at worst biased. But for students of popular culture, national identity, and cultural industries this is but one of the many thousand daily occurrences which exemplify the dynamic complexity of the concept of "americanization."

Embedded within it are at least two notions; the American presence and the presence of an American. In this news story, both notions are at work. On the one hand, the viewer is made aware of the American presence, the influence of American technology on this remote society, through the reference to the snowmobile. (Although the inventor lived and worked in Quebec, Canada, the fact that the Detroit born American puts the snowmobile on the same footing as the automobile implicitly makes it an American invention.) On the other hand, the viewer sees and hears the American instructor.

It is the first form of presence that usually defines the concept of americanization. It usually refers to the presence of American products and technology and it is against this presence that most critics argue. Surprisingly, few argue against the presence of Americans. As individuals, Americans are well liked and friendly; it is the presence of their way of life, of their culture, that makes americanization such an ugly word. Others like them but do not want to be like them; this is the basic attitude in opposition to americanization.

One is led to believe that s/he will become an American, will be americanized, not by interacting with citizens of the United States but by using American products, eating American (fast) food, and enjoying American cultural artifacts. One can go so far as to live and work in the United States while remaining staunchly Canadian or Australian or British, as many artists who have succeeded in the American music and film industries remind us. The danger of becoming americanized seems greater, however, if one stays in the comfort of home enjoying American cultural products such as magazines, novels, movies, music, comics, television shows and news, or computer software and games.

While these two embedded notions, the presence of Americans and the American presence, make for a fascinating debate, the concept of americanization conceals the parallel dual notion of "the host." Hosting the American presence seems to be more prevalent and more americanizing than hosting Americans themselves. To be a host is to make the visitor feel welcome, to make the visitor seem familiar, non-threatening, at home. In this case, to be a host is to be a consumer, to be a friendly user. To become americanized it is presumed not only that one consumes a steady diet of readily accessible made-in-the-U.S. products, but also consumes these cultural products with ease, i.e. as would any American.

American products are distributed internationally but are not made for international markets: they are made for the U.S. market, by, for, and about Americans. Thus, one can conclude, to enjoy these easily accessible products one must be or become American and the more one consumes, the more one becomes American, thereby enabling increasing pleasure and ease in this consumption. Americanization is a case in point of a basic process of acculturation. It results in sounding the alarms of cultural imperialism and cultural alienation: you become what you consume, because in order to consume you must become the targeted consumer. This is the equivalent of saying: because science (as we believe we know it) is a product of Western European civilization, then to become a scientist one must become westernized, i.e. adopt Western mores, values, and ways of thinking.

In most host countries in the world there is an overwhelming presence of American products. The pull and pressure of those products must not be underestimated. Still, the news story of the Inuit mechanic and the Detroit igloo builder serves as a reminder that culture, or at least certain types of culture, are less bound by the economics of their technological environment and modes of production than was once assumed and theorized.

The fact that the Inuit travel on snowmobiles, live in suburban dwellings, watch a great deal of television, and have forgotten how to build igloos does not necessarily make them more americanized when compared with the Detroit born teacher, who is made no less American by his ability to build an igloo. Skills, products, and ideas take root in historically given contexts: they bear witness to their times. When they travel, they bring with them elements of their place of origin. To use these ideas and products, one must have an understanding of their historical background or context, of their original intent and of their mode of operation. If the invention and the corresponding mode of production of goods and ideas are context bound, so too are their uses and in many cases these have an impact on the very nature of products and ideas. This perspective leads to a better understanding of americanization.

Undoubtedly American composers, playwrights, and various other artists have affected the popular arts of the world. With the same degree of certitude, one can proclaim that American entrepreneurs and American entrepreneurship have affected the cultural industries the world over. But perhaps the most profound impact of this particular

historical culture and its modes of production, is found in the social uses American society has made of these cultural products. If one wishes to speak of americanization in the realm of popular (or mass) culture, one must focus on the social uses of industrially produced and commercially distributed sounds and images. To show American-made movies in local theaters, to watch American sitcoms on the television set, to listen to American music on the radio—or to use copycat versions of any of these materials—is not, necessarily, to become americanized. To build into the local social fabric a permanent presence of these sounds and images, *is* to become americanized but not necessarily American.

To have a *permanent* background of American images and sounds (for example, television sets turned on all day, ads overflowing in print, on buses, on T-shirts, talk radio, Walkmans, etc.) means to live and work and play in a permanent kaleidoscope world plugged into a never ending soundtrack. *This*, it can be argued, is to become americanized.

The *Dallas* imperialism syndrome, and its legitimate heir, the O.J. Simpson Trial, are good illustrations of this. The debate surrounding *Dallas* rekindles the debate which greeted the American penny press and Hollywood cinema. Its central question: is communication technology a threat to basic (Western) values, local cultures, and the human psyche? *Dallas* symbolized this ongoing debate, a debate central to Western culture. But *Dallas* also symbolized a social evolution which has not received the attention it deserves. The worldwide popularity of *Dallas* revived the paradigm of the "magic bullet" theory of direct media effects, a theory suggesting that media content and style can be "injected" into the cultural life system, infecting and contaminating the "healthy" cultural body. It also revived discussions of cultural imperialism, but in a more sophisticated fashion and on a much grander scale. And it also raised the counter paradigm of the uses and gratifications model in communication studies.

Many researchers were eager to publish their claims that *Dallas* did not magically turn all its viewers into Americans, but that the program signified many things to many viewers. Moreover, they pointed out that, on the whole, national cultural products (including television programs) still outsold imported American ones. And if they did not, they certainly enjoyed more popular support and provided more enjoyment.

Forgotten in this foray was the fact that *Dallas* symbolized the popularization and the banalization of television viewing, its normal integration within the activities of everyday life, its quiet nestling in the central foyer of the household environment. Television viewing, a remarkable new social practice in many locations, quickly and quietly became, inside and outside academia, a major source of everyday conversation, the measuring stick of many moral debates, the epitome of modern living. In so doing television viewing displaced the boundaries of centuries-old institutions such as family, work, school and religion. The *Dallas* syndrome symbolized the fact that in a large number of host countries, communication technology had become a permanent part of the everyday social environment, that its messages had become a permanent part of the social fabric and that its spokepersons had joined the public club of opinion makers.

While one can debate the pros and cons of this social fact, one can also speculate that television is not the revolution that many of its critics as well as admirers had hoped or feared. It did not destroy a sacred treasure of Western values based on the technology of the written word. Rather it revealed a blind spot among many social thinkers: the constructed centrality of the spoken word in modern societies. Television possibly revealed to the most industrialized society of the postwar era, the United States, that it was and still is, by and large, an oral society.

Communication technology did not trigger a revolution, social, moral, or sexual; it became part of the establishment in every way, shape, and form. And just as U.S. cultural industries have become an American institution, a part of the social order and a sustainer of culture in American society, so too have cultural industries in many other societies. In this sense, other societies have become americanized. Americanization is not to be found in the consumption of American cultural products. It lies in the establishment of a particular social formation. This formation is, to be sure, defined in part by the use of the products of national cultural industries. But it is also defined by alterations in patterns of everyday life and by the emergence of "new" voices that take their place among existing relations and structures of power. The uses of television throughout the world are both cause and effect within these cultural and social shifts

Thus americanization is neither a boon nor a threat—it is a cultural and economic fact of life in most (Western) countries. The debate then, is not over whether to stop or to hasten the consumption of American cultural products. It should instead be centered on the impact of specific social uses of industrially mass-produced cultural products, whether foreign or national. For better or worse, the socialization of sounds and images, and socialization *through* sounds and images, have made more visible, and more mainstream, the oral traditions and the tradition of orality not only in American society but also in all (Western) americanized societies.

It matters little whether television, and other technologically based cultural industries, were invented by the Americans or not. What they invented was a particular social use of these technologies: the massification of pro-

duction, distribution, and consumption and the commodification of industrially produced cultural products. In return, this particular social use revealed to American society, and to other industrialized societies which followed suit, the forgotten presence of traditional, non-national, oral cultures. Cultural industries, and television in particular, revealed that print technology (the written word) had not subverted oral technology (the spoken word); it had only partially silenced it by making it less "visible." Television made words and sound once again "visible" and "audible" to the eyes and ears of the mind. In doing so it also revealed to the heavily industrialized, print oriented, Western societies that they were blinded by their most popular visual aid, television.

—Roger De La Garde

FURTHER READING

Liebes, Tamar and Elihu Katz. *The Export of Meaning: Cross Cultural Readings Of "Dallas."* Cambridge, England: Polity, 1990.

Lull, James. *China Turned on: Television, Reform, and Resistance.* London: Routledge, 1991.

Negrine, Ralph, and S. Papathanassopoulos. *The Internationalization Of Television.* London: Pinter, 1990.

Nordenstreng, Kaarle, and Tapio Varis. *Television Traffic— A One-Way Street? A Survey and Analysis of the International Flow of Television Programme Material* (reports and Papers on Mass Communication, No. 70.) Paris: UNESCO, 1974.

Schiller, Herbert. *Mass Media and the American Empire.* New York: Augustus M. Kelly, 1969.

Sepstrup, Preben. *Transnationalization of Television in Europe.* London: John Libbey, 1990.

Smith, Anthony. *The Age of Behemoths: The Globalization of Mass Media Firms.* New York: Priority Press, 1991.

Tunstall, Jeremy. *The Media Are American: Anglo-American Media in the World.* London: Constable, 1977.

Varis, Tapio. *International Flow of Television Programs* (reports and Papers on Mass Communication, No. 100.) Paris: UNESCO, 1986.

Wasko, Janet. *Hollywood in the Information Age: Beyond the Silver Screen.* Austin, Texas: University of Texas Press, 1994.

Wells, A.F. *Picture Tube Imperialism? The Impact of US Television on Latin America.* New York: Orbis, 1972.

See also Audience Research

AMERICA'S FUNNIEST HOME VIDEOS

U.S. Reality Program/Comedy

A peculiar variant of reality-based television programming, *America's Funniest Home Videos* (AFHV), first aired as a Thanksgiving special in 1989, and later debuted on 14 January

1990 as a regular series on ABC. The show still maintains respectable ratings in its sixth season and is due for syndication in 1995 by MTM Television Distribution. The program's simple premise—to solicit and exhibit a series of humorous video clips shot by amateurs who compete for cash prizes—has had a surprisingly enduring run in its half-hour slot at 7:00 P.M. in the Sunday night schedule.

Rooted generally in the sub-genre of its comical, voyeuristic predecessors, such as *Candid Camera, TV's Bloopers and Practical Jokes,* and *Life's Most Embarrassing Moments, AFHV* more particularly owes its genesis to a weekly variety show produced by the Tokyo Broadcasting Company, *Fun with Ken and Kato Chan,* which featured a segment in which viewers were invited to mail in their home video clips. Vin Di Bona, who had earlier success with other TBC properties, eventually purchased U.S. rights to the Japanese concept. As executive producer, Di Bona expanded the segment into a half-hour hybrid of home video, variety show, stand up comedy, and audience participation synthesized to fit the ABC profile of family viewing.

Although indebted to a prevalence of reality-based programs when it debuted, *AFHV* had a far greater and more immediate impact on weekly ratings than any of its predecessors or imitators. Cracking the Nielsen Top 5 after only six episodes, by March 1990 it had become the number one ranked series, temporarily unseating CBS' *60 Minutes,* a feat no other ABC program had been able to achieve in twelve years. Since then, it has regularly won its time period among children, teenagers, and women and men ages 18 to 34.

At the series' peak of popularity, producers reported receiving close to 2,000 video submissions a day. These tapes, eventually sorted out by screeners for broadcast approval, must meet criteria that render them suitable for family audiences. First and foremost, qualifying videos should portray funny, amazing, or unexpected events in everyday life, such as animal antics, blunders at birthday parties, bloopers during wedding ceremonies, and fouled plays at sporting events. Because the series emphasizes the supposed universality and spontaneity of slapstick humor, tapes that depict extreme violence, offensive conduct, and serious physical injury, or that encourage imitative behavior, are strictly forbidden. Deliberately staged videos, such as parodies of advertisements or lip-synching of popular songs, may be accepted, but in general events rigged to look accidental or spontaneous are disqualified (or were reserved for Di Bona's follow-up program, *America's Funniest People,* now defunct, but created especially to accommodate staged video performances).

Once a clip is approved, its creators and performers must sign releases for broadcast authorization. Then follows a process during which clips are adjusted for uniform quality and matched in terms of production values; are embellished with sound effects and wisecracking voice-overs by host Bob Saget; are organized as a montage related to a loose theme (e.g. dogs, talent shows, skiing); and finally, are nestled into the format of the program. Each episode is first taped before a live studio audience, during which the clips are broadcast upon studio monitors so that the series' producers can gauge audience reaction. After subsequent reviews of the taping, producers pass on their recommendations to the staff, who edit out the less successful moments before the program is broadcast nationwide. Although labor-intensive, this

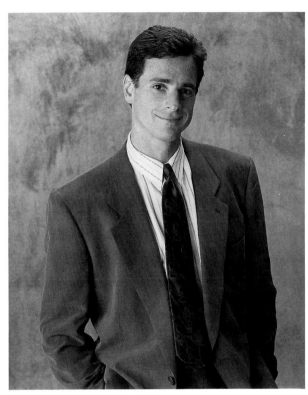

Bob Saget
Photo courtesy of Vin Di Bona Productions

method of television production is a relative bargain, costing less per episode than the average sitcom, and of course was soon imitated (for example, by FOX's *Totally Hidden Video*).

Television critics have been somewhat puzzled by the continued success of *AFHV,* many having panned the series as yet another illustration of the American public's increasing willingness to broadcast their most private and embarrassing moments. Several hypotheses for the series' popularity have been cited: the urge of the viewing public to get on television in order to secure their fifteen minutes of fame; the possibility of winning a $10,000 cash prize; the all expenses paid weekend trip to Hollywood to attend studio tapings; the charisma of host Bob Saget, the first performer since Arthur Godfrey to star in two concurrent, high-rated series (the other being *Full House*); the universal identification with everyday life fundamental to home movies and home video; and the sheer fun of producing television about and for oneself. The series' producers, however, cite the program's humor as the key to its success. Taking the "Bullwinkle approach" that provokes different kinds of laughter from both children and their parents, *AFHV* not only seeks to attract a wide demographic, but self-consciously mocks itself as insignificant, harmless fun.

Despite its overt lack of pretension, *AFHV* remains significant on several accounts, especially its international origins and appeal. Banking upon the perceived cross-cultural universality of home video productions, Di Bona had conceived of the series as international from its inception.

AFHV can be seen in at least 70 countries and in more than a dozen languages (it is rumored to be the favorite show of the sultan of Brunei). Di Bona has subsequently sold the format rights to producers in other nations, at least 16 of which have created their own versions, while others merely replace Saget with indigenous hosts. Most international affiliates also have clip trade agreements; *AFHV* itself liberally blends domestic and imported clips (blurring the title's emphasis on "America" and pointing to television's partnership in global capitalism).

Also significant is the series' premise that the typical consumers of television may become its producers—that the modes of television reception and production are more dialogic than unidirectional. This inversion, as well as the format's unique hybridization of genres, results in peculiar effects worthy of investigation: the professional's commissioning of the amateur for commercial exploitation; the home video's simultaneous status as folk art and mass media; the promise of reward through competition that re-inflects the home mode of production's typical naiveté and non-commercial motivation with formal contrivance and financial incentives; the stress on comedy which excludes the banal everyday activities most typical of home video; and, finally, the format's allowance for a studio audience to vote for and reward their favorite video clip, maintaining the illusion of home video's folksy character, while the ten thousand dollar first prize reifies the slapstick conventions which the producers seek and that keep home viewers tuning in.

—James Moran

HOST
Bob Saget

PRODUCERS   Vin Di Bona, Steve Paskay

PROGRAMMING HISTORY

• ABC
January 1990   Sunday 8:00-8:30

FURTHER READING
"Bob Saget, the Host with the Most on His Busy, Busy Mind." *People Weekly* (New York), 26 March 1990.
Coe, Steve. "Home Is Where the Video Is." *Broadcasting and Cable* (Washington, D.C.), 12 April 1993.

Delsohn, Steve. "The Hip, Low-Key Host of This Season's Most Surprising Hit." *TV Guide* (Radnor, Pennsylvania), 31 March 1990).
Elm, Joanna, and Lisa Schwartzbaum. "Tonight's Hot Story Is Brought To You…By You! How the Camcorder is Changing TV Newscasts." *TV Guide* (Radnor, Pennsylvania), 24 February 1990.
Fore, Steve. "America, America, This Is You!: The Curious Case of *America's Funniest Home Videos*." *Journal of Popular Film and Television* (Washington, D.C.), Spring 1993.
Goldman, Kevin. "*60 Minutes* Show Beaten in Ratings by Home Videos." *Wall Street Journal* (New York), 27 February 1990.
Hiltbrand, David. "*America's Funniest Home Videos*." *People Weekly* (New York), 5 March 1990.
Kaufman, Joanne. "America, Let's Go to Tape!" *People Weekly* (New York), 26 March 1990.
Lippman, John. "ABC to Warn Viewers about Risky Videos; The Network Was Prompted by Mounting Criticism about Safety of Some Acts in its Mega-Hit, *America's Funniest Home Videos*." *Los Angeles Times*, 14 April 1990.
Lyons, Jeffrey. "The Best of *America's Funniest Home Videos*." *Video Review* (New York), August 1991.
Rachlin, Jill. "Behind the Screens at TV's Funniest New Show." *Ladies' Home Journal* (New York), June 1990.
Sackett, Susan. "*America's Funniest Home Videos*." *Prime Time Hits: Television's Most Popular Network Programs, 1950 to the Present.* New York, Billboard Books, 1993.
Sherwood, Rick. "*The Hollywood Reporter* Salutes *America's Funniest Home Videos* on its 100th Episode." *The Hollywood Reporter* (Los Angeles), 19 November 1991.
"That's a Wrap: *America's Funniest Home Videos*: Funniest New TV Show." *U. S. News and World Report* (Washington, D.C.), 9 July 1990.
Waters, Harry F. "Revenge of the Couch Potatoes: The Outrageous Success of *America's Funniest Home Videos* Proves That Any Fool Can Be a Star." *Newsweek* (New York), 5 March 1990.
Zoglin, Richard. "*America's Funniest Home Videos*." *Time* (New York), 5 March 1990.

See also Camcorder

AMERICA'S MOST WANTED

U.S. Reality Program/Public Service

First aired on the seven FOX Stations in February 1988, *America's Most Wanted* is a U.S. reality program featuring segments which reenact crimes of wanted fugitives. Two months later, the show moved to the FOX Broadcasting Corporation and its affiliates. Produced by FOX Television Stations Productions (a unit of FOX Television Stations, Inc.), *America's Most Wanted* may be cited as the first example of the "manhunt" type of reality shows. Consistently winning solid ratings throughout its history, it has also been credited as a television show which doubles as both entertainment and "public-service." Through the use of a toll-free "hotline," it elicits the participation of viewers in helping to capture known suspects depicted on the programme, thus garnering praise and cooperation from law enforcement officials.

As a reality program, the style and content of *America's Most Wanted* closely follows that of other programme types gathered under this broad industry label (e.g., "tabloid" newsmagazines, video-verite and reenacted crime, rescue and manhunt shows, and family amateur video programmes). Central to each of these genres is a visible reference to, or dramatization of, real events and occupations. Thus, while the stories told on *America's Most Wanted* stem from "real life" incidents, they are not comprised of "actual" live footage (with the exception of recorded testimony from the "real" people involved). Rather, incidents of criminality and victimization are reenacted, and in an often intense and involving manner. This dramatic component, particularly as it entails a subjective appeal, is a dominant feature of reality program, which tend to accentuate the emotional for their effectivity. Viewers are thus asked to empathize and identify with the experiences of the people represented on the show, especially insofar as these experiences involve social or moral dilemmas.

Relying upon a structure similar to that used by television newsmagazines—which move back and forth from promotional trailer to anchor to report—each episode of *America's Most Wanted* is divided into a number of segments which retell and reenact a particular crime. Beginning with an up-date on how many viewers' tips have thus far led to the capture of fugitives featured on the show, the program then moves to the host or "anchor," who introduces the program and the first story segment. Using both actors and live footage of the "real people" involved, these story segments are highly dramatized, making liberal use of quick edits, rock music underscoring, sophisticated camera effects and voice-overs. In addition to supplying a narrative function, the voice-overs also include actual testimony of the event from police, victims and the criminals involved, thus emphasizing and appealing to the subjective.

The program resembles the tabloid newsmagazine genre in its often exaggerated language, also used in promotional trailers and by the host to describe the crimes depicted on the show (e.g., "Next, a tragic tale of obsession"). Additionally, and again paralleling qualities of tabloid TV, there are noticeable efforts towards self-promotion or congratulation; the host, law enforcement officials, and even captured fugitives repeatedly hype the policing and surveillance functions of the show. And yet, despite these consistencies with a denigrated tabloid TV genre, *America's Most Wanted* is distinct in its appeal to and affiliation with both "the public" and the police.

The program is hosted by John Walsh, who "anchors" *America's Most Wanted* from Washington, D.C. Given the show's cooperation with federal law agencies, such as the FBI and the U.S. Marshall Service, its broadcast from this loca-

John Walsh
Photo courtesy of John Walsh

tion acts to further associate it with law enforcement institutions. Walsh, whose son was abducted and murdered in 1981, is a nationally-known advocate for missing and exploited children. As part of its program format, *America's Most Wanted* airs a weekly feature on missing children, and has created "The Missing Child Alert," a series of public service bulletins which are made available to all television stations, regardless of network affiliation.

Through its toll-free hotline (1-800-CRIME-TV), which operates seven days and averages 2,500 calls a week, the program has assisted in the apprehension of hundreds of fugitives, and thus earned the appreciation of law enforcement agencies. Additionally, *America's Most Wanted* sees itself as enabling a cathartic process, offering not only legal justice, but psychological resolution to victims of crime. In both these respects, *America's Most Wanted* may be said to move away from much of the fixed voyeurism of reality shows, towards a more active "public" function. And yet, do manhunt shows such as *America's Most Wanted* simply temper the tabloid's spectacle into a new form of "vigilante voyeurism?" Do such shows not only feed into, but actively promote, a public's fears regarding an ever present criminal threat? Such questions, regarding the aims, the intended audience and the effectivity of *America's Most Wanted's* public function, must be addressed.

—Beth Seaton

HOST
John Walsh

PRODUCERS   Lance Heflin, Joseph Russin, Paul Sparrow

PROGRAMMING HISTORY

• FOX

April 1988–August 1990	Sunday 8:00-8:30
September 1990–July 1993	Friday 8:00-9:00
July 1993–January 1994	Tuesday 9:00-10:00
January 1994–	Saturday 9:00-10:00

FURTHER READING

Bartley, Diane. "John Walsh: Fighting Back." *Saturday Evening Post* (Indianapolis, Indiana), April 1990.

Cosgrove, Stuart. "Crime can often Become an Accessory to Fiction on TV." *New Statesman and Society* (London), 7 December 1990.

"F.B.I. Gives Programs Exclusives on Fugitives." *The New York Times*, 15 September 1991.

Finney, Angus. "Gutter and Gore." *New Statesman and Society* (London), 9 September 1988.

Friedman, David. "Wanted: Lowlifes and High Ratings." *Rolling Stone* (New York), 12 January 1989.

Garneau, George. "FBI to Newspapers: Watch Television." *Editor and Publisher* (New York), 21 September 1991.

Nelson, Scott A. "Crime-time Television." *The FBI Law Enforcement Bulletin* (Washington, D.C.), August 1988.

Prial, Frank J. "Freeze! You're on TV." *Reader's Digest* (Pleasantville, New York), March 1989.

"Television: Crime Pays." *The Economist* (London), 10 June 1989.

Thomas, Bill. "Finding Truth in the Age of 'Infotainment.'" *Editorial Research Reports* (Washington, D.C.: Congressional Quarterly, Inc.), 19 January 1990.

White, Daniel R. "America's Most Wanted." *ABA Journal* (Chicago), October 1989.

AMERIKA

U.S. Miniseries

Broadcast on ABC over the course of seven nights in the middle of February 1987, *Amerika* was a controversial 14-and-1/2 hour miniseries. Tom Shales of *The Washington Post* wrote in December 1986 that *Amerika* "could be the hottest political potato in the history of television." It was produced by ABC Circle Films, and written and directed by Donald Wrye, who was also executive producer. This series depicted life as imagined in the United States in the late 1990s, ten years after the Soviet Union took control of America employing a Russian controlled U.N. peace-keeping force.

Some have contended that *Amerika* was produced to provide a television counter to the controversial ABC movie *The Day After*, which depicted nuclear holocaust between the United States and Russia in 1983. The ABC executive responsible for both programs denied this view. Brandon Stoddard, president of ABC Circle films, said on 16 October 1986 at a press tour at the U.N. Plaza Hotel in New York that the idea for *Amerika* "never occurred during the controversy of *The Day After*, had nothing to do with *The Day After*. It happened...the birth of this idea happened substantially later." Stoddard went on to say that a critic of *The Day After*, Ben Stein from the *Herald Examiner* had written something, "at a much later point, a line...that had to do with what would life be like in America in a Russian occupation." Stoddard was stuck, however, thinking about how to do such a television program without getting caught up in the actual struggle of the takeover. Some time later, Stoddard's spouse suggested doing the project at a point in time ten years after the takeover.

At the time, *Amerika* was the most controversial television event ever broadcast by ABC. The network received more mail and phone calls about *Amerika* before it was on

Amerika
Photo courtesy of BBC

the air than the total pre- and post-broadcast viewer reaction of any other program in the history of ABC, including the end-of-the-world story, *The Day After*.

The critics of *Amerika* came from all sides of the political spectrum. Liberals feared the program would antagonize the Kremlin, jeopardize arms control and détente. The right thought the miniseries inadequately portrayed the brutality of the U.S.S.R. The United Nations thought the movie would erode its image.

Despite the pre-broadcast level of controversy, most of the public did not object to the miniseries. Research conducted by ABC before the broadcast indicated that 96% of the population over 18 years old did not object to the program. Most Americans felt strongly that they should have the right to decide for themselves whether they would watch the program.

While almost half the country watched *The Day After* (46.0 rating), *Amerika* was seen in 19% of all TV households. Despite lots of publicity, controversy and viewers, research conducted by Professor William Adams at George Washington University showed that attitudes about the things most critics thought would be influenced by *Amerika* did not change. What Americans thought about the Soviet Union, the United Nations, or U.S.-Soviet relations did not change in before and after surveys.

—Guy E. Lometti

CAST

Devin Milford . . . . Kris Kristofferson
Marion Milford . . . . Wendy Hughes
General Samanov . . . . Armin Mueller-Stahl
Peter Bradford . . . . Robert Urich
Amanda Bradford . . . . Cindy Pickett

Colonel Andrei Denisov . . . . Sam Neill
Kimberly Ballard . . . . Mariel Hemingway
Althea Milford . . . . Christine Lahti
Ward Milford . . . . Richard Bradford
Helmut Gurtman . . . . Reiner Schoene
Herbert Lister . . . . John Madden Towney
Will Milford . . . . Ford Rainey

PRODUCER   David Wrye

PROGRAMMING HISTORY

• ABC

15 February-22 February 1987   9:00-11:00

FURTHER READING

Lometti, G.E. "Broadcast Preparations for and Consequences of *The Day After.*" In, Wober, J.M., editor. *Television and Nuclear Power: Making the Public Mind.* Norwood, New Jersey: Ablex, 1992.

Lometti, G.E. *Sensitive Theme Programming and the New American Mainstream.* New York: American Broadcasting Companies, 1984.

AMOS 'N' ANDY SHOW

U.S. Domestic Comedy

Like many of its early television counterparts, the *Amos 'n' Andy* television program was a direct descendent of the radio show that originated on WMAQ in Chicago on 19 March 1928, and eventually became the longest-running radio program in broadcast history. *Amos 'n' Andy* was conceived by Freeman Gosden and Charles Correll, two white actors who portrayed the characters Amos Jones and Andy Brown by mimicking so-called Negro dialect.

The significance of *Amos 'n' Andy*, with its almost thirty-year history as a highly successful radio show, its brief, contentious years on network television, its banishment from prime-time and subsequent years in syndication, and its reappearance in video cassette format is difficult to summarize in a few paragraphs. The position of the *Amos 'n' Andy* show in television history is still debated by media scholars in recent books on the cultural history of American television.

Amos 'n' Andy, was first broadcast on CBS television in June 1951, and lasted some two years before the program was canceled in the midst of growing protest by the black community in 1953. It was the first television series with an all-black cast (the only one of its kind to appear on prime-time, network television for nearly another twenty years).

The adventures of *Amos 'n' Andy* presented the antics of Amos Jones, an Uncle Tom-like conservative; Andy Brown, his zany business associate; Kingfish Stevens, a scheming smoothie; Lawyer Calhoun, an underhanded crook that no

one trusted; Lightnin', a slow-moving janitor; Sapphire Stevens, a nosey loud-mouth; Mama, a domineering mother-in-law; and the infamous Madame Queen. The basis for these characters was derived largely from the stereotypic caricatures of African-Americans that had been communicated through several decades of popular American culture, most notably, motion pictures.

The program's portrayal of black life and culture was deemed by the black community of the period as an insulting return to the days of blackface and minstrelsy. Eventually, the controversy surrounding the television version of *Amos 'n' Andy* would almost equal that of the popularity of the radio version.

Contemporary television viewers might find it difficult to understand what all the clamor was about. Why did the *Amos 'n' Andy* show go on to become one of the most protested of television programs?

Media historian Donald Bogel notes, "Neither CBS nor the programs' creators were prepared for the change in national temperament after the Second World War....Within black America, a new political consciousness and a new awareness of the importance of image had emerged." Though hardly void of the cruel insults and disparaging imagery of the past, Hollywood of the post-World War II period ushered in an era of better roles and improved images for African-American performers in Hollywood. American motion pictures presented its first

AMOS 'N' ANDY SHOW   65

Amos 'n' Andy

glimpses of black soldiers fighting alongside their white comrades; black entertainers appeared in sequined gowns and tuxedos instead of bandannas and calico dresses. Black characters could be lawyers, teachers and contributing members of society.

Post World War II African-Americans looked upon the new medium of television with hopeful excitement. To them, the medium could nullify the decades of offensive caricatures and ethnic stereotyping so prevalent throughout decades of motion picture history. The frequent appearance of black stars on early television variety shows was met with approval from black leadership.

African-Americans were still exuberant over recent important gains in civil rights brought on by World War II. They were determined to realize improved images of themselves in popular culture. To some, the characters in *Amos 'n' Andy*, including rude, aggressive women and weak black men were offensive. Neither the Kingfish nor Sapphire Stevens could engage in a conversation without peppering their speech with faulty grammar and mispronunciations.

Especially abhorred was the portrayal of black professionals. The NAACP, bolstered by its 1951 summer convention, mandated an official protest of the program. The organization outlined a list of specific items it felt were objectionable, for example, how "every character is either a clown or a crook," "Negro doctors are shown as quacks," and "Negro lawyers are shown as crooks." As the series appeared in June 1951, the NAACP appeared in federal court seeking an injunction against its premiere. To network executives, the show was harmless, not much different from *Life with Liugi, The Goldbergs*, or any other ethnically oriented show.

Moreover, the denunciation of *Amos 'n' Andy* was not universal. With its good writing and talented cast, the show was good comedy, and soon became a commercial success. The reaction of the black community over this well produced and funny program remained divided. Even the *Pittsburgh Courier*, one of the black community's most influential publications, which had earlier led in the protest against the motion picture *Gone With the Wind*, defended the show in an article appearing in June 1951.

In 1953, CBS reluctantly removed the program from the air, but not solely because of the efforts of the NAACP. As mentioned, the period featured a swiftly changing climate for race relations in the United States. Consideration for the southern market was of great concern to major advertisers. In an era when African Americans were becoming increasingly vocal in the fight against racial discrimination, large advertisers were reluctant to have their products too closely associated with black people. Fear of white economic backlash was of special concern to advertisers and television producers. The idea of "organized consumer resistance" caused advertisers and television executives to avoid appearing pro-Negro rights. One advertising agency executive, referring to blacks on television, noted in *Variety*, "the word has gone out, 'No Negro performers allowed.'"

Even with so much contention looming, the *Amos 'n' Andy* show remained in syndication well into the 1960s. Currently, video tape cassettes of the episodes are widely available.

—Pamela S. Deane

CAST

Amos Jones	Alvin Childress
Andrew Hogg Brown (Andy)	Spencer Williams, Jr.
George "Kingfish" Stevens	Tim Moore
Lawyer Algonquin J. Calhoun	Johnny Lee
Sapphire Stevens	Ernestine Wade
Lightin'	Horace Stewart (aka, Nick O'Demus)
Sapphire's Mama (Ramona Smith) . .	Amanda Randolph
Madame Queen	Lillian Randolph

PRODUCERS   Freeman Gosden, Charles Correll

PROGRAMMING HISTORY   78 Episodes

• CBS

June 1951–June 1953   Thursday 8:30-9:00
Widely Syndicated thereafter until 1966

FURTHER READING

Bogel, Donald. *Blacks, Coons, Mullatoes, Mammies and Bucks: An Interpretive History of Blacks in American Film.* New York: Garland, 1973.

———. *Blacks in American Television and Film.* New York: Garland, 1988.

Campbell, Edward D.C., Jr. *The Celluliod South: Hollywood and the Southern Myth.* Knoxville: University of Tennessee, 1981.

Ely, Melvin Patrick. *The Adventures of Amos 'n' Andy: A Social History of an American Phenomenon.* New York: Free Press, 1991.

Friedman, Lester D. *Unspeakable Images: Ethnicity and the American Cinema.* Urbana: University of Illinois Press, 1991.

Gray, Herman. *Watching Race: Television and the Struggle for "Blackness."* Minneapolis: University of Minnesota Press, 1995.

Hughes, Langston. *Fight for Freedom: The Story of the NAACP.* New York: Norton, 1962.

MacDonald, J. Fred. *Blacks and White TV: Afro-Americans in Television Since 1948.* Chicago: Nelson-Hall, 1993.

Marc, David, and Robert J. Thompson. *Prime Time, Prime Movers: From I Love Lucy to L.A. Law, America's Greatest TV Shows and and People Who Created Them.* Boston: Little, Brown, 1992.

Nesteby, James R. *Black Images in American Films 1896–1954: The Interplay Between Civil Rights and Film Culture.* Lanham, Maryland: University Press of America, 1982.

See also Racism, Ethnicity, and Television

ANCHOR

In U.S. television the chief news presenter(s) for network, local, cable and satellite news programming is known as the Anchor. The term distinguishes the presenter-journalist at the newsdesk in the television studio (or above the convention floor, etc.) from the reporter in the field. All news stories in a program are funneled through the anchor as he or she mediates between the public, the network or and other news reporters.

The most commonly cited source of the term is the television news coverage of the 1952 Republican presidential conventions; the metaphor is borrowed, not as one might expect, from the nautical realm, but from the strongest runner of a relay team, the anchorman, who runs the final leg of the race. In the conventional format of broadcast news, when the anchor is not personally delivering a story by directly addressing the viewing audience, or speaking over symbols and visual images of the news, he or she is introducing and calling upon reporters to deliver stories from the field or announcing a commercial break. Moreover, an anchor represents the public and its need to know whenever he or she interrogates and listens to the subject of an interview. National news anchors represent their respective networks and are held accountable for the ratings success of their respective news programs in attracting viewers. In keeping with this serious representational function, the anchor's style of delivery is reserved and his or her appearance is designed to convey credibility. In other words, the anchor is a television host at the top of a hierarchial chain of command with special reportorial credentials and responsibilities centered around "hard" or serious news of the day; celebrity interview and tabloid news shows have hosts, not anchors, even when they are organized similarly in format to network evening news. Journalists in other television news formats without a similar division of labor between studio and field are not anchors strictly speaking.

Being delegated with the daily, prestigious responsibility for presenting national news has brought public exposure that has made some network television news anchors into house-hold names. During his tenure as anchor of the CBS evening news, Walter Cronkite transcended the domain of broadcast news into becoming a widely-admired and "most trusted" national figure, eclipsing the fame of his cohorts, including the NBC newsteam Chet Huntley and David Brinkley; contemporary network anchors ABC's Peter Jennings, CBS' Dan Rather, and NBC's Tom Brokaw are national celebrities and highly-paid television stars. However, the role of the network anchor appears to be declining in cultural significance as the broadcast networks lose their dominance over the industry. The sheer numbers of anchors, for instance, the singles and pairs CNN rotates over its twenty-four hours of news programming, dilutes their potential star power.

Aside from abortive attempts to team Barbara Walters with Harry Reasoner and more recently, Connie Chung with Dan Rather, national news presenting has been a white male preserve. However, local anchor teams have long represented diversity in the community through a news couple of different race and gender, supplemented by reporters on the sports and weather beat and in the field. Even in the local context, however, gender distinctions are vital. The highly publicized case of Christine Kraft, anchor of KMBC-TV in Kansas City, Kansas, illustrates the willingness of executives to dismiss women considered "too old" or "too unattractive" to fill this highly visible role. Such judgments are rarely, if ever, made in cases involving male anchors, who are seen to develop "authority" and "gravity" as their physical glamour fades.

A secondary meaning of anchor comes out of semiology, or the study of signs and meaning. Roland Barthes' "The Rhetoric of the Image" also uses the anchor and relay metaphor to describe two different functions of the caption in relation to a still image: a caption anchors the image when it selectively elucidates its meaning; when it sets out meanings not found in the image itself, it acts as a relay. The television news anchor may be said to function similarly as an "anchor" in this extended sense, by presenting a selection of events as news stories and by providing a framework for the interpretation of their social and cultural meaning.

—Margaret Morse

FURTHER READING

Barnouw, Erik. *Tube of Plenty.* New York: Oxford University Press, 1984.

Barthes, Roland, translated by Stephen Heath. "The Rhetoric of the Image." In, *Image, Music, Text,* New York: Hill and Wang, 1977.

Cunningham, Liz. *Talking Politics: Choosing the President in the Television Age.* Westport, Connecticut: Praeger, 1995.

Fensch, Thomas Fensch. editor. *Television News Anchors: An Anthology of Profiles of the Major Figures and Issues in United States Network Reporting* Jefferson, North Carolina: McFarland, 1993.

Goldberg, Robert, and Gerald J. Goldberg. *Anchors: Brokaw, Jennings, Rather and the Evening News.* Secaucus, New Jersey: Carol Pub. Group, 1990.

Hallin, Dan. *We Keep America on Top of the World: Television Journalism and the Public Sphere.* (London, and New York: Routledge, 1994.

James, Doug. *Walter Cronkite: His Life and Times.* Brentwood, Tennessee: JM Press, 1991.

Matusow, Barbara Matusow. *The Evening Stars: The Making of the Network News Anchor.* Boston : Houghton Mifflin, 1983.

Morse, Margaret. "The Television News Personality and Credibility: Reflections on the News in Transition." In, *Studies in Entertainment: Critical Approaches to Mass Culture.* Bloomington: University of Indiana Press, 1986.

Rather, Dan, with Mickey Herskowitz. *The Camera Never Blinks: Adventures of a TV Journalist.* New York: W. Morrow, 1977.

————. *The Camera Never Blinks Twice: The Further Adventures of a Television Journalist.* New York: W. Morrow, 1994.

Sanders, Marlene, and Marcia Rock. *Waiting for Prime Time: The Women of Television News.* Urbana: University of Illinois Press, 1988.

See also Brinkley, David; Brokaw, Tom; Chung, Connie; Craft, Christine; Cronkite, Walter; Huntley, Chet; Jennings, Peter; Walters, Barbara

ANCILLARY MARKETS

In the American television industry the term "ancillary markets" generally refers to markets for feature films created by new television technologies. Before television, American films played only in motion picture theaters, and the only ancillary markets were found in theaters in international markets around the world. But the rise of commercial television in the 1950s and of pay cable and home video in the 1980s created additional venues for Hollywood product. Today, a feature film first opens in motion picture theaters to establish its box-office value and critical reputation. It is then released to ancillary markets in the following order: (1) home video (videocassette rental); (2)

pay cable (premium cable services such as HBO, Showtime, and Cinemax); (3) network television; (4) cable television; and (5) television syndication. This distribution pattern is designed to maximize the full economic potential of each market, or "window" as it is called in the trade. With the exception of home video, which has a window that remains open almost indefinitely, a new feature is exploited in one market at a time. In each window, the price paid by the consumer to view the picture drops. Economists call this process price tiering: a film is first released to theaters where it is viewed for a period of months at top prices by "high value" consumers, i.e., to those who are most anxious to see the film and are willing to pay $7 and more for a ticket. The film is then released at contractually specified intervals to "lower value" consumers at prices that decline with time. A consumer willing to wait two to three years to view a film can finally receive it "free" over network television. Thus, the distribution pattern taps every segment of the market in an orderly way and at a price commensurate with its demand.

Historically, the first domestic ancillary market for feature films was created in the early 1960s when television networks first scheduled recent vintage Hollywood features in prime time. NBC began this practice on 23 September 1961 by programming "NBC Saturday Night at the Movies." Envious of NBC's successful strategy, ABC became the second network to program a prime time series of features. In 1962 the network launched "Hollywood Special" to bolster its Sunday night ratings with a package of films from United Artists. CBS, the television industry's leading network in this period, did not add a prime time feature film program until 1965 when it moved to strengthen a weak Thursday night.

Feature films had, of course, been a programming staple on television from the early days of the medium. Most of these movies were of pre-1948 vintage, however, and were used mainly to fill fringe time slots, particularly the afternoon and late evening. The first features came from Poverty Row studios, independent producers, and foreign film distributors. But Hollywood soon felt the effects of television's huge popularity. Strapped for cash as a result of the inroads TV had made on motion picture audiences many of the major studios began in 1955 either to sell off their libraries of old films to television syndicators or to create their own separate departments to handle distribution of films to television.

The majors were free to dispose of the pre–1948 films because they controlled television performance rights and all ancillary rights to their pictures. But the Hollywood talent unions, or guilds as they are called, demanded residual compensation to guild members who appeared in features made after 1 August 1948 and subsequently rented to television. Anticipating a boost in demand for recent vintage films when the networks converted to color television, the studios reached a settlement with the guilds in 1960 and began supplying the networks with a steady flow of product

the year round. By the 1960s, the distribution pattern for feature films had thus become, theaters first, then eighteen months after the close of the theatrical run, network television, and then syndicated television.

Pay television and home video opened up still other new opportunities for filmed programming. Pay television came into its own in 1975, when Home Box Office, a venture of Time Inc., offered to cable subscribers, via satellite, the first of the so-called "premium services" consisting of recent, uncut, and uninterrupted films, sports events, and other specially-produced programming. After court battles in which HBO successfully challenged the right of the Federal Communications Commission to protect broadcast television, other premium services such as Showtime, the Movie Channel, and Cinemax entered the business. The distribution pattern in ancillary markets was therefore altered to accommodate these pay-TV services. The premium cable services became the second programming "window," following theatrical release and preceding broadcast network programming.

Although video tape recorders hit the market on the heels of HBO, home video did not become a significant force until the 1980s when Hollywood devised a way to accommodate the new technology. In response to pay-TV's ability to finance its own productions or to form alliances with independent producers, thereby circumventing the established studios, the Hollywood majors decided to release new films to home video prior to their availability on pay-TV. At the same time the studios made thousands of older movie titles available on videocassette. These strategies provided the necessary product diversity to differentiate home video from both the theatrical and pay-TV markets and to enable home video to become Hollywood's premier revenue source.

—Tino Balio

FURTHER READING

Banks, Jack. "The Institutional Analysis of the Pay Cable Market." *Studies in Communication and Culture* (Madison, Wisconsin), Spring 1988.

Lardner, James. *Fast Forward: Hollywood, The Japanese and the Onslaught of the VCR.* New York: Norton, 1987.

Mair, George. *Inside HBO: The Billion Dollar War between HBO, Hollywood, and the Home Video Revolution.* New York: Dodd Mead, 1988.

Valenti, Jack. "Managing Changes in Technology." *Variety* (Los Angeles), 14 January 1987.

Wasko, Janet. *Hollywood in the Information Age: Beyond the Silver Screen.* Austin, Texas: University of Texas Press, 1994.

Wildman, Steven S., and Bruce M. Owen. *Video Economics.* Cambridge: Harvard University Press, 1992.

See also Financial Interest and Syndication Rules; Movies on Television; Reruns; Syndication

THE ANDY GRIFFITH SHOW

U.S. Situation Comedy

The Andy Griffith Show was one of the most popular and memorable comedy series of the 1960s. In its eight years on the air, from 1960 to 1968, it never dropped below seventh place in the seasonal Nielsen rankings, and it was number one the year it ceased production. The series pilot originally aired as an episode of Make Room For Daddy, a popular sitcom starring Danny Thomas. Sheldon Leonard produced both shows for Danny Thomas Productions.

An early example of television's "rural revolution," The Andy Griffith Show was part of a programming trend which saw the development of comedies featuring naïve but noble "rubes" from deep in the American heartland. The trend began when ABC debuted The Real McCoys in 1957, but CBS became the network most associated with it. The success CBS achieved with The Andy Griffith Show provided the inspiration for a string of hits such as The Beverly Hillbillies, Green Acres, Petticoat Junction, and Hee Haw. Genial and comparatively innocuous, these shows were just right for a time when TV was under frequent attack by the Federal Communications Commission(FCC) and Congressional committees for its violent content.

Sheldon Leonard and Danny Thomas designed The Andy Griffith Show to fit the image of its star. Griffith's homespun characterizations were already well-known to audiences who'd seen his hayseed interpretations of Shakespeare on The Ed Sullivan Show and his starring roles in the films A Face in the Crowd (1957) and No Time for Sergeants (1958). On The Andy Griffith Show, he played Sheriff Andy Taylor, the fair-minded and easygoing head lawman of the Edenic small town of Mayberry, North Carolina. Neither sophisticated nor worldly-wise, Andy drew from a deep well of unpretentious folk wisdom that allowed him to settle domestic disputes and outwit the arrogant city folk who occasionally passed through town. When he wasn't at the sheriff's office, Andy, a widower, was applying his old-fashioned horse sense to the raising of his young son Opie (Ronny Howard), a task he shared with his Aunt Bee (Frances Bavier).

Mayberry was based upon Andy Griffith's real home-town, and perhaps this was partially responsible for the strong sense many viewers got that Mayberry was a real place. Over the years the writers fleshed out the geography and character of the town with a degree of detail unusual for series television. The directorial style of the series was also strikingly distinct, employing a relaxed, almost lethargic tone appropriate to the nostalgic settings of front porch, sidewalk, and barber shop. The townspeople, and the ensemble of actors who portrayed them, were crucial to the success of the show. Most of these characters were "hicks," playing comic foils to the sagacious Andy. Gomer Pyle (Jim Nabors) and his cousin Goober (George Lindsey) came right out of the "bumpkin" tradition that had been developed years ago in films, popular literature, and comic strips. Town barber Floyd Lawson (Howard McNear) was a font of

misinformation and the forerunner of Cheers' Cliff Clavin. Otis (Hal Smith), the unrepentant town drunk, was trained to let himself into his jail cell after a Saturday night bender and to let himself out on Sunday morning. Without much real police work to attend to, Andy's true job was protecting these and other citizens of Mayberry from their own hubris, intemperance, and stupidity.

Most of Andy's time, however, was spent controlling his earnest but over-zealous deputy, Barney Fife. Self-important, romantic, and nearly always wrong, Barney dreamed of the day he could use the one bullet Andy had issued to him. While Barney was forever frustrated that Mayberry was too small for the delusional ideas he had of himself, viewers got the sense that he couldn't have survived anywhere else. Don Knotts played the comic and pathetic sides of the character with equal aplomb and was given four Emmy Awards for doing so. He left the show in 1965 and was replaced by Jack Burns in the role of Deputy Warren Furguson.

The Andy Griffith Show engendered two spin-offs. Gomer Pyle, U.S.M.C. was a military sitcom featuring Gomer in the Marines. Mayberry, R.F.D. was a reworking of The Andy Griffith Show made necessary by Griffith's departure in 1968. Like the parent show, the spin-offs celebrated the honesty, the strong sense of community, and the solid family alues supposedly inherent in small town life.

The Andy Griffith Show

By the late 1960s, however, many viewers, especially young ones, were rejecting these shows as irrelevant to modern times. Mayberry's total isolation from contemporary problems was part of its appeal, but more than a decade of media coverage of the civil rights movement had brought about a change in the popular image of the small Southern town. *Gomer Pyle, U.S.M.C.* was set on a U.S. Marine base between 1964 and 1969, but neither Gomer nor any of his fellow soldiers ever mentioned the war in Vietnam. CBS executives, afraid of losing the lucrative youth demographic, purged their schedule of hit shows that were drawing huge but older audiences. *Gomer Pyle, U.S.M.C.* was in second place when it was canceled in 1969. *Mayberry, R.F.D.*, and the rest of the rural comedies, met a similar fate within the next two seasons. They were replaced by such "relevant" new sitcoms as *All in the Family* and *M*A*S*H.*

The Andy Griffith Show remains an enduring favorite in syndicated reruns. New fan books about the program, including a cookbook of favorite dishes mentioned in specific episodes, continued to appear nearly thirty years after the end of the original network run. In 1986, a reunion show brought together most of the original cast and production team. *Return To Mayberry* was the highest-rated telefilm of the season.

—Robert J. Thompson

CAST

Andy Taylor . . . . Andy Griffith
Opie Taylor . . . . Ronny Howard
Barney Fife (1960–65) . . . . Don Knotts
Ellie Walker (1960–61) . . . . Elinor Donahue
Aunt Bee Taylor . . . . Frances Bavier
Clara Edwards . . . . Hope Summers
Gomer Pyle (1963–64) . . . . Jim Nabors
Helen Crump (1964–68) . . . . Aneta Corsaut
Goober Pyle (1965–68) . . . . George Lindsey
Floyd Lawson . . . . Howard McNear
Otis Campbell (1960–67) . . . . Hal Smith

Howard Sprague (1966–68) . . . . Jack Dodson
Emmett Clark (1967–68) . . . . Paul Hartman
Thelma Lou (1960–65) . . . . Betty Lynn
Warren Ferguson (1965–66) . . . . Jack Burns
Mayor Stoner (1962–63) . . . . Parley Baer
Jud Crowley (1961–66) . . . . Burt Mustin

PRODUCERS   Louis Edelman, Sheldon Leonard

PROGRAMMING HISTORY: 249 Episodes

• CBS

October 1960–July 1963   Monday 9:30-10:00
September 1963–September 1964   Monday 9:30-10:00
September 1964–June 1965   Monday 8:30-9:00
September 1965–September 1968   Monday 9:00-9:30

FURTHER READING

Barnouw, Erik. *Tube of Plenty: The Evolution of American Television.* New York: Oxford University Press, 1990.

Beck, Ken, and Jim Clark. *The Andy Griffith Show Book.* New York: St. Martin's, 1985.

Eisner, Joel, and David Krinsky. *Television Comedy Series: An Episode Guide to 153 Sitcoms in Syndication.* Jefferson, North Carolina: McFarland, 1984.

Kelly, Richard. *The Andy Griffith Show.* Winston-Salem, North Carolina: John F. Blair, 1981.

Marc, David. *Comic Visions: Television Comedy and American Culture.* Boston: Unwin Hyman, 1989.

———. *Demographic Vistas: Television in American Culture.* Philadelphia: University of Pennsylvania Press, 1984.

Watson, Mary Ann. *The Expanding Vista: American Television in the Kennedy Years.* New York: Oxford University Press, 1990.

See also Comedy, Domestic Settings; Griffith, Andy

ANNENBERG, WALTER

U.S. Media Executive/Publisher/Diplomat

As a media magnate Walter Annenberg controlled important properties in the newspaper, television, and magazine industries. Perhaps most significantly, he was responsible for the creation of *TV Guide*, the largest circulation weekly magazine in the world, a magazine central to understanding television in America. He was also very active in the arena of American politics, and served as U.S. ambassador to the Court of St. James. In his later life, Annenberg became renowned for his substantial philanthropic activities, which included significant donations to educational institutions and public television.

When his father was imprisoned for tax evasion, Annenberg took over the family publishing business. Triangle Publications, particularly *The Daily Racing Form*, proved to be extremely profitable, and Annenberg looked for ways to expand his company at the time television was beginning to emerge as America's communications medium of the future. Inspired by a Philadelphia-area television magazine called *TV Digest*, Annenberg conceived the idea of publishing a national television feature magazine, which he would then wrap around local television listings. The idea came to fruition when Annenberg purchased *TV Digest*, along with the similar publications *TV Forecast* from Chicago, and *TV Guide* from New York. He combined their operations to form *TV Guide* in 1953, and quickly expanded the magazine by creating new regional editions and purchasing existing television listings publications in other markets.

Annenberg and his aide, Merrill Panitt (who would go on to become *TV Guide*'s editorial director), realized that in order achieve the circulation necessary to make their publication a truly mass medium, they needed to go beyond the fan magazine approach that had been typical of most earlier television and radio periodicals. Because of this desire, they created a magazine that was both a staunch booster of the American system of television, and one of the most visible critics of the medium's more egregious perceived shortcomings. *TV Guide*'s editors often encouraged the magazine's readers to support quality television programs struggling to gain an audience. In fact, *TV Guide*'s greatest accomplishment under Annenberg may have been the magazine's success in walking the fine line between encouraging and prodding the medium to achieve its full potential without becoming too far removed from the prevailing tastes of the mass viewing public. As a consequence, *TV Guide* became extremely popular and widely read, and very influential among those in the television industry. A large number of distinguished authors wrote articles for the magazine over the years, including such names as Margaret Mead, Betty Friedan, John Updike, Gore Vidal, and Arthur Schlesinger, Jr. Many of these writers were attracted by the lure of reaching *TV Guide*'s huge audience; at its peak in the late 1970s, *TV Guide* had a paid circulation of nearly 20 million copies per week.

Annenberg remained supportive of conservative political causes through the years, and his efforts on behalf of Republicans were rewarded with his designation by President Richard Nixon as U.S. ambassador to Great Britain in 1969. The appointment led Annenberg to sell his newspapers and television stations, but he retained *TV Guide* and remained active in managing the publication throughout his five-year tenure as ambassador.

Shortly after the election of his close friend, Ronald Reagan, as president in 1980 (he would endorse Reagan's re-election campaign in 1984 in *TV Guide*, the only such political endorsement ever to appear in the magazine), Annenberg announced a plan to provide the Corporation for Public Broadcasting with $150 million in funds over a fifteen-year period to produce educational television programs through which viewers could obtain college credits. Annenberg's sympathy for educational causes had already been evidenced by his financial support of the Annenberg Schools of Communication at both the University of Pennsylvania and at the University of Southern California. His activities in this regard would grow even more pronounced in the years to come, particularly after his sale of *TV Guide* and Triangle Publications to Rupert Murdoch's News Corporation in 1988 for approximately $3 billion—at the time, the largest price ever commanded for a publishing property.

Annenberg continued to make news after his sale of Triangle because of his many substantial donations to educational causes. In addition, Annenberg was also one of the country's foremost collectors of art, and in 1991, he be-

Walter Annenberg
Photo courtesy of Walter Annenberg

queathed his extensive collection—valued at more than $1 billion—to New York's Metropolitan Museum of Art. His post-Triangle era of charitable activities in the areas of education, art, and television served to further assure Annenberg's lasting legacy to a wide spectrum of American culture.

—David Gunzerath

WALTER (HUBERT) ANNENBERG. Born in Milwaukee, Wisconsin, U.S.A., 13 March 1908. Educated at the Peddie School, Highstown, New Jersey, graduated 1927; attended Wharton School of Finance, University of Pennsylvania, Philadelphia, Pennsylvania, 1927–28. Married: 1) Veronica Dunkelman, 1938 (divorced, 1950); children: Wallis and Roger (deceased); 2) Leonore (Cohn) Rosentiel. Joined father, Moses Annenberg, successful publisher, as assistant in the bookkeeping office, 1928; upon father's death, 1942, assumed leadership of family business, Triangle Publications, Inc., which included the Philadelphia (Pennsylvania) *Inquirer*, the *Daily Racing Form*, the *Morning Telegraph*, and other minor publications; founded *Seventeen* magazine, 1944, and *TV Guide*, 1953; acquired the Philadelphia (Pennsylvania) *Daily News*, 1957; acquired WFIL-AM and FM radio, Philadelphia, Pennsylvania, 1945; expanded station to television outlet, 1947; acquired radio and television stations in Altoona and Lebanon, Pennsylvania, Binghamton, New York, New Haven, Connecticut, and Fresno, California; U.S. ambassador to Great Britain and Northern Ireland, 1968–74; sold Triangle Publications to Rupert Murdoch, 1988. Founder, Annenberg School of Communication, University of Pennsylvania; Annenberg School for Communication, University of Southern California, Los Angeles, California; Annenberg Washington Program in Communication Policy Studies, Washington, D.C.; Annenberg/Corporation for Public Broadcasting Math and Science Project; founder and trustee, Eisenhower Exchange Fellowships, Eisenhower Medical Center, Rancho Mirage, California. Emeritus Trustee, Metropolitan Museum of Art, New York City; Philadelphia (Pennsylvania) Museum of Art; University of Pennsylvania; the Peddie School, Highstown, New Jersey; Churchill Archives Center, Cambridge (England) College. Recipient: Order of the British Empire (Honorary); Legion of Honor (France); Order of Merit (Italy); Order of the Crown (Italy); Order of the Lion (Finland); Bencher of the Middle Temple (Honorary); Old Etonian (Honorary); Freedom Medal for Pioneering Television for Educational Purposes; Gold Medal of the Pennsylvania Society; Linus Pauling Medal for Humanitarianism; George Foster Peabody Award; Ralph Lowell Award, Corporation for Public Broadcasting; Wagner Medal for Public Service, Robert F. Wagner; Award of Greater Philadelphia Chamber of Commerce; Churchill Bell Award.

FURTHER READING

Altschuler, Glenn C., and David I. Grossvogel. *Changing Channels: America in TV Guide.* Urbana, Illinois: University of Illinois Press, 1992.
"Annenberg Gives a Life Injection to Public Television." *New York Times,* 1 March 1981.
Blumenstyk, Goldie. "Annenberg Gives $265-million to 3 Universities." *The Chronicle of Higher Education* (Washington, D.C.), 23 June 1993.
Celis, William. "Annenberg to Give Education $500 Million Over Five Years." *New York Times,* 17 December 1993.
Cooney, John. *The Annenbergs.* New York: Simon and Schuster, 1982.
Fonzi, Gaeton. *Annenberg: A Biography of Power.* New York: Weybright and Talley, 1970.
Grassmuck, Karen. "A $50-million Gift Buoys Black Colleges for Ambitious Drive; Annenberg Makes Big Donation to United Negro College Fund." *The Chronicle of Higher Education* (Washington, D.C.), 14 March 1990.
Nicklin, Julie L. "Annenberg Shifts Priorities" (interview). *The Chronicle of Higher Education* (Washington, D.C.), 12 January 1994.
"A $150 Million Gift for Educational TV." *Newsweek* (New York), 9 March 1981.
Russell, John. "Annenberg Picks Met for $1 Billion Gift." *New York Times,* 12 March 1991.
The Philadelphia Inquirer: The Story of the Inquirer 1829 to the Present. Philadelphia: Triangle, 1956.
Traub, James. "It's Elementary." *The New Yorker,* 17 July 1995.
Wilson, William. "Walter Annenberg Surveys the Land: In Art as in Politics, the Collector and Former Diplomat Knows What He Likes." *Los Angeles Times,* 12 August 1990.

ANTHOLOGY DRAMA

Anthology drama was an early American television series format or genre in which each episode was a discrete story/play rather than a weekly return to the same setting, characters, and stars. In the history of American television the anthology dramas that were broadcast live from New York are often considered the epitome of the genre and of television's "golden age" of the 1950s. While television was otherwise maligned as low-brow and crassly commercial, live anthology dramas represented, at least to some observers, the best of 1950s television. There were, however, several variations on the anthology drama series, and not all were critically acclaimed. A staple of late 1940s and 1950s programming, the last anthology dramas left the airwaves by the mid-1960s.

In 1946–47, a series of monthly dramas were presented on NBC's New York station as *Television Theatre.* However, its schedule was erratic, and it was NBC's *Kraft Television Theatre* that became not only the first weekly anthology drama but the first network television series in 1947. It was followed by several other series in 1948, including *The Ford Television Theater, Studio One, Philco Television Playhouse,* and *Actors' Studio.* These were hour-long dramas broadcast live from New York. Over the next several years, numerous such series appeared on the airwaves, among them, for example, *Robert Montgomery Presents, Celanese Theater,* and *The U.S. Steel Hour.* Critics praised the live, hour-long dramas for their presentations of adapted literary classics, serious dramas, and social relevance. The evocation of Broadway created prestige.

Live half-hour series appeared by 1950, such as *Colgate Theater, Lights Out, Danger,* and *Lux Video Theatre.* Some were thematic, creating continuity and programming niches. For instance, *Danger* and *Lights Out* specialized in suspense. With a few exceptions, these half-hour series were not critically acclaimed. Critics complained of dramas squeezed into half-hours.

The half-hour format quickly became the province of filmed anthology dramas produced in Hollywood. Critics liked these even less. In contrast to the high-brow, Broadway play connotations of the live New York series, critics associated filmed dramas with Hollywood, with low-brow entertainment. But there were all kinds of filmed anthologies just

Playhouse 90: Requiem for a Heavyweight
Photo courtesy of Wisconsin Center for Film and Theater Research

as there were all kinds of live anthologies. The first filmed anthology series was *Your Show Time* in 1949. Lasting only a few months, it was followed that same year by the first successful filmed anthology drama, *Fireside Theatre*. Other network filmed anthology dramas were *Four Star Playhouse*, *The Loretta Young Show*, and *Hollywood Opening Night*. Like some of the live productions, filmed anthologies sometimes also programmed for special interests. *The Loretta Young Show*, for example, was targeted to women. Some filmed anthology dramas were produced specifically for syndication. Examples include *Douglas Fairbanks Presents*, *Death Valley Days*, and *Crown Theatre Starring Gloria Swanson*. *Death Valley Days* was one of the few anthology dramas with a Western theme.

In the earliest years, literary works in the public domain provided the stories for the anthology dramas. There were no experienced television writers and the early industry could not afford experienced writers from other fields. Tele-

vision writers and original television dramas soon appeared, however, and writers as well as critics and audiences recognized the potential power of small-scale, intimate drama created for the new medium. Writers like Rod Serling and Paddy Chayefsky helped refine the form and found critical success writing anthology dramas. Serling would go on to host his own filmed anthology series, *The Twilight Zone*. By the mid-1950s, original television dramas were providing material for feature films. *Marty, 12 Angry Men, No Time for Sergeants, Requiem for a Heavyweight*, and other original television plays were made into motion pictures.

Actors and directors also found opportunities on anthology dramas. At a time when the Hollywood studio system was disappearing, television offered jobs and public exposure. Little-known actors and actresses like Charleton Heston and Grace Kelly, as well as older Hollywood stars like Lillian Gish and Bette Davis, acted in anthology dramas. Some stars of Old Hollywood, such as Loretta Young,

Douglas Fairbanks, and Barbara Stanwyck, had their own anthology series. Directors who would go on to motion picture work include Sidney Lumet and Arthur Penn.

By the later 1950s, competition from the increasingly successful continuing character series filmed in Hollywood led to other innovations in the anthology drama format. *Playhouse 90* presented 90-minute plays. *Matinee Theater* presented live, color dramas five days a week. *Lux Video Theater* and some others switched from live to filmed dramas. Production moved to Hollywood. During its final season in 1957–58, *Kraft Television Theatre* was the last anthology drama broadcast live from New York.

By the end of the decade, the anthology drama was on its way out. A number of factors led to its demise. Coming up with new, quality dramas and characters every week became increasingly difficult. Some anthology dramas had presented controversial episodes, with well-publicized battles with sponsors who wanted to stick with what they considered middle-of-the-road, non-controversial entertainment. Their attitudes, combined with their ultimate power, discouraged some writers and directors from working in the genre. The days of the glamorous Hollywood star as host were also numbered, and anthology dramas like *The Loretta Young Show* and *The Barbara Stanwyck Show* were canceled. Filmed programming, with its possibilities for an economic afterlife in syndication, had greater profit potential than live production. With television production shifting to Hollywood, more action-oriented genres could now be cranked out. And it seemed that audiences (comprising over 90% of American homes by the end of the 1950s) preferred them.

Few examples of the live productions from anthology dramas remain today. Most were not preserved on film and the few that are available were preserved by filming them off of TV screens (kinescopes). Even many of the filmed programs have disappeared. Perhaps the anthology drama legacy remains today in the made-for-TV movie.

—Madelyn Ritrosky-Winslow

FURTHER READING

Averson, Richard and David Manning White, editors. *Electronic Drama: Television Plays of the Sixties*. Boston, Massachusetts: Beacon Press, 1971.

Gianakos, Larry James. *Television Drama Series Programming: A Comprehensive Chronicle, 1947–1959*. Metuchen, New Jersey: Scarecrow Press, 1980.

Hawes, William. *The American Television Drama: The Experimental Years*. University, Alabama: University of Alabama Press, 1986.

Sturcken, Frank. *Live Television: The Golden Age of 1946–1958 In New York*. Jefferson, North Carolina: McFarland, 1990.

Wilk, Max. *The Golden Age of Television: Notes From the Survivors*. New York: Dell, 1977.

See also Advertising, Company Voice; *Alcoa Hour*, *Armstrong Circle Theater*, Brodkin, Herbert; *Fireside Theater*; *General Electric Theater*, "Golden Age" of Television; *Hallmark Hall of Fame*, *Kraft Television Theatre*; Mann, Abby; Robinson, Hubbell; Rose, Reginald; Schaffner, Franklin; *Playhouse 90*; *Studio One*, *Wednesday Play*; *Westinghouse-Desilu Playhouse*

ARBITRON

U.S. Ratings Service

Arbitron is the name for a media research product developed by the American Research Bureau (ARB), a company which became a major institution in developing television ratings. The company's founders were Jim Seiler and Roger Cooper. Prior to 1950 when about 10% of U.S. homes had television, Seiler was experimenting on the East coast to develop a satisfactory method for measuring television audiences. Around the same time, Cooper was also testing methods to develop audience data for TV station and advertiser use in the Los Angeles area.

At the time television viewing was being measured by several different groups using varied techniques such as telephone coincidentals (calls made to viewers during television broadcasts), recalls (telephone calls made on days subsequent to broadcasts), and even door-to-door questionnaires. The common element that brought Cooper and Seiler together was that each found that distributing a viewing diary had distinct advantages in developing audience ratings for this new medium. View-

ARBITRON

Courtesy of Arbitron

ers could be measured from early morning to late night without being bothered by telephone. Moreover, audience composition, as well as household ratings, could be developed. Audiences outside normal dialing areas could be measured and net weekly cumulative audiences could be produced.

The two researchers joined forces, incorporated and established headquarters in Washington, D.C. At about the same time, John Landreth formed a company called Television National Audience Measurement Service. In 1951 he was directed to ARB and after a meeting with Seiler and Cooper, became the third partner in the research endeavor.

ARB developed its own methodology for audience measurement. First, a random sample of homes was drawn from telephone directories of the area surveyed. These households were then contacted to determine whether or not a TV was present. One diary, with an explanatory letter, was mailed to the chosen respondents. Each television set in the house was monitored with a separate diary. The diary keeper in the home would record television viewing at fifteen minute periods day-by-day for seven days and then return the diary. It was determined that four weekly samples would be the basis for each market research report. Diaries were tabulated manually and a simple report was prepared on a program-by-program basis during prime time. A Monday-Friday combination report was prepared for daytime programming.

In the early 1950s ARB was ready to expand its operation. The Federal Communications Commission (FCC) lifted its 1948 freeze on new station license allocations in July 1952 and many new stations began telecasting. Advertising agencies needed a service to measure viewing in the increasing number of rapidly developing television markets. In 1952 ARB was measuring 15 TV markets. In order to position itself as the industry leader, the organization took a quantum leap and expanded to 35 markets. Ad agency support and useage of the company's TV market reports followed and enabled ARB to be a pioneering leader in the exciting new field of audience measurement.

By the late 1950s, it became obvious that a better way had to be found to develop the diary data. Manual tabulation of the data from diaries was impossibly slow. ARB moved its headquarters to Beltsville, Maryland and installed a UNIVAC tabulation method and report preparation. The newly utilized system almost put the company out of business.

The first reports produced by the system were woefully late; in some markets the reports made no sense. Gradually the company worked its way out of its dilemma. By the 1961-62 television year, ARB was on a better footing and had generally solved the problems it had endured. The new computer equipment gave the company the capability to expand its market reports to include needed data on specific demographic groups, making them invaluable tools for advertisers and their agencies to buy and sell spot television time.

By the early 1960s, homes owning a TV set had increased dramatically and hundreds of additional television stations had begun telecasting. Hundreds of thousands of diaries were being placed in American homes each year. By 1967 ARB had clearly defined 225 television markets. It produced television market reports called "sweeps" twice per year for every television market, and from four to seven times a year for the larger major markets. The sweeps provided comparative cumulative data for an entire week. TV's advantage as an advertising medium was thus well documented and appreciated; hundreds of millions of dollars were pouring into station and network coffers.

At this time, as a result of demands from advertising agencies, a new and exclusive market definition was introduced in ARB reports called the "Area of Dominant Influence." The ADI was a collection of counties in which the viewing of particular stations in the market was dominant. Some station executives violently objected complaining the new ratings did not reflect the true size of their station's reach. To counter this, ARB continued to report total homes viewing the station and demographic characteristics of the total audience.

From its inception, ARB's major competitor was the A.C. Nielsen Company. In the local market field, ARB was usually considered the innovative force, normally reacting quickly to what the ad agencies needed in the report. Although many advertising agencies subscribed to both rating services, ARB usually had a larger list of user agencies. In the larger TV markets a majority of stations were subscribers to both rating services.

During the decade of the 1980s, the two services were caught up in a rapidly changing electronic media market place. Arbitron delivered reports on cable penetration and cable viewing within specific markets. A large investment was made in ScanAmerica, a unique service that combined viewing estimates with product purchase surveys. Additional investments were made to change methods of measurement. In larger markets diary surveys were converted to an automated system that used a sample in which special equipment was attached to the television set. Viewing data from the meter was carried through telephone lines to an electronic data center. In the larger TV markets metered research provided reports on a more timely basis; indeed, even overnight program ratings were now available.

These very sophisticated research methods were not only costly to install but also expensive to maintain. This resulted in substantial increases in the cost of market reports. TV stations had always borne most of the cost for the audience research. Both Arbitron and the Nielsen Company charged agencies a token amount for the complete package of all market reports produced.

In the competition Arbitron began losing market share. By the end of the decade it had 19 metered markets, to Nielsen's 29 and ARB had a declining number of TV stations subscribing to market reports based on the viewing diary.

Finally, in the fall of 1993, Arbitron president Stephen Morris declared that his company was out of the television measuring business citing a marketplace that would not support, as in the past, two rating services. It was revealed that approximately 275 stations subscribed to both Arbitron and Nielsen local market reports. But Arbitron's lists of exclusive station subscribers had dwindled to 180 clients while Nielsen could claim 359 exclusive subscribers.

As a company, Arbitron is still in existence. It continues to successfully measure radio listening audiences, using the personal diary, and its research reports are widely used in the radio industry. According to Mr. Morris, Arbitron would continue to provide specialized TV audience research for television stations and advertising agencies. But for the first time in nearly forty years, the sales offices of TV stations and the research departments of ad agencies were dependent on a single source of local market research reports.

—C.A. Kellner

FURTHER READING

"Ailing Oligopoly: TV Station Rating Business: New Petry Study Confirms that more Stations Are Giving up either Arbitron or Nielsen." *Broadcasting* (Washington, D.C.), 23 April 1990.

Arbitron Replication: A Study of the Reliability of Broadcast Ratings. New York: American Research Bureau, 1974.

Beville, Hugh Malcolm. *Audience Ratings: Radio, Television, and Cable.* Hillsdale, New Jersey: L. Erlbaum, 1988.

Carter, Bill. "Arbitron Is Closing Down National Ratings Service." *New York Times* , 3 September 1992.

Inside the Arbitron Television Report. New York: American Research Bureau, 1977.

Standard Errors and Effective Sample Sizes as Reported for Broadcast Audience Measurement Surveys. New York: Broadcast Ratings Council, 1970.

Webster, James G., and Lawrence W. Lichty. *Ratings Analysis: Theory and Practice.* Hillsdale, New Jersey: L. Erlbaum, 1991.

See also Advertising; Market; Ratings; Share

ARCHIVES FOR TELEVISION MATERIALS

The study of television has long been hampered by the lack of sufficient archival resources, and this difficulty is indicative of larger social and cultural attitudes toward the medium. Long seen as culturally suspect if not defined outright as "inferior," television was considered unworthy of preservation. This situation has been most acute in the United States, where the identification of TV with commercial culture led to the notion that the material could simply be thrown away with no loss. Indeed, when television networks found themselves short of vault and storage space, the destruction of television on videotape or film was seen as profitable.

In those countries whose television systems were grounded in notions of public service circumstances have been somewhat different. The National Film and Television Archive in the United Kingdom has been more active in preserving television materials, for instance. Even in these countries, however, the lack of full sets of programs, the difficulties encountered in funding storage and preservation, and an almost complete disregard for such ancillary materials as corporate records and production notes, make it difficult to study television, prepare its histories, or understand its development and change.

This situation is changing, however, throughout the world. More and more producers, companies, distributors and exhibitors are coming to value the works they create and disseminate. Scholarly and critical attention to the medium—as well as the economic usefulness of "vintage" television has led to more and more attention to the TV past. Collectors and archivists alike have now begun to gather and make available more television material, some thought lost.

U.S. television material is archived at a number of government, private, corporate, and university sites. The Library of Congress in Washington, D.C., contains within its Division of Motion Pictures, Broadcasting and Recorded Sound approximately 80,000 television programs, with a particular emphasis on prime-time entertainment series. The NBC Collection at the Library of Congress is made up

The archives of the Museum of Broadcast Communications
Photo courtesy of the Museum of Broadcast Communications

of programming from 1948 to 1977 in a wide variety of genres including sports, game shows, children's programs and daytime television, excluding news. The NET (National Educational Television) Collection is a repository of over 10,000 titles from early non-commercial U.S. television.

The Film and Television Archives at the University of California at Los Angeles (UCLA) houses one of the nation's preeminent collections of media materials. The television collections, which date from 1947, are particularly focused on drama, and include episodes of *The Jack Benny Show*, *Texaco Star Theatre*, *The Colgate Comedy Hour*, and *The Smothers Brothers Comedy Hour*. The Paramount Television collection is made up of programs from the early 1960s to the present. Most national and local Emmy Award-winning programs can be found in the UCLA Archives.

The Academy of Television Arts and Sciences in North Hollywood, California, a co-sponsor of the UCLA archives, also houses an archive of tapes, kinescopes, and films from the earliest days of television to the present. The academy also provides information about Emmy Awards, prime-time credits and biographies of performers, directors, producers and agents. Most services are available only to academy members.

The Archives of Performing Arts at the University of Southern California, also in Los Angeles, contain numerous programs and scripts from the "golden age" of U.S. television, as well as more contemporary materials.

The Wisconsin Center for Film and Theatre Research in Madison, Wisconsin, was one of the pioneer collections in television, and has extensive holdings of original kinescopes, scripts, still photographs, and production information. The ZIV Television Collection contains nearly 2,000 shows produced between 1948 and 1962 by one of the most successful producers of dramatic programs for first-run syndication use in early television. The Fred Coe collection contains copies of successful anthology dramas such as *Playhouse 90* and *Goodyear Playhouse*. There are prints of many of the Ed Sullivan variety programs and MTM Enterprises shows such as *The Mary Tyler Moore Show* and *Bob Newhart*.

The Museum of Television and Radio (MTR) in New York City houses approximately 25,000 programs from network, cable, and local broadcasts. The collection is made up of material from 1939 to the present. Users of the MTR are able to access a computerized database to select programs they wish to view, screen them in individual carrels without ever handling the videotape. A separate area is set aside for scholars and researchers.

The Museum of Broadcast Communications (MBC) in Chicago works in a similar manner, providing a computerized database, individual viewing arrangements and a staff available for questions or special requests. The MBC collections include extensive materials related to local Chicago programming and the "Chicago School" of television with shows by Studs Terkel, Dave Garroway, and Burr Tillstrom. Other special features include collections of ABC-TV programs such as *Wide World of Sports*, episodes of American

Bandstand found in the Dick Clark collection, the Steve Allen Collection focusing on Allen's work, the Chicago Television News Archive, and special collections of award-winning children's programming. Documentaries, television westerns such as *Gunsmoke* and *Bonanza*, and popular comedy programs from the 1950s to the 1990s can be found in the collection.

The Vanderbilt University Television News Archive in Nashville, Tennessee, was founded in 1968 to systematically preserve the most widely-viewed television newscasts, and contains news material from ABC, CBS, NBC, and CNN. The archive also maintains an on-line database.

The George Foster Peabody Collection at the University of Georgia in Athens contains copies of all submissions to the annual competition for the prestigious Peabody Awards for Excellence in Broadcasting. Documentary, entertainment, news, public service, children's, and educational television programs are held in the collection and represent not only United States, but international entries.

The WGBH Educational Foundation Archives in Boston were organized in 1979 to store and preserve program materials produced by the Boston PBS affiliate. The archives represent one of the largest collections of public television programming in the country.

The ABC Library News Information Department in New York maintains a collection of television news material produced by the network. Particular emphasis is given to broadcasting during World War II, the Cold War, and the Vietnam War era. Similarly, the NBC News Archival Services in New York provide scholarly access to news and documentary material from 1940 to the present. In addition, Worldwide Television News (WNT) in New York maintains the film and videotape libraries of British Pathe News (1896–1966), United Press International (UPI) News Films (1963–67), and UPITN (WTN, 1967-present).

In the United Kingdom, the National Film and Television Archive in London houses the most prominent collection of television archival material and receives particular funding for the preservation of ITV and Channel 4 programs.

In Canada, television archives are maintained at the Canadian Broadcasting Corporation Program Archives in Toronto, and the Public Archives in Ottawa, which contain over 30,000 Canadian film and television programs.

Australian materials may be found in two major locations. For historical material from the 1950s to around 1980, the best collection of video material is housed at the National Film and Sound Archives, McCoy Circuit, Acton, Australian Capital Territory. For television documentaries, telemovies, drama series and serials from 1980 onwards, the Library of the Australian Film, Television and Radio School in North Ryde, New South Wales holds the primary collection.

As more and more scholars and researchers recognize that television has been central to the social and cultural history of this century, it is likely to be the case that more careful attention will be given to the preservation of televisual materials. Fortunately, newer technologies, such as digital recording offer advantages both in matters of storage space and longevity and ease of access for the materials. While it is unlikely that the record of television content can ever be reconstructed with the degree of thoroughness long available for the written record, it is likely that a more complete accounting will be available in the future.

—Diane M. Negra

FURTHER READING

Ballantyne, James, editor. *The Researcher's Guide to British Film and Television Collections.* London: British Film and Video Council, 1993.

Davies, Brenda, editor. *International Directory of Film and TV Documentation Sources.* New York: FIAF, 1980.

Godfrey, Donald G. *Reruns on File: A Guide to Electronic Media Archives.* Hillsdale, New Jersey: Lawrence Erlbaum, 1992.

Mehr, Linda Harris, editor. *Motion Pictures, Television and Radio: A Union Catalogue of Manuscript and Special Collections in the Western United States.* New York: FIAF, 1977.

Rowan, Bonnie G. *Scholars Guide to Washington, D.C. Film and Video Collections.* Washington D.C.: Smithsonian Institution Press, 1980.

ARGENTINA

Argentina is one of the most important television and cable markets in Latin America. After Brazil and Mexico, it has the largest number of television receivers in the region (7,165,000 receivers/4.6 persons per receiver, according to the *Britannica Book of the Year,* 1994). Its cable penetration is the highest in Latin America (52%, according to *Producción and Distribución,* 1995). Domestic programmes actively compete with foreign productions, and popular genres include variety shows, sitcoms, telenovelas, and sports and children's programs. The history of television in this country is characterized by cyclical patterns of state and private media ownership which parallel the changes occurring in the political and economic arena.

Argentine television began its transmissions in 1951 through channel 7, during the presidency of Juan Domigo Perón. Jaime Yankelevitch, a pioneer of the medium in the country, was a local radio entrepreneur who traveled to the United States to buy the equipment needed for television broadcasting. Initially, the transmitters were operated by the Ministry of Public Works, and the legal framework established the state as the owner of the broadcasting service. During this time, the government had absolute control over television, even though advertising spots were sold to commercial advertisers from its inception.

The military government of Pedro Eugenio Aramburu that overthrew Perón instituted private television in 1957 through the enactment of the decree 15,460. With the intention of controlling the dissemination of messages, this decree-law also prohibited the existence of broadcasting networks in the country. The stations in Buenos Aires could not send signals to the rest of the country, and as a result many independent stations with limited coverage emerged throughout the country. The first pay-TV systems were founded in 1962–63. They used CATV technology, coaxial cables, and inexpensive equipment, and bought most of their programming from the broadcast stations in Buenos Aires. Ironically, the pay-TV stations that resulted from the 1957 prohibition stand at the root of the high cable penetration and the economic boom in the Argentine cable business today.

The first private channels in the capital city of Buenos Aires started operating in 1960—channels 9, 13, and 11. Though Argentine law prohibited foreign ownership of TV channels, at first the American networks managed to make "back-door" deals with the local stations by creating parallel production companies. Foreign investment could flow to these companies because they were not limited in terms of ownership. Thus the American television corporation NBC invested in channel 9 through the production company Telecenter, ABC invested in channel 11 through Telerama, and CBS and Time-Life invested in channel 13 through Proartel. In this way the American networks became partners of the private Argentine channels.

The founder of channel 13 was Goar Mestre, a famous Cuban broadcasting entrepreneur who left Cuba when Fidel Castro came to power in 1959 and emigrated to Argentina. Because Mestre was married to an Argentine, his wife was able to become the owner of the license for channel 13. At the same time, Mestre established a financial arrangement with CBS and Time-Life in which he owned 60% of Proartel (Producciones Argentinas de Televisión), channel 13's production company. As Elizabeth Fox argues in *Media and Politics in Latin America* (1988), the entrance of foreign capital had a strong impact on national broadcasting, by exposing Argentina to large investments in advertising and driving the development of mass consumption markets.

In the mid-1960s national entrepreneurs invested in the majority stocks of the three private channels, and the American networks withdrew from the market. In 1965, Alejandro Romay bought channel 9. In the early 1970s, the Vigil family, owner of the publisher Editorial Atlántida, invested in channel 13, and Héctor Ricardo García, from the publisher Editorial Sarmiento, invested in channel 11. In *Quien te ha visto y quién TV* (1988), Argentine television expert Pablo Sirvén considers the sixties the best years of private television, a period characterized by the high competition between the stations, and the success of their programming.

Yet this golden period came to an end in 1974 when the third Peronist government decided that the private licenses should return to the state and expropriated the major television stations. Silvio Waisbord indicates that the rationale for deciding not to renew their commercial licenses was based on the defense of the national interest, the elimination of commercialism, and the advancement of cultural goals. However, the state's appropriation of private channels brought no major changes because the stations continued to be supported by advertising and the programming was produced by the same production companies as before. The government did not fulfill its promise to support the national industry and no cultural programming was produced. As re-runs of old programs and movies became commonplace, both audiences and advertising declined and the stations needed additional state support to continue operating.

The fact that all television channels were state-owned played directly into the hands of the military dictatorship during the period from 1976 to 1983. The military exercised tight ideological control over the content of all programming, and there were "black lists" with the names of prestigious producers, scriptwriters, and actors who could not work in television. The 22,285 broadcasting law enacted during this period dealt extensively with the content of the programming. Any appeal to violence, eroticism, vice, or crime was prohibited, as well as any content that challenged the ethical, social, or political norms of the country. During this period, in 1980, the first color transmissions began for the national market.

During the dictatorship, all state units, including all television stations, were allocated one-third to the army, one-third to the navy, and one-third to the air-force. Channel 9 went to the army, channel 11 to the air force, channel 13 to the navy, and channel 7 to the Presidency. While the military government managed to keep an intense ideological control over the content of the programs, their poor administration of the stations indebted them to the point of bankruptcy. For instance, in order to compete with each other, each of the three branches of the armed forces paid enormous sums of money to hire famous stars. Yet the revenues generated by advertising were not enough to cover these expenses.

The military regime was in principle against any kind of state intervention in the economy. Unlike previous governments that had tried to promote the national industry, the last military government eliminated all tariffs and protectionistic measures impeding the free flow of goods in the marketplace. However, in the area of communication their free-market policies were not so clear. Oscar Landi writes in *Devórame Otra Vez* (1988) that the military intended to privatize the channels while keeping them under their ideological control at the same time. Given this ambivalence, the process of privatization undertaken during this period with the enactment of the 1980 Broadcasting Law was intentionally slow, and started with the smaller stations in the provinces. Only in 1984, during the democratically elected government of Raúl Alfonsón, did the wave of privatization reached Buenos Aires. It was at this point that channel 9 returned to its previous owner, Alejandro Romay.

Notwithstanding the elimination of all censorship and "black lists," the communication sector inherited by Alfonsón still operated under the legal legacy of the military regime and was highly inefficient. As a result, cable television, particularly in the interior of the country, developed without regulation, and television channels continued to violate the legal limit of advertising time. Despite many attempts, the Alfonsón administration did not succeed in reforming the broadcast sector. This failure is generally attributed to the gridlock resulting from the strong economic and political pressures that operated during the transition to democracy.

President Menem learned his lesson from Alfonsón's experience, and early in his administration implemented by decree the "Law of State Reform" which included, among other state enterprises, the privatization of channel 11 and channel 13 in December 1989. At this point the deregulation of broadcasting acquired full force. Today there are five superstations in Buenos Aires, four of them are privately owned (channels 2, 9, 11, and 13) and one remains public (channel 7/Argentina Televisora Color).

The loosening of cross-media ownership allowed for the emergence of national media conglomerates. Publishers had extensively lobbied for this measure. Channel 13 was licensed to the conglomerate Clarón, the owner of the largest circulation newspaper in the country; ARTEAR, a film and television production company; two radio stations, Radio Mitre and FM100; a publishing company, Editorial Aguilar; an expanding MSO, Multicanal (400,000 subscribers); three satellite-delivered channels; and one of the partners of a newsprint factory, Papel Prensa, and the national news agency, Diarios y Noticias (DyN). Channel 11 was licensed to Telefé, a consortium integrated by the publisher Editorial Atlántida which also owns Produfé, a program production and distribution company, and at present controls 15 cable systems (200,000 subscribers). ARTEAR and Telefé are the channels that dominate the broadcast landscape and fiercely compete for top ratings.

Towards the end of the 1980s, the number of cable operators in the country reached about 2000. The main players were Video Cable Comunicación (VCC) and CableVisión. In the early 1990s new operators linked to Clar'n and Telefé entered the market and gradually began to buy up cable franchises from smaller operators across the country. At present cable ownership is concentrated in the following four groups: Video Cable Comunicación, CableVisión, Clarón, and Telefé. These companies are also investing in fiber optic cable and are implementing Multi-Channel Multipoint Distribution Services (MMDS) to distribute their signals across areas that cannot be reached by cable. Another player in the cable business is Imagen Satelital, a company that supplies Argentine cable systems with five in-house channels (Space, I-Sat, Infinito, Universo, and Jupiter), and distributes nine additional signals, among them Televisa's Eco Noticias, Bandeirantes from Brazil, and Much Music from Canada. Argentine signal distributors and programmers have grown rapidly since the launching of the domestic satellite

Nahuel in 1992. This satellite's footprint covers the northern part of Argentina, the Western part of Brazil, and most of the territory of Chile, Paraguay, and Uruguay.

During the years following the privatization of television channels, advertising expenditures have more than quadrupled. Television and cable operators pay an 8% tax on advertising revenues to the National Broadcasting Committee (COMFER), which supports the government channel 7/Argentina Televisora Color. Currently the COMFER also directs 25% of this income to the National Film Institute for the subsidy of local film production.

Further trends toward deregulation of communications resulted in the signing of a bilateral accord between Argentina and the United States in September 1994 which allows for American investment in Argentine broadcast and cable operations. American capital entered the market soon afterwards, when TCI Inc. and Continental Cable invested in the two largest cable system operators in Argentina, CableVisión and Video Cable Comunicación (VCC) respectively.

For about U.S. $35 a month, cable subscribers in Argentina receive a varied menu of about 65 channels, which includes (in addition to the domestic superstations): European channels (e.g. RAI from Italy, TV5 from France, TVE from Spain, and Deutsche Welle from Germany); Latin American channels (e.g. Globo TV, Manchete, and Bandeirantes from Brazil, Inravisión from Colombia, ECO from Mexico, and Venevisión from Venezuela); and American channels (FOX, USA, CNN, ESPN, The Discovery Channel, Cartoon Network, MTV, Nickelodeon, HBO Olé, etc.). At present no premium cable channels are offered in Argentina, and all the services are included in the basic subscription package.

Variety shows are among the most popular programs. They are scheduled at different times throughout the day, often in the early afternoon (1:00 to 2:00 P.M.) or during the peak of prime-time (8:00 to 9:00 P.M.). The Argentine version of a variety show features a combination of musicals, interviews, comic skits, and games in which the audience participates by calling the host of the program, who frequently is a famous national actor or actress. An example of a daily variety show that has reached top ratings since 1984 is *Hola Susana*, hosted by actress Susana Giménez. Another popular variety show is *Videomatch*, hosted by Marcelo Tinelli. His program starts at midnight, targets a young, 15 to 30-year-old audience, and includes video-clips, bloopers, and sports.

In general, *telenovelas* are shown from Monday through Fridays in the afternoon (1:00 to 4:00 P.M., depending on the channel) and early prime-time (6:00 to 8:00 P.M.). The former are targeted at women, while the latter are targeted at a young adult audience. Weekly drama series broadcast after 10:00 P.M. are also popular. These attempt to reach an adult audience by dealing with socially controversial themes such as corruption, drugs, homosexuality, etc.

A typical TV prime-time evening starts at 6:00 P.M. with light *telenovelas*, variety-shows, or game-shows. These programs precede the one-hour newscasts that are scheduled in different time-slots in each channel. Channel 11 and ATC/channel 7 broadcast their evening news programs at 7:00 P.M., channel 2 at 9:00 P.M., and channel 9 and channel 13 compete on the news front at 8:00 P.M. From 10:00 P.M. to midnight viewers may opt for movies (which are usually imported), weekly drama series, or public affairs programs led by well-known national journalists and political pundits.

Sports programs are generally scheduled during weekends. They cover different matches and report on the result of national, regional, or world championships. Soccer is the sport followed by the largest audience; the broadcast of a soccer cup final never fails to reach top ratings. But popular sports programs also include tennis, box, motoring, and rugby.

Unfortunately, there is no recent data on the proportion of imported programs available in this country. Early studies on the world flow of television programs conducted by Tapio Varis (1974) show that in 1971 channel 9 and channel 11 respectively imported 10% and 30% of their programming. A decade later, Varis (1984) found that channel 9 imported 49% of its programming. Considering the changes in the Argentine television landscape since 1989 (i.e. privatization, liberalization, the growth of cable, etc.), those partial figures cannot be considered a reliable estimate of the proportion of the current imported/domestic programming. Nevertheless, rating figures show that in general the Argentine audience prefers domestic productions. For instance, in August 1994, according to data from the market research company IBOPE (TV International, 1994), the five programs with the highest ratings were: soccer championship *Copa Libertadores* (13.0 of rating); variety show *Hola Susana* (12.6); family sitcom *¡Grande Pá!* (12.6); movie cycle *Cine ATP* (11.3); and *The Simpsons* (11.2).

—Jaqui Chiemelesky

FURTHER READING

Fox, E. "Nationalism, Censorship, and Transnational Control." In, Fox, E., editor. *Media and Politics in Latin America.* London: Sage, 1988.

Morgan, Michael. "Television and the Cultivation of Political Attitudes in Argentina." *Journal of Communication* (New York), Winter 1991.

Muraro, H. "Dictatorship and Transition to Democracy: Argentina 1973–86," In, Fox, E., editor. *Media and Politics in Latin America.* London: Sage, 1988.

Salwen, M. B. and B. Garrison. *Latin American Journalism.* Hillsdale, New Jersey: Lawrence Erlbaum, 1991.

"Shining Star of South America's Southern Cone Lures New Investors." *TV International.* 24 October, 1994.

Varis, T. "Global Traffic in Television." *Journal of Communication* (Philadelphia),1974.

———. "The International Flow of Television Programs." *Journal of Communication* (Philadelphia), 1984.

Zuleta-Puceiro, E. "The Argentine Case: Television in the 1989 Presidential Election." In, Skidmore, Thomas E., editor. *Television, Politics, and the Transition to Democracy in Latin America.* Washington, D.C., and London: Woodrow Wilson Center Press, 1993.

ARLEDGE, ROONE

U.S. Media Producer/Executive

Roone Arledge, president of ABC News, has had a more profound impact on the development of television news and sports programming and presentation than any other individual. In fact, a 1994 *Sports Illustrated* magazine ranking placed Arledge third, behind Muhammad Ali and Michael Jordan, in a list of 40 individuals who have had the greatest impact on the world of sports in the last four decades. In addition, a 1990 *Life* magazine poll listed Arledge as among the "100 Most Important Americans of the 20th Century."

In 1960, Arledge defected from NBC to join a struggling ABC. Later, in his role as vice president of ABC Sports, Arledge created what would become the longest running and most successful sports program ever, *ABC's Wide World Sports*. He brought his production specialty to ABC, and overhauled sports programming, including introduction of such techniques as slow motion and instant replays. These production techniques enabled Arledge to create a more exciting and dramatic sports event. He combined his production skills with "up close and personal" athlete features, which changed the way the world viewed competing athletes. He was one of the first users of the Atlantic satellite, enabling him to produce live sporting events from around the world.

Arledge's success in sports resulted in his promotion to president of the sports division in 1968, where he served until 1986. Shortly after his promotion, he again elevated ABC's sports prominence with *NFL Monday Night Football*. This prime-time sports program gave ABC the lock on ratings during its time slot, and earned Arledge even greater respect.

Under Arledge's lead, ABC Sports became the unchallenged leader in network sports programming. Arledge's innovations on *Wide World* were also successful for the ten Olympic games he produced. Inducted into the Olympic Hall of Fame for his commitment to excellence, Arledge was later bestowed the Medal of Olympic Order by the International Olympic Committee, making him the first television executive and one of a select group of Americans to receive this prestigious award.

Despite his successful transformation of ABC Sports, his promotion to president of ABC News came as a surprise to many individuals because Arledge had no formal journalistic training. He was president of ABC Sports and ABC News for nearly ten years.

With the development of shows such as *20/20*, *World News Tonight*, and *Nightline*, ABC was soon on the top of the network news battle. Among his greatest skills is identification of potential stars. Arledge successfully recruited the strongest and most promising journalists for his news team, including *World News Tonight* star Peter Jennings. Arledge recognized Jennings' talent and cast this once-defeated *ABC Evening News* anchor in the spotlight, and it worked. Arledge's team includes

Roone Arledge
Photo courtesy of ABC

David Brinkley, Diane Sawyer, Sam Donaldson, Ted Koppel, Barbara Walters and Hugh Downs.

Arledge put news on the air in non-traditional formats and at non-traditional times, and received high ratings. In its 15 years, *Nightline* has battled entertainment personalities such as Johnny Carson, David Letterman and Jay Leno for ratings, and in 1995 it was the highest rated late-night program. From its first show with Ali Agah, Iranian affairs leader, and Dorothea Morefield, wife of American hostage Richard Morefield, *Nightline* has been the leader in international affairs reporting.

Arledge's other news show creations include *Prime Time Live*, with Diane Sawyer and Sam Donaldson; *This Week with David Brinkley*, *World News Now*, a 2:00 to 6:00 A.M. Monday through Friday overnight news program; and numerous *ABC News Presents* specials, such as *Turning Point* and *Viewpoint*. Arledge also designed inventive news broadcasts such as *Capital to Capital*, the first satellite news series to promote discussion between the United States and Soviet legislators.

His shows have received virtually every broadcasting honor possible. In 1995, ABC News was the first news organization to receive the Alfred I. duPont-Columbia University Award, given for the network's overall commitment to excellence.

In a speech following his appointment at ABC, Arledge declared, "We (ABC) will be setting the standards that everyone will be talking about and that others in the industry will spend years trying to equal." It is clear, based on the success of ABC Sports and ABC News, that Arledge lived up to his immodest words.

—John C. Tedesco

ROONE ARLEDGE. Born in Forest Hills, New York, U.S.A., 8 July 1931. Educated at Mepham High School, Merrick, New York; Columbia College, New York, B.A. 1952. Married: Joan Heise, 1953 (divorced, 1971); children: Elizabeth Ann, Susan Lee, Patricia Lu, and Roone Pinckney. Served in United States Army, 1953–1955. Production assistant, DuMont Television Network, 1952; producer-director, Radio Public Relations Spots for U.S. Army, 1953–55; stage manager, director, and producer, NBC Television, 1955–60; joined ABC Television, field producer, NCAA Television, 1960; producer, *ABC's Wide World of Sports,* 1961; vice president, ABC Sports, 1965, president, 1968; created *NFL Monday Night Football,* 1969; president, ABC News, 1977; group president, ABC News and Sports, 1985–90; president, ABC News, since 1987. Recipient: 36 Emmy Awards; four George Foster Peabody Awards; two Christopher Awards; Broadcast Pioneers Award; Gold Medal, International Radio and Television Society; Distinguished Service to Journalism Honor Medal, University of Missouri; John Jay Distinguished Professional Service Award, Columbia University; Distinguished Achievement Award, University of Southern California Journalism Association; Founders Award, Academy of Television Arts and Sciences; Grand Prix, Montreaux Television Festival; Olympic Order, Medal of the International Olympic Committee; Grand Prize, Cannes Film Festival; Man of the Year, National Association of Television Program Executives; Academy of Television Arts and Sciences Hall of Fame, 1990; U.S. Olympic Hall of Fame, 1989; duPont-Columbia Award, 1995.

FURTHER READING

Cosell, Howard. *Like It Is.* Chicago: Playboy Press, 1974.

Flander, Judy. "Rooneglow." *Washington Journalism Review* (Washington, D.C.), July-August, 1990.

Goldenson, Leonard. *Beating the Odds.* New York: Scribners, 1991.

Gunther, Marc. *The House That Roone Built: The Inside Story of ABC News.* Boston: Little, Brown, 1994.

———. "Blue Roone." *American Journalism Review* (College Park, Maryland), April 1994.

Gunther, Marc, and B. Carter. *Monday Night Mayhem: The Inside Story of ABC's Monday Night Football.* New York: William Morrow: 1988.

O'Neil, Terry. *The Game Behind the Game: High Pressure, High Stakes in Television Sports.* New York: Harper and Row, 1989.

Patton, Phil. *Razzle Dazzle: The Curious Marriage of Television and Professional Football.* Garden City, New York: Dial Press, 1984.

Powers, John. "Roone Arledge." *Sport* (New York), December 1986.

Rader, Benjamin G. *In Its Own Image: How Television Has Transformed Sports.* New York: Free Press, 1984.

Roberts, Randy. "Roone Arledge and the Rise of Televised Sports." *USA Today* (New York), January 1992.

"Roone Arledge on ABC's Wide World of News" (interview). *Broadcasting and Cable* (Washington, D.C.), 10 October 1994.

Rushin, Steve. "Roone Arledge (Forty for the Ages)." *Sports Illustrated* (New York), 19 September 1994.

Spence, Jim, with Dave Giles. *Up Close and Personal: The Inside Story of Network Television Sports.* New York: Athaneum, 1988.

Sugar, Bert Randolph. *The Thrill of Victory: The Inside Story of ABC Sports.* New York: Hawthorne, 1978.

Waters, Harry F. "A Relish for Risks; The Ups and Downs of ABC's Roone Arledge." *Newsweek* (New York), 15 June 1987.

See also American Broadcasting Company; News; Olympics; Sports on Television; Sportscasters

ARMED FORCES RADIO AND TELEVISION SERVICE

Armed Forces Radio and Television Service (AFRTS) comprises the primary communication media of the American Forces Information Service (AFIS), a unit of the Department of Defense (DOD). AFRTS provides radio and television news, information, sports and entertainment programming to U.S. military personnel and their families stationed at U.S. military installations and seacraft worldwide.

AFRTS programming, acquired and distributed by the AFRTS Broadcast Center in Los Angeles, is selected from popular commercial and public programming found in the United States (though commercials are replaced by DOD information and spot announcements). Most AFRTS pro-

gramming is acquired with little or no charge thanks to industry cooperation dating back to the AFRTS's beginnings during World War II.

Radio news programming is transmitted by the International Satellite (INTELSAT) and International Maritime Satellite (INMARSAT), which replaced AFRTS's previous short-wave broadcast service in 1988. Programming includes news and commentary from the major U.S. networks and syndicators. Music and entertainment programming is mailed in weekly program units for use by outlets in producing local programming. Television news, information, sports, and other timely programming is distributed by the AFRTS Satellite Network (SATNET). Most entertainment programming, however, is provided by mail, and normally includes over 90% of the top rated programs in the United States. About 63% of AFRTS programming comes from the commercial networks, comprised largely of news and sports. The balance comes from the major entertainment distributors and producers in the United States. Unlike AFRS during its formative years, AFRTS does not produce its own entertainment shows for television.

As of 1992, according to AFIS sources, AFRTS uses nine satellites in providing service to over 450 outlets in more than 130 countries and U.S. territories worldwide. Over 300 military ships at sea also receive programming. By 1985, the AFRTS had become the largest radio and television network in the world.

AFRTS broadcasts also reach a substantial "shadow" audience of U.S. citizens living abroad and citizens of host nations who view or listen to the programming. Though no official figures exist for the size of the "shadow" audience worldwide, one study of the audience in Japan found that 21% of the local population (approximately 25 million people) listened to AFRTS radio at least once a week. One could safely conclude that the enormous presence of AFRTS broadcasts has probably played an important role in informal English language instruction and, relatedly, fostering a general acceptance of U.S. cultural products worldwide—currently the number one export of the United States.

AFRTS's history can be traced to several small radio stations established by servicemen in Panama, Alaska, and the Philippines near the start of World War II. Following the success and popularity of these small operations, the Armed Forces Radio Service (AFRS) was established by the War Department on 26 May 1942, with the expressed intent of improving troop morale by giving service members a "touch of home." The military also sought to provide a source of information to U.S. servicemen that would counter enemy propaganda (such as that found in the broadcasts of Axis Sally and Tokyo Rose), though it denied the move was an attempt at counter-propaganda.

AFRS programs during the war proved enormously popular with the troops, and were made financially possible largely through the contributions of radio and film stars who donated their time regularly without charge. Two of the more popular programs included *Command Performance* and *Mail Call*, which presented such stars as Bob Hope, Jack Benny, Clark Gable, Red Skelton, Bing Crosby, Dinah Shore, and the Andrews Sisters, among many others. Though these stars unselfishly gave of their time to contribute to the patriotic war effort, their careers most certainly didn't suffer from the exposure of a somewhat captive audience. By the end of the war, there were nearly 300 AFRS radio stations operating worldwide (though that number had decreased to only sixty some four years later). Since that time, the number of stations continues to increase and decrease, depending on the level of U.S. military commitments worldwide.

Courtesy of Armed Forces Radio and Television Service

Television came relatively late to the AFRS, considering the enormous impact it was having on American society. The impetus to introduce television, in fact, came from the need to address serious morale problems in the Strategic Air Command. Armed Forces Television (AFT) got its start at Limestone Air Force Base, Maine, in 1953, and after much success in helping to reduce AWOLs, court martials, and the divorce rate at this military installation, AFT was officially joined with the AFRS in 1954 to become the AFRTS—the Armed Forces Radio and Television Service. AFRTS introduced color television in the early 1970s and was one of the first broadcasters to began using satellites for live news and sports as early as 1968.

The AFRTS maintains that its programming is provided "without censorship, propagandizing, or manipulation." The first notable exceptions to that claim surfaced during the Vietnam War period. From 1963 to 1967, AFRTS was instructed by Defense Secretary Robert McNamara to broadcast United States Information Agency (USIA)-produced news analysis programs—material that was widely recognized as propaganda. The more serious challenge to AFRTS's non-interference claims came from broadcast outlets and journalists in Vietnam itself. Though AFRTS and various military policy makers maintained that censorship of programming was prohibited, numerous controversies arose (both public and internal) over news, quotes, and specific words and phrases that were kept off the air due to AFRTS guidelines. According to a history of the AFRTS commissioned by the service for its fiftieth anniversary, such restrictions even included "the editing of President Johnson's comments that the command believed were inaccurate." Justifications for such restrictions most often included the desire to avoid injuring troop morale, helping the enemy, or offending the host nation's sensitivities.

Though AFRTS still maintains its claim to no censorship, it also adamantly defends the altering of programming that might offend the sensitivities of host nations. The direct broadcasting of American news programming via SATNET has increased the problems for AFRTS broadcasters in nations that are particularly sensitive to criticism (such as Korea and the Philippines, in recent years). AFRTS also defends its review of music lyrics and feature films for similar reasons.

—Jeffrey P. Jones

FURTHER READING

American Forces Information Service and Armed Forces Radio and Television Service. *History of AFRTS: The First 50 Years.* Washington, D.C.: U.S. Department of Defense, 1992.

ARMSTRONG CIRCLE THEATRE

U.S. Dramatic Anthology

Armstrong Circle Theatre, which premiered in the summer of 1950, joined thirteen other anthology programs already on the air, but went on to become one of the longest-running anthology series in television history. It aired for fourteen seasons, first in a one-half hour format and later expanding to one-hour. *Armstrong Circle Theatre* was produced by Talent Associates, Ltd., the agency formed by David Susskind and Alfred Levy, which also produced the *Kaiser Aluminum Hour* and individual productions for the *DuPont Show of the Month, Kraft Television Theatre,* and the *Philco Television Playhouse.*

What differentiated the *Armstrong Circle Theatre* from other anthology series was the show's change in focus after its first few seasons. Initially, *Armstrong Circle Theatre* presented typical, formula dramas, with little to distinguish it from other anthologies. In 1952, producers decided to change their approach. With the aid of an advertising agency that gathered scripts from all sources, including first-time writers, producers opted for "quality dramas" that emphasized characterization over pure plot devices. The new stories presented on *Armstrong Circle* attempted a continuity of mood, theme, and style from production to production without presenting the same type of protagonist in varying situations. Some critics described the stories as sentimental with a "pleasantly related moral" as their thematic approach. One example of this "family type" dramatic style was *The Rocking Horse,* a tender story about a reunion between mother and son.

In 1955, when *Armstrong Circle Theatre* expanded to one hour, the series continued its emphasis on the story and presented the earliest form of the docudrama (fact-based dramatizations). Executive Producer David Susskind and producer Robert Costello de-emphasized the role of actors and made the story the "star". According to Costello, their aim was "to combine fact and drama—to arouse interest, even controversy, on important and topical subjects." Using a news story or idea was not enough: the series also had to "be able to present some potential solution, some hope for your citizens to consider, to think about." Examples of these fact-based dramas include *S.O.S. from the Andrea Doria* and *Lost: $2,000,000,* a drama about the effect of Hurricane Diane on a small town in Connecticut.

The docudrama format was enhanced by having a news anchor serve as the host/narrator for the program, and, for this task, NBC hired news anchorman John Cameron Swayze. When the series switched from NBC to CBS in 1957, Swayze was replaced by CBS news anchor Douglas Edwards. Edwards was subsequently removed by CBS when network executives felt his credibility as a news anchor would be diminished by hosting a non-news program. He was replaced by reporter Ron Cochran, formerly of ABC.

At the time its format was lengthened to one hour, *Armstrong Circle Theatre* alternated with *Playwrights '56.* Problems arose between the two series because each was sponsored by a different company with different advertising aims. Pontiac, sponsor of *Playwrights '56,* wanted a very distinct sales message aimed at a large audience. Armstrong Circle desired strong sponsor identification with its special type of programming. Although *Playwrights '56* produced a number of distinctive dramas, they were not as critically

Armstrong Circle Theatre: Battle of Hearts
Photo courtesy of Wisconsin Center for Film and Theater Research

successful as other anthologies. Pontiac considered the ratings for the show too low and withdrew its sponsorship at the end of the season. The next season, *Armstrong Circle* alternated with *The Kaiser Aluminum Hour*, also produced by David Susskind's Talent Associates, Ltd. In 1957, *Armstrong Circle Theatre* switched to CBS and alternated with *The U.S. Steel Hour* until the end of its television run.

—Susan R. Gibberman

HOST/NARRATOR   Nelson Case (1950–1951), Joe Ripley (1952–1953), Bob Sherry (1953–1954), Sandy Becker (1954–1955), John Cameron Swayze (1955–1957), Douglas Edwards (1957–1961), Ron Cochran (1961–1962), Henry Hamilton (1962–1963)

PRODUCERS   Robert Costello, Jacqueline Babbin, George Simpson, Selig Alkon, Ralph Nelson

PROGRAMMING HISTORY

• NBC

June 1950–June 1955   Tuesday 9:30-10:00
September 1955–June 1957   Tuesday 9:30-10:30

• CBS
October 1957–August 1963   Wednesday 10:00-11:00

FURTHER READING

Adams, Val. "An Original Approach to TV Drama." *New York Times,* 16 November 1952.

Gast, Harold. *Full Disclosure, As Presented on the Armstrong Circle Theatre.* Larchmont, New York: Argonaut, 1961.

Gianakos, Larry James. *Television Drama Series Programming: A Comprehensive Chronicle, 1947–1959.* Metuchen, New Jersey: Scarecrow, 1980.

———. *Television Drama Series Programming: A Comprehensive Chronicle, 1959–1975.* Metuchen, New Jersey: Scarecrow, 1978.

Settel, Trudy S., and Irving Settel. *The Best of Armstrong Circle Theatre.* New York: Citadel, 1959.

Shaw, Myron Berkley. *A Descriptive Analysis of the Documentary Drama Television Program, 'The Armstrong Circle Theatre' 1955–1961* (Doctoral dissertation, University of Michigan, 1962).

See also Advertising, Company Voice; Anthology Drama; "Golden Age" of Television

ARMY-MCCARTHY HEARINGS

U.S. Congressional Inquiry

Broadcast "gavel to gavel" on the ABC and DuMont networks from 22 April to 17 June 1954, the Army-McCarthy hearings were the first nationally televised congressional inquiry and a landmark in the emergent nexus between television and American politics. Although the Kefauver Crime Committee hearings of March 1951 can claim priority as a congressional TV show, and subsequent political spectacles (the Watergate hearings, the Iran Contra hearings, the Thomas-Hill hearings) would rivet the attention of later generations of televiewers, the Army-McCarthy hearings remain the genre prototype for sheer theatricality and narrative unity.

Ostensibly, the Army-McCarthy hearings convened to investigate a convoluted series of charges leveled by the junior Republican senator from Wisconsin, Joseph R. McCarthy, at the U.S. Army and vice versa. In November 1953, a consultant on McCarthy's staff named G. David Schine was drafted into the Army. Even before Schine's formal induction, Roy M. Cohn, McCarthy's chief counsel, had begun a personal campaign to pressure military officials—from the secretary of the Army on down to Schine's company commander—into giving Private Schine special privileges. When on 11 March 1954 the Army issued a detailed chronology documenting Cohn's improper intrusions into Schine's military career, McCarthy responded by claiming the Army was holding Schine "hostage" to deter his committee from exposing communists within the military ranks. To resolve the dispute, the Senate Permanent Subcommittee on Investigations, of which McCarthy was chair, voted to investigate and to allow live television coverage of the inquiry. McCarthy relinquished the chairship to Karl Mundt (Republican, South Dakota) to become, with Cohn, contestant and witness in a widely anticipated live television drama.

Throughout the thirty-six days of hearings, 188 hours of broadcast time were given over to telecasts originating from the Senate Caucus Room. The network "feed" came courtesy of the facilities of ABC's Washington, D.C., affiliate, WMAL-TV. Initially, all four networks where expected to carry the complete hearings live, but NBC and CBS balked at the loss of revenues from commercial programming. With an eye to its profitable daytime soap opera line-up, CBS opted out before the hearings began, leaving NBC, ABC, and DuMont formally committed to coverage. On the second day of hearings, however, after a particularly tedious afternoon session, NBC announced it was bailing out. Henceforth NBC, like CBS, broadcast nightly round-ups edited from kinescopes of the daytime ABC telecasts. CBS broadcast from 11:30 P.M. to 12:15 A.M., so when NBC followed suit, it counter-programmed its recaps from 11:15 P.M. to 12:00 midnight. Looking for a way to put his third-string news division on the map, ABC's president Robert E. Kintner stuck with his decision to broadcast the entire event live, jettisoning the network's daytime program-

Senator Joe McCarthy and Roy Cohn
Photo courtesy of AP/ World Wide

ming for continuous coverage, gavel to gavel. Even so, some major markets in the United States (Los Angeles for one) were deprived of live coverage when local affiliates chose not to take the network feed.

In televisual terms, the hearings pitted a boorish McCarthy and a bleary-eyed Cohn against a coolly avuncular Joseph N. Welch of the Boston law firm of Hale and Dorr, whom the Army had hired as its special counsel. Welch's calm patrician manner served as an appealing contrast to Cohn's unctuous posturing and McCarthy's rude outbursts (the senator's nasal interjection "Point of order!" became a national catchphrase). Senators, military men, and obscure staffers on the McCarthy Committee became household names and faces, among them chain-smoking committee counsel Ray H. Jenkins, Secretary of the Army Robert T. Stevens, and, hovering in the background, a young lawyer for the committee Democrats named Robert F. Kennedy. Along with an often partisan gallery in the

packed, smoke-filled hearing room, an audience of some twenty million Americans watched the complicated testimony, a crossfire of mutual recriminations over monitored telephone conversations, doctored photographs, and fabricated memoranda.

The afternoon of 9 June 1954 brought the emotional climax of the hearings, an exchange replayed in myriad Cold War documentaries. Ignoring a pre-hearing agreement between Welch and Cohn, McCarthy insinuated that Fred Fischer, a young lawyer at Hale and Dorr, harbored communist sympathies. Welch responded with a righteous outburst that hit all the hot buttons: "Until this moment, senator, I think I never gauged your cruelty or recklessness....Have you no sense of decency, sir, at long last? Have you left no sense of decency?" When McCarthy tried to strike back, Welch cut him off and demanded the chair "call the next witness." Pausing just a beat, the hushed gallery erupted in applause. The uncomprehending McCarthy, shot dead on live TV, turned to Cohn and stammered, "What happened?"

What happened was that television, whose coverage of McCarthy's news conferences and addresses to the nation had earlier lent him legitimacy and power, had now precipitated his downfall. Prolonged exposure to McCarthy's odious character and ill-mannered interruptions was a textbook demonstration of how a hot personality wilted under the glare of a cool medium. Toward the close of the hearings, Senator Stuart Symington (Democrat, Missouri) underscored the lesson in media politics during a sharp exchange with McCarthy: "The American people have had a look at you for six weeks. You are not fooling anyone."

The Army-McCarthy hearings were a television milestone not only because of the inherent significance of the event covered but because television coverage itself was crucial to the meaning, and unfolding, of events. Moreover, unlike many historic television moments from the 1950s, the hearings have remained alive in popular memory, mainly due to filmmaker Emile de Antonio, who in 1962 culled from extant kinescopes the landmark compilation film *Point of Order!*, the definitive documentary record of America's first great made-for-TV political spectacle.

—Thomas Doherty

FURTHER READING

de Antonio, Emile, and Daniel Talbot. *Point of Order! A Documentary of the Army-McCarthy Hearings.* New York: Norton, 1964.
Straight, Michael. *Trial by Television.* Boston: Beacon, 1954.

ARNAZ, DESI

U.S. Actor/Media Executive

Desi Arnaz is best known for his role as Ricky Ricardo in the early television situation comedy, *I Love Lucy.* The series, which starred his wife, Lucille Ball as his fictional wife, Lucy Ricardo, appeared weekly on CBS. The show originally ran from the fall of 1951 through the 1957 season, and during this time ranked consistently among the top three national programs. In addition to this recognition of Arnaz as perfect comic straight-man for Ball's genius, however, he was one of Hollywood's most perceptive and powerful producers in television's early years. His shrewd business skills and his realization of particular combinations of the television's technological and cultural connections enabled him to develop aspects of the medium that remain central to its economic and cultural force.

Arnaz began his show business career in 1935. After singing and playing guitar with the Xavier Cugat orchestra, Desi toured with his own rumba band, but his big break was being cast in the Broadway show, *Too Many Girls,* in 1939. He met Lucille Ball in Hollywood the next year when both had roles in the movie version of the play. They were married in 1940 and continued their careers, Ball in motion pictures and radio, and Arnaz in music.

Ball had also gained success with her CBS radio program, *My Favorite Husband,* in which she starred as the wife of a banker, played by Richard Denning. CBS was interested in creating a television version of the show, but when Ball insisted that Arnaz play her husband, the network felt that viewers would not be attracted to a show not easily related to their own lives. Executives at CBS were skeptical about whether Arnaz, a Cuban band leader, would be believable and readily accepted by viewers as Ball's husband. In order to prove the network wrong, the couple set out on a nationwide stage tour to designed to gauge public reaction to their working together in a comedy act. CBS was impressed with the positive public response to the couple as well as with a sample script for a TV series developed by the writers from *My Favorite Husband.*

The basics were there, including Arnaz as Ricky Ricardo, a struggling band leader, and Ball as Lucy, a housewife with little talent but a giant yearning to break into show

Desi Arnaz with Lucille Ball

business. This homey battle-of-the-sexes premise for the show convinced the network that viewers could relate, and a pilot version of the program impressed the Philip Morris Company, which agreed to sponsor thirty-nine programs for the 1951–52 season on the CBS network Monday nights at 9:00 P.M. Arnaz and Ball insisted on producing the show in California so they could work together and live at home, an arrangement which had been impossible with Ball acting in films an on radio while Arnaz toured with his band, a situation which had strained their marriage. The idea of recording *I Love Lucy* on film was directly related to the couple's desire to work together in show business as a family and to live in their home in California.

In 1951, before the perfection of video tape, nearly all television shows were live productions, fed from the East Coast because of time-zone differences. Philip Morris approved the idea of filming *I Love Lucy*, but the sponsor wanted a live audience, which had been effective on radio. Arnaz and cinematographer Karl Freund, a veteran of pre-World War II German expressionist cinema working in Hollywood, devised a plan for staging the show as a play, performing each act before an audience, and simultaneously filming with three or four cameras stationed in different locations. Because this technique increased network production costs, CBS asked that Arnaz and Ball take a cut in salary to compensate for the increase. In negotiation, Arnaz agreed, providing Desilu, a company he and Ball had created, would then own the shows after the broadcasts. A few years later the couple sold the films back to CBS for more than four million dollars, a sum that provided the economic base for building what became the Desilu empire. The practice of filming television episodes also paved the way to TV re-runs and syndication. After *I Love Lucy* was established as a hit, Desilu applied its multi-camera film technique to the production of other shows, such as *Our Miss Brooks, December Bride,* and *The Lineup.* By 1957, Desilu was so successful that additional facilities were needed and it bought RKO Studios from the General Tire and Rubber Company.

Desilu had become the world's largest studio. But as the business grew ever larger, Arnaz and Ball drifted apart, ending their 20-year marriage in 1960, and splitting their interests in Desilu. In 1962, Ball bought Arnaz's share in the company, and he retired for a short time to his horse-breeding farm. Both later married others, and Arnaz returned to television, forming an independent production company and making occasional guest appearances. Desilu was purchased by Gulf Western Industries in 1967. Arnaz died in 1986 and Lucille Ball in 1989. *I Love Lucy* is still popular with television audiences today, thanks to the pioneering production techniques of Desilu.

—B. R. Smith

DESI (DESIDERIO ALBERTO, III) ARNAZ (Y DE ACHA). Born in Santiago, Cuba, 2 March 1917. Attended Colegio Delores, Jesuit Preparatory School, Santiago, Cuba. Moved with family to the United States, 1930s. United States Medical Corps., 1943–45. Married: 1) Lucille Ball, 1940 (divorced, 1960); children: Lucie Désirée and Desiderio Alberto, IV (Desi, Jr.); 2) Edith Mack Hirsch. Began entertainment career as singer, with Xavier Cugat Band, 1935–36; formed own band at the Conga Club, Miami, Florida, 1938, height of the "conga craze"; Broadway musical debut, *Too Many Girls,* 1939; RKO film version of the musical, 1940; music director, the Bob Hope radio show, 1946–47; performed with Ball in radio show, *My Favorite Husband,* 1947–50; produced pilot for *I Love Lucy* with own funds, 1951; performed as Ricky Ricardo, *I Love Lucy,* 1951–57; president and co-founder, Desilu Productions, 1951–62. Recipient: Best Performance of the Month, *Photoplay Magazine,* 1943. Died in Del Mar, California, 2 December 1986.

TELEVISION

1951–57   *I Love Lucy* (actor, producer)
1958–60   *Westinghouse Playhouse* (producer)
1962–65, 1967 *The Lucy-Desi Comedy Hour* (actor, producer)

FILMS

Too Many Girls ,1940; *Father Takes a Wife* , 1941; *The Navy Comes Through,* 1942; *Four Jacks and a Jill,* 1942; *Bataan,* 1943; *Holiday in Havana,* 1949; *Cuban Pete,* 1950; *The Long, Long Trailer,* 1954; *Forever Darling,* 1956; *The Escape Artist,* 1982.

PUBLICATION

A Book by Desi Arnaz. New York: Morrow, 1976.

FURTHER READING

Anderson, Christopher. *Hollywood/TV.* Austin: University of Texas Press, 1994.

Andrews, Bart. *The "I Love Lucy" Book.* New York: Doubleday, 1985.

Andrews, Bart, and Thomas J. Watson. *Loving Lucy.* New York: St. Martin's, 1980.

Brady, Kathleen. *Lucille: The Life of Lucille Ball.* New York: Hyperion, 1994.

Firmat, Gustavo Perez. *Life on the Hyphen: The Cuban-American Way.* Austin: University of Texas Press, 1994.

Harris, Warren G. *Lucy and Desi: The Legendary Love Story of Television's Most Famous Couple.* New York: Simon and Schuster, 1991.

Higham, Charles. *Lucy: The Life of Lucille Ball.* New York: St. Martin's, 1986.

Sanders, Coyne Steven, and Tom Gilbert. *Desilu: The Story of Lucille Ball and Desi Arnaz.* New York: Morrow 1993.

Schatz, Thomas. "Desilu, I Love Lucy, and the Rise of Network TV." In, Thompson, Robert, and Gary Burns, editors, *Making Television: Authorship and the Production Process.* New York: Praeger, 1990.

See also Ball, Lucille; *I Love Lucy,* Independent Production Companies; *Westinghouse-Desilu Playhouse*

THE ARSENIO HALL SHOW

U.S. Talk Show

The Arsenio Hall Show, a syndicated late-night talk show starring African American stand-up comedian Arsenio Hall, ran from January 1989 to May 1994. Paramount Domestic Television's syndicated division produced and distributed the show which aired primarily on stations affiliated with FOX Broadcasting. During its five-year run, the show peaked at a 3.9 national rating in February 1990, an amazing feat for a syndicated show that had access to fewer TV stations than network programs and did not have a specific airing time across the nation (though it usually aired sometime between 11:00 P.M. and 1:00 A.M.).

Hall had his first break in late-night television when he became a guest hosts on FOX's The Late Show with Joan Rivers. After Rivers departed in May 1987, the show had a rotating series of guest hosts which included Hall. After fronting the show for several nights, Hall was invited to stay for thirteen weeks. That time permitted Hall to develop as a talk-show host while solidifying his position as a well-known popular entertainer. Although both Hail and the show were doing moderately well, FOX decided to cancel The Late Show and replaced it with The Wilton North Report. During that time, when Hall was without a regular television job, Paramount approached him with a multi-film deal, a deal eventually re-negotiated to include a talk show. Yet, Hall was still under contract with FOX. In order to prevent a legal suit against both Hall and Paramount, FOX affiliates were used as the main venue for Hall's talk show.

The format of The Arsenio Hall Show followed traditional structures set by other late-night talk shows—entrance and rapport with the band and the studio audience, the host's initial monologue at the center of the stage, interviews with guests (usually two to three) in the sitting area, and a musical number by an invited artist. Hall nevertheless brought some changes (sometimes quite subtle), in order to provide a more informal mood for his show. There was no desk in the sitting area where interviews were conducted, so he could be closer to his guests. Hall did not have a sidekick on the show. The set had an area at the stage left of the band designated as the "dog pound" where a group of guests would sit and cheer Hall with barks ("Woof, Woof, Woof!") while moving their right fists in circles above their heads. These more informal elements of the show were attuned with Hall's agenda of providing an alternative kind of entertainment to the traditional late night scene.

From the outset, The Arsenio Hall Show distinguished itself by targeting audiences that have been largely ignored by other late-night talk shows: African Americans, and Latinos, as well as the younger generation of television viewers which he identified on several occasions as the "MTV generation." Hall reached these audiences through a hip and casual approach to the show, strongly informed by his talent as a stand-up comedian as well as by tales of

Arsenio Hall

his childhood experiences in a Cleveland lower-middle-class community. In fact, Hall constantly invoked stories about being someone who left the ghetto for another type of life but who was still emotionally and politically connected to it. The strategy kept his television persona grounded at a level closer to audiences.

Another technique Hall used to reach a multi-ethnic younger audience was showcasing a wide variety of artists, comedians, and performers, especially those who were less mainstream and, thus, not usually invited to participate on other talk-shows. In terms of entertainment, some of the Arsenio Hall Show's highlights included a whole night dedicated exclusively to musical performances by the reclusive artist Prince, a surprise visit in 1992 by (then) presidential candidate Bill Clinton (who performed two songs on the saxophone), and the taping of his thousandth show at the Hollywood Bowl and starring Madonna.

Although entertainment was a priority for Hall, he also conceived of his show as a space where audiences, especially youth, could be educated. For example, he had a special show with Jesse Jackson as well as a night dedicated to commemorating the figure of Martin Luther King Jr. Furthermore, Hall became a spokesperson for "Safer Sex/AIDS Awareness" mainly due to his close friendship with basketball star Magic Johnson. In fact, Johnson chose *The Arsenio Hall Show* as the venue for his first public discussion about AIDS after announcing that he was HIV positive.

The Arsenio Hall Show also had its moments of controversy. Twice, for example, Hall invited the infamous comedian Andrew Dice Clay, notorious for his sexist, racist, and homophobic jokes. On the second visit, members of the gay and lesbian groups Queer Nation and ACT UP showed up on the program in order to voice their disapproval of the guest as well as of Hall for having him. In fact, these organizations had already confronted Hall during an earlier show, both for not having gay and/or lesbian guests as well as for ridiculing homosexuals through one of his recurring impersonations. The visit of the Nation of Islam's leader, Louis Farrakahn, created another controversial moment for the show and Hall was severely criticized for not being aggressive in his interview. In fact, Hall's laudatory attitude towards most of his guests was constantly criticized by the popular press.

The Arsenio Hall Show can be regarded as an example of a syndicated show which was able to succeed temporarily by targeting an audience largely ignored by other late-night shows, the multi-ethnic youth. In fact, in its most popular days, *The Arsenio Hall Show* was able to rank second in the late night rating race, just behind *The Tonight Show Starring Johnny Carson.*

—Gilberto M. Blasini

HOST
Arsenio Hall

PRODUCERS   Arsenio Hall, Marla Kell Brown

MUSIC
The Michael Wolff Band

PROGRAMMING HISTORY   1,248 Episodes
Syndicated Only 1989–1994

FURTHER READING
Freeman, Michael. "Rivals Circle *Arsenio* Slot." *MediaWeek* (Brewster, New York), 26 April 1994.
King, Norman. *Arsenio Hall.* New York: William Morrow, 1993.

See also Talk Shows; Race, Ethnicity and Television

ARTHUR, BEATRICE

U.S. Actor

Bea Arthur stands five-foot-nine-and-a-half inches tall in her stocking feet, and has a voice that one reviewer characterized as "deep as a pothole." Her formidable stature and booming vocal register made her an unlikely leading lady in an industry driven by a narrow regime of feminine beauty. But as character traits for Maude Finley, they proved to be the perfect foil for the sexist bravado of Archie Bunker in Norman Lear's 1970s sitcom, *All in the Family,* in which Arthur first appeared in the role. The spin-off series *Maude* was created for her virtually overnight. As opinionated and caustic in her own way as Archie, Maude Finley was, a crusader for women's liberation, the woman in charge. And in the nascent gender consciousness of the 1970s, the women's movement's fictional spokeswoman had to be big and booming.

Television viewers' love affair with the character Arthur created in Maude has resulted in a struggle with the actors' nemesis—typecasting. She was a recognized actress on Broadway before making the move to television, appearing in, among others, *Fiddler on the Roof, The Threepenny Opera,* and *Mame,* for which she won a Tony Award, but Arthur is nevertheless most remembered as the bombastic caricature of a liberated woman on the small screen. Upon leaving *Maude* in 1978, Arthur took a four-year hiatus before accepting another television series, in hopes the Finley character would fade in the public mind. When she reappeared on the short-lived *Amanda's* in 1983, playing the owner of a seaside hotel, it was as a physically thinner person. Yet

Beatrice Arthur

despite the actress' attempt at transformation, audiences and reviewers alike found it hard to shake their favorite character. "Bea has shed so many pounds she is scarcely recognizable as the imposing, flotilla-like Maude," wrote one reviewer. Arthur responded to the evocation of her prior character, "what can you do? I'm still five feet nine and my voice is still deep. But I'm not going to cut off my legs or change my voice." Arthur's typecasting continued on the hit series, *Golden Girls*, first aired in 1985. Playing alongside well-established actresses, Rue McClanahan, Betty White, and Estelle Getty, only Arthur seemed rooted in a past performance. Her character, Dorothy Zbornak, was a continuation of the Maude character—loud, worldly, flippant—a Maude approaching old age.

Whether as Maude, breaking television's mold of female beauty, or as Dorothy, challenging the omnipotent image of youth, Arthur's roles on the two hit series were instrumental in broadening television representation. She has been recognized for her work in television with two Emmys, for *Maude* and *Golden Girls*, and has five times been nominated for an American Comedy Award's "Lifetime Achievement Award."

—Lisa Anne Lewis

BEATRICE ARTHUR. Born Bernice Frankel in New York City, New York, U.S.A., 13 May 1926. Attended Blackstone College, Blackstone, Virginia; Franklin Institute of Science and Arts, Philadelphia, Pennsylvania, degree in medical technology; studied acting with Erwin Piscator at the Dramatic Workshop, New School for Social Research, New York. Married: actor and theater director Gene Saks, 1950 (divorced); children: Matthew and Daniel. Began career in theater and nightclub performance, New York City, 1947, and thereafter appeared frequently in summer stock, 1951-53; on the New York stage, 1947-66; guest appearance as Maude Findlay in *All in the Family*, September, 1971; starring role in the series *Maude*, 1972-78; co-star, *The*

Golden Girls, 1985-92. Recipient: Tony Award, *Mame*, 1966; Emmy Award, 1977 and 1988.

TELEVISION SERIES

1971–83	*All in the Family*
1972–78	*Maude*
1983	*Amanda's*
1985–92	*The Golden Girls*

TELEVISION SPECIALS

1980	*The Beatrice Arthur Special*
1986	*Walt Disney World's 15th Birthday Celebration* (host)
1987	*All Star Gala at Ford's Theater* (host)

STAGE (selection)
Lysistrata, 1947; *The Dog Beneath the Skin*, 1947; *Yerma*, 1947; *No Exit*, 1948; *The Taming of the Shrew*, 1948; *Six Characters in Search of an Author*, 1948; *The Owl and the Pussycat*, 1948; *Le Bourgeois Gentilhomme*, 1949; *The Creditors*, 1949; *Yes Is for a Very Young Man*, 1949; *Heartbreak House*, 1949; *Personal Appearance, Candle Light, Love or Money, The Voice of the Turtle* (summer stock), 1951; *The New Moon, Gentlemen Prefer Blondes* (summer stock), 1953; *The Threepenny Opera*, 1954; *Shoestring Revue*, 1955; *Seventh Heaven*, 1955; *What's the Rush* (touring), 1955; *Mistress of the Inn* (stock), 1956; *Nature's Way*, 1957; *Ulysses in Nighttown*, 1958; *Fiddler on the Roof*, 1964; *Mame*, 1966.

FURTHER READING
"Bea Arthur's Having a Ball at the Opera." *Chicago Tribune*, 21 March 1994.
Rose, Linda. "Actresses' Roles Continue to Evolve." *Daily Variety* (Los Angeles), 6 June 1996.

See also *All in the Family, Golden Girls*; Lear, Norman; *Maude*

ARTHUR GODFREY SHOWS (VARIOUS)

U.S. Variety/Talent/Talk

Arthur Godfrey's shows helped define the first decade and half of TV history in the United States. While there were a number of television shows on which Godfrey appeared, his fame, fortune, and pioneering activities centered on two variety shows presented on the CBS-TV network: *Arthur Godfrey's Talent Scouts* and *Arthur Godfrey and His Friends*. These two proved so popular that during the 1950s they served as a cornerstone of the CBS-TV network's programming strategies.

In December 1948, after more than a decade on radio, principally for CBS, Arthur Godfrey ventured onto primetime TV by simply permitting the televising of his radio hit *Arthur Godfrey's Talent Scouts*. On TV *Arthur Godfrey's*

Talent Scouts ran until July 1958 on Monday nights at 8:30 P.M. for a half hour and proved Godfrey's best venue on television. Fans embraced this amateur showcase, and during the 1951–52 TV season it reached number one in the ratings. Next season *I Love Lucy* vaulted into first place, but thereafter through most of the 1950s *Arthur Godfrey's Talent Scouts* regularly finished in TV's primetime top ten.

The formula for *Arthur Godfrey's Talent Scouts* was simple enough. "Scouts" brought on their discoveries to a converted New York theater to perform before a live studio audience. Most of these "discoveries" were in fact struggling professionals looking for a break, and so the quality of the talent was quite high. At the program's conclusion, the studio audience selected the winner by way of an applause meter.

In his day Godfrey significantly assisted the careers of Pat Boone, Tony Bennett, Eddie Fisher, Connie Francis, Leslie Uggams, Lenny Bruce, Steve Lawrence, Connie Francis, Roy Clark, and Patsy Cline. His "discovery" of Patsy Cline on 21 January 1957 was typical. Her scout, actually her mother Hilda Hensley, presented Patsy, who sang her recent recording *Walkin' After Midnight.* Though this was heralded as a country song, and recorded in Nashville, Godfrey's staff insisted Cline not wear one of her mother's hand, crafted cowgirl outfits but appear in a cocktail dress. The audience's ovations stopped the meter at its apex, and for a couple of months thereafter Cline appeared regularly on Godfrey's radio program. In short although Cline had been performing for nearly a decade, and had been recording and appearing on local Washington, D.C., TV for more than two years, it is Godfrey, because of the great ratings and fame *Arthur Godfrey's Talent Scouts,* who is heralded as making Patsy Cline a star. Yet Godfrey proved fallible. He turned down both Elvis Presley and Buddy Holly!

His other top ten TV hit was *Arthur Godfrey and His Friends,* which premiered in January 1949. On Wednesday nights Godfrey hosted this traditional variety show, employing a resident cast of singers which over the years included Julius La Rosa, Frank Parker, Lu Ann Simms, Pat Boone, and the Cordettes. Tony Marvin, as he was on *Arthur Godfrey's Talent Scouts,* served as both announcer and Godfrey's "second banana." The appeal of the hour long *Arthur Godfrey and His Friends* rested on the popularity of the assembled company of singers, all clean cut young people, and guest stars. Godfrey played host and pitchman.

Indeed to industry insiders, Godfrey ranked as television's first great salesman. He blended a Southern folksiness with enough sophistication to sell almost anything. As he had long done on radio, Godfrey frequently kidded his sponsors, but always "sold from the heart," only hawking products he had actually tried and/or regularly used. Godfrey made it sound like he was confiding to you and to you alone, and early television viewers listened to Godfrey's rich, warm, resonant descriptions and went out and purchased what he endorsed.

During the early 1950s Godfrey seemed unable to do anything wrong, despite a press that could find little reason for his vast popularity. He began a fall from grace began in October 1953 when he fired the then popular La Rosa—on the air. Because of the negative fallout, Godfrey thereafter regularly feuded with a host of powerful newspaper columnists including Dorothy Kilgallen and John Crosby.

By the end of the 1950s Godfrey's ratings were falling and his brand of variety show was giving way to action and comedy series made in Hollywood. Still, through the 1960s CBS unsuccessfully sought new ways to showcase Godfrey. He flopped on *Candid Camera,* but out came regular specials: *Arthur Godfrey in Hollywood* which aired on 11 October 1963, *Arthur Godfrey Loves Animals* on 18 March 1963,

Arthur Godfrey

and so on once or twice a season. His final television special came on 28 March 1973.

Television in the United States is most dependent on the star system, and Arthur Godfrey, despite common sense declarations that he had "no talent," must be counted as one of television's greatest stars. Prior to 1959 there was no bigger TV draw than this freckled-face, ukulele-playing host. There was something about Godfrey's wide grin, his infectious chuckle, his unruly shock of red hair that made millions tune in not just once, but again and again.

—Douglas Gomery

ARTHUR GODFREY AND HIS FRIENDS

HOST
Arthur Godfrey

REGULAR GUESTS
Tony Marvin
The Chordettes (1949–53)
    (Virginia Osborn, Dorothy Schwartz, Carol Hagedorn, Janet Ertel)
Janette Davis (1949–57)
Bill Lawrence (1949–50)
The Mariners (1949–55)
    (Jim Lewis, Tom Lockard, Nat Dickerson, Martin Karl)
Haleloke (1950–55)

Frank Parker (1950–58)
Marion Marlowe (1950–55)
Julius LaRosa (1952–53)
Lu Ann Simms (1952–55)
The McGuire Sisters (1952–57)
        (Christine, Dorothy, Phyllis)
Carmel Quinn (1954–57)
Pat Boone (1955–57)
The Toppers (1955–57)
Miyoshi Umeki (1955)
Frank Westbrook Dancers (1959–59)

ORCHESTRA
Archie Bleyer (1949–54)
Jerry Blesler (1954–55)
Will Roland and Bert Farber (1955–57)
Bernie Green (1958–59)

PROGRAMMING HISTORY

• CBS

January 1949–June 1957   Wednesday 8:00-9:00
September 1958–April 1959   Tuesday 9:00-9:30

ARTHUR GODFREY'S TALENT SCOUTS

HOST
Arthur Godfrey

ANNOUNCER   Tony Marvin

ORCHESTRA
Archie Bleyer (1948–1954)
Jerry Bresler (1954–1955)
Will Roland and Bert Farber (1955–1958)

PROGRAMMING HISTORY

• CBS

December 1948–July 1958   Monday 8:30-9:00

FURTHER READING
Castleman, Harry, and Walter Podrazik. *Watching TV: Four Decades of American Television.* New York: McGraw-Hill, 1982.

See also Godfrey, Arthur

THE ASCENT OF MAN

British Documentary Series

Born in Poland in 1908, Jacob Bronowski belongs as much to the scattering of central Europe in the wake of pogroms, revolutions and nazism as he did to the easy learning and liberal and humane socialism of the post-war consensus in Britain. A mathematician turned biologist, with several literary critical works to his name, he was a clear choice to provide David Attenborough's BBC2 with the follow-up to the international success of Kenneth Clarke's *Civilisation.*

By Bronowski's testimony, work began on the program in 1969, though the 13-part series only arrived on screen in 1973. Intended as a digest of the history of science for general viewers, and to match the claims of the Clarke series, it actually ranged further afield than the eurocentric *Civilisation,* although Bronowski retained a rather odd dismissal of pre-Colombian science and technology in the New World. The series faced, however, perhaps a greater challenge than its predecessor, in that the conceptual apparatus of science is less obviously telegenic than the achievements of culture. Nonetheless, the device of the "personal view" which underpinned BBC2's series of televisual essays gave the ostensibly dry materials a human warmth that allied them successfully with the presenter-led documentaries already familiar on British screens.

The Ascent of Man covers, not in strict chronological order but according to the strongly evolutionary model suggested in the title, the emergence of humanity, the agri-

cultural revolution, architecture and engineering, metallurgy and chemistry, mathematics, astronomy, Newtonian and relativistic mechanics, the industrial revolution, Darwinism, atomic physics, quantum physics, DNA and, in the final program, what we would now call neurobiology and cognitive science and artificial intelligence. As well as a generous use of locations, the series boasted what were then extremely advanced computer graphics, largely refilmed from computer monitors, and an appropriate delight in the most recent as well as the most ancient tools, skills, crafts and technologies.

Bronowski's scripts, reprinted almost verbatim as the chapters of the eponymous book accompanying the series, display his gift for inspired and visual analogies. Few have managed to communicate the essence of the special theory of relativity with such eloquence as Bronowski aboard a tram in Berne, or of Pythagorean geometry by means of the mosaics in the Alhambra. A decision made early in the filming process, to use sites which the presenter was unfamiliar with, perhaps explains some of the air of spontaneity and freshness which other presenter-led blockbuster documentaries buried beneath the modulated accents of expertise. Though sometimes gratuitous, the use of locations assured more than the visual interest of the series: it at least began the process of drawing great links between the apparently disparate cultures contributing to the development of the modern world view, from hominid skulls in the Olduvai gorge, by way of Japanese swordsmiths and Inca buildings to the splitting of the atom and the unraveling of DNA.

That profound belief in progress which informs the series, its humanism and its faith in the future, seem now to date it. But Bronowski's facility in moving between social, technological and scientific history makes his case compelling even now. His account of the industrialisation of the West, for example, centres on the contributions of artisans and inventors, emphasising the emergence of a new mutuality in society as it emerges from the rural past. On the other hand, the attempt to give scientific advance a human face has a double drawback. First, it privileges the role of individuals, despite Bronowski's attempts to tie his account to the greater impact of social trends. And second, as a result, the series title is again accurate in its gendering: not even Marie Curie breaks into the pantheon.

But it is also the case that *The Ascent of Man*, in some of its most moving and most intellectually satisfying moments, confronts the possibility that there is something profoundly amiss with the technocratic society. For many viewers, the most vivid memory of the series is of Bronowski at Auschwitz, where several members of his family had died. For Bronowski, this is not the apogee of the destructive bent of a dehumanising secularism, but its opposite, the triumph of dogma over the modesty and even awe with which true science confronts the oceanic spaces of the unknown.

In some ways, *The Ascent of Man* stands diametrically opposed to the patrician elegance of Clarke's *Civilisation*. The elegy to Josiah Wedgewood, for example, is based not on his aristocratic commissions but on the simple creamware which transformed the kitchens of the emergent working classes. For all his praise of genius, from Galileo to von Neuman, Bronowski remains committed to what he calls a democracy of the intellect, the responsibility which knowledge brings, and which cannot be assigned unmonitored into the hands of the rich and powerful. Such a commitment, and such a faith in the future, may today ring hollow, especially given Bronowski's time-bound blindness to the contributions of women and land-based cultures. Yet it still offers, in the accents of joy and decency, an inspiration which a less optimistic and more authoritarian society needs perhaps more than ever.

—Sean Cubitt

PRESENTER
Jacob Bronowski

PROGRAMMING HISTORY

• BBC-2
May 5–July 28, 1973

FURTHER READING
Bronowski, Jacob. *The Ascent of Man*. Boston, Massachusetts: Little, Brown, 1974.

ASNER, ED

U.S. Actor

Ed Asner is one of U.S. television's most acclaimed and most controversial actors. Through the miracle of the spin-off, Asner became the only actor to win Emmy Awards for playing the same character in both a comedy and dramatic series. A former president of the Screen Actors Guild (SAG), Asner's mix of politics and acting have not always set well with network executives, corporate sponsors, or the viewing public.

While Asner is best known for his *Mary Tyler Moore Show* supporting character Lou Grant, the role was a departure from his dramatic roots. Asner began his professional career with the Chicago Playwright's Theatre Company, graduating later to off-Broadway productions. Asner came to Hollywood in 1961, where he received a steady stream of roles, including his first episodic work in the series *Slattery's People*, which ran on CBS in the 1964-65 season.

Asner's big break came when he was spotted by MTM Enterprises co-founder Grant Tinker in an ABC made-for-TV movie; Tinker asked *Mary Tyler Moore Show* creators James L. Brooks and Alan Burns to consider Asner for the role of Mary's boss, the gruff-yet-lovable Lou Grant. According to Brooks, Asner gave a terrible first reading; however, Brooks agreed that Asner had a special quality that made him the clear choice for the role.

Although Asner had previously shied away from comedy, he felt that *The Mary Tyler Moore Show* script was the finest piece of writing he had ever seen. The series paid off for Asner, MTM, and the audience. Lou Grant not only became one of the most successful supporting roles in a comedy series, but the prototype for such characters as *Taxi's* Louie DePalma, whose comedy depends on superb timing in the delivery of well-crafted, trick-expectancy dialogue.

After *The Mary Tyler Moore Show* voluntarily retired, Asner became part of another historic TV event when he starred as Captain Davies, a brutal slave trader, in the epic miniseries *Roots*. Meanwhile, James L. Brooks, Allan Burns and *M*A*S*H* executive producer Gene Reynolds began adapting the Lou Grant character to a dramatic role for CBS, in which Asner would star as the crusading editor of the fictional *L.A. Tribune*. Despite a shaky start, the beloved comic character gradually became accepted in this new venue. More than just moving to the big city and losing his sense of humor, however, Asner's more serious Grant become a fictional spokesperson for issues ignored by other mass media venues, including the mainstream press. At the same time, the dramatic narrative offered opportunities for exploring the character more deeply, revealing his strained domestic relationships and his own complex emotional struggles. These revelations, in turn, complicated the professional persona of Lou Grant, the editor.

Like his character, Asner could also be outspoken. His first brush with politics occurred when he became a labor rights activist during the 1980 strike by the Screen Actors Guild (SAG), which delayed the 1980–81 TV season. Asner's work on behalf of the actors helped make him a viable candidate for the SAG presidency, which he received in 1981. Asner's political agenda widened, and, in the face of a growing right-wing national sentiment highlighted by the 1980 presidental election of Ronald Regan, Asner became increasingly vocal against U.S. public policy, including that affecting U.S. involvement in Latin America.

Through *Lou Grant*, Asner's own popularity was growing, leading to appearances in the 1980 film *Fort Apache, The Bronx*, and the 1981 TV movie *A Small Killing*. This level of success was soon to crumble, however, when Asner took part in a fund raiser to send medical aid to El Salvador rebels who were fighting against the Reagan-supported regime. Most disturbing to conservative minds was Asner's direct-mail letter on behalf of the aid organization, which began with, "My name is Ed Asner. I play Lou Grant on television." Conservative SAG members, including Charleton Heston, rose up in arms over Asner using his character to support his own political agenda (of course, one can argue that Heston is so closely associated with his own on-screen persona that his links to conservative causes are just as manipulative).

In his essay on MTM drama, Paul Kerr quoted Allan Burn's assessment of the ensuing anti-Asner onslaught: "I've never seen anybody transformed so quickly from being everyone's favorite uncle to a communist swine." Within weeks, *Lou Grant* was canceled. While CBS maintains the cancellation was based on dwindling ratings, Asner, and others on the *Lou Grant* production team, feel this was swift punishment for Asner's political beliefs. Interestingly enough, Howard Hesseman, star of *WKRP in Cincinnati*, was also involved with the Asner-supported El Salvador rally; *WKRP* and *Lou Grant* were canceled the same day.

It was not until 1985—the year Asner resigned as SAG president—that he obtained another episodic role on TV, this time playing the grouchy co-owner of a L.A. garment factory in the ABC series *Off the Rack*. After 12 years of quality scripts from his MTM days, Asner's *Off the Rack* experience can be viewed as paying penance for his perceived crimes. In 1988, however, he was back in a more serious role in the short-lived NBC series *The Bronx Zoo*, which focused on the problems faced by an inner-city high school. Ironically, Asner later landed the role of a conservative ex-cop who often confronted the liberal heroine in *The Trials of*

Ed Asner

Rosie O'Neill, which starred Sharon Gless as a crusading public defender. Asner has since continued to play a variety of supporting roles in various sitcoms, yet none as weighty or as important as *Lou Grant*.

—Michael B. Kassel

EDWARD ASNER. Born in Kansas City, Missouri, U.S.A., 15 November 1929. Attended University of Chicago, Illinois, 1947–49. Married: Nancy Lou Sikes, 1959; children: Matthew, Liza, Kathryn, and Charles. U. S. Army Signal Corps, 1951–53. Professional debut, Playwright's Theatre, Chicago, 1953; Broadway and off-Broadway productions and television guest appearances, 1950s and 1960s; prominent as Lou Grant in *The Mary Tyler Moore Show*, 1970–77, and as the title character in *Lou Grant*, 1977–82. President, Screen Actors Guild, 1981-85. Recipient: five Golden Globe Awards; seven Emmy Awards; Fund for Higher Education Flame of Truth Award, 1981.

TELEVISION SERIES

1964–65	*Slattery's People*
1970–77	*The Mary Tyler Moore Show*
1977–82	*Lou Grant*
1985	*Off the Rack*
1987–88	*The Bronx Zoo*
1990–91	*The Trials of Rosie O'Neill*
1992–93	*Hearts Afire*
1994–95	*Thunder Alley*

TELEVISION MINISERIES

| 1976 | *Rich Man, Poor Man* |
| 1977 | *Roots* |

MADE-FOR-TELEVISION MOVIES

1966	*The Doomsday Flight*
1969	*Doug Selby, D.A.*
1969	*Daughter of the Mind*
1969	*The House on Greenapple Road*
1970	*The Old Man Who Cried Wolf*
1971	*They Call It Murder*
1971	*The Last Child*
1971	*Haunts of the Very Rich*
1973	*The Police Story*
1973	*The Girl Most Likely to...*
1975	*Twigs*
1975	*The Imposter*
1975	*Hey, I'm Alive!*
1975	*Death Scream*
1977	*The Life and Assassination of the Kingfish*
1977	*The Gathering*
1979	*The Family Man*
1981	*A Small Killing*
1981	*The Marva Collins Story* (narrator)
1983	*A Case of Libel*
1984	*Anatomy of an Illness*
1985	*Vital Signs*
1985	*Tender is the Night*
1986	*Kate's Secret*
1986	*The Christmas Star*
1987	*Cracked*
1988	*A Friendship in Vienna*
1990	*Not a Penny More, Not a Penny Less*
1990	*Happily Ever After* (voice)
1990	*Good Cops, Bad Cops*
1991	*Yes Virginia, There Is a Santa Claus*
1991	*Switched at Birth*
1991	*Silent Motive*
1992	*Cruel Doubt*
1993	*Gypsy*
1994	*Heads*
1996	*Gone in the Night*

FILMS

The Slender Thread, 1965; *The Satan Bug*, 1965; *Peter Gunn*, 1967; *El Dorado*, 1967; *The Venetian Affair*, 1967; *The Todd Killings*, 1970; *Halls of Anger*, 1970; *Change of Habit*, 1969; *They Call Me Mister Tibbs*, 1970; *Skin Game*, 1971; *Gus*, 1976; *Fort Apache, The Bronx*, 1980; *O'Hara's Wife*, 1982; *Daniel*, 1983; *Pinocchio and the Emperor of the Night* (voice), 1987; *Moon Over Parador*, 1988; *JFK*, 1991; *Earth and the American Dream* (voice), 1993; *Gargoyles: The Heros Awaken* (voice), 1994; *Cats Don't Dance* (voice), 1994.

FURTHER READING

Dane, Clark. "The State vs. Asner in the Killing of Lou Grant." *Journal of Communication Inquiry* (Iowa City, Iowa), 1987.

Daneil, Douglass K. *Lou Grant: The Making of TV's Top Newspaper Drama.* Syracuse, New York: Syracuse University Press.

Feuer, Jane, Paul Kerr, and Tise Vahimagi. *MTM: "Quality Television."* London: British Film Institute, 1984.

Gitlin, Todd. *Inside Prime Time.* New York: Pantheon, 1984.

See also *Lou Grant; Mary Tyler Moore Show*

ASPER, IZZY

Canadian Media Executive

Izzy Asper is chair and chief executive officer of CanWest Global Communications Corporation, a western-based Canadian programming service which supplies an informal "network" of independent stations with originally-produced and syndicated international content. CanWest Global intends to become the third English-language Canadian television network and is developing a growing international presence.

Asper's career began in law and politics. In 1964, he was called to the Manitoba bar and established himself as an expert on tax law. From 1966 to 1977, Asper wrote a nationally-syndicated newspaper column on taxation and in 1970 authored a book critical of the federal government's tax reform proposals. He remains legal counsel to the firm of Buchwald, Asper, and Henteleff, and was named Queen's Counsel in 1975. Asper also pursued a political career. From 1970 to 1975, he was leader of the Manitoba Liberal Party and from 1972 to 1975 sat in opposition as a member of the Manitoba Legislative Assembly.

In the early 1970s, Asper turned to broadcasting as he and partner Paul Morton set up Winnipeg independent television station CKND. In 1974, Asper became involved in a financial package to salvage a Toronto-based station, Global Television. As Global's fortunes rose during the late 1970s, so did Asper's financial stake. He extended his broadcast holdings in Western Canada. Asper and his partners were successful in building a string of Western independent stations.

Global Television, located in the Toronto-Hamilton corridor, Canada's richest media market, soon became the flagship of a new programming service. Global's originally-produced content was sold to the string of independents controlled by Asper and his partners. Global also acquired top-rated U.S. shows which it syndicated across Canada. The profits from this were reinvested in original production. Global also sought to reduce its reliance on expensive U.S. shows by developing Canadian content capable of gaining a following. Finally, Global increasingly sought to market its content and expertise internationally.

By 1986, however, disputes had erupted between Asper and his partners, and these in turn led to lawsuits. The disputes were resolved in 1989 when the Manitoba Court of Queen's Bench ordered that the contentious partnerships be dissolved and the assets auctioned to the former partners. Asper emerged victorious from this "corporate shoot-out" as head of a new entity called CanWest Global Communications Corporation.

Since assuming control of CanWest Global, Asper has acquired international interests. CanWest Global now owns 57.5% of the Australian Ten Network, exercises operational control of New Zealand's TV3 (despite owning only 20%), and controls 50% of Chile's La Red network. CanWest Globalis also currently the leading bidder for Britain's fifth television network. CanWest seeks to extend its reach into Quebec and the Maritime provinces.

Asper's broadcasting career has been characterized by two major tendencies. The first is the attempt to move the overall broadcasting system away from Central Canada (Toronto and Montreal) towards the west. This is achieved in the structure of CanWest Global, whose main station and facilities are located in Toronto but whose command centre lies in Winnipeg. The second has been the belief that Canadian content can profitably replace much American content which is over-valued for the Canadian market because of competitive network bidding and regulatory distortions. To that end, CanWest Global has produced and co-produced content which has achieved a degree of success: the highly rated *Global News*, the weekly comedy/drama *Ready or Not*, the weekly "reality" series *Missing Treasures: The Search For Our Lost Children*, and several TV movies. These tendencies, however, are tempered by market realism. Hence, like Canadian broadcasters generally, CanWest Global also uses U.S. shows to subsidize Canadian production, seeks out the largest population centres, and attempts to develop international markets.

—Paul Attallah

IZZY ASPER (Israel Harold Asper). Born in Minnedosa, Manitoba, Canada, 11 August 1932. Educated at the University of Manitoba, B.A. 1953; LL.B. 1957, LL.M. 1964. Married: Ruth Bernstein, 1956; children: David, Leonard, and Gail. Newspaper columnist on taxation, 1966-77; leader of the Liberal Party in Manitoba, 1970-75; sat in Manitoba Legislative Assembly, 1972-75; counsel to the law firm of Buchwald, Asper, and Henteleff; named Queen's Counsel, 1975; acquired ownership of a string of independent stations, 1970s; partner, Global Television programming service; head of CanWest Global Communications Corporation and CanWest Capital Group Inc., since 1989. Address: 1063 Wellington Crescent, Winnipeg, Manitoba, Canada R3N 0A1.

ASSOCIATION OF INDEPENDENT TELEVISION STATIONS

The Association of Independent Television Stations, known as INTV, began 10 November 1972. It's purpose was to promote the needs of local telecasters throughout the United States that had no network affiliation. At first, the organization served about 70 stations, mostly located in large markets, and worked primarily to solve the economic problems encountered by small stations trying to buy costly shows to fill their programming schedules. One special effort involved attempts to both lower the cost and simplify transmission of programs to non-network stations by means of AT and T's "longlines." When the Federal Communications Commission (FCC) deregulated satellite access to national programming in 1975 this problem was eliminated, and much of the recent increase in the profitabiltiy of independent television stations can be attributed to reliance on satellite technology. In this same period the FCC also began to allow more station licenses and frequencies per market.

One area of FCC regulation supported by INTV involved the Financial Interest and Syndication rules. These rules restricted network ownership and future syndication rights to the programs they broadcast and gave

Courtesy of INTV

those rights to the shows' producers. The restrictions created an aftermarket for network shows which could not be controlled by ABC, CBS or NBC. With access to satellite distribution independent stations had easier ways to purchase and receive shows and to reach new markets. Due to these changes, INTV's number of member stations—and its power—grew.

In the context of American broadcasting, largely defined by networked stations, independent stations had three obstacles to overcome. The first was the ability to obtain programming at a reasonable cost and in spite of competition from richer affiliate stations in the same local market. INTV eventually advocated support of the Primetime Access Rule (PTAR), which strengthened the syndication industry and made more shows available for independent stations. The PTAR required an hour each day for local programming and succeeded partially because of INTV lobbying efforts. With the implementation of this rule, every type of station, whether network affiliate or independent, had a scheduling space in which independent producers could place shows.

The second obstacle was related to advertising, lifeblood of the American broadcasting industries. Independent stations generally provided advertisers with a "spot" market based on demographics rather than on audience size. But the advertisers had routinely placed national commercials with the national programmers who delivered the huge mass audience. Sponsors were unaware, in some ways, of the profit available from wooing audience segments defined by shared age, wealth or product purchasing characteristics. This obstacle was exacerbated in 1970 when Congress banned cigarette advertising on television. This greatly reduced the advertising revenue available to electronic media and remaining dollars were keenly sought by all operating stations.

The third obstacle was the audience itself. Independent stations had to provide viewers with shows as compelling as network programs. In addition, UHF stations had to make audiences aware of their very existence and their program schedules. In 1978, only 91 independent stations aired programming, but this mushroomed to 321 by the close of 1988. Most of these stations telecast on newly allocated UHF frequencies with less signal strength and poorer picture quality than the network affiliates making their identity problems even more difficult. At first, many independents schedules followed a similar format: movies each night during primetime, network reruns during the day, strong news hours at primetime access and religious programming on weekends.

By 1980, INTV's members looked toward the burgeoning cable television industry as a way to increase both viewership reach and advertising revenues. Instead, however, cable providers offered new options for the viewer and actually hurt independent stations in local markets. Independent stations began legal battles, seeking to require local cable operators to carry their signal on local systems, an issue not resolved until 1992.

The entire landscape for independent television stations in the United States changed in 1985 when Rupert Murdoch purchased 20th Century-Fox Studios from Marvin Davis. Murdoch appointed Barry Diller, formerly of ABC Television and Paramount Studios, to head the venture. Diller believed enough unaffiliated stations existed to support a fourth television network. Murdoch then purchased the Metromedia Corporation with its owned independent stations in the largest U.S. cities, a foundation of that allowed Diller and Murdoch to begin the FOX Broadcasting Company.

The new FOX network satisfied INTV stations' needs for regular access to relatively inexpensive programming from Hollywood suppliers. This programming also attracted national advertisements and appealed to the local audience. In signing its new affiliates FOX recruited heavily from INTV member stations, and for the next few years, INTV held its annual conventions in tandem with FOX affiliate meetings in Los Angeles. These meetings had a profound impact upon the burgeoning fourth network. At the 1988 meeting, the INTV/FOX affiliates made FOX change its operations strategy. Instead of seeking the best producers, who would design programs according to their own tastes and interests, the network now sought to satisfy its member stations. The first result was the cancellation of FOX's short-lived late night replacement show, *The Wilton North Report.* INTV's leader, Preston Padden, worked closely with FOX executives to institute the pro-affiliate change.

But INTV made a philosophical break from FOX and began focusing its service on non-FOX members. As FOX's early a-few-days-a-week schedule increased, the organization showed signs of becoming a network as defined by the FCC rather than a conglomeration of truly independent stations. In 1990, when 30% fewer station members attended the annual INTV meeting, syndicators began curtailing their presence at the organization's conventions. As a result, INTV began holding its conventions in conjunction with NATPE (National Association of Television Programming Executives), a meeting that attracted far more syndicators than did the FOX affiliate's meeting. FOX hired Padden away from INTV to become its senior vice president for affiliate relations and later, vice president of government relations.

Presently, INTV has welcomed the advent of still more new-network-start-up programming services from Warner Brothers and Paramount studios. The new arrangements have once again provided greater advertising revenue and easier program acquisition for the INTV members affiliated with the new networks. But these affiliations have not lessened the power or interests of INTV. Currently, association leaders are looking toward telephone companies for video dialtone possibilities and as a means for greater audience access to television programming.

As of March 1995, only 84 stations in the United States had no program provider affiliation, according to David Donovan, vice president of legal and legislative affairs for INTV. Of the other 301 stations considered independent, FOX Broadcasting Company had 150 as affiliates, United Paramount Network had 96, Warner Brothers had 45 and 10 stations have combined alliances with both FOX and UPN.

—Joan Stuller-Giglione

FURTHER READING

Dempsey, John. "Syndex, Must-Carry, Show Costs are Issues Confronting INTV." In, Matelski, Marilyn J. and Thomas, David O., editors, *Variety Broadcast-Video Sourcebook I 1989–1990.* Boston: Focal Press, 1990.

Harris, Paul. "Campaign to Ballyhoo Free TV Launched at NAB Confab." In, Matelski, Marilyn J. and Thomas, David O., editors, *Variety Broadcast-Video Sourcebook I 1989–1990.* Boston: Focal Press, 1990.

McClellan, Stephen. "Raining on INTV's Parade." *Broadcasting* (Washington, D.C.), 7 January 1991.

———. "Some Syndicators Cutting Back on INTV presence." *Broadcasting* (Washington, D.C.), 3 September 1990.

ATKINSON, ROWAN

British Actor

By the mid-1990s Rowan Atkinson had achieved a certain ubiquity in British popular-cultural life, with comedy series (and their reruns) on television, character roles in leading films, and even life-size cutouts placed in branches of a major bank—a consequence of his advertisements for the bank. Yet, despite Atkinson's high profile, his career has been one of cautious progressions, refining and modestly extending his repertoire of comic *personae.* As one of his regular writers, Ben Elton, has commented, Atkinson is content to await the roles and vehicles that will suit him rather than constantly seek the limelight.

After revue work at the Edinburgh Fringe Festival and London's Hampstead Theatre in the 1970s, Atkinson first achieved prominence as one quarter of the team in the BBC's satirical review *Not the Nine O'Clock News* (broadcast on BBC2 while the *Nine O'Clock News* occupied BBC1). After a decade in which British satire had diminished, in the wake of the expiration of the *Monty Python* series, a "second wave" was thereby ushered in just as a new Conservative Government took power in 1979. The four performers—also including Mel Smith and Griff Rhys Jones, who later formed a successful production company together, and talented comedienne Pamela Stephenson—had similar university backgrounds to those of the earlier generations of British television satire since *Beyond the Fringe.* But the show's rapid-sketch format, often accompanied by a driving soundtrack, was less concerned with elaborate deflations of British political and social institutions or *Python*esque surreal narratives; instead, it was rather more a combination of guerilla sniping and playful parody, loosely held together by fake news announcements (the most political and topical parts of the programme). Though the quality of the writing varied hugely, Atkinson succeeded most clearly in developing an individual presence through what were to become his comic trademarks—the gawky physicality, the abundance of comic facial expressions from sneering distaste to sublime idiocy, his shifting mood changes and vocal registers from nerdish obsequiousness to bombast, and his ability to create bizarre characterisations, such as his ranting audience member (planted among the show's actual studio audience) or his nonsense-speaker of biblical passages.

From being the "first among equals" in *Not the Nine O'Clock News* Atkinson moved centre stage to play Edmund Blackadder in the highly innovative *Blackadder* (also for the BBC), co-written by Elton and Richard Curtis, the latter a writer of Atkinson's stage shows. The first series was set in a medieval English court, with Edmund Blackadder as a hapless prince in waiting; subsequent series travelled forwards in time to portray successive generations of Blackadders, in which Edmund became courtier in Elizabethan England, then courtier during the Regency period, and finally Captain Blackadder in the trenches of World War I. With a regular core cast, who constantly refined their performances as the writers honed their scripts, the series combined, with increasing success, a sharpening satirical thrust with an escapist, schoolboyish sense of the absurd. The format served Atkinson extremely well in allowing him to play out variations on a character-theme, balancing consistency with change. While all the incarnations of Edmund Blackadder

Rowan Atkinson
Photo courtesy of the British Film Institute

pitted the rational, frustrated, and much put-upon—though intellectually superior—individual against environments in which the insane, tyrannical, and psycopathic vied for dominance, the youthful, gawky Prince of the first series evolved through the wishful, self-aggrandising courtier of the 1800s, to the older, moustachioed, world-weary soldier attempting merely to stay alive amid the mayhem of war. While the *Blackadder* series undoubtedly took time to find its feet, the attention to detail in all matters, from script to opening credits and period pastiche music, produced in the World War I series a highly successful blend of brilliantly conceived and executed characterisations, a situation combining historical absurdity and tragedy, and a poignant narrative trajectory towards final disaster: in the last episode, Blackadder and his entourage finally did go "over the top" into no man's land and to their deaths, as in one last trick of time the trenches dissolved into the eerily silent fields that they are today. In his portrayal of the cynical yet basically decent Captain Blackadder, Atkinson created a kind of English middle-class version of Hasek's Schweik, whose attempts to evade pointless self-sacrifice turn him unwittingly into a "little-man" hero in a world of pathological generals and power brokers. Atkinson's own career write-up describes *Blackadder* as a "situation tragedy", and though the comment may be meant humorously, the phrase neatly summarises the series' genre-transgressing qualities.

If *Blackadder* exploited Atkinson's skills at very English forms of witty verbal comedy and one-upmanship, his persona in the *Mr. Bean* series linked him with another tradition—that of silent film comics, notably Buster Keaton. Though silent-comedy "specials" have made occasional appearances on British television, this was an innovative attempt to pursue the mode throughout a string of episodes. Inevitably, Atkinson also became, to a much greater extent than previously, conceiver and creater of a character, though Curtis again had writing credits. In *Mr. Bean* Atkinson portrays a kind of small-minded, nerdish bachelor, simultaneously appallingly innocent of the ways of the world, yet, in his solipsistic lifestyle, deeply selfish and mean-spirited: the pathetic and the contemptible are here closely allied. It is a comedy of ineptitude, as Bean's attempts to meet women, decorate his flat, host a New Year's Eve party, and so on, all become calamitous, his incapabilities compunded by a seemingly malevolent fate. With its sources in some of his earlier characterisations, Atkinson has been able to exploit his physical gawkiness and plunder his repertoire of expressions in the role. While *Blackadder*'s university wit achieved popularity with mainly younger audiences, the *Mr. Bean* format of eccentric protaganist in perpetual conflict with his intractable world took Atkinson fully into the mainstream, with its appeal to all ages. And, though having some specific resonances for British audiences in its ambience of drab bed-sitter life, its deliberate and almost Beckettian reductionism—man versus the world (and the word) and its objects—has meant the series has translated to other cultures, and has been commercially successful around the world. At the time of writing, a feature-film version is in the making by Atkinson's own production company.

Atkinson's latest television role has been a kind of merging of the otherworldliness of *Mr. Bean* with the witty barbs of *Blackadder*. He plays a middle-ranking, idealistic, uniformed policeman, with an absolute respect for the values of the law and the job, often ridiculed by his more cynical colleagues. This new series, widely seen as writer Ben Elton's attempt to create a character-based comedy in similar vein to the classic *Dad's Army* (much-adored by Elton and many others), has thus far received mixed reviews. Since the gentler, insinuating humour of such comedy by its nature takes time to have its effects, as audiences need to build up sufficient familiarity with the charcters and their traits and foibles, it is at present too early to tell whether this bold attempt to reinvigorate an older formula will succeed in terms of ratings or critical estimation. For Atkinson, though, it is something of a logical progression—a variation not a revolution, and a further integration into the comic mainstream.

So far Atkinson has given no sign of any desire to break out of the character portrayals for which he is renowned. Though his film work has included some strongly defined subsidiary roles (such as his bumbling *ingénu* vicar in *Four Weddings and a Funeral*), he has not attempted to make the move into serious drama, and has never had call to portray genuine and serious emotions. (Indeed, almost all of his comic characters exude a separateness from other human beings—Blackadder is generally uninterested in women, Bean cannot make contact with prospective partners or friends, and Atkinson's policeman has a fragile relationship with a female colleague constantly undermined by his feebleness and passionlessness.) This apparent avoidance of roles demanding emotional display may indicate limitations in his acting range. But Atkinson himself may well regard it more as a choice to concentrate on a steady perfection and crafting of the kind of comic characterisation now so closely identified with him.

—Mark Hawkins-Dady

ROWAN (SEBASTIAN) ATKINSON. Born in Newcastle-upon-Tyne, England, 6 January 1955. Attended Durham Cathedral Choristers' School; St. Bees School; Newcastle University; Queen's College, Oxford BSc, MSc. Married: Sunetra Sastry, 1990; one son. Launched career as professional comedian, actor and writer after experience in university revues; established reputation in *Not the Nine O'Clock News* alternative comedy series and later acclaimed as the characters Blackadder and Mr. Bean; youngest person to have a one-man show in London's West End, 1981; runs Tiger Television production company. Recipient: Variety Club BBC Personality of the Year Award, 1980; BAFTA Best Light Entertainment Performance Award, 1989. Address: PBJ Management Ltd, 5 Soho Square, London W1V 5DE, England.

TELEVISION SERIES

1979	*Canned Laughter*
1979–82	*Not the Nine O'Clock News* (also co-writer)

1983	*The Blackadder*
1985	*Blackadder II*
1987	*Blackadder the Third*
1989	*Blackadder Goes Forth*
1990–91	*Mr. Bean* (also co-writer)
1991–94	*The Return of Mr. Bean* (also co-writer)
1991–94	*The Curse of Mr. Bean* (also co-writer)
1995	*The Thin Blue Line*

TELEVISION SPECIALS

| 1987 | *Just for Laughs II* |
| 1989 | *Blackadder's Christmas Carol* |

FILMS

The Secret Policeman's Ball (also co-writer), 1981; *The Secret Policeman's Other Ball*, 1982; *Never Say Never Again*, 1983; *The Tall Guy*, 1989; *The Appointment of Dennis Jennings*, 1989; *The Witches*, 1990; *Camden Town Boy*, 1991; *Hot Shots! Part Deux*, 1993; *The Lion King* (voice only), 1994; *Four Weddings and a Funeral*, 1994.

STAGE

Beyond a Joke, 1978; *Rowan Atkinson*, 1981; *The Nerd*, 1984; *The New Revue*, 1986; *The Sneeze*, 1988.

FURTHER READING

O'Connor, John J. "Mr. Bean." *The New York Times*, 2 April 1992.
O'Steen, Kathleen. "Mr. Bean." *Variety* (Los Angeles), 6 April 1992.
Schine, Cathleen. "Blackadder." *Vogue* (New York), February 1990.

ATTENBOROUGH, DAVID

British Producer/Host/Media Executive

David Attenborough joined the BBC's fledgling television service in 1952, fronting *Zoo Quest*, the breakthrough wildlife series that established the international reputation of the BBC Natural History Unit at Bristol. The first of these, *Zoo Quest for a Dragon*, established Attenborough as an intuitive performer, so prepossessed by his fascination with the subject at hand and unconcerned for his own dignity in front of the camera that he seemed to sweat integrity. A sense of daring has always surrounded him: even in this early outing, the massive Komodo Dragon, object of the quest through Borneo, looked as ferocious as its name portends, and Attenborough's presence seemed to prove not only the reality and size of his specimens, but a kind of guarantee that we too were part of this far-flung scientific endeavour, the last credible adventure in the period which witnessed the demise of the British Empire. Moreover, *Zoo Quest* engaged, albeit in an entertainment format, a far higher level of scientific seriousness than more child-oriented and anthropomorphic competitors from Europe and the United States. Perhaps only Jacques Cousteau was so resistant to the temptation to cuteness.

Despite this rare skill, shared only by a handful of his fellow scientists, mainly in weather reporting, Attenborough was promoted to senior management at the BBC, where he served for 15 years. As controller of BBC2, he oversaw (and introduced on screen) the arrival of colour on British screens on 1 July 1967. He is credited with turning BBC2 around to an attractive, varied and increasingly popular alternative to the main channels. His skill as scheduler was evidenced in the "common junctions" scheduling policy, which allowed announcers on the two BBC channels to introduce a choice of viewing, a practice which opened the corporation up to charges of unfair advantage from the commercial broadcasters and contributed indirectly to the pressure for a fourth, commercial channel. Attenborough introduced popular sports like snooker as well as *The Forsyte Saga*, and he pioneered the blockbuster, personality-presenter documentaries like Kenneth Clark's *Civilisation*, Jacob Bronowski's *The Ascent of Man*, Alistair Cooke's *America*, J.K. Galbraith's *The Age of Uncertainty* and his own *Life on Earth*. Common

David Attenborough
Photo courtesy of David Attenborough

to these expensive and risky projects was a faith in television as a medium for quite complex historical, cultural and scientific ideas. Even those series which were less popular achieved the talismanic status of the kind of programmes license fees should be used to make. Promoted to deputy controller of programmes for the whole network, third in the BBC's hierarchy, he was hotly tipped for the post of director general. But he abandoned management because, he said, "I haven't even seen the Galapagos Islands". However, he continued to speak passionately in defence of the public service ethos in many public fora.

Life on Earth, for which over 1.25 million feet of film were shot in over thirty countries, subsequently sold in 100 territories and was seen by an estimated 500 million people worldwide. Though Attenborough has always claimed modestly that photographing animals will always bring in an audience, the accumulated skills of naturalists and wildlife cinematographers, as well as enormous planning, are required to reach remote places just in time for the great wildebeest migration, the laying of turtle eggs, or the blooming of desert cacti, scenes which have achieved almost mythic status in the popular history of British television. The multimillion pound sequels to *Life*, *The Living Planet* and *The Trials of Life* created, through a blend of accessible scholarship and schoolboyish enthusiasm, the archetypal middlebrow mix of entertainment and education that marked the public service ethos of the mature BBC. Throughout the trilogy, the developing techniques of nature photography, allied with a sensitive use of computer-generated simulations, produced a spectacular intellectual montage, driven by the desire to communicate scientific theories as well as a sense of awe in the face of natural complexity and diversity. Though it is possible to be irritated by the lack of concern for the human populations of exotic countries (for example, the absence of local musics from the soundtrack), Attenborough's combination of charm and amazement has been profoundly influential on a generation of ecologically-aware viewers.

The Private Life of Plants, devoted to the evolution and adaptation of flora worldwide, was another spectacular success in the old mould, involving Attenborough popping up beside the world's oldest tree, hanging precariously in the jungle canopy, or seeking out the largest flower in existence by sense of smell. Honoured by the academy, respected by his peers and loved by audiences, Attenborough's retirement leaves the BBC with a major problem in finding a replacement. Since the pioneering work of Brian Moser on Anglia TV's *Disappearing World*, competitors have dispensed with onscreen presentation entirely, and in Moser's case opted for subtitled translations from local people rather than Western experts. Attenborough may be not only the first, but the last of a disappearing species.

–Sean Cubitt

DAVID (FREDERICK) ATTENBOROUGH. Born in London, England, 8 May 1926, brother of actor Sir Richard Attenborough. Attended Wyggeston Grammar School for Boys, Leicester; Clare College, Cambridge. Married Jane Elizabeth Ebsworth Oriel, 1950; one son and one daughter. Served in Royal Navy, 1947–49. Worked for educational publishers, 1949–52, joined BBC as trainee producer, 1952; host, long-running *Zoo Quest*, 1954–64; controller, BBC2, 1965–68; director of programmes, BBC, 1969–72; returned to documentary-making in 1979 with *Life on Earth* wildlife series; has since made several more similarly acclaimed nature series. D.Litt.: University of Leicester, 1970; City University, 1972; University of London, 1980; University of Birmingham, 1982. DSc: University of Liverpool, 1974; Heriot-Watt University, 1978; Sussex University, 1979; Bath University, 1981; University of Ulster, 1982; Durham University, 1982; Keele University, 1986; Oxford University, 1988; Plymouth University, 1992. LLD: Bristol University, 1977; Glasgow University, 1980. D.Univ.: Open University, 1980; Essex University, 1987; Antwerp University, 1993. ScD: Cambridge University, 1984. DVetMed: Edinburgh University, 1994. Honorary Fellow: Manchester Polytechnic, 1976; University of Manchester Institute of Science and Technology, 1980; Clare College, Cambridge, 1980. Fellow: British Academy of Film and Television Arts, 1980; Royal Society, 1983; Royal College of Physicians, 1991. Honorary Freeman, City of Leicester, 1990. Commander of the British Empire, 1974; Commander of the Golden Ark (Netherlands), 1983; knighted, 1985; Commander of the Royal Victorian Order, 1991. Member: Nature Conservancy Council, 1973–82; corresponding member, American Museum of Natural History, 1985; president, British Association for the Advancement of Science, 1990–91; president, Royal Society for Nature Conservation, since 1991. Trustee: Worldwide Fund for Nature U.K., 1965–69, 1972–82, 1984–90; Worldwide Fund for Nature International, 1979–86; British Museum, since 1980; Science Museum, 1984=-87; Royal Botanic Gardens at Kew, 1986–92. Recipient: Society of Film and Television Arts Special Award, 1961; Royal Television Society Silver Medal, 1966; Zoological Society of London Silver Medal, 1966; Society of Film and Television Arts Desmond Davis Award, 1970; Royal Geographical Society Cherry Kearton Medal, 1972; UNESCO Kalinga Prize, 1981; Boston Museum of Science Washburn Award, 1983; Philadelphia Academy of Natural Science Hopper Day Medal, 1983; Royal Geographical Society Founder's Gold Medal, 1985; Encyclopedia Britannica Award, 1987; International Emmy Award, 1985; Royal Scottish Geographical Society Livingstone Medal, 1990; Royal Society of Arts Franklin Medal, 1990; Folden Kamera Award, Berlin, 1993. Address: 5 Park Road, Richmond, Surrey TW10 6NS, England.

TELEVISION (writer, presenter)

1954–64	*Zoo Quest*
1975	*The Explorers*
1976	*The Tribal Eye*
1977–	*Wildlife on One*
1979	*Life on Earth*
1984	*The Living Planet*

1987	*The First Eden*
1989	Lost Worlds, Vanished Lives
1990	*The Trials of Life*
1993	*Wildlife 100*
1993	*Life in the Freezer*
1995	*The Private Life of Plants*

PUBLICATIONS

Zoo Quest to Guiana. n.p., 1956.
Zoo Quest for a Dragon. n.p., 1957.
Zoo Quest in Paraguay. n.p., 1959.
Quest in Paradise. n.p., 1960.

Zoo Quest to Madagascar. n.p., 1961.
Quest under Capricorn. n.p., 1963.
The Tribal Eye. New York: Norton, 1976.
Life on Earth. Glasgow: Collins and Sons, 1979.
The Living Planet. Boston: Little, Brown, 1984.
The First Eden. Boston: Little, Brown, 1987.
The Trials of Life. n.p., 1990.
The Private Life of Plants. New Jersey: Princeton University Press, 1994.

See also *Ascent of Man; Civilisation*

AUBREY, JAMES T.

U.S. Media Executive

James T. Aubrey was president of CBS from 1959 until 1965. He later headed MGM studios, from 1969 to 1973, under studio owner Kirk Kerkorian, then finished his career as an independent producer. While he is remembered in some circles as the man who oversaw the dismantling of much of MGM's heritage in an effort to save the failing studio from financial ruin, it was his tenure at CBS that earned him his place in the annals of entertainment history.

Aubrey began his broadcasting career as a salesman for CBS' Los Angeles radio station, KNX, in 1948. Aubrey also worked with CBS' new television station, KNXT, and soon advanced into the ranks of the network's West Coast programmers, where he was largely responsible for the development of the offbeat Western series *Have Gun, Will Travel.* Aubrey left CBS in 1956 to join ABC, where he was made head of programming, and while there was responsible for scheduling such shows as *77 Sunset Strip, The Real McCoys, The Rifleman, Maverick,* and *The Donna Reed Show.* He was lured back to CBS in 1958, and shortly thereafter was named president of the network, succeeding Lou Cowan.

In this position Aubrey's star shined. He assumed complete control over the network's programming decisions, and added shows to the CBS schedule that would become staples for the next decade, including CBS' famed lineup of "rural comedies." Among the programs for which Aubrey can be credited as the overseer of development were *The Beverly Hillbillies, The Andy Griffith Show, The Dick Van Dyke Show, Mr. Ed, Petticoat Junction,* and *The Munsters.* He also unsuccessfully urged CBS Chairman William S. Paley to purchase a Paramount Pictures package of theatrical films to air on the network; the decision to stay away from theatricals returned to haunt CBS, for it allowed NBC to enjoy a substantial advantage in programming feature films throughout the 1960s.

While many critics saw Aubrey's lowbrow programming tastes as tarnish on CBS' "Tiffany" reputation for quality programs, no one could question his knack for

finding shows that met with enormous commercial success. By the 1963-64 season, CBS had 14 of the 15 highest-rated programs in prime time, and dominated the daytime ratings in a similar fashion. CBS' net profits doubled in kind during Aubrey's tenure, from $25 million a year in 1959 to $49 million in 1964.

Aubrey's downfall at CBS came quickly, and for a number of reasons. CBS started the 1964–65 season slowly, and its once seemingly insurmountable lead over NBC and ABC was in danger. Aubrey likely would have been given

James T. Aubrey

more time to correct the situation had it not been for other factors weighing against him in the minds of Paley and his right-hand man, Frank Stanton. For one, Aubrey's brusque and sometimes ruthless style often alienated his allies as well as his foes, and earned him the nickname, "The Smiling Cobra." His abrupt and arrogant manner in dealing with people proved especially troublesome when he treated CBS talent in the same way. At various times, he had run-ins with stars such as Jack Benny (whose long-running program was cancelled by Aubrey), Lucille Ball, Garry Moore, and others. Also contributing to Aubrey's demise at CBS were questions of improprieties in the handling of his business and personal affairs, including allegations that he gave special consideration to certain program producers in exchange for personal favors and gifts. These factors combined with the downturn in CBS' programming fortunes and led Paley and Stanton to fire Aubrey from his post in February 1965. Evidence of Aubrey's impact on CBS, at least in the minds of Wall Street financial executives, came in the immediate nine-point drop in CBS' stock price that followed his dismissal.

Aubrey's reputation as a hard-fighting, hard-living executive would follow him for the rest of his life, thanks in part to his immortalization as a leading character in a number of non-fiction and fiction books. He was featured prominently and unflatteringly in Merle Miller's best seller about the television industry, *Only You, Dick Daring!*, while Jacqueline Susann acknowledged patterning the ruthless character of Robin Stone after Aubrey in her 1969 novel, *The Love Machine*. Among Aubrey's credits in his later career as an independent producer was that of co-executive producer of the highly rated and critically blasted 1979 ABC made-for-television movie, *The Dallas Cowboys Cheerleaders*.

—David Gunzerath

JAMES AUBREY, JR. Born James Thomas Aubrey, Jr., 14 December 1918, in La Salle, Illinois, U.S.A. Graduated from Princeton, New Jersey, B.A. cum laude 1941. Married Phyllis Thaxter, 1944 (divorced, 1963); children: Schuyler and James Watson. Served in U.S. Air Force as test pilot, 1941–45. Started post-war career selling advertising space, Street and Smith and Condé Nast publications, 1946–48; account executive, CBS affiliate KNX, Los Angeles, 1948, and KNXT, 1951; sales manager, then general manager, KNXT and CTPN, 1952–55; manager, CBS television's West Coast network programming (where he and Hunt Stromberg, Jr., wrote the outline, based on an idea by other writers, originating the hit television series *Have Gun, Will Travel*), 1956; vice-president in charge of programs and talent, ABC, 1956–58; with ABC president Oliver Treyz, initiated *The Real McCoys, Maverick, The Donna Reed Show, 77 Sunset Strip*, and *The Rifleman*; vice-president in charge of creative services, CBS television, 1958; appointed executive vice-president

of the CBS television network, 1959; CBS network president, December 1959; launched many successful series, notably *The Beverly Hillbillies, Mr. Ed, Gomer Pyle, The Munsters, My Favorite Martian, Route 66*, and *The Defenders*, and *The Dick Van Dyke Show*; abruptly dismissed by Dr. Frank Stanton, president of CBS, Inc., and William S. Paley, chair of the board, 27 February 1965; headed Aubrey Productions, 1965–69; president, MGM, 1969–73; independent producer, from 1973–94. Died in Los Angeles, California, 3 September 1994.

TELEVISION SERIES

1956   *Have Gun, Will Travel*

MADE-FOR-TELEVISION MOVIES

1979   *The Dallas Cowboys Cheerleaders*

FILMS

Futureworld, 1976; *The Hunger*, 1983

FURTHER READING

Bart, Peter. *Fade Out: The Calamitous Final Days of MGM*. New York: William Morrow, 1990.

Hay, Peter. *Epilogue. MGM: When the Lion Roars*. Atlanta: Turner Publishing, 1991.

Metz, Robert. *CBS: Reflections in a Bloodshot Eye*. Chicago: Playboy, 1975.

Miller, Merle, and Evan Rhodes. *Only You, Dick Daring!: Or How to Write One Television Script and Make $50,000,000*. New York: William Sloane, 1964.

"No. 1 Supplier of TV Viewers." *Business Week* (New York), 25 April 1964.

"Only You, Jim Aubrey." *Newsweek*(New York), 15 March 1965.

Oulahan, Richard, and William Lambert. "The Tyrant's Fall that Rocked the TV World." *Life* (New York), 10 September 1965.

Pace, Eric. "James Aubrey Jr., 75, TV and Film Executive." *New York Times*, 12 September 1994.

Paley, William S. *As It Happened: A Memoir*. Garden City, New York: Doubleday, 1979.

Paper, Lewis J. *Empire: William S. Paley and the Making of CBS*. New York: St. Martin's, 1987.

Rosenfield, Paul. "Aubrey: A Lion in Winter." *Los Angeles Times*, 27 April 1986.

Shales, Tom. "The Hazzards of James Aubrey: Barefooted Slob Heroes Running on TV." *Washington Post*, 21 January 1979.

Smith, Sally Bedell. *In All His Glory: The Life of William S. Paley, the Legendary Tycoon and His Brilliant Circle*. New York: Simon and Schuster, 1990.

See also Columbia Broadcasting System

AUDIENCE RESEARCH

The history of media audience studies can be seen as a series of oscillations between perspectives which have stressed the power of the text (or message) over its audiences and perspectives which have stresses the barriers "protecting" the audience from the potential effects of the message. The first position is most obviously represented by the whole tradition of effects studies, mobilising a "hypodermic" model of media influence, in which the media are seen to have the power to "inject" their audiences with particular "messages", which will cause them to behave in particular ways. This has involved, from the Right, perspectives which see the media as causing the breakdown of "traditional values" and, from the Left, perspectives which see the media causing their audience to remain quiescent in political terms, inculcating consumerist values, or causing then to inhabit some form of false consciousness.

One of the most influential versions of this kind of "hypodermic" theory of media effects was that advanced by Theodor Adorno and Max Horkheimer, along with other members of the Frankfurt School of Social Research. Their "pessimistic mass society thesis" reflected the authors' experience of the breakdown of modern Germany into fascism during the 1930s, a breakdown which was attributed, in part, to the loosening of traditional ties and structures— which were seen as then leaving people more "atomised" and exposed to external influences, and especially to the pressure of the mass propaganda of powerful leaders, the most effective agency of which was the mass media. This "pessimistic mass society thesis" stressed the conservative and reconciliatory role of "mass culture" for the audience. Mass culture was seen to suppress "potentialities", and to deny awareness of contradictions in a "one-dimensional world"; only art, in fictional and dramatic form, could preserve the qualities of negation and transcendence. Implicit here, was a "hypodermic" model of the media which were seen as having the power to "inject" a repressive ideology directly into the consciousness of the masses.

However, against this overly pessimistic backdrop, the emigration of the leading members of the Frankfurt School (Adorno, Marcuse, Horkheimer) to America, during the 1930s, led to the development of specifically "American" school of research in the forties and fifties. The Frankfurt School's "pessimistic" thesis, of the link between "mass society" and fascism, and the role of the media in cementing it, proved unacceptable to American researchers. The "pessimistic" thesis proposed, they argued, too direct and unmediated an impact by the media on its audiences; it took too far the thesis that all intermediary social structures between leaders/media and the masses had broken down; it didn't accurately reflect the pluralistic nature of American society; it was—to put it shortly—sociologically naive. Clearly, the media had social effects; these must be examined and researched, but, equally clearly, these effects were neither all-powerful, simple, nor even necessarily direct. The nature of this complexity and indirectness also needed to be demonstrated and researched. Thus, in reaction to the Frankfurt School's predilection for critical social theory and qualitative and philosophical analysis, American researchers, such as Herta Herzog, Robert Merton, Paul Lazarsfeld and, later, Elihu Katz began to develop a quantitative and positivist methodology for empirical audience research into the "Sociology of Mass Persuasion".

Over the next twenty years, throughout the 1950s and 1960s, the overall effect of this empirically grounded "Sociology of Mass Persuasion" was to produce a much more qualified notion of "media power", in which, media consumers were increasingly recognized to not be completely passive "victims" of the culture industry.

Among the major landmarks here were Merton's *Mass Persuasion* and Katz and Lazarsfeld's *Personal Influence,* in which they developed the concept of "two step flow" communication, in which the influence of the media was seen as crucially mediated by "gatekeepers" and "opinion leaders", within the audience community.

Looking back at these developments, in the early 1970s, Counihan notes the increasing significance of a new perspective on media consumption-the "uses and gratifications" approach, largely associated in the United States with the work of Elihu Katz and, in Britain, with the work of Jay Blumler, James Halloran and the work of the Leicester Centre for Mass Communications Research, during the 1960s. Within that perspective, the viewer came to be credited with an active role, so that there was then a question, as Halloran (1970) put it, of looking at what people do with the media, rather than what the media do to them. This argument was obviously of great significance in moving the debate forward—to begin to look to the active engagement of the audience with the medium and with the particular television programmes that they might be watching. One key advance which was developed by the uses and gratifications perspective, was that of the variability of response and interpretation. From this perspective, one can no longer talk about the "effects" of a message on a homogenous mass audience, who are all expected to be affected in the same way. Clearly, uses and gratifications did represent a significant advance on effects theory, in so far as it opens up the question of differential interpretations. However, critics argue that the limitation is that the perspective remains individualistic, in so far as differences of response or interpretation are ultimately attributed solely to individual differences of personality or psychology. From this point of view the approach remains severely limited by its insufficiently sociological or cultural perspective.

It was against this background that Stuart Hall's "encoding/decoding" model of communication was developed at the Centre for Contemporary Cultural Studies, as an attempt to take forward insights which had emerged within each of these other perspectives. In subsequent years, this model has come to be widely influential in audience studies. It took, from the effects theorists, the notion that mass communication is a structured activity, in which the institutions which produce the messages do have the power to set agendas, and to define issues. This is to move away from the idea of the power of the medium to make a person behave in a certain way (as a direct effect, which is caused by a simple stimulus, provided by the medium), but it is to hold onto a notion of the role of the media in setting agendas (cf. the work Bachrach and Baratz on the media's agenda-setting functions) and providing cultural categories and frameworks within which members of the culture will tend to operate. The model also attempted to incorporate, from the uses and gratifications perspective, the idea of the active viewer, making meaning from the signs and symbols which the media provide. However, it was also designed to take on board concerns with the ways in which responses and interpretations are socially structured and culturally patterned at a level beyond that of individual psychologies. The model was also, critically, informed by semiological perspectives, focusing on the question of how communication works drawing on Umberto Eco's early work on the decoding of TV as a form of "semiological guerrilla warfare". The key focus was on the realisation that we are, of course, dealing with signs and symbols, which only have meaning within the terms of reference supplied by codes (of one sort or another) which the audience shares, to some greater or lesser extent, with the producers of messages. In this respect, Hall's model was also influenced by Roland Barthes' attempts to update Ferdinand de Saussure's ideas of semiology—as "a science of signs at the heart of social life" by developing an analysis the role of "mythologies" in contemporary cultures.

The premises of Hall's encoding/decoding model were:

- The same event can be encoded in more than one way.
- The message always contains more than one potential "reading". Messages propose and "prefer" certain readings over others, but they can never become wholly closed around one reading: they remain polysemic (i.e. capable, in principle, of a variety of interpretations).
- Understanding the message is also a problematic practice, however transparent and "natural" it may seem. Messages encoded one way can always be decoded in a different way.

The television message is treated here as a complex sign, in which a "preferred reading" has been inscribed, but which retains the potential, if decoded in a manner different from the way in which it has been encoded, of communicating a different meaning. The message is thus a structured polysemy. It is central to the argument that all meanings do not exist "equally" in the message: which is seen to have been structured in dominance, despite the impossibility of a "total closure" of meaning. Further, the "preferred reading" is itself

part of the message, and can be identified within its linguistic and communicative structure. Thus, when analysis shifts to the "moment" of the encoded message itself, the communicative form and structure can be analysed in terms of what the mechanisms are which prefer one, dominant reading over the other readings; what are the means which the encoder uses to try to "win the assent of the audience" to his preferred reading of the message.

Hall assumes that there will be no necessary "fit" or transparency between the encoding and decoding ends of the communication chain. It is precisely this lack of transparency, and its consequences for communication which we need to investigate, Hall claims. Having established that there is always a possibility of disjunction between the codes of those sending and those receiving through the circuit of mass communications, the problem of the "effects" of communication could now be reformulated, as that of the *extent* to which decodings take place within the limits of the preferred (or dominant) manner in which the message has been initially encoded. However, the complementary aspect of this problem, is that of the extent to which these interpretations, or decodings, also reflect, and are inflected by, the code and discourses which different sections of the audience inhabit, and the ways in which this is determined by the socially governed distribution of cultural codes between and across different sections of the audience; that is, the range of different decoding strategies and competencies in the audience. In this connection, the model draws both on Frank Parkin's work on "meaning systems" and on Pierre Bourdieu's work on the social distribution of forms of cultural competence.

In parallel with Hall's development of the encoding/decoding model at the course for contemporary cultural studies, in Birmingham, England, the growing influence of feminism during the 1970s led, among other effects, to a revitalisation of interest in psychoanalytic theory, given the centrality of the concern with issues of gender, within psychoanalysis. Within media studies, this interest in psychoanalytic theories of the construction of gendered identities, within the field of language and representation, was one of the informing principles behind the development of the particular approach to the analysis of the media (predominantly the cinema) and its effects on its spectator, developed by the journal *Screen*, which was, for a time in the late 1970s, heavily influential in this field, particularly in Britain, within film studies, in particular.

Screen theory was centrally concerned with the analysis the effects of cinema (and especially, the regressive effects of mainstream, commercial, Hollywood cinema) in "positioning" the spectator (or subject) of the film, through the way in which the text (by means of camera placement, editing and other formal characteristics) "fixed" the spectator into a particular kind of "subject-position", which it was argued, "guaranteed" the transmission of a certain kind of "bourgeois ideology" of naturalism, realism and verisimilitude.

Screen theory was largely constituted by a mixing of Lacan's rereading of Freud, stressing the importance of language in the unconscious, and Althusser's early formulation of the "media" as an "Ideological State Apparatus" (even if operating in the private sphere) which had the principal function of securing the reproduction of the conditions of production by "interpellating" its subjects (spectators, audiences) within the terms of the "dominant ideology". Part of the appeal of this approach to media scholars rested in the weight which the theory gave to the ("relatively autonomous") effectivity of language—and of "texts" (such as films and media products), as having real effects in society. To this extent, the approach was argued to represent a significant advance on previous theories of the media (including traditional Marxism), which had stressed the determination of all superstructural phenomena (such as the media) by the "real" economic "base" of the society—thus allowing no space for the conceptualisation of the media themselves as having independent (or at least, in Althusser's terms "relatively autonomous") effects of their own.

Undoubtedly, one of screen theory's great achievements, drawing as it did on psychoanalysis, Marxism and the formal semiotics of Christian Metz, was to restore an emphasis to the analysis of texts which had been absent in much previous work. In particular, the insights of psychoanalysis were extremely influential in the development of later feminist work on the role of the media in the construction of gendered identities and gendered forms of spectatorship (see, inter alia, Mulvey, 1981; Brunsdon, 1981; Kuhn, 1982; Modleski, 1984; Mattelart, 1984; Gledhill, 1988; Byars, 1991).

Proponents of screen theory argued that previous approaches had neglected the analysis of the textual forms and patterns of media products, concentrating instead on the analysis of patterns of ownership and control—on the assumption, crudely put, that once the capitalist ownership of the industry was demonstrated, there was no real need to examine the texts (programmes or films) themselves in detail, as all they would display would be minor variations within the narrow limits dictated by their capitalist owners. Conversely, screen theory focused precisely on the text, and emphasised the need for close analysis of textual/formal patterns—hardly suprisingly, given the background of its major figures (MacCabe, 1974; Heath, 1977-78) in English studies. However, their arguments, in effect, merely inverted the terms of the sociological/economic forms of determinist theory which they critiqued. In screen theory, it was the text itself which was the central (if not exclusive) focus of the analysis, on the assumption that, since the text "positioned" the spectator, all that was necessary was the close analysis of texts, from which their "effects" on their spectators could be automatically deduced, as spectators were bound to take up the "positions" constructed for them by the text (film).

The textual determination of screen theory, with its constant emphasis on the "suturing" (cf. Heath) of the spectator, into the predetermined subject position constructed for him or her by the text, thus allocated central place in media analysis to the analysis of the text. As Moores puts it, "the aim was to uncover the symbolic mechanisms through which cinematic texts confer subjectivity upon readers, sewing them into the film narrative, through the production of subject positions" on the assumption that the spectator (or reading subject) is left with no other option but, as Heath suggests, to "make...the meanings the film makes for him/her."

Although the psychoanalytic model has continued to be influential in film studies (which has been usefully developed by Valerie Walkerdine, in a way that attempts to make it less universalist/determinist), within communication and media studies, Hall's encoding/decoding model has continued to set the basic conceptual framework for the notable boom in studies of media consumption and the media audiences which occurred during the 1980s. To take only the best-known examples, the body of work produced in that period included Morley's study of the "Nationwide" audience, Hobson's study of Crossroads viewers, Modleski's work on women viewers of soap opera, Radway's study of readers of romance fiction, Ang's study of Dallas viewers, Fiske's study of Television Culture, Philo and Lewis' studies of the audience for television news, Jhally and Lewis' study of American audiences for The Cosby Show, and the work of Schroder, and Liebes and Katz on the consumption of American TV fiction in other cultures. Towards the end of the decade, much of the most important new material on media consumption was collected together in the published proceedings of two major conferences on audience studies—Drummond and Paterson's collection Television and its Audience, bringing together work on audiences presented at the International Television Studies Conference in London in 1986, and Seiter's collection Remote Control: Television, Audience's and Cultural Power, based on the influential conference of that name held in Tubingen, Germany, in 1987.

During the late 1980s, a further new strand of work developed in audience studies, focusing on the domestic context of television's reception within the household, often using a broadly ethnographic methodology and characteristically focusing on gender differences within the household or family in TV viewing habits. The major studies in this respect are Morley's Family Television, James Lull's Inside Family Viewing, Ann Gray's Video Playtime, Roger Silverstone's Television and Everyday Life, and, from a historical perspective, Lynn Spigel's Make Room for TV. Much of this work can be situated within the broad framework of reception analysis research as discussed in the "Analysis Research" entry.

—David Morley

FURTHER READING

Adorno, T., and M. Horkheimer. "The Culture Industry: Enlightenment as Mass Deception." In, Curran, J., with others, editors. Mass Communication and Society. London: Edward Arnold, 1977.

Althusser, L. "Ideological State Apparatuses." In, Althusser, L. *Lenin and Philosophy*. London: New Left Books, 1971.

Ang, I. *Watching "Dallas."* London: Methuen, 1985.

Blumler, J., with others. "Reaching Out: A Future for Gratifications Research." In, Rosengren, K., with others, editors. *Media Gratification Research*. Beverly Hills, California: Sage, 1985.

Bourdieu, P. *Distinction*. London: Routledge, 1984.

Brunsdon, C. "*Crossroads*, Notes on a Soap Opera." *Screen* (London), 1981.

Budd, B., with others. "The Affirmative Character of American Cultural Studies." *Critical Studies in Mass Communication*, (Annandale, Virginia) 1990.

Byars, J. *All That Hollywood Allows*. London: Routledge, 1991.

de Certeau, M. *The Practice of Everyday Life*. Berkeley, California: University of California Press, 1984.

Condit, C. "The Rhetorical Limits of Polysemy." *Critical Studies in Mass Communications* (Annandale, Virginia), 1989.

Corner, J. "Meaning, Genre and Context." In, Curran, J., and M. Gurevitch, editors. *Mass Media and Society*. London: Edward Arnold, 1991.

Curran, J. "The 'New Revisionism' in Mass Communication Research." *European Journal of Communication* (London), 1990.

Drummond, P., and Paterson, R., editors. *Television and its Audiences*. London: British Film Institute, 1988.

Evans, W. "The Interpretive Turn in Media Research." *Critical Studies in Mass Communication* (Annandale, Virginia), 1990.

Fish, S. *Is There a Text in this Class?* Cambridge, Massachusetts: Harvard University Press, 1980.

Fiske, J. *Television Culture*. London: Methuen, 1987.

Gledhill, C. "Pleasurable Negotiations." In, Pribram, E., editor. *Female Spectators*. London: Verso, 1988.

Gray, A. *Video Playtime: The Gendering of a Leisure Technology*. London: Routledge, 1992.

Gripsrud, J. *The Dynasty Years*. London: Routledge, 1995.

Hall, S. "Encoding and Decoding in the TV Discourse." In, Hall, S., with others, editors. *Culture, Media, Language*. London: Hutchinson, 1981.

Halloran, J. *The Effects of Television*. London: Panther, 1970.

Heath, S. "Notes on Suture." *Screen* (London), 1977–78.

Hobson, D. *Crossroads*. London: Methuen, 1982.

Iser, W. *The Implied Reader*. Baltimore, Maryland: Johns Hopkins University Press, 1974.

———. *The Act of Reading*. Baltimore: Johns Hopkins University Press, 1976.

Jauss, H. R. "Literary History as a Challenge to Literary Theory." *New Literary History* (Baltimore, Maryland), Autumn 1970.

Jensen, K.B. "Qualitative Audience Research." *Critical Studies in Mass Communication* (Annandale, Virginia), 1987.

Jensen, K. B., and K. E. Rosengren. "Five Traditions in Search of an Audience." *European Journal of Communication* (London), 1990.

Jhally, S., and J. Lewis. *Enlightened Racism*. Boulder, Colorado: Westview Press, 1992.

Katz, E., and P. Lazarsfeld. *Personal Influence*. Glencoe, Illinois: Free Press, 1955.

Kuhn, A. *Women's Pictures*. London: Routledge, 1982.

Lewis, J. *The Ideological Octopus*. London: Routledge, 1991.

Liebes, T., and E. Katz. *The Export of Meaning*. Oxford: Oxford University Press, 1991.

Lull, J. *Inside Family Viewing*. London: Routledge, 1991.

MacCabe, C. "Realism and the Cinema." *Screen* (London), 1974.

———. "Days of Hope." In, Bennet, T., with others, editors. *Popular TV and Film*. London: British Film Institute, 1981.

Mattelart, M. *Women, Media, Crisis*. London: Comedia, 1984.

Merton, R. *Mass Persuasion*. New York: Free Press, 1946.

Metz, C. "The Imaginary Signifier." *Screen* (London), 1975.

Modleski, T. *Loving with a Vengeance*. London: Methuen, 1984.

Moores, S. *Interpreting Audiences*. London: Sage, 1993.

Morley, D. *Family Television*. London: Comedia, 1986.

———. *Television, Audience and Cultural Studies*. London: Routledge, 1992.

———. *The Nationwide Audience*. London: British Film Institute, 1980.

Parkin, F. *Class Inequality and Political Order*. London: Paladin, 1973.

Radway, J. *Reading The Romance*. Chapel Hill: University of North Carolina Press, 1984.

Rosengren, K. E. "Growth of a Research Tradition." In, K.E.Rosengren, with others, editors. *Media Gratifications Research*. Beverly Hills, California: Sage, 1985.

Schroder, K. "Convergence of Antagonistic Traditions?" *European Journal of Communications* (London), 1987.

Seaman, W. "Active Audience Theory: Pointless Populism." *Media, Culture and Society* (London), 1992.

Seiter, E., with others, editors. *Remote Control*. London: Routledge, 1989.

Silverstone, R. *Television and Everyday Life*. London: Routledge, 1994.

Spigel, L. *Make Room for TV*. Chicago: University of Chicago Press, 1992.

Tomkins, J., editor. *Reader Response Criticism*. Baltimore, Maryland: Johns Hopkins University Press, 1980.

Walkerdine, V. "Video Replay." In, Donald, J., with others, editors. *Formations of Fantasy*. London: Methuen, 1987.

See also Americanization; Children and Television; Demographics; Market; Ratings; Share; Violence and Television

AUDIENCE RESEARCH: CULTIVATION ANALYSIS

The stories of a culture reflect and cultivate its most basic and fundamental assumptions, ideologies, and values. Mass communication is the mass production, distribution, and consumption of cultural stories. Cultivation analysis, developed by George Gerbner and his colleagues, explores the extent to which television viewers' beliefs about the "real world" are shaped by heavy exposure to the most stable, repetitive, and pervasive patterns that television presents, especially in its dramatic entertainment programs.

Cultivation analysis is one component of a long-term, ongoing research program, called cultural indicators, which follows a three-pronged research strategy. The first, called "institutional process analysis," investigates the pressures and constraints that affect how media messages are selected, produced, and distributed. The second, called "message system analysis," quantifies and tracks the most common and recurrent images in television content. The third, cultivation analysis, studies whether and how television contributes to viewers' conceptions of social reality.

First implemented in the late 1960s, by the mid–1990s the bibliography of studies relating to the cultural indicators project included over 300 scholarly publications. Although early cultivation research was especially concerned with the issue of television violence, over the years the investigation has been expanded to include sex roles, images of aging, political orientations, environmental attitudes, science, health, religion, minorities, occupations, and other topics. Replications have been carried out in Argentina, Australia, Brazil, Canada, England, Germany, Hungary, Israel, the Netherlands, Russia, South Korea, Sweden, Taiwan, and other countries.

The methods and assumptions of cultivation analysis were designed to correct for certain blind spots in traditional mass communication research. Most earlier studies looked at whether individual messages or genres could produce some kind of change in audience attitudes and behaviors; in contrast, cultivation sees the totality of television's programs as a coherent *system* of messages, and asks whether that system might promote stability (or generational shifts) rather than immediate change in individuals. Whereas most research and debate on, for example, television violence has been concerned with whether violent portrayals make viewers more aggressive, Gerbner and his colleagues claimed that heavy exposure to television was associated with exaggerated beliefs about the amount of violence in society.

Cultivation analysis is not concerned with the impact of any particular program, genre, or episode. It does not address questions of style, artistic quality, aesthetic categories, high vs. low culture, or specific, selective "readings" or interpretations of media messages. Rather, cultivation researchers are interested in the aggregate patterns of images and representations to which entire communities are exposed—and which they absorb—over long periods of time.

Cultivation does not deny the importance of selective viewing, individual programs, or differences in viewers' interpretations; it just sees these as different research questions. It focuses on what is most broadly shared, in common, across program types and among large groups of otherwise heterogeneous viewers. No matter what impact exposure to genre X may have on attitude Y, the cultivation perspective argues that the consequences of *television* cannot be found in terms of isolated fragments of the whole. The project is an attempt to say something about the more broad-based ideological consequences of a commercially-supported cultural industry celebrating consumption, materialism, individualism, power, and the status quo along lines of gender, race, class, and age. None of this denies the fact that some programs may contain some messages more than others, that not all viewers watch the same programs, or that the messages may change somewhat over time.

The theory of cultivation emphasizes the role that storytelling plays in human society. The basic difference between human beings and other species is that we live in a world that is created by the stories we tell. Great portions of what we know, or think we know, come not from personal or direct experience, but from many forms and modes of story-telling. Stories—from myths and legends to sitcoms and cop shows—tend to express, define, and maintain a culture's dominant assumptions, expectations, and interpretations of social reality.

Television has transformed the cultural process of story-telling into a centralized, market-driven, advertiser-sponsored system. In earlier times, the stories of a culture were told face-to-face by members of a community, parents, teachers, or the clergy. Today, television tells most of the stories to most of the people, most of the time. Story-telling is now in the hands of global commercial conglomerates who have something to sell. Most of the stories we now consume are not hand-crafted works of individual expressive artists, but mass-produced by bureaucracies according to strict market specifications. To be acceptable to enormous audiences, the stories must fit into and reflect—and thereby sustain and cultivate—the "facts" of life that most people take for granted.

For the cultural indicators project, each year since 1967, week-long samples of U.S. network television drama have been recorded and content analyzed in order to delineate selected features and trends in the overall world television presents to its viewers. In the 1990s, the analysis has been extended to include the FOX network, "reality" programs, and various new cable channels. Through the years, message system analysis has focused on the most pervasive content patterns that are common to many different types of programs but characteristic of the system of programming as a whole, because these hold the most significant potential lessons television cultivates.

Findings from the analyses of television's content are then used to formulate questions about people's conceptions of social reality, often contrasting television's "reality" with some other real-world criterion. Using standard techniques of survey methodology, the questions are posed to samples of children, adolescents, or adults, and the differences (if any) in the beliefs of light, medium, and heavy viewers, other things held constant, are assessed. The questions do not mention television, and respondents' awareness of the source of their information is seen as irrelevant.

The prominent and stable over-representation of well-off white males in the prime of life pervades prime time. Women are outnumbered by men at a rate of three to one and allowed a narrower range of activities and opportunities. The dominant white males are more likely to commit violence, while old, young, female, and minority characters are more likely to be victims. Crime in prime time is at least 10 times as rampant as in the real world, and an average of five to six acts of overt physical violence per hour involve well over half of all major characters.

Cultivation researchers have argued that these messages of power, dominance, segregation, and victimization cultivate relatively restrictive and intolerant views regarding personal morality and freedoms, women's roles, and minority rights. Rather than stimulating aggression, cultivation theory contends that heavy exposure to television violence cultivates insecurity, mistrust, and alienation, and a willingness to accept potentially repressive measures in the name of security, all of which strengthens and helps maintain the prevailing hierarchy of social power.

Cultivation is not a linear, unidirectional, mechanical "effect," but part of a continual, dynamic, ongoing process of interaction among messages and contexts. Television viewing usually relates in different ways to different groups' life situations and world views. For example, personal interaction with family and peers makes a difference, as do real-world experiences. A wide variety of socio-demographic and individual factors produce sharp variations in cultivation patterns.

These differences often illustrate a phenomenon called "mainstreaming," which is based on the idea that television has become the primary common source of everyday culture of an otherwise heterogeneous population. From the perspective of cultivation analysis, television provides a relatively restricted set of choices for a virtually unrestricted variety of interests and publics; its programs eliminate boundaries of age, class, and region and are designed by commercial necessity to be watched by nearly everyone.

"Mainstreaming" means that heavy television viewing may erode the differences in people's perspectives which stem from other factors and influences. Mainstreaming thus represents a relative homogenization and an absorption of divergent views and a convergence of disparate viewers. Cultivation researchers argue that television contributes to a blurring of cultural, political, social, regional, and class-based distinctions, the blending of attitudes into the television mainstream, and the bending of the direction of that mainstream to the political and economic tasks of the medium and its client institutions.

Cultivation has been a highly controversial and provocative approach; the results of cultivation research have been many, varied, and sometimes counterintuitive. The assumptions and procedures of cultivation analysis have been vigorously critiqued on theoretical, methodological, and epistemological grounds; extensive debates and colloquies (sometimes lively, sometimes heated) continue to engage the scholarly community, and have led to some refinements and enhancements.

Some researchers have looked inward, seeking cognitive explanations for how television's images find their way into viewers' heads, and some have examined additional intervening variables and processes (e.g., perceived reality, active vs. passive viewing). Some have questioned the assumption of relative stability in program content over time and across genres, and emphasized differential impacts of exposure to different programs and types. The spread of alternative delivery systems such as cable and VCRs has been taken into account, as has the family and social context of exposure. Increasingly complex and demanding statistical tests have been applied. The paradigm has been implemented in at least a dozen countries besides the United States.

The literature contains numerous failures to replicate its findings as well as numerous independent confirmations of its conclusions. The most common conclusion, supported by meta-analysis, is that television makes a small but significant contribution to heavy viewers' beliefs about the world. Given the pervasiveness of television and even light viewers' cumulative exposure, finding any observable evidence of effects at all is remarkable. Therefore, the discovery of a systematic pattern of small but consistent differences between light and heavy viewers may indicate far-reaching consequences.

In sum, cultivation research is concerned with the most general consequences of long-term exposure to centrally-produced, commercially supported systems of stories. Cultivation analysis concentrates on the enduring and common consequences of growing up and living with television: the cultivation of stable, resistant, and widely shared assumptions and conceptions reflecting the institutional characteristics and interests of the medium itself and the larger society. Understanding the dynamics of cultivation can help develop and maintain a sense of alternatives essential for self-direction and self-government in the television age. The cultivation perspective will become even more important as we face the vast institutional, technological, and policy-related changes in television the 21st century is sure to bring.

—Michael Morgan

FURTHER READING

Bryant, Jennings. "The Road Most Traveled: Yet Another Cultivation Critique." *Journal of Broadcasting and Electronic Media* (Washington, D.C.), 1986.

Carlson, James M. *Prime Time Law Enforcement: Crime Show Viewing and Attitudes Toward the Criminal Justice System.* New York: Praeger, 1985.

Gerbner, George. "Toward 'Cultural Indicators': The Analysis of Mass Mediated Message Systems." *Audio Visual Communication Review* (Washington, D.C.), 1969.

————. "Communication and Social Environment." *Scientific American* (San Francisco, California), 1972.

————. "Cultural Indicators: The Third Voice." In, Gerbner, G., L. Gross, and W.H. Melody, editors. *Communications Technology and Social Policy.* New York: John Wiley, 1973.

Gerbner, George, and Larry Gross. "Living with Television: The Violence Profile." *Journal of Communication* (Philadelphia, Pennsylvania), 1976.

————. "Editorial Response: A Reply to Newcomb's 'Humanistic Critique.'" *Communication Research* (Beverly Hills, California), 1979.

Gerbner, George, Larry Gross, Michael Morgan, and Nancy Signorielli. "A Curious Journey into the Scary World of Paul Hirsch." *Communication Research* (Beverly Hills, California), 1981.

————. "Charting the Mainstream: Television's Contributions to Political Orientations." *Journal of Communication* (Philadelphia, Pennsylvania), 1982.

————. "Growing Up with Television: The Cultivation Perspective." In, Bryant, J. and D. Zillmann, editors. *Media Effects: Advances in Theory and Research.* Hillsdale, New Jersey: Lawrence Erlbaum, 1994.

————. "The 'Mainstreaming' of America: Violence Profile No. 11." *Journal of Communication* (Philadelphia, Pennsylvania), 1980.

Hawkins, Robert P., and Suzanne Pingree. "Television's Influence on Social Reality." In, Pearl, D., L. Bouthilet, and J. Lazar, editors. *Television and Behavior: Ten Years of Scientific Progress and Implications for the 80s: Volume II, Technical Reviews.* Rockville, Maryland: National Institute of Mental Health, 1982.

Hirsch, Paul. "The 'Scary World' of the Nonviewer and Other Anomalies: A Re-analysis of Gerbner et al.'s Findings of Cultivation Analysis." *Communication Research* (Beverly Hills, California), 1980.

Melischek, Gabriele, Karl Erik Rosengren, and James Stappers, editors. *Cultural Indicators: An International Symposium.* Vienna, Austria: Verlag der Osterreichischen Akademie der Wissenschaften, 1984.

Newcomb, Horace. "Assessing the Violence Profile of Gerbner and Gross: A Humanistic Critique and Suggestion." *Communication Research* (Beverly Hills, California), 1978.

Morgan, Michael, and James Shanahan. *Democracy Tango: Television, Adolescents, and Authoritarian Tensions in Argentina.* Cresskill, New Jersey: Hampton Press, 1995.

Ogles, Robert M. "Cultivation Analysis: Theory, Methodology, and Current Research on Television-influenced Constructions of Social Reality." *Mass Comm Review* (Philadelphia, Pennsylvania), 1987.

Potter, W. James. "Cultivation Theory and Research: A Conceptual Critique." *Human Communication Research* (New Brunswick, New Jersey), 1993.

————. "Cultivation Theory and Research: A Methodological Critique." *Journalism Monographs* (Austin, Texas), 1994.

Signorielli, Nancy, and Michael Morgan, editors. *Cultivation Analysis: New Directions in Media Effects Research.* Newbury Park, California: Sage, 1990.

AUDIENCE RESEARCH: EFFECTS ANALYSIS

Among matters of scholarly concern about television effects studies have been both tendentious and critical. Their relative importance is reflected in the following from a 1948 paper by Harold Laswell: "A convenient way to describe an act of communication is to answer the following questions: **Who** Says **What** in **Which Channel** to **Whom** with **What Effect?**"

The question as it is applied to television typically becomes either how is society different because television is part of it?, or how are individuals or specific groups of people different because they live in a world where television has been provided? The first of these questions may be thought of as a matter of media effect upon society; the second, a matter of media effect upon the development or status of individual people.

Effects of television then may be social or psychological and developmental. They may also be short-term and long term. Walter Weiss, writing in the second edition of the *Handbook of Social Psychology* (1969), discussed effects literature under ten headings: (1) cognition, (2) comprehension, (3) emotional arousal, (4) identification, (5) attitude, (6) overt behavior, (7) interests and interest-related behavior, (8) public taste, (9) outlook and values, (10) family life.

For the most part, such effects, however they are characterized, have been studied in the haphazard fashion characterized by the funding priorities of governments and non-profit foundations. For example, there have been many efforts to assess the effect of the availability of television upon the developmental processes in children. In 1963, for instance, the British Home Office established its Television Research Committee with sociologist J. D. Halloran as its secretary. The effects of television were to be studied as both immediate and cumulative, with separate attention paid to perceptions of TV, its content and its function for viewers.

One area that has been heavily studied and produced an extensive research literature addresses the specific issue of violence, especially the connection between television treatment of violence and its manifestation in society. This work addresses the issue: will portrayals of violent behaviors result in members of the viewing audience becoming more violent in their relationships with others? This issue is often related to other presumed connections between the models projected by television and various modes of perception and behavior. Thus the way that women and minorities are presented in various television programs may be connected by some researchers to the ways these groups are perceived by viewers in other groups and by the group members themselves.

Just as the presence or absence of a medium or some particular of program content (e.g. violence) can be considered capable of producing effects in an audience, so can such technological innovations as pay-per-view, satellite delivery, three dimensional presentation, stereo sound, interactive television, etc. Any of these technological innovations may be linked in a research question with special viewing populations and special samples of program materials in attempts to determine whether or not the shift in technology has an effect on subsequent behavior or attitude.

Effects research is grounded in various forms of social scientific analysis and often depends on such techniques as controlled experiments, surveys, and observations. As a result, findings are often in dispute. Challenges to methods or design or sample size are used to call results into question and clear, incontrovertible conclusions are difficult to establish. Particularly with regard to research focused on children, or on the role of televised violence, these philosophical and scientific difficulties have made it almost impossible to develop broadcasting policies based on research findings.

—James E. Fletcher

FURTHER READING

Alexander, Alison, James Owers, and Rod Carveth, editors. *Media Economics: Theory and Practice.* Hillsdale, New Jersey: Lawrence Erlbaum, 1993.

Baran, Stanley J., and Dennis K. Davis. *Mass Communication Theory: Foundations, Ferment, and Future.* Belmont, California: Wadsworth, 1995.

Beville, Hugh Malcolm, Jr. *Audience Ratings: Radio Television, Cable.* Hillsdale, New Jersey: Lawrence Erlbaum, 1988.

Brooks, Tim, and Earle Marsh, editors. *The Complete Directory to Prime Time Network TV Shows—1948-Present.* New York, Ballantine, 1981.

Dominick, Joseph R., and James E. Fletcher, editors. *Broadcasting Research Methods.* Newton, Massachusetts: Allyn and Bacon, 1985.

———. *Handbook of Radio and TV Broadcasting: Research Procedures in Audience, Program and Revenues.* New York: Van Nostrand Reinhold, 1981.

Fletcher, James E., editor. *Broadcast Research Definitions.* Washington, D. C.: National Association of Broadcasters, 1988.

Lindzey, Gardner, and Elliot Aronson, editors. *Applied Social Psychology, Volume V of The Handbook of Social Psychology.* Reading, Massachusetts: Addison-Wesley, 1969.

Schramm, Wilbur, and Donald F. Roberts, editors. *The Process and Effects of Mass Communication.* Chicago: University of Chicago Press, 1971.

AUDIENCE RESEARCH: INDUSTRY AND MARKET ANALYSIS

The television audience is the commodity that stations and networks sell to advertisers. Television audiences are bought and sold and audience research is the currency, if you will, that the industry relies upon to make these transactions. From the television side of the business, the goal is to sell as many ads as possible while at the same time charging as much as advertisers are willing to pay. From the advertiser's perspective, the goal is to buy time in programs whose audience contains as many people as possible with the demographic characteristics most desired by the advertiser. Advertisers want to buy these audiences as efficiently as possible. In order to accomplish this task the industry usually describes audiences and their prices in terms of costs per thousand. This is simply the cost to purchase one or more ads divided by an estimate of the number of people in thousands. For example, if the cost for one advertisement is $300,000 and the program audience estimate is 40,000,000 women, 18 to 49 years old, then the cost-per-thousand is $300,000/40,000=$7.50. There are 40,000 one-thousands in 40,000,000. In this example, an advertiser will spend $7.50 for every 1,000 women 18 to 49 years old who watches the program in which the ad will be placed. Audience research provides the estimates of the size and characteristics of the audience that the industry buys and sells.

The A. C. Nielsen Company provides the audience estimates to stations, networks, program producers, advertisers and advertising agencies. Employing probability sample survey research methodology, Nielsen identifies which programs people watch and how long they watch them. Printed reports and on-line computer access allow Nielsen's clients to examine a detailed picture of television audiences.

Advertisers use this research information to locate the programs, stations and networks that have large numbers of viewers with demographic characteristics they desire. These characteristics are based upon other market research that indicates the factors like age, sex, income, household size, and geographic location of people who are most likely to purchase and use their products or services. As they identify the significant users and purchasers of their products, advertisers look for television viewers with similar characteristics. These target audiences become the focus of the deals that buyers and sellers make. The audience research data helps identify the number of and characteristics of the audience as well as the efficiency of a particular advertising buy.

Television stations and networks approach this equation from the other side. They use market research to identify the characteristics of users and purchasers of products and services to whom they hope to sell advertising. TV sales executives then employ Nielsen audience research to find the programs these target audiences watch. They will then do competitive analyses to compare the size and composition of other station and or network program audiences. They will use this data to convince advertisers that they can deliver more of the target audience at a better price than their competition.

Audience research is an integral part of this business ritual. It really is a starting place for the negotiations in which buyers and sellers engage. As in any business deal there are many other factors that will determine the price. Supply and demand, personal relationships, and other intangibles affect prices, but in the television industry, audience research plays an important role in how business is conducted.

—Guy E. Lometti

FURTHER READING

Lometti, G.E. "Measuring Children's Television Viewing." *Children's Research*. New York: Advertising Research Foundation, 1988.
Stipp, H., and Schiavone, N. "Research at a Commercial Television Network: NBC 1990." *Marketing Research* (Chicago), September 1990.

AUDIENCE RESEARCH: RECEPTION ANALYSIS

Despite the (implicit) nominal link to the work on what is also called "Reception Theory", within the field of literary studies, carried out by Wolfgang Iser, Hans Jauss and other literary scholars (particularly in Germany), the body of recent work on media audiences commonly referred to by this name, has on the whole, a different origin, although there are some theoretical links (cf., the work of Stanley Fish) than the work in literary theory. In practice, the term "reception analysis", has come to be widely used as a way of characterising the wave of audience research which occurred within communications and cultural studies during the 1980s and 1990s. On the whole, this work has adopted a "culturalist" perspective, has tended to use qualitative (and often ethnographic) methods of research and has tended to be concerned, one way or another, with exploring the active choices, uses and interpretations made of media materials, by their consumers.

As indicated in the previous discussion of "The Media Audience", the single most important point of origin for this work, lies with the development of cultural studies in the writings of Stuart Hall at the Centre for Contemporary Cultural Studies at the University of Birmingham, England, in the early 1970s and, in particular, Hall's widely influential "encoding/decoding" model of communications (see the discussion of "The Media Audience" for an explanation of this model). Hall's model provided the inspiration, and much of the conceptual framework, for a number of the centre's explorations of the process of media consumption, notably David Morley's widely cited study of the cultural patterning of differential interpretations of media messages among The 'Nationwide' Audience and Dorothy Hobson's work on women viewers of the soap opera *Crossroads*. These works were the forerunners of a blossoming of cultural studies work focusing on the media audience, throughout the 1980s and 1990s, including,

among the most influential, from a feminist point of view, the work of Tania Modleski and Janice Radway on women consumers of soap opera and romance, and the work of Ien Ang, Tamar Liebes and Elihu Katz, Kim Schroder and Jostein Gripsrud on international cross cultural consumption of American drama series, such as *Dallas* and *Dynasty*.

Much of this work has been effectively summarised and popularised, especially, in the United States by John Fiske, who has drawn on the theoretical work of Michel de Certeau to develop a particular emphasis on the "active audience", operating within what he terms the "semiotic democracy" of postmodern pluralistic culture. Fiske's work has subsequently been the object of some critique, in which a number of authors, among them Budd, Condit, Evans, Gripsrud, and Seamann have argued that the emphasis on the openness (or "polysemy") of the message and on the activity (and the implied "empowerment") of the audience, within reception analysis, has been taken too far, to the extent that the original issue—of the extent of media power—has been lost sight of, as if the "text" had been theoretically "dissolved" into the audience's (supposedly) multiple "readings" of (and "resistances" to) it.

In the late 1980s, there were a number of calls to scholars to recognise a possible "convergence" of previously disparate approaches under the general banner of "reception analysis" (cf. Jensen and Rosengren), while Blumler have claimed that the work of a scholar such as Radway is little more than a "re-invention" of the "uses and gratifications" tradition—a claim hotly contested by Schroder. More recently, both Curran and Corner have offered substantial critiques of "reception analysis"—the former accusing many reception analysts of ignorance of the earlier traditions of media audience research, and the latter accusing them of retreating away from important issues of macro-politics and power into inconsequential micro-ethnographies of domestic television consumption. For a reply to these criticisms, see Morley, 1992.

—David Morley

FURTHER READING

See "Audience Research" general entry.

AUSTRALIA

Australian television may be said to show a pattern of "historical modernity." The key features of this pattern are as follows: a dual or mixed television system consisting of private, commercial television broadcast networks as well as a public service television broadcast sector; a heavy reliance on American-style programming practices; and, initially at least, equally heavy reliance on imported programs from America to fill the television schedule; the start-up of local programs on the commercial networks which when coupled with imported programs guarantees the overall viewing popularity of this sector; a relatively weak public service sector, perpetually caught in the dilemma of attempting to hold its traditional minority audiences with innovative, local programs and attracting larger, entertainment-oriented audiences with more main stream programs, often imported. While this pattern has been generally true for Australian television, it has not, however, been a static one. In particular Australian television has followed a classic economic tendency of "import substitution" whereby, after an initial high noon of imported American programs, locally produced popular television programs soon appeared that displaced imported programs in the Australian television schedule. In other words, American imported program played an important role in the creation of a local television production industry. The germ of this situation is there in the second television program broadcast on the opening night of regular television broadcasting on 16 September 1956. *Name That Tune* was an Australian "vernacularisation" of a game show that had first been broadcast on American television in 1953.

These features then of the Australian television situation—vigorous private commercial networks, weakened public service sector; the progressive substitution of locally produced programs for imported ones are part of a more general international and historical pattern that is repeated elsewhere in more recent times (for example, Western Europe in the 1980s). Thus there is a good deal of interest for television scholars elsewhere in the historic trajectory of Australian television both for its own sake and also for the comparative opportunities it offers for understanding developments elsewhere. Marshall McLuhan once claimed that Canadian media developments were an "early warning system" for trends that would later appear elsewhere and Richard Collins has recently embraced this claim, warning pessimistically of the possible "Canadianization" of television in Europe and elsewhere. However, the Australian experience has been at once more complex, more interest-

ing and more positive. Given the linguistic and cultural barriers at work in countries in Europe and in other parts of the world, there are strong grounds for believing that "Dallas-ization" of international television was in fact a passing phase and that the Australian experience of television, most especially that of "import substitution" is, likely to be being repeated.

Structure

Australian television broadcasting began in the 1950s (Sydney and Melbourne in 1956 and Brisbane and Adelaide in 1959) a date that links it with other "major minor" economies such as Canada, Italy and the Netherlands, whereas major economies such as the United States and the United Kingdom, Germany and Japan had all inaugurated television broadcasting in the 1930s and 1940s. The structure of the Australian television system was established in 1950 when the newly elected conservative federal government reversed the decision of the post-war socialist government that television was to be a monopoly in the hands of a public service broadcaster. Instead the 1950 decision decreed that television was to be a dual system containing a private, commercial sector as well as a public service sector. This decision could be justified on the structural grounds that Australian radio had been a dual system since 1932 when the Australian Broadcasting Commission had been established. (In point of fact the development of the Australian Broadcasting Commission [ABC] in 1932 had been intended to create a unitary, public service broadcasting system, an outcome thwarted when private, commercial broadcasters had bought out community radio licenses after they had surrendered their own licenses to the government.)

The dual system of Australian television was to remain in place from the beginning of broadcasting in 1956 until the licensing of community television stations in the most populous cities in 1992–93. This is not however, to suggest that the channel choice of viewers remained the same over this period. In 1956 viewers in the larger cities had two commercial and one public service channels to choose from. By 1964–65 there were three commercial services available. In 1980 a second public service channel went on the air while the community channel of 1992–93 signals both the advent of a third sector as well as the sixth channel in the system. In deciding on the shape of the commercial services the initial consideration was technical: how many transmitting frequencies could be made available in each centre of population? The answer generally was one, although in larger centres it was two.

Commercial television licenses were awarded to two operators in the state capitals of Sydney, Melbourne, Brisbane and Adelaide, and one in Canberra, Perth and Hobart. One commercial license was awarded in smaller cities and towns. This development occurred in several stages and followed the Development of Television Services Plan, an engineering plan devised by engineers at the broadcasting regulatory body, the Australian Broadcasting Control Board (ABCB). By 1965 nearly 80% of the country came within the net of television.

The granting of two licenses in the four most populous cities facilitated the development of networking arrangements. It also allowed for a much weaker network arrangement elsewhere. Networking in Australian commercial television between 1956 and 1987 was a combining together of local interests for the purposes of cost sharing, on program buying and program production. With newspaper companies securing major shares in several of those stations, the first metropolitan networking arrangements built on long term associations between different capital city newspapers which were already in place. Thus, for example, Frank Packer's TCN Channel 9 Sydney had links with HSV Channel 7 Melbourne from 1956 to 1960. However, Packer had ambitions to establish a television network chain, applying unsuccessfully for commercial licenses in Brisbane and in country areas of New South Wales. In 1960 he bought GTV Channel 9 in Melbourne and the Nine Network came into being. Sydney and Melbourne with some 35% of the national population were the hub of the network with Brisbane and Adelaide as satellites. The commercial stations with the designation "7" were forced into partnership but, lacking a common owner, the Seven Network (which emerged later in the decade) was always a looser association.

The Packer buyout was permitted under the two station ownership rule contained in the Broadcasting and Television Act and the Melbourne purchase highlighted the dominance of newspaper interests in Australian commercial television. Until the rule was changed in 1987, the Packer Consolidated Press group controlled TCN 9 and GTV 9, the *Herald* and *Weekly Times* group operated HSV 7 while John Fairfax and Sons controlled ATN 7. The other notable press entrant was the young Rupert Murdoch, owner of the afternoon *Adelaide News*, who in 1958 served the license for one of the first two commercial Adelaide Television stations, NWS Channel 9.

In 1953 the Royal Commission had recommended that the ABC run the public service television service. The government accepted this advice and allocated one channel to the ABC. The public sector radio broadcaster, the ABC was unaffected by these developments. Single ABC television stations began in Sydney and Melbourne in late 1956 and early 1957 respectively and other ABC stations rippled out across the country over the next nine years. Under its long-serving general manager, Sir Charles Moses, the ABC gave little thought to its new television service. By and large, it was television as an extension of radio, along lines generally pioneered by the BBC. Thus by 1964 when Moses retired, the ABC's audience share was below 10% and badly in need of a shake up.

Programs

Early television owners and executives did not give a great deal of thought to programs, concerned as they were with the capital cost of establishing and operating stations. Although several would-be licensees expressed commitment to the idea of locally produced programs both during the hearings of the Royal Commission and the License Inquiries (1955–59), their early practice did not encourage local production. Fortunately for them, the early 1950s had seen American television switch from the live production of network programs, especially drama, in New York and Chicago, to filmed production in Hollywood. By 1956 when Australian television began, there was a plentiful supply of cheap imported American programs available and these soon dominated local prime time programming on the commercial networks. Thus commercial owners and operators offset the initial establishment and operating capital costs against the relatively cheap costs of the imported material. The imported programs also subsidised the production of local programs in a variety of genres. Variety/light entertainment programs represented an important investment in the early years of Australian television and programs such as the *Johnny O'Keefe Show, In Melbourne Tonight* and the *Bobby Limb Late Show* rated extremely well in prime time. Other genres of local production included news, game shows and sporting broadcasts. There was also a small amount of drama produced in this period although, generally, it did not rate sufficiently well to justify the relatively heavy costs involved. The most interesting area of local production was however, that of television commercials. In 1960 the government issued a requirement that 100% of all commercials be locally produced. Even more than the "vernacularising" of formats and formulas, already underway in game shows and light entertainment, this protectionist measure signaled that the import substitution was underway and would shortly spread to drama.

The initial role of Australian television stations was one of both distribution/exhibition of programs. The blueprint for such a role lay in the vertically integrated structure of the Hollywood motion picture companies of the studio era. In the Australian situation, the creation of television production sound stages was necessary because the fragile Australian film production industry of the 1950s, mostly lacked such infrastructure. In addition owning these facilities would give television operators a power over advertisers that their counterparts in radio had, often to their cost, lacked.

The most notable of the stations for in-house production were ATN Channel 7 in Sydney, GTV Channel 9 in Melbourne and the ABC in those two cities. GTV Channel 9 continued with its successful *In Melbourne Tonight* until

1965. ATN persisted with in-house production until 1970, while the ABC only opened its doors to independent producers (packagers) in 1986.

Development

Television is a complex entity (economic enterprise, technology, entertainment medium, political platform, advertising vehicle and so on) and, thus, at any time in its history it is likely to show quite different features in different shapes and combinations. Thus in order to survey developments in Australian television, its particular features and details may be divided into four periods, each lasting for approximately a decade: this coincidence highlights their classificatory convenience.

In the period up to 1965, Australian television, like television in general, was bounded in part by its technology. The programs were either imported and therefore on film, put live to air or else kinescoped as a filmed record of a live broadcast. The first video recorder was imported by Channel 7 Sydney in 1958, but, until around 1965, when other stations and production companies had video playback and editing facilities, this first machine made little difference to the practice of 'live' television. A second technical feature of the period was the local or regional character of television in Australia. Until 1964 there were no cable facilities that allowed the transmission of television signals from one capital city to another. Thus the continent consisted of a series of discrete, isolated television markets that often saw different local programs, regional schedules and frequently geographically distinct commercials.

News programs, soap opera and some early teenage music programs were fifteen minutes in length, although most programs ran for half an hour. A few imported drama series, plays and variety programs were longer, running sixty or ninety minutes. The programming schedule was dominated by half-hour programs such as *The Mickey Mouse Club, The Lone Ranger, Sergeant Bilko, Hancock's Half Hour, I Love Lucy* and and others. The dominant drama genres were imported westerns, crime and situation comedies. This period was also marked by the popularity of the one-off television play. There were two kinds of play; the first, emanating from the BBC, was dominated by a West End conception of drama and theatre. It favoured theatrical works of famous British playwrights such as Shakespeare, Shaw and in the modern period, Coward and Rattigan. This model was the one adopted by ABC television. From the late 1950s it combined BBC imports with television versions of some famous Australian plays, essentially, for the latter, adapting pre-existing theatrical materials to television. The other kind of play came from U.S. television. In the early 1950s, in programs such as *The U.S. Steel Hour* and *Playhouse 90*, playwrights such as Silliphant, Chayefsky and Mosel had written a series of original social realist plays for television including *Marty, The Miracle Worker,* and *Requiem for a Heavyweight.* The *Playhouse 90* model was adopted in Australian television by ATN Channel 7 and its

partner station, first GTV Channel 9 and then HSV Channel 7, under the sponsorship of both Shell and General Motors. Notable plays written for television under the aegis of these sponsors include *Other People's Houses, Tragedy in a Temporary Town* and *Thunder of Silence.*

Current Affairs were absent from television in this early period. *Four Corners,* modeled on the BBC's *Panorama,* did not begin on the ABC until 1961. In its earliest form it was more of a newsreel or news digest program, with several items in each episode, rather than the hard-hitting investigative program it would later become. Its first producer, Bob Raymond, left the ABC in 1963 and began *Project 63* on TCN Channel 9. These programs were forerunners to the kind of current affairs television that blossomed on Australian television in the later 1960s and 1970s.

There was little in the way of locally oriented documentary films on Australian television at this time. The ABC did not establish a production facility (teams of cameramen available to news, documentary and drama), until 1959. There was, instead, especially in news, an enormous reliance on overseas material.

Any "Australian content" in this period, occurred in lower-cost production genres such as variety and quiz shows. Indeed there was a boom in local variety shows. Programs such as *In Melbourne Tonight, In Sydney Tonight, Revue 60/61, Bandstand, Six O'Clock Rock, The Bobby Limb Late Show, Tonight with Dave Allen* and the *Johnny O'Keefe Show* were important landmarks. In Brisbane and Adelaide local "tonight shows" were hosted by figures such as George Wallace Junior, Gerry Gibson and Ernie Sigley. Early successful local quiz shows included *Concentration* and *Tic-Tac-Dough,* all packaged for TCN Channel 9 by Reg Grundy.

A related feature of this period was that of switching various formats, programs and personalities that had worked well in radio across to the new medium. Australian examples included *Consider Your Verdict, Pick A Box* and *Wheel of Fortune* made successful transitions to television. There was also an attempt to move soap opera from radio to television in the late 1950s when ATN Channel 7 produced *Autumn Affair* and *The Story of Peter Gray.* These failed to find either sponsors nor audience. And although several radio personalities including Bob Dyer and Graham Kennedy moved successfully across, a notable casualty of the new medium was Jack Davey.

The local successes in variety game shows and to a lesser extent, drama, meant that, despite the overwhelming presence of American and British programs, Australian programs had a distinct place in the television schedule. It was through the presence of this variety cycle that Australian television was given a local look or flavour and developed a deliberate programming mix between overseas drama and local variety. But variety shows often had international guests, so that even if they qualified under ABCB regulations as Australian content, they had a distinctly international flavour.

The period from 1964 to 1976 was marked by a good deal of stability. The novelty of television was at an end.

Television was increasingly a national service, a part of everyday life, and increasingly—a mirror for the nation to see itself. Between 1963 and 1965 new commercial stations appeared in Sydney, Melbourne, Brisbane, Adelaide and Perth. The new stations were partly brought about by federal government's desire to introduce new players into the field of commercial television station ownership. Ansett, a major transportation group, secured the licenses of ATV 0 Melbourne and TVQ Brisbane while amalgamated wireless Australasia, a telecommunications manufacturing group, obtained the license of Ten 10 Sydney. The new stations formed themselves into the 0-10 Network, so that east coast Australia now had three commercial networks. The 0–10 Network was the weakest in terms of audience ratings—so much so that in 1973 a new federal Labor government briefly contemplated removing the licenses.

The advent of the new network meant that there was barely enough imported program material for the commercial networks and the ABC. This was an important factor in the sudden rise of local television drama production. A new drama cycle began with the unexpected success of the police series *Homicide*, which Crawford Productions in Melbourne began producing in late 1964. By the end of the 1960s there were three Crawford police series—*Homicide, Division 4* and *Matlock Police*—on the different commercial networks and a fourth local series, *Contrabandits*, on the ABC.

There are at least four significant reasons for claiming *Homicide* as the most important drama production in the history of Australian television. *Homicide* ushered in a new production system that saw the integration of indoor electronic recording and outdoor filming that has become a mainstay of local television production. It signaled that the independent packagers now had a permanent place in the Australian industry with networks now farming out production and themselves concentrating on distribution. Thirdly, *Homicide* would help create a drama production industry which in turn became the endorsement for a state supported feature film industry and fourthly *Homicide*, not least through import-substitution, would help create "a vernacular literature" of the small screen which in turn would help a new Australian nationalism.

Homicide ushered in a new look to Australian television. It presented audiences with a different, more factual, image of Australia, especially urban landscapes, than anything hitherto. The increased use of Australian film footage in news programs assisted the factual tone and the authenticity of location and detail. This *mise en scene* could be found across a wide range of locally produced television drama such as *Bellbird, You Can't See Round Corners, My Name's McGooley, The Battlers* and *Dynasty* all produced in those years and all signs of an expanding television drama production industry. These programs were made with Australian audiences in mind. Because they were in black and white and shot on an integrated basis they did not export particularly well. Thus their producers worked very much to Australian audiences in terms of the rendition of language, accents, references and visual icons.

However, the popularity of local drama series resulted in an equally dramatic downturn in variety programs. From 1965 variety production effectively ceased in Brisbane, Adelaide and Perth. Fewer shows came out of Sydney and Melbourne and Graham Kennedy and Bobby Limb, the biggest stars in the variety cycle, were seen infrequently.

The development of a "vernacular literature" was not confined to drama but also occurred in current affairs and documentary. The importance of current affairs and documentary television increased markedly also. After a shaky start, the weekly *Four Corners* settled down to a new kind of investigative journalism. In 1967 the ABC started the daily current affairs *This Day Tonight (TDT)*, modeled on the BBC series *Today Tonight*. The program had a hard-hitting journalistic drive that examined political and social issues in ways never imagined by earlier programs. It was a very big success for the ABC and markedly improved its ratings performance.

TDT and *Four Corners* were enormously influential in extending the range of current affairs television, on the ABC and commercial stations. In the 1970s many ABC journalists and reporters, of whom Mike Willesee was the most famous, would move to current affairs programs on commercial stations. This takeup of current affairs is one of the few instances where, contrary to the ABC's claims, the ABC has actually influenced commercial television in Australia. Documentary series also brought the life of the nation within their scope. The ABC's *Chequerboard* introduced *cinema verite* into Australian television, significantly expanding the range of social concerns and issues that could be examined in the medium of television. A second documentary series, *A Big Country* also enlarged the audience's sense of what constituted the nation.

However, one program, the family series *Skippy*, anticipates the next stage of Australian television. *Skippy* was produced in colour on film and featured a bush kangaroo. The program included familiar international icons of Australia including beaches, bush and fauna and was consciously made with exports in mind. In the event the program did enormously well and pointed out the international sales opportunity for Australian programs.

With the rise in popularity of Australian programs there was a shift in the economies of local commercial television. Earlier cheap television imports subsidised the capitalisation, equipping and maintenance of new stations; they now allowed the commercial stations and networks to underwrite the cost of local productions. It was on the basis of their Australian programs that the commercial stations rose or fell in the ratings.

The state, through the ABC played a part in securing the place of Australian content on television in this period. The first content regulations (effective from 1956 to the early 1960s) required stations to, whenever possible, employ Australians for the production and transmission of programs. But this regulation was too general to be enforceable; as imported programs were pre-recorded it was irrelevant. In 1965 the ABCB introduced a quota system for Australian content. Stations were required to screen three hours per week of Australian content in prime time. A precedent for the program quota had been set by the ABCB 1960 requirement whereby all television commercials had to be Australian.

Three hours a week was a fairly limited quota which the commercial stations had little difficulty in meeting. The quota rose slowly throughout the rest of the 1960s. In 1972 it stood at ten hours per week during prime time. In 1973 the ABCB introduced a "points system", which still operated on a quota basis but attempted to discriminate in favour of more expensive program forms such as drama. However, these measures did not cause the big upsurge in Australian television production that began in 1965. They did though set a minimum threshold for the scheduling of local productions, below which commercial stations could not fall. In other words, the quota and points system helped guarantee at least part of the market for Australian producers.

While the commercial television stations between 1964 and 1972 switched to using independent production packagers, the ABC continued its in-house production. However, with the retirement of Sir Charles Moses in 1965 and following comparable moves some years earlier at the BBC, a major restructuring of ABC television and radio took place. Television drama severed many of its links with the Australian theatre. Following a BBC example, the ABC Drama Department was organised into three strands—series, serials and plays. The series strand produced several successful series including *Contrabandits* and *Delta*. The success of British soap operas, most especially *Coronation Street*, also struck a chord with the ABC. By 1967, the serial strand had initiated *Bellbird*, an ongoing serial set in a rural Australian town and the most successful serial to play on Australian television up to that point. It ran for more than 10 years. In 1973 it was joined by another ongoing serial, produced by the ABC in Sydney, *Certain Women*. The play strand was of lesser importance. It was most active in the late 1960s when it produced several successful seasons of *Australian Playhouse*, an anthology series of one-off hour and half-hour plays written for television.

The range of viewer choice was extended between 1976 and 1986 with the advent of new services and technologies. A new network, the Special Broadcasting Services (SBS) came on the air in 1980, at first serving only Sydney and Melbourne but gradually spreading to the other capital cities. SBS Television was designed to increase the media services available to ethnic Australians and it did this with multilingual programming. But SBS, with developing strengths in the areas of news, current affairs, documentary and foreign films, also appealed to English-language viewers. As a second public service television broadcaster, it considerably extended the range of choice of traditional ABC viewers, giving them an option to the ABC just as commercial viewers had been given an option to the Nine and Seven Networks in the mid 1960s.

This extra choice was fortuitous as the fortunes of the ABC declined between 1976 and 1986. Its operating budget suffered constant government pruning from 1975 onwards, and the national broadcaster steadily lost staff, program ideas and ratings to the commercial networks. In 1983 the ABC was reconstituted as a corporation following the passage of a new act through the federal parliament but these moves did little to arrest this process of decline. The output of ABC TV Drama suffered badly during this period, falling to as low as 40 hours total output in 1984–85. Despite this downturn, the ABC did produce some notable work including *Power Without Glory, Spring and Fall, Scales of Justice* and *Sweet and Sour.*

If things were gloomy at the ABC, commercial television was booming. The other major move at this time was the reinvigoration of the Ten Network thanks to Rupert Murdoch's News Limited purchase of ATV Channel 0 Melbourne in 1978, and Ten Channel 10 Sydney in 1979. Determined to increase the network's ratings, Murdoch increased Ten's program budget considerably. The network programmed heavily in the area of miniseries and feature films. Many fine miniseries—including *Water Under the Bridge, The Dismissal, Waterfront, Return to Eden,* and *Vietnam*—were produced for Ten, which helped push the network ahead of Nine and Seven in the ratings.

A more dramatic technological change was the introduction of colour transmission in 1975. Colour proved a boon for the commercial networks. Advertisers were eager to show their products in colour and station finances rose considerably. Viewers also obtained what was, in effect, a movie channel with the advent of the domestic VCR and the mushrooming availability of feature films on video. The video boom from 1980 to 1985 offered viewers an alternative to broadcast television and constituted a sixth channel in cities such as Sydney and Melbourne and a third channel in regional Australia. It also offered viewers an alternative relationship with broadcast television by making it possible to time shift, zap commercials and store programs. A related, and, as far as networks and advertisers were concerned, equally pernicious technology was the television/radio remote control, which first appeared in 1980. The control enabled viewers to flip channels, and avoid commercials.

The period also saw a new regulatory regime with the abolition in 1976 of the ABCB and its replacement by the Australian Broadcasting Tribunal (ABT). The ABCB had been an advisory body but the ABT was given the power to award radio and television licenses after a public enquiry. This feature, together with the early recognition of the right of public groups to be part of the licensing process represented a community-based broadcasting policy on the part of the government. However, the ABT also moved towards industry deregulation by giving commercial licensees control of such areas as program standards and advertising standards and scheduling. Although the stations were meant to be publicly accountable for their actions, in practice they were not. Australian content levels remained regulated under the points system although stations lobbied vigorously to be allowed to set their own content levels. One other gain for program-makers and audience was the introduction by the ABT of the C classification for children's programs in 1978 and a C quota in 1984.

Following developments in America, Australian television in the mid to late 1970s saw the emergence of two new dramatic forms owing much to the cinema. The first Australian telemovie, a television program with the running time of a feature film, was produced in 1976 with the film *Polly My Love*. The miniseries, a consecutive narrative intended for screening in large time blocks over a short period, came to television in 1978 with *Against the Wind*. The telemovie and miniseries considerably extended the scheduling possibilities of television: series pilots could be screened in one or other form, while features could be reconstituted as mini-series.

By the early 1980s Australian film producers as various as Paul Barron, McElroy and McElroy, and Kennedy-Miller had all moved into television, although without relinquishing their commitment to cinema. After the collapse of the Australian period feature film at the box office, producers found television to be secure financially. They could pre-sell the latter programs to the Australian television networks, thereby considerably diminishing the overall financial risks in their production operation.

The cinematisation also meant that television was now a textually worthy object. Whereas in the 1960s and 1970s, Australian television had been subjected to cautious attention by psychologists and social scientists such as R.J. Thompson, David Martin and Fred Emery, who were anxious to gauge its possibly harmful audience effects, now media researchers such as Stuart Cunningham, John Fiske and John Tulloch celebrated the textual sophistications of Australian television, especially the miniseries.

These structural changes did much to foster drama production particularly in the areas of the serial, the miniseries and children's drama. Although drama serials had proved their ratings worth on commercial television from as early as 1972 with the success of *Number 96*, it was from 1976 that serials became part of the backbone of the program schedule. Serials such as *The Sullivans*, *The Restless Years*, *Prisoner*, *A Country Practice*, *Sons and Daughters* and *The Flying Doctors* ensured a solid audience for the networks other programs. Starting around 1982, and drawing in part on the recent international success of Australian cinema, Australian television programs, including serials, began to sell particularly well overseas. The move to colour substantially increased television's international sales opportunities as did the Australian stockpiling of episodes. When *The Young Doctors,* for example, went on sale internationally in 1983, Grundy had over 1,000 half-hour episodes on offer.

The richest crop in these golden years of Australian television drama lay in the miniseries. After the American and international success of *Roots*, Australian networks and producers made the miniseries a permanent feature in their schedule. Between 1978 and 1987 more than 100 miniseries ranging in running time from four to 13 hours were produced locally. The miniseries as special event television was one important counter to the lure of the VCR, and several miniseries—such as *The Dismissal* and *Bodyline*—pulled very large audiences for the duration of their screening. Notable miniseries include *Vietnam, Return to Eden, The Timeless Land, A Town Like Alice* and *The Great Bookie Robbery.* The miniseries, and, to a lesser extent, the telemovie, were also an important stage in increasing the power of packagers vis-à-vis the networks. Piggybacking on the generous tax concessions, introduced in by government in 1981 to bolster a faltering feature film production industry, the packagers found that they could make deals for the international sale of their products. Initially these sales were secondary to Australian sales but from 1985 on, they were more important. This "internationalisation" of the Australian miniseries could be seen in the shift away from Australian historical situations, issues and figures to more contemporary dramas, frequently located off-shore, and including figures from various nations.

Children's series also blossomed in this general upswing of drama which had previously mostly been the domain of the ABC. The C classification and quota had the effect of making this area more financially attractive for producers than it had once been. Among producers who partially or completely specialised in this area were the Tasmanian Film Corporation, Barron Films, the Australian Children's Television Foundation and Revcom. Many entertaining series for children and young people were produced including particularly innovative work such as *Home, Sweet and Sour,* and *Dancing Daze.* With general international shortage of good children's material, this drama exported particularly well.

In 1987 the federal government made a series of important amendments to the Broadcasting and Television Act. Under the new rules, cross-ownership among the different media sectors (print, radio, television and film) was forbidden. The two-station rule was abandoned in favour of limits based on total audience size. Regional commercial television, a loose "network" of single stations that enjoyed a commercial monopoly in their local area, was also re-organised and under the title of "equalisation", capital city television networking was extended into rural Australia. Thus over 90% of the Australian population now gradually came within reach of the three capital city commercial networks. Divestiture and the extension of networking would, it was hoped, bring new players into commercial television. Such hopes were soon realised with all three networks being sold in 1987—Nine to the Bond Corporation, Seven to Qintex and Ten to Northern Star. However, unable to meet their bank interest charges, all of the new owners lost control of their networks in 1990. The Nine Network returned to the control of Kerry Packer while the other two networks were in the hands of the banks. By 1994-95 Rupert Murdoch and Telecom, the Australian telecommunications carrier, had bought 20% shares in the Seven network, seeking to add broadcast television to their Asian satellite ventures. If television was once perceived as a license to print money, it was no longer the case. Instead it was clear that it would be some time before commercial television might again be a solidly prosperous sector of the media.

Although the networks claimed that their audience had remained mostly intact despite the VCR boom, nevertheless the advent of remote controls for VCRs and television sets led advertisers to look at some other advertising media, including direct mail. The stock market crash of October 1987 and the recession of the late 1980s caused a contraction in advertising budgets. In addition, the advent of people metres in 1991 indicated to advertisers that the television audience was far more mobile in shifting programs and channels than the diary method of gathering audience information had suggested.

The first AUSSAT satellite had been launched in 1986. Although much of its capacity was set aside for telecommunications, the satellite did symbolise the possibility of satellite delivered pay TV. After a protracted series of inquiries, ministerial statements, recommendations and policy changes, pay TV began as a new six channel service in Sydney and Melbourne in 1994.

The ABC also underwent upheaval after 1987. It had become a corporation in 1983 but even under a new administration its budgets still declined. In 1986–87 the new Head of TV Drama, decided, in line with the general moves by the national broadcaster towards corporatism, to farm out much of ABC's television drama requirements to independent or overseas packagers. Thus the ABC now makes little drama in-house, but is in the business of co-productions, supplying production facilities as its contribution to the making of miniseries, series and telefilm. In return for this investment the ABC secures rights to the Australian screening of the program. The packaging partner secures rights to the overseas distribution.

The wind-down of the generous tax concession in 1986 and the economic crises of the networks in 1989 also reduced drama and documentary. Producers increasingly target overseas market for finance and distribution with some companies such as Grundy, Kennedy-Miller and Beyond International relocating their headquarters off-shore. Such moves are indicative both of the internationalisation of markets as well as the continued depression of the Australian television program market. Indeed with production levels in the industry back to what they were around 1965, Australian television was witnessing the development of "underdevelopment".

The final feature of the present era in Australian television has been the creation of a new bureaucratic environment with the replacement of the ABT by the Australian Broadcasting Authority in 1992 and the creation of a new broadcasting bill, the Broadcast Services Act also in 1992. The two measures signified government commitment both to managerialism, new technology and liberal economic doctrines. The measures considerably lessened "public interest" as a factor in broadcasting policy and instead made technological innovation and economic viability of operators the most important criteria in the new broadcasting environment.

In summary then certain key features in the structure and development of Australian television are worth reiterating. Australia has in the past been relatively slow to innovate various technologies associated with television including the broadcast service itself, colour transmission and multi-channel pay services. Nevertheless despite these time-lags, the system has exhibited a "historical modernity" in terms of its dual sections, weak public service and strong independent commercial. Import substitution has occurred leading to a vigorous television production industry which by the 1980s became a significant export earner. In the process the system spawned a number of successful companies and groups such as Packer, Murdoch's News Limited and the Grundy Organisation which are important players not only by local but also by international standards. In recent years Australian television has been increasingly internationalised at a series of levels including ownership, program content and technology. This has also been a period of upheaval and transition and is still without an end in sight.

In 1987 the Australian Broadcasting Tribunal was abolished and the Broadcasting Services Act was introduced. The Australian Broadcasting Authority, introduced in 1992, heralded the beginning of a new regulatory era.

—Albert Moran

FURTHER READING

Agardy, Susanna, and David Bednall. *Television and the Public: National Television Standards Survey.* Melbourne: Australian Broadcasting Tribunal, 1982.

Beck, Christopher, editor. *On Air: 25 Years of TV in Queensland.* Brisbane, Australia: One Tree Hill Publishing, 1984.

Beilby, Peter, editor. *Australian TV: The First 25 Years.* Melbourne: Nelson, 1981.

Bell, Philip, with others. *Programmed Politics: A Study of Australian Television.* Sydney: Sable, 1982.

Brown, Allan. "The Economics of Television Regulation: A Survey with Application to Australia." *Economic Record* (Melbourne), December 1992.

Collins, Richard. "National Broadcasting and the International Market: Developments in Australian Broadcasting Policy." *Media, Culture and Society* (London), January 1994.

Cunningham, Stuart, and Toby Miller, with David Rowe. *Contemporary Australian Television.* Sydney: University of New South Wales Press, 1994.

Hall, Sandra. *Supertoy: 20 Years of Australian Television.* Melbourne: Sun Books, 1976.

An Inquiry into Australian Content on Commercial Television. Sydney: Australian Broadcasting Tribunal 1991–1992.

Jacka, Elizabeth. *The ABC of Television Drama.* Sydney: Australian Film, Television and Radio School, 1991.

Johnson, Nicholas, and Mark Armstrong. *Two Reflections on Australian Broadcasting.* Bundoora, Victoria, Australia:

Centre for the Study of Educational Communication and Media, La Trobe University, 1977.

MacCallum, Mungo, editor. *Ten Years of Television.* Melbourne: Sun Books, 1968.

Moran, Albert. *Images and Industry: Television Drama Production in Australia.* Sydney: Currency Press, 1985.

———. *Moran's Guide to Australian TV Series.* Sydney: Australian Film, Television and Radio School, 1993.

O'Regan, Tom. *Australian Television Culture.* St. Leonards, New South Wales: Allen and Unwin, 1993.

———, with others. *The Moving Image: Film and Television in Western Australia, 1896–1985.* History and Film Association of Australia, 1985.

Seymour-Ure, Collin. "Prime Ministers' Reactions to Television: Britain, Australia, and Canada." *Media, Culture and Society* (London), July 1989.

Tulloch, John, and Graeme Turner. editors. *Australian Television: Programs, Pleasures and Politics.* Sydney and Boston, Massachusetts: Allen and Unwin, 1989.

TV 2000: Choices and Challenges. (Report of the Proceedings of the Australian Broadcasting Tribunal Conference Held at the Hilton Hotel, Sydney, 16-17 November, 1989.) Sydney: ABC Tribunal Conference, 1990.

See also Australian Production Companies; Australian Programming

AUSTRALIAN PRODUCTION COMPANIES

The leading Australian television production companies in the 1990s are the Australian Broadcasting Corporation (ABC), the Grundy Organisation, Village Roadshow and Roadshow, Coote and Carroll, Crawfords, the Beyond International Group, Southern Star, Film Australia, the Seven Network, and the Australian Children's Television Foundation. Other production concerns, such as Yoram Gross Film Studios, JNP, and Gannon Television, are more closely associated with one successful series and/or a set of spin-offs.

The Australian Broadcasting Corporation (ABC)

As Australia's main public service broadcaster, the ABC has always played a leading role in local program production, and is arguably the single most significant force in Australia in one-off television drama, in documentary, in nature programming and even, perhaps, in children's programming.

The ABC was virtually unrivalled in any category of drama until the mid-1970s. The period from 1968 until 1975 is often referred to as the "golden era" of the ABC, the time of long-running and popular series or acclaimed miniseries like *Bellbird, Contrabandits, Certain Women, Rush, Marion, Ben Hall* and *Power Without Glory.* Until the late 1980s, the ABC, like other public broadcasters around the world, was a vertically integrated producer-broadcaster. With the exception of a few co-productions, mainly with the BBC, all its production was initiated, financed and produced in-house. In the 1980s *Patrol Boat, 1915, Spring and Fall, Scales of Justice, Palace of Dreams* and *Sweet and Sour* broke new ground in Australian television drama and provided an arena for trying out new writers and attempts at formal or conceptual innovation. Innovative comedy, such as *Mother and Son,* strong investigative journalism, such as the weekly current affairs program, *Four Corners* (in production since 1961), and quality drama, continue to attract critical and audience approval.

In 1986, after a period of confusion and demoralization in the wake of a major review—the Dix Report—in the early 1980s, the ABC head of drama, Sandra Levy, initiated a "revival" in network drama content, the aim of which was to increase output to at least 100 hours a year. A decision was made to move more towards the "popular" end of the drama spectrum and away from what was seen as more esoteric, eccentric or specialised. At the same time, it was decided that the way to get quantity, quality and spread was by concentrating on a mixture of long-running series and miniseries and by eschewing one-offs which are too expensive when related to the audience they are likely to attract. And finally, it was also decided that the only way to increase drama hours was by entering into co-production arrangements with local producers who could raise cash from the "10BA" tax relief scheme and other government assistance schemes and from overseas presales, with the ABC contributing facilities and technical staff and as little cash as possible.

This strategy was immediately successful at least in quantity and audience terms. Close to 100 hours was achieved by 1988 and there was an immediate improvement in the ratings for miniseries and series, notably, in the latter category, the prime-time medical soap *GP.*

In the period 1988–91 a large number of prestigious miniseries were produced and broadcast; all were co-produced with local and overseas partners. Titles from this period include: *Act of Betrayal* (with TVS), *A Dangerous Life* (with HBO in the United States and Zenith in the United Kingdom), *Eden's Lost* (with Central TV), *The Leaving of Liverpool* (with the BBC), *The Paper Man* (with Granada). It is also the period when *GP* began to be sold to a number of overseas buyers although it has never achieved a large success in foreign markets. And the ABC's most successful situation comedy, both domestically and overseas, *Mother and Son,* was also sold during this period.

Since 1992 the possibilities for financing programs in the British market have diminished and the ABC has begun to swing back towards the production of programs fully financed in-house. Examples are *Phoenix I* and *II, Seven*

Deadly Sins, The Damnation of Harvey McHugh, Heartland and *Janus*. Amongst miniseries in-house titles are *Come in Spinner* and *True Believers*, whereas other parties hold the major rights to around 20 titles, including *Bodysurfer, Brides of Christ, Children of the Dragon, Frankie's House* and *The Leaving of Liverpool*, most of which were co-produced with U.K. partners.

The Grundy Organisation

Although it was bought in 1995 by the U.K. publishing and media conglomerate Pearsons, the history of the Grundy organisation is predominantly Australian and its Australian operations remain the single biggest national contribution to its overall activities. The history of Grundys is of a radio game show producer in the 1950s which transformed into a television game show producer for the local market during the 1960s. The 1970s brought considerable expansion as a local drama producer along with the consolidation of its reputation as a leader in light entertainment.

Without maintaining any particular link to any one network, Grundys has built up a substantial catalogue of game shows like *Celebrity Squares, Wheel of Fortune, Family Feud, Price Is Right, Blankety Blanks* and *Sale of the Century* (now in its fifteenth year of production) as well as highly successful drama programs like *Young Doctors, Number 96, The Restless Years, Prisoner, Sons and Daughters* and its flag-ship soap, which celebrated ten years of production in 1994, *Neighbours*.

Grundys experienced a breakthrough success with *Neighbours* both in Australia and in Britain from the mid-1980s. While that platform was the base on which a number of Grundys and other Australian serials and series were sold into the British market, it also was the impetus to develop the key globalising strategy which Reg Grundy, founder and chairman, dubbed "parochial internationalism." Grundys sets up wholly-owned local production companies to make programs that feature local people and are made by local Grundy staff who are nationals of the country in which the program is made.

By the mid-1990s, Grundys was producing about 50 hours of television a week worldwide. It sells into over 70 countries worldwide, employs around 1200 people in production and administration functions, and claims to be the second largest television light entertainment producer in the world, and, until its takeover by Pearson, one of the world's largest independent production organisations. While Europe as a whole generates more production throughput for the organisation, Australia remains the largest single country for production operations.

Criticisms levelled at Grundys have included that they have remained committed to innocuous formats (games and quiz) and safe drama renditions. However, programs like *Prisoner* and the New Zealand soap opera *Shortland Street* were risky and innovative for their time and places of production, while a program like *Man O Man* represents an equally risky strategy in light entertainment.

Village Roadshow and Roadshow, Coote and Carroll

The Village Roadshow group of companies has been unique in Australia. First established in the 1950s as a drive-in theater operator, it is now the only completely integrated audiovisual entertainment company, having involvement in studio management, production of both film and television, film distribution and exhibition, television distribution, video distribution and movie theme park management. The conglomerate is also moving into multimedia development and exhibition holdings in south east Asia. Its approach to internationalisation is also unique in that the main thrust of its strategy is to attract offshore productions to its Warner Roadshow Movieworld Studios near the Gold Coast in southeast Queensland.

The studios were kicked off in 1988–89 by housing two off-shore television productions for the Hollywood studio Paramount. These were *Dolphin Bay* and *Mission: Impossible*. It is estimated that an hour of series drama can be made here at a cost about 30% lower than a comparable hour made in Hollywood.

Since 1989, the studio has attracted part or whole production of several feature films, a mixture of Australian and overseas productions, including *The Delinquents, Blood Oath, Until the End of the World* and *Fortress*. It has also hosted a number of U.S. series, most of which haven't been shown in Australia, including *Animal Park, Savage Sea* and a new production of *Skippy*. In 1992–93 it housed the major U.S. series *Time Trax*, which, unlike *Mission: Impossible,* used a considerable number of Australian creative personnel, including directors and post-production people. It is, how-ever, conceived, scripted in and entirely controlled from Hollywood.

Until 1995, Village Roadshow had a satellite produc-tion company, Roadshow Coote and Carroll (RCC), an outstanding boutique producer of mid-range budget televi-sion such as *GP* and *Brides of Christ*. RCC has been critically and culturally successful both locally and internationally, but it was not economically significant in the context of the whole conglomerate. This is because the huge investment in the studios depends totally on the success of Village Road-show Pictures in attracting production to them. RCC is a very small organisation with very little fixed infrastructure and finally broke away from the parent company in 1995 so that its principal Matt Carroll could pursue wholly indepen-dent projects.

The strategy, scale and philosophy of RCC were at the opposite end of the spectrum from its parent company. Founded in 1984, it has chalked up an impressive list of television drama—*True Believers, Barlow and Chambers: A Long Way From Home, The Paper Man, Brides of Christ* and *Frankie's House*, as well as the long running ABC series *GP*. Many of its projects have been co-produced with the ABC. It is a marriage made in heaven: the expertise of RCC combined with the reputation of the facilities-rich ABC.

RCC's bigger budget productions which cost about A$1.2 million an hour were typically financed one quarter through Australian presale (usually the ABC), one quarter FFC investment, one third U.K. presale, and about one sixth other investors (including the ABC).

Brides of Christ exemplifies this. It rated 30 in Australia making it, in ratings terms, the most successful drama ever broadcast by the ABC. The repeats did almost as well (it had a third run on the Ten network) and it sold well on video. It also received uniform critical approval. In the United Kingdom, it also rated extremely well on Channel 4, gaining an audience of 6 million. Apart from Brenda Fricker (and an Irish orchestra playing the soundtrack music), all other aspects of the program were Australian. While its theme and mode of telling remained unambiguously Australian and the idiom and cultural feel of it were very local, its story of moral upheavals in the Catholic Church in the 1960s, set against the wider changes that were occurring, was recognisable enough in other places for it to gain wide acceptance internationally.

Brides of Christ, however, was an expensive miniseries set up when the European television market was still buoyant. The changed European environment has since meant that RCC now orients itself towards cheaper 13, 26 and 39 part series. While continuing with *GP*, they also developed *Law of the Land* for the Nine Network.

Crawfords

With a track record of more than 50 years, Crawfords is one of the oldest production companies in Australia, and in its time, the most respected. Before starting in television in 1954, it was Australia's most important producer of radio serials.

In the first 30 years of its existence as a television production company, Crawfords occupied a central place in Australian television. It pioneered popular police shows like *Homicide, Division 4, Matlock Police* in the 1960s and early 1970s; it made an early entry into soap opera with the long-running serial, *The Box* (1974); in 1976 it innovated again with the second world war serial, *The Sullivans*, which ran for 520 episodes and raised long-form drama to new heights of production values and cultural authenticity; and Crawfords was one of the earliest production companies to see the potential of 10BA as a vehicle for high quality miniseries with *All the Rivers Run* (1982). The company sailed through the early to mid-1980s on the back of productions like the glamorous *Carson's Law* and *Cop Shop*, another successful police serial, and further 10BA miniseries. Much of the Crawfords catalogue has great staying power; for example, both *The Sullivans* and *All the Rivers Run* continue to perform well around the world.

The company has always had its own extensive production facilities, unlike many a newer production company. In the more postfordist times that came in the late 1980s, the necessity to keep the facilities occupied became something of an albatross for Crawfords and recent further investment in new studios may have been ill-advised given the constant pressure of keeping the existing facilities occupied. This was

the height of the company's prosperity of recent times; *The Flying Doctors* was making excellent overseas sales (it was voted most popular drama in the Netherlands in 1992) and the Crawfords catalogue had been sold to the Kirch Group and to other territories with a view to the company diversifying into co-productions with overseas partners, game shows, sitcoms and telemovies.

The results of this strategy include the popular and ground-breaking multicultural sitcom, *Acropolis Now*, the game show *Cluedo*, produced in association with Zenith Productions of the United Kingdom; a co-produced package of six telemovies, called *The Feds*, with pre-sales to the Nine Network, TVNZ and a U.K. distribution guarantee; and the children's series, *Halfway Across the Galaxy and Turn Left*, a 1991 co-production with one of the Kirch subsidiaries, Beta-Taurus. The series became one of the most popular children's television programs on British television.

Despite the success of some of these programs, the cancellation of *The Flying Doctors* by the Nine Network in 1992, when it was still doing well in overseas markets, was a severe blow. It had a temporary stay of execution in 1993 when Crawfords were given a chance to revamp it as *RFDS* (for Royal Flying Doctor Service). The changes, though thoroughgoing, were not enough to save it, and without the fallback of "volume television" like that produced by Grundys, the viability of Crawfords has been questioned, at least temporarily.

The Beyond International Group

A young company among leading Australian television producers, the Beyond International Group (BIG) began in 1984 when the public service broadcaster, the ABC, axed *Towards 2000*, a four-year-old popular science and technology program, because it was becoming too expensive. An independent production company was set up and the new program, *Beyond 2000* was sold to the Seven Network in 1984 and then the Ten Network in 1993.

Beyond has progressed into a highly focused boutique production and distribution house whose corporate portfolio also includes merchandising, music publishing, corporate video and separate media production groups in the United States and New Zealand. It is a public unlisted company with approximately 200 employees, almost half of whom work on the production of *Beyond 2000*. Its international profile is by necessity as well as design. They concentrate on combining a training in solid craft skills and serious information programming with entrepreneurial ambition.

From the mid-1980s, what became Beyond International produced in differing formats, participated in international co-productions and became involved in distribution domestically and internationally, but its resounding success is the *Beyond 2000* format which, since 1985, has been sold in over 90 countries, has been dubbed in 10 languages and has an international audience reach of 50 million.

BIG has also involved itself in predominantly European co-production partnerships. In 1989, Beyond and the BBC embarked upon the co-produced *Climate in Crisis* and then the four part series *Great Wall of Iron*, a documentary about the Chinese military. Beyond has also ventured into the production of drama series, miniseries and children's programming, with somewhat less success. The children's series *Bright Sparks* typifies the Beyond International strategy—animated robots take journeys around the world exploring science and technology. *Chances*, an adult drama series featuring nudity and outlandish storylines, was a failure. Its forays into local feature filmmaking virtually began and ceased with *The Crossing* in 1989. The failure of this film led the company to emphasise the more stable activity of distribution, and the distribution arm which began operation in 1990 became, along with Southern Star Distribution, one of two significant Australia-owned independent international distributors.

Southern Star

Southern Star is a lean, diversified operation with an integrated approach to production and distribution through film, television and video, and merchandising. Like most front-running independents, this enables Southern Star to balance higher against lower risk ventures. After a management buyout of the Taft-Hardie Group (whose major shareholders included the Great American Broadcasting Co. and James Hardie Industries) in 1988 by Neil Balnaves, Southern Star reorganised into six operating units including a distribution arm; a Los Angeles-based animation unit responsible for programs such as *Berenstein Bears* and *Peter Pan and the Pirates* made for the FOX Network; a video and audio tape duplication division; a merchandising arm handling BBC, Colombia Tri-Star and Paramount material; and a home video division.

Southern Star Entertainment is a broad corporate umbrella for established independent producers: Errol Sullivan/Southern Star Sullivan, Hal McElroy/Southern Star McElroy and Sandra Levy and John Edwards/Southern Star Xanadu. The production arms run as partnerships with Southern Star meeting all running costs, producer and staff salaries, finance and administration as well as publicity. McElroy and McElroy's *Last Frontier* (1986) was a model for programs that travelled internationally and promoted growth across the company through video release and a 22-hour series spin-off.

A good deal of Southern Star's major co-productions have been with the ABC and the BBC, including *Four Minute Mile* (1988), *Children of the Dragon* (1991) and *Police Rescue* (1990). The *Police Rescue* pilot was originally made for the BBC. The program is a co-production between Southern Star Xanadu and the ABC, with pre-sale to the BBC, who makes a substantial contribution to the current $7 million budget. For their initial financial contribution to the series in 1990, the BBC maintained script, director and cast control. The program is driven by its ongoing success in Australia and its success has been built on a recognised format, a variation of the cop show, but with a 1990s balance between action and personal storylining, that

showcases the natural and built environment of Sydney, and the star profile of Gary Sweet.

In 1993 the Southern Star Group was responsible for a new successful long-running series, *Blue Heelers*, set around a country police station in Victoria. The general feel of the program is very much *A Country Practice* revisited and this seems to be succeeding with audiences all over again and it is in 1994 the highest rating Australian drama across all channels.

Film Australia

Currently a government-owned enterprise which is expected to generate up to two thirds of its own revenue, Film Australia started life in 1911 as a production unit within the Federal Government, before becoming a government-owned film production company in 1945. In the period after 1945 it nurtured the documentary tradition, and a significant number of film-makers who went on the play important roles in the film and television industries, were trained there. In 1976 the Commonwealth Film Unit became a branch of the Australian Film Commission and took on its present name, Film Australia. In 1987, it was made a government-owned business enterprise working under the stricture to become partly self-sufficient from government.

The mission to produce films and programs "in the national interest" continues and this is represented by the government's continuing to fund Film Australia under the so-called National Interest Program (NIP). This program is the core of Film Australia's business, and the reason for it being a government owned company. Both *Mini-Dragons* and *The Race to Save the Planet* used NIP money.

Outside of NIP projects, *The Girl From Tomorrow*, a fantasy science fiction children's series, is one of Film Australia's most successful exports and many countries which bought it also bought the sequel, *Tomorrow's End*. The pre-school children's series *Johnson and Friends* has sold exceptionally well and in addition has become an international marketing phenomenon. Film Australia also does well with the nature programs like *Koalas – The Bare Facts,* and the series *Great National Parks*. Other good sales have come from documentaries with an environmental or scientific angle like *After the Warming, The Loneliest Mountain, Mini-Dragons* and *Roads to Xanadu*.

Teachers of the World was a 1992 seven-part documentary series which dealt with the life of a teacher in each of the contributing countries, Australia, Canada, the United States, Korea and Poland. As a result of the *Teachers of the World* co-production, some of the partners came together again to produce a special documentary series called *Family* to celebrate the Year of the Family in 1994.

Film Australia's success lies in part in its specialisation in those program categories with greatest international currency—nature, environmental and science documentaries and children's programming—and it has had the foresight to focus on the burgeoning markets of Asia with product that doesn't confront too many cultural hurdles. In addition it is blessed with good facilities and the safety net of government funding.

The Seven Network

The Seven and Nine Networks were the two original commercial broadcasters in Australia and until the late 1980s enjoyed stable ownership and management, which allowed them to build up a high degree of programming expertise and audience loyalty. One of Seven's greatest strengths has been its commitment to drama, whereas the Nine Network has been stronger in news and current affairs and sport, which are far less internationally tradeable.

With its traditional emphasis on drama, the Seven Network was well positioned to take advantage of 10BA and during the 1980s produced a number of high quality miniseries with local and overseas partners. Series and serials sold by Seven on behalf of itself and the independent producers involved include *Rafferty's Rules*, *Skirts* and *A Country Practice*. Some of the programs from the 1980s which were sold that way (and which still sell today) were *Land of Hope* and *The Fremantle Conspiracy*, *Jackaroo*, *Sword of Honour* and *Melba*.

Two of the most successful programs of the early 1990s were *Home and Away* (still in production after seven years) and *Hey Dad* (which ran for seven years until 1994). The first is produced in-house by the Seven Network, the second produced by Gary Reilly and Associates and sold jointly by them and the Network through RPTA.

Home and Away was developed in-house as an immediate response to the success of *Neighbours* on the Ten Network. Ironically the latter had originally begun on Seven in 1985 but after indifferent ratings they let it go. When it achieved such success on Ten, Seven realised the potential for youth-oriented soap. *Home and Away* has gone on to achieve great popularity in both Australia, where it outrates its rival *Neighbours*, and in the United Kingdom, where in 1994 it was achieving audiences of 12 million for ITV versus 14 million for *Neighbours*.

By the mid 1990s, the Seven Network seemed well positioned to continue its strong record in commissioning and producing programs with strong export potential. The free-to-air service is flourishing, and Seven is exploring new markets in Asia and Eastern Europe which, while not lucrative in the short term, have great potential in the future. Seven is also exploring pay television and other broadband services and it is safe to predict that it will remain a force in the Australian entertainment industry at the turn of the millennium.

Children's Television Producers

Australia is a significant player in world children's television. Most major children's programs made in Australia recently have enjoyed international sales success and critical acclaim for Australian programs is a regular occurrence.

The structure of regulation and production in Australia for children has strengths which in some respects are unmatched elsewhere in the world. Within the general liberalisation of broadcasting regulation seen in the Broadcasting Services Act 1992, the only mandated regulations that continued from the old ABT were those for Australian content and children, so that in the new regime, the most detailed imposed regulations pertain to children.

The Australian Children's Television Foundation (ACTF) dominates the field of Australian children's television. A body established as a result of both federal and Victorian government support and incorporated in 1982, the ACTF produces, commissions and distributes children's television programming as well as acting as a kind of think-tank and clearing house for children's television advocacy. ACTF has produced more than 115 hours of programming which has been screened in more than 90 countries, and it has received many international awards. *Lift Off*, *Round the Twist* and *Round the Twist 2* were all high-profile ACTF series which were very popular in the United Kingdom and *Sky Traders* has sold into a diverse range of territories.

Western Australia-based Barron Films concentrates on quality children/family television series as well as social realist films and adult television drama, having made *Falcon Island*, *Clowning Around,* and *Ship to Shore*. Yoram Gross Film Studios, an established specialist producer of animated children's films, has crossed successfully to television with the production and distribution of a 26-part television series based on its *Blinky Bill* films. Jonathan Shiff/Westbridge has specialised in children's television since 1988, its biggest production being the $3 million series *Ocean Girl* which sold to Disney in the United States and to the BBC for a record sum for a children's series in the United Kingdom. Roger Mirams/Pacific Productions, a Sydney-based producer of children's programming since the 1950s, shot the $8 million *Mission Top Secret* in seven countries. Pacific Productions made *South Pacific Adventures* in 1990 and Media World Features, another company involved in animated features, made a miniseries based on their animated film *The Silver Brumby*.

Beyond International produces *Deepwater Haven*, a children's drama series with a curious mix of French and New Zealand actors, in Auckland. Millennium Productions made *Miraculous Mellops*, a fantasy science fiction family series, and Warner Roadshow has produced *The Adventures of Skippy* and *Animal Park*.

Other Production Companies

JNP Productions established its reputation almost solely on its long-running and well-regarded series, *A Country Practice*. The program ran as one of the major Seven Network dramas from 1981 to 1993, before being bought by the Ten Network in 1994. Despite a reworked format and setting, the new series on Ten failed; JNP has yet to produce anything as remotely successful.

Like JNP, Gannon Television/View Films has built its name on one major television product, *Heartbreak High*, a youth-oriented series noted for its high production values and its treatment of youth issues. The series suffered from scheduling changes imposed by the Ten Network, but has picked up important sales in the lucrative markets of the United Kingdom, France and Germany to the extent that the series is now produced on the basis of these sales, without any current Australian network deal. In addition to several feature films, View Films has also produced two television miniseries, *Shout! The Story of Johnny O'Keefe* (1985) for the Seven Network and *Shadow of the Cobra* (1988) for Zenith in the United Kingdom, the BBC and the Seven Network.

—Stuart O. Cunningham

FURTHER READING

"Film Funder (Film Finance Corp.) Under Review, Oz Edgy." *Variety* (Los Angeles), 27 April 1992.

Groves, Don. "Aussies Target U.S. for Partners, Growth." *Variety* (Los Angeles), 16 January 1995.

Harris, Mike. "TV Travelling Well to Europe." *Variety* (Los Angeles), 31 October 1994.

———. "Lean Times for Drama Down Under." *Variety* (Los Angeles), 23 March 1992.

———. "Local Programs Give Aussie Nine Its Shine." *Variety* (Los Angeles), 27 April 1992.

Margolis, Irwin. "Crocodile Dundee's Aussie Pack Invades British Television." *Television-Radio Age* (New York), 23 November 1987.

Murdoch, Blake. "Looking Up Down Under [Special Report: Australia]." *Variety* (Los Angeles), 26 April 1993.

"The New Global Order: Site Purchase Instills Faith in Global TV's Future." *Variety* (Los Angeles), 31 October 1994.

See also Crawford, Hector; Grundy, Reg; Gyngell, Bruce; Murdoch, Rupert

AUSTRALIAN PROGRAMMING

The peculiarly Australian television program is still in the minority on Australian television screens which remain dominated by the Hollywood product. Yet, compared with the situation of only a decade ago, Australian television programs today vie with Australian films in the search for markets worldwide. Australian soap operas such as *Neighbours* and *Home and Away* have achieved high ratings in such countries as England and Ireland. And while the Grundy Organization, Australia's largest producer of television shows, began by "borrowing" concepts and formats from American game shows, it has progressed to making a profitable business by selling recycled and rejuvenated American shows back to the country of their origin. *Sale of the Century* and *Wheel of Fortune* today typify this genre. While the ultimate ownership of the Australian companies is today increasingly in the hands of multinational corporations, the Australian character of their television programs now seems established and production resides in Australia.

To outline the origin of this national character, however, one must examine the antecedent media. As in any other national context, television programming in Australia can only be understood by examining its origins in radio and film. As in the American experience, and unlike the British, the major impetus to radio programming in Australia came from the commercial sector with the explosive growth of commercial radio in the 1930s. The Australian experience mimicked the American from the soap opera to the singing commercial. While, as the American critic Norman Corwin has observed, Australia is one of the few places on the globe where radio drama was considered as an art form, the vast bulk of commercial radio dramatic product was of the soap opera variety. In its heyday, it succeeded brilliantly by its own commercial standards, meeting not only a domestic niche, but also providing a steady stream of programs for export. It employed a small army of professional writers and production people who formed the nucleus of writers, actors and producers for the infant Australian television industry when it began in the mid-1950s.

Unlike the American, and like the British experience, however, since the beginning of the 1930s, Australia has also had a powerful national, publicly-owned non-commercial broadcasting entity, the Australian Broadcasting Commission. (After 1983, "Commission" became "Corporation.") This corporation is recognized as the primary culture-making force in Australian national life. The ABC has, in fact, sponsored many non-broadcasting aspects of public culture, from the establishment of symphony orchestras in all states, involvement in children's clubs, sporting activities, advice to farmers through specialized agricultural service, and comment on markets and weather, to the explorations of the culture of the rural environment.

Still, it must be pointed out that despite the widespread misconception by commentators, the Australian Broadcasting Commission did not owe its origins to a simple amalgamation of the "good points" of American and British thinking. Rather it arose from the exigencies of the indigenous experience—an Australian response to an Australian requirement. Given its origins and its mandate, the programming from the ABC provided a contrast to the commercial television stations.

The early British broadcasting experience, was, however, very important in the formative years of the ABC. The BBC's "Reithian ethic" of high moral purpose, nation building, and elevating popular tastes, can, in hindsight, hardly be overestimated. High culture was encouraged by classical music programs and community building by popular music programs which often featured Australian musicians performing the latest popular songs from overseas. Sporting programs such as the dominant national pastime of horse racing and test cricket (in the early days especially with England) was a broadcasting staple from the 1930s to the present time. These broadcasts set the pattern of national participation by the time television arrived in 1956, and the various programming categories and genres can be seen to derive from them.

Local programming by independent stations reached its heyday in the decade of the 1980s and exhibited patterns similar to that in other countries. It was relatively common for local stations to do a program on a local event or a car club rally. But local stations became "aggregated" by government policy into a networks not unlike the American commercial system. Local programming then found it necessary to appeal to a geographically wider-spread audience, and by the 1990s began to fade away.

The generalization that the British programming on Australian television tends to be mostly on the ABC is valid. Commercial stations, on the other hand sometimes take British programs, which have proven to be popular from ABC exposure, and rebroadcast them to achieve higher ratings. A range of programs from the ubiquitous *Yes, Minister* series to the more vulgar *Are You Being Served?* type vie with David Attenborough nature documentaries and similar British fare as might appear on PBS in America.

In sum, Australian television programming bears the marks of several systems which preceded it. But like many other systems it continues to mold those influences in its own ways. Whether the specifically "Australian" character of television can withstand an onslaught from new economic configurations and new technologies that transcend national boundaries remains to be seen.

Non-Fiction Programming

Talk shows, music, morning programs, sports, news, and current affairs programs are all represented in the Australian television line-up, and again, all derived from radio antecedents. As far as television is concerned little about them is specifically Australian.

In the light entertainment talk shows, for example, the programming is decidedly derivative. *Tonight Live* with Steve Vizard in the early nineties betrayed its lineage to David Letterman and Johnny Carson. Admittedly, there was an Australian strain of boyish irreverence inherited from the Australian stars such as Graham Kennedy and Bert Newton, but the sets, presentation, and overall style would be easily recognized by an American viewer. Most importantly, in the commercial medium, Vizard's success was due to the economic fact that his popularity allowed the Seven network to extend prime time and charge premium rates for what was, comparatively, an inexpensively produced program.

Music

High culture is typically provided on television with opera or symphony concerts simulcast on Sunday night by the ABC. At the other end of the scale, the ABC provides, in early morning hours, a simulcast of Triple J, the youth national radio network, which broadcasts rock music accompanied by exceptionally raunchy dialog.

Music videos are broadcast at various times on both commercial and national television.

Morning Television

In the very early morning hours, the ABC provides very high quality instructional television which can be correlated with written instruction and tutorial interaction and taken for college credit. Language, biology, business and other Open Learning subjects provide the casual viewer with exceptional, totally involving informational programming, most often of American origin.

Predictably, in the 1980s and 1990s, on Channel 9, the Australian *Today* show with one male and female compere, provided a mixture of news, interviews, sports and weather in a well-tested format. Variations of this theme have come and gone on competing networks. By the mid 1990s, for example, in the 9:00 A.M. slot, morning television featured *Good Morning Australia* with Bert Newton, another reference to an American programming format. Again, the interview is the feature of choice, with perhaps a lighter vein to vary the flavor. At least one station usually counterprograms these shows with cartoons for kids.

Sports

While sports-watching on television had long been a favorite Australian pastime, the connection between sports and advertising was traditionally not as strong in Australia as in the United States. However, the televised presentation of sporting events is increasingly influenced by American programming strategies. The broadcasting industry had long been poised for intensive activity surrounding the business of sports on television, and media moguls Kerry Packer and Rupert Murdoch vied (and collaborated on occasion) for various contracts with players, licenses and outlets for the advertising dollars and pay television subscriptions.

In cricket, for example, the tradition had been inherited from the British Empire, where white-suited cricketers (divided into "gentlemen" who were amateurs, and "professionals" who were paid) took days to play a "test" match. By the 1970s, media mogul Kerry Packer was credited with promoting a game more suited to television coverage: played in one day, with colorful costumes, showbiz accouterments and players exhibiting enthusiasm rather than the old British "stiff upper lip." Similar transformations occurred in tennis, football, hockey, soccer, netball and other sports. And the trend toward Americanization was markedly increased with the introduction of Rupert Murdoch's Superleague, an entirely new combination of Rugby League teams and with Pay TV sports programs which were becoming more prevalent by 1995.

Through all these changes, the scheduling strategies have remained quite the same. A typical week's viewing would begin with the traditional Saturday afternoon when all channels present one sport or another. The same pattern holds for Sunday afternoon, with one commercial channel starting sports programming at 9:00 A.M. (The ABC has counterprogrammed a high culture arts ghetto on Sunday afternoons, and SBS also tends to eschew sports on Sunday afternoon). The regular television news on Sunday nights tends to increase its sports coverage beyond the acceptable thirty per cent for Australian television newscasts, and there are also irregular sports specials on at various prime time slots.

While special football games of various codes are broadcast during one or two week nights in Australia, American football tends to be consigned to late-night taped presentations on the ABC, except for the Super Bowl which is broadcast live. Basketball is the fastest growing sport in Australia, and thanks to television, in one celebrated 1994 survey 11 year-old Australians considered Michael Jordan as the Best Sportsman.

The television sporting scene is also affected by the specialized narrowcasting of events to pubs and clubs across the nation by satellite transmission. Horse racing is perhaps the sport most associated with gambling, but with the advent of new technologies, and especially with the advent of sports on pay-TV, the ubiquitous TAB's or gambling shops will undoubtedly evolve to exploit the new media.

With the Olympic Games scheduled for Sydney in 2000, the influence of television on the world of sports in Australia will undoubtedly reach a zenith.

News

Australian Radio news was available in the early days in a prototypal form with the stories taken from the newspapers. The newspaper proprietors, already having demonstrated their political clout by keeping the ABC from commercial taint (and revenues), were able to stifle radio news until the war years (1939–45). During World War II, a coalition government, pressured by the imminence of a Japanese invasion, decided that the ABC radio was crucial to the war effort. Once established, ABC news became one of the world's most professional news broadcasting services with bureaux worldwide.

Typically, the ABC television nightly news is of half-hour duration, is presented from each individual state with common stories from overseas feeds, and is followed by a current affairs program. The presenter is of the BBC "Newsreader" variety, and is not typically a practicing journalist. Richard Morecroft, who fronts the ABC TV 7:00 P.M. news in New South Wales (the state with the largest population), is perhaps the best exemplar of the ABC style.

The format is boiler plate: Local, state, national, international, sports and weather. The commercial stations tend to have similar formats, with quicker pacing and a more lurid selection of topics. Australian newscasts typically devote six or seven minutes of a thirty-minute slot to sport, a proportion far greater than typical in the United States. Brian Henderson, the anchor of the Channel Nine (commercial) news, is the long-time champion in the news ratings and provides his network with the coveted high-rated lead-in position for the rest of the night. Another veteran news anchor is his rival Roger Climpson, who fronts for the (also highly profitable) Seven network.

The Special Broadcasting Service, often admired for the quality of its television news, has an unmatched foreign coverage, and tends to longer and more comprehensive stories. Besides the nightly news there are shorter programs throughout the broadcast day, some being short updates.

Documentary and Current Affairs

The prototypal Australian television documentary (or current affairs) program is the long-running *Four Corners* program which is an institution on its Monday night slot at 8:30. Perhaps the finest hour in Australian television was the broadcast of "The Moonlight State" on 11 May 1987 when Australia's premier investigative journalist, Chris Masters, demonstrated on film the illegal booze joints, the prostitution, and the gambling dens whose existence had been long denied by the self-righteous government of the state of Queensland. Senior police officers went to jail and a government was overthrown following the subsequent inquiry triggered by the program.

Channel Nine presents a prestigious current affairs program *Sunday* on Sunday morning, and from time to time other commercial concerns have attempted to match Nine and the ABC with serious public affairs programming, but their efforts seem to vanish as management turns to more profitable programming.

SBS and the ABC program several high quality documentaries in any broadcasting week. Typical titles, chosen at random for illustration only, are: *The Big Picture, That Was Our War, Documentary, Australian Biography, Great Books* and *A Most Remarkable Planet.*

While a number of these presentations move toward television that is distinctively Australian, it is in fictional programming that the clearest and most powerful explorations of a national character and mode of representation have been established.

Fictional Programming

Although the Gorton Liberal (conservative) government in the early 1970s began the process, the great national renaissance in motion picture and television programming began with the free-spending Whitlam Labor government of 1973-75. Because the same people worked in film as worked in television, it is hard to separate out the stories of the different media. The technical infrastructure for movies was aided by the fact that since 1960 imported television commercials were banned. This meant that in the capital cities, especially in Sydney and Melbourne, motion picture laboratories developed a steady business and the technical expertise required to provide high quality professional product in the advertising arena. Until the advent of ENG (electronic news gathering) in the 1970s, when tape was used instead of film, television news, shot on 16mm film also provided a steady demand to supplement the work of the film labs.

The topics of television programming echoed those covered in the motion pictures. Australia, before the 1930s, had an economically viable silent film industry which did not survive the advent of sound and the economic depression of the 1930s. Hollywood (and to a lesser extent British) product then dominated Australian cinema screens. Because film is a cultural artefact as well as being a salable commodity, the Australian audiences became saturated with American culture. Almost ten years after the advent of television in Australia, the American authority Wilson Dizard could make his famous statement: "The daily schedule of a typical Australian television station, particularly in prime listening hours, is virtually indistinguishable from that of a station in Iowa or New Jersey." And as late as 1967, the Australian Broadcasting Control Board required that only two hours of Australian drama be broadcast per month in prime time.

Thus deprived of Australian stories on the screen, when the 1970s Renaissance occurred, the subject of the programming tended to be the indigenous classics, and contemporary themes which depended on a distinctly Australian flavor. In 1976, the government decreed (with a "points system") that there be a 50% Australian content between the hours of 4:00 P.M. and 10:00 P.M., and demanded compliance of commercial licensees. Despite their early protests, the commercial stations found that the Australian programs were very popular with Australian audiences.

Available for television a year or so after cinema release, Australian films became an important part of the indigenous programming, but the epitome of television programming art was seen to be in the miniseries.

Miniseries

The miniseries brought important national myths and icons to the television screen. The quintessential Australian nation-building myth is that of ANZAC (Australian and New Zealand Army Corps). The ANZAC story is one of volunteer soldiers, who, in 1915, on behalf of the British war effort against Germany, invaded Turkish territory on the Gallipoli peninsula. The campaign was a defeat, but the valor of the soldiers, celebrated in a national day of commemoration (ANZAC day, 25 April), became a central theme of the Australian nation as a cause worth any sacrifice. The television miniseries *Anzacs* thus complemented the major motion picture *Gallipoli* to tell the ANZAC story.

Similarly, following the nationalistic, nostalgic (and essentially mythic) impetus, another miniseries, *The Last Outlaw*, told the story of arguably the most famous Australian folk hero, Ned Kelly. Ned Kelly is (literally) an Australian icon, because in his self-made steel body armour, he looked like a medieval knight with six guns. Like his American contemporary, Jesse James, he was a highway robber, but unlike James, his behavior elicited considerable public sympathy with large crowds protesting his hanging in 1880. Today his story is all-pervasive in Australian culture with the Ned Kelly icon appearing in the high culture of Sidney Nolan paintings in the National Gallery in Canberra, and the armour and six guns feature as a logo for a brand of sliced bread. Yet beyond the Australian version of the Robin Hood image lies an historical reality. Because Ned Kelly epitomized the rebellious Irishman persecuted by British rule, his story tied in neatly with a long tradition of Republicanism which is becoming more potent at the turn of the millennium.

The television miniseries *Against the Wind* depicted another important facet of Australian history which had been ignored while American stories had dominated the Australian television screens. It, too, harked back to mythic origins, as Australia's convict past was evoked by the story of a spirited Irish lass who was transported to Australia as a political prisoner. She falls in love with a fine upstanding convict unjustly treated by a vicious system. The settings of the program owe more to the Disney studios than the squalor portrayed by recent historical accounts of the eighteenth century settlement, but the program fulfilled the requirements of standard founding myths which are requisite in all cultures.

The 19th century depiction of a family saga, *Seven Little Australians*, provided a local version of the American *Little House on the Prairie* or Canadian *Anne of Green Gables* genre. Other miniseries covered well-known Australian legends, such as those relating to the sporting stories between the wars. *Bodyline* portrayed unsportsmanlike Englishmen attacking stalwart and long-suffering Australians when playing the extremely popular sport of cricket. The title, *Bodyline*, described a tactic of aiming at the batsman's body, rather than at the wicket—a tactic that worked. The English won the test series in 1936 and a number of Australians were, in fact, injured. The other casualty was Australian good feeling for the British, although the Australians took the high moral ground and did not reciprocate with the "bodyline" tactic. This material, clearly restricted in commercial terms to the "old empire" of cricket players, is the stuff of myth and legend, and as such proved popular with its intended market.

Similarly, the mythic imperative of coming to grips with former enemies was handled with the miniseries *Cowra Breakout*. In 1944, Japanese prisoners of war "broke out" of a prisoner of war camp in the remote Australian town of Cowra. By the early 1980s, when the program was made, Japan and Australia had experienced a quarter century of mutual economic interest as trading partners, and Japan was the most important Australian market by far. The deaths of the brave, but culturally incomprehensible Japanese, were treated in this series in a way not unlike that of the pacifist film of the 1930s *All Quiet on the Western Front*.

Clearly, this outpouring of depictions of Australian history and culture resulted in part because of government production subsidies, provided as partial support for the requirement that holders of the lucrative television licenses broadcast Australian content. But when the ratings demonstrated that these Australian stories were very popular with Australian audiences, it seemed tangible proof that a cultural imperative was also inherent in their acceptance by the indigenous audience.

By the 1980s, however, the economic climate changed. Broadcasting seemed dominated by takeovers of the major television networks. Furthermore, deregulation and privatization rather than activist nationalistic initiatives seemed to capture the governmental imagination. Thus by the end of the decade, the traditional mythical Australian themes of the tragic losers—Ned Kelly, the ANZACS, the bodyline cricketers, Les Darcy the boxer, and even Phar Lap the racehorse—were being superseded by a new type of Australian story. The audiences, satisfied by the availability of their indigenous stories, began to demand a change of programming and the program makers began to look beyond the most obvious indigenous themes.

By the 1990s, the motion picture industry was tackling contemporary themes presented with high production values. For example, *The Heartbreak Kid* concerned an affair between a high school student and his young teacher. The milieu of Greek culture in Melbourne provided a conflict intermingling male dominance (the teacher's fiancé resorts to violence, and her father's role is stereotypical) and a depiction of conflicting loyalties. The television serial spin-off was called *Heartbreak High*, with the same young male lead and an approximation of the cinematic verisimilitude in the sets. Produced at the same time was *Paradise Beach*, in the tradition of *Baywatch*, with Surfers Paradise in Queensland standing for the Californian coast.

Traditional themes, however, remained a staple. For example, *The Man From Snowy River*, a motion picture derived from a poem by Banjo Patterson, the author of "Waltzing Matilda" (the Australian national song) had been a success in the 1980s. By 1994, a 13-part television miniseries entitled *Banjo Patterson's The Man from Snowy River* continued the genre. It is perhaps a sign of the maturity of the industry in Australia that the subjects and formats which secured the initial popularity for Australian programs with Australian viewers now are merely one type of program amongst many.

Soaps

As in the United States soap operas are programmed during the day, and the typical commercial offering has a mixture of American programming (*Days of Our Lives, The Bold and the Beautiful, The Young and the Restless*), interspersed with Australian soap operas such as *Home and Away, Echo Point* and *Neighbours*. The basic rules of the daytime serials which were established in the 1930s radio era still apply, regardless of the racier themes and more topical situations. Perceptions of "Australianness" of the indigenous soap operas vary, and provide interesting perspectives on cultural productions. The general Australian opinion is that the lives of the protagonists in Australian soaps are more ordinary, everyday and working-class. Yet to European observers, the Australian soap opera is characterized by relatively healthy, happy beings who endure their endless travails in a fortunate sun-drenched situation. Regardless of these "Australian" traits, the Australian soap opera remains true to type, exhibiting, most significantly, the "endless narrative" which characterizes the genre worldwide.

Comedy

Much of Australia's television comedy is derivative. At 7:30 P.M. on the Nine Network, for example, *Australia's Funniest Home Video Show* uses the standard American formula.

Perhaps with a more indigenous flavor, the family situation comedy *Hey Dad* (in daytime reruns by the mid-1990s), followed the U.S. sitcom formula but focused on the same everyday working-class context as presented in the Australian soap operas. *Acropolis Now* (also in reruns), a politically incorrect sitcom, made gentle fun of Australia's ethnic communities placed within a dominant Anglo culture.

On the ABC in the mid-1990s, *Mother and Son* presented a genuinely challenging comic world. Veteran actors Ruth Cracknell and Gary Macdonald explored the tribulations of a man taking care of his mother—who is afflicted with Alzheimer's disease. And the cult comedy, *Frontline*, starred Rob Sitch as Mike More, an unhinged, venal, television talking head. A send-up of a television current affairs program, this show was generally considered to be thinly disguised social commentary.

Police Procedurals

The police serial in Australia began with Crawford's, a major production company in Melbourne. Crawford's came to prominence with *Homicide* and established a format with *Cop Shop*. Today, the Australian police show genre can be exemplified by considering two programs, *Police Rescue* and *Blue Heelers*. *Police Rescue*, with its star Gary Sweet as the ("hunk") lead Mickey, takes place in an urban setting. With high production values (as befits its ABC origins and overseas co-producers), the story lines deal with tensions of contemporary life in a city which is not necessarily recognizably Australian.

Blue Heelers, on the other hand, is set in mythical, bucolic, small town Australia. Produced for Channel Seven, *Blue Heelers* is constrained by a modest budget monitored by the creative guiding hand of leading Australian writer, Tony Morphett. The program is clearly indigenous, and not as accessible to overseas audiences as *Police Rescue*. The very name *Blue Heelers* plays a word game recognizable to Australian audiences, yet which would escape viewers unaware of Australian nuances. It refers simultaneously to the standard blue uniforms which color-code police in the English speaking world and to a breed of cattle-dog, the Queensland blue, notorious for sneaking behind unsuspecting people and nipping at their ankles. The star, John Wood, is positively avuncular, although the show has elements of action-drama. While Australians are among the most urbanized people on earth, the call of the small town, as exemplified by the long-running program *A Country Practice*, seems to provide an appeal in national escapism as provided by television.

Both *Blue Heelers* and *Police Rescue* aim at a family audience at eight thirty at night. Both present continuing characters who constitute a "family" in the workplace. Both offer the usual recipe of conflict, violence, sexual attraction and humor. Nevertheless, the program set in the country is much more clearly mythical, Australian, and designed to reassure its audience. While Australian viewers, as the ratings attest, enjoy the restless camera and edgy performances of the American offering *NYPD Blue,* just as they enjoyed *Hill Street Blues,* Australian producers seem to have stayed with less gritty serials. On the other hand, police-based short series such as *Janus,* produced by the ABC from its Melbourne studios, have explored a much darker vision for the policing profession than that exemplified by the prototypal *Blue Heelers* and *Police Rescue.*

—Myles P. Breen

FURTHER READING

Agardy, Susanna, and David Bednall. *Television and the Public: National Television Standards Survey.* Melbourne: Australian Broadcasting Tribunal, 1982.

Bell, Philip, with others. *Programmed Politics: A Study of Australian Television.* Sydney: Sable, 1982.

Breen, Myles. "National Mythology on Film and Television: The Australian Experience." *Communication,* 1989.

———. "Television News is Drama." *Media Information Australia,* 1983.

Brown, Allan. "The Economics of Television Regulation: A Survey with Application to Australia." *Economic Record* (Melbourne) December 1992.

Burke, Jacinta, Helen Wilson, and Susanna Agardy. "*A Country Practice*" and the Child Audience: A Case Study. Melbourne: Australian Broadcasting Tribunal, 1983.

Collins, Richard. "National Broadcasting and the International Market: Developments in Australian Broadcasting Policy." *Media, Culture and Society* (London), January 1994.

Cunningham, Stuart, and Toby Miller, with David Rowe. *Contemporary Australian Television.* Sydney: University of New South Wales Press, 1994.

Hall, Sandra. *Supertoy: Twenty Years of Australian Television.* Sydney: Sun Books, 1976.

Henningham, John. *Looking at Television News.* Melbourne: Longman Cheshire, 1988.

Inglis, Kenneth S. *This is the ABC: The Australian Broadcasting Commission 1932-1983.* Melbourne: Melbourne University Press, 1983.

An Inquiry into Australian Content on Commercial Television. Sydney: Australian Broadcasting Tribunal, 1991–1992.

Johnson, Nicholas, and Mark Armstrong. *Two Reflections on Australian Broadcasting.* Bundoora, Victoria: Centre for the Study of Educational Communication and Media, La Trobe University, 1977.

MacCallum, Mungo, editor. *Ten Years of Television.* Melbourne: Sun Books, 1968.

Mitchell, Tony. "Treaty Now! Indigenous Music and Music Television in Australia." *Media, Culture and Society* (London), April 1993.

———. "Wogs Still Out of Work: Australian Television Comedy as Colonial Discourse." *Australasian Drama Studies* (St. Lucia, Queensland), April 1992.

Moran, Albert. "Interview: Writing Television Comedy." *Australasian Drama Studies* (St. Lucia, Queensland), October 1983.

———. *Images and Industry: Television Drama Production in Australia.* Sydney: Currency Press 1985.

O'Regan, Tom. *Australian Television Culture.* St. Leonards, New South Wales: Allen and Unwin 1993.

———, with others. *The Moving Image: Film and Television in Western Australia, 1896–1985.* History and Film Association of Australia, 1985.

Rowe, David, and Geoff Laurence, editors. *Sport and Leisure: Trends in Australian Popular Culture.* Sydney: Harcourt Brace Jovanovich, 1990.

Seymour-Ure, Collin. "Prime Ministers' Reactions to Television: Britain, Australia, and Canada." *Media, Culture and Society* (London), July 1989.

Tulloch, John, and Graeme Turner, editors. *Australian Television: Programs, Pleasures and Politics.* Sydney and Boston: Allen and Unwin, 1989.

TV 2000: Choices and Challenges; Report of the Proceedings of the Australian Broadcasting Tribunal Conference Held at the Hilton Hotel, Sydney, 16–17 November, 1989. Sydney: ABC Tribunal, 1990.

Williams, Kerry L. "The Cure for Women in Comedy: History as TV Talk Show Therapy." *Australasian Drama Studies* (St. Lucia, Queensland), April 1993.

See also *Country Practice; Four Corners; Heartbreak High; Hey Hey It's Saturday; Homicide; Neighbours; Power Without Glory; Prisoner; Sale of the Century; Sex; Sylvania Waters*

AUSTRALIAN PROGRAMMING (ABORIGINAL)

Although in some ways Australian television has provided little representation of that continent's Aboriginal inhabitants, in others it is impossible to overstate the importance of Aboriginality to the medium. As with many areas of Australian culture, the indigenous inhabitants have been co-opted here in the formation of an Australian sense of identity. It is unusual to watch an evening's television in Australia without encountering some representation of Aboriginality—in an advertizement for the Mitsubishi Pajero; a trailer for a Yothu Yindi concert; or a news item on Aborigines' attempts for land rights. Aboriginal characters and issues have appeared in most genres of Australian television. Soap operas such as *Neighbours, Home and Away* and *A Country Practice* have featured Aboriginal characters; as have children's programs such as *Dolphin Cove* and *Kideo;* game shows such as *Wheel of Fortune* and *Family Feud;* and even lifestyle programs, with *The Great Outdoors*, featuring an Aboriginal presenter.

As well as these insistent, unsystematic images of Aboriginality, Australian television features areas where a greater weight of indigenous representation has occurred. This is true both in Aboriginal produced and circulated programming and in the arena of the broadcast mainstream.

In "Mainstream" free-to-air broadcast television there is a fairly consistent representation of Aboriginal people and issues on Australia's news programs. As researchers have noticed, this often involves what are understood to be negative representations—of crime, drunkenness, family problems, victimhood, and helplessness. Defended as realistic by industry insiders, these patterns of representation are clichés, familiar ways of organising and creating stories in order to render them accessible. Another popular pattern of news coverage is to construct stories about land rights claims in terms of white versus black, two equal and opposing sides.

As well as television news programs, most representations of the Aboriginal on Australian mainstream television occur in nonfictional modes. *Four Corners* and *A Big Country*, two well-known (ABC) Australian documentary strands, have both included reports on the "plight" of indigenous Australians over the decades of their production (the former in episodes such as "Black Sickness, Black Cure," 1983; the latter in productions like 1974's "The Desert People").

There have also been avowedly Aboriginal programs on mainstream broadcast television. *First in Line* (SBS, 1989) and *Blackout* (ABC, 1989) are both Aboriginal-produced and -presented magazine-style programs. Again, they largely feature nonfictional material, although the latter has also increasingly involved comedy sketches and music in its mix.

The ABC miniseries *Heartland* (1994) is worth including in a category of its own. This 13-hour long drama is a unique contribution to Australian television. It is the only example of a drama program with an Aboriginal hero. (In 1992, a detective series called *Bony* singularly failed to do the same, taking a series of books with an Aboriginal protagonist and casting a white actor in the lead part.) Over the weeks, *Heartland* presented a series of Aboriginal communities, rural and urban, and a wide range of characters, all contributing to a vastly increased range of available discourses on Aborigines. An entertaining, watchable piece of television, it is truly distinctive in the history of Australian programming.

Ernie Dingo is responsible for a large amount of the Aboriginal representation on Australian television in the early 1990s. As well as starring in *Heartland* and presenting *The Great Outdoors*, he has appeared on programs such as *Dolphin Cove*, *Clowning Around*, *Wheel of Fortune*, *GP*, *The Flying Doctors*, and *Heartbreak High* and many others. His presence is a large part of current Australian Aboriginal programming.

Any consideration of Aboriginal programming must also cover the material which is made and distributed by Aboriginal groups and communities. Broadcasting for Re-

mote Areas Community Scheme (BRACS) is one of a series of projects set up by Australia's federal government to ensure that Aboriginal communities at a distance from the continent's urban centres can have access to broadcast television. BRACS is the successor of such projects as RATS (Remote Area Television Scheme), STRS (Self Help Television Reception Scheme), RUCS (Remote and Underserved Communities Scheme) and the SHBRS (Self-Help Broadcasting Reception Scheme). Funded by the 1987-88 budget of the Federal Department of Aboriginal Affairs, the purpose of BRACS was slightly different from that which had gone before. Rather than simply ensuring reception of broadcast television, BRACS would provide rebroadcasting and production facilities to allow Aboriginal communities to decide for themselves how much of the material received should actually be shown in their communities, and to make their own material to replace that which they did not want. In order to make this possible, BRACS supplies the community with satellite reception equipment, a domestic quality video camera, two domestic video recorders (to allow for basic editing), and the equipment to rebroadcast to the community. The initial idea was that this would allow broadcast in little-used languages (some Aboriginal dialects have less than 100 speakers), and to allow deletion of offensive material.

The scheme has had varying degrees of success. Difficulties have included the lack of well-trained personnel to look after the equipment, the built-in obsolescence of domestic equipment, equipment incompatibility with desert settings; lack of consultation with Aboriginal communities as to whether they wanted the equipment, and limited-range capability of the rebroadcast equipment. However, it seems that the scheme (available to over 80 Aboriginal communities by 1995) has at least taken into consideration the ways in which communities might want to use television. Although the difficulties with lack of training, equipment, and money cannot be ignored, many of the BRACS communities are finding the scheme useful, taking advantage of the chance to produce local material. Programs produced include news, health information, and music request programs: all with an intensely local orientation.

Perhaps the most active examples of such local television production are the Aboriginal communities in Ernabella and Yuendumu. Both of these towns pre-empted the government's BRACS scheme, establishing their own pirate television broadcasting well before BRACS legitimised the idea. In the latter community, the Warlpiri Media Association has produced hundreds of hours of programming: records of community life, travel tapes, and *Manyu Wana*, an Aboriginal version of *Sesame Street* designed to teach local children the Warlpiri language.

There is also Aboriginal video production from a series of media groups. CAAMA (Central Australian Aboriginal Media Association), TAIMA (Townsville and Aboriginal Islander Media Association), TEABBA (Top End Aboriginal Bush Broadcasting Association), WAAMA (Western Australian Aboriginal Media Association) and TSIAMA (Torres

Strait Islander and Aboriginal Media Association) produce video and radio material. The radio programs are often carried on the networks of the Australian Broadcasting Association. Larger organisations than the media producers in the BRACS communities, these groups make material that is less locally oriented, and has an address wider than a single community.

Australia broadcasts commercial television to the inner part of the continent on the satellite Aussat. Several Remote Commercial Television Service (RCTS) licenses were sold on this satellite; one is held by the CAAMA group. All of the bidders for these satellites were required to guarantee that their services would include material specifically commissioned for the Aboriginal people, who formed a relatively high proportion of their audiences (up to 27% in some cases). All did so, but none have done particularly well in keeping to those promises. The Golden West Network has one Aboriginal magazine program, *Milbindi.* Queensland Satellite Television broadcasts material provided by the government Aboriginal and Torres Strait Islander Commission and the Queensland State Government, programs which present carefully positive images of Aboriginality.

Imparja, despite being Aboriginal-owned, has found constraints of economy have made it difficult to produce broadcast-quality Aboriginal material. The amount of indigenous programming on the channel has varied. When it started broadcasting in 1988, Imparja featured an Aboriginal magazine-style program, *Nganampa Anwernekenhe.* By contrast, in 1990, the station's Aboriginal broadcasting consisted only of community service announcements.

There is a vast range of material encompassed by the term Aboriginal broadcasting of Australia: mainstream television on Aboriginal issues; Aboriginal programs broadcast on the mainstream; and Aboriginal-produced and -controlled broadcasting which is allowing Aboriginal groups in Australia to interact assertively with new technologies, negotiating the places these will hold in their communities.

—Alan McKee

FURTHER READING

Jennett, Christine. "White Media Rituals About Aboriginal Media." *Media Information Australia,* November 1983.

Michaels, Eric. *Bad Aboriginal Art: Tradition, Media, and Technological Horizons.* Minneapolis, Minnesota: University of Minnesota Press, 1993; St. Leonards, New South Wales: Allen and Unwin, 1994.

Mickler, Steve. "Visions of Disorder." *Cultural Studies* (London), 1992.

THE AVENGERS

British Thriller

Possibly Britain's most successful television export, *The Avengers* (1961–69) was the last English-made television show to find a prime-time slot on American network television. Initially *The Avengers* was designed to showcase the breakout star of *Police Surgeon* (1960), Ian Hendry, in the role of a doctor who, after the murder of his fiancee, joined forces with mysterious secret agent John Steed (Patrick Macnee). Six episodes were initially scheduled: twenty-six were made (three were videotaped) before Hendry left. Macnee continued to star in *The Avengers* for another eight years (136 episodes), finally resuming his role in 1976 in *The New Avengers* (produced by Fennell and Clemens). During the subsequent five seasons, he was teamed with three female sidekicks—Cathy Gale (Honor Blackman), a widowed, leather clad, martial arts expert with a Ph.D.; Mrs. Emma Peel (Diana Rigg), an aristocratic young widow, successful industrialist, psychologist and skilled fighter; and finally, Tara King (Linda Thorson), a young professional secret agent with less charisma or self-reliance than her amateur predecessors.

Once Macnee was teamed with Blackman, the show started to develop its characteristic flavor. Steed became more upper-class, dressed in increasingly dandified Edwardian fashion, while Gale represented a new vision of the strong, intelligent, active, and equal woman. Shot on multiple camera video, these episodes did not display the same flair for the fantastic as the later filmed series (indeed, they

The Avengers

look very much like the period's realistic "kitchen sink" dramas), although narratives started to flirt with the bizarre and unexpected.

During this same period (1962–64), there was increasing American interest in *The Avengers,* culminating in 1964 when ABC bought the series for the fall 1965 season. The network wanted a filmed series, so the show went on hiatus for nearly a year, reappearing on ITV in 1965 with new star Diana Rigg. ABC chose to wait until 1967 when color episodes would be available rather than risk showing an imported black-and-white series while the American networks were converting to all-color TV. After two seasons, Rigg left and was replaced by Linda Thorson (1968–69). ABC canceled the show in 1969 because audiences sharply declined after it was scheduled against the new hit *Rowan and Martin's Laugh-In.* Although it continued to top ratings in Britain and throughout Europe, production stopped (it was never officially canceled) because the production company, Associated British, now relied on American money.

While *The Avengers* is often considered part of the James Bond/Cold War cycle of espionage thrillers, it actually dealt less with international issues and more with changes in modern Britain. Narratives explicitly engaged with questions of colonialism, national heritage, and questions of imperial British history, often parodying the nation's past, its institutions and its stock stereotypes like the English Gentleman and the Retired Army Major. This humorous reflection on national identity was combined with a fascination with space age technology and an emphasis on modern femininity, a juxtaposition that recalled Britain's own long emergence out of postwar deprivation into the new, trend-setting world represented by Carnaby Street and the Beatles.

—Moya Luckett

CAST

John Steed . . . . Patrick Macnee
Dr. David Keel . . . . Iain Hendry
Carol Wilson . . . . Ingrid Hafner
One Ten . . . . Douglas Muir
Cathy Gale . . . . Honor Blackman
Venus Smith . . . . Julie Stevens
Dr. Martin King . . . . Jon Rollason
Emma Peel . . . . Diana Rigg

Tara King . . . . Linda Thorson
"Mother" . . . . Patrick Newell
Rhonda . . . . Rhonda Parker

PRODUCERS   Leonard White, John Bryce, Julian Wintle, Albert Fennell, Brian Clemens

PROGRAMMING HISTORY   161 50-minute episodes

• ITV

7 January 1961–30 December 1961
29 September 1962–23 March 1963
28 September 1963–21 March 1964
2 October 1965–26 March 1966
14 January 1967–6 May 1967
30 September 1967–18 November 1967
25 September 1968–21 May 1969

U.S. PROGRAMMING HISTORY

CAST

Jonathan Steed . . . . Patrick McNee
Emma Peel (1966–1968) . . . . Diana Rigg
Tara King (1968–1969) . . . . Linda Thorson
"Mother" (1968–1969) . . . . Patrick Newell

• ABC

March 1966–July 1966	Monday 10:00-11:00
July 1966–September 1966	Thursday 10:00-11:00
January 1967–September 1967	Friday 10:00-11:00
January 1968–September 1968	Wednesday 7:30-8:30
September 1968–September 1969	Monday 7:30-8:30

FURTHER READING

Buxton, David. *From The Avengers to Miami Vice: Form and Ideology in Television Series.* Manchester: Manchester University Press, 1990.
Miller, Toby. *The Avengers.* London: British Film Institute, 1996.
Rogers, Dave. *The Complete Avengers.* New York: St. Martin's, 1989.

See also Lumley, Joanna; Rigg, Diana; Spy Programs;

AZCARRAGA, EMILIO, AND EMILIO AZCARRAGA MILMO

Mexican Media Moguls

There are two Emilio Azcarragas, both equally significant in the history of television in Mexico: Emilio Azcarraga Viduarreta, the William Paley of Mexican broadcasting, and his son and heir, Emilio Azcarraga Milmo, the principal owner of the Mexican entertainment conglomerate Televisa. The elder Azcarraga created the first Mexican radio station in 1930, and soon took on a leading role in the

development of Latin American broadcasting. He convened meetings of fledgling Latin American broadcasting entrepreneurs where it was decided that the region would follow the U.S. commercial model and not the non-commercial, government supported, public service British model. Azcarraga, already the sole Mexican agent for Victor/RCA Records and a successful theater owner, promoted Mexican artists (who were under exclusive contract to him) through his growing chain of radio stations, which included several along the U.S.-Mexican border. In 1950, he created Mexico's first television station and a decade later, the first U.S. Spanish language television stations. The Televisa radio and television networks have, since their inception, been characterized by their close association with the Mexican ruling party, known by its Spanish initials, PRI. Televisa produces conservative, nationalistic entertainment programming and fawning, uncritical news coverage of the Mexican government. Partly as a result of this comfortable relationship, broadcasting in Mexico is virtually unregulated.

This situation has continued through the stewardship of the second Emilio Azcarraga, known in Mexico as *El Tigre* (the tiger), as much for the white streak in his hair as for his reputedly ferocious manner. Azcarraga has expanded Televisa's monopolistic hold on Mexican broadcasting by buying media properties in other Latin American countries and selling Televisa programming throughout the world. For example, a Televisa *telenovela* (soap opera) was a huge hit in Moscow in the early l990s. In 1993 Azcarraga acquired controlling interest of PanAmSat, a hemispheric communications satellite, further consolidating Televisa's position as the world's largest producer of Spanish language television programming. In one of the few setbacks suffered by the Televisa owner, in 1986 Azcarraga was forced to sell Televisa's U.S. subsidiary when it was found to be in violation of U.S. laws restricting foreign ownership. Just six years later, Azcarraga bought 25% of the U.S. network, while continuing to provide the majority of its programming. In Mexico, Azcarraga has diversified his holdings to include the largest stadium in the hemisphere, sports teams, publishing and recording companies, and even Mexico City real estate. Azcarraga maintains offices and homes in New York and Los Angeles, as well as Mexico City, and was featured on the cover of *Fortune's* 1994 issue on the world's richest men.

—America Rodriguez

EMILIO AZCARRAGA VIDUARRETA. Married: Laura, children: Emilio, Laura, Carmela. Representative for Victo-

ria/RCA Records; began radio station XEW, Mexico City, Mexico, 1930; built Churrubusco Studios, 1940s; creator and owner of Channel 2, 1950; became the first president of Telesistema Mexicano, 1955; involved in 92 different businesses by 1969; established Televisa, a production company for his stations. Died 1972.

EMILIO AZCARRAGA MILMO. Born August 1930. Educated at Culver Military Academy, graduated 1948. Married four times; fourth wife: Paula Cusi; children include Emilio Azcarraga Jean. Worked in various positions in television; owner, Univision, a twelve-station Spanish-language, U.S. network, 1960s and 1970s; controlling shareholder of Televisa, S.A.; owner of *The National* sports daily, 1990-91; owner of major Mexican television stations; chair, Galavision; also involved in publishing, video, and real estate ventures. Address: Televisa, S.A., Avda Chapultepec 28, 06724 Mexico City DF, Mexico.

FURTHER READING

Andrews, Edmund L. "FCC Clears Hallmark Sale of Univision TV Network." *The New York Times*, 1 October 1992.

Besas, Peter. "Dynastic Quarrels Undo Mex Media Mix." *Variety* (Los Angeles), 24 December 1990.

Deutschman, Alan. "Reclusive Tiger." *Fortune* (Chicago), 12 February 1990.

Fisher, Christy. "Azcarraga Again Prowls U.S. Media." *Advertising Age* (New York), 1 February 1993.

Malkin, Elisabeth. "The Rupert Murdoch of Mexico? Televisa's Azcarraga Wants to Crash the Global Major Leagues." *Business Week* (New York), 11 December 1995.

Millman, Joel. "El Tigre Pounces Again." *Forbes* (New York), 6 January 1992.

Stilson, Janet. "Hispanic Stations in Jeopardy: Staving Off Loss of TV Licenses." *Variety* (Los Angeles), 15 January 1986.

See also Mexico; Spanish International Network; Univision

B

BAIRD, JOHN LOGIE

Scottish Inventor

John Logie Baird pioneered early television with the mechanical scanning system he developed from 1923 to the late 1930s. He is remembered today as an inventor (178 patents) with considerable insight, who was in many ways ahead of his time. Among his pioneering ideas were early versions of color television, the video disc, large screen television, stereo television, televised sports, and pay television by closed circuit. But he is also a tragic figure who often worked alone for lack of financial backing and lived to see his technical ideas superseded. He was forgotten by the time he died at the age of 58.

Baird did not select television as a field of endeavor so much as he backed into it. As a teen, he had toyed with the notion of pictures by wireless, as had others fascinated with the new technology. Later, having unsuccessfully tried innovation in several more mundane fields (socks, jams, glass razors, shoe soles), Baird traveled to Hastings (on England's south coast) in 1923 to see if the sea air would aid his always marginal health. During a series of long walks there, his mind returned to his earlier notions of how to send wireless images. But he was not well trained in electronics, and this lack of basic knowledge often limited his thinking and experiments.

Beginning in 1923 and continuing until 1939, Baird produced a series of mechanical video systems that could scan (and thus transmit and receive) moving images. These offered a crude picture (about 30 lines of definition from 1929 to 1935, improving to about 240 before he broke off development) by means of a cumbersome system of large rotating discs fitted with lenses. Baird promoted initial public interest in television with the first public demonstrations (one in a London department store window) in 1925 to 1926, and long-distance transmissions by wire (between London and Glasgow in 1926) and short-wave (trans-Atlantic from London to New York in 1927). By 1928 he was experimenting with "phonovision," a means of recording his crude images on a phonograph-like disc. His efforts at promotion and sale of "televisor" devices created considerable controversy among experts as to whether television was sufficiently developed to promote public viewing and purchase of receivers.

For many years, the British Broadcasting Corporation (BBC) resisted his efforts to utilize their frequencies and studio facilities in his work. Under pressure from the British Post Office (then in charge of all wire and wireless transmission), the

John Logie Baird
Photo courtesy of the British Film Institute

BBC reluctantly began to work with Baird in 1930. Several years of experiments culminated in a regular daily broadcast comparison of his 240-line system with an RCA-like all-electronic 405-line system developed by Marconi-EMI in 1936–1937. Baird's now outmoded approach was soon dropped in favor of the latter's vastly superior electronic system.

Baird continued developmental work on color television, now making use of cathode-ray technology, and achieved 600-line experimental color telecasts by 1940. He continued his effort to perfect large-screen projection color television during the war, along with some apparent work for the British military. But his health, never strong, gave out and he died in 1946.

Did Baird "fail?" He ignored or denied the growing value of the cathode ray tube for too long (until the late 1930s), and held on to hopes for his mechanical alternative. His companies did not develop sufficient engineering depth and research capability beyond Baird himself. He kept no regular laboratory notes or records, making support for some of his claims difficult to find. And—perhaps most important as an indicator of impact—he achieved little commercial success. Still, there is growing appreciation of his pioneering if limited role amongst scholars of British television.

—Christopher H. Sterling

JOHN LOGIE BAIRD. Born in Helensburgh, Dumbartonshire, Scotland, 13 August 1888. Attended Royal Technical College, Glasgow, and Glasgow University. Served as superintendent, Clyde Valley Electric Power Company; helped pioneer television transmission, successfully transmitting image of a Maltese cross several feet, 1924; gave scientists a demonstration of "Noctovision," a form of infra-red television imaging, 26 January 1926; succeeded with world's first transatlantic television transmission from London to New York, and produced first television images in natural color, 1928; experimented with stereoscopic television; the BBC adopted his 30-line, mechanically-scanned system, 1929, used for the first televising of the Derby from Epsom, 1931. Recipient: first gold medal of the International Faculty of Science given to an Englishman, 1937; Gold Medal of the International Faculty of Science, 1937. Died in Bexhill, Sussex, England, 14 June 1946.

PUBLICATION

Sermons, Soap and Television: Autobiographical Notes. London: Royal Television Society, 1988.

FURTHER READING

Baird, Margaret. *Television Baird.* Cape Town, South Africa: Haum, 1973.
Burns, R. W. *British Television: The Formative Years.* London: Peter Peregrinus, 1986.
Exwood, Maurice. *John Logie Baird: 50 Years of Television.* London: Institution of Electronic and Radio Engineers History of Technology Monograph, 1976.
Hallett, Michael. *John Logie Baird and Television.* Hove, England: Priory, 1978.
McArthur, Tom, and Peter Wedell. *Vision Warrior: The Hidden Achievement of John Logie Baird.* Glasgow, Scotland: Scottish Falcon Books, 1990.
Moseley, Sydney. *John Baird: The Romance and Tragedy of the Pioneer of Television.* London: Odhams, 1953.
Percy, J.D. *John L. Baird: The Founder Of British Television.* London: Royal Television Society, 1950; Revised, 1952.
Rowland, John. *The Television Man: The Story of John L. Baird.* New York: Roy Publishers, 1966.
Tiltman, Ronald F. *Baird of Television: The Life Story of John Logie Baird.* London: Seeley Service, 1933; reprinted, New York: Arno Press, 1974.

See also Television Technology

BAKEWELL, JOAN

British Broadcast Journalist

Joan Bakewell has been one of the most respected presenters and commentators on British radio and television, with a career that spans more than thirty years. At the start of her career in the 1960s, she was one of the first women to establish a professional reputation in what had previously been an almost exclusively male preserve. She has since consolidated her status as one of the more serious-minded and thoughtful of television's "talking heads," making regular appearances both with the BBC and the independent companies and also becoming a regular writer for leading British broadsheet newspapers such as *The Times* and *The Sunday Times.*

Early appearances on such programmes as BBC2's *Late Night Line Up* provided evidence of her understanding of a range of subjects and her ability to extract from complex arguments the crucial issues underlying them. She also profited by her youthful good looks, which were to earn her the unwanted tag (initially bestowed by humorist Frank Muir) "the thinking man's crumpet." Gradually, though, Bakewell shook herself free of the limitations of her physical description and went on to present a wide range of programmes from current affairs, discussions of the arts and questions of public and private morality (notably in her long-running

Joan Bakewell
Photo courtesy of the British Film Institute

series *The Heart of the Matter*) to the less intellectual territory inhabited by, for instance, *Film 73* and *Holiday*.

Always calm, Bakewell has sometimes been accused of having a somewhat "dour" and even cold personality; viewers have complained that only rarely has she been seen to smile with any conviction. Intent on getting to the bottom of a particular issue, she is never distracted by opportunities for light relief or lured into exploring the possibilities of a colourful tangential course. Even when presenting holiday reports from various exotic parts of the globe she never gave the impression she was ready to abandon herself to anything resembling relaxed frivolity or other conventional "holiday-making" (she was consequently usually dispatched to report back from destinations with obvious cultural and artistic links).

This seriousness of purpose is, however, arguably dictated largely by the material Bakewell is usually associated with—weighty matters of relevance to consumers, voters and enthusiasts of the arts and so on. Her unflurried, concerned tone of voice enables the viewer to concentrate upon the intellectual questions being raised during discussions of such emotional topics as providing funds for the treatment of terminally ill children—questions that in less practiced hands could otherwise all too easily be swamped by sentimentality. There is nonetheless a lighter side to Bakewell's character, amply demonstrated by her contributions to the jovial BBC radio programme *Newsquiz*, among other humorous productions.

—David Pickering

JOAN (DAWSON) BAKEWELL. Born in Stockport, Cheshire, England, 16 April 1933. Attended Stockport High School for Girls, Stockport, Cheshire; Newnham College, Cambridge, B.A. Married 1) Michael Bakewell, 1955 (divorced, 1972); children: Matthew and Harriet; 2) Jack Emery, 1975. Joined BBC radio as studio manager; subsequently hosted numerous arts, travel, and current affairs programmes; television critic, *The Times*, 1978–81; associate, 1980–81, associate fellow, 1984–87, Newnham College, Cambridge; columnist, *Sunday Times*, since 1988; BBC television arts correspondent, 1981–87; has also written for *Punch* and *Radio Times*; President, Society of Arts Publicists, 1984–90; member, governing body, British Film Institute, since 1994. Address: Knight Ayton Management, 70A Berwick Street, London W1V 3PE, England.

TELEVISION SERIES

1962	*Sunday Break*
1964	*Home at 4.30*
1964	*Meeting Point*
1964	*The Second Sex*
1965–72	*Late Night Line Up*
1968	*The Youthful Eye*
1971	*Moviemakers at the National Film Theatre*
1972	*Film 72*
1973	*Film 73*
1973	*For the Sake of Appearance*
1973	*Where Is Your God?*
1973	*Who Cares?*
1973	*The Affirmative Way*
1974–78	*Holiday*
1974	*What's It all about?*
1974	*Time Running Out*
1974	*Thank You, Ron* (producer, writer)
1974	*Fairest Fortune*
1974	*Edinburgh Festival Report*
1976	*Generation to Generation*
1976	*The Shakespeare Business*
1976	*The Brontë Business*
1976–78	*Reports Action*
1977	*My Day with the Children*
1979	*The Moving Line*
1980	*Arts UK: OK?*
1988–	*The Heart of the Matter*

RADIO

Away from It all, 1978–79; *PM*, 1979–81; *Newsquiz*, *There and Back* (play; writer); *Parish Magazine* (play; writer).

STAGE

Brontës: The Private Faces (writer), 1979.

PUBLICATIONS

The New Priesthood: British Television Today, with Nicholas Garnham. London: Allen Lane, 1970.

A Fine and Private Place, with John Drummond. London: Weidenfeld and Nicholson, 1977.

The Complete Traveller. London: Sidgwick and Jackson, 1977.

BALL, LUCILLE

U.S. Actor and Comedienne

Lucille Ball was one of television's foremost pioneers and, quite likely, the preeminent woman in the history of television. As a young contract player for MGM, Ball began her career as a Goldwyn Girl, eventually moving up to become a moderately respected star of "B" movies. She came to television after nearly 20 years in motion pictures, having undergone a gradual transformation from a platinum blonde sex symbol to a wise-cracking redhead.

Her first television program, *I Love Lucy*, premiered 15 October 1951, and for the next 25 years Lucille Ball virtually ruled the airwaves in a series of situation comedies designed to exploit her elastic expressions, slapstick abilities and distinct verbal talents. A five-time Emmy Award winner, the first woman inducted into the Television Academy's Hall of Fame, recipient of a Genii Award and a Kennedy Center Honor, Lucille Ball was perhaps the most beloved of all television stars, and certainly the most recognizable.

In all of her television series, the protagonist she played was at once beautiful, zany, inept and talented. Her comedic skills were grounded in the style of the silent comics, and Buster Keaton, with whom she once shared an office at MGM, seems to have been particularly influential in the development of Ball's daring exploits, hang-dog expressions, and direct looks at the audience. Although she personally fueled the myth that much of her performance was ad-libbed, in actuality, every move was choreographed. An accomplished perfectionist, she spent days practicing a particular routine before incorporating it into her programs. So distinct were her rubbery facial expressions that scriptwriters for *I Love Lucy* referred to them with specific code word notations. For example, the cue "puddling up" directed the star to pause momentarily with huge tear-filled eyes and then burst into a loud wail. "Light bulb" was an indication to portray a sudden idea, while "credentials" directed the star to gape in astonished indignation. Her importance for future comediennes such as Mary Tyler Moore, Candice Bergen, and Cybill Shepard was paramount; Ball demonstrated that a woman could be beautiful and silly, and that she could perform the most outrageous of slapstick routines and still be feminine. Ball's unusual use of props and her imaginative escapes from the most implausible of situations influenced future sitcom stars such as Penny Marshall, Bronson Pinchot, Ellen Degeneris, and Robin Williams, whose comedic styles and series' storylines echoed her own.

But while her acting contributions are singularly laudable, it was Ball's role in re-defining the very structure of television programming that makes her noteworthy. Her independence, popularity, and determination, coupled with her husband's technical and financial savvy, resulted in their co-ownership and control of one of the most successful television production studios in history.

I Love Lucy was unique in that it was one of the first television series to be produced live on film, using a multiple camera technique in front of a studio audience. The filmed nature of the program granted it a permanency which allowed Ball and her husband, Desi Arnaz, to profit from re-runs, syndication and foreign distribution. The program was incomparably successful, reaching the number one position by February of its first season and remaining number one for four of its six years on the air, averaging a 67 share. Aired in over 100 countries, the series quite literally financed the creation of Desilu Studios, where Ball and her husband reigned as vice president and president respectively. Desilu went on to become the production headquarters of many of the greatest hits of 1950s and 1960s television programs, including *Our Miss Brooks*, *Make Room for Daddy*, *The Dick Van Dyke Show*, *The Untouchables*, *Mission Impossible*, *Mannix* and *Star Trek*.

Lucille Ball

Indeed, it was Ball's clout with the CBS network that convinced them to pick up the latter three pilots.

Ball's first success with *I Love Lucy* allowed her a power denied most entertainers. She was one of the few 1950s television stars to successfully fight the Communist witch hunts of HUAC, when a 1953 Walter Winchell program attempted to derail her career. Established film stars, such as Orson Welles, William Holden and Joan Crawford, who had previously shunned television, made guest-appearances for the sake of appearing with the queen of prime time. Ball's popularity with the press and her fans forced CBS executives to acquiesce to her decision to reveal her real-life pregnancy during the show's second season. This television first was monitored carefully by a trio of clergy who oversaw each script. While timid CBS executives insisted the word "expectant" be substituted for "pregnant," seven episodes detailed the fictional Lucy's pregnancy in near symmetry with the actress's own physical condition. Backlogging five episodes for use while she convalesced from delivery, the program worked around Ball's due date, so that her real life Caesarean delivery coincided with the airing of her television delivery. The episode set a rating record of 71.1, with more viewers tuning in to witness the fictional Lucy Ricardo give birth than had seen Eisenhower's inauguration.

With her 1962 buyout of Desilu from her by then ex-husband Desi Arnaz, Ball became the first woman to head a major television production studio. Through the mid-1970s she starred in three additional series for CBS, with her third series, *The Lucy Show,* earning the highest initial price ever paid for a thirty-minute series ($2.3 million dollars for 30 episodes). In the mid-1960s, she sold Desilu to Gulf and Western for $17 million, and she went on to form Lucille Ball Productions with her second husband, Gary Morton, as vice president. Her final CBS series, *Here's Lucy,* while not as critically acclaimed as her previous ventures, was responsible for launching the careers of her children Lucie and Desi Arnaz, Jr., and for bringing Elizabeth Taylor and Richard Burton into situation comedy.

By the mid-1970s the diffused lighting, the surgical tape "face lifts," the skilled makeup and bright wig could not hide her diminishing physical flexibility or her increasing reliance on cue-cards. A 1986 ABC series, *Life with Lucy,* seemed forced and stodgy and lasted a mere 13 weeks. But even in her decline there were flashes of brilliance. In 1985 she surprised critics and fans with her appearance as a homeless woman in the CBS made-for-tv movie *Stone Pillow.* With her death in 1989, she was eulogized by fans, network executives, and even the president of the United States, as "the first woman of television."

For all her impact upon the very nature of television production, Ball is most vividly recalled as a series of black-and-white images. To remember Lucille Ball is to recall a profusion of universal images of magical mayhem—a losing battle with a candy conveyor belt, a flaming nose, a slippery vat of grapes—images which, contrary to most American situation comedy, transcend nationalities and generations, in an absolute paradigm of side-splitting laughter.

—Nina C. Leibman

LUCILLE (DÉSIRÉE) BALL (Lucy Montana, Diane Belmont). Born in Jamestown, New York, U.S.A. 6 August 1911. Attended John Murray Anderson-Robert Milton Dramatic School, New York City. Married: 1) Desi Arnaz, 1940 (divorced, 1960); children: Lucie Désirée and Desi, Jr.; 2) Gary Morton, 1961. Began her performing career in the 1920s under the name Diane Belmont, being hired for, then quickly fired from, Earl Carroll's *Vanities* and the Shuberts' *Stepping Stones*; had a walk-on role in *Broadway Thru a Keyhole,* 1933; selected as a "Goldwyn Girl" for film *Roman Scandals,* 1933; signed with Columbia, 1934; under contract to RKO, from 1935; moved to MGM 1943–46; played role on CBS radio program *My Favorite Husband,* 1947–50; co-starred with Bob Hope in *Sorrowful Jones,* 1949, and *Fancy Pants,* 1950; with husband Desi Arnaz established Desilu Productions, which began producing the *I Love Lucy* television series, 1951–57, and later series such as *The Ann Sothern Show* and *The Untouchables*; with Arnaz, bought RKO studios and lot in 1957,; debuted on Broadway in *Wildcat,* 1960; bought Arnaz's share of Desilu, 1962, which she managed until 1967; sold Desilu to Gulf and Western Industries, 1967; formed and managed Lucille Ball Productions, 1968; starred in film *Mame,* 1974; played a Manhattan bag lady in made-for-television movie *Stone Pillow,* 1985; starred in series *Life with Lucy,* 1986. Recipient: 5

Emmy Awards; Golden Apple Award, 1973; Ruby Award, 1974; Entertainer of the Year, 1975; Television Academy Hall of Fame, 1984. Died in Los Angeles, 26 April 1989.

TELEVISION SERIES

1951–57	*I Love Lucy*
1957–60	*The Lucille Ball and Desi Arnaz Show*
1962-65, 1967	*The Lucy-Desi Comedy Hour*
1962–68	*The Lucy Show*
1968–74	*Here's Lucy*
1986	*Life with Lucy*

MADE-FOR-TELEVISION MOVIES

1974	*Happy Anniversary and Goodbye*
1976	*What Now, Catherine Curtis?*
1985	*Stone Pillow*

TELEVISION SPECIALS

1975	*The Lucille Ball Special Starring Lucille Ball and Dean Martin*
1975	*The Lucille Ball Special Starring Lucille Ball and Jackie Gleason*
1977	*Bob Hope's All-Star Tribute to Vaudeville*

FILMS

Bulldog Drummond, 1929; *Broadway Thru a Keyhole,* 1933; *Blood Money,* 1933; *Roman Scandals,* 1933; *The Bowery,* 1933; *Moulin Rouge,* 1934; *Nana,* 1934; *Bottoms Up,* 1934; *Hold That Girl,* 1934; *Bulldog Drummond Strikes Back,* 1934; *The Affairs of Cellini,* 1934; *Kid Millions,* 1934; *Broadway Bill,* 1934; *Jealousy,* 1934; *Men of the Night,* 1934; *Fugitive Lady,* 1934; *The Whole Town's Talking,* 1934; *Carnival,* 1935; *Roberta,* 1935; *Old Man Rhythm,* 1935; *The Three Musketeers,* 1935; *Top Hat,* 1935; *I Dream Too Much,* 1935; *The Farmer in the Dell,* 1936; *Chatterbox,* 1936; *Follow the Fleet,* 1936; *Bunker Bean,* 1936; *That Girl from Paris,* 1936; *Winterset,* 1936; *Don't Tell the Wife,* 1937; *Stage Door,* 1937; *Go Chase Yourself,* 1938; *Joy of Living,* 1938; *Having Wonderful Time,* 1938; *The Affairs of Annabel,* 1938; *Room Service,* 1938; *The Next Time I Marry,* 1938; *Annabel Takes a Tour,* 1939; *Beauty for the Asking,* 1939; *Twelve Crowded Hours,* 1939; *Panama Lady,* 1939; *Five Came Back,* 1939; *That's Right, You're Wrong,* 1939; *The Marines Fly High,* 1940; *You Can't Fool Your Wife,* 1940; *Dance, Girl, Dance,* 1940; *Too Many Girls,* 1940; *A Girl, a Guy and a Gob,* 1941; *Look Who's Laughing,* 1941; *Valley of the Sun,* 1942; *The Big Street,* 1942; *Seven Days' Leave,* 1942; *Dubarry Was a Lady,* 1943; *Best Foot Forward,* 1943; *Thousands Cheer,* 1943; *Meet the People,* 1944; *Ziegfeld Follies,* 1944 (released 1946); *Without Love,* 1945; *Bud Abbott and Lou Costello in Hollywood,* 1945; *The Dark Corner,* 1946; *Easy to Wed,* 1946; *Two Smart People,* 1946; *Lover Come Back,* 1946; *Lured,* 1947; *Her Husband's Affairs,* 1947; *Sorrowful Jones,* 1949; *Easy Living,* 1949; *Miss Grant Takes Richmond,* 1949; *A Woman of Distinction,* 1950; *Fancy Pants,* 1950; *The Fuller Brush Girl,* 1950; *The Magic Carpet,* 1951; *The Long, Long Trailer,* 1954; *Forever, Darling,* 1956; *Critic's Choice,* 1963; *A*

Guide for the Married Man, 1967; *Yours, Mine and Ours*, 1968; *Mame*, 1974.

RADIO

Phil Baker's show, 1938; Jack Haley's *Wonder Bread Show*, 1938; *Lux Radio Theatre*; *Suspense*; *Screen Guild Playhouse*; *My Favorite Husband*, 1947–50.

STAGE

Dream Girl, 1947–48; vaudeville tour with Desi Arnaz, 1950; *Wildcat*, 1960.

FURTHER READING

Andrews, Bart. *Lucy and Ricky and Fred and Ethel*. New York: Dutton, 1976.

———. *The "I Love Lucy" Book*. Garden City, New York: Doubleday, 1985.

Andrews, Bart, and Thomas Watson. *Loving Lucy: An Illustrated Tribute to Lucille Ball*. New York: St. Martin's, 1980.

Arnaz, Desi. *A Book by Desi Arnaz*. New York: Morrow, 1976.

Brochu, Jim. *Lucy in the Afternoon: An Intimate Memoir of Lucille Ball*. New York: William Morrow, 1990.

Dinter, Charlotte. "I Just Couldn't Take Any More." *Photoplay* (New York), June 1960.

Higham, Charles. *Lucy: The Life of Lucille Ball*. New York: St. Martin's, 1986.

"Lucille Ball" (interview). *Dialogue on Film* (Beverly Hills, California), May-June 1974.

Morella, Joe, and Edward Epstein. *Lucy: The Bittersweet Life of Lucille Ball*. Secaucus, New Jersey: L. Stuart, 1986.

Nugent, Frank. "The Bouncing Ball." *Photoplay* (New York), September 1946.

Shipman, David. *The Great Movie Stars: The Golden Years*. New York: Crown, 1970.

See also Arnaz, Desi; Comedy, Domestic Settings; *I Love Lucy*; Gender and Television; Independent Production Companies

BARBERA, JOSEPH See HANNA, WILLIAM, AND JOSEPH BARBERA

BASSETT, JOHN

Canadian Media Executive

Few individuals in the history of Canadian television have inspired as much controversy as John Bassett, a founder of Toronto station CFTO and key figure in the formation of the CTV network, Canada's first privately-owned television network. Bassett parleyed a career in journalism and his financial connections into a major ownership role in Canadian commercial television. Media historian Paul Rutherford identifies him as one of the architects of Canadian television.

When in 1959 the Board of Broadcast Governors (BBG), reflecting the views of the recently elected Conservative government of John Diefenbaker, decided to allow an expansion of private telecasting in Canada, the most coveted market was Toronto, seen correctly as a potential gold mine. Many prominent business groups wanted the license and nine eventually applied. Bassett joined the Eaton family, owners of a large department store chain, and others in an enterprise known as BATON Broadcasting, which was awarded the Toronto rights. When the winner was announced, the decision was roundly criticized. Some critics alleged that Bassett, a party insider and (unsuccessful) candidate for the Progressive Conservative party, had capitalized on his political connections and personal relationship with the prime minister. The new licensee also owned the Toronto *Telegram*, an unashamedly right-wing supporter of the

John Bassett
Photo courtesy of the National Archives of Canada

party. This connection also aroused concerns about cross-media ownership. Bassett may have had some influence on the Diefenbaker government's decision to weaken the television monopoly held by the public network. However, historians report no evidence that the prime minister personally intervened in the BBG decision to award the license to BATON.

Conflict of interest was also suspected when the rights to televise Canadian professional football games went to BATON, rather than to the CBC with its national audience. Bassett also owned the Toronto club in the league at the time. Initially cool to Spence Caldwell's CTV network, Bassett was forced to come to an agreement with CTV—and the CBC—to reach a national audience for the then highly popular Canadian Football League telecasts. The national championship, known as the Grey Cup game, was a major national event, important to viewers and profitable for broadcasters with a national audience. Once in the fold, Bassett came to dominate the private network.

With its prime-time schedule filled with American imports, CFTO was soon accused of reneging on its promises during the license hearings to promote Canadian content. Similar allegations were levelled at the entire CTV network, and the BBG was seen as either gullible or politically motivated in failing to enforce promises made during application hearings. During the BBG hearings, the BATON group had promised to fight the "battle of Buffalo," appealing to Canadian cultural concerns about American domination. Bassett's promise was to compete with Buffalo, New York, television stations for Toronto viewers, many of whom had been watching American programming for some years before Canadian stations came on the air.

Making matters worse, BATON agreed to sell stock to the American network ABC, a move endorsed by the BBG in 1961. Condemnation of the sale was fierce and sustained. The BBG retracted its decision, but Bassett engineered a different arrangement whereby ABC would make a substantial loan to CFTO in return for a contract to provide "management services" and personnel. This issue arose from concerns about undue American influence in the operation and development of Canadian television.

CFTO went on the air on 1 January 1961 and by the early 1970s was extremely profitable. BATON was clearly the key force behind CTV and provided production services through Glen Warren Productions. Toronto was the center for CTV's limited Canadian production activities and Bassett and his partners began to purchase other media assets, including shares in other CTV affiliates. At times BATON's ambitions have collided with other partners in the network. This produced friction with other ambitious owners.

Bassett ran BATON from its inception until 1979, when he turned the day-to-day operations over to his son, Douglas, who has overseen further expansion of BATON's activities. Well over six feet tall and projecting a "tough, arrogant" image, John Bassett was a major player in the development of commercial television in Canada and the erosion of the dominance of the publicly-owned Canadian Broadcasting Corporation. Perhaps not surprisingly, given his newspaper background, Bassett's stations made their greatest contributions in news and public affairs programming.

—Frederick J. Fletcher and Robert Everett

JOHN BASSETT. Began career in journalism; owner of CFTO-TV, Toronto, and the Toronto *Telegram;* significant leader in CTV, Canadian commercial television network co-operative from 1966; chairman of the Toronto Argonauts football team.

FURTHER READING
Desbarats, Peter. *Guide to Canadian News Media.* Toronto: Harcourt Brace Jovanovich, 1990.
Levine, Allen. *Scrum Wars: The Prime Ministers and the Media.* Toronto: Dundurn, 1993.
Rayboy, Marc. *Missed Opportunities: The Story of Canada's Broadcasting Policy.* Montreal: McGill-Queen's University Press, 1990.
Siggins, Maggie. *Bassett.* Toronto: Lorimer, 1979.

BATMAN

U.S. Adventure Parody

Batman was created by Bob Kane in 1939 as a comic book hero. During his long career he was featured in the *Superman* radio series and in two movie serials produced during World War II. In 1966 the ABC network decided to produce the first *Batman* television series and it became an immediate hit. Initially, the show aired twice a week. On Wednesdays, Batman and his sidekick Robin would confront one of their archenemies and would end the episode in horrible danger, only to save themselves at the beginning of the next episode on Thursdays. These cliffhangers closely followed the tradition created by Kane in the comic books.

The television series also followed the comic books' plot. Bruce Wayne (played by Adam West) was orphaned in his teens when criminals killed his parents. He inherited a huge fortune and, obsessed with fighting the evil-doers who plagued Gotham City, became Batman, the Caped Crusader. Under his mansion, Batman constructed the Batcave, an elaborate laboratory used to fight crime. His young ward, Dick Grayson (played by Burt Ward), also orphaned due to evil-doers, became Robin, the Boy Wonder, under Batman/Wayne's tutelage. Together they defended the city against the sick minded criminals that populated the underworld. The only person who knew their identity was Alfred (Alan Napier), Wayne's butler who raised Bruce after his parents were killed. In the Batlab, and at the Batcave, Batman and Robin were helped by the most advanced technology to fight their enemies. Police Commissioner Gordon (Neil Hamilton) could ask Batman for help either through the use of a searchlight, the Batsignal, or the Bat-phone, a direct line between the Police Station and Bruce Wayne's mansion. To defeat their enemies, Batman and Robin also used the Batmobile, their utility belts and other Batdevices.

The success of the series attracted several famous actors and actress to play the villains. Among the most famous enemies were the Riddler (played first by Frank Gorshin and then John Astin), the Penguin (Burgess Meredith), the Joker (Cesar Romero), King Tut (Victor Buono), Egghead (Vincent Price) and Catwoman (played at different times by Julie Newmar, Lee Ann Meriwether, and Eartha Kitt).

Batman incorporated the expressive art and fashion of the period in its sets and costumes. It also relied excessively on technological gadgetry transforming the show into a parody of contemporary life. It was this self-reflexive parody-camp of the comic character that boosted the ratings of the program to the top ten during its first season. The show was not to be taken seriously. The acting was intentionally overdone and the situations extremely contrived. In the fight scenes animated "Bangs," "Pows," and "Bops" would fill the screen every time a blow was struck. These characteristics, besides displeasing the "organized vocal Batman fans," were not enough to save the show (Boichel, 1991).

Batman came to television under a massive advertising campaign followed by heavy merchandising placement. Directed towards adults and children, this campaign reached the millions of dollars (McNeil, 1991). Originally scheduled to start at the fall of 1966, the show debuted earlier in the middle of the spring season. ABC aired Batman on prime-time from 12 January 1966, to 14 March 1968. By fall 1966, ratings were already falling. To offset this trend, in the fall season of 1967, the show was cut to once a week and Batgirl was introduced. This time she came to save the show from falling ratings and not to protect Batman and Robin against accusations of a homoerotic relationship, as was the case for her creation by the comic book writers in the mid-1950s. Batgirl (Yvonne Craig), the daughter of Commissioner Gordon and a librarian, fought crime on her own and was many times paired with the Dynamic Duo. Her debut, however, was not enough to save the series. The producers tried to spice the plots with the new sexy heroine, but it did not work and *Batman* went off the air in mid-season in the spring of 1968.

In September 1968 CBS produced an animated version of *Batman* in which the super Duo shared one hour with Superman (in separated segments). Even though the program introduced a less camp version of Batman and Robin, possibly in response to fan criticisms to the prime-time serial, the program lasted only two seasons. Between February and

Batman

September 1977 CBS broadcast an animated version with the voices of Adam West and Burt Ward. In September of that year, CBS changed the *New Adventures of Batman* to *The Batman/Tarzan Hour*, in which Batman and Tarzan shared one hour back to back, in separated segments.

In the fall of 1992 FOX television released a new animated series capitalizing on publicity for the movie, *Batman Returns*. This new series followed the stylistic changes in the comic book hero. The FOX series earned critical and popular acclaim for its high-quality graphics and action-packed storylines. Interestingly, as in the two Batman movies released in the 1990s, this new animated series erased Robin from the scene, possibly responding to criticisms of the homoerotic subtext between the two heroes. Originally shown every afternoon, the FOX series moved to the Saturday morning FOX line-up in the spring of 1994. At the same time the series also brought Robin back, possibly responding to the word that a new Batman, film to be released in 1995, would again include Robin in its plot.

—Antonio C. Lapastina

CAST

Bruce Wayne (Batman)	Adam West
Dick Grayson (Robin)	Burt Ward
Alfred Pennyworth	Alan Napier
Aunt Harriet Cooper	Madge Blake
Police Commissioner Gordon	Neil Hamilton
Chief O'Hara	Stafford Repp
Barbara Gordon (Batgirl) (1967–68)	Yvonne Craig

PRODUCERS   William Dozier, Howie Horwitz

PROGRAMMING HISTORY   120 Episodes

• ABC

January 1966–August 1967
                                    Wednesday and Thursday 7:30-8:00
September 1967–March 1968   Thursday 7:30-8:00

FURTHER READING

Grossman, G. *Saturday Morning TV.* New York: Arlington House, 1987.

Pearson, R., and W. Uricchio, editors. *The Many Lives of Batman: Critical Approaches to a Superhero and his Media.* New York: Routledge, 1991.

Reynolds, R. *Super Heroes: A Modern Mythology.* London: Batsford, 1992.

BBC See BRITISH TELEVISION

THE BEACHCOMBERS

Canadian Family Drama Series

The *Beachcombers*, in production for 19 years, was the longest running series drama in Canadian television history. Developed by Marc Strange, producer Phil Keately, and a string of very good West Coast writers, this family series turned on the adventures of an ensemble of characters. Nick Adonidas (Bruno Gerussi) was a licensed beachcomber on the North West Coast of British Columbia. He was primarily involved with his young Native partner Jesse (Pat Johns) and his unscrupulous adversary and rival beachcomber Relic (Robert Clothier). Working out of the port of Gibson's Landing, Nick runs the *Persephone* into the inlets of the Sunshine coast, a setting filled with rugged individuals. The combination of characters, locations, and events strongly appealed to audiences abroad and was a driving force of the show's plot.

The format focused on physical action—boat chases, storms, rising tides, various rites of passage, a long-distance swim, taming a wild dog, a vision quest, but violence was largely confined to physical objects which break up or blow up or somehow threaten the characters. Comedy was part of almost every episode, and there was often a documentary flavour to the scenes of fishing, logging, and beachcombing. The show also used Canada's multi-cultural diversity. Germans, Italians, Japanese, Dutch, East Indians, Swedes, and even a Colonel Blimp from England, all provided opportunities for new plot developments.

Well-loved characters from the early seasons included the two children, Margaret and her older brother Hughie, and their "gran" who owned "Molly's Reach." As Jesse matured he was joined by a small sister, Sara, who also grew up on the show. He then married a widow, Laurel, whose son, Tommy, became the series' resident child. In *Beachcombers*, children of both sexes were respected as human beings who had much to learn and to share. Other running characters were Gus McLoskey, Captain Joe, and teenaged homeless lad, Pat O'Gorman. Constable John, the well-meaning, slightly klutzy member of the RCMP (Royal Canadian Mounted Police) was one of the most popular of the continuing characters. He very seldom pulled a gun or even made an arrest.

The basic premise of *The Beachcombers* demanded that Nick remain a volatile Greek, unattached and available for many interesting women. Relic was his clever, unscrupulous, abrupt, antagonist for 19 years. Early on, his misanthropy was given a context in one of the best episodes, "Runt o' the Litter," written by Merv Campone. Born to a loveless Welsh coal-mining family, Relic is despised by his father—the father for whom he has nevertheless built fantasies of wealth in letters home. In this episode Relic's "Da," is present, and in some sort of doomed attempt to win back the family's honour, challenges Nick, 30 years younger, to an anchor pull. Others look on in horror as "Da" collapses in the sand, humiliated by yet another "failure." Relic, full of hatred and contempt, yet disappointed—every emotion to be read on the actor's face—grabs the rope, hauls the anchor across the line and says bitterly to his father "go home." The old man weeps. The episode is a miniature tragedy. Such ambiguity and ambivalence appeared regularly in the show's early years, and writers and producers occasionally used non-comedic endings, cutting against the grain of the genre.

The best episodes of the later years used two narrative strategies. The first was to continue the introduction of topical issues—the recurring issue of the confiscation of Japanese fishing boats during World War II, clear-cutting logging practices, or First Nations' land claims. This last topic was treated primarily in stories involving "The Reach," enabling writers to focus the issue in familiar terms using Laurel and Jesse, characters whom viewers knew well. Nick's fictional surrogate family and the show's viewers were disturbed—and informed. The second narrative strategy of the series' later period continued to revolve around conflicts between Relic and various other characters. As the 1980s brought increasing awareness of cultural appropriation and rising political tensions, however, this distinctive thread almost disappeared.

In a late attempt to boost ratings, a displaced urban mom, Dana, and her son, Sam, took over "The Reach." But conflicts constructed around urban/small-town, or capable Westerner/effete Easterner seemed not to interest the audience. The writing became tired, the plots full of action sequences. The series ended with an elegiac but rather lifeless one-hour special. To this day, however, the reruns and world-wide syndication of *Beachcombers* represent Canada and Canadians to millions of viewers around the world.

—Mary Jane Miller

CAST

Nick Adonis . . . . Bruno Gerussi
Molly . . . . Rae Brown
Hughie . . . . Bob Park
Margaret . . . . Nancy Chapple
Jesse . . . . Pat Johns
Relic . . . . Robert Clothier
Constable John . . . . Jackson Davies

PRODUCERS   Philip Keatley, Elie Savoie, Hugh Beard, Bob Fredericks, Don S. Williams, Brian McKeown, Gordon Mark, Derek Gardner

PROGRAMMING HISTORY

• CBC

324 Episodes
November 1972–October 1983   Sunday 7:00-7:30
November 1983–October 1989   Sunday 7:30-8:00
November 1989–April 1990   Wednesdays 7:00-7:30

FURTHER READING

Miller, Mary Jane. *Turn Up the Contrast: CBC Drama Since 1952.* Vancouver, Canada: University of British Columbia Press, 1987.
———. *Rewind and Search.* Montreal: McGill-Queen's University Press, 1996.

See also Canadian Programming in English; Gerussi, Bruno

BEATON, NORMAN

British Actor

Norman Beaton was one of those unique actors who managed to scale classical roles, yet excel in light comedies. From 1989 to 1994 he enjoyed nationwide popularity on British television with Channel 4's highly successful situation comedy series *Desmond's*. This show was described as an African-Caribbean equivalent of America's *The Cosby Show*. With sharp scripts by young black writer Trix Worrell, Beaton gave a brilliant performance as the manic owner of a South London barbershop.

Born in Guyana (then British Guiana), Beaton came to Britain in 1960. His reputation as an actor grew steadily. He progressed from regional theater to leading roles at the Old Vic, the National Theatre (where he played Angelo in a blackcast version of Shakespeare's *Measure for Measure* in 1981) and the Royal Court Theatre. Apart from Shakespeare, his theater roles also encompassed Pinter, Beckett, Gilbert and Sullivan, Brecht, Moliere, and pantomime. In 1974 he established the Black Theatre of Brixton, which was instrumental in developing black theatre in Britain. During this period he also became one of Britain's leading television actors. Among his biggest successes were dramatic roles in *Afternoon Dancing* (1974); *Black Christmas* (1977); *Empire Road* (1978-79), Britain's first all-black soap opera; *Play for Today's* "Easy Money" (1981); *Nice* (1984); *Dead Head* (1986); *Playing Away* (1986); *Big George is Dead* (1987); *When Love Dies* (1990); and *Little Napoleons* (1993). He was also interviewed in the documentary *Black and White in Colour* (1992), a history of black people in British television.

Norman Beaton
Photo courtesy of the British Film Institute

Alongside Lenny Henry, Norman Beaton was the star of British television's first black situation comedy series, *The Fosters,* which ran for two series in 1976-77. But the actor will be best remembered for *Desmond's.* As a result of its popularity, African-American television star Bill Cosby invited him in 1991 to make a couple of guest appearances in *The Cosby Show.* Beaton readily accepted a role as a cricket-loving doctor, and Cosby was so taken by the actor that he wore Beaton's gift of a *Desmond's* baseball cap in the show. Shortly after he died in 1994 at the age of 60, Channel 4 aired *Shooting Stars* in the series *Black Christmas* with a memorable appearance by Beaton reading a sonnet by Shakespeare.

—Stephen Bourne

NORMAN (LUGARD) BEATON. Born in Georgetown, British Guiana (now Guyana), 31 October 1934. Attended local schools in Georgetown. Married and divorced three times; children: Jeremy, Norman, Jayme and Kim. Made debut as actor while at teacher training college, 1956; enjoyed success as singer and recording artist, becoming Guyana Calypso Champion, 1956; settled in Britain, 1960, and worked as teacher, Liverpool; appeared in repertory theatre, Liverpool, Bristol and Worthing, late 1960s, made television debut, 1966; subsequently stage, television and radio performer; chair: Black Theatre of Brixton, 1975; events subcommittee (U.K.), World Black and African Festival of Arts and Culture, 1976; Minorities Arts Advisory Service, 1979; artistic director, Ira Aldridge Memorial Theatre Company, 1983. Member: Consultative Committee for the Arts Britain Ignores, 1975; Afro-Asian subcommittee, British Actors Equity, 1979; West Midlands Arts and Drama Advisory Panel, 1979. Recipient: Variety Club of Great Britain Film Actor of the Year Award, 1978; *Caribbean Post* Golden Sunshine Award, 1978. Died 13 December 1994.

TELEVISION SERIES

1976–77	*The Fosters*
1978–79	*Empire Road*
1985	*Dead Head*
1989–94	*Desmond's*
1994	*Little Napoleons*

MADE-FOR-TELEVISION MOVIES

1977	*Black Christmas*
1980	*Growing Pains*
1986	*Playing Away*

FILMS (selection)

Two for a Birdie, Pressure, 1975; *Black Joy,* 1977; *Barbados,* 1978 (narrator); *Eureka,* 1982; *Real Life,* 1983.

RADIO

I Come from the Sun, 1966; *Blues for Mister Charlie,* 1974; *Finding Manbee,* 1974; *Home Again,* 1975; *Carnival in Trinidad,* 1975; *Margie,* 1975; *Pantomime,* 1978; *Play Mas,* 1979; *Alterations,* 1980; *The Fast Lane,* 1980; *Remembrance,* 1981; *The British Empire Part 2,* 1982; *The Comedians,* 1984; *No Get Out Clause,* 1985; *Ascension Ritual,* 1985; *Still Life,* 1985; *Cricket's a Mug's Game,* 1985.

RECORDING (selection)

Come Back Melvina, 1959.

STAGE

Le Bourgeois Gentilhomme (composer), 1956; *Jack of Spades,* 1965; *Cleo* (composer and narrator), 1965; *Bristol Fashion* (composer and narrator), 1966; *A Tale of Two Cities* (composer and narrator), 1966; *The Ticket-of-Leave Man,* 1968; *Richard Three* (composer and narrator), 1968; *The Merchant of Venice,* 1968; *Shylock X,* 1968; *Sit Down Banna* (writer); *The Country Wife* (also composer and narrator), 1968; *Bakerloo to Paradise,* 1968; *So You Think You're One of Us,* 1968; *The Tempest,* 1970; *Prometheus Bound,* 1971; *Arrest,* 1971; *Murderous Angels,* 1971; *Pirates,* 1971; *Tyger,* 1971; *The National Health,* 1971; *Cato Street,* 1971; *Two for a Birdie,* 1971; *The Threepenny Opera,* 1972; *Up the Chastity Belt,* 1972; *Signs of the Times,* 1973; *Talk Shop,* 1973; *Mind Your Head,* 1973; *Larry and Marian,* 1973; *Play Mas,* 1974; *Anansi and the Strawberry Queen* (director), 1974; *Jumbee Street March* (director), 1974; *The Black Mikado,* 1975; *Rum and Coca-Cola,* 1976; *Seduced* (director), 1978; *Sergeant Ola and His Followers,* 1979; *Nice,* 1980; *Samba,* 1980; *Measure for Measure,* 1981; *The Caretaker,* 1981; *The Night of the Day of the Imprisoned Writer,* 1981; *In the Mood,* 1981; *The Miser,* 1982; *The Sol Raye Variety Gala* (also director), 1982; *You Can't Take It With You,* 1983; *Cargo Kings,* 1983; *Jackanory,* 1983; *Blues for Railton,* 1985; *The Black Jacobins,* 1986.

PUBLICATION

Beaton But Unbowed (autobiography). London: Methuen, 1986.

FURTHER READING

Bourne, Stephen. *Black in the British Frame—Black People in British Film and Television 1896–1996.* London: Cassell, 1996.

Pines, Jim, editor. *Black and White in Colour—Black People in British Television Since 1936.* London: British Film Institute, 1992.

See also *Desmond's*

BEAVIS AND BUTT-HEAD

U.S. Cartoon

Beavis and Butt-head was first aired on the U.S. cable network MTV in March 1993. This show, which combined animation and music videos, was an example of the unique programming that MTV has consistently provided for its youthful demographics. The half-hour program alternated between a simple narrative, which focused on the exploits of two low-life adolescents, and clips from music videos, which the two teens commented on. Creator Mike Judge had penned the aimless duo for a festival of animation when Abby Turkuhle, MTV's senior vice president picked up an episode for the network's animated compendium *Liquid Television*. MTV immediately contracted for 65 episodes from Judge, with Turkuhle as producer, and placed *Beavis and Butt-head* in the 7:00 and 11:00 P.M. week-day time slots.

The characters, Beavis and Butt-head, are rude, crude, and stupid, and can be placed in the "dumb comedy" tradition, which includes Abbott and Costello, the Three Stooges, Cheech and Chong, *Saturday Night Live's* Wayne and Garth, and FOX's *The Simpsons*. When the show debuted, television critics differed in their opinions, with some praising the show for daring to present the stupidity of male "metalheads" who watch too much television (effectively satirizing the core MTV audience), and others categorizing *Beavis and Butt-head* as another example of television's declining quality. *Beavis and Butt-head* did find an audience and began pulling in MTV's highest ratings. But the show was also quite controversial, instigating heated public debate on the interconnected issues of representations of violence in the media and generational politics surrounding youth subcultures.

In October 1993 a two-year-old Ohio girl was killed in a fire lit by her five-year-old brother. The children's mother said that her son was inspired by the pyromaniac proclivities of *Beavis and Butt-head*. This real life event sparked the ire of media watchdog groups, who claimed that there was a direct link between the television show and the violent act of this impressionable child. One psychiatrist proclaimed *Beavis and Butt-head* a "Sesame Street for psychopaths." Concurrent Senate hearings on television violence placed these issues at the forefront of American cultural politics. Because of this incident, and given the cultural climate, MTV eliminated all references to fire, pulled four episodes off the air, and moved the cartoon to 10:30-11:30 P.M. only. MTV insisted that they changed the time slot, not because they believed the show was directly responsible for the incident, but because they felt that it was designed for an older audience, and that a different time slot would allow them to target that audience more effectively. Claiming that 90% of its audience was over 12 years of age, MTV attempted to move the discussion away from the children's television debate.

Beavis and Butt-head, they found, was especially popular with those in their twenties. It turned out to be bother-

some to many that young people enjoyed the show and laughed at its two imbecilic boys, even if these fans were much more intelligent and much less grating than Beavis and Butt-head. In this sense, *Beavis and Butt-head* raised the issue of generational taste cultures. Definitions of "taste," Pierre Bourdieu notes, "unite and separate, uniting those who are the product of similar conditions but only by distinguishing them from all others. And taste distinguishes in an essential way, since it is the basis of all that one has—people and things—and of all that one is for others, whereby one classifies oneself and is classified by others." To the degree that taste cultures agree, they are brought together into a subcultural formation; but to this degree they are also separated from those with whom they differ. It was the "bad taste" of *Beavis and Butt-head's* audience which bothered many, and this brings to the surface another one of the reasons why *Beavis and Butt-head* was so controversial.

Cultural critics, educators, and concerned parents gathered skeptically, sternly, and anxiously in front of the television set and passed judgment upon the "tasteless" *Beavis and Butt-head* show. And in an ironic reversal, *Beavis and Butt-head* countered by ascending the cultural hierarchy. The two youths channel-surfed, looking for videos that didn't suck (i.e. those with heavy metal or hardcore rap, those that contained violence, or encouraged genital response). In becoming the self-proclaimed Siskel and Ebert of music video,

Beavis and Butt-head

they served to evaluate pop culture with an unencumbered bottom line—does a music video "suck" or is it "cool?" *Beavis and Butt-head* as a television show, was certainly towards the lower end of traditional scales of cultural "quality." But these two animated "slackers" evaluated other media, and so pronounced their own critical opinions and erected their own taste hierarchies. Beavis and Butt-head had their own particular brand of "taste:" they determined acceptability and unacceptability, invoking, while simultaneously upending, notions of "high" and "low" culture. In this, they entered that hallowed sphere of criticism, where they competed with others in overseeing the public good and preserving the place and status of artistic evaluation. They disregarded other accepted forms of authority, refusing to acknowledge their own limited perspectives. But like other critics, this was an important part of their appeal. After all, critics are sought out for straightforward opinion, not muddled oscillation.

In this recuperation of the critical discourse, Beavis and Butt-head joined with their audience, approximating the contradictory impulses of contemporary cynical youth, who mixed their self-delusion with self-awareness. In the case of fans of *Beavis and Butt-head*, these lines of demarcation indicated both a generational unity and the generation-based barriers between the baby boomers and the "baby busters." The reputed cynicism of the "twentynothings" was on view as *Beavis and Butt-head* evoked both a stunted adolescence which was long past and an unsure and seemingly inaccessible future.

—Paul J. Torre

VOICES
Beavis, Butt-head . . . . Mike Judge

PRODUCERS Abby Turkuhle, Mike Judge

PROGRAMMING HISTORY

• MTV

March 1993–   Various Times

FURTHER READING

Barrett, Wayne M. "*Beavis and Butt-Head*: Social Critics or the End of Civilization as We Know It?" *USA Today Magazine* (New York), September 1994.
Gardner, James. "*Beavis and Butt-head*." *National Review* (New York), 2 May 1994.
Hudis, Mark. "Heh-Heh. Heh-Heh. That's Cool. So You Thought *Ren and Stimpy* was Tasteless. MTV's *Beavis and Butt-head* Go Beyond Tasteless and Crude." *MediaWeek* (Brewster, New York), 2 August 1993.
Hulktrans, Andrew. "MTV Rules (For a Bunch of Wussies)." *Artforum* (New York), February 1994.
Katz, Jon. "Animated Arguments: Why the Show's Critics Just Don't Get It." *Rolling Stone* (New York), 24 March 1994.
Leland, John. "Battle For Your Brain." *Newsweek* (New York), 11 October 1993.
Mandese, Joe. "Job is All Fun and Games for MTV New Media Exec: Del Sesto Interacts with *Beavis and Butt-head*." *Advertising Age* (New York), 7 February 1994.
Young, Charles M. "Meet the Beavis! The Last Word From America's Phenomenal Pop Combo." *Rolling Stone* (New York), 24 March 1994.
Zagano, Phyllis. "*Beavis and Butt-head*, Free Your Minds!" *America* (New York), 5 March 1994.

See also Music Television

BELL CANADA

Canadian Telecommunications Company

Bell Canada, a subsidiary of BCE Inc. of Montreal, is the largest of Canada's telecommunications companies. It provides telephone service to about 9 million customers in the provinces of Ontario and Quebec, and in portions of the Northwest Territories. Bell was created by federal Act of Parliament in 1880 and since 1906 has been subject to regulation by a succession of federal regulatory agencies, currently by the Canadian Radio-television and Telecommunications Commission (CRTC).

Bell Canada's involvement in broadcasting type services dates back to the earliest years of telephony in Canada. Bell's predecessor companies, controlled by Alexander Melville Bell (father of Alexander Graham Bell), offered point-to-mass content services over telephone lines as early as 1877: songs, duets, glees, and sermons, for example, were transmitted for reception by subscribers using ordinary telephone instruments as receivers. As in other jurisdictions, these experimental closed-circuit content services dwindled

Courtesy of Bell Canada

within a few years, to re-emerge only in the 1950s with the advent of cable television.

Bell entered Canadian broadcasting in 1922 by securing licenses for radio stations in Toronto and Montreal. These one year licenses were allowed to lapse in 1923, however, when Bell signed a patent sharing agreement with radio set manufacturers (Canadian Westinghouse, International Western Electric, and Canadian General Electric) and with a radio telegraph company (Marconi) whereby the signatories agreed to split the fields into exclusive domains: Bell henceforth was not to engage in broadcasting or in radio telegraphy, while the other parties agreed not to compete with Bell in telephony.

Resulting from this 1923 contract bifurcating communication into distinct broadcasting and telephone (telecommunication) sectors, unique regulatory frameworks arose for each. Broadcasting companies came to be regulated under the provisions of a succession of *Broadcasting Acts,* requiring that licensed broadcasting undertakings contribute to the Canadian cultural and political identity. Broadcasting undertakings, furthermore, were to retain full responsibility for all programming carried; as a practical matter this meant that broadcasting organizations or their affiliates produced themselves a large portion of their Canadian content.

The legal/regulatory paradigm governing the telephone industry differed markedly from that for broadcasting. Telephone companies, as common carriers, came to be precluded from influencing message content; their mandate, rather, was simply to relay any and all messages on a non discriminatory basis upon the request of clients and upon payment of government-approved tariffs. As well, telephony, unlike broadcasting, was presumed to be a "natural monopoly," whose prices and profits needed to be subject to regulatory supervision and approval.

Although precluded from engaging directly in broadcasting, telephone companies nonetheless figured prominently in the provisioning indirectly of broadcasting services. With the advent of network broadcasting, for example, telephone companies such as Bell Canada provided inter-urban transmission facilities interlinking stations regionally, nationally and internationally. Telephone companies also served the cable television industry by providing independent cable firms with poles, ducts, rights-of-way, and with certain essential equipment such as coaxial cables. Initially telephone companies forced upon cable firms highly restrictive contracts intended to foreclose all possibility of competition in the provisioning of two-way, point-to-point telecommunication services. By the late 1970s the CRTC had overturned most of these restrictive contractual provisions, however, requiring telephone companies under its jurisdiction to provide reasonable access to telco poles and rights-of-way.

Under Canadian law, cable TV constitutes a component of the broadcasting system, and the CRTC to date (April 1995) has been unable and unwilling to license tele-

phone companies to provide cable-type services. Bell Canada and other Canadian telephone companies for many years argued, however, that they should be permitted to own exclusively any and all communication wires into the home or office, including the cable TV connection. Telephone companies proposed leasing portions of the bandwidth of their (to be acquired) broadband facilities to licensed cable entities that would thereby provide cable TV service in the mode of a value-added carrier. These proposals have never met with government approval.

More recently Canadian telephone companies led by Bell, as part of an "information highway" initiative, have argued that the technological convergence of broadcasting, telecommunications, and computer communications not only erodes previously distinct industry demarcations, but as well makes anachronous regulatory policies premised on such distinctions. Bell has argued further that telephone companies should now be permitted to enter directly the cable television industry, whether by leasing bandwidth from cable companies or by interconnecting their own coaxial or fibre optic facilities with those of cable companies, in order to receive signals for retransmission from cable headends. Telephone companies have argued further that cable systems, if they should choose so to do, should be permitted to enter the domain of the telephone companies in the provisioning of two-way, point-to-point telecommunications services. Telephone companies wish also to engage in video program creation, distribution, storage and related activities, for example the sale of advertising, long associated with broadcasting, and as well to enter emerging interactive, multimedia services.

Allowing telephone companies to enter cable TV and other content services would appear to be the likely next step in the CRTC's "pro-competitive" policy stance toward telecommunications. Indeed in September 1994 the commission published its "Review of Regulatory Framework" decision, wherein it announced its intention to promote "open entry and open access" to the greatest extent possible for "all telecommunications services." In March 1995, in response to a request from the Canadian federal government, the CRTC held public hearings concerning, in part, the terms under which telephone companies should be allowed to enter cable and content services.

As competition increasingly penetrates more and more areas of communication, venerable regulatory techniques, principles and goals are threatened. The principle of common carriage and the separation of content from carriage, for example, will be undermined if and when telephone companies are allowed to enter cable TV and other content creation markets. Likewise, the historical goal of safeguarding and promoting Canadian culture through broadcasting will prove to be increasingly illusive as internationally interconnected information highways are put in place. Information highway is the apotheosis of convergence, and hence of deregulation, but in Canada market forces historically have militated against indigenous program production and distribution. A deregulated information highway, whether controlled or not by erstwhile telephone companies enhances the power of those who would further commoditize information, as opposed to formulating information policy for social, political and cultural purposes.

—Robert Babe

FURTHER READING

Babe, Robert E. *Telecommunications in Canada: Technology, Industry, and Government.* Toronto, Canada; Buffalo, New York: University of Toronto Press, 1990.

———. *Communication and the Transformation of Economics: Essays in Information, Public Policy, and Political Economy.* Boulder, Colorado: Westview, 1995.

BELLAMY, RALPH

U.S. Actor

Ralph Bellamy, the well-known stage and film "character" actor, began his career in 1922 when he joined a traveling troupe of Shakespearean players. Later that same year, Bellamy performed in stock and repertory theaters with the Chautauqua Road Company. In 1929, he made his broadway debut in *Town Boy,* followed by a screen debut in 1931 in *The Secret Six.* In 1948 he made his a television debut in the *Philco Television Playhouse.* He then went on to star in one of the medium's first crime series, *Man Against Crime,* from 1949 to 1955.

In a career that spanned six decades on stage and screen, Bellamy played roles that fell into three broad categories: 1) the rich, reliable, but dull figure who is jilted by the leading lady, 2) the detective who always finds his prey, and 3) the slightly sinister but stylish villain. Usually appearing in supporting roles, Bellamy acted in over 100 films. He starred in several "B" movies, notably four in which he portrayed the detective Ellery Queen. Bellamy often said he never regarded himself as a leading man, so no one else did either. He is best remembered on film and television as the "dull other man." It was on the stage that Bellamy made his mark as a strong actor in plays such as *Tomorrow the World, State of the Union* and, the most noteworthy, *Sunrise at Campobello.* It was in the latter play that Bellamy built his reputation as an actor by portraying Franklin Delano Roosevelt. By delving into the history of FDR the man and the politician, he came to an understanding of the personality and psyche of the character. He then spent weeks at a rehabilitation center learning how to manage braces, crutches, and a wheelchair, so that his portrayal of FDR, after he was stricken with polio, would be realistic and accurate. It can be said that character acting was defined and perfected by Ralph Bellamy. He won the Tony and New York's Critics Circle Award as best actor in *Sunrise at Campobella* and starred in the subsequent film version in 1960.

Bellamy appeared in several television series during the 1960s and 1970s such as *The Eleventh Hour* (1963-1964), *The Survivors* (1969), *The Mostly Deadly Game* (1970), and *Hunter* (1976). He returned true to his roles as detective, villain, and other man in each of these series. It was in 1969 that Bellamy made a radical character shift by playing a diabolist in *Rosemary's Baby.* More recently he played a benevolent shipping magnate in the 1990 movie *Pretty Woman,* and a millionaire in *Trading Places* (1983). He recreated his performance as FDR in the 1988 television miniseries *War and Remembrance.*

Best remembered by his fellow actors as a champion of actors' rights, Bellamy founded the Screen Actors Guild and served four terms as president of the American Actors' Equity between 1952 and 1964. He doubled the equity's assets within six years and established the first actors' pension fund. Bellamy guided the Actors' Equity through the political blacklisting of the McCarthy era by forming a panel that established ground rules to protect members against unproved charges of Communist Party membership or sympathy. He also actively lobbied for the repeal of theatre

Ralph Bellamy

admission taxes and for income averaging in computing taxes for performers.

"B" movie actor, the Ellery Queen of the 1940s, champion of actors' rights, a well-known name in the film and television industries, the FDR of the 1950s and the 1980s, Ralph Bellamy is best remembered as the "nice but bland other man."

—Gayle M. Pohl

RALPH BELLAMY. Born in Chicago, Illinois, U.S.A., 17 June 1904. Attended New Trier High School, Wilmette, Illinois. Married: 1) Alice Delbridge, 1922 (divorced, 1931); 2) Catherine Willard, 1931 (divorced, 1945), children: Lynn and Willard; 3) Ethel Smith, 1945 (divorced); 4) Alice Murphy, 1949. Formed acting troupe, North Shore Players, 1922; stage manager, Madison Stock Company, 1922–24; formed Ralph Bellamy Players, stock company, Des Moines, Iowa (later moved to Nashville, Tennessee), 1927; appeared on broadway in *Town Boy*, 1929; founding member and member, first Board of Directors, Screen Actors Guild; president for twelve years of Actors' Equity; appeared in film, theater, and radio, 1940s; began television career in *Man Against Crime*, live production, 1949–54. Presidential appointee, National Board of the United Service Organization (U.S.O.), 1958–60; chair, New York Regional National Council of Christians and Jews Brotherhood Week, 1963; Member: Presidential Commission on the 50th Anniversary of the Department of Labor, 1962; founding member, California Arts Commission; member, board of directors, People to People, Project Hope, Theatervision, 1972–73; Board of Governors, Academy of Motion Picture Arts and Sciences, 1982. Recipient: New York Drama Critics Award, 1958; Tony Award, 1959; Honorary Academy Award, 1986. Died 29 November 1991.

TELEVISION SERIES

1949–54	*Man Against Crime*
1957–59	*To Tell the Truth* (quiz show panelist)
1961	*Frontier Justice* (host)
1963–64	*The Eleventh Hour*
1969–70	*The Survivors*
1970–71	*The Most Deadly Game*
1977	*Hunter*
1985–86	*Hotel*
1989	*Christine Cromwell*

TELEVISION MINISERIES

1976	*Once an Eagle*
1976	*Arthur Hailey's the Moneychangers*
1977	*Testimony of Two Men*
1978	*Wheels*
1985	*Space*
1989	*War and Remembrance*

MADE-FOR-TELEVISION MOVIES

1967	*Wings of Fire*
1969	*The Immortal*
1970	*The Most Deadly Game*
1972	*Something Evil*
1974	*The Missiles of October*
1975	*Search for the Gods*
1975	*Murder on Flight 502*
1975	*The Log of the Black Pearl*
1975	*Adventures of the Queen*
1976	*Return to Earth*
1976	*Nightmare in Badham County*
1976	*McNaughton's Daughter*
1976	*The Boy in the Plastic Bubble*
1977	*Charlie Cobb: Nice Night for a Hanging*
1978	*The Millionaire*
1978	*The Clone Master*
1979	*The Billion Dollar Threat*
1980	*Power*
1980	*The Memory of Eva Ryker*
1980	*Condominium*
1984	*Love Leads the Way*
1985	*The Fourth Wise Man*
1989	*Christine Cromwell: Things That Go Bump in the Night*

TELEVISION SPECIALS

1961	*Brief Encounter*
1962	*Saturday's Children*
1975	*The Devil's Web*

FILMS (selection)

The Narrow Corner, 1933; *Hands Across the Table*, 1935; *His Girl Friday*, 1940; *Dance Girl Dance*, 1940; *Sunrise at Campobello*, 1960; *Rosemary's Baby*, 1968; *Oh, God!*, 1977; *Trading Places*, 1983; *Coming to America*, 1988; *Pretty Woman*, 1990.

STAGE (selection)

Town Boy, 1929; *Tomorrow the World; State of the Union; Sunrise at Campobello*, 1958–59.

PUBLICATION

When the Smoke Hit the Fan. Garden City, New York: Doubleday, 1979.

FURTHER READING

Clarke, Gerald. "The $40 Million Gamble." *Time* (New York), 7 February 1983.

"The Talk of the Town." *The New Yorker* (New York), 9 April 1990.

See also Detective Programs

BEN CASEY

U.S. Medical Drama

Ben Casey, a medical drama about the "new breed" of doctors, ran on ABC from October 1961 to May 1966. James Moser, who also created the Richard Boone series *Medic*, created *Ben Casey* and Matthew Rapf produced the program for Bing Crosby Productions. The show was very successful for ABC and broke into the Top Twenty shows for its first two years. A 1988 made-for TV movie, *The Return of Ben Casey*, enjoyed only moderate success.

Ben Casey was one of two prominent medical dramas broadcast during the early 1960s. In *The Expanding Vista* (1990), Mary Ann Watson characterizes this show as a "New Frontier character drama." Indeed, the title character often stood as a metaphor for the best and the brightest of his generation. Often the ills to which Casey attended were stand-ins for the ills of contemporary society. Symbolism was the stock-in-trade of *Ben Casey* as evidence by its stylized opening: a hand writing symbols on a chalk board as Sam Jaffe intoned, "Man, woman, birth, death, infinity."

County General Hospital was the setting for the practice of its most prominent resident in neurosurgery, Ben Casey, played by Vince Edwards. Edwards had been discovered by Bing Crosby who saw to it that his protege had a suitable vehicle for his talents. As Casey, Edwards was gruff, demanding, and decisive. Casey did not suffer fools lightly and apparently had unqualified respect only for the chief of neurosurgery, Dr. David Zorba (Sam Jaffe). The only other colleagues from whom he would seek counsel were anesthesiologist Dr. Maggie Graham (Bettye Ackerman) and Dr. Ted Hoffman (Harry Landers). Both Hoffman and Graham provided counterpoints of emotion and compassion to the stolid Casey. Virtually every episode in the entire first season of *Ben Casey* involved a patient with a brain tumor. But the nature of the malady was merely a device that allowed Casey to interact with a panoply of individuals with unique problems—only one of which was their illness. Like many shows of its era (*Route 66, The Fugitive*), the core of *Ben Casey* could be found in the development and growth of the characters in any given episode. It was what Casey brought to a person's life as a whole that really drove the show.

Patients were not the only ones with problems. In *Ben Casey* the limits of medicine, the ethics of physicians, and the role of medicine in society were examined. The hospital functioned as a microcosm of the larger society it served. The professionals presented in *Ben Casey* were a tight group sworn to an oath of altruistic service. The majority of physicians in the employ of County General were not terribly inflated with self-importance. Their world was not so far removed from the world inhabited by those they helped. The problems that plagued the world outside the walls of County General could often be found within as well. During their work at County General, Casey and his colleagues came into contact with representatives from every level of society. Part of that contact was learning

about and making judgments on certain societal issues and problems. Racial tension, drug addiction, the plight of immigrants, child abuse, and euthanasia were a few of the issues treated in *Ben Casey*.

The series followed an episodic format for its first four years. But the final season saw Dr. Zorba replaced by Dr. Freeland (Franchot Tone) and a move to a serial, soap opera-like story structure. In so doing, *Ben Casey* moved away from the examination and possible correction of society's problems and moved toward a more conventional, character-driven drama. Vince Edwards, hoping to flex his creative muscles, directed several of the episodes of the last two seasons. Chiefly in these ways, *Ben Casey* departed from the characteristics of the "New Frontier character drama" and more closely resembled an ordinary medical melodrama. In March 1966, ABC cancelled the show.

The real value of *Ben Casey* was in its presentation of maladies of the body and mind as representative of larger problems that existed in our society. The show was one of Hollywood's reactions to FCC Chairman Newton Minnow's plea for better television. With the character of Ben Casey at the center of each episode, the show presented (often quite skillfully) the interrelationship of mental, physical, and societal health.

—John Cooper

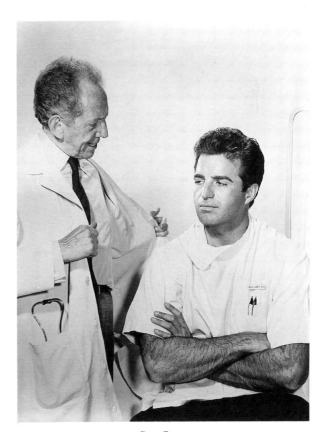

Ben Casey

CAST

Dr. Ben Casey	Vince Edwards
Dr. David Zorba (1961–65)	Sam Jaffe
Dr. Maggie Graham	Bettye Ackerman
Dr. Ted Hoffman	Harry Landers
Nick Kanavaras	Nick Dennis
Nurse Wills	Jeanne Bates
Jane Hancock (1965)	Stella Stevens
Dr. Mike Fagers (1965)	Ben Piazza
Dr Daniel Niles Freeland (1965–66) . . .	Franchot Tone
Dr. Terry McDaniel (1965–66)	Jim McMullan
Sally Welden (1965–66)	Marlyn Mason

PRODUCERS   James E. Moser, John E. Pommer, Matthew Rapf, Wilton Schiller, Jack Laird, Irving Elman

PROGRAMMING HISTORY   153 Episodes

• ABC

October 1961–September 1963	Monday 10:00-11:00
September 1963–September 1964	Wednesday 9:00-10:00
September 1964–March 1966	Monday 10:00-11:00

FURTHER READING

Alley, Robert S. "Media, Medicine, and Morality." In, Adler, Richard P., editor. *Understanding Television.* New York: Praeger, 1981.

Turow, Joseph. *Playing Doctor.* New York: Oxford University Press, 1988.

Watson, Mary Ann. *The Expanding Vista: Television in the Kennedy Years.* New York: Oxford University Press, 1990.

See also Workplace Programs

BENNETT, ALAN

British Actor

Alan Bennett has been a household name in British theatre ever since he starred in and co-authored the satirical review *Beyond the Fringe*, with Dudley Moore, Peter Cooke, and Jonathan Miller, in 1960 at the Edinburgh Festival. Later, the same show played to packed houses in London's West End and in New York. Although Bennett started by writing and acting for the stage, he very soon turned his attention to writing plays for television.

Bennett's career, though less spectacular than those of his *Fringe* companions, has displayed great diversity and solid achievement. To many he is regarded as perhaps the premiere English dramatist of his generation. This is all the more surprising given the low-key themes and understated expression of the "ordinary people" who populate his dramatic world. Like the poetry of Philip Larkin, another Northerner whose writings he admires, his work frequently focuses on the everyday and the mundane: seaside holidays, lower-middle class pretensions, obsessions with class, cleanliness, propriety, and sexual repression. Like Larkin, Bennett casts a loving but critical eye on the objects of his irony, revealing what underlies the apparently trivial language of his protagonists. In "Say Something Happened," the clichéd expression of Dad is shown to be more constructive than the social work jargon of his interviewer June, since it functions to set at ease his gauche interlocutor. While June clings to lexical propriety, Dad attends to the much more important level of the speech act. In *Kafka's Dick* and *Me—I'm Afraid of Virginia Woolf*, Bennett pokes mischievous fun at Wittgenstein and the ordinary language philosophy of Austin, but his ear for telling dialogue reveals that he shares with those philosophers an awareness that language is a series of games, operating at different levels, whose rules can only be

inferred from within. We cannot assume that we know what people mean by reference to our own usage.

Bennett's dramas are easier to enjoy than to categorize and the writer himself is a dubious guide. In the introduction to the five teleplays written for London Weekend Television in 1978–79, *The Writer in Disguise*, Bennett identifies the silent central character in three of them as "the writer in

Alan Bennett
Photo courtesy of Alan Bennett

disguise." To the five plays written for the BBC in 1982 Bennett supplies a title *Objects of Affection*, but immediately disclaims he felt any such theme at the time of writing. The writer is not the centre of attention: Trevor in *Me—I'm Afraid of Virginia Woolf* is pathologically obsessed with not being noticed and yet somehow becomes the centre of others' attentions. He becomes an absent centre through whom other characters seek to make sense of their lives. Similarly, the perambulant chinese waiter Lee, sent on a wild goose chase in search of a female admirer by a cruel fellow-worker, is a device to exhibit the casual xenophobia and fear of intimacy of the English lower-middle classes. The occasion for a Bennett play is often a holiday, or at least a break from routine: these are suggested in the titles of *All Day on the Sands, One Fine Day, Afternoon Off*, "Our Winnie,"*A Day Out*, and even "Rolling Home." The break serves to highlight the peculiar nature of ordinary living by providing a distanced view of it: in extreme instances the distance indicates a near breakdown, as the estate agent Phillips in *One Fine Day* takes to living in a tower block he is unable to let, overwhelmed by the inauthenticity of the language and values of his employment. Hospitals figure in "Rolling Home," "Intensive Care" and "A Woman of No Importance:" here too, it is the intrusion of death which leads to a search for the significance of life, though frequently it is the lives of the visitors, not the patient, that are subjected to scrutiny, and Bennett's irony militates against any portentousness about "Life."

"A Woman of No Importance" marks an important step in Bennett's development: it is the first play featuring a single actress (Patricia Routledge), speaking directly to camera and with minimal scene changes which anticipates the format adopted for the six monologues of *Talking Heads*. The play is essentially a character study of a boring woman whose life revolves around the minutiae of precedence and status of canteen groupings. Peggy sees herself as creating happiness, order, and elegance in a shabby world: we see her as bossy, insensitive, and narrow-minded. Bennett's critique is subtle and sensitive as the gap between her and our vision of the world progressively narrows. Peggy is half-aware of the futility of her life which endows her struggle to make significance out of trivia with a heroic pathos. A more blinkered version of this character is to be found in Muriel in "Soldiering On" in *Talking Heads* who refuses to acknowledge her son's embezzlement and husband's incest. Here, our sympathy for her gradual social and economic privation is offset by the damage to the family of her collusive blindness to its shortcomings. The most successful of *Talking Heads* is probably "Bed Among the Lentils," the narrative of an alcoholic vicar's wife (brilliantly played by Maggie Smith) who is restored to some sense of self-worth by an affair with an Asian shopkeeper. Possessed of greater intelligence and insight than her husband and his adoring camp-followers, she is, despite her wit and perceptiveness, a figure of pathos: marooned in a marriage and a social role she despises but lacking the courage to abandon them or the

belief that real change is possible. In Bennett's world those who succeed do so by unselfconscious egoism, energy, and lack of imagination, but are marginal to our attention; conversely, the failures exhibit insight, and wit, but a crippling self-awareness that inhibits action.

While Bennett's "Englishness" and "Northerness" (terms by no means synonymous) are evident to see, they are no more nationalistic nor restricting than Chekhov's "Russianness." The characters he writes about are rooted in a particular social environment but the issues they raise are of more universal appeal: the essential isolation of human beings within the protective social roles they have adopted or had thrust upon them, the gap between self-awareness and the capacity to change, the crippling power of propriety. All of these themes are relayed through a tone that is simultaneously ironic and tender.

—Brendan Kenny

ALAN BENNETT. Born in Leeds, Yorkshire, England, 9 May 1934. Attended Leeds Modern School, 1946–52; Exeter College, Oxford, 1954–57, B.A. 1957. National service with Joint Services School for Linguists, Cambridge and Bodmin, 1957–59. Temporary junior lecturer in history, Magdalen College, Oxford, 1960–62. Stage debut at Edinburgh Festival, 1959; subsequently wrote and appeared in acclaimed comedy revue *Beyond the Fringe*, 1960; has since worked as writer, actor, director, and broadcaster for stage, television, radio, and films. D.Litt.: University of Leeds, 1990. Honorary Fellow, Exeter College, Oxford, 1987. Trustee, National Gallery, since 1994. Recipient: *Evening Standard* Awards, 1961, 1968, 1971, and 1985; Tony Award, 1963; Guild of Television Producers Award, 1967; Broadcasting Press Guild Awards, 1984 and 1991; Royal Television Society Awards, 1984 and 1986; Hawthornden Prize, 1989; Olivier Award, 1990. Address: Peters, Fraser, and Dunlop Group, 503/4 The Chambers, Chelsea Harbour, Lots Road, London SW10 0XF, England.

TELEVISION SERIES

| 1966–67 | *On the Margin* (also writer) |
| 1987 | *Fortunes of War* |

TELEVISION SPECIALS

1965	*My Father Knew Lloyd George* (also writer)
1965	*Famous Gossips*
1965	*Plato—The Drinking Party*
1966	*Alice in Wonderland*
1972	*A Day Out* (also writer)
1975	*Sunset Across the Bay* (also writer)
1975	*A Little Outing* (also writer)
1978	*A Visit from Miss Prothero* (writer)
1978	*Me—I'm Afraid of Virginia Woolf* (writer)
1978	*Doris and Doreen* (*Green Forms*) (writer)
1979	*The Old Crowd* (writer)
1979	*Afternoon Off* (writer)
1979	*One Fine Day* (writer)

1979	*All Day On the Sands* (writer)
1982	*Objects of Affection* ("Our Winnie," "A Woman of No Importance," "Rolling Home," "Marks," "Say Something Happened," "Intensive Care") (also writer)
1982	*The Merry Wives of Windsor*
1983	*An Englishman Abroad* (writer)
1986	*The Insurance Man* (writer)
1986	*Breaking Up*
1986	*Man and Music* (narrator)
1987	*Talking Heads* ("A Chip in the Sugar," "Bed Among the Lentils," "A Lady of Letters," "Her Big Chance," "Soldiering On," "A Cream Cracker Under the Settee") (also writer)
1987	*Down Cemetery Road: The Landscape of Philip Larkin* (presenter)
1988	*Dinner at Noon* (narrator)
1990	*Poetry in Motion* (presenter)
1990	*102 Boulevard Haussmann* (writer)
1991	*A Question of Attribution* (writer)
1991	*Selling Hitler*
1992	*Poetry in Motion 2* (presenter)
1994	*Portrait or Bust* (presenter)
1995	*The Abbey* (presenter)

FILMS

Long Shot, 1980; *A Private Function* (writer), 1984; *Dreamchild* (voice only), 1985; *The Secret Policeman's Ball*, 1986; *The Secret Policeman's Other Ball*, 1982; *Pleasure at Her Majesty's*; *Prick Up Your Ears* (writer), 1987; *Little Dorrit*, 1987; *Parson's Pleasure* (writer); *The Madness of King George* (writer), 1995.

RADIO

The Great Jowett, 1980; *Dragon*, 1982; *Uncle Clarence* (writer), 1986; *Better Halves* (narrator), 1988; *The Lady in the Van* (writer, narrator), 1990; *Winnie-the-Pooh* (narrator).

STAGE

Better Late, 1959; *Beyond the Fringe* (also co-writer), 1960; *The Blood of the Bambergs*, 1962; *A Cuckoo in the Nest*, 1964; *Forty Years On* (also writer), 1968; *Sing a Rude Song* (co-writer), 1969; *Getting On* (writer), 1971; *Habeas Corpus* (also writer), 1973; *The Old Country* (writer), 1977; *Enjoy* (writer), 1980; *Kafka's Dick* (writer), 1986; *A Visit from Miss Prothero* (writer), 1987; *Single Spies* (*An Englishman Abroad* and *A Question of Attribution*) (also writer and director), 1988; *The Wind in the Willows* (writer), 1990; *The Madness of George III* (writer), 1991; *Talking Heads* ("A Chip in the Sugar," "Bed Among the Lentils," "A Lady of Letters," "Her Big Chance," "Soldiering On," "A Cream Cracker Under the Settee") (also writer), 1992.

PUBLICATIONS (selection)

Beyond the Fringe with Peter Cook, Jonathan Miller, and Dudley Moore. London: Souvenir Press, 1962; New York: Random House, 1963.

Forty Years On. London: Faber, 1969.

Getting On. London: Faber, 1972.

Habeas Corpus. London: Faber, 1973.

The Old Country. London: Faber, 1978.

Enjoy. London: Faber, 1980.

Office Suite. London: Faber, 1981.

Objects of Affection (five teleplays). London: BBC Publications, 1982.

A Private Function. London: Faber, 1984.

The Writer in Disguise (five teleplays and introduction). London: Faber, 1985.

Prick Up Your Ears. London: Faber, 1987.

Two Kafka Plays. London: Faber, 1987.

Talking Heads (collection of six monologues). London: BBC Publications, 1988; New York: Summit, 1990.

Single Spies. London: Faber, 1989.

The Wind in the Willows. London: Faber, 1991.

Forty Years On and Other Plays (collection). London: Faber, 1991.

The Madness of George III. London: Faber, 1992.

Writing Home. London: Faber, 1994.

FURTHER READING

Bergan, Roland. *Beyond the Fringe...and Beyond: A Critical Biography of Alan Bennett, Peter Cook, Jonathan Miller, and Dudley Moore.* London, 1990.

Kendle, Burton S. "Alan Bennett." In, Berney, K.A., editor. *Contemporary Dramatists.* London and Detroit, Michigan: St. James, 1973; 5th edition, 1993.

Wu, Duncan. *Six Contemporary Dramatists: Bennett, Potter, Gray, Brenton, Hare, Ayckbourn.* London: St. Martin's, 1995.

BENNY, JACK

U.S. Comedian

Jack Benny was among the most beloved American entertainers of the 20th century. He brought a relationship-oriented, humorously vain persona honed in vaudeville, radio, and film to television in 1950, starring in his own television series from that year until 1965.

The comedian grew up in Waukegan and went on the vaudeville stage in his early teens playing the violin. The instrument quickly turned into a mere prop, and his lack of musicianship became one of the staples of his act. Benny's first major success was on the radio. He starred in a regular radio program from 1932 to 1955, establishing the format and personality he would transfer almost intact to television. Most of his films capitalized on his radio fame (e.g., *The Big Broadcast of 1937*), although a couple of pictures, *Charley's Aunt* (1941) and *To Be or Not to Be* (1942), showed that he could play more than one character.

Benny's radio program spent most of its run on NBC. In 1948, the entertainer, who had just signed a deal with the Music Corporation of American (MCA) that allowed him to form a company to produce the program and thereby make more money on it, was lured to CBS, where he stayed through the remainder of his radio career and most of his television years.

His television program evolved slowly. Benny made only four television shows in his first season. By the 1954–55 season, he was up to 20, and by 1960–61, 39. The format of *The Jack Benny Show* was flexible. Although each week's episode usually had a theme or starting premise, the actual playing out of that premise often devolved into a loose collection of skits.

Benny played a fictional version of himself, Jack Benny the television star, and the program often revolved around preparation for the next week's show—involving interactions between Benny and a regular stable of characters that included the program's announcer, Don Wilson, and its resident crooner, Dennis Day. Until her retirement in 1958, Benny's wife, Mary Livingstone, portrayed what her husband termed in his memoirs "a kind of heckler-secretary," a wise-cracking friend of the family and the television program.

The main point of these interactions was to show off Benny's onscreen character. The Jack Benny with whom viewers were familiar was a cheap, vain, insecure, untalented braggart who would never willingly enter his fifth decade. Despite his conceit and braggadocio, however, Jack Benny's video persona was uniquely endearing and even in many ways admirable. He possessed a vulnerability and a flexibility few male fictional characters have achieved.

His myriad shortcomings were mercilessly exposed every week by his supporting cast, yet those characters always forgave him. They knew that "Jack" was never violent and never intentionally cruel—and that he wanted nothing (not even money) so much as love. The interaction between this protagonist and his fellow cast members turned the Jack Benny Show into a forum for human absurdity and human affection.

"Human" is a key word, for the Benny persona defied sub-categorization. Benny had shed his Jewish identity along with his Jewish name on his way from vaudeville to radio. The character he and his writers sustained on the airwaves for four decades had no ethnicity or religion.

He had no strongly defined sexuality either, despite his boasts about mythical romantic success with glamorous female movie stars and his occasional brief dates with working-class women. In minimizing his ethnicity and sexuality, the Benny character managed to transcend those categories rather than deny them. Beneath his quickly lifted arrogant facade lurked an American Everyperson.

The Jack Benny Show further crossed boundaries by being the only program for decades that consistently portrayed Americans of mixed races living and working side by side. Jack Benny's ever-present butler/valet/nanny, Rochester (portrayed by Eddie Anderson), had first appeared on the Benny radio program as a Pullman porter but had pleased audiences so universally that he moved into Benny's fictional household. Unlike the popular African-American radio characters Amos and Andy, Rochester was portrayed

Jack Benny

by a black actor, Eddie Anderson, rather than a white actor in blackface.

Rochester's characterization was not devoid of racism. As Benny's employee he was, after all, always in a nominally subservient position. Nevertheless, neither Rochester nor his relationship with his employer was defined or limited by race. Like the other characters on the program, Rochester viewed Benny with slightly condescending affection—and frequently got the better of his employer in arguments that were obviously battles between peers. He was, in fact, the closest thing the Benny character had to either a spouse or a best friend.

The complex relationship between the two was typical of the Benny persona and its fictional formula, which relied on character rather than jokes. Benny sustained the persona and the formula, in his regular half-hour program and in a series of one-hour specials, until both wore out in the mid-1960s. He returned to television from time to time thereafter to star in additional specials but never dominated American ratings as he had in the 1950s, when he spent several years in the Neilsen top 20s and garnered Emmy Awards year after year.

Offscreen, Benny was apparently ambivalent about television. In his memoirs, *Sunday Nights at Seven*, posthumously published with his daughter as co-author in 1990, he wrote, "By my second year in television, I saw that the camera was a man-eating monster. It gave a performer close-up exposure that, week after week, threatened his existence as an interesting entertainer." Despite this concern, Jack Benny and American television clearly did well by each other.

—Tinky "Dakota" Weisblat

JACK BENNY. Born Benjamin Kubelsky in Waukegan, Illinois, U.S.A., 14 February 1894. Married: Mary Livingstone (Sayde Marks), 1927. Served in U.S. Navy, World War I. Worked in vaudeville as violinist in orchestra pit, 1909–14; after military service in World War I, returned to vaudeville, touring as comic and dancer under name Ben K. Benny; small-part actor in Broadway musicals during the 1920s; first film appearance, *Bright Moments* (short), 1928; role as the emcee in feature film *The Hollywood Revue of 1929*, 1929; worked on Broadway in successful *The Earl Carroll Vanities*, 1930; radio debut, *The Ed Sullivan Show*, 1932; own radio series, *The Jack Benny Show*, 1933–41; starring film roles in *Buck Benny Rides Again*, 1940, *Love Thy Neighbor*, 1940, and *Charley's Aunt*, 1941; notable perfor-

mance in film *To Be or Not to Be*, 1942; had own television series *The Jack Benny Show*, 1950–64 (CBS), 1964–65 (NBC); later guest roles in films. Died in Beverly Hills, California, U.S.A., 26 December 1974.

TELEVISION SERIES

| 1950–64 | *The Jack Benny Show* |
| 1964–65 | *The Jack Benny Show* |

FILMS

Bright Moments (short), 1928; *The Hollywood Revue of 1929*, 1929; *Chasing Rainbows*, 1930; *Medicine Man*, 1930; *Mr. Broadway*, 1933; *Transatlantic Merry-Go-Round*, 1934; *Broadway Melody of 1936*, 1935; *It's in the Air*, 1935; *The Big Broadcast of 1937*, 1936; *College Holiday*, 1936; *Artists and Models*, 1937; *Manhattan Merry-Go-Round*, 1937; *Artists and Models Abroad*, 1938; *Man About Town*, 1939; *Buck Benny Rides Again*, 1940; *Love Thy Neighbor*, 1940; *Charley's Aunt*, 1941; *To Be or Not to Be*, 1942; *George Washington Slept Here*, 1942; *The Meanest Man in the World*, 1943; *Hollywood Canteen*, 1944; *It's in the Bag*, 1945; *The Horn Blows at Midnight*, 1945; *Without Reservations*, 1946; *The Lucky Stiff*, 1949; *Somebody Loves Me*, 1952; *Who Was That Lady?*, 1962; *It's a Mad, Mad, Mad, Mad World*, 1967; *A Guide for the Married Man*, 1967; *The Man*, 1972.

RADIO

The Jack Benny Show, 1933–41.

STAGE

The Earl Carroll Vanities, 1930.

PUBLICATION

Sunday Nights at Seven: The Jack Benny Story, with Joan Benny. New York: Warner, 1990.

FURTHER READING

Fein, Irving. *Jack Benny: An Intimate Biography*. New York: Putnam, 1976.
Jack Benny: The Radio and Television Work (published in conjunction with an exhibition of the same title at the Museum of Television and Radio, New York). New York: Harper, 1991.
Josefberg, Milt. *The Jack Benny Show*. New Rochelle, New York: Arlington House, 1977.

See also *Jack Benny Show*

THE BENNY HILL SHOW

British Comedy Program

Thanks to his work in television, especially *The Benny Hill Show*, Benny Hill is the most universally recognised of British comedians. However, what most audiences outside of the United Kingdom know as *The Benny Hill Show*, was in fact a compilation series of 111 half-hour episodes, composed of sketches and numbers drawn from his British ITV series, produced over a 20-year period from 1969 to 1989, and syndicated on American television from 1979 onward.

This series picked up a cult following, making Hill one of the most popular British comedians to appear on U.S. television. The compilation series was sold in over 90 foreign language markets, including Russia and China, which normally did not buy British comedy. However, so much of Hill's series was based on sight gags and humour that audiences in many parts of the world could appreciate the comedy. The early series of *The Benny Hill Show* appeared on the BBC. Hill's television career was launched in 1955 and his show ran, off and on, on the BBC until 1968 with a brief season with ATV in 1967. In 1969 he moved to Thames Television and stayed through the end of the series in 1989.

His early work was inventive and local in its references. Some of the BBC shows are remembered for Hill's many inspired and usually hilarious impersonations of such icons of British television such as Hughie Green (of the talent series *Opportunity Knocks*) and Alan Wicker of the travel/foreign correspondent series *Wicker's World*. The Thames series was quintessential Benny with the cherubic/budgy Hill dominating sketches, slapstick routines, and silent-film type pantomimes of comedy and sight gags. Hill was adept at buffoons, who on a slightly closer inspection, turned out to be both sly and lecherous. Indeed, lechery and smuttiness were a hallmark of many of the shows, in which tall, beautiful girls were constantly being chased or ogled by Hill and a group of stereotypical males such as Henry McGee, Bob Todd, Jackie Wright, and Nicholas Parsons. Wright in particular, as the small, bald man, invariably cropped up in a comic fire brigade or as a cowboy in various of the slapstick sketches. Hill himself often played a series of stock figures such as the short-sighted Professor Marvel, a cowboy, Captain Fred Schutle and a member of the fireman's choir. His characteristic trademarks included a broad accent, whether American Southern, Devon, or other British versions, an oafish salute, and often a jacket buttoned too tightly across the chest. His songs and rhymes were rendered with the look of a happy idiot that constantly broke into a leer.

Although all his material was original, Hill nevertheless owed a comic debt to U.S. entertainer, Red Skelton. Like Skelton, Hill worked in broad strokes and sometimes in pantomime with a series of recurring comic personae. Hill even adopted Skelton's departing line from the latter's 1951-71 network program: "Good night, God bless." However, Hill was without Skelton's often maudlin sentimentality, substituting instead a ribald energy and gusto.

—Albert Moran

PERFORMERS

Benny Hill
Henry McGee
Bob Todd
Jackie Wright
Nicholas Parsons

PROGRAMMING HISTORY

- BBC

1955–1968	Irregular Schedule

- ATV

1967	Irregular Schedule

- ITV

111 Episodes	
1969–1989	Irregular Schedule

FURTHER READING

"Benny Hill, R.I.P." *The National Review* (New York), 11 May 1992.

The Benny Hill Show
Photo courtesy of DLT Entertainment Ltd.

Johnson, Frank. "Wink, Wink, Nudge, Nudge." *The National Review* (New York), 25 May 1992.

Johnson, Terry. *Dead Funny.* London: Methuen Drama, 1994.

Smith, John. *The Benny Hill Story.* New York: St. Martin's, 1989.

See also Hill, Benny

BENSON

U.S. Situation Comedy

Benson premiered in August 1979 on ABC, a spin-off of the popular program, *Soap*, which ran from 1977 to 1981. Robert Guillaume resumed the title role in the new series joining a new cast of characters and moving from the home of a wealthy (if utterly absurd) family to a butler's position in a governor's mansion. The series ran for seven consecutive seasons with a few minor cast changes and with Benson's promotions from his first assignment, to state budget director, and finally, to lieutenant governor.

Although the story lines and the character poke fun at the incompetence of those in positions of wealth and power, the portrayal of an African American man as a butler remains a strong stereotype that serves to uphold racial power relations and reinforce social values in the neo-conservatist 1970s and 1980s America. Despite conscious efforts of writers and actors, the main character's role remains a problem: Why in contemporary television is an African American man still portrayed as a servant? However light-hearted and fictitious *Benson* may be, its significance in television history is both serious and real.

Comedy has long been a way to represent characters of color in both American film and television. Hollywood film picked up where minstrel shows left off: using extreme stereotypes (and often white actors in "blackface" makeup) to connote African American characters. One stereotype in particular that became nearly omnipresent in many classic Hollywood films is the figure of the black servant, a remnant of the ante-bellum American South. This stereotypical trope of the servant is seen time and time again, subtly suggesting the superior status of whites and simultaneously dictating to the viewing audience the position of African Americans in society. The persistence of such representation in contemporary television demonstrates the continuing use of characters of color for racial demarcation and for comic relief.

Benson as a source of humor is historically significant in television. Few American programs featuring characters of color have been dramas. Instead, beginning with *Beulah* and *Amos 'n' Andy* in the 1950s and continuing into the present, this tradition has been continuously practiced, and most programs have fallen into the genre of situation comedy. Issues of race are to be dealt with, it seems, through laughter. Although the character of Benson is indeed allowed to rise through the occupational ladder, this advancement is carefully contained within the realm of comedy. It is also controlled by the narrative, as evidenced in a 1983 episode in which the ghost of Jessica Tate comes back to haunt Benson and remind him of how far he has come.

The premise in this half-hour situation comedy is that Benson, who worked for the Tate household in the parodic *Soap*, has been "loaned" by Jessica to her cousin, Governor James Gatling, after his wife has passed away. This loan becomes permanent as Benson's utility becomes indispensable. Through his service in the governor's mansion—saving the governor from political blunders, managing both the political and domestic staff, and helping to raise the governor's daughter, Katie—Benson is seen not only as the source of composure and wisdom, but also of warmth. At the same time, he is famous for his sharp wit, often expressed at the expense of other characters on the show.

The critical view of *Benson* has generally been positive and, moreover, addresses the issue of Benson as a butler by arguing his is a "dignified" portrayal. Nevertheless, the limitations of the role are clearly set in the way in which he is characterized. For example, the headlines of some reviews instruct their readers in specific ways: "*Benson* Moves Out and Up," "Benson Butlers His Way Into a Sensational Spinoff," "ABC May Clean Up With *Benson.*" One critic describes Benson as the "smug, cocky and perennially bored black butler." These descriptions and plays on words only emphasize the position that Benson is expected to occupy—his rise "out and up" are deemed unusual, irreverent, and ultimately funny. In this light, a "cocky" servant who is smarter than his masters is not a subversive portrayal as some may wish to believe, but rather, is exactly the opposite. The often overdetermined praise of Benson's independence and sophistication perhaps reveals the effort on the part of critics to compensate for the fact that Benson is a servant. Unfortunately, arguing that these characteristics of an African American man/butler are exceptional only further dictates what his place is supposed to be. To be uppity or insolent, as Benson is sometimes described, implies that he must somehow be put back down where he belongs.

This contradiction—Benson as the defiant yet also stereotypical character—seemed to have confused audiences as well. Although *Benson* was not among the top 10 shows (it was in the top 25 in its first year only), the program lasted for seven seasons. And although Robert Guillaume was nominated several times for an Emmy Award for Best Leading Actor, he won only in the category of Best Supporting

Benson

Actor for his work in *Soap*. While the producers and writers of the show worked consciously with Benson's character in light of the strides in civil rights that were made in the previous decades, they still chose to use the stereotype of the black servant. Hence, though far lower-rated, the fact that *Benson* far outlasted such programs as *Taxi* and even its parent program, *Soap*, might suggest that American television audiences were ultimately sustaining and supporting the status quo.

Guillaume has taken a critical stance toward his own role, saying variously, "I will not go back to 1936"; "This is not going to be one of those plantation-darky roles"; "It was employer-employee, not master-servant." Still, despite Guillaume's talent and his determined attempts to bring substance and accuracy to his role, the long-standing cultural connotations of an African American servant predominate. *Benson* is not derogatory or inflammatory and, in fact, can be quite entertaining. Nevertheless, the program stands as part of an on-going practice of representing people of color in subordinate positions. Though liberal, the television industry is by no means revolutionary. Accordingly, *Benson* attempts to portray the life of an African American in a progressive and "dignified" manner, yet cannot escape the trappings of a deeply embedded cultural classification.

—Lahn S. Kim

CAST

Benson DuBois	Robert Guillaume
Gov. James Gatling	James Noble
Katie Gatling	Missy Gold
Gretchen Kraus	Inga Swenson
Marcy Hill (1979–81)	Caroline McWilliams
John Taylor (1979–80)	Lewis J. Stadlen
Clayton Endicott III (1980–88)	Rene Auberjonois
Pete Downey (1980–85)	Ethan Phillips
Frankie (1980–81)	Jerry Seinfeld
Denise Stevens Downey (1981–85)	Didi Conn
Mrs. Cassidy (1984–88)	Billie Bird
Sen. Diane Hartford (1985–88)	Donna Laurie

PRODUCERS   Paul Junger Witt, Tony Thomas, Susan Harris, Don Richetta

PROGRAMMING HISTORY   158 Episodes

• ABC

September 1979–July 1980	Thursday 8:30-9:00
August 1980–March 1983	Friday 8:00-8:30
March 1983–April 1983	Thursday 8:00-8:30
May 1983–March 1985	Friday 8:00-8:30
March 1985–September 1985	Friday 9:00-9:30
October 1985–January 1988	Friday 9:30-10:00

January 1986–August 1986   Saturday 8:30-9:00

FURTHER READING

Bretz, Mark. "Robert Guillaume Keeps Rolling Along as TV's Smug, Cocky *Benson.*" *St. Louis (Missouri) Globe-Democrat,* 24–25 July 1982.

Gelman, Steve. "*Benson* Soft-Soaps No One." *TV Guide (Radnor, Pennsylvania),* 15 September 1979.

Holsopple, Barbara. "*Benson* Moves Out and Up." *Pittsburgh (Pennsylvania) Press,* 22 July 1979.

Krupnick, Jerry. "Benson Butlers His Way Into a Sensational Spinoff." *(Newark, New Jersey) Star-Ledger,* 13 September 1979.

Miller, Ron. "*Benson.*" *San Jose (California) Mercury News,* 24 January 1985.

Torrez, Frank. "ABC May Clean Up with *Benson.*" *Los Angeles (California) Herald Examiner,* 13 September 1979.

See also Racism, Ethnicity and Television, *Soap*

BERG, GERTRUDE

U.S. Actor/Writer/Producer

Gertrude Berg was perhaps the only woman to reach a status on prime-time network television during the 1950s as the creator, principle writer and star of her own weekly situation comedy, *The Goldbergs.* When the show came to television she was already thoroughly identified in the public mind with her life-long dramatic persona, Molly Goldberg, a Jewish-American mother she had developed into a quintessential stereotype on a long-running radio series. Public familiarity with the Molly character tended to obscure her career as a remarkably prolific writer.

Berg began writing and performing skits at her father's resort hotel in the Catskill Mountains, later studying playwriting at Columbia University. After selling several dramatic scripts to radio, her big break came in 1929 with the debut of her own series on NBC, *The Rise of Goldbergs* (later shortened to *The Goldbergs).* It was among the most popular programs of the radio era, often rivaling *Amos 'n' Andy,* another NBC series based on racial stereotypes, at the top of the national ratings. Fifteen-minute episodes of *The Goldbergs* aired Monday through Friday, placing the form of the program somewhere between the contemporary parameters of situation comedy and daytime soap opera. Berg wrote most of the episodes which, after a twenty-year production run, numbered over 5,000. A pioneer in product tie-in concepts, the writer-performer capitalized on the Molly Goldberg phenomenon with short stories, stage plays, a feature film and even a cookbook.

The Goldbergs premiered on television as a CBS sitcom in 1949. During its five-season production run, the show would move around the dial to NBC, DuMont and first-run syndication. A sentimentalized vision of melting-pot assimilation, *The Goldbergs* was "pure schmaltz," a mythic idealization of the American dreams and aspirations of a lower-class Jewish family in the Bronx. The differences between traditional shtetl values and middle-American values are consistently exposed as merely stylistic. The older members of the family, including Molly, her husband Jake and Uncle David, all speak with thick Yiddish accents, while Molly's children, Rosalie and Sammy, sound more like the voices heard on *Ozzie and Harriet.* When it was becoming clear in the mid-1950s that ethnic sitcoms of this type were on the way out, Berg revamped the show by moving the family to the suburbs, renaming the series *Molly* (1954–55) and offering it in first-run syndication. These changes, however, could not save it.

For the next five years Berg was a frequent guest on comedy-variety shows, appearing with Perry Como, Kate Smith, Ed Sullivan and others. She also played several dramatic roles on anthology showcases, such as *The U.S. Steel Hour* and *The Alcoa Hour.* In 1961, Berg attempted to return to situation comedy with *Mrs. G Goes to College* (also called *The Gertrude Berg Show)* on CBS. It was the first time she had appeared on

Gertrude Berg

series television as any character other than Molly Goldberg. The old assimilationist themes remained at the heart of Berg's work; she plays Sarah Green, an elderly widow pursuing the education denied her by a poverty-stricken youth. Once again, Jewish values and American values are portrayed as distinguishable only in matters of style.

Berg's autobiography, *Molly and Me*, was published in 1961. Her papers, including many of her radio and television scripts, are collected at the George Arents Research Library at Syracuse University. It is worth noting that Berg took a stand against the blacklist in 1951, refusing to fire her long-time co-star Philip Loeb (Loeb resigned to prevent the show's cancellation and later committed suicide).

—David Marc

GERTRUDE BERG. Born Gertrude Edelstein in New York City, New York, U.S.A., 3 October 1899. Extension courses in playwriting at Columbia University. Married: Lewis W. Berg, 1918; children: Harriet and Cherney Robert. First radio script, *Effie and Laura*, 1927; wrote, starred in and produced the NBC radio series situation comedy, *The Rise of the Goldbergs*, starting 1929; *The Rise of the Goldbergs* cast and Goldberg toured vaudeville, 1934–36; half-hour radio serial *The House of Glass*, 1935; first film, *Make a Wish*, 1937; wrote and starred in Broadway reworking of the Goldberg saga, titled *Me and Molly*, 1948; wrote and starred in *The Goldbergs*, CBS television, 1949–54; with N. Richard Nash co-wrote the movie version, *Molly*, starring in the title role, 1951; starred in *The Goldbergs*, NBC-TV, 1952 and the summer of 1953, then locally on WABD (Channel 5), 1954; appeared in MGM's *Main Street to Broadway*, 1953; acted in non-Molly Goldberg roles in stage plays, from 1956; starred in television series *Mrs. G Goes to College*, later retitled *The Gertrude Berg Show*, 1961–62. Recipient: Federation of Jewish Philanthropies of New York Award, 1949; Emmy Award, 1950; Girls Clubs of America Radio and TV Mother of the Year; Antoinette Perry Award, 1959. Died in New York City, 14 September 1966.

TELEVISION SERIES (as writer, star and producer)
1949–54   *The Goldbergs* (*The Rise of the Goldbergs*)
1954–55   *Molly*
1961–62   *The Gertrude Berg Show*
              (originally titled *Mrs. G Goes to College*)

FILMS
Make a Wish (writer), 1937; *Molly*, 1951; *Main Street to Broadway*, 1953.

RADIO
Effie and Laura (writer only), 1927; *The Rise of the Goldbergs* (star, producer), 1929–45; *The House of Glass* (star, producer), 1935.

STAGE
Me and Molly, 1948; *The Solid Gold Cadillac*, 1956; *The Matchmaker*, 1957; *A Majority of One*, 1959; *Dear Me, The Sky Is Falling*, 1963.

PUBLICATIONS
The Molly Goldberg Cookbook. Garden City, New Jersey: Doubleday, 1955.
Molly and Me. New York: McGraw-Hill, 1961.

See also *Goldbergs*

BERLE, MILTON

U.S. Comedian/Actor

Milton Berle's career is one of the longest and most varied in show business, spanning silent film, vaudeville, radio, motion pictures, and television. He started in show business at the age of five, appearing as a child in *The Perils of Pauline* and *Tillie's Punctured Romance*. Through the 1920s, Berle moved up through the vaudeville circuit, finding his niche in the role of a brash comic known for stealing the material of fellow comedians. He also became a popular master of ceremonies in vaudeville, achieving top billing in the largest cities and theaters. During the 1930s, Berle appeared in a variety of Hollywood films and further polished his comedy routines in night clubs and on radio.

Berle is best known for his role as host of *Texaco Star Theater*, television's most popular program during its early years. The show had begun on the ABC radio network in the spring of 1948, and Berle took part in a television test version for Texaco and NBC in June of that year. He was selected as host, and the first East Coast broadcast of the TV series began in September. Within two months, Berle became television's first superstar, with the highest ratings ever attained and was soon referred to as "Mr. Television," "Mr. Tuesday Night," and "Uncle Miltie." Restaurants, theaters, and nightclubs adjusted their schedules so patrons would not miss Berle's program at 8:00 P.M. on Tuesday nights. Berle is said to have stimulated television sales and audience size in the same way *Amos 'n' Andy* had sparked the growth of radio.

Although the budget for each program was a modest $15,000, many well-known entertainers were eager to appear for the public exposure *Texaco Star Theater* afforded, providing further viewer appeal and popularity for the program. The one-hour live shows typically included visual vaudeville routines, music, comedy and sketches. Other regular features included the singing Texaco station attendants and the pitchman commercials by Sid Stone. Berle was noted for interjecting himself into the acts of his guests, which, along with his opening appearance in outlandish costumes, became a regular feature. His use of sight gags, props, and visual style seemed well-suited for the TV medium. In 1951, Berle signed a contract with NBC granting him $200,000 a year for 30 years, providing he appear on NBC exclusively.

His was one of the first television shows to be promoted through merchandising, including Uncle Miltie tee-shirts, comic books and chewing gum. When other programs evolved to compete with Berle's popularity, his dominance of the television audience began to wane, and Texaco ended its sponsorship. In the 1953–54 season, the *Buick-Berle Show*, as it was retitled, was set into the 8:00 P.M. Tuesday time slot. Facing greater competition and sensing the need for more determined effort to compensate for the dwindling novelty of both the program and the medium, Berle's staff and writers changed focus from the zany qualities of the show's early days to a more structured format. Berle continued to attract a substantial audience, but he was dropped by the sponsor Buick at the end of the season in 1955. Hour-long variety shows had become more difficult to orchestrate due to higher costs, increasing salary demands, and union complications. Also, Berle's persona had shifted from the impetuous and aggressive style of the *Texaco Star Theater* days to a more cultivated, but less distinctive personality, leaving many fans somehow unsatisfied. The show was produced in California for the 1955-56 season, but it failed to capture either the spirit or the audience of Uncle Miltie in his prime. Berle was featured on *Kraft Music Hall* in the late 1950s and *Jackpot Bowling*, a 1960s game show. In 1965, Berle renegotiated his 30-year contract with NBC, allowing him to appear on any network. He later made guest appearances in dramas as well as comedy programs. In addition to television, Berle's career in the later years included film, night clubs, and benefit shows. He has been the subject of nearly every show business tribute and award, including an Emmy and TV specials devoted to his contributions and legacy in broadcasting.

—B.R. Smith

MILTON BERLE. Born Mendel Berlinger in New York City, New York, U.S.A., 12 July 1908. Attended Professional Children's School. Married: 1) Joyce Mathews (twice; divorced, twice); two children; 2) Ruth Gosgrove Rosenthal, 1953; children: Vicki and Billy. Began career by winning contest for Charlie Chaplin imitators, 1913; childrens' roles in Biograph silent film productions; cast member E.W. Wolf's vaudeville children's acts; in theater since *Floradora*, Atlantic City, New Jersey, 1920, debuted in New York City with *Floradora*, 1920; in radio, 1930s; toured with Ziegfeld Follies, 1936; television series and specials from 1948; lyricist of more than 300 songs; contributor to *Variety* magazine. Honorary H.H.D., McKendree College, Lebanon, Illinois, 1984. Member: ASCAP; American Guild of Authors and Composers; Grand Street Boys; Recipient: Yiddish Theatrical Alliance Humanitarian Award, 1951;

Milton Berle

Look magazine TV Award, 1951; National Academy of Arts and Sciences Award, Man of the Year, 1959; AGVA Golden Award, 1977; Special Emmy Award for Lifetime Achievement, 1978–79. Address: c/o Sagebrush Enterprises, 151 El Camino Boulevard., Beverly Hills, California 90212 U.S.A.

TELEVISION SERIES

1948–56	*Texaco Star Theater* (later called *The Milton Berle Show* and *Buick-Berle Show*)
1958–59	*Milton Berle Starring in the Kraft Music Hall*
1960–61	*Jackpot Bowling*
1966–67	*The Milton Berle Show*

MADE-FOR-TELEVISION MOVIES

1969	*Seven in Darkness*
1972	*Evil Roy Slade*
1975	*The Legend of Valentino*
1988	*Side by Side*

TELEVISION SPECIALS

1950	*Uncle Miltie's Christmas Party*
1950	*Show of the Year* (host)
1951	*Uncle Miltie's Easter Party*
1955	*The Big Time* (co-host)
1959	*The Milton Berle Special*
1959	*The Milton Berle Special*
1961	*The Chrysler Television Special*

1962	*The Milton Berle Special*
1972	*Opening Night: U.S.A.*
1973	*A Show Business Salute to Milton Berle*
1975	*Milton Berle's Mad Mad Mad World of Comedy*
1976	*The First 50 Years* (co-host)
1978	*A Tribute to "Mr. Television" Milton Berle*
1986	*NBC's 60th Anniversary Celebration* (co-host)

FILMS (selection)

Various Biograph silent productions; *New Faces of 1937*; *Radio City Revels*, 1938; *Tall, Dark, and Handsome*, 1941; *Sun Valley Serenade*, 1941; *Rise and Shine*, 1941; *A Gentleman at Heart*, 1942; *Over My Dead Body*, 1942; *Whispering Ghosts*, 1942; *Margin for Error*, 1943; *Always Leave Them Laughing*, 1949; *Let's Make Love*, 1960; *It's a Mad, Mad, Mad, Mad World*, 1963; *The Loved One*, 1965; *The Oscar*, 1966; *The Happening*, 1967; *Who's Minding the Mint?*, 1967; *Where Angels Go, Trouble Follows*, 1968; *For Singles Only*, 1968; *Can Hieronymous Merkin Ever Forget Mercy Humppe and Find True Happiness?*, 1969; *Lepke*, 1975; *The Muppet Movie*, 1979; *Broadway Danny Rose*, 1984; *Driving Me Crazy*, 1992; *Storybook*, 1995.

RADIO (selection)

Texaco Star Theater, 1939–48; *The Milton Berle Show*, 1939; *Stop Me if You've Heard This One* (co-host); *Let Yourself Go*, 1944; *Kiss and Make Up*, 1946.

STAGE

Floradora, 1920; *Earl Carroll Vanities*, 1932; *Saluta*, 1934; *Life Begins at 8:40*, 1935; *See My Lawyer*, 1939; *I'll Take the High Road*, 1943; *Spring in Brazil*, 1945; *Seventeen*, 1951; *Top Banana*, 1963; *The Goodbye People*, 1968; *Two by Two*, 1971; *The Milton Berle Show*, 1971; *Last of the Red Hot Lovers*, 1970-71; *Norman, Is That You?*, 1973-75; *The Best of Everybody*, 1975; *The Sunshine Boys*, 1976.

PUBLICATIONS

Laughingly Yours. New York, Los Angeles: Samuel French, 1939.

Out of My Trunk. Garden City, New York: Blue Ribbon Books, 1945.

Earthquake. New York: Random House, 1959.

Milton Berle: An Autobiography with Haskel Frankel. New York: Delacourte, 1974.

B.S. I Love You. New York: McGraw-Hill, 1987.

Milton Berle's Private Joke File. New York: Crown, 1989.

More of the Best of Milton Berle's Private Joke File. New York: William Morrow, 1993.

FURTHER READING

Allen, Steve. *The Funny Men*. New York: Simon and Schuster, 1956.

Bester, Alfred. "The Good Old Days of Mr. Television." *Holiday* (New York), February 1958.

"The Child Wonder." *Time* (New York), 16 May 1949.

Glut, Donald F., and Jim Harmon. *The Great Television Heroes*. New York: Doubleday, 1975.

"Milton Berle: Television's Whirling Dervish." *Newsweek* (New York), 16 May 1949.

Sylvester, Robert. "The Strange Career of Milton Berle." *The Saturday Evening Post* (Philadelphia, Pennsylvania), 19 March 1949.

See also *Milton Berle Show*, Variety Programs

BERLUSCONI, SILVIO

Italian Media Mogul and Politician

While still a student, Silvio Berlusconi, the son of a Milan bank official, displayed two of the main qualities that marked his later career as a media tycoon: business acumen and a penchant for performing. While preparing a dissertation on "The Newspaper Advertising Contract", for his honours degree in law from Milan University, he helped finance his studies by working as a crooner on cruise ships.

On graduating, he was quick to recognise the entrpreneurial opportunities opened up by the wave of post-war affluence that rolled across Italy in the 1960s. He moved into the booming contruction sector, and in 1969 borrowed 3 billion lire to build a prestigious dormitory suburb, Milano 2, on the edge of the city. His decision to install a cable network in the complex in 1974, was his first entry into a television marketplace that was about to undergo a massive expansion.

The historic monopoly over national broadcasting enjoyed by the public sector organisation, RAI (Radio Televisione Italiana) had been confirmed by Law 103, passed in 1975. But the following year, the Constitutional Court ruled that it did not extend to the local level. This decision legitimated the mushrooming "pirate" television operators and attracted new investors with around 700 commercial stations springing up around the country. Berlusconi was quick to see the enormous potential in this explosion of activity and in 1975 he set up a holding company, Fininvest, to manage his expanding interests. In 1979 he established a major film library, renting titles to stations on the condition that they carried advertising purchased through his Publitalia subsidiary. He rapidly became the dominant force in a market that saw television increase its share of national advertising from 15% in 1976 to nearly 50%, ten years later. By 1983, Publitalia's advertising revenues had overtaken those of RAI and by the end of the decade they accounted for around 70% of all television advertising expenditure.

His power within the new commercial television marketplace was further cemented by his own moves into station ownership. Between 1977 and 1980, he created a nationwide network, Canale 5, creating the illusion of a single channel by dispatching video tapes by courier for simultaneous transmission. Programming was unashamedly populist relying heavily on imported films and soap operas and home produced game shows. In 1981, the Constitutional Court revised its earlier decision and ruled in favour of national private networks providing there were strong anti-trust provisions. Berlusconi took full advantage of this opening, buying out one of his main competitors, Italia 1, in 1982, and acquiring his only other serious challenger, Rete 4, in 1984. These moves confirmed his domination of commercial television earning him the nickname Su' Emittenza ("His Transmitter-ship", a pun on the traditional title for a cardinal).

His power did not go unopposed however. In October 1984 magistrates ruled that his channels breached RAI's monopoly right to broadcast a simultaneous national service, and shut them down. But he had powerful political friends, including the prime minister, Bettino Craxi, who returned from overseas early to sign a decree re-opening them. Even in a climate of growing enthusiasm for deregulation no other European government had allowed a single individual to accumulate such concentrated control over terrestial television. This political support established an effective duopoly in national television for the rest of the decade, giving Fininvest's three commercial networks and RAI's three public channels an overall share of between 40 to 45% each.

Reviewing this situation in 1988, the Constitutional Court sent a warning to parliament urging them to introduce strong anti-trust provisions at the earliest opportunity. Parliament's response, the Broadcasting Act of 1990 (known as the "Mammi Act" after the Post and Telecommunications Minister who presented it) fell way short of this. The parliamentary debate was bitter with the former chair of the Constitutional Court arguing that the Act disregarded the Court's anti-trust instructions and was far too sympathetic to private television power. The new law legitimated the status quo. Berlusconi was allowed to keep his three broadcasting networks and Publitalia's domination of the television advertising market remained untouched. However, new cross ownership rules did require him to sell 90% of his shares in the country's first pay-TV venture, Telepiu, and to divest his majority stake in the Milan daily newspaper, *Il Giornale Nuovo*, which passed to his brother Paolo. Critics of his communicative power were unimpressed and in 1992 media workers mounted a strike to protest against Finivest's domination of the advertising market.

Renewed pressure for tougher anti-trust legislation concided with a worsening fiancial situation within Finivest, as the group absorbed the costs of recent acquisitions. In 1986, Berlusconi had bought the football club AC Milan and spent substantial sums on making it into the most sucessful Italian club of all time. In 1988, he acquired the La Standa department store chain, one of largest in Italy. And, after an expensive and bitterly fought contest with Carlo de Benedetti of the computer company Olivetti, in 1990, he had made a major move into newspaper, magazine and book publishing with the purchase of the Mondadori group, giving him control of 20% of the domestic publishing market. These outlays led to a 12-fold increase in the group's debt, which stood at $2 billion by 1994.

Faced with continuing demands for the break-up of his television empire, he siezed the political initiative and at the beginning of 1994, announced that he would contest the forthcoming general election. Luciano Benetton, head of the clothing group, spoke for many when he wryly observed that, "Silvio Berlusconi's love of politics is motivated by fear of loosing his television interests." His vehicle was an entirely new party, Forza Italia (named after the football chant "Go Italy") in coalition with the federalist Northern League and the remnants of the neo-fascist MSI movement, renamed the National Alliance. During the campaign he relied heavily on orchestrated support from his press and television interests leading the distinguished journalist, Indro Montanelli, to resign the editorship of *Il Giornale* in protest. He projected an image of a man untouched by the old corruption, in touch with the aspirations of young Italy, and in favour of low taxation, free markets and personal choice.

His coalition of the Right won 43% of the popular vote in the March 1994 poll and formed a government with Berlusconi as Prime Minister. There were immediate allegations of conflicts of interest. He had tried to forstall these at the start of his election campaign by resigning from all managerial positions and handing chairmanship of his major company to his old piano accompanist, Fidele Confalonieri. But since he and his family still held 51% of the group's shares, critics were unconvinced. These suspicions, coupled with the defection of the Northern League, led to the fall of his administration after nine months.

His exit from office coincided with other shifts in his personal circumstances. In July 1995 he announced that he had sold a 20% stake in his new subsidiary, Mediaset (covering his television, advertsing, film and record interests) to three outside investors (including the German media magnate, Leo Kirch) for $1.1 billion. More shares were sold later to banks and other institutions, reducing his holding to 72%. Then, two days before the April 1996 election, he announced a public flotation that would eliminate his majority control.

His political standing was also under threat. His carefully cultivated image of a man outside the corrupt old guard had been dented by revelations that in 1978 he had joined the secretive masonic lodge, P2 (Propaganda 2) that had formed a powerful state within a state with connections to the armed forces, secret services, banks and government.

Then in January 1996 he was called before magistrates in Milan to answer charges that he had bribed financial police to present a favourable tax audit of his corporate accounts.

This helped to sour his return to politics in the general election in April 1996. Although he was elected as a member of parliament, his right wing bloc was forced to conceed control of government to the Olive Tree Alliance, Italy's first successful centre-left coalition since the war.

Whether he remains a central figure in Italian politics and business in the future, Berlusconi will be remembered as the man who in the space of just 25 years built a conglomerate that rose to dominate Italian commercial television, and to become Europe's second largest media empire (after Bertelsmann of Germany) and Italy's third biggest private company, and the man who used his communicative power and his flair for showmanship to launch a new political party that gathered enough votes to secure his election as Prime Minister in just four months. Overall, his career over the last 25 years stands as an impressive illustration and warning of the power of concentrated media ownership in a lightly regulated marketplace.

—Graham Murdock

SILVIO BERLUSCONI. Born in Milan, Italy, 29 September 1936. Educated at Milan University, degree in law 1971. Married: 1) Carla Dall'Ogglio (divorced), children: Marina and Pier; 2) Veronica Lario, 1990. Founded real estate development companies Cantieri Riuniti Milanesi, 1962, and Edilnord, 1963; financed construction of suburbs Milano 2, 1969, and Milano 3, 1976; created Telemilano cable television system, 1974; established Canale 5 television network 1977-80; purchased television networks Italia 1, 1982, Rete 4, 1984; purchased movie theater chain, 1985; purchased Milan AC soccer club, 1986; acquired the La Standa department store chain, 1988; acquired interests in publishing conglomerate Arnoldo

Mondadori Editore S.p.A., 1990; formed political party Forza Italia, 1994; Prime Minister of Italy, 1994. Member: Masonic lodge Propoganda 2, 1978 (disbanded, 1981); Confindustria (Italian Manufacturers' Association). Honorary degree in managerial engineering from Calabria University, 1991. Recipient: Cavalliere del Lavoro, 1977; named Man of the Year by the International Film and Programme Market of Television, Cable, and Satellite, 1991.

FURTHER READING

"Blind Trust—In Berlusconi: Italy." *The Economist* (London), 30 April 1994.

Emmrich, Stuart. "Don Silvio." *Mediaweek* (Brewster, New York), 25 February 1991.

Fisher, William and Mark Shapiro. "An InterNation Story: Four Titans Carve Up European TV." *The Nation* (New York), 9 January 1989.

Henderson, David. "Berlusconi at Bay." *New Statesman and Society* (London), 9 December 1994.

"The Lord of the Transmitters." *The Economist* (London), 22 August 1992.

Lottman, Herbert. "Italy's Berlusconi Extends Media Grasp." *Publishers Weekly* (New York), 21 November 1994.

"Playing Silvio's Song: Italian Television." *The Economist* (London), 29 July 1995.

"Unstoppable." *The Economist* (London), 22 July 1995.

Walter, David. "Winner Takes All." *Index on Censorship* (London), September-October 1994.

"The Way Things are in Italy." *The Economist* (London), 17 June 1995.

Zucconi, Vittorio. "White Stallion of TV." *New Perspectives Quarterly* (Los Angeles, California), Summer 1994.

See also Italy

BERNSTEIN, SIDNEY

British Media Executive

Sidney Bernstein was one of Britain's first television "barons", the least flamboyant but probably the most enduringly influential of a select number of show-business entrepreneurs who won the first independent commercial television franchises in the 1950s. As founding chair of the London-based Granada Group, and later of its famous subsidiary the Granada Television Network Ltd., Bernstein earned a considerable reputation as a man sensitive to the frequently contradictory ideals of popular entertainment and public service. Today, Granada Television continues to thrive, some 40 years after its creation, reconciling its twin roles as a powerful purveyor of regional culture and a senior participant in a vigorous national network. It is one of the most profitable and highly respected television companies in Europe and the only British Channel 3 contractor still

surviving in anything like its original form. In 1956, the first year of Granada's transmissions, the Granada Group posted pre-tax profits of £218,204; by 1980 that figure had grown to over £43 million. Sidney Bernstein, Socialist millionaire and "benevolent despot", is the visionary who brought this empire into being.

Bernstein had developed a considerable show-business organisation long before his controversial entry into television. Inheriting from his father a modest interest in a handful of small London cinemas while in his early twenties, he went on to build, with his brother Cecil, a successful circuit of some 60 cinemas and theatres on the way to creating a diversified leisure group with interests in publishing, property, motorway services, retail shops and bowling alleys, as well as the hugely profitable business of television rentals. It is said he chose the name Granada for his cinema chain, and later for his television company, because its Spanish reference connoted sun-drenched gaiety and flamboyance, the qualities he sought to have associated with his entertainment establishments, which tended in the early days of cinema to be decorated in the Spanish baroque style. Another story suggests that Bernstein, rambling in Andalucia while looking for a name for his company, visited the city of Granada and its exotic splendour suggested the name. Always considering himself first and foremost an unashamed showman (an attitude underlined by his unqualified admiration for Phineas T. Barnum whose portrait hung symbolically in various parts of the Granada empire), Bernstein nevertheless possessed a seriousness of purpose. He introduced serious foreign films into his cinemas at a time when distribution outlets for them were scarce and was a founder of the British Film Society. More significantly for the future of independent television, he fought a crusade to equate popularity and accessibility with quality and depth.

Bernstein had been aware of the commercial potential of television from an early stage but his Socialist principles prevented him from questioning the BBC's monopoly. From 1948 he had been lobbying the government to give the cinema industry the right to produce and transmit television programmes, not to individual homes as the BBC did, but to collective audiences in cinemas and theatres. Indeed, the evidence of Granada Theatres Ltd. to the Beveridge Committee of Enquiry into Broadcasting (report published 1951), fully acknowledged the sanctity of the public monopoly principle in respect of domestic broadcasting. All the same, Granada and Bernstein were quick to overcome their reservations when the resulting Television Act of 1954 signalled the end of the BBC's monopoly and permitted private companies to apply for the first regional commercial franchises.

The London-based Granada group surprised the establishment by bidding, not for a lucrative contract in the affluent Southeast, but for the northern weekday licence centred on Manchester in the industrial north and embracing an area which then extended geographically right across the north of England and Wales. Granada's evidence to the Pilkington Committee of Enquiry into Broadcasting in 1961, justified this decision thus: "The North and London were the two biggest regions. Granada preferred the North because of its tradition of home-grown culture, and because it offered a chance to start a new creative industry away from the metropolitan atmosphere of London." Bernstein himself shrewdly put it another way: "the North is a closely knit, indigenous, industrial society; a homogeneous cultural group with a good record for music, theatre, literature and newspapers, not found elsewhere in this island, except perhaps in Scotland. Compare this with London and its suburbs—full of displaced persons. And, of course, if you look at a map of the concentration of population in the North and a rainfall map, you will see that the North is an ideal place for television."

So, indeed, it proved. Despite certain objections to a commercial franchise being awarded to a company with overtly left-wing leanings, Granada commenced broadcasting from Manchester in May 1956, proudly proclaiming its origins with the slogan "From the North" and labelling its new constituency "Granadaland". The first night's programming began, at Bernstein's insistence, with a homage to the BBC, whose public broadcasting pedigree he had always admired, and closed with a worthy, public-spirited statement of advertising policy which suggested an initial ambivalence surrounding the commercial imperative. Already by January 1957, Granada was responsible for all the top ten rated programmes receivable in its region and, in 1962, it became the first station to screen the Beatles to the British television audience. Bernstein's company soon came to be regarded as one of the most progressive of the independent television contractors and more consistently identifiable than most with the aspirations of its region. Its reputation for quality popular drama in the long-running serial *Coronation Street* and for high-profile current affairs and documentary in programmes like *World in Action* and *What the Papers Say* gave it early prestige and aligned it unmistakably with the ideals of its founder.

In the 1970s, Lord Bernstein finally relinquished stewardship of the television company and moved over to the business side of the Granada Group. He retired, after a long career, in 1979, and died in 1993, aged ninety-four.

—Tony Pearson

Sidney Bernstein
Photo courtesy of the British Film Institute

SIDNEY LEWIS BERNSTEIN. Born in Ilford, Essex, England, 30 January 1899. Married: Sandra Malone (died, 1991); children: one son and two daughters. Inherited control of cinema chain from his father, 1921; founding member, British Film Society, 1924; introduced Saturday morning film matinées for children, 1927; acquired control of some 30 cinemas by late 1930s; chair, Granada Group, encompassing films, television, and publishing, 1934–79; film adviser to British Ministry of Information, 1940–45; posted to British Embassy, Washington, D.C., 1942; chief of film section, allied forces in North Africa, 1942–43, allied forces in Europe, 1943–45; collaborated as producer with film director Alfred Hitchcock, 1948–52; founder, with his brother Cecil, of Granada Television, part of Granada Entertainment Group, 1956; governor, Sevenoaks School, 1964–74; lecturer on film and international affairs, New York University and Nuffield Foundation, 1965–72; president, Granada Group, 1979–93; chair, Royal Exchange Theatre, Manchester, 1983–93. Fellow, British Film Insti-

tute, 1984. Created Baron Bernstein of Leigh, 1969. Recipient: International Emmy Directorate Award, 1984. Died 5 February 1993.

FILMS

Rope, 1948; *Under Capricorn*, 1949; *I Confess*, 1952.

FURTHER READING

Black, Peter. *The Mirror in the Corner: People's Television.* London: Hutchinson, 1971.
British Film Institute. *Granada: The First 25 Years* (BFI Dossier No. 9). London: British Film Institute, 1981.
Tinker, Jack. *Television Barons.* London: Quartet Books, 1980.
Year One: The Story of the First Year of Granada TV Network. Manchester, England: Granada, 1958.

See also British Programme Production Companies

BERTELSMANN AG

Bertelsmann AG is the one of the largest media corporations in the world (third as of 1995). Headquartered in Gutersloh, Germany, Bertelsmann is an international media conglomerate with major investments in book and magazine publishing, records and music publishing, broadcasting, on-line services, and other allied entertainment and information products.

A privately owned corporation dating back to 1835, Bertelsmann was revived after World War II by Reinhard Mohn, a fifth generation member of the founding family. In the 1950s, Bertelsmann established itself as a major publisher through its book clubs. To this day, publishing remains the center of Bertelsmann's profitability (and accounts for 55% of total sales). That profitability was enhanced in the 1970s with the purchase of a 74.9% interest in Gruner + Jahr, the German newspaper and magazine publisher of such titles as *Stern* and *Geo*, and the 1986 purchase of Bantam Doubleday Dell, the second largest trade publisher in the United States. Book clubs continue to be an important growth area for Bertelsmann, as the corporation recently expanded into Eastern Europe, China, and Latin America.

Bertelsmann also has major investments in the music industry, handled by its entertainment arm based in New York, Bertelsmann Music Group (BMG) Entertainment. In 1986, Bertelsmann made a major move into the entertainment industry with its purchase of RCA records. Also owners of the Arista and Ariola labels, BMG has become the second largest record club operator in the United States. BMG has sought to use its position in the music industry to expand further into other forms of media entertainment—namely music television. Bertelsmann was recently a partic-

Courtesy of Bertelsmann, Inc.

ipant in a joint venture with Rupert Murdoch's Star TV satellite broadcast system in Asia, forming Channel V, a music video channel that replaced Viacom's MTV on the satellite feed. And though plans were later canceled, Bertelsmann had announced that it was joining with Tele-Communications Inc. (TCI, America's largest cable television provider) in offering a hybrid music-video, home shopping cable channel to compete with MTV and VH-1 in the United States.

Ever since the German television market opened its previous public-based system to commercial competition in 1985, Bertlesmann's strong financial position in the media marketplace has allowed it to become one of the two dominant forces in the commercial television market (the other being the Kirch Group). Bertelsmann is part owner (39%) of RTL Plus, Germany's most successful and profitable commercial channel, which has recently developed several spin-off channels and has established itself as a major player in television production circles in Cologne. Bertelsmann also teamed with France's Canal Plus to launch Germany's first pay television movie channel, Premiere.

Not all Bertelsmann television ventures, however, have been so successful. In 1993, the company launched an infotainment channel, Vox, which has generally been a disaster. After only 15 months of operation, the company said it would shut down operations at Vox. The channel was saved, however, by substantial investments made by Rupert Murdoch (49.9%) and Canal Plus (24.9%). Bertelsmann blames such flagging performance on German licensing and anti-trust regulations, and on the low levels of advertising allowed by law. Indeed, German law has generally slowed the pace at which large media concerns such as Bertelsmann have been able to dominate the market. As a result, Bertelsmann has sought to develop joint ventures with other German and foreign media firms.

Bertelsmann has joined with Canal Plus in a programming venture to jointly fund the purchase of program and movie rights, as well as create a Europe wide network for pay television. In addition to owning several film and television production companies, including Ufa Film und Fernsehen, Stern-TV, and GEO-film, Bertelsmann has also formed a production company with the U.S. ABC Television Network. And though Bertelsmann has also shown substantial interest in purchasing a movie studio, it has made no offers. The industry press reports that management at Bertelsmann believes the company must make the transition from print to audio-visual based media products if the company is to continue to be successful in the future.

Another area of diversification for Bertelsmann is on-line services. The company recently bought a five per-cent stake in America On-line (AOL), and has begun a joint venture with AOL in Europe. Finally, Bertelsmann had planned a joint venture with the Kirch Group and the state telephone monopoly to provide video on demand and other pay services for television—plans that were denied authorization by the European Commission in Brussels. In short, while Bertelsmann's current financial strength derives from its publishing and music related businesses, the company continues to advance its interest in the growing markets of television, film, and computer based technologies, and should continue to be a major force in those areas for years to come.

—Jeffrey P. Jones

FURTHER READING

Bagdikian, Ben H. "Conquering Hearts and Minds: The Lords of the Global Village." *The Nation* (New York), 12 June 1989.

Burke, Justin. "Commercial TV Struggles With Tight German Laws." *Christian Science Monitor* (Boston, Massachusetts), 4 May 1994.

Dempsey, Judy. "Going Online for European Expansion." *Financial Times* (London), 5 May 1995.

Kleinsteuber, Hans J., and Bettina Peters. "Media Moguls in Germany." In, Tunstall, Jeremy and Michael Palmer, editors. *Media Moguls.* New York: Routledge, 1991.

Smith, Anthony. *The Age of Behemoths: The Globalization of Mass Media Firms.* New York: Priority Press Publishers, 1991.

BERTON, PIERRE

Canadian Journalist/Broadcast Personality

Pierre Berton is one of Canada's best known personalities and arguably Canada's best-known living writer. He has also been an important television presence since the earliest days of Canadian television. For more than 30 years, he was rarely absent from the nation's television screens and by the 1970s was correctly described as "clearly Canada's best-known and most respected TV public affairs personality" by Warner Troyer in *The Sound and the Fury: An Anecdotal History of Canadian Broadcasting.* He was also one of most highly paid personalities. During his career as a columnist and commentator, he has been a tireless defender of public broadcasting and the importance of Canadian content. In all of his many public roles, he has been a prodigious popularizer of the Canadian experience. He may be remembered most for his many books, mostly popular histories, but he has long had an arresting television presence.

Berton's first TV appearance was probably in 1952, as a panellist on *Court of Opinion,* soon after he arrived in Toronto from Vancouver, where he got his start as a student newspaper editor (*The Ubyssey*) and daily newspaper writer. Always well informed and opinionated, he provided a strong journalistic thrust to various CBC public affairs programs. In 1957, he became the host of the interview show *Close-Up* and joined the panel of *Front Page Challenge,* a long-running program that featured "mystery guests." The guests were connected with stories in the news and the task of the panel was to identify them by asking questions and then to conduct a brief interview with the guest. After a long run, the program was finally cancelled in 1995. In 1963, on the newly formed private network, CTV, he premiered *The Pierre Berton Show* (also known as the *Pierre Berton Hour*) another talk show, which ran until 1973.

Berton's commitment to popular history led in 1974 to *My Canada* on a new, private television service, Global. The program made use of his formidable talents as a story teller to present Canadian history viewers. The program had few props and relied on Berton's ability to hold an audience with the story. Later, from 1986 to 1987, he was host of *Heritage Theatre* on CBC television, a series of dramatizations of true Canadian stories.

Among his major television triumphs was the 1974 CBC production of *The National Dream.* Based on his books, *The National Dream* and *The Last Spike*, the drama-documentary series consisted of eight hour-long programs on the opening of the Canadian West and the building of the Canadian Pacific Railway. Berton wrote the series outline and served as on-air guide to the documentary and drama segments. The series premiered at 9:00 P.M., Sunday, 3 March 1974 and had 3.6 million viewers, a very large audience in English Canada, where, at that time, the average audience was 3.1 million.

Over his career, Berton made a major contribution to Canadian television. Not surprisingly, he has been an ardent champion of public broadcasting and the CBC. Closely involved with the Canadian Radio and Television League, he helped found a successor organization, the Friends of Canadian Broadcasting, which has been a critical supporter of the CBC and Canadian production. As a Canadian cultural nationalist, Berton has made a major contribution to the development of a distinct Canadian approach to television.

—Frederick J. Fletcher and Robert Everett

PIERRE BERTON. Born in Yukon Territory, Canada, 1920. Married: Janet; six children. Began career as reporter, the *Vancouver Sun*; managing editor, *Maclean's* magazine, 1947; editor/columnist, *Toronto Star* newspaper, 1958–62; writer of documentaries and plays for TV, film and radio, revue sketches and musical comedy for theatre; author of 36 books. Member: Canadian New Hall of Fame. Recipient: Companion of the Order of Canada, three Governor General Awards for Creative Non-fiction; two National Newspaper Awards; two ACTRA Awards for broadcasting.

TELEVISION (selection)

1957–95	*Front Page Challenge* (weekly panelist)
1957–63	*Close-Up* (host)
1963–73	*The Pierre Berton Show* (host)
1974	*The National Dream* (writer/narrator; series in 8 parts)
1976	*Greenfell*
1979	*The Dionne Quintuplets* (writer)
1984–87	*Heritage Theatre* (story editor/host)
1985	*Spirit of Batoche*
1988	*The Secret of My Success* (writer/interviewer)

FILM

Klondike (writer), 1960.

PUBLICATIONS (selection)

"Make Way for the One-Eyed Monster." *Maclean's* (Toronto), 1 June 1949.

"Everybody Boos the CBC." *Maclean's* (Toronto), 1 December 1950.

The Mysterious North. New York: Knopf, 1956.

The Klondike Fever: The Life and Death of the Last Great Gold Rush. New York: Knopf, 1958.

Adventures of a Columnist. Toronto: McClelland and Stewart, 1960.

Pierre Berton
Photo courtesy of Pierre Berton

The Comfortable Pew. Toronto: McClelland and Stewart, 1965.

Les Biens-pensants or The Smug Minority. Montreal: Editions de l'Homme, 1968.

The Last Spike. Toronto: McClelland and Stewart, 1971.

Drifting Home. Toronto: McClelland and Stewart, 1973.

Canadian Food Guide. Toronto: McClelland and Stewart, 1974.

The Dionne Years: A Thirties Melodrama. Toronto: McClelland and Stewart, 1977.

My Times: Living with History. Toronto: Doubleday Canada, 1995.

FURTHER READING

Gould, Terry. "Front Page Challenged: Aging Panelists Were One Thing, Then They Got Grumpy." *Saturday Night* (Toronto), July/August 1995.

"A Star is Born: In His New Memoirs, Pierre Berton Describes How TV Bought Him Fame and Fortune." *Maclean's* (Toronto), 11 September 1995.

Stewart, Sandy. *Here's Looking at Us: A Personal History of Television in Canada.* Toronto: CBC Enterprises, 1986.

Troyer, Warner. *The Sound and the Fury: An Anecdotal History of Canadian Broadcasting.* Toronto: Wiley, 1980.

See also Canadian Programming in English; *Front Page Challenge*

BETACAM

After its introduction in 1981, Sony's Betacam became the standard professional field camera for location video work. Its adoption on an international scale was no small accomplishment given the brutal competition that characterized the "format wars" in television equipment manufacturing—a high-stakes, capital intensive struggle that produced scores of competing and incompatible high-end recording formats in less than a decade. The Panasonic Recam, Bosch QuarterCam, and RCA Hawkeye "alternatives" all proved costly losers to Sony in the race for the first successful broadcast quality "camcorder," a single unit containing both camera and videocassette recorder.

Before Betacam, electronic news gathering (ENG) utilized the 3/4" U-matic cassette format introduced in 1973. While 3/4" tape economies made 16mm newsfilm obsolete in the late 1970s, the video format was actually a step backwards in terms of portability and ease of use. While 16mm newsfilm cameras like the CP16R combined a magnetic sound recording head within the camera head, 3/4" videotape shooting required a separate video cameraperson, sound recordist and VCR (videocassette recorder) operator—all tethered together by multi-pin camera/sound cables in a cumbersome relationship that made moving shots extremely difficult. The 20-30 pound weight of each loaded VCR and camera in the late 1970s tethered sytem made logistics and transportation crucial in any location news assignment. Add to this the fact that 3/4" videotape was only marginally "broadcastable," and the system's limitations are apparent. While Ampex marketed a true broadcast-quality portable 1" system in the early 1980s (the 53 pound VPR-20) and producers had used AC-powered 1" type-C VTRs housed in trucks in the field, neither proved adequate solutions for those who sought to cover fast-breaking, spontaneous stories without being intrusive. At a mere 17.7 pounds, and in a configuration that combined both 1/2" VCR and camera in an integrated unit on the shoulder of a single camera operator, the BVW-1 Betacam was widely hailed as a revolution.

Betacam's significance came in three areas: in new technologies that the format introduced; in broader technical improvements that Betacam simply incorporated; and in a number of new practices that developed alongside widespread adoption of the format. First, Betacam's defining edge resulted from rejecting the dominant system of "composite" recording—where all electronic information is recorded as part of *one* fluctuating signal. Betacam was grounded in "component" recording. By recording and manipulating luminance (brightness) and chrominance (color) information separately throughout the production process, component recording aimed to "solve" one of the built-in flaws of the American NTSC broadcast standard. Historically, NTSC was standardized for black-and-white recording and was more than adequate for live transmission. Color, as approved by the Federal Communications Commission (FCC) in the late 1940s, was a troubling afterthought for the NTSC system. Engineers struggled to "fit" color information onto its existing and very limited black and white composite signal. The resulting "compromise" meant that interference between chroma and luminance, and color instability due to multiple generations or amplifications, became synonymous with the NTSC standard. Component engineers argued that the production process should not remain hostage to the limited bandwidth of broadcasters, but could take advantage of superior—even if incompatible—alternatives, as long as the endproduct was compressed back to NTSC before broadcasting. Component recording, then, emerged as a production, rather than transmission, format. By maintaining the integrity of signal components throughout production Betacam eliminated the cross-interference that degrades NTSC composite image quality, even as Sony hyped a "field look" that rivaled 1" or 2" "studio quality."

Apart from logistical benefits that came with Betacam's size and portability, and the enhancements that came with its shift to component processing, the camcorders that followed the BVW-1 and BVW-3 became, in the next fifteen years, a veritable index of historical improvements in video technology. In 1983, for example, NEC first introduced charged coupled device (CCD) camera sensors. These solid state chips eliminated the aberrations of traditional camera pickup "tubes": blooming, burning, image variability, bulkiness, and high-light levels. It was Sony, however, that quickly exploited the breakthrough. Upgraded with CCDs, Betacams became even smaller, yet allowed videographers film-quality contrast at extremely low-light levels. Sony made the format "dockable" with high-end Ikegami cameras, added metal tape and the processing designation "SP" (for superior performance), and increased the camera resolution to 700+ lines. Betacam SP's visual sophistication made it the dominant rental camera in commercial production in the 1990s. The format was widely used in the field, in multi-camera shoots and in microwave uplinks for live news coverage.

Betacam also led to important changes in video postproduction. First, the advantages of component recording were only fully realized in editing systems that were also entirely component. While the shift was expensive, the 1980s saw widespread changeover to all-component processing in editing suites across the country. Second, the emergence of Betacam encouraged the development of "interformat" editing systems as well. Before Betacam, system source decks and master recorders typically utilized the same format. After the arrival of Betacam source tapes that equalled the quality of 1" online systems, however, "bumping" tapes up to 1" made no sense given the inevitable loss in quality that resulted from copying. Third party engineers quickly customized interformat suites that could exploit first generation Betacam quality for 1" program masters. With an eye on the digitalization of post-production and to the future of field imaging, Sony aggressively marketed its next "breakthrough" in 1994: Betacam Digital. Made to compete with Panasonic's D-3 and D-5 digital tape formats, analysts speculated that Sony's existing market share and Betacam "branding" would insure the format's future.

While Betacam can be seen as a barometer of technical developments, the unit is also symptomatic of aesthetic changes in the medium. Betacam emerged along with a number of new genres in the late 1980s. Its accessible "broadcast quality" gave half-hour "infomercials" the affordable wall-to-wall quality control that the form needed. Its extreme low-light capability provided the gritty street-look of the new "reality shows" that emerged in 1988–90 (*COPS, Rescue 911, America's Most Wanted*). Its portability and collapsed crew size provided ample fragmentary fodder for the new tabloid shows (*Hard Copy, A Current Affair*). Even "higher" journalistic forms that disdained the tabloids—such as the primetime news magazines that experienced explosive growth in 1993–94 (*First Person, 20/20, Dateline*)—made Betacam a bottom-line workhorse to fill primetime hours. When several Betacams were stolen from the frenzied corps that covered the O.J. Simpson trial in 1995, police quickly theorized that the gear—essentially low-cost studios-in-a-package—was probably already being used in the pornographic video industry that flourished in the San Fernando Valley area near Los Angeles. Technologies do not "cause" changes in narrative or genre, but Betacam's proliferation in the 1980s and 1990s—alongside economic and institutional shifts—suggests that the system helped comprise the technical preconditions for one of television's most volatile stylistic periods.

The fate of Betacam is directly tied to the future of three alternative imaging systems: film, digital video, and HDTV (High Definition Television). Low budget feature films have been shot on Betacam, printed on film, and distributed theatrically. Yet even the best Betacam Digital system cannot replicate the tonality of film negative—at least acccording to the Eastman Kodak Company. HDTV has been touted as a step closer to true film quality, a next generation camera system, but the best HDTV cameras are cumbersome compared to Betacam. Finally, the future of Betacam may have as much to do with the survival of videotape as with anything else. When Avid and Hitachi announced the joint development of a RAM (random access memory) disk-based portable camera system at the convention of the National Association of Broadcasters (NAB) in 1995 the implications were far from subtle: digital computer storage may revolutionize and render obsolete tape-linked camera technologies to the same extent that nonlinear editors and video servers have altered the practice of video post-production.

—John Thornton Caldwell

FURTHER READING

Denison, D.C. *As Seen on TV: An Inside Look at the Television Industry.* New York: Simon and Schuster, 1992.

Gross, Lynne, and Larry Ward. *Electronic Moviemaking.* Belmont, California: Wadsworth, 1994.

Matthias, Harry, and Richard Patterson. *Electronic Cinematography.* Belmont, California: Wadsworth, 1985.

Patterson, Richard, and Dana White, editors. *Electronic Production Techniques.* Los Angeles: American Society of Cinematographers, n.d.

Ward, Peter. *Basic Betacam Camerawork.* Boston, Massachusetts: Focal Press, 1994.

BETAMAX CASE

U.S. Legal Decision

Universal City Studios, Inc. et al. v. Sony Corporation of America Inc. et al., commonly known as the Betamax case, was the first concerted legal response of the American film industry to the home video revolution. After nearly a decade of announcements and false starts by one American company or another, Sony, the Japanese electronics manufacturing giant, introduced its Betamax video tape recorder to the U.S. consumer market in early 1976 at an affordable price. In its marketing strategy Sony promoted the machine's ability to "time shift" programming—that is, to record a television program off the air even while watching another show on a different channel.

The plaintiffs, Universal and Walt Disney Productions on behalf of the Hollywood majors, charged that the ability of the Betamax to copy programming off air was an infringement of copyright and sought to halt the sale of the machines. The studios were ostensibly trying to protect film and television producers from the economic consequences of unauthorized mass duplication and distribution. However, Universal might have also wanted to prevent Betamax from capturing a significant segment of the fledgling home video market before its parent company, MCA, could introduce its DiscoVision laserdisc system, which was to scheduled for test marketing in the fall of 1977.

The Betamax case was filed in the U.S. Federal District Court of Los Angeles in November 1976 and went to trial on 30 January 1979. In its defense, Sony asserted that a consumer had the absolute right to record programs at home for private use. It drew an analogy to the audio cassette recorder, which was introduced in the 1960s and had made music tapers out of millions of American teenagers. Although the practice had not been tested in the courts, Sony believed a tradition had been established.

Handing down its decision in October 1979, the U.S. District Court ruled in favor of Sony, stating that taping off air for entertainment or time shifting constituted fair use; that copying an entire program also qualified as fair use; that set manufacturers could profit from the sale of VCRs; and that the plaintiffs did not prove that any of the above practices constituted economic harm to the motion picture industry.

These rulings pertained to the court's interpretation of the fair use doctrine as it pertained to consumers. Addressing the matter of retailing of videocassettes, the court let stand the First Sale Doctrine of the 1976 Copyright Act, which stated that the first purchaser of a copyrighted work (e.g. a motion picture on videocassette) could use it in any way the purchaser saw fit as long as copyright was not violated by illegal duplication, etc. This right extended to the rental of videocassettes purchased from Hollywood studios. Until the arrival of the VCR, film companies had received a portion of the box-office or a fee each time one of their films was shown. As holders of copyright on their pictures, the studios by law were entitled to these forms of remuneration. Since the court's interpretation of the First Sale Doctrine threatened to undermine Hollywood's control over the use of its product, Universal appealed the decision.

Although the U.S. Court of Appeals reversed the lower court's decision in October 1981, the decision, if it were to stand, would have been impossible to enforce. The home video market had been expanded enormously since the start of the case; VCR sales had increased from 30,000 sets a year in 1976 to 1,400,000 a year in 1981. Meanwhile, Sony lost the lead to its Japanese rival Matsushita, which introduced a competing format—VHS (for "video home system")—recorder in 1977. Normally, Sony and Matsushita cross-licensed recording and playback equipment, but for the home video market, the two Japanese companies went their separate ways by marketing systems that were incompatible.(The VHS cassette was larger than the Beta and had a longer recording capability.) VHS overtook Beta as the preferred format for home video and by 1981 more than six Japanese manufacturers had entered the business both in their own names and as suppliers of VHS machines to American firms. Starting out at around

$1,300, the price of the machine had been dropping steadily, enabling it to become a standard appliance for most middle-class Americans.

The Betamax case went all the way to the Supreme Court, which reversed the appeals court decision on 17 January 1984. By 1986, VCRs had been installed in 50% of American homes and annual videocassettes sales surpassed the theatrical box-office. At first, the major studios believed that the only logical way to market videocassettes was direct sales, reasoning that consumers wanted to buy cassettes and create "libraries" in much the same way as they acquired record albums. But people preferred renting to buying and as the situation stood, retailers and not film producers initially wrung most of the profits from the market. After purchasing a cassette for around $40 wholesale, a retailer could rent it over and over at a nominal charge. In contrast, the film company's profit would be small, less than a few dollars after materials, duplication, and distribution costs had been covered.

In their struggle with retailers to capture a dominant share of the home video market, the major Hollywood companies formulated a two-tiered pricing policy. For the first six months after a new movie went on sale, it would be priced relatively high on the assumption that the overwhelming majority of transactions would consist of sales to video stores for rental purposes. Then as demand began to ebb, the same movie would be reissued at a much lower price to stimulate home sales. The majors used similar strategies overseas and soon became the principal beneficiaries of the new distribution technology.

—Tino Balio

FURTHER READING

Harris, Paul. "Supreme Court O.K.'s Home Taping: Approve 'Time Shifting' for Personal Use." *Variety* (Los Angeles), 18 June 1984.
Lardner, James. "Annals of Law; The Betamax Case: Part 1." *The New Yorker*, 6 April 1987.
———. "Annals of Law; The Betamax Case: Part 2." *The New Yorker*, 13 April 1987.

See also Time Shifting; Videocassette; Videotape

BEULAH

U.S. Situation Comedy

Beulah, the first nationally broadcast weekly television series starring an African American in the leading role, ran on ABC from 1950 to 1953. The role had originally been created by white, male actor Marlin Hurt for the *Fibber McGee and Molly* radio program and the character was spun off onto "her" own radio show in 1945. After Hurt's untimely death in 1946, Hattie McDaniel played the role on radio until her death in 1953. Ethel Waters played the

character on television during its first two seasons and Louise Beavers in its third year.

A half-hour situation comedy, the program revolved around the whimsical antics of a middle-aged black domestic, Beulah, the so-called "queen of the kitchen," and the white family for whom she worked—Harry and Alice Henderson and their young son, Donnie. Beulah's boyfriend Bill Jackson ran a fix-it shop, but managed to spend most of his time hanging around Beulah's kitchen. Beulah's other black companion was Oriole, a feather-brained maid who worked for the white family next door. Storylines tended to involve Beulah coming to the rescue of her employers, by providing a great spread of Southern cuisine to impress Mr. Henderson's business client, teaching the awkward Donnie how to dance jive and impress the girls, or saving the Henderson's stale marriage. Beulah's other major obsession was trying to get Bill to agree to marry her. A regular comedic feature of the show involved Bill hyperbolically proclaiming his devotion to Beulah, while always finding a reason why the two could not wed just yet.

As one of the very few images of African-Americans on prime-time television in this period, the program came in for a certain amount of criticism for perpetuating comic black stereotypes. The show was panned in *The New York Times* and condemned by widely syndicated television critic John Crosby who singled out Ethel Waters for censure. Waters achieved great renown as a vocalist, actress (particularly for her work in the Broadway production, *A Member of the Wedding*), and as an author with her brutally honest rags-to-riches autobiography. Yet her work in *Beulah* was considered by Crosby—and some critics in the black press—as a betrayal of her other exemplary accomplishments. Actor Bud Harris, who had been contracted to play the role of Bill, quit the series a few months into its run, complaining that the show's writers were forcing him to play the character as an "Uncle Tom" and engage in comic activity he found degrading to his race.

Despite these examples of controversy, *Beulah* never generated the amount of heated debate that *Amos 'n' Andy* provoked. The latter series joined the television airways a year after *Beulah* and became a flashpoint for organized protest. The National Association for the Advancement of Colored People (NAACP), at its June 1951 annual convention, condemned both shows for depicting black people in a derogatory manner which "tends to strengthen the conclusion among uninformed or prejudiced peoples that Negroes and other minorities are inferior, lazy, dumb and dishonest." The organization, however, chose to engage in a consumer boycott only of *Amos 'n' Andy*'s sponsor, and not Procter and Gamble, the sponsor of *Beulah*.

Beulah is significant in that it was part of a phenomenon in early entertainment television programming which saw more diversity in ethnic and racial depictions than would be seen again at any time until the late 1960s. The portrayals may have been stereotyped—as they were in other early 1950s ethnic sitcoms such as *The Goldbergs* and *Life with Luigi*—but at least African Americans were visible in prime-time hours. After *Beulah* left the air in September 1953, no programme would star a black woman again until fifteen years later in 1968 when *Julia* appeared.

—Aniko Bodroghkozy

CAST

Beulah (1950–52) . . . . Ethel Waters

Beulah *(Louise Beavers)*

Beulah (1952–53) . . . . Louise Beavers
Harry Henderson (1950–52) . . . . . . William Post, Jr.
Harry Henderson (1952–53) . . . . David Bruce
Alice Henderson (1950–52) . . . . Ginger Jones
Alice Henderson (1952–53) . . . . Jane Frazee
Donnie Henderson (1950–52) . . . . Clifford Sales
Donnie Henderson (1952–53) . . . . Stuffy Singer
Oriole (1950–52) . . . . Butterfly McQueen
Oriole (1952–53) . . . . Ruby Dandridge
Bill Jackson (1950–51) . . . . Percy (Bud) Harris
Bill Jackson (1951–52) . . . . Dooley Wilson
Bill Jackson (1952–53) . . . . Ernest Whitman
Alice's Mother . . . . Madge Blake
Harry's Mother . . . . Ruth Robinson

PRODUCER   Roland Reed

PROGRAMMING HISTORY

• ABC

October 1950–September 1953   Tuesday 7:30-8:00

FURTHER READING

Dates, Jannette L., and William Barlow, editors. *Split Image: African Americans in the Mass Media*. Washington, D.C.: Howard University Press, 1990.
Kolbert, Elizabeth. "From Beulah to Oprah: The Evolution of Black Images on TV." *New York Times*, 15 January 1993.

MacDonald, J. Fred. *Blacks and White TV: Afro-Americans in Television Since 1948*. Chicago: Nelson-Hall, 1983.
Steenland, Sally. *The Unequal Picture: Black, Hispanic, Asian, and Native American Characters on Television.*

Washington, D.C.: National Commission on Working Women, 1989.

See also Waters, Ethel

THE BEVERLY HILLBILLIES

U.S. Situation Comedy

The Beverly Hillbillies (1962–71, CBS) was the brainchild of Paul Henning, the cracker-barrel surrealist also responsible for *Petticoat Junction, The Real McCoys*, and, notably, *Green Acres*. Certainly the most popular sitcom in television history, and quite possibly the most successful network series ever, it ran more than 200 episodes, clocking in as the top-rated show of its premier season, and remaining in the top ten throughout its nine-year tenure. Individual episodes almost always placed in the Nielsen Top 20 and, on occasion, rivaled the ratings of Super Bowls.

As explained in the opening montage and cadenced theme song, Jed Clampett (Buddy Ebsen) is an Ozarks mountaineer who, through epic fortuity and sheer ineptitude rather than the Protestant work ethic, falls into unfathomable wealth with the discovery of oil beneath his worthless Arcadian scrub oak. When a roving petrochemical concern gets wind, they buy him out for $25 million, whereupon town sophisticate Cousin Pearl (Bea Benaderet) convinces him fabled Beverly Hills might provide: (a) a suitable beau for his daughter Elly May (Donna Douglas) and (b) career opportunities for his wayward nephew Jethro Bodine (Max Baer, Jr.). Taking their cue from *The Grapes of Wrath* (Steinbeck via John Ford), they load up the truck and move to Beverly—replete with a rocking chair up top to house Granny (Irene Ryan), the family's reluctant matriarch.

Despite his mystification at the newfangled trappings of luxury, and the craven depths to which almost everyone around him sinks, Jed remains a bastion of homespun wisdom—very much the Lincolnesque backroads scholar. Virtually recycling his George Russel character, the sidekick in Disney's *Davy Crockett* series from the mid-1950s, Ebsen eventually carried the Lincoln conceit over into his private life, authoring a stage play in 1966 titled *The Champagne Generation*, in which he starred as the late president. (When Nancy Kulp, the birdwatching Vassar grad Miss Jane Hathaway, ran for a Congressional seat from Pennsylvania in the early 1980s, she only lost when Buddy Ebsen, a lifelong Republican, stepped in to actively campaign against her.)

Despite the silliness of much of its humor, *The Beverly Hillbillies* managed to bolster its credibility among its core audience with a kind of hillbilly authenticism. Bluegrass avatars Lester Flatt and Earl Scruggs were enlisted for the theme song, which quickly became a number-one hit on country-western charts, and they frequently appeared on the show as themselves (long before their music was appropriated for its native exoticism by the film *Bonnie and Clyde*). Cousin Pearl was a textbook recreation of Grand Ol' Opry

mainstay Minnie Pearl, and Roy Clarke was an occasional guest before inheriting the show's constituency with his 20-year stint as host of *Hee Haw*. Even the series name was taken from a bluegrass band of the 1930s. And, of course, the characters of Jethro, Elly Mae, and Granny seemed to borrow more than casually from Li'l Abner, Daisy May, and Mammy Yokum, respectively.

Yet turning up in the fall of 1962 as they did, the paradigmatic arrivistes, the Clampetts seemed to mirror almost perfectly another eccentric clan of uninvited backwoods arrivals, one which was thrust into the national spotlight—decisively and distastefully—with the Kennedy assassination. Suddenly, instead of glamorous Brahmins dictating the national agenda, we had Texas crackers straight off the farm (whose political fortunes could be traced back to Texas Tea of their own). And long before Lyndon Johnson was known for his consummate political savvy and rattlesnake ruthlessness, he entered the popular culture as a national embarrassment, remembered and endlessly ridiculed for turning off the lights in the White House to save electricity, or showing an incredulous nation his gall bladder scar.

By extension, the show became in certain quarters something of a public embarrassment as well, emblematic of the nation's having slipped another notch into pandering anti-intellectualism, a pervasive "bubbling crude" which stained all in its wake. By the time television had caught up with the changing times—the fall of 1971—youth culture and its built-in consumer demographic looked far more appealing to advertisers on the professional rut, and *The Beverly Hillbillies*, while still vastly successful, was caught in the same network purge which claimed Jackie Gleason, Red Skelton, and rural mainstays such as *Mayberry RFD* and Henning's own *Green Acres*. This is the same changing of the guard which ushered in *The Mary Tyler Moore Show, All in the Family, M*A*S*H*, and, ostensibly, social realism and the death of the 1960s. A Made-for-Television movie appeared on CBS in 1981, without Baer, and the series was later remade as a feature film in 1993 by the makers of *Wayne's World*, but neither did justice to the original.

—Paul Cullum

CAST

Jed Clampett	Buddy Ebsen
Daisy Moses (Granny)	Irene Ryan
Elly May Clampett	Donna Douglas
Jethro Bodine	Max Baer, Jr.

The Beverly Hillbillies

Milburn Drysdale . . . . Raymond Bailey
Jane Hathaway . . . . Nancy Kulp
Cousin Pearl Bodine (1962–63) . . . . . Bea Benaderet
Mrs. Margaret Drysdale (1962–69) . Harriet MacGibbon
Jethrene Bodine (1962–63) . . . . Max Baer, Jr.
John Brewster (1962–66) . . . . Frank Wilcox
Edythe Brewster (1965–66) . . . . Lisa Seagram
Jasper DePew (1962–63) . . . . Phil Gordon
Ravenswood, the butler (1962–65) . Arthur Gould Porter
Marie, the maid (1962–63) . . . . Sirry Steffen
Sonny Drysdale (1962) . . . . Louis Nye
Janet Trego (1963–65) . . . . Sharon Tate
Lawrence Chapman (1964–67) . . . . . . Milton Frome
Studio Guard (1964–66) . . . . Ray Kellogg
John Cushing (1964–67) . . . . Roy Roberts
Dash Riprock (nee Homer Noodleman)(1965–69) . . . .
. . . . Larry Pennell
Homer Cratchit (1968–71) . . . . Percy Helton
Elverna Bradshaw (1969–71) . . . . Elvia Allman
Shorty Kellems (1969–71) . . . . George "Shug" Fisher
Miss Switzer (1969–70) . . . . Judy Jordan
Helen Thompson (1969–71) . . . . . . Danielle Mardi
Miss Leeds (1969) . . . . Judy McConnell
Susan Graham (1969–71) . . . . Mady Maguire
Gloria Buckles (1969–71) . . . . Bettina Brenna
Shifty Shafer (1969–71) . . . . Phil Silvers
Flo Shafer (1969–71) . . . . Kathleen Freeman
Joy Devine (1970–71) . . . . Diana Bartlett

Mark Templeton (1970–71) . . . . Roger Torrey

PRODUCERS   Paul Henning, Al Simon, Joseph DePew, Mark Tuttle

PROGRAMMING HISTORY   216 Episodes

• CBS

September 1962–September 1964   Wednesday 9:00-9:30
September l964–September 1968   Wednesday 8:30-9:00
September 1968–September 1969   Wednesday 9:00-9:30
September 1969–September 1970   Wednesday 8:30-9:00
September 1970–September 1971   Tuesday 7:30-8:00

FURTHER READING

Marc, David. *Demographic Vistas: Television in American Culture.* Philadelphia: University of Pennsylvania Press, 1984.
———. *Comic Visions: Television Comedy and American Culture.* Boston: Unwin Hyman, 1989.
Marc, David, and Robert J. Thompson. *Prime Time, Prime Movers: From I Love Lucy to L.A. Law, America's Greatest TV Shows and the People Who Created Them.* Boston: Little Brown, 1992.
Story, David. *America on the Rerun: TV Shows That Never Die.* Secaucus, New Jersey: Carol, 1993.

See also Comedy, Domestic Settings

BEVERLY HILLS 90210

U.S. Serial Drama

Despite a slow start in its inaugural season on FOX in fall, 1990, *Beverly Hills 90210* quickly became an important fixture on the network and in the popular discourse of adolescents and young adults. In that first season the show's main characters (Dylan, Kelly, Donna, Steve, David, Andrea and twins Brandon and Brenda) all attended West Beverly Hills High School (zip code 90210). Brandon and Brenda Walsh and their parents, transplants from Minneapolis, were the stable nuclear family with strong values; their home was a safe haven for the whole gang and the center of much of the drama. By its third season the show's popularity had soared, and in 1993 it became available in syndication both in the United States and internationally. In 1996 the show's ratings were still high, the teens had graduated from high school, and some were attending California University. A number of the original characters had literally graduated from the show by then, and new characters introduced. But despite those changes, *Beverly Hills 90210* continually attracted a loyal viewership.

Produced by Aaron Spelling, who has seemed to have his finger on the pulse of popular television taste since the 1960s, *Beverly Hills 90210,* was the first in a string of programs on Fox geared toward adolescent and young adult audiences who were attracted to glamour and attention to certain issues. For both reasons, *90210's* popularity catapulted. Not long after the first season, cast members were interviewed regularly on other television programs and in such magazines as *TV Guide, Seventeen, Rolling Stone,* and *Ladies' Home Journal.* Soon, *Beverly Hills 90210* dolls, books and fan clubs were everywhere. The show set clothing and hairstyle trends for both male and female youth. Young women regularly sent letters to the character Brenda Walsh, asking her advice on their dating and other personal problems. Because the show dealt with topics of concern to adolescents in a way unlike any other teen drama to date, it was soon taken seriously by parents, educators and scholars as well. Some of the issues dealt with on the program included learning disabilities, prejudice, divorce, date rape, sexuality, alcoholism and drug use. One of the main characters, Dylan, had recurring drug and alcohol problems; another, Kelly, had a drug and alcohol abusing mother in recovery. Donna learned to overcome a learning disability, and several others struggled through parental divorce and remarriage. Many of the show's main characters were sexually active, and issues concerning safe sex and contraception were openly discussed on the program. Because it dealt with these realistic issues, the show was attractive to youth.

But not everyone considered it realistic. Some criticisms aimed at the show centered on unreal or stereotypical representations. The cast and the setting of the show were almost completely white, upper income. Non-whites appeared almost exclusively in episodes dealing with prejudice or difference. They were also almost always lower income, from a zip code outside Beverly Hills. Of the main characters, Andrea was the only Jewish female. She was portrayed as the brainy, less attractive female compared to Kelly, Donna and Brenda, who were sexier and less intellectual. Most viewers could not identify with the high income, WASP background of the Beverly Hills teens. Yet in spite of criticisms and differences, *Beverly Hills 90210* retained a diverse youth audience.

Hoping to capitalize on the early success of *90210* other Fox-Spelling collaborations followed. The first, *The Heights*, which was less glamorous but featured the same age group, did not last. Neither did the later *Models, Inc.*, set in the fashion industry. *Melrose Place*, however, did become a hit. That program, also set in southern California, featured a cast in their twenties, working on careers and later life issues like marriage and divorce. *Melrose Place* differed from *Beverly Hills 90210* in that it was far less sincere or moralistic in treating issues. *Melrose Place* relationships and plots were more sensationalized in a manner reminiscent of early 1980s prime time serials, *Dynasty* and *Dallas*. In early 1996 Aaron Spelling introduced another crowd of rich adolescents in the program *Malibu Shores*.

The rise of *Beverly Hills 90210* and its ilk coincided with changes in the broadcast network television in an era of increased competition from cable television. Network program narrowcasting to the youth market represented an attempt to remain competitive with other television distribution outlets. It also signaled a renewed effort to take seriously issues of importance to young people, a large and lucrative niche market.

—Katherine Fry

Beverly Hills 90210

CAST

Brandon Walsh	Jason Priestley
Nikki Witt (1992)	Dana Barron
Brenda Walsh (1990–94)	Shannen Doherty
Iris McKay	Stephanie Beacham
Valerie Malone (1994–)	Tiffani-Amber Thiessen
Samantha Sanders	Christina Belford
Kelly Taylor	Jennie Garth
Dylan McKay (1990–95)	Luke Perry
Rick (1992–93)	Dean Cain
Clare Arnold (1993–)	Kathleen Robertson
Donna Martin	Tori Spelling
Steve Sanders	Ian Ziering
Andrea Zuckermann (1990–95)	Gabrielle Carteris
Mrs. Teasley (1992–93)	Denise Dowse

Jesse Vasquez (1994–95)	Mark D. Espinoza
Emily Valentine (1991–)	Christine Elise
David Silver	Brian Austin Green
Ray Pruit (1994–)	Jamie Walters
Stuart Carson (1993–94)	David Gail
Scott Scanlon (1990–91)	Douglas Emerson
Jim Walsh (1990–95)	James Eckhouse
Cindy Walsh (1990–95)	Carol Potter
Jackie Taylor	Ann Gillespie
John Sears (1993–94)	Paul Johansson
Mel Silver	Matthew Laurance
Nataniel "Nat" Basigio	Joe E. Tata
Sue Scanlon (1992)	Nicholle Tom
Rush Sanders	Jed Allen
Joe Bradley (1995–)	Cameron Bancroft
Felice Martin (1991–)	Katherine Cannon
Susan Keates	Emma Caulfield
Mr. Martin	Michael Durrell
Antonia Marchette (1995)	Rebecca Gayheart
Celeste Lundy (1993–94)	Jennifer Grant
Suzanne Steele (1993–94)	Kerrie Keane
LuAnn Pruit	Caroline McWilliams
Chancellor Arnold (1993–)	Nicholas Pryor
Jake Hanson (1992)	Grant Show
Ryan Sanders (1996–)	Randy Spelling
Mr. McKay	Josh Taylor
Alpha Sorority Alumni person	Brooke Theiss

Erica Steele (1993–94) . . . . Noley Thornton
Colin (1995–) . . . . Jason Wiles
D'Shawn Hardell (1993–94) . . . . . . Cress Williams

PRODUCERS   Jessica Klein, Larry Mollin, Jason Priestley, Aaron Spelling, E. Duke Vincent, Paul Waigner, Steve Wasserman

PROGRAMMING HISTORY

• FOX

October 1990–August 1992	Thursday 9:00-10:00
July 1992–May 1993	Wednesday 8:00-9:00
June 1993–August 1993	Tuesday 8:00-9:00
September 1993–	Wednesday 8:00-9:00

FURTHER READING

Fitzgerald, Kate. "*90210* Promo ZIP: Marketers Hitch a Ride as Show Goes Worldwide." *Advertising Age* (New York), 6 September 1993.

Freeman, Mike. "Worldvision Pitches Reps on Strength of *90210*." *Broadcasting and Cable* (Washington, D.C.), 22 March 1993.

Rapping, Elayne. "The Year of the Young." *The Progressive* (Madison, Wisconsin), February 1993.

Roberts, Donald F. "Adolescents and the Mass Media: From *Leave it to Beaver* to *Beverly Hills 90210*." *Teachers College Record* (New York), Spring 1993.

Simonetti, Marie-Claire. "*Degrassi Junior High* and *Beverly Hills 90210*." *Journal of Popular Film and Television* (Washington, D.C.), Spring 1994.

BEWITCHED

U.S. Situation Comedy

Bewitched, a fantasy situation comedy featuring the suburban life of a witch housewife married to a mortal, aired on ABC from 1964 to 1972. In its first season, it was the highest rated of all the new series and for its first five seasons, the program found itself consistently in Neilsens' Top Twelve. By 1968, its re-runs had sold to ABC for nine million dollars.

Set in Westport, Connecticut, *Bewitched* chronicles the difficulties Samantha (Elizabeth Montgomery) has negotiating her supernatural powers and her role as the suburban housewife of advertising executive Darrin Stevens (Dick York, replaced by Dick Sargent after the fifth season). Other major characters include Samantha's mother, Endora (Agnes Moorehead), who enjoys employing meddling witchcraft to complicate her daughter's marriage, a suspicious neighbor named Gladys Kravitz (Alice Pearce, later replaced by Sandra Gould) and Darrin's neurotic boss Larry Tate (David White). Sporadically, Elizabeth Montgomery would appear as her cousin, Serena, embodied as a teeny-bopper, counter-culture type, with a knack for free-spirited and manipulative sorcery. Eventually, Samantha and Darrin have a daughter, Tabitha, and a son, Adam, both of whom display witchly powers. (In 1977, ABC attempted a spin-off called *Tabitha*, where the now grown witch [Lisa Hartman] works as assistant producer for a California news program—with Robert Urich as the anchorman. The spin-off failed before season's end.)

Bewitched's formula typically involves a disruption created by either Samantha or Darrin's family, or Darrin's boss Larry. Samantha's responsibility to keep up the family harmony comes into conflict with her vow not to exercise witchcraft. Usually the resolution does come about with witchcraft, but Samantha's role as a "good" wife undergoes re-inscription because she performed her spells for the sake of her family (Morey, 1993).

Samantha generally exercises her witchcraft by twitching her nose and mouth (known at the time of the show as the "witch twitch") or casting verbal spells. Either method may result in making objects and people disappear or appear, granting unearthly powers to herself or others, or turning herself or others into various kinds of animals. She constantly subordinates her supernatural powers at the request of her husband—he is particularly adamant that she not cheat her domestic duties. Samantha could easily have the entire house cleaned and dinner on the table with a single "witch twitch" but, for Darrin's sake, she chooses to perform the labor of housework herself.

At the same time, Samantha takes a keen interest in Darrin's job and gets him out of many a campaign jam with her "imagination" and "intuition"—sometimes attributed to her witchcraft, sometimes not. She often saves Darrin's job by producing sales concepts on the spot for his clients or sometimes even going to the extent of turning his clients into animals to prove a point or buy him time. Her mastery in this area includes shoring up Darrin's ego and making him feel that it was *his* ideas that saved the day. In this way, *Bewitched* brings forward a host of questions pressing mid-1960s middle class culture such as anxieties about women's place in the public and private spheres and general mistrust between the sexes: What is the appropriate woman's role? How should a woman exercise her own agency to the best of her abilities? What do we do with female power since it has been relegated to a place outside of culture for so long? Toward the end of the run of *Bewitched*, Samantha often travels to far away places and times or interacts with historical figures, somewhat displacing the centrality of the home and middle-class suburban life.

Notably, Elizabeth Montgomery's real-life husband was William Asher, the director of the series (who also

Bewitched

directed *I Love Lucy, Danny Thomas,* and *Patty Duke*). Asher and Montgomery owned a percentage of profits of *Bewitched* as well as a percentage of the merchandising rights which involved the conception of a Samantha doll, jewelry, cosmetics, and a flavor of *Bewitched* ice cream. The couple's first child was born three weeks before the production of the first episode, leading much of the popular press at the time to refer to the initiation of the show as a birthing process.

That series premier remains one of the series' most memorable episodes in many ways. When Samantha reveals to Darrin that she is a witch, he seeks the advice of others (best friend, doctor, bartender), each of whom refuses to take him seriously. So he returns home, resolving, "So my wife's a witch. Every married man has to make some adjustments." His conclusion rings true, and continues to define much of the series—marriage may not be what it appears on the

surface and the commitment to marriage and family, certainly in late 20th-century America, means confronting male fears about women's sexuality and otherness, women's power, and the changing social and cultural significance of domestic institutions.

—Christina Lane

CAST

Samantha Stephens/Serena	Elizabeth Montgomery
Darrin Stephens (1964–69)	Dick York
Darrin Stephens (1969–72)	Dick Sargent
Endora	Agnes Moorehead
Maurice	Maurice Evans
Larry Tate	David White
Louise Tate (1954–55)	Irene Vernon
Louise Tate (1955–72)	Kasey Rogers
Tabitha Stephens (1966–72) . . .	Erin and Diane Murphy

Adam Stephens (1971–72) . . David and Greg Lawrence
Abner Kravitz . . . . George Tobias
Gladys Kravitz (1964–66) . . . . Alice Pearce
Gladys Kravitz (l966–72) . . . . Sandra Gould
Aunt Clara (1964–68) . . . . Marion Lorne
Uncle Arthur (1965–72) . . . . Paul Lynde
Esmerelda (1969–72) . . . . Alice Ghostley
Dr. Bombay (1967–72) . . . . Bernard Fox

PRODUCERS   Harry Ackerman, William Froug, Danny Arnold, Jerry Davis, Bill Asher

PROGRAMMING HISTORY   306 Episodes

• ABC

September 1964–January 1967   Thursday 9:00-9:30
January 1967–September 1971   Thursday 8:30-9:00
September 1971–January 1972   Wednesday 8:00-8:30
January 1972–July 1972   Saturday 8:00-8:30

FURTHER READING

Amory, Cleveland. "Bewitched." *TV Guide* (Radnor, Pennsylvania), 24 October 1964.

Asimov, Isaac. "Beware of Bewitched." *TV Guide* (Radnor, Pennsylvania), 22 March 1969.

Marc, David. *Comic Visions: Television Comedy and American Culture.* Boston: Unwin Hyman, 1989.

———. "Every Witch Way but Loose." *Village Voice* (New York) 20 August 1985.

Pilato, Herbie J. *The Bewitched Book: The Cosmic Companion to TV's Most Magical Supernatural Situation Comedy.* New York: Dell, 1992.

Spigel, Lynn. "From Domestic Space to Outer Space: The 1960s Fantastic Family Sit-Com." In, Penley, Constance, Elisabeth Lyon, Lynn Spigel, and Janet Bergstrom, editors. *Close Encounters: Film, Feminism, and Science Fiction.* Minneapolis: University of Minnesota Press, 1991.

Stang, Joanne. "The Bewitching Miss Montgomery." *New York Times*, 22 November 1964.

BILLY GRAHAM CRUSADES

U.S. Religious Program

Billy Graham is often at pains to distinguish himself from the band of preachers known as "televangelists," and his programs have typically been formulaic in the extreme. Still, no evangelist has used television as efficiently, effectively, and, ultimately, as creatively as has Billy Graham.

The legendary preacher's initial experiment with television occurred in 1951, when he attempted to take his phenomenally successful radio program, *The Hour of Decision*, to the new medium. Some programs featured filmed segments from live crusades, where Graham was at his best, but most were studio productions that showed him in a study or living-room setting. They often included obviously rehearsed interviews and did not allow him to preach with the kind of intensity and effectiveness he could manifest before a large crowd. The program ran for nearly three years on the fledgling ABC network, but neither Graham nor his associates have ever regarded it as a particularly memorable effort. Years later, he told an interviewer, "They are interesting films, but I can't find anyone who ever saw one! Prime time on Sunday nights on network TV, and no one remembers."

Graham's next attempt to fulfill the Great Commission via the cathode ray tube came in 1957, during his summer-long crusade in Madison Square Garden. At ABC's invitation, and with J. Howard Pew's financial guarantees, Graham began airing his Saturday-night services live from the Garden. The first broadcast, on 1 June, posted an 8.1 Trendex rating, which translated into approximately 6.4 million viewers, more than enough to convince the evangelist of television's great promise as a vehicle for the gospel. A Gallup poll taken that summer revealed that 85 % of Ameri-

cans could correctly identify Billy Graham, and three-quarters of that number regarded him positively. In an

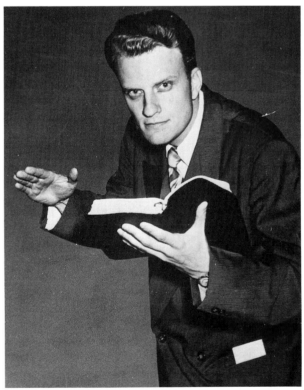

Billy Graham
Photo courtesy of the Billy Graham Evangelistic Association

innocent masterpiece of understatement, *Christian Life* magazine cautiously observed, "Undoubtedly, this fact will affect Graham's ministry."

Those first telecasts were quite simple. Cliff Barrows led a huge chorus in familiar hymns. George Beverly Shea sang "How Great Thou Art," a celebrity or two gave a testimony of the power of Christ in his or her life, Billy Graham preached, and hundreds of people streamed toward him when he offered the invitation at the conclusion of his sermon. Remarkably, Graham has stuck to that same prosaic formula for nearly forty years. To be sure, production values have improved dramatically, viewers are sometimes treated to a brief tour of the host city, Graham has adjusted his speaking style and bodily movements to the smaller screen, and the programs are aired weeks after the crusades end rather than live, but the basic elements remain the same.

One key to Graham's success in using television was an early decision not to attempt a weekly Sunday-morning program. As years of Nielsen and Arbitron ratings have demonstrated, the audiences for his programs, usually aired in prime time in groups of three on a quarterly basis, are far larger than those for the syndicated Sunday programs of other religious broadcasters. This larger audience also appears to contain far more un-churched people than do the Sunday shows. No less important, twelve programs a year, filmed while he is doing what he would be doing anyway, cost less than a weekly studio program, minimize the risk of overexposure, and cause far less drain on the evangelist's time and energy. In recent years, the production team has filmed all services in a crusade, then blended the best segments into three composite programs.

In addition to reaching for a mass audience with an edited product, Graham has long used the medium to carry crusade services live to audiences in locations far from the central arena. In 1954, during a twelve-week effort that packed London's Harringay Arena, the sound from the crusade was carried to various sites by landline relay. Twelve years later, during his 1966 visit to London, Graham used Eidophor projection equipment to supply a television feed to beam his message into auditoriums and stadiums in British cities where the ground had been prepared as if he were going to be present for a full-scale live crusade. A similar effort, also in London, followed in 1967. In 1970, he used an ambitious and innovative television relay system to transmit a crusade in Dortmund, Germany, to theaters, arenas, and stadiums throughout Western Europe and into Yugoslavia—"unscrambling Babel," as one aide put it—to reach speakers of eight different languages in ten nations.

In recent years, many of Graham's crusades, especially those outside the United States, have used satellite technology to elaborate on this means of multiplying the effectiveness of his crusades. Interestingly, the number of "inquirers" responding to Graham's invitation almost always match or exceed those registered at the central site. Encouraged by such results, the Billy Graham Evangelistic Association launched an ambitious effort to reach virtually the entire world in a series of transmissions. In 1989, Graham preached from London to more than 800,000 people gathered at 247 "live-link" centers throughout the United Kingdom and the Republic of Ireland, and to an astonishing 16,000 sites in 13 nations of Africa. In most cases, the down-link was effected by means of low-cost portable satellite dishes. Another 20 African nations received the program by videotape a week or two later, usually after translation into one of nine different languages. The aggregate attendance at the African sites exceeded 8 million. In 1990, similar technology was used to beam Graham's sermons from Hong Kong to an estimated 100 million souls assembled at 70,000 locations in 26 countries of Asia. In 1991, a Buenos Aires satellite mission reached 5 million people at 850 locations in 20 countries.

The climax to these efforts and, in all probability, to Billy Graham's 50-year ministry, came in March 1995, when the 76-year-old evangelist's distinctive voice and familiar message soared upward from his pulpit in Puerto Rico to a network of 30 satellites that bounced it back to receiving dishes in more than 165 countries. Plausible estimates indicate that, when network television telecasts and delayed videotape presentations were included, as many as one billion people heard at least one of Graham's sermons during this campaign, aptly titled "Global Mission." Graham sees no contradiction between "the old, old story" and the newest means to transmit it. "It is time," he observed, "for the church to use the technology to make a statement that in the midst of chaos, emptiness and despair, there is hope in the person of Jesus Christ."

—William Martin

FURTHER READING

Frady, Marshall. *Billy Graham: A Parable of American Righteousness.* Boston: Little, Brown, 1979.

Martin, William C. *A Prophet with Honor: The Billy Graham Story.* New York: William Morrow, 1991.

Morgan, Timothy C. "From One City to the World." *Christianity Today* (Carol Stream, Illinois), 24 April 1995.

Muck, Terry, and Harold L. Myra. "William Franklin Graham: Seventy Exceptional Years (interview)." *Christianity Today* (Carol Stream, Illinois), 18 November 1988.

Neff, David. "Personal Evangelism on a Mass Scale." *Christianity Today* (Carol Stream, Illinois), 8 March 1993.

Pollock, John Charles. *To all the Nations: The Billy Graham Story.* Cambridge, Massachusetts: Harper and Row, 1985.

Rosell, Garth M. "Grace under Fire." *Christianity Today* (Carol Stream, Illinois), 13 November 1995.

Streiker, Lowell D., and Gerald S. Strober. *Religion and the New Majority: Billy Graham, Middle America, and the Politics of the 70s.* New York: Association Press, 1972.

Thomas, William. *An Assessment of Mass Meetings as a Method of Evangelism: Case Study of Eurofest '75 and the Billy Graham Crusade in Brussels.* Amsterdam, The Netherlands: Redopi, 1977.

See also Religion on Television

BLACK AND WHITE IN COLOUR

British Documentary

In 1992, BBC Television broadcast a season of programmes celebrating the contribution which black and Asian people have made to British television. Prior to the five consecutive evenings' special screenings, BBC2 broadcast *Black and White in Colour* (26 June/3 July 1992), a two-part documentary tracing black participation in British television. The programmes resulted, in part, from the BFI (British Film Institute) Race and Ethnicity Project. This began in 1985 and aimed, through archival research, to examine black people's involvement in British television, both on and off the screen. The research emerged at a time when the debate about race and cultural representation was at its peak, and when there was increasing criticism of images of blackness on British television.

Black and White in Colour is a British Film Institute production, directed by the black British filmmaker, Isaac Julien. It examines both the socio-political context and on-screen developments and in so doing, effectively traces the shifts and contours of black British television history. The documentary, which uses rare archive footage, is narrated by Professor Stuart Hall and includes interviews with actors, actresses, cultural critics, directors and other key players in the making of black British television history.

The first part of *Black and White in Colour* begins by noting black American performers' contribution to British variety in the 1930s and 1940s. American entertainers such as Adelaide Hall, Buck and Bubbles and Elisabeth Welch were some of the first images on TV that British people saw of black people. Compared to other genres, light entertainment was significantly advanced in celebrating black performers such as Harry Belafonte and Shirley Bassey. *Black and White in Colour* goes on to discuss how the image of black person as social problem was developed in the post-war years, particularly in news and documentary programming. The late 1950s saw the emergence of some innovative drama which focused on race and the black British experience, for example, John Elliot's *A Man from the Sun* (1956) and John Hopkin's *Fable* (1965). What *Black and White in Colour* highlights is that in most pre-1970s programming black people were quite clearly spoken about and referred to rather than directly addressed.

The second part of *Black and White in Colour* concentrates on black representation on British television from 1962 to 1992. It begins by describing how Enoch Powell and his 1968 "rivers of blood" speech influenced perceptions of black British people. The most popular programme on British television at this time was Johnny Speight's sitcom *Till Death Us Do Part,* which, although it rarely featured black characters, gave space to the blatantly racist views of Alf Garnett (often described as

Powell's alter-ego). *Black and White in Colour* points out that, generally speaking, the first part of the 1970s was an uncreative time in terms of images of blackness. A number of situation comedies during the 1970s, such as *Love Thy Neighbour, Mind Your Language* and *Mixed Blessings,* claimed that they were diffusing racial tension by laughing at racism, but in fact developed their own set of racist stereotypes. During the same period, the first programmes which featured predominantly black casts began to emerge. *Empire Road* (1978–79) was the first black soap opera to be made for British television screens. *Black and White in Colour* also examines off-screen developments at this time, when many black artists were beginning to complain and campaign for better roles on television. For example, the Equity's Coloured Artists Committee was established in 1974. In 1979, the Campaign Against Racism in the Media critically assessed television's representation of race in *It Ain't Half Racist Mum.*

Black and White in Colour examines the impact of Channel 4 and the black British independent film movement on black cultural representation during the 1980s. Black programming was built into the structure of Channel 4, which began in 1982. Subsequently, black audiences were offered their own magazine programmes such as *Eastern Eye* and *Black on Black* and comedies such as *No Problem!, Tandoori Nights* and *Desmonds.* The specifically black programmes of the 1980s, triggered off a number of debates about black audiences, race and television.

Although *Black and White in Colour* traces a history which reveals an improvement in images of blackness on British television since 1936, the analysis makes it clear that representations of black people are far from perfect and that many of the early patterns are still apparent. In that sense, the two-part documentary is more a retrospective than a celebration. Most importantly perhaps, *Black and White in Colour* manages to illustrate how much black artists and practitioners have had to struggle to gain access to the British television institution.

—Sarita Malik

PROGRAMMING HISTORY   Documentary aired in two parts

• BBC

26 June 1992
3 July 1992

FURTHER READING

Dhondy, Farrukh. "Black and White in Colour in the U.K." *Intermedia* (London), August 1992.
Pines, Jim, editor. *Black and White in Colour: Black People in British Television Since 1936.* London: British Film Institute, 1992.

THE BLACK AND WHITE MINSTREL SHOW

British Music/Variety/Minstrel Show

One hundred years after the "Nigger Minstrel" enter-tainment tradition had begun in London's music-halls, the convention was revived on television in the form of *The Black and White Minstrel Show*. This variety series was first screened on BBC Television on 14 June 1958 and it was to stay on air for the next two decades. *The Black and White Minstrel Show* evolved from the "Swannee River" type minstrel radio shows. One year before it was first broadcast on television, George Inns produced the *1957 Television Minstrels* (BBC TV 2, September 1957) as part of the National Radio Show in London.

The occasional television specials soon developed into a regular series with a forty-five minute non-stop format of Mississippi tunes and Country and Western songs. The series was devised and produced by Inns and featured music conducted by George Mitchell and the Television Toppers

Dance Troupe. The series showcased the Mitchell Minstrels as well as solo performances from entertainers such as Tony Mercer, John Boulter and Dai Francis. During the early years, various comedians such as Lesley Crowther, Stan Stennett and George Chisholm acted as "fillers" between the slick song and dance routines.

The Black and White Minstrel Show won the 1961 Golden Rose of Montreux. The variety series could almost always guarantee an audience of at least 16 million, but frequently managed to top 18 million viewers. At a time when the variety show was a popular television genre for the whole family, *The Black and White Minstrel Show* established itself as one of the world's greatest musical programmes on television. The music from the show broke sales records and the stage show was equally popular. Robert Luff's production opened at the Victoria Palace

The Black and White Minstrel Show
Photo courtesy of the British Film Institute

Theatre in 1969 and established itself in *The Guinness Book of Records* as the stage show seen by the largest number of people. At this time, the creation had gained considerable international respect and kudos. *The Black and White Minstrel Show*'s success was marked by its regular Saturday night transmissions over a vast period. The programme managed to maintain its freshness, its manic pace and its nostalgic premise on a weekly basis.

What accounts for such immense popularity? Part of the explanation was undoubtedly the pleasure many got from the programme, with its meticulously choreographed dance routines and popular songs and melodies. George Inns combined white dancers with black-faced singers and this was believed to be visually striking, particularly when colour television was introduced in 1967. *The Black and White Minstrel Show* harked back to a specific period and location—the Deep South where coy white women could be seen being wooed by docile, smiling black slaves. The black men were, in fact, white artists "Blacked-up." The racist implications of the premise of the programme were yet to be widely acknowledged or publicly discussed. But it was this which largely led to the programme's eventual demise.

Many felt that a large part of "minstrel humour" was based on caricaturing black people and depicting them as being both stupid and credulous. This image was felt to be insensitive and inappropriate in an increasingly multi-racial and multi-cultural Britain. *The Black and White Minstrel Show* is important in the context of British television because it outlines how racist representations became part of public debate and how performance was linked to social context. The programme revealed a tension between the television

controllers, critics and audience. Many were angry at the fact that during this time there were very few other representations of black people on British television. On 18 May 1967, the Campaign Against Racial Discrimination delivered a petition to the BBC signed by both black and white people, which requested that the programme be taken off television. Despite the controversy, the programme continued until 1 July 1978. Ultimately, its removal from the air coincided with the demise of the popularity of the variety genre on British television.

—Sarita Malik

REGULAR PERFORMERS
Leslie Crowther
George Chisholm
Stan Stennett

SINGERS
The Mitchell Minstrels

SOLO PERFORMERS
Tony Mercer, Dai Francis, John Boulter

DANCERS
The Television Toppers

PRODUCER   George Inns

PROGRAMMING HISTORY

• BBC
June 1958–July 1978

BLACK ENTERTAINMENT TELEVISION

U.S. Cable Network

Black Entertainment Television (BET) is the first and only television network in the United States primarily devoted to the attraction of African American viewers. Launched with a paltry $15,000 investment in 1980, the black-owned, basic-cable franchise had grown into a diversified, $61 million media enterprise by late 1993. Despite this rather phenomenal growth, however, BET's audience reach continues to be overshadowed by larger cable industry players (e.g., Turner Broadcasting Systems [TBS], Home Box Office [HBO], and ESPN).

Based in majority-black Washington, D.C., BET has added about 2 million subscriber homes per year since 1984, reaching more than 40 million cable households in 2500 markets by 1995. Moreover, the network has more than tripled revenues since 1985; it reported profits for the first time in 1986, when it finally hit A.C. Nielsen ratings charts and attracted major advertisers. In 1991, BET Holdings, Inc.—BET's parent company—became the first black-

owned company to be traded on the New York Stock Exchange.

From the very beginning, the heart and soul of BET programming was the music video. Predating MTV by a year, BET has offered as much as eighteen hours of music

Courtesy of BET

videos a day, prompting many to perceive the 24-hour network as essentially a black-oriented music video service. Thus while MTV was being criticized in 1983 for excluding black artists from its playlist (Tina Turner and the interracial group English Beat excepted), many viewers were tuning into BET for such offerings. Indeed, the network's flagship program, *VideoSoul*, has became a household word in many black communities.

But as BET grew, the network began to diversify its program offerings and image. By its tenth anniversary in 1990, the network had initiated several original programs/projects, including: *For the Record*, featuring members of the Congressional Black Caucus; *Teen Summit*, a Saturday noon show for youth; *Black Agenda 2000*, a series of forums on issues of interest to the black community; *Conversation with Ed Gordon*, an interview program with contemporary newsmakers; *Inside Studio A*, concerts and interviews taped before a live audience; *Personal Diary*, one-on-one interviews with prominent blacks; *On Stage*, plays written and performed by blacks; and *Our Voices*, a daily talk show.

More recent BET program schedules have included: *ComicView*, a stand-up comedy review; *Screen Scene*, a black-oriented entertainment journal; *Jazz Central*, a jazz music program; and *Rap City*, a rap video program. From time to time, BET also airs sporting events featuring teams from historically black colleges and universities, and rounds out its schedule with reruns of popular black-oriented shows such as *Sanford and Son*, *What's Happening*, *Frank's Place* and *Roc*. News and public affairs programs tend to be relegated to the weekends.

BET was the brainchild of Robert L. Johnson, who developed the idea for the network in 1979 while serving as vice president for governmental relations at the National Cable Television Association. Johnson, an African American, noted in 1989 that BET "should be for black media what Disney is to the general media or what Motown was to music." Industry observers have applauded Johnson's efficient management style and his aggressive plans to expand the company's product base and consumers. Johnson currently owns 52 percent of BET, while HBO, Tele-Communications Inc., and Great American Broadcasting each own 16 percent.

Echoing others who point to unique obstacles in the path of black business, Johnson argued in 1989 that industry racism had stunted BET's growth. In particular, he noted that many cable operators have been slow to carry BET (e.g., BET was carried on only 1,825 of the nation's 7,500 systems in 1989), and that BET has been saddled with some of the lowest subscriber fees in the industry (e.g., BET earned only about five cents per subscriber in 1989, while other cable services typically earned between fifteen to twenty cents per subscriber). Some analysts

agreed with Johnson's charges of industry racism, but noted that many of BET's problems were due to the network's lack of resources and Johnson's corresponding inability to adequately market it.

Nonetheless, BET has become much more than just a basic-cable network since its humble beginnings. By 1995, BET Holdings owned and operated a broad array of black-oriented media products, including: Black Entertainment Television, the basic-cable network; *YSB (Young Sisters and Brothers)*, a magazine targeted at black youths; *Emerge*, a magazine offering analysis and commentary on contemporary issues facing black America; Action Pay-Per-View, a national, satellite-delivered, pay-per-view movie channel based in Santa Monica, California; BET International, a provider of BET programming throughout Africa and other foreign markets; Identity Television, a London-based cable service targeting Afro-Caribbean viewers; BET Productions, a subsidiary providing technical and production services to outside companies; BET Radio Network, a radio service providing news and entertainment packages to affiliated stations across the U.S.; and BET Pictures, a joint venture with Blockbuster Entertainment Corporation to produce and distribute black, family-oriented films.

—Darnell M. Hunt

FURTHER READING

Brown, Joe. "Toasting a Sure BET: Black Network Links to New Satellite." *Washington Post*, 16 August 1982.

Hall, Carla. "Birth of a Network: Salesman and Stars at a Kickoff for BET." *Washington Post*, 25 January 1980.

Little, Benilde. "Robert Johnson: The Eyes Behind BET." *Essence* (New York), November 1990.

Margulies, Lee. "Black Cable TV Network Grows." *Los Angeles Times*, 8 December 1981.

Osborne, Karen. "BET: Tuning Into Viewers." *Black Enterprise* (New York), April 1989.

Shales, Tom. "Beyond 'Benson': Black-Oriented Channel from a Cable Pioneer." *Washington Post*, 30 November 1979.

Stein, Lisa. "Getting BETter: After 10 Years, TV's Black Network Comes of Age." *TV Guide* (Radnor, Pennsylvania), 16 June 1990.

Sturgis, Ingrid. "The BE 100s: BET Expands into Pay-Per-View." *Black Enterprise* (New York), September 1993.

Watson, John G. "Black Network Debuts on Cable." *Los Angeles Times*, 29 January 1980.

Williams, Christopher C. "A Black Network Makes its Move: Cable's BET Puts Plenty of Ambitionin into its Fall Schedule." *New York Times*, 17 September 1989.

See also Cable Networks

BLACKLISTING

Blacklisting is the practice of refusing to hire or terminating from employment an individual whose opinions or associations are deemed politically inconvenient or commercially troublesome. In the U.S. tradition, the term is forever linked to the fervent anti-communism of the Cold War era, a time when government agencies, private newsletters, and patriotic organizations branded selected members of the entertainment industry as (variously) card-carrying communists, fellow travelers, pinkos, or unwitting dupes of Moscow. The rubric "McCarthyism" is often used as shorthand for the reckless accusations and limitations on free expression during the Cold War, but from a media perspective the term is something of a misnomer. The period of the blacklist pre-dated and post-dated the junior senator from Wisconsin's reign and McCarthy himself evinced little interest in the entertainment industry: his targets of choice were the Department of State and the U.S. Army. The blacklisting of directors, writers, and performers in film, radio, and television was the project of a much wider coalition of anti-communist forces, a web of interlocking agents that included government investigators (the FBI), legislative committees (the House Committee on Un-American Activities and the Senate Internal Security Subcommittee), private interest groups (American Business Consultants, AWARE, Inc.) and patriotic organizations (the American Legion, the Veterans of Foreign Wars). They applied pressure on, and worked in concert with, fearful and compliant studio heads, network executives, sponsors, and advertising agencies to curtail the employment opportunities and civil rights of targeted undesirables.

The convergence of two cultural historical factors abetted the blacklist. One of the legacies of World War II was a heightened sensitivity to the political impact of the popular media; one of the coincidences of history was that television's early days paralleled precisely the escalating intensity of the Cold War in the years from 1946 to 1954. The contest between East and West, Soviet Communism and American Democracy, found its domestic expression in impassioned debates over the subversive influence of the mass media. In June 1950, the atmosphere reached fever pitch with the arrest of the atomic spies Julius and Ethel Rosenberg and the outbreak of the Korean War. That same month the editors of *Counterattack*, a four page "newsletter of facts on communism," issued a special report entitled *Red Channels, The Report of Communist Influence in Radio and Television*, a listing of 151 names of performers deemed to be communist party members or to have like-minded opinions and associations (called "fellow travelers" in the argot of the day). The *Red Channels* report formalized an informal practice in effect since at least November 1947 when representatives from the major Hollywood studios pledged they would "not knowingly employ a communist" and "take positive action" on "disloyal elements." Though the scholarship of *Red Channels* was slipshod—the actors listed

ranged from unapologetic Communist Party members, to mainstream liberals, to bewildered innocents—its impact was immediate and long-lasting. CBS instituted in-house loyalty oaths; the advertising firm of Batten, Barton, Durstine, and Osborn recruited executives to serve as security officers. A study on blacklisting in the entertainment industry published by the Fund for the Republic in 1956 concluded that *Red Channels* put in black and white what was previously an *ad hoc* practice and thus "marked the formal beginning of blacklisting in the radio-TV industry."

As an emergent medium subject to government oversight by the Federal Communications Commission, television was the most timorous of the mass media when confronted by state power. The scrutiny of legislative bodies concentrated the minds of network executives powerfully, notably the hearings held by the House Committee on Un-American Activities in November 1947 and throughout 1951 and 1952 and a kindred set of hearings on the "Subversive Influence of Radio, Television, and the Entertain-

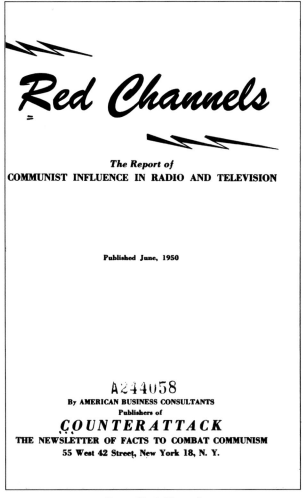

Cover of Red Channels
Courtesy of Wisconsin Center for Film and Theater Research

ment Industry" held by Senator McCarran's Internal Investigatory Subcommittee in 1951. Moreover, as an advertiser supported medium still in embryonic development, television was especially susceptible to protests from special interest groups threatening product boycotts, pickets, or public censure. Casting the widest commercial net possible, the networks aimed for "100% acceptability" and assiduously avoided alienating any group of potential viewers.

Though the effect of the blacklist was punitive, its rational was preemptive. From the perspective of the networks, its purpose was less to rid the medium of subversive content than to avoid the controversy that ensued upon the appearance of a suspect individual. Rather than canceling the appearance of announced performers or firing known talent, the blacklist tended to operate off-camera, behind the scenes, by deleting or clearing talent in advance. Though the list in *Red Channels* was the founding document, other lists and publications (not to say rumors and innuendo) might also render an individual politically radioactive in the eyes of any one of the networks, sponsors, or advertising agencies.

For talent tainted with the communist brush, the path to vindication was tortuous. Once accused, actors might suffer in silence, defy the accusations, or engage in rituals of public recantation or denial ("clearance") either before Congress, in the public press, or at the offices of *Counterattack* itself. Given the difficulty of proving a negative, the total number of people burned by the blacklist—careers permanently derailed, jobs lost, or energies squandered—is difficult to gauge, but hundreds were listed and investigated and thousands were singed by paranoia. Even allowing for the vagaries of memory and self-romanticization, the blacklist traumatized a generation of artists in the entertainment industry. One particularly tragic case may stand for many. Listed in *Red Channels*, Philip Loeb, who played the warm Jewish patriarch in *Molly* on radio and in the show's first television season in 1950–51, was replaced in the show's second season after General Foods withdrew its sponsorship. An embittered and unemployed Loeb committed suicide in 1955.

In the wake of the TV-inspired downfall of McCarthy in 1954, some of the pressure to purge alleged subversive from the airwaves lifted, but the blacklist—both as a formal, institutionalized procedure and as an informal gentleman's agreement—endured well into the next decade. The motion picture industry began gingerly defying the blacklist in the late 1950s and by 1960 was giving screen credit to once-blacklisted writers. By contrast, television, ever cautious, kept well back in the ranks of defiance. Not until the fall of 1967, on *The Smothers Brothers Comedy Hour*, was blacklisted folk singer Pete Seeger finally "cleared" for a return to network television.

—Thomas Doherty

FURTHER READING

Bentley, Eric. *Are You Now or Have You Ever Been: The Investigation of Show Business by the Un-American Activities Committee, 1947–1958.* New York: Harper and Row, 1972.

Burton, Michael C. *John Henry Faulk: The Making of a Liberated Mind.* Austin, Texas: Eakin Press, 1993.

Ceplair, Larry. *The Inquisition in Hollywood: Politics in the Film Community, 1930–1960.* Garden City, New York: Anchor Press/Doubleday, 1980.

Cogley, John. *Report on Blacklisting.* New York: Fund for the Republic, 1956.

Faulk, John Henry. *Fear on Trial.* New York: Simon and Schuster, 1964.

Foley, Karen Sue. *The Political Blacklist in the Broadcast Industry: The Decade of the 1950s.* New York: Arno, 1979.

Navasky, Victor S. *Naming Names.* New York: Viking, 1980.

Red Channels: The Report of Communist Influence in Radio and Television. New York: American Business Consultants, 1950.

Vaughn, Robert. *Only Victims: A Study of Show Business Blacklisting.* New York: Putnam, 1972.

See also Censorship

BLEASDALE, ALAN

British Writer

Alan Bleasdale is one of the most successful and influential writers working in British television today. Drawing on the traditions of realist television drama, he has created powerful but darkly comic television plays and miniseries set in the depressed cities of the north of England.

Bleasdale's first success as a writer came with the development of the character of Scully, a Liverpool youth whose anarchic adventures challenge the authority of those responsible for the impoverished society in which he lives. A series of stories about Scully was broadcast on BBC Radio

Merseyside in 1971 while Bleasdale was still earning his living as a teacher. From 1974 to 1979 Bleasdale presented the *Franny Scully Show* on Radio City Liverpool, while the character also appeared in a touring theater show, a television play called *Scully's New Year's Eve* broadcast by the BBC in 1978, and two novels which became the basis of a Granada television series in 1984.

The ability to create characters who capture the popular imagination was also apparent in *Boys from the Blackstuff*, the series which firmly established Bleasdale as a key figure in British television in the 1980s. This project had its roots in a single play called *The Black Stuff*, broadcast by the BBC in 1980, dealing with the disastrous money-making efforts of a gang of road workers from Liverpool. With the support of producer Michael Wearing, Bleasdale was able to create a five-part series dealing with the effects of unemployment on the "boys" and their families after their return to Liverpool.

Boys from the Blackstuff was first shown in a late-night time-slot on BBC2 in 1982 but proved so popular that it was quickly repeated in prime-time on BBC1 in January 1983. Each episode centered on a different character, but their paths frequently crossed and the action built toward the final episode in which they all came together at the funeral of an old worker whose socialist ideals no longer inspire the men of Margaret Thatcher's Britain. The impact of the series grew out of its commitment to showing the experience of unemployment from the point-of-view of the unemployed. It drew on the conventions of northern working-class realism prevalent in British cinema and television since the 1960s but also included elements of black comedy, derived from Liverpool's traditional "scouse" humor, and grotesque nightmare images that expressed the psychological pressures of unemployment. This mixture of elements created an unsettling effect but, despite its bleak vision, *Boys from the Blackstuff* promoted a sense of solidarity in viewers who faced similar problems. Catchphrases from the series were incorporated into chants by the supporters of the Liverpool soccer team.

Bleasdale has continued to write for television, as well as for film and theater, but the closest he has come to repeating the success of *Boys from the Blackstuff* has been with *GBH*, a seven-part serial broadcast on Channel 4 in 1991. Dealing with the takeover of a northern English city by a fascist organization, *GBH* was related to earlier serials, such as Troy Kennedy Martin's *Edge of Darkness* (1985) and Alan Plater's *A Very British Coup* (1988), which blended science-fiction and political thriller to address growing fears that the British democratic system was threatened with collapse. Bleasdale's political message was more explicitly stated here than in *Boys from the Blackstuff*, but the fiction was once again enriched by grotesque comedy, largely associated with the casting of Michael Palin, a member of the Monty Python troupe, as an unassuming school teacher who inadvertently becomes a symbol of resistance to the new order.

In 1994 Bleasdale took on a new role as producer of series on Channel 4 called *Alan Bleasdale Presents*, using the influence made possible by the popular success of his work to give young writers a chance to demonstrate their talents. While the dramas presented in this series have adopted a variety of approaches, they owe much to Bleasdale's own achievement, grounded in the tradition of "naturalism" in British television drama but creating compelling fictions by gradually introducing disruptive elements drawn from popular genres.

—Jim Leach

Alan Bleasdale
Photo courtesy of the British Film Institute

ALAN BLEASDALE. Born in Liverpool, Lancashire, England, 23 March 1946. Attended St. Aloysius Roman Catholic Infant and Junior Schools, Huyton, Lancashire, 1951–57; Wade Deacon Grammar School, Widnes, Lancashire, 1957–64; Padgate Teachers Training College (Teacher's Certificate), 1967. Married Julia Moses: 1970; children: two sons and one daughter. Teacher, St. Columbus Secondary Modern School, Huyton, Lancashire, 1967–71, King George V School, Gilbert and Ellice Islands, 1971–74, and Halewood Grange Comprehensive School, Lancashire, 1974–75; resident playwright, Liverpool Playhouse, 1975–76, Contact Theatre, Manchester, 1976–78; joint artistic director, 1981–84, and associate director, 1984–86, Liverpool Playhouse. Liverpool Polytechnic, D.Litt. 1991. Recipient: Broadcasting Press Guild Television Award for Best Series, 1982; British Academy of Film and Television Arts Writers' Award, 1982; Royal Television Society Writer of the Year, 1982; Pye Television Award, 1983; Toronto Film Festival Critics' Award, 1984; *London Standard* Best Musical Award, 1985; ITV Best British TV Drama of the Decade Award, 1989; Broadcasting Press Guild Television and Radio Award, 1991. Address: Lemon Unna and Durbridge Ltd, 24 Pottery Lane, Holland Park, London W11 4LZ, England.

TELEVISION SERIES

1982	*Boys from the Blackstuff*
1984	*Scully*

| 1991 | *GBH* |
| 1994 | *Alan Bleasdale Presents* (producer) |

TELEVISION SPECIALS

1975	*Early to Bed*
1976	*Dangerous Ambition*
1978	*Scully's New Year's Eve*
1980	*The Black Stuff*
1981	*The Muscle Market*
1986	*The Monocled Mutineer*

FILM

No Surrender, 1986.

STAGE

Fat Harold and the Last 26, 1975; *The Party's Over*, 1975; *Scully* (with others), 1975; *Franny Scully's Christmas Stories* (with Kenneth Alan Taylor), 1976; *Down the Dock Road*, 1976; *It's a Madhouse*, 1976; *Should Auld Acquaintance*, 1976; *No More Sitting on the Old School Bench*, 1977; *Crackers*, 1978; *Pimples*, 1978; *Having a Ball*, 1981; *Young People Today*, 1983; *Are You Lonesome Tonight?*, 1985; *Love Is a Many Splendoured Thing*, 1986; *On the Ledge*, 1993.

PUBLICATIONS

Scully (novel). London: Hutchinson, 1975.
Who's Been Sleeping in My Bed? (novel). London: Hutchinson, 1977.
No More Sitting on the Old School Bench (play). Todmorden, Yorkshire: Woodhouse, 1979.
Love Is a Many Splendoured Thing (play), in David Self and Ray Speakman, *Act I*. London: Hutchinson, 1979.

Scully (play), with others. London: Hutchinson, 1984.
Scully and Mooey (revised version of *Who's Been Sleeping in My Bed?*). London: Corgi, 1984.
Boys from the Blackstuff (television play). London: Hutchinson, 1985.
Are You Lonesome Tonight? (musical). London: Faber, 1985.
It's a Madhouse/Having a Ball (plays). London: Faber, 1986.
The Monocled Mutineer (television play). London: Hutchinson, 1986.
No Surrender: A Deadpan Farce (screenplay). London: Faber, 1986.

FURTHER READING

Millington, Bob. "Boys from the Blackstuff." In Brandt, George W., editor. *British Television Drama in the 1980s.* Cambridge: Cambridge University Press, 1993.

Millington, Bob, and Robin Nelson. *Boys from the Blackstuff: The Making of TV Drama.* London: Comedia, 1986.

Paterson, Richard. "Restyling Masculinity: The Impact of Boys from the Blackstuff." In Curran, James, Anthony Smith, and Pauline Wingate, editors. *Impacts and Influences: Essays on Media Power in the Twentieth Century.* London: Methuen, 1987.

Paterson, Richard, editor. *Boys from the Blackstuff.* London: British Film Institute, 1984.

Saynor, James. "Clogging Corruption." *Sight and Sound* (London), July 1991.

Tulloch, John. *Television Drama: Agency, Audience and Myth.* London: Routledge, 1990.

See also *Boys from the Blackstuff*

BLUE PETER

British Children's Programme

Blue Peter is one of British television's longest running programmes, regularly reaching 5 to 6 million children and teenagers. It takes its name from the blue and white flag hoisted by a ship leaving port on a voyage. The originator of the programme wanted this to suggest the voyage of discovery that it would provide for its young viewers. The programming has a magazine format that involves a combination of studio presentation, interview, and demonstration with additional film report items. It is transmitted live from the BBC's Television Centre after hectic rehearsal. The programme was launched with its catchy "Barnacle Bill" signature tune in 1958 as a fifteen-minute slot, involving two presenters, described by Barnes and Baxter as "Chris Trace playing with trains and Lelia Williams playing with dolls." It became a twice-weekly, 30-minute programme in 1963. A third presenter was later introduced and its Monday/Thursday slots were changed to thrice-weekly transmission (Monday/Wednesday/Friday) in 1965. *Blue Peter* runs for a 40-week season from autumn to early summer with a ten-week break in which special overseas items are filmed. The programme is broadcast between 17:05 and 17:35 hours, a bridging slot taking teenagers into an Australian soap opera and into "adult" early evening news. It has won over twenty major television awards, including from BAFTA, the Sun Television, and the National Viewers and Listeners Association for excellence in children's programming.

It is successful as a programme because it has remained true to the basic format of its original creator, John Hunter Blair, but has accommodated itself to the social change that has taken place over two generations of television viewing. Editorial continuity was achieved by the singular influence of long-standing editor Biddy Baxter, who worked on *Blue Peter* between 1962 and 1988. Baxter was a liberal, inventive, but demanding leader of the programme team with a very shrewd sense of how the developing medium could best be harnessed for a young audience. In the best tradition of British public service broadcasting, *Blue Peter* aims to inform, educate, and stimulate its target viewers with enter-taining content and it remains one TV programme that parents encourage their children to watch. In the 1960s many of the programme's innovations were quickly imitated by rivals or adapted in later programmes such as ITV's *Magpie*, aired from 1968 to 1980. In 1965, for instance, *Blue Peter* introduced a puppy to the programme and then asked its viewers to send in suggestions for its name. Petra became the nation's first TV pet. Phenomenally popular, other pets, including cats and tortoises, were added to the programme so that respect for animals and pet care tips could be passed on. The programme actively encouraged the participation of its viewers by instituting a *Blue Peter* badge scheme (awarded for appearances on the programme or special achievements), regular competitions and an annual Christmas Appeal to raise money for charity. The studio items very often involve presenters trying new hobbies, cooking, making home-made toys from household rubbish (washing-up liquid bottles, wire coat-hangers, and "sticky-backed plastic" being fa-voured materials), or bringing talented youngsters into the studio to make their achievements more widely known. The overall ethos of the programme encourages children by the example of the adult presenters to "have a go", to try something new and be inquisitive about the world around them. *Blue Peter* presenters with strong personalities in-volved in unforgettable exploits have impressed themselves on the popular memory of television viewers. The phrases of their scripted cookery demonstrations ("here's one I made earlier") and idiosyncratic expressions ("get down, Shep!") have become clichés and are parodied in pop songs. The show remains "live," which means that unplanned incidents occur, much to the delight of the viewers. One such moment has gone down in British television lore. It involved a baby elephant ("Lulu") departing from the script by defecating in the studio and running amok with its elderly zoo keeper as the transmission came to a close.

Today's presenters follow in a long line of enthusiastic personalities who have played no small part in shaping the views of generations of viewers. Critics of the programme suggest that *Blue Peter*'s format, content and presentation epitomise a "safe" agenda of middle-class attitudes, that it is patronising towards young people, replicating a dominant ideology. The programme's own audience research would suggest that on the whole its target audience do not feel patronised. Given the centrality of *Blue Peter* to its schedul-ing area, it is not surprising that it tends to reflect the values and aspirations of the institution from which it originates. It is more accurate to see *Blue Peter* as a barometer of social values and cultural change in Britain over the extended period of its existence. Like all successful programmes, *Blue Peter* has had to deal with change and be flexible to a degree, but this has been uneven. Lewis Bronze, who succeeded Baxter in 1988, introduced Diane-Louisi Jordan, a black presenter, in 1990. The editorial team was quietly accepting and supportive of the unmarried status of Janet Ellis, who became pregnant, but shaken to find out that one of its

Blue Peter
Photo courtesy of the British Film Institute

ex-presenters, Michael Sundin, turned out to be gay. The significance of *Blue Peter* within British television history resides in its longevity, continued popularity, and institu-tional centrality. Within Children's BBC, *Blue Peter* is still, in the words of Anna Home, head of Children's Television, "very deliberately chosen as one of the foundation stones upon which the rest of the schedule can be built."

—Lance Pettitt

PRESENTERS
Christopher Trace, Leila Williams, Valerie Singleton, Peter Purves, John Noakes, Diane Louisi-Jordan, Janet Ellis, Mi-chael Sundin, and others

PRODUCER   John Hunter Blair

PROGRAMMING HISTORY

• BBC
Various Times, from 1958

FURTHER READING
Baxter, B., and E. Barnes. *Blue Peter: The Inside Story.* London: BBC Books, 1989.
The Blue Peter Annual. London: BBC, 1964–.
Ferguson, Robert. "Black Blue Peter." In, Masterman, L., editor. *Television Mythologies.* London: Comedia, 1984.

THE BOB NEWHART SHOW/NEWHART

U.S. Situation Comedy

The Bob Newhart Show and Newhart are both prime examples of the ensemble comedy that came into vogue in U.S. television during the 1970s and enjoyed continued popularity in the 1980s and 1990s. The two shows had much else in common (in addition to their star, Bob Newhart); both had sharp writing, well-drawn characters, and a distinctive style of humor that was intelligent and sophisticated, yet just a bit off the wall.

As with many 1970s ensemble sitcoms, such as *The Mary Tyler Moore Show*, *The Bob Newhart Show* focused on career-oriented adults, mostly single, related by circumstance rather than blood. Newhart played Dr. Bob Hartley, a psychologist practicing in Chicago. He treated a variety of patients whose problems, no matter how eccentric, were played for laughs; the star among them was the misanthropic Elliott Carlin (Jack Riley). Bob's office mate was Dr. Jerry Robinson (Peter Bonerz), an orthodontist and typical 1970s "swinging single"; they shared the services of a quick-witted secretary-receptionist, Carol Kester (Marcia Wallace). Bob's wife, Emily—smart, funny, sexy—was played by Suzanne Pleshette. The couple's neighbor and closest friend in their high-rise apartment building was Howard Borden (Bill Daily), a childlike airline navigator who ate most of his meals with the Hartleys and had them water his plants even when he was home; he was, in effect, the offspring they didn't have.

"That guy could lose an argument with a fern," was the caustic Carlin's comment on Howard.

A few lines and situations illustrate the show's deft and daft humor: Bob and Emily have a bicentennial party in 1976 and invite Carlin because, according to Bob, "He says he gets lonely every bicentennial"; Howard explains how spilling salt could be fatal—after Bob nearly falls down an elevator shaft and becomes obsessed with death; the Hartleys send Howard to a psychologist so he can become independent and responsible—but then want the old Howard back; Jerry comes into money, gives up his practice, and turns into "the village coot," who wants to do nothing but whittle and watch the sunrise.

These characters, even if defined by their specific quirks, developed and grew throughout the show's long run. Emily began as a substitute teacher, became a full-time teacher and moved up to vice principal; Carol married a travel agent and also tried out some other careers, but always came back to Bob and Jerry; Howard was engaged for a time to Bob's sister Ellen, a newspaper reporter, but she went out of his life and off the show when she moved to Cleveland for a better job (and after she had a flirtation with Howard's visiting brother, game warden Gordon Borden). The show made creative use of running gags such as Bob's one-sided telephone conversations, which had been a popular part of

The Bob Newhart Show

Newhart

Newhart's standup act; his habit of trying to explain situations by using analogies no one understood; and his bedtime conversations with Emily, as each could turn back on the light, and make one more comment.

When Newhart retired the show, by choice, he expressed misgivings about the direction of situation comedy as the 1970s gave way to the 1980s. Broad physical comedy and obvious jokes seemed to be pushing out wit and sophistication. The subsequent success of *Newhart*, however, showed there was still a place for intelligent, eccentric comedy. In this series Newhart played Dick Loudon, a writer of how-to books who moved from New York to Vermont to realize his dream of running a country inn. His wife, again smart, funny, and sexy, was named Joanna and was played by Mary Frann. Again there were numerous quirky supporting characters. Tom Poston, who had frequently guested on the earlier show, portrayed the inn's unhandy handyman, George Utley. Julia Duffy played the hilariously vain and spoiled Stephanie Vanderkellen, an heiress working as a maid at the inn (Stephanie replaced her less interesting cousin, Leslie, after the first season). Stephanie's boyfriend, Michael Harris (Peter Scolari), was an insufferable yuppie and producer of a local TV show, *Vermont Today*, which Dick began hosting a few years into *Newhart*'s run. Perhaps the most memorable, and certainly the most unusual, characters were three bizarre backwoodsmen, of whom only one ever spoke (until the final episode). "I'm Larry, this is my brother Darryl, and this is my other brother Darryl," was their stock introduction. They could always be counted upon to enjoy any activity that would disgust most people. The show, like Newhart's earlier sitcom, weeded out weak characters and developed the strong ones as it went along.

Newhart closed its successful eight-year run with one of the best final episodes of any series. It involved everyone in town—except the Loudons—selling their property to a Japanese corporation, included a parody of *Fiddler on the Roof*, and ended with Newhart waking up in bed with Suzanne Pleshette, the woman who portrayed his wife on his previous show, and explaining that he'd had a very strange dream (a parodic reference to the famous 1986–87 season of *Dallas*).

As this ending indicates, the 1970s *Bob Newhart* show is especially fondly remembered and there have been several other tributes to its enduring popularity. Marcia Wallace made a guest appearance on *Taxi* as the dream date of cabby Jim Ignatowski, who had nearly memorized every episode of *The Bob Newhart Show*. (Many members of the creative staff of *Taxi* had begun their careers at MTM Entertainment, Inc., the company that produced *The Bob Newhart Show*.) Newhart reprised Dr. Bob Hartley on a *Saturday Night Live* segment in the 1990s, with Hartley being the only voice of reason on a talk-show panel. And when TV character Murphy Brown (as part of a continuing joke on the show of the same name) was finally assigned a competent secretary, it was again Marcia Wallace, playing Carol. At the end of the episode, however, Newhart showed up as Bob Hartley and, after reducing himself to begging, won her back from Murphy.

—Trudy Ring

THE BOB NEWHART SHOW

CAST

Robert (Bob) Hartley	Bob Newhart
Emily Hartley	Suzanne Pleshette
Howard Borden	Bill Daily
Jerry Robinson	Peter Bonerz
Carol Kester Bondurant	Marcia Wallace
Margaret Hoover (1972–73)	Patricia Smith
Dr. Bernie Tupperman (1972–76)	Larry Gelman
Ellen Hartley (1974–76)	Pat Finley
Larry Bondurant (1975–77)	Will McKenzie
Eliot Carlin	Jack Riley
Mrs. Bakerman	Florida Friebus
Miss Larson (1972–73)	Penny Marshall
Michelle Nardo (1973–76)	Renee Lippin
Mr. Peterson (1973–78)	John Fiedler
Mr. Gianelli (1972–73)	Noam Pitlik
Mr. Vickers (1974–75)	Lucien Scott
Mr. Herd (1976–77)	Oliver Clark

PRODUCERS Tom Patchett, Jay Tarses, David Davis, Lorenzo Music, Michael Zinberg

PROGRAMMING HISTORY   138 Episodes

• CBS

September 1972–October 1976	Saturday 9:30-10:00
November 1976–September 1977	Saturday 8:30-9:00
September 1977–April 1978	Saturday 8:00-8:30
June 1978–August 1978	Saturday 8:00-8:30

NEWHART

CAST

Dick Loudon	Bob Newhart
Joanna Loudon	Mary Frann
Kirk Devane (1982–84)	Steven Kampmann
George Utley	Tom Poston
Leslie Vanderkellen (1982–83)	Jennifer Holmes
Stephanie Vanderkellen (1983–90)	Julia Duffy
Larry	William Sanderson
First Darryl	Tony Papenfuss
Second Darryl	John Voldstad
Jim Dixon	Thomas Hill
Chester Wanamaker	William Lanteau
Cindy Parker Devane (1984)	Rebecca York
Michael Harris (1984–90)	Peter Scolari
Harley Estin (1984–88)	Jeff Doucette
Elliot Gabler (1984–85)	Lee Wilkof
Bev Dutton (1984–88)	Linda Carlson
Constable Shifflett (1985–89)	Todd Susman

J.J. (1985–87) . . . . Fred Applegate
Bud (1985–90) . . . . Ralph Manza
Paul (1988–90) . . . . Cliff Bemis
Prudence Goddard (1989–90) . . . . Kathy Kinney
Art Rusnak (1989–90) . . . . David Pressman

PRODUCERS Barry Kemp, Sheldon Bull

PROGRAMMING HISTORY 182 Episodes

• CBS

October 1982–February 1983	Monday 9:30-10:00
March 1983–April 1983	Sunday 9:30-10:00
April 1983–May 1983	Sunday 8:30-9:00
June 1983–August 1983	Sunday 9:30-10:00
August 1983–September 1986	Monday 9:30-10:00
September 1986–August 1988	Monday 9:00-9:30
August 1988–March 1989	Monday 8:00-8:30
March 1989–August 1989	Monday 10:00-10:30
August 1989–October 1989	Monday 10:30-11:00
November 1989–April 1990	Monday 10:00-10:30
April 1990–May 1990	Monday 8:30-9:00
May 1990–July l990	Monday 10:00-10:30
July 1990–August 1990	Friday 9:00-9:30
September 1990	Saturday 9:00-9:30

FURTHER READING

Hammamoto, Darrell Y. *Nervous Laughter: Television Situation Comedy and Liberal Democratic Ideology.* New York: Praeger, 1989.

Marc, David. *Comic Visions: Television Comedy and American Culture.* Boston, Massachusetts: Unwin Hyman, 1989.

———. *Demographic Vistas: Television in American Culture.* Philadelphia: University of Pennsylvania Press, 1984.

Mayerle, Judine. "The Most Inconspicuous Hit on Television: A Case Study of Newhart." *Journal of Popular Film and Television* (Washington, D.C.), Fall 1989.

"*Newhart* Gets Early Airing on Some Stations in 'Surprise' Option Plan." *Television-Radio Age* (New York), 27 June 1988.

Sorenson, Jeff. *Bob Newhart.* New York: St. Martin's, 1988.

See also Newhart, Bob

BOCHCO, STEVEN

U.S. Writer and Producer

Steven Bochco has become a brand name for American quality television in the 1980s and 1990s. With a reputation for not contenting himself with given formats or standard practices, Bochco has developed a unique style, perhaps several unique styles, for his work. His firm's logo—a concert violinist playing a short section of Vivaldi's "Four Seasons"—constantly reminds us of Bochco's creative intentions and artistic higher aims while at the same time indicating his roots in a more traditional humanistic education. Bochco's father Rudolph was a concert violinist, and his mother, Mimi Bochco, a painter.

He began writing for television after he finished college. He always considered himself to be a writer, and when, in the 1960s, MCA gave writing grants to theater departments around the country, he jumped at the occasion. As he puts it in a 1988 interview with Michael Winship: "I had an MCA writing fellowship when I was in college, and I used that to sort of con my way into a summer job at Universal Studios between my junior and senior years. They put me in the story department as an assistant to its head, and at the end of that summer, they invited me to come back permanently when I graduated." Mike Ludmer, then head of Universal's story department, made sure everyone on the lot got to know the talented young man with no writing experience at all. Bochco's first writing credit (with Harry Tatelman) came with a segment of the *Bob Hope Presents the Chrysler Theater* called "A Slow Fade to Black", starring Rod Serling.

Bochco stayed twelve years with Universal, working his way up from writer to story editor (for the Robert Stack segments in the adventure drama series *The Name of the Game,* which aired from 1968 to 1971, and later for *Col-*

Steven Bochco
Photo courtesy of Steven Bochco

umbo). He went on to produce, starting with "Lt. Shuster's Wife", a Movie of the Week for ABC, starring Lee Grant. He also had to learn how to handle flops: *Griff*, made for ABC, was supposed to become a post-*Bonanza* vehicle for Lorne Greene. The series lasted a only few days into 1974. The same experience occurred with his next series, *The Invisible Man*, an update of the classical H.G. Wells story for NBC (1975–76). *Delvecchio*, made for CBS in 1976, bloomed one full season before being canceled in June 1977. Bochco was co-producer and wrote eight of the twenty scripts eventually broadcast. On *Delvecchio* he met Michael Kozoll, with whom he later co-created and co-wrote *Hill Street Blues*. Both Charles Haid and Michael Conrad were regulars of the show, and both would later find themselves among the regular cast of *Hill Street Blues*.

While at Universal, Steven Bochco wrote episodes for *McMillan and Wife* and *Ironside* as well as other series. He was involved in different movie projects, such as *The Counterfeit Killings* (1968) and *Silent Running* (1972), both for theatrical release, and *Double Indemnity* for ABC (1973). His last project for Universal was *Richie Brockelman, Private Eye* (NBC, 1978), starring Dennis Dugan, Robert Hogan and Barbara Bosson, Steven Bochco's wife, a short-lived spin-off to Stephen J. Cannell and Roy Huggins' successful detective drama *The Rockford Files*.

Bochco left Universal in 1978 for MTM Enterprises. One of the reasons he left was his apparent wish to break new ground, both inside and outside the confined world of action-adventure drama series. He also felt there was more to learn about producing than what Universal had to offer. His first MTM venture was a Movie of the Week called *Vampire*, co-written with Michael Kozoll. Then came *Paris*, a police drama series (CBS, 1979) which lasted, again, just a few days into 1980. *Paris* was interesting in terms of quality writing. There were unusual stories, focused on a black police captain moonlighting as a criminology-teacher at a nearby university. The impressive cast was headed by James Earl Jones as Woody Paris. But there was, or so it seemed, just not enough old-fashioned "spice" to attract a larger audience.

In January 1980, NBC asked MTM if Bochco and Kozoll could come up with something for them. Vague ideas about an ensemble piece set in a hotel lobby led nowhere. (The concept would later be developed by Aaron Spelling to become *Hotel*.) What NBC wanted was a cop melodrama, a cop ensemble piece. Bochco and Kozoll agreed under two conditions: total creative control and a meeting about network standards. The result of that meeting was *Hill Street Blues*, a cop show setting new rules for almost every aspect of the action-adventure formula. As David Marc and Robert J. Thompson put it, *Hill Street Blues* set standards for "multiple centers of audience identification; complicated personal lives; overlapping dialogue; hand-held camera shots; busy, crowded mise-en-scènes." The show also established its own realistic, "dirty" look and

defined a fictional world, "the Hill," that could be understood as a metaphorical melting pot, a community (or family) consisting of members of almost any nation and race that had ever set foot in America. These elements could later be recognized, in a more accented and refined matter, in many drama series developed in the 1990s, set in police precincts (*NYPD Blue*, and *Hill Street Blues*) or hospitals or courtrooms.

Hill Street Blues earned its creators several Emmies (for "Outstanding Drama Series" and "Outstanding Writing", among others) and a Golden Globe for "Best Television Drama Series". Still, MTM remained somewhat unhappy about its prestige object, which was very expensive and never able to pay off financially. *Hill Street Blues* lasted from 1981 well into 1987; Bochco was fired in 1985, after the disastrous short run of another of his (and MTM's) high-brow series projects, *The Bay City Blues* (NBC, 1983). Later, for Twentieth Century-Fox, Bochco developed another long-running hit, a legal drama called *L.A. Law* (NBC, 1986–94). On this project he served as co-producer with Terry Louise Fischer. As often noted, *L.A. Law* looked very similar to *Hill Street Blues* set in a fancy law office, with many characters and stories intertwined in each episode. Bochco himself pointed out the differences between the two shows, however, describing *L.A. Law* as "populated by people who are infinitely more successful. They make more money, they drive nicer cars, they have prettier girlfriends, they're possibly smarter, and they win more." But the series maintained its "bluesy" feeling, a certain notion of the world being a much too complicated and absurd place to live in, with rules no one would ever really understand.

Besides crime and courtroom dramas (*Civil Wars*, dealing with divorce cases, lasted from 1991 to 1993), Bochco developed one quite successful half-hour comedy drama, together with David Kelley. *Doogie Howser, M.D.* (ABC, 1989–93) told the improbable story of perhaps the youngest doctor ever to do medical examinations on-screen. The mild-mannered youngster was only sixteen years old when his professional career began. Bochco wouldn't be Bochco without at least one taboo being broken. Here, Neil Patrick Harris hit the news when his character lost his virginity, in one of the later episodes of the series.

The wish to break new ground on prime time, in terms of content as well as in aesthetic matters, has become even more apparent in Bochco's television productions for the 1990s. Some of these attempts were flops. The infamous experiment attempting to combine the cop show with a musical in *Cop Rock* (ABC, 1990) lasted for only a few weeks.

NYPD Blue (ABC, 1993–), however, earned its cast and crew six Emmies in 1994 alone. It was basically another ensemble piece, set in a police precinct right in Bochco's childhood home, New York. With *NYPD Blue*, Bochco tried to expand the limits of network standards even further, experimenting with gritty realism, or documentarism, filmed in a highly stylized, self-reflexive manner. The show was controversial even before its appearance on the schedule because Bochco had announced that he would include far coarser language and some nudity in his move toward realism.

Bochco has earned a reputation for re-inventing the formula of the cop-show with *Hill Street Blues* and *NYPD Blue*. He certainly has introduced a new understanding of television realism, complete with partial nudity and four-letter words, into prime time—despite network Standards and Practices and actual boycotts of advertisers and network affiliates around the country in the case of *NYPD Blue*. Thanks to him, the term "teamwork" has taken on new meaning in television producing: it means quality writing, and it means intriguing, interesting stories of human bonding and struggle which drive the actors, individually and collectively, to give their best. Bochco has thus succeeded in integrating different aspects and perspectives into what seems (or seemed) to be one and the same story.

New projects in the post-O.J.Simpson-era continue his tendency toward innovation in the area of narrative structure. A new courtroom drama, *Murder One* (1995–), follows a single murder trial for an entire season, interweaving personal and professional lives of a large cast of characters.

—Ursula Ganz-Blaettler

STEVEN BOCHCO. Born in New York City, New York, U.S.A. 16 December 1943. Attended High School of Music and Art, Manhattan, New York; New York University, Manhattan; Carnegie Institute of Technology (now Carnegie-Mellon University), B.F.A. in Theater 1966. Married Barbara Bosson, 1969; children: Jeffrey and Melissa. Assistant to head of story department, Universal Television, 1966; and subsequent writer of various other Universal television series; joined MTM Enterprises as writer-producer, 1978; formed Steven Bochco Productions and entered into production deal with Twentieth Century-Fox and ABC, 1987. Recipient: Emmy Awards, 1971, 1972, 1981, 1982, 1983, 1984, 1987, 1989.

TELEVISION SERIES (writer)

1967-75	*Ironside* (writer)
1968–71	*The Name of the Game* (writer)
1968-71	*The Game of the Game*
1971	*Columbo* (story editor, only)
1971–76	*McMillan and Wife*
1973-74	*Griff* (also producer)
1975–76	*The Invisible Man*
1976–77	*Delvecchio* (also co-producer)
1978	*Richie Brockelman*
1979	*Turnabout*
1979–80	*Paris* (also executive-producer)
1981–87	*Hill Street Blues* (also executive-producer)
1983	*The Bay City Blues* (also executive-producer)
1986–94	*L.A. Law* (also executive-producer)
1987	*Hooperman* (also executive-producer)
1989–93	*Doogie Howser, M.D.* (also executive producer)
1990	*Cop Rock* (also executive-producer)
1991–93	*Civil Wars* (also executive-producer)
1993–	*NYPD Blue* (also executive-producer)
1995–	*Murder One* (also executive-producer)

PUBLICATIONS

"Steven Bochco" (interview). *American Film* (Washington, D.C.), July-August 1988.

"Steven Bochco: Taking Risks with Television." (interview), *Broadcasting* (Washington, D.C.), 6 May 1991.

FURTHER READING

Christensen, Mark. "Bochco's Law." *Rolling Stone* (New York), 21 April 1988.

Coe, Steve, and Harry A. Jessel. "'NYPD Blue': Rocky Start, On a Roll" (includes interview with Steven Bochco). *Broadcasting and Cable* (Washington, D.C.), 1 November 1993.

Feuer, Jane, Paul Kerr, and Tise Vahimagi, editors. *MTM: Quality Television*. London: British Film Institute, 1984.

Gitlin, Todd. *Inside Prime-Time*. New York: Pantheon, 1983.

Levinson, Richard, and William Link. *Off Camera: Conversations with the Makers of Prime-Time Television*. New York: New American Library, 1986.

Marc, David, and Robert Thompson. *Prime Time, Prime Movers: From I Love Lucy to L.A. Law—America's Greatest TV Shows and the People who Create Them*. Boston, Massachusetts: Little, Brown, 1992.

Rensin, David. "Hitmaker Steven Bochco Defends Adult Drama." *TV Guide* (Radnor, Pennsylvania), 14-20 April 1993.

Selnow, Gary W., and Richard R. Gilbert. *Society's Impact on Television: How the Viewing Public Shapes Television Programming*. London: Westport, 1993.

Span, Paula. "Bochco on the Edge." *Esquire* (New York), May 1990.

Stempel, Tom. *Storytellers to the Nation. A History of American Television Writing*. New York: Continuum 1992.

"Steven Bochco." *Esquire* (New York), June 1988.

"20th Century's Bochco: Selling the Cerebral." *Broadcasting* (Washington, D.C.), 30 May 1988.

Zoglin, Richard. "Changing the Face of Prime Time: Trendsetting Producer Steven Bochco Turns Out Hits by Rocking the Boat." *Time* (New York), 2 May 1988.

———. "Bochco Under Fire." *Time* (New York), 27 September 1993.

See also *Hill Street Blues, NYPD Blue*

BOGART, PAUL

U.S. Director

Paul Bogart has enjoyed a career as a director in almost every medium of visual communication. Bogart is one of a handful of individuals who has directed live television productions of the "Golden Age", the telefilm, the made-for-television movie, and the feature film.

Bogart's career began as a puppeteer and actor with the Berkeley Marionettes in 1946. From there he went on to be stage manager and associate director at NBC, working on such "Golden Age" cornerstones as *Kraft Television Theater*, *Goodyear Playhouse*, and *Armstrong Circle Theater*. During the 1955-1956 season, when *Goodyear Playhouse* was known as the *Alcoa Hour-Goodyear Playhouse*, Bogart directed an episode entitled "The Confidence Man" and an award-winning partnership began. This was the first time Bogart had directed for producer Herbert Brodkin. Bogart would go on to direct many episodes of Brodkin's *The Defenders*, one of television's most honored series, and garner his first Emmy Award for directing "The 700-Year Old Gang," a two-part *Defenders* episode. Bogart worked almost exclusively for Brodkin series during the early to mid-1960s (*The Defenders*, *The Nurses*, *The Doctors and Nurses*, and *Coronet Blue*).

After *The Defenders* period, the larger part of Bogart's work was in long form—either television specials, television movies, or feature films. His work for *CBS Playhouse* was particularly noteworthy. Under that banner, Bogart won Emmys for his direction of "Dear Friends" (again with Brodkin producing) and "Shadow Game." During this period Bogart produced the 1966 television series *Hawk*, starring Burt Reynolds; he also directed the pilot and a handful of episodes for the series. For theatrical release he directed *Halls of Anger* (1968), *Marlowe* (1969), and *The Skin Game* (1971).

In the mid-1970s, Bogart began another long-term relationship with a single production unit. He directed scores of episodes of *All in the Family* for Norman Lear and Bud Yorkin's Tandem Productions and in 1978 earned another Emmy for his work on the series. *The Golden Girls* brought Bogart yet another Emmy in 1986. In 1986 he directed *The Canterville Ghost* for television and *Torch Song Trilogy* for theatrical release.

Bogart has said that, in an ideal world, the feature film is his form of choice because the time constraints of television production are absent. Still, he is a singular talent among television directors. He has expressed a partiality for strong characters over a strong story. This preference takes advantage of the intimacy of the television medium, and allows those characters to reveal themselves to viewers through the nuance and subtlety of staging and blocking. These qualities are at a premium in entertainment television today, but because Bogart's aesthetic sensibilities were developed early, in the theater and live television, the episodes he directs are graced by excellent staging and movement of characters. One need only carefully watch Bogart's work for

Paul Bogart
Photo courtesy of the Academy of Motion Picture Arts and Sciences

The Defenders, *All in the Family*, or *Nichols* to understand that this ability to place characters for the camera is one of the strongest characteristics of his work.

A second characteristic is that he directs like an editor. Bogart begins a directing assignment with a very clear idea of what the program should look like. He then creates the images he needs and pays particular attention to the way those images are linked to make a program. He has stated that, in his view, one of the most important aspects of visual expression is how one image follows another and contributes to the cumulative effect of those joined images. Bogart understands that the power of emotions and ideas can be reinforced or defeated by the manner in which shots are linked. The result is a directorial style which draws on the best elements of the editor's art—the linking of carefully composed images for emotional and dramatic emphasis.

In 1991, Bogart was awarded the French Festival Internationelle Programmes Audiovisuelle at Cannes, one of the few television directors to be recognized for a remarkable body of work. Many directors working in television today are members of a generation raised on television. The better of these directors are those who paid attention to the work of Paul Bogart.

—John Cooper

PAUL BOGART. Born in New York City, New York, U.S.A. 13 November 1919. Attended public schools in New York City. Married: Jane, 1941; children: Peter, Tracy, and Jennifer. Served in U.S. Army Air Force, 1944–46. Puppeteer-actor with the Berkeley Marionettes, 1946–48; TV stage manager and associate director, NBC television, 1950–52; director, installments of various live television dramas, 1950s–1960s; director, telefilm series and made-for-television movies, from 1960s. Recipient: Emmy Awards, 1965, 1968, 1970, 1978, 1986; Christopher Awards, 1955, 1973, and 1975; Golden Globe, 1977; French Festival Internationale Audiovisuelle, Cannes, 1991. Address: Office—760 N. La Cienega Boulevard, Los Angeles, California 90069, U.S.A. Agent—Contemporary Artists Agency, 1888 Century Park East, Los Angeles, California 90067, U.S.A.

TELEVISION SERIES (selection)

1947–58	*Kraft Television Theater*
1949–55	*One Man's Family*
1950–63	*Armstrong Circle Theatre*
1951–60	*Goodyear Playhouse*
1953–63	*U.S. Steel Hour*
1961–65	*The Defenders*
1962–65	*The Nurses*
1966–76	*Hawk*
1971–83	*All in the Family*
1985–92	*The Golden Girls*

MADE-FOR-TELEVISION MOVIES

1966	*Evening Primrose*

1970	*In Search of America*
1972	*The House Without a Christmas Tree*
1974	*Tell Me Where It Hurts*
1975	*Winner Take All*
1980	*Fun and Games*
1986	*The Canterville Ghost*
1987	*Power, Passion and Murder*
1987	*Natica Jackson*
1991	*Broadway Bound*
1994	*The Gift of Love*

TELEVISION SPECIALS

Ages of Man; Mark Twain Tonight; The Final War of Ollie Winter; Dear Friends; Secrets; Shadow Game; Look Homeward Angel; The Country Girl; Double Solitaire; The War Widow; The Thanksgiving Treasure; The Adams Chronicles.

FILMS

Halls of Anger, 1968; *Marlowe*, 1969; *The Skin Game*, 1971; *Class of '44*, 1973; *Mr. Ricco*, 1975; *Oh, God! You Devil*, 1984; *Torch Song Trilogy.*

FURTHER READING

Wicking, Christopher, and Tise Vahimagi. *The American Vein: Directors and Directions in Television.* New York: Dutton, 1979.

See also *All in the Family*, Anthology Drama; "Golden Age" of Television

BOLAM, JAMES

British Actor

James Bolam has proved one of the most popular and enduring character stars of British television comedy and drama, capitalizing on his northern background and on his natural, pugnacious charm in a variety of roles over a 30-year period. Bolam had the good fortune to begin his screen career at a time when there was a tremendous vogue in British theatre, film, and television for working-class northern drama. With his punchy but vulnerable Geordie persona and undisguised accent, Bolam was a natural choice for such worthy though relatively plodding films as *The Kitchen*, which was based on the play by Arnold Wesker, and John Schlesinger's North Country feature *A Kind of Loving*. Subsequently, among other films, he supported fellow-northerner Tom Courtenay in *Otley* and played second lead to Alan Bates in Lindsay Anderson's *In Celebration* (a David Storey play set in the mining towns of Nottinghamshire in which he and Bates had already appeared on the Royal Court stage).

It was as a favourite of television comedy and period drama audiences, however, that Bolam (a former trainee chartered accountant) was destined to make his mark. Cast as the girl-chasing, anti-establishment cynic Terry Collier opposite Rodney Bewes's diffident and socially-aspiring Bob Ferris in the long-running and warmly realistic comedy series *The Likely Lads* (1964–66), written by Ian La Frenais and Dick Clement, Bolam cut a fine line between pathos and brash northern cockiness. In his scorn for Bob's middle-class pretensions, Bolam's work-shy proletarian Terry typified northern prejudice and aggression, but in his overt sensitivity to any rejection by his aspiring childhood friend and drinking partner, he became both endearing and sympathetic, as much a victim of a hostile class system as his soul companion. The friendship between the two characters was in many situations their only defence, coupled with a shared nostalgia for time-honoured northern ways. The series, which relied heavily on the writing of Le Frenais and Clements as well as upon the innate charm of Bolam and Bewes, was significant in that it raised issues of greater relevance to the viewing public than was attempted by virtually any other sitcom of the time (and, indeed, by many in succeeding decades).

The underlying theme of nostalgia for the values of the old north, and the comedy inherent in two northern lads trying to keep their friendship alive while coming to terms with the realities of life, was underlined in the even better later series, *Whatever Happened to the Likely Lads?* (1973–74), in which the pathos was strengthened by an awareness of time passing. This revival, which took up the lives of the two friends after Terry's return from four years in the army and Bob's assumption of bourgeois respectability (and engagement to the self-willed Thelma, played by Bridgit Forsyth), proved as well written and as pointed as the first series, the friendship tottering and swaying as the two men argued heatedly about their conflicting views on such issues as class, sexual equality, and self-advancement.

Though identified primarily with northern working-class characters, Bolam has managed to vary his diet by escaping from the straitjacket of television comedy on several occasions. Particularly notable was his success as the indomitable entrepreneur Jack Ford in the long-running between-the-wars period drama set in South Shields, *When the Boat Comes In*, which extended to four series and finally ended with Ford's death in the Spanish Civil War. Jessie Seaton, women's campaigner and Ford's love interest in the series, was played by Bolam's off-stage wife, Susan Jameson.

To underline Bolam's versatility, he also appeared with success in a BBC production of William Shakespeare's *As You Like It*, and in the 1980s forged a new variation on the sympathetic but single-minded northerner theme as Trevor Chaplain, the inquisitive jazz-loving schoolteacher investigating corruption in Alan Plater's *The Beiderbecke Affair* and its sequels.

A long-established favourite of low-brow television comedy, since the days of *The Likely Lads*, Bolam has continued to enjoy success in such unchallenging fare as *Only When I Laugh*, an unexceptional hospital sitcom that nevertheless lasted four series, *Room at the Bottom, Andy Capp, Executive Stress, Sticky Wickets*, and, most recently, *Eleven Men Against Eleven* (1995)—a comedy thriller in which Bolam played the beleaguered manager of an ailing Premier Division football team, under crooked chairman Timothy West.

—David Pickering

JAMES BOLAM. Born in Sunderland, Tyne and Wear, England, 16 June 1938. Attended Bede Grammar School, Sunderland; Bemrose School, Derby. Married: Susan Jameson; one child: Lucy. Trained as actor at Central School of Speech and Drama, London; stage debut, Royal Court Theatre, London, 1959; established reputation as television star in the long-running series *The Likely Lads*, 1964–66, and the sequel *Whatever Happened to the Likely Lads?*, 1973–74; subsequently consolidated reputation as popular star of situation comedy as well as playing straight roles and acting in films. Address: Barry Burnett Organization Ltd, Suite 42–43, Grafton House, 2–3 Golden Square, London W1, England.

James Bolam
Photo courtesy of the British Film Institute

TELEVISION SERIES

1964–66	*The Likely Lads*
1973–74	*Whatever Happened to the Likely Lads?*
1976–81	*When the Boat Comes In*
1979	*The Limbo Connection*
1979–83	*Only When I Laugh*
1985	*The Beiderbecke Affair*
1986	*Executive Stress*
1987	*The Beiderbecke Tapes*
1987	*Room at the Bottom*
1987	*Father Matthew's Daughter*
1988	*The Beiderbecke Connection*
1988	*Andy Capp*
1991–93	*Second Thoughts*
1994	*Sticky Wickets*
1995	*Eleven Men Against Eleven*

FILMS

The Kitchen, 1961; *A Kind of Loving*, 1962; *The Loneliness of the Long Distance Runner*, 1962; *HMS Defiant*, 1962; *Murder Most Foul*, 1965; *Half a Sixpence*, 1967; *Otley*, 1968; *Crucible of Terror*, 1971; *Straight on Till Morning*, 1972; *O Lucky Man!*, 1973; *In Celebration*, 1974; *The Likely Lads*, 1976; *The Great Question*, 1982; *The Plague Dogs*, 1982 (voice only); *Clash of Loyalties*, 1983.

RADIO

Second Thoughts, 1988.

STAGE (selection)

The Kitchen, 1959; *Events While Guarding the Bofors Gun,* 1966; *In Celebration,* 1969; *Veterans,* 1972; *Treats,* 1976; *Who Killed 'Agatha' Christie?,* 1978; *King Lear,* 1981; *Run For Your Wife!,* 1983; *Arms and the Man,* 1989; *Who's Afraid of Virginia Woolf?,* 1989; *Victory,* 1989; *Jeffrey Bernard is Unwell,* 1990; *Glengarry Glen Ross,* 1994.

FURTHER READING

Grant, Linda. "The Lad Most Likely to..." *The Guardian* (London), 12 August 1995.
Ross, Deborah. "What Really Happened to the Likely Lad?" *Daily Mail* (London), 17 July 1993.

See also *Likely Lads*

BONANZA

U.S. Western

Bonanza, the first Western televised in color, premiered on a Saturday night in the fall of 1959. After *Gunsmoke,* *Bonanza* was the longest-running and most successful Western in U.S. television, airing for fourteen seasons. The series related the story of Ben Cartwright (Lorne Greene) and his three sons, Adam (Pernell Roberts), Hoss (Dan Blocker) and

Little Joe (Michael Landon), prosperous ranchers in the vicinity of Virginia City, Nevada, in the mid 1800s, during the Civil War years and the discovery of the Comstock Silver Lode. The show was designed to appeal to a broad audience, crossing age and gender groups. The action characteristics catered to a more traditional audience for Westerns, while

Bonanza

dramatic issues and family values expanded the show's popularity to a more general audience. The careful photography presented beautiful scenery and interiors resembled movies more than other contemporary television shows.

The Cartwrights were not a traditional nuclear family. The patriarch was a three-time widower, with a son from each wife. In the first few seasons, personality differences between the sons motivated most of the plot conflicts. Two years after its debut, *Bonanza* moved to Sunday night and its popularity soared. By this time, the three sons had worked out most of their differences and the show was about the dealings of a well-integrated all male family as well as their problems with mining and ranch interests. Other characters would wander into the community causing conflict, leading the members of the family individually or communally as a group to restore the order. The oldest son, Adam, was the most serious of the three brothers, the potential patriarch. Middle son, Hoss was the Buffoon type, big and friendly, naive yet explosive. Little Joe was the impulsive and romantic type in the family.

Bonanza differs from other Westerns in its relative use violence and "shoot-outs". Conflicts were resolved through dialogue between the main characters and guest stars. Generally, this one-hour show tackled topical issues (i.e., racial discrimination, voting, religion). Famous guest stars such as Yvonne De Carlo, Ida Lupino, Barry Sullivan, Ricardo Cortez and Jack Carson added to the show's popularity. *Bonanza* was also the first show to introduce the ranch, in this case the thousand-acre Ponderosa, as an important element in the narrative, the fifth character, as producers referred to it. Brauer and Brauer (1975) argue that this emphasis on the "piece of land" was symbolic of a shift in emphasizing mobility, the lone wanderer, with his gun and horse to a focus on the settle landowner. These changes also led to a restructuring of the leading characters' role in the community.

The cook at Ponderosa was Hop Sing (Victor Sen Yung), a Chinese immigrant. He was presented in the traditional subservient role reserved for minorities in the period the show was produced. He spoke with a heavy accent, wore generic Asian clothes and long, braided hair, and he always delivered words of wisdom. In several episodes the family engaged in various conflicts with outsiders to protect Hop Sing against discrimination. In doing so, the show foregrounded the racial discrimination in the historical period as well as the ongoing racial conflicts in the 1960s.

Between 12 September 1959 and 16 January 1973 a total of 440 episodes were produced. Those years witnessed several cast changes. Pernell Roberts left the series at the end of 1964–65 season calling it "Junk TV" and complaining about the glorified portrayal of wealthy ranchers. His character was eliminated from the series. Dan Blocker died before the beginning of the 1972–73 season. After his death the show's ratings started to fall, and it was canceled in 1973. A change from the traditional slot on Sunday to Tuesday

evening, after 11 years on the air might. also have caused the demise of the show. Even before the show was canceled it was already being rerun under the name *Ponderosa* by NBC on Tuesday evenings. *Bonanza* was exported throughout out the world, and it has been in syndication for several years in the United States.

In the mid-1980s there was an attempt to revive the series with a made-for-television movie entitled *Bonanza: The Next Generation*. None of the original cast of the series appeared in the show. Greene's death forced the producer to cast another actor. John Ireland, playing Ben Cartwright's brother, became the patriarch of Ponderosa. He could not control the ranch and it was almost taken over by miners and oil speculators. It is only when the sons of Little Joe and Hoss returned that the ranch experienced a new Bonanza.

—Antonio Lapastina

CAST

Ben Cartwright	Lorne Greene
Little Joe Cartwright	Michael Landon
Eric "Hoss" Cartwright (1959–72)	Dan Blocker
Adam Cartwright (1959–65)	Pernell Roberts
Hop Sing	Victor Sen Yung
Sheriff Roy Caffee (1960–72)	Ray Teal
Candy (1967–70, 1972–73)	David Canary
Dusty Rhoades (1970–72)	Lou Frizzel
Jamie Hunter (1970–73)	Mitch Vogel
Griff King (1972–73)	Tim Matheson
Deputy Clem (1961–73)	Bing Russell

PRODUCERS   Richard Collins, David Dortort, Robert Blees

PROGRAMMING HISTORY   440 Episodes

• NBC

September 1959–September 1961	Saturday 7:30-8:30
September 1961–September 1972	Sunday 9:00-10:00
May 1972–August 1972	Tuesday 7:30-8:30
September 1972–January 1973	Tuesday 8:00-9:00

FURTHER READING

Brauer, R., and Brauer, D. *The Horse, the Gun and the Piece of Property: Changing Images of the TV Western.* Bowling Green, Ohio: Bowling Green University Popular Press, 1975.

Jackson, R. *Classic TV Westerns.* New York: Citadel, 1994.

Kirkley, D. *A Descriptive Study of the Network Television Western during the Seasons 1955–56—1962–63.* New York: Arno, 1979.

MacDonald, J. Fred. *Who Shot the Sheriff? The Rise and Fall of the TV Western.* New York: Praeger, 1987.

See also Greene, Lorne; Westerns

BOONE, RICHARD

U.S. Actor

Richard Boone was one of the television acting profession's gladiators, a craggy, determined and almost menacing figure among the actors and directors who worked with him. His uncompromising commitment to his work often brought him into conflict with his fellow players and was as well a constant source of frustration to the directors and producers who tried to control him. That his work for television eventually brought him critical acclaim and viewer popularity while he simultaneously alienated certain sections of the industry may be, perhaps, the hallmark of his genius.

In 1947 he travelled to New York and joined the well-known Actor's Studio (where his classmates included such then unknowns as Marlon Brando, Karl Malden, Eva Marie Saint and Julie Harris). He got his growth, he claimed, as an actor in some 150 live TV shows in New York between 1948 and 1950, after which he returned home to California. He is also reported as being a regular on the CBS children's program *Mr. I. Magination* in 1947 (when the program was a local New York show) and also appeared as one of the reporters in *The Front Page* series (1949–50) during its early days. Back in Los Angeles he was put under contract to 20th Century-Fox and his first feature film was *Halls of Montezuma*, directed by Lewis Milestone in 1950 (Milestone would later be invited to direct episodes of *Have Gun, Will Travel* and *The Richard Boone Show*). While at Fox he was also working for Jack Webb in his radio *Dragnet* when, still as an unknown bit player, around the summer of 1950, he did a single radio drama called *The Doctor* (written by *Dragnet* writer James Moser). This radio show turned out to be the forerunner of Boone's first starring TV role, *Medic*.

By 1954 his Dr. Konrad Styner, host, narrator and frequent participant of *Medic* (1954–56), which had been created and written by Moser, had made him a household name. *Medic* employed a dramatic-documentary style, factual and educational in content but with a dramatic impact that few if any physician centered programs achieved until the advent of *Ben Casey* in 1961. With Moser writing and generally steering the series, *Medic* developed a highly effective semi-documentary technique similar to TV's popular *Dragnet*. The program took its stories from the files of the L.A. County Medical Association, real medical case histories showing inherent drama. Boone's stolid underplaying heightened the dramatic force of the series but there were critics and viewers at the time who thought his character too dour and gruff. When *Medic* came to an end Boone found other parts elusive; although this had been his first real doctor role casting directors had come to see him as a "doctor" character and his strong screen association with the role of Dr. Styner left him typecast in the "he always plays doctors" file.

His most memorable TV role, however, was set in a completely different genre and featured Boone as a 1870s

Richard Boone

San Francisco gentleman-adventurer who hired himself out as a mercenary gunslinger. As the impassive troubleshooter Paladin in the post Civil War West of *Have Gun, Will Travel* (1957–63), Boone helped push the series to top-ten positions in the Nielsen ratings (numbers 3 and 4) during its first four seasons. The part was originally offered to Randolph Scott, who at the time had other commitments. After first turning down Boone for the role, CBS made a five-minute test film for New York executives still pepared to type-cast him as a physician—and then signed him to a five-year contract. While *Have Gun, Will Travel* and Boone's popularity rose in the ratings and in the esteem of fans, his standing among people in the industry dropped significantly. His strict dedication to his work, which he also demanded of everyone around him, saw him all but legally take over the CBS production; scripts, actors, directors, even costumes, all had to receive his personal approval. From 1960 onwards Boone was particularly active in the series' director's chair, directing almost one in four episodes himself. "When I direct a show, I'm pretty arbitrary," he commented to *TV Guide* magazine in early 1961. "If I have a fault, it's that I see an end and go for it with all my energy; and if I'm bugged with people who don't see it or won't go for it, it looks as though I'm riding all over them."

During this time of course he also continued appearing in multiple TV plays. Notable performances during this period came with David Shaw's acclaimed "The Tunnel" (1959; for *Playhouse 90*), in *The Right Man* (1960), for which he delivered a fine performance as Lincoln, and with his work as narrator for Stephen Vincent Benet's Pulitzer Prize-winning poem *John Brown's Body* (1962).

The Richard Boone Show repertory theatre idea was first proposed by Boone in 1960 to CBS. When CBS executives suggested that they might find a slot for such a program among their Sunday afternoon schedules Boone put the idea on a back-burner until he had acquired his "go-to-hell money", as he put it, from the millions he made during his years in *Have Gun, Will Travel*, and to a lesser extent from *Medic*. It was not until his idea received the enthusiasm and support of the distinguished playwright Clifford Odets, the Goodson-Todman production company and NBC president Robert Kintner that the television repertory company series started becoming a reality. *The Richard Boone Show* (1963–64) featured a workshop of ten actors whom Boone considered the best in the business: Robert Blake, Lloyd Bochner, Laura Devon, June Harding, Bethel Leslie, Harry Morgan, Jeanette Nolan, Ford Rainey, Warren Stevens and Guy Stockwell. Boone himself, of course, starred at times and served as the regular host. With Odets as the program's script editor, the series' prestige was almost guaranteed. Unfortunately, after completing much of the preliminary work for the series, Odets died in August 1963. Before the 24 episodes had completed their run (and despite having just been voted "the best dramatic program on the air" in the 15th Annual Motion Picture Daily poll) the program was cancelled in January 1964. Boone took the news hard. It had after all been a very personal project and—the result of a premature NBC press office release—he learned of his program's demise in a morning trade paper. Still, his anger was tempered by the knowledge that he was by that time already receiving $50,000 a year for 20 years after selling out his interest in *Have Gun, Will Travel*; he was also to receive a reported $20,000 a week for his now-defunct show, also on a deferred payment basis.

From 1964 to 1971 he lived a very comfortable life with his family in Honolulu, travelling to the mainland only for the occasional movie such as *Hombre* (1966) and *The Kremlin Letter* (1969). He also helped induce producer Leonard Freeman to film *Hawaii Five-O* in Honolulu instead of the intended San Pedro; Freeman even offered him the leading part of McGarrett which he declined.

In 1971 Boone was offered the lead role in Universal TV/Mark VII's *Hec Ramsey* (1972–74) series (two seasons as one of four rotating 90-minute TV-movies). The program, about a grizzled turn-of-the-century lawman with a fascination for the new science of criminology, was in its way, perhaps, a gentle monument to Boone's earlier TV performances: Hec Ramsey was Paladin grown older, with an accumulation of artfulness and astuteness along with a stockpile of barely contained impatience.

The latter part of his career was taken up with such diverse made-for-TV movie plots and themes as the elaborate murder set-up of *In Broad Daylight* (1971), the espionage tale of *Deadly Harvest* (1972), the period private-eye spoof *Goodnight, My Love* (1972), the Depression-era drama *The Great Niagra* (1974) and the rather sorry fantasy adventure *The Last Dinosaur* (1977).

With his dedication to his work in television Boone always gave an extraordinarily commanding performance, always straightforward, always the center of interest.

—Tise Vahimagi

RICHARD (ALLEN) BOONE. Born in Los Angeles, California, U.S.A. 18 June 1917. Attended military school; Stanford University, 1934-37. Married: 1) Jane Hopper, 1937 (divorced, 1940); 2) Mimi Kelly, 1949 (divorced, 1950); 3) Claire McAloon, 1951; children: Peter. Served in U.S. Navy, 1941–45. Oilfield worker, 1930s; painter and short story writer, 1930s; after World War II, studied acting at the Neighborhood Playhouse and Actors Studio; studied modern dance with Martha Graham; stage debut as soldier, and as understudy to John Gielgud's Jason in Broadway staging of *Medea*, 1947; acted in radio drama *The Halls of Montezuma*, 1950; led to role in the movie version, 1951; film actor, 1951–79; starred in television series *Medic*, 1954–56; starred in CBS Television's *Have Gun, Will Travel*, 1957–63; developed and directed repertory theater-style television series, *The Richard Boone Show* (also host and often the lead), 1963–64; in Hawaii, after *The Richard Boone Show* cancelled, established movie company Pioneer Productions, and taught acting; starred in NBC Television's *Hec Ramsey*, one of four rotating series comprising the *Sunday Night Mystery Shows*, 1972–73; lectured on acting at Flagler College. Member: Academy of Television Arts and Sciences; Academy of Motion Picture Arts and Sciences. Recipient: three American Television Critics Best Actor Awards. Died in St. Augustine, Florida, 10 January 1981.

TELEVISION SERIES

1954–56	*Medic*
1957–63	*Have Gun, Will Travel*
1963–64	*The Richard Boone Show* (also director)
1972–74	*Hec Ramsey*

MADE-FOR-TELEVISION MOVIES

1971	*In Broad Daylight*
1971	*A Tattered Web*
1972	*Goodnight, My Love*
1972	*Deadly Harvest*
1974	*The Great Niagra*
1977	*The Last Dinosaur*

FILMS

The Halls of Montezuma, 1951; *Call Me Mister*, 1951; *Rommel, Desert Fox*, 1951; *Kangaroo*, 1952; *Return of the Texan*, 1952; *Red Skies of Montana*, 1952; *Way of a Gaucho*, 1952;

Man on a Tightrope, 1953; *City of Bad Men*, 1953; *Vicki*, 1953; *The Robe*, 1953; *Beneath the 12-Mile Reef*, 1953; *The Siege at Red River*, 1954; *Dragnet*, 1954; *The Raid*, 1954; *Man Without a Star*, 1955; *Ten Wanted Men*, 1955; *Robbers' Roost*, 1955; *Battle Stations*, 1956; *Star in the Dust*, 1956; *Away All Boats*, 1956; *Lizzie*, 1957; *The Garment Jungle*, 1957; *The Tall T*, 1957; *I Bury the Living*, 1958; *The Alamo*, 1960; *A Thunder of Drums*, 1961; *Rio Conchos*, 1964; *The War Lord*, 1965; *Hombre*, 1966; *The Arrangement*, 1968; *Kona Coast*, 1968; *The Night of the Following Day*, 1969; *The Kremlin Letter*, 1969; *Madron*, 1970; *Little Big Man*, 1970;

Big Jake, 1971; *The Big Sleep*, 1971; *The Last Dinosaur*, 1971; *The Shootist*, 1976; *Winter Kills*, 1979.

RADIO

The Halls of Montezuma, 1950; *The Doctor*, 1950.

STAGE

Medea, 1947; *Macbeth*, 1948; *The Man*, 1950; on tour, *The Hasty Heart*, 1959; *The Rivalry*, 1959.

See also Anthology Drama; *Have Gun, Will Travel*; *Medic*

BOYLE, HARRY

Canadian Writer/Media Executive

Harry Boyle made his career in broadcasting, but, given the ephemeral nature of radio and television productions, he may be remembered more as an author and humorist. Television historians, however, will likely see his accomplishments as a broadcast regulator as the most significant aspects of his long career. Boyle started his career on a radio station in Wingham, Ontario, and after a brief detour into the newspaper business he joined the Canadian Broadcasting Corporation (CBC) in 1943 as a farm commentator. He advanced rapidly into executive ranks and joined the television service in the 1960s, serving as program director and executive producer. In both radio and television, he established a reputation as a creative programmer who launched the careers of many talented broadcasters, such as the comedy team of Wayne and Shuster, and the eclectic Max Ferguson. He was known for defending the independence of producers against management restrictions.

Boyle's career as a regulator began in 1967. While serving as program supervisor at CBC-Toronto, he was appointed by the Board of Broadcast Governors (BBG) to an eleven-member consultative committee on program policy, the only member from the CBC. The committee issued its report in 1968, just as the BBG was abolished by the 1968 Broadcasting Act, to be replaced by a new, more powerful regulatory body, the Canadian Radio-Television Commission (CRTC), later called the Canadian Radio-Television and Telecommunications Commission.

Boyle was appointed vice chair of commission, led by the formidable Pierre Juneau. He served with Juneau until Juneau resigned in 1975. Boyle was named acting head and then confirmed in the role in 1976, but he left after a year, by some accounts disenchanted with his limited influence on programming.

Throughout his career, Boyle promoted a vision of Canadian identity as an expression of a sense of place, best realized in specific communities. He argued that the CBC, and Canadian broadcasting generally, neglected local, regional and multi-cultural programming in pursuing national audiences. In a recent interview, Boyle commented that he agreed to the

CRTC appointment in the hope of pushing the CBC into providing such coverage. The team of Juneau, dapper and precise, and Boyle, rumpled and disorganized, accomplished much more than anyone expected in carrying forward the ambitious goals of the 1968 Broadcasting Act. They safeguarded domestic ownership of Canada's broadcasting industry, produced a strong set of Canadian content quotas for television (regulations that contributed significantly to the development of Canada's independent television production industry), supported the extension of the private network CTV,

Harry Boyle
Photo courtesy of the National Archives of Canada

and formulated the first rules for the cable TV industry. Though rendered increasingly obsolete by new broadcast technologies, these initiatives provided important opportunities for Canadian expression.

Boyle's most controversial legacy was a report tabled by the Committee of Inquiry into the National Broadcasting Service in 1977. Boyle presided over the inquiry, which was launched shortly after the 1976 Quebec election, in which a party dedicated to a sovereign Quebec received a majority. Not surprisingly, the event added to concerns about Canadian unity and led to accusations that the French-language news services of the CBC were biased in favor of Quebec independence. It has been suggested that Boyle accepted the task to forestall a more politically-motivated investigation. He may also have been motivated by the fact that the committee's mandate reflected his much-quoted view that Canada "exists by reason of communication." The report expressed concern about the centralization of the Canadian television system, the lack of programming from regions outside central Canada and, in particular, the gulf between French and English audiences. Although supportive of the CBC, Boyle also expressed the hope that new communications technologies, formats and programming would bridge the divisions in Canadian society. One example was the multichannel possibilities presented by cable television and pay-per-view programming. The report, with others, helped to lay the foundation for the expansion of cable services.

With respect to content, the report characterized the CBC as "biased to the point of subversiveness" for its failure, in the committee's view, to promote communication among the country's regional and linguistic communities. The report was not received favorably by CBC journalists—who felt it was inaccurate and unfair—but it was successful in turning attention away from accusations of "separatist bias" to the extent to which the English and French networks reflected Canada as a whole. Debate about the latter issue has continued. In the politically charged atmosphere of 1977, however, the tack taken by Boyle helped to defuse French-English tensions a little.

Boyle's substantial personal archives have been deposited with York University in Toronto and will attract scholars interested in making sense of a crucial time in the development of Canadian television.

—Frederick J. Fletcher and Robert Everett

HARRY BOYLE. Born in St. Augustine, Ontario, Canada, 7 October 1915. Attended St. Jerome's College in Kitchener, Ontario. Married: Marion McCaffery, 1937; children: Patricia and Michael. Worked for radio station CKNX, Wingham, Ontario, 1936-41; writer, *Beacon-Herald*, Stratford, Ontario, 1941–42; farm broadcaster, CBC, Toronto, Ontario, 1943; supervisor of farm broadcasts, 1943–45; program director, Trans-Canada Network, 1946–52; regional program director, radio and television, 1952–55; supervisor of radio features, from 1955; television executive producer, from 1963; weekly columnist, *Toronto Telegram*, 1956–68; author of numerous books, since 1961; vice chair, Canadian Radio-Television Commission, 1968–75; chair, 1976–77; columnist, *Montreal Star* from 1978. Recipient: Stephen Leacock Medal for Humour, 1964; John Drainie Award, Association of Canadian Television and Radio Artists, 1970; named to Canadian Newspaper Hall of Fame, 1979; Jack Chisholm Award, Canadian Film and TV Directors' Association, 1980.

PUBLICATIONS (selection)

With a Pinch of Sin. Garden City, New York: Doubleday, 1966.

Memories of a Catholic Boyhood. Garden City, New York: Doubleday, 1973.

FURTHER READING

Peers, Frank W. *The Public Eye: Television and the Politics of Canadian Broadcasting, 1952–68*. Toronto: University of Toronto Press, 1979.

Raboy, Marc. *Missed Opportunities: The Story of Canada's Broadcasting Policy*. Montreal, Quebec: McGill-Queen's University Press, 1990.

BOYS FROM THE BLACKSTUFF

British Drama Series

Boys from the Blackstuff, the first television series by Liverpool playwright Alan Bleasdale, was a technical and topical triumph for BBC English Regions Drama, capturing the public mood in 1982, at a time of economic recession and anxiety about unemployment. Set in a grimly recognisable Liverpool, it chronicled the disparate and sometimes dissolute attempts of five former members of a tarmac gang to find work in a city hit hard by mounting unemployment and depression. As an outwardly realist intervention into a serious social problem, its impact, sustained through its dramatic power and emotional truth, was comparable to

that of *Cathy Come Home* fifteen years earlier. With its ostensibly sombre subject matter leavened by passionate direction and flashes of ironic Scouse wit, *Boys from the Blackstuff* overcame its regional setting and minority channel scheduling (on BBC2) to receive instant critical acclaim, winning an unprecedented repeat run only nine weeks later on BBC1 and a BAFTA award for best drama series of 1982.

Bleasdale (who described it as "an absurd, mad, black farce") originally conceived *Boys from the Blackstuff* in 1978 during filming for *The Black Stuff* (D. J. Goddard), his single play introducing the Boys as a tarmac gang (hence the title)

Boys from the Blackstuff
Photo courtesy of the British Film Institute

and culminating in their sacking for "doing a foreigner" (non-contract job). But whilst technically a sequel, *Boys from the Blackstuff* was a deeper and darker investigation of character and circumstance consisting of five linked plays of varying lengths (from 55 to 70 minutes). As such, it proved difficult to fit into the production and budgetary system of English Regions Drama. However, the delay to the production which this caused contributed significantly to the strength and originality of the final work as well as providing a timely conjunction between its transmission and the apex of British unemployment.

To cut costs the production was budgeted across two financial years using newly available lightweight video equipment except for one episode ("Yosser's Story") made on film with the unit's annual film budget. Unusually for the time, the video episodes were edited in post-production and the series' filmic qualities were further enhanced by Ilona Sekacz's specially-composed music and by the replacement of Goddard (no longer available) with Philip Saville, through whose elegant and inventive shooting style Liverpool's dereliction took on a crumbling grandeur.

Of the five central characters, Chrissie (Michael Angelis) was the most ordinary (standing, perhaps, for Bleasdale himself), desperate for legitimate work and increasingly soured by the indignity and insecurity of life on the dole. Loggo (Alan Igbon), more defiant, stood as an ironic observer least affected by the experience. Dixie (Tom Georgeson), once the gang's foreman, had become embittered and unforgiving, his pride as a working man shattered. George (Peter Kerrigan), much the oldest, represented the dignity of labour, wise and greatly respected as a trade union official, refusing to give up hope even on the remarkable wheelchair ride through the decaying Albert Dock which precedes his death—a scene which includes an emotional speech based partly on Kerrigan's own experiences as a docker. But it was Bernard Hill's maniacally self-destructive Yosser, a colossal performance of incoherence, savagery and pathos, who captured the public imagination. Deprived of his dignity and eventually of his children, he is reduced to butting authority figures with the bewildered declaration: "I'm Yosser Hughes!" Yosser's head-butts and his woeful "gizza job" became totems in the popular press.

The delay in production also benefitted the series in enabling the script to develop through ruthless changes initiated by producer Michael Wearing. In the most extreme case, lamenting the absence of female and domestic perspectives on unemployment, Wearing returned the original episode 3 with an instruction to "write Angie". In the rewrite, Angie (Julie Walters), Chrissie's wife, emerged as a pivotal character. In an emotionally-charged performance she uttered the lines which seemed to sum up the series' message about Liverpool and the dole:

"It's not funny, it's not friggin' funny. I've had enough of that 'if you don't laugh you'll cry'. I've heard it for years. This stupid soddin' city's full of it... Why don't you fight back, you bastard. Fight back."

As well as pricking the national conscience (helping to dissolve the popular characterisation of the unemployed as "scroungers"), *Boys from the Blackstuff* confirmed Bleasdale as one of the nation's leading writers for stage and television, although his subsequent television work (most notably the self-produced *GBH*) might have benefitted from the editorial influence of Wearing. Equally important, it helped to establish Liverpool as a dramatic location of special significance, where brutality, decay and poverty could serve as a backdrop for the expression, through darkly defiant wit, of the resilience and spirit of ordinary people. Its indirect influence is detectable in the proliferation of Liverpool-based television and film drama of the 1980s, including the sitcom *Bread*, resembling a travestied *Boys from the Blackstuff*

stripped of its social conscience, and the long-running soap *Brookside*, which inherited its shooting style (single camera shooting on lightweight video) as well as part of its milieu.

—Peter Goddard

CAST

Chrissie Todd	Michael Angelis
Loggo	Alan Igbon
Dixie Deans	Tom Georgeson
George Malone	Peter Kerrigan
Yosser Hughes	Bernard Hill
Angie Todd	Julie Walters

PRODUCERS   Alan Bleasdale, Michael Wearing

PROGRAMMING HISTORY   Five episodes of varying length

• BBC
10 October 1982–7 November 1982

FURTHER READING

Millington, Bob, and Robin Nelson. *"Boys from the Blackstuff": The Making of TV Drama*. London: Comedia, 1986.
Paterson, Richard, editor. *BFI Dossier 20: "Boys from the Blackstuff"*. London: British Film Institute, 1983.

See also Bleasdale, Alan

THE BOYS OF ST. VINCENT

Canadian Docudrama

The *Boys of St. Vincent* (1993), directed by John N. Smith for the National Film Board of Canada, is a two-part docudrama which caused considerable controversy when it first appeared. At the time of its release, the criminal trials of several brothers from Mount Cashel Orphanage in Newfoundland were in progress. The Canadian Broadcasting Corporation (CBC) was not allowed to broadcast the film in Ontario and western Quebec in case it should in some way interfere with the trial—even though a disclaimer, saying that the film is loosely based upon several different events and not any real individuals, was added. Part one of *The Boys of St. Vincent* deals with the brutalization and sexual molestation of several orphans under the care of a group of priests headed by brother Peter Lavin (Henry Czerny). Part Two, which takes place fifteen years later, concerns the events surrounding Lavin's trial and the lives of the boys, who are now adults. *The Boys of St Vincent* is a powerful, adult docudrama about a painful and largely repressed part of Canadian history.

The critic John Caughie locates the specificity of docudrama in the integration of two distinct discourses: that of the realist narrative drama (which I would call melo-

drama), and that of the Griersonian documentary, from which the docudrama adopts two aspects, a strong desire for social education presented in a palatable form, and the need to reveal repressed histories. The melodramatic aspect attracts an audience and the documentary aspect serves to keep the narrative truthful. In effect, the documentary acts to detrivialize the melodrama—an essential function if its moral point is to be taken seriously. Some critics, such as Elaine Rapping, have taken the made-for-television movie seriously, but it is still widely castigated for its overly emotional representation of domestic disasters.

Unlike most American-made telefeatures, *The Boys of St. Vincent* does not have a hero. The two main characters, Kevin Reeny, who is one of the abused children, and Peter Lavin, the head of the orphanage, are not really figures with whom the audience can identify easily. In Part One Reeny is a badly abused child who barely speaks. Smith builds up tremendous sympathy for Reeny in Part One, showing the child's desperate attempts to avoid the priest and escape from the orphanage. His youthfulness makes him an object of our compassion, particularly as he struggles to free himself and stand up to the predatory Lavin. Audience identification is much stronger with him in this part of the film. In Part Two Reeny becomes a troubled man, unable to deal with his past. A loner given to bouts of violence, and clearly troubled in his relationship with his girlfriend, he is a closed and emotionally withdrawn character with whom it is possible to sympathize, but not really identify.

Peter Lavin is certainly the centre of the film's controversy and also its insightful and troubling depiction of child molestation. The fact that Lavin is a handsome, intelligent and charismatic man, as well as a brutal and overbearing pedophile is part of what makes *The Boys of St. Vincent* such a complex experience. In many child molestation films the child molester is a villain, pure and simple. This is never the case with the Smith film. The film in fact asks the audience to understand Lavin, and even gives the audience his point of view as he molests Kevin. This is a shocking moment in the narrative. As the first scene of molestation begins, the camera is placed in an observer's position. But as the sequence develops, the camera moves close to Lavin's point of view as he fondles Kevin's body. When Kevin refuses the priest's advances, he is severely beaten, and a statue of a wounded Jesus juts into the frame as if to comment upon what is taking place. The next morning as Brother Lavin watches the boys shower, the camera shows an aesthetically pleasing and sensuous depiction of their naked bodies. How is the spectator expected to respond to those pictures of desire—when the object of that desire is a beautiful, nude ten-year-old boy seen through the eyes of a pedophile? This highly charged and controversial sequence was cut when *The Boys of St. Vincent* was shown on the A and E channel in the United States. This excision, however, undermines Smith's attempt to ask the audience to understand a pedophile rather than merely condemning him or turning him into a melodramatic villain.

Of further significance in *The Boys of St. Vincent* is Smith's critique of patriarchy as a whole, with its patterns of dominance and submission worked throughout the educational system and the religious and governmental orders. We are shown boys literally owned by the church, brutalized not only physically, but intellectually through the fear and guilt instilled in them in both church and classroom. Lessons are taught by hypocritical and tedious rote, and the boys are harshly disciplined for seemingly minor infractions. *Boys* is nothing if not a thorough critique of middle-class, patriarchal capitalism in its most brutalizing form. Interestingly, Smith shows that both the boys and the priests are all victims of this system, that in fact this kind of behaviour is institutionalized and even traditional in orphanages.

Except for one of the older boys, the janitor and one policeman, no one is much outraged by what has gone on. Through *The Boys of St. Vincent* we are kept thoroughly off balance, not only by Smith's style, which tends to throw us into situations with few establishing shots, but also by the difficulty of identifying with any of the damaged characters in the fiction. Nor does the ending of the film bring any relief. Although the priests are brought to trial, Brother Lavin is neither healed nor forgiven; ironically, he is only able to confess his sins in the confessional, where he may in fact, be confessing to another child molester, and his confession never becomes public. We are never shown whether he has confessed his problems to his psychiatrist, and because the film ends before the verdict is given, we do not have the satisfaction of knowing what will happen to him. The film ends with Lavin's wife demanding to know if he has molested his own sons—and no answer is forthcoming here either. Kevin Reeny, who has resisted all attempts to speak up at the trial, finally manages to testify, but we are left with no sense or either triumph or revenge. One of the other boys, who has become a prostitute and a drug addict, overdoses and dies before the trial is complete. This film does not offer us any comfortable assurances about the future, and by avoiding closure, it implies that this kind of crime does not go away. In a film that consistently violates convention, this may be the most difficult of all to face, since no morally reassuring note is sounded at the film's conclusion.

The Boys of St. Vincent fully develops the potential of the made-for-television movie. Although it has a high-concept plot and is based upon a sensational news story, it

The Boys of St. Vincent
Photo courtesy of Tele-Action

violates many of the conventions of the U.S. telefeature. *Boys* mounts a damning condemnation of both the Catholic Church and the government of Newfoundland. It asks the audience to consider a child molester as a human being, not merely a depraved monster. By controlling the worst excesses of the melodrama and adopting documentary techniques, it manages to become a believable and powerful depiction of a serious social problem, proving that the simplicity of the made-for-television movie does not have to equal simple-mindedness, and that made-for- television movies can become sites for significant, but accessible social critique.

—Jeannette Sloniowski

CAST

Peter Lavin . . . . Henry Czerny
Kevin Reeny . . . . Johnny Morina
Kevin Reeny (at age 25) . . . . Sebastian Spence
Brian Lunny . . . . Ashley Billard
Brian Lunny (at age 30) . . . . Timothy Webber
Billy Lunny . . . . Jonathon Hoddinott
Steven Lunny . . . . Brian Dodd
Steven Lunny (at age 25) . . . . David Hewlett
Sheilah . . . . Kristine Demers

Detective Noseworthy . . . . Brian Dooley
Commission Lawyer . . . . Sheena Larkin
Chantal . . . . Lise Roy
Lenora . . . . Mary Walsh

PRODUCERS   Sam Grana, Claudio Luca

PROGRAMMING HISTORY

• CBC
1993

FURTHER READING

Caughie, John. "Progressive Television and Documentary Drama." In, Bennett, Tony, with others, editors. *Popular Film and Television.* London: British Film Institute, 1981.

Goodwin, Andrew, with others. *Drama-Documentary.* London: British Film Institute, 1983.

Rapping, Elaine. *The Movie of the Week: Private Stories, Public Events.* Minneapolis: University of Minnesota Press, 1992.

See also Canadian Programming in English; Docudrama

THE BRADY BUNCH

U.S. Situation Comedy

When it premiered on ABC in 1969, *The Brady Bunch* garnered mostly negative reviews. From that date until 1974, its entire network run, the series never reached the top ten ranks of the Nielsen ratings. Yet, the program stands as one of the most important sitcoms of American 1970s television programming, spawning numerous other series on all three major networks, as well as records, lunch boxes, a cookbook, and even a stage show and feature film.

In an era in which situation comedies emphasized how social climes were changing, *The Brady Bunch* was one of the few series that hearkened back to the traditional family values seen in such sitcoms as *Leave it to Beaver* and *Father Knows Best.* Executive producer Sherwood Schwartz conceived of the premise: a widower, father of three boys, marries a widow, mother of three girls. The concept worked as a springboard for dramatizations of an array of childhood and adolescent traumas. The cluster of children—Greg (Barry Williams), Marcia (Maureen McCormick), Peter (Christopher Knight), Jan (Eve Plumb), Bobby (Mike Lookinland) and Cindy (Susan Olsen)—provided a male and female version for three separate stages of youth. With this group the show managed to portray the typical crises of orthodonture, first crushes, neighborhood bullies and school plays, as well such homebound issues as sibling rivalry and problems with parental restrictions. Father Mike Brady

(Robert Reed) was always there with a weekly homily that would explain to the children the lessons they had learned. Although mother Carol Brady (Florence Henderson) was initially written as a divorcee, and episodes of the first season did deal with the problems of children getting used to a new mother or father, the half-hour show repeatedly and firmly upheld the family as a tight unit of support, love and understanding.

Unlike *All in the Family* or even *Julia, The Brady Bunch* tried to steer clear of the political and social issues of the day. Rarely were non-white characters introduced into the series. Women's liberation and gender equality were boiled down to brother-sister in-fighting. The counterculture of the 1960s was represented in random minor characters portrayed as buffoons—or in Greg trying to impress a girl with hippie jargon.

The representation of childhood in the series as a time of blissful innocence was in marked contrast to what was happening off camera. Many of the boys and girls playing the Brady children dated each other secretly, making out in their trailers or in the doghouse of the Brady's pet, Tiger. Oldest boy Barry Williams attempted to date Florence Henderson and filmed at least one episode while high on marijuana. All these incidents (as well as Robert Reed's homosexuality) occurred behind closed doors, coming to light only a decade after the series originally aired.

The Brady Bunch

The decided emphasis of the series on the Brady children made it very popular among younger audiences. ABC capitalized on this appeal, programming the show early on Friday evenings. This popularity also resulted in various attempts to create other profitable spin-off products: "The Brady Kids," a pop rock group (patterned on "The Archies" and "The Partridge Family"), a Saturday morning cartoon called *The Brady Kids* (1972–74), and regular appearances of the young actors and actresses (particularly Maureen McCormick and Christopher Knight), in teen fan magazines.

Following its initial network run, *The Brady Bunch* became inordinately popular in rerun syndication. This success can be attributed in part to children's afternoon-viewing patterns. Often programmed as a daily "strip" in after-school time periods, the show found new viewers who had not previously seen the series. The age distribution of the cast may have created appeal among a range of young viewers, and as they aged they were able to take a more ironic viewing stance toward the entertainment of their childhood.

The ongoing success of the Brady characters has continually brought them back to television. *The Brady Bunch Hour*, produced by Sid and Marty Krofft from 1976 to 1977 on ABC, had the family hosting a vividly-colored disco-oriented variety series. *The Brady Brides*, on NBC in 1981, was a half-hour sitcom about Marcia and Jan as they dealt with their new husbands and the trials of being married. In December 1988, CBS aired the TV-movie *A Very Brady Christmas*, which became CBS' highest-rated TV-movie that season. This led in 1990 to a short-lived hour-long dramatic series called simply *The Bradys*.

Although the dramatic series faded quickly, a live-stage parody of the original series quickly became a national sensation after its debut in Chicago in 1990. Playing the original scripts as camp performance, "The Real Live Brady Bunch" seemed to tap into viewers' simultaneous love for and cynicism towards the values presented by the series. The stage show and the subsequent film *The Brady Bunch Movie* (1995) reveled in the kitsch taste of 1970s culture, complete with "groovy" bell bottoms and day-glo orange and lime-green color schemes. Yet, although the stage production and the film gleefully deconstructed the absurdity of the wholesomeness of the Brady family, an admiration remained. Many children who grew up with the show came from families of divorce, or were "latch-key" children with both parents working. Consequently, some of those amused at the naiveté of the series also admittedly envy the ideal nuclear family that they never had and that the Bradys represent.

Much like *Star Trek*, another Paramount-produced television series of the late 1960s, *The Brady Bunch* was underappreciated by critics and network executives, but fan loyalty has made the series a franchise for book deals, memorabilia and feature films. A cultural throwback even in its time, the family led by "a lovely lady" and "a man named Brady" has become celebrated in part precisely for its steadfast obliviousness to societal change.

—Sean Griffin

CAST

Mike Brady	Robert Reed
Carol Brady	Florence Henderson
Alice Nelson	Ann B. Davis
Marcia Brady	Maureen McCormick
Jan Brady	Eve Plumb
Cindy Brady	Susan Olsen
Greg Brady	Berry Williams
Peter Brady	Christopher Knight
Bobby Brady	Mike Lookinland

PRODUCERS Sherwood Schwartz, Lloyd J. Schwartz, Howard Leeds

PROGRAMMING HISTORY 117 Episodes

• ABC

September 1969–September 1970	Friday 8:00-8:30
September 1970–September 1971	Friday 7:30-8:00
September 1971–August 1974	Friday 8:00-8:30

FURTHER READING

Bellafante, Gina. "The Inventor of Bad TV: What Would the '70s Have Been without Sherwood Schwartz? (interview)." *Time* (New York), 13 March 1995.

Briller, Bert. "Will the Real Live Brady Bunch Stand Up?" *Television Quarterly* (New York), Spring 1992.

Steele, Scott. "Bringing Up Brady." *Maclean's* (Toronto, Canada), 7 February 1994.

Williams, Barry, with Chris Kreski. *Growing Up Brady: I Was a Teenage Greg*. New York: Harper Perennial, 1992.

Zeman, Ned. "Seventies Something; The Era that Gave Us Bell-Bottoms, Abba and *The Brady Bunch* Is Coming Back. Have a Nice Decade." *Newsweek* (New York), 10 June 1991.

See also Comedy, Domestic Settings

BRAGG, MELVYN

British Media Executive/Personality/Author

Melvyn Bragg has become the most articulate spokesman for the arts on Independent Television (ITV) in Britain. As presenter and editor of *The South Bank Show* since 1978 and head of arts for London Weekend Television from 1982 to 1990 (since 1990 controller of arts), Bragg has attained the same fame as an arts expert for ITV that Huw Wheldon enjoyed in the 1960s for the BBC TV arts program *Monitor* in the 1960s. Both Wheldon and Bragg became senior management administrators because of their successful role as arts presenters and both became articulate authors who wrote extensively about the directions in which television should develop.

Bragg was a working-class boy who went to Wadham College, Oxford. After Oxford he joined the BBC as a radio and later television producer, but he never forgot his origins, and viewers shared with him his genuine delight in new artistic discovery. At the BBC he worked for the *Monitor* program under Huw Wheldon, and became widely respected for his arts reporting. In 1967 Bragg became a freelance writer and broadcaster, working as producer and editor of *New Release* and *Writers' World*, and later presenting the BBC series *Second House* and *Read all about It*. Interviewed in 1970, he explained that when he worked for the BBC in the sixties he had wanted to make arts programs current; he added that he wanted to put on the arts because "I think it's the only way that People, with a capital P, are going to find out about the things that I particularly like. Missionary is too strong a word for it and propaganda is the wrong word—but it's certainly to do with the fact that the people I was born and brought up among very rarely read books, but all of them look at television."

Bragg's tenure as the anchor of the BBC Radio 4 program *Start the Week*, as well as being editor of *The South Bank Show*, has given him a role as "Arts Tsar" or "Arts Supremo." Critics have suggested that "any traffic between high art and mass taste had to pass through Bragg's custom post", as Henry Porter wrote in the *Guardian*. Bragg replied that in England if people get too big for their boots they get cut off at the knees. His long tenure as presenter of *The South Bank Show* has kept the flag flying for the arts on ITV, and at times the program has achieved greatness, especially with Bragg's portrait of the English film director David Lean. His arts stories have been sold worldwide, and history will see his contribution to *The South Bank Show* to be as remarkable as Huw Wheldon's to *Monitor*.

Bragg is also a prolific writer with fifteen novels to his credit, some depicting his working-class background in Cumbria; his 1990 novel *A Time to Dance* was televised in 1992. He has written two stage musicals: *Mardi Gras* in 1976 and *The Hired Man* in 1984. His screenplays include *Isadora, Jesus Christ Superstar* and, with Ken Russell, *Clouds of Glory*. Bragg is also a prolific journalist, and has written for the *Guardian*, the *Daily Mail* and the *Evening Standard* and other English newspapers.

As chair of the ITV program contractor Border Television since 1990, Bragg's views are heard with respect. Without his skills and dedication, it is possible that arts programs on ITV might have been marginalized in the same way that ITV religious programs have been. His presence has ensured good time slots and good ratings for *The South Bank Show*. And his clear-sighted integrity has endeared him to television makers, artists and politicians alike.

Established as an outstanding arts presenter, Bragg is also seen as a wise elder statesman commenting on the future of ITV. In the 1980s his *Guardian* article in July 1984 on ITV's identity crisis was a timely warning of ITV's future problems. In the 1990s he warned the government that British television is being turned into a two-tier system, "telly for nobs and telly for slobs", and that it was being destroyed by a "class and cash system" whereby satellite and cable television systems were able to syphon off prime material. Every newspaper reported his speech, and the *Daily Telegraph* devoted an editorial to the subject. Such leadership, all too rare in the independent sector, suggests that Melvyn Bragg will be remembered as one of the greatest of the ITV leaders in the 1980s and 1990s.

—Andrew Quicke

MELVYN BRAGG. Born in Carlisle, Cumberland, England, 6 October 1939. Attended Nelson-Thomlinson Grammar School, Wigton, Cumberland, 1950–58; Wadham College, Oxford, 1958–61, M.A. honours 1961. Married: 1) Marie-Elisabeth Roche, 1961 (died, 1971), one daughter; 2) Catherine Mary Haste, 1973, one daughter and one son. General trainee, BBC, 1961; producer and presenter numerous arts programmes, 1963–67; writer and broadcaster, 1967–78; editor and presenter of *The South Bank Show*, from 1978; head of arts, London Weekend Television, 1982–90; deputy chair, Border Television, 1985–90; presenter, BBC Radio's *Start the Week*, since 1988; controller of arts, London Weekend Television, since 1990; chair, Border Television, Carlisle, since 1990. D.Litt: University of Liverpool, 1986; University of Lancaster, 1990; Council for National Academic Awards, 1990; D.Univ.: Open University, Milton Keynes, Buckinghamshire, 1987; LLD, University of St. Andrew's, 1993; DCL, University of

Melvyn Bragg

Northumbria, 1994. Fellow: Royal Society of Literature, 1970; Royal Television Society; Lancashire Polytechnic, 1987; St. Catherine's College, Oxford, 1990. Member: Arts Council (chair, Arts Council Literature Panel, 1977–80); Cumbrians for Peace (president, since 1982); Northern Arts (chair, 1983–87); National Campaign for the Arts (chair, since 1986). Recipient: Writers Guild Screenplay Award, 1966; Rhys Memorial Prize, 1968; Northern Arts Association Prose Award, 1970; Silver Pen Award, 1970; Broadcasting Guild Award, 1984; Ivor Novello Musical Award, 1985; British Academy of Film and Television Arts Dimbleby Award, 1986. Address: 12 Hampstead Hill Gardens, London NW3 2PL, England.

TELEVISION SERIES

1963–65	*Monitor* (producer)
1964–70	*New Release/Review/Arena* (editor)
1964–70	*Writers' World* (editor)
1964–70	*Take It or Leave It* (editor)
1971	*In the Picture* (presenter)
1973–77	*Second House* (presenter)
1976–77	*Read all about It* (editor and presenter)
1978–	*The South Bank Show* (editor and presenter)
1989–	*The Late Show* (presenter)

TELEVISION SPECIALS (selection; editor, presenter, and writer)

Maria Callas: An Operatic Biography; The Literary Island: Land of the Lakes; Richard Burton: In from the Cold; Paris Live! The French Revolution Bicentennial.

TELEVISION SPECIALS (writer)

1965	*The Debussy Film* (with Ken Russell)
1970	*Charity Begins at Home*
1972	*Zinotchka*
1977	*Orion* (with Ken Howard and Alan Blaikley)
1990	*A Time to Dance*

FILMS (writer)

Play Dirty, with Lotte Colin, 1968; *Isadora*, with Clive Exton and Margaret Drabble, 1969; *The Music Lovers*, 1970; *Jesus Christ Superstar*, with Norman Jewison, 1973; *Clouds of Glory* (with Ken Russell), 1978; *Marathon: The Flames of Peace*, 1992.

FILM (actor)

The Tall Guy, 1989.

RADIO

Robin Hood (writer), 1971; *Start the Week* (presenter), since 1988.

STAGE (writer)

Mardi Gras, with Alan Blaikley and Ken Howard, 1976; *The Hired Man*, with Howard Goodall, 1984; *King Lear in New York*, 1992.

PUBLICATIONS (selection)

For Want of a Nail (novel). London: Secker and Warburg, 1965; New York: Knopf, 1965.

The Second Inheritance (novel). London: Secker and Warburg, 1966; New York: Knopf, 1967.

Without a City Wall (novel). London: Secker and Warburg, 1968; New York: Knopf, 1969.

The Hired Man (novel). London: Secker and Warburg, 1969; New York: Knopf, 1970.

A Place in England (novel). London: Secker and Warburg, 1970; New York: Knopf, 1971.

The Nerve (novel). London: Secker and Warburg, 1971.

The Hunt (novel). London: Secker and Warburg, 1972; New York: Knopf, 1972.

Josh Lawton (novel). London: Secker and Warburg, 1972; New York: Knopf, 1972.

The Silken Net (novel). London: Secker and Warburg, 1974; New York, Knopf, 1974.

Speak for England: An Essay on England 1900–1975. London: Secker and Warburg, 1976; as *Speak for England: An Oral History of England 1900–1975*, New York: Knopf, 1977.

A Christmas Child (children's fiction). London: Secker and Warburg, 1976.

Autumn Manoeuvres (novel). London: Secker and Warburg, 1978; New York: Knopf, 1978.

Kingdom Come (novel). London: Secker and Warburg, 1980.

My Favourite Stories of Lakeland, editor. Guildford, Surrey: Lutterworth Press, 1981.

Love and Glory (novel). London: Secker and Warburg, 1983.

Land of the Lakes. London: Secker and Warburg, 1983; New York: Norton, 1984.

The Cumbrian Trilogy (collection). London: Coronet, 1984.

Laurence Olivier. London: Hutchinson, 1984; New York: St. Martin's Press, 1985.

Cumbria in Verse, editor. London: Secker and Warburg, 1984.

The Hired Man (play). London: French, 1986.

The Maid of Buttermere (novel). London: Hodder and Stoughton, 1987; New York: Putnam, 1987.

Rich: The Life of Richard Burton. London: Hodder and Stoughton, 1988; as *Richard Burton: A Life*, Boston: Little Brown, 1989.

A Time to Dance (novel). London: Hodder and Stoughton, 1990; Boston: Little Brown, 1991.

Credo (novel). London: Sceptre, 1996.

FURTHER READING

Field, Michele. "Melvyn Bragg: The Author of a Biography of Richard Burton Finds that his own Background Has Much in Common with that of His Subject." *Publishers Weekly* (New York), 3 February 1989.

BRAMBELL, WILFRID

British Actor

British character actor Wilfrid Brambell became nationally famous late in his career as Albert Steptoe in the BBC's most popular and successful sitcom, *Steptoe and Son*, although the character he played was considerably older than he was. He was never one for starring roles, but supplied reliable support in a variety of stage, screen and television roles before Albert Steptoe thrust him into the limelight. Television appearances included a variety of parts in adaptations of classic texts, including *The Government Inspector* (1958), *Bleak House* (1959) and *Our Mutual Friend* (1959), all for the BBC.

Writers Ray Galton and Alan Simpson wanted to use straight actors, rather than comedians, when casting the leads for their new BBC comedy *Steptoe and Son* in 1962. Harry H. Corbett was cast as Harold Steptoe and Brambell given the role of his father Albert. Over the years to follow, the actors and writers together were to develop characters which found their way into the national consciousness.

Albert Steptoe is an old-time rag-and-bone man who inherited the family business of the title from his father and now runs it with his son, Harold. Harold goes out on the cart to collect the junk, while Albert remains at home, ostensibly to run the administrative side of the business, but, in reality, to take it easy or go out to the cinema. Albert is a widower. He still has an eye for the ladies, and for the main chance, though generally espousing an old-fashioned morality. He is a veteran of the Great War and bemoans declining standards, but his own behaviour is often gross and earthy in the extreme. He rarely washes and, when he does, is liable to eat his evening meal in the bath. His language and behaviour are, in Harold's eyes in particular, uncouth, prompting the description, "You dirty old man!", the series' only catchphrase.

Brambell played Albert Steptoe as a grumpy old curmudgeon, capable of resorting to the most pathetic pleading to get his own way. The role of the scruffy old man could not have been further from the rather suave and cultured person Brambell was in real life.

Steptoe and Son ran for four series between 1962 and 1965. It regularly attracted audiences of over 20 million, from all sectors of society, and in 1963 a *Steptoe and Son* sketch was performed by Brambell and Corbett as part of that year's Royal Variety Performance. Between series, and after Galton and Simpson brought it to an end, both Brambell and Corbett were in demand for movie parts because of their great popularity. Amongst Brambell's roles was that of Paul McCartney's grandfather in the Beatles film *A Hard Day's Night* and the White Rabbit in Jonathan Miller's 1966 television version of *Alice in Wonderland*.

Steptoe and Son was revived, in colour, by the BBC in 1970 and ran for another four series between then and 1974. There were also two spin-off feature films. The characters and situations had not changed—nor had the quality of writing and performance or the popularity of the show.

—Steve Bryant

WILFRID BRAMBELL. Born in Dublin, Ireland, 22 March 1912. Attended schools in Dublin. Married: Molly (divorced, 1955). Stage debut as a child, entertaining troops during World War I, 1914; began professional acting career as an adult at the Gate Theatre, Dublin; toured with ENSA during World War II; first appearance on London stage, 1950; single appearance on Broadway, 1965; played character parts in theater and films before achieving fame as Albert Steptoe in long-running *Steptoe and Son* comedy series, 1962–74. Died in London, 18 January 1985.

TELEVISION SERIES
1962–65,
    1970–74   *Steptoe and Son*

FILMS
The 39 Steps, 1935; *Odd Man Out*, 1946; *Another Shore*, 1948; *Dry Rot*, 1956; *The Story of Esther Costello*, 1957; *The Salvage Gang*, 1958; *The Long Hot Summer*, 1958; *Serious Charge*, 1959; *Urge to Kill*, 1960; *The Sinister Man*, 1961; *Jack's Horrible Luck*, 1961; *Flame in the Streets*, 1961; *What a Whopper!*, 1961; *The Grand Junction Case*, 1961; *In Search of the Castaways*, 1962; *The Boys*, 1962; *The Fast Lady*,

Wilfrid Brambell
Photo courtesy of the British Film Institute

1962; *The Small World of Sammy Lee*, 1963; *Crooks in Cloisters*, 1963; *The Three Lives of Thomasina*, 1963; *Go Kart Go!*, 1963; *A Hard Day's Night*, 1964; *San Ferry Ann*, 1965; *Alice in Wonderland*, 1966; *Where the Bullets Fly*, 1966; *Mano di Velluto*, 1966; *Witchfinder-General*, 1968; *Lionheart*, 1968; *Cry Wolf*, 1968; *The Undertakers*, 1969; *Carry On Again, Doctor*, 1969; *Some Will, Some Won't*, 1970; *Steptoe and Son*, 1972; *Steptoe and Son Ride Again*, 1973; *Holiday on the Buses*, 1973; *The Adventures of Picasso*, 1978; *High Rise Donkey*, 1980; *Island of Adventure*, 1981; *Death and Transfiguration*, 1983; *Sword of the Valiant*, 1983; *The Terence Davies Trilogy*, 1984.

RADIO
Steptoe and Son.

STAGE (selection)
Blind Man's Buff; Stop It, Whoever You Are; The Canterbury Tales; The Ghost Train; Kelly; A Christmas Carol.

PUBLICATION
All Above Board (autobiography). London: Allen, 1976.

FURTHER READING
Burke, Michael. "You Dirty Old Man!" *The People* (London), 9 January 1994.
"How We Met: Ray Galton and Alan Simpson." *The Independent* (London), 11 June 1995.

See also *Steptoe and Son*

BRAZIL

Brazil has one of the world's largest and most productive commercial television systems. Its biggest television network, TV Globo, is the fourth largest commercial network in the world. Brazil is also one of the largest television exporters within Latin America and around the world, particularly of *telenovelas*, the characteristic Latin American prime time serials, which have become popular in a many countries.

Though Brazilian television began in 1950, it remained urban and elitist. Sets were expensive, programs were broadcast live, and transmitters covered only major centers. As in many other settings, that era of early television produced quite a bit of classic drama, and during this period local traditions in variety, news, drama and *telenovelas* were established. The advent of videotape around 1960 opened Brazil to imported programs. Again, typical of countries then developing their television systems, the imports dominated programming for much of the decade, but their presence also stimulated some efforts at creating local networks. Two major early networks, TV Tupi and TV Excelsior, operated at that time.

Television became a truly mass medium in Brazil earlier than in most developing countries. The military governments which took power in 1964 saw televisual communication as a potential tool for creating a stronger national identity, creating a broader consumer economy, and controlling political information. The military pushed television deeper into the population by subsidizing credit for set sales, by building national microwave and satellite distribution systems, and by promoting the growth of one network they chose as a privileged partner. TV Globo, which also started in 1964, created the first true national network by the late 1960s. Censorship of news was extensive under the military governments between 1966 and 1978, but they also encouraged national television program production. In the early 1970s, several government ministers pushed the commercial networks hard to develop more Brazilian programming and reduce reliance on imported programs, particularly those that contained violence.

The 1960s represented a formative period for genre development. Brazilian *telenovelas* had largely been patterned after those in other Latin American countries, even using imported scripts, but during these years they were developed into a considerably more sophisticated genre by TV Excelsior in São Paulo and TV Globo in Rio. A key turning point was the 1968 *telenovela*, *Beto Rockefeller*, a well-produced story reflecting a singular Brazilian personality, the Rio good-lifer or *boa vida*. By the 1970s, *telenovelas* were the most popular programs and dominated prime time on the major networks, TV Globo and TV Tupi. TV Globo, in particular, began to attract major writers and actors from both film and theater to also work in *telenovelas*. The Brazilian *telenovelas* became good enough, as commercial television entertainment, to be exported throughout Latin America and into Europe, Asia and Africa.

Another major genre of the 1960s was the *show de auditório*, a live variety show mixing games, quizzes, amateur and professional entertainers, comedy, and discussion. The *shows de auditório* have been extremely popular with the lower-middle and lower-classes, and, according to analyses such as Sérgio Miceli's 1972 *A Noite da Madrinha* (*Evening with the Godmother*), played an extremely important role in drawing them into television viewing.

The years 1968 to 1985 constitute Brazilian television's second phase. In this period TV Globo dominated both the audience and the development of television programming. It tended to have a 60-80% share of the viewers in the major cities at any given time. TV Globo was accused during this period of representing the view of the government, of being its mouthpiece. Other broadcast television networks found themselves pursuing smaller, more specific audience segments largely defined by social class. SBS (Sílvio Santos) targeted a lower middle class, working class and poor audience, mostly with variety and game shows. The strategy gained it a consistent second place in ratings in most of the 1980s and 1990s. TV Manchete targeted a more elite audience initially, with news, high budget *telenovelas*, and imported programs, but found the segment too small to gain adequate advertiser support. TV Bandeirantes tended to emphasize news, public affairs and sports. All three ultimately wished to pursue a general audience with general appeal programming, such as *telenovelas*, but generally discovered that such efforts still did not gain an audience sufficient to pay for the increased programming costs.

Brazilian television since 1985 has gone through a third phase, marked by its role in the transition to a new civilian republic. In 1984, TV Globo initially supported the military government against a campaign for direct election of a civilian government, while other media, including other television networks, many radio stations, and most of the major newspapers supported the change. Perceiving that it might literally lose its audience to the competition, Globo switched sides and supported transition to a civilian regime, which was indirectly elected in a compromise situation. The new political circumstances immediately reduced political censorship and pressure on broadcasters.

The fourth phase of Brazilian television has been its internationalization. The importation of television programs into Brazil declined from the 1970s through the 1980s, as Brazilian networks produced more of their own material. TV Globo often filled 12-14 hours a day with indigenous productions. TV Globo and other networks also began to export programs, particularly *telenovelas*, and Brazilian exports of programming to the rest of the world soon became economically and culturally significant. Brazilian exports reached over a hundred countries and the programs have often proved great international successes. This is particularly the case with historical *telenovelas* such as *A Escrava Isaura* (*Isaura the Slave*), about the abolition of slavery in Brazil, a hit in countries as diverse as Poland, China, Cuba and most of Latin America.

The recent fifth phase of Brazilian television is marked by the appearance of some new video distribution systems. The first new technology to diffuse widely in Brazil was the home videocassette recorder (VCR), which largely gave the middle and upper classes greater access to imported feature films. The new technology with most effect on Brazilian electronic media, however, is the satellite distribution of television to small repeaters throughout the country. In the 1980s, thousands of small towns in rural Brazil purchased satellite dishes and low power repeaters to bring in Brazilian television networks, effectively extending television to 99% of the population. Recent studies show that over 90% of the population probably has television sets. New video technologies entered the Brazilian television market in the 1990s, offering focused or segmented programming through additional advertising supported UHF

(ultra high frequency) channels or pay-TV systems such as subscription television (STV), cable TV systems, multichannel multipoint distribution systems (MMDS) and direct satellite broadcasting (DBS).

In this most recent period three main approaches have so far been used to support programming and distribution: Advertising supported UHF, exemplified by the Brazilian adaptation of MTV, which features about 10-20% Brazilian music; over-the-air pay-TV systems, which usually rely on imported channels like CNN, ESPN and HBO; and DBS (Direct Broadcast Satellite) systems, which require subscription. So far only MTV has gained even a small share of the audience. Studies to date indicate that most satellite dishes and many cable connections are being used to secure better reception of Brazilian channels.

Even though the new technologies seem to threaten to bring in a new wave of largely U.S. programming, then, the audience studies so far do not indicate a strong audience response to them, except perhaps among a globalized elite and upper middle class. The dominant characteristic of Brazilian television still seems to be that of a strong national system with a distinct set of genres very popular with its own audience and in export.

—Joseph Straubhaar

FURTHER READING

Fachel Leal O. "Popular Taste and Erudite Repertoire: The Place and Space of Television in Brazil." *Cultural Studies* (London), 1990.

Kottak, C. P. *Prime Time Society—An Anthropological Analysis of Television and Culture.* Belmont, California: Wadsworth, 1990.

Lima, V. A. "Television and the Brazilian Elections of 1989." In Skidmore, Thomas, editor. *Television, Politics and the Transition to Democracy in Latin America.* Washington, D.C.: Woodrow Wilson Center/Smithsonian Institution Press, 1993.

Lins da Silva, C. E. "Transnational Communication and Brazilian Culture." In Atwood, R., and E. G. McAnany, editors. *Communication and Latin American Society—Trends in Critical Research, 1960–1985.* Madison, Wisconsin: University of Wisconsin Press, 1986.

Mattelart, M., and A. Mattelart. *The Carnival of Images: Brazilian Television Fiction.* New York: Bergin and Garvey, 1990.

Mattos, S. "Advertising and Government Influences on Brazilian Television." *Communication Research* (Newbury Park, California), 1984.

McAnany, E. G. "The Logic of Cultural Industries in Latin America: The Television Industry in Brazil." In Mosco, V., and J. Wasco, editors. *Critical Communications Review.* Norwood, New Jersey: Ablex, 1984.

Oliveira, O. S. "Brazilian Soaps Outshine Hollywood: Is Cultural Imperialism Fading Out?" In Nordenstreng, Kaarle, and Herbert Schiller, editors. *Beyond National Sovereignty: International Communication in the 1990s.* Norwood, New Jersey: Ablex, 1993.

Sarti, I. "Communication and Cultural Dependency: A Misconception." In Mosco, V., and J. Wasco, editors. *Communication and Social Structure*. New York: Praeger, 1981.

Straubhaar, J. "The Development of the Telenovela as the Paramount Form of Popular Culture in Brazil." *Studies in Latin American Popular Culture* (Las Cruces, New Mexico), 1982.

———. "The Decline of American Influence on Brazilian Television." *Communication Research* (Newbury Park, California), 1984.

———. "The Reflection of the Brazilian Political Opening in the Telenovela, 1974-1985." *Studies in Latin American Popular Culture* (Las Cruces, New Mexico), 1988.

———. "Beyond Media Imperialism: Asymmetrical Interdependence and Cultural Proximity." *Critical Studies in Mass Communication* (Annandale, Virginia), 1991.

Vink, N. *The Telenovela and Emancipation—A Study on TV and Social Change in Brazil.* Amsterdam: Royal Tropical Institute, 1988.

BRIDESHEAD REVISITED

British Miniseries

Brideshead Revisited was made by Granada television, scripted by John Mortimer and originally shown on ITV in October 1981. The eleven episode adaptation of Evelyn Waugh's novel of the same name helped set the tone of a number of subsequent screen presentations of heritage England, such as *Chariots of Fire* (1981), *The Jewel in the Crown* (1982), *A Passage to India* (1984), and *A Room with a View* (1986). These "white flannel" dramas, both on television and on the big screen, represented a yearning for an England that was no more, or never was. *Brideshead Revisited* opens in England on the eve of the World War II. Charles Ryder (played by Jeremy Irons), the main character and narrator, is presented as a rather incompetent officer in the British Army. He stumbles upon an English country house, which he has visited more than twenty years before. Upon seeing the house, Charles begins to tell the story of his years at Oxford, his meeting with Sebastian Flyte (Anthony Andrews) and his love for Julia (Diana Quick). This retrospective narrative is nostalgic in two senses. It is concerned with Charles' nostalgia for his affairs in the interwar period. But it is also concerned with a nostalgia for a time before World War I—a longing for a lost way of life, for an Edwardian England.

The first five episodes focus on Charles' relationship with Sebastian, dealing candidly with homosexual passion. Parts six to eight portray Charles' "dead years," his ties to the Flyte family apparently severed. His growing love for Julia returns him to Brideshead. The final three parts follow the development and decline of this relationship and the death of Lord Marchmain.

The locations are centrally important in the drama. In the early episodes of the serial Charles recounts his years at university in Oxford. Establishing shots of "dreaming spires" and college courtyards paint a picture of opulent, languid, summer days. Likewise Brideshead Castle, the home of Sebastian and Julia, presents in stark symbolic form the once commanding heights of a now declining aristocracy. The stately home was actually Castle Howard in Yorkshire, the home of the then BBC chair, George Howard. These were

deliberate signs of "quality". *Brideshead Revisited* visually displayed all the hallmarks of "quality television". The serial, which lasted over twelve hours in total, was officially costed by Granada television at £4.5 million, but other estimates put the figure closer to £11 million. Granada was committed to capturing an accurate atmosphere of Waugh's original novel and the high production values signaled a desire for authenticity. For example, filming on board the ocean liner the *Queen Elizabeth II* cost £50,000 per eight minutes of film. Other rich backdrops were provided by expensive location filming in Venice, Malta, and the island of Gozo. The large budget was justified by artful creation: "every frame a Rembrandt," as Mike Scott put it. Viewers, taken with the obvious prestigious connotations of the production, frequently mistook the serial as originating from the British Broadcasting Corporation.

The visual lushness of the serial was matched by the excessive decadence of Sebastian and his various friends. Waugh's misogyny is revealed and we are delivered a gathering of aristocratic men accustomed to each others' company rather than to women. The myth of Edwardian England is fashioned through their clothes and manners. Sebastian is styled in cricket whites, Charles in tweed. The foppishness of their character is matched by the flow of their loose fitting wardrobe. Altogether, we are presented with a 1920s version of the Edwardian dandy—"tastefully" homoerotic. Sebastian's Teddy Bear, Aloysius, which is closely clutched in the early episodes, became a popular icon in the early 1980s of a new breed of white flannelled men. As the drama unfolds Charles is caught within a more engulfing family romance. As Charles comes to know the family and as his love for Julia grows, Sebastian grows more melancholy and the idyllic images of Oxford and Brideshead Castle give way to a more disturbing ambiance of loss and mourning.

The elegance and nostalgia, the longing for a bygone "Englishness" of empire and perceived stability led to *Brideshead* being widely attacked in cultural criticism. It was seen as a "Thatcherite text", part of a resurgence of regressive nationalism. It was criticised for its slow, reverential pace,

Brideshead Revisited

for wallowing in inherited wealth, for being a glorified "soap". Nevertheless, the production is seen internationally as an example of what the British do best, a large-scale "quality" production of television drama.

—David Oswell and Guy Jowett

CAST

Charles Ryder . . . . Jeremy Irons
Lady Julia Flyte . . . . Diana Quick
Sebastian Flyte . . . . Anthony Andrews
Edward Ryder . . . . John Gielgud
Anthony Blanche . . . . Nikolas Grace
Nancy Hawkins . . . . Mona Washbourne
Boy Mulcaster . . . . Jeremy Sinden
Jasper . . . . Stephen Moore
Sergeant Block . . . . Kenneth Graham
Barber . . . . John Welsh
Commanding Officer . . . . John Nettleton
Lord Marchmain . . . . Laurence Olivier

Cara . . . . Stephane Audran
Lady Marchmain . . . . Claire Bloom
Brideshead . . . . Simon Jones
Cordella . . . . Phoebe Nicholls
Samgrass . . . . John Grillo
Wilcox . . . . Roger Milner
Hayter . . . . Michael Bilton
Rex Mottram . . . . Charles Keating
Nanny . . . . Mona Washbourne
Nurse . . . . Mary McLeod
Hooper . . . . Richard Hope
Dr. Grant . . . . Michael Gough

PRODUCERS   Michael Lindsay-Hogg, Derek Granger

PROGRAMMING HISTORY   11 Episodes

• Granada Television
12 October–22 December 1981

FURTHER READING

Brunsdon, Charlotte. "Problems with Quality." *Screen* (London), Spring 1990.

Wollen, Tana. "Over our Shoulders: Nostalgic Screen Fictions for the 1980s." In, Corner, John, and Sylvia Harvey, editors. *Enterprise and Heritage: Crosscurrents of National Culture.* London: Routledge, 1991.

See also Adaptations; British Programming; *Jewel in the Crown*; Miniseries

BRIGGS, ASA

British Historian

Asa Briggs is the most important broadcasting historian in Britain. By writing about broadcasting as part of modern British social history, he has become a powerful advocate for the continuation of the British Broadcasting Company (BBC).

A Victorian historian of considerable note, Asa Briggs began his great work *The History of Broadcasting in the United Kingdom* in the 1960s. The first volume, entitled *Birth of Broadcasting*, was published in 1961, and contained a marvelously evocative description of the birth of the BBC, and its founder John Reith, through 1927. The second volume, *Golden Age of Wireless*, published in 1965, covered the period from 1927 to 1939, and received very favorable reviews. Volume three, *War of Words*, covered the war years, 1939 to 1945. The fourth volume, entitled *Sound and Vision*, covered the period from 1945 to 1955, and the final volume, *Competition*, from the end of the BBC monopoly in 1955 to the mid-1970s.

Because independent television was not created until 1955, Briggs is primarily a historian of the BBC. However, in 1985 Briggs was commissioned by the independent companies to write with Joanna Spicer an account of the way the Independent Broadcasting Authority organized awarding franchises in 1980. In this book *The Franchise Affair* his normal Olympian detachment from the politics of broadcasting was dropped in a fascinating and often critical account of the development of independent TV. Cynics pointed out that Briggs had been a director of Southern Television, one of only two companies whose franchise was arbitrarily removed in 1980. *The Franchise Affair* was published by Hutchinson, a wholly owned subsidiary of London Weekend Television, which was re-awarded its franchise.

Made Baron Briggs of Lewes in 1976, Briggs is often seen as an establishment figure keen on preserving the status of the BBC. But readers of his 1985 compilation volume, *The BBC: The First 50 Years*, were delighted to find that Briggs was not uncritical of the organization that sponsored his mammoth *History of Broadcasting in the United Kingdom* and paid for his offices in London.

Perhaps Briggs' greatest contribution to British broadcasting may not be his history books; it could be his role as chancellor of the Open University from 1978 to 1994, a non-residential institution which provides primary contacts with its students through radio and television broadcast. The Open University has grown to become a major educational institution, awarding degrees for low fees, while maintaining high intellectual standards. Briggs has spent some of his prodigious energies fostering the growth of similar Open Universities of the Air in countries of the British Commonwealth.

As a member of the Campaign for Quality Television, Briggs has been a great defender of the BBC's charter, which came up for renewal in 1996. Thanks to the many defenders of the BBC's position in British society, not least to the Campaign for Quality Television, the BBC had its charter renewed for a further 15 years. Briggs is well satisfied with the result. Thanks to his influence, perhaps in the future some historian will be able to write a history of the First Hundred Years of the BBC. Briggs' contribution to broadcasting is that of historian and advocate. He has skillfully narrated the story of the most important of all British media enterprises.

—Andrew Quicke

ASA BRIGGS. Born in Keighley, Yorkshire, England, 7 May 1921. Attended Keighley Grammar School; Sidney Sussex College, Cambridge, 1941; University of London, First Class BSc in Economics 1941. Married: Susan Anne

Asa Briggs
Photo courtesy of Asa Briggs

Banwell, 1955; children: Katharine, Daniel, Judith and Matthew. Served in Intelligence Corps, 1942–45. Fellow, Worcester College, Oxford, 1945–55; professor of history, Leeds University, 1955–61; professor of history, later vice-chancellor, Sussex University, 1961–66; provost, Worcester College, Oxford, 1976–91; chancellor, Open University, Milton Keynes, 1979–94. Made Baron Briggs of Lewes, East Sussex, 1976. President: Social History Society, from 1976; Victorian Society, from 1983; Ephemera Society, from 1984; British Association for Local History, 1984–86; Association of Research Associations, 1986–88. Chair: Standing Conference for Study of Local History, 1969–76; European Institute of Education and Social Policy, Paris, 1975–90; Commonwealth of Learning, Vancouver, 1988–93; Advisory Board for Redundant Churches, 1983–89. Governor: British Film Institute, 1970–77. Trustee: Glyndebourne Arts Trust, 1966–91; International Broadcasting Institute, 1968–87; Heritage Education Group, 1976–86; Civic Trust, 1976–86. Member: American Academy of Arts and Sciences, 1970. Fellow: Sidney Sussex College, Cambridge, 1968; Worcester College, Oxford, 1969; Saint Catherine's College, Cambridge, 1977; British Academy, 1980. Numerous honorary degrees. Recipient: Marconi Medal for Communication History, 1975; Médaille de Vermeil de la Formation, Fondation de l'Académie d'Architecture, 1979; Royal College of Anaesthetists Snow Medal, 1991. Address: The Caprons, Keere Street, Lewes, Sussex, England.

PUBLICATIONS (selection)

History of Broadcasting in the United Kingdom, 5 vols. Oxford: Oxford University Press, 1961–95.

Governing the BBC. London: British Broadcasting Corporation, 1979.

The BBC: The First Fifty Years, with Joanna Spicer. Oxford: Oxford University Press, 1985.

The Franchise Affair: Creating Fortunes and Failures in Independent Television. London: Hutchinson, 1986.

BRINKLEY, DAVID

U.S. Broadcast Journalist

David Brinkley and Chet Huntley debuted NBC's *The Huntley—Brinkley Report* in October 1956. A few months earlier NBC producer Reuven Frank had put them together as a team to anchor the network's television coverage of the Democratic and Republican presidential nominating conventions. Network news would never be the same. Nor would Sunday mornings a quarter of a century later when Brinkley introduced on ABC, *This Week with David Brinkley.* Since the mid-1950s Brinkley has not only reported the news; he has also helped to shape the industry of television news. His renowned wit, his singular delivery, and his superb TV news writing style have made him an institution in broadcast journalism.

Brinkley's story is as interesting as any he has ever covered. It begins in a small North Carolina town in 1920, and takes him to the pinnacle of media stardom, a solid journalist with enormous credibility who has also been so famous that he was once more recognizable than John Wayne and the Beatles. And the media world has informally named him one of the "Magnificent Seven" (which also includes Barbara Walters, Peter Jennings, Sam Donaldson, Hugh Downs, Ted Koppel, and Diane Sawyer—all of ABC).

But Brinkley was no star when he first went to NBC radio in 1943. His talent for strong and clear writing became evident as he continually struggled to write for announcers who read only the words and seemed to miss the meaning. He also began to gain experience as a newscaster when he did ten-minute newscasts for the network. Nor was he famous when he became the Washington reporter for John Cameron Swayze's *Camel News Caravan*, NBC's early TV news effort. But as the 1956 political conventions came into focus for the U.S. TV audience, they came to see, hear, and to know Brinkley as a new breed of TV journalist.

David Brinkley
Photo courtesy of ABC

Brinkley was one of the first journalists to be absolutely comfortable with this new medium of TV. As his boss at NBC, Reuven Frank, has often said, Brinkley had wit, style, intelligence, and perhaps most importantly, a lean writing style filled with powerful declarative sentences which is very effective in TV news. And Brinkley was aware that TV was made up of pictures and corresponding sounds. He understood that the reporter had to stop talking and let the news footage tell the story. "Brinkley writes silence better than anyone else I know," says Frank. And when this natural TV journalist was teamed with the California reporter Chet Huntley, they literally took TV audiences by storm.

TV news before Huntley and Brinkley was a combination of dull film reports, similar to movie theater newsreels of the 1940s, and a radio reporting style similar to the World War II era. But Huntley and Brinkley took TV news into a new age of electronic journalism. According to one of their main competitors, Don Hewitt of CBS who produced Walter Cronkite and later *60 Minutes*, "They came at us like an express train." When Huntley spoke, it was clear the story was a global story. When Brinkley spoke, it was clear it was a story about Washington. They began with a 15-minute newscast, and in 1963 increased to 30 minutes per night. Audiences in the 1990s take for granted seeing different journalists in different cities talking to each other on TV. But it was *The Huntley-Brinkley Report* that began such techniques. And this switching back and forth between Huntley in New York and Brinkley in Washington created the now famous final exchange from every newscast: "Good night, David"..."Good night, Chet." The order of the exchange alternated night by night—until their last newscast together in 1970 when Huntley's "Good night, David" brought the response, "Good-bye, Chet."

In that year Huntley retired to a Montana ranch, and Brinkley became progressively restless at NBC. His important role in *The Huntley-Brinkley Report* could not be matched, and he did not continue producing the excellent documentaries on *David Brinkley's Journal*. He became known as the grumpy older newsman in the NBC family. He did a series of programs for NBC, including *NBC Nightly News* and *NBC Magazine with David Brinkley*. But he hated to go to New York to do the news, since he saw his news beat as Washington. Finally, in 1981 Roone Arledge hired Brinkley for ABC. All the years with *The Huntley-Brinkley Report* had made Brinkley into the absolute Washington insider. When ABC gave him the Sunday program *This Week with David Brinkley*, he and his guests could talk among themselves and with all the other Washington insiders about the week's news event.

Brinkley asked his friend George Will to join him on *This Week with David Brinkley*. ABC reporter Sam Donaldson joined as the resident "liberal" to confront Will's avowed "conservative" stance. Besides the guests who were interviewed every week, other reporters such as NPR's Cokie Roberts have joined Brinkley, Will, and Donaldson. By some critics the program has been deemed opinionated,

referred to as ABC's Op-Ed page. But there has traditionally been very little interpretation of news on U.S. TV, and *This Week with David Brinkley* seems to have partially filled the void. Because of Brinkley's strong Washington ties, the show has at times appeared to be one group of Washingtonians talking to another. But criticisms aside, with ABC's *This Week with David Brinkley*, Brinkley's enormous talents and his many decades of TV news experience have been given free reign.

Brinkley has received many awards, most notably the Presidential Medal of Freedom by President George Bush. But when asked what he thought his legacy to TV news would be, Brinkley told *Broadcasting* magazine, "(E)very news program on the air looks essentially as we started it (with *The Huntley-Brinkley Report)*. We more or less set the form for broadcasting news on television which is still used. No one has been able to think of a better way to do it."

—Clayland H. Waite

DAVID BRINKLEY. Born in Wilmington, North Carolina, U.S.A., 10 July 1920. Attended New Hanover High School, Wilmington. Special student in English, University of North Carolina, Chapel Hill, 1939–40; special student in English, Emory and Vanderbilt universities, 1941–43. Married: 1) Ann Fischer, 1946 (divorced); children: Alan, Joel, and John; 2) Susan Melanie Benfer, 1972; children: Alexis. Served in U.S. Army, 1941–43. Reporter at Wilmington, North Carolina *Star-News*, 1938–41; reporter, bureau manager, United Press news service (later United Press International), various southern cities, 1941–43; radio news writer and non-broadcast reporter, NBC, Washington, D.C., 1943; NBC-TV, from 1946; Washington correspondent, NBC, 1951–81; co-anchor, with Chet Huntley, *The Huntley-Brinkley Report*, 1956–70; correspondent, commentator, *NBC Nightly News*, 1971–76; co-anchor, *NBC Nightly News*, 1976–79; anchor, ABC's *This Week with David Brinkley*, from 1981. Member: Cosmos Club, Washington; National Press Club, Washington; trustee, Colonial Williamsburg. Recipient: DuPont Award, 1958; Golden Key Award, 1964; Peabody Award, 1961; Emmy Award, 1963; Scholastic Bell Award; Presidential Medal of Freedom, 1992. Address: ABC News, 1717 DeSales Street, N.W., Washington, D.C. 20036-4407, U.S.A.

TELEVISION SERIES

1951–56	*Camel News Caravan* (correspondent)
1956–70	*The Huntley-Brinkley Report*
1961–63	*David Brinkley's Journal*
1971–76	*NBC Nightly News* (commentator only)
1976–79	*NBC Nightly News* (co-anchor)
1980–81	*NBC Magazine with David Brinkley*
1981–	*This Week with David Brinkley*
1981–	*ABC's World News Tonight* (commentator)

PUBLICATIONS

David Brinkley: A Memoir. New York: Knopf, 1995.

"Pull the Plug" (editorial). *The New Republic* (Washington, D.C.), 7 May 1990.

FURTHER READING

Cook, P., D. Gomery, and L. Lichty, editors. *The Future of News: Television-Newspapers-Wire Services- Newsmagazines.* Washington, D.C.: The Woodrow Wilson Center Press, 1992.

Frank, Reuven. *Out of Thin Air: The Brief Wonderful Life of Network News.* New York: Simon and Schuster, 1991.

Gunther, M. *The House that Roone Built: The Inside Story of ABC News.* Boston: Little, Brown, 1994.

See also Anchor; Huntley, Chet; News (Network)

BRITISH ACADEMY OF FILM AND TELEVISION ARTS

The British Academy of Film and Television Arts, (BAFTA) developed from the British Film Academy (founded 1947) and the Guild of Television Producers and Directors (founded 1953). The two organizations amalgamated as the Society of Film and Television Arts in 1958 which assumed its present identity as BAFTA in 1976. One of the Guild's stated aims was to provide awards of merit for outstanding work in television. The first of the Guild award ceremonies was held at the Television Ball of the Savoy Hotel in October 1954. The awards on this occasion were six in number, presented to actors (2 awards), writer, producer, designer, and a "personality" award. In 1957 the number of awards was expanded to nine to accommodate entries from Independent television, including one for "Light Entertainment Artist" which went to Tony Hancock. In 1960 the Desmond Davis award for "outstanding service to television" was added to commemorate a founding member and past chairman. The first recipient was the broadcaster Richard Dimbleby. The number and the categories covered increased and varied over the years, and by 1967 there were 17 Guild awards and 3 additional awards presented under the aegis of the Guild by Mullard Ltd., Shell International and the National Institute of Adult Education. The total had swelled by 1993 to 32 television and 21 film BAFTA awards.

BAFTA consists of approximately 3000 members in the United Kingdom with branches in Manchester, Scotland, Wales and Los Angeles. Any person working within the film and television industries in Britain is eligible to join. The organization prides itself on its democratic principles and has developed voting procedures with checks and balances to ensure that awards are allocated on a combination of popular vote and expert opinion. Nominations are collected direct from the members throughout a year. Broadcast companies are permitted to add programmes to the final members' lists in the television categories. Members then vote directly to select the Best Film as well as all the Film and Television Performance awards.

The Production and Craft Awards are decided by peer-group juries (the chairman appointed by the Council has absolute discretion to select experts of diverse interests whether members or non-members). The jury panel reaches its decision following viewings of the short-listed candidates' work.

The Film Committee determines the nominations for the Alexander Korda Award for the Best British Film and the Council of the Academy selects the winner. The Michael Balcon, the Alan Clarke, the Dennis Potter and the Richard Dimbleby Awards, the Foreign Television Programme, the Television Award for Originality, the Academy Fellowship and any special awards are awarded by the Council of Management.

These built-in safeguards in the award process ensure a balance between respect for democracy and professionalism. It has also resulted in high credibility and prestige attaching to BAFTA awards which, though not as influential as the American Academy Awards, are increasingly seen as enhancing the subsequent commercial success of films and programmes. Televising of the Award Ceremony in Britain is a media event second only to that for the Oscars, and keeps BAFTA awards in the public eye. Despite the benefits of

British Academy of Film and Television Arts
Courtesy of BAFTA

awards, there has been little evidence in Britain of any lobbying to influence panel decisions.

Television awards are primarily devoted to British television, although there is a category for the best programme not in English and for Best Foreign Television. As yet there have been no submissions by satellite channels, but these are eligible to submit and are likely to do so in the near future. New categories of award are constantly emerging in response to developments within the media: a recent addition has been the Lew Grade Award for Significant and Popular Television and under consideration is an award for best interactive video production.

Film awards are international, although there is one reserved for best British film—the Alexander Korda Award. This category is increasingly difficult to determine given the prevalence of co-production arrangements, films made for television with prior release to cinema audiences (e.g. *Film on Four* by Channel 4) and films made in Britain with American backing.

As a registered charity BAFTA supports a wide range of educational and training initiatives for young people (e.g. the Carl Foreman Award) provides a scholarship to study script writing in the University of California.

Among distinguished contributors to the shaping of the organization have been: Richard Cawston, Lord Attenborough, Sir Sydney Samuelson and Sir David Puttnam. The current chairman is Edward Mirzoeff CVO.

—Brendan Kenny

The author would like to thank the following BAFTA personnel for their generous assistance: Doreen Dean, Harry Manley and Peter Morley.

BRITISH PROGRAMME PRODUCTION COMPANIES

The British government has always played a key role in the development of broadcasting policy, which has direct implications for the production of television programmes in the United Kingdom. No significant structural changes have taken place without the report of a major government committee followed by a parliamentary act. Some of the more significant reports and acts are:

- the Selsdon Committee Report (1935) on the development of television and the relative merits of the different technical systems available;
- The Hankey Committee Report (1945) on postwar television in Britain;
- the Beveridge Committee (1949–51), the result of which was the Broadcasting Act of 1954 which recommended the creation of commercial TV;
- the Pilkington Committee (1960–62), which led to the Broadcasting Act of 1964 and the creation of BBC2;
- the Annan Committee (1974–77), which led to the Broadcasting Act of 1980 and the creation of Channel 4;
- The Hunt Report (1982), which led to Cable and Broadcasting Act 1984 setting up the new cable authority to oversee the selection and monitoring of the operations of the new cable operators;
- the Peacock Report published in July 1986, which reinterpreted the role of the market in broadcasting, argued against introducing advertising on the BBC system but recommended a quota for independent production;
- the Broadcasting Act of 1990, which restructured the Independent Broadcasting Authority (IBA) as the Independent Television Commission (ITC), incorporating the cable authority and also restructured the ITV franchise system;
- 1995 BBC Charter Renewal.

The BBC History

By far the largest and still in many ways the most interesting producer of television in the United Kingdom is the British Broadcasting Corporation itself. The BBC is a public corporation which operates under a Royal Charter of Incorporation (first granted on 1 January 1927 when the BBC was a radio organisation) and funded through a license fee system. The corporation now supplements this income from foreign sales and cable and satellite contracts. It is a national broadcaster, based in London with eight regional TV studios in England and further studios in Wales, Scotland, and Northern Ireland. The government appoints, on a five-year rolling basis, a board of 12 governors to oversee the running of the corporation.

John (later Lord) Reith was the first managing director of the BBC when it was founded in 1922 as the British Broadcasting Company, and was eventually named director general. In his 16 years at the BBC he exerted the greatest direct influence on attitudes about broadcasting in the United Kingdom, and, indirectly influenced the development of public service broadcasting in Canada, Australia, and New Zealand. Reith gave rise to the original principle of public service broadcasting "to inform, educate and entertain." Public service broadcasting is a much debated principle and includes attitudes about the responsibility to be objective and balanced when reporting events in news, current affairs, and documentary programmes.

Following World War II, BBC Television resumed transmissions on 7 June 1946 and enjoyed a monopoly of TV broadcasting until Associated Rediffusion made the first commercially-funded transmission at 7:15 P.M. on 22 September 1955. A second BBC TV service, called BBC2, was launched in April 1964. The channel had a more specialized and cultural focus.

There have been 11 director generals since Reith. Perhaps the most famous has been Hugh (later Sir Hugh) Carleton Greene, brother of novelist and film critic Graham Greene. He defended the BBC against criticism of some of its most exciting and daringly satirical productions (*That Was The Week That Was*), that reflected the shifting moral and political climate of the "permissive" and "swinging" 1960s. Director General John Birt is noted for his role in restructuring the BBC and its practices in the mid-1990s in order to make the corporation more financially and administratively efficient and smaller in scale. Whilst not responsible for the 1991 system of "Producer Choice," John Birt developed a notoriety for implementing a more wide-ranging version of the controversial system whereby all producers have total control over an individual programme budget and don't have to use the internal technical facilities. Instead they are encouraged to hire outside technical facilities with the lowest bid on a project.

The BBC World Service is one of the oldest and most respected services globally, a reputation which was established during World War II. It is the only section of the BBC not funded from the license fee—the bulk of the income comes from the Foreign Office—and it launched BBC World Service TV in October 1991.

The BBC has also established significant operations which lie outside mainstream broadcasting. These include BBC Enterprises which was set up to market BBC programmes internationally and has become one of the key wings of the whole operation, and the BBC's Open University operation which has transmitted OU television and radio programmes since 1971.

Commercial Television History

In the mid-1950s, commercial television began in the United Kingdom. A new group of broadcasters emerged, who were also to be heavily involved in original programming for television. In setting up commercial television, the government established the Independent Television Authority (ITA) on 30 July 1954 by an act of parliament. The ITA later became the Independent Broadcasting Authority (IBA), when commercial radio was introduced in 1972. The ITA/IBA fulfilled four functions:

- to build, operate and own the transmitters;
- appoint the independent programme companies;
- supervise programmes; and
- controll advertising.

The purpose of ITA/IBA was to ensure that the commercial companies observed a broad public service broadcasting policy, and as balanced a schedule of programmes as the BBC. Independent television broadcasters were also required to provide fair, objective, and balanced reporting in news, current affairs, and documentary programmes. Similarly to the BBC, the ITA/IBA had a board of 12 governors appointed by the government. The first chair was Sir Kenneth Clarke and the first director general was Sir Robert Fraser, both appointed on 3 August 1954.

The 1990-restructured organization, now named the Independent Television Commission (ITC), periodically organises the reallocation of commercial television franchises as a way of encouraging companies to maintain and improve standards. After the founding companies were established in 1955, franchise reallocations took place in 1968, 1982, and 1990. Most of the companies maintain their franchises, but over the years, there were notable changes.

Commercial TV is funded by advertising and overseas sales and, more recently, through sponsorship, cable, and satellite deals. Until 1990, the commercial companies paid an annual fee to the ITA/IBA to finance that operation and also a levy to the Exchequer which, for many years, amounted to 66.6% of all profits.

Commercial TV is structured regionally with two companies serving London (one weekdays, and the other weekends) and 13 others serving the rest of the United Kingdom. The companies jointly owned a company which was a national news provider, Independent Television News (ITN). The commercial companies did not compete with each other for advertising revenue but instead worked in consort to compete with the BBC for audience share. After a financially disastrous first year of operation the commercial companies established the "Network" where the five largest companies met regularly to organise the schedule for prime-time viewing (i.e. 7:30-10:30 P.M). Between these hours programming across the United Kingdom is identical. For the rest of the schedule there are regional variations and "opt-outs."

Traditionally the companies fell into three groups:

(1) The "Big Five" covered the four most densely populated parts of England—London (two companies), the Midlands, the northwest, and Yorkshire. These companies provided the bulk of the domestically-produced programmes for the network. The companies have changed over the years but the most influential have been: in London, Thames Television and London Weekend Television; in the Midlands, Central TV; in the northwest, Granada TV; and in Yorkshire, Yorkshire TV.

(2) The middle five (sometimes called the "mini-majors") covered the less populated areas and produced perhaps two hours of network programming a week, plus a range of regional programmes. The regions are: south and southeast England; east of England; northeast England; central Scotland; and Wales and the west of England.

(3) The smallest five cover the remote and least populous areas of the United Kingdom. They make an average of one hour a day of local programming. The regions are: southwest England; the Borders (south Scotland and the Isle of Man); north Scotland; Northern Ireland; and the Channel Islands.

Channel Four

A second commercial channel—Channel Four—began transmission on 2 November 1982. This national channel, a wholly owned subsidiary of the ITC, is also funded by advertising but has a specialized, minority interest. Channel Four has a radically different structure to the other TV organisation in the United Kingdom and was set up as a result of the Annan Commission Report. Published in March 1977, the report recommended that a fourth channel be run by an Open Broadcasting Authority on a publishing model.

In addition to mainstream programming, it encourages programmes which reflect the concerns of minority groups (blacks, the disabled), disadvantaged groups (women, the working class), and political parties, broadcasting partisan programmes. Individual programmes are allowed to display bias and offer controversial views as long as the overall schedule reflects a balanced range of positions.

Channel Four does not make its own programmes but commissions independent producers and production companies (including commercial ITV companies) to make programmes and is therefore considered to function more like a book publisher. This structure encouraged the development of small independent television production companies in the early 1980s.

Wales has its own Channel Four called Sianel Pedwar Cymru (S4C) which began transmission on 1 November 1982 and transmits a significant percentage of its programmes in Welsh. It also transmits BBC Welsh language programmes, making it the only commercial channel to schedule BBC programmes.

Breakfast Television

Breakfast TV was not introduced until 1983. The IBA created a franchise for a national station to run for three hours each morning. It was awarded to TV-AM, a new TV company which featured on screen the Famous Five: David Frost, Michael Parkinson, Robert Kee, Anna Ford, and Angela Rippon. TV-AM promised to offer a dynamic and exciting news service and took to the air with a self-declared "mission to explain." The BBC decided to establish its own five-days-a-week breakfast news service (*Breakfast Time*, renamed *Breakfast News* in 1989), which went on air two weeks earlier (17 January 1983), thereby making the competition tough for the fledgling commercial station which began transmission on 1 February 1983.

Viewer ratings for TV-AM's *Good Morning Britain* were disastrous and, in less than three months, four of the "Five," plus the chair and chief executive Peter Jay, resigned. Timothy Aitkin and, eventually, Bruce Gyngell took over, making a commercial success of the station. During the 1991 franchise renewals, TV-AM lost its license, when it was outbid by Sunrise Television (later renamed GMTV).

Shortly afterwards Channel 4 started its own breakfast service, which provided a high-powered news and business information service. Since 1982 it has offered a kid's show produced by Bob Geldorf's Planet 24.

The Main Commercial Television Companies

Thames Television won the London weekday franchise on 29 July 1968, and was formed by the merger of the American Broadcasting Corporation (ABC) and Associated Rediffusion, the first company to begin commercial TV transmissions in 1955. For many years Thames was the largest and wealthiest of the ITV companies and built a reputation for producing a wide range of high quality programmes with a particular emphasis on contemporary drama. Jeremy Isaacs, director of programmes in the 1970s, became the first chief executive of Channel 4 and was dubbed "the finest Director General the BBC never had." Thames TV also owned the highly successful film production company Euston Films, which produced many major dramas including *The Sweeney, Minder, Out, Fox Widows,* and *Reilly–Ace of Spies.* Surprisingly, given the success of the company, it lost its franchise in 1991 when it was outbid by Carlton Communications. Since then Thames has concentrated on programme production and has also helped to establish the satellite channel U.K. Gold, which broadcasts archive Thames material alongside old BBC favourites.

London Weekend Television (LWT) obtained the franchise for weekend transmissions in London in 1967 and went on air on 2 August 1968, replacing Associated Television (ATV—the only company which held franchises in two regions). The company is well known for its light entertainment productions, current affairs coverage with *Weekend World* and *Walden,* and the longest running arts programme, Melvyn Bragg's *The South Bank Show* (launched in 1978).

Central Independent Television went on air on 1 January 1982, and covers the East and West Midlands region. Lord Grade of Elstree (Lew Grade) was, for many years, chief executive of ATV and the most powerful personality in British TV. He was also chair of Associated Communications Corporation which was Britain's only fully-fledged entertainment conglomerate. He was also, from the 1950s, the most successful exporter of British TV programmes to the United States including series such as *The Saint, The Persuaders, The Julie Andrews Show* and *The Muppets.* In 1991 Central retained its franchise with a bid of just £2,000 (there were no competitors) and was subsequently taken over by Carlton Communications.

Granada Television Network covers the northwest of England and began transmission on 5 May 1956. One of the most influential people in the early days of British television was Granada's chair Sidney Bernstein, who *The Observer* described in 1959 as "the celebrated Socialist millionaire, Sidney Bernstein, the Mr. Culture of TV." Granada TV Network Ltd was born out of the 22-year-old Granada Group which ran a chain of cinemas and theatres. Granada TV built a solid reputation as one of the most important contributors to the ITV network particularly in current affairs, drama, and regional programming. Its two most famous and longest-running shows are the current affairs programme *World in Action* (from January 1963 to present day) and the first British television soap opera *Coronation*

Street (from December 1960 to the present day). Granada is the longest surviving ITV company and in the 1990s took over LWT and also bought shares in Rupert Murdoch's satellite channel, BSkyB.

Independent Television News (ITN), established as a specialist news company in 1955, is a wholly owned subsidiary of the ITV companies. Its first bulletin was transmitted on 22 September 1955. Following the regulations of the 1990 Broadcasting Act, ITN was refounded as a profit-making news business with commercial contracts to the ITV companies and other broadcasters. It is owned by a consortium of Carlton, Central, Granada, LWT, Reuters (all 18%) and Anglia and STV (both 5%).

Until the creation of Channel Four, virtually all domestic television was produced by either the BBC or the ITV companies. Furthermore, strict controls were placed on the importation of foreign programming. Basically, 84% of all television transmitted had to be domestically produced. There was a proliferation of new small independent production companies, fueled by the Channel Four commissions, and the 1990 Broadcasting Bill that required both the BBC and ITV companies to commission at least 25% of their programmes from independent producers by 1993.

Alternate Delivery Systems

Cable television (using coaxial cable) began in the late 1940s as a master antenna system for communities that had poor reception signals due to buildings, topographical problems, or distance from relay antenna. In 1972 Britain's first local cable station was inaugurated by Greenwich Cablevision on 3 July with a programme entitled *Cable Town*. This station was followed by five others: Bristol Channel, Sheffield Cablevision, Swindon Viewpoint, Cablevision (Wellingborough) Ltd, and Milton Keynes' Channel 40, with two experiments taking place in Scotland.

Five Direct Broadcasting by Satellite (DBS) channels were allocated to Britain at the World Administrative Radio Conference (WARC) in 1977. Two of these channels were allocated exclusively to the BBC in 1982, the year that

Rupert Murdoch's Sky Channel in Europe was launched. Sky used existing telecommunication satellites to broadcast to cable stations and by the time the Astra satellites went into orbit, Sky was able to broadcast four satellite channels directly into peoples' homes.

Also in 1982 the British government accepted the Home Office recommendation that the new D-MAC technical format be adopted. Thus committed to this format British Satellite Broadcasting (BSB) won the DBS contract in 1986 and, after many financial and technical setbacks, the service was officially launched in April 1990. However Sky had already launched service using conventional television standards. Both companies experienced serious financial difficulties, Sky announcing operating losses in 1990 of £95,000,000 with £121,000,000 start-up costs. However, BSB's problems were even greater. On 2 November 1990 the merger of the two companies was formally announced. The new company was called BSkyB, trading as Sky. Sky offered nine of its own channels and marketed a range of other channels in its Sky Multi-Channel package.

Both cable and satellite have been slow to develop in the United Kingdom. A number of reasons have been suggested for this seeming lack of interest in these "new" delivery systems, including the generally high quality and wide variety of terrestrial television—despite the limit of four channels—resulting in overall audience satisfaction. In the 1990s cable was finally beginning to take off, and satellite "sports wars" got more people to subscribe to satellite channels.

However, a significant reason for the slow development of cable and satellite has been the undoubted success of video in the U.K. market, with one of the highest levels of video penetration in the world. The technology is used extensively for time-shift viewing—another indicator of audience satisfaction with British TV—but also for video rental which is particularly strong among the large ethnic communities, such as those from the Indian sub continent, where video is used to maintain cultural cohesion through the viewing of Asian films and TV programmes.

—Manuel Alvarado

BRITISH PROGRAMMING

There are a few points to note about British television programming. The first is that it is not uncommon for certain programmes—particularly, but not solely, light entertainment ones—to change production base and transmission channel. The second is that all domestic programmes not listed here as BBC productions have been produced either by one of the ITV companies or an independent commercial TV production company. The third is that production information about U.S. shows and those from

other countries, which air in the United Kingdom, are not indicated in this history.

The BBC provided the world's first public high-definition regular domestic television service from 3:00 P.M. on 2 November 1936. After the initial introductory speeches the first programme began with a cinema newsreel, followed by an international variety show involving British, American, and Chinese performers. After closing down at 4:00 P.M., the service resumed for another hour at 9:00 P.M.

when a short documentary and a magazine programme were screened, then the newsreel was repeated. In the three years until the closedown of British television on 1 September 1939 (due to the announcement of Britain entering World War II) a complete range of television programmes had been transmitted on the fledgling service. These included newsreels, documentaries, dramas, magazine shows, light entertainment, and children's programmes. Drama productions were almost solely theatrical productions of classics; on 28 March 1938, Cecil Madden established the Sunday night TV drama, beginning with the transmission of Pirandello's *Henry IV.*

From the earliest days, a mobile broadcast unit was utilized. The coronation of King George VI was covered in 1937, with a viewing audience of more than 10,000 people. The unit also covered other public occasions such as the Lord Mayor's Show, the Armistice Day Service, and a range of sporting events such as Wimbledon (tennis) and the FA Cup Final (association football). Undoubtedly the most popular offering was the twice-weekly one-hour magazine programme of topical and general interest, *Picture Page*, which ran from 1936 to 1939 and then returned in 1946 for a further 300 editions until 1954.

The immediate post-war years saw the continuation of *Picture Page* and the broadcast of events such as the Victory Parade (8 June 1946), and royal and sporting events such as tennis and test cricket. The largest such coverage of the 1940s was the televising of the XIVth Olympiad held in London in 1948.

Many plays were transmitted—including some written especially for TV—although very few films and filmed newsreels were broadcast due to industry fears of supporting the competition. The few films that were shown were recognised classics such as D. W. Griffiths' *The Birth of a Nation* (1915), Josef von Sternberg's *Der Blaue Engel* (*The Blue Angel*, 1930), Sergei Eisenstein's *Alexander Nevsky* (1938), and Marcel Carne's *Les enfants du paradis* (1945). The introduction of a ballroom dancing competition programme entitled *Come Dancing*, began in 1949 and is still running.

The early 1950s saw a rapid expansion of TV-set ownership, with the broadcast of the 1953 coronation of Queen Elizabeth II often cited as one of the driving causes. More than 2 million licenses were registered in 1953 (approximately 20% of all households). Licenses rose to over 10 million by the end of the decade. The coronation was broadcast for seven hours; it is estimated that 20 million people in the United Kingdom saw it before it was shipped for screenings in Europe, North America, and across the Commonwealth.

In the 1950s the BBC's monopoly of TV broadcasting ended. The government ushered in television funded through the sale of advertising revenue at the end of July 1954, with transmissions starting on 22 September 1955. Commercial TV transformed the safe, traditional, and cosy world depicted in many programmes produced by the BBC.

The early part of the 1950s saw the production of the United Kingdom's longest running police series, *Dixon of Dock Green* (BBC, 1955–76), created by Ted Willis, one of the world's most prolific creators of television series. *The Good Old Days* (BBC), an Edwardian style variety show ran from 1953 to 1983. *What's My Line?* (BBC, 1951–62, 1973–74; Thames, 1984–90) could be characterised as a quiz show but belongs to a typically British radio and TV genre which continues to this day. This genre is best described as a parlour game show played by guest celebrities. Other examples include *Face the Music* (BBC 1967–84), *A Question of Sport* (BBC, 1970–), *Celebrity Squares* (ATV/Central, 1975–79; 1993–), *Call My Bluff* (BBC 1965–88), *Give Us a Clue* (Thames 1979–91).

Commercial television introduced new ideas and many new areas of programming. British television drama, for instance, was transformed by *Armchair Theatre* (ABC, 1956–69, Thames, 1970–74), which served as an umbrella programme for different productions by new writing talent, particularly under Canadian producer Sidney Newman. A more North American-style entertainment was also produced, such as the variety show *Sunday Night at the London Palladium* (ATV, 1955–67, 1973–74), and game shows such as *Double Your Money* (A-R, 1955–68) and *Take Your Pick* (A-R 1955–68). One example of the BBC buying an American format was *This Is Your Life* (BBC, 1955–64), although Thames took it over from 1969 to the present day.

A very popular production was the science fiction/horror serial *The Quatermas Experiment* (BBC, 1953) from which there have been a number of spin-offs. It was the half-hour filmed period action series which became the most popular drama. These included *The Adventures of Robin Hood* (ABC/Sapphire/ITP, 1955–59), *The Adventures of Sir Lancelot* (Sapphire, 1956–57), *The Adventures of William Tell* (ITC-NTA, 1958–59), *The Count of Monte Cristo* (Vision Productions, 1958), *Ivanhoe* (Sydney Box Prods.-Screen Gems/ITC, 1958).

In comedy, the first edition of *The Benny Hill Show* was produced by the BBC in 1955. The BBC continued to produce it, with a one year gap in 1967, until 1968. Thames (ITV) took it over in 1969 and ran it for the next 20 years. *Hancock's Half Hour* (1956-60) showcased the talents of Britain's best-loved radio comic, Tony Hancock, and Alfie Bass and Bill Fraser, the two main characters of the situation comedy *The Army Game* (Granada, 1957–61). The American shows *The Phil Silvers Show* and *I Love Lucy* were very popular.

In the 1950s, ITV established the practice of buying American shows to supplement its own production. The most popular purchases were traditionally American genres: westerns such as *Gunsmoke/Gun Law, Wagon Train, Cheyenne, The Lone Ranger, Rawhide,* or fast-moving police series such as *Highway Patrol* and *Dragnet.* Gradually British TV began to imitate such police series and the first of these was *No Hiding Place* (A-R, 1959–67). *The Alfred Hitchcock* shows were also popular (*Alfred Hitchcock Pres-*

ents and *The Alfred Hitchcock Hour*). In light entertainment, *The Black and White Minstrel Show* (BBC 1958–78) ran for 20 years until eventually the offensiveness of white performers "blacking up" was finally acknowledged. *Opportunity Knocks!* (A-R, 1956; ABC, 1964–67; Thames, 1968–78) was a talent show—a genre which has continued in many guises since.

Popular music shows began with *Six-Five Special* (BBC, 1957–58) and was followed by *Oh Boy!* (ABC, 1958–59), *Juke Box Jury* (BBC, 1959–67; 1979; 1989–90), *Thank Your Lucky Stars* (ABC, 1958–59). The notorious *Eurovision Song Contest* began in 1956 and the United Kingdom has broadcast it from 1957 to the present day.

The first twice-weekly soap opera was set in a hospital (*Emergency Ward 10*, ATV, 1957–65) and was soon followed by the popular American import *Dr. Kildare*.

Current affairs began to develop as a key area of television broadcasting in the 1950s with the introduction of an early evening five-nights-a-week programme *Tonight* (BBC, 1957–65). General arts programmes were launched with *Monitor* (BBC, 1958–65). The 1950s also saw the introduction of a number of programmes that still ran 40 years later. These include *Grandstand* (BBC, 1958–), the longest running live sports series on TV; *The Sky at Night* (BBC, 1957–), which is an astronomy programme presented by Patrick Moore; and the range of programmes with many titles fronted by Alan Whicker offering his idiosyncratic travelogues of the world. The children's programme *Blue Peter* (BBC) also enjoyed surprising longevity, running from 1958 until the present day.

On 21 April 1964, the BBC launched its second channel—BBC2. To the annoyance of the commercial TV companies (who were not allocated their second channel, Channel 4, for nearly two decades), the BBC could schedule some of its more specialist programming to this "minority" channel and therefore compete more directly with ITV by running the most popular programming on BBC1.

To further restrict the commercial companies, in August 1965 the ITA instructed that from 8:00 to 8:55 P.M. Monday through Friday no more than two of five programmes could be from the United States, and no more than three could be crime or western series. This was followed by the rule whereby only 14% of output could be originated in the United States with a further 2% allowed from the Commonwealth and 1.5% from Europe. These proportions were not changed until the development of cable and satellite in the 1980s, and still pertain to broadcast television.

The largest national audience in British broadcasting history watched the final of the World Cup 1966 in which England beat West Germany 4-2 at Wembly. It is estimated that more than 33 million people watched the final.

On 2 December 1967 colour TV was officially introduced on BBC2. It is generally considered that the 1960s saw some of the most innovative and imaginative programming in the history of broadcasting in Britain. In the field of drama the BBC introduced *The Wednesday Play* (BBC,

1964–70), which, like *Armchair Theatre*, was innovative and commissioned a number of controversial and subsequently famous plays. These included Jeremy Sandford's *Cathy Come Home* (1966), Nell Dunn's *Up the Junction* (1965) and Dennis Potter's *Vote, Vote, Vote for Nigel Barton* (1965). Peter Watkins' *Culloden* (1964) covered an important battle in Scottish history and *The War Game* (1966) dealt with the devastating results of nuclear war. *The War Game* was not transmitted for 25 years because it was considered too distressing. On the popular drama front, one of the most enduring shows was the espionage series *The Avengers* (ABC, 1961–69). Popular too was the BBC's production of the French novelist George Simenon's *Maigret* (BBC, 1960–63) and the medical series set in rural Scotland *Dr. Finlay's Casebook* (BBC, 1962–71), which STV began as a new series in 1993.

The BBC also introduced a new form of gritty realism with the creation of *Z Cars* (BBC, 1962–78), a police show, which was supported with the spin-off *Softly, Softly* (BBC, 1966–70). Another highly successful espionage series was *Danger Man* (ATV/ITC, 1960–61; 1964–67), starring Patrick McGoohan. As a result of this success, McGoohan was allowed to produce the enigmatic *The Prisoner* (Everyman/ATV, 1967–68) which, although only 17 episodes long, became one of the great cult series. Roger Moore starred in two "mid-Atlantic" thrillers, *The Saint* (ATV, 1962–69), which was followed in the 1970s by the unsuccessful series, *The Persuaders!* (Tribune/ITC, 1971–72), co-starring Tony Curtis.

BBC's most successful series *Doctor Who* (1963–89), a science fiction programme about a time lord who travels through time, was designed for children but developed a cult status enjoyed by a huge and faithful adult audience. This was also the decade in which some major soap operas were created. In 1960 Granada TV launched *Coronation Street,* a representation of daily life in a northern working-class community, in the northwest but it was soon networked across the country. It still remains at the top of the audience ratings after over 35 years and transmissions have been increased from twice to four times a week.

In 1964 ATV introduced the highly popular *Crossroads,* a soap set in a Midlands motel, which ran for 24 years. Until 1985 when the BBC introduced the highly successful *EastEnders*, the BBC did not fare well with its soaps. Two were experimented with: *Compact* (1962–65) was set in the offices of a magazine, and *The Newcomers* (1965–69) presented the story of a London family that moved to a country town.

In the 1960s *Comedy Playhouse* (BBC, 1961–74) was created. This was a premiere comedy showcase in which pilots written by writers such as Alan Simpson and Ray Galton were televised. A number of the pilots went on to become some of the best loved comedy series on British TV. They included *Steptoe and Son* (BBC, 1962–65; 1970; 1972, 1974), and *Till Death Us Do Part* (BBC, 1966–68; 1972; 1974–75, which later became *In Sickness and in Health*, BBC 1985–). In the 1960s there was a rise of satirical shows such as *That Was the Week That Was* (BBC, 1962–63) and *Not Only –But Also...* (BBC, 1965–66; 1970), innovative shows such as *Monty Python's Flying Circus* (BBC, 1969–70; 1972–73), and the enduring favourite *Dad's Army* (BBC, 1968–77)—a sitcom about a partially geriatric Home Guard in the early days of the World War II. A number of Gerry Anderson's puppet productions were also produced: *Supercar* (ATV/AP/ITC, 1961–62) *Fireball XL5* (AP/ATV/ITC, 1962–63); Stingray (AP/ATV/ITC, 1964–65), *Thunderbirds* (ATV/AP/ITC, 1965–66) and *Captain Scarlett* and *The Mysterons* (ITC/Century 21 TV Prod, 1967–68).

Eric Morecambe and Ernie Wise grew in popularity to the level of national institution. Their show, under different titles, ran from 1961 to 1983, regularly changing channels. In the pop music field, *Thank Your Lucky Stars* (ABC, 1961–66), *Ready, Steady Go!* (A-R, 1963–66) and the BBC's *Top of the Pops* was launched in 1964 and continued through the 1990s.

In the nonfiction field, a number of notable series were broadcast. In 1967, the BBC initiated David Attenborough's long-running *The World about Us* (BBC, 1967–86), a natural history series which resulted in the creation of the BBC's natural history unit at their Bristol studios. Sir Kenneth Clark's renowned *Civilization* (BBC 1969) charted the history of western culture from the collapse of Greece and Rome to the 20th Century.

A number of series were initiated which continue to this day. ITN created the first half-hour evening news bulletin, *News at Ten*, in 1967; Granada TV's pathbreaking current affairs series *World in Action* was first transmitted in 1963; the BBC's science series *Horizon* began in 1964; the BBC's science futures programme *Tomorrow's World* started in 1965; and the BBC's seasonal weekly football magazine *Match of the Day* was first broadcast in 1964.

Television in the 1970s moved away from the experiments of the 1960s into safer territory. For example, apart from *Play for Today* (BBC, 1970–84), original TV drama was replaced with period- and novel-based serials. These included such series as *The Six Wives of Henry VIII* 1970), *Upstairs Downstairs* (LWT, 1971–75). It was also the decade of the major, solemn documentary series such as *The World at War* (Thames, 1973–74), *The Ascent of Man* (BBC, 1973), and *Life on Earth* (BBC, 1979).

Comedy moved more into the fairly bland with *Are You Being Served?* (BBC, 1973–83). There were, however, some notable exceptions such as *Fawlty Towers* (BBC, 1975; 1979), *Porridge* (BBC, 1974–77), *Some Mothers Do 'Ave 'Em* (BBC, 1973–75; 1978), *Rising Damp* (YTV, 1974–78), *The Fall and Rise of Reginald Perrin* (BBC, 1976–79), *The Liver Birds* (BBC 1969–79), and *The Last of the Summer Wine* (BBC, 1973–). There was also the zany *The Goodies* (BBC, 1970–77; 1980) and the perennially popular *The Two Ronnies* (BBC, 1971–86).

American westerns virtually disappeared in the 1980s and American crime series were in ascendance. However, programmes such as *Kojak* were influential, and indirectly encouraged the development of more action-oriented Brit-

ish crime series. One company in particular—Euston Films Limited (a subsidiary of Thames TV)—developed a portfolio of such programmes for the ITV network. These included *Van der Valk* (Thames, 1972–73; Euston 1977; Thames 1991–92), *The Sweeney* (Euston, 1975–78), *Minder* (Euston, 1979–85; 1988–), *Widows* (Euston 1983; *Widows II* 1985), *Reilly—Ace of Spies* (Euston, 1983). Series from other commercial companies included *The Professionals* (LWT, 1977–83) and two grittily realistic and much applauded serials made by the BBC, *Gangsters* (1976; 1978) and G. F. Newman's four-part *Law and Order* (1978).

There were also a number of highly successful drama series two of which focused on court-room situations—the day-time (three days a week) *Crown Court* (Granada, 1972–84), and the immensely popular *Rumpole of the Bailey* (Thames, 1978–79; 1983; 1987-88; 1991–present day). There was also a highly successful serial set in a secondary school, *Grange Hill* (BBC, 1978–), devised by the ex-teacher Phil Redmond (who went on to found Mersey Productions and to produce Channel 4's equally successful soap *Brookside*.

On the soap front, Yorkshire TV produced a rural daytime serial, *Emmerdale Farm*, which began in 1972 and became increasingly popular as *Emmerdale*. The BBC also experimented with an all black soap (written by a black author), *Empire Road* (1978–79).

In light entertainment, there was Bruce Forsyth's *Generation Game* (BBC, 1971–77), a very popular format which has continued on and off (with Larry Grayson taking over his role); the chat show *Parkinson* (BBC, 1971–82) featuring Michael Parkinson; the long-running *That's Life* (BBC, 1973–94); *Jim'll Fix It* (BBC, 1975–); *The Muppet Show* (ATV/Central, 1976–81); *Blankety Blank* (BBC, 1979–89). There were quiz shows ranging from *Mastermind* (BBC, 1972–) where contestants compete for a title by answering complex general-knowledge questions and obscure questions about specialist areas of knowledge they possess through *Sale of the Century* (Anglia, 1972–83) to the banal *Mr. and Mrs.* (ATV/Border, 1972–88).

There was a great deal of television activity in the 1980s. The commercial second channel was launched on 2 November 1982; Breakfast TV was introduced on three of the four channels; there was a massive growth in video recorder ownership; and cable and satellite networks were established. American soaps such as *Dallas* and *Dynasty* dominated the ratings, media coverage, and popular debate. Possibly the most disastrous attempt to compete with the United States head on was the production of *Chateauvallon* (1985), where five European networks attempted to produce a competitive equivalent to *Dallas*.

In programming terms, the 1980s represented a period when some very expensive classic drama was produced. This included *Death of a Princess* (ATV, 1980) which gained notoriety because it was about the public beheading of a Saudi princess and her lover. The Saudi government tried to stop its transmission, and banned its importation to Saudi Arabia. Because of video technology, it was being clandestinely viewed in Saudi Arabia within 24 hours of first transmission in the United Kingdom. Almost as controversial was the BBC's *Boys from the Blackstuff* (BBC, 1982) about unemployment in Liverpool. Granada TV produced the hugely expensive, highly successful 13-part series *The Jewel in the Crown* (1984), which was shot entirely in India. The BBC also produced the film-noir-style six-part drama, *Edge of Darkness* (1985), about the attempt to sabotage a nuclear power station.

Police dramas proliferated in the 1980s. Both the BBC and ITV had female detectives—*Juliet Bravo* (BBC, 1980–85) and *The Gentle Touch* (LWT, 1980-84) respectively; there was a black detective—*Wolcott* (ATV 1981); a local radio detective, *Shoestring* (BBC, 1979–80); a Chinese detective, *The Chinese Detective* (BBC, 1981–82); a Scottish detective, *Taggart* (STV, 1983–); the long-running series set on the island of Jersey, *Bergerac* (BBC, 1981–91); and the highly acclaimed series set in Oxford starring John Thaw, *Inspector Morse* (Central, 1987–92); and literary private detectives: *The Adventures of Sherlock Holmes* (Granada, 1984–85; *The Return of Sherlock Holmes*, 1986–88; *The Casebook of Sherlock Holmes*, 1991; *Sherlock Holmes*, 1993) with Jeremy Brett offering what is currently considered to be the definitive performance of the great detective; and two famous Agatha Christie detectives—the BBC-produced *Miss Marple* (1984–92) and ITV's *Poirot* (LWT/Carnival 1989–).

Popular non-crime series included the BBC's *A Very Peculiar Practice* (1986 and 1988), set in a university health centre; and two highly realistic long-running series, one based in a fire station, *London's Burning* (LWT, 1988–), and the other an equally long-running hospital series, *Casualty* (BBC, 1986–).

A number of new soap operas started in the 1980s. First there was Scottish TV's daytime soap *Take the High Road* (1980–); Channel 4's *Brookside* (Mersey, 1982–); the BBC's first successful soap which rivaled *Coronation Street* in the audience ratings *EastEnders* (1985–); and a police soap, *The Bill* (Thames, 1984–).

In the 1980s a range of highly successful and, in some cases long-running sitcoms developed. There was Carla Lane's long-running *Bread* (BBC, 1986–) and *Yes, Minister* (BBC, 1980, 1982) was successful enough for Paul Eddington (the minister) to return as the prime minister in *Yes, Prime Minister* in 1986 and 1988. *Hi-De-Hi!* (BBC, 1981–88); *'Allo, 'Allo* (BBC, 1984–92) and *Only Fools and Horses* (BBC, 1981–) are long-running series that, like *Dad's Army* and *Fawlty Towers*, continue to be regularly repeated. Over the decades the BBC has always been more successful with sitcoms than the ITV companies, but in the 1980s ITV enjoyed significant success in this field with Rik Mayall's *The New Statesman* (Yorkshire, 1987–92).

In the 1980s U.K. TV produced its first all-black sitcom, *No Problem!* (C4, 1983–85), Rowan Atkinson in *Blackadder* (BBC, 1983–) and Peter Fluck and Roger Law's award winning satirical puppet show *Spitting Image* (Central, 1984–). This last show has enjoyed significant international format sales.

In the area of light entertainment the BBC's *The Lenny Henry Show* (BBC, 1984–85; 1987–88) and French and Saunders (BBC, 1987–88) were very successful and Channel 4 enjoyed success with the innovative pop music show *The Tube* (Tyne, Tees 1982–87) and the even more original *Max Headroom* (Chrysalis, 1985).

A number of new game shows were introduced in the 1980s. *Bullseye* (ATV, 1981–), a show based on the game of darts and Channel 4's *Countdown* (Yorkshire, 1982–), a word game with which C4 opened transmissions. Two American formats were hugely successful, *The Price Is Right* (Central, 1984–88) and *Blind Date* (LWT, 1985–). In current affairs, the BBC introduced *Newsnight* (1980–) and LWT made the first ethnic minority current affairs programmes for Channel 4, *Black on Black* (1982–85) and *Eastern Eye* (1982–85).

In the 1980s programmes about cooking, e.g. *Food and Drink* (BBC/Bazal, 1982–) and holidays, e.g. *Holiday* (BBC, 1969–), which has a number of rivals including ITV's *Wish You Were Here...?* (Thames, 1976–) proliferated and became hugely popular.

The 1990s saw the development of the satellite companies and the financial battle over the rights to major world sporting events, with Rupert Murdoch seeming to win most of the battles. It was also the decade that the Australian soaps such as *Neighbours* and *Home and Away* dominated the U.K. daytime schedules.

The major drama successes were *Prime Suspect* (Granada, 1991–95), *The Darling Buds of May* (Yorkshire, 1991–), *Oranges Are not the only Fruit* (BBC, 1990) and *Jeeves and Wooster* (Granada, 1990–93), starring Hugh Laurie and Stephen Fry.

The BBC made another foray into soap territory with a spectacular failure set on the Costa del Sol, *Eldorado* (Cinema Verity/J Dy T, 1992–93) which ironically was just beginning to significantly improve its audience ratings when it was cut from broadcast.

Successful sitcoms included *One Foot in the Grave* (BBC, 1990–), Channel 4's set in a TV newsroom *Drop the Dead Donkey* (Hat Trick, 1990–) and *Absolutely Fabulous* (BBC, 1992–). However, probably the most acclaimed comedy show of the decade was the wickedly funny *Have I Got News For You?* (Hat Trick, 1990–) which is a panel game recorded the day before transmission to ensure its biting satire is completely topical.

—Manuel Alvarado

FURTHER READING

Alvarado, Manuel, and John Stewart. *Made for Television: Euston Films Limited*. London: British Film Institute, 1985.

Davis, Anthony. *Television: The First Forty Years*. London: Severn House, 1976.

Halliwell, Leslie, with Philip Purser. *Halliwell's Teleguide*. London: Granada Publishing, 1979. *Halliwell's Television Companion*, 3rd edition, London: Grafton, 1986.

Kingsley, Hilary, and Geoff Tibbals. *Box of Delights: The Golden Years of Television*. London: Macmillan, 1989.

Vahimagi, Tise, editor. *British Television: An Illustrated Guide*. Oxford: Oxford University Press, 1994.

BRITISH SKY BROADCASTING

International Satellite Broadcasting Service

British Sky Broadcasting (BSkyB) is the first entrepreneurial venture of any significance to have challenged the hitherto closely regulated, four-channel, public service character of British television. As part of the international media empire that includes the FOX network and Star TV, BSkyB has rapidly become a major player in the world broadcasting market-place. It is a large commercial satellite network, available principally to viewers in the British Isles but capable of reception anywhere within the European ASTRA satellite system footprint.

Forty per cent owned by News International and successfully floated on the British Stock Exchange as a public company at the end of 1994, BSkyB is instantly associated with the name of Rupert Murdoch who invested heavily in the venture from 1983, accepting enormous initial losses while waiting for satellite television in Britain to become profitable. Although many other satellite services are available to British audiences, the wide choice offered by BSkyB's continually expanding package of channels is undoubtedly the main incentive to satellite antenna acquisition; the network has come to be regarded by the terrestrial broadcasting sector as the true commercial competition. In just over a decade from its inception, BSkyB has firmly established itself as the third force in British broadcasting.

The inauspicious origins of BSkyB can be traced to Rupert Murdoch's purchase in 1983 of a 65% share (subsequently increased to 82%) in a fledgling London-based operation called Satellite Television Ltd which, as the first European satellite television channel, had been transmitting programmes for about a year to small audiences in Western Europe over one of the earliest EUTELSAT satellites. Murdoch, who has described satellite television as "the most important single advance since Caxton invented the printing press", re-launched the company as Sky Channel and commenced broadcasting a new programming mix in January 1984, receivable in Britain only by cable households (at that time no more than about 10,000). By 1987 Sky had achieved an 11.3% share of viewing in those homes capable of receiving it and had raised some £28 million in rights issues to fund its planned expansion into direct-to-home delivery.

Sky's expansion, widely criticised at the time as irresponsibly risky, began in February 1989 when the company's new three-channel package went on air over the first Luxembourg-owned ASTRA satellite. Indeed, since U.K. broadcasting legislation did not then permit a satellite undertaking to uplink signals from British soil, Sky was only legally able to do so by virtue of its non-British transmission source. At first available unscrambled and free-of-charge, the original Sky package consisted of a premium film channel (Sky Movies), a 24-hour news channel (Sky News) and a general entertainment family channel (Sky One). This package, however, experienced a very slow initial take-up by the British public for a number of reasons, the main one being

that many potential customers were holding back pending the heavily advertised launch of the rival satellite service, British Satellite Broadcasting (BSB), which promised subscribers an attractive range of alternative benefits with a distinctly British cultural emphasis.

The rise and fall of BSB represents something of a fiasco in broadcasting deregulation, but in retrospect can be seen as an unprecedented opportunity for the entrepreneurship of Rupert Murdoch's Sky. This organisation, specially provided for in the British Government's Broadcasting Act of 1990, was licensed as the official Direct Broadcast by Satellite (DBS) provider, legally enabled to uplink from British soil and established as the direct competitor of Sky. BSB was claimed to possess an enormous technological advantage over its rival in that it would use a much higher powered satellite with the more technically sophisticated D-MAC transmission standard delivering a higher fidelity TV picture than Sky's inferior (but more affordable) PAL standard. BSB's two Marco Polo satellites (at an astronomical cost of some £500 million each) were duly launched from Cape Kennedy by Space Shuttle between August 1989 and early 1990, by which time Sky had been consolidating its audience for over a year. After several embarrassing delays, BSB launched on 29 April 1990 and its five-channel service competed uneasily with Sky throughout the summer and autumn of 1990 but was even slower than Sky to attract consumer interest. On 2 November 1990 (ironically the day after the Broadcasting Act was finally passed), BSB suddenly collapsed, recognising that the market could not sustain two such capital-intensive satellite operations in competition. Without the permission of the Independent Broadcasting Authority, Sky immediately announced a merger with BSB to form the BSkyB network. Though this was, in effect, a serious breach of BSB's contract, the merger (in effect, a take-over) was allowed to proceed in the best interests of viewers and transitional arrangements were put in hand to compensate dispossessed BSB subscribers so that a five-channel service would continue to be available to them via Marco Polo until the end of 1992 but provided by the new BSkyB organisation.

Freed from non-terrestrial competition, BSkyB was now in a position to rationalise its activities, especially in the area of subscription services. It immediately re-launched BSB's Movie Channel, having acquired the rights to an expanded cartel of Hollywood feature films, thus giving itself greater flexibility and market domination in movie scheduling. In October 1992, the company replaced a short-lived Comedy Channel experiment with a third movie channel, Sky Movies Gold, dedicated to classic films. Then, in September 1993, BSkyB introduced its most aggressive market move to date when it announced the "Sky Multi-channels" subscription package with various price options to suit viewer preference. By now a Sports Channel had been added to the network, later to be followed by Sky Sports 2, Sky Travel and Sky Soaps. Interestingly, the Multichannels package also included a number of competing English language ASTRA channels, such as Discovery, Bravo, Children's Channel, Nickolodeon and QVC which pay BSkyB a premium for the use of its patented Videocrypt™ decoding technology. Hence, BSkyB cleverly generates revenue, not only from its own programmes but also from those of its immediate competitors.

Rupert Murdoch initially regarded the Sky satellite venture as a five-year risk to profitability from 1988. After gigantic early losses which would have deterred more timid investors, the company had already begun to move into profit by early 1992 and has since built itself into an extremely valuable and powerful business. In the five months between June and November 1993 alone, BSkyB experienced an impressive 30% increase in its operating profit and has continued to thrive with the gradual increase in satellite dish penetration. More recently, much to the chagrin of terrestrial broadcasters, the network has concentrated on purchasing exclusive rights to major sporting events in the hope of attracting many new subscribers. In the late 1990s, digital television will undoubtedly offer BSkyB new opportunities but it is also likely to usher in serious competition from new satellite ventures. BSkyB has, however, become so well established as part of an enormous vertically-integrated international media empire that it will probably continue to maintain its market advantage unless cross-media ownership rules eventually place debilitating constraints on its potential.

—Tony Pearson

FURTHER READING

Chippindale, Peter. *Dished: The Rise and Fall of British Satellite Broadcasting.* London: Simon and Schuster, 1991.

Collins, Richard. *Satellite Television in Western Europe.* London: John Libbey, 1990.

———. "The Language of Advantage: Satellite Television in Western Europe." In, Collins, Richard, editor. *Television: Policy and Culture.* London: Unwin Hyman, 1990.

———. "The Prognosis for Satellite Television in the U.K." In, Collins, Richard, editor. *Television: Policy and Culture.* London: Unwin Hyman, 1990.

———. *The Second Generation: The Lessons of Satellite Television in Western Europe.* (PICT Policy Research Paper, No. 12.) London: Economic and Social Research Council (ESRC), 1991.

———. *Direct Broadcasting by Satellite in the U.K.—From Sky to BSkyB.* (PICT Policy Research Paper, No. 15.) London: Economic and Social Research Council (ESRC), 1991.

Crouch, Colin. "The Perversity of Television Markets (Monopoly and Regulation in British Broadcasting)." *Political Quarterly* (London), January-March 1994.

"In a Hole." *The Economist* (London), 17 June 1995.

"The Nimbleness of Murdoch." *The Economist* (London), 20 May 1995.

See also Murdoch, Rupert; Satellite

BRITISH TELEVISION

British television is impossible to pigeonhole. Eminently capacious, it has increasingly been open to multiple goals, forces and programming approaches. It has responded to new demands more often by accretion and absorption than by re-direction. Though innundated with public service principles, these have periodically been retuned to chime both with shifting social needs and with more pragmatic imperatives. British television has simultaneously pursued intrinsic communication purposes (enriching viewers, serving society) and extrinsic ones (organisational survival, earnings, power).

It also tends to be taken seriously. For many Britons, broadcasting is a social pillar that closely affects the well-being of other key institutions—not only the crown, Parliament and the church but also sport, education, theater, the arts and film. Much valued, much debated, often officially enquired into, and much criticised, it is treated as both a national asset and a national scapegoat. Its present and future condition are therefore thought to matter greatly. In 1990s television, however, the British way of managing the tensions of continuity vs. change is being severely tested.

Television in the United Kingdom has historically been a highly regulated public service system that has periodically admitted, while striving to contain, commercially competitive impulses. Three of its four core terrestrial channels still have public service remits (BBC-1, BBC-2 and Channel 4) and the other significant public service requirements (channel 3 of Independent Television). Whereas BBC-2 and Channel 4 have predominantly catered for minority and specialist tastes (each attracting around 10 to 12% of viewers), competition for larger audiences has been waged between BBC-1 and ITV's Channel 3 (with the latter usually gaining a somewhat greater share).

Although until recently the notion of "public service" was nowhere explicitly defined, it was widely understood to embrace purposes of programming range, quality, and popularity with the general viewing audience. Other emphases have included: universality of reception; reflection of national identity and community; provision of a civic forum; special regard for minorities; respect for children's all-round personality and development needs; due impartiality in coverage of controversial issues; avoiding offense to law and order, taste and decency; and the editorial independence of program makers within the overall regulatory framework.

The sway of the public service idea helps to explain many past programming strengths of British television:

- Heavy investment in news and current affairs, including treatment of election campaigns as transforming civic events.

- An impressive tradition of children's television, including a wide range of entertainment, information, drama and animation, not only on Saturday mornings but also on mid-afternoon weekdays on BBC-1 and Channel 3.

- Provision of a very wide range of drama in format, subject matter and cultural level.

- Leading soap operas frequently laced with explorations of significant social issues and moral dilemmas.

- Vigorous documentary strands, especially on BBC-2 and Channel 4.

- The cultural patronage role of arts coverage, including BBC funding of a chorus and five large orchestras and commissioning of feature films by Channel 4 and BBC-2.

- Well-resourced programming in natural history, popular science and technology.

- Investment in a wide range of educational television (for schools, further and adult education, the Open University and prime-time public awareness campaigns), social action programs, public access programs and programs for immigrant communities.

Three organisations have been central in the governance of British television. First, government responsibility for broadcasting is lodged with the Department of the National Heritage (succeeding the Home Office in 1992, which had previously taken over from the Postmaster General). This appoints the members of all regulatory bodies, oversees policy development (sometimes jointly with the Department of Trade and Industry), and initiates legislation and debates in Parliament.

Second, a board of 12 governors is required to direct the British Broadcasting Corporation (BBC) in the public interest. The BBC is a large organisation of approximately 25,000 employees and a £2 billion annual income, the bulk of which comes from a licence fee that is levied on every household with a television set. Fixed by negotiation between the BBC and the government, the level of the fee has broadly kept pace with the retail price index since the mid-1980s. The BBC's obligations are outlined in a charter and agreement, the present terms of which will run until 2006 (although BBC finance will be reviewed in 2001). For the first time, these spell out in some detail both its public service programming role and the governors' supervisory duties as well as authorising BBC involvement in commercial activities. The governors appoint the BBC director-general and, in consultation with him, other members of a board of management. Traditionally, management decided most matters of BBC policy and programming with the governors serving more as a sounding board and ultimate authorizer, commenting only after the fact on individual broadcasts of which they approved or disapproved. From the

1970s, however, the governors became increasingly active and in the late 1980s were even a spur for fundamental organisational reform.

Third, all advertising-financed television is under the jurisdiction of the Independent Television Commission (ITC; known in previous incarnations as the Independent Broadcasting Authority and the Independent Television Authority). Its writ runs over Independent Television, a federal grouping of 15 regionally-based companies, plus companies of national news and breakfast television, which jointly schedule the nationally networked portion of Channel 3; Channel 4, a non-profit "publisher-broadcaster" (commissioning and scheduling but not making programs), which is legally required to be innovative and to cater for different interests and tastes from those served by Channel 3; Channel 5, a new terrestrial service that will cover approximately two thirds of the country from 1997; and cable and satellite services originating in Britain. The ITC will eventually be responsible as well for any channels of digital terrestrial television that may be introduced.

The ITC's duties are set out in the Broadcasting Act of 1990, and its 12 members are appointed by the government. The main tasks are to franchise the commercial television companies by a process of first tendering for and then auctioning the licences and to enforce the licence conditions thereafter. The act posits a "quality threshold", which all applying companies must cross before being admitted to the auction itself, at which the highest bidder would normally be the winner. Since 1993, when the new Channel 3 licensees took over, the ITC has been a relatively resolute regulator, holding the companies to their obligations (through directives, warnings and fines as necessary) and annually reporting on their programming performance.

Three further features of the system should also be mentioned. First, the opening of Channel 4 in 1982 encouraged the growth of a large sector of some 900 independent program-making companies of diverse sizes and production specialisms. This was strengthened by the Broadcasting Act of 1990, which obliged all terrestrial broadcasters to commission at least 25% of their output from such sources, and will be further boosted by many commissions from Channel 5.

Second, elaborate codes of practice have been evolved to cover a wide range of matters on which programs could cause offense. The ITC has drawn up four such codes—on program sponsorship; advertising standards and practices; advertising breaks; and the Program Code—for their conformity to which the ITV companies are required to introduce effective compliance procedures. The BBC has developed a 300-page booklet of Producers' Guidelines, oversight of which is vested in a four-person Editorial Policy Unit. In addition, for the specific areas of violence, sexual display, taste, decency and bad language, the government in 1988 established a Broadcasting Standards Council to issue the Code of Practice that all broadcasters must take into account and in light of which viewers may submit complaints.

Third, public expectations of broadcasting and options for its future development have been shaped in the past by a series of comprehensive reviews by independent Committees of enquiry appointed by the government. (Their main reports are listed in the suggestions for further reading accompanying this essay).

In recent times, however, all these structures have been buffeted by both internal and external pressures to change. Within British broadcasting, technological developments are paving the way for new program-delivery systems, multichannel expansion and intensified competition for viewers' attention. Television finance is becoming much tighter, as production costs escalate (responding to competition for top performers, programs and sporting events) beyond the general inflation rate. External markets—as arenas of sales, imports, co-production and international rivalry—are becoming more salient. To cope, revamped organisational structures, program commissioning strategies, scheduling practices, accounting systems and managerial skills are all required. In commercial television the rules on concentration of ownership are also being relaxed to encourage the emergence of "national champions" in global markets.

Admittedly, adaptation to change has been eased by the relatively slow diffusion of multichannel offerings to the British audience. Although cable franchises cover 70% of the population, not all are up and running, and only one in five households passed have subscribed. Satellite television, provided by BSkyB (40% owned by Rupert Murdoch's News International Corporation), has been more successful, gaining over 3 million subscribers to packages of up to 28 channels, and profiting especially from people's willingness to pay extra for premium sports and movie channels. But with cable and satellite services in only about a fifth of British homes and attracting an overall audience share under 10%, the multichannel revolution is seeping into British television instead of taking it by storm.

Nevertheless, around broadcasting, the values, expectations and ways of life of British viewers are also changing. The advance of consumerism breeds a more choosy and critical audience. The advance of social complexity multiplies sub-group tastes and identities and fragments moral and political opinion. Leaders in many spheres face waning respect for and growing scepticism toward their claims and credentials. The brokerage role of programming between elite perspectives and mass interests has been disrupted.

In these conditions, British television resembles a large ocean-liner, fashioned by a master ship-builder and serving many classes of passengers in a host of compartments, which is sailing through ever stormier seas that may—or may not—tear it apart! How did it get that way? From its inception British television has progressed through five overlapping phases.

First, up to 1955, development of the medium was subordinated to the needs of radio. Having provided sound broadcasting since 1922, the BBC inaugurated the world's first television service in 1936, shut it down during World War II, and reopened it in 1946. In the early post-war years, however, television enthusiasts waged an uphill battle against those in higher BBC echelons who saw it as a cultural Trojan horse—committed predominantly to entertainment, brash and childish, not very civilised, and conducive to audience passivity. The balance began to shift in 1952, first, after the appointment as director-general of Sir Ian Jacob, who realised that television had to be taken more seriously, and secondly, with the striking success in June of that year of the televising of the Coronation of Queen Elizabeth—as a spectacle with great symbolic impact, audience reach and appeal.

This phase came to an end through a characteristic political development, one that aimed to reconcile a cultural mission for broadcasting with chances to exploit the advertising potential of television and to upgrade the claims of popular taste. The Television Act of 1954 authorised creation of a new advertising-financed service, to be called Independent Television (purposely not "Commercial Televison"), in competition with the BBC. Although the Beveridge Committee enquiry (1951) had recommended renewal of the BBC's monopoly, the incoming conservative government of 1951 adopted a minority report that proposed "some element of competition" in television. Bitterly fought inside and outside Parliament, the government had to concede crucial safeguards against rampant commercialism: no sponsorship; only time spots of controlled length and frequency would be sold to advertisers who would have no say in program content; and creation of a new public corporation, an Independent Television Authority, to appoint the companies and supervise their performance in light of requirements specified in the act.

A second phase followed from the mid-1950s to the early 1960s of vigorous but creative competition between an insurgent ITV and a threatened BBC, which, though it aroused doubts, fear and dismay among some at the time, is now widely regarded as having advanced the medium's programming powers and viewers' all-round enjoyment. From the outset, ITV set its cap at neglected mass tastes, especially for entertainment, while cultivating a more informal and accessible presentation style and celebrating what one executive termed "people's television". After experiencing a dramatic loss of viewers (down to a 28% share at the nadir), the BBC fought back hard all across the programming board.

Many achievements ensued. Since ITV was based on separate companies in London and other parts of the country, British television catered for the first time to diverse regional interests in addition to metropolitan ones. Television news was transformed—with named news readers, pace, incisiveness and eye-catching pictures. Inhibitions on political and election coverage were shed. Saturday afternoons were devoted to coverage of top sporting events. A host of memorable children's programs were developed. New forms of television drama were pioneered. New comedy stars (e.g. Tony Hancock, Jimmy Edwards, Charlie

Duke) were born, served by high-profile writers. The BBC created an early evening topical magazine, *Tonight*, the sprightliness and irreverence of which broke sharply with its traditions. Yet the flag of authoritativeness was also flown in its weekly current affairs program, *Panorama*, a new arts magazine, *Monitor*, and an in-depth interview program, *Face to Face*.

In this phase, the British concern to blend potentially opposed impulses in its television system remained strong. For its part, the BBC had to become more competitive and seek a larger audience share to sustain its claim to licence fee funding and its status as Britain's national broadcaster. But this was not to be its sole aim and was to be achieved through high standards of quality across a broad range of programming. Endorsing its record, the Pilkington Committee enquiry (1962) recommended that the BBC be awarded a second channel (BBC-2, which opened in 1966). Finding that ITV programming had become too commercial, trivial and undemanding, the committee proposed stronger regulatory powers and duties for the ITA. The next television act accordingly instructed the Authority to ensure a "proper balance and wide range of subject matter having regard both to the programmes as a whole and also to the day of the week on which, and the times of day at which, the programmes are broadcast" as well as "a wide showing of programmes of merit." The ITV companies were also obliged to submit their program schedules for advance approval to the ITA, who could direct the exclusion of any items from them.

In much of the 1960s and early 1970s, a third phase ensued, as hierarchical and consensual ties loosened and traditional institutions were criticised more often in the name of modernisation. Broadcasters became concerned to portray the different sectors of a pluralist society realistically in both fictional and factual programs and to be more probingly critical themselves. For Hugh Greene, BBC director-general from 1960 to 1969, public service implied putting an honest mirror before society, reflecting what was there, whether it was "bigotry...and intolerance or accomplishment and inspiring achievement". He also believed broadcasters had a duty to take account of changes in society, the challenges and options they posed and where they might lead. He even regarded impudence as an acceptable broadcasting quality (a far cry from founding father John Reith's stress on dignity). Illustrative of this spirit were hard-hitting satire (*That Was the Week That Was*), anarchic comedy (*Monty Python*), more forceful political interviewing, series set in northern towns (*Coronation Street*, *The Likely Lads*), realistic police series (*Z Cars*), social-issue drama (*Cathy Come Home*) and socially conscious comedy (*Til' Death Us Do Part*, featuring a Cockney racist, and *Steptoe and Son*, featuring a rag-and-bone man and his son).

In a fourth phase throughout much of the 1970s, British television increasingly acquired the image of an over-mighty subject, attracting unprecedentedly sharp criticism and pressure to mend its ways. On balance, more of the fire was directed at factual than fictional programming.

In 1971, politicians of all parties had been outraged by a BBC program about labour in opposition, *Yesterday's Men*, deploring its flippant tone, lack of openness when interviewees were briefed about the intended approach, and questions put to former Prime Minister Harold Wilson that seemed beyond the pale (e.g. about earnings from his memoirs). Thereafter, the political establishment became more assertive of its interests, more organised in their pursuit and more vocal in their complaints. Spokespersons of other groups also voiced dissatisfaction over stereotypical portrayals and limited access. Traditional moralists (like the members of Mary Whitehouse's Viewers' and Listeners' Association) were deeply unhappy about what they regarded as increasingly permissive depictions of sex and violence in programs. Media sociologists chipped in with a series of studies purporting to undermine the pretensions of broadcasters to impartiality and objectivity and to demonstrate how news coverage of social conflicts supported the ideological status quo. Other critics perceived a middle-ground convergence in BBC and ITV output that excluded unconventional perspectives and opinions. Behind these otherwise different reactions, there was also a shared concern over the difficulties of holding broadcasters to account for their policies and performance.

Structural responses to this chorus of criticism included some tightening of editorial controls; creation by the BBC of a Community Programming Unit to help groups to present their ideas on their own terms in a new strand of access broadcasting; and establishment of a Programme Complaints Board by the BBC to consider complaints against producers of unfair representation and invasions of privacy. The most important outcome, however, was the creation in 1982 of Channel 4 with its brief to be different, experimental and heterodox. Although commercials would be sold on the channel, pains were taken to avoid competition for advertising with ITV. Its budget was therefore fixed by the IBA on the basis of funds it levied from the ITV companies, who were allowed to sell (and keep the revenues from) its advertising. Thus, a viable source of funding would be tapped, the Channel would be guaranteed sufficient resources for its tasks, and its innovative efforts would be insulated from advertisers' conformist pressures.

Beginning in the mid-1980s, the fifth phase of British television has been dominated by issues of structure and finance. In this period, all British broadcasters have had to adjust to a new and less supportive political mood—one that regards television more as an industry than a cultural agency and its institutions as badly in need of a shake-up. A tide of radically revisionist commercialism was unleashed, which effected major changes but was also resisted and curbed at key points.

The curtain-raiser was appointment in 1985 of the Peacock Committee on Financing the BBC to consider alternative sources of revenue to the licence fee, including advertising and sponsorship. Its 1986 report condemned the existing system as a cosy and overly "comfortable duopoly", lacking financial disciplines to keep costs down in both the BBC and ITV; it defined the fundamental aim of broadcasting as increasing through competition "the freedom of choice of the consumer and the opportunities available to offer alternative wares to the public"; and it proposed that "public service" in British television be scaled down from a full-blown to a market-supplementing model. Yet the committee also counselled against the sale of commercials by the BBC, since competition for advertising would narrow its range of programming. But although the government accepted this last recommendation, it drew heavily on the committee's rationale for its policies to overhaul British television.

The government acted directly on the advertising-financed sector through three significant features of the 1990 Broadcasting Act. One was the introduction of competition for advertising by requiring Channel 4 to sell its own commercials and authorising a fifth commercial channel. Another was the new franchising system of auctioning licences to the highest bidder among qualified applicants. A third was a change in status of the regulator, whereby the new ITC lost the old IBA's broad powers to preview programs and schedules in advance; hereafter it could only enforce company compliance to specific obligations defined in law and licences after the fact.

Even so, a full-scale commercialism was avoided. Channel 4 was given a safety net, whereby it would be subsidised by the Channel 3 companies should its advertising income fall below 14% of the total advertising and sponsorship income of Channels 3 and 4. And in a period of intense debate while the act was passing through Parliament, the "quality threshold" for franchise applicants was much strengthened. Companies would have to give a "sufficient amount of time" to a series of mandated programs—which included national and regional news, current affairs, religion and children's television; cater for a variety of tastes; and give a "sufficient amount of time" to "programmes that are of high quality". Moreover, the ITC fleshed out some of these requirements in precise quantitative terms, specifying, for example, that companies would have to offer 90 minutes of high-quality current affairs programs weekly, at least two hours of religious programs and 10 hours a week of children's television, including a range of entertainment, drama and information.

The government promoted change at the BBC by conveying its expectation of far-reaching reforms, appointing a forceful chair of the Board of Governors (Marmaduke Hussey) who shared its priorities, and implying that the terms of the next BBC Charter (to take effect in 1996) were at stake in the process. Led by director-generals Michael Checkland (from 1987) and John Birt (from 1991), the BBC's managerial structure was overhauled. Overheads were cut, axing more than 2,000 jobs. Most important from the government's standpoint were two steps. An internal market (known as Producers' Choice) was introduced in relations between program producers and providers of technical facilities. And an aggressive policy was adopted of BBC entry into international markets of multichannel television, program sales and co-production. Nevertheless, the BBC also undertook a fundamental review of the meaning and implications of "public service" in multichannel conditions, the results of which appeared in *Extending Choice* (1992) and *People and Programmes* (1995). Concentrating mainly on future directions and roles, the former proposed three priority purposes: "informing the national debate"; "expressing British culture and entertainment"; and "creating opportunities for education". More attuned to the modern choosy audience member, the latter stressed themes of relevance and accessibility and the need for program makers in all fields to take greater account of popular interests, tastes and attitudes.

New conditions have made it more difficult to classify and give an appropriate label to the British television system. The public service element remains pervasive but is less influential and stable than formerly. Significant elements of competition have been injected but have not been given their full head. The British pattern is nowhere near the U.S. model—an essentially commercial system with a marginal public service to pick up its slack. Neither is it even a compartmentalised half-and-half system, pitting a ratings-sensitive sector against a quality-sensitive public service sector. What seems to be emerging in Britain is a thoroughly mixed television system. Competitive populism is advancing everywhere in it, but public service is nowhere denied. The impulses are not segregated in separate camps. Instead, they are commingled in every service, albeit in different balances and gradations—with social responsibilities most influential in the programming of BBC-2 and Channel 4, next at BBC-1 and least so (but still a presence) at Channel 3.

Three further features dominate. First, the BBC is still a major force in British television, now officially confirmed as such by the government, but is also a rather torn force. Charged with multiple tasks and a focus of numerous expectations, the BBC is having to ride many horses at once. For its *raison d'être* in a multichannel system, it must offer distinctive programs (ones the market will not supply), though to justify its claim to licence fee support from all viewers in the land, it must engage in head-to-head competition with ITV for the mass audience. Although the government says that as the U.K.s' main public service broadcaster, its primary role should be making programs for the domestic audience, it also urges the BBC "to increase its income from its commercial activities" (to contribute to U.K. exports, to ensure that a distinctive British culture is spread in world markets and to generate more income for program making). It must reconcile its reputation for quality, responsibility, seriousness and high standards with recognition of the fact that when people have a lot of choice, excellence and authority may not be enough to bring home the bacon. It must keep the creative juices flowing within a framework of much closer budgetary and managerial control. It must reconcile its tradition of editorial independence with demands for increased public accountability.

Time will tell whether this can be accomplished. In high policy terms, however, one BBC endeavour to do so should be noted—in its present emphasis on yet more extended broadcasting range. The thrust for each main area of production is to offer a full mix of programs from the demanding to the easy-to-take, the more esoteric to the most popular. "Distinctiveness" may then be satisfied at one end (say, with lavish classic serials or extensive election coverage), while mass appeal can be sought elsewhere (even by inserting programs into the schedules that would not have previously made it to the screen, such as chat, game and blind-dating shows).

Second, in Britain's gradually emerging multichannel system, the force of audience competition, even if still controlled, is reshaping everything it touches. Competitive scheduling has become more concerted and aggressive on all channels. Initiative and power have shifted to the schedulers, to whose more formed requirements creative staffs must tailor their work. Their audience targets and expectations have become more definite; audience research and other data are being articulated more systematically to their needs. Calculations of costs-by-viewers-reached are playing a bigger part. Competitive bidding between BSkyB, the BBC and ITV for coverage rights to major sporting events has heated up, and Parliament has keenly debated proposals to guarantee access for terrestrial channels against exclusive satellite deals. When Channel 5 opens in 1997, able to counter-program against the established services, all these pressures will be exacerbated.

One consequence of such a situation is that the competition for viewers becomes more of a struggle to be noticed. More favored are strategies of immediate attention gaining and qualities of pace, impact, brevity, the arresting, and personal stories with which ordinary people can identify. A new-found populism has come into vogue—with talk shows, studio audiences, phone-ins (even e-mail-ins!), after-discussion polls, clips from viewers' home videos and camcorders all on the increase. Overall, more money and screen time are being devoted to program promotion. Even Channel 4 (so successful in selling its own advertising that its safety net will be phased out) has not been immune to these tendencies. Though praised by the ITC for fulfilling its remit with "general distinction", some of its recent output has appeared to equate innovation with outrageousness and sensationalist taboo-breaking.

Third, both continuing commitment and increasing uncertainty attend some of the programming areas on which Britain's public service tradition was based. The presence of two well-supported and widely viewed lesser channels—BBC-2 and Channel 4—sustains the production bases of minority genres that might otherwise go to the wall. Nevertheless, some of those genres are now under a degree of strain:

- Children's television: despite a continuing commitment to range, relying more on animation and on licensing products from program spin-offs.
- Documentaries: treatments tending to focus less on socio-political issues and more on slices of popular life in modern society.

- Current affairs: still impressive for extent and breadth of significant issues covered, but party politicians appear less often (except in Sunday morning interview programs).
- Arts programming: some strands have been moved out of peak time and popular culture is receiving more attention.
- Soap operas: scheduled in the early evening, some of these bear heavy competitive responsibilities, with more episodes per week scheduled and more melodramatic story lines plotted.
- Other drama: more reliance on high-profile stars and actors and an increase in serials based on crime, law and order, hospital settings, emergency services and urban grittiness.

Of course evaluations of such a mixed and fluid system will vary. It is less "priestly" and sometimes more flashy than in the past. Some observers perceive a gradual erosion of standards of quality, and some top writers and producers have complained of more bureaucratic interference in the creative process. As evidence that British broadcasting is artistically still in fine shape, however, others point to the recent appearance of such outstanding programs: *Pride and Prejudice* (classic serial), *The Borrowers* (children's serial), *Our Friends in the North* (socio-political drama), *Have I Got News for You* (inventive comedy quiz), *Rory Bremner Who Else?* (satire), *Newsnight* and Channel 4 News. Even if the world is spinning away from public service as it used to be conceived, British television still differs greatly from U.S. television in important ways:

- Its network news bulletins are models of solidity.
- It has no tabloid magazines, heavy on emotion-packed tales (such as *A Current Affair*).
- It does not treat children predominantly as mere excitement-loving consumers.
- Its resort to violence in programs is measurably less.
- It has not killed off the documentary tradition.
- It continues to support drama of social relevance.
- Advertising on the main commercial channels is limited to seven minutes per hour, and product placement is strictly prohibited.

—Jay G. Blumler

FURTHER READING

Barnett, Steven, and Andrew Curry. *The Battle for the BBC: A British Broadcasting Conspiracy?* London: Aurum Press 1994.

Blumler, Jay G. "The British Approach to Public Service Broadcasting: From Confidence to Uncertainty." In, Avery, Robert K., editor. *Public Service Broadcasting in a Multichannel Environment.* New York and London: Longman, 1993.

———. "United Kingdom." In, Bertelsmann Foundation and European Institute for the Media, editors. *Televi-*

sion *Requires Responsibility*. Gutersloh, Germany: Bertelsmann Foundation Publishers, 1994.

Briggs, Asa. *The History of Broadcasting in the United Kingdom*. Volumes 1-5, Oxford and New York: Oxford University Press, 1961, 1965, 1970, 1979, 1995.

———. *Governing the BBC*. London: British Broadcasting Corporation, 1979.

———. *The BBC: The First Fifty Years*. Oxford, and New York: Oxford University Press, 1985.

Burns, Tom. *The BBC: Public Institution, Private World*. London: MacMillan, 1977.

Extending Choice: The BBC's Role in the New Broadcasting Age. London: BBC, 1992.

Hearst, Stephen. "Broadcasting Regulation in Britain." In, Blumler, Jay G., editor. *Television and the Public Interest: Vulnerable Values in West European Broadcasting*. London, Newbury Park and New Delhi: Sage, 1992.

Nossiter, T. J. "British Television: A Mixed Economy." In, Blumler, Jay G., and T. J. Nossiter, editors. *Broadcasting Finance in Transition: A Comparative Handbook*. Oxford, U.K. and New York: Oxford University Press, 1991.

Paulu, Burton. *British Broadcasting in Transition*. London: MacMillan, 1961.

People and Programmes: BBC Radio and Television for an Age of Choice. London: BBC, 1995.

Potter, Jeremy. *Independent Television in Britain*. Volumes 3 and 4, London and Basingstoke: MacMillan, 1989 and 1990.

Sargant, Naomi. "United Kingdom." In, Mitchell, Jeremy and Jay G. Blumler, editors. *Television and the Viewer Interest: Explorations in the Responsiveness of European Broadcasters*. London: John Libbey, 1994.

Sendall, Bernard. *Independent Television in Britain*. Volumes 1 and 2, London and Basingstoke: MacMillan, 1982 and 1983.

Wedell, E. G. *Broadcasting Policy in Britain*. London: Michael Joseph, 1968.

Wilson, H. H. *Pressure Group: The Campaign for Commercial Television*. London: Secker and Warburg, 1961.

OFFICIAL ENQUIRY COMMITTEE REPORTS

The Sykes Report. Cmnd. 1951. London: His Majesty's Stationary Office: 1923.

The Crawford Report. Cmnd. 2599. London: His Majesty's Stationary Office, 1926.

The Selsdon Report. Cmnd. 4793. London: His Majesty's Stationary Office, 1935

The Ullswater Report. Cmnd. 5091. London: His Majesty's Stationary Office, 1936.

The Beveridge Report. Cmnd. 8116. London: His Majesty's Stationary Office, 1951.

The Pilkington Report. Cmnd. 1753. London: Her Majesty's Stationary Office, 1962.

The Annan Report. Cmnd. 6753. 1977. London: Her Majesty's Stationary Office, 1977.

The Peacock Report. Cmnd. 9824. London: Her Majesty's Stationary Office, 1986.

BRITTAIN, DONALD

Canadian Documentary Filmmaker

Donald Brittain is well known for his National Film Board documentaries, all shown on Canadian Broadcasting Corporation (CBC) television. In the 1980s Donald Brittain directed *Running Man*, an early exploration of homosexuality in the CBC's topical anthology *For the Record*. He then created two biographical docudramas: one about mobster and union boss Hal Banks in the two-hour docudrama special *Canada's Sweetheart: The Saga of Hal C. Banks* (1985), the other about Prime Minister William Lyon MacKenzie King, in a six-hour miniseries, *The King Chronicles* (1987).

In *Canada's Sweetheart* Brittain shows us, through the lens of the Seafarers' International Union, the primitive state of labour-management relations in Canada from the late 1940s to early 1960s. In *The King Chronicles* he explores Canadian political culture from the days following World War I to the wrenching changes in society in the aftermath of World War II. Brittain spells out Canadian complicity in the activities of both men—an imported thug who controlled Great Lakes shipping and a prime minister who, to quote Brittain's narrative, was "a

creature who cast no shadow though he ruled the land of the midnight sun."

Canada's Sweetheart incorporated interviews with survivors from those years, stills, newsreels, and dramatisation. Brittain uses full colour for the dramatised Royal Commission hearings, the interviews with real people and some of the flashbacks. Black-and-white scenes include Banks' quiet entrance into Canada and his equally surreptitious exit, and union leader Jim Todd's futile challenge to an executive in a packed meeting hall. Some scenes which are particularly violent or menacing are given a specifically *film noir* treatment.

The film is also quite self-reflexive. Todd, recalls how Banks' bully-boys came to his house one night while his wife was in the kitchen. The camera then discloses the hitherto silent Mrs. Todd who tells us that "Friday is fish and chips night" and that when she heard a commotion she went into the living room with a full pan of boiling fat in her hand. At her firm word "that dinner was ready", the thug left. Her understated telling of the situation is far more effective than a dramatisation would be, a strong illustration of what happened when ordinary seamen and lock masters had finally had enough. In another sequence Jack Pickersgill, a cabinet minister in St. Laurent's government, is filmed with a pet dog in his lap—a nicely ironic touch. He damns himself without knowing it. The episodic narrative then turns into one of the oldest forms of dramatic confrontation—the trial. However, in typically Canadian fashion, the drama ends not with the damning report of the Royal Commission but with Banks slipping out of the country with the implicit cooperation of cabinet ministers.

In *The King Chronicles* Brittain dramatises both the public records and the private diaries of Prime Minister King. As with Hal Banks, the public King is represented by news footage intercut with drama, often with ironic effect. For the private life of King (who was discovered, after his death, to have been a spiritualist who talked to his dead mother and his dead dog), Brittain uses recurring, visually lyrical motifs. Less successfully, he also uses grotesque fantasy sequences for King's visions.

The primary focus in each film is on power: how it is used for a variety of purposes, and how it changes the men who use it. Throughout both films Brittain shows his viewers how Hal Banks and Willie King grappled with the necessity of maintaining an acceptable public face and how they managed to hide both their goals and methods and their eccentric and dangerous private personae.

Of course, he shows us King the manipulator, the obsessively vain and insecure politician, object of a hundred political cartoons, editorials and sardonic poems. Yet there are enough glimpses of the man's ability to surprise us throughout the miniseries. Maury Chaykin as Banks and Sean McCann as King gave superb performances full of subtextual nuance covering a wide range of emotions. Each actor was physically brilliant in his gestures and body language.

Brittain has said he enjoyed "the tone of someone's voice combined with a certain visual setup against something that went before," an effect achieved in post-production. Editorial decisions such as splicing are crucial to his work. Brittain includes a sense of scale and of social context, a feel for curious juxtapositions, a sense of ironic detachment and black humour, and what has been called his signature, a "tart historical narrative".

In both these films Brittain provides almost continuous voice-over, counterpointing the images on the screen with a highly personal interpretation of events. This ironic inflection of the "voice of god" convention of early National Film Board of Canada documentaries was intended to signify an objective, omniscient perspective. These two films also stand within a tradition of docudrama at the CBC, one that included the very controversial modern adaptation of the Easter story told in the style of direct cinema, *The Open Grave* (1964), as well as massive 1970s projects like the six-hour *The National Dream* and the critical look at Canada's *October Crisis*. Brittain was one of the few who used television to tell memorable tales which redefined the life and times of the viewers.

—Mary Jane Miller

Donald Brittain
Photo courtesy of the National Archives of Canada

DONALD BRITTAIN. Born in Ottawa, Ontario, Canada, in 1928. Attended Queen's University, Kingston, Ontario. Journalist for the *Ottawa Journal*, member, National Film Board of Canada, 1954-68; worked for the Fuji Group, Japan, 1968; independent producer, from 1970; director, producer, and writer of theatrical and TV films of documentary and dramatic nature. Recipient: fifteen Genie and CFA awards; ACTRA Awards, 1981 and 1983; two Geminis, 1985, 1985, and 1986; Died in Montreal, Quebec, Canada, July 1989.

FILMS AND MADE-FOR-TELEVISION MOVIES (selection; as writer, director, and producer)

1963	*Bethune* (writer and co-producer)
1965	*Ladies and Gentlemen...Mr. Leonard Cohen* (writer and co-director)
1975	*His Worship, Mr. Montréal*
1976	*Henry Ford's America*
1978	*The Dionne Quintuplets* (director and producer)
1979	*Paperland: The Bureaucrat Observed*
1981	*The Most Dangerous Spy*
1981	*A Blanket of Ice*
1983	*The Accident* (director)
1983	*Something to Celebrate*
1984	*The Children's Crusade*
1985	*Canada's Sweetheart: The Saga of Hal C. Banks*
1986	*The Final Battle* (also narrator)
1987	*The King Chronicles*
1988	*Family: A Loving Look at CBC Radio*
1991	*Brittain on Brittain*

FURTHER READING

Boone, Mike. "Great Brittain: Witness Series Focuses on Documentary Film Genius." *Montreal* (Quebec) *Gazette*, 12 December 1992.

"A Day with Donald Brittain." *Globe and Mail* (Toronto), 24 July 1989.

"Donald Brittain: Green Stripe and Common Sense." In, Feldman, Seth, and Joyce Nelson, editors. *Canadian Film Reader*. Toronto: Peter Martin, 1977.

"Donald Brittain's Precious Legacy is a National Treasure." *Montreal* (Quebec) *Gazette*, 24 July 1989.

Dwyer, Victor. "A Fond Farewell: Donald Brittain's Last Film Eyes CBC Radio." *Maclean's* (Toronto), 10 June 1991.

Johnson, Brian D. "A Chronicler for a Nation *(The King Chronicles)*." *Maclean's* (Toronto), 28 March 1988.

Kolomeychuk, Terry, editor. *Brittain: Never the Ordinary Way*. Toronto: National Film Board Publication, 1990.

See also Canadian Programming in English

BROADCAST PROMOTION AND MARKETING EXECUTIVES

PROMAX International (formerly BPME—Broadcast Promotion and Marketing Executives) is the trade organization for media promotion and marketing professionals. Founded in the United States in 1956 as the Broadcast Promotion Association (BPA), its name changes tellingly reflect the substantial changes experienced by the media industries in the last four decades.

Initially, broadcast promotion was the term for media efforts conducted by television and radio stations to maximize the size of audiences and the numbers of advertisers. These efforts largely consisted of date/time program announcements on the station's own air coupled with print advertisements in the local media (particularly *TV Guide* in the case of television promotion). More elaborate promotion campaigns were usually handled by the networks. Sweeping industry changes in the 1970s and 1980s—including among others the lessening of the dominance of the commercial networks, the growing importance of locally-produced news, the rise of cable and pay-TV services, increases in program production costs, and the growth of syndicated programming—resulted in a significantly more complex media environment and led to the need for more sophisticated promotion techniques. Consequently, in 1985, the organization changed its name to Broadcast Promotion and Marketing Executives (BPME) to reflect the increasing importance of marketing principles such as the use of consumer research, competitive positioning, long range planning, and audience segmentation. An ever-more-rapidly changing media scene in the late 1980s and early 1990s—including the growth of non-broadcast program distribution channels and increasingly international webs of participation—led to a second major name change to PRO-MAX International in 1993.

PROMAX, a loose acronym for Promotion and Marketing Executives in the Electronic Media, employs a full time paid president and staff and receives oversight from a volunteer board of directors comprised of industry personnel. Focussing on the fields of broadcast and cable television, radio, entertainment, and emerging technologies, the organization supports a wide range of related activities including promotion, market-

Courtesy of Promax International

ing, advertising, public relations, design, sales, and community service. Among its services to members are: the quarterly magazine *Image*, which reports on industry events and developments, key issues, notable campaigns, and new products, services, and techniques; *PromoFax*, a weekly newsletter faxed directly to members; an annual directory/promotion planner which lists members and suppliers, including key industry dates and events; the Resource Center, located in the organization's Los Angeles headquarters, which houses an extensive collection of videotapes, printed materials, and publications; and a Job Line, which provides information on available positions and job seekers (a key service in a field noted for advancement across rather than within markets). Perhaps the most notable service is the organization's annual seminar where members meet for workshops, demonstrations, presentations, and general networking. Suppliers of promotion materials demonstrate their products and services in an exhibit hall, and networks, group owners, and other industry organizations host suites for special presentations. The culmination of the seminar is an awards ceremony recognizing creative excellence, for many years hosted by the popular film critics Gene Siskel and Roger Ebert.

In addition to ongoing member services, PROMAX awards several academic scholarships in cooperation with sponsoring industry groups. In 1980 the organization published a college text, *Broadcast Advertising and Promotion: A Handbook for Students and Professionals*. It has also conducted numerous surveys over the years on salaries, budgets, staff size, and other departmental measures, which help promotion executives gauge their status and performance according to industry standards.

—Jerry Hagins

FURTHER READING

Eastman, Susan Tyler, and Robert A. Klein. *Strategies in Broadcast and Cable Promotion.*Belmont, California: Wadsworth Publishing, 1982.

Webster, Lance. "The Growth Years: BPA to BPME." *BPME Image*, April 1991.

BROADCASTING STANDARDS COUNCIL/COMMISSION

British Regulatory Commission

Television has been described as a battle ground for rival sets of moral perspectives and disputed assessments of the medium's power to influence its audiences. It enters the home, may trade in vivid and unexpected images, and appeals greatly to children. It presents both reassuring and disturbing impressions of values and behaviors prevalent in society. The propriety of its program standards is therefore continually debated in many countries.

In Britain, the government responded to perceived public concerns of this kind by establishing a Broadcasting Standards Council, on a pre-statutory basis in 1988 and as a statutory body under the Broadcasting Act of 1990. Its remit covers the portrayal in television and radio programs and advertising of violence, sexual conduct and matters of taste and decency. The council has five main tasks:

- To draw up a code of practice in consultation with the broadcasting authorities and others, which broadcasting organisations must "reflect" (not adopt) in their own codes and program guidelines. Initially published in 1989, the code was revised in 1994.
- To monitor programs and make reports in the areas of its remit.
- To commission research and enquiries in those areas.
- To consider and make findings on complaints about programs and advertisements.
- To represent the United Kingdom on international bodies involved in setting standards for broadcasting.

The BSC is not an instrument of censorship, for it has no authority to consider programs before transmission. Since its findings are essentially subjective judgments (not determinations of fact within a framework of law), neither is it a judicial body. Its powers are relatively limited. It may require broadcasters to supply tapes of programs and statements in response to complaints about them. It publishes its findings in a Complaints Bulletin (which is widely reported in the press) and in serious cases may require the offending broadcaster to do so on air or in print as well. The council is made up of eight members, including a chairman and seputy, appointed by the secretary of state for the Department of National Heritage. It has been served by a staff of 15 full-time posts, including a director and deputy; and had a budget of £1,375,000 in 1994–95.

The council's role and approach may be summarised in five features: First, its remit is more wide-ranging than might be supposed. Although it covers the three main areas of violence, sexual conduct and bad language, its 56-page Code of Practice also deals with the stereotyping of women, men, the elderly, and ethnic minorities; disparaging treatments of the disabled and mentally ill; depictions of death, grief and bereavement, suicide, disasters, respect for victims and intrusions into privacy; and responsible presentations of alcohol, drugs and smoking.

Second, the council's "philosophy" of standards is not one-sidedly illiberal. It aims to balance the claims of creativity and explorations of contemporary reality against those of respect for audience sensitivities.

Third, the council does not apply the simple precepts of a black-and-white morality. Its Code of Practice reads more like a guide to editorial responsibility than a set of proscriptions. Very little is ruled out *per se*, and most code provisions and findings are couched in a spirit of context-sensitivity. Conditioning factors may include the time of scheduling, the program genre and viewers' expectations of what it tends to present, likely audience composition at the time, whether advance warnings of sensitive material have been given, and the role of such material in the overall flow of the story or report. Among the contextual influences, much weight is given to a 9:00 P.M. "watershed", before which nothing that is unsuitable for children should be shown and after which it is acceptable to move to a more adult type of material. But even after 9:00 P.M., carte blanche is not envisaged, and broadcasters are expected to move only gradually into more challenging waters.

Fourth, although the council has had to deal with an increasing volume of complaints (rising from 512 in 1990–91 to 1,473 in 1993–94 and 2,032 in 1994–95), its approach has not been draconian. In most years, only about 20% of complaints have been upheld.

Fifth, the council has largely based its work on an understanding of the broad limits and tolerances of British public opinion (including how these are evolving). To that end, it consulted approximately 100 organisations when drawing up its Code of Practice. Its members periodically travel on "road shows" to meet diverse groups in different parts of the country, exchanging views on broadcasting standards. Above all, it has commissioned and published the results of a great deal of high-quality, often cited and well-regarded research.

This has included broad surveys over time of both program content and audience attitudes in the key remit areas. The results have drawn attention to the diversity of public opinion about the boundaries between acceptable and unacceptable treatments of violence, sex and other matters and have done justice to the complexity of people's views. This has supported the council's emphasis on "context" when dealing with complaints. Other projects have included a review of research findings on violence and pornography effects, an enquiry into the future of children's television, an international review of approaches to media education, a study of delinquents' media use patterns, and in-depth studies of interpretations of screened violence by women, men and victims of actual violence; children's cognitive and emotional responses to diverse program materials; the portrayal of ethnic minorities; and perspectives on the portrayal of disabilities by both disabled and able-bodied viewers. The council has also co-sponsored a large-scale enquiry into children's uses of the television screen in the new media environment and commissioned an independent analysis of the representativeness of those who submit complaints to it. On the whole, the latter suggested that complainants come from a relatively broad spectrum of the audience.

Critics occasionally object to the council's role on one of three grounds: for inducing caution among broadcasters; for imposing fuddy-duddy restrictions on a medium of expanding diversity and choice; and for a confusing overlap of jurisdiction with other authorities like the Independent Television Commission and a Programme Complaints Commission. Such objections do not seem widely shared or politically weighty, however, and much of the early suspicion of the council as a prospective agent of right-wing or puritanical control has been disarmed by its record. Indeed, Mary Whitehouse (past leader of the Viewers' and Listeners' Association and once a forceful lobbyist for a body of standards control) has complained about its failure to stand up to broadcasters' permissiveness.

In 1996, a bill was introduced into Parliament to merge the BSC with the Programme Complaints Commission, which, since its statutory establishment in 1982, had considered complaints arising from alleged unfairness toward people appearing in or dealt with in programs and alleged invasions of privacy. The new body is to be called the Broadcasting Standards Commission.

—Jay G. Blumler

FURTHER READING

Annual Reports. London: Broadcasting Standards Council, 1990–91 to 1995–96.

Annual Research Reviews (numbers 1-6). London: John Libbey and Broadcasting Standards Council, 1990–96.

Blumler, Jay G. *Television and the Public Interest: Vulnerable Values in West European Broadcasting.* London, and Thousand Oaks, California: Sage, 1992.

A Code of Practice. London: Broadcasting Standards Council, 1994.

Coleman, Francis. "All in the Best Possible Taste: The Broadcasting Standards Council, 1989–92." *Public Law* (London), Autumn 1993.

Gauntlett, David. *A Profile of Complainants and their Complaints* (Research Working Paper 10). London: Broadcasting Standards Council, 1995.

Shaw, Colin. "Taste, Decency, and Standards in Television." In, Smith, Anthony, editor. *Television: An International History.* Oxford, and New York: Oxford University Press, 1995.

See also British Television

BRODKIN, HERBERT

U.S. Producer

Herb Brodkin enjoyed a singular career in television because of his insistence on quality, his uncompromising standards, and his longevity. Brodkin, who served as executive producer or producer on some of television's finest moments, began his television career producing live television in its Golden Age, and produced until his death in 1991.

Brodkin came to television with a background in theater and scenic design. He began working as a set designer for CBS in 1950. After three years he was handling the production chores for no less than three anthology dramas. Brodkin continued to work in the anthology format during what has been generally termed the "golden years of television." These dramas, such as *Playhouse 90* and *Studio One*, were splendid vehicles for Brodkin's broad and varied theatrical experience. One telecast in particular would prove fortuitous for Brodkin and others. "The Defender" (28

February and 4 March 1957), starring Ralph Bellamy and William Shatner, would serve as a model for one of Brodkin's cornerstone filmed series.

When the telefilm began to flourish in the 1950s and most filmed production came from Hollywood, Brodkin remained in New York although he, too, changed from the live format to film. Brodkin brought a great deal of technical expertise to telefilm production, for he had made dozens of films for the Army Signal Corps. His first series, *Brenner*, focused on a father/son team of cops and was scheduled sporadically by CBS. But Brodkin's next series was the landmark *The Defenders.* The series was based on the *Studio One* show and featured E.G. Marshall and Robert Reed as a father/son team of lawyers. The "Brodkin approach" of treating controversial issues with intelligence and dispassion, developed during the live years, translated well to the filmed medium of television. Brodkin had always held the script in the highest esteem and consistently used writers of excellence—Ernest Kinoy, Robert Crean, and Reginald Rose. Though television was and is a medium that appeals largely to the emotions, Brodkin's productions consistently asked the viewer to think, to consider, and to weigh. Issues considered taboo, such as abortion, euthanasia, racial prejudice, and blacklisting, were familiar ground to Brodkin. CBS constantly battled affiliates that refused to clear *The Defenders* and the network endured some financial hardship due to advertiser pull-out from the series. Nevertheless, the hallmark of every Herb Brodkin production was a thoughtful and even-handed examination of an issue in a dramatic context. *The Defenders* enjoyed a four-year run in which it garnered every major award for television drama.

Brodkin's filmed series work often used the settings of the legal and medical profession to explore a variety of very contemporary controversies. The series also used the convention of the mentor/student relationship. In *The Defenders* as well as *Brenner* the protagonists are father and son. In the unsold pilot *The Firm*, written by long-time Brodkin associate Ernest Kinoy, the protagonists are father and daughter. Brodkin, and those who wrote for him, proved especially adept at balancing the maturity of the mentor and the intellectual enthusiasm of the student as a framework for examining the issues of the day.

In 1965, Brodkin shifted his attention from his Plautus Productions to his newly created Titus Productions (formed with Robert Berger), under whose banner some of his most memorable dramatic specials were produced. This was also the year of one of Brodkin's more metaphorical productions. *Coronet Blue* was a short series run by CBS in the summer of 1967. It chronicled amnesiac Michael Alden's search for his identity while being pursued by a shadowy band of assailants. The only clue to Alden's identity was the cryptic phrase, "coronet blue." The character of Alden can be seen as a metaphor for the angst-ridden youth of the 1960s. His search mirrored the search of the "counterculture" for its identity, its place in the world. The series was fairly well-received but could not be revived for regular production because Frank Converse, who played Michael Alden, was already signed for another series.

In 1981, Titus Productions was acquired by the Taft Entertainment Company. Both Brodkin and Berger remained to produce dramatic specials for Taft. Notable among those specials was *Skokie*, starring Danny Kaye as a Holocaust survivor who fights to keep a group of neo-Nazis from marching in Skokie, Illinois, and the HBO special *Sakharov*, which featured Jason Robards and Glenda Jackson as Soviet dissident Andrei Sakharov and his wife Elena Bonner. In 1985, the Museum of Broadcasting in New York mounted a retrospective of Herbert Brodkin's career. In the words of television curator Ronald Simon, "the ouevre of Herb Brodkin is an impressive collection of socially significant dramas." Herb Brodkin died in 1991 leaving a legacy of creative and intellectual integrity unparalleled in the annals of television.

—John Cooper

Herbert Brodkin
Photo courtesy of Broadcasting and Cable

HERBERT BRODKIN. Born in New York City, New York, U.S.A., 9 November 1912. University of Michigan, B.A. 1934, Yale Drama School, M.A. 1941. Served in U.S. Army, 1943–46. Began career in theater as scene designer, Bucks County Playhouse, Pennsylvania, 1946–48; production manager, director, scenery designer, Westport Country Playhouse, Connecticut, 1946–50; set designer, City Center and Theatre Guild, New York, 1946–50; opera set designer, City Center, New York, 1946–50; began television career as producer and designer, *Charlie Wild, Private Detective*, 1950–52; producer of numerous live television productions; *The Defenders*, 1961–64; producer of made-for-television movies, from 1970s. Died 1991.

TELEVISION

1950–52	*Charlie Wild, Private Detective*
1953–55	*ABC Album*
1953–55	*The TV Hour*
1953–55	*The Motorola TV Hour*
1953–55	*Center Stage*
1953–55	*The Elgin Hour*
1955–56	*The Alcoa Hour*
1955–56	*Goodyear Playhouse*
1957	*Studio One*
1958–60	*Playhouse 90*
1959–64	*Brenner*
1961–64	*The Defenders*
1962–65	*The Nurses*

| 1966 | *Shane* |
| 1967 | *Coronet Blue* |

TELEVISION MINISERIES

| 1978 | *Holocaust* |

MADE-FOR-TELEVISION-MOVIES

1970	*The People Next Door*
1981	*Skokie*
1982	*My Body, My Child*
1983	*Ghost Dancing*
1984	*Sakharov*
1985	*Mandela*

| 1988 | *Stones for Ibarra* |
| 1990 | *Murder Times Seven* |

FURTHER READING

Barnouw, Erik. *Tube of Plenty*. New York: Oxford University Press, 1975; 2nd revised edition, 1990.

Produced by . . . Herb Brodkin. New York: Museum of Broadcasting, 1985.

Watson, Mary Ann. *The Expanding Vista: Television in the Kennedy Years*. New York: Oxford University Press, 1990.

See also *Defenders*

BROKAW, TOM

U.S. Broadcast Journalist

Tom Brokaw serves as anchor and managing editor of *NBC Nightly News*. Sole anchor of the program since 1983, he had previously been anchor of NBC News' *Today Show* from 1976 to 1982 and had worked in a series of increasingly prominent assignments for NBC News. Brokaw's distinctively smooth style and boyish charm have made him a well-recognized star through the shifting stakes in television news in the 1980s and 1990s.

After an early position in Sioux City, Iowa, Brokaw's career in broadcast news began in earnest in 1962 when he worked in Omaha, Nebraska. He moved to Atlanta, Georgia, in 1965 to report on the Civil Rights Movement, then joined NBC in Los Angeles as a reporter and anchor in 1966. From the West Coast, Brokaw moved to Washington, eventually becoming NBC's White House correspondent during the Watergate era. In 1976 and 1980 he was a member of NBC News' team of floor reporters for the Democratic and Republican conventions. In 1984 and 1988 he served as anchor of all NBC News' coverage of the primaries, national conventions, and election night, a role he repeated in 1992. In the fall of 1987 Brokaw scored a number of high profile successes, interviewing Mikhail Gorbachev in the Kremlin, Ronald Reagan in the White House, and in December 1987 moderating a live, televised debate from Washington among all declared candidates for the presidential nomination from both parties. He also moderated the first debate among the declared Democratic candidates for president in December 1991.

Brokaw's opportunity to serve as anchor arose when, after being courted by ABC, NBC countered by teaming him with Roger Mudd (apparently attempting to replicate the Chet Huntley-David Brinkley pairing), and the two went on the air as co-anchors in April 1982. Mudd was soon dropped by NBC, and Brokaw took over as sole anchor in August 1983. At CBS Dan Rather had replaced Walter Cronkite in 1981, at ABC Peter Jennings, who had anchored from 1965 to 1968, returned to that position in 1983, and thus a three-man race was

put in place which continues to structure the national nightly news. When each of the networks was bought by a large conglomerate in the mid-1980s (ABC by Capital Cities, CBS by Laurence Tisch's Loews Corporation, and NBC by General Electric), network news divisions became cost-accountable in new ways that also impinged on the importance of the anchor.

Tom Brokaw
Photo courtesy of NBC

While budgets and staffs were cut, promotional campaigns were expanded, and increasingly, the center of those campaigns was the persona of the news anchor, who became a virtual corporate symbol.

Brokaw has been one of the most well-recognized participants in the trend toward expanding the role of the news reader into a prominent position of creative control and celebrity. Along with Rather and Jennings, Brokaw has emerged in the 1990s as a kind of living logo, the image taken to be representative of an entire news organization. A number of critics have raised questions about the quality and integrity of news presentation in this increasingly star-driven climate, charging that on the national news broadcasts, journalism has become subordinate to entertainment. Brokaw was reportedly the model for William Hurt's Tom Grunick, the protagonist in James L. Brooks' 1987 film *Broadcast News.*

As an anchor, Brokaw is renowned for his globetrotting, and he has provided live coverage of such important recent events as the dismantling of the Berlin Wall. In addition to *NBC Nightly News,* Brokaw has anchored, with Katie Couric, the nighttime program. *Now with Tom Brokaw and Katie Couric* as well as the short-lived *Expose,* a news magazine show on the order of *60 Minutes.* He has also anchored a series of periodic prime-time specials.

—Diane M. Negra

TOM (THOMAS JOHN) BROKAW. Born in Webster, South Dakota, U.S.A. 6 February 1940. Educated at University of South Dakota, B.A. in political science 1962. Married: Meredith Lynn Auld, 1962; children: Jennifer Jean, Andrea Brooks, and Sarah Auld. Began career as newscaster, weatherman, and staff announcer KTIV, Sioux City, Iowa, 1960–62; morning news editor KMTV, Omaha, Nebraska, 1962–65; editor for 11:00 news, WSB-TV, Atlanta, Georgia, 1965–66; joined NBC news as anchor, KNBC-TV, Los Angeles, California, 1966; anchor, NBC, since

1966. Honorary degrees: University of South Dakota; Washington University; Syracuse University; Hofstra University; Boston College; Emerson College; Simpson College; Duke University, 1991; Notre Dame University, 1993. Recipient: duPont Award, 1987; Peabody Award, 1988.

TELEVISION
1973–76	*NBC Saturday Night News* (anchor)
1976–82	*Today Show* (host)
1982–	*NBC Nightly News* (anchor)
1991	*Expose* (anchor)
1992–	*Dateline NBC* (co-anchor)
1993–94	*Now with Tom Brokaw and Katie Couric* (co-anchor)

TELEVISION SPECIALS (selection)
1987	*To Be a Teacher*
1987	*Wall Street, Money, Greed and Power*
1987	*A Conversation with Mikhail S. Gorbachev*
1988	*Home Street Home*
1988	*To Be An American*

FURTHER READING
Corliss, Richard. "Broadcast Blues." *Film Comment* (New York), March-April, 1988.
Goldberg, Robert, and Gerald Jay Goldberg. *Anchors: Brokaw, Jennings, Rather and the Evening News.* New York: Birch Lane, 1990.
Jones, Alex S. "The Anchors: Who They Are, What They Do: The Tests They Face." *The New York Times,* 27 July 1986.
Kaplan, James. "Tom Brokaw: NBC's Air Apparent." *Vogue* (New York), April 1988.
Westin, Av. *Newswatch: How TV Decides the News.* New York: Simon and Schuster, 1982.

See also Anchor, News (Network)

BROOKE-TAYLOR, TIM

British Comedian/Writer

Tim Brooke-Taylor has established himself as a familiar face on British television since making his first appearances in the early 1960s, when he was one of a celebrated generation of young new comedians and comedy writers to emerge from the famous Cambridge University Footlights Revue.

Brooke-Taylor began his television career working for *On the Braden Beat,* which was one of a flood of innovative new comedy shows to be created around 1962 to 1964. Subsequently he teamed up as a writer with star Eric Idle on *The Frost Report* and also contributed as writer and performer to the spin-off series *At Last the 1948 Show,* on which his collaborators were John Cleese, Marty Feldman, Graham Chapman and Aimi Macdonald, under the leadership of David Frost as producer. This last

show was a significant step in British television comedy, having a distinctly surreal air with its unconnected sketches and eccentric, often slapstick humour, which paved the way for the *Monty Python* series, among other successors.

After teaming up as straight man to Marty Feldman on *Marty,* Brooke-Taylor entered upon the most successful collaboration of his television career to date, completing a highly popular comedy trio with Graeme Garden and Bill Oddie in *The Goodies.* Oddie, Garden, and Brooke-Taylor had in fact already worked together once before with some success, first developing their sparky three-man act in the series *Twice a Fortnight* in 1967. Anarchic, weird, and often hilarious, *The Goodies* sought to save the world from such bizarre threats as a marauding giant kitten and a plague of Rolf Harrises. Pedalling into action on a beflagged three-seater bicycle, the trio were purveyors of a more slapstick, lighthearted brand of comedy than their counterparts in *Monty Python* and consequently appealed to a wider age range, with many fans in their teens or even younger.

Much of the humour evolved from the contrasting, and ludicrous, personalities of the three heroes. While Graeme Garden was the obsessive scientist who dreamt up all manner of wacky schemes to save the world and Bill Oddie was a short, scruffy hippy with a strong cynical streak, Tim Brooke-Taylor was the clean-cut patriot in union jack waistcoat, always ready with a rousing Churchillian speech when things looked bleak but first to bolt when danger reared its head. Targets of the humour included a range of contemporary fads and issues, from satirical swipes at the science-fiction adventure serial *Dr. Who* to take-offs of the Hollywood western.

The series was hugely successful, but ultimately it fell victim to the BBC's indecision about whether it should be scheduled for adult or younger audiences (despite pleas from the performers themselves, it was broadcast relatively early in the evening, thus restricting the adult content of the material). The team switched to London Weekend Television in 1981 in the hope that they might fare better there, but there was no real improvement and no more programmes were made after 1982.

After *The Goodies* the three stars went their more or less separate ways, Tim Brooke-Taylor managing to maintain the highest profile in subsequent years. As well as establishing himself as a prominent panellist on such long-running radio programmes as *I'm Sorry, I Haven't a Clue*, he also developed a second television career in situation comedy, starring in several efficient but fairly unremarkable series in the 1980s and early 1990s. Perhaps the most successful of these latter efforts was *Me and My Girl*, in which Brooke-Taylor gave support as best friend (Derek Yates) to Richard Sullivan, an advertising executive struggling to bring up a teenage daughter on his own. Typical of other series that were greeted with only lukewarm praise was *You Must Be the Husband*, in which Brooke-Taylor was the startled uptight husband of a woman newly revealed as the bestselling authoress of salacious romantic novels.

—David Pickering

TIM(OTHY JULIAN) BROOKE-TAYLOR. Born in Buxton, Derbyshire, England, 17 July 1940. Attended Cambridge University. Married: Christine Wheadon, 1968; children: Ben and Edward. Actor, Cambridge Footlights Revue while at university; writer, various 1960s comedy series, co-star, *The Goodies*, 1970–80, 1981–82; later appeared in situation comedies and consolidated reputation as radio performer. Address: Jill Foster Ltd, 3 Lonsdale Road, London SW13 9ED, England.

TELEVISION SERIES (selection)

1962–67	*On the Braden Beat*
1966–67	*The Frost Report* (co-writer)
1966–67	*At Last the 1948 Show* (also producer)

Tim Brooke-Taylor
Photo courtesy of the British Film Institute

1970–80,	
1981–82	*The Goodies*
1984–88	*Me and My Girl*
1987	*You Must Be the Husband*

FILMS

Twelve Plus One; The Statue; Willy Wonka and the Chocolate Factory.

RADIO

I'm Sorry, I'll Read That Again; I'm Sorry, I Haven't a Clue; Hello Cheeky; Does the Team Think?; Loose Ends; The Fame Game; Hoax.

RECORDINGS

Funky Gibbon; The New Goodies LP; The Goodies' Beastly Record; The Least Worst of Hello Cheeky; The Seedy Sounds of Hello Cheeky.

STAGE (selection)

The Unvarnished Truth; Run for Your Wife; The Philanthropist.

PUBLICATIONS

Rule Britannia; Tim Brooke-Taylor's Golf Bag; Tim Brooke-Taylor's Cricket Box.

See also Cleese, John

BROOKS, JAMES L.

U.S. Writer/Producer/Director

James L. Brooks is one of television's most outstanding and successful writer-producers. He is also one of the few who have become highly successful screenwriters and directors of feature films. His work in both media has been recognized with numerous awards from peers and critics, and both television programs and films have been acclaimed by audiences.

Brooks career in television began, however, in a very different arena. He was a writer for CBS News in New York from 1964 to 1966. In 1966 he moved to Los Angeles and became a writer and producer of documentaries for David Wolper at Wolper Productions. By 1968, however, Brooks and his partner, Allan Burns, had created the hit television show *Room 222*, where they served as executive story editors. This program broke new ground for television by focusing on the career of a black high-school teacher, Pete Dixon (Lloyd Haynes). The show tackled tough issues such as drug use and racial conflict in a concerned, humane manner and won an Emmy as Outstanding New Series in 1969.

Much of the same style and tone carried over into Brooks and Burns next success, *The Mary Tyler Moore Show*. At MTM Entertainment Brooks and Burns were among the first members of a large group of extremely talented individuals, all working in a creatively charged atmosphere established by executive producer Grant Tinker. Tinker's philosophy was to acquire the services of creative individuals and then assist them in every way possible to become even more productive. Brooks and Burns thrived under the system, working first on *The Mary Tyler Moore Show*, then creating or co-creating, *Rhoda, Paul Sand in Friends and Lovers, Taxi, The Associates,* and *Lou Grant*. On the basis of these successes, the team of Brooks and Burns became known as members of a new group of Hollywood television producers, often referred to as the *auteur* producers. They were the creative force behind their shows, imparting a recognizable, distinctive style and tone. Indeed, programs created at MTM have been referred to as the defining examples of "quality television."

The programs were noted not only for their wit and quick jokes, but for establishing a focus on character. Most were built around groups of characters related by circumstance or profession rather than by family relations. They were quickly recognized by critics as something different from the earlier forms of television comedy focused either on zany "situations" or on domestic settings. These new programs were among the first and strongest of the "ensemble comedies" that were to dominate television for decades to come. Human frailty and the comfort of friends, professional limitations and the joy of co-workers, a readiness to take one's self too seriously at times, matched by a willingness to puncture excessive ego—all these are hallmarks of the Brooks style of ensemble comedy. While social issues might come to the foreground in any given episode, they were always subordinate to the comedy of human manners, to character. In this way, the MTM shows were distinguished from the more overtly issue-oriented style of Norman

James L. Brooks
Photo courtesy of Broadcasting and Cable

Lear. This focus on character and ensemble has been passed down through professional and industrial relationships into the work of other producer-writers in shows as diverse as *ER* and *Hill Street Blues*, and programs such as *Cheers, Murphy Brown* or *Seinfeld* are clear descendants of the work of Brooks and his various partners.

In 1978 Brooks began to shift his work toward feature films. He worked as writer and co-producer on the film *Starting Over* and in 1983 he wrote, produced, and directed *Terms of Endearment*, a highly successful film in terms of both box office and critical response.

In 1984 Brooks founded Gracie Films, his own production company, to oversee work on film and television projects. To date, the best known television programs developed at Gracie Films have been *The Tracey Ullman Show* and its immensely popular spin-off, *The Simpsons*. With some degree of irony, given Brooks' career, these two shows are marvelously skewed views of television comedy. *The Tracey Ullman Show* was replete with send-ups of American TV "types," the housewife-mother, the bored "pink collar" worker, the prime-time vamp. And *The Simpsons*, using all the cartoon techniques at its disposal, pokes fun at, the idealized version of domestic comedy that has long been a television staple. While Brooks' involvement with these shows remains primarily at the level of executive producer, the style and attitude he developed throughout his years in television comedy is clearly at work. In some ways he might be said to have inherited the mantle of Grant Tinker, discovering new talent, making a space for creative individuals, and changing the face of television in the process.

—Horace Newcomb

JAMES L. BROOKS. Born in Brooklyn, New York, U.S.A., 9 May 1940. Attended New York University, New York City, 1958-60. Married: 1) Marianne Katherine Morrissey, 1964 (divorced), child: Amy Lorriane; 2) Holly Beth Holmberg. Began career at CBS television Sports division; writer/producer, David Wolper Productions, 1966; co-creator, with Alan Burns, *Room 222*; writer/producer, MTM; founder, Gracie Films, 1984; film writer, producer and director. Recipient: numerous Emmy Awards; Golden Globe Awards; Peabody Awards; Humanitas Awards; Directors Guild Awards; Writers Guild of America Awards.

TELEVISION

1968–69	*Room 222*
1970-77	*The Mary Tyler Moore Show*
1974	*Paul Sands in Friends and Lovers*
1974–75	*Rhoda*
1976	*The New Lorenzo Music Show*
1977–82	*Lou Grant*
1978–83	*Taxi*
1978	*Cindy*
1979	*The Associates*
1986–90	*The Tracy Ullman Show*
1990–	*The Simpsons*
1994–	*The Critic*

MADE FOR TELEVISION MOVIE

1974	*Thursday's Game* (writer-producer)

FILMS

Starting Over (writer, producer), 1979; *Modern Romance* (actor), 1981; *Terms of Endearment* (director, writer, producer), 1983; *Broadcast News* (director, writer, producer), 1987; *Big* (producer), 1988; *The War of the Roses* (producer), 1989; *Say Anything...* (executive producer), 1989; *I'll Do Anything* (director, writer), 1994; *Bottle Rocket* (executive producer), 1996.

FURTHER READING

Alley, Robert S., and Irby B. Brown. *Love Is All Around: The Making of The Mary Tyler Moore Show*. New York: Delta, 1989.

Corliss, Richard. "Still Lucky Jim? Comedy Czar James L. Brooks Tries to Fix the Movie That Used To Be A Musical." *Time* (New York), 31 January 1994.

Feuer, Jane, Paul Kerr, and Tise Vahimagi. *MTM: "Quality Television."* London: British Film Institute Publications, 1985.

Lovece, Frank. *Hailing Taxi*. New York: Prentice Hall, 1988.

Mitchell, Sean. "James L. Brooks (Don't Worry Be Unhappy)." *American Film* (Washington, D.C.), May 1989.

Newcomb, Horace, and Robert S. Alley. *The Producer's Medium: Conversations with Creators of American TV*. New York: Oxford University Press, 1983.

Orth, Maureen. "Talking To...James Brooks" (interview). *Vogue* (New York), April 1988.

Tinker, Grant. *Tinker in Television: From General Sarnoff to General Electric*. New York: Simon and Schuster, 1994.

Zehme, Bill. "The Only Real People On T.V. (The Simpsons)." *Rolling Stone* (New York), 28 June 1990.

See also *Mary Tyler Moore Show; Simpsons*

BROOKSIDE

British Soap Opera

Brookside, produced independently by Mersey Television, is inextricably linked to the history of the British independent publishing channel, Channel Four. Founded in 1982, Channel Four's remit was to attract audiences not already catered for by other channels, and to innovate in form and style. In particular, *Brookside* attracted a young audience who were essential to its success.

Unlike earlier serial dramas, *Brookside* avoids the traditional television studio; the show filmed on a small housing estate, built as part of a Liverpool housing redevelopment. The structure of the close itself, with small "two up, two down" working-class accommodation next to large detached houses for wealthier occupants, set the stage for confrontation between classes, with politically contentious issues dealt with in an upfront manner.

Whereas its competitor soaps are perceived to be "character-based," *Brookside's* initial aim was a realism that directly tackled the social and political problems apparent in the Britain of the 1980s. This approach has been followed by the BBC's *Eastenders*, which also copied *Brookside's* "weekend omnibus repeat" format. More recently, the pressing concerns of audience maximisation have led to a more sensationalist approach to social issues, with British television's first "on-screen" lesbian kiss, and a recent story line focusing on an incestuous affair between brother and sister. These developments have led to suggestions that *Brookside*, in particular its Saturday omnibus edition, is unsuitable for "family audiences."

One crucial difference between the *Brookside* of the 1980s and other British soaps was the lack of a central community meeting point such as a public house or corner shop, forcing characters to interact either on the close itself, or in scenes shot on location in and around Liverpool. However, the addition of a shopping development to the set, has led to more traditional interactions over the counter of a pizza parlour, and at the bar of Brookside's nightclub, La Luz.

Many of the main changes in *Brookside* are symbolised by the fate of the Grant family. Moving onto the close at the start of the programme, the Grants symbolised the expansion in working-class property ownership encouraged by the Conservative governments of the 1980s. Bobby Grant, a trade unionist with a fierce line in socialist rhetoric, suffered unemployment, Damon Grant was murdered in London (with the death filmed as part of a *Brookside* spin-off entitled *Damon and Debbie*, a format copied by Granada's *Coronation Street*); Karen Grant left home to study at university, and Sheila Grant left Bobby, symbolising the breakdown of the traditional post–World War II family unit. Barry Grant gradually developed the role of a ruthlessly competitive young entrepreneur, encouraged by the boom-bust cycle of the British economy during the 1980s and 1990s. He continued with the series into the 1990s, but gradually disappeared after murdering the wife and child of his lifelong best mate, Terry Sullivan. Murder and violence are no strangers to the *Brookside* set, which, since its inception, has seen two armed sieges, the murder of a child-abusing father, a violent rape, and a fatal cocaine-fueled car accident.

Channel Four broadcasts three episodes a week of the soap, and *Brookside* is invariably the channel's most popular programme, giving it a greater scope for minority-oriented programming elsewhere in the schedule. Still shot film-style with one camera, the contemporary *Brookside* retains many of the formal qualities of its 1980s twice-weekly version. However, gritty social realism has gradually given way to a more populist approach; whereas early episodes did their best to reflect the specific concerns of the northwest of England, nowadays *Brookside* rarely references its Liverpudlian roots.

—Stuart Borthwick

CAST

Roger Huntingdon	Rob Spendlove
Heather Huntingdon	Amanda Burton
Sheila Grant	Sue Johnston
Bobby Grant	Ricky Tomlinson
Damon Grant	Simon O'Brien
Karen Grant	Shelagh O'Hara
Barry Grant	Paul Usher
Jean Crosbie	Marcia Ashton
Anabelle Collins	Doreen Sloane
Paul Collins	Jim Wiggins
Lucy Collins	Katrin Cartlidge
Gordon Collins	Nigel Crowley
Gavin Taylor	Daniel Webb
Petra Taylor	Alexandra Pigg
Debbie McGrath	Gillian Kearney
Audrey Manners	Judith Barker

Brookside
Photo courtesy of Channel Four

Emma Piper	Paula Belle
Sarah Banks	Andrea Marshall
Rosie Banks	Susan Twist
Eddie Banks	Paul Broughton
Carl Banks	Stephen Donald
David Crosbie	John Burgess
Rachel Jordache (1993–)	Tiffany Chapman
Beth Jordache (1993–)	Anna Friel
Mandy Jordache (1993–)	Sandra Maitland
D-D Dixon	Irene Morot
Ron Dixon	Vince Earl
Mike Dixon	Paul Byatt
Mick Johnson	Louis Emerick
Patricia Farnham	Gabrielle Glaister
Jackie Corkhill	Sue Jenkins
Jimmy Corkhill	Dean Sullivan
Mo McGee	Tina Malone
Kevin	Terry Melia
Max Farnahm	Steven Pinder
Sinbad	Michael Starke
Viv	Kerrie Thomas
Bev McLoughlin (1993–)	Sarah White

PRODUCER   Mel Young

PROGRAMMING HISTORY

- Channel Four (Brookside Productions)

1982–

FURTHER READING

Brown, Mary Ellen. *Soap Opera and Women's Talk: The Pleasure of Resistance.* Thousand Oaks, California: Sage, 1994.

Geraghty, Christine. *Women and Soap Opera: A Study of Prime Time Soaps.* Cambridge: Polity Press, 1991.

Kilbourn, R.W. *Television Soaps.* London: Batsford, 1992.

See also Soap Opera

BUREAU OF MEASUREMENT

The Bureau of Measurement is a cooperative, non-profit Canadian audience research organization, which has struggled to survive in the face of increasing competition from the American-based A. C. Nielsen company, advances in electronic systems of audience measurement, and ambivalent support from the major Canadian broadcasters. It was created on 11 May 1944, on the recommendation of the Canadian Association of Broadcasters, and granted a government charter a year later. Originally called the Bureau of Broadcast Measurement (BBM), its first president was Lew Phenner of Canadian Cellucotton Products. It had no paid staff initially, but received administrative assistance from the Association of Canadian Advertisers and technical support from the Canadian Broadcasting Corporation. Its primary purpose in the beginning was to provide radio stations with reliable coverage estimates so that they could compete with the print media for advertising. The first BBM survey, released in October 1944, was conducted by the private ratings company Elliott-Haynes using the unaided mail ballot technique developed by CBS; instead of checking stations from a prepared list, participants compiled their own lists of stations to which they had listened.

Although financed largely by broadcasters, BBM was controlled for many years by advertising interests; of the nine positions on the original board of directors, three were filled by advertisers, three by advertising agencies, and three by broadcasters. Shortly after the creation of BBM, a similar organization called the Broadcast Measurement Bureau (BMB) was established in the United States. As a result of the efforts of Horace Stovin, chairman of BBM's technical committee, the two organizations worked in concert for a few years, using the same mail ballot technique and running their surveys simultaneously. This enabled advertisers to operate on either side of the border with equal facility. However, BMB was criticized for its methods, plagued by high costs, and thrown into disarray by the resignation of its president, Rugh M. Feltis. In 1950 it threw in the towel and left the American station coverage field to A. C. Nielsen, which used an interview-aided recall method.

By the end of Phenner's presidency in 1951, BBM had increased the number of areas surveyed, introduced bilingual ballots in some areas, and more than doubled its broadcasting membership. But a number of stations still refused to join, and in 1956 the CBC withdrew because of dissatisfaction with BBM's surveys. The same year, BBM began Producing time-period ratings for radio and television using a panel-diary method pioneered in Canada by International Surveys Limited. The new surveys were initially conducted every spring and fall with each member of participating households keeping a week-long diary of listening and viewing by half-hour periods. At the same time, the circulation surveys were increased from every other year to twice a year. However, the CBC remained critical of BBM operations

BBM Bureau of Measurement

Courtesy of BBM

and subscribed instead to Nielsen, ISL, and McDonald Research. A 1962 CBC report criticized BBM's surveys for their "non-coverage, biased selection procedure, low response and poor quality of response." By then BBM was also coming under strong criticism from both advertisers and private broadcasters, and there was a danger that it might collapse.

Under Bill Hawkins of CFOS Owen Sound, BBM began to put its house in order. It revised its constitution so as to increase the representation of broadcasters, and in 1964 became the first ratings service in the world to introduce computerized sample selection. It also increased the number of surveys, redesigned the bilingual household diary, and switched its premium from a card of safety pins to a 50-cent coin. In terms of winning back confidence in the validity of its surveys, the most important step was taken in 1967 when BBM decided to switch from household diaries, which had usually been kept by the harried home-maker, to personal diaries sent to selected members of households—including children, although their diaries were filled out by an adult. This change increased the response rate for mailed diaries to almost 50% and facilitated the acquisition of demographic data. Within a few years, BBM became the only audience measurement service for radio in Canada, and in television the competition was reduced to Nielsen. Between 1963 and 1968, BBM increased its membership from 357 to 534 or about 90% of the broadcasting industry, including the CBC.

Unlike the original household diary, the new personal diary was used for both radio and television, largely for reasons of cost. In theory, however, the most reliable diary is the single-medium personal diary. In addition, the use of dual-media diaries irritated radio broadcasters, who argued that they provided BBM with twice as much revenue as television broadcasters but only received the same benefits. In 1975, therefore, following several studies and considerable debate, BBM adopted separate diaries for each medium, including different samples and survey dates. This move greatly increased survey costs, however, so that in the mid-1980s BBM implemented household flooding or saturation sampling for both radio and television. Ironically, this development brought BBM almost full-circle back to its original household diary technique and illustrated the fact that audience measurement methods generally are determined as much by economic considerations as by the requirements for scientific validity.

In the mid-1970s, BBM began investigating electronic measuring systems. A committee was set up to develop a proposal for a meter-based system for television, and a contract was signed with Torpey Controls Ltd. for a prototype using existing circuitry and the vertical blanking interval. Despite successful test results, however, the cost of switching from diaries to meters was considered prohibitive, especially since diaries would still be required for radio and to supplement the data gathered for television. It was not until the advent of "electronic diaries" or people meters by Nielsen and others in the early 1980s that BBM gave serious consideration to replacing its traditional diary system for television. Unlike the original Nielsen audimeter, the people meter measured viewing rather than mere tuning and could track audience flow much more precisely.

In 1984, while still testing its new meter technology in the United States, Nielsen announced its intention to launch a people meter service in Canada. In response, BBM turned initially to Audits of Great Britain for help, but then decided to invite bids from other companies as well, including Niel-

sen. In November 1985, Nielsen and BBM reached a tentative agreement by which Nielsen would provide BBM with people meter data from 1,800 Canadian households, which it could then market as it saw fit. The agreement later fell through, however, and in September 1989 Nielsen launched a people meter service for network television in Canada on its own. BBM tried to develop its own electronic television audience measurement or TAM system in conjunction with Les Entreprise Videoway, but the tests results were unsatisfactory. Late in 1990, BBM and Nielsen resumed talks for a joint venture to extend people meters from the national network level to local and regional broadcasting. But the following year, a proposed deal again fell apart because of the concerns of local and regional broadcasters about costs and various technical matters. Since then, BBM has continued to use its diary method of audience measurement for both radio and television.

—Ross A. Eaman

FURTHER READING

Blankenship, A.B., C. Chakrapani, and W.H. Poole. *A History of Marketing Research in Canada.* Toronto: Professional Marketing Research Society, 1985.

Eaman, Ross A. *Channels of Influence: CBC Audience Research and the Canadian Public.* Toronto:University of Toronto Press, 1994.

BURNETT, CAROL

U.S. Comedienne

The many honors awarded Carol Burnett attest to the approbation of her peers and the love of her public. Burnett has been Outstanding Comedienne for the American Guild of Variety Artists five times and recipient of five Emmys. She received *TV Guide*'s award as Favorite Female Performer for three consecutive years in the early 1960s, and a Peabody award in 1963. The Academy of Television Arts and Sciences proclaimed her Woman of the Year; a Gallup Poll found her to be one of America's 20 Most Admired Women in 1977. She received the first National TV Critics Circle Award for Outstanding Performance, the first Ace Award for Best Actress, and the Horatio Alger Award, conferred by the Horatio Alger Association of Distinguished Americans. The latter is, in many ways, most significant, as Burnett's personal style and endearing "everywoman" qualities resulted from a life filled with emotional abuse and the ravages of poverty. She was inducted into the Television Hall of Fame in 1985.

Her grandmother wanted her to go to secretarial school, with the objective of marrying a rich executive. Burnett wanted college, and a degree in journalism. The odds were slim against her finding tuition and carfare of over fifty dollars at a time when the family's rent was thirty-five dollars per month. When an anonymous donor placed a fifty dollar bill in the mailbox,

Carol Burnett
Photo courtesy of Carol Burnett

she enrolled at University of California, Los Angeles, quickly switching from journalism to theater arts. Eventually, she joined a musical comedy/opera workshop where she honed her skills in characterization, comic music, and acting. She became a campus star. But her family's poverty made her dreams of moving to New York City and playing on Broadway seem unattainable. A performance at a professor's home in a skit from the musical *Annie Get Your Gun* in 1954 offered her an unexpected break. A party guest gave Burnett and her boyfriend, Don Saroyan, each a grant of one thousand dollars designed to jump-start their careers. Her benefactor attached four stipulations to the money: she must never reveal his identity, she must move to New York City to try her luck; she had to repay the loan within five years; and she was honor-bound to help other young people attain careers in the entertainment business. Within eighteen months, she managed to fulfill two of these criteria. While living at New York's Rehearsal Club, the hotel haven for aspiring actresses that had inspired the movie *Stage Door*, she made her own break by organizing the First Annual Rehearsal Club Revue, which showcased the myriad talents of her housemates. While others gained varying opportunities from the program, Burnett signed with the William Morris Agency and rapidly found outlets for her comedic and singing talents.

The Winchell-Mahoney Show, Paul Winchell's children's program, was her first break in television; for 13 weeks in 1955 she played comic foil for his ventriloquist dummies, where she sang, but did little comedy. She played Buddy Hackett's girlfriend in NBC's short-lived 1956 sitcom, *Stanley*. A comedic nightclub act and her collaboration with writer/composer Ken Welch gave her more opportunities for exposure to television audiences. Welch wrote a song spoofing the Elvis craze; Burnett's rendition of "I Made a Fool of Myself over John Foster Dulles" led to appearances on *The Tonight Show* with Jack Paar, *Toast of the Town* with Ed Sullivan, and an amazing amount of publicity as the dour Secretary of State fielded questions regarding his "relationship" with Burnett. In 1956, she appeared on CBS-TV's morning show with Garry Moore, and from 1959 to 1962, became a regular on Moore's eponymous prime-time program. Critical and popular praise followed, as Burnett portrayed as many as five or six characters an hour in each show; ranked as America's Favorite Female Performer of 1961-62 by *TV Guide*, that season she received her first Emmy. She also made a television special based on her successful 1959-61 portrayal of Princess Winnifred, the gangly, sensitive heroine of the off/on Broadway musical, *Once Upon a Mattress*. She and Julie Andrews made an Emmy-winning special, *Julie and Carol at Carnegie Hall*. Her popularity amply confirmed, CBS negotiated a ten-year contract which required her to perform in specials and guest appearances for the first five years. During the remaining five, Burnett was to dedicate herself to her own show.

The Carol Burnett Show debuted on 11 September 1967, and ran for eleven seasons. It gave Burnett the opportunity to integrate a vaudeville-inspired melange of guest stars, music, and various comedic styles with her own unique blend of sophisti-

cation and folksiness. By filming the show live, with an in-studio audience and a recurring ensemble cast, *The Carol Burnett Show* fused the aura of live performance with the benefits of filmed production. Burnett's opening question-and-answer session with audience members showcased her congenial, unpretentious persona, and illustrated her astonishing spontaneity in dealing with the unexpected. Bits and pieces of her life experience found their way into the show: her signature ear-tug, originally a signal to her grandmother, the working-class grace of her Charwoman character, her childhood fascination with movies and stars, and the painfully funny relationship between Burnett's Eunice character and Vicki Laurence's Mama in "Family" sketches. The show reached its ratings peak in 1972, but remained popular enough to carry it through 1978, when Burnett terminated the program before it became too stale.

After *The Carol Burnett Show*, Burnett continued to perform in all aspects of the entertainment industry, from television to Broadway. Highlights of her television career include the made-for-television movie, *Friendly Fire* (1979), which examined issues confronting families with sons in Vietnam, the miniseries *Fresno* (1986), which lampooned popular night-time soap operas like *Dallas* by presenting comedic elements as if they were serious drama, and musical/opera specials with stars as diverse as Beverly Sills and Dolly Parton. Burnett-as-performer is also known as Burnett-the-Crusader: in 1981, she won a lawsuit against *The National Enquirer* tabloid, which had slandered her in 1976 with an article suggesting that she was drunk and rowdy at a gathering of celebrities and international political figures. Burnett's diverse list of credits continue to grow, and even after a lifetime of success, this consummate professional remains true to the pledge she made to her anonymous benefactor—a lecture given for the Actors' Studio in New York City is scheduled for airing in 1996 on the *Bravo* Arts network, as Burnett helps others find their way into television, motion pictures, and legitimate theater.

—Kathryn C. D'Alessandro

CAROL BURNETT. Born in San Antonio, Texas, U.S.A. 26 April 1933. Attended the University of California, Los Angeles (UCLA), 1951–54. Married: 1) Don Saroyan, 1955 (divorced, 1962); 2) Joe Hamilton, 1963 (divorced, 1984); children: Carrie Louise, Jody Ann, and Erin Kate. UCLA summer stock, summer 1952 and 1953; moved to New York, 1954; hatcheck girl, 1954–55; signed with William Morris Agency, 1955; in television from 1955; debuted on Broadway as lead in *Once Upon a Mattress*, 1959; recorded first solo record album, 1961; toured Midwest in concert, summer 1962; signed with CBS-TV, 1962; in film, from 1963, debute, *Who's Been Sleeping in My Bed?*, 1963. Recipient: 5 Emmy Awards, 1962–91; 5 American Guild of Variety Artists Awards; TV Guide Award, 1961, 1962 and 1963; Peabody Award, 1963; National Television Critics Circle Award, 1977; San Sebastian Film Festival Award for Best Actress, 1978; 12 People's Choice Awards; 2 Photoplay Gold Medals; 8 Golden Globe Awards; Academy of Television Arts and Sciences Woman of the Year; Ace Award, 1983; Television

Hall of Fame induction, 1985; Horatio Alger Award, 1988. Address: c/o International Creative Management, 8899 Beverly Boulevard, Los Angeles, California 90048, U.S.A.

TELEVISION SERIES

1950–63	*Pantomime Quiz*
1953–64	*The Garry Moore Show*
1955	*The Winchell-Mahoney Show*
1956	*Stanley*
1964–65	*The Entertainers*
1967–78	*The Carol Burnett Show*
1990–91	*Carol and Company*
1991	*The Carol Burnett Show*

TELEVISION MINISERIES

1986	*Fresno*

MADE-FOR-TELEVISION MOVIES

1974	*6 RMS RIV VU*
1975	*Twigs*
1978	*The Grass Is Always Greener Over the Septic Tank*
1979	*Friendly Fire*
1979	*The Tenth Month*
1982	*Life of the Party: The Story of Beatrice*
1983	*Between Friends*
1985	*Laundromat*
1988	*Hostage*
1994	*Seasons of the Heart*

TELEVISION SPECIALS

1962	*Julie and Carol at Carnegie Hall*
1963	*Calamity Jane*
1963	*An Evening with Carol Burnett*
1964	*Once Upon a Mattress*
1966	*Carol and Company*
1967	*Carol + 2*
1969	*Bing Crosby and Carol Burnett—Together Again for the First Time*
1971	*Julie and Carol at the Lincoln Center*
1972	*Once Upon a Mattress*
1975	*Twigs*
1976	*Sills and Burnett at the Met*
1978	*A Special Carol Burnett*
1979	*Dolly and Carol in Nashville*
1982	*Eunice*

1982	*Hollywood: The Gift of Laughter* (co-host)
1984	*Burnett "Discovers" Domingo*
1985	*Here's TV Entertainment* (co-host)
1987	*Plaza Suite*
1987	*Carol, Carl, Whoopi, and Robin*
1987	*Superstars and Their Moms*
1988	*Superstars and Their Moms*
1989	*Julie and Carol—Together Again*
1991	*The Funny Women of Television*
1991	*The Very Best of the Ed Sullivan Show* (host)
1993	*The Carol Burnett Show: A Reunion*
1994	*A Century of Women*
1994	*Men, Movies, and Carol*

FILMS

Who's Been Sleeping In My Bed?, 1963; *Pete 'n' Tillie*, 1972; *The Front Page*, 1974; *A Wedding*, 1978; *Four Seasons*, 1981; *Chu Chu and the Philly Flash*, 1981; *H.E.A.L.T.H.*, 1982; *Annie*, 1982; *Noises Off*, 1992.

STAGE

Once Upon a Mattress, 1959; *Fade Out—Fade In*, 1964; *Plaza Suite*, 1971; *I Do! I Do!*, 1973; *Same Time Next Year*, 1977; *Love Letters*, 1990.

PUBLICATIONS

One More Time: A Memoir. New York: Random House, 1986.

Purdum, Todd S. "Carol Burnett Comes Round to Where She Started From" (interview). *The New York Times*, 24 September 1995.

"The Serious Business of Being Funny" (interview). *The New Yorker*, 21 August 1995.

FURTHER READING

Marc, David. "Carol Burnett: The Last of the Big-time Comedy-Variety Stars." *Quarterly Review of Film Studies* (Chur, Netherlands), July 1992.

O'Connor, John J. "Funny Women of Television: A Museum of Television and Radio Tribute." *The New York Times*, 24 October 1991.

Taraborrelli, J. Randy. *Laughing Till It Hurts: The Complete Life and Career of Carol Burnett.* New York: Morrow, 1988.

See also *Carol Burnett Show*, Variety Programs

BURNS, ALLAN

U.S. Writer/Producer

Allan Burns moved to Los Angeles in 1956 intending to pursue a career as a cartoonist or commercial artist. After being laid off from his job as a page at NBC, he did begin earning a living as a cartoonist for greeting cards. He soon moved to television, employed in 1962 by Jay Ward on the cartoon series, *Rocky and his Friends* and *The Bullwinkle Show*. Burns then formed a partnership with Chris Hayward and they created *The Munsters*, perhaps an obvious next step for a cartoonist. He then moved on to the comedy series, *He and She*, where he won the first of six Emmy Awards for his writing. Of that series Burns says, "That was my first great experience, creating character rather than gimmicks." On *He and She* Burns met Jay Sandrich, who was directing the show.

Hayward and Burns then became story editors for *Get Smart*, where they worked with Mel Brooks and Buck Henry and where Sandrich also worked for a time as a producer. Following that experience the Burns-Hayward partnership dissolved and in 1969 Burns saw the pilot of *Room 222*, created by James L. Brooks, liked it, and began to write for the show. When Brooks took a leave to do a movie, Grant Tinker, the executive in charge of programming, asked Burns to produce *Room 222*.

At about this same time Tinker received a 13-week commitment from CBS for an undeveloped series starring Mary Tyler Moore, to whom he was then married. CBS agreed that the project was to be under the complete control of Tinker and Moore; Tinker approached Burns and Brooks and asked them to collaborate to develop a show. As Burns remembers, "We had this remarkable situation where we had an office and an on-air commitment and nothing else."

The group rejected the idea of a domestic comedy and determined to portray a woman who was 30 years old, unmarried, and employed "somewhere." Burns recalls that they had to explain "30 and unmarried" to the network, so "We thought, 'Ah! here is our chance to do a divorce.'" CBS would have no part of that idea and the executives in New York sent word to Tinker, "Get rid of those guys." He refused. Instead, the creators changed the plot to begin with Mary having just ended a failed love affair. The pilot was made, with Jay Sandrich directing, and one of television's landmark series, *The Mary Tyler Moore Show*, was on its way.

In 1977 when the show concluded after 168 episodes most of the writing staff moved to Paramount with long term contracts. Burns, however, decided to stay with Tinker and joined with Gene Reynolds to create *Lou Grant*. Despite the fact that it essentially re-invented the Lou Grant character, the series was a major success, and soon became part of the CBS Monday night response to ABC football.

Burns also directed his talent to the writing of feature films, one being the highly praised *A Little Romance*, starring Laurence Olivier, for which he received an Oscar nomination for Best Screenplay Adaptation. Burns left MTM in 1991 after developing several other TV series.

Calm and persuasive, Allan Burns combines outstanding talent with an ability to work extremely well with a variety of competing personalities. Observing him on the set of a series in production one senses that he quickly commands both trust and respect from those with whom he collaborates. Director Jay Sandrich sums it up well, "Allan is the best."

—Robert S. Alley

Alan Burns
Photo courtesy of Alan Burns

ALLAN BURNS. Born in Baltimore, Maryland, U.S.A., 18 May 1935. Attended University of Oregon, 1953-56. Married: Joan Bailey, 1964, children: Eric C. and Matthew M. Screen and television writer from 1964. Recipient: Emmy Awards, 1968, 1971, 1977, 1974, 1976, 1977; Writers Guild Award, 1970.

TELEVISION SERIES

1964–66	*The Munsters* (co-creator)
1965–70	*Get Smart* (head writer)
1967–68	*He and She* (head writer)
1969–74	*Room 222* (also director, and producer)
1970–77	*The Mary Tyler Moore Show* (also creator)
1974–75	*Paul Sand in Friends and Lovers* (creator and producer)
1974–78	*Rhoda* (also creator)
1977–82	*Lou Grant* (also creator)
1984	*The Duck Factory* (also creator)
1988	*Eisenhower and Lutz* (also creator)

FILMS

Butch and Sundance: The Early Days, 1979; *A Little Romance*, 1979; *I Won't Dance*, 1983; *Just the Way You Are*, 1984; *Just Between Friends* (also director and co-producer), 1986.

FURTHER READING

Newcomb, Horace, and Robert S. Alley. *The Producer's Medium: Conversations with Creators of American TV*. New York: Oxford University Press, 1983.

See also *Mary Tyler Moore Show*, *Lou Grant*

BURNS, GEORGE

U.S. Comedian and Actor

George Burns moved in the course of his lengthy career from serving as a vaudeville straight man to being one of the grand old men of American show business—and an expert on the history of entertainment in the United States. The television program he shared with his wife, comedienne Gracie Allen, for eight years (1950 to 1958 on CBS) was central to Burns' professional life, chronologically and symbolically.

According to accounts of his early life (all of which originate from Burns himself), he was drawn to show business as a small child, singing on street corners with friends for pennies, and never seriously considered any other calling. Burns floundered in vaudeville for years, changing his act with great frequency, until he met Allen in 1922 (or 1923; accounts vary), and the couple inaugurated the straight-man/"Dumb Dora" pairing they would enact for more than four decades. The team moved successfully into film and radio in the early 1930s and finally into television in October 1950.

In *The George Burns and Gracie Allen Show*, Burns and Allen played versions of themselves, a show-business couple living in Beverly Hills, California. As she had throughout their joint career, Allen acted as the comedian of the two, creating chaos through her misunderstandings of the world about her, while Burns served as her straight man. He helped establish her elaborate humorous situations, set the timing for their conversations, and lovingly extricated his partner and wife from the fictional consequences of her "zany" personality—all the while maintaining a deadpan stance.

The pair were supported by Bea Benaderet playing their neighbor Blanche Morton, by a series of actors portraying Blanche's husband Harry, by their announcer (first Bill Goodwin, later Harry von Zell) playing himself, and eventually by their son Ronnie. The program was playful and sophisticated, relying more on linguistic than on physical humor. Although the character of Gracie was dumb in many ways, she never lost the respect and affection of her fellow cast members, particularly not of her husband. Her mistakes were never unkind, and her dumbness was in its own way brilliant. Perhaps more than any other couple-oriented situation comedy of its day, *Burns and Allen* presented an egalitarian marriage—in large part because George Burns as straight man was always dependent on his partner's comic abilities.

Burns used the new medium of television to expand his straight-man role, however. In *Gracie: A Love Story*, a 1988 biography of Allen, he jokingly explained his function in planning the show: "My major contribution to the format was to suggest that I be able to step out of the plot and speak directly to the audience, and then be able to go right back into the action. That was an original idea of mine; I know it was because I originally stole it from Thornton Wilder's play *Our Town*."

George Burns

Burns thus moved from merely setting up his partner's jokes to interpreting them, and indeed the entire action of the program, to the audience. Eventually the program's writers (of whom Burns himself served as the head) gave the character George-as-narrator additional omniscience by placing a magic television set in his den. This device enabled him to monitor and comment on the plot even when he was not directly involved in it.

Television gave additional responsibilities to the offscreen George Burns as well as to his onscreen counterpart. Like many video stars of the 1950s, Burns owned the program in which he starred. His production company, McCadden, also produced or co-produced a number of advertisements and two other situation comedies—*The Bob Cummings Show* (1955–1959) and *The People's Choice* (1955–1958).

The ever-busy Burns also used the *Burns and Allen* years to become an author. He produced his first volume of memoirs, *I Love Her, That's Why!*, with Cynthia Hobart Lindsay in 1955. The book enhanced Burns' reputation as a raconteur and staked his claim to authorship of the Burns and Allen team.

Unfortunately for Burns, he was soon to discover that he was still not the star of that team. When Allen retired from their act and from show business in 1958, he immediately reassembled his writers and his cast to churn out

The George Burns Show, a situation comedy featuring all of Burns and Allen's characters except Allen. The show foundered after one season.

Burns persevered, trying nightclub work alone and with other actresses. In the fall of 1964, attempting to recover from Allen's death earlier that year, he returned to television, co-starring in *Wendy and Me* with Connie Stevens and producing *No Time for Sergeants*. Neither program lasted beyond the first season. The following year, he was back producing another short-lived program, *Mona McCluskey*.

Burns continued to move along on the edges of American show business until 1975, when, after the death of his close friend Jack Benny, he was given Benny's part in the film version of Neil Simon's comedy *The Sunshine Boys*. His success in this role led to other film work (including portrayal of the almighty in three *Oh, God!* pictures), television specials, and contracts for several more books—mostly memoirs.

His final book, *100 Years, 100 Stories*, was published in 1996. In many ways, this small and entertaining volume summed up the life and career of George Burns. It consisted of a number of often retold, highly repolished jokes. Its origins, like Burns' own ethnic roots, were obscured but oddly irrelevant-seeming. (Burns himself was in such poor health during the book's production that he clearly played little part in it; nevertheless, the stories were ones he had told for years and years.) Years after her death, it still depended heavily for its meaning on Burns' relationship with Allen, who figured prominently in many of the stories. And coming out as it did in the weeks between its author's 100th birthday in January of 1996 and his death in March, this final volume exhibited the sort of timing for which George Burns was justly renowned.

—Tinky "Dakota" Weisblat

GEORGE BURNS. Born Nathan Birnbaum, in New York City, New York, U.S.A. 20 January 1896. Married: Gracie Allen, 1926 (died, 1964); children: Sandra Jean and Ronald Jon. Early career in vaudeville as singer in children's quartet, then as dancer, roller skater, and comedian; formed comedy partnership with Gracie Allen, 1923; co-starred with Allen in radio program, 1932–50; partnership moved to television in *The George Burns and Gracie Allen Show*, 1950-58; continued as star of *The George Burns Show*, 1958–59; after death of Allen in 1964, continued to work in film, notably in *The Sunshine Boys*, 1976. Honorary degree: University of Hartford, 1988. Recipient: Academy Award, 1976; Kennedy Center Honor, 1988. Died in Beverly Hills, California, 9 March 1996.

TELEVISION SERIES
1950–58	*The George Burns and Gracie Allen Show*
1958–59	*The George Burns Show*
1964–65	*Wendy and Me*
1985	*George Burns Comedy Week*

TELEVISION SPECIALS (selection)
1959	*George Burns in the Big Time*
1976	*The George Burns Special*
1977	*The George Burns One-Man Show*
1981	*George Burns in Nashville*
1981	*George Burns Early, Early, Early Christmas Show*
1982	*George Burns 100th Birthday Party*
1982	*George Burns and Other Sex Symbols*
1983	*George Burns Celebrates 80 Years in Show Business*
1983	*Grandpa, Will You Run with Me?*
1984	*George Burns: An Hour of Jokes and Songs*
1984	*George Burns' How to Live to Be 100*
1986	*George Burns' 90th Birthday Party— A Very Special Special*
1988	*Disney's Magic in the Kingdom* (host)
1991	*George Burns' 95th Birthday Party*

FILMS
Lamb Chops, 1929; *Fit to be Tied*, 1930; *Pulling a Bone*, 1930; *The Antique Shop*, 1931; *Once Over, Light*, 1931; *One Hundred Per Cent Service*, 1931; *The Big Broadcast of 1932*, 1932; *Oh My Operation*, 1932; *The Babbling Book*, 1932; *Hollywood on Parade A-2*, 1932; *International House*, 1933; *Love in Bloom*, 1933; *College Humor*, 1933; *Patents Pending*, 1933; *Let's Dance*, 1933; *Walking the Baby*, 1933; *Six of a Kind*, 1934; *We're Not Dressing*, 1934; *Many Happy Returns*, 1934; *Here Comes Cookie*, 1935; *Love in Bloom*, 1935; *The Big Broadcast of 1936*, 1936; *College Holiday*, 1936; *The Big Broadcast of 1937*, 1937; *A Damsel in Distress*, 1937; *College Swing*, 1938; *Many Happy Returns*, 1939; *Honolulu*, 1939; *Two Girls and a Sailor*, 1944; *Screen Snapshots No. 224*, 1954; *The Solid Gold Cadillac* (narrator only), 1956; *The Sunshine Boys*, 1975; *Oh God!*, 1977; *Sgt. Pepper's Lonely Hearts Club Band*, 1978; *Going in Style*, 1979; *Just You and Me, Kid*, 1979; *Two of a Kind*, 1979; *Oh God! Book Two*, 1980; *Oh God, You Devil!*, 1984; *Eighteen Again*, 1988; *Radioland Murders*, 1994.

RECORD ALBUMS
I Wish I Was Young Again, 1981; *George Burns in Nashville*, 1981; *George Burns—Young at Heart*, 1982; *As Time Goes By* (with Bobby Vinton), 1993.

PUBLICATIONS
I Love Her, That's Why!, with Cynthia Hobart Lindsay. New York: Simon and Schuster, 1955.
Living It Up, or, They Still Love Me in Altoona. New York: Putnam, 1976.
How to Live to Be 100: Or More!, The Ultimate Diet, Sex and Exercise Book. New York: Putnam, 1983.
Dear George: Advice and Answers from America's Leading Expert on Everything from A to Z. New York: Putnam, 1985.
Gracie: A Love Story. New York: Putnam, 1988.
All My Best Friends, with David Fisher. New York: Putnam, 1989.
Wisdom of the 90s, with Hal Goldman. New York: Putnam, 1991.
100 Years, 100 Stories. New York: Putnam, 1996.

FURTHER READING

"Burns." *The New Yorker*, 15 March 1976.

"Burns without Allen." *Time* (New York), 3 March 1958.

Blythe, Cheryl, and Susan Sackett. *Say Goodnight Gracie! The Story of Burns and Allen.* New York: Dutton, 1986.

Leerhsen, Charles. "Grace after Gracie; George Burns Carries on with a Best Seller and a Love Affair with Showbiz." *Newsweek* (New York), 26 December 1988.

Maynard, John. "George Burns—New TV Tycoon." *Pictorial Review* (New York), 8 December 1957.

McCollister, John. "George Burns: An American Treasure." *Saturday Evening Post* (Indianapolis, Indiana), May/June 1987.

See also Allen, Gracie; *George Burns and Gracie Allen Show*

BURNS, KEN

U.S. Documentary Film Maker

Ken Burns is one of public television's most celebrated and prolific producers. He has already fashioned a record of nine major Public Broadcasting System (PBS) specials, addressing a wide range of topics from American history, such as *The Brooklyn Bridge* (PBS, 1982), *The Shakers: Hands to Work, Hearts to God* (PBS, 1985), *The Statue of Liberty* (PBS, 1985), *Huey Long* (PBS, 1986), *Thomas Hart Benton* (PBS, 1989), *The Congress* (PBS, 1989), *The Civil War* (PBS, 1990), *Empire of the Air* (PBS, 1992), and *Baseball* (PBS, 1994), which have all won various awards and recognitions from both professional and scholarly organizations and at international film festivals.

Burns is a 1975 graduate of Hampshire College in Amherst, Massachusetts, where he studied under still photographers, Jerome Liebling and Elaine Mayes, and received a degree in film studies and design. Upon graduation, he and two of his college friends started Florentine Films and struggled for a number of years doing freelance assignments, finishing a few short documentaries before beginning work in 1977 on a film based on David McCullough's book, *The Great Bridge* (1972). Four years later, they completed *The Brooklyn Bridge*, which won several honors including an Academy Award nomination, thus ushering Burns into the ambit of public television. While editing *The Brooklyn Bridge* in 1979, Burns moved Florentine Films to Walpole, New Hampshire, surviving on as little as "$2,500 one year to stay independent."

Much about Ken Burns's career defies conventional wisdom. He operates his own independent company in a small New England village more than four hours north of New York City, hardly a crossroads in the highly competitive and often insular world of corporately funded, PBS-sponsored productions. His television career is a popular and critical success story in an era when the historical documentary generally holds little interest for most Americans. His PBS specials so far are also strikingly out of step with the visual pyrotechnics and frenetic pacing of most reality-based TV programming, relying instead on techniques that are literally decades old, although Burns reintegrates these constituent elements into a wholly new and highly complex textual arrangement.

Beginning with *The Brooklyn Bridge* and continuing through *Baseball*, Burns has intricately blended narration with what he calls his "chorus of voices," meaning readings from personal papers, diaries, and letters; interpretive commentaries from on-screen experts, usually historians; his "rephotographing" technique which closely examines photographs, paintings, drawings, daguerreotypes, and other artifacts with a movie camera; all backed with a musical-track that features period compositions and folk music. The effect of this collage of techniques is to create the illusion that the viewer is being transported back in time, literally finding an emotional connection with the people and events of America's past.

Ken Burns
Photo courtesy of Lisa Berg/General Motors/Florentine Films

At first, it may appear that he has embraced a wide assortment of subjects—a bridge, a 19th-century religious sect, a statue, a demagogue, a painter, the congress, the Civil War, radio, and the national pastime—but several underlying common denominators bind this medley of Americana together. Burns's body of work casts an image of America which is built on consensus and is celebratory in nature, highlighting the nation's ideals and achievements. He suggests, moreover, that "television can become a new Homeric mode," drawing narrative parameters which are epic and heroic in scope. The epic form tends to celebrate a people's shared tradition in sweeping terms, while recounting the lives of national heroes is the classical way of imparting values by erecting edifying examples for present and future generations.

In this way, Burns's chronicles are populated with seemingly ordinary men and women who rise up from the ranks of the citizenry to become paragons of national (and occasionally transcendent) achievement, always persisting against great odds. *The Brooklyn Bridge,* for example, described by the film's "chorus of voices" as "a work of art" and "the greatest feat of civil engineering in the world," is the "inspiration" of a kind of "Renaissance man," John A. Roebling, who died as the building of the bridge was beginning, and his son, Washington Roebling, who finished the monument 14 years later through his own dogged perseverance and courage, despite being bedridden in the process.

Along with being an outstanding documentarian and popular historian, Burns, like all important cultural voices, is also a moralist. Taken as a whole his series of films stand as morality tales, drawing upon epic events, landmarks, and institutions of historical significance. They are populated by heroes and villains who allegorically personify certain virtues and vices in the national character as understood through the popular mythology of our modern memory. At the beginning of *Empire of the Air,* for instance, Jason Robards' narration explains how Lee DeForest, David Sarnoff, and Edwin H. Armstrong "were driven to create [radio] by ancient qualities, idealism and imagination, greed and envy, ambition and determination, and genius." And Burns himself describes Huey Long as "a tragic almost Shakespearean story of a man who started off good, went bad, and got killed for it."

Burns is best known, of course, for his 11-hour documentary series, *The Civil War.* The overwhelming popularity of this program, aired in September 1990, made him a household name. Much of the success of the series must be equated to the extent with which Burns makes this 130-year-old conflict immediate and comprehensible to a contemporary audience. He adopted a similar strategy with *Baseball.* "Baseball," he says, "is as much about American social history as it is about the game," as it examines such issues as immigration, assimilation, labor and management conflicts, and, most importantly, race relations. Burns explains that "Jackie Robinson and his story are sort of the center of gravity for the film, the Gettysburg Address and Emancipa-

tion Proclamation rolled into one." This 19-hour history of the sport debuted over nine evenings in September 1994, lasting nearly double the length and costing twice the budget ($7 million) of *The Civil War.*

Burns is now executive producer on two additional projects for PBS. He has next committed to a 10-hour, seven-part multicultural history of the American West, which is scheduled to inaugurate the public television season during the fall of 1996. He also has an agreement with General Motors to oversee a series entitled *American Lives,* in which various documentarians, including himself, will film brief biographies of important historical figures, such as Thomas Jefferson, Susan B. Anthony, and Mark Twain. His involvement with *American Lives* ensures that Burns will be a fixture at PBS into the next century.

Despite his long-standing affiliation with non-commercial television in the U. S., Burns still remembers his boyhood dream of becoming the next John Ford. As he recalls, "I had always wanted to be a Hollywood director. I think as I look back now in retrospect, I realize how my whole body of work is a kind of documentary version of Ford—that is a real love for American mythology." Burns is once again exploring a subject that is intimately related to John Ford's filmic legacy in *The West.* Ford was a visual poet of the first order; he was also a populist, stressing a respect for the past and the lessons it can teach. Burns shares a similar style and outlook in his documentaries: "All my work is animated by the question 'who are we?' that is to say who are we as a people? What does it mean to be an American? And all of these questions are not necessarily answered by these investigations as the questions are themselves deepened." In this respect, no one has ever done a better job of probing and revivifying the past for more Americans through the power and reach of prime-time television than Ken Burns.

—Gary R. Edgerton

KEN BURNS. Born in Brooklyn, New York, U.S.A., 29 July, 1953. Educated at Hampshire College, B.A. in film studies and design, 1975. Married: Amy Stechler, 1982, children: Sarah and Lily. Cinematographer, BBC, Italian television, and others; president and owner, Florentine Films, since 1975; producer, cinematographer, and director of documentaries, since 1977. Member: Academy of Motion Picture Arts and Sciences; Society of American Historians; American Antiquarian Society; Massachusetts Historical Society; Walpole Society for Bringing to Justice Horse Thieves and Pilferers. Honorary degrees (selection): University of New Hampshire, L.H.D., Notre Dame College, Litt.D., Amherst College, Litt.D., 1991, Pace University, L.H.D., Bowdoin College, L.H.D., 1991, and CUNY, Ph.D. Recipient: Christopher Awards, 1973, 1987, 1990; two Erik Barnouw Awards; eight CINE Golden Eagle Awards; Producer's Guild of America's Producer of the Year Award, 1990; two Emmy Awards, 1991; People's Choice Award, 1991. Address: P.O. Box 613, Walpole, New Hampshire 03608, U.S.A.

TELEVISION (producer, director, cinematographer)

1982	*Brooklyn Bridge*
1985	*The Shakers: Hands to Work, Hearts to God* (also co-writer)
1985	*The Statue of Liberty*
1986	*Huey Long* (also co-writer)
1989	*The Congress*
1989	*Thomas Hart Benton*
1990	*Lindbergh* (executive producer only)
1990	*The Civil War* (also co-writer)
1991	*The Songs of the Civil War*
1992	*Empire of the Air*
1994	*Baseball*

PUBLICATIONS

The Shakers: Hands to Work, Hearts to God, with Amy Stechler Burns. New York: Aperture Foundation, 1987.

The Civil War: An Illustrated History, with Ric Burns and Geoffrey Ward. New York: Knopf, 1990.

Baseball: An Illustrated History, with Geoffrey Ward. New York: Knopf, 1994.

Cripps, Thomas. "Historical Truth: An Interview with Ken Burns." *American Historical Review* (Washington, D.C.), June 1995.

FURTHER READING

Edgerton, Gary. "Ken Burns's America: Style, Authorship, and Cultural Memory." *Journal of Popular Film and Television* (Washington, D.C.), Summer 1993.

————. "Ken Burns's American Dream: Histories-for-TV from Walpole, New Hampshire." *Television Quarterly* (New York), Winter 1994.

"Film Maker Opposes Disney Theme Park." *The New York Times*, 20 May 1994.

Leventhal, Larry. "One Man's 'Civil War' Is Another's Foundation." *Variety* (Los Angeles), 21 September 1992.

Thomson, David. "History Composed with Film." *Film Comment* (New York), September-October 1990.

Tibbetts, John C. "The Incredible Stillness of Being: Motionless Pictures in the Films of Ken Burns." *American Studies* (Lawrence, Kansas), Spring 1996.

See also *Civil War*

BURR, RAYMOND

U.S. Actor

Raymond Burr is so associated with his characterization of television lawyer/detective *Perry Mason* that his rich and varied career in film, radio, and television is often ignored. His face, in the words of *Perry Mason* creator Erle Stanley Gardner, is cow-eyed. He is broad shouldered, heavy, robust, but excelled at playing introverted rather than extroverted characters. This may be, in part, why Burr accomplished the rare television feat in which actor becomes almost thoroughly identified with character, the performer inseparable from the role. Just as William Shatner is James Kirk, Peter Falk is Columbo, and Carroll O'Connor is Archie Bunker, Burr is Perry Mason.

Burr began as a stage actor who performed small roles in radio. His early film work was remarkable only in the sense that he rarely played anything other than the villain in such films as *Raw Deal* (1948). Burr even managed to play the "heavy" in comedies, such as the Marx Brothers' *Love Happy* (1949). When he was in the courtroom drama *A Place in the Sun* (1951), he assumed the role of the relentless district attorney. During these movie years Burr continued to work in several radio series such as *Pat Novak for Hire* (1949) and *Dragnet* (1949–1950). In 1954 he confirmed his villainous persona with his appearance as the menacing wife-killer Lars Thorwald in Alfred Hitchcock's *Rear Window* (1954).

In 1955 when he learned that the lawyer/detective drama *Perry Mason* was being cast for television, Burr was requested to audition—but for the part of district attorney Hamilton Burger, another "villain". As the story goes the producers at Paisano Productions (the *Perry Mason* produc-

tion company) allowed Burr to try for the title role simply to secure his audition for Burger. Erle Stanley Gardner,

Raymond Burr

author of the original Mason novels and co-creator of the television series, is said to have taken a look at Burr during the audition and declared "He's Perry Mason." This was the role Burr played from 1957 to 1966 and reprised in a successful series of made-for-television movies from 1985 until his death in 1993.

At the time of *Perry Mason*'s popularity Burr was one of the highest paid actors in series television, commanding a yearly salary of $1 million. Yet he was well known for his philanthropy. Between television production seasons he would take the time to journey to Vietnam on his own—not to perform but to meet and visit with those serving on the front lines. Burr was comfortable with self-depreciating humor and appeared in numerous television send-ups of his own career and characters on shows such as *The Jack Benny Show* and *The Red Skelton Show*.

What happened to Burr was a classic case of an actor being blended with a character he or she successfully plays. During his time on *Perry Mason*, Burr and his character gradually merged so much that when the series was recast in 1973 with Monte Markham in the title role the audience refused to accept anyone else as Mason. The Markham version was canceled after 15 unsuccessful episodes. The Burr/Mason association was so strong that Burr even received an honorary law doctorate from the McGeorge School of Law in Sacramento, California.

This connection between character and actor was a burden to Burr. He continued to be associated with Mason, even when he starred as a wheelchair-bound policeman in another successful series, *Ironside* (1967–75). In this series, Burr portrayed Chief of Detectives Robert Ironside, crippled by an assassin's bullet in the pilot episode. Although urged to retire, Ironside worked to ferret out criminals—this time from the prosecution's side. The show was pure crime drama common to the late sixties, mixed with "hip" dialogue and situations relevant to the time. As Richard Meyers argues in *TV Detectives* (1988), Ironside was the perfect "armchair detective." It was still rational detection, in the *Perry Mason* mode, that was his strongest asset.

Burr tried several other series, but after the twin successes of *Perry Mason* and *Ironside* he was unable to capture the unity of character that a television series needs. In 1976 he had the title role of a lawyer in *Mallory: Circumstantial Evidence*, a pilot that never went to series. Next he played an investigative reporter in *Kingston*, which aired as a series for less than a season 1977, and another lawyer in *The Jordan Chance* (1978), also a failed pilot. Through the early to middle 1980s Burr was a pitchman for a number of products such as the Independent Insurance Agents association.

Only when he returned to the role of Mason in the made-for-television movie *Perry Mason Returns* (1985) was he able to renew his success in American television. He also reprised his role as Chief Ironside in *The Return of Ironside* in 1993. The original cast returned for what was planned to be a new series of made-for-television movies, but only the first movie was completed. Burr finally succumbed to cancer on 12 September 1993.

To every character, Burr brought a cool calculation and intensity. In his three most notable roles—as Lars Thorwald in Hitchcock's *Rear Window*, Perry Mason and Robert Ironside—his acting is introspective and low-key. He portrayed Thorwald as stony-faced and deliberate, thoroughly menacing. That same focus was present in his Mason and Ironside but transformed Burr into the hero rather than the villain. While his Thorwald could level a stare across a courtyard to frighten voyeurs looking out their rear window, his Mason could stare down a witness and bring a quick and heartfelt confession. Burr's stare still reveals more than the ranting and pacing of most other actors.

—J. Dennis Bounds

RAYMOND BURR. Born in New Westminster, British Columbia, Canada, 21 May 1917. Attended Stanford University, University of California, Columbia University, and University of Chungking. Married: 1) Annette Sutherland, 1941 (died, 1943); children: Michael and Evan (died, 1953); 2) Isabella Ward, 1947 (divorced); 3) Laura Andrina Morgan, 1953 (died, 1955). Served in California Conservation Corp. and Forestry Service. Began stage career as teenager, eventually performing on Broadway in *Crazy with the Heat*, 1941, and *The Duke in Darkness*, 1944; director, Pasadena Community Playhouse, 1943; started film career in 1946; cast often as villain, notably in *A Place in the Sun*, 1951, and *Rear Window*, 1954; television actor, appearing as title character in *Perry Mason*, CBS, 1957–66, and *Ironside*, NBC, 1967–75; returned to television as Perry Mason in 1985–86 made-for-television movie, which led to 25 subsequent Perry Mason made-for-television movies on NBC; started Royal Blue Ltd., television production company with business partner Robert Benevides, 1988. Recipient: Emmy Awards, 1959 and 1961. Died, in Dry Creek, California, 12 September 1993.

TELEVISION SERIES

1957–66	*Perry Mason*
1967–75	*Ironside*
1977	*Kingston: Confidential*

TELEVISION MINISERIES

1977–79	*Park Ave*
1978	*Centennial*
1978	*The Bastard*

MADE-FOR-TELEVISION MOVIES

1967	*Ironside: Split Second to an Epitaph*
1971	*The Priest Killer*
1976	*Mallory: Circumstantial Evidence*
1977	*Kingston* (pilot)
1978	*The Bastard* (narrator)
1978	*The Jordan Chance*
1979	*Love's Savage Fury*
1979	*Disaster on the Coastliner*

1980	*Curse of King Tut's Tomb*
1980	*The Night the City Screamed*
1981	*Peter and Paul*
1985	*Perry Mason Returns*
1986	*Perry Mason: The Case of the Notorious Nun*
1986	*Perry Mason: The Case of the Shooting Star*
1987	*Perry Mason: The Case of the Lost Love*
1987	*Perry Mason: The Case of the Murdered Madam*
1987	*Perry Mason: The Case of the Scandalous Scoundrel*
1987	*Perry Mason: The Case of the Sinister Spirit*
1988	*Perry Mason: The Case of the Avenging Ace*
1988	*Perry Mason: The Case of the Lady in the Lake*
1989	*Perry Mason: The Case of the All-Star Assassin*
1989	*Perry Mason: The Case of the Lethal Lesson*
1989	*Perry Mason: The Case of the Musical Murder*
1990	*Perry Mason: The Case of the Desperate Deception*
1990	*Perry Mason: The Case of the Poisoned Pen*
1990	*Perry Mason: The Case of the Silenced Singer*
1990	*Perry Mason: The Case of the Defiant Daughter*
1991	*Perry Mason: The Case of the Maligned Mobster*
1991	*Perry Mason: the Case of the Ruthless Reporter*
1991	*Perry Mason: The Case of the Glass Coffin*
1991	*Perry Mason: The Case of the Fatal Fashion*
1992	*Perry Mason: The Case of the Fatal Framing Grass Roots*
1992	*Perry Mason: The Case of the Reckless Romeo*
1992	*Perry Mason: The Case of the Heartbroken Bride*
1993	*The Return of Ironside*
1993	*Perry Mason: The Case of the Telltale Talk Show Host*
1993	*Perry Mason: The Case of the Skin-Deep Scandal*
1993	*Perry Mason: The Case of the Killer Kiss*

FILMS

Without Reservations, 1946; *San Quentin,* 1947; *Code of the West,* 1947; *Desperate,* 1947; *I Love Trouble,* 1947; *Fighting Father Dunne,* 1948; *Pitfall,* 1948; *Raw Deal,* 1948; *Ruthless,* 1948; *Sleep My Love,* 1948; *Station West,* 1948; *Walk a Crooked Mile,* 1948; *The Adventures of Don Juan,* 1948; *Abandoned,* 1949; *Black Magic,* 1949; *Bride of Vengeance,* 1949;

Love Happy, 1949; *Red Light,* 1949; *Borderline,* 1950; *Key to the City,* 1950; *Unmasked,* 1950; *Bride of the Gorilla,* 1951; *His Kind of Woman,* 1951; *M,* 1951; *The Magic Carpet,* 1951; *New Mexico,* 1951; *A Place in the Sun,* 1951; *The Whip Hand,* 1951; *Horizons West,* 1952; *Mara Maru,* 1952; *Meet Danny Wilson,* 1952; *Bandits of Corsica,* 1953; *The Blue Gardenia,* 1953; *Fort Algiers,* 1953; *Serpent of the Nile,* 1953; *Tarzan and the She-Devil,* 1953; *Casanova's Big Night,* 1954; *Gorilla at Large,* 1954; *Khyber Patrol,* 1954; *Passion,* 1954; *Rear Window,* 1954; *Thunder Pass,* 1954; *Count Three and Pray,* 1955; *A Man Alone,* 1955; *They Were So Young,* 1954; *You're Never Too Young,* 1955; *The Brass Legend,* 1956; *A Cry in the Night,* 1956; *Godzilla: King of the Monsters,* 1956; *Great Day in the Morning,* 1956; *Please Murder Me,* 1956; *Ride the High Iron,* 1956; *Secret of Treasure Mountain,* 1956; *Affair in Havana,* 1957; *Crime of Passion,* 1957; *Desire in the Dust,* 1960; *P.J.,* 1968; *Tomorrow Never Comes,* 1977; *The Return,* 1980; *Out of the Blue,* 1980; *Airplane II: The Sequel,* 1982; *Godzilla 1985,* 1985; *Delirious,* 1985.

STAGE

Night Must Fall; Mandarin; Crazy with the Heat, 1941; *The Duke in Darkness,* 1944.

FURTHER READING

Hill, Ona L. *Raymond Burr: A Film, Radio and Television Biography.* Jefferson, North Carolina: McFarland, 1994.

Kelleher, Brian, and Diana Merrill. *The Perry Mason Show Book.* New York: St. Martin's, 1987.

Margolick, David. "Raymond Burr's Perry Mason was Fictional, But He Surely Was Relevant and, Oh, So Competent." *The New York Times,* 24 September 1993.

Martindale, David. *The Perry Mason Casebook.* New York: Pioneer, 1991.

Meyers, Richard. *TV Detectives.* San Diego: A. S. Barnes, 1988.

See also *Perry Mason*

BURROWS, JAMES

U.S. Director/Producer

James Burrows is one of the few television directors who has made the successful transition to producer. He became one of the top sitcom directors at MTM Productions, the company founded by Mary Tyler Moore and Grant Tinker. Later, as well working as the resident director for *Taxi,* Burrows helped form the independent production company responsible for the long-running NBC series *Cheers.* His critically acclaimed directing and production talents have won numerous awards, including seven Emmies.

One of Burrow's first goals was to establish an identity separate from that of his famous father, Abe, who had written the books for a number of successful musicals, including *Guys and Dolls* and *How to Succeed in Business Without Really Trying.* Ironically, the senior Burrows had also written for the popular 1930s radio series *Duffy's Tavern,* which, like *Cheers,* was set in a bar. While this did not inspire the younger Burrows to duplicate that situation in *Cheers,* his father's work on a stage adaptation of Truman

Capote's *Breakfast at Tiffany's*, which starred Mary Tyler Moore, did lead James Burrows to an informal meeting with MTM President Grant Tinker. At that time, the younger Burrows was known simply as "Abe's kid."

In 1974, while directing theater in Florida, Burrows asked Tinker for a job at MTM and was hired him to observe other MTM sitcom directors, with his first assignment being *The Bob Newhart Show*. Tinker recounts in his autobiography, *Tinker in Television*, that as Burrows became more comfortable with his role as observer, he began drawing closer to action on the *Bob Newhart* set, causing Newhart to turn to his producer and demand, "Get that guy out of here. He makes me nervous."

This incident marked a significant turning point in Burrows' career, for Tinker responded by teaming Burrows with MTM's veteran director Jay Sandrich. The two hit it off immediately, and Burrows proved a quick study. Today he is considered as accomplished a director as Sandrich himself. Like Sandrich, he developed a directing style sensitive to the specific needs of the weekly sitcom format, which includes actors who already have a deep understanding of the characters they portray. Burrows' goal is to make his actors "director proof," so that subsequent directors do not erode the developed, established personae.

Burrows stayed with MTM until 1977, gaining directing experience on every sitcom they produced, including *The Bob Newhart Show*. He then joined MTM alumni James L. Brooks, Stan Daniels, David Davis and Ed Weinberger on the series *Taxi*, for which he directed 76 episodes. Because *Taxi* had such a large set, Burrows became one of the first directors to use four cameras simultaneously, an adaptation of the three-camera system that had been a staple of sitcom production since *I Love Lucy*. A testament to his talent, Burrows won Emmies in both 1980 and 1981 for his *Taxi* efforts.

In 1982, Burrows, along with Glen and Les Charles, formed the Charles-Burrows-Charles Company, and then created and produced *Cheers*. Lasting into the 1990s, *Cheers* allowed Burrows, now in the role of producer, to carry on the tradition of quality television established two decades earlier at MTM. Although the Charles-Burrows-Charles Company disbanded after *Cheers* voluntarily retired, Burrows has continued working as a director for such sitcoms as *Wings*, *Flesh 'N' Blood*, *Friends*, and *News Radio*.

—Michael Kassel

JAMES BURROWS. Born in Los Angeles, California, U.S.A., 30 December 1940. Education: Oberlin College, B.A.; Yale University, M.F.A. Director, some off-Broadway productions; worked at MTM Productions, 1974–77, directed episodes of *The Mary Tyler Moore Show*, *The Bob Newhart Show*, *Rhoda*, *Phyllis*, *Taxi*, *Lou Grant*; *Dear John* (pilot), *Night Court*; with Glen and Les Charles, formed Charles-Burrows-Charles Company, 1982; co-creator and co-executive producer, as well as director of *Cheers*; further directing credits include *Wings* (pilot); *Roc* (pilot); episodes of *Flesh 'N' Blood*, *Friends*, and *News Radio*. Recipient: Directors Guild of America award for comedy direction, 1984; seven Emmy Awards 1979–80, 1980–81, 1982–83, 1990–91; 1982–83, 1983–84, 1989–90. Address: c/o Paramount TV Productions 5555 Melrose Avenue, Los Angeles, California 90038, U.S.A.

TELEVISION SERIES (as director of various episodes)

1970–71	*The Mary Tyler Moore Show*
1972–78	*The Bob Newhart Show*
1974–78	*Rhoda*
1975–77	*Phyllis*
1977–82	*Lou Grant*
1978–83	*Taxi*
1982–93	*Cheers* (also co-creator, co-executive producer)
1984–92	*Night Court*
1987–90	*The Tracy Ullman Show*
1988	*Dear John* (pilot)
1990	*Wings* (pilot)
1990	*The Simpsons*
1991	*Flesh 'N' Blood*
1994–	*Friends*
1995–	*Caroline in the City*
1995–	*News Radio*
1995	*Partners*

MADE-FOR-TELEVISION MOVIES

1978	*More Than Friends*

FILM (director)
Partners, 1982.

FURTHER READING

Lovece, Frank, and Jules Franco. *Hailing Taxi*. New York: Prentice Hall, 1988.
Sackett, Susan. *Prime Time Hits*. New York: Billboard, 1993.
Sorensen, Jeff. *The Taxi Book*. New York: St. Martin's, 1987.
Tinker, Grant, with Bud Rukeyser. *Tinker in Television*. New York: Simon and Schuster, 1994.
Van Hise, James. *Cheers: Where Everybody Knows Your Name*. Las Vegas: Pioneer, 1993.

See also *Bob Newhart Show*, *Cheers*; *Mary Tyler Moore Show*; *Taxi*

C

CABLE NETWORKS

Cable networks are programming services that deliver packages of information or entertainment by satellite to local cable television systems. The cable systems then redistribute the network programs, through wires, to individual residences in their local franchise areas. The number of cable networks carried by any particular cable system varies, and is based on the channel capacity of the system. Older cable systems may have as few as twenty channels while newer ones may have more than 150 channels. Cable system managers decide which cable networks will be carried. Their decisions are based on analyses of the requirements of their franchise agreement with the local community they serve, on their own economic needs and abilities, and on local audience needs and wishes. Cable networks can be divided into three major types: basic, pay, and pay-per-view.

Basic Networks

The majority of channels on most cable systems are devoted to basic cable networks. These are termed "basic" because the subscriber can obtain a large number of them for a low price. There are over sixty basic networks including:

Arts and Entertainment (A and E)—cultural fiction and non-fiction.

Black Entertainment Television (BET)—talk shows, children's programs, game shows and other fare particularly aimed at people of color.

Bravo—cultural programming.

Cable News Network (CNN)—24 hours a day of news and information.

Consumer News and Business Channel (CNBC)—primarily business news.

Comedy Central—situation comedies, stand-up comedians, comedy movies and similar fare.

Courtroom Television—coverage of cases being tried in the courts.

C-SPAN—coverage of Congress and other political bodies and events.

The Discovery Channel—documentaries and informational programming.

E! Entertainment TV—programming by and about entertainment.

ESPN—24 hour sports programming.

The Family Channel (formerly CBN, the Christian Broadcasting Network)—wholesome programming including reruns of older commercial TV series.

Courtesy of A and E Networks

Courtesy of CourtTV

Courtesy of Discovery Networks

Courtesy of the Disney Channel

Courtesy of HSN

Courtesy of Lifetime

Home Shopping Network—demonstrations of products people can buy by calling the network.

The Learning Channel—formal college credit courses and general education material.

Lifetime Television—information and entertainment shows aimed primarily at women.

MTV—music videos and music-related material aimed at teenagers.

Nickelodeon—children's and family programming.

Nostalgia Television—TV programming from the past, particularly old commercial network series.

QVC Network—a home shopping service.

TNN: Nashville Net—music and other country related programming.

Turner Network TV (TNT)—old movies and some original programming.

Univision—a general Spanish language service.

USA Network—a general service that includes network reruns, children's programs, and originally produced material.

VH-1—primarily music videos for people who are older than teenagers.

The Weather Channel—24 hours a day of weather information.

Most basic cable networks charge the cable systems for their service. The fee is based on the number of subscribers the cable system has. A typical basic network charges a cable system an amount between 3 and 25 cents per month per subscriber, depending on its popularity. ESPN, for example, can charge more than Nostalgia Television.

The systems must recoup their expenses, and potentially garner some profit, by selling the cable TV service to consumer households. Most cable systems offer a "basic service" as a package to their subscribers. This includes all local origination and public access channels, all local broadcast stations, and all basic networks for a cost of about $15 a month. Some cable

Courtesy of Playboy Entertainment Group

Courtesy of USA Networks

Courtesy of USA Networks

Courtesy of Showtime Networks, Inc.

SHOWTIME NETWORKS INC.

systems divide this basic package into two or more "tiers." They offer local origination, public access, local broadcast stations, and some of the public service and less glamorous basic networks (C-SPAN, the Learning Channel) for a very inexpensive price, about $5. The second, and more expensive, tier may include MTV, ESPN, USA, A and E, and other more entertainment-oriented basic networks.

Most basic networks sell advertising. As a result they have two sources of income—cable system subscriber fees and fees paid by advertisers. Cable advertising rates are not as high as those for commercial networks such as NBC, ABC, or CBS because audiences are not as large. Most cable networks are delighted if they obtain a rating of 4, whereas commercial network program ratings tend to be in the 11-15 range. One reason cable network audiences are low is that many cable networks program for relatively specific audiences—Lifetime to women, ESPN to sports fans, Nickelodeon to children. These and other program suppliers were created specifically as cable television entities.

Superstations, however, such as WTBS from Atlanta, WGN from Chicago, and WWOR from New York, are a special type of basic service. They are not really networks. Rather they are local television stations that have been placed on the satellite for national distribution. The stations themselves do not

earn direct money from becoming a superstation. They are placed on the satellite by other companies such as United Video. These companies collect the fees from the cable systems. The superstations make additional money because they can set advertising rates based on a national rather than local audience.

Among the more than 60 basic networks, there is considerable variation in operating procedure. C-SPAN, which features the proceedings of the House and Senate, is non-commercial. All revenue comes from money paid to it by the cable systems. The home shopping networks, which make their money because viewers call in and buy the products shown, are usually provided to cable systems free of charge. As an initial enticement to try its material, networks sometimes pay systems to carry their programming. If the system later decides to carry the network on a regular basis it must start paying the networks.

In addition to "moving picture" networks, other services are offered to cable systems as part of the basic package. These include digital sound services such as Home Music Store and electronic text services such as news bulletins from Associated Press and Reuters.

Some basic channels produce most of their own programming. ESPN, for example, provides its own coverage of sporting events, and CNN produces its own newscasts. The same applies to C-SPAN, Courtroom Television, the

Weather Channel, and the home shopping channels. Many networks, however, acquire programming from other sources. Lifetime, the Family Channel, Nickelodeon and others often contract with independent producers to develop movies or series for them. Other channels obtain movies from the major motion picture studios. A and E and Discovery buy some of their programming from the British Broadcasting Corporation. Many channels program old commercial network series. USA Network, for example, has programmed *Murder, She Wrote*, and Lifetime has used *Cagney and Lacey*. In a few instances cable networks have picked up commercial series canceled by the major broadcast networks (*Paper Chase, The Days and Nights of Molly Dodd*), produced new episodes, and aired them as a series.

Pay Networks

Pay cable networks, such as HBO, the Movie Channel, Showtime, Cinemax, and the Disney Channel, do not sell advertising. They derive all income from the cable systems that carry them. The systems, in turn, charge consumers subscription fees for each pay network, usually at a rate of $10 to $20 per month per pay service. In other words, the pay services are on a more expensive tier than basic services. The systems and the networks divide the consumer fee, usually about 50-50, but this ratio is subject to negotiation. Consumers who do not subscribe to the pay services receive scrambled signals on channels occupied by those services. To justify their additional monthly fees, pay channels must offer subscribers programming or services they can not receive for free. Most of these channels present feature films. The networks purchase rights from motion picture studios allowing them to show feature films shortly after their theatrical runs and prior to their availability to broadcast networks. They show the films uncut and without commercial interruptions. To many viewers this programming policy is worth the extra dollars they pay each month. Some pay channels also offer commercial-free specials such as sporting events, documentaries, miniseries, comedy specials, musical concerts, and original movies created for the pay service. Some of the channels, primarily HBO and Showtime, produce their own television series. These programs usually contain language or themes that commercial networks do not present to their larger, general audiences. Some of these original programs are created by network personnel, some by outside production companies.

Pay-per-View Networks

Of all forms of cable networks, pay-per-view networks are the newest, and therefore the most unsettled. With these systems, subscribers pay only for those programs they actually watch. If they have not paid for a particular program, a scrambled signal appears on the pay-per-view channel. The network and the system divide the subscriber fees, based on a negotiated percentage. The subscriber pays what the market will bear. Movies can be seen for a few dollars, while major sports events may have a price tag in the $20 to $50 range.

Most cable systems that offer pay-per-view programming employ addressable technology that allows for interaction. Viewers who want to see a particular program can press a button on a remote control device that sends a signal back through the wire to the cable system. The program is then unscrambled or otherwise made viewable by the consumer. A computer also notes that the subscriber should be billed for the program and this amount is added to the monthly amount the subscriber must pay. Systems without addressable technology can operate pay-per-view options by having subscribers call an 800 number to order a particular program, but the instant access provided by the remote control works better.

The two main pay-per-view services, Request Television and Viewer's Choice, program twenty-four hours a day. Their staple programming is newly released hit movies, but they also present sports and entertainment specials. Both these services provide multiple channels that repeatedly run the same movie (or the same ten or fifteen movies). The fundamental plan of pay-per-view television is to compete with the video rental business. Pay-per-view services want to enable viewers to see movies at their convenience without having to leave their homes.

Playboy at Night cablecasts each evening and is the oldest of the services that are now pay-per-view. Originally a pay cable service, many community groups objected to the "adult entertainment" content of the material. They pointed out that if parents subscribed to the Playboy Channel on a monthly basis, unsupervised children could easily tune in—accidentally or on purpose. As a pay-per-view option, each Playboy program must be specifically requested.

Other pay-per-view networks do not cablecast on a regular basis—they feature special events, primarily sports and concerts. TVKO, for example, programs a boxing event the second Friday of each month. The Wrestling Federation supplies occasional wrestling matches. And Forum Boxing shows events from the Los Angeles Great Western Forum.

Regional Networks

Regional networks that supply programming to a limited geographic area are fairly numerous in the cable world. Almost all of them are sports or news oriented (e.g. Home Team Sports, Prime Ticket, Madison Square Garden Network, and Orange County Now). Sports networks are active only when games are in progress, but most of the news services provide 24 hours a day of regional news information. Some of these news services are operated in conjunction with a local newspaper or local TV station.

Some regional sports networks are considered pay or pay-per-view services even though they contain advertisements. Usually the placement of such sports channels in the "basic" or "pay" category depends on the particular system. Some systems juggle regional sports networks between basic and pay. If the system can obtain greater revenue by offering a pay service, it may do so. If there is little interest among consumers, the network is placed in the basic tier.

History

The first cable network was Home Box Office (HBO). This service was established in 1972 by Time, Inc., as a movie/special service for Time's local cable system in New York City. The company then decided to expand the service to other cable systems and set up a traditional broadcast-style microwave link to a cable system in Wilkes-Barre, Pennsylvania. In November of 1972, HBO sent its first programming from New York to Wilkes-Barre. During the next several years HBO expanded its microwave system to include about fourteen cable companies The venture was not overly successful, nor was it profitable for Time.

In 1975, however, shortly after domestic satellites were launched, Time used satellite transmission from Manila to program the Muhammad Ali-Joe Frazier heavyweight championship match for two of its U.S. cable systems. The experiment was technically and financially successful and HBO decided to distribute all its programming by satellite. The satellite distribution system was easier and cheaper than the microwave system. It also made it possible for HBO signals to be received throughout the country by any cable system willing and able to buy an earth station satellite receiving dish.

HBO began marketing its service to cable systems nationwide, but initially was not very successful. Few local systems were willing to pay the almost $150,000 required for the technology required to receive the signal. But satellite technology changed quickly, and by 1977 dishes sold for less than $10,000. Other pricing and programming problems had to be overcome as well. But once the service reached consumers, it was readily accepted. Viewers were willing to pay to watch uncut movies without commercial interruptions. By October of 1977, Time was able to announce that HBO had turned its first profit.

Shortly after HBO beamed onto the satellite, Ted Turner, who owned WTBS, a low-rated UHF station in Atlanta, Georgia, decided to put his station's signal on the same satellite as HBO. Cable operators who had installed a receiving dish for HBO could now also place Turner's station, complete with network reruns and the Atlanta Braves baseball games, on one of their channels. This placement created the first superstation. A company transmitting the station charged cable operators ten cents a month per subscriber for the signal, but the systems provided WTBS free to their subscribers. The rationale for presenting the superstation in this manner was that the extra program service would entice more subscribers. The charge to the cable companies did not cover WTBS's own costs, but the station was now able to set higher advertising rates because its audience was spread over the entire country.

With two successful programming services on the satellite, the floodgates opened and many other companies set up cable networks. Viacom launched a pay-cable service,

Showtime, to compete with HBO. Like Time, Viacom owned various cable systems throughout the country and had been feeding them movies and special events through a network that involved shipping the tapes by mail for microwave relay. Following the launching of Showtime, Warner Amex began the Movie Channel, a pay service that provided movies 24 hours a day. Not to be outdone, Time established a second network, Cinemax, a service that consisted mostly of movies programmed at times complementary to HBO. Other pay services that sprung up were Galavision, a Spanish-language movie service; Spotlight, a Times-Mirror movie service; Bravo and the Entertainment Channel, both cultural programming services; and Playboy, an adult service that entered the cable business by joining forces with an already established network, Escapade.

Services that accepted commercials (later to be known as basic services) also exploded in number. ESPN was an early entry, and its sports programming was much in demand. Other basic services that appeared by the early 1980s were CNN (also owned by Turner), the Christian Broadcasting Network (CBN), USA, MTV, and C-SPAN. Two basic cultural services were formed. One, owned by ABC, was called ARTS. The other was CBS Cable, a service very expensive for its broadcast network owner because it featured a great deal of originally-produced material. Satellite News Channel (SNC), a twenty-four hour news joint venture between Westinghouse and ABC was established to compete with CNN. Daytime was a service geared toward women, and Cable Health Network programmed material dealing with physical and mental health. The number of superstations also grew as WGN in Chicago and WWOR in New York joined WTBS.

For several years in the early 1980s, both new pay and basic networks were announced at a rapid rate—sometimes several in one day. Some of these never materialized, some existed only for short periods, but many showed signs of longevity. The entire cable TV industry was growing. Revenues and profits increased over 100% a year.

Of course, this could not last forever. In the mid-1980s cable growth began to decline and the entire cable industry went through a period of retrenchment. Many cable networks consolidated or went out of business. Both Galavision and Bravo converted from pay services to basic services. Spotlight went out of business. The Entertainment Channel turned its pay programming over to the basic network ARTS, which then became Arts and Entertainment. The Playboy Channel shifted programming between hard-core and soft pornography, caught between angry citizens who objected to televised nudity and a small but loyal group of viewers who wanted access to it. This shifting strategy angered its partner, Escapade, and the two parted company with Playboy paying Escapade $3 million dollars. MTV's ownership changed from Warner-Amex to Viacom, as did Nickelodeon's. Getty Oil, which owned ESPN, was purchased by Texaco. The new owner had no interest in the sports network and sold it to ABC. CBN changed from a strictly religious format to a broader, family-oriented format, and became the Family Channel. Daytime and Cable Health Network joined to form Lifetime.

The most highly touted failure was that of the CBS-owned cultural channel, CBS Cable, which ended programming in 1983 after losing $50 million. The service did not receive sufficient financial support from either subscribers or advertisers. Its demise was almost applauded by some cable companies who resented the encroachment of the broadcast networks into their business. Another well-publicized coup occurred when Ted Turner's Cable News Network bought out the Westinghouse/ABC Satellite News Channel. This meant less competition for CNN, which proceeded on less tenuous financial footing. The Turner organization then established CNN2, a headline service that used the same writers and reporters as the original CNN.

Very few new cable networks were introduced in the mid to late 1980s, in part because many cable systems had filled all their channels and had no room for newcomers. One notable exception was the Discovery Channel, launched in 1985, which became quite successful.

The cable network landscape changed somewhat in the 1990s. The downsizing of the late 1980s allowed for moderate growth in the next decade. In addition, in 1992, Congress passed a bill requiring cable networks to sell their programming to services in competition with cable, such as direct broadcast satellite (DBS) and multichannel multipoint distribution services (MMDS). Prior to this time, cable systems had tried to keep cable network programming to themselves. In fact, many cable system owners also owned all or part of cable networks, making it convenient and financially rewarding to make sure their cable networks provided content for their own cable systems. For example, TCI (Telecommunications, Inc.), the largest cable system owner, had a financial stake in American Movie Classics, Black Entertainment Television, CNN, the Discovery Channel, the Family Channel, QVC Home Shopping, Turner Network TV, and WTBS.

Probably the greatest threats to the cable system structure (but not necessarily the cable networks) are Congressional actions of the 1990s that have opened the door for telephone companies to enter the cable TV business. Phone companies hope to become the "one wire into the home." If this happens, cable systems will suffer, or perhaps disappear. But the phone companies will have to turn somewhere for programming, no doubt to entities that closely resemble the present cable networks.

Technology also improved in the 1990s, and the prospect of digital signals delivered over fiber optic lines meant cable systems (or phone companies) would be able to deliver more than 500 channels to the home. All these channels would need programming.

With new markets and new technologies in mind, a number of companies launched new networks. NBC started Consumer News and Business Channel (CNBC) in 1991, and was followed by Courtroom TV and two new Turner services, TNT (Turner Network Television) and the Cartoon Channel. Several comedy channels started and eventually merged into Comedy Central. A science fiction network, a game show network, a history network, and many others appeared.

The proposed change in programming most likely to affect cable networks is video-on-demand (VOD). This type of distribution allows consumers to select and view a program or movie at any time. Now in the experimental stage, this process will probably involve a system that can receive and store an entire movie in a device in or on the TV set and play it from there at the viewer's convenience. Closer to reality is near-video-on demand (NVOD). A cable system with 500 channels could easily devote twelve channels to one two-hour movie and start the movie on a different channel every ten minutes. In this way any viewer could have the movie within ten minutes of when he or she wanted it. Twenty or thirty movies could be running this way at the same time. The present pay-per-view services engage in a limited version of near-video-on-demand, but true VOD might very well change the nature of both pay and pay-per-view services.

These changes in both technology and policy will continue to keep cable television services at the center of issues surrounding television. Just as early cable networks transformed the meaning and experience of television programming and viewing, the newer practices will undoubtedly continue to alter our understanding and use of the medium.

—Lynn Schafer Gross

FURTHER READING

Adler, Richard, editor. *The Electronic Box Office: Humanities and Arts on the Cable.* New York: Praeger, 1974.

Flower, Joe. *Prince of the Magic Kingdom: Michael Eisner and the Re-Making of Disney.* New York: Wiley, 1991.

Goldberg, Robert, and Gerald Jay Goldberg. *Citizen Turner: The Wild Rise of an American Tycoon.* New York: Harcourt Brace, 1995.

Jones, Felecia G. "The Black Audience and the BET Channel." *Journal of Broadcasting and Electronic Media* (Washington, D.C.), Fall 1990.

Lamb, Brian, and the Staff of C-Span. *C-SPAN: America's Town Hall.* Washington, D.C.: Acropolis, 1988.

Liska, A. James. "Is there any such Thing as Black Programming? Hollywood Producers and Actors Speak on Blacks' Image and Hiring On Web TV." *Television-Radio Age* (New York), 26 October 1987.

Mair, George. *Inside HBO: The Billion Dollar War between HBO, Hollywood and the Home Video Revolution.* New York: Dodd, Mead, 1988.

Straub, Gerard Thomas. *Salvation for Sale: An Insider's View of Pat Robertson.* Buffalo, New York: Prometheus, 1988.

Tyler, Ralph. "The Network that 'Listens' to Children Marks Decade as Kidvid Leader." *Variety* (Los Angeles), 5 April 1989.

Whitmore, Hank. *CNN, The Inside Story*. Boston: Little, Brown, 1990.

See also American Movie Classics; Black Entertainment Television; Cable Networks; Canadian Cable Television Association; Cable News Network; Direct Broadcast Satellite; Distant Signal; Federal Communications Commission; Geography and Television; Home Box Office; Association of Independent Television Stations; Levin, Gerald; Mergers and Acquisitions; Midwest Video Corporation Case; Music Television; Must Carry Rules; Narrowcasting; National Cable Television Association; National Telecommunications and Information Administration; News Corporation; Pay Cable; Pay Television; Pay-Per-View Cable; Prime Time Access Rule; Public Access Television; Satellite; Scrambled Signals; Star-TV (Hong Kong); Super Station; Telcos; Time Warner; Translator; Turner, Ted; Turner Broadcasting Systems

CABLE NEWS NETWORK

U.S. Cable Network

The Cable News Network (CNN) ranks as one of the most important, indeed perhaps the most important, innovation in cable television during the final quarter of the 20th century. In 1984 CNN first began to earn wide-spread recognition and praise for its nearly around the clock coverage of the Democratic and Republican conventions. By 1990 Ted Turner's 24 hour-a-day creation had become the major source for breaking news. Praise became so routine that few were surprised when a mid-1990s Roper survey found viewers ranked CNN as the "most fair" among all TV outlets, and the Times Mirror's Center for the People and the Press found viewers trusted CNN more than any television news organization.

But success did not come overnight. Launched in June 1980 by the then tiny Turner Broadcasting of Atlanta, in the beginning CNN (mocked as the "Chicken Noodle Network") accumulated losses at the rate of $2 million a month. Ted Turner transferred earnings from his highly profitable superstation to slowly build a first rate news organization. CNN set up bureaus across the United States, and then around the world, beginning with Rome and London. Yet at first Turner and his executives were never sure they would even survive the stiff competition from rival Satellite NewsChannel, a joint venture of Group W Westinghouse and ABC. In January 1982 Turner let Satellite News Channels know he was serious and initiated a second CNN service, "Headline News." Through 1982 and most of 1983 CNN battled SNC. In October 1983 ABC and Westinghouse gave up and sold their news venture to Turner for $25 million, ending effective competition for CNN in the United States.

CNN then took off. By 1985 it was reaching in excess of 30 million homes in the United States and had claimed its first profit. Turner added bureaus in Bonn, Moscow, Cairo and Tel Aviv, and in the years before Court TV alone televised celebrated trials such as the Claus von Bulow murder case. In 1987 when President Ronald Reagan met Mikhail S. Gorbachev at a summit that would signal the end of the Cold War, CNN was on the air continuously with some seventeen correspondents on site. By 1989 CNN had 1600 employees, an annual budget was about $150 million, and was available in 65 countries with such specialized segments such as a daily entertainment report, *Show Biz Today*, and a nightly evening newscast, *The World Today*. Larry King had moved his interview show to CNN and become famous for attracting ambitious politicians and infamous celebrities. In 1991, as the only TV network in the world operating live from the very beginning of Operation Desert Storm, CNN reported everything the military permitted—from the first bombing of Baghdad to the tank blitz that ended the conflict. Indeed, at a press conference after the initial air bombing runs by the U.S. Air Force, Defense Secretary Richard B. Cheney and General Colin L. Powell, chairman of the Joint Chiefs of Staff, admitted that they were getting much of their war information from CNN.

But the fame of CNN's Gulf War coverage did not turn into corporate fortune because the costs of coverage of a wide ranging set of battles had risen faster than advertising revenues. The crest came on the night of the invasion of Kuwait by Iraq when CNN captured 11% of the audience as compared to the usual 1 or 2% normal audience shares. Advertising time had already been sold. Still, as the late 1980s and early 1990s provided regular disasters, wars, and "media

Courtesy of CNN

events," CNN was able to experience surges in interest and thus take in ratings binges around the fascination peaked by the confrontations at Tiananmen Square, the calamities of the San Francisco earthquake, and the long awaited announcement of the verdict in O. J. Simpson's "trial of the century."

Whatever the news mix, CNN's prestige never stopped rising. It became a basic component of how the new global village communicated. When United States troops invaded Panama in 1989, the Soviet foreign ministry's first call did not go to its counterpart in the United States diplomatic corps, but to the Moscow bureau of CNN—a statement could be read on camera condemning the action. Ted Turner proudly told anyone who would listen that Margaret Thatcher, Francois Mitterrand, Nancy Reagan, and Fidel Castro all had declared themselves faithful viewers of CNN. But as CNN moved well past 50 million households reached in the United States (and millions more abroad), all was not calm inside the organization. Staffers began to grumble about low wages and pressure not to unionize. And by the early 1990s Ted Turner seemed to lose his innovative magic. In 1992 he heralded and launched an "Airport Channel," and a "Supermarket Channel," but neither added much in the way of new audience or profits. And as CNN reached over more and more of the world, indigenous local news organizations began to publicly label Ted Turner a "cultural imperialist."

Yet there was no doubt that as CNN turned fifteen in June 1995 it had surely become a prosperous and important part of the new world of cable television. Yearly revenues neared one billion dollars, but growth stalled as advertisers realized that the CNN audience was "too old" and "not as affluent" as could be found elsewhere. The year 1995 was most eventful. First Ted Turner sold his complete operation, including CNN, to mega-media giant Time Warner and skeptics grumbled that a serious news organization would have difficulty trying to function as part of such a corporate colossus. At the end of the year Microsoft announced it would ally with NBC to form MSNBC to directly challenge CNN. Rupert Murdoch's News Corps., Inc., and Capital Cities/ABC also promised future 24-hour news services to contest CNN around the world. Whatever the future held by the mid-1990s CNN had become the stuff of legend. Ted Turner had forever changed the history of television news with his innovation of CNN.

—Douglas Gomery

FURTHER READING

Bibb, Porter. *It Ain't as Easy as It Looks: Ted Turner's Amazing Story.* New York: Crown, 1993.
Picard, Robert G., editor. *The Cable Networks Handbook.* Riverside, California: Carpelan, 1993.
Whittemore, Hank. *CNN: The Inside Story.* Boston: Little Brown, 1990.

See also Cable Networks; News (Network); Superstation; Turner, Ted; Turner Broadcasting Systems

CAESAR, SID

U.S. Comedian

Son of a Yonkers restaurant owner, Sid Caesar learned first-hand the variety of dialects and accents he would later be known to mimic as a comedian. But his first performing interest was as a musician. He studied saxophone at Julliard, and later played with nationally famous bands (Charlie Spivak, Claude Thornhill, Shep Fields, Art Mooney). During World War II, Caesar was assigned as a musician in the Coast Guard, taking part in the service show "Tars and Spars," where producer Max Liebman overheard him improvising comedy routines among the band members, and switched him over to comedy. Caesar went on to perform his "war" routine in the stage and movie versions of the review, and continued in Liebman's guidance after the war, appearing in theatrical reviews in the Catskills and Florida.

Liebman cast Caesar in the Broadway review *Make Mine Manhattan* in 1948, and in 1949 brought him to star on television in the big-budget variety show *Admiral Broadway Review*, which was simultaneously broadcast on both the NBC and DuMont networks. Caesar had appeared on Milton Berle's *Texaco Star Theater* the previous fall, but became an enormous success on his own program, starring with the multi-talented and splendid comedienne Imogene Coca (who had appeared on TV as early as 1939), Mary McCarty, Marge and Gower Champion, and Bobby Van, among others. The series, produced and directed by Liebman, adopted the format of a Broadway review, with top-name guest stars in comedy skits and big production numbers. It also introduced a savvy genre-bending that would help to characterize Caesar's programs: the opening show closed with an elaborate parody of both opera and Billy Rose, called "No, No, Rigoletto." Seen in every city with television facilities in the United States (either live or by filmed kinescope), the show dominated Friday night viewing, the way Berle did on Tuesday and Ed Sullivan on Sunday. Its sponsor, Admiral, was a major manufacturer of television sets. Running an hour in length, the show lasted only seventeen weeks, from January to June 1949.

Its successor, *Your Show of Shows*, was a Saturday night fixture for four years, adopting a similar format of comedy monologues, skits, and parodies of movies and plays. But this program was less a showcase for guest stars than for Caesar and Coca, ably supported by Carl Reiner (who replaced Tom Avera after the first season) and Howard

Morris (who joined a season later). Writers Mel Tolkin, Lucille Kallen, and Mel Brooks, choreographer James Starbuck, set designer Frederick Fox, and conductor Charles Sanford were all *Admiral* alumni; the other writers completed a Who's Who of post-World War II American comedy—Larry Gelbart (*M*A*S*H*, TV series), Bill Persky and Sam Denoff (*The Dick Van Dyke Show*), Neil Simon, and also Joe Stein (*Fiddler on the Roof*) and Mike Stewart (*Hello, Dolly* and *Bye, Bye Birdie*). The writing sessions were reputedly raucous and sometimes even violent, splitting up into groups of two or three who competed with one another, all fighting for attention and success—with the possible exception of Simon, whispering his suggestions to Reiner, who would repeat them to the group. It has long been reported that Woody Allen worked on the show, though this has recently been suggested to be untrue.

The show included a large cast of regular singers and dancers, and was originally the New York half of a larger overall show, NBC's *Saturday Night Revue*. (Jack Carter hosted a Chicago portion an hour earlier.) At the end of the first season, Carter and the umbrella title were dropped, and Caesar and company went on to perform some 160 telecasts—all live, original comedy. Both raucous and urbane, combined revue and sketch comedy with a rather sophisticated sense of satire and parody, especially for early TV: how many other programs of this era would have conceived a spoof of Italian neorealist cinema?

Caesar, notorious for his deviations from the script, was skilled at mime, dialects, monologues, foreign language double-talk, and general comic acting. Whether alone, paired with Coca, or part of the four-man repertory group, he excelled. Not a rapid-fire jokester like Berle or Fred Allen, Caesar was often compared in the press to the likes of Chaplin, Fields, or Raimu. The 90-minute show usually featured a guest host (who played a minor role), at least two production numbers, sketches between Caesar and Coca, the showcase parody of a popular film (e.g., "Aggravation Boulevard," "From Here to Obscurity"), further sketches (as many as ten per show), Caesar in monologue or pantomime (e.g., an expectant father in the waiting room, the autobiography of a gum-ball machine), and the entire company in a production number. The most famous characters included Charlie and Doris Hickenlooper, a mis-matched married couple; the Professor, a Germanic expert scientist in everything and nothing; storyteller Somerset Winterset; jazz musicians Cool C's and Progress Hornsby; and the mechanical figures of the great clock of Baverhoff, Bavaria, striking one another in addition to the hour.

In the fall of 1954, Leibman went on to produce "Spectaculars" for NBC, Caesar began *Caesar's Hour* (with Reiner, Morris, and Nannette Fabray), which lasted three seasons, while Coca had her own half-hour show, lasting one season. Caesar and Coca reunited in 1958 on the short-lived *Sid Caesar Invites You.*

Building on the interest generated by a 1972 *Esquire* article about the show, Liebman compiled routines of

Sid Caesar
Photo courtesy of Sid Caesar

several programs from 1950 to 1954 into a feature film, *Ten from Your Show of Shows* (1973). NBC had thrown away their copies of the program, but Caesar and Liebman had retained their kinescopes made during the show's original run. A series of 90-minute TV specials anthologized from the original shows were syndicated in 1976. By the mid-1970s, Caesar was seen only in occasional guest appearances, and later in diverse TV series and films (*Grease*, 1978). His autobiography, *Where Have I Been?*, was published in 1983. Caesar and *Your Show of Shows* served as the not-so-thinly-veiled inspiration behind the film *My Favorite Year* (1982).

—Mark Williams

SID CAESAR. Born in Yonkers, New York, U.S.A., 8 September 1922. Graduated Yonkers High School, 1939. Married: Florence Levy, 1943; children: Michele, Richard, and Karen. Studied saxophone and clarinet, New York City; played in small bands, then the orchestras of Charlie Spivak, Shep Fields, and Claude Thornhill; toured theaters and nightclubs as a comedian; appeared in film, on Broadway and television, from 1945; starred in several TV shows; returned to Broadway as star of *Little Me*, 1962-63; appeared in such films as *It's a Mad, Mad, Mad, Mad World*, 1963, *Silent Movie*, 1975, and *Grease*, 1978; appeared in opera *Die Fledermaus*, 1987. Recipient: Best Comedian on TV Award from *Look* magazine, 1951 and 1956; Emmy Award, 1956; Sylvania Award, 1958. Named to U.S. Hall of Fame, 1967.

TELEVISION SERIES

1949	*Admiral Broadway Review*
1950–54	*Your Show of Shows*
1954–57	*Caesar's Hour*
1958	*Sid Caesar Invites You*
1962–63	*As Caesar Sees It* (syndicated)

MADE-FOR-TELEVISION MOVIES

1976	*Flight to Holocaust*
1977	*Curse of the Black Widow*
1981	*The Munsters Revenge*
1983	*Found Money*
1985	*Love is Never Silent*
1988	*Freedom Fighter*
1988	*Side By Side*
1988	*Nothing's Impossible*

TELEVISION SPECIAL

1959	*The Sid Caesar Special*

FILMS

Tars and Spars, 1945; *The Guilt of Janet Ames*, 1947; *It's a Mad, Mad, Mad, Mad World*, 1963; *The Busy Body*, 1966; *The Spirit is Willing*, 1966; *A Guide for the Married Man*, 1967; *Ten From Your Show of Shows*, 1973; *Airport 1975*, 1974; *Silent Movie*, 1975; *Fire Sale*, 1977; *Barnaby and Me*, 1977; *Grease*, 1978; *The Cheap Detective*, 1978; *The Fiendish Plot of Dr. Fu Manchu*, 1980; *History of the World, Part I*, 1981; *Grease 2*, 1982; *Over the Brooklyn Bridge*, 1983; *Cannonball Run II*, 1983; *Stoogemania*, 1985; *The Emperor's New Clothes*, 1987; *The South Pacific Story*, 1991.

STAGE

Make Mine Manhattan, 1948; *Little Me*, 1962-63; *Die Fledermaus* (opera), 1987; *Does Anobody Know what I'm Talking About?*, 1989.

PUBLICATIONS

"What Psychoanalysis Did For Me." *Look* (New York), 2 October 1956.

Where Have I Been? New York: Crown, 1983.

FURTHER READING

Adir, Karen. *The Great Clowns of American Television*. Jefferson City, North Carolina: McFarland, 1988.

Bester, Alfred. "The Two Worlds of Sid Caesar." *Holiday* (New York), September 1956.

Davidson, Bill. "Hail Sid Caesar!" *Colliers* (New York), 11 November 1950.

Myers, Deb. "The Funniest Couple in America." *Cosmopolitan* (New York), January 1951.

Robbins, Jhan, and June Robbins. "Sid Caesar: 'I Grew Up Angry.'" *Redbook* (New York), November 1956.

Sennett, Ted. *Your Show of Shows*. New York: Macmillan, 1977.

See also "Golden Age" of Television; Kinescope; Variety Programs; *Your Show of Shows*

CAGNEY AND LACEY

U.S. Police Series

Cagney and Lacey, a U.S. police procedural with pervasive melodramatic overtones, is, deservedly, one of the most widely discussed programs in television history. The series aired on the CBS television network from 1982 to 1988 and presented a set of bold dramatic combinations, blending and bending genre, character, and narrative strategies. Though rated in the list of top 25 programs only once during those years, the show drew critical acclaim—and controversy—and established a substantial audience of fiercely loyal viewers who, on at least one occasion, helped save the program from cancellation by the network. As demonstrated by television scholar Julie D'Acci's outstanding study, *Defining Women: Television and the Case of Cagney and Lacey*, the history of *Cagney and Lacey* provides a textbook case illustrating many issues pervasive in the U.S. television industry as well as that industry's complicated relationship to social and cultural issues.

Created in its earliest version by writer-producers Barbara Corday and Barbara Avedon in 1974, *Cagney and Lacey* was first designed as a feature film. Unable to sell the project, the women presented it to television networks as a potential series.

Rebuffed again, they finally brought *Cagney and Lacey* to the screen as a 1981 made-for-television movie, co-produced by Barney Rosenzweig, then Corday's husband. The movie drew high ratings and led to the series, which premiered in 1982. The difficulties involved in the production history to this point was indicative of struggles encountered by women writers and producers in the film and television industries—especially when their work focuses on women. Those difficulties, however, were merely the beginning of continuing contests.

As put by D'Acci, "the negotiation of meanings of *women*, *woman*, and *femininity* took place among a variety of vested interests and with considerable conflict." Throughout the run of the series the "negotiations" continued, and the interests included the creative team for the series—producers, writers, actors, directors. They also included network executives and officials at every level, television critics, special interest groups, and the unusually involved audience that actively participated in ongoing discussions of the series' meanings and directions.

While many of these controversies took place on sets, in writer's meetings, and in board rooms, one of the earliest spilled over into public discussion in newspapers, magazines, and letters. In the made-for-television movie, the character of Christine Cagney was played by Loretta Swit, that of Mary Beth Lacey by Tyne Daly. Unavailable to take on the Cagney role in the series because of her continuing work in *M*A*S*H*, Swit was replaced by Meg Foster. Almost immediately discussion at CBS and in some public venues focused on potential homosexual overtones in the relationship between the two women. Foster, who had played a lesbian in an earlier television role, was cited as "masculine" and "aggressive," and after considerable argument CBS threatened to cancel the series, made Foster's removal and replacement a condition of continuing the show, and the fall 1982 season began with Sharon Gless, presumably more conventionally feminine and heterosexual, portraying Cagney.

Similar, though not so visible, conflicts and adjustments continued throughout the history of the series. Questions of appearance—dress, body weight, hair styles—were constantly under consideration and negotiation. Story material, particularly when focused on issues of vital concern to women—rape, incest, abortion, breast cancer— often proved controversial and led to continuing battles with the network standards and practices offices. Daly reported that even in the matter of sexual relations with her fictional husband, Harvey (John Karlin), differences of opinion flared into argument over how to present domestic sexual behavior.

In the spring of 1983 CBS executives had more straightforward matters to present to the producers of *Cagney and Lacey;* pointing to low audience ratings, they canceled the program. By this time, however, the producers and the production company for the series had mounted an impressive public relations campaign and letter-writers from across the country mailed their protests to the company, the network, the producers—to anyone who would read and make use of them. The National Organization of Women took a lead role in the publicity campaigns. Newspaper critics called attention to the campaign. The series won numerous awards, Daly's Emmys for Best Actress in 1982-83 and 1983-84 among them. In the fall of 1983, CBS announced it would program seven "trial episodes" beginning in March 1984. *Cagney and Lacey* was back and remained on the air four more seasons.

All of these difficulties were played out as the series developed narrative strategies that took best advantage of U.S. commercial television's abilities to present serious social and personal issues in the context of genre fiction. Two factors stand out among the techniques that distinguish *Cagney and Lacey*. One strategy, evidenced in many of the conflicts described above, is the series' ability to blend three areas of concern into single dramatic productions. First, most episodes of *Cagney and Lacey* dealt with the on-going difficulties encountered by two women in a male-dominant profession. This entailed far more than simply presenting gender conflicts in the work place, though certainly there

Cagney and Lacey
Photo courtesy of Orion Pictures Corporation

were many of those. Rather, this dramatic structure required a reconsideration of the entire generic structure of the "cop show." As the two women dealt with issues such as violence, guns, male criminals, or the streets-—all elements of police fiction—writer-producers as well as audiences were required to reflect on new resonances within the genre.

Second, each narrative usually focused on a particular crime and criminal investigation. The generic modifications were intertwined with rather conventional police matters, and the sense of strangeness caused by the gender shift was combined with the familiarity of crime drama.

Third, each story usually linked the crime drama to a social problem, the kinds of issues often explored in television drama throughout the history of the medium. Thus, the issues cited above, often, though not always definable as "women's issues," formed a third aspect of the narrative triad structuring individual episodes.

The series was at its best when these elements were "balanced," that is, when it was not overly didactic regarding the social issue, nor utterly conventional as a police drama, nor submerged in the exploration of gender inflected genre. If, as sometimes happened, one of these aspects did "take over" the story, the result was often a very thin examination of the element.

The second major narrative strategy of the series militated against this imbalance. This was the establishment of

Cagney and Lacey as a "cumulative narrative." Unlike serial dramas such as *Hill Street Blues*, or, in the more strictly melodramatic vein, *Dallas*, *Cagney and Lacey* did usually bring each episode to closure. Criminals were caught. Cases were solved. Sometimes, even the particular gender-related work place issue was brought to a satisfactory solution.

But beneath these short term narrative aspects of the series, the long-term narrative stakes were continually explored. More important, each of the closed episodes shed light on those ongoing matters. Thus, as viewers watched the Lacey children move from childhood into adolescence, they also saw strains appear in the Lacey marriage, and the toll that strain took on professional commitments, and the conflicts the strain caused in the interpersonal relationship of the two women, and so on. Similarly, each small development could lead to new story possibilities, new inflections of character. Elements from past episodes could be brought into play. Features of character biographies could be revealed to explain events in a particular episode, then used to develop further characteristics in future episodes.

The cumulative narrative, one of television's strongest forms, was put to near perfect use in *Cagney and Lacey*. Evidence of the utility of this strategy, and the ways in which its methods of story elaboration can appeal to viewers, came in the latter years of the series. Though some critics see the series as diminishing its stronger feminist tonality in this period, it is also possible to see the growing emphasis on the "personal" and "the domestic" as a fuller union of public and private.

One of the most significant developments in the series in this period was the exploration of Christine Cagney's alcoholism. In addition to their own focus on this topic, producer-writers have cited viewer letters calling attention to the fact that Cagney often turned to alcohol in times of stress. In a harrowing, two-part, award-winning performance, Sharon Gless portrayed Cagney's descent into "rock bottom" alcoholic behavior. What is significant about the development is that it altered not only the series present and future, but its history as well, and simultaneously altered the "triadic" structure of social issue, personal problem, and police drama.

Cagney and Lacey left network program schedules in 1988. But it continued for some time as a staple for the Lifetime network's programming aimed at female audiences. Critical and viewer responses to the series continue to be mixed even now. Most recently the series characters have been resurrected in the form of several made-for-television movies. Older, physically changed, perhaps "wiser," these fictional characters and the narratives in which they appear continue to explore complex issues and themes, and to experiment with narrative forms.

—Horace Newcomb

CAST

Detective Mary Beth Lacey	Tyne Daly
Detective Chris Cagney (1982)	Meg Foster
Detective Chris Cagney (1982–88)	Sharon Gless
Lieutenant Bert Samuels	Al Waxman
Detective Mark Petrie	Carl Lumbly
Detective Victor Isbecki	Martin Kove
Detective Paul La Guardia (1982–85)	Sidney Clute
Deputy Inspector Marquette (1982–83)	Jason Benhard
Desk Sergeant Ronald Coleman	Harvey Atkin
Harvey Lacey	John Karlin
Harvey Lacey, Jr.	Tony La Torre
Michael Lacey	Troy Slaten
Sergeant Dory McKenna (1984–85)	Barry Primus
Inspector Knelman (1984–88)	Michael Fairman
Detective Jonah Newman (1985–86)	Dan Shor
David Keeler (1985–88)	Stephen Macht
Alice Lacey (1985–87)	Dana and Paige Bardolph
Alice Lacey (1987–88)	Michele Sepe
Detective Manny Esposito (1986–88)	Robert Hegyes
Detective al Corassa (1986–88)	Paul Mantee
Josie (1986–88)	Jo Corday
Kazak (1986–87)	Stewart Coss
Beverley Faverty (1986–87)	Beverley Faverty
Tom Basil (1986–88)	Barry Laws
Verna Dee Jordan (1987–88)	Merry Clayton

PRODUCERS Barney Rosenzweig, Barbara Corday, Barbara Avedon, Richard Rosenbloom, Peter Lefcourt, Liz Coe, Ralph Singleton, Patricia Green, P.K. Knelman, April Smith, Joseph Stern, Steve Brown, Terry Louise Fisher, Georgia Jeffries, Jonathan Estrin, Shelly List

PROGRAMMING HISTORY   125 Episodes

- CBS

March 1982–April 1982	Thursday 9:00-10:00
October 1982–September 1983	Monday 10:00-11:00
March 1984–December 1987	Monday 10:00-11:00
January 1988–April 1988	Tuesday 10:00-11:00
April 1988–June 1988	Monday 10:00-11:00
June 1988–August 1988	Thursday 10:00-11:00

FURTHER READING

Brower, Susan. "TV ' Trash and Treasure': Marketing Dallas and *Cagney and Lacey*." *Wide Angle* (Athens, Ohio), 1989.

Clark, Danae. "*Cagney and Lacey*: Feminist Strategies of Detection." In, Brown, Mary Ellen, editor. *Television and Women's Culture: The Politics of the Popular*. Newbury Park, California: Sage, 1990.

D'Acci, Julie. *Defining Women: Television and the Case of Cagney and Lacey*. Chapel Hill: University of North Carolina Press, 1994.

Fiske, John. *Television Culture*. London: Methuen, 1987.

Mayerle, Judine. "Character Shaping Genre in Cagney and Lacey." *Journal of Broadcasting and Electronic Media* (Washington, D.C.), Spring 1987.

McHenry, Susan. "The Rise and Fall—and Rise of TV's *Cagney and Lacey*." *Ms.* (New York), April 1984.

Montgomery, Kathryn C. *Target Prime Time: Advocacy Groups and the Struggle over Entertainment Television*. New York: Oxford University Press, 1989.

Rosen, Marjorie. "*Cagney and Lacey*." *Ms.* (New York), October 1981.

See also Daly, Tyne; Gless, Sharon; Gender and Television; Police Programs; *Prime Suspect*

CALL SIGNS/LETTERS

U.S. Broadcasting Policy

Call letters are used by television stations to identify themselves to the TV audience. The call letters usually consist of various combinations of four letters, sometimes followed by the suffix—TV; for example, WAAA-TV. Since many of the early television stations shared common ownership with radio stations, they often shared the same call letters. If the radio station call letters were WBBB, the TV station simply became WBBB-TV.

Federal Communications Commission regulations require that each TV station identify itself at least once each hour by call letters and by city of license. The announcement should be made at or close to the hour during a natural break in programming and can be made either visually or aurally. Stations have the option to insert their channel numbers between the call letters and the city of license, and virtually all stations follow this practice; e.g., KRON-TV, channel four, San Francisco. In advertising and promotional announcements, stations generally promote their channel assignments more vigorously than their call letters.

Some of the more ingenious call letters actually identify the channel either by word or by Roman numeral. These include K*TWO*, Casper, Wyoming: K*FOR*, Oklahoma City; W*TEN*, Albany, New York; and K*TEN*, Ada, Oklahoma. Two Roman numeral examples include WIXT, Syracuse, New York; and KXII, Ardmore, Oklahoma. Two other stations, WPVI, Philadelphia; and KPVI, Pocatello, Idaho, both use a P for their respective cities followed by Roman numerals to indicate their channel six assignments.

The procedures for assigning call letters have their origin in the earliest days of radio. Blocks of initial letters were assigned to various countries following the London International Radiotelegraph Conference of 1912. The letters W, K, N, and A were assigned to the United States. W and K were used to designate commercial broadcasters, while N and A were allocated to military users of the radio spectrum. The initial letters C and X were assigned to Canada and Mexico, respectively, and are still used today to identify Canadian and Mexican television stations.

The first U.S. radio stations were allowed to select their own call letters beginning with either a W or a K. Also, early radio stations could select either a three-letter or a four-letter combination. Later, around 1928, the Federal Radio Commission formalized rules which required that all stations use four-letter combinations. Further, those stations east of the Mississippi were required to use an initial W while those stations west of the Mississippi were required to use an initial K.

Stations already on the air were allowed to keep their call letters regardless of number or location. Radio and later television stations such as KDKA, Pittsburgh, Pennsylvania; WGN, Chicago; WHO, Des Moines, Iowa; and WOW, Omaha, Nebraska, demonstrate their pioneer status and their unbroken ownership by being notable exceptions to the current rules. When WOR-TV, New York, was acquired by a new owner it was required to adhere to the four-letter requirement and became WWOR-TV.

Call letters often tell something about station ownership. New York stations WABC-TV, WCBS-TV, and WNBC-TV are each owned and operated by the respective networks contained within their call letters. So too are Los Angeles stations KABC-TV, KCBS-TV, and KNBC-TV. Ted Turner's WTBS (Turner Broadcasting System) is still another example. A change in ownership will often, but not always, bring a change in call letters. When Philadelphia TV station WTAF was sold by Taft Broadcasting to another owner, it became WTXF.

Some TV call letters trace their origins to the slogans of their radio station predecessors. Examples include WGN (World's Greatest Newspaper), the Chicago station owned by the *Chicago Tribune*; WLS (World's Largest Store), the Chicago station originally owned by Sears Roebuck; WSM (We Shelter Millions), the Nashville station originally owned by an insurance company; and WSB (Welcome South, Brother), the Atlanta station that conveys regional boosterism in its call letters.

Public television stations have continued this tradition. Chicago's WTTW (Windows to the World) and Philadelphia's WHYY (Wider Horizons for You and Yours) are two examples. Both WQED, Pittsburgh, and KQED, San Francisco, use the abbreviation for the Latin phrase *Quod Erat Demonstrandum*, "which was to be proven," in their call letters.

The growth of cable has increased the promotional value of call letters since some cable systems re-transmit TV signals "off-channel." For example, a VHF station that broadcasts on channel ten might be carried on cable channel five; a UHF station that broadcasts on channel forty-eight might be carried on channel thirteen. As a result, many TV stations continue to identify themselves by channel assignments, but also promote their call letters more extensively than in the past.

—Norman Felsenthal

FURTHER READING

Barnouw, Erik. *A History of Broadcasting in the United States; Volume I, A Tower in Babel.* New York: Oxford University Press, 1966.

Inglis, Andrew F. *A History of Broadcasting: Technology and Business.* Boston: Focal Press, 1990.

Sterling, Christopher H. and John M. Kitross. *Stay Tuned: A Concise History of American Broadcasting.* Belmont, California: Wadsworth, 1990.

See also United States: Networks

CAMCORDER

The "Camcorder" is a commercial name for professional and home video cameras that combine a camera and video recorder in one unit. Since the introduction of this technology in 1981, camcorders have become the tool of choice for local and national Electronic News Gathering (ENG). Consumer camcorders, introduced by Sony in 1985, have rendered Super-8 film for home movies obsolete. Moreover, some critics and academic media theorists claim the camcorder has democratized the media, as well.

Professional and consumer camcorders are based on several, non-compatible formats. Ed Beta and MII are popular professional formats, while VHS, Compact VHS, and ultra-compact 8mm dominate among consumers. The 8mm format led to significantly smaller cameras that can be operated with one hand (Sony uses the trade name *Handycam* to describe their 8mm models). Super VHS (S-VHS) and Hi-8, which are compatible with their lower resolution counterparts, offer higher definition and color control when used with high resolution playback equipment. S-VHS and Hi-8 are used by high-end consumers, as well as academic and industrial videographers. The camcorder has also led to a growing sophistication in ancillary equipment for the home video market, with numerous titlers, editors, and mixers available to both average and high-end users. Computer-based multimedia allows camcorder images to be incorporated in computer presentations for business and instructional use.

The camcorder came into prominence in early 1991, when Hollywood plumbing store manager George Holliday focused his camcorder on the beating of Rodney King by members of the Los Angeles Police Department. The tape, which Holliday submitted to KTLA, received international attention, and showed the power amateur video can wield over the national, indeed, world psyche. Previous to this, local stations, as well as cable news giant CNN, had solicited and used newsworthy amateur video. The popular ABC series *America's Funniest Home Videos* and similar television programs throughout the world are based on the existence of camcorders, as well.

The camcorder has also become an icon of numerous dramas and sitcoms, which commonly frame home and family scenes within the confines of a camcorder viewfinder, replacing the very notion of "home movies" as a form of expression.

—Michael B. Kassel

FURTHER READING

Aufderheide, Pat. "Vernacular Video: For the Growing Genre of Camcorder Journalism, Nothing Is too Personal." *Columbia Journalism Review* (New York), January-February 1995.

Berko, Lili. "Video: In Search of a Discourse." *Quarterly Review of Film Studies* (Chur, Netherlands), April 1989.

Brodie, John. "Hi8: Expanding the Role of TV Reporter." *Columbia Journalism Review* (New York), September-October 1991.

Dullea, Georgia. "Camcorder! Action! Lives Become Roles." *New York Times*, 15 August 1991.

Hedgecoe, John. *John Hedgecoe's Complete Guide to Video.* New York: Sterling, 1992.

Luft, Greg. "Camcorders: When Amateurs Go after the News." *Columbia Journalism Review* (New York), September-October, 1991.

Metz, Holly. "Camcorder Commandos." *The Progressive* (Madison, Wisconsin), April 1991.

Mouzard, Froncois. *Camcorder = Camscope.* Ottawa, Canada: Department of the Secretary of State of Canada, 1991.

A VHS camcorder
Photo courtesy of Magnavox

Oulette, Laurie. "The (Video) Revolution Will Be Televised." *Utne Reader* (Minneapolis, Minnesota), March-April 1992.
———. "Will the Revolution be Televised? Camcorders, Activism, and Alternative Television in the 1990s." In, d'Agostino, Peter, and David Tafler, editors. *Transmission: Toward a Post-Television Culture.* Thousand Oaks, California: Sage, 1995.
Slouka, Mark Z. "'Speak, Video': Life, Death, and Memory in the New Age." *The Georgia Review* (Athens, Georgia), Summer 1993.

Talty, Stephen. "Family Record." *Film Comment* (New York), May-June 1991.
Warren, George. "Big News: Little Cameras." *Washington Journalism Review* (Washington, D.C.), December 1990.
Weiss, Michael J. "Camcorder Consumers." *American Demographics* (Ithaca, New York), September 1994.

See also Experimental Video; Home Video; Public Access Video; Videocassette; Videotape

CAMERON, EARL

Canadian News Reader

Earl Cameron was English Canada's first noteworthy TV news anchor, once known as "Mr. CBC News." Unlike his successors, however, Cameron was a presenter in the British tradition, not a journalist in the American tradition, and he fell victim to the professionalization of television news during the 1960s.

The news service of the Canadian Broadcasting Corporation (CBC) was created in the early years of World War II and modeled on the style of the British Broadcasting Corporation. The key figure was Dan McArthur, the first chief news editor, who believed that broadcast news should be delivered in a calm, neutral fashion, free of any showmanship or editorializing. McArthur wanted the news to appear "authoritative": meaning the news reader must act as an impersonal presenter of the news text.

Cameron was trained in this tradition. He had begun to deliver the National News Bulletin in 1944, the year he joined the CBC, and remained a top CBC radio announcer throughout the 1950s. Although he had little or no experience in television, he succeeded to the job of reading the nightly 11:00 P.M. TV news in 1959, probably because of his reputation as a top announcer.

For the next seven years Cameron was almost unchallenged as the voice of the news, since the rival CTV News, born in 1962, lacked the resources to match the quality of CBC's *The National* (then called *CBC Television News*). He obeyed the rules laid down long ago by McArthur—he appeared solid, even bland, and spoke in measured, careful tones that avoided all hint of emotion or bias. "No matter what Earl Cameron reads," noted one critic, "he makes it sound less alarming than it sounds coming from someone else." Within a few years, *The National* had earned a reputation as more being reliable and believable than newspapers and radio.

But as the 1960s progressed, Cameron looked increasingly outdated. He was not, in any sense of the word, a journalist: "I just read the words," he once told Knowlton Nash, who would later anchor *The National*. Such an attitude did not sit well with the new people who had entered the ranks of CBC news. First, Cameron was pro-hibited from narrating commercials, a task that had been common amongst staff announcers as a source of extra revenue. His participation in such a crass business as selling toothpaste apparently undermined the credibility of the news. Then Bill Cunningham, the executive producer of news and an admirer of Walter Cronkite, proposed a sweeping change in the character of the CBC news service along the lines common in the United States. He urged a longer newscast, eighteen minutes instead of thirteen during the week, more pictures and less talking heads, more coverage over Canada (rather than just Ottawa, Montreal, and Toronto), and above all more "pizzazz." The changes would require that *The National* be delivered by a newsperson: only a journalist could properly convey the significance of the news to the viewing audience.

The argument was not wholly specious: it was true that viewers expected the anchor to understand the news. But the key was the performance of the anchor, his or her ability to act as a storyteller, to present the news items in a coherent and organized fashion that would serve to make clear what happened. This crucial task could be carried out by an announcer as well, or better, than by a journalist. Whatever the merits of Cunningham's argument, it apparently swayed CBC management. Cameron was replaced in 1966 by an actual journalist. Ironically, union regulations prevented his frustrated successor from writing or editing *The National*, a situation which was not remedied until many years later. Only a few of the recommendations of Cunningham's report were effectively implemented, and he himself was soon removed as executive producer.

Cameron did not immediately disappear from Canadian screens. He became the host of *Viewpoint*, a talking-head program that ran for about five minutes after *The National* as a vehicle for individual opinions on public issues. But, according to one of his compatriots, he remained unhappy over his treatment and eventually took early retirement from the CBC, a victim of changing fashions.

—Paul Rutherford

EARL CAMERON. Born in Canada, 1915. Began career as radio news announcer, 1944; moved to television as news reader for *The National*, 1959–66; host of *Viewpoint* (a five-minute commentary).

TELEVISION
1959–66   *The National*

FURTHER READING
Lochead, Richard, editor. *Beyond the Printed Word: The Evolution of Canada's Broadcast News Heritage.* Kingston, Canada: Quarry, 1991.

Nash, Knowlton. *Prime Time at Ten: Behind-the-Camera Battles of Canadian TV Journalism.* Toronto: McClelland and Stewart, 1987.
Rutherford, Paul. *When Television Was Young: Primetime Canada 1952-1967.* Toronto: University of Toronto Press, 1990.
Trueman, Peter. *Smoke and Mirrors: The Inside Story of Television News in Canada.* Toronto: McClelland and Stewart, 1980.

See also Canadian Programming in English; *National*

CANADA

The story of Canadian television begins in 1952, with the launching of bilingual French-English broadcasts by the Canadian Broadcasting Corporation (CBC) in Montreal. Within a year, the CBC was well on its way to establishing two national television networks.

The CBC had been charged with setting up a public service television system following the study carried out by a wide-ranging royal commission on the arts, letters and sciences, which reported in 1951. This procedure followed the tradition of an earlier royal commission on radio, which had recommended establishing a public broadcasting corporation along the lines of the BBC model, and had led to the creation of the CBC in 1936. But radio in Canada developed during the 1930s and 1940s under "mixed" ownership, with public and private stations co-existing in a single system, and competing for advertising. This model was to be repeated in television. While the CBC would enjoy a virtual monopoly for most of television's crucial first decade in Canada, private commercial television appeared in 1960. As of 1961 CTV, a national network linking private television stations, was on the air competing vigorously with the CBC.

The 1950s were critical in setting the tone for Canadian television, in both English and French. Distinctive Canadian news and current affairs formats were developed and, in French particularly, popular dramatic serials known as *téléromans* were established. *Hockey Night in Canada*, programmed in both official languages, became a national ritual which continues unto this day. But as in most other television systems, some important genres, such as live theatre, remain strictly in the memory of the ageing.

The basic legislation governing Canadian broadcasting was rewritten in 1958, following the election of a Conservative government friendly to the interests of the private broadcasting industry. Responding to a long-standing demand of the Canadian Association of Broadcasters (CAB), an independent regulatory authority, the Board of Broadcast Governors (BBG) was created, removing the regulation of private broadcasting from the respon-

sibility of the CBC. Shortly thereafter, the BBG began to license private television stations.

Meanwhile, CBC faced a series of political crises. On the English side, attempts by the government to interfere with programming led to massive resignations among current affairs staff in 1959. In the same year, a strike by French-language Radio-Canada producers paralysed the French television service for over two months, and became an important symbolic reference point for the emerging Quebec nationalist movement.

During the 1960s, news and information programming continued to be a source of friction both within the CBC and in the corporation's relationship with the government. The unorthodox weekly program *This Hour Has Seven Days*, which rated the highest audience "enjoyment index" of any CBC show, provoked an internal management and authority crisis that eventually toppled CBC's senior management while redefining Canadian television journalism. During the same period, French service news programs infuriated the government by paying serious attention to Quebec separatist politicians and issues, and in 1968 the law was rewritten, albeit with little effect, obliging CBC to "contribute to national unity".

While CBC led the way in Canadian programming, private television was slowly and steadily carving a place for itself, building an audience by consistently offering the most popular U.S. programs, competing with CBC for the broadcasting rights to Canadian sports classics such as football's annual Grey Cup Game, and emulating the CBC's successes in news and current affairs. By the late 1980s, the CBC's share of the Canadian television audience was down to around 20% in English and 30% in French.

The issue of maintaining a balance between Canadian and U.S. programs was tackled by the regulatory authority early on. Beginning in 1960, Canadian television broadcasters were required to offer 55% Canadian programs. (In 1970, the regulation was stiffened to 60% in prime time.) Canadian content regulations remain a controversial and ongoing issue in Canadian television up to the present. Aside from the philosophical question surrounding the legitimacy of intervening in audience "choice", the effectiveness of content quotas in bringing Canadian programs to the screen and getting Canadians to watch them has been a subject of continual debate. Since the 1960s, however, there has been a general consensus that without Canadian content requirements commercial broadcasters would have no incentive to produce Canadian programs when they could acquire U.S. exports for as little as one-tenth the cost.

The 1968 reform of the Broadcasting Act replaced the BBG with the Canadian Radio-Television Commission, or CRTC (which became the Canadian Radio-Television and Telecommunications Commission in 1976). The CRTC spent most of the 1970s developing a regulatory framework for the rapidly expanding cable industry, which had emerged in the 1950s as community antenna television serving remote areas. By retransmitting signals picked out of the air from U.S. border-town transmitters (for which they paid no license fees until 1989), the Canadian cable industry built an attractive product for the Canadian television audience, which quickly developed a taste for the best of both worlds. To paraphrase the 1929 royal commission on broadcasting, Canadians wanted Canadian programming, but they wanted U.S. programming too.

Aware that the increasingly widespread cable model was undermining its policy to support and promote Canadian content, the CRTC moved to ensure that cable, as well, contributed to the overriding policy objective of delivering Canadian television to Canadians. Must-carry provisions ensure that every available Canadian over-the-air signal in any area is offered as basic service, along with a local community channel. But in exchange, cable companies were authorised to distribute the three U.S. commercial networks plus PBS. This was, for many years, the basic cable package available to Canadian cable subscribers, and on this basis, cable penetration grew to 76% of Canadian homes by 1992.

The CRTC was also charged with putting in place Canadian ownership regulations, limiting foreign participation in Canadian broadcasting companies to 20%. This policy has resulted in the fact that Canadian television today is 100% Canadian owned, with only a handful of operations having any proportion of foreign ownership at all. It has not affected the rise of Canadian media conglomerates along the lines of those known elsewhere, however, and the Canadian television industry is characterised by a high degree of concentration of ownership. The trend since the mid-1980s is towards the take-over of private television outfits by cable companies, creating multi-media conglomerates which, in some cases, verge on monopoly. The best known examples are the Quebec cable enterprise Vidéotron, which also owns Canada's main French-language network, TVA; and Rogers Communications, Canada's largest cable company, which acquired the Maclean-Hunter publishing, television and cable conglomerate in 1994.

An important shift in the ecology of Canadian television occurred in the 1970s, when the CRTC began to license second private stations in large metropolitan markets. Regional networks such as Global (in southern Ontario) and Quatre Saisons (in Quebec) grew out of this policy, which also saw the establishment of independent stations in many cities, including Toronto's highly successful CITY-TV. The resulting audience fragmentation contributed to further eating away at the CBC's audience share. Consequently, it also weakened important arguments for legitimating the spiralling cost of public broadcasting to the public purse.

Although advertising had always been a component of CBC television, basic funding was provided by an annual grant from Parliament. By the late 1980s, this grant had risen to over $1 billion CAN annually. Advertising, meanwhile, represented over 20% of the budget—enough to be an important consideration in every programming decision, but not nearly enough to take the pressure off the public treasury. The CBC's dilemma, particularly for services provided in English, has been how to maintain a distinctive television profile while competing commercially, and how to respond to the vast demands of an encompassing mandate in a context of government cutbacks. It has not been an easy process.

Private television, meanwhile, after two lucrative decades in the 1960s and 1970s, also began to experience the financial doldrums of a weak market in the 1980s. As a period of stagnating advertising revenues followed the earlier licensing boom, many private television operations became ripe for takeover, especially by cable companies.

Conventional broadcasters faced a further challenge with the introduction, in 1982, of pay-tv and later, in 1987, of a series of Canadian speciality channels. The CRTC had resisted pressure from the cable industry to allow the importation of the new U.S. services such as HBO that came on the market in the mid-1970s. The Commission opted instead to promote development of Canadian services along the same lines. In most cases, such as movies, sports and rock videos, the Canadian services provide a range of programs similar to that of their American counterparts, but they are Canadian-owned, subject to CRTC licensing, and they do offer at least a window for Canadian programs. In some cases, such as the CBC's 24-hour news service, *Newsworld*, or the international francophone channel, *TV5*, the first generation of Canadian speciality services licensed in 1987 represented a distinctive addition to the program offerings.

The financing of Canadian pay-tv and speciality channels provides an instructive example in the problems of competing with globally distributed television products in a small domestic market. The regulatory justification for creating Canadian pay-tv in 1982 was to provide an additional vehicle for Canadian feature films but the actual percentage of Canadian films offered has never been statistically significant. At the same time, weak penetration of the cable market by film channels made them commercially unviable. Thus, when the CRTC decided to license a new series of speciality channels in 1987, it chose a different funding formula. This time, cable operators were authorised to provide the new range of services to all subscribers in their territory, and charge accordingly. The discretionary aspect was thus shifted from the consumer to the cable operator, who could calculate the economics of the deal with great precision. The cost to the consumer for each additional service was relatively low, and as rates were regulated, the market mechanism was essentially removed. At the same time, cable operators could still offer the available Canadian discretionary pay-tv channels which they were by now packaging along with a range of authorised American services not considered to be competitors of the Canadian offerings.

Since 1987, then, Canadian cable subscribers in most markets have received a 24-hour CBC news channel (in English), channels featuring music videos, sports, weather, and children's programming (in either English or French), and the international francophone channel *TV5*. In addition, they could choose to subscribe to pay-tv movie channels, specialised channels in the other official language, and, depending where they lived, a range of American channels including CNN (but not, for example, MTV, which was a direct competitor of the new Canadian equivalent).

By the early 1990s, combined viewing of all of these services accounted for somewhat under 20% of the overall audience share. But pressure to establish even more Canadian services continued. It was grounded in discussions of the coming "500-channel universe" and the perceived need to maintain the attractiveness of a cable subscription for Canadian viewers and forestall their defection to direct broadcast satellites. Thus, as of 1 January 1995, a cabled Canadian household (now up to 76%) can receive, in addition to everything mentioned previously, a French-language CBC news channel, arts-and-entertainment channels in English or French (depending on the market), a science channel, a women's channel, a lifestyle channel, a Canadian country music channel, and a channel featuring old programs. The specific offer and funding formulas have become extremely complicated, and vary from territory to territory according to the leeway provided by the CRTC to each cable operator. The initial response from consumers has been laced with confusion and frustration, for despite the concept of "consumer sovereignty" that supposedly accompanies increased channel capacity, the consumer finds that he or she is not really the one who has the choice.

In the mid-1990s, Canadian television was struggling to adjust to the new technological and economic environment characterised by the metaphor of the "information highway". The CRTC's regulatory regime was under review, the CBC faced increasingly radical budgetary restrictions, and private broadcasters were competing for dwindling advertising revenue. As in other western countries, the conventional model of generalist television was increasingly in a state of siege. However, Canadian distribution undertakings—still protected from U.S. dominance under the cultural industries exemption within the North American Free

Trade Agreement—were well-positioned in the Canadian market. And across the range of channels available, Canadian independent productions were finding an audience.

In addition, Canadian television provided some unique programming services in the form of its provincial government-supported educational broadcasters, community broadcasters, and autonomous undertakings run by northern and native broadcasters. In all its facets, Canadian television constituted a complex system which, in the spirit of the Broadcasting Act, was seen as "a public service essential to the maintenance and enhancement of national identity and cultural sovereignty".

—Marc Raboy

FURTHER READING

Audley, Paul. *Canada's Cultural Industries: Broadcasting, Publishing, Records and Film.* Toronto: James Lorimer, 1983.

Broadcasting Act. Statutes of Canada, 1991.

Collins, Richard. *Culture, Communication and National Identity: The Case of Canadian Television.* Toronto: University of Toronto Press, 1990.

Miller, Mary Jane. *Turn Up the Contrast: CBC Television Drama Since 1952.* Vancouver: University of British Columbia Press, 1987.

Nash, Knowlton. *The Microphone Wars: A History of Triumph and Betrayal at the CBC.* Toronto: McClelland and Stewart, 1994.

Peers, Frank W. *The Public Eye: Television and the Politics of Canadian Broadcasting, 1952–1968.* Toronto: University of Toronto Press, 1979.

Raboy, Marc. *Missed Opportunities: The Story of Canada's Broadcasting Policy.* Montreal: McGill-Queen's University Press, 1990.

Report, Task Force on Broadcasting Policy. Ottawa: Ministry of Supply and Services, 1986.

Rutherford, Paul. *When Television Was Young: Primetime Canada 1952–1967.* Toronto: University of Toronto Press, 1990.

Skene, Wayne. *Fade to Black: A Requiem for the CBC.* Vancouver: Douglas and McIntyre, 1993.

Smythe, Dallas W. *Dependency Road: Communications, Capitalism, Consciousness, and Canada.* Norwood, New Jersey: Ablex, 1981.

Woodcock, George. *Strange Bedfellows: The State and the Arts in Canada.* Vancouver: Douglas and McIntyre, 1985.

See also Bureau of Broadcast Measurement; *CBC News World*; Canadian Cable Television Association; Canadian Commercial Television Network; Canadian Film and Television Production Association; Canadian Production Companies; Canadian Programming in English; Canadian Programming in French; Citytv; First People's Broadcasting in Canada; Telecomm Canada; Telefilm Canada; Television Northern Canada

CANADIAN BROADCASTING CORPORATION NEWSWORLD

Canadian News Channel

Canada's English-language all-news 24-hour channel, Canadian Broadcasting Corporation Newsworld, followed CNN as the second such network in the world when it went on the air in August 1989. News has historically been a strong suit on Canadian television, with many innovative programs including *CBC Newsmagazine, This Hour Has Seven Days,* and *The Journal.* Canadian audiences have consistently demonstrated a taste for news produced indigenously, reflecting local concerns, as well as for Canadian perspectives on international events. Unlike other areas of television, such as drama and situation comedy, news programming has been able to draw significant and reliable audience numbers. Consequently, the availability of only the U.S.-based CNN during the 1980s sparked an interest in the formation of a similar Canadian 24-hour news network.

The Canadian Broadcasting Corporation (CBC) won the license for the all-news network in November 1987. Private broadcasters fought this decision made by the Canadian Radio-television and Telecommunications Commission (CRTC). In particular, Allarcom Ltd., whose own bid lost to CBC, felt that there was undue favoritism towards the national public broadcaster. After a tough challenge in a conservative parliament sympathetic to Allarcom's charges, the CRTC's decision was finally accepted, though not without delaying the network's start date for over a year. Federal cabinet actions, however, modified the conditions of the license by insisting that CBC Newsworld involve the private sector in their operations and that they develop a similar French-language service.

The perception that CBC has a central Canadian bias, and therefore that it does not adequately reflect the diverse interests and locations of the nation as a whole, also surfaced as a criticism of the CRTC decision. In a bid to address the issue of CBC's centralization in Toronto, CBC Newsworld began by situating its broadcast centres in Halifax, Winnipeg and Calgary.

CBC Newsworld's financing is entirely separate from that of CBC. Its revenue comes from advertising and "pass-through" cable fees. As part of basic cable service, the pass-through fee meant that all cable subscribers had to pay for the service, whether they wanted it or not. The monthly cost to cable subscribers was 44.5 cents (CDN) in 1989, increased to 55 cents (CDN) in 1992. Some cable operators, particularly around Montreal, initially refused to accept the service because the pass-through fee for an English-language service made no sense to their majority francophone subscribers.

The network's annual budget is $20 million, which makes its operation roughly one-tenth the size of CNN in terms of both budget and staff. Thus, CBC Newsworld relies heavily upon other news-gatherers (e.g. local CBC reporters, CBC national news, and internationally packaged programming from BBC, ITN and CNN). As such, it has become essentially a news re-broadcaster. This need for inexpensive programming has led toward the news-panel and phone-in format for many of their productions (e.g. *Sunday Morning Live, Petrie in Prime, On the Line with Patrick Conlon,* and *Coast to Coast). Rough Cuts, The Passionate Eye,* and *Witness* are prominent windows for documentary film, the latter being a rebroadcast from CBC. In 1994, the CBC French-language all-news service received its licence. *Le Reseau de l'information* (RDI) went on the air in 1995, and like CBC Newsworld, it is part of the basic cable service in Canada.

— Charles Acland

FURTHER READING

Allen, Glen. "News around the Clock: CBC's Newsworld Takes to the Air." *Maclean's* (Toronto), 7 August 1989.
Corelli, Rae. "A Committed News Junkie: Head of Newsworld, Joan Donaldson." *Maclean's* (Toronto), 7 August 1989.
———. "The CBC's Future: Budget Cuts Have Plunged the CBC into the Worst Crisis of its 52-year History." *Maclean's* (Toronto), 7 August 1989.
Ellis, David. *Split Screen: Home Entertainment and the New Technologies.* Toronto: Lorimer, 1992.
Jensen, Holger. "Growing Pains: Newsworld's Debut is Shaky but Promising." *Maclean's* (Toronto), 14 August 1989.

See also Canadian Programming in English

CANADIAN CABLE TELEVISION ASSOCIATION

In 1957, Canada's fledgling cable operators formed the National Community Antenna Television Association of Canada to represent their collective interests to the public and various government bodies. In 1968, after the passage of the Broadcasting Act and the creation of the Canadian Radio-television and Telecommunications Commission, the cable industry changed the name of its umbrella organization to the Canadian Cable Television Association (CCTA). Over the last three decades Canada's cable operators have certainly dramatically altered the character of Canadian television services, by extending the range of programming and services available to Canadians and opening the door to the "500 channel universe."

The first Canadian cable television system was established in London, Ontario, in 1952 (though it was preceded by a Montreal cable system that delivered audio-only service until later the same year). Cable's original purpose was simply to improve the quality of over-the-air reception from local and regional TV stations. In London, Ontario, in 1952 the cable TV system delivered the CBC signal from Toronto and the U.S. networks from border cities. In 1963, Canadian cable TV operators began using microwave technology to deliver services to rural and remote communities.

In the 1970s cable subscriptions rose sharply. By 1977, the number of households subscribing to cable passed 50%. Currently 95% of Canadian TV households are passed by cable and 81% of those households subscribe to cable services. Through microwave relay and satellite systems, cable TV services are available in more than 2,000 small and rural communities across Canada.

The cable business has been extremely lucrative for most CCTA members. Between 1983 and 1993, cable rates rose an average of 80% compared to a 31% increase in local telephone rates and a 47% increase in the consumer price index. Moreover, the CRTC only regulates the basic subscription rate charged by cable operators, but 96% of subscribers chose a package of channels known as extended basic whose rate is unregulated.

Like other media industries, cable is now characterised by a significant level of corporate concentration; the largest nine companies account for 80% of total subscribers. With over 30% of all Canadian cable subscribers, and close to 45% of all English-Canadian subscribers under its corporate banner, Rogers Communications is the dominant national firm. In Quebec, Le Groupe Videotron accounts for close to 60% of all subscribers.

The expansion of cable in Canada in the 1970s can be attributed to a number of regulatory decisions made by the Canadian Radio-television and Telecommunications Commission (CRTC). In 1969, after much public pressure and lobbying from the CCTA, the CRTC permitted cable systems operating at a distance from the U.S. border, as in Edmonton and Ottawa, to use microwave distribution technology to gather U.S. broadcast signals. Cable's success as a distribution technology was directly related to its ability to provide Canadian households with U.S. signals they either could not otherwise receive or received poorly with conventional roof-top antennae. In 1975, the CRTC declared that cable was a "chosen instrument of public policy" and developed detailed regulations concerning the signals and services that cable companies can or must provide, the rates charged subscribers, the provision of a community channel, and more.

In many respects, cable was the first of the much ballyhooed new technologies. Aside from its early use of microwave technology, Canadian cable TV initiated the use of satellite-delivered services when in the 1970s it offered the House of Commons proceedings to subscribers across the country. Cable companies also developed the first alpha-numeric television services in Canada. Home shopping and real estate services have been available in larger centers for several

years. Some cable systems also offer travel information, electronic mail, video games, and instructional services. Cable companies are involved in a number of field-trials to deliver broadband, interactive home services.

At the local level, the member companies of the CCTA have supported community channels for over 25 years. In 1993, 225 community channels across the country provided more than 235,000 hours of programming. For all but the smallest cable companies, community channels are a condition of their license to operate. Cable companies must make available both space and equipment to community groups and individuals interested in producing television programming; the cable operators are legally responsible for all the material broadcast on the community channels. Although they were initially envisioned as a great experiment in citizen participation and democratic communication, the community channels have by and large developed into rather paternalistic institutions that avoid controversial and politically-charged programming. Instead, local council meetings, local sports events, and multicultural information programming make up the bulk of the offerings on most community channels.

As Canada moves forward into age of interactive information and entertainment services, the CCTA must contend with the looming possibility of competition from Canada's telephone companies. The CCTA has argued repeatedly that cable operators are better suited to providing Canadians with access to the information superhighway. CCTA companies are currently engaged in an elaborate project to improve the interactive, multimedia, transactional capabilities of cables systems, including a plan to establish national interconnection via cable. The CCTA has also maintained that, unlike the telephone companies, cable operators are committed to protecting and supporting the production of Canadian material in the interests of reinforcing Canadian sovereignty and cultural identity.

—Ted Magder

FURTHER READING

Babe, Robert E. *Cable Television and Telecommunication in Canada: An Economic Analysis.* East Lansing, Michigan: Michigan State University, 1975.

Brady, Diane. "Competing Channels: Regulators Debate Television's Future." *Maclean's* (Toronto), 22 March 1993.

Cable Television. Ottawa: Statistics Canada, 1971–.

Cable Television in Canada. Ottawa: Canadian Radio-Television Commission, 1971.

Freeman, Mike. "Canada Test Angers Border Broadcasters." *Broadcasting* (Washington, D.C.), 8 June 1992.

Hollins, Timothy. *Beyond Broadcasting: Into the Cable Age.* London: British Film Institute, 1984.

Murray, Karen. "Canadian Co-op Combats Yank Satellite Attack." *Variety* (Los Angeles), 17 May 1993.

————. "Striking Out at TV Violence." *Variety* (Los Angeles), 17 May 1993.

See also Canada

CANADIAN FILM AND TELEVISION PRODUCTION ASSOCIATION

The Canadian Film and Television Production Association (CFTPA) is a national, non-profit association of over 300 companies in Canada's independent production industry. The CFTPA is Canada's only national film producers' association, bringing together entrepreneurial companies engaged in film, television and video production, in distribution, and in the provision of facilities and services to the independent production industry. Member companies include Canada's leading independent film and television producers, such as Alliance, Atlantis, Nelvana, Paragon and Cinar.

The CFTPA promotes the interests of its members by lobbying government on policy matters, negotiating labor agreements on behalf of independent producers (including a low-budget production agreement which entitles CFTPA members to discounts on ACTRA performers), sponsoring conferences, seminars and/or workshops, and publishing a variety of material to assist CFTPA members. The CFTPA is also the founding member of the Canadian Retransmission Collective, the body that claims royalties from Canadian cable companies on behalf of program creators.

The CFTPA is the latest incarnation of voluntary organizations that have represented Canada's independent film and television producers. The first such organization, the Association of Motion Picture Producers and Laboratories of Canada (AMPPLC) was established in 1948. The AMPPLC focused its lobbying efforts on reducing the role of the National Film Board of Canada (NFB), and expanding the opportunities for Canada's independent producers. Throughout the 1950s and into the early 1960s, the AMPPLC challenged what it described as the NFB's "expansionist, monopolistic psychology" and repeatedly called for the contracting-out of government film work. By the 1960s, the AMPPLC had also joined the growing chorus of organizations and individuals making the case for government subsidies for the production of private-sector feature films.

Since the 1960s, and especially since the establishment of the Canadian Film Development Corporation (now Telefilm Canada), the independent sector for film and television production in Canada has grown substantially. The industry employs more than 31,000 Canadians and its direct impact on Canada's GDP is over $800 million a year. Exports of Canadian film and television productions are now valued at well over $150 million a year, more than double the value of exports in 1986.

CFTPA members benefit from a number of government programs and regulations designed to stimulate independent film and television production in Canada. Since 1968 the Canadian Film and Development Corporation has offered a combination of loans, subsidies and grants to private-sector feature film production. In 1983,

Telefilm Canada initiated the Canadian Broadcast Program Development Fund earmarked especially for Canadian television productions. CFTPA members also make use of a wide range of provincial funding sources, the largest of which is the Ontario Film Development Corporation. As of 1993, the total annual amount of government funds available for private-sector film and television productions was $340 million.

Aside from the availability of government funds to "prime-the-pump" of independent film and television production, CFTPA members also benefit from the Canadian-content regulations that are a condition of license for all Canadian broadcasters. Administered by the Canadian Radio-television and Telecommunications Commission, the Canadian-content regulations ensure that Canadian broadcasters do not operate merely as conduits for foreign programming which is much cheaper to acquire. Since the early 1980s, traditional over-the-air broadcasters, such as CTV and Global, have made much greater use of product from the independent sector to fulfill their Canadian-content responsibilities.

CFTPA members have also benefited considerably from the licensing of new specialty cable and pay-TV channels in the 1980s. Indeed, the global expansion of new outlets for television programming has greatly enhanced the fortunes of CFTPA members. CFTPA members now export their product to markets around the world and many of the larger firms have developed effective working relationships with foreign partners. Joint ventures with U.S. firms have become a mainstay of the industry, in part because of the savings in production costs that result from the relative value of the Canadian dollar.

The CFTPA plays a crucial role in ensuring a stable business climate for its members. In the midst of political pressure to reduce the level of government spending, the CFTPA has repeatedly lobbied on behalf of the efforts of Telefilm Canada, the provincial fund agencies, and the Canadian Broadcasting Corporation (which is the major buyer of independent TV programs in Canada). The CFTPA has also been at the forefront of efforts to establish a refundable tax credit system for Canadian producers. Aside from issues related directly to the production of Canadian film and television production, the CFTPA is also a vocal proponent of the need to maintain regulations that ensure a minimum level of Canadian content on new and proposed delivery systems, such as the information highway. Relatedly, the CFTPA has argued repeatedly for legislation that would enhance the role of Canadian film distributors by making it impossible for U.S. film distributors to treat Canada as part of their domestic market.

—Ted Magder

FURTHER READING

Ayscough, Suzan. "Factions Fracture Pic Funds." *Variety* (Los Angeles), 16 November 1992.

Clanfield, David. *Canadian Film.* Toronto, Canada: Oxford University Press, 1987.

Eisner, Ken. "B.C. to Prairies: Film Biz Boom." *Variety* (Los Angeles), 24 April 1995.

Film and Video. Ottawa:Statistics Canada, 1988–89.

Johnson, Brian D. "Successes on the Screen: Canada Develops Its Film Industry." *Maclean's* (Toronto), 10 September 1990.

Lyon, S. Daniel. *Public Strategy and Motion Pictures: The Choice of Instruments to Promote the Development of the Canadian Film Production Industry.* Toronto: Ontario Economic Council, 1982.

Magder, Ted. *Canada's Hollywood: The Canadian State and Feature Films.* Toronto: University of Toronto Press, 1993.

Pendakur, Manjunath. *Canadian Dreams and American Control: The Political Economy of the Canadian Film Industry.* Detroit, Michigan: Wayne State University Press, 1990.

Posner, Michael. *Canadian Dreams: The Making and Marketing of Independent Films.* Vancouver, Canada: Donglas and McIntyre, 1993.

Wallace, Bruce, Joseph Treen, and Robert Enright. "A Campaign in Support of Entertainment." *Maclean's* (Toronto), 17 March 1986.

Winikoff, Kenneth. "They Always Get Their Film: The Canadian Government Has Sired a National Cinema, But Can a Film Industry Thrive When Every Taxpayer is a Producer?" *American Film* (Washington, D.C.), July 1990.

See also Telefilm Canada

CANADIAN MORNING TELEVISION

Canadian Morning Television is partially defined by the perception that audiences use television differently at that time of day. Much morning programming is designed to fit into the patterns of everyday rituals: the discrete nature of programs and content that often defines prime time programming breaks down in the patterns of morning television.

Historically, morning TV in Canada has been the location of the marginalia of television culture. Farm reports were regular features of morning television after the sign-on of local stations in the early 1960s, and some local religious programming was part of early regional television in a rotation that covered the principal Christian denominations. After 6:00 A.M., television became the province of news or children's programming. Children's programming generally divided along the lines of syndicated American situation comedies and cartoons with live hosts who catered to the local market. In commercial television the early morning hours were the province of the local station and rarely determined by network time organization. This resulted in a great variety of programs across the country. A morning movie could be part of one television market, while the *Junior Forest Rangers* part of another. Because the CBC partially operated on a network of commercial affiliates, the early morning hours were generally not programmed with CBC network feeds. One of the principal changes of early morning television that moved it closer to its contemporary form was the shift away from this local focus to network programming.

In 1972 CTV, a private network established in 1960 introduced *Canada A.M.*, a program modeled on the long-running American NBC *Today* show. This news and chat show—with regular bulletins of news, sports, and weather—begins

each day at 6:30 and runs until 9:00 A.M. In its live presentation and with its relatively relaxed hosts who move seamlessly into softer news stories and entertainment gossip, *Canada A.M.* attempts to be an ambient program designed to be used during other preparations for the workday. CBC also launched *CBC Morning News* which provides a similar diet of bulletins and easy-listening banter among hosts and guests. Regional networks such as Global in Ontario have counter-programmed against this style of "flow" television with either reruns of children's cartoons such as the *CareBears* (which provides needed Canadian content) or religious programming drawn from both Canadian and American sources.

The pattern of morning network television shifts quite dramatically after 9:00 A.M.; the news flow model organized for the working audience transforms into something that targets those connected neither to work nor school, and the divide between the commercial stations and the public broadcasters becomes more obvious. Public stations generally engage in children's educational programming aimed primarily at the preschool age group. The provincially-funded education networks such as TVO in Ontario and the Knowledge Network in British Columbia vary this diet with programs aimed at older students within the school and university system. With its larger mandate, CBC's programs operate commercial-free, providing a series of critically acclaimed and internationally successful children's series, which have included the long-running *Mr. Dress Up, Fred Penner's Place, Under the Umbrella Tree,* and *Theodore Tugboat.* These programs have followed in the tradition of *Chez Helene* (1959-72) and the *Friendly Giant* (1958-85) as staples of childhood experience in Canada. A Canadian version of *Sesame Street* has run on CBC since 1973, and inserts of Canadian puppets and stories (including French language

Canada A.M.
Photo courtesy of CTV

training) derived from Canadian city and country land-scapes have increased from 5 minutes to 25% of the program content of this American program. *Sesame Street* provides the end of morning shows on the CBC.

In contrast, the commercial free-to-air stations provide almost exclusively adult-oriented programming during this same time period with talk and game shows predominating in the schedule. *Dini*, an hour-long talk show hosted by Dini

Petty in the tradition of *Oprah* and *Donahue*, has had a successful Canadian run on CTV and BBS, and made a brief appearance in the American market. *Supermarket Sweep* is the latest of the scaled-down (in terms of the size of prizes) Canadian versions of American game shows shown on day-time television. Peppered into the schedule are imported American programs such as *Regis and Kathy Lee*, that provide talk-celebrity shows better connected to the Hollywood circuit of stars, or issue talk shows such *Sally Jesse Raphael.* Exercise programs have on occasion been successful at either the pre or post-9:00 A.M. slot. The most successful in terms of Canadian and American syndication was the 1980s Citytv production *The Twenty-minute Workout,* which featured three female models performers aerobics routines to a *Miami Vice*-like synthesized backbeat soundtrack. *Body Moves* is a current fitness program that continues this tradition.

Religious programming is also presented on Canadian television to some degree. The most prevalent Canadian program which competes with American productions is *100 Huntley Street.* Like the "infomercials," religious programs often buy blocks of time directly from the station and use it for their own forms of promotion. Because they are often out of the general flow of morning television they are also placed further to the margins of early morning.

Weekend morning television presents another principal distinction in Canadian programming. On both Saturday and Sunday mornings, the commercial stations expand their children's programming to include virtually the entire time period. This focus on cartoons and hosted programs aimed at children gradually dissolves by late morning into sports programming. Sunday morning is divided among a variety of Canadian and American-based religious programs and children's television. The religious programs are further subdivided between local production and more slickly produced syndicated shows.

The expansion of Canadian television channels in the 1980s and 1990s has made the temporal designations in programming—such as the category of morning television—less valid. The patterns of morning television have instead been expanded into actual channels, where the former marginalia of television populate the entire broadcast day. For instance, CBC Newsworld, the 24 hour news channel does alter its content throughout the day, but the general pattern resembles breakfast television news programs that predated the channel's launch. Subtle differences can be seen in channels producing what could be described as micro-genres. Muchmusic, the nationally distributed cable music channel, organizes its morning into *Videoflow* and the retro-oriented mid-morning *ClipTrip.*

These channel orientations are complicated, however, by technological factors. Satellite distribution, unless it delays the signal—as it does for the more traditional networks of CTV and CBC—means that programming strategies of the cable-to-satellite channels break down in their attempts to match the temporal flows of their viewers. Programming designed for morning television in Toronto would appear in its satellite feed as very early morning television in Vancouver. Partly as a result of these difficulties, one can discern a slight tendency to program for the most populous part of the country connected to Montreal-Ottawa-Toronto eastern time zone.

Nevertheless, what can be identified more generally is that morning television, as it is now presented through the 40 or more channels available through Canadian television, may be slipping into programs associated with other day parts and even other generations, or "eras," from previous years of television. Past television becomes the domain of channels such as Bravo and the distinction between morning and prime time appears to dissolve. Cable channel advertising decisions now rotate commercials through the entire day of programming. Such a strategy indicates that the newer cable channels aim to gather their target audience through cumulative reach, rather than with the purchase of a particular prime time moment at a premium rate.

Morning television, then, does continue to provide particular categories of viewing practices and has produced associated genres connected to this marginalized part of television. The emerging reality of multi-channel television in Canada has made this sense of Canadian morning television and its connection to a temporal identification less distinct, but it is nevertheless a clear and continuing pattern in both programming and production practices.

—P. David Marshall

CANADIAN PRODUCTION COMPANIES

Most Canadian production companies are relatively recent phenomena. Indeed, prior to 1983 and the creation of Telefilm Canada, the independent production sector was either extremely weak or virtually non-existent. Since 1983, however, the sector has blossomed and Canada now has a number of financially sound production companies. Besides the CBC, the largest production companies are Alliance Communications Inc., Astral Communications Inc., Atlantis Communications Inc., and Paragon Entertainment Corporation. Other companies include Nelvana Ltd., Cinar Films, TeleScene Films, Primedia Productions, Sullivan Films, and Salter Street Films. The most unanticipated addition to the sector occurred in 1995 when Seagram Company Ltd. of Montreal acquired Hollywood-based MCA.

Pre-Telefilm

From 1952 to 1982, television production was dominated by the television networks themselves. This was especially true of the CBC which produced almost entirely in-house and which was, until 1961, the only network. The dominance of network production arises from three main factors. First, unlike U.S. networks, Canadian networks are restricted neither from owning all of their affiliates nor from producing all of their content. The CBC therefore is an integrated production, distribution, and broadcasting enterprise. As the owner of its affiliates, it naturally seeks to fill their air time with content which it produces in its fully-owned facilities. Second, there existed in Canada no film industry similar to Hollywood on which the nascent television networks could draw for content, expertise, or ideas. Third, CBC television adopted its operational methods from CBC radio where in-house production was the norm.

Consequently, the CBC, and to a lesser extent private networks after 1961, filled the need for content themselves. The CBC became therefore Canada's first major television production company, a role which it maintains to the present though on a reduced scale. However, until the early 1980s, the CBC dwarfed competitors and collaborators alike in terms of both the quantity and quality of its output.

The sheer volume of CBC production cannot adequately be characterized. It is possible, however, to point to certain structural elements. As a public network, the CBC's production activities necessarily occur within the framework of its parliamentary mandate which enjoins it to "reflect Canada and its regions to national and regional audiences, while serving the special needs of those regions" and to "contribute to shared national consciousness and identity". Hence, CBC production must provide for both mass and specialized audiences while being "distinctively Canadian". Second, as the CBC is only partially reliant upon commercial revenues, it has traditionally enjoyed the freedom to experiment and schedule material which is either challenging or of limited audience appeal. Third, its heavy reliance on in-house production has resulted in a recognizable network style across all program categories. This style, derived from the CBC's expertise in news and documentaries, has at times been called awkward, and has been blamed for a tendency to turn even drama into fictionalized news accounts.

Nonetheless, since its inception, the CBC has produced not only news and public affairs, for which it has earned a well-deserved reputation, but also drama (*CBC Playbill, On Camera, For the Record*), variety (*Don Messer's Jubilee, The Tommy Hunter Show, Rita and Friends*), comedy (*Wayne and Shuster, Kids in the Hall*), science (*The Nature of Things*), game shows (*Front Page Challenge, Reach for the Top*), weekly serials (*RCMP, Wojeck, Street Legal*), talk shows (*Take 30, 90 Minutes Live*), children's shows (*The Friendly Giant, Chez Hélène, Fred Penner's Place*), miniseries (*The Whiteoaks of Jalna, Empire Inc.*), arts programming (*Adrienne Clarkson Presents*), religious programming (*Man Alive*), cooking shows, do-it-yourself shows, numerous sports shows, and so on.

Four major aspects of CBC production stand out. The first is its stability. For example, whereas other North American broadcasters have abandoned variety and prime time game shows, the CBC continues to produce both. Additionally, many CBC shows have been in continual production for over 20 or 30 years. Both *Front Page Challenge* and *The Nature of Things* debuted in 1956 and are still in production. Comedians Wayne and Shuster performed on CBC televi-

sion from 1952 until well into the 1980s. The nature/adventure drama *The Beachcombers* ran uninterruptedly for 18 years from 1972 to 1990. CBC production, then, runs on a longer cycle than American production largely because it is responsive to social and cultural imperatives rather than simply to commercial and economic imperatives.

The second aspect is its variety. The CBC clearly attempts to produce for a much broader range of audience tastes and interests than virtually any other North American broadcaster. As a result, its production slate is perhaps the most highly varied though not the most watched in North America.

The third aspect concerns the nature of in-house production. This practice effectively precluded the emergence of an independent production sector. The CBC felt no need to call upon outside resources since everything could be done in-house. Likewise, outside resources had few opportunities to break into the business since the CBC would not buy from them. As a result, the independent sector languished and CBC production, despite its abundance and variety, acquired a recognizable look. Independent producers were forced to depend upon private broadcasters who were financially weak and slow to develop. However, the 1983 requirement that the CBC purchase dramatic content from independent producers both altered the look and feel of CBC programming and greatly assisted the independent production sector.

The fourth aspect concerns the way in which CBC programs attempt to meet the requirements of the Broadcasting Act. Systematically, they appeal to varied and various audiences, cover topics of broad appeal and specialist interest, are set in various regions of the country, cover different types of interest, are overwhelmingly pro-social, and deal with recognizably Canadian characters and situations.

In this respect, the most typical CBC genre may be the nature/adventure drama of which outstanding examples include *The Forest Rangers* (1963–66), *Adventures in Rainbow Country* (1970), *The Beachcombers* (1972–90), *Ritter's Cove* (1979–91), *Danger Bay* (1984–90), and others. The genre is highly durable and usually features children or adolescents surrounded by caring adults in a nature or wilderness setting. Each week, a problem arises which the young people attempt to solve through their own resources and the help of authoritative others, typically parents, the local RCMP detachment, or a native person. Favourite animals may also figure prominently as companions.

The genre corresponds well to the objectives of the Broadcasting Act. By decentralizing production to non-urban locations, it shows Canada to Canadians and gives all regions a sense of representation. It also appeals to parents as non-violent programming with potentially educational benefits. Furthermore, the genre's lower costs coincide with the resources of Canadian producers. Finally, as the child audience is both very forgiving and constantly renewed, the same programs can be constantly reissued, thereby building up a profitable backlog of shows. For all of these reasons, independent producers have also shown a proclivity for this genre or elements of it.

The CBC's French-language network, SRC (Société Radio-Canada), shares certain of the above characteristics. Like the CBC, the SRC was until 1961 virtually the only French-language producer in Canada and, like the CBC, produced huge quantities of programs across an enormous range of categories. It was likewise bound by budgetary constraints due to the size of its market (approximately six million viewers concentrated mainly in Quebec) and by the Broadcasting Act. However, it evolved quite differently.

Television in Quebec was immediately embraced as a tool for shaping a cultural community. As a result, French-language productions enjoy a popularity and cultural status unimaginable for English-language productions. The very rapid development of an indigenous star system and advertising culture further reinforced their appeal. They therefore address a loyal and voracious audience and are less concerned with "showing Canada to Canadians" than with representing and affirming their own culture. Hence, there is little crossover between French- and English-language productions.

The most popular and enduring genre of French-language TV is the *téléroman*. It is highly comparable to both the South American *telenovela* and the Australian *soapie*, and is a cross between American daytime soap opera, for production values, and prime time drama, for audience interest, cultural impact, and prestige. *Téléromans* are frequently written by leading authors or playwrights and may possess a cultural status similar to an important play or novel. They frequently broach topical issues or deal with significant historical and political themes though many are merely family sagas.

Private networks began to go to air in 1961. Their production activities, however, were much more limited than those of the CBC and tended to resemble the patterns of American TV. They typically produced news and sports but called upon outside producers to provide games shows (*It's Your Move, The Mad Dash*), the occasional sitcom (*The Trouble With Tracy, Pardon My French, Snow Job*), and some drama (*The Littlest Hobo, The Starlost*). They heavily supplemented their schedules with U.S. imports. On the French-language side, importation was more difficult and broadcasters soon became producers. Hence, the French-language TVA network became an important production company in its own right, duplicating much of SRC's output though with a heavier emphasis on the demotic and the inexpensive. Significantly, TVA has also come to rely on the *téléroman*, a genre pioneered by the public network.

The market represented by private networks, however, was sufficiently small that only very few independent production companies could co-exist. As a result, the private networks tended to draw heavily upon a very small number of independent producers thereby reproducing in the private sector a situation analogous to the public sector's use of in-house production.

This entire period is characterized, therefore, by the dominance of public networks, the prevalence of in-house

production or its analogue, a relatively small number of private broadcasters relying on U.S. imports, and the absence of a syndication market. Beginning in the early 1980s, the situation changed.

Post-Telefilm

In 1983, the federal government established Telefilm Canada. Telefilm administers two funds, the Feature Film Fund (FFF) and the Canadian Broadcast Program Development Fund (CBPDF), each worth approximately C$60 million per year. This money is available for independent producers and Telefilm invests in all phases of production: scriptwriting and pre-production, production, post-production, dubbing, marketing, test-marketing, and distribution.

To receive Telefilm funding, a project must be certified as "Canadian" according to the "points system" administered by CAVCO (the Canadian Audio-Visual Certification Office). In the first instance:

- the material must be produced by a Canadian citizen or landed immigrant
- its copyright must be owned by a Canadian citizen
- 75% of remuneration must be payable to Canadians
- 75% of aggregate costs for services must be payable to Canadians

Additionally, the content must obtain six points on the following scale:

- two points each for director and screenwriter
- one point each for highest paid actor
- one point each for second highest paid actor
- one point each for art director, music composer, picture editor, director of photography

Private investors participating in certified projects may also receive tax benefits. Additionally, provincial governments have instituted parallel structures to support film and television production and to attract activity to their territory. To date, Vancouver, Toronto, and Montreal have emerged as the centres of a vigorous independent film and television production industry.

Telefilm essentially provided a new source of funding for independent producers. However, it worked in conjunction with three other factors: the widening of the Canadian television industry, the emergence of a U.S. syndication market for Canadian content, and the development of a system of international co-productions.

The television market was widened in several ways. First, in 1983 the CBC was ordered to acquire entertainment programming from outside sources. It did, and by 1990, 50% of its entertainment content came from independent producers. The CBC has therefore been transformed from a producer to a purchaser of programming, thereby creating opportunities for the independent production sector. Amongst the highly successful independent productions acquired by the CBC are the made-for-TV miniseries *Ann of Green Gables* (Sullivan Entertainment) which earned the highest ratings of any television show in Canada to that time (5.8 million viewers) and was subsequently turned into a weekly series, *Road to Avonlea* (Sullivan Entertainment), *Kids in the Hall* (Broadway Video), *North of 60* (Alliance), *Babar* (Nelvana), *Wimzie's House* (Cinar), and numerous made-for-TV movies including the highly acclaimed *The Boys of St. Vincent* (Alliance).

Second, since 1982, the CRTC has licensed over 20 specialty and pay-TV channels. These channels not only require but also frequently demand highly specialized content, thereby requiring diversification within production companies or the emergence of parallel specialized producers. For example, the two music video channels, MuchMusic and MusiquePlus, obviously require musical content and a fund, VideoFax, has been set aside for the production of Canadian music videos. The sports channel requires news and information in addition to sports content. The movie channels require a certain number of Canadian movies. The Discovery Channel has an appetite for science and documentary. YTV, the youth channel, has likewise spawned shows aimed at its target audience. All of these channels also provide a second life to many older shows, thereby capitalizing the earlier investments of production companies.

Third, the CRTC has maintained its Canadian content quotas. These quotas effectively create a permanent domestic market for Canadian content. However, in order to avoid situations in which broadcasters program Canadian content in off-peak hours or fund only the cheapest types of content, the CRTC has also attached conditions to the licenses of virtually all the major broadcasters, whether they be over-the-air, cable networks, or independent television stations. The conditions vary from broadcaster to broadcaster but overall require that specified sums be spent on high profile content.

Fourth, U.S. cable networks have also emerged as a syndication market for Canadian content. Although they have insatiable appetites, they also tend to have smaller budgets than the major U.S. networks. As a result, they need content which is more affordable while still possessing acceptable production values. Consequently, they have turned to Canadian production companies and it is estimated that up to 30% of their original programming comes from Canadian producers.

The success of cable networks using Canadian content has convinced not only the major U.S. networks but also major U.S. production companies to begin investing in Canada where many American shows are now produced. As a result, CBS scheduled in 1994 the first non-American prime time series ever to air in the United States, *Due South* (Alliance). As well, Spelling Productions and Stephen J. Cannell productions have both set up shop in Vancouver. U.S. shows produced in Canada currently include *The X-Files*, *The Commish*, *Top Cops*, and others.

Several conditions have, therefore, combined to transform the fortunes of Canadian production companies. On the one hand, new sources of funding have been created through the establishment of Telefilm Canada and tax deductions. Furthermore, the regulatory environment has contributed to Canadian production through the maintenance of content quotas, the attachment of conditions of license, and the CAVCO certification procedure. Finally, the market has expanded through the licensing of new channels and the emergence of a U.S. syndication market. Even the presence of American productions has created opportunities for Canadian producers by affording them high profile exposure which they might not otherwise obtain. Together, they have given Canadian production companies two things they never before possessed: a track record and a backlog of marketable product.

However, the Canadian television market remains too small and too fragile to support the current scale of Canadian production. Indeed, Atlantis Communications Inc. reported in January 1995 that fully 80% of its license fees came from outside Canada. Hence, access to the wider North American and international markets constitutes the key to continued viability for Canadian production companies. They are therefore driven to seek additional sources of funding through international partnerships and Canada has developed a highly elaborate system of "international co-productions".

Co-productions involve partners from Canada and another country contributing to the manufacture of a single film or television program. They occur within the framework of treaties signed by the governments of both countries and covering financial participation, mutual tax concessions, national treatment, creative control, and copyright. Canada has over thirty such treaties and is the world's leading co-producer.

The advantage of co-productions are higher production values, access to foreign markets, and opportunities for on-going business relations. Their disadvantages are that they also create opportunities for conflict over financial and creative control, can be nightmares to administer, and can result in culturally unspecific content. The success of co-productions in their various markets is, of course, extraordinarily variable but they have served the fundamental purposes of broadening the financial base of production companies and giving them international reach.

Structure of a Production Company

An examination of some of the leading companies reveals strategic differences and similarities.

Astral Communications Inc. of Montreal was founded in 1962 as a photographic store but incorporated under its current name in 1974. It owns over 100 photographic stores, distributes film, television, and video, and has a library of 2000 titles. For Astral, production refers to the physical process of handling raw material and distributing content rather than to the combination of ideas, money, and talent to form a television program. It provides video duplication, post-production, and dubbing services, and owns a motion picture laboratory in downtown Montreal. It also participates in production and has long-standing relationships with Walt Disney Company, Warner Brothers Inc., Columbia Pictures, Universal Studios, and Hearst Entertainment, as well as others. For example, Astral and Twentieth Century-Fox have together formed Fox Astral Television which develops and finances international co-productions and distributes *NYPD Blue*, *The Simpsons*, *The American Music Awards*, and others. Astral also controls seven Canadian specialty channels: the Movie Network, Viewer's Choice, Family Channel, SuperEcran, Canal Famille, Moviepix, and Arts et divertissement. Finally, it manufactures up to 32 million CDs per year for music, education, and video. Astral invests, manufactures, and distributes. Its strength, therefore, lies not in the content which it produces but in the distribution networks which it controls and in its ability to market across media. Finally, as with many Canadian production companies, Astral handles both film and television productions for both the English- and French-language markets.

Alliance Communications Corporation of Toronto was incorporated in 1985 and is involved in both film and television production and co-production. Although Astral is Canada's largest entertainment enterprise, Alliance is definitely its most successful and its president, Robert Lantos, is currently the most important producer in Canada. Alliance has broken itself down into separate operating units: Alliance Releasing which handles distribution, Alliance Productions, the production arm, Alliance International, which distributes to Europe, Latin American, Asia, and the Pacific Rim, and Alliance Equicap, its financial and brokerage arm. Alliance produced two "breakthrough" programs in the late 1980s, *Night Heat*, a police drama, and *E.N.G.*, about the daily life of a television station. Not only did they sell internationally but they also achieved extremely good ratings in Canada, demonstrating that Canadian content could be popular (even in Canada) and that Canadian production companies used the highest production values. Alliance also landed the first regular prime time Canadian series on a U.S. network, *Due South*, and is currently developing several other projects. It also produced *Mrs. Harris Goes to New York*, *To Save the Children*, *Woman on the Run*, *Family of Strangers*, *Counterstrike*, *Bordertown*, *Diamonds*, and others. Alliance has heavily used the co-production treaty system in order to gain expertise and entry into various markets although it is tending increasingly towards purely private investment. Alliance's long-term strategy has been to invest in more modest projects budgeted at under $30 million and to finance only part of them. Alliance also owns 55% of the Showcase Network, a specialty cable channel which serves as an outlet for its catalogue. Like Astral, Alliance is involved in both film and television and produces and co-produces for both the English- and French-language markets.

Paragon Entertainment Corporation, though based in Toronto, has located its CEO and chairman, Jan Slan, in Los Angeles. Paragon's strategy is not to rely on the Canadian market but to produce for the North American and international markets. It wants to be in the right place at the right time and to be independent of Canadian financing. It sees itself as a production company on the international scene which just happens to be Canadian. It has been reasonably successful and has produced *Forever Knight*, *Lamb Chop's Play-Along*, *Sherlock Holmes Returns*, and *Blood Brothers*. The "Canadian" element of these programs lies in their financial and creative control rather than in their thematic or stylistic content.

Atlantis Communications Inc. of Toronto has a varied production slate including *Lost in the Barrens*, *Ray Bradbury Theatre*, *Tekwar*, *The Twilight Zone*, *Maniac Mansion*, *Adrift*, *Journey into Darkness: The Bruce Curtis Story*, *Kurt Vonnegut's Monkey House*, and *Race to Freedom: The Underground Railroad*. Like many other production companies, Atlantis produces for both the film and TV markets. Atlantis also owns a cable channel, the Life Network, as well as 28% of YTV. It intends to launch a science-fiction channel in order to capitalize on its expertise and backlog in the genre and to acquire another permanent outlet for its production.

Nelvana Ltd. of Toronto has specialized in the traditional Canadian niches of animation and children's programming. Its recent productions include *Babar*, *Tales From the Cryptkeeper*, *Cadillacs*, *Dinosaurs*, and *Tintin*. *Babar* in particular yielded profitable marketing tie-ins (toys, posters, etc.).

Cinar Films of Montreal has likewise targeted children with *Wimzie's House/ La maison de Ouimzie*, a program aimed at four-year-old children from which it expects marketing tie-ins. It has also sold *The Busy World of Richard Scarry*, based on the popular children's book known around the world, and produced *Are You Afraid of the Dark?*, a horror/fantasy show for young people, for both Nickelodeon and YTV. Its has also produced the TV-movie *Million Dollar Babies*, about the Dionne quintuplets.

Independent producer Kevin Sullivan has enjoyed enormous success, first with the two-part miniseries *Anne of Green Gables*, then with the weekly series *Road to Avonlea*, which ran for seven seasons, and finally with his TV movie, *Butterbox Babies*. All three ranked amongst the highest rating Canadian television programs.

Interestingly, many independent production companies have attempted to locate at least some of their output in an area of traditional Canadian strength, the "family drama", which both incorporates and transforms elements of the nature/adventure genre. Like nature/adventure shows, family dramas usually involve children and families, though they possess few of the precocious or saccharine characteristics of U.S. sitcoms. They also systematically eschew violence in favour of cleverness or circumstance and foreground pro-social values. However, unlike nature/adventure shows, they freely mix humour with drama, often fail to end happily, and jettison the requirement for wilderness settings and animals in favour of urban and frequently highly ironic plot lines.

The most celebrated example is probably *The Kids of Degrassi Street* (Playing with Time Productions) which spawned both *Degrassi Junior High* and *Degrassi High*. Like nature/adventure shows, the Degrassi series is aimed squarely at a family audience, features young people, and involves weekly dilemmas, but these are now cast in an urban setting with frequently unforeseen results and are neither clearly drama nor comedy. *Mom P.I.* (Atlantis) involves a mother whose job as a waitress forces her to moonlight as a detective; *My Secret Identity* (Sunrise Films) concerns a teenage boy with super powers; *Max Glick* (Glick Productions Inc.) follows the early-1960s adventures of the young title character.

Astral has been a publicly traded company since 1974, however, Alliance, Paragon, Atlantis, and Cinar all went public in 1993. Another factor which most of these companies have in common is their effort to acquire existing film libraries to feed their distribution channels. Finally, virtually all of them have major deals underway with U.S. networks and all of them maintain offices around the world.

Canadian production companies are, therefore, relatively recent phenomena. They produce for both film and television. They increasingly attempt to control distribution outlets thereby tending to make them integrated production/distribution houses on the CBC model. They increasingly attempt to acquire film libraries to feed their distribution networks and to market internationally alongside their own material. They rely heavily upon international markets although they rely less and less upon public money. Their content is frequently "Canadian" from the point of view of creative and financial control rather than from the perspective of tehmatic and stylistic content.

—Paul Attallah

FURTHER READING

Ayscough, Susan. "The Experiment that Spawned an Industry (Telefilm Canada at 25)." *Variety* (Los Angeles), 16 November 1992.

"Canada's Who's Who in Film and TV." *Variety* (Los Angeles), 22 November 1989.
Eisner, Ken. "B.C. to Prairies: Film Biz Boom." *Variety* (Los Angeles), 24 April 1995.
Kelly, Brendan. "Facing Up to the Future: Canadians View Expo as Great Meeting Place." *Variety* (Los Angeles), 16 January 1995.
———. "Focus Sharpens on Production (Special Report: Canada)." *Variety* (Los Angeles), 22 November 1993.
———. "Light Turns Green in Canada." *Variety* (Los Angeles), 11 April 1994.
———. "More Homegrown Up There." *Variety* (Los Angeles), 24 April 1995.
———. "The Year of Maturity: TV Biz Leads Growth as Firms Go Public and International (Special Report: Canada)." *Variety* (Los Angeles), 22 November 1993.
Lorimer, Rowland M., and Donald C. Wilson, editors. *Communication Canada: Issues in Broadcasting and New Technologies.* Toronto: Kagan and Woo, 1988.
Magder, Ted. *Canada's Hollywood: The Canadian State and Feature Films.* Toronto: University of Torono Press, 1993.
Murray, Karen. "Local Fare Finds Hungrier Palates South of the Border." *Variety* (Los Angeles), 16 November 1992.
———. "Paragon Slate Sees Yank Nets Head North." *Variety* (Los Angeles), 16 March 1992.
Pendakur, Manjunath. *Canadian Dreams and American Control: The Political Economy of the Canadian Film Industry.* Detroit, Michigan: Wayne State University Press, 1990.
Rainsberry, F.B. *A History of Children's Television in English Canada, 1952–1986.* Metuchen, New Jersey: Scarecrow Press, 1988.

See also *Boys of St. Vincent*; *Degrassi*; *Kids in the Hall*; *North of 60*; *Road to Avonlea*; Telefilm Canada

CANADIAN PROGRAMMING IN ENGLISH

The term "Canadianization" is used by some Europeans as a metonym for their fear of the audience fragmentation new satellite technologies would bring to their orderly systems of state supported public service broadcasting. But if the presence of alternative programming choices is this powerful, how did distinctive Canadian programming survive alongside the largest and most enclosed media giant in the world? Decades before cable and satellite the majority of Canadians could flick a dial and find ABC, NBC and CBS, plus dozens of local American stations. In the 1970s and 1980s Canadians had a cornucopia of specialty channels on cable, albeit the mix was controlled by the CRTC (Canadian Radio-Television and Telecommunications Commission).

By the mid-1970s, parts of Southern Ontario rivaled New York City for television choices. Yet here stands Canada—its electronic frontier as permeable as the world's longest unguarded border, still a separate nation-state. Canada's response to and appropriation of other sources of television may serve more as a success story for other national contexts than a model of dire consequences.

In 1952, when the Canadian Broadcasting Company (CBC) first went to air, thousands of Canadians along the border from coast to distant coast had already set their aerials to receive signals from the many American stations within range. And it is true that even in those early days, American television genres shaped the expectations of Canadian viewers about the conventions of television. At the same time, these types of programmes were beginning to differ significantly from the radio prototypes—variety shows, soaps, quiz and game shows—which had also been familiar beyond the northern border. Viewers were also enjoying the more televisual treatment of sports, documentaries and dramas.

On American television, these programme genres were usually clearly separated. However, the multi-talented first CBC head of programming, Mavor Moore, and his producer/directors (who were drawn from the National Film Board, the theatre, radio and off the street) were interested in experimenting with the forms of television. For example, on series like *Horizon* and anthologies like Robert Allen's *Scope/Folio/Festival,* Daryl Duke's *Q for Quest* and Mario Prizek's *Eyeopener,* they combined dramatization with panel discussions or documentaries or interviews.

But after the early years of experimentation the genres for the most part settled back into their self-defined places and thus the history of Canadian broadcasting can be summarised in terms of separate compartments, reflecting not only the sharpened distinctions made for the viewers but also the developing administrative empires.

In the first 15 years of CBC TV arts and drama producers broadcast the first full-length opera, programmed evenings of jazz, poetry and avant-garde drama (the outlawed American play *The Brig,* and scripts by Pinter, Albee, Beckett, Arrabal Anouilh). They adapted Shaw and Chekov. They broadcast live the family serial *The Family Plouffe* in both French and English, wrote and broadcast musicals for television (*Anne of Green Gables* is still performed on stage) and trained writers new to television on half-hour adaptations of Stephen Leacock's *Sketches of a Sunshine Town.* They produced ballet, Gilbert and Sullivan shows, regular classical music, folk and jazz concerts and made a quite successful *Hamlet* under severe limitations imposed by a tiny drama studio. Until 1967 almost all of the output was in black and white—colour came late to Canada—and live or live to tape until the late 1960s. They stirred up a major controversy (duplicated in the United Kingdom when the BBC bought the film) with Ron Kelly's direct cinema experimental drama, *The Open Grave.* Kelly had the nerve to treat the Resurrection as a breaking news story, full of interruptions and improvisations, using familiar reporters from CBC news and the following scenario: the previous Friday, Joshua Corbett had been hanged for alleged terrorism, though in fact he has disrupted the war industries with his pacifist ideas. Now his grave is empty and neither Mary Morrison, a ravaged, rather vague middle-aged prostitute, nor any of his other friends know where he is. The film, intended for broadcast on Easter Sunday, made the headlines for weeks.

Although in the United States, series from radio (soaps, westerns, cop shows and situation comedies) were transferred to television, for many years series were not made by the CBC. On American television viewers saw 1950s television anthologies like *Playhouse 90* and *Studio One* fade to black in the 1960s under the tide of strippable series filmed by major studios or independent producers in Hollywood. In the 1960s the CBC did introduce *RCMP (Royal Canadian Mounted Police)* and *Seaway,* two moderately successful independent productions for an adult audience. These were followed in 1966 by Ron Weyman's hugely successful and innovative in-house CBC series about a coroner, *Wojeck.* However the CBC also kept anthology drama alive for another three decades. With neither the inclination nor the resources to succumb to the "disease of the week" nor "murder of the week" staples of the popular American movies of the week the CBC preferred to put a significant portion of its revenue into drama specials and the long running topical drama anthology, *For the Record.* This program was followed in the late 1980s and 1990s by explorations of the country's regions with *The Way We Are,* and ethnic communities with *Inside Stories.* Anthology disappeared, at least to this date, in 1993.

Sports

Hockey Night in Canada was a staple of Saturday night radio in the 1930s and 1940s with the well-loved voice of Foster Hewitt shouting "He shoots . . .He Scores ! ! !" from the gondola in Toronto's Maple Leaf Gardens. When hockey came to television it continued to be a consistent ratings winner right up to the mid-1990s. What began as the "hot stove league" (commentary occurring between playing periods), became weekly tirades by the much-loved-or-hated Don Cherry. Initially, the expert camera work and the on-air commentary spoiled Canadians for coverage from the expansion teams but the gaps have closed—although Canadian viewers are bemused by the electronic pucks, cartoons and other "explanations" of the game by the U.S. FOX network.

Coverage of the short season of then immensely popular Canadian Football League (CFL) contests, including the Grey Cup Championship Game, began in 1952. CFL survival, now tied to television revenues as well as an ill-advised expansion, is in doubt in the 1990s. The national curling bonspiels were another regular sports feature. A much loved drama by W. O. Mitchell called *The Black Bonspiel of Wullie MacRimmon,* first seen CBC in 1955, is still produced in theatres around the country 40 years later, reflecting the Canadian affection for this purely amateur winter sport

Baseball came late to national Canadian television first with the Montreal Expos and then the Toronto Blue Jays—who, though in two different leagues, still echo the traditional winter hockey rivalry of the two cities—and languages. As the Olympic coverage has expanded, other sports receive more regular coverage: from skiing and gymnastics, which are a natural for television, to track and field, swimming and rowing. There are also annual events such as the rodeo competitions at the Calgary Stampede and the Queen's Plate, the oldest horse race on the continent. Women are used as colour commentators in many of these sports—but they are also authoritative voices in both gendered sports and horse racing, dressage and show jumping where both sexes appear in one field of competitors.

In recent years with the introduction of hemi-demi-semi finals which create a Hockey season extending into June, many Canadians viewers have complained that sports is dominating not only Saturday afternoons and nights and Sunday afternoons, but too much week night CBC prime time as well. Private broadcasters repeatedly urge the CRTC and the government to force the CBC out of this lucrative field. The CBC reply is direct. Government revenues have been cut in constant dollars from 1982 onwards. Professional Sports programming, particularly hockey gets ratings, makes money—and subsidises the coverage of amateur sports which CTV and Global/Canwest will not cover. The policy of displacing all other programming for 10 weeks when the hockey "finals" get under way in April continues. The 1995 Juneau report on the mandate of the CBC recommends that the CBC scrap the early rounds and get out of sports broadcasting except, of course, hockey coverage.

A cross-over between Sports and Entertainment has been the very successful skating specials pioneered by Toller Cranston in the early 1980s with *Strawberry Ice*. Brian Orser, Elizabeth Manley, Kurt Browning, Elvis Stojko, and pairs champions Eisler and Brasseur, have followed with specials which offer a little narrative, a lot of music and spectacle, other international medal-winning skaters and non-skating stars and superb special effects to complement the skating.

Religion

From the mid 1930s to 1995, both the CBC and the private networks were explicitly forbidden to sell time to radio and television evangelists. The result was that the CBC offers weekly a church service drawn from a variety of denominations and that individual stations program local church services or sell time to a few evangelists on late night or early-morning television. In 1995, the CRTC did license a small evangelical station in Lethbridge, Alberta.

In the 1950s and early 1960s the CBC broadcast specific words and music or drama programming keyed to Christmas and Easter, notably the innovative drama *The Hill* and *The Open Grave*. In these more ecumenical and culturally diverse times, such specific observances outside of the church or synagogue have disappeared. Surviving for many years however has been the popular, cheaply produced and musically impeccable *Hymn Sing. Man Alive*, the 25-year-old programme on ethical and moral issues, continues and is widely sold abroad.

A broadcasting initiative unique to Canada is Vision, a network run by a consortium of several faiths. It is financed by sales of weekend time to all kinds of groups from Jimmy Swaggart to Ba'hai. This "Mosaic" programming, so identified, must conform to Canadian laws regarding defamation, and a few programs have been pulled from the air. Vision's weekday and primetime programming offers a mix of documentaries, news, commentary, controversy, films and series from other countries, and programmes made by the marginalised, most of which offer an ethical perspective on the issues of the day as well

as addressing more permanent issues raised by the human condition. These programmes usually present more questions than answers. The network is provided on basic cable and also depends on viewer donations

News and Current Affairs

Unlike their American cousins who spare only a half hour (including commercials) for the national and, too seldom, international news, Canadians take their news, news analysis, current affairs and documentaries very seriously. They demand the best and they often get it. Since 1980 significant numbers have been willing to watch an hour of CBC news analysis and documentaries from 10-11:00 P.M. then switch to CTV at 11:00 P.M. for another half hour. CTV depends more on American and British feed that the CBC and too often neglects the regions outside of central Canada but on national stories they often do as well or better, finding fresh information or a different angle. Both newscasts attract significant numbers. However, when a national crisis such as the 1995 referendum looms, the CBC and CBC Newsworld, a separate all-news and features network, combine forces to bring Canadians detailed and comprehensive coverage and analysis. In those circumstances, as the ratings indicate, the CBC is the first choice.

If someone from another country asks who are the Canadian TV "stars" the candidates are likely to appear among the following lists of reporters and anchors rather than from the leads of a sitcom or cop show. They are also likely to be told how Knowlton Nash resigned as anchor of *The National* so that Peter Mansbridge would stay home to replace him rather than taking up a far more lucrative offer in the United States. And yet no one, anchor or reporter, could ever be said to have influenced a country's opinion on a national issue as Walter Cronkite is said to have done with the Vietnam War. Canadians accord no individual in broadcasting that kind of influence or impact, not even the late and much lamented anchor of *The Journal*, Barbara Frum.

Throughout its history, Canadian television, particularly the CBC, as part of its mandate, has emphasised News and Current Affairs. The nightly newscasts began in the early 1950s—with film clips rapidly gaining prominence. Anchors, many of whom were also reporters have included Earl Cameron, Larry Henderson, Stanley Burke, Knowlton Nash, Peter Mansbridge, Lloyd Robertson at both CBC and then CTV, Sandie Renaldo, Hana Gartner, Alison Smith, Pamela Wallin and Sheldon Turcotte.

In the 1970s the CBC and latterly CTV have used men and women in all the hot spots and on most beats. Well-known reporters include Peter Kent reporting from Cambodia, Anne Medina, an American who became an incisive Canadian voice from Lebanon, Brian Stewart from Ethiopia and Rwanda, Joe Schlosinger from all over the world, Bill Cameron, Anna-Maria Tremonti from Russia and Bosnia, senior Ottawa correspondents Jason Moscowitch and David Halton, Terry Malewski, Mary-Lou Finlay, Ian Hanomansing, Eve Savory on social policy and Der Ho Yen on economic policy.

Well known CBC current affairs and features series have included *Close-up, Telescope Quarterly Report* and the much admired and feared 1960s "gotcha" journalism of *This Hour Has Seven Days* whose cancellation lead to debate in Cabinet, a crisis in confidence between management and producers and a chilling effect on current affairs. After a hiatus in the late 1960s the news and current affairs department came back strongly with *the fifth estate*. CTV answered with W5 (*with Eric Mallins* was added in the 1980s). Among the widely acclaimed 1960s documentaries were Beryl Fox's cinema verite treatment of Vietnam, *The Mills of the Gods*, and Larry Gosnell's *Air of Death* on air pollution. For over 25 years the CBC has also offered a variety of analytical as well as descriptive programming about science and the natural world on the weekly series *The Nature of Things*.

Morning, Noon and Night Shows

Until quite recently CTV has had the only national "morning show" with *Canada AM.*—where lighter fare, news and national weather was the backdrop for incisive questioning of national and international figures. Norm Perry, Pamela Wallin, Valerie Pringle and Keith Morrison gave a jump-start to sluggish viewers heading out for work or into the day's work at home. In the 1980s Citytv (Toronto) and some other local stations offered a lighter version of "breakfast television". *Newsworld* offers full news and analysis to the country, updated hourly.

The CBC, again unlike the American networks, did not leave the afternoons completely to the soap opera and the rerun. From the early 1960s *Take 30* used the considerable journalistic talents of hosts like Adrienne Clarkson and Paul Soles to provide women at home with a daily half hour of news, current affairs, personalities, reviews, interviews and regular features, including by far the most thorough coverage at the time of the Royal Commission on the Status of Women. The program was replaced in 1994 by *Midday,* an hour at noon for the same audience, updated to include regular gardening features, analysis of popular culture and mini-documentaries. It is even more likely than its predecessor to examine the topical serious issues of the day from Quebec separation to the collapse of the fishing stock on both coasts.

Tabloid was an early (1953–63) national supper hour show which featured personalities from politics and entertainment. With a chalk-tossing weatherman, Percy Saltzman, the show was hosted by the genial Dick MacDougal and hostess Elaine Grand, and later Joyce Davidson. For the most part, however, supper hour shows of news, weather sports and features have been the territory of local stations. Under severe financial constraints and in some haste, the CBC closed some local stations in the late 1980s and ordered the stations which survived to cover a wider market with their supper hour shows—a decision which devastated morale and resulted in much lower ratings in some areas. The policy has since been reversed.

Basically all stations in Canada, independently or publicly owned or part of a network provide supper hour shows

and news, weather and sports at 11:00 P.M. The quality varies enormously but Toronto stations (with a potential market of 3 million) will cover transit policy, policing in the suburbs and "what's on" in the nightclubs while CKNX Wingham (pop. 10,000 with a market of 50,000) will cover the day's prices for cattle, the problems of the Saugeen Valley water authority and the "snowfest" in Durham.

Children's Programming

Programming for children is specifically mentioned in the existing CBC mandate. The CBC has offered very creative commercial-free, non-violent programming on weekday mornings since its inception. Ed McCurdy, Raffi, Sharon Lois and Bram, Fred Penner brought all kinds of music to kids. Puppets like *Uncle Chichimus* and his friend *Hollyhock* were followed by somewhat more sophisticated, much loved and very long lived series such as *Mister Dress-up* with his puppet friend Casey and *The Friendly Giant* with Rusty and his silent pal, the giraffe Jerome. *Romper Room* on CTV and *Polka Dot Door* on TVO (the Ontario educational network) were other popular programmes for young children. Special segments in both French and English were made in Canada as inserts for *Sesame Street.* Since its inception in 1970, TVO has devised all kinds of award winning children's series.

For older children viewing in prime-time there were 1960s adventure series on CBC like *Adventures in Rainbow Country* and *The Forest Rangers.* Both series were set in Canada's wilderness and structured around the usual gaggle of boys—and a girl or two—who get in and out of trouble, very little of it violent, with the help of parents or adult friends. Both are still in reruns.

The 1970s and 1980s belonged to *The Edison Twins* who used science to solve domestic puzzles, CTV's well-written family series *The Campbells,* set just before the Rebellion of 1837, and the three CBC *Degrassi* series which followed basically the same group of young actors through three series as they grew up. Using workshops and improvisational exercises, the series developed characters and plots reflecting their own lives until the "kids" graduated from high school This success lead to the more gritty *Northwood* and Global's *Madison* as well as the excellent "tween" show *Ready or Not.*

A much more complex concept for the 1990s is the CBC's *The Odyssey* which takes its viewer from the regular "Upworld" of school and work where Jay, the protagonist lies in a coma into the "Downworld," inhabited entirely by children. Downworld is full of great adventures (and wildly imaginative designs) which mirror and sometimes parody, as a dream might, the world of consciousness. The basic quest narrative (Jay seeks his absent father) has evolved over the seasons into more interaction between the worlds.

Variety

In the 1950s and 1960s variety shows combined singers, dancers, puppet shows, acrobats, animal acts and comedy sketches—including recurring favourites on *The Ed Sullivan*

Show like *Wayne and Shuster*. In Canada there were copies of American programs such as *Cross-Canada Hit Parade*, and *Show-time*, country and western shows like *Holiday Ranch* and then for twenty-five years *The Tommy Hunter Show*. Light music shows starred home-grown favourites like everyone's "pet *Juliette*" who sang pop favourites and ballads and always said good night to her mom. CTV responded to Canadian content regulations requiring cultural diversity with an imitation English pub *The Pig and Whistle* and the home-grown *Ian Tyson Show*.

A special case was the much loved down East fiddle music of *Don Messer's Jubilee*. With Marg Osborne and Charlie Chamberlain, Don Messer and his Islanders flourished for years on radio and then on television—until the late 1960s music "revolution" persuaded the executives in Toronto to cancel it for a limp imitation of similar American shows called *Hullabaloo*. Re-edited for the 1990s, *Don Messer's Jubilee* was surprise hit.

The CBC also discovered that in the 1990s an eclectic mix of every style of Canadian music from grunge rock to Buffy Ste. Marie, hosted by Cape Bretoner, Rita MacNeil is a major ratings winner. Running against an American trend to narrowcasting, musical variety at least has returned to Canadian prime-time.

Talk Shows and Game Shows

The nearly forty-year run of *Front Page Challenge* reflected the Canadian preference for hybrid form and an emphasis on current affairs. Part quiz, part-current affairs show, its guests included domestic and foreign prime ministers, sports and entertainment celebrities and ordinary citizens who had made the headlines. Most other Canadian quiz shows have been "Canadian Content fillers," (produced to meet requirements for Canadian content), and were merely less expensive imitations of American game shows. On CTV *Shirley, Dini Petty*, and in a more serious vein *Jane Hawtin Live* are successful day-time talk shows. *Pamela Wallin Live* on Newsworld is a 1990s prime-time success story with a very wide range of guests and subjects and a few callers. Other cross-country call-in shows on Newsworld are oriented toward public affairs. Neither public nor private television has been successful with late night talk shows

Comedy Shows

For 50 years Canadians have excelled in developing small companies who perform satirical, usually topical revue comedy on radio and television. The grandfather of them all was *Wayne and Shuster*. The grandmother was the annual theatrical revue *Spring Thaw*. The proud children were *SCTV* in the 1970's and *The Royal Canadian AirFarce* still going strong on radio and television. The grandchildren are *CODCO* (and its stepchild *This Hour Has 22 Minutes)* and *Kids in the Hall*. With their gentle, literate yet often slapstick parodies of both high and popular culture, edited reruns of *Wayne and Shuster* were popular in many countries. *SCTV* (also in reruns) was so self-reflexive that it became a cult favourite with a younger media literate generation as did

Kids whose executive producer, Canadian Lorne Michaels was so closely connected to *Saturday Night Live*. In contrast to *Kids in the Hall*, *CODCO*'s much harder hitting satire and complex, sustained characterisations were informed by the eloquence of Newfoundland speech and a more distinctly Canadian sense of values. Some of *CODCO*'s original members now turn their biting wit on the week's news in *This Hour Has 22 Minutes*.

Drama

For the first twenty years of CBC TV drama, in the absence of any strong professional theatre, the general policy was that it should entertain, inform, and reflect national and regional concerns (intermittently and with significant gaps). It should experiment with television as a medium, show Canadians what classical and contemporary world theatre looked like and explore the relationship of the documentary and the fictional. In the 1960s, the drama department was also expected to inflect some forms of American popular culture (cop shows, mysteries, sitcoms) and ignore others like soaps; and until 1992 continue with anthology drama. Finally, in very occasional miniseries or films, the "single" play, whether a light comedy, a theatre adaptation, a docudrama or an intensely personal vision, would find a home.

Biographies

Throughout its history the CBC has explored various dramatic forms to produce biographies. A mixture of voice-over commentary, selections from the works of fiction or the paintings etc., sustained satire, even musical numbers have been used to produce a non-standard series of biographies: the mix of drama, documentary and commentators in *The Baron of Brewery Bay* with John Drainie playing Stephen Leacock; the lives of artists Tom Thompson and Emily Carr; Kate Reid as suffragette Nellie McLung; three versions of the life of feminist Emily Murphy; Prime Ministers John A. Macdonald (several times) and William Lyon MacKenzie King (once as a satire, *Rexy*, once as a miniseries by Donald Brittain). Others less well known included Brittain's *Canada's Sweetheart the Saga of Hal Banks* (the imported thug who ran the waterfronts of Canada), colourful newspaper editors and columnists like Bob Barker and "Ma" Murray. The CBC also presented the trials of the assassin of D'Arcy McGee twice and rebel/martyr Louis Riel three times: first as a two part drama, then as an opera and finally as a lavish, revisionist miniseries, shot in both languages in 1979.

The lives of explorers, politicians, financiers and engineers were treated in the hugely successful five part adaptation of Pierre Berton's trilogy *The National Dream*. The miniseries combined contemporary narrative, shot by Berton on locations across the country, with dramatizations of the men who made it happen. In the 1980s *Some Honourable Gentlemen* also depicted a wide variety of historical figures—not all of them heroes.

Two successful experiments on the private networks include *The Life and Times of Edwin Alonzo Lloyd* (with veteran actor Gordon Pinsent) and Pierre Berton's inexpensive and fascinating half-hour vignettes on *Heritage Theatre*.

Soap Opera

Some of the most popular U.S. genres have never appeared on Canadian television. Unlike every other developed country and despite successful efforts in 1940s and 1950s radio, until the 1990s, there were no soap operas, no *teleromans* (a francophone long serial form at which SRC excels) on English Canadian television. There was only one brief though seminal fling in the 1960s at short serials on film. There is a very straightforward reason for this. In the early days the CBC had no interest. When CTV arrived in the early 1960s, soaps were "too expensive" since they involved a sustained commitment to TV drama. In the 1970s CBC TV tried the longer serial form using Mazo de la Roche's widely popular Whiteoaks novels. *Jalna* was shot using experimental techniques, multiple story and time lines—and failed. In the same decade, the CBC also tried a twice weekly night soap called *House of Pride*. Reflecting the CBC mandate to show Canadians the five "Regions"—a largely fictional but still potent set of geopolitical myths consisting of "the Atlantic provinces", Quebec, Ontario, "the West" and British Columbia—*House of Pride* was set and taped in five cities across the country. Although ahead of its time (*Dallas* was five years away) logistics and problems with the story lines killed it.

After a hiatus of more than ten years two half hour daytime soaps appeared on the private networks. Whether Global's early 1990s *A Foreign Affair* or CTV's *Family Passions,* both co-produced with several other countries, will survive long enough to be the training ground and cash cow that Canadian television, both public and private, needs remains to be seen. Perhaps because they are international co-productions they seem to be more hodgepodge than tasty puddings.

Canada's Exports: People

Canadians take rueful pride in the export of talent that has happened throughout their broadcast history: host Bernard Braden, many producers including Sydney Newman to the United Kingdom; actors Raymond Massey, Leslie Nielsen, Lorne Green, William Shatner, John Colicos, Martin Short and John Candy, producer Lorne Michaels, writers Bernard Slade, Arthur Hailey, Anna Sandor and Bill Gough and literally dozens of others to the United States. In the 1980s the independently made satire *The Canadian Connection,* using several expatriates explored the theory that Canadians were involved in a conspiracy to take over Hollywood—and thus all of American culture. It has been rerun several times.

Programmes

Why didn't Canada simply export some of its entertainment programming to the United States instead of its talent? The answers are many. First, there was no star system in English Canadian TV until the mid 1970s and then only fitfully—

no actor was bankable. Since its beginning, Canadian television could not retain some of its major talent because it paid much less than competitors in other countries. When talented individuals stay—and many do—it is because of the life in Canada and the opportunities to do a very different kind of work. Still, Canadian television has been shaped from the beginning by a steady exodus. An American network bought the concept, writer, star and much of the technical team of *Wojeck* which, after being run through the network blender came as the barely recognisable *Quincy*.

Nearly 20 years later a summer prime-time run of the fairly gritty and not overtly Canadian CTV cop show *Sidestreet* (which had been scheduled by CBS at midnight, though run in Canada at 10:00 P.M.) meant American stars had to appear as guests. More to the point, the scripts had to be more straightforward with less allusion and ambiguity. In the case of *Danger Bay,* in the 1980s a popular family/adventure series set in part at the Vancouver aquarium, the CBC and their independent partner had to struggle with co-producers from Disney to allow a scene and a story line featuring the live birth of a whale. One of the CBC's most successful exports, *Road to Avonlea* has featured at least one American or British star for an episode or two because Disney was co-producer.

Docudrama

The perception that current events are raw material for the by now thoroughly debased U.S. "docudrama" permeates U.S. society. In the North American context of the 1990s it may be one of the most distinctive things about Canadian culture that front page events are not yet seen as fodder for the movie-of-the-week mill, nor Canadians, as they live their lives, as featured players for next week's video releases.

In fact Canadians still care very much about the differences between evidence, argument, reenactment and the "make it up or leave it out, whichever makes a more entertaining television movie" approach. Canadian audiences can still distinguish between docudrama (real people are characters), topical drama (foregrounding a contemporary issue) or historical drama (a mixture of real and fictional characters set in a time when most viewers will not have first-hand knowledge of the "history" portrayed). The example of the very controversial co-production with the National Film Board (NFB), *The Valour and the Horror,* illustrates the difference. It is unimaginable that Americans in the United States would argue strenuously for months on end about the verisimilitude of both the documentary and dramatized segments of three programs about the World War II. Jeanine Locke, a writer-producer of period and topical dramas made many distinctive drama specials like *Chautauqua Girl* (which looked at both 1930s prairie populism and the Chautauqua circuit), *You've Come a Long Way Katie* (about alcoholism—Katie dies) and *The Greening of Ian Elliot* (which combined the debate about the ordination of homosexual ministers in the Unified Church and the fight against the Aleimeda-Rafferty Dam).

From 1976–85 the CBC presented an anthology of what R.L. Thomas, the first executive producer called "journalistic dramas". Searching, topical, often controversial, innovative in subject matter and not usually too didactic, *For the Record* attracted the best talent in the country, in front of and behind the cameras. Some of the most notable productions were *A Far Cry From Home, Ready for Slaughter, Blind Faith, Every Person is Guilty, I Love a Man in Uniform, Maria, One of Our Own,* and *The Winnings of Frankie Walls.* Subjects included unemployment, the economic troubles of family farms, euthanasia, aboriginal injustice, televangelism, wife abuse, and a Francophone/Anglophone marriage at the time of the 1980 referendum.

When the CBC made *The Scales of Justice* a series of drama specials about well known, (sometimes sensational, sometimes only half-remembered) legal cases, they hired a well-known criminal lawyer to advise on the scripts and serve as an on-camera/voice-over guide through the intricacies of the law. The parts of the script based on testimony and those based on speculation, as well as the contradictions, are explicitly pointed out. *The Scales of Justice* appears two or three times a year, presenting Canadian judicial and social history without losing track of the ethical questions involved in docudrama.

In the late 1980s and 1990s miniseries the voice is also distinctive, however dissonant to the English Canadian culture under scrutiny: producer Bernie Zukerman's *Love and Hate,* explored the personalities involved and also the cultural context of the terrorising and murder of the wife of a well known Saskatchewan political family. His *Conspiracy of Silence: The Story of Helen Betty Osborne* is a searching account of the racism in a northern community. *Liar, Liar* looked at the possibility that a child may lie about child abuse and *Life with Billy* examined once again wife and child abuse. *Butter Box Babies* recreated a period tale of neglect in an orphanage and Adam Egoyan's *Gross Misconduct* was an unsparing (and experimental) look at the destruction of a hockey star. Many of these have been ratings hits on American prime-time.

Of them all, John Smith's *The Boys of St. Vincent,* a 1993 CBC/NFB collaboration is the best example of the survival of a distinctive English Canadian television voice. It is also worth noting that, like *The Valour and the Horror, The Boys of St. Vincent* eluded efforts at censorship through a court injunction in Ontario and parts of Quebec because the NFB (partnered with an independent company with a broadcast window and input from the CBC) had the conviction and the resources to put these programs on cassette for sale or loan. The miniseries had a Canada-wide airing a few months later.

No such "State" institutions exist in the United States. More important is the fact that the commercial constraints on the independent television film-makers and the American networks would have ensured that such programs are not made. When shown on A and E in 1994, some of the scenes from *The Boys of St. Vincent,* scenes which made the

viewer a potentially complicit spectator—a point vital to the moral challenge of the work—were simply cut. Unfortunately this masterwork was not shown on the CBC without commercials on the "publicly owned broadcasting system". The effect was very damaging to the integrity of the work.

Series

Most Canadian series are produced by the CBC and are inflections or sometimes hybrids of U.S. genres. Yet they show a different legal or medical system, different urban landscapes (no mean streets), very different ethnic mixes and attitudes, and are less violent. They are also often less confrontational, although not always, as illustrated by *Streetlegal* and its mid–1980s rival, CTV's only high quality series *E.N.G.* In most of these series we see actors who are comfortable working in ensemble, usually performing in less extroverted ways than their U.S. cousins. The writers, producers and executives have always been more comfortable with ambiguity in characterisation, literate dialogue, sometimes open endings and often complex subtext.

The fact is, that if Canadians created many clones of a U.S. genre like CTV's action adventure series *Counterstrike* they could not compete with the production values or the stars and would not be worth watching when the originals are a channel changers' zap away. But it is also true that Canadians are utterly delighted that the huge neighbour to the south broadcast in primetime 1994—and then renewed mid-season 1995–96 CTV's *Due South,* the "odd couple" comedy/cop show which features a Mountie from the far north displaced to the streets of Chicago and Ray, his cynical side-kick. Both cultures are satirised, but Canadians, saturated in U.S. popular culture get all the jokes. Americans may well miss many of them.

It is true that Canadian popular drama has always been competitive with "theirs" when time and money is spent on it. Note the success of *Wojeck, The Manipulators,* the much loved period series *A Gift to Last, The Great Detective* and sitcoms like *King of Kensington, Hangin' In, Max Glick,* and the wonderful hybrid mystery show *Seeing Things.* Co-producers David Barlow and Louis DelGrande inflected the cop show to produce a protagonist, Louie Ciccone, a short-sighted newspaper reporter with glasses who has visions of murders he would much rather ignore, doesn't drive or know which end of a gun is which, is rescued by a flying puck, a cake and often by his wife Marge. Yet the series had a strong moral centre, a lot of culturally specific topical satire and also worked as a good whodunnit.

Francophone and First Nations

The French fact in Quebec, the million francophones outside Quebec and the aboriginal nations, who are scattered throughout Canada and dominant in the north, have all been visible intermittently in English Canada's television drama. *La famille Plouffe* (1953–59 on CBC, 1952–59 on Radio Canada) was broadcast live, sequentially, in both languages. There were also a few efforts to reflect each culture to the other in the arts. *Festival* presented in English a handful of Quebec playwrights including Michel Tremblay's *Les Belles Soeurs*. But *For the Record* produced just one contemporary drama, *Don't forget: Je me souviens* in 1980. There has been no other drama on this subject on the CBC in the last 16 years. Yet television fiction is the site where the conflicting discourses of society are made concrete, sometimes mediated and sometimes exposed as unresolved.

As the CBC itself admitted in its submission to the CRTC in 1978 "the perception of the need to reflect the two linguistic communities to one another emerged in the CBC at about the same time as it emerged in the country—gradually over the last half of the 1960s and then early 1970s and then abruptly in the mid-1970s". Yes, the CBC presented our fractious politics at length in the 1980s on *The Nation* and *The Journal* in all kinds of specials during recurrent crises—but not in fiction.

On the other hand, Radio-Canada created its own mythology by decontextualizing and repeating months later, over and over, the "red-necks stomp on the Quebec flag episode" during the Meech Lake Accord fiasco. Radio-Canada also regularly ignores the Arts in the rest of Canada as well as most anglophone popular culture, with a nationalist fervour that also creates a deafening silence.

There were a few "cross-cultural" dramas during and after the first Quebec referendum in 1980. Miniseries such as the French *Duplessis*, the very successful English *Empire Inc.* and the less successful *Chasing Rainbows* (all set in Montreal, all lavish period pieces) were dubbed into the other language. However, *Lance et Compte (He shoots! He Scores!)* (1987) which was shot in both languages, turned into a litmus test of both cultures. *Lance et Compte* started on SRC with a million viewers and soon nearly tripled to 2.7 out of a total viewing population of 6 million. There were T-shirts, mugs, a fan magazine, a book, even sweat suits over its three year run. Yet the same scripts in English using the same actors, directors, producer and crew drew, at its peak in a hockey obsessed culture, only 750,000 viewers.

It is safe to say that at no time in its history did CBC English Television depend on a soupcon of French for a distinctive flavour to its stew. Although efforts in news and current affairs continue, if Quebec leaves Canada the opportunities for shared music, drama, news reporting, sportscasts and documentaries on a daily basis which have been wasted over the previous four decades may be one of the clearest discernible reasons for the divorce.

A more consistently distinctive motif in Canadian television has been the representation of aboriginal peoples. The subject was first fully explored by Philip Keately (producer/director) and Paul St. Pierre (writer) who created a 1960s anthology with recurring characters *Cariboo Country*, a contemporary television "western" which was as far away as it could get from the U.S. TV Westerns so popular at the time. The motif reappeared sporadically in other places

throughout the 1970s and 1980s: Claude Jutra's *Dreamspeaker*, *Where the Heart Is*, *A Thousand Moons*, many episodes of *Beachcombers*, a few episodes of *Danger Bay*, all of the short series for children *Spirit Bay*, and most notably and controversially in 1989 *Where the Spirit Lives*, a historical drama about residential schools which was sold to PBS and around the world and rebroadcast in Canada four times.

Since 1992 the CBC presented four full seasons of *North of 60*, set on a reservation in the North West Territories. Unlike *Northern Exposure*, the U.S. cult hit to which it is sometimes so inappropriately compared, *North of 60* does not use aboriginal people as an exotic back-drop. In its third and fourth seasons all but one of the leading characters have been native. The series has presented complex and sustained examinations of alcoholism, the effect of residential schools and forced acculturation on individuals and families, internal feuds and band politics, interference from government, anthropologists and ill-informed animal rights activists, the ongoing friendships and resentments between white band manager, storekeeper and nurse and the chief, treatment centre staff, visiting artists etc. There were also the drama specials *Spirit Rider* and *Medicine River*, based on a novel by aboriginal writer Thomas King. However stereotypes can still be found in reruns of the late 1980s *Bordertown*, the CTV "western" about a Mountie, a U.S. marshal and a woman doctor from France (the series is a co-production with France), or Global's steamy *Destiny Ridge*, and in the CBC's 1994 *Trial at Fortitude Bay*.

Nevertheless, since the OKA crisis of 1990 and in the midst of an ongoing debate about cultural appropriation, Canadians have changed what they watch and how they watch it. Meanwhile, the long-running and evolving aboriginal motif has now been claimed by those whose lives it reflects. Slowly the fresh perceptions which can arise from First Nations writers, directors and producers are making their way into the main stream of CBC drama.

The future of the CBC as it is now constituted is as uncertain as the composition of the country as it is now constituted. Yet despite its proximity to the biggest media giants in the world, its "mixed" structure and its inevitable ups and downs Canadian television and the CBC in particular has retained a distinctive voice supporting, amplifying and sometimes defining a distinctive national culture.

—Mary Jane Miller

FURTHER READING

Collins, Richard. *Culture, Communication and National Identity: The Case of Canadian Television*. Toronto: University of Toronto Press, 1990.

Miller, Mary Jane. *Turn up the Contrast: CBC Television Drama Since 1952*. Vancouver: University of British Columbia Press, 1987.

————. *Rewind and Search: Makers and Decisionmakers of CBC Television Drama*. Montreal: McGill-Queens University Press, 1996.

Nash, Knowlton. *The Microphone Wars: A History of Triumph and Betrayal at the CBC.* Toronto: McLelland and Stewart, 1994.

Peers, Frank W. *The Public Eye: Television and the Politics of Canadian Broadcasting, 1952–68.* Toronto: University of Toronto Press, 1979.

Raboy, Marc. *Missed Opportunities: The Story of Canada's Broadcasting Policy.* Montreal and Kingston: McGill-Queens University Press, 1990.

Rutherford, Paul. *When Television Was Young: Primetime Canada 1952–1967.* Toronto: University of Toronto Press, 1990.

See also Canadian Programming in French; Canadian Production Companies, *CODCO; Beachcombers; Boys of St. Vincent; Cariboo Country; Degrassi; E.N.G.; Family Plouffe; Fifth Estate; For the Record; Front Page Challenge; Hockey Night in Canada; Kids in the Hall; Man Alive; Market Place; National; Nature of Things; North of 60; Quentin Durgens, M.P.; Road to Avonlea; Second City TV; Street Legal; This Hour Has Seven Days; Tommy Hunter Show; Valor and the Horror; Wayne and Shuster; Wojeck*

CANADIAN PROGRAMMING IN FRENCH

Television was embraced by French-language viewers more quickly than any other group in Canada. They bought TV sets more rapidly and watched more television than did their English-speaking counterparts. A majority of television households were concentrated among the working-class families of Montreal. From the beginning, La Societé Radio-Canada, Canada's public francophone broadcaster, was the center of French programming in Canada and the company strategy was to attempt to be all things to all people.

As the only francophone television broadcaster, it enjoyed a monopoly position. Because it faced no competition either inside or outside Canada, and because it had to produce over 75% of its own programming, Radio-Canada was able to craft programs intended to enlighten and educate as well as entertain its captive audience. The power of television was very quickly understood by Quebec's creative community and, unlike comparable groups in anglophone Canada, television production in Quebec drew upon some of the most creative and inventive minds in French Canadian society. Historians and commentators generally describe francophone television's early years from 1952 to 1960 as a "golden age." Leading academics, artists, intellectuals, and cultural heroes were quick to embrace this new medium, making television a powerful force in Quebec's Quiet Revolution.

In the realm of news and information, Radio-Canada was determined to keep its public well-informed—not only about the country but about the entire world. Journalists such as Gerard Pelletier and André Laurendeau argued that television could be an instrument of modernity which would not only introduce the rest of the world to Quebec but which would serve to improve knowledge and raise the sense of national pride. Pelletier hosted *Les idées en marche* (1955–61), a public affairs show which featured debates and interviews with prominent intellectuals on domestic and international issues. Laurendeau presided over *Pays et merveilles* (1953–61), a world-travel series which featured film footage and guests who would discuss such issues as the Middle East. Other popular news information shows included *Carrefour* (1958–59) and *Premier Plan* (1959–60) which were interview shows. But the most critically-acclaimed news and information program was *Point de Mire* (1957–59), hosted by René Lévesque, the future premier of Quebec. This show attempted to popularize international issues such as the Algerian crisis, and used maps, charts, film footage, even a blackboard, to educate and inform viewers. Only occasionally did the show address Quebecois or Canadian themes.

Other shows like *Panoramique* (1958–59) a series of historical documentaries from the French division of the National Film Board of Canada, drew viewers attention to Canadian and Quebec historical issues. *Le roman de la science* was a docudrama about major scientific discoveries throughout history. *Je me souviens/Dateline* was a bilingual informational program on Quebec and Canadian history. *Explorations* (1956–61) was another history series which tried to bridge the Canadian cultural and linguistic divide. One segment from the series, "Two Studies of French Canada," was run on the English-language CBC. Hosted by Lévesque this program tried to explain to anglophone Canadian the recent history and aspirations of French Canadians.

Variety and musical programs also carried an international flavour. *Music Hall* (1955–65), Quebec's alternative to *The Ed Sullivan Show*, hosted a line-up of international francophone stars which included Maurice Chevalier, Edith Piaf, and Charles Aznavour as well as well-known Canadian singers such as Monique Leyrac and Denise Filiatrault.

Radio-Canada provided a broad range of variety programs to suit all tastes. *Feu de joie* featured jazz, *Dans tous les cantons* ran traditional French-Canadian folk music, *Chansons vedettes* and *Chansons canadiennes* showcased contemporary popular artists. Despite this impressive line-up with extravagant costumes and lavishly produced numbers, the shows did not attract viewers. Variety programming was the least popular of all the types of television produced by Radio-Canada in the 1960s and, unlike the CBC, the system never had a truly popular program such as those hosted on the CBC by Don Messer or Tommy Hunter. The only light entertainment show which developed any following was the comedy-sketch series, *Quelles nouvelles*, which had been a popular radio series and starred Jean Duceppe and Marjolaine Hébert.

Comedy was, however, a central feature of game shows. Cheap and easy to design and produce—particularly since they involved little prize money—quiz shows like *Le nez de Cléopâtre* (1953–57) and *Point d'interrogation* (1956–62) featured panels of well-known personalities given a limit of twenty questions in which to identify a person or object. Other shows like *Chacun son métier* (1954-59) was a French version of the popular American program *What's My Line?*

Radio-Canada's real strength was the novelty or fun show. Shows such as *La clef des champs* (1955–59) and *Le club des autographs* (1957–62) were popular with audiences as much for their comedy as for their contests. Both were based on simple premises; *La clef des champs* was a charades game but the actor and comedians competed more for laughs than for prizes, while *Le club des autographs* invited celebrities to twist and shake in a comical dance contest. The audience's favorite and the most extreme example of this kind of programming was *La rigolade* (1955–58). Referring to itself as the "least serious broadcast on the air," it invited ordinary people to test their skills at the silliest contests the producers could invent. As the contests became zanier, critics decried it as a scandalous spectacle and it was pulled off the air after only three seasons despite being among the top-ranked shows on Radio-Canada.

Francophone programmers were continually faced with trying to balance such popular programs with its cultural and educational mandate. Any kind of spectacle seem to have a large audience. *La Lutte* (1952–59) and *La Boxe* (1952–55) broadcast weekly prize fights which attracted a large following (even among women). Sports were consistently in demand, especially *La soirée du hockey*, the most popular program on television. Though hockey had always been popular in Quebec, television made players like Rocket Richard, the star of the Montreal Canadiens, into national heroes. As many as two million fans watched each Canadiens' game. Richard had become such a cultural icon that when he was suspended from the playoffs in the spring of 1995, the city exploded into rioting. It was no accident that Richard made public television appeals to induce the crowds to end the violence.

This incident only added to the dilemma facing programmers as more and more viewers demanded more sports while the elites and the clergy condemned television for inciting and promoting violence. Television programmers tried to counteract these charges in the 1950s by scheduling most of its sportscasts on the weekends and by increasing its broadcast of the performing arts.

Radio-Canada had always believed that television could stimulate and educate the viewer. Music, ballet, opera, and drama were presented several times a week in various anthologies. *L'heure du concert* (1954–66) was devoted to concerts, opera, and ballet. Initially, it offered a series of excerpts from various productions and provided brief lectures on various art forms. Theatre also occupied the most prominent place in Radio-Canada's early programming, and despite the challenges and difficulties and production costs involved with live television drama, CBFT produced as much as two dramas a week throughout the 1950s. A demand for local productions fuelled an enormous expansion in the development of Quebecois literature. Initially, great classical works such as Cocteau's *Oedipe-Roi* had been presented, but these were quickly replaced with local works. Soon short stories and even novels had to be adapted for television as more traditional works were soon exhausted. Eventually, Quebecois authors were commissioned to write specifically for television.

Between 1952 and 1960, Radio-Canada aired 435 plays, 80% of which were originally written or adapted by popular Quebecois writers such as Marcel Dubé, Hubert Aquin, Françoise Loranger, and Felix Leclerc. The majority of teleplays were showcased in *Le Teletheâtre de Radio-Canada* (1953–66) which presented more than 160 works and *Théâtre populaire* (1956–58) which presented more than 100 plays. Other series included *Théâtre d'été* (1954–61) and *En première* (1958–60), *Théâtre du dimanche* (1960–61), *Jeudi Théâtre* (1961–62), and *Théâtre d'une heure* (1963–1966).

While the teleplays received great critical acclaim, they were far less popular than the *téléromans*, televised serials adapted from popular novels. Since the debut of Roger Lemelin's *La famille Plouffe* (1953–59), this television genre has been a mainstay of francophone programming. Usually broadcast in half-hour episodes in peak hours over the fall/winter schedule, the stories would generally be completed in two or three seasons, but two series lasted much longer than the norm. *Les Belles Histoires des pays d'en haut* went on for 14 years while *Rue des Pignons* continued for 11 years. Other popular téléromans included: *Quartorze, rue de Galais* (1954–57), *Le Survenant* (1954–57, 59–60), *Cap-aux-sorciers* (1955–58), *La Pension Velder* (1957–61), *La Côte de sable* (1960–62), *De 9 à 5* (1963–66), and *Septième nord* (1963–67).

A producer's strike at CBFT in Montreal from December 1958 to March 1959 brought serious disruption to francophone programming and an end to the "golden age" of French-Canadian broadcasting. Not only did popular shows like *Point de Mire* and *La famille Plouffe* end their run, many critically-acclaimed programs were never to return to the airwaves. The strike has become part of the annals of Quebec's Quiet Revolution. Some of the province's most popular television personalities like René Lévesque abandoned careers in broadcasting, in Levesque's case to launch himself into politics.

The strike and its aftermath reflected the changing realities that television faced. In 1960, Radio-Canada faced competition from a private broadcaster. Télé-Métropole, "le 10," promoted itself as the station for ordinary people. In

1971 it became part of the Télé-Diffuseurs Associés (TVA) network. Its programming relied heavily on foreign movies and dubbed American drama series. Quiz shows like *Quiz-O* and *Télé-poker* became mainstays on the schedule, along with hockey broadcasts and variety programs which show-cased Quebec's popular comedians and singers such as Robert Charlebois and Yvon Deschamps.

"Le 10" did produce a daily serial, *Ma femme et moi,* which ran in 1961 but it was only with *Cré Basile* (1965–68) that Télé-Métropole and the TVA network found critical acclaim for its television dramas. *Cré Basile* was Quebec's first sitcom and for the first time comedy was to become an integral part of francophone television drama. Télé-Métropole went on to develop other popular burlesque comedies *Lecoq et fils* (1967–68), *Symphorien* (1974–78), *Les Brillant* (1979–80), and situation comedies *Dominique* (1977–80) and *Peau de banane* (1982–87). Télé-Métropole's programming was immediately popular. By 1966 it had 23 out of the top 25 shows and in turn, spurred Radio-Canada to change many of its programs.

With competition, advertising revenues and sponsor-ships began to play a larger role in determining the television schedule. Radio-Canada's own internal surveys taken in 1960 had shown that viewers were little affected by the interruption in programming save for the loss of the téléromans. Feature films which had occupied much of the 1959–60 schedule had drawn as large an audience as its regular line-up. American imports were now available on film and could be easily translated and dubbed for a franco-phone audience. Not only were they cheaper than locally made productions, they were watched by more people and generated more revenue for their broadcasters. By the mid-1960s, Radio-Canada had virtually abandoned its notion of public service in favour of a more stream-lined and enter-taining schedule.

Performing arts broadcasts were the first victims of this change. *L'heure du concert* was cut back to bi-monthly broadcasts and presented only one performance per episode as it dropped all pretensions of educating the public. Tele-plays were confined to 90 minutes per week or appeared only in summer anthologies. From a high of almost 100 broadcast hours per year, theatre drama had dropped to 20 hours per year in the mid-1960s. By 1966, all music, opera, ballet and theatrical programs were combined in the two-hour anthol-ogy *Les beaux dimanches* which has remained as part of the Sunday line-up.

A shift to lighter programming affected all genres. Pub-lic affairs programming reflected this change with the intro-duction of *Appelle-moi Lise,* a late-night talk show with host Lise Payette which became the new model for the interview format. Sports gained more prominence and give-away shows such as *La poule aux oeufs d'or* (1958–65) which had replaced *La rigolade* were modelled on American quiz shows such as *The $64,000 Question.* It was later joined by *Tous pour un* (1963–64) which became the most watched pro-gram on Tuesday nights.

Téléromans which had always been successes remained as the backbone of Radio-Canada's production. They were joined by locally-made comedies and sitcoms as the public broadcaster sought to win back viewers. *Moi et l'autre* (1966–71), *La p'tite semaine* (1972–76), *Du tac à tac* (1977–81), and *Poivre et sel* (1983–87) were just some of the lighter television series which competed with the private network.

When TVA launched its celebrated *Les Berger* (1970–78) series, francophone television added the new family saga genre to its drama repertoire. *Rue des Pignons* (1970–77), *Grand-Papa* (1976–85), and *Terre humaine* (1978–84) were part of the regular of Radio-Canada which competed with TVA's *Le Clan Beaulieu* (1978–82), *Marisol* (1980-83), and *Les Moineau et le Pinsons* (1982–85).

A growing concern over the sharp decline in educational and cultural programming as well as a sharp increase in dubbed American imports, prompted the Quebec provincial government to launch its own public broadcaster, Radio-Québec in 1968. Its programming was, and still is, devoted to providing educational and cultural programs which re-flect Quebecois society. Largely a community-based system, it did not begin to broadcast in the evening until the 1972–73 season. Its programming featured many documen-taries, nature, and science shows as well as broadcasts of the proceedings of the legislative assembly. In recent years, it too has developed its own series such as *Avec un grand A* (1985–1992). It has also showcased some English-made series such as *Degrassi* but has remained committed to its educational mandate. Over half of its programming is educational and very few of its programs are American imports.

With the development of cable systems and more private stations, fears that the airwaves would be overrun with Ameri-can programming once again became an issue. Although stud-ies had shown that only about 20% of all programming were foreign imports, they also showed that local productions were dominant only in the informational, sports, and educational genres. More alarming was the fact that over 80% of all drama and comedies were American-made imports.

This led to a call for a stronger commitment on the part of the province's two public broadcasters to strengthen their commitment to producing more local dramas since the studies also indicated that, when given a clear choice be-tween imports and local shows, Quebecois viewers prefer to see their own artists and programs. Many Quebecois pro-grams rank consistently in the top ten lists. The recent success of the drama series like *Lance et compte, Les Filles du Caleb,* and the comedy hit *La Petite vie,* which have had huge followings both domestically and internationally, attest to Quebecois television's vitality and creativity.

Francophone television has always offered the Québecois a vivid expression of their own unique history and places. Its public affairs, sports, and popular drama have not only mirrored society's growth, they have mirrored the development of television itself. Despite a variety of changes and the proliferation of choices available to the average viewer, the Quebecois remain avid television fans. They spend more time watching television than any other activity, other than sleeping and working. Though no longer a "captive audience," they remain enthusiastic about their own brand of programming. Television still remains an integral part of Quebecois cultural life as it still strives to be all things to all people.

—Manon Lamontagne

FURTHER READING

Collins, Richard. *Television and Culture.* London: Unwin Hyman, 1990.

Raboy, Marc. *Missed Opportunities: The Story of Canada's Broadcasting Policy.* Montreal: McGill Queen's University Press, 1990.

Rutherford, Paul. *When Television Was Young: Primetime Canada 1951–1967.* Toronto: University of Toronto Press, 1990.

Trofimenkoff, Susan. *The Dream of Nation.* Toronto: Gage, 1983.

See also Canadian Programming in English; *Family Plouffe;* Teleroman

CANADIAN TELEVISION NETWORK

Canadian Television Network Ltd.(CTV) was incorporated in 1961 as Canada's first private television network. Unlike other North American networks, CTV has no owned and operated stations and controls no production facilities. Instead, CTV consists of major independent stations located in cities throughout Canada. As a result, it has a unique network structure which strongly affects its operations.

CTV is the most popular Canadian network with over 20% of the English-speaking audience, although this figure has tended to decline in the 1980s. It has also been accused by cultural nationalists and regulatory agencies of airing U.S. imports in prime time and relegating its few often inexpensive Canadian productions to off-peak hours. Although the network has produced relatively little drama or comedy, it has achieved some notable programming successes. In 1967, CTV launched the news magazine *W5* which still enjoys excellent ratings. In 1972, it launched *Canada AM* which became the prototype for ABC's *Good Morning America.* Its news and sports programs have also enjoyed steady success, even at times surpassing the CBC. In the mid to late 1980s, CTV co-produced such highly successful drama as *Night Heat* and *E.N.G.* Ultimately, CTV's protestations that its achievements are under appreciated must be balanced against the view that it has failed to contribute fully to the development of national culture.

CTV's network structure has moved through three distinct phases. From 1961 to 1965, CTV was controlled principally by its founder, Spencer Caldwell. Having won the original licence, he planned to supply affiliates with ten hours of programming per week: content acquired internationally, original content produced in the affiliates' stations, and content controlled by the affiliates but offered to the network. Caldwell hoped to increase the weekly hours until CTV rivalled the CBC.

Three factors prevented the realization of this plan. First, Caldwell underestimated the technological startup costs and was forced to seek loans from the affiliates. Second, the affiliation agreements worked to the detriment

of the network since affiliates could demand network compensation even if the network had not managed to sell all of its air time. Third, as CTV supplied only 10 hours per week, the affiliates established a parallel acquisition service to fill another 24 hours. The ITO (Independent Television Organization) effectively competed against CTV and drove up prices.

By 1965, on the brink of bankruptcy, Caldwell sold out to the affiliates. Until 1993, CTV operated as a cooperative. As such, each affiliate became a shareholder in the network, each shareholder sat on the board of directors, and each held the power of veto over board decisions. Additionally, the network now provided 39.5 hours of programming per week, thereby obviating the need for the ITO which was abolished in 1969. Finally, affiliates could no longer demand compensation for unsold air time.

This structure introduced new tensions. First, the affiliates served highly differentiated markets and held correspondingly divergent views on appropriate programming. Second, as major local independents, affiliates derived as much profit from local market dominance as from network affiliation. Hence, they tended to their own profitability

Courtesy of CTV

before the network's health, treating it at times as a necessary evil and approving only minimal operating budgets. Third, although the larger affiliates attracted a larger share of the audience, and therefore contributed proportionally more to network profits, they had only one vote and could be overruled. Four, some shareholders acquired more than one affiliate but were nonetheless restricted to a single vote. As a result, some shareholders lobbied for changes to the network structure. Finally, some shareholders owned stations unaffiliated with CTV thereby creating potential conflicts of interest, especially as these stations sometimes competed against CTV for both program acquisition and market share.

CTV therefore failed to develop as a powerful network. Its weakness as a network curtailed its ability to produce Canadian content and therefore to meet the expectations of the Broadcasting Act.

In 1986, CTV's corporate structure came to the attention of the CRTC which introduced new conditions at the network's licence renewal hearings. For example, between 1987 and 1994, the CRTC instructed CTV: (a) to spend $C403 million on Canadian programming, (b) to schedule 120 hours of Canadian dramatic features, miniseries and limited series in prime time, (c) to provide 24 hours of Canadian musical programming, and (d) to provide a minimum of 1.5 hours of regularly scheduled Canadian programming in prime time rising to 3.5 hours per week. CTV spent $C417 million, scheduled 126 hours of dramatic features, programmed 40 hours of musical content, and (e) requested that the minimum number of regularly scheduled dramatic hours not exceed three per week.

In January 1993, CTV instituted a new corporate structure. The network now operates under the Canadian Business Corporations Act. It consists of seven shareholders who have each invested $2 million into the network. Board decisions are taken by majority vote with no party having a veto. Shares may be sold and transfered so long as they are first offered to the other shareholders. The network also provides 42.5 hours of programming per week and purchases air time from affiliates for a fixed annual sum.

This structure brings CTV closer to the American network model while maintaining some earlier features. For example, although CTV now compensates affiliates at a fixed rate, it still has no owned and operated stations. Indeed, it is the shareholders who control chains of stations and who are in the best position to operate as U.S.-style networks. Indeed, CTV's largest shareholder, Baton Broadcasting Inc., which owns 20 stations, has proposed to buy the network outright. In the absence of a positive response, Baton has created its own Ontario-based network, ONT (Ontario Network Television), and has taken away from CTV the rights to certain highly prized sporting events.

At this time, CTV's future appears uncertain as its strongest parts may strike out on their own. This possibility coincides with the accelerated fragmentation of the television audience. In 1990-91, CTV registered its first and only annual loss. Nonetheless, CTV is turning towards more Canadian production and "big event" programming in the belief that these will emerge as distinguishing features in a television universe characterized by 500 or more channels.

—Paul Attallah

FURTHER READING

Building Partnerships: Television in Transition. Reports Produced Following the Television Industry Summit of December 1991. Ottawa: Supply and Services Canada, 1992.

Caplan, Gerald, and Florian Sauvageau. *Report of the Task Force on Canadian Broadcasting*. Government of Canada: Ottawa, 1986.

Communications Department of Telefilm Canada. *Directory, Canadian Film, Television, and Video Industry*. Ottawa: Canada Communication Group Publishing, 1994.

CANDID CAMERA

U.S. Humor/Reality Program

Candid Camera, the first and longest running reality-based comedy program, premiered on ABC 10 August 1948 under its original radio title *Candid Microphone*. The format of the program featured footage taken by a hidden camera of everyday people caught in hoaxes devised by the show's host Allen Funt. In the world of *Candid Camera* mailboxes talked to passers-by, cars rolled along effortlessly without engines, little boys used x-ray glasses, and secretaries were chained to their desks—all to provoke a reaction from unsuspecting mechanics, clerks, customers and passers-by. In a 1985 *Psychology Today* article, Funt explained his move to television by saying that he "wanted to go beyond what people merely said, to record what they did—their gestures, facial expressions, confusions and delights."

The program ultimately changed its name to *Candid Camera* when it moved to NBC in 1949, but did not gain a permanent time slot until it finally moved to CBS in 1960. For the next seven years it was consistently rated as one of television's top ten shows before it was abruptly canceled. Funt was frequently joined by guest hosts such as Arthur Godfrey, Durward Kirby and Bess Meyerson. A syndicated version of the program containing old and new material aired from 1974 to 1978. Aided by his son Peter, Funt continued to create special theme episodes (e.g., "Smile, You're on Vacation," "Candid Camera goes to the Doctor," etc.) for CBS until 1990 when *The New Candid Camera*, advised by Funt and hosted by Dom DeLuise, went into syndication. Low ratings finally prevented King Productions from renewing the show for the 1992–93 season.

The scenarios designed and recorded by Funt and his crew were unique glimpses into the quirks and foibles of human nature never before deliberately captured on film. The average scenario lasted approximately five minutes and was based on one of five strategies. These "ideas" included reversing normal or anticipated procedures, exposing basic human weaknesses such as ignorance or vanity, fulfilling fantasies, using the element of surprise or placing something in a bizarre or inappropriate setting. As Funt noted, "You have to make lots of adjustments to create viewer believability and really involve the subject. You need the right setting, one in which the whole scenario will fit and make sense to the audience even when it doesn't to the actor." Finding the right setting, and the right people for *Candid Camera* stunts was not always an easy task.

Early attempts to film *Candid Camera* were hampered by technical, logistical and censorship difficulties. While they appeared simple, the staged scenes took many hours to prepare and success was far from guaranteed. Approximately fifty recorded sequences were filmed for every four to five aired on the program. Funt and his crew had to contend with burdensome equipment that was difficult to conceal. The cameras were often hidden behind a screen, but the lights needed for them had to be left out in the open. Would-be victims were told that the lights were part of "renovations." Microphones were concealed in boxes, under tables and, in a number of episodes, in a cast worn by Funt himself. In his book *Eavesdropping at Large* (1952), Funt also described his battles with network censors and sponsors who had never before confronted this type of programming and were often fickle in their decisions about what was and was not acceptable material for television at the time. Funt himself destroyed any material that was off color, or reached too deeply into people's private lives. A hotel gag designed to fool guests placed a "men's room" sign on a closet door. The funniest, but ultimately unaired reaction, came from a gentleman who ignored the obvious lack of accommodations and "used" the closet anyway.

Candid Camera's unique approach to documenting unexpected elements of human behavior was inspired in part by Funt's background as a research assistant at Cornell University. Here Funt aided psychologist Kurt Lewin in experiments on the behaviors of mothers and children. He also drew on his experiences in the Army Signal Corps where he was responsible for recording soldier's letters home. *Candid Camera* was different from other programming because of its focus on the everyday—on the extraordinary things that happen in ordinary, everyday contexts. "Generations have been educated to accept the characterizations of the stage and screen," Funt noted in his chronicle of the program's history. "Our audiences have to unlearn much of this to accept candid studies, although anyone can verify our findings just by looking around and listening."

Candid Camera spawned a new genre of "reality programming" in the late 1980s, including such shows as *America's Funniest Home Videos* and *Totally Hidden Video*. Television audiences were forced to become reflexive about

Candid Camera
Photo courtesy of Bob Banner Associates

their own role in the production of comedy and in thinking about the practices of everyday life. "We used the medium of TV well," Funt commented, "There were close ups of people in action. The audience saw ordinary people like themselves and the reality of events as they were unfolding. Each piece was brief, self-contained and the simple humor of the situation could be quickly understood by virtually anyone in our audience." Conceived in a less complex era free of camcorder technology, *Candid Camera* brought insight and humor into understanding both the potential of television and the role of the TV audience.

—Amy W. Loomis

HOST
Allen Funt

CO-HOSTS
Arthur Godfrey (1960–61)
Durward Kirby (1961–66)
Bess Myerson (1966–67)
Peter Funt (1990)

PRODUCER   Allen Funt

PROGRAMMING HISTORY

• ABC

August 1948–September 1948   Sunday 8:00-8:30
October 1948   Sunday 8:30-8:45
November 1948–December 1948   Friday 8:00-8:30

• NBC
May 1949–July 1949   Sunday 7:30-8:00
July 1949–August 1949   Thursday 9:00-9:30

• CBS
September 1949–September 1950   Monday 9:00-9:30

• NBC
June 1953   Tuesday 9:30-10:00
July 1953   Wednesday 10:00-10:30

• CBS
October 1960–September 1967   Sunday 10:00-10:30
July 1990–August 1990   Friday 8:30-9:00

FURTHER READING

Brooks, T., and E. Marsh. *The Complete Directory to Prime Time TV Shows: 1946-present.* New York: Ballentine, 1992.

Carey, P. "Catching Up with Candid Camera," *Saturday Evening Post* (Indianapolis, Indiana), 1992.

Funt, A. *Eavesdropping at Large: Adventures in Human Nature with Candid Mike and Candid Camera.* New York: Vanguard Press, 1952.

Zimbardo, P. "Laugh Where We Must, Be Candid Where We Can," *Psychology Today* (New York), 1985.

CANNELL, STEPHEN J.

U.S. Producer and Writer

Stephen J. Cannell emerged as one of television's most powerful producer-writers in the 1980s. A prolific writer, he would eventually also become a series creator, an executive producer, a director, a station owner, and the head of his own studio He specializes almost exclusively in crime shows and action-adventures, and his work, by its sheer volume, played a significant role in redefining the parameters of those genres. Early in his career, he created and produced programs with such other crime show auteurs as Jack Webb, Roy Huggins, William Link and Richard Levinson, and Steven Bochco.

Like many other aspiring television artists in the 1960s, Cannell got his start at Universal Television, where he joined the writing staff of *Adam-12* in 1970. After a few years of writing for several of the company's other series, he began to create and produce his own shows for Universal, including *Chase, Baretta, Baa Baa Blacksheep, Richie Brockelman, Private Eye, The Duke,* and *Stone. The Rockford Files,* which won an Emmy for Outstanding Drama in 1978, was by far his most commercially and critically successful series of this period. The show exhibited all the trademarks of the Cannell style: a facile blending of comedy and drama, up-to-the-minute contemporary vernacular dialogue, and a protagonist who was a likable outsider, in this case an ex-convict.

In 1979 Cannell left Universal to form Stephen J. Cannell Productions. He won a Writers Guild Award for *Tenspeed and Brownshoe* and achieved some modest ratings success for *The Greatest American Hero*, but it was *The A-Team* that established the company as a major force in Hollywood in 1983. Adding a heavy dosage of cartoon-like action to the familiar Cannell themes, *The A-Team* made Nielsen's top ten in its debut season. Three years later, Cannell had six series on the network prime-time schedule, including *Hunter, Riptide,* and *Hardcastle and McCormick.*

Many critics who had praised *The Rockford Files* rejected this latest batch of Cannell's series, complaining that they were juvenile and overly formulaic. With the debut of *Wiseguy* in 1987, however, one of Cannell's shows once again earned critical respect for its intelligent dialogue, complex characterization, and occasional treatment of

Stephen J. Cannell
Photo courtesy of Stephen J. Cannell Productions, Inc.

timely issues. *Wiseguy* also employed an innovative new narrative structure, the "story arc," whereby the season was in effect divided into several multi-part episodes.

In an effort to lower production costs, Cannell opened a major studio facility in Vancouver, British Columbia, toward the end of the 1980s. One of the first series shot there was *21 Jump Street*, the highest-rated show of the new FOX network's first season. *Scene of the Crime*, a mystery anthology series for CBS' late-night schedule, was also filmed in Vancouver and was hosted by Cannell himself.

—Robert J. Thompson

STEPHEN J. CANNELL. Born in Los Angeles, California, U.S.A., 5 February 1941. University of Oregon, B.A. 1964. Married: Marcia C. Finch, 1964; children: Derek (deceased), Tawnia, Chelsea, Cody. Began career as television writer in late 1960s, selling story ideas to Desilu Productions; head writer, Universal Studios, *Adam 12*, 1970; creator, writer, producer of other Universal action-adventure programs, through 1970s; founder, Stephen J. Cannell Productions, 1979. Recipient: Mystery Writers Award; four Emmy Awards; four Writers Guild of America Awards.

TELEVISION SERIES (writer-producer)

1970	*Adam-12*
1973	*Chase*
1973–74	*Toma*
1974–80	*The Rockford Files*
1976–78	*Baa-Baa Blacksheep* (*The Blacksheep Squadron*)
1978	*Richie Brockleman, Private Eye*
1979	*The Duke*
1980	*Tenspeed and Brownshoe*
1980	*Stone*
1981–83	*The Greatest American Hero*
1982	*The Quest*
1983–84	*The Rousters*
1983–86	*Hardcastle and McCormick*
1983–87	*The A-Team*
1984–86	*Riptide*
1984–91	*Hunter*
1986	*The Last Precinct*
1986–87	*Stingray*
1987–88	*J.J. Starbuck*
1987–90	*21 Jump Street*
1987–89	*Wiseguy*
1988	*Sonny Spoon*
1989	*Unsub*
1991	*The Commish*
1991–94	*Scene of the Crime*
1995	*Marker*
1996	*Profit*

FURTHER READING

Christensen, Mark, and Cameron Stauth. *The Sweeps.* New York: Willlam Morrow, 1984.

Fanning, Deirdre. "What Stuff Are Dreams Made of?" *Forbes* (New York), 22 August 1988.

Freeman, Mike. "Man of the Hours" (interview). *Broadcasting* (Washington, D.C.), 25 January 1993.

Perry, Jeb. *Universal Television: The Studio and Its Programs, 1950–1980.* Metuchen, New Jersey: Scarecrow, 1983.

Shindler, Merill. "Okay, Cannell, Come Clean." *Los Angeles Magazine,* October 1983.

Thompson, Robert J. *Adventures on Prime Time: The Television Programs of Stephen J. Cannell.* New York: Praeger, 1990.

Wicking, Christopher, and Tise Vahimagi. *The American Vein: Directors and Directions in Television.* New York: Dutton, 1979.

See also Bochco, Steven; Huggins, Roy; *Rockford Files*

CAPTAIN VIDEO AND HIS VIDEO RANGERS

U.S. Children's Science-Fiction Program

Captain Video and His Video Rangers, which premiered 27 June 1949 on the DuMont Network, was the first science-fiction, space adventure program on television and was to inspire a spate of similar offerings. Although it combined many of the early staples of children's programming, such as the inclusion of inexpensive film clips and pointed moral lessons, *Captain Video* capitalized upon the public fascination with science and space and the technical elements of the new television medium to create the longest running science-fiction show in early television.

Captain Video was the creation of James L. Caddigan, a DuMont vice president. Set in the year 2254, the show was an ambitious undertaking—it was live, technically demand-ing, and programmed as a continuing serial appearing every evening from 7:00 to 7:30 P.M. The show was designed to take advantage of the new technology; dissolves, superimpositions, and crude luminance key effects were utilized to place Captain Video in fanciful surroundings and allow him to travel through space and time. Without the luxury of video tape and editing, however, scripts, written by Maurice C. Brock (a veteran radio scriptwriter for *Dick Tracy* and *Gangbusters*), had to contain a great deal of exposition to allow time to set-up for short bursts of action.

The lack of sustained action was the reason given by creator Caddigan for using clips from the DuMont film library. In a typical program, as the conflict subsided for a moment, Captain Video (played by Richard Coogan, who later portrayed U.S. Marshal Matt Wayne on *The Californians*) would turn to his Remote Tele-Carrier, or inexplicably the show would switch to Ranger Headquarters, to show the exploits of other rangers (often cowboys such as Bob Steele and Sunset Carson in Western films). These clips always involved action-oriented sequences and helped to pick up the pace of the show and allow time for the production crew to change sets and set up special effects.

Other breaks between scenes were filled with Ranger Messages. While messages on other children's programs would focus on children's issues such as safely crossing the street, Ranger Messages dealt with more global issues such as freedom, the Golden Rule, and nondiscrimination. The sophistication of these messages seemed to anticipate an adult audience, but the shifts between space and Western adventures were incomprehensible to many adults. The show was most popular with children and by 1951 was carried by 24 stations and seen by 3.5 million viewers, outdrawing its nearest competitor, *Kukla, Fran and Ollie.*

As the "Master of Science," Captain Video was a technological genius, who invented a variety of devices including the Opticon Scillometer, a long-range, X-ray machine used to see through walls; the Discatron, a portable television screen which served as an intercom; and the Radio Scillograph, a palm-sized, two-way radio. With public concerns about violence in television programming, Captain Video's weapons were never lethal but were designed to capture his opponents (a Cosmic Ray Vibrator, a static beam of electricity able to paralyze its target; an Atomic Disintegrator Rifle; and the Electronic Strait Jacket, which placed captives in invisible restraints). In testimony before Senator Estes Kefauver's subcommittee probing the connection between television violence and juvenile delinquency, Al Hodge, who had previously starred in radio's *Green Hornet* and became Captain Video in 1951, noted that he did not even use the word "kill" on the show.

In addition to the futuristic inventions, the plots featured sharply drawn distinctions between good and bad science. Although Captain Video, with the fifteen-year-old Video Ranger (played by Don Hastings, who later appeared in *The Edge of Night* and *As the World Turns*), battled a wide array of enemies, the most clever and persistent was the deranged scientist Dr. Pauli (originally portrayed by Bram Nossem who could not sustain the grueling live schedule and was replaced by Hal Conklin). The battles were originally earthbound with Captain Video circling the globe in his X-9 jet to thwart the plans of Dr. Pauli who joined forces with other villains, such as the evil Heng Foo Sueeng. However, in response to other newly created science-fiction competitors, in 1951 Captain Video began to patrol the universe and battle aliens in the spaceship Galaxy under the auspices of the Solar Council of the Interplanetary Alliance. He encountered such notable villains as clumsy McGee, (played by Arnold Stang) an inept Martian, Norgola (played by Ernest Borgnine) who turned the sun's energy into magnetic forces, and television's first robot, Tobor ("robot" spelled backwards), played by Dave Ballard.

Captain Video and His Video Rangers

The audience was exceptionally involved in the show, often writing to oppose plot developments or to suggest new inventions. For example, Tobor and Dr. Pauli were destroyed when their schemes backfired; however, the opposition of the viewers was great enough to bring them back in later episodes. Young viewers were also encouraged to join the Video Rangers Club and to buy Captain Video merchandise, including helmets, toy rockets, games, and records although the show not as extensively merchandised as some of its competitors. The show was supported, however, by large sponsors such as Skippy Peanut Butter and Post Cereals. Fawcett also published six issues of *Captain Video Comics* in 1951. A fifteen-chapter movie serial, *Captain Video, Master of the Stratosphere* (released by Columbia Pictures in 1951, starring Judd Holdren and Larry Stewart) was the first attempt by Hollywood to capitalize on a television program. DuMont also attempted to build on the popularity of the show by developing *The Secret Files of Captain Video*, a thirty-minute, weekly adventure complete within itself which ran concurrently with the serial from September 1953 until May 1954.

However, although Captain Video was "The Guardian of the Safety of the World," he was not able to escape the economic necessities of the industry nor prevent the demise of the DuMont network. When Miles Laboratories, Inc., canceled its sponsorship of the Morgan Beatty news program, *Captain Video* remained as DuMont's only sponsored program between 7:00 and 8:00 P.M. Unfortunately the income was not large enough to justify the rental of the coaxial cable, and *Captain Video* left the air 1 April 1955, with DuMont folding that same year.

—Suzanne Hurst Williams

CAST

Captain Video (1949–1950)	Richard Coogan
Captain Video (1951–1955)	Al Hodge
The Ranger	Don Hastings
Dr Pauli (1949)	Bran Mossen
Dr. Pauli (later)	Hal Conklin

PRODUCERS Olga Druce, Frank Telford, James L. Caddigan, Al Hodge

PROGRAMMING HISTORY

• DuMont

June 1949–

August 1949	Tuesday/Thursday/Friday 7:00-7:30
August 1949–September 1953	Monday-Friday 7:00-7:30
September 1953–April 1955	Monday-Friday 7:00-7:15
February 1950–September 1950	Saturday 7:30-8:00
September 1950–November 1950	Saturday 7:00-7:30

FURTHER READING

Adams, Val. "'Space Opera' Hero" *New York Times,* 26 March 1950.
"Captain Video!" *TeleVision Guide* (Radnor, Pennsylvania), 6-12 August 1949.
"'Captain Video' Doomed." *New York Times,* 16 March 1955.
"Captain Video." *Variety* (Los Angeles), 13 July 1955.
Fischer, Stuart. *Kids TV: The First Twenty-Five Years.* New York: Facts on File Publications, 1983.
Gould, Jack. "Captain Video." *New York Times,* 20 November 1949.
Grossman, Gary H. *Saturday Morning TV.* New York: Dell, 1981.
Hamburger, Philip. "Now I Lay Me Down to Sleep." *The New Yorker* (New York), 22 December 1951.
Houston, David. "The 50s Golden Age of Science Fiction Television." *Starlog* (New York), December 1980.
"7 M.P.S; Zero 3." *Time* (New York), 25 December 1950.
"Speaking of Pictures." *Life* (New York), 13 September 1954.
Van Horne, Harriet. "Space Rocket Kick." *Theatre Arts* (New York), December 1951.

CAPTIONING

Captioning is the display, in writing, of dialogue, narration or other unspoken information on the screen. As an audiovisual medium, television makes extensive use of writing. Captions usually appear in two to three lines at the bottom of the screen.

Captions used for translating a foreign-language text or program are usually called subtitles. While such "translation subtitling" is rarely used in some countries including the United States, captioning in the same language is indispensable especially in information programs such as news, documentaries and weather reporting, or entertainment programs such as game shows. Captions are also used when intelligibility is reduced by poor voice quality, dialectalism, colloquialism or other features of speech. Commercials make extensive use of captioning, sometimes with calligraphic expression. The written element either enhances the spoken, visual, graphic, sound and musical components of an advertisement, or provides additional information.

Captions are either "open," i.e. appear on the screen without viewer control of their display, or "closed," i.e. available for display at viewer's choice; closed captions can be "opened" with a decoder. An increasingly important use of closed captions is for making the spoken language of television available to the hearing impaired and hard-of-hearing audiences. The first experiments with such captioning were initiated by the PBS in the early 1970s, and approved by the Federal Communications Commission

(FCC) in 1976. The PBS's Boston station, WGBH-TV, established a Caption Center which set standards for captioned programming. Although a real success with hearing-impaired viewers who lobbied for more, the hearing audience complained about the distraction of open captions. The problem was solved when it became possible to assign line 21 of the "vertical-blanking interval" for hiding captions, which could be conveniently opened up by a decoder. The non-profit National Captioning Institute, formed in

An example of captioning
Photo courtesy of the Caption Center

1981, promoted the service and tried to gradually meet viewers' demands. In Britain, the 1990 Broadcasting Act stipulated the captioning of a minimum of fifty percent of all programs by 1998. In Canada, broadcasters raised public interest in this service by opening closed captions during a Captioning Awareness Week in 1995. In the United States, all television sets with screens larger than 13 inches produced after 1993 were required to be equipped with decoders.

Non-standardized technology is an obstacle to transnational exchange of closed caption programs in countries speaking the same language. By the mid-1990s, there were some 3,000 captioned videos in the United States. However, NCI captioned products in Britain could be viewed only with a decoder because the VBI lines used in the two countries are not compatible.

In both film and television, captioning began as a post-production activity. Technological advances as well as a growing demand by hearing-impaired viewers have made it possible to provide real-time captioning for live broadcasting. This is done with the aid of a court-room stenograph or short-hand machine; a high-speed stenographer can type no less than 200 words per minute, which is adequate for keeping up with the speed of normal conversation. Stenographed texts are not readable, however, because words are abbreviated or split into consonant and vowel clusters. While the stenographer strikes the keyboard, a computer transforms them into captions and delivers them to the transmitting station, making it possible for the viewers to read the words seconds after they are spoken. Stenocaptioning was first tried in the early 1980s in Britain and the United States. The improved system was in use in North America in the mid-1990s, although alternative technologies were being developed in Europe.

While captioning allows millions of deaf and hard-of-hearing citizens access to television, it usually involves heavy editing of the spoken language. Screen space is limited and captions can be displayed for only a few seconds. Thus, in order to allow viewers enough time to read the captions and watch the pictures, the dialogue or narration must be summarized; such editing entails change of meaning or loss of information. However, refined, though not yet standardized, styles are developed to help the viewer get a better grasp of the spoken language. When more than one speaker is present, the captions may either be placed next to each speaker or marked by different colours. Moreover, codes or brief comments are used to indicate the presence of some features of the speech, music and sound effects.

Captioning is a useful teaching aid in second language learning, child or adult acquisition of literacy, and in most types of educational programming. It also has a potential for creating new television genres and art forms.

—Amir Hassanpour

FURTHER READING

Clark, Joe. "Typography and TV Captioning." *Print* (New York), January-February 1989.
"Closed Captioning: Between the Lines." *The Economist* (London), 7 May 1994.
Neuman, S. B., and P.S. Koskinen. *Using Captioned Television to Improve the Reading Proficiency of Language Minority Students.* Falls Church, Virginia: National Captioning Institute, 1990.

CARIBOO COUNTRY

Canadian Drama Series

Cariboo Country, one of the most imaginative, innovative, and evocative series ever broadcast by the CBC, was a hybrid of anthology and series programming originating in Vancouver. It appeared on the CBC as a summer replacement from 1960 to 1967, and was among the first Canadian television dramas to be filmed on location. This meant that the team of producer Philip Keately and writer Paul St. Pierre, as well as the actors whose characters appeared in various episodes, all received direct and timely reactions from the ranchers and First Nations' peoples of the Cariboo whose lives the series explored.

The series was a deliberate antithesis to the dominant North American television genre of the 1960s—the television western. It was set in the Chilcotin region of modern British Columbia. Guns were used for hunting only and were seldom seen. Horses and overused tractors shared the fields. The stories were told by a gently humourous narrator who ran the general store. Reflecting Canada's different culture and history, there were no stagecoach robberies, range wars, or wagon trains fending off hostile Indians with the help of the cavalry. When the Royal Canadian Mounted Police were introduced in one episode they were parodied. There were no prim school marms or whores with hearts of gold. The women were occasionally in the foreground but only as full partners to the men—and they never needed rescue.

The series introduced actor Chief Dan George as "Ol' Antoine," and was distinguished in the 1960s by the fact that all actors representing Indian characters were members of the First Nations. *Cariboo Country* was shot in black-and-white in documentary style without programmatic music or rapid edits. It used laconic but superbly allusive dialogue, marked by silences and honed by St. Pierre's ear for dialect.

Notable episodes included the historical flashback called *The Strong Ones,* about the reaction of a young man to the fact that his Indian mother and her children—who are involved in an "up country" relationship with a successful rancher—are suddenly displaced by a "suitable" bride from the East. Another episode, *One Small Ranch,* documents the struggles of Smith, a recurring character, and his wife to survive harsh weather, low prices, and government interference on their marginal ranch. It also explains with ironic humour why they refuse to sell it to wealthy hunters from "outside." In *Sarah's Copper,* a young couple eventually refuse to sell a precious artifact—a "copper" which signifies for Northwest Coast aboriginal peoples wealth, prestige, and an honourable history—to a white collector for his apartment wall. Their choice is made more difficult because it means they will have to do without a new truck. *All Indian,* like Keatley's *Beachcombers,* tried to be authentic and responsive to concerns about cultural appropriation long before the term was widely used. This episode refuted the myth that "all Indians are the same" by showing a cross-cultural conflict between a husband from the Cariboo and his coast Salish wife who is "kidnapped" by her people to become a spirit dancer. The episode included a trailer which pointed out that none of the dances shown were authentic. Other episodes looked at an old rancher who competes in the rodeo until it kills him, and at the conflict between a metis and his wife who bears him an imperfect child and then leaves him. Like most of the episodes of *Cariboo Country,* few of these had linear plots or neatly wrapped endings.

Two hour-long specials were developed from the series. The award-winning *The Education of Phylistine* (pulled together from two half-hour episodes), not only explains the roots of the heedless racism which drives an Indian child out of a small rural school, but also explores the relationship between the child and Ol' Antoine, her grandfather. The second, *How to Break a Quarterhorse,* was commissioned for the prestigious anthology, *Festival,* during the 1967 Centennial. It is a story of justice Cariboo style—the recent history of exploitation and racism which motivates a murder is taken into account when a fugitive surrenders after ten years on the run, and he is aquitted by a Cariboo jury. The story's other plot line focuses on how Smith, Ol' Antoine's old friend, gets involved in the outcome of the case. After a less successful third drama special, *Sister Balonika,* Keately moved on to *Beachcombers* while St. Pierre continued to write short stories about the Cariboo.

St. Pierre and Keately enjoyed the freedom of being away from Toronto, production headquarters of English Canada, and were thus able to make filmed drama when it was not usually done. *Cariboo Country* was broadcast for several summers on CBC-owned stations only, and then was presented as part of *The Serial* (despite the fact that each episode was self-sufficient). It remains one of the very best works of televison created in English Canada on the CBC or the private networks.

—Mary Jane Miller

CAST (irregular)

Arch MacGregor	Ted Stidder
Ken Larsen	Wally Marsh
Mr. Smith	David Hughes
Norah Smith	Lillian Carlson
Morton Dillonbeigh	Buck Kendt
Mrs. Dillonbeigh	Rae Brown
Ol' Antoine	Chief Dan George
Walter Charlie	Merv Campone
Sarah	Jean Sandy
Johnny	Paul Stanley
Frenchie	Joseph Golland

PRODUCERS   Philip Keatley, Frank Goodship

PROGRAMMING HISTORY

• CBC

July-September 1960	Thirteen half-hour episodes
May 1965	Two Episodes
Februrary 1966	One Episode
January 1967	One Episode

FURTHER READING

Mary Jane Miller. "Cariboo Country: The CBC Response to the American Television Western." *The American Journal of Canadian Studies,* Fall 1984.

See also Canadian Programming in English

CARNEY, ART

U.S. Actor

Art Carney's many noteworthy achievements as an actor will always be overshadowed by one role: Ed Norton. Carney made his reputation as the loyal but dopey neighbor, Ed Norton, opposite Jackie Gleason's Ralph Kramden in the classic sketches and series *The Honeymooners.* So complete was Carney's transformation into the loose-limbed, bumbling sewer worker that he won five Emmy Awards for his work with Gleason, including three consecutive awards as best supporting actor from 1953 to 1955.

Carney got his start in show business doing imitations and comedy bits with Horace Heidt's orchestra. Stints in radio and bit parts in films led to Carney's first regular role on television on *The Morey Amsterdam Show.* When Jackie Gleason took over as host of the DuMont network's *Cavalcade of Stars,* Carney became a principal supporting player. He moved with the show to CBS in 1952 where it was rechristened *The Jackie Gleason Show* and "The Honeymooners" became a regular sketch.

Ed Norton may have been second banana to Ralph Kramden, but Carney's performance never took a back seat to Gleason's. Indeed, the pair created a symbiosis of comic styles so unique that when Carney left the show in 1957 "The Honeymooners" went on hiatus until his return almost ten years later. In contrast to Gleason's broad, blustery Kramden, Carney's Norton was the personification of nonchalance. His casual delivery could make any statement sound vacuous. Even his typical greeting, "Hey-hey, Ralphie boy," announced Norton's child-like amicability as well as his lack of brains. Carney's face drooped into a slackjawed expression that was perpetually blank. Coupled with his feeble-minded manner was a body like a rubber band. It could be as slouched as the hat that was always perched on his head at one moment, then snapping into improbable contortions the next. Carney seemed to make up for Ed's lack of intelligence by investing the character with a host of broad physical tics that could turn a game of pool, a few moments on a pinball machine, or a mambo step, into a comic ballet. Much like the great silent comedians, Carney created an wholly original character who was recognizable at a glance. In Ed Norton we find the pathos of Chaplin, the earnestness of Lloyd, and the physical grace of Keaton.

Even though the *Gleason Show* and the role of Ed Norton cemented Carney's success as a comedian, he was never content to be known as merely a comic actor. When the program moved to CBS, Carney's agent negotiated for the actor to have three out of every thirteen weeks off to perform in noncompetitive shows. Carney built up a solid background as a dramatic performer on episodes of *Studio One, Suspense, Kraft Television Theatre,* and *Playhouse 90,* and in special events like a telecast of Thornton Wilder's *Our Town.* By the latter part of the decade critics had come to take the excellence of Carney's dramatic performances for granted. When he appeared in the lead in Rod Serling teleplay "The Velvet Alley" on *Playhouse 90,* the *Variety* review of 28 January 1959 commented, "Carney achieved considerable stature as a dramatic actor with his remarkable performance."

In 1966 Carney returned to *The Jackie Gleason Show,* and the role of Norton. That same year, he captured one of the coveted slots as a guest villain ("The Archer") in ABC's wildly popular *Batman* series. He had achieved success on Broadway, creating the role of Felix Unger in the original run of Neil Simon's *The Odd Couple.* And he was maturing as an actor. Lacking any formal training in the profession, Carney drew from his own life to build performances. Overcoming battles with alcoholism and depression seemed to add depth and wisdom to his characterizations. His ability to convey a sense of loneliness and world-weary resignation tended to belie his relative youth. This was evident in his film work, including his Academy Award winning portrayal as an old man traveling across the country with his cat in *Harry and Tonto* (1974), and as the aging hardboiled detective in *The Late Show* (1977). He also had impressive performances in television movies, such as his low-key portrayal of Robert Stroud, "The Birdman of Alcatraz" in

Art Carney

Alcatraz: The Whole Shocking Story (1980). Despite a flourishing career for theatrical features Carney continually returned to the medium that made him a star. He took the lead in the short-lived series *Lanigan's Rabbi* (1977), did guest appearances on shows like *Alice* and *Fame,* and was featured in specials and telefilms. He won a sixth Emmy in a heartfelt performance as the loyal caretaker of an elderly boxing champion (played by Jimmy Cagney in his last role), in *Terrible Joe Moran* (1984).

Constant re-runs of *The Honeymooners* and the packaging of the so-called lost "Honeymooners" sketches from *The Jackie Gleason Show* have guaranteed Art Carney's place in the pantheon of television comedians. But to be given his full due Carney must be recognized as one of the most accomplished and multi-faceted actors to emerge during television's "golden age."

—Eric Schaefer

ART CARNEY (Arthur William Matthew Carney). Born in Mount Vernon, New York, U.S.A., 4 November 1918. Attended A.B. Davis High School, Mount Vernon, New York. Married: Jean Myers, 1940 (divorced, 1965); children: Ellen, Brian, Paul; remarried Jean Myers, 1977 (divorced); Barbara Isaac. United States Army, 1944–45. Began entertainment career as member of the Horace Heidt

Orchestra, 1936–39; vaudeville and club performer, 1939–40; radio performer, 1942–44, 1945–49; began television career on *The Morey Amsterdam Show*, 1948; featured performer in various versions of *The Jackie Gleason Show*, 1952-70; various guest performances in television series from 1950s. Recipient: six Emmy Awards; two Sylvania Awards; Academy Award, 1974; Best Actor, National Society of Film Critics, 1977.

TELEVISION

1948–50	*The Morey Amsterdam Show*
1952–59,	
1966–70	*The Jackie Gleason Show*
1955–56	*The Honeymooners*
1966–68	*Batman*
1977	*Lanigan's Rabbi*
1986–89	*The Cavanaughs*

MADE-FOR-TELEVISION MOVIES

1972	*The Snoop Sisters*
1975	*Katherine*
1975	*Death Scream*
1976	*Lanigan's Rabbi*
1979	*Letters from Frank*
1980	*Alcatraz: The Whole Shocking Story*
1980	*Fighting Back*
1981	*Bitter Harvest*
1984	*Terrible Joe Moran*
1984	*The Night They Saved Christmas*
1984	*The Emperor's New Clothes*
1984	*A Doctor's Story*
1985	*The Undergrads*
1985	*Izzy and Moe*
1985	*The Blue Yonder*
1986	*Miracle of the Heart: A Boys Town Story*
1990	*Where Pigeons Go to Die*

FILMS

Pot of Gold, 1941; *The Yellow Rolls-Royce*, 1965; *A Guide for the Married Man*, 1967; *Harry and Tonto*, 1974; *W.W. and the Dixie Dancekings*, 1975; *Won Ton Ton, the Dog Who Saved Hollywood*, 1976; *Scott Joplin*, 1977; *The Late Show*, 1977; *Movie Movie*, 1978; *House Calls*, 1978; *Sunburn*,

1979; *Ravagers*, 1979; *Going in Style*, 1979; *Steel*, 1980; *Roadie*, 1980; *Defiance*, 1980; *Take This Job and Shove It*, 1981; *St. Helens*, 1981; *Better Late Than Never*, 1982; *The Naked Face*, 1984; *The Muppets Take Manhattan*, 1984; *Firestarter*, 1984; *Night Friend*, 1987; *Last Action Hero*, 1993.

STAGE

The Rope Dancers, 1957; *Harvey*, 1956; *The Rope Dancers*, 1957; *Take Her, She's Mine*, 1961; *The Odd Couple*, 1965; *Lovers*, 1968; *The Prisoner of Second Avenue*, 1972; *The Odd Couple*, 1974; *The Prisoner of Second Avenue, Long Island, New York*, 1974.

FURTHER READING

Bishop, Jim. *The Golden Ham: A Candid Biography of Jackie Gleason.* New York: Simon and Schuster, 1956.
Crescenti, Peter. *The Official Honeymooners Treasury: To the Moon and Back with Ralph, Norton, Alice, and Trixie.* New York: Perigee, 1990.
Hall, Jane. "Reunited for a Made-for-TV Movie, Jackie Gleason and Art Carney Savor a Wacky Second Honeymoon." *People Weekly* (New York), 23 September 1985.
Henry, William A. *The Great One: The Life and Legend of Jackie Gleason.* New York: Doubleday, 1992.
Marc, David. *Comic Visions: Television Comedy and American Culture.* Boston: Unwin Hyman, 1989.
McCrohan, Donna. *The Honeymooners' Companion: The Kramdens and the Nortons Revisited.* New York: Workman, 1978.
McCrohan, Donna, and Peter Crescenti. *The Honeymooners Lost Episodes.* New York: Workman, 1986.
Meadows, Audrey. *Love Alice: My Life as a Honeymooner.* New York: Crown, 1994.
Mitz, Rick. *The Great TV Sitcom Book.* New York: R. Marek, 1980.
Waldron, Vince. *Classic Sitcoms: A Celebration of the Best of Prime-time Comedy.* New York: Macmillan, 1987.
Zolotow, Maurice. "The All-out Art of Art Carney." *Reader's Digest* (Pleasantville, New York), October 1989.

See also Gleason, Jackie; *Honeymooners*

THE CAROL BURNETT SHOW

U.S. Comedy/Variety Show

When *The Carol Burnett* show aired in September 1967 on CBS, no one expected it to run eleven years. The show gave Carol Burnett, along with regulars Harvey Korman, Vicki Lawrence, Lyle Waggoner (who left in 1974), and Tim Conway (whose occasional guest appearances became permanent in 1975) an opportunity to fuse the best of live vaudeville-style performance with the creative benefits of time and

tape. Burnett's ensemble quickly bonded into a tight unit of professionals who looked and acted as if performing on *The Carol Burnett Show* was the best fun an entertainer could have. In reality, the meticulously-structured, musical-comedy program became one of the last, and one of the finest, prime-time variety shows to link the modern television age with Tin Pan Alley and the golden ages of motion pictures and television.

The show brought Carol Burnett's working-class persona into a unique relationship with her audience. There was a glamorous, celebrity-brushed side to her work: Burnett could wear exclusive Bob Mackie gowns, banter with popular celebrities, and illustrate her brilliant talent for physical and intellectual comedy in cleverly written and produced skits. Her musical abilities ranged from Shubert's Alley to more refined venues, and her voice could amuse and inspire. She vamped with Hollywood royalty: Lucille Ball, Liza Minnelli, Sammy Davis, Jr. Even California governor Ronald Reagan joked and performed. On the other hand, Burnett's charwoman character, her dysfunctional and beleaguered "family" member, Eunice, her zestful Tarzan call, and her weekly question-and-answer sessions with the studio audience gave her an accessibility and down-to-earth warmth that firmly reinstated her within the world of her viewers. The dichotomy between the two Carols—one homespun, the other neon-minted—gave *The Carol Burnett Show* a flavor and personality that showcased the idiosyncrasies of its eponymous star. Only later did Burnett reveal the source of that working-class quality—the talented comedienne had lifted herself from appalling poverty, a dysfunctional family, and emotional abuse to become a beloved star. One of Burnett's insightful actions, as she constructed her characters and her persona, was to draw on the contradictions that informed her artistic evolution.

Throughout the show's run, Burnett maintained, and increased, her creative input and control. She worked closely with a team of writers, among them Ken Welch and his wife, Mitzi, who had a strong sense of Burnett's attributes and strengths. (Ken Welch had written the famous "I Made a Fool of Myself over John Foster Dulles" routine which had catapulted comic chanteuse Burnett to fame in 1956.) The show combined musical comedy with humorous sketches, using the ensemble of players as well as weekly guest stars, such as Jim Naybors, Cher, and Julie Andrews.

Burnett's three-tiered abilities—singer, actress, comedienne—allowed the writers to create and sustain characters throughout the 11-year-run. The charwoman, whose pantomimed mishaps often brought her into the shadow of greatness, became the show's trademark; a caricature of the dusty maid adorned credits and teasers for the program. Eunice, who was always under the abusive power of her mama, blended the kind of sharply-sketched comedy and tragedy that marks the finest comedic characters. Eunice, Mama, and the rest of the working-class family members insulted, demeaned, and belittled one another, in acrimonious skits that revealed the dark heart of a family in turmoil. Critics complained that Eunice became more disturbing, rather than amusing, as the show progressed. Eventually, the family skits were spun off into a situation comedy, without Burnett, entitled *Mama's Family*, in which Vicki Lawrence reprised her role as the bilious Mama.

The show centered on Burnett, but its enduring qualities also arose from its talented ensemble of players, whose interactions contributed to the overwhelming sense of "live" performance exuded by the show. Vicki Lawrence was fresh out of

The Carol Burnett Show

high school when her resemblance to Burnett won her a role; her transformation from sprightly youth to dour Mama astonished and delighted audience and cast. The infamous comic rivalry between perennial bemused Harvey Korman and the irrepressible Tim Conway remains one of the show's most distinctive features, as Conway's scripted and ad-libbed high jinks forced Korman to battle uncontrollable laughter during skits. Bits would halt as Korman struggled to stay in character; Conway would continue to pile on more egregious additions, trying to break up his costar. While the other cast members joined in unexpected break-ups, the anarchic camaraderie of Korman and Conway became legendary.

These refreshing ad-libs often appeared during movie parodies, another of the show's trademarks. Burnett had been deeply influenced by classical Hollywood films during her childhood, and she and her writers drew from a copious knowledge of motion pictures to design film-related skits. Nothing was sacred: genres, films, actors, and characters from familiar and obscure pictures provided fodder for the ensemble. A take-off of *Gone with the Wind* ("Went with the Wind") found Burnett dressed in Bob Mackie window drapes, complete with curtain rods doubling as shoulder pads, rolling down the stairs as she deconstructed one of the film's most famous moments, Scarlett's miscarriage during a fight with Rhett. "From Here to Maternity," "Sunnyset Boulevard," "Lovely Story": Burnett and her ensemble paid tribute to a bygone golden age with arch and loving comic elegies.

The show ended in 1978, still attaining decent ratings at a time when variety shows no longer attracted large audiences. Burnett wished to go on to other projects, and wanted to close *The Carol Burnett Show* while it could still entertain its viewers. The show periodically appears in syndication as *Carol and Company*; in 1992, *Carol Burnett: A Reunion* brought highlights of the run back to CBS prime time, where the special did well in the ratings. Ultimately, *The Carol Burnett Show* represents a sophisticated fusion of music, comedy, drama, celebrity, parody, and slapstick which both resurrected and archived the traditions of America's vaudeville-variety past.

—Kathryn C. D'Alessandro

REGULAR PERFORMERS
Carol Burnett
Harvey Korman (1967–77)
Lyle Waggoner (1967–74)
Vicki Lawrence
Tim Conway (1975–79)
Dick Van Dyke (1977)
Kenneth Mars (1979)
Craig Richard Nelson (1979)

MUSIC
The Harry Zimmerman Orchestra (1967–71)

The Peter Matz Orchestra (1971–78)

DANCERS
The Ernest Flatt Dancers

PROGRAMMING HISTORY

• CBS

September 1967–May 1971	Monday 10:00-11:00
September 1971–November 1972	Wednesday 8:00-9:00
December 1972–December 1977	Saturday 10:00-11:00
December 1977–March 1978	Sunday 10:00-11:00
June 1978–August 1978	Wednesday 8:00-9:00

• ABC
| August 1979–September 1979 | Saturday 8:00-9:00 |

FURTHER READING

Marc, David. "Carol Burnett: The Last of the Big-time Comedy-Variety Stars." *Quarterly Review of Film Studies* (Chur, Netherlands), July 1992.

O'Connor, John J. "Funny Women of Television: A Museum of Television and Radio Tribute." *The New York Times*, 24 October, 1991.

See also Burnett, Carol; Variety Programs

CARSEY, MARCY

U.S. Producer

Marcy Carsey, one of the most successful situation comedy producers of the 1980s and 1990s, is co-owner of the Carsey-Werner Company, an independent television production company responsible for two of the most highly rated and longest running sitcoms on TV, *The Cosby Show* and *Roseanne*. Carsey has a number of notable accomplishments in the television industry: she developed the concept of building a sitcom around a single standup comedian: she established one of the first successful production companies to operate independently of the networks; she is frequently named one of the most powerful women in show business.

Carsey began her career in television in the 1960s as a tour guide at NBC, later becoming a story editor for the Tomorrow Entertainment company. In 1974 she joined ABC as a program executive concentrating on comedy programming, rising, to senior vice president of prime-time series in 1978. While at ABC, she developed some of the most successful shows of that era, including *Mork and Mindy, Soap*, and *Happy Days*. In 1980 she left ABC and in 1982 started Carsey Productions, an independent production company. She was joined in this venture a year later by Tom Werner who had worked with her at ABC. They remain equal partners in the Carsey-Werner Company.

The programs produced by Carsey-Werner have been notable for their innovation in pushing the boundaries of traditional sitcom fare. *The Cosby Show*, the first sitcom about an African-American family to sustain wide, diverse and enduring popularity, consistently led in the ratings for several years. It was Carsey-Werner's first hit show, employing the formula that helped to establish them as a television production powerhouse: building a family-based situation comedy around a popular, established standup comedian. *Cosby* aired in prime time for eight seasons and is currently in worldwide syndication. With virtually no track record when they sold *Cosby* to NBC, the company's success was firmly established, as well as its reputation as a source of programming.

In *Roseanne*, Carsey-Werner continued the concept of a show starring a well-known comedian, in this case Roseanne (then Roseanne Barr). *Roseanne* has been a centerpiece of the ABC programming schedule since it was introduced in 1988. In contrast to *Cosby*, which was about an upper-middle-class family, *Roseanne* featured a working-class woman with husband and children, a perspective not usually found in prime-time sitcoms. The character Roseanne is closely based on the persona evident in Barr's stand-up performances, which she derived from her personal experi-

Marcy Carsey with Tom Werner
Photo courtesy of the Carsey-Werner Company

ences. Not only is the main character relatively authentic, the program has received critical acclaim for the topics it addresses and the quality of the writing. It has gained a reputation for scathing dialogue and controversial plotlines, while sustaining high ratings.

In addition to *Cosby* and *Roseanne,* Carsey and Werner have a number of other popular situation comedies to their credit, including *Grace Under Fire, A Different World,* and *Cybill.* Beginning with *The Cosby Show,* Carsey Werner programs have emphasized non-mainstream, non-traditional, and ethnic family groupings. This can be seen in the flops as much as the hits—shows like *Chicken Soup* starring Jewish comedian Jackie Mason, and *Frannie's Turn* based on the life of a single working-class mother.

Carsey and Werner have led the wave of independent production companies in the 1980s that resist affiliation with a major network or distributor. Carsey-Werner shows have appeared on all three major broadcast networks. They retain (or have repurchased) control of syndication rights for re-runs of their hit shows and have produced original programming for syndication, for example a revival of the Groucho Marx quiz show, *You Bet Your Life* hosted by Bill Cosby, which aired briefly in the early 1990s. In 1995, Carsey-Werner ventured into the feature film industry by founding Carsey-Werner Moving Pictures. Carsey has been quoted as saying that the secret of the success of Carsey-

Werner's shows has to do with their preference for thinking up "people and ideas together" and for "atypical casting."

Carsey has been touted as one of the few women in high-level executive positions in television and one of the most successful American business women in show business. She has been on the board of directors of the Academy of Television Arts and Sciences and on the board of the Film School at the University of Southern California.

—Kathryn Cirksena

MARCY CARSEY (Marcia Lee Peterson). Born in South Weymouth, Maine, U.S.A., 1944. Attended the University of New Hampshire, Durham, New Hampshire, B.A. in English literature 1966. Married: John Carsey, 1969; children: Rebecca and John. Program supervisor, William Esty advertising agency, 1960s; story editor, Tomorrow Entertainment, Los Angeles, 1971–74; program executive, later senior vice president for prime-time series, ABC Television, 1974–80; founder, Carsey Productions, Los Angeles, 1982; co-owner, Carsey-Werner Productions, Los Angeles, from 1982; producer of numerous prime-time television series, including *The Cosby Show, A Different World,* and *Roseanne,* from 1982.

TELEVISION (producer)
1983   *Oh, Madeline*

FURTHER READING

"Carsey-Werner: The Little Programming Engine That Did." *Broadcasting* (Washington, D.C.), 18 July 1988.

Gerard, Jeremy. "What Have They Done for Us Lately?" *The New York Times Magazine*, 25 November 1990.

Grover, Ronald. "Can This TV Team Go Five for Five?" *Business Week* (New York), 19 June 1989.

Walley, Wayne. "Carsey-Werner: Cosby's Co-Pilots Stay Small and Lean." *Advertising Age* (New York), 16 June 1986.

See also *Cosby Show; Different World; Roseanne*

CARSON, JOHNNY

U.S. Comedian/Talk Show Host

Johnny Carson is best known as America's late night king of comedy. For thirty years he hosted NBC television's *Tonight Show;* his topical monologues, irreverent characters, comical double takes and frivolous sketches entertained more people than any other performer in history. His late-night arena provided plugs for untold books, films and products, created a springboard to stardom for an infinite number of new performers, and, more than occasionally, offered a secure refuge for aging legends.

Carson began performing professionally at the age of fourteen as a magician-comic, "The Great Carsoni," for the local Rotary Club in his hometown of Norfolk, Nebraska. After a two-year stint as a Navy Ensign during World War II, and four years as a radio-drama major at the University of Nebraska, he plunged headfirst into the world of broadcasting as a radio announcer-disc jockey. When WOW in Omaha began television operations in 1949, Carson was there to host his first video program, *The Squirrel's Nest*, a daily early afternoon show. The young performer told jokes, conducted humorous interviews and staged various skits with wacky comic characters and premises. *Squirrel's Nest* gave Carson the opportunity to develop a good portion of his public persona and adjust his performance style to the intimate visual medium.

Relocating to Hollywood in the early 1950s, Carson's television career took a step forward with his weekly low-budget series, *Carson's Cellar*, on CBS' KNXT. Performing monologues and satirical sketches reminiscent of his later work, Carson attracted the attention of such stars as Fred Allen, Groucho Marx and Red Skelton—all of whom dropped by to appear on the local show at no charge. Based on his work with *Carson's Cellar*, a more sophisticated *Johnny Carson Show* was created for regional broadcasts in the western United States. This proved unsuccessful and Carson subsequently began work for *The Red Skelton Show* as a writer.

Casting about for new on-air opportunities, Carson's first prime-time network television exposure happened in May 1954, as host of the short-lived quiz show, *Earn Your Vacation*. Fortunately, working for Skelton provided more of a career boost. When Skelton was injured during a show rehearsal, the young Carson was thrust instantly into the limelight as substitute host. On the strength of this appearance, CBS created a new prime-time *Johnny Carson Show*, a traditional potpourri of comedy, music, dance, skits and monologues. Working through seven writers and eight directors in thirty-nine weeks, the troubled show left the air due to poor ratings.

As quizmaster of the ABC-TV daytime show, *Who Do You Trust?*, in 1957, Carson's career again took an upward turn. This highly rated daytime entry allowed Carson to display his engaging personality and quick wit through five years of continual give and take with a wide variety of guests. During this time, he also worked at extending his reputation and base of experience by appearing on a number of television musical variety shows and game shows, on Broadway and as a guest actor in live television plays. Most importantly, Carson's successes brought him offers to substitute for Jack Paar as guest host on *The Tonight Show* and ultimately to replace Paar when the temperamental emcee retired.

On 1 October 1962, Carson broadcast his first *Tonight Show* as permanent host. Less excitable and emotional than his predecessor, Carson's relaxed pace, more casual interviewing style, impeccable timing and ability to play straight for other guests proved instantly popular with his viewing audience. Comparing differences between Paar and Carson, *Time* magazine reported on 28 May 1965 that "Paar's emotionalism had made the show the biggest sleep stopper since caffeine. By contrast, Carson came on like pure Sanka. But soon his low-key, affable humor began to prove addictive. Paar generated new interest, but Carson is watched."

Within four months of assuming *Tonight Show* reins, Carson surpassed Paar's old record night-time ratings by nearly a half million viewers, adding approximately twenty stations to the NBC network—this despite heavy CBS com-

Johnny Carson
Photo courtesy of Carson Productions

petition from former *Tonight Show* host Steve Allen. Incredibly, over a fifteen-year period, with continual competitive threats from CBS and ABC, the *Tonight Show* doubled its audience. Observed Kenneth Tynan in his *New Yorker* portrait of Carson on 20 February 1978, this was "a feat that, in its blend of staying power and mounting popularity, is without precedent in the history of television."

Despite occasional contract squabbles, criticism over his numerous days off, marital conflicts and assorted family problems, Carson continued to outdistance his competition for an additional fifteen years. Without losing his timing, his unpredictability or his perfectionist work ethic, for thirty years he kept his finger on the pulse of mainstream America's moods, attitudes and concerns. Combining his verbal dexterity with a well-stocked supply of facial expressions and gestures, he became the acknowledged master at lampooning the pretentious, salvaging the boring or sharpening a nervous guest's performance for maximum effect.

Through the years, Carson hosted a number of network television specials, including the Academy Awards and Emmy Awards, and performed stand-up comedy at the top hotels in Las Vegas. But it was *The Tonight Show* that guaranteed his place in American history. For thirty years, he entered our homes to provide commentary on the day's news, to help determine our next day's conversational agenda and, of course, to entertain. Over time, his mild-mannered midwestern brand of humor became more politically biting and sexually frank but never demeaning or offensive. His well-known characters, like Carnac, Aunt Blabby, and Art Fern, so familiar to multiple generations of American families, remained brash, silly and, somehow, consistently funny.

On 22 May 1992, at the age of sixty-six, Johnny Carson left the *Tonight Show*—a remarkable thirty-year run in more than a half century of comedy performance that raised him to the level of national court jester and national treasure.

—Joel Sternberg

JOHNNY (JOHN WILLIAM) CARSON. Born in Corning, Iowa, U.S.A., 23 October 1925. Attended the University of Nebraska, Lincoln, Nebraska, B.A. 1949. Ensign, U.S. Navy, World War II. Married: 1) Jody Wolcott, 1948 (divorced, 1963), children: Chris, Ricky, Cory; 2) Joanne Copeland, 1963 (divorced); 3) Joanna Holland, 1972 (divorced, 1983); 4) Alexis Maas, 1987. Began career as radio announcer, KFAB, Lincoln, Nebraska, 1948; announcer, WOW and WOW-TV, Omaha, Nebraska; announcer, KNXT-TV, Los Angeles, California, 1950; began television with *Carson's Cellar*, a comedy-variety-talk show, KNXT-TV, 1951; writer, *The Red Skelton Show*, on air as replacement for the injured Skelton, 1954; host-star of quiz show, *The Johnny Carson Show*, 1955–56; succeeded Jack Paar as host of *The Tonight Show*, 1 October 1962; last telecast 22 May 1992. Recipient: four Emmy Awards; Friar's Club Entertainer of the Year Awards, 1965, 1969; Harvard Hasty Pudding Club Man of the Year, 1977.

TELEVISION

1951–52	*Carson's Cellar*
1954	*Earn Your Vacation*
1955–56	*The Johnny Carson Show*
1957–62	*Who Do You Trust?*
1961–62	*To Tell the Truth*
1962–92	*The Tonight Show Starring Johnny Carson*

MADE-FOR-TELEVISION MOVIE

| 1993 | *The Positively True Adventures of the Alleged Texas Cheerleader-Murdering Mom* |

FILM

Looking for Love, 1965.

PUBLICATIONS

Happiness Is...A Dry Martini. New York: Doubleday, 1965.
Unhappiness Is...A Blind Date. New York: Doubleday, 1967.
"The Last Monologue: Nostalgia and a Few Political Digs" (transcript). *The New York Times*, 23 May 1992.
"Notes and Comment: Johnny Carson on *Tonight*." *The New Yorker*, 1 June 1992.

FURTHER READING

Bark, Ed. "So Long, Johnny." *Dallas* (Texas) *Morning News*, 17 May 1992.

Bart, Peter. "We Hardly Knew Ye." *Variety* (Los Angeles), 18 May 1992.
Corkery, Paul. *Carson: The Unauthorized Biography*. Ketchum, Idaho: Randt, 1987.
Cox, Stephen. *Here's Johnny!: Thirty Years of America's Favorite Late-night Entertainment*. New York: Harmony, 1992.
de Cordova, Fred. *Johnny Came Lately: An Autobiography*. New York: Simon and Schuster, 1988.
Du Brow, Rick. "This Is It . . . Maybe, Says Johnny Carson." *Los Angeles* (California) *Times*, 23 April 1991.
"The Great Carsoni." *Time* (New York), 28 May 1965.
Higgins, Robert. "August 31, 1968: Johnny Carson." In, Harris, Jay S., editor. *TV Guide: The First 25 Years*. New York: New American Library, 1980.
Knutzen, Erik. "Celebs Say Thanks, Johnny." *Boston* (Massachusetts) *Herald*, 21 May 1992.
Leamer, Laurence. *King of the Night: The Life of Johnny Carson*. New York: Morrow, 1989.
McMahon, Ed, with Carroll Carroll. *Here's Ed: The Autobiography of Ed McMahon*. New York: Berkley Medallion, 1976.
Metz, Robert. *The Tonight Show*. Chicago: Playboy, 1980.
"Midnight Idol." *Time* (New York), 19 May 1967.
Ostrow, Joanne. "Lights Out for Johnny." *Denver* (Colorado) *Post*, 17 May 1992.
Rosenfield, Paul. *The Club Rules: Power, Money, Sex, and Fear: How It Works in Hollywood*. New York: Warner, 1992.
Smith, Ronald L. *Johnny Carson: An Unauthorized Biography*. New York: St. Martin's, 1987.
Tynan, Kenneth. "Profiles: Fifteen years of the Salto Mortale." *The New Yorker*, 20 February 1978.
Van Hise, James. *40 Years at Night: The Story of the Tonight Show*. Las Vegas, Nevada: Pioneer, 1992.
Wilde, Larry. *The Great Comedians Talk About Comedy*. New York: Citadel, 1968.
———. "Johnny We Hardly Knew Ye!" *Washington* (D.C.) *Times*, 17 May 1992.
Zoglin, Richard. "And What a Reign It Was: In His 30 Years, Carson Was The Best." *Time* (New York), 16 March 1992.

See also Talk Shows; *Tonight Show*

CARTIER, RUDOLPH

British Producer/Director

When Rudolph Cartier died in June 1994 his obituaries unanimously credited him as the "inventor of television drama" and "a television pioneer". He was a television drama director at the BBC from 1952 to the late-1960s (although the BBC preferred the title "producer" for their directors until the 1960s) and he was one of first innovative television stylists working in British television during this period. The range of his 120 television productions (all for the BBC) stretched from the science fiction serial (*The Quatermass Experiment*, 1953; *Quatermass II*, 1955; *Quatermass and the Pit*, 1958), drama documentary (*Lee Oswald—Assassin*, 1966), adaptations of classics

(*Wuthering Heights,* 1953; *Anna Karenina,* 1961), to crime serials (*Maigret,* 1961 and *Z Cars,* 1963) and opera.

He was born Rudolph Katscher in Vienna, 1904, and studied to be an architect, before attending classes given by Max Reinhardt which had an important impact upon him. In 1929 he submitted a script to a film company in Berlin which was accepted and he was enrolled as a staff writer (paired with Egon Eis) scripting low-budget crime movies. He later moved on to writing for UFA and directed his first movie, *Unischtbare Gegner* in 1931. Cartier emigrated to Britain in 1935, but it was not until 1952 that he began work as a BBC television drama director. From this point until the mid-1960s he directed over 120 separate productions, most of them live studio plays, although he also had a penchant for televised opera adaptations.

Cartier did not expand the spectrum of BBC TV drama single-handedly, but he did offer some innovations both stylistically and thematically. Before Cartier's arrival on the scene BBC TV drama production has been perceived as consisting largely of adaptations of West End successes: theatrical, static stage performances respectfully and passively relayed by efficient BBC personnel. This is a false perception, although it captures the sense of impasse felt by a drama department which, during the late 1940s, was starved of funds, studio space and equipment. The transformation of BBC drama in the early 1950s was the result of various factors, not simply Cartier's fortuitous arrival. By 1951 the expansion of television was underway: threats of a commercial competitor, and increased funding for the TV department meant that new studios were acquired and re-fitted with fresh equipment (new camera mountings, cranes, etc.). The largely ad hoc manner of production and training was formalised: training manuals and production courses were established.

The appointment of Michael Barry (a former drama director, and innovative in his own way—he had directed the first documentary-drama for the BBC) as Head of Drama established a continuity of drama policy that was to last a decade until Barry was replaced by Sydney Newman. Unlike his predecessors Barry was convinced that TV drama had to rely less on dialogue, more on the "power of the image": that television had to be visibly televisual, not a discrete passive relay medium. It was into this new fertile environment that Cartier was employed, and he quickly took full advantage, "I said [to Barry] that the BBC needed new scripts, a new approach, a whole new spirit, rather than endlessly televising classics like Dickens or familiar London stage plays." Barry was initially receptive to these suggestions (drama directors were given a relative amount of freedom in the selection of their material).

One way of changing traditional approaches to drama direction was to change the material: instead of using current or recent West End successes, Cartier drew upon the science-fiction genre and European modernist theatre as well as the pulp detective genres he had worked on in Germany. Initially Cartier directed more unconventional, European modernist drama: Brecht, Sartre, Anouihl; later he developed a partnership with the newly appointed BBC staff writer Nigel Kneale, and directed works specifically written by Kneale for the medium, including the three *Quatermass* serials. Later Kneale adapted Orwell's *Nineteen Eighty-Four* for television and Cartier directed.

The impact of that play (transmitted live and repeated live a few days later, as was the norm) cannot be overstated. Produced in 1954, as Cold War ideologies were being constructed and reinforced, the play's landscapes of totalitarian control achieved a massive resonance with the public, both celebratory when perceived as an anti-Soviet piece (an editorial in *The Times* praised the play for clarifying the "Communist practice of making words stand on their heads" for the British public) and disgusted by the graphic depiction of torture (one letter to the BBC reads, "Dear Sir, *Nineteen Eighty-Four* was unspeakably putrid and depraved"). Questions were asked in Parliament about the tendency for BBC drama to "pander to sexual and sadistic tastes" and Cartier himself received death threats from those who considered the play anti-fascist (the BBC provided bodyguards for him).

Hidden behind the furor is an important point. If the 1953 BBC live broadcast of the coronation proved that television had a mass audience which could be united by a spectacle of national re-birth, Cartier's *Nineteen Eighty-Four* proved television's ability to influence, and frighten a mass audience (one *Daily Express* headline read, "Wife Dies as She Watches"). It was the beginning of television's role as an agency of pernicious influence.

The power of that production rests with Cartier's explicit desire to influence and manipulate the television audience. *Nineteen Eighty-Four* is an exemplary instance of his technique: the mixture of powerful close-up and expanded studio space. Writing in 1958, Cartier cites the close-up as a key tool of the TV director, "When the viewer was watching these 'horrific' TV productions of mine, he was, completely in my power."

Another important element was his use of filmed inserts. The restrictive space of the Lime Grove studios meant that filmed inserts were usually location scenes introduced into the live studio action. In this way scenery, camera and costume changes could be made in the studio. But Cartier took this further: instead of filmed inserts for entire scenes, he often used telecine inserts *between shots* hence expanding the apparent studio space.

For example, a minor, almost unnoticeable case in *Nineteen Eighty-Four:* Winston Smith (Peter Cushing) is walking down a corridor past another employee working at a console. This movement consists of three shots. The first, live in the studio, Winston walks past. The second, a filmed insert, Winston walks past another console (in fact the same one, filmed earlier with another actor). And the third—with Cushing having the chance to re-position—Winston walks past the same console again: the corridor appears to be long, but takes only a few steps to complete! This is a minor example of how confident Cartier was combining both live and telecine material seamlessly.

One criticism of this technique made by television purists at the time was that the expansion of space gave the plays a cinematic rather than a strictly televisual feel: one critic described his plays as "the trick of making a picture on a TV screen seem as wide and deep as Cinemascope". And Cartier's desire to expand the scale of television often brought him into conflict with Barry.

In 1954 Barry sent Cartier a warning that his productions were becoming ambitious and, more importantly, expensive. He cites Cartier's recent version of *Rebecca:*

> I am unable to defend at a time when departmental costs and scene loads are in an acute state the load imposed by *Rebecca* on Design and Supply and the expenditure upon extras and costumes ... the leading performances were stagey and very often the actors were lost in the setting.
>
> Occasionally there were fine shots such as when Max was playing the piano with his wife beside him, and the composition of figures, piano top and vase made a good frame, but the vast area of the hall and the stairway never justified the great expenditure of effort required in building and one is left with a very clear impression of reaching a point where the department must be accused of not knowing what it is doing.

Michael Barry to Rudolph Cartier, memo, 12 October 1954,
BBC Written Archives Centre, File number T5/424

In effect Barry is judging Cartier by the model of the small-scale "intimate style" espoused by many critics and television producers of the time—for them television plays should be small with few characters, and nice close shots, "Max playing the piano with his wife beside him". Cartier's television style was radically different: large spaces, long shots *and* close-ups. Cartier's response to Barry is that "the set should be large enough so that the small Mrs. de Winter should feel 'lost' enough and not 'cosy'". Packed into this observation is the contrast between the early BBC drama style of directors such as Fred O'Donovan, George More O'Ferrall, Jan Bussell and Royston Morley (longer-running shots, close-ups, the study of one or two characters) and Cartier and Kneale's conception of a wider canvas of shooting styles, a more integrated mixture of studio and film, larger sets, multi-character productions.

Cartier's difference from other directors did not simply lie in a greater use of film. It was a refusal to confine television within one essentialist style which required constant reference to its material base (intimate because the screen was small, the audience was at home, urgent because it was live, etc.). It was a use of film not primarily dependent on the limitations of what could be achieved during live studio production, a use as a material which could expand the space of the production.

Cartier never saw himself as a film director constrained by an imperfect medium: he preferred television production (although he returned once to cinema in 1958 to direct a striking melodrama, *The Passionate Summer*). Writing in 1958, when his stature was confirmed, he noted, "If the TV director knows his medium well and handles it skillfully, he can wield almost unlimited power over his mass audience; a power no other form of entertainment can give him—not even cinema."

—Jason J. Jacobs

RUDOLPH CARTIER. Born Rudolph Katscher in Vienna, Austria, 17 April 1904. Attended the Vienna Academy of Music and Dramatic Art (Max Reinhardt's master-class). Married: Margaret Pepper, 1949; two daughters. Film director and writer, Berlin; emigrated to the United Kingdom, 1935; joined BBC, 1952, and remained for 25 years as producer and director. Recipient: Guild of Television Producers and Directors Award, 1957. Died in London, 7 June 1994.

TELEVISION SERIES

1953	*The Quatermass Experiment*
1955	*Quatermass II*
1958-59	*Quatermass and the Pit*
1961	*Maigret*
1962-78	*Z Cars*
1974	*Fall of Eagles*

TELEVISION PLAYS (selection)

1951	*Man With the Twisted Lip*
1952	*Arrow to the Heart*
1952	*Dybbuk*
1952	*Portrait of Peter Perowne*
1953	*It is Midnight, Doctor Schweitzer*
1953	*L'Aiglon*
1953	*Wuthering Heights*
1954	*Such Men are Dangerous*
1954	*That Lady*
1954	*Rebecca*
1954	*Captain Banner*
1954	*Nineteen Eighty-Four*
1955	*Moment of Truth*
1955	*The Creature*
1955	*Vale of Shadows*
1955	The Devil's General
1955	*Thunder Rock*
1956	*The White Falcon*
1956	*The Mayerling Affair*
1956	*The Public Prosecutor*
1956	*The Fugitive*
1956	*The Cold Light*
1956	*The Saint of Bleecker Street*
1956	*Dark Victory*

1956	*Clive of India*
1956	*The Queen and the Rebels*
1957	*Salome*
1957	*Ordeal by Fire*
1957	*Counsellor-at-Law*
1958	*Captain of Koepenick*
1958	*The Winslow Boy*
1958	*A Tale of Two Cities*
1958	*A Midsummer Night's Dream*
1959	*Philadelphia Story*
1959	*Mother Courage and Her Children*
1959	*Otello*
1960	*The White Guard*
1960	*Glorious Morning*
1960	*Tobias and the Angel*
1961	*Rashomon*
1961	*Adventure Story*
1961	*Anna Karenina*
1961	*The Golden Fleece*
1961	*Liars*
1961	*Cross of Iron*
1962	*The Aspern Papers*
1962	*Doctor Korczuk and the Children*
1962	*Sword of Vengeance*
1962	*Carmen*
1963	*Anna Christie*
1963	*Night Express*
1963	*Stalingrad*
1963	*Peter the Lett*
1964	*Lady of the Camellias*
1964	*The Midnight Men*
1964	*The July Plot*
1965	*Wings of the Dove*

1965	*Ironhand*
1965	*The Joel Brand Story*
1966	*Gordon of Khartoum*
1966	*Lee Oswald—Assassin* (also writer)
1967	*Firebrand*
1967	*The Burning Bush*
1968	*The Fanatics*
1968	*Triumph of Death*
1968	*The Naked Sun*
1968	*The Rebel*
1969	*Conversation at Night*
1969	*An Ideal Husband*
1969	*Shattered Eye*
1970	*Rembrandt*
1970	*The Bear*
1970	*The Year of the Crow*
1971	*The Proposal*
1972	*Lady Windermere's Fan*
1973	*The Deep Blue Sea*
1976	*Loyalties*
1977	*Gaslight*

Films

Unsichtbare Gegner, 1931; *Corridor of Mirrors* (producer and writer), 1948; *Passionate Summer* (director), 1958.

FURTHER READING

Cartier, Rudolph. "A Foot in Both Camps." *Films and Filming* (London), September 1958.

Myles, L., and J. Petley. "Rudolph Cartier." *Sight and Sound* (London), Spring 1990.

See also *Quatermass, Z Cars*

CARTOONS

Cartoons have long existed on the periphery of broadcast television, consigned to the shadowy regions of weekday afternoons and Saturday mornings. The networks' evening programming has been remarkably empty of cartoon series. Indeed, there have been only a pair of prime-time series that have lasted more than two seasons: *The Flintstones* and *The Simpsons.* Many of the "television" cartoon characters with which we are the most familiar (Bugs Bunny, Mickey Mouse, Daffy Duck, Popeye) were not actually designed for television, but, rather, were initially exhibited in cinema theaters. On any given day one may view a short history of theatrical film animation on television—as cartoons from the 1930s and 1940s are juxtaposed with more recent offerings. This results in some odd cultural gaps, such as when a viewer born in the 1980s watches cartoons making jokes about 1930s movie stars and politicians.

Cartoons initially evolved in the teens, but their development was slowed by their prohibitive cost. After all, 24

entire pictures had to be drawn for every second of film. Animation became more economically feasible in 1914 when Earl Hurd patented the animation cel. The cel is a sheet of transparent celluloid that is placed on top of a background drawing. By using cels, the animator need only re-draw the portions of the image that move, thus saving considerable time and expense. The acceptance of the cel was slowed by legal wrangling, however, and comparatively few silent cartoons were made.

At the same time that sound and color film technologies were popularized, studios also found ways to streamline the animation process by using storyboards (small drawings of frames that represented different shots in the cartoon) to plan the cartoon and departmentalizing the steps of the process. Thus, something resembling an assembly line was created for animation, making it much more cost effective. Producer Walt Disney was a leader in using these technologies and devising an efficient mode of cartoon production.

Batman: The Animated Series

Steamboat Willie (1928) was the first significant cartoon with synchronized sound and *Flowers and Trees* (1932) was the first to use the three-color Technicolor process (which became the cinema's principal color process in the late 1930s). Disney was so protective of these new technologies that he negotiated an exclusive deal with Technicolor; for three years, no other animators could use it.

The final key to the success of the cartoon was an effective distribution system. During the silent era, cartoons had been created by small studios with limited access to cinema theaters. In the 1930s, major studios such as Paramount, Warners, Universal, and MGM each signed distribution deals with the cartoon studios, or they created their own cartoon departments—the output of which they then distributed themselves. Since the studios also owned the preeminent theaters and since the standard way of exhibiting films at the time was two feature-length films separated by a newsreel and a cartoon, the animation studios and departments had a steady, constant demand for their product. The late 1930s to 1950s were a "golden era" for the cartoon and it is from this era that most theatrical cartoons on television are drawn.

Cartoons started their emigration to television in the late 1940s when one of the smaller studios (Van Beuren) began marketing their catalogue to early children's programs such as *Movies for Small Fry*. Other, larger studios were slower to take advantage of the electronic medium. In 1948 the major studios were forced by the U.S. Supreme Court to divest themselves of their theaters—which greatly weakened their ability to distribute their product. In this weakened state, they also had to compete with television for viewers. Disney, however, was among the first of the major cartoon studios to develop a liaison with television networks. Its long-running programs, *Disneyland* (later known as, among other things, *The Wonderful World of Disney*) and *The Mickey Mouse Club*, included cartoons among live action shorts and other materials when they premiered in the mid-1950s. The other studios soon followed suit and, by 1960, most theatrical films and cartoons were also available to be shown on television.

Concurrent with these critical and, for the film studios, disastrous changes in the entertainment industry were significant transformations in the aesthetics of animation. Up until the 1950s cartoonists, especially those with Disney, had labored under a naturalistic aesthetic—striving to make their drawings look as much like real world objects as was possible in this medium. The apotheosis of this was Disney's *Snow White* which traced the movements of dancer Marge Champion and transformed her into Snow White. But post-World War II art movements such as abstract expressionism rejected this naturalistic approach and these avant-garde principles eventually filtered down to the popular cartoon. In particular, United Productions of America (UPA), a studio which contained renegade animators who had left Disney during the 1941 strike, nurtured an aesthetic that emphasized abstract line, shape, and pattern over naturalistic figures. UPA's initial success came in

Huckleberry Hound

The Jetsons

1949 with the *Mr. Magoo* series, but its later, Academy Award-winning *Gerald McBoing Boing* (1951) is what truly established this new style.

The UPA style was characterized by flattened perspective, abstract backgrounds, strong primary colors, and "limited" animation. Instead of using perspective to create the illusion of depth in a drawing, UPA's cartoon objects looked flat, like the blobs of color that they were. Instead of filling in backgrounds with lifelike detail as in, say, a forest scene in *Bambi*, UPA presented backgrounds that were broad fields of color, with small squiggles to suggest clouds and trees. Instead of varying the shades and hues of colors to imply the colors of the natural world, UPA's cartoons contained bold, bright, saturated colors.

Most importantly for the development of television cartoons, UPA used animation that was limited in three ways. First, the amount of movement within the frame was substantially reduced. Rather than have a cartoon woman move her entire head in a shot, a UPA cartoon might have her just blink her eyes. Second, in limited animation figure movements are often repeated. A character waving good-bye, for instance, might contain only two distinct movements which are then repeated without change. Full animation, in contrast, includes many unique movements. Third, limited animation uses fewer individual frames to represent a movement. If, for example, Yosemite Sam were to hop off his mule in a movement that takes one second, full animation might use 24 discrete frames to represent that

movement. Limited animation, in contrast, might cut that number in half. The result is a slightly jerkier movement.

UPA's changes in animation appear to have been aesthetically inspired, but they also made good business sense. Flattened perspective, abstract backgrounds, strong primary colors, and limited animation result in cartoons that are quicker and cheaper to produce. When animators began creating programs specifically for television, they quickly adopted these economical practices, jettisoning UPA's aesthetics in the process.

The first successful, designed-for-television cartoon was not created for a TV network, but rather was released directly into syndication. *Crusader Rabbit*, created by Jay Ward (of *Rocky and Bullwinkle* fame) and Alexander Anderson, was first distributed in 1949. Network television cartooning came along eight years later. The networks' first cartoon series was *The Ruff and Reddy Show*, which was developed by the most successful producers of television cartoons, Bill Hanna and Joe Barbera. *The Ruff and Reddy Show* was also the first made-for-TV cartoon show to be broadcast nationally on Saturday mornings; its popularity helped established the feasibility of Saturday morning network programming. Hanna-Barbera was also responsible for bringing cartoons to the prime-time network schedule—though its success in prime-time did not result in a trend. Hanna-Barbera's *The Flintstones* (1960) was prime-time's first successful cartoon series. It was also prime-time's last successful series until the premiere of *The Simpsons* in 1989.

With *Crusader Rabbit, The Ruff and Reddy Show,* and *The Flintstones,* the characteristics of the made-for-TV cartoon were established. UPA-style aesthetics (especially limited animation) were blended with narrative structures that developed in 1950s television. In particular, *The Flintstones* closely resembled live-action situation comedies and was often compared to Jackie Gleason's *The Honeymooners.* One final characteristic of the made-for-TV cartoon that distinguishes it from the theatrical cartoon is an emphasis on dialogue. Often dialogue in *The Flintstones* re-states that which is happening visually. Fred will cry out, "Pebbles is headed to the zoo" over an image of Pebbles' baby carriage rolling past a sign that reads, "Zoo, this way." In this way, television reveals its roots in radio. There is an reliance on sound that is missing from, say, *Roadrunner* cartoons in which there is no dialogue at all. Made-for-TV cartoons are often less visually oriented than theatrical cartoons from the "golden era."

Since the early 1960s, when cartoons became an established television feature, they have been the source of two major controversies: commercialization/merchandising and violence. These two issues have taken on special significance with the cartoon since so many of its viewers are impressionable children.

Commercialization and merchandising have been a part of cartooning since comic strips first began appearing in newspapers. The level of merchandising increased in the 1980s, however, as several cartoon programs were built around already existing commercial products: *Strawberry Shortcake, The Smurfs,* and *He-Man.* Unlike the merchandising of, for instance, Mickey Mouse, these cartoon characters began as products and thus their cartoons were little more than extended commercials for the products themselves. It became more and more difficult for child viewers to discern where the cartoon ended and the commercial began. The degree of cartoon merchandising did not lessen in the 1990s—as the popularity of the *Mighty Morphin Power Rangers* attested—but broadcasters did add short intros to the programs to try to better distinguish cartoon from commercial.

The complicated issue of violence on television and its potential impact on behavior has yet to be resolved, but in response to critics of cartoon violence broadcasters have censored violent scenes from many theatrical films shown on television. Oddly enough, scenes that were considered appropriate for a general audience in a theater in the 1940s are now thought to be too brutal for today's Nintendo-educated children.

TV cartoons in the 1990s were dominated by the phenomenal success of Matt Groening's *The Simpsons,* which thrived after its series premiere in 1989 (first appearing in 1988, in short form, on *The Tracey Ullman Show*). Its ratings triumph was largely responsible for establishing a new television network (FOX) and launching one of the biggest merchandising campaigns of the decade. In 1990, Bart Simpson was on T-shirts across the United States declaring, "Don't have a cow, man!" And yet, despite the trappings of success, *The Simpsons* was often a sly parody of popular culture, in general, and television cartoons, in particular—as was to be expected from Groening, who established himself as the artist of the *Life in Hell* comic strip. The recurrent feature of *The Itchy and Scratchy Show,* a cartoon within *The Simpsons,* allowed the program to critique violence in cartoons at the same time it reveled in it. And in one episode, *The Simpsons* retold the entire history of cartooning as if Itchy and Scratchy had been early Disney creations.

—Jeremy G. Butler

FURTHER READING

Brasch, Walter M. *Cartoons Monickers: An Insight Into the Animation Industry.* Bowling Green, Ohio: Bowling Green University Popular Press, 1983.

Butler, Jeremy G. *Television: Critical Methods and Applications.* Belmont, California: Wadsworth, 1994.

Cawley, John, and Jim Korkis. *Cartoon Superstars.* Las Vegas, Nevada: Pioneer, 1990.

Crafton, Donald. *Before Mickey: The Animated Film, 1889–1928.* Cambridge, Massachusetts: MIT Press, 1982.

Erickson, Hal. *Television Cartoon Shows: An Illustrated Encyclopedia, 1949–1993.* Jefferson City, North Carolina: McFarland, 1995.

Grossman, Gary H. *Saturday Morning TV.* New York: Dell, 1981.

Herdeg, Walter. *Film and TV Graphics; An International Survey of Film and Television Graphics.* Zurich, Switzerland: W. Herdeg, Graphis Press, 1967.

Lenberg, Jeff. *The Encyclopedia of Animated Cartoons.* New York: Facts on File, 1991.

Maltin, Leonard, with Jerry Beck. *Of Mice and Magic: A History of American Animated Cartoons.* New York: New American Library, 1980.

Seiter, Ellen. *Sold Separately: Children and Parents in Consumer Culture.* New Brunswick, New Jersey: Rutgers University Press, 1993.

Smoodin, Eric. *Animating Culture: Hollywood Cartoons from the Sound Era.* New Brunswick, New Jersey: Rutgers University Press, 1993.

United States Congress Senate Committee on Commerce, Science, and Transportation: Subcommittee on Communications, Education, Competitiveness and Children's Television. *Hearings Before the Committee,* 12 April 1989. Washington, D.C.: Congressional Sales Office, 1989.

Woolery, George W. *Children's Television, The First Thirty-Five Years: 1946–1981.* Metuchen, New Jersey: Scarecrow, 1985.

See also *Beavis and Butt-head;* Hanna, William, and Joseph Barbera; *Flintstones;* Park, Nick, *Simpsons, Watch with Mother*

CASUALTY

British Hospital Drama

Since it was launched in autumn 1986 as a 15-part series, the hospital drama *Casualty* has grown into one of the BBC's most successful programmes. Eventually running to 24 episodes a year (plus a repeat season), and with ratings second only to those for soap operas *EastEnders* and *Neighbours*, it was to become a linchpin of the schedule and crucial to the corporation's confidence in the run up to the renewal of its charter in 1996.

The series began as the brainchild of Jeremy Brock, a young BBC script editor, and Paul Unwin, a director at the Bristol Old Vic Theatre. A visit to a Bristol accident and emergency ward and conversation with one of the charge nurses prompted the idea of a series which would deal with the working lives of casualty staff but which would also have a campaigning edge at a time when the National Health Service in Britain was under increasing financial and political pressure. The proposal was taken up by the head of BBC drama, Jonathan Powell, who was convinced that a medical series was essential to a healthy schedule. The Bristol hospital became Holby General and the nurse, Peter Salt, one of the programme's medical advisors and a model for the longest serving central character, charge nurse (later nursing manager) Charlie Fairhead.

The foregrounding of a male nurse was one of several ways in which *Casualty* set out to contest the traditional values of hospital drama. The gender stereotyping associated with sluice room romances of popular medical fiction was inverted (if not always subverted) in storylines such as Charlie's passionate involvement with a female house officer, and the protracted consequences of nursing officer Duffin's pregnancy by a feckless doctor. The series has also attempted to address racial underrepresentation by placing black characters at the centre of the drama and has carried storylines on racial prejudice and abuse.

What *Casualty* sought to achieve in its first series was a gritty realism, bordering on documentary authenticity, capable of dealing with the day-to-day stresses of front-line emergency care, and the further difficulties of working in a system coming apart at the seams. Brock claimed to have been influenced by the high-octane style of MTM Entertainment Inc. shows, especially *Hill Street Blues*, with their overlapping narratives and dialogue, their rapid cutting and their wry humour, though the series never went for the sort of élan found in its U.S. counterparts. It began on a modest budget, and was shot exclusively on video, with lightweight cameras to give it pace and fluidity: the technique of following dialogue down corridors and picking up on several overlapping conversations within the same take was to become a hallmark of the emerging production style.

The central storyline for the first two series was the campaign to keep the night shift open at Holby in the teeth of funding cuts. The shift also provided the setting and time frame for each episode and, improbably, a justifica-

tion for focusing on the same eight members of staff. By the end of the first series, although another was in production, there was talk of *Casualty* being axed. There had been criticism of the show's stress-laden relentlessness and press coverage of protests from the medical professions about the disreputable image of staff conduct, though there was considerable support for the series' representation of health service conditions. The programme also came under attack from the ruling Conservative Party for its stand against such key Thatcherite policies as funding cuts and the contracting out of services and, along with news coverage of the bombing of Tripoli and the drama *The Monocled Mutineer*, was held up as an example of alleged left-wing bias at the BBC.

However, as audience figures for the second series began to climb to eight million, the BBC started to invest more in it. New characters were brought in and a sharper style began to emerge, particularly in the cross-weaving of storylines and the more honed gallows humour. By 1991, *Casualty* had an audience of 12 to 13 million and the formula was securely established: a basic structure created by the 10 main characters' continuing stories, a major accident interwoven with 6 to 8 further parallel storylines and up to 80 short scenes per episode, a real-time feel based on the single-shift setting, sharp cutting, mobile single-camera work, no background music, realistic lighting, an army of trauma-specific extras and models, and a range of 30-40 guest actors per series. The casting of familiar, high-caliber performers in cameo roles was, for some time, one of the series' main attractions, along with its growing reputation for graphic authenticity in the depiction of injuries and their treatment. The series also shed its regional identity: although still shot in and around Bristol, this was no longer its ostensible setting and the characters came to reflect a more general population mix. A proposal by Powell, by now controller of BBC1, to go to a twice weekly, early-evening slot was rejected but by this time, many would argue, the show had already softened into a standardized predictability. By 1993, audiences were peaking at 15.47 million and the programme was tentpoling the Saturday evening schedule. A ruling in that year by the Broadcasting Standards Council concerning the pre-watershed unsuitability of a storyline about rent boys and male rape and further controversy over an episode showing teenagers rioting and burning down the ward forced the new BBC1 controller, Alan Yentob, into a promise of greater "responsibility" in the handling of topical material. A year later, audiences stood at 17.2 million.

Against the claim that *Casualty* has lost its earlier political abrasiveness, the producers would argue that public opinion had caught up with the programme, that the once controversial claims had become fact and the issues were more subtly woven into the fabric of the stories. By

1995, however, the series seemed to reach a final transformation into soap opera. It was the human interest vignettes imported with each casualty case which now dominated, along with the lives and loves of the regular medical staff. Yet the storylines have never fully lost contact with the fabric of contemporary life, one of the series' recurring concerns being the social cohesion of the world beyond the hospital doors.

Casualty is a classic example of the intergeneric development of formula-based television fiction. All the attractions of hospital drama are there: life, death, and human vulnerability; institutional hierarchy; and the personal and professional tension. The show also chimes in with the ascendancy in the 1990s of a new genre of emergency service narrative on British television, from Carlton's drama, *London's Burning,* to reconstruction programmes like the BBC's *999.* Beneath the surface, however, the fictional structure rests on foundations tried and tested in the cop-shop police drama, and it is no coincidence that the background of founding producer Geraint Morris lay with series such as *Softly Softly* and *Juliet Bravo.* The accident and emergency ward, in particular the waiting area that provides the focal point of the production set, operates here as a classic front line—a site of friction between the hospital community and life on the street, and a liminal space into which hundreds of individual cases are drawn, to be returned, in varying states of social and psychological repair, to the world beyond.

—Jeremy Ridgman

CAST

Charlie Fairhead	Derek Thompson
Lisa Duffin	Catherine Shipton
Megan Roach	Brenda Fricker
Clive King	George Harris
Ewart Plimmer	Bernard Gallagher
Elizabeth Straker	Maureen O'Brien
Karen Goodlife	Suzanna Hamilton
Cyril James	Eddie Nestor
Dr. Andrew Bower	William Gaminara
Martin Ashford	Patrick Robinson
Adele Beckford	Dona Croll
Helen Chatsworth	Samantha Edmonds
Mr. Mike Barratt	Clive Mantle
Maxine Price	Emma Bird
Kenneth Hodges	Christopher Guard
Sandra Nicholl	Maureen Beattie
Dr. Robert Khalefa	Jason Riddington
Mr. Julian Chapman	Nigel le Vaillant
Dr. Beth Ramanee	Mamta Kaash
Dr. Lucy Perry	Tam Hoskyns
Dr. David Rowe	Paul Lacoux
Dr. Mary Tomlinson	Helena Little
Dr. Barbara "Baz" Samuels (Hayes)	Julia Watson
Alex Spencer	Belinda Davidson
Karen O'Malley	Kate Hardie
Andrew Ponting	Robert Pugh
Sandra Mute	Lisa Bowerman
Shirley Franklin	Ella Wilder
Keith Cotterill	Geoffrey Leesley
Frankie Drummer	Steven O'Donnell
Susie Mercer	Debbie Roza
Mie Nishi-Kawa	Naoko Mori
Josh Griffiths	Ian Bleasdale
Jane Scott	Caroline Webster
Liz Harker	Sue Devaney
Norma Sullivan	Anne Kristen
Kuba Trzcinski	Christopher Rozycki
Jimmy Powell	Robson Green
Kelly Liddle	Adie Allen
Trish Baynes	Maria Freedman
Rachel Longworth	Jane Gurnett
Kate Wilson	Sorcha Cusack
Jude Kocarnik	Lisa Coleman
Daniel Perryman	Craig Kelly
Laura Milburn	Lizzy McInnerny
Matt Hawley	Jason Merrells
Valerie Sinclair	Susan Franklyn
Kate Miller	Joanna Foster
Simon Eastman	Robert Dawe
Mark Calder	Oliver Parker

PRODUCER Geraint Morris

PROGRAMMING HISTORY

- BBC

1986–

FURTHER READING

Kerr, Paul. "Drama Out of a Crisis." *The Listener* (London), 4 September 1986.

Kingsley, Hilary. *Casualty: The Inside Story.* London: BBC Books, 1993.

Lustig, Vera. "Emergency Ward Tenable?" *The Listener* (London), 20 September 1990.

Saynor, James. "Doctor, It's Something Up My Nose." *Guardian* (Manchester), 22 February 1993.

Smith, David James. "Close to the Bone." *7 Days* (London), 3 September 1989.

CATHY COME HOME

British Docudrama

Cathy Come Home was screened by BBC1 on 16 December 1966, within the regular *Wednesday Play* slot. The program is a "drama-documentary" concerning homelessness and its effect upon families. Written by Jeremy Sandford, produced by Tony Garnett and directed by Ken Loach, the programme has become a British TV "classic," regularly referred to by critics and researchers as well as by programme-makers themselves. Part of the status accorded to *Cathy* is undoubtedly due to its particular qualities of scripting, direction and acting, but part follows from the way in which has been seen to focus and exemplify questions about the mixing of dramatic with documentary material and, more generally, about the public power of television in highlighting social problems. After the screening, the issue of homelessness, and of various measures adopted by local authorities to deal with it, became more prominent in public and political discussion and the housing action charity "Shelter" was formed. The more long-term consequences, in terms of changes to the kinds of conditions depicted in the film, remain much more doubtful, of course.

Cathy is organised as a narrative about a young woman who marries, has children and who then, following an accident to her husband which results in his loss of job and the following family poverty, suffers various states of homelessness in poor or temporary accommodation until her children are taken into care by the social services. The programme adopts an episodic structure, depicting the stages in the decline of Cathy and her family across a number of years. Both as a play and as a kind of documentary, it is held together by the commentary of Cathy herself, a commentary which is given in a self-reflective past-tense and which not only introduces and ends the programme but is heard regularly throughout it, providing a bridge between episodes and a source of additional explanation to that obtained by watching the dramatic action.

The "documentary" element of *Cathy* is a matter of depictive style. But is also partly a matter both of the large amount of research on the problem of homelessness which went into the writing of the script and the amount of time the script gives to depicting aspects of this problem as it advances the storyline concerning Cathy and her family.

Stylistically, the programme has a number of scenes which are shot in the documentary mode of action-led camera, with events appearing to develop spontaneously and to be "caught" by the filming. The resultant effect is one of high immediacy values, providing the viewer with a strong sense of "witness." Where the script broadens its scope to situate Cathy's story in the context of the more general problem, camerawork and sound-recording produce a scopic field and address to the viewer which is that of conventional reportage. So, for instance, in a scene in a crowed tenement block, we hear the anonymous voices of occupants on the soundtrack whilst various shots are com-

Cathy Come Home
Photo courtesy of BBC

bined to produce a montage of "place," of "environment." Similarly, when towards the end of the film Cathy and her children enter the lowest class of Hostel accommodation, the camera not only situates them in the crowded dormitory they have entered but offers "snapshot" case-histories of some of the other women who are living there. Some of this information comes through voice-over, some in speech to camera, as if addressed to Cathy herself. The documentarist element is more directly present in the use of commentary and brief "viewpoint" voice-over at several points in the film. These moments offer statistics on the housing situation and allow various perspectives on it to be heard in a manner which directly follows conventional documentary practice.

Therefore *Cathy* plays with the codes of reportage and merges them with those of realist drama. The developing story, however, often shown through an exploration of private, intimate space, requires that the film be organised principally as narrative fiction, moving outwards to establish a documentary framing of context at a number of points and then closing back in on "story." Since the story is a *particularization* of the general problem, however, movement between "story" and "report" often involves no sharp disjunctions, substantive or stylistic.

The initial critical response to the programme was generally positive but public discussion tended to circulate around two issues—the possibility of the audience being deceived into according a greater "truth" to it than was warranted by its fictional status, and the way the account was a "biased" one, depicting officials as uncaring and often hostile in a way which would have been unacceptable in a conventional documentary.

It is hard to imagine a viewer so unskilled in the conventions of television as to believe that *Cathy* was "actuality" footage, so extensively is it conceived of in terms of narrative fiction. However, doubt clearly existed in some viewers' minds as to whether it was a story based directly on a real incident, or whether (as was actually the case) Cathy's tale was a construction developed from a range of research materials. The legitimacy of combining the dramatic license to articulate a viewpoint through character and action with the documentary requirement to be "impartial" was queried by several commentators, often with a certain amount of naiveté about the veracity of "straight documentary."

Against these complaints, other critics defended the programme-makers' right to use dramatic emotional devices in order to engage the viewer with public issues, pointing to the way in which the programme's view of officialdom was essentially the view of Cathy herself—in their eyes, a perfectly proper use of character viewpoint from which audience members could measure their own empathetic distance.

In British television history, then, *Cathy Come Home* remains an important marker in the long-running debate about television and truth. This should not be allowed to overshadow its own qualities as a work of social imagination, however, and as an exploration in "hybridized" forms which sometimes brilliantly prefigures much later shifts in the modes of address of factual television.

—John Corner

CAST

Cathy . . . . Carol White
Ray . . . . Ray Brooks

PRODUCER   Tony Garnett

PROGRAMMING HISTORY

• BBC

16 December 1966

FURTHER READING

Brandt, George, editor. *British Television Drama*. London: Cambridge University Press, 1981.
Petley, Julian. "Why Cathy Will Never Come Home Again." *New Statesman and Society* (London), 2 April 1993.
Sanford, Jeremy. *Cathy Come Home*. London: Boyars, 1976.

See also Docudrama; Garnett, Tony; Loach, Ken; Sanford, Jeremy; *Wednesday Play*

CAVALCADE OF AMERICA

U.S. Anthology Drama

Cavalcade of America pioneered the use of anthology drama for company voice advertising. A knock-off of sponsor E.I. DuPont de Nemours and Company's long running radio program, television's *Cavalcade* celebrated acts of individual initiative and achievement consistent with its sponsor's "Better things for better living" motto. The historical-documentary format especially fit the politically conservative DuPont Company, whose own history in America dated to 1802. The *Cavalcade* frequently touched upon science and invention, often focusing its free enterprise subtext upon the early American republic. "Poor Richard," its first telecast 1 October 1952, dramatized the wit and inventiveness of Benjamin Franklin. Developed from a back catalog of radio plays judged to have "picture qualities," the drama sent the "old and obstinate" Franklin to delay American surrender talks with the British, thereby allowing General George Washington to escape capture to fight another day. The denouement found Franklin "on his knees praying for Liberty and Peace and the ability to deserve them." Other first season telecasts reprised *Cavalcade* favorites Samuel Morse in "What Hath God Wrought," electric motor inventor Thomas Davenport as "The Indomitable Blacksmith,"

Samuel Slater in "Slater's Dream" and Eli Whitney as "The Man Who Took a Chance."

For many viewers the *Cavalcade of America* was history on the air. DuPont Company publicist Lyman Dewey confidently asserted that the typical viewer "abstracts (sic) the meaning for himself" without explicit statement from the company, identifying DuPont with the "rugged scene of America's struggle." Program specialists exercised the format's malleable historical and dramatic properties under maximum editorial control. A complete reliance upon telefilms ensured the prescribed interpretation of scripts, expanded the scope of production limited by the television studio, and lent programs a finished look that specialists felt reflected the company's stature. The use of telefilms allowed for additional economies in the rebroadcast and syndication of programs. Shorn of the "Story of Chemistry" commercials that concluded each program, telefilms were then placed in circulation on the club-and-school circuit. Merchandising directed to the general viewing public leavened the series' educational purpose with entertainment values. Promotional material accompanying the *Cavalcade's* second telecast entitled "All's Well with Lydia," for example, described "the Revolutionary War story of Lydia Darragh, American patriot and Philadelphia widow, who by her cleverness gained information instrumental in an American victory." Spot announcement texts supplied to local stations read "Was she minx or patriot?" A second exclaimed, "Lydia Darragh's receptive ear, ready smile and pink cheek are more dangerous to British hopes than a thousand muskets!"

In a bid to freshen up the series' historical venue with the trend toward "actuals" then in favor on *General Electric Theater* and *Armstrong Circle Theatre,* during the 1954-55 television season, *Cavalcade* introduced contemporary story subjects: "Saturday Story," with the Cleveland Browns' Otto Graham, who played himself; "Man on the Beat," a police drama; "The Gift of Dr. Minot," the story of the 1934 Nobel Laureate in Medicine and his treatment of anemia; and "Sunrise on a Dirty Face," a juvenile delinquent drama. The favorable reception of stories of "modern American life" led to a change of title for the 1955–56 television season. Retaining an option on the historical past, the new *DuPont Cavalcade Theater* debuted with "A Time for Courage," the story of "Nancy Merki and the swimming coach who led her to victory over polio and to Olympic stardom." In subsequent weeks the *Cavalcade* featured a contemporary, historical story mix including "Toward Tomorrow," a biography of Dr. Ralph Bunche; "Disaster Patrol," an adventure story about the Civil Air Patrol; "The Swamp Fox," featuring Hans Conried in the role of General Francis Marion; and "Postmark: Danger," a police drama drawn from the files of U.S. postal investigators.

DuPont's new interest in contemporary relevance, however, was occasionally misread by Batten, Barton, Durstine and Osborn, its Madison Avenue advertising agency and program producer. Rejecting a *Cavalcade Theater* script entitled "I Lost My Job," a DuPont Company official testily explained to agency producers that "on *Cavalcade* or in any other DuPont advertising, we do not want to picture business in a bad light, or in any way that can be interpreted as negative by even a single viewer. It just seems axiomatic that we'd be silly to spend advertising money to tear down the very concept we're trying to sell." By the 1956-57 television season that sale had moved to new settings and locations far from the *Cavalcade's* capsule demonstrations of free enterprise at work. Spurred by an editorial confidence in the value of entertainment, the newly renamed *DuPont Theatre* all but abandoned the historical past, at least as an educational prerequisite for an evening's entertainment. The following season the *DuPont Show of the Month* confirmed the trend with a schedule of 90-minute spectaculars, some in color, debuting 29 September 1957 with "Crescendo," a musical variety program co-starring Ethel Merman and Rex Harrison.

—William L. Bird Jr.

PRODUCERS Maurice Geraghty, Armand Schaefer, Gilbert A. Ralston, Arthur Ripley, Jack Denove, Jack Chertok

PROGRAMMING HISTORY

• NBC
October 1952–June 1953   Wednesday 8:30-9:00

• ABC
September 1953–June 1955   Tuesday 7:30-8:00
September 1955–June 1957   Tuesday 9:30-10:00

FURTHER READING
Hawes, William. *The American television Drama: The Experiemntal Years.* University, Alabama: University of Alabama Press, 1986.
Sturcken, Frank. *Live Television: The Golden Age of 1946–58 In New York.* Jefferson, North Carolina: McFarland, 1990.

See also Advertising, Company Voice; Anthology Drama; *Armstrong Circle Theatre; General Electric Theater*

CENSORSHIP

Conceptions of censorship derive from Roman practice in which two officials were appointed by the government to conduct the census, award public contracts and supervise the manners and morals of the people. Today the scope of censorship has been expanded to include most media and involves suppressing any or all parts deemed objectionable on moral, political, military and other grounds.

With regard to television in the United States, censorship usually refers to the exclusion of certain topics, social groups or language from the content of broadcast programming. While censorship has often been constructed against the explicit backdrop of morality, it has been implicitly based on assumptions about the identity and composition of the audience for American broadcast television at particular points in time. Different conceptions of the audience held by broadcasters have been motivated by the economic drive to maximize network profits. At times, the television audience has been constructed as an undifferentiated mass. During other periods, the audience has been divided into demographically desirable categories. As the definition of the audience has changed over time, so has the boundary between appropriate and inappropriate content. At times, different sets of moral values have often come into conflict with each other and with the economic forces of American broadcasting. The moral limits on content stem from what might be viewed as the social and cultural taboos of specific social groups, particularly concerning religious and sexual topics.

During the 1950s and 1960s, the networks and advertisers measured the viewing audience as an undifferentiated mass. Despite the lumping together of all viewers, broadcasters structured programming content around the "normal," dominant, values of white, middle-class Americans. Therefore, content centered around the concerns of the nuclear family. Topics such as racism or sexuality which had little direct impact on this domestic setting were excluded from content. Indeed, ethnic minorities were excluded, for the most part, from the television screen because they did not fit into the networks' assumptions about the viewing audience. Sexuality was a topic allocated to the private, personal sphere rather than the public arena of network broadcasting. For example, the sexual relationship between Rob and Laura Petrie in *The Dick Van Dyke Show* during the mid-1960s could only be implied. When the couple's bedroom was shown, twin beds diffused any explicit connotation that they had a physical relationship. Direct references to non-normative heterosexuality were excluded from programming altogether. In addition, coarse language which described bodily functions and sexual activity or profaned sacred words were excluded from broadcast discourse.

However, conceptions about the viewing audience and the limits of censorship changed drastically during the early 1970s. To a large degree, this shift in censorship came about because techniques for measuring the viewing audience became much more refined at that time. Ratings researchers began to break down the viewing audience for individual programs according to specific demographic characteristics, including age, ethnicity, education and economic background. In this context, the baby boomer generation—younger, better educated, with more disposable income—became the desired target audience for television programming and advertising. Even though baby boomers grew up on television programming of the 1950s and 1960s, their tastes and values were often in marked contrast to that of their middle-class parents. Subjects previously excluded from television began to appear with regularity. *All in the Family* was the predominant battering ram that broke down the restrictions placed on television content during the preceding twenty years. Frank discussions of sexuality, even outside of traditional heterosexual monogamy, became the focal point of many of the comedy's narratives. The series also introduced issues of ethnicity and bigotry as staples of its content. Constraints on the use of profanity began to crumble as well. Scriptwriters began to pepper dialogue with "damns" and "hells," language not permitted during the more conservative 1950s and 1960s.

While the redefinition of the desirable audience in the early 1970s did expand the parameters of appropriate content for television programming, the new candor prompted

reactions from several fronts, and demonstrated larger divisions within social and cultural communities. As early as 1973 the Supreme Court emphasized that community standards vary from place to place: "It is neither realistic nor constitutionally sound to read the First Amendment as requiring that people of Maine or Mississippi accept public depiction of conduct found tolerable in Las Vegas or New York City." Clearly such a ruling leaves it to states or communities to define what is acceptable and what is not, a task which cannot be carried out to everyone's satisfaction. When applying community standards, the courts must decide what the "average person, in the community" finds acceptable or not and some communities are clearly more conservative than others. These standards are particularly difficult to apply to television programming which is produced, for economic reasons, to cross all such regional and social boundaries.

In part as a result of these divisions, however, special interest or advocacy groups began to confront the networks about representations and content that had not been present before 1971. For some social groups which had had very little, if any, visibility during the first twenty years of American broadcast television, the expanding parameters of programming content were a mixed blessing. The inclusion of Hispanics, African-Americans, and gays and lesbians in programming was preferable to their near invisibility during the previous two decades, but advocacy groups often took issue with the framing and stereotyping of the new images. From the contrasting perspective, conservative groups began to oppose the incorporation of topics within content which did not align easily with traditional American values or beliefs. In particular, the American Family Association decried the increasing presentation of non-traditional sexual behavior as acceptable in broadcast programming. Other groups rallied against the increased use of violence in broadcast content. As a result, attempts to define the boundaries of appropriate content has become an ongoing struggle as the networks negotiate their own interests against those of advertisers and various social groups. Whereas censorship in the 1950s and 1960s was based on the presumed standards and tastes of the white middle-class nuclear family, censorship in the 1970s became a process of balancing the often conflicting values of marginal social groups.

The proliferation of cable in the 1980s and the 1990s has only exacerbated the conflicts over programming and censorship. Because of a different mode of distribution and exhibition—often referred to as "narrowcasting—cable television has been able to offer more explicit sexual and violent programming than broadcast television. To compete for the viewing audience that increasing turns to cable television channels, the broadcast networks have loosened restrictions on programming content enabling them to include partial nudity, somewhat more graphic violence and the use of coarse language. This strategy seems to have been partially successful in attracting viewers as evidenced by the popularity of adult dramas such as *NYPD Blue*. However, this programming approach has opened the networks to further attacks from conservative advocacy groups who have increased the pressure for government regulation, i.e. censorship, of objectionable program content.

As these issues and problems indicate, most Americans, because of cherished First Amendment rights, are extremely sensitive to any forms of censorship. Relative to other countries, however, the United States enjoys remarkable freedom from official monitoring of program content. Negative reactions are often expressed toward imported or foreign programs when they do not reflect indigenous norms and values. "Cutting of scenes" is practiced far more in developing countries than in western countries. And Americans may find it interesting to note that even European countries consider exposure to nudity and sex to be less objectionable than abusive language or violence.

Head, et al. (1994), point out that the control of media and media content is also related to the type of government in power within a particular country. They identify four types of governmental philosophy related to the issue of censorship; authoritarian, paternalistic, pluralistic and permissive. Of the four types, the first two are more inclined to exercise censorship because they assume they know what is best for citizens. Anything that challenges this exclusive view must be banned or excluded. Since most broadcasting in such countries is state funded, control is relatively easy to impose. Exclusionary methods include governmental control of broadcast stations' licenses, jamming external broadcasts, promoting indigenous programming, imposing restrictions on imported programs, excluding newspaper articles, cutting scenes from films, shutting down printing presses, etc.

Pluralistic and permissive governments allow for varying degrees of private ownership of broadcasting stations. Such governments assume that citizens will choose what they consider best in a free market where competing media companies offer their products. Such an ideal can only be effective, of course, if the competitors are roughly equal and operate in the interests of the public. To maintain this "balance of ideas" in the United States, the Federal Communications Commission (FCC) established rules which control the formation of media monopolies and require stations to demonstrate they operate in the interests of their audiences' good. Despite such intentions, recent deregulation has disturbed the balance, allowing powerful media conglomerates to dominate the market place and reduce the number of voices heard.

Pluralistic and permissive governments also assume that competing companies will regulate themselves. Perhaps the most well known attempt at self regulation is conducted by the Motion Picture Association of America (MPAA), which rates motion pictures for particular audiences. For example, the contents of "G" rated movies are considered suitable for all audiences, "GP" requires parental guidance, "R," "X," and "NC17" are considered appropriate for adults. These standards are offered as a guide to audiences and have never been strictly enforced. Parents may take children to see X-rated movies if they so desire.

In the past one of the arguments against censorship has been freedom of choice. Parents who object to offensive television programs can always switch the channel or choose another show. Unfortunately, parental supervision is lacking in many households. In the 1990s this problem, coupled with political and interest group outrage against media producers has opened the possibility of a self imposed television rating system similar to that of the MPAA. To counter conservative criticism and government censorship, producers and the networks have agreed to begin a ratings system which could be electronically monitored and blocked in the home. Thus, parents could effectively censor programming which they found unsuitable for their children while still allowing the networks to air adult-oriented programming.

In the 1970s an early attempt at a similar sort of regulation came when the FCC encouraged the television industry to introduce a "family viewing concept," according to which television networks would agree to delay the showing of adult programs until children were, presumably, no longer among the audience. The National Association of Broadcasters (NAB) willingly complied with this pressure but in 1979 a court ruled that the NAB's action was a violation of the First Amendment.

In the late 1990s, as networks relaxed corporate restrictions on content in their competition with cable and satellite programming, the early evening hours once again took on special importance. In mid-1996 more than 75 members of the U.S. Congress placed an open letter to the entertainment industry in *Daily Variety*. The letter called on the creative community and the programmers to provide an hour of programming each evening that was free from sexual innuendo, violence, or otherwise troublesome material. Clearly, the question of censorship in television continues to vex programmers, producers, government officials, and viewers. No immediate solution to the problems involved is apparent.

However, the debate and struggle over censorship of programming will more than likely continue into the next century, as social groups with diverse values vie for increased influence over program content.

—Richard Worringham and Rodney A. Buxton

FURTHER READING

Brown, Les. *Television: The Bu$iness Behind the Box*. New York: Harvest Book/Harcourt Brace Jovanovich, 1971.

Cowan, Geoffrey. *See No Evil: The Backstage Battle over Sex and Violence on Television*. New York: Simon and Schuster, 1979.

Cripps, Thomas. "*Amos 'n' Andy* and the Debate Over American Racial Integration." In, O'Connor, John E., editor. *American History/American Television: Interpreting the Video Past*. New York: Frederick Ungar, 1985.

Head, Sydney, Christopher Sterling, and Lemuel Schofield. *Broadcasting in America: A Survey of Electronic Media.* Boston: Houghton Mifflin, 1972; 7th edition, Princeton, New Jersey: Houghton Mifflin, 1994.

Marin, Rick. "Blocking the Box." *Newsweek* (New York), 11 March 1996.

Montgomery, Kathryn C. *Target: Prime Time Advocacy Groups and the Struggle over Entertainment Television.* New York and Oxford: Oxford University Press, 1989.

See also Family Viewing Time

CENTRAL EUROPE

Television in Central Europe has undergone major changes in the last decade. Up until 1989, all of the countries of the region, with the exception of Austria, were ruled by Communist governments. These governments attempted, with varying degrees of success, to exercise a complete monopoly over economic, political, and symbolic power. They thus had television systems which were very different from that existing in the United States and Western Europe. Since 1989, with the collapse of Communist rule and the establishment of a variety of new governments in the region, television has been both a contributory factor to political transformation and has, in its turn, been itself transformed.

There is a well-known model of the "Soviet-Communist media system" which dates from the depths of the Cold War. In this model, the Communist political elite regarded media as an instrument of social engineering and used a considerable battery of powers to ensure that it voiced nothing which would cast doubt on their vision of a rosy Communist future. Media also played a role in the construction of the Communist human psychology which would flourish in the new world. The media was thus closely controlled politically and didactic in its intent, both in news and entertainment.

By the end of the 1980s, this model was seriously at odds with the reality of the television systems of Central Europe. Even if it had ever been accurate, it was certainly now false. There was no single "Soviet-Communist" model. On the contrary, broadcasting differed considerably from country to country.

At one extreme stood Romania, where many of the features of the classic model could still be observed in action and where the combination of political tyranny and economic disaster had brought the television system very close to collapse. Another example of a tightly controlled system was that in Czechoslovakia. After the Russian invasion of 1968, a conservative Stalinist government was imposed, putting an end to all of the previous manifestations of liberalism. Television was amongst the new government's chief targets. Direct political control continued to be exercised up to the fall of the regime in the Velvet Revolution of 1989.

Even in Czechoslovakia, however, despite continual policy statements that entertainment should reflect Communist values, the buyers of television imports found it impossible to reach their quotas of programs from other Communist countries. There was a continual inflow of programs from the capitalist west, and these often accounted for a majority of imported programs.

This inability to control the symbolic landscape was widespread in Central Europe. In many cases, it is difficult to find evidence that, by the 1980s, there was any serious will on the part of the political leadership, either in government or in television, even to attempt to enforce media control. By the mid-1980s, for example, the three largest suppliers of imported programs to Hungarian television (MTV) were, in order of numbers of programs supplied, the United Kingdom, West Germany, and the United States. All of these provided many more programs than the USSR.

Political control was more sustained in news and current affairs, but even in those areas observers detected a shift of emphasis in the course of the 1980s. In Poland, after the banning of Solidarity and the imposition of martial law in December 1981, there was a return to close control of the news. By the middle of the decade, however, the government spokespersons increasingly were prepared to engage in indirect debates in the media with the representatives of the opposition. One Polish spokesperson even won a small propaganda victory by demanding to be allowed to broadcast on Radio Free Europe and then claiming capitalist censorship when refused. The general tone of the news and current affairs programming gradually shifted from proclaiming the glories of Communist construction to accepting the simple fact of Communist rule and the impossibility of replacing it while the Russian veto remained.

Because of these developments, it is profitable to think about the television systems in Central Europe not as examples of the Communist media system but as one version of a more general type. They may be considered as examples of state-controlled television, similar to RTVE in Spain under Franco or the ORTF in France under de Gaulle. In each case, there was a different degree of ideological control over the output of the stations, but they all had in common the fact that there were obvious and direct links between the television system and the government in power. The distance from, and attempt to balance between, the major political parties which are marked features of the public service broadcasters of northwestern Europe and the U.S. commercial system, were here quite absent.

Television has not been a simple and direct beneficiary of the new freedom and independence. On the contrary, in many countries, broadcast media continues to have a subordinate relationship to politics in general and to the governing parties in particular. There have indeed been considerable changes to the broadcasting systems, but there have also been marked continuities.

The politicians and broadcasters of Central Europe have been deluged with advice from well-paid western experts. Some of these have advocated the adoption of a version of the U.S. system, in which the central place is held by commercial companies. Others have advocated the Western European model in which state broadcasters hold a central role. In general, a mixed system of broadcasting is emerging in Central Europe in which ownership is more based on the European model than the U.S. model. There is, generally, a large state broadcaster at the center of the system, with an increasing number of franchised and supervised commercial channels emerging to compete with them.

There is, however, little evidence that this restructuring of television is producing a solution to the problem of political subordination. In the extreme cases like Croatia and Serbia, political control of television remains as tight, or possibly even tighter, than it was in the last days of the Communist regimes. In most other cases, the new political elites have been less successful in their attempts to control broadcasting, despite sometimes vigorous efforts in that direction.

The most dramatic case was that of the Hungarian "media wars." As part of the preparations for the first democratic elections in 1990, the main political forces agreed on new heads for Hungarian Radio and Hungarian Television (MTV). These were appointed by a process which involved the consent of both the governing party and the opposition. The intention was to make broadcasting independent of pressure from political parties. The situation was seen by all parties as an interim one, since the new appointees headed organizations that operated under media laws inherited from the Communist regime. The new director's task was to ensure that the transition to a new broadcasting system was a smooth one, unmarked by partisan strife.

The man appointed to head MTV was an eminent sociologist and longtime opponent of the old regime, Elemer Hankiss. Opinions as to the merits of his leadership vary widely, even amongst those who count themselves his strong supporters, but there is no doubt that he pursued a line independent of the Hungarian Democratic Forum (MDF) government which emerged as a result of the first election.

The MDF party was concerned about two things. Firstly, it perceived that the bulk of the printed press supported opposition parties both during the election and in the aftermath. It therefore wished to use broadcasting as a counterweight to this bias, and to ensure that TV and radio gave a full and favorable account of the government's point of view. It was particularly concerned that the main news and current affairs programs reflect this orientation and be staffed by people it considered politically reliable.

The second major issue stemmed from the fact that the MDF was a strongly nationalist party, which included a right-wing which voiced xenophobic and anti-Semitic views. The party as a whole was strongly committed to rebuilding and sustaining a sense of Hungarian national identity. They saw television as a major element in helping form this national consciousness, and were therefore very concerned that it reflected what they said were the "genuine" Hungarian concerns and cultural values.

The government was further concerned that large numbers of ethnic Hungarians lived outside the contemporary borders of Hungary. These Hungarian minorities have often experienced oppression at the hands of the majority in the states in which they live. The MDF government wished to provide cultural resources for these people, and television programming was one important element they attempted to make available.

Hankiss, and many professional broadcasters, resisted the pressure to turn TV into an MDF fiefdom. The government responded with three forms of pressure to force broadcasters into line. The first was to restrict the government subsidy to MTV, thus provoking a financial crisis. The money saved was used to launch a satellite channel, Duna TV, directed at the nonresident Hungarian populations. Secondly, they mobilized their followers in street demonstrations against the leadership of radio and television. Thirdly, they attempted to sack the existing directors.

In the short term, these pressures proved inadequate. Hankiss countered the financial squeeze by greatly increasing the advertising revenues of MTV. Supporters of the opposition parties organized their own street demonstrations in favor of the existing directors. The president of the Republic, legally responsible for their appointment, refused to sign the dismissal notices and the sackings became bogged down in legal and constitutional wrangling.

The matter was not soon resolved, however, since the Parliament was unable to reach a quick decision on the form of a new broadcasting law. The interim arrangements persisted for much longer than was originally envisaged. In the long term, though, the government was able to wear down the resistance of Hankiss and his colleagues. In December 1992 they were interrogated by a parliamentary inquiry into allegations that they had mismanaged the funds of MTV. Although they were able successfully to defend themselves, the strain proved too much, and in January 1993 both Hankiss and the director of radio resigned. The government was not constitutionally able to replace them, since that power lay with the president. Instead, it appointed its own supporters, already installed as deputy directors, as acting directors, thus effectively bypassing the legal process.

The new acting directors carried out a series of political purges of the broadcasting organizations, particularly the news sections. They managed to ensure that the key posts were held by individuals loyal to the MDF. By the elections of 1994, MTV was effectively a propaganda weapon for the MDF government. The election was a crushing defeat for the MDF, and a big win for the Hungarian Socialist Party, the main successor to the Communists. The election also helped support a suspicion long held by scholarly observers, but persistently disbelieved by politicians around the world, that there is no simple and direct connection between control of television and electoral success.

In 1995, five years after the first democratic elections, there was no new comprehensive television law in Hungary. Broadcasting still operated under a legal framework which is, in essence, inherited from the Communist regime. The new government has been less aggressive in its attempts to control television, and its threats of mass sackings are motivated more by the need to cut costs than to remove political opponents from editorial positions. It has still found it convenient, though, to preside over a television system whose basic structure remains untransformed.

Other countries have made more progress in installing new legal regimes for broadcasting and in awarding licenses for commercial broadcasters. This does not mean, however, that elsewhere the process has been free of political interference. In the new Czech Republic (Czechia) and Slovakia, which issued from the collapse of the old Czechoslovak Federal Republic at the end of 1992, and in Poland the new laws grant a measure of independence from the government to broadcasting councils. In all three cases, leading politicians have been reluctant to accept that they cannot interfere in the direction of television. One of the major tasks of the new broadcasting councils is to allocate the new commercial franchises, and this has often proved politically contentious.

These new commercial stations were envisaged not merely as commercial ventures but as a prime mechanism by which the political culture of Central Europe could be brought closer to the norms of western capitalist countries. It was argued in Central Europe that the only way out of the trap of government intervention in television, which turned every attempt to create Western European-style public service broadcasters into the mere mouthpieces of the ruling party, was to establish a commercial system. The pursuit of profit would lead to an attempt to maximize audiences in order to maximize advertising revenue, and this in turn would lead to the adoption of a neutral political position in order to avoid alienating any large section of the potential audience.

The argument had a considerable persuasive force. This was partly due to the positive example of the well-documented development of U.S. print journalism toward objectivity as a result of similar economic factors. In a negative sense, it was partly due to the continuing pervasive interference of governments in the running of the would-be public service broadcasters.

Two factors have conspired to undermine the appeal of the case. In the first place, the career of Sylvio Berlusconi in Italy was widely noted in Central Europe. In direct contradiction to the Hungarian example, this seemed to demonstrate that, at least under some circumstances, the control of television could be a major factor in political success. Further, it demonstrated that partisan television was as possible in a commercial system as in a state one.

The second factor is that, at least in countries emerging from a long period of repressive government, economic groupings are often closely aligned with different political factions. Whatever may be the reality, political leaders as diverse as Walensa in Poland, Meciar in Slovakia, and Klaus in Czechia are convinced that it is important to their political future that the new commercial licences are awarded to people whose views they believe they can rely on.

A good example is provided by Czechia, whose government is the most free-market oriented of the region. The first commercial licence was awarded the first national commercial television licence to a North-American-owned company, Central European Television. This provoked an angry attack from the governing party, who believed that many of the local collaborators of the new station (TV Nova) were its political opponents, if not actually former supporters of the Communist regime.

The power to grant licences for commercial operators was granted to the National Broadcasting Council under the new broadcasting law rushed through parliament at the birth of the new state. This body is independent of parliament and the government, although its members are appointed by the parliament. The only power that parliament retains over the council is the ability to reject its annual report. In the event of that happening, the council members must resign and a new council is appointed.

In both 1993 and 1994, the governing party attempted to reject the annual report, but narrowly failed to command a majority. In 1993, the vote was tied and the political pressure was so great that the chair of the council felt obliged to resign as an individual. Subsequently, in the course of 1995, the parliament launched a new offensive, this time concentrating on the holders of radio licences, whom it alleged paid for their franchises and stations with funds acquired illegally under the old regime.

Up until 1996, then, the broadcasting systems of Central Europe remained highly politicized. In this, they display a marked continuity with the old order. It is important, however, to note that while there is no apparent transformation in the nature of the systems, there has been a major change in the degree of control. The old Communist systems were, in principal, unified. Whatever the constitution may have said, the Central Committee reached all of the important decisions, including those on television. That is not to say that there were not struggles in Communist societies. Quite apart from those between the bureaucrats and the workers and peasants they ruled, there were, in reality, bitter fights within the bureaucracy itself, which sometimes found expression in different nuances in the mass media. All of these differences, and indeed their expression, were contained within the Communist system itself. They were never subject to the popular will. Consequently, the degree of direct political control was very high.

In the new, post-Communist, systems of Central Europe there is a plurality of parties and of economic forces. Political disputes are now between parties and take place in public, and there are occasions upon which the popular will is expressed, in however distorted a form. Attempts by the government to control the mass media therefore face much greater obstacles. They are contested by other parties and by journalists and other media workers. It is extremely difficult for any of the new governments to have the same sort of complete and stable control over the whole of the mass media as did the old Communist regimes. This new contestation of political control, and the consequent spaces which open up for oppositional voices, is the major shift in the political aspect of television since the collapse of Communism, and it is a great gain for democracy.

Some of the other major issues in Central European television are local variations of more general themes. The first of these concerns the relationship between state-based broadcasting services and the increasingly internationalised world television industry. Many of the new governments in Central Europe have adopted strongly nationalistic policies and, as a consequence, have written into their broadcasting acts restrictions on the ownership and direction of commercial broadcasters. They often have specific instructions about the amount of nationally-originated material that must be broadcast, either included in the broadcasting acts themselves or in the licences to broadcast awarded to commercial companies.

These measures are under pressure from two directions. In the first place, a number of transnational media enterprises view the emerging markets of Central Europe as important and seek to position themselves strongly in terms of ownership of media industries. At the same time, the would-be local commercial broadcasters are often lacking in the technical skills of running profitable channels and, above all, in the capital needed to establish such channels. There is thus a constant tendency for the restrictions on ownership to be challenged.

One of the allegations directed by Polish President Lech Walensa against the winner of the first Polish national commercial franchise, Polsat, was that it was secretly controlled by Rupert Murdoch. This charge was probably advanced as a cover for more directly political objections. On the other hand, there is no doubt that Murdoch, Hersant, Bertelsmann, Berlusconi, and almost every other large international player has, at one time or another, attempted to gain entry to the local television market.

The most successful so far of these companies is Central European Television, which already controls TV Nova in Czechia and which is likely to be granted a licence in Hungary in the course of 1995. This is not a major media concern, being effectively controlled by an heir to the U.S. Lauder cosmetics fortune.

Its activity in the region is interesting for two reasons. In the first place, it is an example of what may be termed "missionary capitalism." According to its most prominent figure, the interest in the region is only partly commercial and springs in part from Lauder's rediscovery of his family roots. That is not to say that its operation is not run as an aggressive commercial venture interested in maximizing revenue and return on capital, but that its path into the ownership of television is a different one from the normal pattern.

The second reason the success of this company is interesting is that it is a reflection, in part at least, of the close link between political and economic power in the region. Its most prominent negotiator is Mark Palmer, former U.S. ambassador to Hungary, who is extremely well-known to all of the major political figures, both former Communists and former oppositionists, in the region.

The other factor which bears upon the relationship between nationalism and the world market is the question of imported programming. The broadcast of imported programs is no novelty in most regions. Previously, the main constraint was often a shortage of the hard currency needed to buy them. That has now been lifted, and there has been a considerable increase in the number of imported programs, particular from the United States. This irritates the more nationalist-minded politicians because they would prefer the population to be watching material which more closely reflects their view of the local cultural values. On the other hand, imported programming has initially proved very popular with the audiences, and is relatively cheap to acquire. All of the states in Central Europe lack the resources of the major U.S. networks, or the BBC. The choice, therefore, was often not between broadcasting good local programs with a strong "national" content and good imported programs, but between cheap local programs with a strong "national" content and good imported programs. The latter produced good audiences and cost little, and so was popular with broadcasters as well as audiences.

There have been suggestions that the audiences in Central Europe are becoming "standardized" in their tastes. After the initial period in which anything from the West, and particularly from the United States, was regarded as automatically better, audiences are apparently starting to discriminate between good and bad imported programs. They may also be starting to express preference for good local programs over good imported programs. Some broadcasters are attempting to meet this demand. Given the poverty of resources, it is unlikely that they will be able to produce a full schedule of high quality education, information, and entertainment, but there are plans to try to go as far as possible. The other open question is whether popular local programming will be of a kind to satisfy the definition of "national" advanced by politicians. In some cases, their view of properly national television consisted of church services and folk dancing. Whether this kind of programming could prove enduringly popular is a matter of some doubt. It is more likely that broadcasting in the region will tend to follow the more general European pattern in which, at least in prime time, the programming tends increasingly to be local in origin. Very often it is of a franchised nature and is dominated by the cheaper kinds of programming like games and quizzes.

The final factor to consider is the funding of television. Internationally, funding systems may be arranged on a spectrum. At one extreme there is the system of competing private channels financed more or less entirely out of advertising revenue. The United States is the best-known example of this pattern. At the other extreme is the broadcaster dependent upon state funds. The BBC is the best-known example of this pattern, even though its funds are mediated through a licence fee. In between, there are a number of variants. One which has been popular in Europe is the state broadcaster which is, either wholly (Spain) or partly (Germany) dependent upon advertising. Up until the 1970s, the state broadcasters were the only television providers and faced no competition for advertising revenue. In these circumstances, the commercial revenue provided a welcome source of additional funding independent of politicians, which could be generated without excessive concessions to commercial programming. The introduction of private broadcasting everywhere produced a crisis in this model of funding.

The state broadcasters of Central Europe generally combine revenue sources. They enjoy state funding, either directly, through a budget subsidy, or indirectly, through a licence fee. They also enjoy advertising revenue. So long as there were no commercial competitors, this advertising revenue was very valuable. It supplemented shrinking state funding. It permitted a measure of political independence, as in the case of Hungary. It seemed a perfect source of funding.

The entry of commercial competitors has begun to change this situation. In the Czech case, for example, TV Nova very rapidly gained large audiences and has been able to use these to win a large share of advertising revenue. Even though the total amount of advertising revenue available in Czechia is growing quite quickly, the impact of competition upon the state broadcaster has still been quite marked. The state broadcaster is further handicapped, as is common in Central Europe, by regulations which restrict the amount of advertising time that they can sell to below that permitted to the commercial broadcasters.

The dilemma faced by the state broadcaster is increasingly the one which is familiar from Western Europe. On the one hand, there is the possibility of meeting the commercial challenge head on. While this will almost certainly mean an improvement in some aspects of programming, it will also mean the acceptance of the dominance of commercial goals in production, purchase, and scheduling. This runs counter to any attempt to develop a public-service-type broadcasting policy. On the other hand, the state broadcaster could accept a much smaller audience share and consequently less revenue from advertising. This would not only lead to a decline in the available budgets for production and purchase, but would also throw the broadcasters upon the mercy of the politicians. The political culture in Central Europe is not one in which the government is likely to increase the subsidy to television without demanding concessions in return. This, in turn, would defeat any attempt at constructing a public-service-type broadcaster.

It has here been argued that, during the Communist era, broadcasting in Central Europe was best understood as one extreme version of a more common European type of state intervention. As the legacy of Communism recedes into the past,

this European dimension becomes ever more clear. Increasingly, the dilemmas and problems of television in Central Europe are clearly variants, albeit often extreme variants, of dilemmas and problems faced more widely in Europe, and perhaps beyond.

—Colin Sparks

FURTHER READING

Casmir, Fred L., editor. *Communication in Eastern Europe: The Role of History, Culture, and Media in Contemporary Conflicts.* Mahwah, New Jersey: L. Erlbaum, 1995.

Elam, Peter. "Hoist on its own Media (Hungary)." *Index on Censorship* (London), July-August 1994.

Gersh, Debra. "U.S. Government Sponsors Fund for Eastern European Media." *Editor and Publisher* (New York), 15 September 1990.

Giorgi, Liana, with Ronald J. Pohoryles. *The Post-socialist Media: What Power the West? The Changing Media Landscape in Poland, Hungary, and the Czech Republic.* Aldershot, England, and Brookfield, Vermont: Avebury, 1995.

Hankiss, Elemer. "The Hungarian Media's War of Independence: A Stevenson Lecture, 1992." *Media, Culture and Society* (London), April 1994.

Hester, Al, L. Earle Reybold, and Kimberly Conger, editors. *The Post-Communist Press in Eastern and Central Europe: New Studies.* Athens, Georgia: James M. Cox, Jr., Center for International Mass Communication Training and Research, 1992.

Jakubowicz, Karol. "Equality for the Downtrodden, Freedom for the Free: Changing Perspectives on Social Communication in Central and Eastern Europe." *Media, Culture and Society* (London), April 1994.

———. "Media within and without the State: Press Freedom in Eastern Europe." *Journal of Communication* (New York), Autumn 1995.

King, Sarah Sanderson, and Donald F. Cushman. *Political Communication: Engineering Visions of Order in the Socialist World.* Albany, New York: State University of New York Press, 1992.

"Read, Write, Disbelieve: Eastern Europe's Media." *The Economist* (London), 8 January 1994.

"Romania." *IPI (International Press Institute) Report* (Zurich, Switzerland), December 1994.

Sparks, Colin. "Understanding Media Change in East Central Europe." *Media, Culture and Society* (London), April 1994.

Splichal, Slavko, Andrew Calabrese, and Colin Sparks, editors. *Information Society and Civil Society: Contemporary Perspectives on the Changing World Order.* West Lafayette, Indiana: Purdue University Press, 1994.

Splichal, Slavko. *Media Beyond Socialism: Theory and Practice in East-Central Europe.* Boulder, Colorado: Westview, 1994.

———. "Media Privatization and Democratization in Central-Eastern Europe." *Gazette,* January-March 1992.

Volgyes, Ivan. *Political Socialization in Eastern Europe: A Comparative Framework.* New York: Praeger, 1975.

CHANNEL FOUR

British Programming Service

The fourth British channel arrived on the scene in 1982 after extensive debate between proponents of public service television on the one hand and of commercial broadcasting on the other. The timing was crucial, for the commercially funded ITV network was starting to outstrip combined BBC1 and BBC2 in terms of audience numbers. Channel Four (C4) was a compromise between the two principles: it was to be financed by advertising revenue from the existing private companies, but governed independently from them, with a brief to provide minority and complementary programming to the three existing channels. It would make none of its own programming, but rather "publish" work produced by outside production companies, and indeed, a host of small independent producers sprung up in its wake, peddling their ideas to a group of "commissioning editors". It would be innovative in program styles and working practices and would find new audiences.

Piloted in its first years by Jeremy Isaacs, a veteran of documentary and current affairs television production who had given a noteworthy speech about his vision at an Edinburgh Television Festival, C4 saw its role as being "different, but not too different". It would stake its claim to being "alternative" by pioneering material new to British television (access, community, youth and minority programs), by catering for as-yet-untelevised sports and hobby enthusiasts (cycling, basketball, chess), and by giving new life to threatened genres like documentary, arts features and independent film. Risk-taking would include the first hour-long TV news and the first overtly "committed" current affairs magazines *(The Friday Alternative)*. Dubbed "Channel Bore" by early critics put off by earnest late-night intellectual discussions, and afflicted with occasional censorship battles over certain programs that appeared overly partisan (toward the left), the channel saw its audience share gradually creep upward—though it never attained the 10% share it sought in a national television landscape as yet untouched by cable and satellite. Associated with yuppie and liberal values, it boasted a 90% satisfaction rate among its selective audience.

Channel Four did not neglect popular genres, creating its own early evening serial *(Brookside,* Liverpool-set, remains its most popular program), and launching *Max Headroom* and other avant-garde—or at least less classical than existing—series. It showed quality series imported from the United States like *Hill Street Blues* and *Cheers* and launched some of Britain's alternative comedians *(Comic Strip Presents...).*

But its main success has been its feature film production; Channel Four revitalized a moribund British film industry. It invested in a third of the feature films made in Britain in 1984, financing a number of low budget films like Stephen Frears' *My Beautiful Launderette* (shot on 16-mm in 1985) and co-producing medium budget ones

Courtesy of Channel Four

like *The Draughtsman's Contract* (Peter Greenaway) and *Dance with a Stranger* (Mike Newell). "Film on Four", under David Rose, wooed writers like David Hare and directors like Mike Leigh from the BBC, and attracted new ones like Neil Jordan and Derek Jarman. In contrast to the BBC, C4 policy has been to address contemporary issues and use experimental storytelling. It has backed a number of projects aimed at the European art film market: Wim Wender's *Paris, Texas,* Agnes Varda's *Vagabond,* Andre Tarkovsky's *The Sacrifice,* Neil Jordan's *The Crying Game.* "Film Four International" showcases independent filmmakers from around the world.

In 1988 chief executive Isaacs stepped down and was replaced by Michael Grade, formerly controller of BBC1 and scion of a family distinguished in commercial entertainment. Despite fears that he would be forced by commercial pressures to take the channel down a vulgarian path Grade proved a populist in the best sense of the word, importing more U.S. shows (e.g., *Oprah Winfrey, Roseanne, ER),* although the gamble on American content did not always pay off *(Tales of the City).* The 1990 Broadcasting Act refined its remit to be "distinctive", that is, to include proportions which are European and are supplied by independent producers. More importantly, the act spun C4 off from the ITV companies by giving it the right to market its own advertising. Funding, like distribution, became a problem: Channel Four has been so successful at marketing itself that subsidy is flowing the other way, as a share of its profits instead reverts back to the ITV companies' coffers—£ 38 million in 1994.

Channel Four's 1993 audience share of 5.4 % reflected a quality market for advertisers (BBC1 had 19.9%

at the time). But despite its international reputation as a model for innovative television, some critics questioned whether it had indeed been a life-saving transfusion to the British film industry or even to the independent film and video sector, as many of the workshops folded, more of the commissions settled on a few strong production companies, and as BBC2 responded to C4's innovations. The inherent tension between the channel's public service and commercial objectives seemed to tilt increasingly toward the latter.

—Susan Emmanuel

FURTHER READING

Isaacs, Jeremy. *Storm Over Four: A Personal Account.* London: Weidenfeld and Nicholson, 1989.

Pym, John. *Film on Four, 1981–1991.* London: British Film Institute, 1992.

Stoneman, Rod. "Sins of Commission." *Screen* (London), Summer 1992.

Wyver, John. "The English Channel." *American Film* (Washington, D.C.), July-August 1986.

See also British Television; *Film on Four*

CHANNEL ONE

U.S. Proprietary Programming Service

Channel One is a twelve-minute television news program targeted to teenagers and distributed via satellite to over 12,000 middle and high schools across the United States each school day morning. This represents an audience of over eight million students, with thousands of other schools currently on a waiting list to receive the program. *Channel One* became, almost from its inception, a highly controversial educational program offering, primarily because two minutes of each program are devoted to advertising.

Channel One began its pilot phase in January 1989 originally as a production of Whittle Communications, Inc. in Knoxville, Tennessee, and was heavily promoted by the company's founder, Christopher Whittle. In 1995, Whittle Communications, Inc. closed, and sold *Channel One* to K-III Communications Corporation, a large diversified communications company focused on education, information and magazine publishing. Among its titles are *Weekly Reader, Funk and Wagnell's New Encyclopedia*, and *Seventeen* magazine.

In order for a school to receive *Channel One*, it must sign a three-year agreement to carry the program in its entirety each school day, and make the telecast available to at least 90% of the student body. In return, each school receives a satellite dish (TVRO), two videocassette recorders, one 19-inch television set per classroom and all of the necessary cabling. No money is exchanged.

Channel One news content is geared to teenagers, and delivered by anchors and reporters typically in their early to mid-20s. Program content includes the latest news as well as week-long series for more depth on such topics as jobs, drug abuse, science and technology and international politics. According to *Channel One*, its news programming has "five educational goals":

1. To enhance cultural literacy
2. To promote critical thinking
3. To provide a common language and shared experience
4. To provide relevance and motivation

5. To strengthen character and build a sense of responsibility

Channel One has received many awards including the Advertising Council's Silver Bell Award for "outstanding public service" and a George Foster Peabody Award for the series "A Decade of AIDs."

In addition to the daily *Channel One* news program, schools are also provided with approximately 250 hours per school year of noncommercial educational programming (through an agreement with Pacific Mountain Network) that is designed to serve as a supplemental teaching tool to support existing curricula.

Many in the educational community and elsewhere have decried *Channel One* on the basis that it commercializes the classroom environment, and some have expressed concern that there may be an implicit endorsement of the products shown. *Channel One* characterizes its role as a

Photo courtesy of Channel One

positive partnership between the educational and business communities. They cite, for example, a three-year study of *Channel One* by a team, commissioned by Whittle, from the University of Michigan. Among the study's findings were apparent increases in awareness and knowledge of current events by the audience, and the judgment by a majority of teachers surveyed that they would recommend the program to other teachers. Other studies have found that *Channel One's* stated commitment to community service is evidenced by a high percentage (about 15%) of the commercial time being given to public service announcements. And in a 1993 report published in *Educational Leadership*, 90% of teachers thought *Channel One* included the "most important events of the previous day." Others teachers, critics, and evaluators, however, still find the idea of students viewing advertising in the classroom anathema. The debate continues.

—Thomas A. Birk

FURTHER READING

Greenberg, B.S., and J.E. Brand. "Television News and Advertising in Schools: The *Channel One* Controversy." *Journal of Communication* (New York), 1993.

Thomas, L. R. "Whittle Pleased by its Study of *Channel One*." *The Knoxville News-Sentinel* (Knoxville, Tennessee), 4 February 1994.

Tiene, D. "Channel One: Good or Bad News for Our Schools?" *Educational Leadership* (Alexandria, Virginia), May 1993.

———. "Exploring the Effectiveness of the *Channel One* School Telecasts." *Educational Technology* (Englewood Cliffs, New Jersey), May 1993.

Wulfemeyer, K. T., and B. Mueller. "*Channel One* and Commercials in Classrooms: Advertising Content Aimed at Students." *Journalism Quarterly* (Urbana, Illinois), 1992.

CHARLES, GLEN AND LES

U.S. Writers and Producers

When Glen and Les Charles watched television comedies in the early 1970s, they saw more than just clever entertainment and escape—they saw an opportunity to leave their unsatisfying jobs and become part of show business. While many people might share this dream, the Charles brothers had the talent, dedication, and luck to move from their sofa to behind the scenes of some of the most successful comedies in television history.

The Charles were raised Mormon near Las Vegas, exposed to the glitz of their hometown while absorbing their family's emphasis on education. They both received a liberal arts education at University of Redlands in Los Angeles. Les Charles followed in his mother's footsteps by teaching public school, while Glen Charles attended law school, and eventually worked as an advertising copywriter. Neither brother was content in his job and both dreamed of something more. So on a Saturday night in 1974, they were watching their favorite night of television and they became inspired—instead of just watching CBS' Saturday line-up of *All in the Family*, *M*A*S*H*, *The Bob Newhart Show*, and *The Mary Tyler Moore Show*, they would write episodes for these television comedies.

They started by writing an episode of their favorite, *The Mary Tyler Moore Show*, and sending it to MTM Productions. After receiving no response, they persisted, writing a sample episode of every television comedy they enjoyed and sending it to the producers on spec. Confident in their talents, they both quit their jobs to dedicate more time to their writing; Les Charles and his wife were living out of their van when the Charles brothers received notification of their first sold script. They lived off the money and excitement generated from seeing their episode of *M*A*S*H* on the air, but no jobs followed immediately. Finally after two years and dozens of unsolicited scripts, they received the phone call they'd been waiting for—the producers at MTM had read their first script at last and offered them jobs as staff writers on the spin-off *Phyllis*.

Often referred to MTM Television University, MTM Productions was a training ground for young writers in the 1970s, offering a supportive atmosphere that emphasized talent and quality over commercial success and popularity. The Charles brothers quickly climbed up the ranks in MTM, moving from story editors to producers at *Phyllis* and eventually getting the opportunity to produce one of the programs that had first inspired them, *The Bob Newhart Show*. While at *Phyllis*, the brothers met a colleague with whom they would form a long fruitful working partnership—James Burrows. The Charles brothers and Burrows "graduated" from MTM together when four MTM veterans created *Taxi* and hired this team to oversee the daily production of the show. Glen and Les Charles left MTM to become writer-producers for *Taxi*, while Burrows directed the series.

Taxi brought both success and acclaim to the Charles brothers, winning Emmy Awards for their writing in addition to TV's top honor in their category—Outstanding Comedy Series. But Glen and Les Charles and Jim Burrows all wanted to work on a series that was uniquely their own, not the concept of other writers and producers. So after three highly successful years at *Taxi*, the trio left the show to form Charles-Burrows-Charles Productions and create their own signature brand of television comedy. Luckily for them, Grant Tinker had just taken over NBC and was looking for "quality" programming to fill out the last-place network's schedule. Without even a concept or script in hand, Tinker gave Charles-Burrows-Charles a deal to produce a new comedy for NBC.

All three partners were fans of the British comedy *Fawlty Towers* and thought that setting the series in a hotel would be a good choice. Like the British series, theirs would feature odd guests passing through and associating with the series regulars. But after sketching out their ideas, they realized that most scenes took place in the hotel bar and they could streamline the show by eliminating the hotel altogether. Unlike the seedy atmosphere commonly associated with bars, they envisioned a classy neighborhood tavern based on a Boston pub. To avoid any implication that they were glorifying drinking they made the owner of the bar a recovering alcoholic. After casting a group of unknowns, many of whom had been guest stars on *Taxi*, *Cheers* was born.

While *Cheers* certainly bore many of the marks of MTM shows and *Taxi*, there were aspects distinct to Charles Burrows Charles. Unlike most MTM shows, there were no well-known actors on the show, which relyied solely on the comedic talent of the cast and writing to draw in audiences. While *Taxi* had moved away from the middle-class and optimistic settings of MTM programs and toward a grittier and more pessimistic view of the world, *Cheers* found a middle-ground—while no characters were truly happy with their jobs or circumstances, there was a contentedness in the bar where "everybody knew your name" that was never present in *Taxi*. The major adjustment the Charles brothers brought to *Cheers* was the presence of a long-term narrative arc concerning the tempestuous romance between Sam Malone and Diane Chambers; Glen and Les Charles wrote this aspect of the series in direct reaction to the static relationship between Mary Richards and Lou Grant, which never changed through the course of the *The Mary Tyler Moore Show*.

Luckily for the Charles brothers, Tinker was willing to give *Cheers* a chance to develop this long-term arc. The program's first season ratings were horrible (77th place), but both Tinker and his programming head Brandon Tartikoff were fans of *Cheers* and subsequently gave the show another chance. Emmy Awards followed, word of mouth grew, and the show gained in the ratings, but it wasn't until *The Cosby Show* found its place in the lead-off slot of NBC's Thursday night line-up that *Cheers* turned into a blockbuster show. The Charles brothers moved away from writing individual episodes and served as general overseers of the program from their executive producer chairs. They attempted to develop a stable of programs by introducing the *Cheers* spin-off *The Tortellis* and *All Is Forgiven*, but both shows bombed; after this failure, Glen and Les Charles decided that they were not the "comedy

factory" type of producers. They needed direct day-to-day control of their programs. They stuck with *Cheers* as executive producers throughout its eleven-year run and returned to the writing table to script the series' final episode. Since *Cheers*, the Charles brothers have been fairly inactive, working on a few unproduced film scripts and other projects. But even if they never write another script for television, their rise from comedy fans to creators of one of the most successful and acclaimed television series ever should be enough for a valued place in television history.

—Jason Mittell

GLEN CHARLES. Born in Henderson, Nevada, U.S.A. Attended University of Redlands, California, B.A. in English; San Francisco State University. Advertising copywriter; began television career as writer, with brother Les Charles; writer-producer, *The Bob Newhart Show*; formed Charles-Burrows-Charles production company with television director, James Burrows, 1977; creator-producer, *Taxi*, *Cheers*.

LES CHARLES. Born in Henderson, Nevada, U.S.A. Attended University of Redlands, California, B.A. in English. High-School English teacher; began television career as writer, with brother Glen Charles; writer-producer, *The Bob Newhart Show*; formed Charles-Burrows-Charles production company with television director, James Burrows, 1977; creator-producer, *Taxi*, *Cheers*.

TELEVISION (Glen and Les Charles)

1972–78	*The Bob Newhart Show*	(writer-producers)
1972–83	*M*A*S*H*	(writers)
1975–77	*Phyllis*	(writers)
1978–83	*Taxi*	(writers, co-producers)
1982–93	*Cheers*	(writers, co-producers)
1986	*All Is Forgiven*	(co-producers)
1987	*The Tortellis*	(co-producer)

FURTHER READING

Greenberg, Keith Elliot. *Charles, Burrows and Charles: TV's Top Producers* (children's book). Woodbridge, Connecticut: Blackbirch Press, 1995.

Sorensen, Jeff. *The Taxi Book*. New York: St. Martin's, 1987.

Waldron, Vince. *Classic Sitcom*. New York: MacMillan, 1987.

See also *Cheers*

CHARLIE'S ANGELS

U.S. Detective Drama

Charlie's Angels, the critically panned female detective series that heralded the age of "jiggle TV," aired on ABC from 1976 to 1981. The show, which featured three shapely, often scantily clad women solving crimes undercover for a boss they knew only as a Godly voice from a phone speaker, was an immediate sensation, landing the number five spot in the Nielsen ratings during the 1976-77 TV season. (This premiere-season record would remain unbroken until 1994-95, when NBC's new medical drama *ER* finished number two for the year.) In its second year, following the departure of its most popular star, *Charlie's Angels* tied for number four with, ironically, the critically acclaimed *60 Minutes* and *All in the Family.* But by its third season, *Charlie's Angels'* slipped out of the top ten. And in 1980-81, the show's novelty had worn as thin as the Angels' slinky outfits, and *Charlie's Angels,* placing 59 out of 65 shows, was cancelled after 115 episodes.

Deemed sexploitation by its detractors, *Charlie's Angels* was the brainchild of producer Aaron Spelling, who in the early 1970s had found success in the TV detective genre with *The Mod Squad* and *The Rookies,* hip series shooting for young-adult audiences. With *Charlie's Angels,* Spelling spun a new formula that would attract desirable demographics among young men and women: he combined detective drama with the glamorous fantasy that would become his staple in the 1980s with *Dynasty* and the 1990s with *Beverly Hills, 90210* and *Melrose Place.* Not only were his Angels beautiful and sexy, they were smart and powerful heroines who used provocative attraction (and feminine, often feigned, vulnerability) to lure and capture unsuspecting male criminals. Though *Charlie's Angels* was among TV's first dramas to instill female characters with typically male "powers" via a dominant subject position, the show's critics, including infuriated feminists, countered that *Charlie's Angels* was little more than a patriarchal production that sexually objectified its characters.

Charlie's Angels' premise placed its feminine heroes in a male-dominated work place and a woman-as-victim society. The Angels—once "three little girls who went to the police academy"—worked under the auspices of a patriarchal, narrative voice they called Charlie (the never-seen John Forsythe), who ran from remote locations the Charles Townsend Detective Agency in Los Angeles. Bosley, Charlie's asexual (and thus unthreatening) representative (played by David Doyle), helped direct the Angels meet Charlie's desired ends. Working undercover in women's prison camps, as showgirls, as prostitutes, and in other sexually suggestive locales and professions, the Angels inevitably found themselves in jeopardy each week, victimized either by evil men or unattractive (which in Spelling's lexicon meant "bad") women who underestimated the Angels' smarts and strengths as beautiful, seemingly frail decoys.

The three original Angels included two decoys—brunette Kelly Garret (played by Jaclyn Smith, the only Angel

Charlie's Angels

to remain through the series' entire run) and blonde Jill Munroe (played by Farrah Fawcett, whose fluffy, feathered hairstyle became a nationwide 1970s fad and whose sexy posters became bestsellers). By contrast, the third, less glamorous Angel, Sabrina Duncan (played by Kate Jackson, who also starred in Spelling's *The Rookies*), became known as "the smart one." Sabrina's impish qualities—independence, athleticism, adventurism and asexuality—often kept her working behind the scenes with Bosley, helping to rescue other Angels, and consequently often kept her out of the bikinis, braless t-shirts and tight dresses with plunging necklines that her co-workers opted to wear. Sabrina, Jill and Kelly (a martial arts expert) all participated in the show's choreographed violence, which included karate chops, kicks to the groin and other sanitized brutality (guns seldom were fired).

Fawcett (then Farrah Fawcett-Majors during her brief marriage to *Six Million Dollar Man* star Lee Majors) broke her contract and left the series after one season to become a movie star. She was replaced by blonde actress Cheryl Ladd, who played Jill's younger sister, Kris, also a decoy character. (As part of her exit agreement, Fawcett was forced to make guest appearances through the show's fourth season.) After two seasons and struggles to insert more meaningful characterizations into the show, Kate Jackson also retired her wings. She was replaced in 1979 by blonde actress Shelley Hack, who in 1980 was replaced by brunette actress Tanya Roberts for the show's final season. Throughout these cast changes, the formula remained consistent, save the loss of the impish Sabrina.

All six Angels, especially Fawcett, Smith, Jackson and Ladd, became media icons whose faces—and heavenly bodies—were plastered on magazine covers, posters, lunch boxes and loads of other toys and related merchandise. *Charlie's Angels* was undoubtedly a fantasy whose trappings appealed to males and females, young and old. Whether the show ultimately helped or hurt female portrayals in TV drama remains debatable. But as pure camp, the show, highlighted by episodes with titles like "Angels in Chains," remains a cult classic. As the omniscient Charlie would say, "Good work, Angels."

—Chris Mann

CAST

Sabrina Duncan (1976–79)	Kate Jackson
Jill Munroe (1976–77)	Farrah Fawcett-Majors
Kelly Garrett	Jaclyn Smith
Kris Munroe (1977–81)	Cheryl Ladd
Tiffany Welles (1979–80)	Shelley Hack
Julie Rogers (1980–81)	Tanya Roberts
John Bosley	David Doyle
Charlie Townsend (voice only)	John Forsythe

PRODUCERS   Leonard Goldberg, Aaron Spelling, Rich Husky, David Levinson, Barney Rosenzweig, Ronald Austin, James David Buchanan, Edward J. Lasko, Robert Janes, Elaine Rich

PROGRAMMING HISTORY   108 Episodes
• ABC

September 1976–August 1977	Wednesday 10:00-11:00
August 1977–October 1980	Wednesday 9:00-10:00
November 1980–January 1981	Sunday 8:00-9:00
January 1981–February 1981	Saturday 8:00-9:00
June 1981–August 1981	Wednesday 8:00-9:00

FURTHER READING

D'Acci, Julie. *Defining Women: Television and the Case of Cagney and Lacey.* Chapel Hill: University of North Carolina Press, 1994.

Fiske, John. *Television Culture.* New York: Routledge, 1987.

Meehan, Diana. *Ladies of the Evening: Women Characters of Prime-Time Television.* Metuchen, New Jersey: Scarecrow, 1983.

See also Gender and Television; John Forsythe; Detective Programs

CHAYEFSKY, PADDY

U.S. Writer

Sydney "Paddy" Chayefsky was one of the most renown dramatists to emerge from the "golden age" of American television. His intimate, realistic scripts helped shape the naturalistic style of television drama in the 1950s. After leaving television, Chayefsky succeeded as a playwright and novelist. He won greatest acclaim as a Hollywood screenwriter, receiving Academy Awards for three scripts, including *Marty* (1955), based on his own television drama, and *Network* (1976), his scathing satire of the television industry.

Chayefsky began his television career writing episodes for *Danger* and *Manhunt* in the early 1950s. His scripts caught the attention of Fred Coe, the dynamic producer of NBC's live anthology drama, the *Philco Television Playhouse* and the *Goodyear Television Playhouse,* alternating series. Chayefsky's first script for Coe, *Holiday Song,* won immediate critical acclaim when it aired in 1952. Subsequently, Chayefsky bucked the trend of the anthology writers by insisting that he would write only original dramas, not adaptations. The result was a banner year in 1953. Coe produced six Chayefsky scripts, including *Printer's Measure* and *The Reluctant Citizen.* Chayefsky became one of television's best-known writers, along with such dramatists as Tad Mosel, Reginald Rose, and Rod Serling.

Chayefsky's stories were notable for their dialogue, their depiction of second-generation Americans, and their infusions of sentiment and humor. They frequently drew on the author's upbringing in the Bronx. The protagonists were generally middle-class tradesmen struggling with personal problems: loneliness, pressures to conform, blindness to their own emotions. The technical limitations of live broadcast suited these dramas. The stories took place in cramped interior settings and were advanced by dialogue, not action. Chayefsky said that he focused on "the people I understand; the $75 to $125 a week kind"; this subject matter struck a sympathetic chord with the mainly urban, middle-class audiences of the time.

Marty, a typical Chayefsky teleplay and one of the most acclaimed of all the live anthology dramas, aired in 1953. Rod Steiger played the lonely butcher who felt that whatever women wanted in a man, "I ain't got it." When Marty finally met a woman, his friends cruelly labeled her "a dog." Marty finally decided that he was a dog himself and had to seize his chance for love. The play ended happily, with Marty arranging a date. Critics compared *Marty* and other Chayefsky teleplays to the realistic dramas of Arthur Miller and Clifford Odets. In Chayefsky's plays, however, positive endings and celebrations of love tended to emerge from the naturalistic framework. The Chayefsky plays also steered clear of social issues, like most of the anthology dramas.

After *Marty* enjoyed phenomenal success as a Hollywood film, Chayefsky left television in 1956. His exit narrowly preceded the demise of the live dramas, as sponsors began to prefer pre-recorded shows. Even while the live dramas were declining, however, Chayefsky's teleplays found new life. Simon and Schuster published a volume of Chayefsky's television plays. And three of them, in addition to *Marty*, became Hollywood films: *The Bachelor Party* (1957) and *Middle of the Night* (1959), adapted by Chayefsky, and *The Catered Affair* (1957), adapted by Gore Vidal.

In the 1960s, Chayefsky abandoned the intimate, personal dramas on which he had built his reputation. His subsequent work was often dark and satiric, like the Academy-Award winning film, *The Hospital* (1971). *Network*, Chayefsky's send-up of television, marked the apex of his satiric mode. He depicted an institution that had sold its soul for ratings and become "a goddamned amusement park," in the words of news anchor Howard Beale, the movie's main character. Before Chayefsky's death in 1981, he wrote one more screenplay, *Altered States* (1980), based on his own novel. He refused a script credit, however, due to disagreements with the film's director, Ken Russell.

Chayefsky wrote only one television script after 1956, an adaptation of his 1961 play *Gideon*. His reputation as a television dramatist rests on the eleven scripts he completed for the *Philco* and *Goodyear Playhouse* series. His influence on the live anthologies was considerable, but he is just as notable for the career he forged after television.

—J.B. Bird

PADDY CHAYEFSKY (Sidney Chayefsky). Born in Bronx, New York, U.S.A., 29 January 1923. City College of New York, B.S.S. 1943; studied languages, Fordham University, New York. Married Susan Sackler, 1949; one son. Served in U.S. Army 1943–45. Dramatist from 1944; printer's apprentice, Regal Press (uncle's print shop), New York City, 6 months in 1945; wrote short stories, radio scripts full-time, late 1940s; gag writer for Robert Q. Lewis, late 1940s; with Garson Kanin, wrote documentary, *The True Glory*, his first film, uncredited, 1945; first screenplay credit for *As Young as You Feel*, 1951; adapted plays for *Theatre Guild of the Air*, 1952-53; first television script, *Holiday Song*, 1952; *Marty*, 1953; screenplay, *Marty*, 1955 (Oscar for Best Screenplay and Best Picture); president, Sudan Productions, 1956; president, Carnegie Productions, from 1957; president S.P.D. Productions, from 1959; president, Sidney Productions, from 1967; president of Simcha Productions, from 1971; last screenplay, *Altered States*, credited under nom de plume Aaron Sydney, 1980. Member: New Dramatists' Committee, 1952–53; Writers Guild of America; Screen Writers Guild; American Guild of Variety Artists; American Guild of Authors and Composers; Screen Actors Guild; Council, Dramatists Guild, from 1962. Recipient: Purple Heart, 1945; private fellowship from Garson Kanin, 1948; Sylvania Television Award, 1953; Screen Writers Guild Awards, 1954 and 1971; Academy Awards, 1955, 1971, and 1976; Palm d'Or, Cannes Film Festival, 1955; *Look Magazine* Award, 1956; New York Film Critics Awards, 1956, 1971 and 1976; Venice Film Festival Awards, 1958; Edinborough Film Festival Award, 1958; Critics' Prize, Brussels Film Festival, 1958; British Academy Award, 1976. Died in New York City, 1 August 1981.

Paddy Chayefsky
Photo courtesy of Wisconsin Center for Film and Theater Research

TELEVISION SERIES

1948–55	*Philco Television Playhouse*
1950–55	*Danger*
1951–52	*Manhunt*
1951–60	*Goodyear Television Playhouse*

TELEVISION PLAYS (as episodes of anthology series, selection)

1952	*Holiday Song*
1953	*The Reluctant Citizen*
1953	*Printer's Measure*
1953	*Marty*
1953	*The Big Deal*
1953	*The Bachelor Party*
1953	*The Sixth Year*
1953	*Catch My Boy On Sunday*
1954	*The Mother*
1954	*Middle of the Night*
1955	*The Catered Affair*
1956	*The Great American Hoax*

FILMS

The True Glory (uncredited, with Garson Kanin), 1945; *As Young as You Feel*, with Lamar Trotti, 1951; *Marty*, 1955; *The Catered Affair*, 1956; *The Bachelor Party*, 1957; *The Goddess*, 1958; *Middle of the Night*, 1959; *The Americanization of Emily*, 1964; *Paint Your Wagon* (with Alan Jay Lerner), 1969; *The Hospital*, 1971; *Network*, 1976; *Altered States*, 1980.

RADIO PLAYS (adapter)

The Meanest Man in the World, Tommy, Over 21, 1951-52, for *Theater Guild of the Air* series.

STAGE

No T.O. for Love, 1944; *Fifth from Garibaldi*, ca. 1944; *Middle of the Night*, 1956; *The Tenth Man*, 1959; *Gideon*, 1961; *The Passion of Josef D* (also director), 1964; *The Latent Heterosexual*, 1967.

PUBLICATIONS

"'Art Films', They're Dedicated Insanity." *Films and Filming.* (London), May 1958.
Altered States (novel). New York: Harper and Row, 1978.

FURTHER READING

Brady, John. *The Craft of the Screenwriter.* New York: Simon and Schuster, 1981.
"Chayefsky, Paddy." *Contemporary Authors.* New Revision series, volume 18. Detroit, Michigan: Gale Research, 1983.
Clum, John M. *Paddy Chayefsky.* Boston, Massachusetts: Twayne, 1976.
Considine, Shaun. *Mad as Hell: The Life and Work of Paddy Chayefsky.* New York: Random House, 1994.
Frank, Sam. "Paddy Chayefsky." *Dictionary of Literary Biography*, volume 44. Detroit: Gale Research, 1986.
Horowitz, S. "P.C. Speaks Out." *Saturday Review* (New York), 13 November 1976.
Marc, David, and Robert J. Thompson. *Prime Time, Prime Movers.* Boston, Massachusetts: Little, Brown, 1992.
Sturcken, Frank. *Live Television: The Golden Age of 1946–1958 in New York.* Jefferson, North Carolina: McFarland, 1990.

See also Anthology Drama; Coe, Fred; Golden Age of Television; Robinson, Hubble; Writing for Television

CHEERS

U.S. Situation Comedy

Cheers, NBC's longest running comedy series, aired from 1982 to 1993, at 9:00 P.M. Thursdays. The show narrowly escaped cancellation during its first season and took several years to develop a strong following. By 1985, however, *Cheers* was one of television's most popular shows. It garnered top ten ratings for seven of its eleven seasons and often earned the number one ranking in the weekly Nielsens. The final episode, aired 20 May 1993, received the second-best Nielsen ratings of all-time for an episodic program. Numerous awards complemented *Cheers'* commercial success and the show boosted the careers of all its stars.

This popular situation comedy is often cited for successfully blending elements of romance and soap opera into the sitcom format. Fans of the show enjoyed its witty dialogue and comic situations, but also followed the twists and turns in the lives of the main characters. Would Sam and Diane get together? Would Rebecca marry Robin? These sorts of plot questions strung together episodes and whole seasons, which often ended with summer cliffhangers, a rare device for television comedy.

The show was set at Cheers, the Boston bar "where everybody knows your name." Bar owner Sam Malone (Ted Danson), a former Red Sox pitcher and an irascible womanizer, served up beers and traded one-liners with regular customers Cliff (John Ratzenberger) and Norm (George Wendt). Carla (Rhea Perlman), a feisty waitress with a weakness for hockey players, kept the men in check with her ascerbic comments. Bartender "Coach" (Nicholas Col-

Cheers

assanto) was the slow-witted and ironically funny straight man of the ensemble cast. When Colassanto passed away in 1985, Woody Harrelson joined the cast as Woody, a young bartender who took slow-wittedness to new heights.

Sam's on-again, off-again romance with cocktail waitress Diane (Shelly Long) exemplified the show's serial-comedy mix. In the first season, Diane despised Sam and constantly rejected his come-ons. In the second season, she started a torrid affair with him. They broke it off in the third season, and Diane took up with a neurotic psychiatrist, Frasier Crane (Kelsey Grammer). Diane almost went back to Sam after the fourth season, but then rejected his marriage proposal. The ongoing romantic tension allowed Sam and Diane to develop as characters. Flashbacks and references to past episodes gave the show a sense of continuous history, like an evening soap. Over the years, other characters developed their own plot lines. Rebecca (Kirstie Alley), who replaced Diane when actress Shelly Long left the show in 1987, pursued a futile romance with Robin, a corporate raider who briefly owned the bar. Woody dated Kelly (Jackie Swanson), a wealthy socialite who matched him in naiveté. Frasier married Lillith (Bebe Neuwirth), an ice-cold psychiatrist who matched him in neurosis. Only Cliff and Norm remained essentially static, holding down the bar with their mutual put-downs.

The creators of *Cheers*, Glen Charles, James Burrows, and Les Charles, previously worked on various MTM sitcoms, such as *The Mary Tyler Moore Show, Phyllis*, and *The Bob Newhart Show*. Like *Taxi*, another of their creations, *Cheers* inherited the MTM emphasis on character development. Upscale audiences appreciated this emphasis—and advertisers appreciated the upscale audiences. *Cheers* was not politically correct: the main character was a womanizer; Rebecca pretended to be a career woman but really just wanted a rich husband; and the collegial atmosphere centered around drinking. Though several of the characters were working-class, the show completely avoided social issues. And *Cheers* never preached to its audience on any subjects whatsoever. Even the poignant moments of personal drama that quieted the set from time to time were quickly counter-balanced by sardonic one-liners before any serious message could take hold.

In 1993 Paramount announced that *Cheers* would go off the air. The show was still highly rated, but production costs had soared to record numbers—$65 million for the 1991–92 season. Star Ted Danson, reportedly in on the decision to cancel, was earning $450,000 per episode. The network orchestrated a rousing finale, which garnered a 45.5 rating and a 64-audience share. On the evening of the finale, many local newscasts aired segments from bars, where fans saluted *Cheers* from an appropriate setting. In 1994, Kelsey Grammer launched a spin-off, *Frasier*, and George Wendt tried his own series, *The George Wendt Show*. Woody Harrelson landed starring roles in Hollywood, following in the footsteps of his *Cheers* co-stars Alley and Danson.

Over the years *Cheers* received 26 Emmy Awards and a record 111 Emmy nominations. In 1995 it rivaled *M*A*S*H* and *Roseanne* on the rerun circuit and showed all signs of continuing to be a major hit in syndication. As an inheritor of the MTM character-comedy tradition, *Cheers* pushed the "serialization" of sitcoms to new levels and was one of the most successful shows from the 1980s.

—J.B. Bird

CAST

Sam Malone . . . . Ted Danson
Diane Chambers (1982–97) . . . . Shelley Long
Carla Tortelli Lebec . . . . Rhea Perlman
Ernie "Coach" Pantusso (1982–85) . Nicholas Colasanto
Norm Peterson . . . . George Wendt
Cliff Clavin . . . . John Ratzenberger
Dr. Frasier Crane (1984–93) . . . . . Kelsey Grammer
Woody Boyd (1985–93) . . . . Woody Harrelson
Rebecca Howe (1987–93) . . . . Kirstie Alley
Dr. Lilith Sternin (1986–93) . . . . . Bebe Neuwirth
Evan Drake (1987–88) . . . . Tom Skerritt
Eddie LeBec (1987–89) . . . . Jay Thomas
Robin Colcord (1989–91) . . . . Roger Rees
Kelly Gaines (1989–93) . . . . Jackie Swanson
Paul (1991–93) . . . . Paul Willson
Phil (1991–93) . . . . Philip Perlman

PRODUCERS   Glen Charles, Les Charles, James Burrows

PROGRAMMING HISTORY   274 Episodes

• NBC

September 1982–December 1982	Thursday 9:00-9:30
January 1983–December 1983	Thursday 9:30-10:00
December 1983–August 1993	Thursday 9:00-9:30
February 1993–May 1993	Thursday 8:00-8:30

FURTHER READING

Brooks, Tim. *The Complete Directory to Prime-Time Network TV Shows*. New York: Ballantine, 1992.

Carter, Bill. "Why 'Cheers' Proved so Intoxicating." *New York Times*, 9 May 1993.

Feuer, Jane. "Genre Study and Television." In, Allen, Robert C., editor. *Channels of Discourse, Reassembled*. Chapel Hill: University of North Carolina Press, 1992.

Hamamoto, Darrell Y. *Nervous Laughter: Television Situation Comedy and Liberal Democratic Ideology*. New York: Praeger, 1989.

Long, Rob. "Three Cheers." *National Review* (New York), 7 June 1993.

Marc, David. *Comic Visions*. Boston: Unwin-Hyman, 1990.

Marc, David, and Robert J. Thompson. *Prime Time, Prime Movers*. Boston: Little, Brown, 1992.

Papazian, Ed. *Medium Rare: The Evolution, Workings and Impact of Commercial Television*. New York: Media Dynamics, 1991.

Sackett, Susan. *Prime-Time Hits: Television's Most Popular Network Programs*. New York: Billboard, 1993.

See also Burrows, James; Charles, Glen and Les; Comedy, Workplace

CHEYENNE

U.S. Western

*C*heyenne was the first successful television series to be produced by the motion picture studio, Warner Brothers. Originally one of the three rotating series in the studio's showcase series, *Warner Brothers Presents, Cheyenne* emerged as the program's breakout hit and helped to fuel ABC's ratings ascent during the mid-1950s. ABC had fewer national affiliates than CBS and NBC, but in markets with affiliates of all three networks, *Cheyenne* immediately entered the top ten; by 1957, it had become the number one program in those markets. Although clearly successful, *Cheyenne* never stood alone as a weekly series, but alternated bi-weekly with other Warner Brothers series: *Casablanca* and *King's Row* in *Warner Brothers Presents* (1955–56), *Conflict* (1956–57), and two spin-off series, *Sugarfoot* (1957–61) and *Bronco* (1958–62). *Cheyenne's* eight-year run produced only 107 episodes, an average of thirteen per season.

Early network television was staked out by refugees from Hollywood's B-western backlots who salvaged their careers by appealing to a vast audience of children. Cowboy stars Gene Autrey, Roy Rogers, and William "Hopalong Cassidy" Boyd made their fortunes in television with inexpensive little westerns made from noisy gunfights and stock-footage Indian raids. As television westerns were made to appeal to younger viewers, the movie industry shifted in the opposite direction, toward "adult" westerns in which the genre's familiar landscape became the setting for psychological drama or mythic allegory, as in *High Noon* (1952) and *The Searchers* (1956). With the 1955 premieres of *Cheyenne*, *Gunsmoke* (1955–75), and *The Life and Legend of Wyatt Earp* (1955–61), the networks attempted to import the "adult" western into prime time by infusing the genre with more resonant characters and psychological conflicts.

Cheyenne starred Clint Walker as Cheyenne Bodie, a former frontier scout who drifts through the old West, traveling without any particular motivation from one adventure to another. Along the way he takes a number of jobs, working on ranches or wagon trains, taking part in cattle drives or protecting precious cargo. Sometimes he works for the federal government; at other times he finds himself deputized by local lawmen. Essentially, the producers of *Cheyenne* changed the character's circumstances at will in order to insert him into any imaginable conflict. Indeed, several *Cheyenne* episodes were remakes of earlier Warner Brothers movies like *To Have and Have Not* (1944) and *Treasure of the Sierra Madre* (1948) with the character of Cheyenne Bodie simply inserted into the original plot.

With Walker as a lone redeemer wandering from community to community, *Cheyenne* had a thin, though ex-tremely adaptable, premise for generating episodic stories. With its virtually unrelated individual episodes, this type of series bears many similarities to the anthology format. In *Cheyenne*, each episode featured a new conflict involving new characters, with only the recurring character of Cheyenne Bodie to connect one episode with another. Each time Cheyenne enters a new community, he either witnesses or provokes a new story in which he can participate to varying degree—though he is the force of moral order able to resolve any conflict. This structure is particularly suited to the western's violent resolutions, since only one continuing character must remain alive when the dust settles.

The series was held together not so much by its premise as by its charismatic star, Clint Walker, who rose from obscurity to become one of the icons of the TV western. With his powerful physique and towering height, Walker commanded the small screen through sheer presence; his

Cheyenne

performance gained gravity simply from the way his body dominated the screen. Walker's personal strength extended beyond the screen to his dealings with Warner Brothers, which exercised tight control over its contract performers. In battling the studio, Walker made *Cheyenne* one of the more tempestuous productions in the history of television.

For the 1957–58 season ABC offered to purchase a full season of thirty-nine episodes of *Cheyenne*, but Warner Brothers declined. Since each hour-long episode took six working days for principle photography alone, the studio couldn't supply a new episode each week. Because Walker appeared in virtually every scene, it was also impossible to shoot more than one episode at a time. Consequently, Warner Brothers developed a second series, *Sugarfoot*, to alternate with *Cheyenne*.

In a gesture that would characterize creativity at Warner Brothers, the studio designed *Sugarfoot* as only a slight variation on the *Cheyenne* formula. In *Sugarfoot*, Will Hutchins played Tom Brewster, a kind-hearted young drifter who travels the West while studying to become a lawyer. Toting a stack of law books and an aversion to violence, he shares Cheyenne Bodie's penchant for meddling in the affairs of others. But whereas Cheyenne usually dispatches conflicts with firepower, Tom Brewster replaces gunplay with a gift for rhetoric—though he knows how to handle a weapon when persuasion fails. The series was more light-hearted than *Cheyenne*, but otherwise held close to the formula of the heroic loner.

In May 1958 Clint Walker demanded to renegotiate his contract before returning for another season. Walker had signed his first contract at Warner Brothers in 1955 as a virtual unknown and had received an initial salary of $175 per week, which had risen gradually to $1250 per week. After the second season of *Cheyenne*, Warner Brothers capitalized on Walker's rising popularity by casting him in a feature film, *Fort Dobbs* (1958), and by releasing a musical album on which he sang. But Walker was still merely a contract performer who worked on the studio's terms. Walker timed his ultimatum carefully, assuming that he had acquired some leverage once *Cheyenne* finished the 1957–58 season as ABC's second-highest-rated series. He requested more freedom from his iron-clad contract, particularly the autonomy to decide which projects to pursue outside the series. "Television is a vicious, tiring business," he informed the press, "and all I'm asking is my fair share."

When Warner Brothers refused to negotiate, Walker left the studio and did not return for the entire 1958-59 season. After meeting with ABC and advertisers, Warner Brothers decided to continue the *Cheyenne* series without its star. In his place the studio simply substituted a new charismatic drifter, a former Confederate captain named Bronco Layne (Ty Hardin). Warner Brothers received some puzzled fan mail, but the studio sustained an entire season without Walker—and finished among the top twenty programs—by interspersing Bronco Layne episodes with reruns of Walker episodes from previous seasons. If there was a difference between episodes of *Bronco* and *Cheyenne*, it was solely in the stars; otherwise, *Bronco* was a nearly identical clone.

Warner Brothers finally renegotiated Walker's contract after his boycott, and *Cheyenne* resumed with its star for the 1959-60 season. *Bronco* survived as a stand-alone series and alternated with *Sugarfoot* for the season. During the following season, the three shows alternated in *The Cheyenne Show*; occasionally the characters would crossover into episodes of the other series.

By the end, the actors were numbed by the repetition of the scripts and by the dreary, taxing routine of production on series in which one episode was virtually indistinguishable from another. Even after returning from his holdout, Walker disliked working on *Cheyenne* and complained to the press that he felt "like a caged animal" pacing back and forth in a zoo. "A TV series is a dead-end street," he lamented. "You work the same set, with the same actors, and with the same limited budgets. Pretty soon you don't know which picture you're in and you don't care." Will Hutchins admitted hoping that *Sugarfoot* would be canceled. Its episodes, he complained, "are pretty much the same after you've seen a handful. They're moneymakers for the studio, the stations, and the actors, but there's a kind of empty feeling when you're through."

—Christopher Anderson

CAST

Cheyenne Bodie . . . . Clint Walker
Toothy Thompson . . . . Jack Elam

PRODUCERS   William T. Orr, Roy Huggins, Arthur Silver, Harry Foster

PROGRAMMING HISTORY   107 Episodes

• ABC

September 1955–September 1959	Tuesday 7:30-8:30
September 1959–December 1962	Monday 7:30-8:30
April 1963–September 1963	Friday 7:30-8:30

FURTHER READING

Anderson, Christopher. *Hollywood TV: The Studio System in the Fifties*. Austin: University of Texas Press, 1994.

Jackson, Ronald. *Classic TV Westerns: A Pictorial History*. Seacaucus, New Jersey: Carol, 1994.

MacDonald, J. Fred. *Who Shot The Sheriff? The Rise and Fall of the Television Western*. New York: Praeger, 1987.

West, Richard. *Television Westerns: Major and Minor Series, 1946–1978*. Jefferson, North Carolina: McFarland, 1987.

Woolley, Lynn, Robert W. Malsbary, and Robert G. Strange, Jr. *Warner Bros. Television: Every Show of the Fifties and Sixties, Episode by Episode*. Jefferson, North Carolina: McFarland, 1985.

Yoggy, Gary A. *Riding the Video Range: The Rise and Fall of the Western on Television*. Jefferson, North Carolina: McFarland, 1994.

See also *Warner Brothers Presents*, Westerns

CHICAGO SCHOOL OF TELEVISION

During the late 1940s and early 1950s, broadcast television emanating from Chicago was noted for its original ideas, inventive production techniques and significant contributions to the development of the new visual medium. Paying close attention to the problems of adjusting personal styles of writing, direction, and performance to television, and to the more theoretical questions of how television actually worked, Chicago broadcasters developed a style or technique that came to be known as the Chicago School of Television.

While all Chicago stations contributed to the school, most success with the distinctive approach to programming is attributed to the NBC owned and operated station, WNBQ. Under the leadership of station manager Jules Herbuveaux and program manager Ted Mills, the NBC outlet went further in developing formats and ideas that would capitalize on television's idiosyncrasies.

Simply stated, the Chicago School worked at creating inventive programs different from both New York's theatrical offerings or Hollywood's screenplay based productions. Utilizing an almost totally scriptless-improvisational approach reliant on interpretive camera work and creative use of scenery, costumes, props, and lighting, Chicago School practitioners produced successful programs in limited spaces with local talent and small budgets. Herbuveaux provided the freedom for his staff to create and Mills theorized and experimented with a variety of ideas including Chinese Opera, commedia dell'arte and Pirandellian forms of reality in his search for new and effective television forms.

By late 1949, Chicago's low-cost television packages were making a ratings impact with such offerings as NBC's *Kukla, Fran and Ollie*, ABC's *Super Circus* and the piano talents of DuMont's Al Morgan. By spring, 1950, the major body of Chicago School work focused on such NBC-WNBQ variety offerings as *Garroway at Large*, the *Wayne King Show*, *Hawkins Falls*, and *Saturday Square*. Children's shows consisted of an extraordinary number of award winning entries including *Zoo Parade, Quiz Kids, Mr. Wizard,*

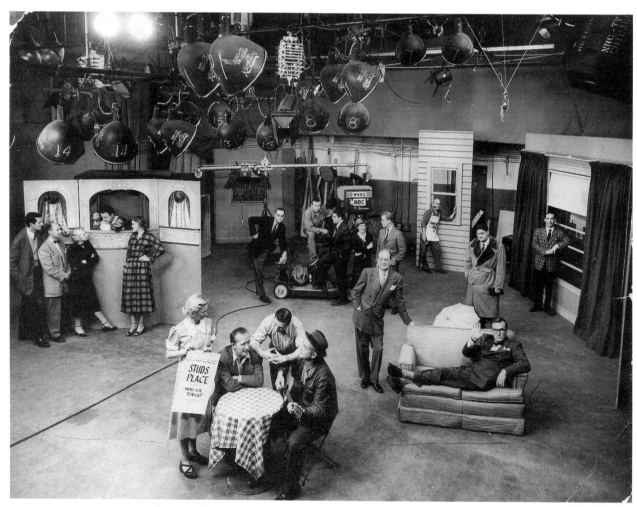

(foreground from left) Kukla, Fran and Ollie; Studs' Place; Garroway at Large

Ding Dong School, Pistol Pete and Jennifer and the highly rated-low budgeted cowboy film series, *Cactus Jim*. For comedy and drama there was Studs Terkel's *Studs' Place, Portrait of America, Crisis,* and *Reported Missing*. Actuality programming featured *Walt's Workshop, The Pet Shop* and *R.F.D. America*. Local news offered the unique *Five Star Final* with weatherman Clint Youle, news anchor Clifton Utley, Dorsey Connors with consumer tips, sportscaster Tom Duggan and, reflecting Herbuveaux's sense of showmanship, Herbie Mintz with musical nostalgia.

As critically acclaimed as it proved to be, elements of the Chicago School's decline were seen as early as 1950. Chicago programs were shortened and/or removed from network schedules. Key personnel left Chicago to pursue more lucrative careers in New York and Los Angeles and, in 1953, with the opening of the coast-to-coast network cable, there was less and less need for Chicago productions. In 1953, thirteen network programs originated from Chicago. By 1955, no Chicago produced programs appeared on the DuMont network. CBS and NBC had no Chicago network originations except occasional newscasts and a network radio farm program. The Chicago School of Television was becoming just a fond memory.

—Joel Sternberg

FURTHER READING

"Chi Network Originations." *Variety*, (Los Angeles), 27 May 1953.

"The Chicago School." *Time* (New York), 11 September 1950.

"The Chicago Touch: It May Give You the Show You Need." *Sponsor*, 5 April 1954.

Davis, J. Hugh E. "Are Chi Network TV Originations Dying?" *The Billboard* (New York), 5 April 1952.

Fay, Bill. "Top TV Town." *Collier's* (New York), 17 March 1951.

Herbuveaux, Jules. "Chi TV Parlays a Myth into B.O. Inventiveness." *Variety* (Los Angeles), 27 May 1953.

Kupcinet, Irv. "Windy City Nominated as Nation's TV Centre; Home of 'Relaxed' Video." *Variety* (Los Angeles), 10 January 1951.

Mabley, Jack. "When Chicago TV Was Young, Bright, and Fun." *Chicago's American Magazine* (Chicago), 19 November 1967.

"NBC's Chi Staffers Miffed Over 'Orphan' Status; Blame N.Y. Relations." *Variety* (Los Angeles), 29 November 1950.

Nielsen, Ted. "Television: Chicago Style." *Journal of Broadcasting*, Fall, 1965.

Oboler, Arch. "Windy Kilocycles." *Theatre Arts* (New York), July 1951.

Olson, John. "The Reward of Being Local, Live, Lively." *Broadcasting* (Washington, D.C.), 24 May 1954.

"School's Out." *Time* (New York), 10 September 1951.

Shayon, Robert Lewis. "A Deadly Calm in the Windy City." *Saturday Review of Literature* (New York), 5 September 1959.

———. "Chicago's Local TV Corpse." *Saturday Review of Literature* (New York), 11 October 1958.

———. *Open to Criticism*. Boston, Massachusetts: Beacon Press, 1971.

———. "Toynbee, TV, and Chicago." *The Christian Science Monitor* (Boston, Massachusetts), 5 June 1950.

Sternberg, Joel. "Television Town." *Chicago History* (Chicago), Summer, 1975.

"Telefile: Creative Programming Highlights WNBQ (TV) Success." *Broadcasting* (Washington, D.C.), 9 January 1950.

Terkel, Studs. "Chi's TV Imagination Vs. Radio City Panjandrums." *Variety* (Los Angeles and New York), 27 May 1953.

"TV Chicago Style." *Television Magazine* (New York), March 1951.

Van Horne, Harriet. "The Chicago Touch." *Theatre Arts* (New York), July 1951.

Wolters, Larry. "Television News and Views," *Chicago Tribune*, 4 January 1952.

See also Allison, Fran; *Garroway at Large;* "Golden Age" of Television; *Kukla, Fran and Ollie;* Tillstrom, Burr

CHILDREN AND TELEVISION

Children devote much of their free time to watching television—seemingly enamored of the screen—and continuous contact is thought to influence the way they understand and interpret both television and the world in which they live. Although children have everyday contact with other media and many other forms of expression and communication, visual media alone are seen as speaking a "universal language," accessible regardless of age. In the United States questions about program content and its use by children, about television's influence on children's attitudes, knowledge and behavior, and about the appropriate public policy toward children's television have been central to the discussion of this medium throughout its half century as the electronic hearth.

Children's Programming

In the 1950s, children's programs and the benefits that television could presumably bring to the family were highly touted selling points for television sets. By 1951, the networks' schedules included up to 27 hours of children's programs. Like much of television programming, offerings for children continued radio's tradition of action-adventure themes and a pattern of late afternoon and evening broadcasts. An early reliance on movies as a program staple was

Barney and Friends

lessened in favor of half-hour live-action shows such as *The Lone Ranger*, *Sky King*, or *Lassie*, and host/puppet shows such as *The Howdy Doody Show* and *Kukla, Fran and Ollie*. By the mid-1950s programs had found their place on Saturday morning, and by decade's end the thirty-minute, once-a-week format was established.

Captain Kangaroo
Photo courtesy of Bob Keeshan

Ding Dong School

During the 1960s almost all other forms gave way to animation. Reduced costs resulting from limited action animation techniques, and the clear appeal of cartoons to children, transformed scheduling, and the institutionalization of Saturday morning cartoons became complete—an unexpected lucrative time slot for the networks. Popular shows included *The Flintstones, The Jetsons, Bullwinkle,* and *Space Ghost.*

The 1970s have been described as a video mosaic in which sixty- or ninety-minute shows incorporated a number of segments under umbrella labels such as *The New Super Friends Hour* or *Scooby Laff-a-Lympics.* These extended shows were designed to increase audience flow across the entire morning.

Children's programming in the 1980s was influenced by the "television revolution" as the growth of cable and VCR penetration began to erode the network audience, and international co-ventures began to change the production process. Cartoons remained the standard children's fare, but live action shows began to increase in number. Cable networks such as Nickelodeon and Disney, devoted primarily to children, as well as cable networks with extensive children's programming like Discovery, Learning Channel, USA, TBS, the Family Channel and Lifetime, have experimented extensively in programming for children. They have produced live-action programs, including game shows, puppet shows, magazine format news and variety programs, and

live action drama/adventures shows frequently incorporating anthropomorphic creatures into the storyline.

The 1990s have been influenced by the Children's Television Act with many educational shows joining the available programming. Since 1990, for example, eight of the nine Peabody Awards for children's programs were for informational or educational programs.

While it is the case that most of the television viewed by children is of programs not specifically considered "children's shows," the production of children's programming is big business, often defined by the ways in which "children's shows" are distinctive. "Children's shows" are those which garner a majority of a child audience, traditionally the Saturday morning programs. These shows are almost always profitable. Because the child audience changes rapidly, and because children do not seem to mind watching reruns, the programs are shown as many as four times a year, a factor that reduces production costs without reduction in program availability or profitability. Moreover, a strong syndication market for off-network children's shows adds to the profits.

For many of these reasons the major networks have traditionally exerted strong control over production in the five or six production houses they routinely use. Each network has a vice president for children's programming who uses other advisors and often relies on extensive marketing research, as do the Children's Television Workshop and the Nickelodeon cable network.

Both those who purchase and those who produce children's programs operate with assumptions about the child audience that, although changing, remain important. They assume, for example, that there are gender differences in preferences, but an important corollary is the assumption that, while girls will watch "boys' shows," boys will not watch "girls' shows." They assume that older children control the set, an assumption related to the axiom that younger children will watch "up" (in age appeal) but that older children will not watch "down." Producers and purchasers assume that children have a short attention span, that repetition is a key to education and entertainment, and that children prefer recognizable characters and stories.

The body of television content emerging from these economic and industrial practices, and based on these and similar assumptions, has been a central component of "childhood" since the 1950s. Because they are seen as a special "class" or "group" of both citizens and viewers, great concern for the role of television in the lives of children has accompanied the development of the medium. As a result of this concern issues surrounding children and television have often been framed as "social problems," issues of central concern to numerous groups. Large-scale academic research enterprises have been mounted to monitor, analyze, and explain relationships between television and children. Congress, regulatory agencies, advocacy groups, and the television networks have struggled continuously over research findings, public responsibility, and popular response. And significant policy decisions continue to be made based both on that research and on the political and economic power that is brought to bear on these issues.

The Effects of Television Violence

Throughout all these policy debates, citizens' actions, and network responses, the issue of violence in television programming has been central to concerns regarding children and television. As an aspect of television content, violence has traditionally been measured quantitatively by researchers who count incidents of real or threatened physical injury. Gerbner and his colleagues have conducted such analyses yearly since 1967. Their violence index shows a fairly stable level of prime-time violence over the past 25 years. The question then becomes what is the effect of this type of programming on children.

In the 1960s researchers used experimental methods to investigate the impact of media violence. Albert Bandura's social learning theory (also called observational learning or modeling theory) argued that children could easily learn and model behaviors observed on film or television. Sometimes known as the "Bobo doll" studies, these experiments demonstrated that children who viewed filmed violent actions were as likely to imitate those actions as were children who saw live modeling of those actions. Many extensions of this basic finding established that modeling was influenced by other attributes of the children such as their prior level of aggressiveness. Context and message, specifically the punish-

ment or reinforcement of the filmed aggressor, and the presence of an adult in the viewing or imitation context, emerged as other significant factors in the modeling behavior. Later laboratory studies used more realistic measures of aggression and programming that more closely resembled primetime television. Field experiments were also conducted, in which viewing in real life situations (home, camps, schools) was manipulated.

In a series of experiments, two opposing theories, catharsis and stimulation, were investigated. Catharsis holds that viewing violence purges the individual of negative feelings and thus lessens the likelihood of aggressive behavior. Stimulation predicted the opposite. No support for the catharsis theory emerged from the research; stimulation was found to be more likely.

Taken together, the experimental studies demonstrated that the process of televisual influence on children is indeed complicated. Still, the results from laboratory experiments do demonstrate that shortly after exposure to violent programming, children are more likely to show an increase in their own levels of aggression. But how would these laboratory findings translate into real life?

Correlational studies, surveys, tell little about cause and effect, but they do avoid the artificiality of laboratory studies. If viewing is associated with television violence, then individuals who watch a great deal of violent television should also score high on survey scales that measure aggressive behavior. The results from a large number of such surveys are remarkably consistent: there is a small but consistent association between viewing violent television and aggressive tendencies. Yet another form of survey research, panel studies, tackles the question of causality by looking at the same individuals over time. In the case of television violence, the question is: does television viewing at Time 1 relate to aggression at Time 2; or, conversely, could the causal linkage be reversed, suggesting that aggressive behavior leads to a propensity to view violent television content? Only a few such studies exist but, again, the findings are generally consistent. Although the effect is small, watching television violence encourages aggression.

What conclusions can be reached from this large, ongoing body of research? Television does contribute to aggressive behavior—however, television is only one of many causes of aggression. Many other factors unrelated to television influence violence, and the precise impact of televised violence will be modified by age, sex, family practices, and the way violence is presented. One statement is frequently repeated: television has large effects on a small number of individuals, and modest effects on a large number of people. The questions and approaches continue to be refined, and currently, groups funded by both the cable and network industries are studying levels of violence and its appearance in context, in order to provide better information on the type of violence being shown.

Television and Cognitive Development

While televisual violence is often the most visible and debated aspect of questions linking children and television, it is hardly the only topic that concerns researchers. Other inquiries focused on potential effects of the medium on patterns of thinking and understanding has prompted extensive research. Posed negatively, the question is: does television mesmerize attention, promote passive or over-stimulated children, while wrecking creativity and imagination? To explore such concerns, cognitive developmental approaches to television and children have typically examined attention, comprehension, and inference.

Children's attention to television has often been characterized as "active" versus "passive." Popular concern about the "zombie" viewer suggests that children enter some altered stated of consciousness when viewing television. But this generalization has received little research support. However, one notion that seems to underlie many implicit theories of children's attraction to the screen is that children's viewing is governed by the novelty of the visual stimulus, rapid formal features such as movements, visual complexity, cuts, pans, zooms, which produce an orienting reflex.

A theory of active television viewing suggests that attention is linked to comprehension. Thus, when visual or auditory features of television content suggest to the young viewer that it is designed "for children," attention is turned to that content. When material is no longer comprehensible, becomes boring, or when distractions occur, attention is deflected. This theory of child attentional patterns has received substantial support and has indicated specific stages. Attention to television is fragmentary before the age of two; visual attention increases during the preschool years, with a major shift in amount and pattern of attention occurring between 24 and 30 months. Frequently beginning around the age of eight, visual attention to TV decreases (presumably as the decoding of television becomes routine), and the attention pattern begins to resemble that of an adult.

With regard to perception and evaluation of television content, children clearly operate on different dimensions than adults who produce programs. Understanding television programming requires a fairly complex set of tasks for children, including selective attention to the events portrayed, perceiving an orderly organization of events, and making inferences about information given implicitly. Comprehension research has examined both verbal and visual decoding and determined that comprehension is a function of both cognitive development and experience. Younger children have difficulty with a number of tasks involved in understanding television programs: separating central from peripheral content, comprehending the sequence of events, recalling events and segments, and understanding causation. As well, they find it difficult to complete such inferential tasks as understanding intersections of motivation, action, and consequence, or evaluating the "reality" of programs and characters. The comprehension of forms and conventions—sometimes termed "formal features"—is similarly grounded in developmental stages, with surprisingly early recognition of the time and space ellipses of cuts or the part whole relationship of zooms. Such complex storytelling functions as point of view shots or flashbacks, however, are unclear to children through much of the first decade.

Television Within the Family

In most cases, this viewing and the development of skills and strategies occurs within a family context filled with other activities and other individuals. The average child watches television a little more than four hours a day. Childhood viewing peaks somewhere around 12 years of age and declines during adolescence to a little more than three hours per day. Children do most of their viewing during the weekday hours with only 10% of their viewing on Saturday and Sunday mornings. Viewing amount varies by gender and race, with studies showing that blue-collar families averaging more television viewing more than white-collar families and blacks viewing more than whites. Television provides the backdrop for growing up, and studies show that children often play, eat, do homework, and talk while "watching tv."

Viewing is not usually solitary. Children and adults view together and do many other things while watching. The family has a say in creating the context in which television will be consumed, a context involving who decides what to watch, sibling or parental conflict over viewing, and the rules for decision making. Although many families report few rules, there may be subtle as well as direct rules about television use. For example, children may not be allowed to watch until they have completed important tasks such as homework or chores, or there may be a requirement that television must be turned off at a certain time. When parents report rules, they report control of when younger children can watch; older children have rules about what they can watch.

Often this context is modified by processes of "mediation," a term used to refer to the role of social interaction in relation to television's use in the home and the potential impact of television within the family. Some mediation is direct and intentional—parents make specific comments about programs. Other mediation may be indirect or unintentional, as in general comments about alternative activities, discussions of social or personal issues generated by media content, and talk loosely tied to content. Parents and siblings may respond to questions with evaluative comments, interpretive comments, explanations of forms and codes, or discussions of morality or desirability of behavior.

One result related to the complexity of viewing practices has emerged very clearly from research conducted within a number of different contexts: interaction with parents during viewing increases comprehension and learning from television. In middle childhood, peer and sibling co-viewing involves talk about television action and evaluation of that action. Parental comments on the importance, truthfulness, and relevance of media are common at this age.

Learning from Television

In many ways general notions of how children learn from television and specific aspects of educational television were revolutionized by the premier of *Sesame Street* in 1969. Viewed by over 6 million preschoolers every week in the United States and internationally, this production is also one of the most studied television programs. Research focused on *Sesame Street* has provided ample evidence to suggest that young children can learn skills from the show, and that these skills will contribute to their early educational success. Many other programs produced by the Children's Television Workshop, by public broadcasting stations, independent producers, and state departments of education have been constructed to teach educational concepts ranging from reading to international understanding.

Related to these educational programs are pro-social programs which model socially valued responses for viewers. Pro-social behavior is usually defined as "good for persons and society" and may include lessons on the value of cooperation, self-control, helping, sharing, and understanding those who are different. *Mr. Rogers' Neighborhood*, for example, is a classic pro-social program.

Even with the knowledge gained from research focused on television's ability to teach specific skills, the medium is frequently castigated for interfering in the education of children. Achievement, intellectual ability, grades, and reading show complex relationships with television viewing. For example, the relationship between television viewing and academic performance is not clear cut. Children who spend a great deal of time watching television do poorly in school but children who spend a moderate amount of time with TV perform better than non-viewers. The small negative relationship between IQ and television viewing masks some important subgroup differences, such as age (high IQ is positively correlated with viewing until the teens) and gender (with the negative relationship holding stronger for boys than for girls). Reading and television viewing are positively correlated up to a threshold of about ten hours of viewing per week. Only when television viewing rises above a certain level does it seem to be related to less reading. Overall, the data suggest that television has a small adverse effect on learning.

In addition to the many ways in which television can influence the learning of specific educational concepts, or the ways in which basic television behavior affects other forms of learning, the medium can also teach indirect lessons. Socialization, especially sex role socialization, has been a continuing concern because television so frequently presents basic images of gender. In prime-time programming men outnumber women two or three to one. Women are younger than men and tend to be cast in more stereotypical roles, and tend to be less active, more likely to be victimized, less aggressive, and more limited in employment than men. Children's programs are similarly sex-stereotyped; women are generally underrepresented, stereotyped, and less central to the program. Cultivation analysis suggests that a relationship exists between viewing and stereotypical conceptions about gender roles. Nonetheless, some improvement has been made. Research on the impact of gender representation reveals that children do

understand the images and want to be like same sex television characters, and it seems clear that counter-stereotypical images are helpful in combating stereotypes.

Some research examining race role socialization shows similar patterns, suggesting that limited portrayals and stereotyped roles can contribute to skewed perceptions by race. Although African Americans have frequently been portrayed negatively, other minority groups such as Asians and Hispanics have simply been missing from the screen world—a process sometimes called symbolic annihilation.

Beyond the content of fictional representations, parents would agree that children learn from television advertising. Researchers initially assumed children had minimal comprehension of the selling intent of advertising and children verbally described advertisement as an "informational service." Nonverbal measures, however, demonstrated that children understood that commercials persuaded them to buy products. Social scientists have studied a number of potential effects of advertising. These include the frequent requests for products, the modification of self-esteem, the relations of advertising to obesity, and to alcohol and cigarette consumption. This research has been dominated by a deficit model in which children are defined as unable to distinguish selling intent, or as easily misled by what they see.

History and Policy

Such vulnerability on the part of children explains, in part, the designation of "children and television" as a specific topic for political as well as intellectual concern. Politicians and the public worried about the effects of media on children long before television, of course. Novels, movies, music, radio, comic books, all came under scrutiny for their potential negative consequences on the behaviors and attitudes of the young. But in the 1950s, the spotlight turned to television.

The first congressional hearings, predictably, addressed violence on television, and were held in the House Interstate and Foreign Commerce Subcommittee in June 1952. Network representatives were called to testify about television and violence before the Senate Subcommittee on Juvenile Delinquency headed by Estes Kefauver in 1954 and 1955. In 1964 the same committee again held hearings and issued a report critical of television programming and concluding that television was a factor in shaping the attitudes and character of the young people.

In the wake of the urban unrest and violence of the 1960s, a Presidential Commission on the Causes and Prevention of Violence was formed to examine the issues of violence in society. The report, basing its conclusions on a review of existing research, indicted television as part of the problem of violence. At the instigation of Senator John Pastore of Rhode Island, the U.S. Surgeon General commissioned a series of studies of televised violence and its effects on children. This work resulted in what is popularly termed the Surgeon General's Report of 1972, in which 23 research projects in five volumes focused on many issues surrounding television. The committee's main conclusion was that there was a causal link between viewing television violence and subsequent antisocial acts. Despite some initial confused reporting of the findings, the consensus that had emerged among the researchers was made clear in subsequent hearings. In 1982, a ten-year update of the Surgeon General's Report was released. It underscored the findings of the earlier report and also documented other areas in which television was having an impact, particularly on perceptions of reality, social relationships, health, and education.

During this long history of public regulatory debate on television, government commissions and citizen action groups were pursuing related agendas. Key to these interactions were the Federal Communications Commission (FCC), the Federal Trade Commission (FTC), and citizens' advocacy and action groups. Always involved in these disputes, whether directly or indirectly, were the major television networks, their industry associations, usually the National Association of Broadcasters (NAB), and advertisers. Action for Children's Television (ACT) was the citizens' group most directly engaged in legal procedures and policy actions.

Founded in 1968 by Peggy Charren, Action for Children's Television was formed to increase availability of quality programming for children. Unsuccessful at obtaining cooperation from the networks directly, ACT turned to political action. In 1970, the organization presented a petition to the FCC intended to change a number of FCC policies regarding children's programming. A resulting inquiry launched unprecedented response. Hearings were held, and in 1974 the *FCC Children's TV Report and Policy Statement* offered specific guidelines: a limit of nine and a half advertising minutes per hour in children's programs, the use of separation devices indicating divisions between commercials and programs, the elimination of host selling, and the directive that children's programs not be confined to one day—(Saturday morning television had become synonymous with children's television). Later reviews suggested that the networks were not meeting these requirements or their obligations to serve children, but further regulatory action in the 1980s was blocked by the shift toward a deregulatory stance at the FCC and in the courts.

At the Federal Trade Commission ACT was also at work, petitioning for the regulation of advertising directed at children. In 1977 the group presented a petition requesting that advertising of candy in children's programs be banned. The FTC responded with a notice that it would consider rulemaking to ban all ads to audiences too young to understand selling intent, to ban ads for sugared products, or to require that counter and corrective advertising be aired in order to counteract advertising of sugared products. Hearings were held, but lobbying efforts by networks and advertisers were very strong. Congress passed a bill eliminating the power of the FTC to rule on "unfair" practices, and restricting its focus to the regulation of "deceptive" practices. In 1981, the FTC issued a formal report dropping the

inquiry. Throughout the 1970s and 1980s ACT was engaged with the FCC and FTC in many other ways, representing petitions dealing with matters such as the banning of program length commercials (programs designed primarily to provide product exposure and create consumer demand), or the evaluation individual ads deemed deceptive.

Other citizen action groups have also been involved with issues surrounding television. The National Coalition on Television Violence (NCTV) has focused on television violence and efforts to educate the public and curb such content. The National Citizen Committee for Broadcasting monitored programs and identified companies that support television violence. The PTA threatened boycott of products and programs. The Coalition for Better Television (CBTV) was successful in pressuring some advertisers to boycott sponsors of programs with sexual themes.

But by the 1990s, the regulation of children's media was back on the legislative agenda. The 1990 Children's Television Act was the first congressional act that specifically regulated children's television. Most importantly, it imposed an obligation on broadcasters to serve the educational and informational needs of children. These are further defined as cognitive/intellectual or social/emotional needs. Although no minimum number of hours was established as a requirement, the obligation of some regularly scheduled programming specifically designed for children was established. Stations were also mandated to keep a log of that programming and to make the log available in a public inspection file. In a 1992 move widely viewed as an effort to stave off a federally imposed ratings system for violence, the three networks announced new standards, forswearing gratuitous violence; later they agreed to include on-screen advisories prior to the presentation of strong programs. In spite of these proposals all the issues emerged again in the Telecommunications Act of 1996.

A major legislative package that rewrote the 1934 Communications Act, the many provisions of the act will take years to sort out. But, in February 1996 the Telecommunications Act was signed into law. Of relevance to the children and television arena were provisions requiring the installation of an electronic monitoring device in television sets, a "V-chip" which would "read" violence ratings and allow families to block violent programming. Moreover, the networks have been charged with creating a self-designed and regulated ratings system, similar to that used by the Motion Picture Association of America, which would designate specific content depicting degrees of violence, sexual behavior, suitable language, and other controversial content. The bill includes the threat of a governmentally imposed system if the networks do not comply, but concerns about constitutionality and practicality of such a ratings system suggest that the issue will be under debate for many years.

In all these research and policy areas much of what we know comes from the study of children enjoying television as it has existed for almost half a century. But that traditional knowledge, like the traditional definition of television itself, is being challenged by emerging telecommunications technologies. Cable, video games, and VCRs changed the face of television within the home. The Internet, a 500-channel world, increasing international programming ventures, and regulatory changes will change the way children interact with electronic media. The special place of children in human societies assures, however, that the concerns that have surrounded their interaction with television will remain central, even if they are shifted to new and different media.

—Alison Alexander

FURTHER READING

Gunter, Barrie, and Jill L. McAleer. *Children and Television: The One Eyed Monster?* New York: Routledge, 1990.

Liebert, Robert M., and Joyce Sprafkin. *The Early Window: Effects of Television on Children and Youth.* New York: Pergamon, 1973; 3rd edition, 1988.
Signorielli, Nancy. *A Sourcebook on Children and Television.* New York: Greenwood, 1991.
Van Evra, Judith. *Television and Child Development.* Hillsdale, New Jersey: Erlbaum, 1990.

See also Audience Research; Cartoons; *Blue Peter*; Childen's Television Workshop; Cooney, Joan Ganz; Family Viewing Time; *Grange Hill; Howdy Doody Show; Kukla, Fran and Ollie;* Laybourne, Geraldine; *Muppet Show; Pee-wee's Playhouse; Road to Avonlea; Sesame Street; Watch with Mother*

CHILDREN'S TELEVISION WORKSHOP

U.S. Production Company

Children's Television Workshop (CTW) is a nonprofit organization created in 1967 for the purpose of producing the educational program *Sesame Street.* CTW was headed by Joan Ganz Cooney, a television producer who, with Lloyd Morrisett of the Markle Foundation, attracted funding from federal and private sources, including the U.S. Department of Health, Education, and Welfare, the National Institutes of Mental Health, the Carnegie and Ford foundations, and the Corporation for Public Broadcasting. *Sesame Street,* designed to promote the intellectual and cultural growth of preschoolers, particularly disadvantaged preschoolers, revolutionized children's educational television when it premiered in 1969 and established the CTW model for program development and research regarding children and television.

The CTW model refers to the unique process of educational program development at its workshop. It evolved under the direction of Cooney, Dr. Edward L. Palmer, director of research, and Dr. Gerald S. Lesser, chair of the CTW Board of Advisors. Each CTW series begins with extensive initial planning sessions involving producers, researchers, content experts, and advisors. The concepts developed in these sessions are then translated into program segments and pretested with the target audience. Frequently the testing extends for lengthy periods prior to actual production, so that producers can see how receptive the audience is to the educational messages embedded in the programs. In preparing for *Sesame Street,* for example, the research and design focused on demonstrable ability to attract attention, to appeal to the audience, and to be comprehensible. Researchers assessed the attention-holding power of material by presenting content in competition with potential distractions. The tactics which elicited most interactivity among viewers were explored further. The research concluded with tests for recall by appropriate audiences. As a result of these procedures *Sesame Street* went on air with

very specific attention-holding tactics such as fast movement, humor, slapstick, and animation. It was packaged in

Sesame Street
Photo courtesy of the Children's Television Workshop

a magazine format, and presented a carefully planned curriculum that focused on teaching letters and number skills.

Program development at CTW does not stop when programs are broadcast. In addition to the unusual attention to formative research, the CTW model also includes a strong commitment to summative research; as part of its summative research plan, the Educational Testing Service (ETS) was commissioned to evaluate the program. In a series of studies published by ETS in 1970 and 1972, researchers Ball and Bogatz found significant program-viewing impact and the development of a positive attitude toward school. Cook and Connor in a 1976 summary discovered that parental encouragement was vital to learning and that advantaged families were more likely to watch, thus ironically arguing that the gap between that group and the disadvantaged was not narrowed.

Sesame Street is clearly CTW's outstanding success, broadcast continuously since 1969. From its beginning as a weekday show designed to teach thinking skills and factual knowledge such as letters and number skills, the curriculum has been broadened to include goals such as reasoning, bilingual skills, acceptance of special needs, ecology, and health. The program is viewed by almost half of all U.S. preschoolers on a weekly basis. Internationally it has been broadcast in more than 40 countries and there are at least ten foreign-language versions.

Following the success of *Sesame Street* CTW went on to produce a number of other major educational programs, including *The Electric Company*, which premiered in 1971 and was in production for a decade. *The Electric Company* emphasized symbol and sound analysis and meaning in a half-hour program designed to help slower readers catch up and good readers reinforce their skills. *The Electric Company* used the CTW model, a magazine format, and a variety of entertaining and attention-grabbing production techniques. Formative research for the program included innovative eye movement and eye contact measures of appeal and attention. ETS evaluation found that *The Electric Company* fostered significant positive effects, particularly for the youngest target viewers. *Feeling Good*, a 24-episode experimental series, was programmed in 1974, designed to examine health issues and targeted particularly for young parents and low-income families. Funding difficulties and low ratings forced the program to be produced in stages with considerable format changes. Low public awareness of the program seemed to contribute to lack of demonstrable effects.

3-2-1 Contact, a 65-program series for 8- to 12-year-old children, premiered in 1980 and focused on science and technology. The goals were to promote scientific thinking, participation in science activities, and awareness of science as a career, particularly for women and minority children. It used a magazine format with continuing features such as a mystery adventure dramatic component. Research by Mielke and Chen in 1980 and 1983 found *3-2-1 Contact* attractive to children, with particularly positive responses to the drama format used in the Bloodhound Gang segments.

Square One TV premiered in 1987 with the goal of increasing problem solving ability and positive attitude toward mathematics for 8- to 12-year-old children. Format features include Mathnet, game show parodies, and commercials. The program covers mathematical concepts from estimation through graphics, probabilities, and geometry. CTW research shows increases in problem-solving ability and more positive attitudes toward mathematics in the target age group. *Ghostwriter*, a series focusing on writing skills, premiered in 1992. The series' appeal was built around a computer that provided "ghostlike" clues which enabled a group of young people to solve problems. Of all the CTW programs, only *Sesame Street* is still in production, but because there is always a new audience of children available, most of the programs can still be seen. And these are only a sampling of major CTW projects. The workshop continues with many other projects on the air and in development.

By the 1980s, many of the funds for CTW were generated from *Sesame Street* product sales, the Sesame Place Amusement Park, and from Sesame Street Live, a touring company. CTW became an unhappy participant in the struggles over PBS funding in the mid-1990s when the financial success of *Sesame Street* was used as an example of why public funding was not needed to support educational children's programming. In spite of such difficulties the Children's Television Workshop—and *Sesame Street* in particular—remain a hallmark of children's programming in the United States.

—Alison Alexander

FURTHER READING

Bryant, J., A. Alexander, and D. Brown. "Learning from Educational Television Programming." In Howe, M., editor. *Learning from Television.* London: Academic Press, 1983.

"Children's Learning from Television: Research and Development at the Children's Television Workshop" (special issue). *Educational Technology Research and Development* (Washington, D.C.), 1990.

Clifford, B.R., B. Gunter, and J. McAleer. *Television and Children: Program Evaluation, Comprehension, and Impact.* Hillsdale, New Jersey: Erlbaum, 1995.

Lesser, Gerald S. *Children and Television: Lessons from Sesame Street.* New York: Random House, 1974.

See also Children and Television; Cooney, Joan Ganz; *Sesame Street*

CHINA

China's first TV station, Beijing Television, began broadcasting on 1 May 1958. Within two years, dozens of stations were set up in major cities like Shanghai and Guangzhou. Most stations had to rely on using planes, trains, or cars to send films and tapes from one to another.

The first setback for Chinese television came in early 1960 when the former Soviet Union withdrew economic aid from China. Many TV stations were closed and the number was reduced from 23 to 5. Then came the Cultural Revolution (1966-76), during which television's functions became a single one: to publicize, explain, and express "class struggles." Anti-imperialism, anti-revisionism, and anti-capitalism policies were erected for fulfilling the task of class struggle. Beijing Television's regular telecasting came to a halt on January 1967. Local stations followed its lead. It was not until the early 1970s that television development gradually became normal.

In the reform period starting from the late 1970s, television became the most rapidly growing and advanced medium. On 1 May 1978, Beijing Television changed to China Central Television (CCTV) as the country's only national network with the world's largest audience. In 1994 the country had near 700 stations, with one national, 30 provincial, 300 regional, and 350 local. A total of 220 channels are broadcasting nationwide. The change in TV set ownership is among the fastest in the world's television history. By 1993 China had 230 million TV sets, becoming the nation with the most TV sets in the world. Statistically, every Chinese family now owns a TV set. In 1978 every 100 urban families had only 0.59 color set. The number increased 100 times during the 1980s, rising to 59.04 sets in every 100 urban families. The estimated viewership in 1994 was about 80% of the population, nearly 900 million. They comprised 83% of urban population and 33% of rural population. Television has become the most important medium in people's daily life. About 54% of the people watched TV every day, while 32% read a newspaper and 35% listened to the radio every day.

The growth in TV stations, TV set ownership, and TV audience, demonstrate the extraordinary diffusion of television throughout China. From 1958 to 1984, stations grew in number from two to 683. Set ownership increased from a few thousand to 260 million between 1960 and 1984. And from 1975 to 1984 viewers increased from 18 million to 900 million.

Broadcasting technology also developed quickly. By 1990, 90% of the transmission facilities were manufactured domestically. In the 1960s only 3,000 to 5,000 TV sets were produced annually, a tiny figure compared to a population of seven million at the time. In the 1980s, 50-odd color TV enterprises with nearly 1,000 production lines were in operation. From 1978 to 1992 the output of TV sets increased 55.4 times, leaping from *seventh* to top place in the world,

with the biggest output of black-and-white television sets and third in color-set production.

Structure and System

The only form of television allowed in China is state ownership. No private television ownership is allowed, and no foreign television ownership is permitted. Receiving foreign TV programs via satellite is prohibited. For many years television was financed by the government. There are no license fees or direct charge for television. Television advertising did not exist until the economic reform started in the late 1970s.

Media theories undergirding the organization and uses of Chinese television flow directly from Marxist-Leninist doctrine. Mao Zedong, the founder and late chairman of the Chinese Communist Party, embellished Lenin's concept of media control and stressed that media must be run by the Party and become the Party's "loyal eyes, ears, and tongue." The Party requires that "Broadcasting must keep in line with the Party voluntarily, and serve the main Party objectives of the time."

Television's central task is to serve as the mouthpiece of the leadership, and is regarded as both a political institution and an ideological apparatus. It is used, to the greatest possible extent, by the Party and state command to impose ideological hegemony on the society. It is the Party and government that set the tone of propaganda for television. Although TV stations transmit news, deliver government orders or decrees, provide education and enrich the people's cultural life, in the past decades television was mainly used by the Party and state to popularize policies and directions and motivate the masses in the construction of communism.

A tight control system was maintained to make television function effectively. The Party is concurrently the owner, the manager, and the practitioner of television. Television is under the direct leadership and control of the Party and run by the government. All stations are under the dual jurisdiction of the Party's Central Propaganda Department and the government's Ministry of Radio, Film and Television. The Party's Propaganda Department is under the supervision of the Secretariat and the Political Bureau of the Party's Central Committee. Local supervision comes from the various provincial, municipal, and local Party propaganda departments and the provincial or municipal broadcasting administrative bureaus. The Propaganda Departments set media policies, determine programming content and themes, and issue operational directives. Technological, regulatory and administrative affairs are generally the concern of the government. As a political organ of the Party, virtually no independence of media is envisioned. Open debate on ideology is not allowed, nor is media criticism of the Party, government and high ranking officials, policies and affairs. The self-imposed censorship has long and extensively been used. Every individual in the media circle knows well what he or she can do or cannot do. While routine material does not require approval from Party authorities, important editorials, news stories and sensitive programs all require prior endorsement by the Party authorities.

Programming and Production

Television programs consist of four categories: news (15%), entertainment (50%), feature and service (10%), and education (15%).

Although entertainment occupied the most hours, before the reform there were not many real entertainment programs. Most entertainment consisted of old films, with occasional live broadcast of operas. Newscasts were mostly what the official *People's Daily* reported. Production capability was low, equipment and facilities were simple, broadcasting hours and transmitting scales were limited and usually lasted three hours daily. Between 1958 and 1977 only 74 TV plays were produced.

Television has developed rapidly since the reform. Taboos were eliminated, restrictions lifted, and bold breakthroughs made. Both domestic and foreign news coverage have expanded. News on the frustration of economic reform, opinions from the audience, coverage of disaster, crime reports and human interest stories have been seen on a daily basis. A number of "firsts" have been tried, such as market information programs, sensitive topics, live telecasts of the Party's congress, and VIP interviews. In 1980 CCTV signed an agreement with Visnews and UPITV to receive international news stories via satellite. Now CCTV also receives international news stories from Asiavision, World TV News, and CNN.

Entertainment in the form of soap operas, traditional operas, and foreign feature films has become routine. In 1986 CCTV opened an English-language channel to serve foreigners in China. A dozen municipal and provincial stations now also have their English channels.

Education programs have been expanded to college courses offered by TV universities. More than 5,000 educational ground receiving terminals have been installed, allowing one million college students to study at home. In 20 years, five million people received continuing education through TV networks and 20 million farmers learned practical farming techniques in this way. Currently, two million students get their education or training via TV, including 1.2 million primary and middle school teachers. Service programs now range from commodity advertising, public announcement, weather and traffic reports, to date and stock information.

Production capacity has also been remarkably enhanced since the reform. In 1993 CCTV's news service increased to 11 programs per day, compared to only three before. During the 1960s and 1970s fewer than a dozen TV plays were made annually. In 1990 the number jumped to 1,500. In 1994 domestically produced TV plays reached 5,000. Broadcasting hours increased impressively as well. In an average week of 1980, 2,018 hours of programs were broadcast nationwide. The number went up to 7,698 in 1985 and 22,298 in 1990, a 3.5-fold increase in five years and an 11-fold expansion in ten years. Nationwide, television now broadcasts 30,000 hours per week. Annually, domestic programming has reached 150,000-hours of programming.

Openness in Television

An epochal move towards openness in television has been made in the reform period. It started in economic and technological aspects, but soon was expanded to political and cultural aspects as well.

The first token of openness in television is the change in programming importation. Importation before the reform was quantitatively limited and politically and ideologically oriented. For 20 years, only the national network was authorized to import programs under tight control and restrictions. Programs were imported almost exclusively from socialist countries, and the content concentrated on the Soviet Revolution and their economic progress. Few programs were imported from the West and were restricted to those which exemplified that "socialism is promising, capitalism is hopeless."

In the late 1970s the ban was lifted. In 1986 U.S. Lorimar Productions signed a contract with Shanghai Television, providing 7,500 hours of American shows. Today, with some restrictions, central, regional, and local television stations are all looking to other countries as a source of programs. In the early 1970s imported programming occupied only less than one percent of the total programming. In 1982 the number jumped to eight percent. In 1994 it became 15%.

The second token of openness in television is the organizing of TV festivals. In 1986, STV held China's first international TV festival. Around 40 TV companies from 15 countries attended the festival. In 1994 more than 300 companies from 38 countries were present at the 5th Shanghai TV Festival, which was recognized as the largest TV festival ever held in Asia. Since 1990 another TV festival has been held every two years in Sichuan Province, providing one international TV festival in China every year. At the program market of the 1993 Sichuan TV festival, 1,723 TV serials were imported and 213 exported.

The third token of openness is the resurrection of advertising on television. Advertising was halted for three decades following the Party ascent to power in 1949. Over the last 15 years, economic and political reforms have revived the importance of the market forces and the power of advertising. Both domestic and foreign advertising have been resurrected. The majority of foreign programs were imported on barter agreements. In 1986 the figure went up to 115 million yuan, representing a 30-fold growth. In the 1980s, business increased at an annual rate of 50 to 60%, and reached 561 million yuan in 1990. In 1992 the sale of television advertising jumped to 2,050 million, accounting for over 30% of the country's total advertising revenue.

In recent years television has become the most commercialized and market oriented medium and has attracted the most advertising investment from both domestic and foreign clients. Presently, a large proportion of programming revenue, ranging from 40% to 70%, is being funded by advertising and other trade activities. Recently, a fully commercialized television service, Oriental Television, the first of its kind in China, was established in Shanghai. Its operation is stripping away all state financial support . The greater revenues from this source have not only lessened the government's control on finance, but also lessened its control on programming.

New Policies

These drastic changes in television may be attributed to the Party's new policies, including the modernization policy, decentralization policy, and relaxation and pluralism policy.

Under the modernization policy, the authorities have allocated large appropriations to the television industry. In 1967, the total investment in television was 20 million Chinese yuan, but in 1977 the budget was 50 million. In 1980 the expenditure rose to 670 million yuan. In 1985, the number reached to 1,780 million yuan and in 1989, the number became three billion. Entering the 1990s, television investment has exceeded five billion yuan annually.

The decentralization policy entitled "four-level development and management of radio and television services" was adopted in the early 1980s. The "four levels" refer to the country's system of divided administrative. With the central authority at the top, the other three levels are regions (30), local cities (about 450), and counties (approximately 1,900). This policy aimed particularly at extending television into rural areas and inland provinces. Within ten years a widely-penetrated television system was formulated. In the meantime, the number of relay stations grew to 10,000, a 100-fold increase.

Increasingly, television has played an important role in the people's leisure time. The decades-long preview system has been loosened. Except for some politically sensitive topics, most programs no longer need to be previewed by the authorities. The diversification and pluralism of programming has grown with passage of the reform years.

Satellite Broadcasting and Cable Service

Efforts have been made to develop broadcasting satellites to increase the penetration of television and to improve the quality of transmission. Along with terrestrial broadcasting China launched its first telecommunications satellite in 1970. In 1972 the first ground satellite-reception station was set up to assist in domestic and international program exchanges. During the 1980s, a total of five telecommunications and broadcasting satellites were launched, which made it possible to transmit television and radio programs from Beijing to all parts of the country. In 1992 CCTV opened its fourth channel via satellite, covering Hong Kong and Taiwan as well as the whole mainland. Now, 12 channels are transmitted via satellite. With more than 50,000 ground satellite receiving stations, television broadcasting reaches 81.3% of the population

In 1991 China started cable television. In the past three years more than 15,000 cable TV stations have emerged, with a total subscription of 25 million households. The largest cable TV station is Shanghai Cable TV Station (SCTV) with its coverage of 1.2 million terminal users, making this system the biggest cable TV network in the world. SCTV is the country's first cable TV station to adopt the advanced techniques of combined transmission through optical and power cables. It has 12 channels with 13 sets of programs specialized in entertainment, economic information, news, sports, music, education, public service, and other services.

—Junhao Hong

FURTHER READING

Bishop, R. *Qi Lai!—Mobilizing One Billion Chinese: The Chinese Communication System.* Ames, Iowa: Iowa State University Press, 1989.

Chan, J. "Media Internationalization in China: Process and Tensions." *Journal of Communication* (New York), Summer, 1994.

Chang, W. *Mass Media in China: The History and the Future.* Ames, Iowa: Iowa State University Press, 1989.

Hong, J. "Changes in China's Television News Programming in the 1980s: The Case of Shanghai Television (STV)." *Media Asia* (Singapore), 1991.

_____. "China's TV Program Import 1958-1988: Towards the Internationalization of Television." *Gazette,* 1993.

_____. "CNN Over the Great Wall: Transnational Media in China." *Media Information Australia,* February 1994.

_____. "CNN Sets Its Sights on the Asian Market." *Media Development* (London), 1994.

_____."The Evolution of China's Satellite Policy." *Telecommunications Policy* (Guilford, England), March, 1995.

_____. "The Resurrection of Advertising in China: Developments, Problems and Trends." *Asian Survey* (Berkeley, California), April 1994.

Hong, J., and M. Cuthbert. "Media Reform in China since 1978: Background Factors, Problems and Future Trends." *Gazette,* 1991.

Huang, Y. "Peaceful Evolution: The Case of Television Reform in Post-Mao China." *Media, Culture and Society* (London), 1994.

Lee, C. , editor. *Voices of China: The Interplay of Politics and Journalism.* New York: Guilford Press, 1990.

Lee, P. "Mass Communication and National Development in China: Media Roles Reconsidered." *Journal of Communication* (New York), Summer 1994.

Li, X. "The Chinese Television System and Television News." *The China Quarterly* (London), 1991.

Lull, J. *China Turned On: Television, Reform, and Resistance.* London: Routledge, 1991.

Sun, L. "A Forecasting Study on Chinese Television Development 1986 to 2001." *Media Asia* (Singapore), 1989.

CHINA BEACH

U.S. War Drama

Sitting at the televisual intersection of the soap opera, medical show, and war drama, *China Beach* took the pursuit of serial ensemble dramatism to a self-conscious, provocative extreme. The program's premise was the exploration of personal and professional entanglements among American soldiers and civilians staffing a hospital and entertainment company during the Vietnam War. But the show's hybridization of filmic and televisual genres, its rhetorically complex invocation of popular music, and its pointed mod-

ernist-cum-postmodern reflexivity, eventually shifted the emphasis from the story to the telling. Ultimately the series approached a convergence of televisual narrative association with collectively shared cultural remembrance. *China Beach*'s ensemble, the show ultimately implied, necessarily included the viewer inhabiting post-Vietnam America.

The program depicted issues familiar from dark war comedies like *M*A*S*H* and revisionist allegories like *Apocalypse Now*. Story lines explored the corruption or ineptitude

China Beach

of military authority; soldiers' inability to function in "normal" interaction; the medical staff's necessary posture of mordant irony; or the war's sudden curtailment of friendship or romance.

But the narration profoundly shifted the usual priorities of such plots by focusing on the women at the base, an emphasis fundamentally intended to undermine vainglorious heroism and to portray war instead, through "women's eyes," as a vast and elaborate conceit. Contemporary critics divided between those applauding the program's feminine deflation of war, and those who regarded the characters and their orientations toward war as wholly stereotypical invocations of femininity. John Leonard, writing for *Ms.*, anticipated both camps in an early review: on one hand he identified the show's "war-movie foxhole principle of diversity-as-paradigm, which is to say that if you're stuck with all these women, one must be a Madonna, another a whore, a third, Mother Courage, and a fourth, Major Barbara." On the other hand, he reveled in the power of such stereotypes to multiply dramatic possibilities.

Certainly China Beach's two crucial protagonists amounted to carefully elaborated formulas. The camp's head nurse was the willful Colleen McMurphy, a woman proud of her composure and careful in her moral convictions, compassionate but capable of a scathingly condemning glance. K.C. was the calculating madam, alluring but hard, for whom the war brought nothing but higher profits, better contacts, and escalating entrepreneurial opportunities. These two roles constituted an important dialectic not primarily in character conflict, but in the orientation viewers were asked to take at any given time. They were played by exceptional performers whose portrayals complicated the stereotypes by importing still other formulas. Rather than a distanced Madonna, Dana Delany's McMurphy proved to be a passionate woman who—as a feminized, Irish Catholic version of *M*A*S*H*'s Hawkeye Pierce—found not mere escape, but potential redemption in relationships. Rather than a whore with a heart of gold, Marg Helgenberger's K.C. emerged as chillingly objective, independent, self-isolated and unaccountable—as formidable and unapologetic as any soap opera bitch. If McMurphy sought to discover a sheltering and resilient humanity in the ensemble's reciprocities, K.C.'s continual interest was the manipulation of the ensemble's pitifully predictable foibles from without. McMurphy, K.C., and their supporting characters merged the sentimental education of women's melodrama, the life-and-death ethical discourse of medical dramas, and the lurid bathos of the apocalyptic war story in an ambitious format. Here the simultaneous development of serial plot lines created (as on *St. Elsewhere* and *Hill Street Blues*) an ongoing, organically changing, symbolically charged fictional world.

Both melodramatic sentiment and the psychic dislocation of war were conveyed not only through juxtaposed storylines and generic recombination, but through the show's evocative use of Vietnam-era soul, blues, and rock. *China Beach* frequently used such nostalgic music to frame

the show's events as remembrances, laden with a sense of moral revisitation. Even more ambitiously, the program consistently invoked the audiences' feelings of nostalgic distance from the period in which the songs originated. That separation served as an analog for the feelings of distance which the protagonists, immersed in a war, were likely to feel from the society producing those songs. The viewer, like the dislocated combatant, was asked to yearn for the consolations of everyday 1960s American civilization (an invitation which drew on already prevalent revivals of 1960s counterculture among baby boomers and late 1980s youth).

In its final season, the show's convergence between the viewing audience and the protagonists took a considerable leap. The program now followed the characters into their post-war lives, reconstructing key events at China Beach—and the end of the war itself—through flashbacks. In an especially melodramatic plot, the show's narrative is controlled by the investigative efforts of K.C.'s dispossessed baby, now a film student whose hand-held video camera (an instrument of 1980s culture) becomes the show's eye as she interviews her mother's acquaintances in an attempt to find where K.C. has gone. In this season, the original ensemble has dispersed geographically, historically, and socially. Their separation exacerbates the multiplicity of vantages which gestated at China Beach during the war, and places the characters, sometimes disconcertingly and tragically, in situations which seem approachably contemporary with the viewing audience. Screen time became equally divided between fictive "past" and "present," making the entire narration an uprooted historical rumination. The viewer became implicated, not just in a Rashomon-like reconstruction of the war, but in an equally segmented and self-conscious sense of present American society, and its shared reflections.

Formal complication was not confined to music or narrative. *China Beach* used self-conscious, often expressionist lighting, sets, sound, and camera movement, which could vary dramatically from subplot to subplot. The military company's role as an entertainment unit was sometimes exploited to set characters in ironic plays-within-the-show, or to frame the allegorical dimension of musical performances.

For some critics, *China Beach* comprised, at its moment in the history of television production and viewership, a remarkable case of intrinsically televisual fiction. Others, however, regarded the program's overwrought televisual rhetoric differently. It was seen not as an exploration of the ethical and aesthetic possibilities of one of American culture's key sites for the fictional production of touchstone sentiments; rather, it was a conceited diminishment of history. Richard Zoglin of *Time* (a considerable forge of collective memory in its own right), accurately perceived the show's postmodern efforts to collapse wartime tragedy into contemporary viewers' casual nostalgia. But he seemed to think he was indicting the show by suggesting it reflected "the way dissent [against Vietnam] has become domesticated in America; what were radical antiwar views in the '60s are now mainstream TV attitudes." His assessment was accurate but not necessarily lamentable. *China Beach* demonstrated the historical war's continuing ability to open special sentiments among contemporary audiences.

Zoglin and others' questionable worries over television's historical license were based in the assumption that *China Beach*'s version of the war would remain exclusive, definitive, and unrecognized as fiction. But television, with its multiple representations in fiction, documentary and news programs dealing with Vietnam, clearly continues to deny that assumption.

—Michael Saenz

CAST

Nurse Colleen McMurphy	Dana Delany
Cherry White (1988-1989)	Nan Woods
Laurette Barber (1988)	Chloe Webb
Karen Charlene (K. C.) Koloski	Marge Helgenberger
Pvt. Sam Beckett	Michael Boatman
Dr. Dick Richard	Robert Picardo
Natch Austen (1988-1989)	Tim Ryan
Maj. Lila Garreau	Concetta Tomei
Boonie Lanier	Brian Wimmer
Wayloo Marie Holmes (1988-1989)	Megan Gallagher
Pvt. Frankie Bunsen	Nancy Giles
Dodger	Jeff Kober
Jeff Hyers (1989)	Ned Vaughn
Sgt. Pepper (1989–1991)	Troy Evans
Holly the Donut Dolly (1989–1990)	Ricki Lake

PRODUCERS   John Sacret Young, William Broyles, Jr.

PROGRAMMING HISTORY

• ABC

April 1988	Tuesday 9:00-11:00
April 1988–June 1988	Wednesday 10:00-11:00
August 1988–September 1988	Wednesday 10:00-11:00
November 1988–March 1990	Wednesday 10:00-11:00
April 1990	Monday 9:00-10:00
July 1990–August 1990	Wednesday 10:00-11:00
August 1990–December 1990	Saturday 9:00-10:00
June 1991–July 1991	Tuesday 10:00-11:00
July 1991	Monday 9:00-11:00

FURTHER READING

Auster, Albert. "'Reflections of the Way Life Used to Be': *Tour of Duty, China Beach*, and the Memory of the Sixties." *Television Quarterly* (New York), Fall 1990.

Ballard-Reisch, Deborah. "*China Beach* and *Tour of Duty*: American Television and Revisionist History of the Vietnam War." *Journal of Popular Culture* (Bowling Green, Ohio), Winter 1991.

Hanson, Cynthia A. "The Women of *China Beach*." *Journal of Popular Film and Television* (Washington, D.C.), Winter 1990.

Leonard, John. "Networking: A Not-So-Frank Assessment of Prime-time Women." *Ms.* (New York), October 1988.

Morrison, Mark. "*China Beach* Salutes the Women of Vietnam." *Rolling Stone* (New York), 19 May 1988.

Rasmussen, Karen. "*China Beach* and American Mythology of War." *Women's Studies in Communication* (Los Angeles), Fall 1992.

Schine, Cathleen. "TV's Women in Groups: They Work Together, They Sweat Together, They 'Care' Together." *Vogue* (New York), September 1988.

Vande Berg, Leah R. "*China Beach*, Prime Time War in the Postfeminist Age: An Example of Patriarchy in a Different Voice." *Western Journal of Communication* (Salt Lake City, Utah), Summer 1993.

Zoglin, Richard. "War as Family Entertainment." *Time* (New York), 20 February 1989.

See also Vietnam on Television; War on Television

THE CHRISTIAN BROADCASTING NETWORK/ THE FAMILY CHANNEL

U.S. Cable Network

The Christian Broadcasting Network (CBN) grew from the vision of one man, Pat Robertson, who in 1960 bought a run-down UHF station in Portsmouth, Virginia, for a mere $37,000. While many religious broadcasters relied on sermons to convey their message, Robertson developed a talk show approach on his new station, in which interviews, music, teaching, prayer and healing were all provided in a smoothly produced program format. CBN's first telethon to raise funds in the fall of 1963 was named *The 700 Club* because Robertson asked for 700 people to pledge $10 a month to support the new station and keep it

Courtesy of the Christian Broadcasting Network

on the air. This became the name of Pat Robertson's religious talk show; he became host for the show, and a former Black Muslim Ben Kinchlow became co-host; the show is still running more than thirty years later.

Three innovations adopted by CBN helped the fledgling network grow rapidly to into one of the biggest religious broadcasting networks in the world. The first innovation was CBN's use of the telephone to provide ongoing contact with viewers. *The 700 Club* provides a telephone number on screen so that viewers can call to ask for prayer and counseling during and after each program. Viewers responded warmly to this semi-interactive relationship with the *700 Club* hosts; the hosts would write personalized follow-up letters to those who called. In 1979 sixty counseling centers across the nation were established to respond to calls 24 hours a day. By 1992 over forty million calls had been received; now in 1995 an average of a million calls a year have enabled CBN to meet the spiritual needs of millions, while at the same time, updating its data base of supporters. CBN's second innovation was to follow the lead of HBO and CNN and build its own satellite earth station as early as 1977. When CBN first started buying time on network affiliate stations, it had to transport videotapes of the *700 Club* episodes from station to station, which meant programs were usually days and sometimes weeks old by the time they were broadcast. This new satellite technology enabled CBN to transmit the shows live across the nation either for immediate broadcast, or for rebroadcast later.

CBN's third innovation was to provide 24-hour religious programming to the nation's growing network of cable stations. By 1980 the Continental Broadcasting Network, an alternative name for CBN Cable, provided a 24-hour satellite TV service reaching more than 5 million homes; cable operators were paid a few cents per month per viewer for providing a religious cable channel in their area. CBN Cable moved to become an advertiser-and-cable-system-funded family entertainment channel with limited religious programming. On 1 August 1988 CBN Cable changed its name to the Family Channel; two years later CBN sold the channel to International Family Entertainment to satisfy IRS requirements so that CBN would retain its tax exempt status.

CBN claim that the transaction provided them with more than $600 million in total benefits—everything from cash to airtime. IFE became a publicly held 150 million dollar company when traded on the New York Stock Exchange in 1992. Effectively a small UHF religious station has become a cable programming giant in thirty years.

In 1980 *The 700 Club* changed format from an all religious show to a contemporary talk show with news elements, based on news bureaus in Virginia Beach, Washington D.C., and later in Jerusalem, Israel. *USam,* a morning news show, began in 1981 but was withdrawn after a year. *Another Life,* a daily soap opera featuring the adventures of a Christian family, ran for 800 episodes from 1981 to 1984,

and still airs in many countries around the world. Perhaps the most successful productions were the two animated Bible story series *Superbook* and *Flying House.* These two series were syndicated worldwide and when broadcast in Russia and the Ukraine in 1991 produced more than eleven million requests for gospel literature.

Program content on the *700 Club* stresses a biblical worldview, based on the belief that there exists a set of moral absolutes revealed in scripture that should undergird society's institutions, laws, and public policy. Like other conservative Christians, Robertson sees certain Supreme Court decisions in the 1960s as paving the way for a moral and spiritual decline in American society, and blames secular humanism as the source of the corruption and godlessness that leads to the social ills like abortion and the break-up of traditional families.

During the 1980s the growth of religious television and the resurgence of the New Religious Right in American politics went hand in hand. Historian James Heinz in his book *The Struggle to Redefine America* suggests that conservative evangelicalism won support because "it tapped into symbols that turn out to be powerfully resonant in the lives of many people." Robertson launched a bid for the Republican nomination for president in 1986, but was defeated by George Bush.

International Family Entertainment which owns the Family Channel, is completely separate from the Christian Broadcasting Network. The Family Channel has become a profitable secular family entertainment cable network, which is required to continue to broadcast *The 700 Club* in perpetuity, and will do so as long as it is controlled by the Robertson family through their Class A voting shares. With an assured commercial income from advertising, the future for the Family Channel looks bright. CBN depends heavily on the income of thrice annual fund raising telethons. Total revenues for Fiscal 1993 from donations, earned income and investments were $186.4 million dollars. The significance of CBN is that it provides incontrovertible evidence that a generous section of the American television public continue to want to watch religious TV, and contribute millions of dollars every year to support such broadcasting ventures.

—Andrew Quicke

FURTHER READING

Ableman, Robert, and Stewart M. Hoover, editors. *Religious Television: Controversies and Conclusions.* Norwood, New Jersey: Ablex, 1990.

Armstrong, Ben. *The Electronic Church.* Nashville, Tennessee: Thomas Nelson, 1979.

Aufderheide, Pat. "The Next Voice You Hear." *Progressive* (Madison, Wisconsin), 29 September 1985.

Clark, Kenneth R. "The $70 Miracle Named CBN." *Chicago Tribune,* 26 July 1985.

Ellens, J. Haarold. *Models of Religious Broadcasting.* Grand Rapids, Michigan: Eerdmans, 1974.

Hoover, Stewart M. *Mass Media Religion: The Social Sources of the Electronic Church.* Newbury Park, California:Sage, 1988.

Kabler, Ciel Dunne. *Telecommunications and the Church.* Virginia Beach, Virginia: Multi Media Publishing, 1979.

Peck, Janice. *The Gods of Televangelism: The Crisis of Meaning and the Appeal of Religious Television.* Cresskill, New York: Hampton, 1993.

Schmidt, Rosemarie, and Joseph Kess. *Television Advertising and Televangelism: Discourse Analysis of Persuasive Language.* Amsterdam, The Netherlands and Philadelphia, Pennsylvania: J. Benjamins, 1986.

Straub, Gerard Thomas. *Salvation for Sale: An Insider's View of Pat Robertson.* Buffalo, New York: Prometheus, 1988.

See also Cable Networks; Religion on Television

CHUNG, CONNIE

U.S. Broadcast Journalist

Connie Chung is one of a very small group of women who have achieved prominence in American network news. Along with Barbara Walters, Diane Sawyer and Jane Pauley, Chung is one of the leading female journalists on television. Until 1995 she co-anchored the *CBS Evening News* with Dan Rather, as well as *Eye to Eye with Connie Chung,* a prime-time news hour. Following considerable controversy over her interviewing style and reportorial skills, and during which it was reported that Rather had never been happy with the co-anchor arrangement, Chung parted ways with CBS in 1995.

Chung began her journalism career in 1969 as a copyperson at WTTG-TV, Washington, D.C., a Metromedia affiliate, where she later became a newswriter and on-air reporter. She first joined CBS News in 1971, working as a Washington-based correspondent from 1971 to 1976, covering Watergate, Capitol Hill and the 1972 presidential campaign. In 1976 she joined KNXT (now KCBS-TV), the CBS-owned television station in Los Angeles, working on both local and network broadcasts. In her seven years in Los Angeles, Chung co-anchored three daily newscasts, and was a substitute anchor for the *CBS Morning News* and CBS News' weekend and evening broadcasts. She also anchored CBS News' *Newsbreak* for the Pacific time zones.

Chung left CBS to join NBC News as a correspondent and anchor. Her assignments included anchoring the Saturday edition of the *NBC Nightly News, NBC News at Sunrise, NBC News Digest,* several primetime news specials and the newsmagazine, *1986.* She was also contributing correspondent and substitute anchor on the *NBC Nightly News* broadcast. Chung served as political analysis correspondent and podium correspondent during the 1988 president campaign and political conventions.

When she joined Dan Rather as co-anchor of the *CBS Evening News,* Chung became only the second woman to hold a network anchor job, following Barbara Walters' brief stint as co-anchor with Harry Reasoner on ABC in the mid-1970s. The male-female anchor pairing, already a staple of local news, seemed designed also to capitalize on Chung's recognizability. In the Q-ratings (a set of measurements

Connie Chung
Photo courtesy of Connie Chung/Tony Esparza

provided by a company called Marketing Evaluations, which gauge the popularity of people who appear on television), Chung has always scored extremely high. At the time she was named co-anchor, she had one of the highest Q-ratings of any woman in network news. In 1990 she was chosen "favorite interviewer" in *U.S. News and World Report's* Best of America survey.

In unexpected ways, Chung has foregrounded issues of concern to working women. In 1990, she took the unusual step of announcing plans to postpone her magazine series *Face to Face with Connie Chung* in order to take time to conceive a child with her husband, syndicated daytime television talk-show host Maury Povich.

Chung has also been part of the trend toward using newscast anchors on prime-time programs. Her work on nighttime news shows has sometimes drawn criticism, as when the short-lived *Saturday Night with Connie Chung* was tagged as "infotainment" and charged with undermining the credibility of network news by using controversial techniques such as news re-enactments. Chung was again involved in controversy in early 1995, when in an interview with Kathryn Gingrich, the mother of Speaker of the House Newt Gingrich, Chung urged her subject to whisper her son's comments about First Lady Hillary Clinton "just between us." The whisper was picked up by the microphone and used by Chung for broadcast, drawing attacks on Chung's journalistic integrity. This incident was followed by conflict over Chung's assignment to cover the Oklahoma City bombing incident, CBS' apparent plans to "demote" her to the position of weekend anchor, and possibly to cancel her prime-time program *Eye to Eye with Connie Chung*. Accompanied by an almost palpable strain on the set of the *CBS Evening News*, as well as by the program's declining ratings, these events led to Chung's departure from CBS amidst charges of sexism, and counter-charges of a lack of journalistic seriousness.

—Diane M. Negra

CONNIE CHUNG. Born Constance Yu-Hwa Chung in Washington, D.C., U.S.A., 20 August 1946. Educated at University of Maryland, B.A. in journalism, 1969. Married: Maurice (Maury) Richard Povich, 1984; child: Matthew Jay. Reporter, WTTG-TV, Washington, 1969–71; correspondent, CBS News, Washington, 1971–76; anchor, KNXT-TV (CBS), Los Angeles, 1976–83; anchor, NBC News, 1983–89, and NBC News Specials, 1987–89; anchor, *Saturday Night with Connie Chung*, CBS, *CBS Evening News* (Sunday), 1989–92; co-anchor, *CBS Evening News*, 1993-95; currently developing a news magazine show, with her husband, for DreamWorks SKG, projected to begin fall 1998. Honorary degrees: D.J., Norwich University, 1974; L.H.D., Brown University, 1987. Honorary member: Pepperdine University Broadcast Club, 1981. Recipient: Metro Area Mass Media Award, American Association of University Women (AAUW), 1971; Outstanding Excellence in News Reporting and Public Service Award, Chinese-American Citizens Alliance, 1973; award for best TV reporting, Los Angeles Press Club, 1977; award for outstanding TV broadcasting, Valley Press Club, 1977; Emmy Awards; 1978, 1980, and 1987; Peabody Award, 1980; Newscaster of the Year Award, Temple Emmanuel Brotherhood, 1981; Portraits of Excellence Award, B'nai B'rith, Pacific S.W. Region, 1980; First Amendment Award, Anti-Defamation League of B'nai B'rith, 1981.

TELEVISION SERIES

1983–89	*NBC Nightly News* (anchor and reporter)
1983–89	*News Digest* (anchor and reporter)
1983–89	*NBC News at Sunrise* (anchor and reporter)
1985–86	*American Almanac* (co-host)
1985–86	*1986* (co-host)
1989–95	*CBS Evening News* (reporter)
1989–90	*Saturday Night with Connie Chung* (host)
1990	*Face to Face with Connie Chung* (host)
1993–95	*CBS Evening News* (co-anchor)
1993–95	*Eye to Eye with Connie Chung*

TELEVISION SPECIALS

1980	*Terra: Our World*
1987	*NBC News Report on America: Life in the Fat Lane*
1987	*Scared Sexless*
1988	*NBC News Reports on America: Stressed to Kill*
1988	*Everybody's Doing It*

FURTHER READING

Anderson, Kurt. "Does Connie Chung Matter?" *Time* (New York), 31 May 1993.

Carter. Bill. "Chung to Join Rather." *The New York Times,* 18 May 1993.

Conant, Jennet. "Broadcast Networking: Despite What You've Heard, the Women of TV News Feel a Strong Sense of Solidarity." *Working Woman* (New York), August 1990.

Frank, Reuven. "Connie Chung at the Circus." *The New Leader* (New York), 8 May 1995.

"A Future Affair." *MediaWeek* (Brewster, New York), 10 June 1996.

Hosley, David H., and Gayle K. Yamada. *Hard News: Women in Broadcast Journalism.* New York: Greenwood, 1987.

Reibstein, Larry. "Irreconcilable Ratings." *Newsweek* (New York), 5 June 1995.

Westin, Av. *Newswatch: How TV Decides the News.* New York: Simon and Schuster, 1982.

Wolf, Steve. "Weighing Anchors." *Time* (New York), 15 May 1995.

CITYTV

Canadian Television Station

Citytv, Toronto's fast-paced and image-driven independent television station, first went to air 28 September 1972 as a UHF channel. It was assured of financial security when the Canadian media-giant CHUM Ltd., who had purchased a 45% interest in Citytv from Montreal-based Multiple Access in 1979, acquired the remainder of shares in the struggling station in 1981. ChumCity's total enterprise includes the cable and satellite music-video channels MuchMusic and MusiquePlus (also franchised in Latin America as MuchaMusica); the national arts and culture channel Bravo!; and international syndication sales of Citytv's magazine programmes (such as *The New Music, Fashion Television, Media Television,* or *The Originals*). Citytv is now a consistently top-ranked channel within what is perhaps North America's most competitive market (Toronto has 53 television stations).

Built upon the programming keystones of news, music and movies, Citytv found early notoriety by broadcasting *Baby Blue Movies,* a series of late-night, soft-core porn films. While the "Baby Blues" are now off the air, Citytv still broadcasts an average of five movies a day, many of which are World or Canadian premiers. Similarly innovative in music programming, Citytv first telecast *The New Music,* a forerunner to both MTV and MuchMusic, in 1979. However, Citytv's most notable distinction lies in a conceptual approach which consistently attempts to expand the mobility and function of the medium. As Canada's first all-videotape station, Citytv initiated the practices of Electronic News Gathering and single-person reportage. Such techniques are exercised in the local news programme *CityPulse,* which foregoes anchor desks and news studios for an unconventional and tabloid-like momentum. The emphasis upon process, locality and informal interactivity is particularly evidenced in the ChumCity building, a refurbished 19th century gothic structure in which there are no studios, no sets or control rooms. Instead, the entire complex is wired to "shoot itself" through a series of strategically placed electronic "hydrants". In this manner, cameras are enabled to roam anywhere—the roof , stairwells, or the street—and are often integrated into the shot. Viewers then watch camera operators at work setting up, watch themselves viewing programmes in process through the building's large ground-floor windows, or see an interview through the eyes of an interviewee, via a second Hi-8 camera provided to the story subject. The concept of public access is expanded through *Speaker's Corner,* a video booth where, for a charity-addressed dollar, passers-by may confess their sins, declare their love, or sound off on pet peeves; the best of these are used as shorts between shows or collated into the weekly *Speaker's Corner* programme.

Courtesy of Citytv

Unlike many other Canadian networks or independent stations, Citytv does not bid for dramatic programmes produced in the United States, with the exception of importing the contemporary *Star Trek* series (*The Next Generation, Deep Space Nine,* and *Voyager*), and the occasional made-for-TV movie or miniseries. Citytv does buy syndicated daytime talk shows from the United States, which it airs during its weekday schedule. There are no game shows, children's programmes, soaps, sitcoms or sports on Citytv. Saturday and Sunday morning schedules are given over to community ethnic programming.

While often favoring style and self-promotion over substance and self-reflexivity, Citytv's accomplished characteristic lies in its process-oriented format. This is evident not only within the programmes per se, but the breaks in between programmes: station IDs, interstitials and promotional spots are tailored to intervene, as well as interweave, within the overall affect and tenor of the show. In this respect, Citytv successfully capitalizes upon the capacities of televisual "flow".

—Beth Seaton

FURTHER READING

McDonald, Marci. "The Gospel According to Moses (Znaimer)." *Maclean's* (Toronto), 8 May 1995.

Murray, Ken. "Canadian TV Moguls Rev Engines in Race for U.K.'s Channel 5." *Variety* (Los Angeles), 1 June 1992.

Robins, J. Max. "This Moses May Lead TV to its Promised Land." *Variety* (Los Angeles), 26 July 1993.

See also Canada; Canadian Production Companies; Canadian Programming in English; MuchMusic; Znaimer, Moses

CIVIL RIGHTS MOVEMENT AND TELEVISION

American television coverage of the Civil Rights Movement ultimately contributed to a redefinition of the country's political as well as its televisual landscape. From the 1955 Montgomery bus boycotts to the 1964 Democratic National Convention in Atlantic City, technological innovations in portable cameras and electronic news gathering (ENG) equipment increasingly enabled television to bring the non-violent civil disobedience campaign of the Civil Rights Movement and the violent reprisals of Southern law enforcement agents to a new mass audience.

The NAACP's 1954 landmark Supreme Court case, *Brown v. Board of Education,* along with the brutal murder of 15-year-old Emmet Till in Mississippi and the subsequent acquittal of the two white men accused of his murder marked the beginning of America's modern Civil Rights Movement. The unprecedented media coverage of the Till case rendered it a *cause celebre* that helped to swell the membership ranks of civil rights organizations nationwide. As civil rights workers organized mass boycotts and civil disobedience campaigns to end legal segregation and white supremacist terror in the South, white segregationists mounted a counter-offensive that was swift and too often violent. Medgar Evers and other civil rights activists were assassinated. Black churches, businesses and residences with ties to the movement were bombed. Although this escalation of terror was intended to thwart the Civil Rights Movement, it had the effect of broadening support for civil rights.

These events were unfolding at the same time that the percentage of American homes equipped with television sets jumped from 56 to 92%. This was 1955 and television was securing its place in American society. Network news shows were also beginning to expand from the conventional fifteen to thirty minutes format, splitting the time between local and national issues. From the mid to late 1950s, these social, political, technological and cultural events began to converge. The ascendancy of television as the new arbiter of public opinion became increasingly apparent at this time to civil rights leaders and television news directors alike. Thus television's coverage of the Civil Rights Movement changed considerably, especially as the "anti-establishment politics" of the 1960s erupted. When television covered the consumer boycotts and the school desegregation battles in the early days of the Civil Rights Movement, it was usually in a detached manner with a particular focus on the most dramatic and sensational occurrences. As well, the coverage in the late 1950s was intermittent, with a field reporter conducting a stand-up report from a volatile scene. Alternatively, an in-studio anchor man would narrate the unfolding events captured on film. Rarely, if ever, did black participants speak for themselves or address directly America's newly constituted mass television audience. Nevertheless, civil rights leaders understood how central television exposure was becoming to the success of the movement.

The desire to bring the struggle for civil rights into American living rooms was not limited to civil rights workers, however. The drama and sensationalism of peaceful civil rights protesters in violent confrontation with brutal agents of Southern segregation was not lost on news producers. News programmers needed to fill their expanded news programs with live telecasts of newsworthy events, and the public clashes around the Civil Rights Movement were too violent and too important to ignore.

For example, among the most enduring images telecast from this period were: 1955—shots of numerous boycotted busses driving down deserted Alabama streets; 1957—angry white mobs of segregationists squaring-off against black students escorted by a phalanx of Federal Troops in front of Ole Miss, the University of Mississippi; 1965—Dr. Martin Luther King, Jr., leads a mass of black protesters across a bridge in Selma, Alabama. Most memorable, perhaps, of all these dramatic video images is the 1963 attack on young civil rights protesters by the Birmingham, Alabama, police and their dogs, and the fire department's decision to turn on fire hydrants to disperse the young black demonstrators, most of whom were children. Television cameras captured the water's force pushing young, black protesters down flooding streets like rubbish during a street cleaning. Unquestionably, this was compelling and revolutionary television.

By the early to mid 1960s, television was covering the explosive Civil Rights Movement regularly and forcefully. It was at this time that the young, articulate and telegenic Reverend Martin Luther King, Jr., had emerged from the Southern Christian Leadership Conference as the Movement's chief spokesman. Commenting on King's oratorical skills, one reporter noted that his "message and eloquence were met with rapt attention and enthusiastic support." He was the perfect visual symbol for a new era of American race relations. During this period television made it possible for civil rights workers to be seen and heard on an international scale. Fanny Lou Hamer's televised speech at the 1964 Democratic Convention in Atlantic City signaled a pivotal moment in the history of television's relationship to the civil rights campaign. Hamer's now famous "Is this America?" speech infuriated President Johnson, emboldened the networks, and riveted the nation. Even though Johnson directed the networks to kill the live feed carrying her speech on voting rights on behalf of the African American Mississippi Freedom Democratic Party (MFDP), the networks recognized the speech's powerful appeal and aired Hamer's address in its entirety later that night. Thus Hamer, a black woman and a sharecropper, became one of the first black civil rights activists to address the nation directly and on her own terms. King's historic "I Have a Dream" speech was delivered on 28 August 1963, at the March on Washington rally. King's speech not only reached the 300,000 people from civil rights organizations, church

Dr. Martin Luther King, Jr.

groups and labor unions who gathered at the nation's capital to demonstrate for unity, racial tolerance and passage of the civil rights bill, with the aid of television it reached the nation as well. Later that same year, television covered the assassinations of civil rights leader Medgar Evers, and months later that of President John F. Kennedy. These deaths devastated the civil rights community and television coverage of both events ensured that the nation mourned these losses as well. This phase of the movement also saw an influx of white, liberal college students and

adults from across the country into the deep South during the so-called "Freedom Summer" of 1964.

Civil rights organizers encouraged the participation of white liberals in the movement because organizers understood that the presence of whites would attract the television cameras and, by extension, the nation. No one was prepared for the tragic events that followed. As it turns out, television's incessant probing into the murders and subsequent month-long search for the bodies of two white, Northern civil rights workers, Michael Schwerner and

Andrew Goodman, and black, Southerner James Chaney did have a chilling effect on the nation. With the death of innocent white volunteers, television was convincing its suburban viewers around the country that the Civil Rights Movement did concern them as well. For it was difficult to turn on the television without news of the Schwerner, Chaney and Goodman search. From late June to 4 August 1964, television regularly and consistently transmitted news of the tragedy to the entire nation. Television ultimately legitimated and lent new urgency to the decade-long struggle for basic human and civil rights that the Civil Rights Movement had difficulty achieving prior to the television age. The incessant gaze of the television cameras on the murders and disappearance of Schwerner, Chaney and Goodman, following on the heels of the Evers and Kennedy assassinations, resulted in mobilizing national support for the Civil Rights Movement. In fact, it was television's coverage of the Civil Rights Movement's crises and catastrophes that became a prelude to the medium's subsequent involvement with and handling of the later social and political chaos surrounding the Black Power, Anti-War, Free Speech and Feminist Movements. As veteran civil rights reporters went on to cover the assassinations of Malcom X, Martin Luther King and Robert Kennedy, as well as the ghetto uprisings thereafter, a whole new visual and aural lexicon of crisis-television developed, one that in many ways still defines how television news is communicated.

By 1968, it was clear that television's powerful and visceral images of the civil rights struggle had permeated many levels of American social and political reality. These images had helped garner support for such liberal legislation as the 1964 Voting Rights Act and President Lyndon B. Johnson's "Great Society" and "War on Poverty" programs, all of which are legatees of the Civil Rights Movement. As volatile pictures of Watts, Detroit, Washington, D.C., and other cities going up in smoke hit the television airwaves, they provoked a strong reaction by the end of the decade, marked by the presidential campaign slogans calling for law and order. Consequently, many of the very images that supported the movement simultaneously helped to fuel the national backlash against it. This anti-civil rights backlash contributed to the 1968 presidential election of conservative Republican Richard M. Nixon.

While television news programs strove to cover the historic events of the day, entertainment shows responded to the Civil Rights Movement in their own fashion. With their concern over advertising revenues and corporate sponsorship, television's entertainment divisions decided on a turn to social relevance that did not tackle the controversy and social conflict of the Civil Rights Movement directly. Instead, it took the cautious route of slowly integrating (in racial terms) fictional programming by casting black characters in roles other than the usual domestic and comedic stereotypes. Beloved characterizations of domesticated blacks in such popular television shows as *Beulah, Amos 'n'*

Andy, The Jack Benny Show, and *The Danny Thomas Show,* for example, slowly gave way to integrated cast programs depicting the network's accommodationist position on the "new frontier" ideology of Kennedy liberalism wherein black characters were integrated into American society as long as they supported American law and order. Among these shows were *East Side/West Side* (1963–64), *The Defenders* (1961–65), *Naked City* (1958–63), *The Nurses* (1962–65), *I Spy* (1965–68), *Peyton Place* (1964–69), *Star Trek* (1966–69), *Mission: Impossible* (1966–73), *Daktari* (1966–69), *NYPD* (1967–69) and *Mod Squad* (1968–73), to name but a few. Rather than reflect the intense racial conflicts of bombed-out churches, blacks being beaten by Southern cops and massive demonstrations, these dramatic programs portrayed interracial cooperation and peaceful coexistence between black and white characters. For the first time on network television, many of the black characters in these shows were depicted as intelligent and heroic. While some of these shows were criticized for their lone black characters who staunchly upheld the status quo, these shows, nevertheless, did mark a significant transformation of the televisual universe. And for mass audiences accustomed to traditional white and black shows, the Civil Rights Movement brought a little more color to the television spectrum.

—Anna Everett

FURTHER READING

Brooks, Tim, and Earle Marsh, editors. *The Complete Directory to Prime Time Network TV Shows: 1946-Present.* New York: Ballentine, 1979; 5th edition, 1992.

Gitlin, Todd. *Inside Prime Time.* New York: Pantheon, 1985.

Hampton, Henry. *Voices of Freedom: An Oral History of the Civil Rights Movement from the 1950s through the 1980s.* New York: Bantam, 1990.

Hill, George, with others. *Black Women in Television.* New York and London: Garland, 1990.

Hine, Darlene Clark, with others, editors. *Black Women in America.* Bloomington: Indiana University Press, 1993.

Kellner, Douglas. *Television and the Crisis of Democracy.* Boulder, Colorado: Westview, 1990.

MacDonald, J. Fred. *Blacks and White TV: Afro-Americans in Television Since 1948.* Chicago: Nelson-Hall Publishers, 1992.

———. *One Nation Under Television: The Rise and Decline of Network TV.* New York: Pantheon, 1990.

McNeil, Alex. *Total Television, Including Cable: A Comprehensive Guide to Programming from 1948 to the Present.* New York: Penguin, 1980; 3rd edition, 1991.

Mills, Kay. *This Little Light of Mine: The Life of Fannie Lou Hamer.* New York: Penguin, 1993.

Newcomb, Horace, editor. *Television: The Critical View.* New York: Oxford University Press, 1976; 4th edition, 1987.

O'Connor, John E., editor. *American History/American Tele-vision: Interpreting the Video Past.* New York: Ungar, 1983.

Renov, Michael, editor. *Theorizing Documentary.* New York and London: Routledge, 1993.

Williams, Juan, with the Eyes on the Prize Production Team. *Eyes on the Prize: America's Civil Rights Years, 1954–1965.* New York: Viking Penguin, 1987.

See also Racism, Ethnicity, and Television

THE CIVIL WAR

U.S. Compilation Documentary

The Civil War premiered on the Public Broadcasting Service over five consecutive evenings (23 to 27 September 1990) amassing the largest audience for any series in public television history. Over 39 million Americans tuned into at least one episode of the telecast, and viewership averaged more than 14 million viewers each evening. Subsequent research indicated that nearly half the viewers would not have even been watching television at all if it had not been for *The Civil War.*

The widespread positive reaction to *The Civil War* was generally lavish and unprecedented. Film and television critics from across the country were equally attentive and admiring. *Newsweek* reported "a documentary master-piece"; *Time* "eloquen[t]...a pensive epic"; and *U.S. News and World Report* "the best Civil War film ever made." David Thomson in *American Film* declared that *The Civil War* "is a film Walt Whitman might have dreamed." And political pundit, George Will, wrote: "Our *Iliad* has found its Homer...if better use has ever been made of television, I have not seen it."

Between 1990 and 1992, accolades for Ken Burns and the series took on institutional proportions. He won "Pro-

The Civil War
Photo courtesy of Florentine Films

ducer of the Year" from the Producers Guild of America; two Emmys (for "Outstanding Information Series" and "Outstanding Writing Achievement"); a Peabody; a Du-Pont-Columbia Award; a Golden Globe; a D.W. Griffith Award; two Grammys; a People's Choice Award for "Best Television Mini-Series"; and eight honorary doctorates from various of American colleges and universities, along with literally dozens of other recognitions.

The Civil War also became a phenomenon of popular culture. The series was mentioned on episodes of *Twin Peaks, thirtysomething,* and *Saturday Night Live* during the 1990-91 television season. Ken Burns appeared on *The Tonight Show,* and he was selected by the editors of *People* magazine as one of their "25 most intriguing people of 1990." The series, moreover, developed into a marketing sensation. The companion volume, published by Knopf, *The Civil War: An Illustrated History,* became a runaway bestseller; as did the nine episode videotaped version from Time-Life, and the Warner soundtrack, featuring the bittersweet anthem, "Ashokan Farewell," by Jay Ungar.

Several interlocking factors evidently contributed to this extraordinary level of interest, including its accompanying promotional campaign, the momentum of scheduling Sunday through Thursday, the synergetic merchandising of its ancillary products, and of course the quality of production itself. Most significantly, though, the series examined America's great civil conflict from a distinct perspective. A new generation of historians had already begun addressing the war from the so-called "bottom-up" point of view, underscoring the role of African-Americans, women, immigrants, workers, farmers, and common soldiers in the conflict. This fresh emphasis on social and cultural history had revitalized the Civil War as a subject, adding a more inclusive and human dimension to the traditional preoccupations with "great men," transcendent ideals, and battle strategies and statistics. The time was again propitious for creating a filmed version of the war between the states which included the accessibility of the newer approach. In Ken Burns' own words, "I don't think the story of the Civil War can be told too often. I think it surely ought to be retold for every generation."

Much of the success of Ken Burns' *The Civil War* must be attributed to the ways in which his account makes this nineteenth century conflict immediate and comprehensible in the 1990s. The great questions of race and continuing discrimination, of the changing roles of women and men in society, of big government versus local control, and of the individual struggle for meaning and conviction in modern life, all form essential parts of Burns' version of the war. In his own words, "I realized the power that the war still exerted over us."

To define and present that power on television Burns employed 24 prominent historians as consultants on the project. He melded together approximately 300 expert commentaries and another 900 first-person quotations from Civil War era letters, diaries, and memoirs. Exerpts from these source materials were read by a wide assortment of distinguished performers, such as Sam Waterston, Jason Robards, Julie Harris, and Morgan Freeman, among many others.

Often these remarkable voices would be attached to specific historical characters—foot soldiers from both armies, wives or mothers left behind, slaves who escaped to fight on behalf of their own freedom. One of Burns' extraordinary techniques was to follow some of these individuals through long periods of time, using their own words to chronicle the devastating sense of battle weariness, the loneliness of divided families, and both the pain and joy of specific moments in personal histories.

Just as significantly, he attached pictures to these words. Using a vast collection of archival photographs, some rarely seen, the primary visual production techniques was the slow movement of the camera over the surfaces of still photographs. Audiences were allowed to move in for close-ups of faces and eyes, to survey spaces captured in more panoramic photos, and to see some individuals at different stages of their war experiences. The visual component of *The Civil War* also compared historical photographs of places with contemporary filmed shots of the same locations. The "reality" of bluffs over Vicksburg, a Chancellorsville battlefield, or Appamattox Courthouse was established by these multiple pictorial representations.

All these visual and aural techniques combined in a special sort of opportunity for the audience. The series invited one into a meditation more than an analysis, an intimate personal consideration of massive conflict, social upheaval, and cultural devastation.

Ken Burns, a hands-on and versatile producer, was personally involved in researching, fund raising, co-writing, shooting, directing, editing, scoring, and even promoting *The Civil War.* The series, a production of Burns' Florentine Films in association with WETA-TV in Washington, also boasted contributions by many of the filmmaker's usual collaborators, including his brother and co-producer, Ric Burns, writer Geoffrey C. Ward, and narrator David McCullough. Writer, historian, and master raconteur, Shelby Foote, emerged as the onscreen star of *The Civil War,* peppering the series with entertaining anecdotes during 89 separate appearances.

The Civil War took an estimated five years to complete and cost nearly $3.5 million, garnered largely from support by General Motors, the National Endowment for the Humanities, and the Corporation for Public Broadcasting. By any standard that has gone before, *The Civil War* is a masterful historical documentary.

Burns now laughs about the apprehension he felt on the evening *The Civil War* premiered on prime-time television and changed his life forever. He remembers thinking long and hard about the remarks of several reviewers who predicted that the series would be "eaten alive," going head-to-head with network programming. He recalls being "completely unprepared for what was going to happen" next, as the series averaged a 9.0 rating, an exceptional performance for public television. Ken Burns admits, "I was flabbergasted! I still sort of pinch myself about it. It's one of those rare instances in which something helped stitch the country together, however briefly, and the fact that I had a part in that is just tremendously satisfying."

—Gary R. Edgerton

PRODUCERS   Ken Burns, Ric Burns, Stephen Ives, Julie Dunfey, Mike Hill

PROGRAMMING HISTORY

• PBS

23–27 September 1990

FURTHER READING

Burns, K. "In Search of the Painful, Essential Images of War." *The New York Times*, 27 January 1991.
Censer, J.T. "Videobites: Ken Burns' *The Civil War* in the Classroom." *American Quarterly* (Philadelphia, Pennsylvania), 1992.
"*The Civil War*: Ken Burns Charts a Nation's Birth." *American Film* (Washington, D.C.), September 1990.
DuBois, E. "The Civil War." *American Historical Review* (Washington, D.C.), 1991.
Duncan, D. "A Cinematic Storyteller." *The Boston Globe Magazine*, 19 March 1989.
Edgerton, G. "Ken Burns—A Conversation with Public Television's Resident Historian." *Journal of American Culture* (Bowling Green, Ohio), 1995.
———. "Ken Burns' America: Style, Authorship, and Cultural Memory." *Journal of Popular Film and Television* (Washington, D.C.), 1993.
———. "Ken Burns' American Dream—Histories-for-TV from Walpole, New Hampshire." *Television Quarterly* (New York), 1994.
———. "Ken Burns' Rebirth of a Nation: Television, Narrative, and Popular History." *Film and History* 1992.
Henderson, B. "*The Civil War*: 'Did It Not Seem Real?'" *Film Quarterly* (London), 1991.
Koeniger, A.C. "Ken Burns' *The Civil War*: Triumph or Travesty?" *The Journal of Military History* (Lexington, Virginia), April 1991.
Milius, J. "Reliving the War Between Brothers." *The New York Times,* 16 September 1990.
Powers, R. "Glory, Glory." *GQ* (New York), September 1990.
Purcell, H. "America's Civil Wars." *History Today* (London), May 1991.
Summers, M.W. "*The Civil War*." *The Journal of American History* (Bloomington, Indiana), December 1990.
Thomson, D. "History Composed with Film." *Film Comment* (New York), September/October 1990.
Toplin, Robert Brent, editor. *Ken Burns' The Civil War: Historians Respond.* New York: Oxford University Press, 1996.
Weisberger, B. "The Great Arrogance of the Present is to Forget the Intelligence of the Past." *American Heritage* (New York), September/October 1990.

See also Burns, Ken; Documentary

CIVILISATION: A PERSONAL VIEW

British Arts Programme

Kenneth Clark's 13-part series produced by British Broadcasting Corporation's Channel 2 (BBC-2) in 1969 and released in the United States in 1970 on public television, remains a milestone in the history of arts television, the Public Broadcasting System, and the explication of high culture to interested laypeople. The series offers an extended definition of the essential qualities of Western civilisation through an examination of its chief monuments and important locations. While such a task may seem both arrogant and impossible, Clark's views are always stimulating and frequently entertaining. Civilisation, he suggests, is energetic, confident, humane, and compassionate, based on a belief in permanence and in the necessity of self-doubt.

As Clark would readily acknowledge, civilization is not always all of these things at once, which gives his chronological tour considerable drama inasmuch as episodes speak to each other; Abbot Suger enters into dialogue in the viewer's mind with Michelangelo, Beethoven, and Einstein. A self-confessed hero worshiper, Clark arranged each epi-

Civilisation
Photo courtesy of BBC

sode around one or more important figures, illustrating his Carlylean view that civilisation is the product of great men. Given his exploration of the visual possibilities of television (not always utilized in previous arts programming) and his particular intellectual biases, the programme draws its evidence primarily from art history, but takes a wider view than that description might suggest. In his memoir *The Other Half*, he commented that "I always . . . based my arguments on things seen—towns, bridges, cloisters, cathedrals, palaces," but added that he considered the visual a "poin[t] of departure" rather than a final destination: "When I set about the programmes I had in mind Wagner's ambition to make opera into a *gesamtkunstwerk*—text, spectacle and sound all united."

Clark's qualifications for the series included his position as a leading art historian and, beginning in 1937, his career as a pioneer of British television arts programming. He had also served in the Ministry of Information during World War II, an experience that seems to have contributed to his philosophy of arts television. "The first stage was to learn that every word must be scripted; the second that what viewers want from a programme on art is not ideas, but information; and the third that things must be said clearly, energetically and economically," he wrote. Thus his first successful television series, *Five Revolutionary Painters* (which aired on ITA and which he discusses briefly in *The Other Half*), allowed him to both test his theory that the viewing public wanted to learn about individual artists and serve as a kind of dress rehearsal for the more ambitious *Civilisation*. As Clark noted, "I might not have been able to do the filmed sequences of *Civilisation* with as much vivacity if I had not 'come up the hard way' of live transmission".

Following the social and political upheavals that marked 1968 in both Europe and the United States, *Civilisation* teaches that hard times do not inevitably crush the humane tradition that are central to Clark's view of Western civilisation. Indeed, when David Attenborough suggested the title for the series, Clark's typically self-deprecating response was, "I had no clear idea what [civilisation] meant, but I thought it was preferable to barbarism, and fancied that this was the moment to say so." That the programme offers a personal (and in some ways idiosyncratic) look at nine centuries of European intellectual life is thus a crucial part of its appeal, inasmuch as it argues that to follow cultural matters—and care about them—is within the reach of television viewers.

Clark appreciated the fact that television remains a performer's medium even when it deals with the abstract. This established the pattern for later pundit programmes such as Alistair Cooke's *America* and Jacob Bronowski's *The Ascent of Man*, which were, like *Civilisation*, directed by Michael Gill. In all three programs the cultural cicerone and his locations are the stimulus for the presentation of ideas.

"I am convinced that a combination of words and music, colour and movement can extend human experience in a way words alone cannot do," he remarked in the foreword to the book version of *Civilisation*. His series aired only two years after BBC-2 switched to full-color broadcasting and was intended in part as a dramatic introduction to the possibilities of the new technology.

Civilisation came at an opportune time for American public television, appearing in that venue after the BBC had tried in vain to place the series with the commercial networks. The programme was underwritten by Xerox, which also provided $450,000 for an hour-long promotional programme (produced by the BBC) to drum up business for the multipart broadcast. The nascent Public Broadcasting System received plaudits for carrying the programme, and Clark undoubtedly found his largest audience in the United States. The series' reach in America was demonstrated by the precedent-setting Harper and Row tie-in book, which became a best-seller despite its $15 price tag. Thus in addition to promulgating its comforting message about the survival of a high culture besieged for a millennium by the forces of darkness, *Civilisation* had in the United States the serendipitous effect of demonstrating that high-culture television could in fact draw significant numbers of viewers.

—Anne Morey

HOST

Kenneth Clark

PRODUCERS   Michael Gill, Peter Montagnon

PROGRAMMING HISTORY

- BBC-2

13 Episodes
23 February–18 May 1969

FURTHER READING

Clark, Kenneth. *Civilisation: A Personal View.* New York: Harper and Row, 1969.
———. *The Other Half: A Self-Portrait.* London: John Murray, 1977.
A Guide to Civilisation: The Kenneth Clark Films on the Cultural Life of Western Man. Introduction and notes by Richard McLanathan. New York: Time-Life, 1970.
Secrest, M. *Kenneth Clark: A Biography.* London: Weidenfeld and Nicolson, 1984.
Walker, John A. *Arts TV: A History of Arts Television in Britain.* London: John Libbey and Company, 1993.
———. "Clark's *Civilisation* in Retrospect." *Art Monthly* (London), December-January 1988–89.

See also Attenborough, Richard

CLARK, DICK

U.S. Producer/Media Personality

With a career spanning fifty years, Dick Clark is one of television's most successful entrepreneurs of program production. Often acknowledged more for his youthful appearance than for his business acumen, Clark nevertheless has built an impressive production record since the 1950s with teen dance shows, prime-time programming, television specials, daytime game shows, made-for-television movies, and feature films.

As a teenager, Clark began his career in broadcasting in 1945 in the mailroom of station WRUN in Utica, New York, working his way up to weatherman and then newsman. After graduating from Syracuse University in 1951, Clark moved from radio into television broadcasting at station WKTV in Utica. Here, Clark hosted *Cactus Dick and the Santa Fe Riders*, a country-music program which became the training ground for his later television hosting persona. In 1952, Clark moved to Philadelphia and radio station WFIL as a disc jockey for *Dick Clark's Caravan of Music*. At that time, WFIL was affiliated with a television station which carried *Bandstand*, an afternoon teen dance show. Clark often substituted for Bob Horn, the show's regular host. When Horn was jailed for drunken driving in 1956, Clark took over as permanent host, boosting *Bandstand* into Philadelphia's best-known afternoon show. From that point on, he became a fixture in the American television broadcasting arena.

In 1957, the American Broadcasting Corporation (ABC) picked up the program for its daytime schedule, changing the name to *American Bandstand*. As a cornerstone of the afternoon lineup through 1963, the program was a boon for ABC, an inexpensively produced success for the network's target audience of youthful demographics. From 1963 through 1987, *American Bandstand* ran on a weekly basis to become one of the longest running shows in broadcast television.

In addition to Clark's hosting and producing duties for *American Bandstand*, he began to diversify in the 1950s by moving into the music publishing and recording industries. However, by the end of 1959, the federal government began to scrutinize Clark for a possible conflict between his broadcasting interests and his publishing and recording interests. At that time, payola, the practice of music industry companies paying radio personalities to play new records, was widespread throughout radio broadcasting. Clark, with the cultural scope of his network television program, became the prime target of the Congressional investigation into this illegal activity. Pressured by ABC to make a choice between broadcast and music industry interests, Clark opted for the former, divesting himself of his publishing and recording companies. Even though Clark was cleared of any illegal behavior, he had to testify before the Congressional Committee on payola practices in 1960.

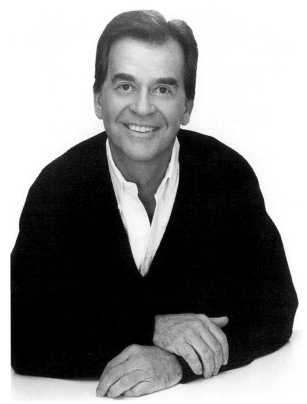

Dick Clark
Photo courtesy of Dick Clark Productions, Inc.

Given the present state of cross-corporate links among the recording, broadcasting, cable and film industries, Clark's persecution would be highly unlikely now. Indeed, even at the time of the payola scandals, the networks and film studios, such as ABC and Disney, were already inextricably connected with program production, broadcasting and profits. In retrospect, Clark's problems stemmed as much from his embrace of a somewhat raucous, interracial youth culture and his involvement in the conflict between ASCAP, representing the old guard of the music publishing business, and BMI, representing the new breed of rock and roll songwriters.

A somewhat tarnished reputation did not hinder Clark's further success in the area of broadcast programming and film production with Dick Clark Productions (DCP). DCP produced *Where the Action Is*, another daily teenage music show, during the late 1960s, as well as feature exploitation films such *Psych-Out*, *The Savage Seven* and *Killers Three*. At this time, Clark also moved into the game show arena with *Missing Links* and *The Object Is*, culminating in the late 1970s with *The $25,000 Pyramid*.

In addition, DCP produced *Elvis*, *Murder in Texas*, and *The Woman Who Willed a Miracle*, made-for-television movies which garnered impressive audience ratings. The latter won an Emmy Award. On a more low-brow level, DCP also introduced *Bloopers and Practical Jokes*, another inexpensive, but extremely popular recurring television special. Clark also produces award shows, the *American Awards* and *The Golden Globe Awards*.

Often criticized for the lack of quality in DCP programs, Clark points to the networks and the audiences as the index of that quality. He gives them what they want. In an interview in *Newsweek* magazine in 1986, Clark points out, "If I were given the assignment of doing a classical-music hour for PBS, it would be exquisite and beautifully done." Despite the boyish good looks and charm that are the identifying characteristics of this American icon, it is Clark's economically efficient business savvy and his uncanny ability to measure the American public's cultural mood that have been his most important assets in television broadcasting.

—Rodney A. Buxton

DICK CLARK (Richard Wagstaff Clark). Born in Mt. Vernon, New York, U.S.A., 30 November 1929. Graduated from Syracuse University, 1951. Married: 1) Barbara Mallery, 1952 (divorced, 1961); child: Richard, Jr.; 2) Loretta Martin, 1962 (divorced, 1971); children: Duane and Cindy; 3) Karen Wigton, 1977. Announcer, station WRUN, Utica, New York, 1945–1950; staff anouncer, station WOLF, Syracuse, New York, 1950; announcer, WRUN, 1951; announcer, station WKTV, Utica, 1951; announcer, station WFIL, Philadelphia, 1952; host, *American Bandstand*, 1956–89; formed Dick Clark Productions, 1956, producing more than 7,500 hours of television programming, including more than 30 series and 250 specials, and more than 20 movies for theatrical release and television. Founder: Dick Clark Media Archives. Inductee: Hollywood Walk of Fame, 1976; Broadcasting Magazine Hall of Fame, 1992; Rock 'n' Roll Hall of Fame, 1993; Academy of Television Arts and Sciences Hall of Fame, 1993. Recipient: Emmy Awards, 1979, 1983, 1985, 1986, and Daytime Emmy, Lifetime Achievement Award, 1994; MTV Award, 1987; Grammy National Trustees Award, 1990; named International Person of Year, NAPTE, 1990; Distinguished Service Award, National Association of Broadcasting, 1991; American D.J. Association, Lifetime Achievement Award, 1995; Person of the Year, Philadelphia Advertising Club. Address: Dick Clark Productions, 3003 West Olive Avenue, Burbank, California 91510-7811, U.S.A.

TELEVISION SERIES (selection)

1951	*Cactus Dick and the Santa Fe Riders* (host)
1956–89	*American Bandstand* (host, executive producer)
1958–60	*The Dick Clark Saturday Night Beechnut Show* (host)
1959	*Dick Clark's World of Talent* (host)
1959	*The Record Years* (host, executive producer)
1964	*Missing Links* (host)
1964	*The Object Is* (host)
1973–74	*Dick Clark Presents the Rock and Roll Years* (host, executive producer)
1973–75	*In Concert* (executive producer)
1973–89	*$10,000 Pyramid* (host)
	$20,000 Pyramid (host)
	$25,000 Pyramid (host)
	$50,000 Pyramid (host)
	$100,000 Pyramid (host)
1981	*The Krypton Factor* (host)
1984–86, 1988	*TV's Bloopers and Practical Jokes* (executive producer)
1985–88	*Puttin' on the Hits* (executive producer)
1988	*Live! Dick Clark Presents* (host, executive producer)
1990–91	*The Challengers* (host, executive producer)
1995–	*Tempestt* (executive producer)

MADE-FOR-TELEVISION MOVIES (executive producer)

1979	*Elvis*
1979	*Man in the Santa Claus Suit*
1979	*Birth of the Beatles*
1981	*Murder in Texas*
1983	*The Demon Murder Case*
1983	*The Woman Who Willed a Miracle*
1985	*Copacabana*
1988	*Promised a Miracle*
1988	*The Town Bully*
1988	*Liberace*
1989	*A Cry for Help: The Tracy Thurman Story*
1991	*Death Dreams*
1993	*Elvis and the Colonel: The Untold Story*
1994	*Secret Sins of the Father*

TELEVISION SPECIALS (selection, executive producer)

1965–67	*Where the Action Is*
1966	*Swinging Country*
1968–69	*Happening*
1970	*Get It Together*
1970	*Shebang*
1972–	*Dick Clark's New Year's Rockin' Eve*
1977	*Dick Clark's Good Ol' Days*
1978	*Dick Clark's Live Wednesday*
1980	*The Sensational, Shocking Wonderful Wacky 70's*
1981	*Whatever Became Of . . .?*
1981	*I've Had It up to Here*
1982	*Inside America*
1983	*Hollywood's Private Home Movies*
1983	*The 1/2 Hour Comedy Hour*
1984	*Hollywood Stars Screen Test*
1984	*You Are the Jury*
1985	*Reaching for the Stars*
1985	*Rock 'n' Roll Summer Action*
1985	*Live Aid—An All-Star Concert for African Relief*

1985	*American Bandstand's 33 1/3 Celebration*
1985	*Dick Clark's Nighttime*
1986	*America Picks the #1 Songs*
1986	*Alabama . . . My Home's in Alabama*
1987	*Keep on Cruisin'*
1987	*Superstars and Their Moms*
1987	*In Person from the Palace*
1987	*Getting in Touch*
1988	*Sea World's All-Star Lone Star Celebration*
1989	*Freedom Festival '89*
1991, 1993	*Super Bloopers and New Practical Jokes*
1992	*1992 USA Music Challenge*
1992	*American Bandstand's 40th Anniversary*
1992	*The World's Biggest Lies*
1992	*A Busch Gardens/Sea World Summer Safari*
1992	*Golden Greats*
1992	*Olympic Flag Jam*
1993	*The Return of TV Censored Bloopers*
1993	*The Academy of Country Music's Greatest Hits*
1993	*The Olsen Twins Mother's Day Special*
1993	*American Bandstand: One More Time*
1993	*Caught in the Act*
1993, 1994	*Sea World/Busch Garden Summer Celebration*
1993-95	*The Jim Thorpe Pro Sports Awards*
1994	*Taco Bell's Battle of the Bands*
1994	*How I Spent My Summer Vacation*
1994	*Chrysler American Great 18 Golf Championships*
1994	*American Music Awards 20th Anniversary Special*
1994	*Golden Globes 50th Anniversary Celebration*
1994	*Hot Country Jam '94*
1994	*American Bandstand's Teen Idols*
1994	*American Bandstand's #1 Hits*
1994	*Universal Studios Summer Blast*
1994, 1995	*Will You Marry Me?*
1995	*We're Having a Baby*
1995	*The Making of the Adventures of Mary Kate and Ashley*
1995	*Christmas at Home with the Stars*
1995	*When Stars Were Kids*
1995	*Rudy Coby: The Coolest Magician in the World*
1995	*Sea World/Busch Gardens Party for the Planet*
1995	*All Star Ultra TV Censored Bloopers*
1995	*TNN Country Series*

FILMS

Because They're Young (actor), 1960; *The Young Doctors,* (actor), 1961; *Wild in the Streets,* 1968. *Killers Three,* 1968; *Psych-Out* (producer), 1968; *The Savage Seven* (producer), 1968; *The Dark* (producer), 1970; *Remo Williams: The Adventure Begins* (producer), 1985.

RADIO

Dick Clark's Caravan of Music; Dick Clark's Music Machine; Dick Clark's National Music Survey, Dick Clark's Rock, Roll and Remember; Dick Clark's U.S. Music Survey.

PUBLICATIONS

Your Happiest Hears. New York: Rosh, 1959.
To Goof or Not to Goof. New York: B. Geis, 1963.
Rock, Roll and Remember, with Richard Robinson. New York: Crowell, 1976.
Dick Clark's Program for Success in Your Business and Personal Life. New York: Cornerstone Library, 1980.
Looking Great, Staying Young, with Bill Libby. Indianapolis, Indiana: Bobbs-Merrill, 1980.
Dick Clark's The First 25 Years of Rock 'n' Roll, with Michael Usland. New York: Dell, 1981.
The History of American Bandstand, with Michael Shore. New York: Ballantine, 1985.
Dick Clark's Easygoing Guide to Good Grooming. New York: Dodd, Mead, 1985.

FURTHER READING

"'Bandstand' Ready to Rock Again." *Broadcasting* (Washington, D.C.), 21 May 1990.
"Dick Clark on Dick Clark: The Flip Side." *Broadcasting* (Washington, D.C.), 1 May 1989.
Miller, Holly G. "Dick Clark's Role After Rock." *Saturday Evening Post* (Indianapolis, Indiana), July-August 1995.
Responsibilities of Broadcasting Licensees and Station Personnel: Hearings before a Subcommittee of the Committee on Interstate and Foreign Commerce, House of Representatives, Eighty-Sixth Congress, Second Session on Payola and Other Deceptive Practices in the Broadcasting Field. Washington: United States Government Printing Office, 1960.
Schipper, Henry. "Dick Clark." *Rolling Stone* (New York), 19 April 1990.

See also *American Bandstand;* Music on Television

CLARKSON, ADRIENNE

Canadian Television Personality

Adrienne Clarkson has been a television personality and major cultural force in Canada for some twenty-five years. She began her career in broadcasting in 1965, as a book reviewer on CBC-TV. She then became interviewer and host of the long-running CBC daytime magazine show *Take Thirty.* After ten years there, she spent seven years as host of *The Fifth Estate*, another long-running magazine program, this one in prime time.

In 1982 Clarkson was appointed agent general for Ontario in France, a high-level government position in which she promoted the province and acted as a cultural liaison between the two countries. When she returned to Canada in 1987, she became president and publisher of McClelland and Stewart, one of Canada's most prestigious publishing firms, where she still maintains her own imprint—"Adrienne Clarkson Books." At the same time, she resumed her work in television as host and executive producer of her own CBC program—*Adrienne Clarkson's Summer Festival*—in 1988. Its successor, *Adrienne Clarkson Presents*, is a prime-time cultural affairs series on which Clarkson offers profiles of Canadian and international figures from the worlds of opera, ballet, folk-singing, and the other arts.

Despite the variety of her work in journalism, news, the arts, and cultural policy, Clarkson is perceived as an elitist. For twelve years, she has been lampooned by Canadian comics such as the *Royal Canadian AirFarce* and *Double Exposure*. In one skit, a haughty, modulated voice introduces itself, "I'M Adrienne Clarkson...and YOU'RE not..." Because her most recent programs have been artsoriented and she has been involved in arts activities and posts of distinction, she is seen as having limited commercial appeal. Indeed, like most arts programs, hers do not garner high ratings but are highly regarded by critics.

Clarkson has won numerous television awards, including three Association of Canadian Television and Radio Artists (ACTRA) awards for *Take Thirty* and *The Fifth Estate*. In 1993, she was the recipient of a Gemini Award (which succeeded the ACTRAs as the national television awards) for Best Host in a Light Information, Variety, or Performing Arts Program for *Adrienne Clarkson Presents*.

In 1992 Clarkson wrote, produced and directed her first film, a full-length drama/documentary for television, called *Artemisia*, about the Seventeenth-century Italian painter, Artemisia Gentileschi, whose rape by an artist friend of her father's informed her work. Clarkson was passionately involved in her production, which was premiered at the 1992 Toronto International Film Festival and was then aired on Clarkson's series.

—Janice Kaye

ADRIENNE CLARKSON. Born in Hong Kong, 10 February 1939. Educated at Trinity College; University of Toronto, B.A. 1960, M.A. 1962; Sorbonne, Paris, France, 1963–64. Lecturer, University of Toronto, 1964–65; host and interviewer, *Take Thirty*, 1965–75; host, *Adrienne at Large*, 1975; host, *The Fifth Estate*, 1975-82; appointed agent general, France, 1982–87; producer and host of her own TV programs, since 1988; president and publisher, McClelland and

Adrienne Clarkson
Photo courtesy of Adrienne Clarkson

Stewart, 1987–88; publisher, Adrienne Clarkson Books, McCelland and Stewart, since 1988. Honorary Degrees: Dalhousie University, Lakehead University, Acadia University. Recipient: Gordon Sinclair Award, 1979; ACTRA Awards, 1974, 1975, 1976; Order of Canada, 1992; Gemini Award, 1993.

TELEVISION SERIES

1965–75	*Take Thirty*
1975	*Adrienne at Large*
1975–82	*The Fifth Estate*
1988	*Adrienne Clarkson's Summer Festival* (became *Adrienne Clarkson Presents*)

TELEVISION SPECIAL

1992	*Artemisia*

PUBLICATIONS

A Lover More Condoling. Toronto: McClelland and Stewart, 1968.
Hunger Trace. New York: William Morrow, 1970.
True to You in My Fashion. Toronto: New Press, 1971.

See also *Fifth Estate*

CLEARANCE

U.S. Broadcasting Policy

The term clearance, as applied in the context of American broadcasting, refers to the acceptance, by a local station, of a program provided by a broadcasting network or a supplier of syndicated programming. Ideally, an affiliate will carry a program when the network specifies. The number of clearances determines the potential audience size of a program. Networks hope to clear their programs with as many stations as possible. This will ensure greater advertising revenues. Clearance of a network program by an affiliate is thus crucial to the network's profitability. Likewise, affiliates who frequently reject network offerings risk their survivability if they are dropped by the network. Networks provide programming sure to compete successfully with programs provided by the other local stations. Moreover, the networks compensate affiliates to carry their programs. The practice of program clearance best illustrates the symbiotic nature of the network/affiliate relationship, a relationship established in law as well as in economic practice.

The Federal Communications Commission (FCC) recognized the problems inherent in "chain broadcasting" as early as 1943 when the Supreme Court attempted to clarify the role of networks as program suppliers in the "Network Case" (*NBC, Inc. et al. v. United States et al.*). To further prevent anti-competitive practices, the FCC implemented rules such as clearance and the Prime Time Access Rule. These regulations grant programming autonomy to affiliate stations, while in practice the stations are dependent on other program suppliers.

Clearances vary by daypart. Prime-time commands the highest number of clearances by affiliates. The stations can charge high rates for advertising time during top-rated network programs. Low-rated programs run a greater risk of being rejected by stations. Because more spots are available in a film, for example, it might be more lucrative for an affiliate to substitute it for the low-rated network offering.

An affiliate station will also sometimes reject a prime-time network program because of controversial subject matter. In order to appease the tastes and attitudes of their local communities, affiliates may not air particular programs, despite their potential for high ratings. In 1993, for example, the program *NYPD Blue* was rejected by 57 ABC affiliates before it aired because of objectionable material. It is an affiliate's legal right to reject any program in an attempt to serve the public interest. The choice to reject a program may prove most profitable to independent stations which opt to carry the "taboo" programs.

Preemption occurs when an affiliate cancels a program it has agreed to carry, or when a network interrupts a "cleared" program to broadcast a special event or breaking news story. Because of lost advertising time such preemptions can prove costly to both parties.

Affiliates give low clearances to network programs during morning, late afternoon, early evening and late night dayparts. During these times the predominant source of programming is syndicated material, often consisting of older network program with proven audience appeal.

Clearance of a syndicated program involves acceptance through purchase. To be truly profitable syndicators must "clear" (sell) a program in enough markets to represent at least 70% of all television households.

—Sharon Zechowski

FURTHER READING

Eastman, Susan Tyler, Sydney W. Head, and Lewis Klein. *Broadcast/Cable Programming: Strategies and Practices.* California.: Wadsworth, 1981; 3rd edition, 1989.

Head, Sydney W., and Christopher H. Sterling. *Broadcasting in America: A Survey of Electronic Media.* 6th edition, Boston: Houghton Mifflin, 1990.

Kahn, Frank J., editor. *Documents of American Broadcasting.* Englewood Cliffs, New Jersey: Prentice-Hall, 1968; 3rd edition, 1978.

See also United States: Networks

CLEESE, JOHN

British Actor

John Cleese belongs to a tradition of university humour which has supplied a recognisable strand of comedy to British television and radio from *Beyond the Fringe* in the late 1950s to *Blackadder* and beyond. The brilliance of his writing, the dominant nature of his performances (due largely to his extraordinary height), and the variety of his successes have made him undoubtedly the most influential figure of this group. He has always shown an unerring instinct for how far to go with any one project or idea, with the result that there is little in his large body of work that could be counted as failure, though he is also highly critical, in hindsight, of anything he regards as not having worked precisely as he might have wanted it to.

Following the success of Cambridge Circus, the Cambridge University Footlights Club revue to which he contributed and which toured Britain and the world between 1963 and 1965, Cleese made his first big impact on television by writing and performing sketches on David Frost's *The Frost Report* (BBC). (He had already written material for *That Was the Week That Was*, the seminal BBC satire show which had launched Frost's career). Fellow performers included Ronnie Barker and Ronnie Corbett, with whom he created the classic "class" sketches, and the show won the Golden Rose of Montreux in 1966. Cleese's written contributions were created in collaboration with his writing partner, Graham Chapman, then still a medical student at Cambridge. At the same time Cleese was also writing and performing in the cult BBC radio series *I'm Sorry, I'll Read That Again*, together with Cambridge Circus colleagues like Tim Brooke-Taylor and Bill Oddie. There were a total of eight series of this show between 1964 and 1973, probably the only thing Cleese ever over-did.

Cleese was now much in demand and his next major project, produced by David Frost for Rediffusion, was *At Last the 1948 Show*, a sketch-comedy series written and performed in collaboration with Chapman, Brooke-Taylor and Marty Feldman, two series of which were transmitted in 1967. Although not seen throughout the country, the show gained a cult following for the brilliance and unpredictability of its comedy and the innovative nature of its structure, in which the show was linked by a dumb blonde called the Lovely Aimi MacDonald. Cleese was now developing a full range of comic personae, including manic bullies, unreliable authority figures (especially lawyers and government ministers) and repressed Englishmen, all of which were later to gel in Basil Fawlty. The quality of invention in *At Last the 1948 Show* was consistently high and it gave the world of comedy one of its most enduring pieces—the "Four Yorkshiremen" sketch. It was also the recognised precursor to the series which remains, in spite of all his own retrospective criticism, Cleese's most significant contribution to television comedy, *Monty Python's Flying Circus* (BBC).

Beginning in 1969, *Monty Python's Flying Circus* teamed Cleese and Chapman with three other university comedians, Michael Palin and Terry Jones, who wrote together and had also contributed to *The Frost Report*, and Eric Idle. The team was completed by American animator Terry Gilliam. Four series were made between 1969 and 1974, though Cleese did not appear in the fourth, contributing only as a writer. This was probably the main reason for the comparative failure of the final series, because Cleese was clearly the dominant figure in the *Python* team and appeared in the sketches which made the greatest impact, thus becoming the figure most associated with the series in the public mind.

Two sketches in particular stand out in this regard: the "Dead Parrot" sketch, in which Cleese returns a defective pet bird to the shop where he bought it; and the "Ministry of Silly Walks" sketch, in which Cleese used his angular figure to startling effect. He was to be constantly exasperated in future years by people asking him to "do the silly walk". In *At Last the 1948 Show*, Cleese's appearances with Marty Feldman have a particular resonance. In *Monty Python's Flying Circus* his work with Michael Palin was similarly memorable.

John Cleese
Photo courtesy of John Cleese

The overall impact and influence of *Monty Python's Flying Circus* is difficult to overestimate. The intricate flow of each show, the abandonment of the traditional "punch line" to a sketch, the knowing experimentation with the medium and the general air of silliness combined with obscure intellectualism set a standard, one which comedians thereafter found hard to get away from. Producers like John Lloyd and writer-performers like Ben Elton acknowledge the enormous influence of *Monty Python's Flying Circus* on their own work. The word "pythonesque" entered the language, being used to describe any kind of bizarre juxtaposition.

Although there were no more series of *Monty Python* on television after 1974, largely because Cleese had had enough, the team continued to come together occasionally to make feature films, of which *Monty Python's Life of Brian* was the best and most controversial, given its religious theme. Cleese's discussion of the film with religious leaders on the chat show *Friday Night...Saturday Morning* in 1979 remains a television moment to cherish. The untimely death of Graham Chapman from cancer in 1989 put an end to the team for good.

By then, Cleese, having altered the world of sketch comedy for ever, had done the same for the sitcom. He was no stranger to sitcom, having written episodes of *Doctor in Charge*, together with Chapman. For *Fawlty Towers* he teamed up with his American wife Connie Booth to create a comedy of character and incident which is almost faultless in its construction. The "situation" is a small hotel in the genteel English resort of Torquay, run by Basil Fawlty (Cleese), his wife Sybil (Prunella Scales), the maid Polly (Booth), and the incompetent Spanish waiter Manuel (Andrew Sachs). Each episode is so packed with comic situations and complex plot developments, often bordering on farce, that it is no surprise that there were, in all, only twelve episodes ever made, in two series of six each from 1975 and 1979. Basil Fawlty is the ultimate Cleese creation—a manic, snobbish, repressed English stereotype with a talent for disaster, whether it be trying to dispose of the dead body of a guest or coping with a party of German visitors.

Cleese's television work after *Fawlty Towers* was sporadic and included the role of Petruchio in Jonathan Miller's production of *The Taming of the Shrew* for the BBC Television Shakespeare series and a guest appearance on the U.S. sitcom *Cheers*, as well as the two funniest *Party Political Broadcasts* (for the Social Democratic Party) ever made. He concentrated more on esoteric projects such as the comic training films he made through his own company, Video Arts, and books on psychotherapy written in collaboration with Dr. Robyn Skinner. He also pursued his work in feature films, enjoying great success with *A Fish Called Wanda*, in which he returned to one of his favourite subjects—the differences between English and American characters—already explored in one memorable episode of *Fawlty Towers*. The film also saw him play the role of a lawyer—the profession he had lampooned throughout his career and which he had originally studied to join.

—Steve Bryant

JOHN (MARWOOD) CLEESE. Born in Weston-super-Mare, Somerset, England, 27 October 1939. Attended Clifton Sports Academy; Downing College, Cambridge. Married: 1) Connie Booth, 1968 (divorced, 1978), child: Cynthia; 2) Barbara Trentham, 1981 (divorced, 1990), child: Camilla; 3) Alyce Faye Eichelberger, 1992. Appeared in London's West End, and later on Broadway, as member of the Cambridge Footlights company, 1963; first appeared on television in *The Frost Report* and *At Last the 1948 Show*, 1966; leading comedy star in *Monty Python* television series and films, from 1969, and subsequently as television's Basil Fawlty, *Fawlty Towers*; founder and director, Video Arts Ltd, company making industrial training films, 1972–89. LLD, University of St. Andrews. Recipient: Golden Rose of Montreux, 1966; *TV Times* Award for Funniest Man on TV, 1978–79; Emmy Award, 1987; British Academy of Film and Television Arts for Best Actor, 1988. Address: David Wilkinson Associates, 115 Hazlebury Road, London SW6 2LX, England.

TELEVISION SERIES

1966–67	*The Frost Report*
1966–67	*At Last the 1948 Show*
1969–74	*Monty Python's Flying Circus*
1975–79	*Fawlty Towers*

TELEVISION SPECIALS

| 1977 | *The Strange Case of the End of Civilization as We Know It* |
| 1980 | *The Taming of the Shrew* |

FILMS

Interlude, 1968; *The Bliss of Mrs. Blossom*, 1968; *The Best House in London*, 1968; *The Rise and Rise of Michael Rimmer* (also co-writer), 1970; *The Magic Christian*, 1970; *The Statue*, 1970; *The Bonar Law Story*, 1971; *And Now For Something Completely Different* (also co-writer), 1971; *It's a 2' 6" Above the Ground World* (*The Love Ban*), 1972; *Abbott and Costello Meet Sir Michael Swann*, 1972; *The Young Anthony Barber*, 1973; *Confessions of a Programme Planner*, 1974; *Romance Wwth a Double Bass*, 1974; *Monty Python and the Holy Grail* (also co-writer), 1975; *Pleasure at Her Majesty's*, 1976; *Monty Python Meets Beyond the Fringe*, 1978; *Monty Python's Life of Brian* (also co-writer), 1979; *Away from It All* (voice only), 1979; *The Secret Policeman's Ball*, 1979; *Time Bandits*, 1981; *The Great Muppet Caper*, 1981; *The Secret Policeman's Other Ball*, 1982; *Monty Python Live at the Hollywood Bowl*, 1982; *Monty Python's The Meaning of Life*, 1983; *Yellowbeard*, 1983; *Privates on Parade*, 1984; *The Secret Policeman's Private Parts*, 1984; *Club Paradise*, 1985; *Gonzo Presents Muppet Weird Stuff*, 1985; *Silverado*, 1985; *Clockwise*, 1986; *S. D. Pete*, 1986; *The Secret Policeman's Third Ball*, 1987; *A Fish Called Wanda* (also executive producer and writer), 1988; *The Big Picture*, 1988; *Erik the Viking*, 1989; *Bullseye!*, 1990; *An American Tail: Fievel Goes West* (voice only), 1991; *Splitting Heirs*, 1992; *Mary Shelley's Frankenstein*, 1994; *Rudyard Kipling's The Jungle Book*, 1995.

STAGE

Cambridge Footlights Revue, 1963; *Half a Sixpence*, 1965.

PUBLICATIONS

The Strange Case of the End of Civilization as We Know It, with Jack Hobbs and Joe McGrath. London: Methuen, 1970.

Fawlty Towers, with Connie Booth. London: Methuen, 1979.

Families and how to Survive Them, with Robin Skynner. London: Methuen, 1983.

The Golden Skits of Wing Commander Muriel Volestrangler FRHS and Bar. London: Methuen, 1984.

The Complete Fawlty Towers, with Connie Booth. London: Methuen, 1988; New York: Pantheon, 1989.

Life and how to Survive It, with Robin Skynner. New York: Norton, 1993.

FURTHER READING

"And Now for Something Completely Different...." *The Economist* (London), 20 October 1990.

Bryson, Bill. "Cleese up Close." *The New York Times Magazine*, 25 December 1988.

"Cleese on Creativity." *Advertising Age* (New York), 4 December 1989.

Gilliat, Penelope. "Height's Delight." *The New Yorker*, 2 May 1988.

Johnson, Kim. *Life (Before and) after Monty Python: The Solo Flights of the Flying Circus.* New York: St. Martin's, 1993.

———. *The First 20 Years of Monty Python.* New York: St. Martin's, 1989.

McCall, Douglas L. *Monty Python: A Chronological Listing of the Troupe's Creative Output, and Articles and Reviews about Them.* Jefferson, North Carolina: McFarland, 1991.

Margolis, Jonathan. *Cleese Encounters.* New York: St. Martin's, 1992.

Sanoff, Alvin P. "And Now for Something Completely Different." *U.S. News and World Report* (Washington, D.C.), 16 October 1989.

Wilmut, Roger. From Fringe to Flying Circus. London: Methuen, 1980.

See also *Fawlty Towers; Monty Python's Flying Circus*

CLOSED CAPTIONING

Closed captioning involves the display of subtitles superimposed over a portion of the television picture. These subtitles or captions are created to represent the audio portion of the television signal. While closed captioning was initially developed for the hearing-impaired, it can also be utilized as a teaching device by viewers for whom English is a second language and by children, and even adults, who are learning to read. It can even be used as a convenience device for viewers who mute their TV to take a phone call but activate closed captioning to continue the program dialogue.

The captions are "closed" to the general viewing audience because television producers believe that a continuous display of alphanumeric data across a TV screen is distracting and bothersome to the majority of viewers who are able to following the dialogue aurally. Any viewer can choose to "open" the closed captioning by activating a switch on newer television sets or utilizing a separate decoder with older television sets that do not include the necessary decoder circuitry.

The decoder circuitry is designed to "read" the closed captions embedded in the vertical blanking interval. The vertical blanking interval is that 21-line portion of the 525-line NTSC television signal which does not contain picture information. Various lines are used to carry technical data and one of these lines is specifically reserved for closed captioning.

Closed captioning is not a new idea. The concept was conceived in 1971 by engineers at the National Bureau of Standards. Further development involved WGBH-TV, the Boston public television station, Gallaudet University, the leading university for the hearing-impaired, and the National Technical Institute in Rochester, New York. In 1976, the Federal Communications Commission formerly authorized the use of line 21, the last line of the vertical blanking interval, for this purpose.

Closed captioning received a major boost with the passage of the Television Decoder Circuitry Act of 1990. This law mandated the inclusion of closed-captioned circuitry in every television receiver with a screen of 13 inches or more that was manufactured, assembled, imported, or shipped in interstate commerce beginning 1 July 1993. Most receivers sold prior to that date did not include the circuitry and viewers who wanted to access closed captions were required to purchase a separate decoder box for approximately $160.

The National Captioning Institute, an independent, non-profit corporation, worked with engineers to develop an inexpensive electronic chip that could perform the same function as the cumbersome decoder boxes. This chip, if included in every TV receiver, would cost as little as $5 and this expense would presumably be absorbed into the total production cost of the sets. Citizen groups representing the hearing-impaired lobbied Congress to enact legislation requiring the inclusion of a decoder chip in all receivers. Some opposition from manufacturers groups was voiced during Congressional hearings, but the overwhelming number of those testifying supported the legislation. The bill passed both house and was signed into law on 15 October 1990.

Closed captioning is program dependent and not all programs are captioned. Most network and syndicated programs are captioned, however, and the percentage continues to grow. Locally produced programs are less likely to be captioned since stations lack the technical and financial resources to provide this service. Most cities do have one or more local newscasts with captions. Typically, the cost of this service is underwritten by a local health care provider or a charitable foundation.

Captions appear in either "roll-up" or "pop-up" fashion. The captions roll up the screen if the program is being aired live. Live captioning is done by skilled professionals using court stenographic techniques who can transcribe speech as rapid as 250 words per minute. The lag time between the spoken word and the caption is one to five seconds. The captions are not always word-for-word transcripts, but they do closely approximate the verbal message.

"Pop-up" captions are used for prerecorded programs and for commercials. These captions can be prepared more leisurely and are timed to match the flow of dialogue on the TV screen. Also, an attempt is made to place the caption under the person speaking at the time. In a two-person dialogue, the caption would pop-up on either the left or right half of the screen depending on the position of the speaker. Various icons are used to symbolize sounds; e.g., a musical note is placed next the caption when a person is singing.

The most challenging captions involve live sports coverage since there is no way to anticipate what program participants will say. Newscasts are less difficult since the same TelePrompTer that cues on-air talent also cues the person preparing the captions.

Since the captions are encoded as part of the electronic signal, a closed captioned program may be transmitted in any form: over-the-air broadcast, satellite, cable, video cassette, or video disc. Programs containing captions are noted with a (CC) following the program title in *TV Guide* and similar listings.

—Norman Felsenthal

FURTHER READING

Fantel, Hans. "Watch Television and Get the Word." *New York Times*, 11 July 1993.

Television Closed Captioning: Hearing Before the Subcommittee on Telecommunications and Finance of the Committee on Energy and Commerce on *H.R. 4267.* U.S. House Of Representatives, One Hundred First Congress, Second Session, 2 May 1990.

See also Language and Television

CLOSED CIRCUIT TELEVISION

Closed Circuit Television (CCTV) is a television transmission system in which live or prerecorded signals are sent over a closed loop to a finite and predetermined group of receivers, either via coaxial cable or as scrambled radio waves that are unscrambled at the point of reception.

CCTV takes numerous forms and performs functions ranging from image enhancement for the partially-sighted to the transmission of pay-per-view sports broadcasts. Although cable television is technically a form of CCTV the term is generally used to designate TV systems with more specialized applications than broadcast or cable television. These specialized systems are not subject to regulation by the Federal Communications Commission (FCC), though CCTV systems using scrambled radio waves are subject to common carrier tarriffs and FCC conditions of service.

CCTV has many industrial and scientific applications, including electron microscopy, medical imaging and robotics, but the term "closed circuit TV" refers most often to security and surveillance camera systems. Other common forms of CCTV include live on-site video displays for special events (e.g. conventions, arena sports, rock concerts); pay-per-view telecasts of sporting events such as championship boxing matches, and "in-house" television channels in hospitals, airports, racetracks, schools, malls, grocery stores, and municipal buildings.

The conception of many of these uses of CCTV technology dates back to the earliest years of television. In the 1930s and 1940s, writers such as *New York Times* columnist Orrin Dunlap predicted that closed circuit TV systems would enhance industry, education, science, and commerce. Dunlap and other writers envisioned CCTV systems for supervising factory workers and for visually coordinating production in different areas of a factory, and anticipated CCTV systems replacing pneumatic tubes in office communications. In the world of science, closed circuit television was heralded as a way of viewing dangerous experiments as they took place; in the sphere of education, CCTV was seen a way of bringing lessons simultaneously to different groups of students in a school or university.

Many of today's CCTV systems were first implemented in the postwar years. For example, pay-per-view closed circuit sports broadcasts can be traced back to a postwar Hollywood invention known as "theater television," a CCTV system used for viewing sports in movie theaters that became a lucrative source of ancillary revenue for boxing promoters in the fifties, sixties, and seventies. With the growth of cable television and satellite delivery systems CCTV telecasts have become an integral part of the business of sports today, not only in the boxing industry but also in horseracing, baseball, and golf.

Educational TV and video advertising in retail stores are other CCTV applications that originate in the postwar period. The controversial Channel One, a now defunct commercial CCTV channel for schools founded in the 1980s, was only the latest of several CCTV experiments in education dating back to the 1950s. Today's "on-site" media industry, which places video advertising monitors in grocery stores, shopping malls, and other retail sites, dates back to a series of tests involving closed circuit advertising in department stores that took place in the 1940s.

A closed circuit television viewing set-up

Although all of these applications of CCTV are fairly common, perhaps the most pervasive use of CCTV is for surveillance. Security cameras are now an ubiquitous feature of many institutions and places, from the corrections facility to the convenience store. In prisons, CCTV systems reduce the costs of staffing and operating observation towers and make it possible to maintain a constant watch on all areas of the facility. CCTV is also used as a means of monitoring performance in the workplace; in 1992, according to an article in *Personnel Journal*, there were ten million employees in the United States whose work is monitored via electronic security systems. Retail stores often install CCTV cameras as a safeguard against theft and robbery, a practice which municipal authorities have adopted as a way of curtailing crime in public housing and even on city streets. In the United Kingdom, for example, police in several cities have installed closed circuit cameras in busy public areas.

These uses of CCTV technology are not neutral; indeed, they are often a matter of some controversy. These controversies center on the status of legal evidence acquired via closed circuit TV, and on the Orwellian implications of constant perceived surveillance. Police use of CCTV security cameras in Britain has led to charges of civil liberties violations. A 1978 survey on the topic of CCTV in the workplace found that 77% of employers interviewed supported the use of CCTV on the job. However, it also found that a majority of employees felt that CCTV in the workplace constituted an unwarranted intrusion, and favored the passage of laws prohibiting such surveillance. Ironically, the ascendancy of more sophisticated electronic employee surveillance technologies such as keystroke monitoring of information workers has rendered CCTV somewhat obsolete as a visual management technology.

In addition to these civil liberties isssues, another controversy surrounding security cameras concerns their effectiveness in crime prevention. The purpose of CCTV surveillance is usually deterrence of, rather than intervention in, criminal acts. Many security cameras go unmonitored and are thus ineffective as a means of halting crimes in progress. This fact was forcefully demonstrated by a highly publicized juvenile murder case in England in 1992. After the discovery of the victim's body and the apprehension of the perpetrators, police discovered that the initial abduction had been recorded by a shopping center's security cameras.

Another controversy surrounding CCTV is its use in the courtroom. In 1985, the state of California passed a law allowing children to testify via CCTV in child molestation cases. In response to a similar ruling, the Illinois Supreme Court ruled that this method of testimony was unconstitutional, as it violated a defendant's right to confront his/her accuser.

Although this particular case reflects a concern that the camera can somehow "lie" and that it is not equivalent to face-to-face interaction, the latest trends in CCTV applications seem to rely precisely on the equation of closed circuit vision with actual presence. New technological developments which seem to base themselves upon this premise include "Teleconferencing," an audiovisual communications form designed to allow individuals in different places to interact via CCTV hookups, and "Virtual Reality," an imaging system which uses CCTV "goggles" in conjunction with advanced computer graphics and input devices to create the illusion of a three-dimensional, interactive envrionment for its viewer.

—Anna McCarthy

FURTHER READING

Borow, Wendy. "Medical Television: Prescription for Progress." *Journal of the American Medical Association*, 6 October 1993.

Clement, Andrew. "Office Automation and the Technical Control of Information Workers." In, Mosco Vincent, and Janet Wasko, editors. *The Political Economy of Information*. Madison, Wisconsin: University of Wisconsin Press, 1988.

Constant, Mike. *The Principles and Practice of Closed Circuit Television*. Borehamwood: Paramount Publishing, 1994.

Dawson,Tim. "Framing the Villains." *New Statesman and Society* (London), 28 January 1994.

Dunlap, Orrin. *The Outlook for Television*. New York: Arno Press and *The New York Times*, 1971 (reprint of 1932 edition.).

_____. *The Future of Television*. New York: Harper, 1947.

Gannon, Mary. "Retail Applications of Television." *Television Magazine* (New York), November 1945.

Genensky, S.M. *Advances in Closed Circuit TV Systems for the Partially-Sighted*. Santa Monica, California: Rand, 1972.

Goldberg, Stephanie. "The Children's Hour." *American Bar Association Journal* (Chicago, Illinois), May 1994.

Gomery, Douglas. "Theater Television: The Missing Link of Technological Change in the U.S. Motion Picture Industry." *Velvet Light Trap* (Austin, Texas) 1985.

Laabs, Jennifer J. "Measuring Work in the Electronic Age." *Personnel Journal* (Santa Monica, California), June 1992.

Levine, Barry. "TV Cameras in Prison: Providing Extra Eyes for Officers." *Corrections Today* (College Park, Maryland), July 1989.

"Safe Testimony." *Time* (New York), 3 June 1985.

Sambul, Nathan J. *The Handbook of Private Television: A Complete Guide for Video Facilities and Networks within Corporations, Nonprofit Institutions, and Government Agencies*. New York: McGraw Hill, 1982.

Stevenson, Richard W. "They're Capturing Suspects on Candid Camera." *The New York Times*, 11 March 1995.

U.S. Congress, Office of Technology Assessment. *The Electronic Supervisor: New Technology, New Tensions*. Washington: D.C.: OTA, 1987.

Zworykin, Vladimir. *Television in Science and Industry*. New York: Wiley, 1958.

COCK, GERALD

British Broadcasting Executive and Producer

Gerald Cock was appointed by the BBC in 1935 to run its first Television Service (under the title director of television). At the time many BBC executives were skeptical about the value and potential of the new medium and Cock's achievement during his short reign—the pre-World War II service began in November 1936 and was closed in September 1939—was to push for the expansion of the television service in the face of the BBC's reluctance to adequately fund what became known as the "Cinderella Service". Unlike many senior BBC executives he regarded television as a natural successor to radio, rather than as a luxury or novelty.

Before joining the BBC during the 1920s Cock spent a colourful youth in the Americas, gold mining and ranching in Alaska, Utah and Mexico; he also worked as an extra in Hollywood. He started working for BBC radio during the 1920s and was appointed director of the Outside Broadcasts Department in 1925, where he encouraged the deployment of new technology and the development of new programme forms, whilst often dealing with a competitive press.

The Selsdon Report of 1935 recommended that the BBC be given responsibility for the development of a regular high-definition television service; at the time television's potential as a medium of live immediacy meant that Cock's experience in the Outside Broadcasts Department—which aspired to be topical and contemporary—made him an obvious choice to head the new division.

The service began regular transmissions in 1936 from Alexandra Palace. Despite few staff and two small studios, Cock was able to build up an effective and successful repertoire of programme achievements—including the live televising of the Coronation of George VI, tennis from Wimbledon, and even a programme where Cock himself answered viewers' phoned-in questions. In fact every type of programme that was to become popular after the war was already tried out during these prewar years, in part the result of the freedom to experiment that Cock allowed his producers.

The programming policy of the prewar service was overseen by Cock. He instigated a policy of "variety and balance" which was coordinated through Cecil Madden, programme organiser and chief liaison with the producers. This policy was congruent with Cock's realisation that television's main attraction was its advantage of allowing the viewer to "see at a distance" contemporary events. For him, this included not only the relay of current showbiz personalities and sporting events but also early television drama. As he put it in a 1939 *Radio Times* article:

> Television is essentially a medium for topicalities . . . An original play or specially devised television production might be a weekly feature. If a National Theatre were in being, close co-operation between it and the BBC might have solved an extremely difficult problem. Excerpts from plays during their normal runs, televised from the studio or direct from the stage, with

perhaps a complete play at the end of its run would have attractive possibilities as part of a review of the nation's entertainment activities. But, in my view television is from its very nature more suitable for the dissemination of all kinds of information than for entertainment.

Cock's view of television is clearly inflected by his previous career as director of Outside Broadcasts for BBC radio, where the broadcasts were conceived as informative and enabling rather than entertainment; hence, the broadcast of "scenes" from current plays, congruent with Cock's overall attitude, served as informative views on the nature of contemporary drama and performance, and also providing a "what's on" function. Cock's own attitude towards television's function was as a relay service, its key benefits and attractions provided by the Outside Broadcast. For Cock, therefore, there was no need for large studios to house spectacular drama productions. However, the "Theatre Parade" relay of "scenes" from the West End theatre was far less popular than the studio production of complete plays. This meant that the demands on studio time and space were heavy, demands which were exacerbated as the ambitions of producers and the length of programmes increased.

Cock's vision for a topical television service was also undermined by underfunding and a general distrust of television by sports promoters and theatre managers; contrary to received history outside broadcasts of West End plays and scenes from plays were the exception after 1937, and the prewar television service largely consisted of what would later be considered studio-based light entertainment.

Unfortunately—and despite Cock's determined enthusiasm—current affairs television was not developed until the mid-1950s, and BBC Television News in vision was not introduced until 1954 (this was because senior executives assumed that seeing the news announcer in vision would distract the viewer from important information).

However, Cock himself is indirectly responsible for the gradual development of current affairs television. When the television service was closed in 1939 Cock went on to work as North American representative for the BBC in New York and California. He later gave evidence to the Hankey Committee, appointed to consider the resurrection of the television service after the war, and he wrote a key 1945 document, "Report on the Conditions for a Post-War Television Service", which stressed that news and current affairs should be "a main feature of the new service". However, senior BBC management were to disregard Cock's suggestions for a further ten years. By the late 1940s Cock was seriously ill. In 1948 a young radio producer, Grace Wyndham Goldie, had been offered a post in the television service; at the time she was working for the prestigious and highbrow Third Programme. Despite discouragement from two senior radio executives, it was Cock who encouraged her to work in television. Goldie was to become the single most important personality in the development of British current affairs television, overseeing the development of programmes such as *Panorama* and *Tonight*—precisely the kind of programmes that Gerald Cock had envisaged as the *sine qua non* of television programming.

—Jason J. Jacobs

GERALD COCK. Born in 1887. Educated at Tonbridge School; Seafield Park. Commissioned Royal Engineers, BEF, France, and Belgium, 1915–20; served as captain, 1917. Traveled in United States, British Columbia, Mexico, working various jobs, including gold mining and ranching, 1909–15; returned to United Kingdom, 1915; conducted business in London, 1920–1924; first director of Outside Broadcasts, BBC, 1925; appointed first director of television, 1935; organized and directed first television service to be established in Europe, 1936–39; served as North American representative, BBC, 1940–41; Pacific Coast representative, BBC, 1942–45; retired, 1946. Member: Reform Club; Royal Victorian Order, 1935. Died 10 November 1973.

PUBLICATION (selection)

"Looking Forward, A Personal Forecast of the Future of Television." *Radio Times* (London), 29 October 1936.

See also British Television

CODCO

Canadian Comedy Revue

CODCO, for Cod Company, is a pun on this theatre troupe's origins. Founded as a theatrical revue in the early 1970s in the maritime island-province of Newfoundland, *CODCO* draws on the province's cultural history of self-deprecating "Newfie" humour, frequently focusing on the cod fishing industry. From these roots, *CODCO* subsequently developed a half-hour, television comedy program of the same name, for national broadcast, produced in the Canadian Broadcasting Corporation's regional studio in Halifax, Nova Scotia, and on location in St. John's, Newfoundland.

Over six seasons of production history on the CBC, *CODCO* underwent two marked changes without losing its satirical edge or drive to endure in another form. Original *CODCO* member Andy Jones left the cast in 1991 to pursue solo theatrical projects. Then, in 1993, just months before Tommy Sexton's death from AIDS-related causes and Greg Malone's departure, *CODCO* went off the air. The death of the boyish, talented Sexton was a subject of national news and reflection on the role of humour in the television and cultural life of Canada. The remaining core members of *CODCO*, Mary Walsh and Cathy Jones, teamed up with two new members, maritime writers-actors Rick Mercer and Greg Thomey, and returned in the 1993-94 season in a half-hour newsmagazine satire, *This Hour Has 22 Minutes*. This foursome also deftly integrated their wacky *22 Minutes* characters to host the Juno Awards (1995), a television special celebrating Canadian popular music.

CODCO's pointed satire takes aim at regional differences, national assumptions, politics, sexism, gender roles, gay codes, and television genres. The general format of *CODCO*'s satire is sketch comedy, with sets, costumes, and make-up that replicate the sources under attack. The *CODCO* members' theatrical roots trained them to shape detailed caricatures, with nuances that dismantle not only the conventions of the source personas and genres but also the ideologies of a medium colonized by commercialism. Spun from the collective writing and acting skills of the members, and ably directed by the experienced John Blanchard and David Acomba, the *CODCO* members' sketches show the tightness of well rehearsed scene studies, rather than the loose burlesque of *Saturday Night Live*.

All four members cross-dress, and their ability to traverse sex roles plays to *CODCO*'s evident interest in social transgression and critique. Cathy Jones and Mary Walsh portray a variety of males, from macho through wimpy, along with their *femme fatales,* "loud feminists," and pesky middle-aged, bingo-bent matrons. The sketches featuring the homely, dateless "Friday Night Girls" satirize the isolation of women in Newfoundland's island life. Walsh's Dakey Dunn, "Male Correspondent," replete with gold chain, hairy chest, cigarette and beer, might explain the dilemma of the "Friday Night Girls"; in one monologue, Dakey admits to not completing high school and, in crude English, lays out a machismo view of economic and cultural matters as if he were in command of Newfiedom. Greg Malone's Queen Elizabeth and his and Tommy Sexton's gay queens share an excessive style and gay-rights politics that only satire can contain on broadcast television. In 1992, Sexton and Malone collaborated with musical theater satirist, John Gray, on a CBC special called *The National Doubt,* which features two mediaeval characters (played by Sexton and Malone) crossing Canada to take the nationalist pulse amid the regional climate that had developed since the Expo' 67 celebrations 25 years earlier in Montreal.

Ivan Fecan, once the CBC's "wunderkind" and former director of television programming, nurtured *CODCO* into a place on the network, first in a late-night slot and later in prime time. Placed back to back with *Kids in the Hall* to comprise an hour of "adult" programming (after 9:00 P.M.), *CODCO*'s satiric authority was enhanced by this yoking with the *Kids*' misbehavior and, in context, with the juxtaposition to the CBC's flagship national newscast, *The National* (later renamed *Primetime News*).

CODCO's transformation into *This Hour Has 22 Minutes* in the CBC's 1993–94 season brought Mary Walsh into her own as head writer and actor, working in collaboration with Cathy Jones, Greg Thomey, Rick Mercer and other writers. The newsmagazine format suits the topical satire of *22 Minutes,* whose title recalls *This Hours Has 7 Days,* a landmark CBC public affairs television program of the 1960s. Dinah Christie sang satirical songs on political and social issues of the day, providing an ironic and entertaining context for the interviews by *7 Days*'hosts-journalists (including the young Pierre Trudeau and Rene Levesque). By its very title, *This Hour Has 22 Minutes* alludes to the shrinkage of content and the prestige of the network since the era of *7 Days. 22 Minutes'* parody of up-to-the minute news of Canadian, American, and international scope obeys the conventions of the contemporary newscast or newsmagazine, but its inventive satire comes from the members' understanding of the unspoken concerns underlying the news, the CBC, the television medium, and the Canadian culture.

As well as playing ever-smiling anchor-journalists, the cast of four portrays a range of continuing and new characters, including obsessive columnists, editorialists of the right and the left, and bizarre interview subjects. Mary Walsh's Marg Delahunty, a self-styled "commentator" with a tacky sense of dress, rails against the codes and inequities of patriarchal culture. Cathy Jones' Babe Bennet, "sexual affairs correspondent," looks and speaks like a hybrid of the late gossip columnist Hedda Hopper and a classic Hollywood screen star of the 1940s. Wearing a persistent smile, suit, hat and white gloves, the "femme" Babe glides through her mansion and verbally skewers men in power (institutional figures such as judges familiar from news items) for bizarre behavior against women. Rick Mercer and Greg Thomey's "The Right Answer" features a fast-talking pair of right-wing "media pundits," Stewart Steed and Steve Steel, who bang a desk bell to punctuate their spitting exchange of prejudices on social and political issues. The pair mimics the rhetoric of shock-talk radio and television figures, with Mercer's character's trademark suspenders specifically suggesting the dress code of the verbose Larry King. As television commentators with licence to pontificate on any subject, Steed and Steel embody media style run amuck.

Television and its cultivation of media personas are under chronic scrutiny in the manic monologues of *22 Minutes,* often delivered distortingly close to the camera lens. The pace and bite of the satire are reminiscent of the wild flights of British television's *Monty Python's Flying Circus* and, later, *Spitting Image.* The frequently employed "in your face" camera technique literalizes the aggression of tabloid TV, and so confronts the unquestioning television viewer by the act of critiquing the uses of the television medium.

Like *CODCO, This Hour Has 22 Minutes* is risk-taking television comedy in that it tests its own satiric boundaries and is not guided by social decorum or by television's laugh meter. Nor does it play up or down to its television or studio audiences—or to other, live audiences. *(22 Minutes* is taped before a studio audience.)

—Joan Nicks

PERFORMERS
Tommy Sexton
Greg Malone
Cathy Jones
Mary Walsh
Andy Jones

PROGRAMMING HISTORY

• CBC

63 Episodes
1987–1994

FURTHER READING
Hluchy, Patricia. "Cold War of the Sexes." *Maclean's* (Toronto), 2 March 1987.
Peters, Helen. "From Salt Cod To Cod Filets." *Canadian Theatre Review* (Guelph, Ontario), Fall 1990.
———. *The Plays of CODCO.* New York: Peter Lang, 1992.

See also Canadian Programming in English

COE, FRED

U.S. Producer

A prolific television, theater, and film producer and director, Fred Coe is closely identified with the "golden age" of live television. His television career started in 1945, when he became production manager for NBC in New York and worked with Worthington Miner on *Studio One.* In 1948, Coe began production of NBC's *Philco Television Playhouse,* a live dramatic-anthology series broadcast on Sunday evenings, from 9:00 to 10:00. From 1951 to 1955, *Philco Television Playhouse* alternated with *Goodyear Television Playhouse* and became one of the top-rated programs of the early 1950s. Live programming of this type was used by NBC's programming chief Pat Weaver to differentiate television from motion pictures, to strengthen ties with its affiliates, and to enlarge the audience for TV sets (manufactured by NBC's parent company, RCA).

Coe was noted for using unknown writers and directors who were able to create works tailored for the new medium: the writers included Paddy Chayefsky, Tad Mosel, Horton Foote, Gore Vidal, J.P. Miller, and Robert Alan Arthur; and the directors included Delbert Mann, Arthur Penn, and Vincent Donehue. Setting anthology drama on a course that established it as the most prestigious format on live television, Coe relied at first on TV adaptations of Broadway plays and musicals, then on literary classics, biographies, and old Hollywood movies, and finally on original television drama. The Philco series opened on 3 October 1948 with a one-hour version of George S. Kaufman and Edna Ferber's *Dinner at Eight.* In 1952, Coe produced the first play of the first playwright to achieve fame in television. The playwright was Paddy Chayefsky, and the play, *Holiday Song.* In 1953, Coe produced Chayefsky's *Marty* with Rod Steiger in the title role. Directed by Delbert Mann, *Marty* became the most popular anthology drama of the period, winning many awards and even initiating a Hollywood production trend of films based on TV drama. *Marty* the film, produced by Harold Hecht and released through United Artists in 1955, won Academy Awards for Best Picture, Best Actor (Ernest Borgnine), Direction (Delbert Mann), and Original Screenplay (Paddy Chayefsky). Other notable Coe productions included Chayefsky's *The Bachelor Party,* Horton Foote's *The Trip to the Bountiful,* and Tad Mosel's *Other People's Houses.* Productions such as these earned Coe and the *Philco Playhouse* the George Foster Peabody Award in 1954 and many other honors.

In 1954, Coe began producing *Producer's Showcase,* a 90-minute anthology series that aired every fourth Monday for three seasons. One aim of the series was to broadcast expensive color spectaculars to promote RCA's new color television system. The best example of this strategy was *Peter Pan,* a successful Broadway production of Sir James M. Barrie's fantasy which Coe brought to television almost intact. Starring Mary Martin, *Peter Pan* was broadcast on 7 March 1955 and was viewed by an estimated 65-75 million people, becoming the highest-rated show in TV's brief history. As a result of this memorable production and adaptations of such plays as Sherwood Anderson's *The Petrified Forest* (1955), which starred Humphrey Bogart and Lauren Bacall in their TV dramatic debuts, and Thornton Wilder's *Our Town,* which starred Paul Newman and Eva Marie Saint, Coe was awarded an Emmy for Best Producer of a Live Series in 1955.

NBC's programming strategies radically changed after 1956 to rely on the routines of series programming produced by West Coast suppliers on film. In 1957, Coe departed the network for CBS, where he produced *Playhouse 90* for three seasons. Among the best productions of the series were *Days of Wine and Roses* (1958), *The Plot to Kill Stalin* (1958), and *For Whom the Bell Tolls* (1959). Thereafter, Coe worked sporadically in television, producing specials for all three networks in the late 1960s and 1970s, and producing and directing several episodes of *The Adams Chronicles* for PBS in 1976.

Fred Coe
Photo courtesy of Wisconsin Center for Film and Theater Research

Anticipating the decline of live anthology drama on television, Coe brought anthology drama to Broadway by producing theatrical versions of TV plays by TV writers, among them William Gibson's *Two for the Seesaw* (1958) and *The Miracle Worker* (1959), Tad Mosel's *All the Way Home* (1960), and Herb Gardner's *A Thousand Clowns* (1962). Coe even converted two TV plays into films— *The Miracle Worker* (1962) and *A Thousand Clowns* (1966). Coe's legacy is a tradition of programming demonstrating television's unique aspects as a medium of dramatic expression.

—Tino Balio

FRED COE. Born in Alligator, Mississippi, U.S.A., 23 December 1914. Attended Peabody Demonstration School, Nashville, Tennessee; attended Peabody College for Teachers, Nashville; studied at Yale Drama School, New Haven, Connecticut, 1938–40. Married: 1) Alice Griggs, 1940 (divorced), children: John and Laurence Anne; 2) Joyce Beeler, 1952; children: Sue Anne and Samuel Hughes. Ran community theater in Nashville; presented radio dramas on station WSM; production manager, NBC, New York (producing more than 500 hour-long teleplays), 1945; producer, *Philco-Goodyear Theater,* NBC, 1948–53; executive producer, *Mr. Peepers* series, 1952–53; producer, *Producers' Showcase,* 1954–55; producer, *Playwrights '56,* 1956; producer and director, *Playhouse 90,* CBS, produced such Broadway shows as *Two for the Seesaw, A Trip to Bountiful,* and *The Miracle Worker,* co-producer and director, various Broadway shows. Recipient: Writers Guild of America Evelyn Burkey Award; Peabody Award, 1954; Emmy Award, 1955. Died in Los Angeles, California, U.S.A., 29 April 1979.

TELEVISION SERIES

1948–53	*Philco Television Theater* and *Goodyear Television Theater*
1952–53	*Mr. Peepers* (executive producer)
1954–55	*Producers' Showcase*
1956	*Playwrights '56*
1956–61	*Playhouse 90* (also director)

MADE-FOR-TELEVISION MOVIE

1979	*Miracle Worker* (producer)

TELEPLAYS (selection)

1949	*Philco Television Playhouse:* "What Makes Sammy Run?"
1949	*Philco Television Playhouse:* "The Last Tycoon"
1953	*Philco Television Playhouse:* "Marty"
1955	*Producers' Showcase:* "Peter Pan"

FILMS

The Left-Handed Gun (producer), 1958; *Miracle Worker* (producer), 1962; *This Property Is Condemned* (writer), 1966

STAGE

Two for the Seesaw; A Trip to Bountiful; The Miracle Worker; All the Way Home (co-producer); *A Thousand Clowns* (co-producer and director).

FURTHER READING

Averson, Richard, editor. *Electronic Drama: Television Plays of the Sixties.* Boston, Massachusetts: Beacon, 1971.

"The Broadcasting and Cable Hall of Fame (Biographies of 17 Inductees)." *Broadcasting and Cable* (Washington, D.C.), 7 November 1994.

Hawes, William. *The American Television Drama: The Experimental Years.* University: University of Alabama Press, 1986.

Kindem, Gorham, editor. *The Live Television Generation of Hollywood Film Directors: Interviews with Seven Directors.* Jefferson, North Carolina: McFarland, 1994.

Sturcken, Frank. *Live Television: The Golden Age of 1946–1958 in New York.* Jefferson, North Carolina: McFarland, 1990.

Wilk, Max. *The Golden Age of Television: Notes from the Survivors.* New York: Dell, 1977.

See also Anthology Drama; Chayefsky, Paddy; "Golden Age" of Television; *Goodyear Playhouse;* Mann, Delbert; *Peter Pan; Philco Television Playhouse; Playhouse 90*

COLE, GEORGE

British Actor

George Cole, in his alter ego of Arthur Daley in the long-running series *Minder,* is to countless British viewers the quintessence of the Cockney spiv, a mischief-causing small businessman always with an eye to the main chance and often caught treading on the toes of the law. Endearingly convinced against all the evidence of his own cunning, and equally often driven to distraction by the comical collapse of his schemes, the irrepressible Daley, with his salesman's patter and naive pretensions as a big-time wheeler and dealer, became an icon for the 1980s, representing the materialist sub-yuppie culture that was fostered under the capitalist leadership of Margaret Thatcher. Every episode of the comedy series, which co-starred Dennis Waterman as his dimwitted but resolutely honest bodyguard-cum-assistant Terry McCann, featured the launch of another of Daley's shady schemes, or "nice little earners" as he called them, and culminated in the hapless secondhand car salesman and would-be executive being exposed for some fiddle or other and having to be rescued from arrest, physical assault, or worse by his long-suffering minder. Other troubles in Daley's life, from which he took refuge in his drinking club, the Winchester, came from "'Er indoors", the formidable Mrs. Daley, who was never seen.

Minder, written by Leon Griffiths and filmed in some of the less picturesque parts of London, was not an instant success. The first two series failed to convince audiences, who welcomed Cole but were confused at the sight of tough-guy Dennis Waterman, fresh from the police series *The Sweeney,* taking a comic part. Thames Television persevered, however, and the public were gradually won over, the two stars becoming the highest-paid television actors in Britain. After six series, each billed as the last, Waterman finally withdrew to concentrate on other work, but Cole continued just a little longer, now with his nephew Ray (played by Gary Webster) as Terry's replacement.

The part of Arthur Daley was perfect for Cole, who had in fact been playing variations of the character for years on both the large and small screen (he made his film debut as early as 1941). He had been schooled in the finer points of comic acting as the protégé of the film comedian Alistair Sim and as a young man made a memorable impression as the cockney spiv Flash Harry, an embryonic Daley figure complete with funny walk, loud suits, catchy signature tune, and suitcase bulging with dodgy merchandise, in the *Saint Trinian's* films of the 1950s. His television career took off in 1960, when he was seen as David Bliss in *A Life of Bliss*, which had started out as a radio series. Subsequently he continued to be associated chiefly with similar cockney roles, as in *A Man of Our Times*, in which he played the manager of a small furniture store, though in reality he has played a much wider variety of parts—including an aspiring playwright in *Don't Forget to Write*, a dedicated communist in *Comrade Dad*, the aristocratic and much put-upon Sir Giles Lynchwood in Tom Sharpe's hilarious *Blott on the Landscape*, and Henry Root in *Root Into Europe*, among other assorted characters.

It is, however, as the ever-likable if sometimes unscrupulous Arthur Daley that George Cole, an Officer of the British Empire, is best known. Such is his identification with the part that the actor reports that he frequently has trouble getting people to accept his cheques, fearing that they will not be honoured by the banks because of his on-screen reputation. The extensive use of cockney rhyming slang by Daley in the 70-odd episodes that were made of *Minder* is also said, incidentally, to have done much to keep this linguistic oddity from extinction.

—David Pickering

GEORGE COLE. Born in Tooting, London, England, 22 April 1925. Attended Surrey County Council Secondary School, Morden. Married: 1) Eileen Moore, 1954 (divorced, 1966); one son and one daughter; 2) Penelope Morrell, 1967; children: Tara and Toby. Served in Royal Air Force, 1943–7. Began career as stage actor in *The White Horse Inn* on tour, 1939; discovered by Alistair Sim in 1940 to play a cockney evacuee in the film *Cottage to Let*, 1941; subsequently specialized in chirpy cockney roles, notably Flash Harry in the *St. Trinian's* films; established reputation on television with the role of David Bliss in *A Life of Bliss*, 1960–61; best-known to television audiences as Arthur Daley in the long-running series *Minder*. Order of the British Empire, 1992. Address: Joy Jameson, 19 The Plaza, 535 King's Road, London SW10 0SZ, England.

George Cole
Photo courtesy of George Cole

TELEVISION SERIES

1960–1	*A Life of Bliss*
1968	*A Man of Our Times*
1977–9	*Don't Forget to Write*
1979–85	*Minder*
1982–3	*The Bounder*
1985	*Blott on the Landscape*
1986	*Comrade Dad*
1988–94	*Minder*

MADE-FOR-TELEVISION MOVIE (selection)

1985	*Minder On the Orient Express*

FILMS

Cottage to Let, 1941; *Those Kids from Town*, 1942; *Fiddling Fuel*, 1943; *The Demi-Paradise*, 1943; *Henry V*, 1944; *Journey Together*, 1945; *My Brother's Keeper*, 1948; *Quartet*, 1948; *The Spider and the Fly*, 1949; *Morning Departure*, 1949; *Gone to Earth*, 1949; *Flesh and Blood*, 1951; *Laughter in Paradise*, 1951; *Scrooge*, 1951; *Lady Godiva Rides Again*, 1951; *The Happy Family*, 1952; *Folly to Be Wise*, 1952; *Who Goes There?*, 1952; *Top Secret*, 1952; *The Clue of the Missing Ape*, 1953; *Will Any Gentleman*, 1953; *Apes of the Rock*, 1953; *The Intruder*, 1953; *Our Girl Friday*, 1953; *Happy Ever After*, 1954; *The Belles of St. Trinian's*, 1954; *An Inspector Calls*, 1954; *Where There's a Will*, 1955; *A Prize of Gold*, 1955; *The Constant Husband*, 1955; *The Adventures of Quentin Durward*, 1955; *It's a Wonderful World*, 1956; *The Weapon*, 1956; *The Green Man*, 1956; *Blue Murder at St. Trinian's*, 1957; *Too Many Crooks*, 1958; *Don't Panic Chaps*, 1959; *The Bridal Path*, 1959; *The Pure Hell of St. Trinian's*, 1961; *The Anatomist*, 1961; *Cleopatra*, 1962; *Dr. Syn Alias the Scarecrow*, 1963; *One Way Pendulum*, 1964; *The Legend of Young Dick Turpin*, 1965; *The Great St. Trinian's Train Robbery*, 1966; *The Green Shoes*, 1968; *The Right Prospectus*, 1970; *The Vampire Lovers*, 1970; *Girl in the Dark*, 1971; *Fright*, 1971; *Take Me High*, 1973; *Gone in 60 Seconds*, 1974; *The Blue Bird*, 1976; *Double Nickels*, 1978; *Perishing Solicitors*.

RADIO

A Life of Bliss (series).

STAGE (selection)

The White Horse Inn, 1939; *Cottage to Let*, 1940; *Goodnight Children*, 1942; *Mr. Bolfry*, 1943; *Dr. Angelus*, 1947; *The Anatomist*, 1948; *Mr. Gillie*, 1950; *A Phoenix too Frequent*,

1951; *Thor with Angels*, 1951; *Misery Me*, 1955; *Mr. Bolfry*, 1956; *Brass Butterfly*, 1958; *The Bargain*, 1961; *The Sponge Room*, 1962; *Squat Betty*, 1962; *Meet Me on the Fence*, 1963; *Hedda Gabler*, 1964; *A Public Mischief*, 1965; *Too True To Be Good*, 1965; *The Waiting Game*, 1966; *The Three Sisters*, 1967; *Doubtful Haunts*, 1968; *The Passionate Husband*, 1969; *The Philanthropist*, 1971; *Country Life*, 1973; *Déjà Revue*, 1974; *Motive*, 1976; *Banana Ridge*, 1976; *The Case of the Oily Levantine*, 1977; *Something Afoot*, 1978; *Brimstone and Treacle*, 1979; *Liberty Hall*, 1980; *The Pirates of Penzance*, 1982; *A Month of Sundays*, 1986; *A Piece of My Mind*, 1987; *Peter Pan*, 1987; *The Breadwinner*, 1989; *Natural Causes*, 1993; *Theft*, 1995.

FURTHER READING

Berkmann, Marcus. "Still a Nice Little Earner." *Daily Mail* (London), 9 October 1993.

Bradbury, Malcolm. "Requiem for an Old Rogue." *Daily Mail* (London), 9 October 1993.

Buss, Robin. "Minder." *Times Educational Supplement* (London), 8 November 1991.

Truss, Lynne. "Television Workhorses Finally Put Out to Grass." *The Times* (London), 10 March 1994.

See also *Minder, Sweeney*

THE COLGATE COMEDY HOUR

U.S. Variety Show

For approximately five-and-a-half seasons, NBC's *Colgate Comedy Hour* presented big budget musical variety television as head-to-head competition for *Ed Sullivan's Toast of the Town* on CBS. Featuring the top names in vaudeville, theater, radio and film, this live Sunday evening series was the first starring vehicle for many notable performers turning to television. Reflecting format variations by host, *The Colgate Comedy Hour* initially offered musical comedy, burlesque sketches, opera and/or night club comedy revues.

In his autobiography, *Take My Life*, comedian Eddie Cantor recalled proposing to NBC that he was prepared to host a television show but only once every four weeks in rotation with other comics. Colgate-Palmolive-Peet picked up the tab for three of the four weeks and *The Colgate Comedy Hour* was born with Cantor, Dean Martin and Jerry Lewis and Fred Allen as hosts. The fourth show of the month was sponsored originally by Frigidaire and appeared for a short time under the title *Michael Todd's Revue* with Todd producing and comic Bobby Clark scheduled to alternate with Bob Hope as host.

Cantor premiered *The Colgate Comedy Hour* on 10 September 1950, to rave reviews. Working the thread of a story line into the show for continuity, the veteran performer took his material out of the realm of vaudeville and turned it into more of a legitimate Broadway attraction. Martin and Lewis met with similar success. Dominating their hour, the energetic duo created a night club setting whose intimacy and ambience the trade press found continuously funny. Allen, on the other hand, found the large scale theatrical nature of the format too demanding and out of character for his more relaxed style of humor. Attempting to transfer elements of his successful radio show to video, he only met with disappointment. This was especially true when the characters of his famous Allen's Alley were foolishly turned into puppets. Allen showed improvement on subsequent

telecasts but was retired from the series after his fourth broadcast. Bitter about his experience, he promised he would not return to television unless provided a low-key format comparable to Dave Garroway's Chicago-based *Garroway at Large*. Clark produced better ratings and reviews

The Colgate Comedy Hour
Photo courtesy of Wisconsin Center for Film and Theater Research

than Allen but ultimately he and the *Michael Todd Revue* suffered a similar fate.

Premiering with Jackie Gleason in its second season, *The Colgate Comedy Hour* was the highest budgeted, single-sponsor extravaganza on television with Colgate-Palmolive-Peet picking up a three million dollar a year talent-production-time tab. Back for their second year were Cantor and Martin and Lewis with Gleason, Abbott and Costello, Spike Jones, Tony Martin and Ezio Pinza slotted as starters. Ratings remained high for the original hosts but the Sullivan show began producing high budget specials that chipped away at the Colgate numbers when the new hosts appeared.

During the second season, *The Colgate Comedy Hour* also became the first commercial network series to originate on the west coast when Cantor hosted his program from Hollywood's El Capitan Theatre on 30 September 1951. Two years later, on 22 November 1953, a Donald O'Connor *Comedy Hour* became the first sponsored network program to be telecast in color. In an FCC-approved test of RCA's new compatible color system, several hundred persons monitored the broadcast in specially equipped viewing booths at a site distant from the Colgate production theater.

Despite an annual budget estimated at more than six million dollars, during the 1953–54 season *The Colgate Comedy Hour* began to experience problems. Many performers, hard pressed to continually generate new material, were considered stale and repetitious. Cantor and Martin and Lewis were still highly rated regulars but Cantor was feeling stressed. The diminutive showman had suffered a heart attack after a *Comedy Hour* appearance in September 1952, and, now nearly sixty years of age, he felt the work too demanding. This would be his last season. To attract and maintain an audience, new hosts, including the popular Jimmy Durante, were absorbed from NBC's faltering *All Star Revue*. Occasional "book" musicals, top flight shows such as *Anything Goes* with Ethel Merman and Frank Sinatra, were produced. The *Comedy Hour* also began to tour providing viewers with special broadcasts from glamorous locations— New York seen from the deck of the *S.S. United States*, among others.

During the 1954–55 season, the Sullivan show made significant inroads on *The Colgate Comedy Hour's* ratings. Martin and Lewis made fewer appearances and an emphasis was placed on performers working in big settings such as the Hollywood Bowl and Broadway's Latin Quarter. During the summer, Colgate collaborated with Paramount Pictures, the latter supplying guest stars and film clips from newly released motion pictures. The show moved away from comedy headliners; actor Charlton Heston hosted as did orchestra leader Guy Lombardo and musical star Gordon MacRae. To reflect these differences the show's name was changed to the *Colgate Variety Hour*, but, despite the changes, for the first time in its history, the series dropped out of the top twenty-five in Nielsen ratings while Sullivan moved into the top five.

A feuding Martin and Lewis kicked off the last season of the *Colgate Variety Hour* to good reviews but subsequent shows proved it had become increasingly difficult to sustain acceptable ratings for a series of this budget magnitude. On 11 December 1955, Sullivan drew an overnight Trendex of 42.6. The *Variety Hour's* salute to theatrical legend George Abbott came in a distant third with a dismal 7.2. Two weeks later, on 25 December 1955 the Colgate series quietly left the air following a Christmas music broadcast by Fred Waring and his Pennsylvanians. Replaced with the poorly conceived *NBC Comedy Hour*, featuring unlikely host Leo Durocher, one of the most lavish, entertaining and at times extraordinary musical variety series in television history was just a memory. In May 1967 NBC presented a *Colgate Comedy Hour* revival but it was a revival in name only—not in format or in star value.

—Joel Sternberg

PRINCIPAL HOSTS

Eddie Cantor (1950–54)
Dean Martin and Jerry Lewis (1950–55)
Fred Allen (1950)
Donald O'Connor (1951–54)
Abbott and Costello (1951–54)
Bob Hope (1952–53)
Jimmy Durante (1953–54)
Gordon MacRae (1954–55)
Robert Paige (1955)

PRODUCERS   Charles Friedman, Sam Fuller

PROGRAMMING HISTORY

• NBC

September 1950-December 1955   Sunday 8:00-9:00

FURTHER READING

"Abbott, Costello into Colgate Hour." *Variety* (Los Angeles), 13 December 1950.

Brooks, Tim, and Earle Marsh. *The Complete Directory to Prime Time Network TV Shows 1946–Present.* New York: Ballantine Books, 1979; 5th edition, 1992.

Cantor, Eddie, with Jane Kesner Ardmore. *Take My Life.* Garden City, New York: Doubleday, 1957.

"Cantor Faces the East as First L.A.-to-N.Y. Com'l TV Show Bows." *Variety* (Los Angeles), 3 October 1951.

Castleman, Harry, and Walter J. Podrazik. *Watching TV: Four Decades of American Television.* New York: McGraw Hill, 1982.

"Colgate Comedy Hour." *Variety* (Los Angeles), 20 September 1950.

"Colgate Comedy Hour." *Variety* (Los Angeles), 27 September 1950.

"Colgate Comedy Hour." *Variety* (Los Angeles), 5 September 1951.

"Colgate Comedy Hour." *Variety* (Los Angeles), 17 May 1967.

"Colgate Looks and Reads Like the Sullivan Show, But Still Takes Beating." *Variety* (Los Angeles), 14 December 1955.

"Colgate Variety Hour." *Variety* (Los Angeles), 15 June 1955.

"Colgate Variety Hour." *Variety* (Los Angeles), 21 September 1955.

"Color TV Review: Colgate Comedy Hour." *Variety* (Los Angeles), 25 November 1953.

"How the New Shows Are Doing." *Television* (New York), November 1950.

"Martin and Lewis Show." *Variety* (Los Angeles), 24 September 1952.

"Martin and Lewis Show (Colgate Comedy Hour)." *Variety* (Los Angeles), 7 October 1953.

"Michael Todd's Revue." *Variety* (Los Angeles), 4 October 1950.

"NBC Comedy Hour." *Variety* (Los Angeles), 11 January 1956.

Rosen, George. "Cantor Sock in Debut on Colgate Airer; Vet Showman a TV Natural." *Variety* (Los Angeles), 13 September 1950.

"Tele Follow-Up Comment." *Variety* (Los Angeles), 20 December 1950.

"Tele Follow-Up Comment." *Variety* (Los Angeles), 29 September 1954.

"Tele Follow-Up Comment." *Variety* (Los Angeles), 6 July 1955.

"Tele Topics." *Radio Daily* (New York), 19 September 1950.

"Television Follow-Up Comment." *Variety* (Los Angeles), 25 October 1950.

Terrace, Vincent. *The Complete Encyclopedia of Television Programs 1947–1979, Vol. 1, A-Z.* New York: Barnes, 1979.

COLLINS, BILL

Australian Television Personality

Bill Collins has been described as "Mr. Movies of Australia". He has presented films on television and on video since 1963 and has come to seem like a trusted and enthusiastic guarantor of whatever film he happens to be presenting. As a high-school English teacher, long interested in the cinema and its possible role in the classroom, he completed a Master's degree in education on the role of film in education and took a position as a lecturer in English at the Sydney Teachers' College. He regularly introduced trainee teachers to the place of film in the high-school English curriculum.

In 1963 he made his first appearance on television, producing and presenting a series of filmed segments on film appreciation. That same year he compiled a weekly column in the better of Australia's television guides, *TV Times*, entitled "The Golden Years of Hollywood". The column consisted of a series of reviews of upcoming Hollywood films to be screened on Australia's three commercial networks as well as the public broadcaster, the ABC. Collins' reviews were invariably to the point and reliable in their production credits at a time when this kind of information was not so easily available as it is nowadays. To write these reviews, Collins was having to preview many of the films. It seemed quite logical, then, when TCN Channel 9 (owned by Consolidated Press who co-published *TV Times* with the ABC) decided to have Collins host a Saturday night movie, with the generic name of *The Golden Years of Hollywood*. Collins continued to host the Saturday night movie on Channel 9 in Sydney until 1975 when he moved to the Seven Network. Channel 9 disputed that Collins had the legal right to call his Saturday night movie program *The Golden Years of Hollywood* and so the Seven program became *Bill Collins' Golden Years of Hollywood*. The change

suited Collins because his career as a movie host was now taking off. His Saturday night movie was now increasingly seen nationally and as his earnings increased Collins quit

Bill Collins
Photo courtesy of Bill Collins

his teaching job to concentrate full time on his television work. At Seven, Collins began to host a Sunday daytime film, *Bill Collins' Picture Time* and also a more general program featuring film clips and promotion for new releases, *Bill Collins' Show Business.*

Collins moved yet again in 1980 in a move that made him even busier. Rupert Murdoch had recently acquired the third commercial network which he renamed Network Ten. The latter had always lagged in the ratings and Murdoch was determined to change this situation even if it meant spending a lot of money—to hire Collins away. Collins now became a national figure to the point that other movie hosts on regional stations ceased to have any importance and little recognition. By this time he seemed to be everywhere. Not only did he host a double feature on a Saturday night under the old title of *The Golden Years of Hollywood,* a double feature on Sunday lunch time and afternoon, the midday movie during the week on a capital city by capital city basis but also an afternoon book review and promotion program. Thanks both to the size of his program budgets as well as his commercial standing, Collins was able to do live interviews with major Hollywood actors including his favourite, Clint Eastwood. He also published two books, lavishly illustrated, on his favourite films. In addition Collins also had his own series of Hollywood feature films on video which he hosted—*Bill Collins' Movie Collection.* Collins also made professional visits to fans across the country, these taking the form of breakfasts and lunches. To carry out these massive commitments, Collins now had a staff of researchers and his own press and publicity agents. In 1987 because of the introduction of new cross-ownership rules in Australia media, Murdoch sold off Network Ten. Collins continued there until 1994. The network suffered from financial problems, so there was a curtailment of his programs. However, in 1995, he, in effect, rejoined the Murdoch camp when he began presenting films on Australia's first cable network,

Foxtel, owned and operated by Murdoch's News Corporation and Telstra Corporation. Collins now hosts films produced by Twentieth Century-Fox on Foxtel Channel.

There is no gainsaying the achievement of Bill Collins. He appeared on Australian television at a time when Hollywood films, not only of the 1930s and 1940s, but also of the 1950s, were becoming available for television programming. He has helped to make Hollywood films popular with generations who were born after the Hollywood studio era. As befits a former teacher, his introductions to particular films are invariably interesting, enthusiastic and well researched. He will often display a still or a poster, brandish the book on which a film is based (he has an extensive collection of these, often extremely rare books), or play some of a film's theme music. All of these ploys are in the service of not only giving the audience particular features to look for in the upcoming film but also contextualising it in terms of such frames as the biography of one of the leading figures. Nor has Collins been afraid to expose his audience to some of the fruits of more critical research with references to such material as a critical study of John Ford or an article in the U.S. film studies journal *The Velvet Light Trap.* Altogether Bill Collins is one of the most durable and valuable figures in the history of Australian television.

—Albert Moran

BILL COLLINS. Born in Sydney, Australia, 1935. Educated at Sydney University, B.A., M.A., DipEd., and M.Ed. Taught in high school for four years; university lecturer; began reviewing movies in print (*TV Times*) and on television (ABC Television), 1963; moved from ABC to commercial station TCN Channel 9, 1967–75; movie host, ATN Channel 7 Sydney, 1975–79; presented movies nationally on the Network Ten, 1980–94; currently presenting movies on the Foxtel movie network.

COLOR TELEVISION

The early stages of color television experimentation in America overlap the technological development of monochromatic television. Color television was demonstrated by John Logie Baird as early as 1928, and a year later by Bell Telephone Laboratories. Experimental color broadcasting was initiated in 1940, when the Columbia Broadcasting System (CBS) publicly demonstrated a field sequential color television broadcasting system. This system employed successive fields scanned one at a time in one of the three primary colors; red, blue, or green. On the receiver end, a mechanical color wheel was used to reconstitute the primary colors in sequence to enable reproduction of the colors in the original scene. In their 1941 report confirming the National Television Systems Committee (NTSC) monochromatic standards, the Federal Communications

Commission (FCC) noted the potential benefits of the CBS color system but concurred with the NTSC assessment that color television required further testing before it could be standardized.

Further refinement of color television was temporarily suspended during World War II. After the war, work on the development of color TV resumed, and engineers were able to design a system that would operate within the 6 MHz channel allocation that had been established for black and white service. In a hearing which began 26 September 1949, and lasted for 62 days, CBS petitioned the FCC for commercialization of their 6-MHz, 405-line, 144-fields-per-second-field sequential color system. Due to the higher scanning rate, such a system was not compatible with the existing monochromatic standard.

The economic costs of adopting an incompatible system were a major factor in the FCC deliberations. If adopted, it appeared that consumers would carry the cost of modifying the existing two million monochrome receivers to follow the higher field-sequential scanning rates and reproduce color signal transmissions in monochrome. The projected costs of this modification varied, with a low figure of about $25. In addition, it was also argued that when broadcasters elected to begin color service, they would lose that portion of the audience had not yet modified their monochrome receivers.

At the hearings, work on several experimental electronic color systems designed to be compatible with the existing monochrome system was presented to the commission. Color Television, Incorporated (CTI) demonstrated their line sequential color system which assigned the color portion of the signal to the successive lines of the image. In the first field, the uppermost line was scanned in green, the next line in blue, the next in red, and so on until the first field was complete. The second field was scanned in a similar manner, and the combination of the two fields produced a complete picture in color. The system operated at 525 lines, and 60 fields a second, corresponding to the existing monochrome service. The Radio Corporation of America (RCA) demonstrated its dot sequential color system in which color is assigned to successive picture elements or dots of the image. With this system, each line of any field is composed of dots in the three primary colors. The scanning system for this color design, (525/60), was also identical to the existing monochrome standard. Both the CTI and RCA color system were formally proposed to the commission as potential standards. In addition to these proposals, preliminary development of several other color systems were also presented. To many of the industry witnesses appearing before the commission, the demonstrations and discussions indicated that a satisfactory compatible system could be developed in a reasonable period of time and they urged that a decision regarding color be postponed.

Examining the various proposed color systems, the FCC determined that the shortcomings of the compatible systems were fundamental and noted that if a viable alternative compatible system could not be developed, and the field-sequential color system was eventually adopted, the costs of modifying an even greater number of monochrome receivers would be prohibitive, denying the public of color service altogether. The commission therefore felt that it was unwise to delay the decision and on 10 October 1950, decided that the adoption of the color field-sequential system proposed by CBS was in the public interest. RCA appealed this decision, all the way to the Supreme Court, but the commission's actions were upheld. The CBS station in New York began regular color broadcasts on 25 June 1951. However, due to the military demands of the Korean War and the reallocation of resources towards the war effort, color receiver production could not be dramatically increased. On 19 October 1951, CBS discontinued color broadcasts due to the limited numbers of color receivers.

It was within this context that the NTSC, the entity which played a key role in setting monochrome standards in the United States, was reactivated to investigate the status of compatible color systems. On 21 July 1953, two years after their first meeting, the second NTSC approved a compatible all electronic color television dot sequential system (a modified version of RCA's system) and petitioned the FCC for adoption. On 17 December 1953 the FCC formally adopted a compatible color standard.

After the color standard was set in 1953, broadcasting stations were fairly quick to upgrade their transmission facilities to provide for color programming. Of the 158 stations operating in the top 40 cities, 106 had adopted color capabilities by 1957. Color programming offerings, however, remained fairly limited for quite some time. Although NBC increased its output of color programming to help its parent company, RCA, sell color receivers, the other major networks were not as supportive of this new innovation. As late as 1965, CBS provided only 800 hours of color programming the entire year and ABC only 600 hours. In addition to the limited programming, early sets were somewhat cumbersome to adjust for proper color reception, receiver prices remained fairly high, and manufacturers were reluctant to promote color receivers until the lucrative black and white market had been saturated. Consequently, consumers were fairly slow to adopt color technology. As of 1965, only 10% of U.S. homes had a color set. It was not until the late 1960s, over a decade after the standard was set, that color TV sales rose significantly. Today, approximately 95% of all U.S. homes have color television.

—David F. Donnelly

FURTHER READING

Crane, Rhonda J. *The Politics of International Standards: France and the Color TV War.* Norwood, New Jersey: Ablex, 1979.

Fink, D., editor. *Color Television Standards: Selected Papers and Records of the National Television System Committee.* New York: McGraw-Hill, 1955.

Radio Corporation of America. *Petition of Radio Corporation of America and National Broadcasting Company, Inc. For Approval of Color Standards For the RCA Color Television System.* New York: Federal Communications Commission, 1953.

Rzeszewski, T., editor. *Color Television.* New York: Institute of Electrical and Electronics Engineers Press, 1983.

Sterling, C., and J. Kittross. *Stay Tuned: A Concise History of American Broadcasting.* Belmont, California: Wadsworth, 1990.

See also Television Technology

COLORIZATION

Colorization is a computerized process that adds color to a black-and-white movie or TV program. The process was invented by Wilson Markle and was first used in 1970 to add color to monochrome footage of the moon from the Apollo mission. In 1983, Markle founded Colorization, Inc. The word "colorization" soon became a generic name for the adding of color to black-and-white footage.

The process of colorizing a movie begins with a monochrome film print, preferably a new print struck from the original negative. From the film print, a high-quality videotape copy is made. Technicians, aided by a computer, determine the gray level of every object in every shot and note any movement of objects within shots. A computer adds color to each object, while keeping gray levels the same as in the monochrome original. Which color to use for which object is determined through common sense (green for grass, blue for the ocean) or by investigation. For example, movie studio photographs or costume vaults may provide guidance as to what color a hat should be. In cases where no such guidance is available, colorists pick their own colors, presumably with some aesthetic sensibility.

Colorization is an expensive and time-consuming process. *Popular Mechanics* reported in 1987 that it cost more than $3,000 per minute of running time to colorize a movie. The economic justification for such an expenditure lay in audience demand. *Variety* estimated in 1988 that while it cost $300,000 to colorize an old movie, the revenue generated by the release of the colorized version was $500,000. This revenue came mostly from television syndication, although videocassette release was also important in some cases. Another important consideration was the opportunity to claim new copyrights on old films, thus extending the film's potential life as a profit center for the owner.

Colorization became extremely controversial in the late 1980s, especially with regard to "classic" monochrome films such as *Citizen Kane* (which ultimately was not colorized), *Casablanca, The Maltese Falcon,* and *It's a Wonderful Life.* With some exceptions, the dispute pitted film directors and critics (who opposed colorization) against copyright owners (who favored it). Among its opponents, TV critic Eric Mink viewed colorization as a "bastardization" of film. The Writers Guild of America West called it "cultural vandalism."

The case against colorization is most often couched in moral terms. According to this reasoning, colorization violates the moral right of the film director to create a work of art that has a final, permanent form and that will not be subject to alteration years later by unauthorized parties. Moral rights of artists, recognized in other countries, have no standing in United States law, which gives preference to the property rights of copyright holders. In film and television, the copyright holder is almost always a large film studio or production company, which employs the director as an author-for-hire, so to speak. To an extent, the battle over colorization was an attempt by directors and other creative

artists to prevent further erosion of their power to control their own work.

This position was often framed, somewhat spuriously, in more high-minded terms. For example, it was argued that colorization is an affront to film history. According to this line of thinking, the color version of a film drives the original monochrome version out of circulation, with the result that some viewers may not understand that *Casablanca* was shot in black and white. Similarly, as Stuart Klawans notes, the viewer might erroneously conclude that a color film such as *Gone with the Wind* was originally shot in monochrome and later colorized. If colorization can deceive to this extent, it must have a fairly convincing appearance, and, indeed, image quality and craftsmanship were probably the least-often-heard objections to colorizing.

As more movie "classics" became involved, the reaction against colorization took on the flavor of a moral panic. With colorization frequently the object of ridicule, the case in favor of the process became largely a defensive one: colorization does not harm the black-and-white original, and in fact encourages restoration of the original film and the striking of new prints; colorization is no more meddlesome than other, generally accepted practices in the televising of movies, such as interruption for commercials, editing for TV, cropping, time compression, and panning and scanning (not to mention the reduction in image size and the possibility of watching a color movie on a monochrome TV set); finally, any viewer who is offended by the color image can turn off the chroma on the TV set and watch in black-and-white.

It is worth emphasizing that the product of colorization is a videotape, not a film print. When a movie is colorized, nothing bad happens to the original film print, and the colorized version can only be watched on TV. Ultimately, the greatest impact of colorization may be upon old, monochrome TV series, if and when colorization loses its stigma. Indeed, one of the original ideas behind colorization was the creation of quasi-new TV series. As Earl Glick put it in 1984, "You couldn't make *Wyatt Earp* today for $1 million an episode. But for $50,000 a segment, you can turn it into color and have a brand new series—with no residuals to pay." As logical as this may sound, only *McHale's Navy* and a few other series have been colorized.

As of 1995, colorization is no longer a hot issue. Demand for colorized movies has shrunk drastically. Ted Turner, owner of hundreds of MGM, Warner Bros., and RKO titles and colorization's most outspoken advocate, has quietly stopped releasing colorized movies. The main legacy of colorization is the National Film Registry, established by Congress in 1988 in response to the colorization controversy. The Registry is a list of films, selected by experts and expanded annually, that, if colorized, will have to be labeled with a disclaimer. As Klawans points out, the hundreds of thousands of dollars spent on compiling the registry would be much better spent on actual film (not to mention television) preservation.

—Gary Burns

FURTHER READING

Cooper, Roger. "Colorization and Moral Rights: Should the United States Adopt Unified Protection for Artists?" *Journalism Quarterly* (Urbana, Illinois), Autumn 1991.

Daniels, Charles B. "Note on Colourization." *British Journal of Aesthetics* (London), January, 1990.

Dawson, Greg. "Ted Turner: Let Others Tinker With the Message. He Transforms the Medium Itself" (interview). *American Film* (Washington, D.C.), Janurary-Februray 1989.

Library of Congress, Copyright Office. *Technological Alterations to Motion Pictures: Implications for Creators, Copyright Owners, and Consumers: A Report of the Register of Copyrights*. Washington, D.C.: U.S. Copyright Office, 1989.

Leibowitz, Flo. "Movie Colorization and the Expression of Mood." *Journal of Aesthetics and Art Criticism* (Cleveland, Ohio), Fall 1991.

Moral rights and the Motion Picture Industry: Hearing Before the Subcommittee on Courts, Intellectual Property, and the Administration of Justice. United States Congress. House of Representatives. Washington, D.C.: U.S. Government Printing Office, 1991.

Sherman, Barry L. "Perceptions of Colorization." *Journalism Quarterly* (Urbana, Illinois), Winter 1988.

Wagner, Craig A. "Motion Picture Colorization, Authenticity, and the Elusive Moral Right." *New York University Law Review* (New York), June 1989.

See also Movies on Television

COLTRANE, ROBBIE

British Actor

Robbie Coltrane is one of Britain's most popular and versatile actors. During the 1980s he became a household name following a succession of spirited comedic stage, cinema, and small screen appearances. In the 1990s Coltrane's celebrity has developed internationally; his acting repertoire has matured to include dramatic roles, as befits his more mellow tremperament and professional confidence.

In the mid-1970s Coltrane became involved in repertory theater in Edinburgh, before a brief stint in New York, where he participated in several experimental films. Returning to England, Coltrane achieved his first major stage success in *The Slab Boys*, a bittersweet trilogy about Glaswegian youth written by ex-collegemate John Byrne. Relocating to London in the early 1980s, Coltrane became associated with the city's burgeoning, politically-charged stand-up comedy movement. There he headlined alongside the likes of Rik Mayall, Jennifer Saunders, Ade Edmondson, and Dawn French—to name only a few of the talents who would soon become, collectively and individually, the core of British broadcasting's "alternative" comedy. Coltrane's first television credits were earned in various programs, taking first sketch then narrative forms, centered around the satirical humor generated by this new wave troupe. He co-starred in *A Kick up the Eighties* and *Laugh??? I Nearly Paid My Licence Fee*, he was a regular in *The Comic Strip Presents*, and frequently appeared as minor characters in shows such as *Blackadder's Christmas Carol*.

Effortlessly humorous, yet sharply critical, Coltrane proved to be an immediate audience favorite. Full-bodied and unpretentious, the Scotsman was often bracketed with his fellow comedic social commentator, Alexei Sayle. But whereas Sayle was manic and edgy, constantly exposing his personal identity, Coltrane's exuberant delivery was channeled into his role-playing and his amazing ability to parody the self-righteous through imitation. The Scot's capacity to produce more mainstream material is evident in his prodigious work record, his marketability as a celebrity endorser

Robbie Coltrane

of commercial products, and his mass appeal across a variety of audiences and age groups.

Coltrane's enthusiasm for his performances is unassailable. His own personal passions and vices—chain-smoking, 1950s cars, American glitz, outrageous figures, an appreciation for the style (if not the substance) of Chandleresque masculinity—have become recurrent motifs that function as backdrops to his stage and screen personae. Since the mid-1980s, Coltrane has rapidly progressed from supporting roles in successful feature films like *Mona Lisa* and *Defence of the Realm* to made-to-measure, screen-stealing leads in *Henry V* (an homage to Orson Welles amidst a tribute to Olivier), *Nuns on the Run*, and *The Pope Must Die!* Occasionally miscast as a genial funnyman, Coltrane has starred in his share of lightweight comedies. But as a known box-office property, he is now able to choose his Hollywood offers more selectively—electing, for instance, to play the villain in the James Bond revival, *Goldeneye*.

Coltrane's thespian maturity has been achieved less in cinema than on the stage and in his television performances, where his ability to convincingly portray complex characters and convey contradictory emotions has more fully developed. His own enigmatic personality (jocular and acutely perceptive, sensitive, forthright, both worldly and down-to-earth), combined with his penchant for panache (with its mixture of grand style and garish display) often surface in his TV roles. As Danny McGlone in the hit 1987 miniseries *Tutti Frutti*, Coltrane portrayed the endearing, egotistical frontman of the Majestics—a group of aging rock 'n' rollers touring Scotland in search of newfound fame and fortune. The critical and popular acclaim accorded this black comedy was due in large measure to the affectionately self-mocking tone of John Byrnes' screenplays; he and Coltrane again collaborated several years later on the serio-comic historical adaptation *Boswell and Johnson's Tour of the Western Isles*. Coltrane's theatrical versatility, comedic range and gallery of accents were evident in his interpretation of Dario Fo's anti-establishment satire, *Mistero Buffo*. Juggling anger, hostility and humor between the numerous characterizations required in this one-man show, Coltrane performed the play at British venues in 1990, prior to its broadcast as a BBC miniseries.

That year marked a turning point for the Scotsman, who married and retreated to the more sedate pace of a converted Stirlingshire farmhouse. Proclaiming his hell-raising years to be over, Coltrane consciously sought dramatic roles. In a part written for him by social realist Jimmy McGovern, Coltrane played Dr. Eddie Fitzgerald, a forensic psychologist for the Manchester police force, in Granada TV's *Cracker*. "Fitz" applies his incredible mental agility to outwit suspects and solve a series of heinous crimes, all the while evidencing shortcomings of his own brought on by personal overindulgence and "deviant" behavior (drinking, smoking, debt, domestic ruin). Extremely well-received in Britain and North America, *Cracker*'s nine stories represent Coltrane's most accomplished screen performance to date—

one rewarded with numerous industry honors, including the British Academy of Film and Television Arts' Award for Best Television Actor in 1995.

—Matthew Murray

ROBBIE COLTRANE. Born Anthony McMillan in Rutherglen, Glasgow, Scotland, 31 March 1950. Attended Trinity College, Glenalmond, Perthshire; Glasgow School of Art. One son with partner Rhona Irene Gemmell. Began career as actor with the Traverse Theatre Company and Borderline Theatre Company, Edinburgh; worked briefly as stand-up comedian in the United States, late 1970s, then returned to England to appear in various alternative television comedy shows and dramas; subsequently established reputation as character actor in films; returned to the U.S. to develop film career, 1989. Recipient: Montreux Television Festival Silver Rose Award, 1987; *Evening Standard* Peter Sellers Award, 1991; British Academy of Film and Television Arts Award, 1993, 1994, 1995; Monte Carlo Silver Nymph Best Actor Award, 1994; BPG Best Actor Award, 1994; Royal Television Society Best Actor Award, 1994; FIPA (French Academy) Best Actor Award, 1994; Cable Ace Best Actor Award, 1994; Cannes Film Festival Best Actor Award, 1994. Address: CDA 17, 47 Courtfield Road, London SW7 4DB, England.

TELEVISION SERIES

1981–84	*A Kick Up the Eighties*
1987	*Tutti Frutti*
1992	*Coltrane in a Cadillac*
1993	*Boswell and Johnson's Tour of the Western Isles*
1993	*Cracker*
1994	*Cracker II*

TELEVISION SPECIALS

1982–92	*The Comic Strip Presents* ("Five Go Mad in Dorset", "Beat Generation", "War", "Summer School", "Five Go Mad on Mescalin", "The Strike", "Gino— Full Story and Pics", "GLC", "South Atlantic Raiders", "Demonella", "Jealousy")
1985	*Laugh??? I Nearly Paid My Licence Fee*
1986	*Hooray for Hollywood*
1988	*Blackadder's Christmas Carol*
1990	*Mistero Buffo*
1992	*Open to Question*

FILMS

Flash Gordon, 1980; *Subway Riders*, 1981; *Krull*, 1983; *Chinese Boxes*, 1984; *Ghost Dance*, 1984; *Loose Connections*, 1984; *Scrubbers*, 1984; *The Supergrass*, 1985; *Revolution*, 1985; *National Lampoon's European Vacation*, 1985; *Defence of the Realm*, 1985; *Mona Lisa*, 1986; *The Secret Policeman's Third Ball*, 1987; *Caravaggio*, 1986; *Absolute Beginners*, 1986; *Eat the Rich*, 1987; *The Fruit Machine*, 1988; *Wonderland*, 1988; *Slipstream*, 1989; *Danny, the Champion of the*

World, 1989; *Lenny —Live and Unleashed*, 1989; *Let It Ride*, 1989; *Henry V*, 1989; *Bert Rigby, You're a Fool*, 1989; *Where the Heart Is*, 1990; *Nuns on the Run*, 1990; *Perfectly Normal*, 1990; *The Pope Must Die!* (U.S.: *The Pope Must Diet!*), 1991; *Triple Bogey on a Par 5 Hole*, 1992; *Oh, What a Night*, 1992; *The Adventures of Huckleberry Finn*, 1993; *Goldeneye*, 1995.

STAGE (selection)
Slab Boys Trilogy, Yr Obedient Servant, 1987; *Mistero Buffo*, 1990.

PUBLICATION
Coltrane in a Cadillac, 1993.

FURTHER READING
Burn, Gordon. "A Nice Glass of Milk with Robbie Coltrane." *The Independent* (London), 3 May 1990.
Cosgrove, Stuart. "History Is Bunk." *New Statesman and Society* (London), 16 February 1990.
Leith, William. "A Big Star, but Shrinking." *The Independent* (London), 16 May 1993.
Linklater, Andro. "On the Road with Johnson and Boswell and Co." *Daily Telegraph* (London), 11 September 1993.
Wilmut, Roger, and Peter Rosengard. *Didn't You Kill My Mother-in-Law?: The Story of Alternative Comedy in Britain from The Comedy Store to Saturday Live*. London: Methuen, 1989.

COLUMBIA BROADCASTING SYSTEM

U.S. Network

The network CBS, traditionally referred to as the "Tiffany network" among major television broadcasting systems, has in recent years come more and more to resemble Wal-Mart. Ironically, this often prestige-laden television institution began almost as an afterthought. In 1927, when David Sarnoff did not see fit to include any of talent agent Arthur Judson's clients in his roster of stars for the new NBC radio networks, Judson defiantly founded his own network—United Independent Broadcasters. Soon merged with the Columbia Phonograph Company, the network went on the air on 18 September 1927 as the Columbia Phonograph Broadcasting Company. Within a year heavy losses compelled the sale of the company to Jerome Louchheim and Ike and Leon Levy, the latter the fiancee of the sister of William Paley. Paley, who had become enamored of radio as a result of advertising the family's La Palina brand cigars over a local station, bought the fledgling network, then consisting of 22 affiliates and 16 employees, for $400,000 on 18 January 1929, and renamed it the Columbia Broadcasting System.

Relatively untested as a business executive, Paley immediately showed himself a superb entrepreneur. He insured the success of the new network by offering affiliates free programming in exchange for an option on advertising time, and was extremely aggressive in gaining advertising for the network. Paley's greatest gift, however, was in recognizing talent. He soon signed singers such as Bing Crosby, Kate Smith and Morton Downey for the network. Unfortunately, as soon as some of them gained fame at CBS they were lured away by the far richer and more popular NBC.

This was not to be the case with news. Starved for programming Paley initially allowed his network to be used by the likes of the demagogic Father Charles Coughlin. But by 1931, Paley had terminated Coughlin's broadcasts, and under the aegis of former *New York Times* editor Edward

Courtesy of CBS

Klauber and ex-United Press reporter Paul White, began building a solid news division.

CBS news did not come of age, however, until Klauber assigned the young Edward R. Murrow to London as director of European talks. On 13 March 1937 at the time of the Anschluss, Murrow teamed with former newspaper foreign correspondent William L. Shirer and a number of others to describe those events in what would become the forerunner of *The CBS World News Roundup*. Subsequently, during World War II, Murrow assembled a brilliant team of reporters, known collectively as "Murrow's Boys," including Eric Sevareid, Charles Collingwood, Howard K. Smith, Winston Burdett, Richard K. Hottelet, and Larry LeSueur.

In 1948, Paley turned the tables on NBC and signed some of its premier talent such as Jack Benny, Red Skelton, and Burns and Allen. He also stole a march on his rival in what they considered their undisputed realm—technology—when his CBS Research Center, under the direction of the brilliant inventor Peter Goldmark, developed the Long Playing phonograph recording technique and color television.

Even with this success Paley was still loathe to enter television broadcasting. But with prodding from Dr. Frank Stanton, whom he had appointed CBS president in 1946, and his growing awareness of how rapidly television was expanding, Paley began increasing CBS investment in television programming. Indeed with the talent that CBS had taken from NBC and homegrown artists and programming such as *I Love Lucy, Ed Sullivan, Arthur Godfrey,* and *Gunsmoke,* CBS dominated the audience rating system for almost twenty years.

The post-war years were hardly an undisturbed triumphal march for CBS. The network found itself dubbed the Communist Broadcasting System by conservatives during the McCarthy era. Nor did it distinguish itself by requiring loyalty oaths of its staff, and hiring a former FBI man as head of a loyalty clearance office. These actions were, however, redeemed to a large extent by Edward R. Murrow's 9 March 1954 *See It Now* broadcast investigating Senator McCarthy. Unfortunately, Murrow's penchant for controversy tarnished him in the eyes of many CBS executives and shortly thereafter, in 1961, he resigned to head the United States Information Agency.

More and more the news division, which thought of itself as the crown jewel at CBS, found itself subordinate to the entertainment values of the company, a trend highlighted at the end of the 1950s by the quiz show scandals. Indeed Paley, who had taken CBS public in 1937, now seemed to make profits his priority. Perhaps the clearest evidence of this development occurred when Fred Friendly, one of Murrow's closest associates and then CBS News division president, resigned after reruns of *I Love Lucy* were shown instead of the 1966 Senate hearings on the Vietnam War.

This tendency was only exacerbated in the sixties when, despite almost universal critical disdain, *The Beverly Hillbillies, Green Acres,* and *Petticoat Junction* were CBS' biggest hits. However, an abrupt shift away from these programs occurred in the early 1970s. Programming executives Robert Wood and Fred Silverman inaugurated a series of sitcoms such as *All in the Family, The Mary Tyler Moore Show,* and *M*A*S*H.* These changes had less to do with any contempt for the rural idiocy of the "barnyard comedies" than the need to appeal to a younger-urban audience with larger disposable incomes. But the newer programs, with their socially conscious themes, garnered both audience and critical acclaim.

During these years profits increased to such an extent that by 1974 the Columbia Broadcasting System had become CBS, Inc., and consisted not only of radio and TV networks but a publishing division (Holt, Reinhart and Winston), a magazine division (*Woman's Day*), a recording division (Columbia Records), and even for a time the New York Yankees (1964–1973). Nevertheless, CBS, Inc., was hardly serene. Indeed it was quite agitated over the question of who would succeed William S. Paley.

In violation of his own rule, Paley refused to retire. He did, however, force the 1973 retirement of his logical heir, Frank Stanton. He then installed and quickly forced the resignation of Arthur Taylor, John Backe, and Thomas Wyman as presidents and chief executive officers of CBS,

Inc. Anxiety about the succession at CBS began to threaten the network's independence. Declining ratings left the company vulnerable. The biggest threat came from a takeover bid by cable mogul Ted Turner. To defend itself against a takeover CBS turned to Loew's president, Lawrence Tisch, who soon owned a 25% share in the company and became president and CEO in 1986.

Within a year Tisch's cuts in personnel and budget, and his sale of assets such as the recording, magazines, and publishing divisions had alienated many. Dan Rather, who had succeeded the avuncular Walter Cronkite as the anchor on the *CBS Evening News* in 1981, wrote a scathing *New York Times* opinion editorial called "From Murrow to Mediocrity." By 1990, the year of Paley's death, *The CBS Evening News,* which had led in the ratings for eighteen years under Cronkite, and for a long period under Rather, fell to number three in the rankings.

After what seemed a brief ratings resurrection resulting from the success of the 1992 Winter Olympics, and the 1993 coup of wresting *The David Letterman Show* away from NBC, CBS was outbid for the television rights to NFL professional football by the fledgling FOX network and watched the defection of twelve choice affiliates to the same company. Despite repeated denials that the company was for sale, Tisch shopped it to perspective buyers such as former Paramount and Fox President Barry Diller. In November 1995 CBS was sold to the Westinghouse Corporation for $5.4 billion, effectively bringing to a close CBS' history as an independent company.

—Albert Auster

FURTHER READING

Benjamin, Burton. *Fair Play: CBS, General Westmorland, and How a Television Documentary Went Wrong.* New York: Harper and Row, 1988.

Gates, Gary Paul. *Air Time: The Inside Story of CBS News.* New York: Harper and Row, 1978.

Goldmark, Peter C. *Maverick Inventor: My Turbulent Years at CBS.* New York: Saturday Review Press, 1973.

Joyce, Ed. *Prime Time, Bad Times.* New York: Doubleday, 1988.

McCabe, Peter. *Bad News at Black Rock: The Sell-out of CBS News.* New York: Arbor House, 1987.

Murray, Michael D. *The Political Performers: CBS Broadcasts in the Public Interests.* Westport, Connecticut: Praeger, 1994.

Paley, William S. *As It Happened: A Memoir.* Garden City, New York: Doubleday, 1979.

Paper, Lewis J. *Empire: William S. Paley and the Making of CBS.* New York: St. Martin's, 1987.

Slater, Robert. *This—Is CBS: A Chronicle of 60 Years.* Englewood Cliffs, New Jersey: Prentice-Hall, 1988.

Smith, Sally Bedell. *In all His Glory: The Life of William S. Paley, the Legendary Tycoon and His Brilliant Circle.* New York: Simon and Schuster, 1990.

Winans, Christopher. *The King of Cash: The Inside Story of Laurence A. Tisch and How He Bought CBS.* New York: J. Wiley, 1995.

COLUMBO

U.S. Police Drama

Columbo is a popular detective series featuring Peter Falk as Lieutenant Columbo. The character (who never had a first name), and the series are a creation of the writing/producing team of Richard Levinson and William Link. *Columbo* ran as a television series from 1971 to 1978, but the character had appeared in a short story, a live-television broadcast, and a stage play before making his first network television appearance in the made-for-television movie *Prescription: Murder* (1968). Originally written for Bing Crosby, the Columbo role went to Falk when Crosby opted not to end his retirement.

The series' original run was not in weekly hour-long episodes, but as a 90-minute "spoke" in the *NBC Mystery Movie* "wheel" concept: each week, one of three different series was shown on a rotating basis. *Columbo* was interspersed with *McMillan and Wife* (starring Rock Hudson and Susan St. James), and *McCloud* (starring Dennis Weaver). This suited Falk and the producers just fine since the pace of production would be much slower than was usually the case with weekly series. The 90-minute program length also allowed each episode to be more intricate than the typical one-hour installment, and intricacy was stock in trade for the character.

Columbo was not a "who-done-it." Indeed, the most distinguishing aspect of the series is the plot structure itself. Although this structure is just as rigid and successful as that in *Perry Mason, Dragnet,* or *The Rockford Files,* each episode is actually an inversion of the classic detective formula. In the classic formula, the crime is committed by an unknown person, a detective comes onto the case, clues are gathered, the detective solves the crime with the aid of his/her assistants, and the ability of the detective is proven true. In each *Columbo* plot, the crime *and* the culprit are shown in great detail. The audience sees the murder planned, committed, and covered up by the murderer. Since the audience knows who did it and how, the enigma becomes "how will Columbo figure it out?" The methods of the murderer are presented with such care that there is little doubt that the horrible crime will go unpunished—little doubt until Columbo comes onto the scene.

With his rumpled overcoat, stubby cigar, tousled hair and (apparently) confused attitude, Columbo rambles around in his old Peugeot, doggedly following the suspect of a homicide. The attitude and behavior, however, are all an act. Columbo is not confused but acutely aware, like a falcon circling its prey, waiting for a moment of weakness. Columbo bumbles about, often interfering with the activities of the uniformed police and gathering what seem to be the most unimportant clues. All the while he constantly pesters the person he has pegged as his central suspect.

At first even the murderer is amused at the lieutenant's style and usually seems inclined to assume that if this is the best the Los Angeles police can offer, the murder will never be found out. But whenever the suspect seems to be rid of the Lieutenant,

Columbo

Columbo turns with a bemused remark, something like "Oh, there's just one more thing ...." By the end of the episode, Columbo has taken an apparently minor discrepancy in the murderer's story and wound it into the noose with which to hang the suspect. Conclusions often feature a weary, yet agreeable, criminal admitting to his or her guilt as Columbo, in the form of some imaginative turnabout, delivers the final blow. If the suspect is a magician, the Lieutenant uses a magic "trick". If the crime was done by knowledge of movie special effects, Columbo uses similar special effects.

Columbo is the only regular character in the series. There is no grizzled police commissioner, no confidant with whom the case could be discussed. For Columbo, each guest villain becomes something of an ironic "Watson". Columbo and the murderer spend most of the story playing off each other. The Lieutenant discusses the twists and turns of the case, the possible motives, the implications of clues with his primary suspect, always rich, powerful, and arrogant, always happy to match wits with the apparently witless policeman on the doorstep. In the end the working-class hero overcomes the wealthy, privileged criminal.

Many influential writers, directors, and producers of the 1980s and 1990s worked on this series. Stephen J. Cannell (*The Rockford Files, The A-Team, Wiseguy*), Peter S. Fisher (*Murder,*

She Wrote), and Steven Bochco (*L. A. Law, Hill Street Blues*) were writers. Dean Hargrove (*Matlock, Perry Mason*) and Roland Kibbee (*Barney Miller*) were producers. The premiere episode was directed by a very young Steven Spielberg. Each episode featured a well-known character actor or minor star as the murderer. Robert Culp and Jack Cassidy had the highest number of returns as guest villain (three each).

Columbo won seven Emmys over the first run of the series, including three for Falk and one for the series itself. *Columbo* spawned only one spin-off, NBC's short-lived, *Mrs. Columbo* (name later changed to *Kate Columbo, Kate the Detective,* and *Kate Loves a Mystery*) with Kate Mulgrew in the title role. This series played against *Columbo* in several ways. Instead of Mrs. Columbo being absent each episode, the lieutenant was "unavailable". And here the plot followed the traditional detective format instead of the inverted one. It is not clear what caused this series to fail, but *Mrs. Columbo* was ill fated and ill advised. Both Link and Levinson disavowed it and Falk disliked the concept.

Following the success of Raymond Burr's return as Perry Mason in a series of made-for-television movies, Falk returned to *Columbo* on 6 February 1989, for a new "mystery wheel" concept (this time on ABC and alternating with Burt Reynolds in *B. L. Stryker* and Lou Gossett, Jr., in *Gideon Oliver*). Just as he left Rock Hudson and Dennis Weaver behind during his original run, the rumpled detective was the only one of the new "wheel" to survive. Indeed, like the character, *Columbo* always seems to be coming back as if to say "Oh, there's just one more thing . . ."

—J. Dennis Bounds

CAST

Lt. Columbo . . . . Peter Falk

PRODUCERS   Richard Levinson and William Link, Dean Hargrove, Roland Kibbee, Richard Alan Simmons

PROGRAMMING HISTORY   43 Episodes in Original Series

• NBC

September 1971–September 1972	Wednesday 8:30-10:00
September 1972–July 1974	Sunday 8:30-10:00
August 1974–August 1975	Sunday 8:30-10:30
September 1975–September 1976	Sunday 9:00-11:00
October 1976–September 1977	Sunday 8:00-9:30

• ABC

February 1989–May 1989	Monday 9:00-11:00
August 1989–July 1990	Saturday 9:00-11:00
August 1990	Sunday 9:00-11:00
January 1992–May 1992	Thursday 8:00-10:00
November 1992–February 1993	Saturday 8:00-10:00

FURTHER READING:

Dawidziak, Mark. *The Columbo Phile: A Casebook.* New York: Mysterious, 1989.

Marc, David, and Robert J. Thompson. *Prime Time, Prime Movers.* Boston: Little, Brown, 1992.

Meyers, Richard. *Murder on the Air: Television's Great Mystery Series.* New York: Mysterious, 1989.

———. *TV Detectives.* San Diego: Barnes, 1988.

Newcomb, Horace, and Robert S. Alley. *The Producer's Medium: Conversations with Creators of American TV.* New York: Oxford University, 1983.

See also Detective Programs; Falk, Peter; Levinson, Richard; Link, William; NBC Mystery Movie

COMEDY, DOMESTIC SETTINGS

Domestic comedy is the term for a generic category coined by Horace Newcomb in his *TV: The Most Popular Art* (1974). In U.S. television the phrase provides a useful means of distinguishing between situation comedy, and the more broad-based, "comedy." Domestic comedies are identified by a character-based humor as opposed to that originating in a series of confusions or complications. Within a domestic comedy, qualities such as warmth, familial relationships, moral growth and audience inclusiveness predominate. In each episode a character experiences some sort of learning experience, often motivated by some ethical trial or test. The humor emanates from the audience's familiarity with the characters and their relationships with one another, and the overwhelming harmony of each story encourages the audience to problem-solve along with the characters.

Originally, domestic comedies were literally housebound, and generally characterized by their stereotypical nuclear family protagonists. Thus 1950s programs like *Leave it to Beaver, The Donna Reed Show,* and *The Adventures of Ozzie and Harriet* were considered seminal examples. Young Beaver, Mary, or Ricky experienced some sort of lightly-depicted minor dilemma (a lost sweater, making two dates for the same night, lying to a pen pal) which Ward, Donna or Ozzie then neatly dispatched of with some well-pointed words of advice. The child learned the moral lesson, only to be confronted with a new predicament the following week.

With time, the definitions of domestic comedy have changed and expanded. First, critical work has begun to explore whether many of these domestic comedies were in fact comedies at all. Nina Leibman has demonstrated in *Living Room Lectures* that despite the presence of a laugh track, most of these programs contained more generic similarity to domestic melodrama than any sort of comedic categories. Programs such as *Father Knows Best*, with their

The Munsters

The Donna Reed Show

Kate and Allie

Home Improvement

hyperbolic acting styles and crises, their reliance upon peripety and coincidence in problem-solving, their thematic and structural dependency on repetitive musical motifs, and their obsession with issues of gender and generational conflict, convincingly associates them more with their 1950s cinematic dramatic counterparts than with their television situation comedy cousins.

Second, Newcomb, Ella Taylor and others have demonstrated that domestic comedies need not take place in a suburban home to claim membership within the domestic comedy genre. Workplace domestic comedies such as *The Mary Tyler Moore Show, Cheers, Murphy Brown,* and *Ellen,* construct character-based comedies out of the ersatz familial relationships of a group of friends or co-workers. As in their more literal family forebears, these comedies place an emphasis on moral growth and development, warmth, and viewer identification in a representational (rather than presentational format).

Generic blends and hybrids cause further evolution of the term. Some programs such as *The Brady Bunch,* originated with a situation-type premise: what happens when a widower with three sons marries a widow with three daughters? Eventually, however (often within the first three episodes), the situation no longer motivates the central narrative and the individual episodes deal with topics that fall more neatly into the domestic comedy camp. For *The Brady Bunch,* then, moral imperatives provide the comedy when Greg tries smoking, Marcia is caught lying about a special prom guest, and Jan's resentment of her prettier, older sister motivates her to experiment with antisocial behavior. Similarly, domestic comedies, such as *The Dick van Dyke Show,* vacillate between outrageous acts of slapstick and confusion (Laura dyes her hair blonde, Laura gets her toe stuck in a bathtub faucet) to more poignant and morally complex episodes (Richie adopts a duck, Buddy gets fired). A program such as this (with stars who excel at physical comedy) might originate as a domestic premise, but then, in light of van Dyke's prowess for farce, reconfigure the narratives into situational exercises of complexity and confusion.

Domestic comedies of the 1970s sprang from two main sources. Norman Lear's were true familial settings in which the ironic familial head, Archie Bunker on *All in the Family,* George Jefferson on *The Jeffersons,* Maude on the program which bears her name, proved both a verbal provocateur and a victim while undergoing subtle moments of moral growth. Grant Tinker's MTM productions was home to a plethora of successful workplace domestic comedies such as *The Mary Tyler Moore Show, The Bob Newhart Show,* and *Rhoda.* Each of these programs reconfigured domestic troubles into professional ones and transformed business relationships into familial ones by ascribing certain familial roles to the office workers—the cranky boss becomes the father, the ditzy newsman becomes a wild brother, etc.

During the 1980s domestic comedies retreated into near extinction, emerging in neoclassical incarnations such as *Family Ties,* and *The Cosby Show.* Like the domestic comedies of the 1950s, these programs seem closer to domestic melodrama, with a particular emphasis on gender and class-based issues. The 1990s entries into the field are a skewed blend of sitcom, domestic comedy and family melodrama. *Roseanne,* and *Grace Under Fire,* for example, tackle the topics of incest, spouse abuse, alcoholism, masturbation, and unemployment within the hyperbolic representational stance of family melodrama. Yet the sarcasm and sheer cynicism of the central characters diffuse any seriousness associated with the problem, moving them out of melodrama and back into the generic sphere of domestic comedy. At the same time, the programs often insert situation comedy routines (drunkenness, mistaken identity, extravagant production numbers) right in the midst of a particularly bleak episode, rendering its generic identity cloudy at best. Domestic comedies remain a staple of series television, but, as with most television genres in an advanced evolutionary phase, the category has been expanded upon and complicated by its fusion with other generic elements.

—Nina C. Leibman

FURTHER READING

Attallah, Paul. "Situation Comedy and 'The Beverly Hillbillies': The Unworthy Discourse." Montreal, Canada: McGill University Graduate Communication Program Working Papers, 1983.

Butsch, Richard. "Class and Gender in Four Decades of Television Situation Comedy: plus ça change...." *Critical Studies in Mass Communication* (Annandale, Virginia), December 1992.

Einstein, Dan, Nina Leibman, Randall Vogt, Sarah Berry, and William Lafferty. "Source Guide to TV Family Comedy, Drama and Serial Drama, 1946–1970." *Camera Obscura: A Journal of Feminism and Film Theory* (Berkeley, California), January 1988.

Frazer, June M., and Timothy C. Frazer. "*Father Knows Best* and *The Cosby Show*: Nostalgia and the Sitcom Tradition." *Journal of Popular Culture* (Bowling Green, Ohio), Winter 1993.

Freeman, Lewis. "Social Mobility in Television Comedies." *Critical Studies in Mass Communication* (Annandale, Virginia), December 1992.

Gray, Frances B. *Women and Laughter.* Basingstoke, England: McMillan, 1994.

Hamamoto, Darrell Y. *Nervous Laughter: Television Situation Comedy and Liberal Democratic Ideology.* New York: Praeger, 1989.

Haralovich, Mary Beth. "Sitcoms and Suburbs: Positioning the 1950s Homemaker." *Quarterly Review of Film and Television* (Los Angeles, California), May 1989.

Horowitz, Susan. "Sitcom Domesticus: A Species Endangered by Social Change." *Channels* (New York), September/October 1984.

Javna, John. *The Best of TV Sitcoms: Burns and Allen to the Cosby Show, The Munsters to Mary Tyler Moore.* New York: Harmony Books, 1988.

Jones, Gerard. *Honey, I'm Home!: Sitcoms, Selling the American Dream.* New York: Grove Weidenfeld, 1992.

Leibman, Nina. *Living Room Lectures: The Fifties Family in Film and Television.* Austin: University of Texas Press, 1995.

Lipsitz, George. "The Meaning of Memory: Family, Class, and Ethnicity in Early Network Television." *Camera Obscura* (Berkeley, California), January 1988.

Marc, David. *Comic Visions: Television Comedy and American Culture.* Boston, Massachusetts: Unwin-Hyman, 1989.

———. *Demographic Vistas: Television in American Culture.* Philadelphia, Pennsylvania: University of Pennsylvania Press, 1984.

Neale, Stephen, and Frank Krutnik. *Popular Film and Television Comedy.* London and New York: Routledge, 1990.

Rowe, Kathleen. *The Unruly Woman: Gender and the Genres of Laughter.* Austin: University of Texas Press, 1995.

Spigel, Lynn. *Make Room for TV: Television and the Family Ideal in Postwar America.* Chicago: University of Chicago Press, 1992.

Taylor, Ella. *Prime-Time Families: Television Culture in Postwar America.* Berkeley: University of California Press, 1989.

See also *Absolutely Fabulous; Adventures of Ozzie and Harriet; All in the Family; Amos 'n' Andy; Andy Griffith Show; Benson; Beulah; Beverly Hillbillies; Bewitched; Brady Bunch; Cosby Show; Dad's Army; Dick Van Dyke Show; Family Ties; Father Knows Best; George Burns and Gracie Allen Show; Goldbergs; Golden Girls; Good Times; Green Acres; Happy Days; Hazel; Honeymooners; I Love Lucy; Jeffersons; Julia; Kate and Allie; Laverne and Shirley; Leave It to Beaver; Life of Riley; Likely Lads; Married...With Children; Maude; My Three Sons; Odd Couple; One Foot in the Grave; Only Fools and Horses; Partridge Family; Rising Damp; Roseanne; Sanford and Son; Seinfeld; Simpsons; Soap; Some Mothers Do 'ave Em; Steptoe and Son; That Girl; Three's Company; Till Death Us Do Part; 227; Wonder Years*

COMEDY, WORKPLACE

Workplace comedies provide a convenient vehicle for the writers/producers of the television program to access all the essential components of series drama. The workplace frame adapts to changes in the production context, gives the characters a continuing mandate for action, provides the dramatic tension of continuing relationships among persons of different backgrounds, and offers the opportunity to introduce additional or visiting characters. The significant structural weakness of the workplace comedy is that it is deprived of the interaction between youth and maturity often central to situation and domestic comedy in television. But even this arrangement can be addressed by creating a work situation devoted to child nurturing, or by introducing the workers' family members who can appear regularly or randomly at the will of producers.

In pragmatic industrial terms, the workplace series provides a flexible format that can adapt to changes in the real world production context. With the workplace series, the departure of a cast member allows a new performer to assume the job responsibility and simultaneously introduce a new interpersonal dynamic to the ensemble—as with the departures of McLean Stevenson (Lt. Colonel Henry Blake) and Wayne Rogers (Capt. John [Trapper John] McKenzie) on *M*A*S*H.* The characters introduced by Harry Morgan (Col. Sherman Potter) and Mike Farrell (Capt. B.J. Hunnicut) did not simply replace the job functions of their predecessors, they created new personalities that varied the mix of relationships within the ensemble. The death of Nicholas Colasanto (Coach) was mourned on *Cheers* and his character was replaced by the much younger Woody Harrelson (Woody Boyd) who

portrayed a naive Indiana farmboy who had been taking a mail order bartending course from the Coach. *Cheers* writers and producers dealt with the departure of Shelley Long (Diane Chambers) with the introduction of Kirstie Alley's Rebecca Howe and an increased emphasis on the Kelsey Grammer (Dr. Frasier Crane) and Bebe Neuwirth (Dr. Lilith Stern) characters.

As these industrial strategies indicate, the humor in the workplace comedy may come from the personalities of the characters, the interaction of the characters, or the situations encountered by the characters. The successful series draw on all these elements, but the balance differs from program to program. Some shows emphasize character relationships, others are best at creating comedic situations, still others offer characters who are individually funny in their own right, often the case when a series is developed specifically to showcase the talents of a stand-up comedian.

Series like *Our Miss Brooks, Newhart, The Andy Griffith Show, The John Larroquette Show, Frasier,* and *The Mary Tyler Moore Show* drew many of their laughs from the antics of a few eccentric characters. Some of the comic characters were objects of ridicule, some were simply out-of-step with their surroundings, and some so superior to their surroundings that they were humorous. Richard Crenna's dimwitted Walter Denton was often a source of amusement on *Our Miss Brooks;* Don Knotts made the bumbling Barney Fife a laugh-getter on *The Andy Griffith Show;* and *Newhart's* Larry, Darryl, and Darryl needed only to appear on screen to draw anticipatory giggles from many viewers. Even *Rhoda's* unseen Carleton the Doorman acquired a unique comedic persona. On *The Mary Tyler Moore Show,* the pompous Ted Baxter, acerbic Sue Ann Nivens, and ditzy Georgette Frank-

Car 54, Where Are you?

Alice

Night Court

WKRP in Cincinnati

lin Baxter were all ridiculous characters who inspired varying degrees of sympathy.

Workplace comedies can also draw on references to the popular forms they parody. The incompetent spy of *Get Smart* and the bumbling policemen of *Car 54, Where are You?* developed the comedy line by contradicting the premise of a strong, competent leading character. *The Wild, Wild West* and *The Rockford Files* parodied the Western and Detective forms so well that they are generally categorized among those forms instead of being regarded as comedies.

Persons in a work situation are granted a franchise to action by the nature of their work—the job requires them to deal with problems or participate in events related to their work. Professions such as law enforcement, medicine, and media provide ready made opportunities to place the characters in varied situations and involve them with a wide range of characters.

WKRP in Cincinnati, Barney Miller, E/R, Taxi, and *Night Court* often found their strength in creating bizarre situations, then letting the established characters play out the story. Episodes such as the *WKRP* Thanksgiving story in which Herb Tarlek and Mr. Carlson dropped live turkeys from a helicopter as a promotional gimmick take logical premises and carry them to illogical extremes.

The workplace setting facilitates interaction among characters of varied origin. Despite their diverse backgrounds, the characters on a workplace comedy are united by a common goal and are required to maintain even difficult relationships. Diahann Carroll's *Julia* was the first series to place a professional black woman in a starring role, but many other series have drawn humor from contrasting characters of different race, gender, ethnicity, regional, or class origin. *Barney Miller's* Ron Glass, as Harris—a literate, urbane black man—constantly reminded his coworkers of racial stereotyping and his own departure from those stereotypes; Jack Soo as Yemana similarly made ironic reference to his Asian background. On *Designing Women* there were frequent references to the "hillbilly" background of Jean Smart's Charlene, and Meschach Taylor's Anthony often made mention of his race. In *M*A*S*H*, Cpl. Walter (Radar) O'Reilly's rural background and Major Charles Emerson Winchester's upper class Boston upbringing were frequent sources of humor.

In some instances, workplace comedies require that individuals who are not merely different, but actually hostile to one another, maintain a relationship and the resultant tension provides humor. In *The Dick Van Dyke Show*, Richard Deacon's character—the pompous producer Mel Cooley—was the butt of endless jokes by the writing staff. Robert Guillaume's *Benson* was constantly engaged in combat with Inga Swenson who portrayed the cook Gretchen, and a truce between Craig T. Nelson's Hayden Fox and the women's basketball coach Judy, in *Coach*, would have removed a consistent source of humor from that series.

The ability to introduce guest or visiting characters is another advantage of the workplace comedy. The criminals and complainants who visited the police station in *Barney Miller* or the varied defendants who appeared in *Night Court* all contributed to the general atmosphere of those series. Similarly, the patients on *The Bob Newhart Show* and *E/R* added interest and facilitated the development of new plotlines. In some cases, guest performers appeared only once; others became semi-regulars who would appear unexpectedly to add further complications to their stories.

In some workplace series, the families and friends of the working group also participate in the storylines. In the case of *The Mary Tyler Moore Show*, Mary's friend Rhoda and landlady Phyllis became such important characters that each was given a spinoff series of her own. *Murphy Brown's* resident housepainter Eldin became a significant component of the series, and *The Andy Griffith Show* drew heavily on Andy's relationships with Aunt Bea and son Opie. Even *Get Smart* assumed a family aspect when Smart and Agent 99 were married and became the parents of twins. The relationship between Gabriel and Julie Kotter was frequently the focus of *Welcome Back, Kotter* episodes, and *The Dick Van Dyke Show* included numerous segments dealing with Rob and Laura Petrie's home life.

The workplace comedy, like the society it portrayed, has both evolved and gone through cyclical changes. The form of the series has definitely evolved. Contrasting one of the earliest workplace comedies, *Private Secretary*, with more recent series shows changes in casting, relationships, and narrative structure. *Private Secretary* centered around the activities of Susie McNamara, a private secretary in a New York City talent agency, a vehicle that provided for the introduction of numerous guest characters who appeared as clients. All the cast members were middle- and upper-middle class whites. Although the relationship between Susie and her boss was congenial, there was no doubt that Susie was by no means as intellectually or emotionally competent as the male authority figure for whom she worked. While the men carried out business, the women worried about relationships—especially that special relationship that would take them out of the office and into a blissful married life. Susie was central to every episode, and each episode came to closure, bringing with it no memory of previous episodes and leaving no character or situation changes to affect subsequent episodes.

By contrast, more recent series portray a broad range of racial and ethnic characters. Members of many races and nationalities pass through the bus terminal on *The John Larroquette Show*, and the majority are working class characters. Most series attempt to offer a broader representation of the population and the awareness of differences within the society has expanded definitions to include persons with disabilities, older and younger individuals, gay and lesbian characters, and people practicing faiths other than Protestant. Job responsibilities and character traits are no longer always assigned on the basis of gender or ethnic stereotypes, and when they are this fact may give rise to more complication and humor.

Along with this broader range of characters comes a broader distribution of storyline emphases. *The Mary Tyler Moore Show* and subsequent MTM productions are often cited as a turning point in the evolution of series structure, with their refinement of the ensemble cast. Rather than focussing every episode on the actions of one clearly defined lead character, the ensemble allows any of several central characters to provide the story focus. In some series—for example, *Murphy Brown*—a central character will provide the stimulus for the actions of the featured character, but that character is still the focus of the storyline.

The narrative structure has made distinct changes with the move to more open stories, allowing growth and change. The series is allowed memory of previous events and stories are no longer required to return the situation to its state at the opening of the play. Episodes no longer require complete closure, and some problems require multiple episodes to reach resolution, or even continue indefinitely.

Topics addressed by the workplace comedy have experienced cyclical popularity, influenced by the dominant concerns of the society and by the economic influence of other popular forms. Comedy has often addressed social concerns, and the workplace comedy has assumed that joint opportunity and responsibility. From direct confrontation—as when Mary Richards learned her male predecessor had been more highly paid—to implicit endorsement of the abilities of under represented groups—as in Benson's steady rise to gubernatorial candidacy—the workplace comedies provide a forum for the expression of social issues and offer opportunities to consider new ideas and challenges to the existing order. At the same time, television comedies are a commercial form, directly influenced by the need to remain commercially viable. Examining the popular topics for the workplace comedy reinforces Steve Allen's charge that "Imitation is the sincerest form of television." Series do tend to borrow ideas from the headlines, from other media, and from one another. These notions receive broad attention for a time, then some are integrated into the form, others disappear. In this process, the television workplace series operates in the same manner as many other elements of modern culture, evolving slowly in the process of contested change.

—Kay Walsh

FURTHER READING

Attallah, Paul. "Situation Comedy and 'The Beverly Hillbillies': The Unworthy Discourse." Montreal, Canada: McGill University Graduate Communication Program Working Papers, 1983.

Butsch, Richard. "Class and Gender in Four Decades of Television Situation Comedy: plus ça change...." *Crit-ical Studies in Mass Communication* (Annandale, Virginia), December 1992.

Feuer, Jane, Paul Kehr and Tise Vahamagi. *MTM: Quality Television. London: British Film Institute*, 1985.

Freeman, Lewis. " Social Mobility in Television Comedies." *Critical Studies in Mass Communication* (Annandale, Virginia) December, 1992.

Hamamoto, Darrell Y. *Nervous Laughter: Television Situation Comedy and Liberal Democratic Ideology.* New York: Praeger, 1989.

Javna, John. *The Best of TV Sitcoms: Burns and Allen to the Cosby Show, The Munsters to Mary Tyler Moore.* New York: Harmony Books, 1988.

Jones, Gerard. *Honey, I'm Home!: Sitcoms, Selling the American Dream.* New York: Grove Weidenfeld, 1992.

Leibman, Nina. *Living Room Lectures: The Fifties Family in Film and Television.* Austin, Texas: University of Texas Press, 1995.

Lipsitz, George. "The Meaning of Memory: Family, Class, and Ethnicity in Early Network Television." *Camera Obscura* (Berkeley, California), January 1988.

Marc, David. *Comic Visions: Television Comedy and American Culture.* Boston, Massachusetts: Unwin-Hyman, 1989.

———. *Demographic Vistas: Television in American Culture.* Philadelphia, Pennsylvania: University of Pennsylvania Press, 1984.

Neale, Stephen, and Frank Krutnik. *Popular Film and Television Comedy.* London and New York: Routledge, 1990.

Rowe, Kathleen. *The Unruly Woman: Gender and the Genres of Laughter.* Austin: University of Texas Press, 1995.

Mellencamp, Patricia. "Situation Comedy, Feminism, and Freud, Discourse of Gracie and Lucy." In, Modleski, Tanya, editor. *Studies in Entertainment: Critical Approaches to Mass Culture.* Bloomington: Indiana University Press, 1986.

Mitz, Rick. *The Great TV Sitcom Book.* New York: Richard Marek, 1980.

Spigel, Lynn. *Make Room for TV: Television and the Family Ideal in Postwar America.* Chicago: University of Chicago Press, 1992.

Taylor, Ella. *Prime-Time Families: Television Culture in Postwar America.* Berkeley, California: University of California Press, 1989.

See also *Amen; Andy Griffith Show; Batman; Bob Newhart Show/ Newhart; Cheers; Dad's Army; Desmonds'; Different World; Fawlty Towers; Frank's Place; Get Smart; It's Garry Shandling's Show/The Larry Sanders Show; M*A*S*H; Mary Tyler Moore Show; Monkees; Murphy Brown; Phil Silvers Show; Room 222; Taxi; Yes Minister*

COMMUNICATIONS SATELLITE CORPORATION

COMSAT, or the Communications Satellite Corporation, was created in 1962 with the passage of the Communications Satellite Act. The act authorized the formation of a private corporation to administer satellite communications for the United States. COMSAT was given responsibility for many activities including the development of a global satellite communications system, the acquisition and maintenance of ground stations around the world, and the development of new satellite technologies. COMSAT is governed by a Board of Directors elected by the company's shareholders and the President of the United States. Half of the company's shares are owned by major communications companies such as AT and T, ITT, and Western Union, and the rest are held by members of the public. COMSAT has offices worldwide and its headquarters are located in Washington, D.C.

COMSAT emerged amidst a public controversy staged in a series of congressional hearings from 1961–62. During these hearings public advocates and private businesses struggled for control over satellite communications in the United States. Senators Morse and Kefauver and Congressman Celler formed an alliance against the privatization of COMSAT and rallied support from the American Communication Association—a union of telecommunications workers—as well as Assistant Attorney General Lee Loevinger and communications scholars Dallas Smythe and Herbert Schiller. Concerned that the privatization of COMSAT would strengthen the private sector's control over public airwaves, they called for further public participation in the hearings and government ownership of satellite communications. Senator Kerr, on the other hand, formed an alliance led by major communications companies such as RCA and AT and T and proposed a bill that called for the privatization of satellite communications. Kerr insisted that space communication offered new business opportunities that would benefit the private sector, the nation and the world. Pressure from both sides ultimately culminated in the creation of a "government corporation" designed to operate as a private business and yet act in the public interest. Throughout its history, COMSAT has faced the difficult challenge of negotiating the often contradictory interests of private enterprise and the public good. The organization has historically favored the business end of its mandate.

COMSAT was established as a "carrier's carrier." This meant that COMSAT could not sell satellite circuits directly to broadcasters, news agencies and other customers for overseas communication. Rather, the company could only sell circuits wholesale to other communications carriers and allow them to resell them. COMSAT must pursue customers to buy satellite time in order to recover the high cost of developing new satellite systems. Its customers range from national governments to common carriers. COMSAT maintains liaisons with private businesses and national governments around the world, and, at the same time, must fill its mandate to conduct business negotiations in the interest of the American public.

Courtesy of COMSAT

In 1964, COMSAT representatives participated in international negotiations that led to the creation of Intelsat—the International Telecommunications Satellite Organization. Intelsat still exists today and is a global satellite network that provides developing nations with access to communications satellites for domestic communications. The United States owns more than 50% of Intelsat, and COMSAT has managed the organization since 1964. In 1965, COMSAT launched Early Bird—the first commercial communications satellite. Early Bird relayed common carrier network traffic, telephone, television telegraph and digital data as well as voice bandwidth analog data such as facsimile and wire photo transmittals. The satellite was deployed to evaluate the viability of synchronous satellites for commercial communications and to supplement the capacity of trans-Atlantic cables. In 1980, COMSAT formed a subsidiary company called the Satellite Television Company (STC) to design and launch the United States' first direct broadcast satellite. Despite the STC's efforts, its domestic satellite system was thwarted when the Federal Communications Commission (FCC) denied its application because of the STC's failure to demonstrate how satellite programming would differ from that offered by cable or network television. Today, COMSAT operates as the United States signatory to Intelsat and Inmarsat (International Maritime Satellite Organization). The company still sells satellite circuits to private companies and governments around the world for national and international communication. COMSAT laboratories located in Clarksburg, Maryland have been responsible for a variety of technical developments in satellite and wireless communications including coding and transmission, networking and multiple access, space-qualified electronics and power sources, antennas, and many others.

—Lisa Parks

FURTHER READING

Kinsley, Michael E. *Outer Space and Inner Sanctums: Government, Business, and Satellite Communication*. New York: Wiley, 1976.

Maddox, Brenda. *Beyond Babel: New Directions in Communications*. London: Andre Deutsch, 1972.

Schiller, Herbert I. *Mass Communications and American Empire*. Boulder: Westview, 1992.

See also Satellite

COMPUTERS IN TELEVISION

The advent of computers has had a tremendous effect on the television and the video industry. Smaller, faster personal computers and computer chips have reduced camera sizes, revolutionized editing, and brought the process of video production to the desktop.

Cameras have benefited from the increased computer power and decreased chip size. Computer chips, called charged coupled devices (CCDs), have replaced tubes as image processing devices in video cameras. Because CCDs are small and provide good resolution, high quality cameras have become smaller, more portable, and better able to provide good pictures in low light situations. Other types of computer chips are also used to control some studio cameras. These cameras have an internal memory which automatically retains the correct camera settings ensuring accurate synchronization between camera and the camera control unit and allowing easy registration and alignment. Other cameras even have remote control capabilities that allow the camera operator to pre-load shots during rehearsal and then recall them at the appropriate moment with the touch of a button.

Computers have also enhanced other production equipment. Still-stores and frame stores, devices that capture one frame of video and store it in memory for future use, rely on computers. Still-stores and frame stores are often used to generate the graphics that accompany news anchors as they introduce news stories. Digital video effects, such as rotating images, morphing (when one image turns into another) and image stretching, previously sent out to specialty shops, can now be done on the premises, for less money, with a computer.

Computer-generated imaging is also on the rise and is used widely in a variety of applications such as computer graphics, titles, paint systems, and three dimensional animation. Technology enables computer-generated images often to look "real" or to be so well integrated in post-production that they appear to be a part of the camera-generated images. This area is likely to continue to increase in sophistication.

Computerization has also allowed more automation. At NBC network studios, satellite feeds to affiliates and master control of programming is largely in the hands of a computer. Some local television stations also use computers to keep track of their air traffic and master control.

Perhaps the biggest change in the television production process has come in post-production. The change began when computers were found to be useful in controlling videotape recorders using timecode. By adding a character generator and a switcher and using a computer-generated edit decision list, a new on-line editing process was born. Timecode and the computer provided an accuracy not achieved before.

Non-linear editing has progressed beyond computer-controlled VTRs. Non-linear editing is performed with a personal computer outfitted with hardware and software

An example of computers used in television production
Photo courtesy of Avid Technology, Inc.

that enable it to digitize the video and audio and store them on computer disk. Non-linear editing is often referred to as "random access editing" because it provides the editor with random access to the source material stored on a computer disk. Therefore, it is not necessary to wait for the source tape to fast forward or rewind to a desired scene. One of the biggest advantages to non-linear editing is that if the timing of an edit is unacceptable, it can be changed easily. Unlike linear editing, segments can be tightened or extended without revising subsequent edit points. Segments can also be effortlessly added, deleted, and moved around within the program. At present, non-linear editing is most often used for off-line editing because a high quality digital to analog converter is needed to convert the finished product to a broadcast quality product. Generally, an edit decision list is generated and on-line editing is done in a computer controlled editing suite. However, companies such as AVID are developing high quality on-line non-linear editing systems.

In general, the introduction of computers to the television and video industry has demystified the industry and made it possible for individuals to produce video at a relatively affordable price. "Desktop video" has become a viable production process especially for independent and corporate producers. Small, portable, high quality cameras and desktop editing systems can cost as little as $10,000 total. Macintosh based systems such as Adobe Premiere and Avid Media Suite Pro provide special effects, transitions, filters and a means for digitizing video. Similar systems exist for other platforms. Of particular note is the Video Toaster, which is on Commodore's Amiga platform and was specifically designed to interface with video systems. This system is capable of performing many functions of traditional video production and does not have the problems with conversion to analog that other systems have. However, because the Commodore is not a popular platform the market for the Toaster is not very large and its future is unclear. What is clear is that the future of desktop video is bright. Television and video are no longer confined to the broadcast industry. It can be expected that video on the computer, in educational settings, games, and other applications, will become more commonplace. As interactive television and the much promised information super highway develop, television, television equipment and television production will continue to change.

—Patti Constantakis-Valdes

FURTHER READING

Borrell, Jerry. "The Future of Television and Computers; In 1991 Computers and Video Are Combining to Create New Media." *Macworld* (San Francisco, California), February 1991.

Churbuck, David C. "Desktop Television." *Forbes* (New York), 7 December 1992.

Noll, M.A. *Television Technology: Fundamentals and Future Prospects.* Norwood, Massachusetts: Artech House, 1988.

Ohanian, T. A. *Digital Non-linear Editing.* Stoneham Massachussetts: Focal Press, 1992.

Smith, C. C. *Mastering Television Technology: A Cure for the Common Video.* Richardson, Texas: Newman-Smith, 1990.

Verna, T. *Global Television: How to Create Effective Television for the Future.* Stoneham, Massachussets: Focal Press, 1993.

Wells, M. *Desktop Video.* White Plains, New York: Knowledge Industry Publications, 1990.

Wurtzel, A., and J.Rosenbaum. *Television Production.* 5th edition, New York: McGraw Hill, 1995.

See also Television Technology

COOKE, ALISTAIR

U.S. Journalist/Television Personality

During some eras of history significant individuals may serve as important cultural and social links of communication between countries. In the years after World War II and for many decades after Alistair Cooke filled such a role. He served as British correspondent for the BBC in the United States, and as host of both British and American shows that revealed some of the finer aspects of American life.

As British correspondent for the BBC, Cooke lived and reported on American affairs, both political and cultural for half a century. In so doing, he became a kind of 20th-century Alexis de Tocqueville—noting those qualities of American life that only a foreigner could describe with such unique insight. And as Tocqueville, in the early 19th century, marveled over a land of wonders where everything was in constant motion, Cooke observed American life with a similar precision, but using tools common to his time, radio and television.

Cooke's first notoriety was in Great Britain with his weekly radio series on the BBC, *Letter from America.* The program continued for many decades, providing British audiences with perspectives unavailable from other sources and perhaps some appreciation for the American ethic. But his real influence came with his efforts to bring a refinement to American television. The program was *Omnibus* and Cooke served as host and narrator. The program turned out to be the longest running cultural series on U.S. commercial television. First seen on CBS in 1952, the show was scheduled for late afternoon and early evening on Sundays. In the era before Sunday afternoon/evening football and other sports *Omnibus* served as a respite from the commercial chatter of the week days. It offered time to reflect in a non-hurried pace on the cultural, historical and artistic heritage of American society, aspects of American life rarely noticed by television.

Later *Omnibus* moved to ABC, which scheduled the program from 9:00-10:00 P.M. on Sunday. Yet later, NBC picked up the series and programmed it earlier, on Sunday afternoons. Cooke remained the host on one of the few programs that made the rounds to all three commercial networks. Although the program never achieved high ratings, it proved that a portion of the American television audiences could appreciate program elements different from most television fare, elements traditionally thought of as part of high culture. *Omnibus* ended in 1961, having established

Alistair Cooke
Photo courtesy of WGBH-Boston

an image of thoughtfulness and wisdom for Cooke and earned him enormous respect.

Cooke returned as narrator and sometimes writer for the NBC program, *America*. The program, a series of 13 one-hour documentaries, told the fascinating story of the growth of a country from its inception during colonial times into the then-current scene of the 1970s. Cooke regarded the series as a "personal history of America," and he told it in a way that was both entertaining as well as educational. He made it a point to examine events, individuals, locations, and controversies from both close and distant perspectives. He insisted on being on the scene, walking the paths where history was made. We see his face, we look at his hands handling objects; it was, indeed, a personal history. It carried his trademarks, his reminiscences, his feelings about his memories and his knowledge.

Cooke also insisted on producing for "the box," for television's small screen. In order for television viewers to see the objects, there were more close-ups. In order for them to understand concepts there were more careful, unhurried examinations of ideas. Cooke brought together the words, sights and sounds in a way that was to be recognized by the industry: he won an Emmy Award in 1973 for "Individuals contributing to Documentary Programs." Later *America* would run on public television, one of the few programs originally produced for U.S. commercial television to do so.

In the meantime, America would overlap with Cooke's other appearances on television—as host for a number of British productions shown on U.S. public television under the umbrella title *Masterpiece Theatre*. The program premiered in the United States in 1971. *Masterpiece Theatre* offered American viewers adaptations of British and American novels (Jane Austen's *Emma*, Henry James' *The Golden Bowl*, for example) as well as original productions such as *Elizabeth R* and *The Six Wives of Henry VIII*. It is often remembered for its popular continuing serials such as *Upstairs, Downstairs*, which ran from 1974 until 1977.

Cooke was there as host who introduced the program, making a few off-the-cuff observations about the style of the production of the ideas of British culture found therein. He referred to his role on *Masterpiece Theatre* as "headwaiter." "I'm there to explain for interested customers what's on the menu, and how the dishes were composed. But I'm not the chef." Nevertheless, he won another Emmy Award for his role on the program as "Special Classification of Outstanding Program and Individual Achievement" in 1974. Cooke remained in this role for twenty-two years, until 1992, when he retired at 83. He planned at that time to continue producing his weekly BBC *Letter from America*.

—Val E. Limburg

ALFRED ALISTAIR COOKE. Born in Manchester, Lancashire, England, 20 November 1908; took U.S. citizenship, 1941. Attended Blackpool Grammar School; Jesus College, Cambridge, B.A. in English 1930; Commonwealth Fund Fellow, Yale University, 1932–33; Harvard University, 1933–34. Married: 1) Ruth Emerson, 1934; one son; 2) Jane White Hawkes, 1946; one daughter. BBC film critic, 1934=-37; BBC commentator on U.S. affairs, from 1938; NBC London correspondent, 1936–37; special correspondent on U.S. affairs, *London Times*, 1938–42; U.S. feature writer, *Daily Herald*, 1941–43; U.N. correspondent, 1945–48, and chief U.S. correspondent, 1948–72, *Manchester Guardian*; best known for *Letter from America*, the world's longest-running solo radio feature programme, first broadcast in 1946. Knight Commander of the Order of the British Empire, 1973. Honor Fellow: Jesus College, Cambridge, 1986. LLD: University of Edinburgh, 1969; University of Manchester, 1973. Litt.D: St Andrew's University, 1976; Cambridge University, 1988; Yale University, 1993. Recipient: Peabody Awards, 1952, 1983; Writers Guild of Great Britain Award for Best Documentary, 1972; Society of Film and Television Arts Dimbleby Award, 1973; Royal Society of Arts Benjamin Franklin Medal, 1973; four Emmy Awards; Yale University Howland Medal, 1977. Address: 1150 Fifth Avenue, New York City; Nassau Point, Cutchogue, Long Island, New York, U.S.A.

TELEVISION SERIES

1938–3	*The March of Time* (narrator)	
1948	*Sorrowful Jones* (narrator)	
1952–61	*Omnibus* (host)	
1957	*Three Faces of Eve* (narrator)	
1961–67	U.N.'s International Zone programme (host and producer)	
1971–92	*Masterpiece Theatre* (host)	
1972–73	*America: A Personal History of the U.S.* (writer and narrator)	
1973	*Hitler* (narrator)	

RADIO
Letter from America, 1946–.

PUBLICATIONS (selection)
Garbo and the Night Watchmen (editor). London: J. Cape, 1937.

Douglas Fairbanks: The Making of a Screen Character. New York: Museum of Modern Art, 1940.

A Generation on Trial: USA v Alger Hiss. New York: Knopf, 1950.

Christmas Eve. New York: Knopf, 1952.

A Commencement Address. New York: Knopf, 1954.

Around the World in Fifty Years. Chicago: Field Enterprises Educational Corp., 1966.

Talk About America. London: Bodley Head, 1968.

Alistair Cooke's America. New York: Knopf, 1973.

The American in Europe: From Emerson to S.J. Perelman. Cambridge: Cambridge University Press, 1975.

Six Men. London: Bodley Head, 1977.

Above London, with Robert Cameron. London: Bodley Head, 1980.

Masterpieces. New York: Knopf, 1981.
The Patient Has the Floor. Franklin Center, Pennsylvania: Franklin Institute, 1986.
America Observed. New York: Collier, 1988.
Fun and Games with Alistair Cooke. New York: Arcade, 1994.

FURTHER READING
Barnouw, Erik. *Tube of Plenty.* New York: Oxford University Press, 1975.
Brozan, Nadine. "Chronicle." *The New York Times,* 22 July 1992.
Fireman, Judy, editor. *TV Book.* New York: Workman, 1977.

COONEY, JOAN GANZ

U.S. Producer/Media Executive

Joan Ganz Cooney is the one of the visionaries and the chief moving force behind the creation of Children's Television Workshop (CTW) and the most successful children's television show in the history of either commercial or educational television, *Sesame Street.* Before *Sesame Street,* successful children's programs were entertainment oriented and appeared on commercial television; educational programs were thought to be boring and pedantic and appeared on public television which garnered a small, more affluent audience. Cooney recognized that television could do more than entertain; it could provide supplementary education at a fraction of the cost of classroom instruction. She demonstrated that quality educational programming could attract and hold a mass audience and established an organization which continues to produce innovative programming for all ages. And, through *Sesame Street,* a larger, more diverse audience discovered public television, bringing it to the forefront of the national consciousness.

Cooney had an early interest in education, earning a B.A. degree in education from the University of Arizona in 1951, but she gravitated toward the mass media in part as a result of the influence of the Christophers, a religious group who emphasize utilizing communication technologies for humanitarian goals. Although she began her career as a reporter for the *Arizona Republic* in 1952, she moved into television in 1954, joining the NBC publicity department in New York. By 1955 she was handling publicity for the prestigious *U.S. Steel Hour.* However, public television offered greater opportunity to do in-depth analyses of major issues, and she moved to the non-commercial WNDT-TV (now WNET-TV) in New York in 1962, where she produced a number of documentaries, including *A Chance at the Beginning,* a Harlem precursor of Project Head Start, and the Emmy-award-winning *Poverty, Anti-Poverty and the Poor.*

At a 1966 dinner party at her apartment, Lloyd N. Morrisett, vice president of the Carnegie Corporation, wondered aloud whether television could be a more effective educator. Realizing that she could continue to produce documentaries without having a lasting effect on the disadvantaged, Cooney undertook a study called "The Potential Uses of Television in Preschool Education." This vision was the genesis of a proposal she submitted to Carnegie in February 1968, a proposal which resulted in the establishment of CTW and the creation of *Sesame Street.* Morrisett was particularly active in developing the proposal and raising the initial funds, and he remains a guiding force of CTW, as chair of the board of directors. But it was Cooney who articulated the creative vision and established the organization that brought it to reality.

Cooney proposed taking advantage of commercial production techniques, such as the fast pacing and repetition of advertisements and the multiple formats of *Rowan and Martin's Laugh-In,* to give life to the curriculum. Although she hoped the program would educate all preschool children,

Joan Ganz Cooney
Photo courtesy of the Children's Television Workshop

she stated that if the needs of disadvantaged children were not met, then the program would be a failure.

Cooney also recognized that educational programs often fail because they are planned by educators and implemented by production personnel. Shortly after the creation of CTW in March 1968, therefore, she established a series of seminars in collaboration with Gerald S. Lesser (a Harvard educational psychologist who became chairman of the board of advisors). Production personnel (under David D. Connell, executive producer) worked with educators, child development experts, and research personnel (under Edward L. Palmer, director of research) to plan the show. Cooney, as executive director of CTW, established the guidelines, stressing the importance of exploiting the unique features of television to present a well-defined curriculum designed to supplement rather than replace classroom activity. She indicated that there was to be no star but rather a multiracial cast including both sexes and that the primary goal was to produce an excellent program not more academic research. The working environment she established was one that fostered mutual confidence and participation among its diverse members.

Once her vision was articulated, Cooney developed an organization that guaranteed the production team the freedom to focus upon the creative task. Although required by funding agencies to establish an affiliation with National Educational Television (NET), CTW remained semi-autonomous and self-contained, utilizing some administrative functions of NET but retaining all rights to the program. Cooney traveled the country, insuring morning air time for the new show. CTW also utilized unprecedented means of informing the potential audience, enlisting commercial networks in promotional efforts. These efforts were coupled with more personal means of reaching disadvantaged families, using sound trucks and door-to-door representatives, for example, in Harlem.

Sesame Street first aired in November 1969, on nearly 190 public and commercial stations, and by all measures has been a continuing success. In large scale studies, the Educational Testing Service of Princeton concluded that *Sesame Street* generally reached its educational goals. The show also rapidly gained a mass audience, which it currently maintains. And, there have been numerous critical measures of success, including a Peabody Award and three Emmys after the first year and fifty-eight Emmys to date.

After the first successful season, CTW dissolved its relationship with NET, and Cooney became its president. The impetus was there to develop other projects, so Cooney guided the fund raising and creative vision for a second show airing in 1971, called *The Electric Company*. This program providing basic reading instruction for eight-to-twelve-year-old children. Although by 1973 Cooney described her work as mostly administrative, her vision of utilizing the unique features of television coupled with methodical planning and research to produce programming to address identified needs was evident in other innovative CTW productions, including *Feelin' Good* (1974), *The Best of Families* (1977), *3-2-1 Contact* (1980), and *Square One TV* (1987).

Since the role of foundations is usually to provide start-up money, and since government support of public television has declined, Cooney has extended the influence of CTW productions and insured the organization's survival by guiding the licensing of an array of commercial products and developing foreign distribution and production agreements. Product and international revenues have often provided as much as two-thirds of the budget, helping to sustain CTW and provide money for new projects. Cooney has also led CTW down the narrow road between commercial and public television, developing tax-paying subsidiaries which operate in commercial broadcasting, such as Distinguished Productions which produced *Encyclopedia* in 1988 in collaboration with HBO.

In 1990 Cooney stepped down as president to become chair of the CTW executive committee, thus allowing her more time for creative development. Still actively involved in the creation of *Sesame Street*, she also focuses upon strategic planning, with more recent projects involving interactive software and a multimedia project entitled *Ghostwriter*, which debuted in 1992.

Cooney has enriched children's television with her vision, has altered public perception and introduced record-setting audiences to public television, and has raised the level of expectation for children entering school. Fittingly, among the many honors that she and CTW have received was a 1970 Christopher Award.

—Suzanne Hurst Williams

JOAN GANZ COONEY. Born in Phoenix, Arizona, U.S.A., 30 November 1929. University of Arizona, B.A. in education 1951. Married: 1) Timothy J. Cooney, 1964 (divorced, 1975); 2) Peter G. Peterson, 1980. Reporter, *Arizona Republic*, Phoenix, 1952–54; publicist, NBC, 1954–55; publicist, *U.S. Steel Hour*, 1955–62; producer, Channel 13, New York City, 1962–67; TV consultant, Carnegie Corporation, New York City, 1967–68; executive director, Children's Television Workshop (producers of *Sesame Street, Electric Company, 321 Contact, Square One TV,* and *Ghostwriter*), New York City, 1968–70; president and trustee, 1970–88, chair and chief executive officer, 1988–90, chair, executive committee, since 1990; director, Johnson and Johnson, Metropolitan Life Insurance Company. Trustee: Channel 13/Educational Broadcasting Corporation; Museum of Television and Radio; Columbia Presbyterian Hospital. Member: President's Commission on Marijuana and Drug Abuse, 1971–73; National News Council, 1973–81; Council Foreign Relations, since 1974; Advance Committee for Trade Negotiations, 1978–80; Governor's Commission on International Year of the Child, 1979; President's Commission for Agenda for the 1980s, 1980–81; Carnegie Foundation National Panel on High Schools, 1980–82; National Organization of Women (NOW), National Academy of Television Arts and Sciences, National Institute Social Sciences, International Radio and TV Society, American Women in Radio and TV. Honorary degrees: Boston College, 1970; Hofstra University, Oberlin College, Ohio Wesleyan University, 1971; Princeton University, 1973; Russell Sage College, 1974; University of Arizona, and Harvard University, 1975; Allegheny College, 1976; Georgetown University, 1978; University of Notre Dame, 1982; Smith College, 1986; Brown University, 1987; Columbia University, and New York University, 1991. Recipient: Christopher Award, 1970; National Institute for Social Sciences Gold Medal, 1971; Frederick Douglass Award, New York Urban League, 1972; Silver Satellite Award, American Women in Radio and TV; Woman of the Decade Award, 1979; National Endowment for the Arts, Friends of Education Award; Kiwanis Decency Award; National Association of Educational Broadcasters Distinguished Service Award; Stephen S. Wise Award, 1981; Harris Foundation Award, 1982; Emmy Award, for Lifetime Achievement, 1989; named to Hall of Fame Academy of Television Arts and Sciences, 1989; Presidential Medal of Freedom, 1995. Address: Children's Television Workshop, One Lincoln Plaza, New York City, New York 10023, U.S.A.

TELEVISION (publicist)
1955–62   *U.S. Steel Hour*

TELEVISION DOCUMENTARIES (producer)
1962–67   *Court of Reason*
             A Chance at the Beginning
             Poverty, Anti-Poverty and the Poor
1968–90   *Children's Television Workshop* (executive)

FURTHER READING
"The First Lady of *Sesame Street*: Joan Ganz Cooney." *Broadcasting* (Washington, D.C.), 7 June 1971.

Gilbert, Lynn, and Gaylen Moore. *Particular Passions: Talks with Women Who Have Shaped Our Times.* New York: Clarkson N. Potter, 1981.
Gratz, Roberta Brandes. "*Sesame*: An Open-End Play Street." *New York Post*, 8 November 1969.
Heuton, Cheryl. "TV Learns How to Teach...." *Channels: The Business of Communication* (New York), 22 October 1990.
Kramer, Michael. "A Presidential Message from Big Bird." *U.S. News and World Report* (Washington, D.C.), 13 June 1988.
Lesser, Gerald. *Children and Television: Lessons from Sesame Street.* New York: Random House, 1974.
Moreau, Dan. "Joan Ganz Cooney Created Sesame Street 20 Years Ago. Now It's an Institution." *Changing Times* (Washington, D.C.), July 1989.
O'Dell, Cary. *Women Pioneers in Television.* Jefferson, North Carolina: McFarland, 1996.
Polsky, Richard M. *Getting to Sesame Street: Origins of the Children's Television Workshop.* New York: Praeger, 1974.
Sheldon, Alan. "Tuning In with Joan Cooney." *Public Telecommunications Review* (Washington, D.C.), November-December, 1978.
Sklar, Robert. "Growing Up with Joan Ganz Cooney." *American Film* (Washington, D.C.), November 1977.
"TV's Switched-on School." *Newsweek* (New York), 1 June 1970.
Tyler, Ralph. "Cooney Cast Light on a Vision." *Variety* (Los Angeles, California), 13 December 1989.

See also Children and Television; Children's Television Workshop; *Sesame Street*

COPRODUCTIONS INTERNATIONAL

Coproduction is a generic term that covers a variety of production arrangements between two or more companies undertaking a television (or film or other video) project. Coproduction International refers to the situation of two or more organizations from different countries undertaking such projects. It encompasses everything from a straightforward co-financing arrangement in which one partner provides partial funding while another company undertakes the actual production, to more complex arrangements that involve joint creative control over projects. In both cases the allocation of distribution rights and other after-market rights is a standard element of the negotiation. More complex coproduction agreements generally involve more permutations in such matters. While coproductions in film have a history dating from the 1920s, in television they were rarely popular until the 1980s. They now appear to be more and more common as the cost of production rises and as international markets for television mature.

Simple coproductions—those that provide financing in return for distribution rights—offer significant advantages to the partners and have been undertaken for many years. Having multiple partners means more money for a project, and in an era of escalating production costs the financial needs of television production can be tremendous, particularly for certain genres. Historically, coproductions have been especially popular with television networks that required programs or films but did not have a sufficiently large budget to produce programs of their own. In the U.S., for example, coproductions became common between the public broadcasting stations in major markets (Boston, Maryland, New York) and the British Broadcasting Company (BBC). Coproductions offered U.S. public television stations the opportunity for high quality product at a fraction of their production cost. In return, the arrangements offered the BBC, with its huge sunk costs in production facilities, a means of stretching its budget with no threat to its other distribution rights or its own primary market, the United

Kingdom. The first such coproduction, a 1971 U.S. public broadcaster-BBC venture called *The First Churchill*, was a BBC period saga that won an Emmy. Since then, such ventures have become common fare for PBS stations and, more recently, for cable services such as A and E (Arts and Entertainment) and Discovery. Popular television fare has included *The Jewel in the Crown* and *Brideshead Revisited* (produced by ITV in Britain), with a typical contribution of about 10% of the BBC production budget from U.S. services.

Many countries maintain coproduction treaties. Such treaties establish terms which, when met, enable productions to qualify for various forms of government support. While the specifics of such treaties vary, they generally ensure that, over time, creative, technical and financial contributions will be balanced among the participating countries; the treaties may scrutinize crew composition, investment, actors, sites, and perhaps even the language of the production. For countries such as Canada, France, or other European Union members, coproduction treaties ensure that the resulting product qualifies as "domestic," a category crucial in meeting legally established quotas determining allowable amounts of imported television content. The treaties also assure that co-produced material is eligible for government financing or investor tax credits in terms of the national policies. The *1995 Coproduction International* handbook identifies the BBC, Italian broadcaster RAI, British Independent Television (ITV), the combined U.S. PBS stations, and British Channel 4 as most active coproducing broadcasters over the past 15 years. (At this writing, the best annual trade review of television coproduction is published jointly by PACT (Producers Alliance for Cinema and Television) of Great Britain in conjunction with Television Business International. Edited by Charles Brown, this compilation, called *Coproduction International 19—*, examines the television production finance structure of many countries, focusing on coproduction. Specific organizations—public and private broadcasters, producers and distributors—are profiled, and their production needs and processes are highlighted.)

As cable networks developed in the United States during the 1980s, and as additional commercial and satellite channels proliferated around the globe, the search for affordable programming has intensified, and coproductions have become even more attractive ways to maximize production and distribution. One result of this development is the clear evidence that the international aspects of television programming now receive greater scrutiny from the outset of program planning. Making television programs that can cater to multiple audiences across national boundaries increasingly requires careful planning and an awareness of audiences as well as broadcasting conventions around the globe.

Another consequence of some concern regards the range of content accommodations coproductions entail when the products must satisfy different national audiences. A great deal of scholarly interest and some attention

by policy makers has been directed at the perceived threat to "national" television that international coproductions may represent. Its most extreme version invokes a scenario of homogeneous, global programs driving out national television production that caters to and captures what is meaningful to local audiences. In a sense, some concern over coproduction joins the worry focused on "Americanization" or "cultural imperialism" of international television programming. Selection of the primary language in which to record dialogue, and the choice to dub or subtitle, also figure into this issue. The response of the European Union (EU) to such problems to date has included a loosely worded 1989 Broadcasting Directive that urged members to insure that at least 50% of their television programming originated from within the EU. The EU has also established several programs (e.g. the MEDIA program) to support and invigorate the production and exhibition infrastructure within member countries.

As a financing vehicle, coproductions have emerged as particularly significant means for smaller market countries to ensure that some local production remains possible. Insofar as the television schedules in many countries rely heavily on films (indeed, in certain countries—France, for example—broadcasters are major investors in film), the financial clout available through coproduction is almost mandatory for film production destined for television airing. The ability to produce high budget feature films is moving out of the reach of single companies, but with partners from several countries or companies the opportunities still exist. The European Council of Ministers created the organization Eurimages to facilitate coproduction among three or more countries, hoping to ensure the vitality of film among all European countries.

One consequence of the demand for more product has been more intense competition for these coproduction partners, a factor that both has driven up the cost of coproductions and threatened arrangements for financially strapped public broadcasting in the United States. Moreover, the process of coproducing is itself not without problems. On the one hand coproductions offer a mechanism for films and higher budget television to garner the capital they require, as well as ways to penetrate other markets, but they may also create production headaches emerging from the very difficult process of being accountable to multiple funders and multiple audiences. And they must encounter and deal with issues related to multiple styles and cultures among the cast and crew. Many efforts have floundered when partners could not agree on script, production technique, cast, or post-production. One of the most notorious failed coproduction efforts was *Riviera*, a $35 million project of several European broadcasters. This soap opera, set on the Cote d'Azur, ultimately pleased none of its backers (nor their audiences), and has gone down in history as a costly lesson in the frailties of joint production efforts.

Coproductions will continue to figure into the growth of international media corporations looking for ways to maximize their investments in productions; partnering with local media companies in various countries has become a way to guarantee broad distribution as well as a method of obviating certain national restrictions on "imported" television product, and that trend shows no evidence of slowing. However, coproduction does seem to be yielding some production lessons, so that partners and contracts are more carefully initiated than was perhaps the case in earlier years. The "Euro-puddings" and failed efforts that garnered trade press headlines in the late 1980s have given way to growing understanding that coproduction makes most sense only under certain conditions, and only for certain types of projects.

Coproduction's partner vehicle, format licensing, also became more popular in the late 1980s and 1990s. Format licensing represents a useful scheme for adapting tested, lower budget formula programming (especially quiz shows and soap operas) for new markets in a way that allows them to be tailored to local tastes and styles. It eliminates many of the production problems coproduction may present, and effectively domesticates a content and a format originated elsewhere.

—Sharon Strover

FURTHER READING

Becker, Jurgen. *European Coproduction in Film and Television: Second Munich Symposium on Film and Media Law. Munich Symposium on Film and Media Law.* Baden-Baden: Verlagsgellschaft, 1989.

Hill, J., Martin McLoone, and Paul Hainsworth, editors. *Border Crossing: Film in Ireland, Britain and Europe.* Belfast Institute of Irish Studies in association with the University of Ulster and the British Film Institute, 1994.

Johnston, C. *International Television Co-Production: From Access to Success.* Stoneham, Massachusetts: Butterworth-Heinemann, 1992.

Moshavi, Sharon D. "Cable's MIPCOM Presence: Networks Are Increasingly Thinking International as They Look Overseas for Coproduction Partners and New Markets for Their Own Fare." *Broadcasting* (Washington, D.C.), 21 October 1991.

Negrine, R., and S. Papathanassopoulos. *The Internationalisation of Television.* London: Pinter, 1990.

Porter, V. "European Co-productions: Aesthetic and Cultural Implications." *Journal of Area Studies*, (London), 1985.

Renaud, J., and B. Litman. "Changing Dynamics of the Overseas Marketplace for TV Programming." *Telecommunications Policy* (Guildford, England), September 1985.

Schlesinger, P. "Wishful Thinking: Cultural Politics, Media and Collective Identities in Europe." *European Journal of Communications* (London), 1993.

Straubhaar, J. "Beyond Media Imperialism: Assymetrical Interdependence and Cultural Proximity." *Critical Studies in Mass Communication* (Annandale, Virginia), 1991.

Strover, S. "Recent Trends in Coproductions: Demise of the National." In, Corcoran, F., and P. Preston, editors. *Democracy and Communications in the New Europe: Change and Continuity in East and West.* Cresskil, New Jersey: Hampton Press, 1995.

Turow, J. "The Organizational Underpinnings of Contemporary Media Conglomerates." *Communication Research* (Newbury Park, California), 1992.

COPYRIGHT LAW AND TELEVISION

Copyright law is the economic linchpin of the television broadcasting business. In nearly every country of the world, the domestic law permits the owner of the copyright in a literary or artistic work to prevent that work from being copied, broadcast or communicated to the public by cable. The right owner can then license other parties to use the work on either an exclusive or a non-exclusive basis. As broadcasting becomes ever more international in scope and reach, the international framework of copyright law has become as important as the national laws themselves.

The International Framework

Nearly every country has ratified the *Berne Convention for the Protection of the Rights of Authors in Literary and Artistic Works*, which was last revised in 1971. This lays down the minimum requirements for the national laws of all signatory states. There is a second international convention, the *Rome Convention for the Protection of Performers, Producers of Phonograms and Broadcasting Organisations*, which dates from

1961 and extends protection to performers, record producers and broadcasters. But this has been ratified by far fewer states. Although both conventions are administered by the World Intellectual Property Organisation, the *Rome Convention* is managed in association with UNESCO and the International Labour Organisation. Finally, a chapter protecting *Trade-Related Aspects of Intellectual Property Rights* (TRIPS) is included in the *WTO Agreement*, which was agreed in 1994 and is administered by the World Trade Organisation.

There are formal linkages between each of the three international legal instruments. A state cannot ratify the *Rome Convention* unless it has also signed the *Berne Convention*; and a country which ratifies the *TRIPS Agreement* must comply with the provisions of the *Berne Convention*, but with one significant exception. It does not have to protect the moral rights of authors to prevent any distortion or other modification of their work which would damage their honour or reputation.

The origins of these three international legal instruments can be traced back to the late eighteenth century. Some countries, with common law systems, such as the United Kingdom and the United States, gave copyright protection to the work itself. But others, whose legal systems were based on Roman law, such as France and most of continental Europe, gave protection to the author of the work. The difference is often insignificant, since in practice it is normally the same for an author to license the economic rights in a work which s/he has authored, as it is for the owner to license the rights in a work for which s/he owns the copyright. Furthermore, the text of the *Berne Convention*, which affords protection of the rights of authors in their literary and artistic works (but not to rights in the literary and artistic works themselves), has been ratified both by countries with common law and those with Roman-law systems. This is because there is no definition of the word "author" in the Convention; and the definition of the phrase "literary and artistic works" has been extremely carefully drafted. A literary and artistic work includes "every production in the literary, scientific or artistic domain, whatever may be the mode or form of its expression, such as ... ." There then follows an extensive list of forms of literary and artistic expression. But although this list includes cinematographic works, it does not include broadcasts. Thus the *Berne Convention* can be ratified both by Roman law countries, where "an author's right" can only be granted to a natural person, and by common law countries, where the copyright in a work can be owned by either a natural or a legal person.

As broadcasters were clearly not natural persons, Roman law countries originally denied them protection as authors. Instead, they awarded a broadcaster a separate, but secondary right, called a neighbouring right. A key reason for negotiating the *Rome Convention* was to afford international protection to holders of neighbouring rights, including broadcasters. But by protecting the rights of performers, as well as those of phonogram producers and broadcasters, the drafters of the *Rome Convention* gave performers rights which many countries, such as the United States, considered excessive. They have therefore declined to ratify the *Rome Convention*. The *TRIPS Agreement* includes some, but not all, the provisions of the *Rome Convention*. It only protects performers against the unauthorised recording and broadcasting of live performances— i.e. bootleg recordings and broadcasts.

However, the main reason for establishing a parallel system of protecting intellectual property rights within the *WTO Agreement* was to strengthen enforcement procedures for protecting intellectual property rights. Each country must ensure that its laws provide enforcement procedures that are backed by rapid and effective action. Judicial authorities must be given powers to serve an injunction requiring an alleged infringer to desist, and to require the destruction of infringing goods, or the tools and materials with which the infringing activities were carried out. They must also require the infringer to pay damages and costs to the right holder. Furthermore, under the most favoured nation clause of the *WTO Agreement*, each country must afford equal immediate and unconditional protection to nationals from all other signatories. Finally, any dispute as to the implementation of the provisions of the *WTO Agreement* must be settled under its Dispute Settlement Procedures. This is a new departure, as there are no enforceable disputes procedures in the *Berne* and the *Rome Conventions*.

Broadcasting Rights in Literary and Artistic Works

The author of every literary and artistic work has the exclusive right to license the work to be broadcast or communicated to the public by wire. As most broadcasts include literary or artistic works, the broadcaster must normally acquire these rights in advance. When recorded music is used, it is also necessary to acquire a separate neighbouring right in the sound recording of the performance; and in many countries the performers also have a separate right in their performance. If a cinematographic recording is used during a broadcast, the broadcaster must also acquire its broadcasting right. By acquiring the broadcasting rights in all the constituent literary or artistic works which are included in a broadcast, the broadcaster can thus protect the broadcast itself from being copied, broadcast or communicated to the public by cable.

The broadcaster has only five key issues to negotiate when acquiring a licence to broadcast a literary or artistic work. They are: (a) the territories for which the right should be acquired; (b) the period of time for which the right should be acquired; (c) whether the right should be licensed on an exclusive or non-exclusive basis; (d) whether to acquire any ancillary rights, such as cable rights; and (e) whether payment to the original right holders should be made immediately, or stage by stage with each successive broadcast. Thus, once the broadcaster has acquired the constituent rights in the broadcast, these can form the basis of protection for the broadcast itself.

The Copyright of Broadcasts

In some broadcasts however, there may be no constituent literary or artistic work. The broadcaster cannot rely therefore on the licences to the constituent works in order to protect the broadcast itself. Two typical examples would be a live broadcast of a sports event or a discussion programme. In common law countries, the broadcaster is normally granted a copyright in the broadcast itself. But in Roman-law countries, a broadcaster is only given a neighbouring right. The international protection afforded by the *Berne Convention* does not extend to these broadcasts therefore.

In order to facilitate international trade in television programmes, a number of European states used the umbrella of the Council of Europe to establish the *European Agreement Concerning Programme Exchanges by Means of Television Films* in 1958 and the *European Agreement to Protect Television Broadcasts* in 1960. But in the following year, broadcasters were also afforded more limited, although more widespread protection by the *Rome Convention for the Protection of Performers, Phonogram Producers and Broadcasting Organisations.* Even so, broadcasters that are established in states which are not signatories to the *Rome Convention,* may have to rely for protection on bilateral agreements between the country where they are established and that where protection is claimed. Elsewhere, the broadcaster's only protection could depend on the terms of the contract between the broadcaster and the foreign user.

Cable Relays of Broadcasts

Once a television programme has been broadcast, it is technically possible to capture it and relay it to new audiences by cable. In the early days, cable was often used to improve signal reception, particularly in the so-called "shadow zones," or to distribute the signal through large buildings. The *Berne Convention* permits states to determine the conditions under which authors of literary and artistic works may exercise their rights to communicate their works to the public by wire, provided that those conditions are prejudicial neither to the moral rights of the author, nor to the right to receive equitable remuneration. Many states therefore impose compulsory licences on the cable rights of literary and artistic works which were incorporated in broadcasts. The *Rome Convention* affords even less protection. It denies a performer the right to prevent a performance from being communicated to the public by cable when the performance is already part of a broadcast; and it only allows a broadcaster a separate cable right in its television broadcasts if they are relayed to places where the public must pay an entrance fee. In many countries therefore, cable operators can relay both domestic and foreign broadcasting services to their subscribers without a sub-license from the original broadcaster.

The U.S. Supreme Court originally held that it was not an infringement of copyright to relay broadcasts to paying subscribers. But the *1976 Copyright Act* drew a distinction between "secondary transmissions" which simultaneously retransmit network programmes or programmes within the local service area of a broadcaster, and the retransmission of far away non-network programmes. The former are deemed to have no adverse economic effect on the copyright owners, whereas the latter are determined to have such an effect, since they distribute the broadcast to a new audience which the original right owner did not anticipate when the works were first licensed. Each distant signal is therefore given a "distant signal equivalent", with different values for independent station networks and educational stations. The total royalty is calculated by applying a formula based on these values to the cable operator's gross receipts. This is then redistributed to the appropriate authors by the Copyright Royalty Tribunal.

In Europe the situation is variable. The United Kingdom permits licensed cable operators to retransmit the broadcasts of British broadcasting organisations. But in Germany, copyright owners are fully protected against their works being retransmitted by cable. In addition, both broadcasters and cable operators have a 25-year neighbouring right against rebroadcasting and retransmission. In Austria, complete and unaltered transmissions of the public broadcaster ORF can be retransmitted throughout the country. On the other hand, cable retransmissions of foreign broadcasts are subject to copyright under a statutory licence which sets out the remuneration criteria.

A cable operator can now pick up a broadcast signal from a foreign satellite and relay it to its domestic subscribers. In its Council Directive on the co-ordination of certain rules concerning copyright and rights related to copyright applicable to satellite broadcasting and cable retransmission (93/83), the European Union harmonised the rules for the internal market between its fifteen member states. When a programme from another member state is retransmitted by cable, the applicable copyrights and related rights must be observed. Any retransmission must be licensed by individual or collective contractual arrangements between cable operators and the relevant right holders. But this provision does not automatically apply to cable retransmissions of broadcasts from countries outside the European Union. Furthermore, although there are several European states that are members of the Council of Europe but not of the European Union, the parallel convention of the Council of Europe—the *European Convention Relating to Questions of Copyright Law and Neighbouring Rights in the Framework of Transfrontier Broadcasting by Satellite*—does not cover the simultaneous, complete and unchanged retransmission of satellite broadcasts by terrestrial means.

The Collective Administration of Rights

For many broadcasters the time and effort in negotiating copyright clearance for all the literary, musical and artistic works used in their broadcasts is potentially extremely expensive and time-consuming. Conversely, many rights owners have neither the means nor the ability to monitor the use of their work by broadcasters. In practice therefore, many rights are collectively administered by collecting societies. These collecting societies are effectively co-operatives between different categories of rights holder. Originally, this form of administration was mainly confined to musical works. But when sound recording and radio broadcasting arrived, composers and music publishers soon realised that the performing rights of their works in gramophone recordings and radio broadcasts would far outstrip sales of sheet music. They therefore transferred the right to authorise the use of their works to a collecting society. The collecting society can, in turn, authorise recording companies and broadcasters to use a wide range of music in one general contract. Depending on the agreement, the fee which the broadcaster has to pay may either be standard, or vary according to some agreed criterion, such as the broadcaster's net advertising revenue. The collecting society then passes its revenues back to its members, after deducting its administration costs. On the other hand, broadcasting licences for cinematographic works or dramatico-musical works are still normally acquired by individual negotiation and the payment of a specific fee.

Since 1926, an international organisation—The International Confederation of Societies of Authors and Composers (CISAC)—has provided an international framework of co-operation and financial exchange between national collecting societies. In many countries, similar collecting organisations, or sometimes the same ones, have also been established to licence the recording rights for musical works. A parallel international bureau of societies administering those rights (BIEM) has also been set up, which negotiates model agreements with broadcasters and others which serve as the basis for licensing recordings throughout many parts of the world. Today collecting societies administer collectively the authors rights and neighbouring rights for radio and television broadcasting, the public reception of broadcasts and cable transmission (including retransmission of broadcasts). Indeed, in Europe, the simultaneous cable transmission of broadcasts, both domestic and foreign, has led to the formation of "super-collectives" which are able to grant licences on behalf of several different collective licensing organisations.

Transfrontier Broadcasting

High power and medium power satellites have now made transfrontier broadcasting possible. In some situations, the signals are broadcast direct to home, elsewhere they are relayed by cable. Some channels, financed by advertising and sponsorship, broadcast open signals. Others, which are financed by subscription, broadcast encrypted signals. But in practice, every transfrontier service also has to negotiate the appropriate copyright clearances, both for the literary and artistic works in the programme and for the broadcast itself.

A key issue which the international community has still to resolve is to agree upon the relevant jurisdiction for a transfrontier broadcast. Is it where the broadcast originates, or where it is received? Although this issue has not been formally resolved at the international level, the international community will probably follow the regional lead which has been given by the European Union (EU), and through them, the EEA. The EU's Directive specifies that the broadcast takes place "where the programme-carrying signals are introduced under the control and responsibility of the broadcasting organisation into an uninterrupted chain of communication leading to the satellite and down towards earth." Thus if a broadcast starts life in country A, but is then relayed by cable to country B, where it is up-linked to a satellite owned by an organisation whose headquarters are registered in country C, using frequencies allocated to country D, the broadcast is deemed to originate in country A.

All EU (and EEA) Member States now provide an exclusive right for the author of a copyright work to autho-

rize the communication to the public by satellite. In countries where there is a collective agreement between a collecting society covering a particular category of works, the law may extend that agreement to right holders of the same category who are not represented by the collecting society, provided that two conditions are met. First, the satellite broadcast must be a simulcast of a terrestrial broadcast by the same broadcaster. But second, an unrepresented right holder may be able to exclude the extension of the collective agreement to cover his works. This provision does not apply to cinematographic works however. Furthermore, broadcasters retain their exclusive right to authorise or prohibit their broadcasts from being rebroadcast or communicated to the public by cable if such communication is made to places where an entrance fee is payable. Finally, they also have the exclusive right to make fixations of their broadcasts available to the public.

Home Taping

The advent of the video recorder means that the ordinary viewer can now tape television programmes off air, to be stored and replayed at a later time. Many educational institutions also tape broadcasts off air for educational use. There is still no firm agreement at the international level as to whether these activities are a breach of copyright. There are two distinct, but related, issues. First, does the act of making a video or audio recording infringe copyright? And second, does the replaying of the recording infringe copyright?

The *Berne Convention* allows countries to permit the reproduction of literary and artistic works "in certain special cases, provided that such reproduction does not conflict with a normal exploitation of the work and does not unreasonably prejudice the legitimate interests of the author;" [art. 9(2)] and there is a parallel provision for broadcasts in the *Rome Convention* [art. 15(2)]. Therefore it is not necessarily an infringement of copyright to make an off air video recording, provided that the manner in which the recording is used does not conflict with the normal exploitation of the work and does not unreasonably prejudice the legitimate interests of the author.

In general, common law countries, such as the United Kingdom and the United States, permit video recording for domestic use, but although most countries in continental Europe consider video recording to be a breach of the author's right, they simultaneously recognise that they cannot prevent the onward march of technology. Many therefore impose a levy, either on the sale of video recorders, or on the sale of blank recording tape, or both, to "compensate" right owners for their "lost" revenues. Conversely, many right owners consider these levies to be a compulsory licence which has been imposed on their right to licence the video recordings of television broadcasts of their works. In some countries however, these levies are also used to subsidise the domestic film production industry. The principles on which these levies have been established and the levels at which they have been set have often been ambiguous.

The regulations governing the educational use of video recordings are even more confused. The *Berne Convention* allows states to permit the use of literary or artistic works by way of illustration in broadcasts or visual recordings for teaching, provided such use is compatible with fair practice. In the United States and the United Kingdom a clear distinction is made between the domestic use of off air recordings which is free, and their educational use which must be paid for. In Germany and the Nordic countries however, schools and universities may use educational broadcasts for educational purposes. In Norway, they pay a nominal fee for educational broadcasts, whereas in Germany, the recordings have to be erased at the end of the following year.

The policy differences between individual states carry significant implications for domestic educational policies, but some degree of international harmonisation may emerge. In the Europe Union, the Commission has prepared a draft directive to introduce a system of blank tape levies in all member states, although at the time of writing, this proposal has not commanded the consent of a qualified majority in the Council of Ministers. Furthermore, a producer state could choose to use the stronger mechanism for resolving international disputes set down in the *WTO Agreement*, in order to challenge a lax interpretation by a user state of the ambiguous provisions in the *Berne Convention* regulating off air recording.

—Vincent Porter

FURTHER READING

Becker, Jurgen, and Manfred Rehbinder, editors. *European Coproduction in Film and Television: Second Munich Symposium on Film and Media Law.* Baden-Baden: Nomos Verlagsgesellschaft, 1989.

Besen, Stanley M. *Copyright Liability for Cable Television: Is Compulsory Licensing the Solution?* Santa Monica, California: Rand Corporation, 1977.

Copyright Broadcast Retransmission Licensing Act of 1992: Hearings Before the Subcommittee on Intellectual Property and Judicial Administration. Washington, D.C.: U.S. Government Printing Office, 1994.

Council of Europe. Committee of Ministers. *Principles Relating to Copyright Law Questions in the Field of Television by Satellite and Cable: Recommendation no. R (86)2.* Strasbourg: Directorate of Human Rights, 1987.

Dittrich, Robert, with others. *Intellectual Property Rights and Cable Distribution of Television Programmes: Report Prepared by a Working Party.* Strasbourg: Council of Europe, 1983.

Mosteshar, Said, and Stephen de B. Bate. *Satellite and Cable Television: International Protection: A Specially Commissioned Report.* London: Longman Professional Intelligence Reports, 1986.

Patrick, Dennis R. "Cable Systems Held Ready for Full Copyright Liability; Consumer Seen Benefiting." *Television-Radio Age* (New York), 29 December 1986.

Pichler, Marie Helen. *Copyright Problems of Satellite and Cable Television in Europe.* London: Graham and Trotman, 1987; Boston: Nijhoff, 1987.

Porter, Vincent. *Copyright and Information: Limits to the Protection of Literary and Pseudo-literary Works in the Member States of the European Communities: A Report Prepared for the Commission of the European Communities (DG IV).* Luxembourg: Office for Official Publications of the European Communities, and Lanham, Maryland : UNIPUB, 1992.

———. "The Re-regulation of Television: Pluralism, Constitutionality and the Free Market in the USA, West Germany, France and the UK."" Media, Culture and Society (London), January 1989.

Satellite Compulsory License Extension Act of 1994: Report (To accompany S. 1485, as amended). United States Congress, Senate. Committee on the Judiciary. Washington, D.C.: U.S. Government Printing Office, 1994.

Veraldi, Lorna. "Newscasts as Property: Will Retransmission Consent Stimulate Production of more Local Television News?" *Federal Communications Law Journal* (Los Angeles), June 1994.

Willard, Stephen Hopkins. "A New Method of Calculating Copyright Liability for Cable Rebroadcasting of Distant Television Signals." *Yale Law Journal* (New Haven, Connecticut), May 1985.

CORBETT, HARRY H.

British Actor

British actor Harry H. Corbett is best remembered for the single role which dominated his career—Harold Steptoe in the BBC's most popular and successful sitcom, *Steptoe and Son.* Corbett added the "H" to his stage name to distinguish himself from the children's entertainer, Harry Corbett, creator of *Sooty*, but did not show any particular leaning towards comedy in his early career, which consisted both of supporting and lead roles in film and television. His bulky frame made him a natural to play tough-guy roles.

Corbett appeared regularly in ABC's ground-breaking anthology drama series, *Armchair Theatre*, contributing at least two performances to each season between 1957 and 1961. Notable productions included the death row drama *The Last Mile* (1957), directed by Philip Saville, and Eugene O'Neill's *The Emperor Jones* (1958).

When creating *Steptoe and Son* in 1962, writers Ray Galton and Alan Simpson wanted to cast straight actors, rather than comedians, in the lead roles of Harold and Albert

Steptoe. Wilfrid Brambell was cast as Albert and Corbett given the role of his son, Harold. Corbett was later to claim credit for altering Galton and Simpson's original conception by lowering the ages of these characters, making Harold a man approaching his forties (his own age).

Albert and Harold Steptoe run the rag-and-bone business of the show's title. Albert is a widower and his son, Harold, does most of the work. But Harold has dreams of betterment—he wants to be sophisticated, to get out of the business he is in, to get married and, most of all, to get away from his father. These remain dreams—he really knows that his life will not change, however much he tries, but the struggle with his father goes on. The pilot episode, "The Offer", ends with Harold pitifully failing to drag his belongings away to a new life on the back of a cart—a heavily symbolic scene which set the tone for the series as a whole. Over the next four years, and four seasons of *Steptoe and Son*, Harold had all his dreams shattered by Albert, whether it be his cultural pursuits—classical music, antiques and foreign films—or his romantic involvements.

Harry H. Corbett brought great dramatic pathos to the part of Harold, creating a character who hit a nerve in the audience. He had ambitions and pretentions beyond his abilities and social position and was often left bitterly disappointed, but remained a decent and honest man despite it all. Corbett enriched Galton and Simpson's wonderful scripts and gave them a character to develop further as the series progressed. His own comic timing also developed with his character, particularly his delivery of the predictable catchphrase, "You dirty old man!", when his father displayed his more earthy characteristics.

Between series and when Galton and Simpson brought *Steptoe and Son* to an end in 1965, both Corbett and Brambell were sought for movie roles because of their popularity, though Corbett's starring roles in *Ladies Who Do*, *The Bargee* and *Rattle of a Simple Man* are scarcely remembered today. Corbett also became a regular on the chat show scene, particularly as a frequent guest on the *Eamonn Andrews Show*. The audience expected him to be funny and he knew it, but his failure only pointed up the fact that Harold Steptoe was his career.

Fortunately, the BBC brought *Steptoe and Son* back for a further four series, in colour, between 1970 and 1974, and there were two *Steptoe and Son* movies as well. The new episodes simply took up where the series had left off and achieved the same level of popularity and quality as before.

—Steve Bryant

HARRY H. CORBETT. Born in Rangoon, Burma, 28 February 1925. Attended schools in Manchester. Married: 1) Sheila Steafel (divorced); 2) Maureen Blott; two children. Served in Royal Marines during World War II. Trained as radiographer before embarking on career as an actor; joined the Chorlton Repertory Company, later recruited by Joan Littlewood's Theatre Workshop in Stratford East, London; acted extensively in the theatre and in films before achieving fame as Harold Steptoe

Harry H. Corbett
Photo courtesy of the British Film Institute

in long-running *Steptoe and Son* comedy series, 1962–65 and 1970–75. Officer, Order of the British Empire, 1976. Died in Hastings, Kent, 21 March 1982.

TELEVISION SERIES

1962–65,	
1970–75	*Steptoe and Son*
1967	*Mr. Aitch*
1969	*The Best Things in Life*
1979–83	*Potter*
1980	*Grundy*

FILMS

The Passing Stranger, 1954; *Floods of Fear*, 1958; *Nowhere to Go*, 1958; *In the Wake of a Stranger*, 1959; *Shake Hands With the Devil*, 1959; *The Shakedown*, 1960; *Cover Girl Killer*, 1960; *The Big Day*, 1960; *The Unstoppable Man*, 1960; *Marriage of Convenience*, 1960; *Wings of Death*, 1961; *Time to Remember*, 1962; *Some People*, 1962; *Sparrows Can't Sing*, 1963; *Sammy Going South*, 1963; *Ladies Who Do*, 1963; *What a Crazy World*, 1963; *The Bargee*, 1964; *Rattle of a Simple Man*, 1964; *Joey Boy*, 1965; *Carry on Screaming*, 1966; *The Vanishing Busker*, 1966; *The Sandwich Man*,

1966; *Crooks and Coronets*, 1969; *Magnificent Seven Deadly Sins*, 1971; *Steptoe and Son*, 1972; *Steptoe and Son Ride Again*, 1973; *Percy's Progress*, 1974; *Hardcore*, 1976; *The Chiffy Kids*, 1976; *Adventures of a Private Eye*, 1977; *Jabberwocky*, 1977; *What's Up Superdoc*, 1979; *Silver Dream Racer*, 1980; *The Moles*, 1982.

RADIO

Steptoe and Son.

STAGE (selection)

Hamlet; The Power and the Glory; The Way of the World.

FURTHER READING

Burke, Michael. "You Dirty Old Man!" *The People* (London), 9 January 1994.
"How We Met: Ray Galton and Alan Simpson." *The Independent* (London), 11 June 1995.

See also *Steptoe and Son*

CORDAY, BARBARA

U.S. Television Producer

Barbara Corday is one of several dozen women who first entered the television business in the early 1970s. She began her entertainment career with a small theatrical agency in New York and later worked there as a publicist. In 1967, she moved to Los Angeles and joined Mann Scharf Associates.

In 1972 she met Barbara Avedon, who had been a television writer for several years, at a political activist group. They began discussing writing and Corday sensed that her experience gave her a certain discipline and ability to tell a story succinctly and "in a kind of a linear fashion." She and Avedon became writing partners and came up with a project that "got us in the door" and that became their calling card. This led to their being hired as a writing team to do several projects, and as free-lance writers they wrote numerous episodes for television series and a few pilots from 1972 to 1979.

It was during that period that the two women developed the idea for their best-known television creation, *Cagney and Lacey*. They began the project in 1974 as a theatrical film intended as a comedy feature. Written in the year when "buddy" movies had become popular, their project was a crazy comedy featuring two women, originally planned as a spoof of the police genre. Unable to get the movie made as a feature, they tried to sell it as a television series—and all three networks rejected it. Nobody wanted a television series about two women cops. But when they tried to sell it as a television movie, CBS said "maybe" and the two women rewrote the script completely, adjusting for budget and language and story. As Corday noted, "Here we had written this insane, irreverent feature with all kinds of chases and things exploding and clearly we couldn't do that for television. We retained a lot of what we thought was the feminist point of view."

But there was a vast difference between what they created in 1974 and what it became by 1982. As Corday commented in an interview, "By the time the show went on as a television series, it was no longer necessary to say a lot of the things we had started out saying; and I think the show became far more intelligent and sensitive and interesting.

The characters deepened and broadened and became much more real." Produced by Barney Rosenzweig, *Cagney and Lacey* first appeared as a TV movie in 1981 and then scheduled as a CBS series beginning in 1982.

In 1979 Avedon returned to freelancing on her own. Corday had by then determined that she was not able to sit down at the typewriter and create without the incentive of a particular show or episode. She liked going into the studio

Barbara Corday
Photo courtesy of Barbara Corday

every day and working on projects that kept her really busy. A neighbor, an executive at ABC, offered her a position at the network. Corday surmised that the company wanted someone experienced in production and writing who could deal with writers and producers making shows for ABC. She took the job as vice president of comedy series development at ABC, where she remained for three years.

In 1982 she was offered a position with Columbia Pictures where she started her own production company, "Can't Sing, Can't Dance Productions." Having demonstrated that she could bring projects to completion, she was appointed president of Columbia Pictures Television in 1984, and in March 1987 took on the additional duties of overseeing another Coca-Cola television subsidary, Embassy Communications. She became president and chief operating officer of Columbia/Embassy Television, overseeing production and development at both units. In October of that same year she resigned as president.

In July 1988 Barbara Corday was named vice president of prime-time programs at CBS. The appointment, announced by network entertainment president Kim LeMasters, placed her in the number two position behind LeMasters in overseeing the prime-time schedule and gave her broader programming responsibilities than any other woman had ever had at one of the three major television networks. By December 1989 Kim LeMasters resigned after CBS failed to climb out of the third place position in the rating and Corday left shortly thereafter.

In the spring of 1992 Lorimar Television hired Corday to be co-executive producer of the CBS evening serial *Knot's Landing*. In the Fall of 1993 she was appointed president of New World Television where she was to create programming for first run syndciation. Following a managerial shakeup Corday resigned after ten months.

Corday is a founding member of the Hollywood Womens' Political Committee and a member of the Board of Governors of the Academy of Television Arts and Sciences. An outspoken advocate of equality in the workplace, she is one of the most articulate television executives. Her perceptive assessment of the role of women in the television industry coupled with her executive skills has earned her wide respect among her peers.

—Robert S. Alley

CORDAY, BARBARA. Born in New York City, New York, U.S.A., 15 October 1944. Married: 1) Barney Rosenzweig, 1979 (divorced, 1990); 2) Roger Lowenstein, 1992. Began career as publicist in New York and Los Angeles; switched to TV writing; vice president for comedy series development, ABC TV, 1979–82; co-creator (with Barbara Avedon), *Cagney and Lacey* TV series; president, Columbia Pictures TV, 1984–87; executive vice president, Primetime Programming, CBS Entertainment, 1988–1990; producer, *Knots Landing* TV series, 1992; president, New World Television, 1993–94. Member: Caucus of Writers, Producers and Directors; founding member, Hollywood Women's Political Committee. Address: 532 South Windsor Boulevard, Los Angeles, California 90020, U.S.A.

TELEVISION

1979	*American Dream* (pilot; writer)
1980	*Cagney and Lacey* (TV movie)
1981	*Cagney and Lacey* (series; co-creator)
1992	*Knots Landing* (producer)

FURTHER READING

Battaglio, Stephen. "Woman of the Year." *Adweek's Marketing Week* (New York), 5 June 1989.

D'Acci, Julie. *Defining Women: Television and the Case of Cagney and Lacey.* Chapel Hill: University of North Carolina Press, 1994.

McHenry, Susan. "Cagney and Lacey" (review). *Ms.* (New York), April 1984.

Tobenkin, David. "Seismic Shift at New World." *Broadcasting and Cable* (Washington, D.C.), 8 August 1994.

Weller, Sheila. "The Prime Time of Barbara Corday." *Ms.* (New York), October 1988.

See also *Cagney and Lacey*

CORONATION STREET

British Soap Opera

Coronation Street, the longest running and most successful British soap opera, was first transmitted on ITV on Friday, 9 December 1960. Made by Granada Television, the Manchester-based commercial company, the *Street*, as it is affectionately known, has been at the top of the British ratings for over thirty years.

The programme is perhaps best known for its realistic depiction of everyday working-class life in a Northern community. Set in a fictional area of Weatherfield in a working class region of north-west England, it grew out of the so-called "kitchen sink" drama style popularized in the late 1950s. The series, originally called "Florizel Street" by its creator Tony Warren, began as a limited thirteen episodes, but its cast of strong characters, its northern roots and sense of community immediately created a loyal following. These factors, combined with skillfully written and often amusing scripts, have ensured its continued success.

From its opening titles with scenes of terraced houses there is a strong sense of regional and local identity which is echoed in the language of its characters. Set in a domestic existence of various homes, the pubs, the shops which are all set out to be part of everyday life, *Coronation Street* is imbued

Coronation Street
Photo courtesy of the Brisith Film Institute

with a definite feeling of community. Through its account of supposedly everyday life, the programme shows a high degree of social realism. A close parallel is made between the fictional world of Weatherfield and the everyday world inhabited by its audience, whose loyalty is encouraged by the sense of close community, the predictability of plot and the regular transmission times.

The storylines of *Coronation Street* tend to concentrate on relationships within and between families rather than on topical or social issues, as is the case with the newer soaps such as *Brookside* and *EastEnders*. Critics might argue that the celebration of a mutually supportive community has more than a touch of nostalgia, whilst its fans would argue that the programme reflects shifts in social attitudes in Britain.

Early episodes were recorded live without editing, requiring a high standard of performance. This theatrical style of production has influenced the character of the programme, resulting in a reliance on good writing and ensemble performance. For many years *Coronation Street* was produced on a studio set and shot on multi-camera with few exterior film inserts. The advent of the social realism soaps and introduction of light-weight video cameras have resulted in a dramatic increase in the number of exterior scenes. The *Street* itself has been expanded to incorporate such filming with a specially constructed exterior set although interior filming is still multi-camera.

The *Street,* in common with other soaps, has always been noted for its independent and assertive women characters, such as Ena Sharples, Elsie Tanner, Annie Walker, and more recently Bet Lynch and Rita Fairclough. Even a more downtrodden character such as Hilda Ogden produced a huge amount of affection from the programme's audience. In contrast the men often seem weak by comparison. The viewer of *Coronation Street* is often encouraged to make a moral judgement on the behaviour of a particular character and it is generally the stronger women characters who set the tone. Tony Warren summed up the programme as "a fascinating freemasonry, a volume of unwritten rules.... *Coronation Street* sets out to explore these values and in doing so, to entertain."

Only two characters have remained in the programme since its launch—Ken Barlow played by William Roache and Emily Bishop, née Nugent, played by Eileen Derbyshire. However, the programme has been the ground for many actors who have gone on to greater fame such as Davy Jones (later of the Monkees), Joanna Lumley and Ben Kingsley. The *Street* has also nurtured many novice writers such as Jack Rosenthal and Jimmy McGovern, while the award-winning, feature-film director Michael Apted has also been part of the production team.

The deaths and departures in recent years of several well-established characters combined with the introduction of *EastEnders*, *Brookside* and the Australian soaps has resulted in a shift towards the lives of its younger characters.

The success of *Coronation Street* has resulted in a series of merchandising and promotional ventures by Granada, many of them focused around the soap's local pub and centre of gossip, the Rover's Return. By providing a secure economic base through high ratings, *Coronation Street* has enabled Granada to build a wide range of programmes. Because of the long-standing cultural ties and familiarity with the world it evokes, *Coronation Street* has also built up a sizable audience in Australia, Canada and New Zealand.

In 1989 the *Street* went from two to three episodes a week, and in the autumn of 1996 this will be increased to four. Granada is confident that a more pressurised production line will not affect *Coronation Street's* reputation for quality writing. Instead, it is planned to develop secondary characters more strongly. *Coronation Street* recently celebrated its 35th anniversary and tops the ratings with an average audience of 16 million. Its longevity and success are testament to the firm place it holds in the hearts of the British public.

—Judith Jones

CAST

Ena Sharples	Violet Carson
Elsie Tanner	Patricia Phoenix
Annie Walker	Doris Speed
Tracy Barlow	Dawn Acton
Florrie Lindley	Betty Alberge
Hilda Ogden	Jean Alexander
Bill Webster	Peter Armitage
Derek Wilton	Peter Baldwin
Janet Reid/Barlow	Judith Barker
Mavis Riley/Wilton	Thelma Barlow
Alec Gilroy	Roy Barraclough
Alma Sedgwick/Baldwin	Amanda Barrie
Harry Hewitt	Ivan Beavis
Denise Osbourne	Denise Black
Tricia Armstrong	Tracy Brabin
Maud Grimes	Elizabeth Bradley
Mike Baldwin	Johnny Briggs
Alan Howard	Alan Browning
Minnie Caldwell	Margot Bryant
Liz McDonald	Beverly Callard
Martha Longhurst	Lynne Carol
Andy McDonald	Nicholas Cochrane
Rosie Webster	Emma Collinge
Linda Cheveski	Anne Cunningham
Vera Duckworth	Elizabeth Dawn
Emily Nugent/Bishop	Eileen Derbyshire
Debbie Webster	Sue Devaney
Betty Turpin/Williams	Betty Driver
Ida Barlow	Noel Dyson
Alan Bradley	Mark Eden
Judy Mallet	Gaynor Faye
Angela	Diane Fletcher
Jamie Armstrong	Joseph Gilgun
Bet Lynch/Gilroy	Julie Goodyear
Irma Ogden/Barlow	Sandra Gough
Steve McDonald	Simon Gregson
Fiona Middleton	Angela Griffin
Josie Clarke	Ellie Haddington
Ernest Bishop	Stephen Hancock
Christine Hardman	Christine Hargreaves
Daniel Osbourne	Lewis Harney
May Hardman	Joan Heath
Norris	Malcolm Hebden
Sean Skinner	Terence Hillyer
Renee Bradshaw/Roberts	Madge Hindle
Don Brennan	Geoffrey Hinsliff
Tina Fowler	Michelle Holmes
Albert Tatlock	Jack Howarth
Eddie Yates	Geoffrey Hughes
Nicky Platt/Tisley	Warren Jackson
Eunice Nuttall/Gee	Meg Johnson
Tricia Hopkins	Kathy Jones
Curly Watts	Kevin Kennedy
Concepta Hewitt	Doreen Keogh
Sarah-Louise Platt	Lynsay King
Deirdre Hunt/Barlow/Rachid	Anne Kirkbridge
Rita Littlewood/Fairclough/Sullivan	Barbara Knox
Raquel Wolstenhulme/Watts	Sarah Lancashire
Jim McDonald	Charles Lawson
Kevin Webster	Michael Le Vell
Jack Walker	Arthur Leslie
Nick Wilding	Mark Lindley
Leonard Swindley	Arthur Lowe
Dennis Tanner	Philip Lowrie
Elaine Perkins	Joanna Lumley
Jenny Bradley	Sally Ann Matthews
Gary Mallet	Ian Mercer
Des Barnes	Philip Middlemiss
Sophie Webster	Ashleigh Middleton
Billy Williams	Frank Mills (II)
Reg Holdsworth	Ken Morley
Alf Roberts	Bryan Mosley
Lucille Hewitt	Jennifer Moss
Suzie Birchall	Cheryl Murray
Roy Cropper	David Neilson
Vicky McDonald	Chloe Newsome

Audrey Potter/Roberts	Sue Nicholls
David Platt	Thomas Ormson
Ester Hayes	Daphne Oxenford
Frank Barlow	Frank Pemberton
Ivy Tilsley/Brennan	Lynne Perrie
Terry Duckworth	Nigel Pivaro
Tanya Pooley	Eve Pope
Brian Tilsley	Chris Quentin
Ken Barlow	William Roache
David Barlow	Alan Rothwell
Alison Dunkley	Maggie Saunders
Fred Eliott	John Savident
Maxine Heavey	Tracy Shaw
Anne Malone	Eve Steele
Phyliss Pearce	Jill Summers
Jack Duckworth	William Tarmey
Percy Sugden	Bill Waddington
Ivan Cheveski	Ernst Walder
Tony Horrocks	Lee Warburton
Sally Webster	Sally Whittaker
Martin Platt	Sean Wilson
Gail Potter/ Tilsley/ Platt	Helen Worth
Stan Ogden	Bernard Youens
Brian Dunkley	Benny Young

PRODUCERS Stuart Latham, Derek Granger, Tim Aspinall, Harry Kershaw, Peter Eckersley, Jack Rosenthal, Michael Cox, Richard Doubleday, John Finch, June Howson, Leslie Duxbury, Brian Armstrong, Eric Prytherch, Susi Hush, Bill Podmore, Pauline Shaw, Mervyn Watson, John G. Temple, Carolyn Reynolds, H.V. Kershaw, Richard Everitt, David Liddiment

PROGRAMMING HISTORY

• Granada Television

1960–

FURTHER READING

Dyer, Richard, with others. *Coronation Street.* London: British Film Institute, 1981.

Geraghty, Christine. *Women and Soap Opera: A Study of Prime-Time Soaps.* Oxford: Basil Blackwell, 1991.

Kilborn, Richard. *Television Soaps.* London: Batsford, 1992.

Nown, Graham, editor. *Coronation Street: 25 Years (1960–1985).* London: Ward Lock, in association with Granada Television, 1985.

See also Soap Opera

COSBY, BILL

U.S. Comedian/Actor

Bill Cosby is a successful comedian, product representative, television producer, story teller, author, and film and television actor. His work in the media has been recognized by his peers and critics, and acclaimed by audiences.

Cosby began his career as a stand-up comedian and in that arena developed his trademark of using raceless humor to capture audience appeal. His "humor for everyone" cast him less as a jokester than as a story teller, commenting on the experiences of life from a personal point of view. Immensely popular on the nightclub circuit, Cosby translated his act to phonograph recordings and won five Grammys and seven gold records for his comedy albums.

His first starring role on television, however, came not in comedy, but in the 1960s action-adventure series, *I Spy* (1965–68). Producer Sheldon Leonard fought network hesitance to cast him as co-star for Robert Culp, making Cosby one of the first African-American players to appear in a continuing dramatic role on U.S. television. More than the faithful sidekick to the star, Cosby's role developed into an equal partner winning him three Emmy awards. His portrayal in this series introduced viewers to an inoffensive African-American feature character who seldom addressed his blackness or another character's whiteness.

When Cosby began to produce his own comedy series, however, this disassociation with black culture ended. The

Bill Cosby

programs were noted not only for their wit, but for introducing a side of African-American life never portrayed on the small screen. Cosby's comedies share several common characteristics. Each has been a trend setter, has included characters surrounded by family and friends, and has specialized in plots with universal themes and multidimensional characters.

As Chet Kincaid in *The Bill Cosby Show* (1969-71) Cosby defied the typical image of the militant black man depicted on 1960s television by exuding his blackness in more subtle, nonverbal ways. Starting with the opening music by Quincy Jones, the program created a black ambience unique to the African-American experience. The character Kincaid wore dashikis, listened to black music, and had pictures of Martin Luther King and H. Rap Brown and prints by black artist Charles White hanging on the walls of his home. He worked with less privileged children and ordered "soul" food in black restaurants. Kincaid was pictured as a colleague, friend, teacher, and member of a close supportive family unit. Audiences experienced his failures and successes in coping with life's everyday occurrences.

Fat Albert and the Cosby Kids (1972–77) was the first cartoon show to include value-laden messages instead of the slapstick humor used in most cartoons to that time. Plots featured Fat Albert and the Kids playing, going to school, and sharing experiences. After the success of *Fat Albert* on CBS, ABC and NBC also added children's shows to the Saturday morning schedule that presented specific value oriented material.

Cosby's most notable success in series television, *The Cosby Show* (1984–92), departed from familiar sitcom formulas filled with disrespectful children and generational conflict; it presented instead a two-parent black family in which both partners worked as professionals. In the Huxtable household, viewers were exposed to the existence and culture of historically black colleges and universities. Prints by black artist Varnette Honeywood decorated the walls. The music of African-American jazz artists was woven into the background or featured for discussion. Events in black history and signs calling for an end to apartheid became elements of plots. Just as Chet Kincaid and the Cosby Kids portray their frailties and personality traits, the Huxtables followed this Cosby pattern by depicting imperfect but likable people in realistic situations.

Even when he turned to the police genre with *The Cosby Mysteries* (1994–95), Cosby continued his exploration and presentation of his fundamental concerns. His use of nonverbal symbols (e.g. pictures, magazines, a fraternity paddle) attached his character, Guy Hanks, a retired criminologist (who recently won the lottery), to African-American culture.

To ensure that universal themes were depicted in his series, Cosby hired professionals to serve as consultants to review scripts. *A Different World* (1987–93) was the spinoff series from *The Cosby Show* that portrayed life on the fictional Hillman College campus. It floundered during its first year on the air, and Cosby hired director and choreographer Debbie Allen to lend her expertise to focus and give direction to writers and actors. The ratings improved significantly and *A Different World* became a top 20 program for the 1991 season.

Commercials began to interest Cosby in the mid-1970s and he has become one of the most respected and believable product spokespersons on television. He has represented Coca-Cola, Jello, Ford Motor Company, Texas Instruments, and Del Monte Foods. The Marketing Evaluation TVQ index, the television industry's annual nationwide survey of a performer's popularity with viewers, as well as the Video Storyboard Tests that rank the most persuasive entertainers in television commercials, rated Cosby the number one entertainer for five consecutive years during the 1980s.

In 1974, he teamed with Sidney Poitier in the film *Uptown Saturday Night.* This duo was so popular with audiences that two sequels followed, *Let's Do It Again* (1975) and *A Piece of the Action* (1977). Cosby also starred in a number of other movies, but his Everyman character, so successful on the small screen, did not translate into box office revenues in theatrical release.

As a creative artist, Cosby's forte is the half-hour comedy. In this form his application and exploration of universal themes and multidimensional characters create situations common to audiences of all ages and races. He counters the accepted practice of portraying African Americans as sterile reproductions of whites, as trapped in criminality, or as persons immersed in abject poverty performing odd jobs for survival. Instead, he creates black characters who are accepted or rejected because they depict real people rather than "types." These characters emanate from his own experience, not through reading the pages of 18th-century literature or viewing old tapes of *Amos 'n' Andy. The Bill Cosby Show* presented a more realistic image of the black male. *Fat Albert* significantly altered Saturday morning network offerings. And with *The Cosby Show,* a standard was set with which all television portrayals of the black family and African-American culture will be compared. Cosby's personal style is stamped on all his products, and his creative technique and signature are reflected in each book he writes or series he produces.

—Bishetta D. Merrit

BILL COSBY. Born in Germantown, Pennsylvania, U.S.A., 12 July 1937. Served in U.S. Navy, 1956–60. Attended Temple University; University of Massachusetts, M.A. 1972, Ed.D. 1977. Married: Camille Hanks, 1965; children: Erika Ranee, Erinn Chalene, Ennis William, Ensa Camille, and Evin Harrah. Worked as stand-up comedian through college; appeared on *Tonight Show,* 1965; starred in TV's *I Spy,* 1965–68; guest appearances on shows, including *The Electric Company,* 1972; host and voices, *Fat Albert and the Cosby Kids,* 1972–79; star and producer, various television programs, since 1984. Recipient: four Emmy Awards; eight Grammy Awards for comedy recordings.

TELEVISION SERIES

1964–65	*That Was the Week That Was*
1965–68	*I Spy*
1969–71	*The Bill Cosby Show*
1971–76	*The Electric Company*
1972–73	*The New Bill Cosby Show*
1972–77	*Fat Albert and the Cosby Kids*
1976	*Cos*
1981	*The New Fat Albert Show*
1984–92	*The Cosby Show*
1987–93	*A Different World* (executive producer)
1992–93	*You Bet Your Life*
1992–93	*Here and Now* (executive producer)
1994–95	*The Cosby Mysteries*
1996	*Cosby*

MADE-FOR-TELEVISION MOVIES

1971	*To all My Friends On Shore*
1978	*Top Secret*
1994	*I Spy Returns*

TELEVISION SPECIALS

1968	*The Bill Cosby Special*
1969	*The Second Bill Cosby Special*
1970	*The Third Bill Cosby Special*
1971	*The Bill Cosby Special, Or?*
1972	*Dick Van Dyke Meets Bill Cosby*
1975	*Cos: The Bill Cosby Comedy Special*
1977	*The Fat Albert Christmas Special*
1977	*The Fat Albert Halloween Special*
1984	*Johnny Carson Presents The Tonight Show Comedians*
1986	*Funny*

FILMS

Hickey and Boggs, 1972; *Man and Boy*, 1972; *Uptown Saturday Night*, 1974; *Let's Do It Again*, 1975; *Mother, Jugs and Speed*, 1976; *A Piece of the Action*, 1977; *California Suite*, 1978; *The Devil and Max Devlin*, 1981; *Bill Cosby, Himself*, 1982; *Leonard: Part VI*, 1987; *Ghost Dad*, 1990; *The Meteor Man*, 1993.

RECORDINGS

Bill Cosby is a Very Funny Fellow... Right!; *I Started Out as a Child*; *Why is There Air?*; *Wonderfulness*; *Revenge*; *To Russell My Brother With Whom I Slept*; *Bill Cosby is Not Himself These Days*; *Rat Own Rat Own Rat Own*; *My Father Confused Me, What Must I Do? What Must I Do?*; *Disco Bill*; *Bill's Best Friend*; *Cosby and the Kids*; *It's True It's True*; *Bill Cosby – Himself*; *200 MPH*; *Silverthroat*; *Hooray for the Salvation Army Band*; *8:15 12:15*; *For Adults Only*; *Bill Cosby Talks to Kids about Drugs*; *Inside the Mind of Bill Cosby*.

PUBLICATIONS

The Wit and Wisdom of Fat Albert. New York: Windmill Books, 1973.

Bill Cosby's Personal Guide to Tennis Power. New York: Random House, 1975.

Fatherhood. Garden City, New York: Doubleday, 1986.

Time Flies. New York: Doubleday, 1988.

Love and Marriage. New York: Doubleday, 1989.

"Someone at the Top Has to Say: 'Enough of this'" (interview). *Newsweek* (New York), 6 December 1993.

FURTHER READING

Adams, Barbara Johnston. *The Picture Life of Bill Cosby*. New York: F. Watts, 1986.

Adler, Bill. *The Cosby Wit: His Life and Humor*. New York: Carroll and Graf, 1986.

Behrens, Steve. "Billion Dollar Bill." *Channels of Communication* (New York), January-February 1986.

Britt-Gibson, Donna. "Cover Story: The Cos, Family Man for the 80s." *USA Today* (New York), 23 December 1986.

Cohen, Joel H. *Cool Cos: The Story of Bill Cosby*. New York: Scholastic, 1969.

Darrach, Brad. "Cosby!" *Life* (New York), June 1985.

Fuller, Linda K. *The Cosby Show: Audiences, Impact, and Implications*. Westport, Connecticut: Greenwood, 1992.

Goodgame, Dan. "'I Do Believe In Control'; Cosby Is a Man Who Gets Laughs and Results—By Doing Things His Way." *Time* (New York), 28 September 1987.

Griffin, Cynthia, and George Hill. "Bill Cosby: In Our Living Rooms for 20 Years." *Ebony Images: Black Americans and Television*. Los Angeles, California: Daystar Publications, 1986.

Jhally, Sut, and Justin Lewis. *Enlightened Racism: The Cosby Show, Audiences, and the Myth of the American Dream*. Boulder, Colorado: Westview, 1992.

Klein, Todd. "Bill Cosby: Prime Time's Favorite Father." *Saturday Evening Post* (Indianapolis, Indiana), April 1986.

Lane, Randall. "Bill Cosby, Capitalist." *Forbes* (Chicago), 28 September 1992.

McClellan, Steve. "Wussler, Cosby Eye NBC Bid." *Broadcasting and Cable* (Washington, D.C.), 19 July 1993.

Merritt, Bishetta D. "Bill Cosby: TV Auteur?" *Journal of Popular Culture* (Bowling Green, Ohio), Spring 1991.

Smith, Ronald L. *Cosby*. New York: St. Martin's, 1986.

See also *Cosby Show*; Racism, Ethnicity, and Television

THE COSBY SHOW

U.S. Situation Comedy

The Cosby Show, one of the biggest surprise hits in American television history, dominated Thursday evenings from 1984 to 1992. Focusing on the everyday adventures of an upper-middle-class black family, the series revived a television genre (situation comedy), saved a beleaguered network (NBC), and sparked controversy about race and class in America.

The Cosby Show premiered on 20 September 1984 and shot to the top of the ratings almost immediately. The series finished third in the ratings its first season (1984-85), and first for the next four seasons. The Cosby Show fell from the very top of the ratings only after its sixth season (1989-90), when it finished second behind another family-oriented situation comedy, Roseanne.

But The Cosby Show was almost not to be. NBC recruited Marcy Carsey and Tom Werner to develop the sitcom after a Bill Cosby monologue about child rearing on NBC's Tonight show impressed the network's entertainment chief, Brandon Tartikoff. However, despite Cosby's widespread popularity— he had registered one of the highest audience appeal ratings in history as a commercial pitchman—programmers initially viewed his star potential with suspicion. His television career history was mixed. After co-starring in the hit series I Spy (1965-68), Cosby appeared in a string of ratings failures: The Bill Cosby Show (1969), The New Bill Cosby Show (1972), and Cos (1976). While NBC fretted over questions concerning Cosby's viability as a television star and situation comedy's status as a dying genre, Carsey and Werner presented the idea to ABC. But that network was not interested. At the last minute, just in time for inclusion in the fall schedule, NBC gave a firm commitment to Carsey and Werner to produce a pilot and five episodes for the sitcom. The extraordinary success of the show quickly propelled also-ran NBC into first-place in the primetime ratings.

Set and taped before a studio audience in Brooklyn, New York, The Cosby Show revolved around the day-to-day situations faced by Cliff (Bill Cosby) and Clair Huxtable (Phylicia Ayers-Allen, later Phylicia Rashad) and their five children. This family was unlike other black families previously seen on television in that it was solidly upper-middle-class—the Huxtables lived in a fashionable Flatbush brownstone, the father was a respected gynecologist, and the mother a successful attorney. Theo (Malcolm Jamal-Warner), the only son, was something of an underachiever who enjoyed a special relationship with his father. The oldest daughter, Sondra (Sabrina LeBeauf), was a college student at prestigious Princeton University. The next daughter in age, Denise (Lisa Bonet), tested her parents' patience with rather eccentric, new-age preoccupations. She left the series after the third season to attend the fictitious, historically black Hillman College; her experiences there became the basis of a spin-off, A Different World (1987–93). The two

younger daughters, Rudy (Keisha Knight Pulliam) and Vanessa (Tempestt Bledsoe), were cute preteens who served admirably as foils to Cosby's hilarious child-rearing routines. Secure in a cocoon of loving parents and affluence, the Huxtable kids steered clear of trouble as they grew up over the series' eight-year run. Indeed, TV Guide compared the Huxtable's lifestyle to that of other black families in America and described the family as the most "atypical black family in television history."

For many observers, The Cosby Show was unique in other ways as well. For example, unlike many situation comedies, the program avoided one-liners, buffoonery and other standard tactics designed to win laughs. Instead, series writers remained true to Cosby's vision of finding humor in realistic family situations, in the minutiae of human behavior. Thus episodes generally shunned typical sitcom formulas by featuring, instead, a rather loose story structure and unpredictable pacing. Moreover, the soundtrack was sweetened with jazz, and the Huxtable home prominently featured contemporary African American art. Several observers described the result as "classy."

In many respects, The Cosby Show and its "classy" aura were designed to address a long history of black negative portrayals on television. Indeed, Alvin Poussaint, a prominent black psychiatrist, was hired by producers as a consultant to help "recode blackness" in the minds of audience members. In contrast to the families in other popular black situation comedies—for example, those in Sanford and Son (1972–77), Good Times (1974–79), and The Jeffersons (1975–85)—the Huxtables were given a particular mix of qualities that its creators thought would challenge common black stereotypes. These qualities included: a strong father figure; a strong nuclear family; parents who were professionals; affluence and fiscal responsibility; a strong emphasis on education; a multigenerational family; multiracial friends; and low-key racial pride.

This project, of course, was not without its critics. Some observers described the show as a 1980s version of Father Knows Best, the Huxtables as a white family in blackface. Moreover, as the show's debut coincided with the President Reagan's landslide reelection, and as many of the Huxtables' "qualities" seemed to echo key Republican themes, critics labeled the show's politics as "reformist conservatism." The Huxtables' affluence, they argued, worked to obscure persistent inequalities in America—especially those faced by blacks and other minority groups—and validate the myth of the American Dream. One audience study suggests that the show "strikes a deal" with white viewers, that it absolves them of responsibility for racial inequality in the United States in exchange for inviting the Huxtables into their living room. Meanwhile, the same study found that black viewers tend to embrace the show for its positive portrayals of blackness, but express misgivings about the Huxtables' failure to regularly interact with less affluent blacks.

The Cosby Show

On an April evening in 1992—when America was being saturated with images of fires, and racial and economic turmoil from Los Angeles—many viewers opted to tune into the farewell episode of *The Cosby Show*. In Los Angeles, at least, this viewing choice was almost not an option. KNBC-TV's news coverage of the civil unrest seemed certain to preempt the show, much as the news coverage of other networks' affiliates would preempt their regular prime-time programming that evening. But as Los Angeles Mayor Tom Bradley worked to restore order to a war-torn Los Angeles, he offered, perhaps, the greatest testament to the social significance of the series: he successfully lobbied KNBC-TV to broadcast the final episode as originally scheduled.

—Darnell M. Hunt

CAST

Dr. Heathcliff (Cliff) Huxtable	Bill Cosby
Clair Huxtable	Phylicia Rashad
Sondra Huxtable Tibideaux	Sabrina Le Beauf
Denise Huxtable Kendall	Lisa Bonet
Theodore Huxtable	Malcolm-Jamal Warner
Vanessa Huxtable	Tempestt Bledsoe
Rudy Huxtable	Keshia Knight Pulliam
Anna Huxtable	Clarice Taylor
Russel Huxtable	Earl Hyman
Peter Chiara (1985–89)	Peter Costa
Elvin Tibideaux (1986–92)	Geoffrey Owens
Kenny ("Bud") (1986–92)	Deon Richmond
Cockroach (1986-87)	Carl Anthony Payne II
Denny (1987–91)	Troy Winbush
Lt. Martin Kendall (1989–92)	Joseph C. Phillips
Olivia Kendall (1989–92)	Raven-Symone
Pam Tucker (1990–92)	Erika Alexander
Dabnis Brickey (1991–92)	William Thomas, Jr.

PRODUCERS   Marcy Carsey, Tom Werner, Caryn Sneider, Bill Cosby

PROGRAMMING HISTORY   200 Episodes

• NBC

September 1984–June 1992	Thursday 8:00-8:30
July 1992–September 1992	Thursday 8:30-9:00

FURTHER READING

Beller, Miles. "*The Cosby Show*." *The Hollywood Reporter* (Los Angeles), 29 September 1986.

Bogle, Donald. *Blacks in American Films and Television: An Encyclopedia*. New York: Fireside, 1988.

Brown, Judy. "Leave it to Bill: The Huxtables, the Cleavers of the '80s." *L.A. Weekly* (Los Angeles), 27 December-2 January 1985.

Cantor, Muriel. "The American Family on Television: From Molly Goldberg to Bill Cosby." *Journal of Comparative Family Studies*, Summer 1991.

Carson, Tom. "Cosby Knows Best." *Village Voice* (New York), 23 October 1984.

Carter, Richard G. "TV's Black Comfort Zone for Whites." *Television Quarterly* (New York), Fall 1988.

Downing, John D. H. "*The Cosby Show* and American Racial Discourse." In, Smitherman-Donaldson, Geneva, and Teun A. van Dijk, editors. *Discourse and Discrimination*. Detroit: Wayne State University Press, 1988.

Frazer, June M., and Timothy C. Frazer. "*Father Knows Best* and *The Cosby Show*: Nostalgia and the Sitcom Tradition." *Journal of Popular Culture* (Bowling Green, Ohio), Winter 1993.

Fuller, Linda K. *The Cosby Show: Audiences, Impact, and Implications*. Westport, Connecticut: Greenwood, 1992.

Gelman, Morris. "Prof Says *Cosby* a Symptom of TV's Impossible Ideals." *Daily Variety* (Los Angeles), 9 June 1987.

Gendel, Morgan. "Cosby and Co.: What Makes the Show a Hit." *Los Angeles Times*, 26 September 1985.

Gray, Herman. "Response to Justin Lewis and Sut Jhally." *American Quarterly* (Philadelphia, Pennsylvania), March 1994.

———. "Television, Black Americans, and the American Dream." *Critical Studies in Mass Communication* (Annandale, Virginia), December 1989.

———. *Watching Race: Television and the Struggle for "Blackness."* Minneapolis, Minnesota: University of Minnesota Press, 1995.

Hill, Doug. "Viacom Pitchmen Got a Record $500 Million for *Cosby* Reruns. Now the Buyers Await the Results of their Expensive Gamble." *TV Guide* (Radnor, Pennsylvania), 7 May 1988.

Inniss, Leslie B. "*The Cosby Show*: The View from the Black Middle Class." *Journal of Black Studies* (Newbury Park, California), July 1995.

Jhally, Sut, and Justin Lewis. *Enlightened Racism: The Cosby Show, Audiences, and the Myth of the American Dream*. Boulder, Colorado: Westview, 1992.

Johnson, Robert B. "TV's Top Mom and Dad." Ebony (Chicago), February 1986.

Kalu, Anthonia C. "Bill Cosby, Blues and the Reconstruction of African-American Literary Theory." *The Literary Griot: International Journal of Black Oral and Literary Studies* (Wayne, New Jersey), Spring-Fall 1992.

Lyons, Douglas C. "Blacks and 50 Years of TV: Ten Memorable Moments." *Ebony* (Chicago), September 1989.

McNeil, Alex. *Total Television*. New York: Penguin, 1991.

Merritt, Bishetta D. "Bill Cosby: TV Auteur." *Journal of Popular Culture* (Bowling Green, Ohio), Spring 1991.

Miller, Jack. "*Cosby* a Big Hit in Canada." *Hollywood Reporter* (Los Angeles), 18 March 1986.

Nelson, Carlos. "White Racism and *The Cosby Show*: A Critique." *The Black Scholar* (Oakland, California), Spring 1995.

Palmer, Gareth. "*The Cosby Show*—An Ideologically Based Analysis." *Critical Survey* (Oxford), 1994.

Payne, Monica A. "The 'Ideal' Black Family? A Caribbean View of *The Cosby Show.*" *Journal of Black Studies* (Newbury Park, California), December 1994.

Real, Michael R. *Super Media: A Cultural Studies Approach.* London: Sage, 1989.

See also Cosby, Bill; Comedy, Domestic Settings; Racism, Ethnicity, and Television

COST-PER-THOUSAND AND COST-PER-POINT

Media Efficiency Measurement Ratios

Cost-Per-Thousand (CPM) and Cost-Per-Point (CPP) are two methods of evaluating media efficiency. CPM is a ratio based on how much it costs to reach a thousand people. CPP is a ratio based on how much it costs to buy one rating point, or 1% of the population in an area being evaluated.

Cost-per-thousand is calculated by using the following formula:

$$CPM = \frac{\text{Cost of advertising schedule purchased}}{\text{Gross Impressions} \quad 1,000}$$

Cost-per-point is calculated by using the following formula:

$$CPP = \frac{\text{Cost of advertising schedule purchased}}{\text{Gross Rating Points (GRPs or "grips")}}$$

Some explanations: The area being evaluated might be a country such as the United States or a television market such as New York. The major networks cover virtually all of the United States, and their audiences are measured by A.C. Nielsen, the company that provides television networks, television stations, and advertisers with the audience measurement, or rating, information.

Television markets typically cover an area inside a circle with a radius of about seventy-five miles from television stations' transmitter sites plus those homes reached by cable television systems that carry local TV station signals. Such an area is referred to as a Designated Marketing Area, or DMA, by A.C. Nielsen. DMAs can encompass several counties and many cities, and are usually designated by the largest city in the area. Hence, the New York market includes Newark in New Jersey, Long Island, White Plains in New York, and Stamford in Connecticut.

The average television network program achieves about an 11.0 rating, which means it reaches 11% of the 94,000,00 homes in America with television sets, or approximately 10,300,000 homes. If an advertiser were to buy ten commercials each with a rating of 11.0 on a network (ABC, for example), then it would make 10 times 10,300,000, or 103,000,000, Gross Impressions. If ABC charged an average of $150,000 per 30-second commercial (the typical television commercial length), the total cost of a ten-commercial

schedule would be $1,500,000. The CPM of the schedule would be:

$$CPM = \frac{\$1,500,000}{103,000 \text{ (103,000,000 Gross Impressions} \div 1,000)}$$

CPM = $14.56 (the cost of making 1,000 impressions)

Advertisers and their advertising agencies and media buying services evaluate television networks based on CPM because it is a good comparative measure of media efficiency across several media. Thus, the efficiency of reaching 1,000 viewers with the above theoretical schedule on ABC could be compared, for example, with how much it cost to reach 1,000 readers with an ad in *Cosmopolitan*.

There are two primary buying methods, or markets, in which advertising time is purchased on network television. These are referred to as the upfront market and the scatter market. The upfront buying market is usually active in the spring of each year. Advertisers place orders for commercials that will appear in television programs run during the television season beginning in the fall of each year. By buying in advance and committing for a full network season (which runs until the second week in April), advertisers are given lower prices than they would pay in the later, scatter, market. The scatter market is active at a period much closer to the actual time the advertising is to appear. Advertisers may purchase time in September, for example, in order for their ads to run during a fourth-quarter schedule, from October through December.

The networks give advertisers CPM guarantees for buying in the upfront market. If a network does not deliver the guaranteed ratings, it will run free commercials, called makegoods, to make up the rating shortfall.

In the past, CPMs for television networks have been based on homes, or households (HHs). The use of newer technologies such as VCRs and cable television networks, however, has increasingly fragmented the television audience. Recognizing this change, advertisers tended to evaluate and compare network schedules based on persons reached rather than on HHs. Even more specifically, they have based their analysis and spending on numbers of persons within demographic groups. The two most desirable demographics for advertisers are women 18 to 49 and adults 25 to 54.

Advertisers evaluate *local* television stations based on Cost-Per-Point (CPP), because the method provides a good comparative measure of media efficiency within a broadcast medium. Rating points are also used by advertising agency media departments as a planning tool to make very rough estimates of how many times an average viewer might be reached by a particular advertisement placed within the television schedule. For example, a media plan might call for 300 rating points to be purchased in a television market with the hope that 100% of the viewers in the market might see a commercial three times (a frequency of three). Thus, using rating points and CPP serves both an evaluative function and a planning function.

—Charles Warner

FURTHER READING

Warner, C., and J. Buchman. *Broadcast and Cable Selling.* Belmont, California: Wadsworth, 1993.

Webster, James G., and Lawrence W. Lichty. *Ratings Analysis: Theory and Practice.* Hillsdale, New Jersey: L. Erlbaum, 1991.

See also Ratings; Share; Market

COUNTRY MUSIC TELEVISION

U.S. Cable Network

Country Music Television (CMT), a twenty-four-hour, advertiser-supported music video channel that airs videos exclusively on basic cable systems, has emerged in recent years as one of the fastest growing cable channels in the United States. In a symbiotic relationship with record companies and radio stations, CMT has become the most influential aspect in the introduction and popularity of new artists in the country music entertainment field. CMT is also credited with creating the "young country" format which many radio stations have adopted, and with shaping other new trends in the country music genre.

The channel went on the air in March 1983 with about 20 videos and a very small audience. Many observers in the country music industry did not take the channel seriously because they were too concerned about the image already created by Music Television (MTV), an image decidedly at odds with that created by the country music establishment in Nashville. After several years of struggle, CMT was acquired in 1991 by Gaylord Communications and Group W Satellite Communications. The 1990s have proved to be both popular and profitable for the channel, which, according to the A.C. Nielsen ratings service, now reaches almost 30% of all U.S. households and 42% of all cable households, numbers that translate into 25 million television homes. In 1992 CMT was launched in Europe and is now seen in more than eight million homes there. CMT went on the air in the Asia-Pacific region in 1994 and in Latin America in 1995.

The popularity of country music was not truly realized until the use of Soundscan, a computerized tabulation technique. This system, which reads a bar-code and counts the actual number of record, cassette, and compact disk sales, is used at discount stores such as Wal-Mart and K-Mart, where the audience for country music is more likely to make purchases than in music stores. A.C. Nielsen reports that CMT is the number one choice for cable programming among women aged 18 to 49. The popularity of country music videos may be attributed to a more sensitive music video genre than its rock music counterparts, and therefore more appealing to female audiences. This sensitivity is created and reinforced through production codes such as camera angles, lighting, and shot sequencing.

CMT has also become a major influence in the success of country music artists and their records. *The Gavin Reports*, a music industry publication, noted that much of the popularity of country music artists is attributed to CMT and the impact it has had on the marketing of country music. Another indication of this effect is evidenced through the tracking of CMT's "pick hits," videos selected each week to receive additional play. In 1993, 68% of the recordings supported by these "pick hit" videos reached the "top ten" charts of *Radio and Records*, a major music industry trade publication.

—Margaret Miller Butcher

A COUNTRY PRACTICE

Australian Drama Series

A *Country Practice*, one of Australia's longest-running and most successful drama series, aired on Australian Television Network (Channel 7) in Sydney and networked stations across Australia from 1981 to 1994. Produced by Sydney-based company JNP, the series consistently drew high ratings in Australia and also screened on the ITV network in Britain, on West German cable television, on the European satellite system Sky TV, as well as in the United States, Italy, Sweden, New Zealand, Ireland, Zimbabwe, Zambia, Malta and Hong Kong. In the mid-1980s, executive producer, James Davern estimated an audience worldwide of between five and six million people.

A Country Practice
Photo courtesy of JNP Films Pty. Ltd.

In their comprehensive book-length treatment of the series, John Tulloch and Albert Moran, identify *A Country Practice* as "quality soap." While produced on a modest budget, it was noted for the high priority given to creative script development and its sometimes provocative treatment of topical social issues. It was particularly important in the context of Australian television for staking a position somewhere between the high-cultural production values of the government-funded Australian Broadcasting Corporation and the often narrow commercialism of Australian drama screened on the privately owned networks.

Set in Wandin Valley, a fictional location in rural New South Wales, the series focused on a small medical practice, a site which provides a window into the life of the wider community. Key founding characters were Dr. Terence Elliott (Shane Porteous), his junior partner Dr. Simon Bowen (Grant Dodwell), the doctors' receptionist Shirley Dean (Lorraie Desmond), and her daughter Vicky (Penny Cook), a local vet. The mainstay of narrative development was romance, the most notable instance being the evolving relationship of Simon and Vicky which culminated, at the high point of the series' ratings, in their wedding in 1983. Against this background and the general peace of the rural community, disruptive and confronting episodes often dealt with illnesses or deaths encountered in the medical practice, but also took up issues such as youth unemployment, the problems of aging, or the position of Aboriginal people in Australian society.

Much of the interest of the series was generated by this ongoing tension between romanticism and realism. On the one hand, it was a conscious policy, as producer James Davern put it, "to reinforce the positive values of human relationships." The series rarely featured violence, frankly presenting itself as an escape from the harsher realities of news and current affairs, and implicitly distancing itself both from the dominant strain in imported U.S.-produced drama and from other long-running Australian series such as *Prisoner* and *Homicide*. The rural setting provided ample opportunity for mid-range shots of outdoor scenes as well as the inclusion of animals. It also established the series within the tradition which has been most successful in giving Australian audiovisual products international exposure, a tradition which includes feature films such as *Picnic at Hanging Rock*, *The Man from Snowy River*, and *Crocodile Dundee*. More recently, the international appeal of Australian settings as a site of innocence and harmonious community has been spectacularly demonstrated by the success of *Neighbours* in the United Kingdom.

On the other hand, the series became widely recognised for its topicality on medical and social issues and responded closely to the immediate concerns of its largely urban audience. Material for episodes was often directly inspired by news or current affairs stories or by suggestions from viewers and organisations such as the Australian Medical Association. Particularly in the medical area, *A Country Practice* was overtly pedagogical, providing basic information on problems such as heart failure, leukemia, epilepsy, alcoholism, and leprosy. Working from the relative safety of this base of technical expertise, it also took positions on more controversial issues, suggesting for example, in one notable episode, that unemployment cannot be blamed on a lack of motivation of the unemployed themselves. The series employed naturalistic dialogue, sets, and action, and strove to avoid what is often identified in Australia as "Hollywood" sentimentality.

A Country Practice ceased production in 1993, largely as a result of staff losses. In the history of Australian television, it remains a landmark for its success in overseas markets and for setting a standard in quality low-budget production.

—Mark Gibson

CAST

Ben Green	Nick Bufalo
Alex Fraser/Elliott	Di Smith
Jo Loveday/Langley	Josephine Mitchell
Cathy Hayden/Freeman	Kate Raison
Matt Tyler	John Tarrant
Lucy Gardiner/Tyler	Georgie Parker
Dr. Chris Kouros	Michael Muntz
Jessica Kouros	Georgina Fisher
Julian "Luke" Ross	Matt Day
Dr. Terence Elliott	Shane Porteous
Sister Shirley Dean/Gilroy	Lorraie Desmond
Sgt. Frank Gilroy	Brian Wenzel
Vet Vicky Dean/Bowen	Penny Cook
Dr. Simon Bowen	Grant Dodwell
Melissa "Molly" Jones	Anne Tenney
Brendan Jones	Shane Withington
Vernon "Cookie" Locke	Syd Heylen
Bob Hatfield	Gordon Piper
Miss Esme Watson	Joyce Jacobs
Nurse Judy Loveday	Wendy Strethlow
Matron Sloan	Joan Sydney

PRODUCERS

James Davern, Lynn Bayonas, Marie Trevor, Bruce Best, Forrest Redlich, Bill Searle, Denny Lawrence, Robyn Sinclair, Peter Dodds, Mark Callam

PROGRAMMING HISTORY

• Seven Network

1,058 Episodes
November 1981–January 1982

Monday/Thursday 7:30-8:30

February 1982–March 1987

Tuesday/Wednesday 7:30-8:30

March 1987–April 1993   Monday/Tuesday 7:30-8:30

• Ten Network

29 Episodes

April 1994–May 1994	Wednesday 7:30-8:30
June 1994–July 1994	Saturday 7:30-8:30
July 1994–November 1994	Saturday 5:30-6:30

FURTHER READING

Tulloch, John, and Albert Moran. *A Country Practice: Quality Soap.* Sydney: Currency Press, 1986.

See also Australian Programming

COURTROOM TELEVISION

The question of whether to permit television coverage of court proceedings in the United States has evolved from the tension created by conflicting rights in the First and Sixth Amendments to the Constitution. Among its several guarantees, the First Amendment assures that Congress shall make no law abridging the freedom of speech, or of the press. In the Sixth Amendment, citizens accused of committing a crime are granted the right to a speedy and public trial by an impartial jury of their peers drawn from the state and district where the crime has taken place. Additionally, the accused is to be informed of the basis for the accusation, allowed to be confronted by any witnesses testifying against her/him, has the right to secure witnesses on their behalf, and have the assistance of legal representation to counsel the defendant's case.

At first examination, these rights may not appear to clash. However, the sensational press coverage practiced by the tabloids during the late 1800s combined with the flash camera's development in the early 1900s and led to the inevitable legal test of these competing rights. Most legal historians refer to the Lindbergh kidnapping trial in 1935 as initiating the hostility to cameras in the courts. Bruno Hauptmann was accused of kidnapping and killing the 18-month-old son of aviation hero, Charles Lindbergh. While only a small number of cameras were actually permitted inside the courtroom and photographers generally followed the court order prohibiting taking pictures while court was in session, a few years after the trial's conclusion, the American Bar Association (ABA) passed Canon 35 of the association's Canons of Professional and Judicial Ethics recommending cameras be banned from trials. Although Canon 35 did not have the weight of law, such ABA recommendations are often consulted by state legislatures, state bar associations, and judges writing case opinions. Radio was similarly barred by the ABA in 1941, and television cameras were added to the list in 1963.

As television became a part of life in the United States in the 1950s and early 1960s, most states continued to prohibit any form of camera coverage in their courts. By 1962, only a couple of states permitted television coverage of courtroom trials. In Texas that year, the pre-trial hearing of accused scam artist Billie Sol Estes played to live television and radio coverage. Broadcast equipment jammed the courtroom to the degree that, by the time Estes' actual trial began, the judge restricted television cameras to a booth in the back of the courtroom. Live coverage was allowed only periodically, and most trial coverage was done during news reports. Despite these precautions, Estes appealed his conviction claiming his Sixth Amendment rights had been denied him because of the broadcast coverage. In 1965, the United States Supreme Court ruled 5-4 in Estes' favor. On retrial, Estes was again convicted.

In *Estes v. Texas* (1965) the court majority ruled the Sixth Amendment guarantee to a fair trial was paramount

The Menendez trial
Photo courtesy of CourtTV

over the press's right to cover the proceeding. Four of the five majority justices wrote they believed the Sixth Amendment was violated simply by the presence of the television cameras. The majority stated cameras caused a distraction, had a negative impact on testimony, presented mental and physical distress for defendants, placed additional burdens on judges, and allowed judges to utilize televised trials for political purposes.

Many of these concerns were evident to the justices the following year when the Supreme Court addressed the negative influence of media coverage in *Sheppard v. Maxwell* (1966). This was the celebrated case in which Dr. Sam Sheppard was accused of murdering his wife in their suburban Cleveland, Ohio, home. Sheppard maintained his innocence throughout, claiming he had wrestled in the bedroom with a shadowy intruder who knocked the doctor unconscious. According to Sheppard, when he awoke his wife was already dead, bludgeoned to death on the bed. The case, and the ensuing nationwide publicity it received later provided the basis for the popular television series *The Fugitive*.

Sheppard was arrested and "tried in the press" even before the coroner's inquest, which was held in a high school gymnasium in front of live broadcast microphones to accommodate media coverage and public interest. The Supreme Court ruled that during both the inquest and trial proceedings, the coroner and judge failed to insure Dr. Sheppard's Sixth Amendment rights by their inability to control the media, jurors, and court officers as well as by allowing the release of information to the press during the actual trial. The judge, who was campaigning for re-election, was also rebuked for failing to shield jurors from pre-trial publicity. While live television coverage of the trial itself was prohibited, the labyrinth of cable and extra lighting needed to cover the trial snaked throughout the courthouse and contributed to the case's "carnival atmosphere."

While the Sheppard courtroom was not affected by television coverage to the degree seen in the Estes case, the

Supreme Court, in an opinion written by Justice Clark, was explicit when it came to setting forth guidelines judges should follow to ensure a fair trial. These instructions provided the foundation for states and their courts to follow in the future to insure proper use of television cameras in courtrooms. As specified by Justice Clark, judges sitting on highly-publicized cases in the future were instructed to adopt strict rules governing courtroom use by the media by considering the following: (1) The number of reporters in the courtroom itself should be limited at the first sign that their presence would disrupt the trial. (2) The court should insulate prospective witnesses from the news media. (3) The court should make some effort to control the release of leads, information, and gossip to the press by proscribing extra-judicial statements by police, counsel for both sides, witnesses, and officers of the court. (4) The judge could continue the case or transfer it to another county whenever "there is reasonable likelihood that prejudicial news prior to trial will prevent a fair trial." (5) The judge should discuss with counsel the feasibility of sequestering the jury. In the end, the United States Supreme Court ruled Dr. Sheppard deserved a retrial. He was eventually found not guilty. In the years following *Sheppard,* television technology improved dramatically as cameras became more portable and required less light to obtain broadcast-quality pictures. While these improvements were being implemented and refined, the United States Supreme Court ruled in 1980 in *Richmond Newspapers v. Virginia* that members of the public and the media have a constitutionally guaranteed right to attend criminal trials. This opinion reflected an ongoing trend in the states to open their courts by experimenting with television coverage. By December 1980, twenty-two states allowed cameras into their court systems to some degree, with twelve more studying such implementation.

In 1976, Florida had led the way by attempting to allow camera coverage of civil and criminal trials. The initial guidelines necessitated agreement from all trial participants, however, and this requirement stifled television coverage in most instances. In July 1977, Florida's State Supreme Court began a one-year study that placed responsibility for opening a trial to television coverage solely on the presiding judge. The state guidelines specified the type of equipment to be used. Additionally, no more than one television camera and camera operator were permitted, and broadcasters could only use a courtroom's existing audio recording system for sound pickup. Broadcast equipment was to remain stationary, no extra lighting beyond existing light in the courtroom was allowed, and film, videotape, and lenses could not be changed while court was in session. The lone camera was to serve as a pool camera if more than one television station desired footage.

After the year-long program was completed, a study discovered that the presence of a television camera was generally not a problem. This conclusion, and the state's guidelines, were challenged by two Miami Beach police officers who had been found guilty of conspiring to burglarize an area restaurant.

Because the case involved two local law enforcement officers who were caught by luck when a local amateur radio operator accidentally overheard them planning the heist, the case drew above-average media attention. The officers' attorney requested Florida's new courtroom rules (Canon 3A[7]) be declared unconstitutional, but the state Supreme Court declined to decide on grounds the rules were not directly relevant to the criminal charges against the officers. Eventually the trial was held and the defendants found guilty. An appeal was filed claiming the officers had been denied a fair trial because of the trial's television coverage. They were denied appeal throughout the Florida system, but the case was scheduled for hearing by the United States Supreme Court. In *Chandler v. Florida* (1981), Chief Justice Warren Burger wrote "the Constitution does not prohibit a state from experimenting with the program authorized by revised Canon 3A(7)." The Florida procedures provided restrictions on television coverage that paired with technological advances to ensure defendants a fair trial and, since the United States Supreme Court found no Constitutional issues threatened by Florida's guidelines, the request for a new trial was found lacking.

Shortly following the *Chandler* decision, the majority of states decided to allow camera coverage of some levels of their court systems. By mid-1993, only three states and the District of Columbia still banned any camera coverage of their courts. Those states allowing coverage have proceeded to address the question of what contexts establish that a camera's presence violates a defendant's rights, especially since this issue was not clarified by the United States Supreme Court in *Estes* or *Chandler.*

Broadcast journalists gained entry to most state courts as a result of the latter decision, but still faced closed doors to the federal court system. On 12 March 1996 the Judicial Conference of the United States voted 14 to 12 to allow cameras to cover federal appeals court cases. The decision allowed each of the thirteen federal appellate circuits to determine whether or not to admit coverage. At the same time the conference voted not to open federal district courtrooms to television. The change of heart by the conference allowed for television coverage of civil cases, but left broadcast journalists uncertain whether or not they could gain access to federal criminal cases.

The United States Supreme Court's decision in *Chandler* came at a time when cable television entered a phenomenal growth phase. As the 1980s progressed, cable television networks were created to serve an increasing variety of programming niches. By the decade's conclusion many cable systems looked like the electronic equivalent of a well-stocked magazine rack providing special interest material on almost any imaginable subject. Such special interest programming was evident in the July 1991 launch of the Courtroom Television Network (Court TV). The brainchild of Steven Brill, legal journalist and editor of *The American Lawyer,* the channel initially programmed its day emphasizing two or three courtroom trials from around the country. During evening prime time, Court TV's schedule provided a summary of the day's court cases and various original material. During the weekend, trial highlights from the preceding week were paired with special programming oriented specifically for lawyers. Criticized by some for its "play-by-play" commentary by the channel's legal experts during trial coverage, the service has developed a reputation for aggressive trial reporting while fulfilling its mission of demystifying the national court system for the public.

While Court TV has established itself as the channel for law buffs, it has yet to reach the number of homes covered by Ted Turner's Cable News Network (CNN). During the 1980s, CNN pioneered cable network presence in well-publicized trials ranging from the case of murder suspect Claus von Bulow and the William Kennedy Smith rape trial to the network's lengthy presentation of the O.J. Simpson case. Taking its cue from the program's creation and popularity during the Simpson coverage, CNN added the legal issues discussion show, *Burden of Proof,* to its schedule of specialty news-related fare. The Simpson case also provided an opportunity for other "specialized" channels to follow courtroom proceedings. One of the most notable of these was coverage of the trial by E! The Entertainment Channel. E!'s approach to the Simpson trial began with a slightly ironic, at times comic, approach, but quickly developed into serious analysis. It was also highlighted by viewer call-ins and fax messages which gave the channel a more participatory profile.

The rise of Court TV, CNN's live coverage of trials, and use of courtroom footage by local and network television news organizations has brought up issues beyond the Constitutional ones posed by the First and Sixth Amendments. Many judges and attorneys still question the effect a television camera's presence has on witnesses, jury members, and counsel during a trial and how these often-subtle nuances contribute to the trial's outcome. Others are concerned that television coverage of cases may be incomplete and contribute to rioting or public misperception and trivialization of crucial issues affecting a case rather than positively informing viewers about the court system. At the same time, court journalists point out their cameras often act as

the public's representative at a trial, while helping the news media provide oversight of the nation's judicial system.

—Robert Craig

FURTHER READING

Bart, Peter. "Trial by Tube." *Variety* (Los Angeles), 27 March 1995.

Cox, Gail Diane. "TV Changed Politics and Football: What Will It Do to Our System of Justice?" *The National Law Journal* (New York), 29 January 1996.

Craig, R. Stephen. "Cameras in Courtrooms in Florida." *Journalism Quarterly* (Urbana, Illinois), Winter 1979.

Denniston, Lyle. "Are Federal Cases Headed for Television." *American Journalism Review* (College Park, Maryland), June 1994.

Diuguid, Carol. "Court Touts Integrity Over Sensationalism." *Variety* (Los Angeles), 11 December 1995.

Drucker, Susan. "Cameras in the Court Revisited." *New York State Bar Journal* (Albany, New York), July-August 1992.

———. "The Televised Mediated Trial: Formal and Substantive Characteristics." *Communication Quarterly* (University Park, Pennsylvania), Fall 1989.

Hernandez, Debra. "Courtroom Cameras Debated." *Editor and Publisher* (New York), 17 February 1996.

Landau, Jack. "The Challenge of the Communications Media." *American Bar Association Journal* (Chicago), 1976.

Minow, Newton, and Fred Cate. "Who is an Impartial Juror in an Age of Mass Media?" *The American University Law Review* (Washington, D.C.), 1991.

Pryor, Bert, with others. "The Florida Experiment: An Analysis of On-the-Scene Responses to Cameras in the Courtroom." *Southern Speech Communication Journal* (Winston-Salem, North Carolina), Fall 1979.

Thaler, Paul. *The Watchful Eye: American Justice in the Age of the Television Trial.* Westport, Connecticut: Praeger, 1994.

See also Cable Networks

COUSTEAU, JACQUES

French Scientist and Television Producer

Jacques Cousteau is television's most celebrated maker and presenter of documentaries about the underwater world. Setting the standard for such programmes for decades to come, he had a profound influence upon succeeding generations of television documentary-makers around the world.

Cousteau was the virtual creator of the underwater documentary, having helped to develop the world's first aqualung diving apparatus in 1943, while a lieutenant in the French Navy, and having pioneered the process of underwater television. The aqualung afforded divers a freedom un-

derwater that they had never hitherto enjoyed and the arrival of equipment to film underwater scenes opened the door to the documentary makers for the first time (he also had a hand in the development of the bathyscaphe, which allowed divers to descend to great depths).

Founder of the French Navy's Undersea Research Group in 1946, Cousteau became commander of the research ship *Calypso* (a converted minesweeper) in 1950 and most of his epoch-making films were subsequently made with this vessel as his base of operations (he made a total of some 30 voyages in all). Cousteau's early films were made for the cinema and he earned Oscars for *The Silent World, The Golden Fish* and *World Without Sun,* as well as other top awards, such as the Palme d'Or at the Cannes Film Festival. Later documentaries were made for television, and such series as *Under the Sea, The World About Us* and *The Cousteau Odyssey* consistently attracted large audiences when shown in the United Kingdom *The World of Jacques Cousteau,* first broadcast in 1966, proved internationally successful, running for some eight years (later retitled *The Undersea World of Jacques-Yves Cousteau*) and drawing fascinated audiences of millions all around the globe. When this series ended in 1976 he concentrated on one-off specials on selected subjects (titles including *Oasis in Space, The Cousteau/ Amazon* and *Cousteau Mississippi*).

The appeal of Cousteau's films was not limited to the subject matter, for Cousteau's narrative, delivered in his distinctive nasal unremittingly French accent, was part of the character of his work. His narration was occasionally humorous and tended to personalize the species under discussion, with fish being described as "cheeky" or "courageous". The inclusion of members of his family, his wife Simone and his two sons (one of whom later died) in his films also added a humanizing touch. Such an approach did much to rouse awareness of the richness of life beneath the waves and underlined the responsibility humankind had towards other species.

The winner of numerous accolades and awards over the years, Cousteau is also respected as a outspoken commentator on a range of environmental issues, particularly noted for his uncompromising stand on such matters as nuclear waste and oil pollution. He has also written numerous books based on his research and was until 1988 director of the Oceanic Museum of Monaco (a similar institution opened in Paris in 1989 failed to prosper and closed its doors two years later).

—David Pickering

JACQUES-YVES COUSTEAU. Born in Saint-Andre-de-Cubzac, Gironde, France, 11 June 1910. Educated at Stanislas Academy in Paris, Bachelier, 1930; Ecole Navale in Brest, France, 1933. Married: Simone Melchior, 1937 (died, 1990); children: Diane, Elizabeth, Pierre-Yves Daniel, Phillipe (died, 1979). Served in the French Navy, entering as a second lieutenant, 1933; assigned to the naval base at Toulon; served as a gunnery officer, 1939–40; active in the French underground resistance; founded and became head of the French navy's Undersea Research Group, 1946; resigned from French Navy, 1956. Co-invented the first aqualung, 1943; set a world's free-diving record, 1947; founded and became president, Campagnes Oceanographiques Francaises, 1950, and the Centre d'Etudes Marines Acancees, 1952; as scientific leader, conducted field expeditions aboard his oceanographic research vessel named *Calypso,* 1950–1996, and *Calypso II,* since 1996; director, Oceanographic Institute and Museum, Monaco, 1957–88; promoted the Conshelf Saturation Dive Program, 1962; general secretary, International Com-

Jacques Cousteau

mission for the Scientific Exploration of the Mediterranean (I.C.S.E.M.), 1966; author of numerous books, since 1953; author and producer of numerous documentary films and television series; environmental advocate; inventor of turbosail system, 1985. Member: National Academy of Sciences; Academie Francaise. Recipient: Academy Awards, 1957, 1959, 1965; Cannes Film Festival, Gold Palm Award, 1959; Potts Medal of the Franklin Institute, 1970; Presidential Medal of Freedom, 1985; inducted into the Television Hall of Fame, 1987; National Geographic Society's Centennial Award, 1988; numerous Emmys; the Legion of Honor.

TELEVISION SERIES

1966–68	*The World of Jacques Cousteau*
1968–76	*The Undersea World of Jacques Cousteau*
1977	*Oasis in Space*
1977–81	*The Cousteau Odyssey*
1982–84	*The Cousteau/Amazon*
1985–91	*Cousteau's Rediscovery of the World I*
1992–94	*Rediscovery of the World II*

TELEVISION SPECIALS (selection)

The Tragedy of the Red Salmon
The Desert Whales; Lagoon of Lost Ships
Dragons of Galapagos; Secrets of the Sunken Caves
The Unsinkable Sea Otter
A Sound of Sea Dolphins
South to Fire and Ice

The Flight of Penguins
Beneath the Frozen World
Blizzard of Hope Bay
Life at the End of the World
Jacques Cousteau's Calypso's Legend
Lilliput Conquers America
Outrage at Valdez

FILMS (selection)
The Silent World, 1956; *The Golden Fish,* 1959; *World Without Sun,* 1965.

PUBLICATIONS (selection)
The Silent World, with Frederic Dumas. New York: Harper, 1952.

The Living Sea, with James Dugan. New York: Harper and Row, 1963.
World Without Sun, with James Dugan, editor. New York: Harper and Row, 1965.
The Shark: Splendid Savage of the Sea, with Phillipe Cousteau. Garden City, New York: Doubleday, 1970.
Jacques Cousteau's Amazon Journey, with Mose Richards. New York: H.N. Abrams, 1984.

FURTHER READING
Dunaway, Philip, and George De Kay, editors. *Turning Point.* New York: Random House, 1958.
Madsen, Axel. *Cousteau: An Unauthorized Biography.* New York: Beaufort, 1986.
Wagner, Frederick. *Famous Underwater Adventurers.* New York: Dodd, 1962.

CRAFT, CHRISTINE

U.S. Broadcast Journalist

Christine Craft is a broadcast journalist who will be remembered not for what she said on the air, but rather for what she said, and was said about her, in a federal district courtroom. It was there that she challenged the different standards by which male and female on-air broadcast news anchors were being judged in the U.S. media industries.

Her broadcast career began in 1974, when, at the age of 29, she took a job as a weather reporter with KSBW-TV in Salinas, California. During her tenure at channel 8 in Salinas, as well as her next position at KPIX-TV, the CBS affiliate in San Francisco, Craft filled every on-air position in the newsroom, from weather to sports to news reporting.

In 1977, Craft was hired by the CBS television network to do features on women athletes for *CBS Sports Spectacular* for the segment entitled "Women in Sports." According to Craft, this was her first experience with being "made over," and she hated it. Among the physical characteristics that were altered was her hair, bleached so that she appeared on-camera as a platinum blonde. After a year at CBS, Craft returned to California where she again worked in several news positions including co-anchor for the ABC affiliate in Santa Barbara, KEYT-TV.

Her life inexorably changed when she received a phone call from the Metromedia, Inc., ABC affiliate in Kansas City, KMBC-TV Channel 9. According to Craft, a consulting firm had made a tape of her without her permission or knowledge and marketed it around the country. Executives at KMBC saw the tape, and called her to Kansas City for an interview and audition. Based on her experience at CBS, Craft states that she told the station management that she "showed signs of her age and experience" and was not willing to be made over. She interviewed and auditioned in the KMBC studios, and was hired as co-anchor with a two-year contract. Eight months later, in July 1981, Craft was in-

Christine Craft
Photo courtesy of Christine Craft

formed that she had been demoted to reporter because focus group research had indicated that she was "too old, too unattractive and wouldn't defer to men." Craft decided to challenge the action of management, and when asked for a comment on why she was no longer anchor, told a Kansas City newspaper what had occurred.

Craft left the station in Kansas City and returned to television news in Santa Barbara, where for two years she prepared a breach of contract lawsuit against Metromedia. In August 1983 a ten-day trial was held at Federal District Court in Kansas City, at the conclusion of which the jury unanimously returned a verdict in favor of Craft, awarding her $500,000 in damages. U.S. District Court Judge Joseph E. Stevens, Jr., then threw out the verdict, and called for a second trial in Joplin, Missouri. After a six-day trial in 1984 in Joplin, the jury again returned a verdict in favor of Craft. Metromedia appealed, and the 8th Circuit Court threw out the second verdict. When the U.S. Supreme Court would not hear the case, Craft's years of litigation ended.

In 1986 Craft wrote *Too Old, Too Ugly, Not Deferential to Men* about her experiences. She continues to appear as a broadcast journalist on both radio and television, most recently in San Francisco.

—Thomas A. Birk

CHRISTINE CRAFT. Born in 1943. Graduated from the University of the Pacific McGeorge School of Law, 1995. Competitive surfer and teacher; weather reporter, KSBW-TV, Salinas, California, 1974; reporter, KPIX-TV, San Francisco; worked at KEYT-TV, Santa Barbara, California; co-anchor, KMBC-TV, Kansas City, Missouri, 1981; returned briefly to KEYT-TV, 1983; lecturer, 1983-84; talk-show host, KFBK-AM, Sacramento, California, since 1991.

PUBLICATIONS

Cristine Craft: An Anchorwoman's Story. Santa Barbara, California: Capra Press, 1986.
Too Old, Too Ugly, Not Deferential to Men. New York: St. Martin's, 1986.

FURTHER READING

Smith, S. B. "Television Executives Upset by Kansas City Finding." *New York Times*, 9 August 1983.
Thornton, M. "Newscaster Wins $500,000." *Washington Post*, 9 August 1983.
"Woman in TV Sex Bias Suit is Awarded $500,000 by Jury." *New York Times*, 9 August 1983.

See also Anchor

CRAIG, WENDY

British Actor

Wendy Craig emerged as one of the most familiar faces of British domestic situation comedy in the 1970s and 1980s, starring in a string of series in which she typically played a self-searching housewife and mother struggling to cope with the various demands made by her family, her home and life in general.

Craig began a career on the stage as a very young child and later entered films before establishing herself as a television performer. *Not in Front of the Children* was the first of the sitcoms in which she was cast in the role of harassed mother, a role she was later to make peculiarly her own. Resilient and yet sensitive (or, according to critics of the programme and its successors, simpering and middle-class), her character, Jennifer Corner, held the family together through crises both trivial and serious. The character appealed to thousands of real women whose days were similarly filled. Newly-widowed Sally Harrison in *And Mother Makes Three* (later retitled *And Mother Makes Five* after Sally remarried) and Ria Parkinson in Carla Lane's *Butterflies* were essentially extensions of the same character, only the members of the families and the details of the kitchen decor changed.

Butterflies, with Carla Lane's fluent scripts, was perhaps the most assured of the sitcoms in which Craig was invited to explore the state of mind of a flustered contem-

porary housewife facing a mid-life crisis. Supported by the lugubrious but always watchable Geoffrey Palmer as her husband and the up-and-coming Nicholas Lyndhurst as one of her two sons (the other was Andrew Hall), Craig played the part at a high pitch—sometimes arguably over-

Wendy Craig
Photo courtesy of the British Film Institute

hysterically—as she debated ways to break out of the confinements of the life imposed upon her by her family (chiefly through seemingly endless contemplation of an affair with the smooth and wealthy businessman Leonard Dunn, played by Bruce Montague). The comedy was often obvious (Ria's failure to cook anything without destroying it risked becoming tiresome), the pathos was sometimes painful, and the central character's self-absorption and inability to help herself was irritating to many more liberated viewers, but the skillful characterizations and the pace at which events were played together with the quality of the support kept the series fresh and intriguing and ensured a large and faithful audience.

Nanny, about the experiences of a children's nanny in the 1930s, represented something of a variation upon the matriarchal roles Craig had become associated with. The story of nanny Barbara Gray, caring for the children of the rich and well-connected, was in fact Craig's own idea, submitted and accepted under a pen name after she got the idea while flicking through advertisements for children's nurses in *The Lady* magazine. It eschewed comedy for a straighter dramatic approach. Comparisons between Craig's enlightened nanny Gray adding a helping hand to obviously dysfunctional upper-crust families and cinema's Mary Poppins were inevitable but did not detract from the success of the series and an increase in the numbers of girls planning careers as nannies was duly reported as a result.

Since the late 1980s, perhaps reflecting changes in society in general, Craig's matriarch has largely disappeared from the screen. *Laura and Disorder*, which Craig and her real-life son had a hand in writing, depicted her as an accident-prone divorcée newly returned from the U.S., but proved weak and was only short-lived. Even more misjudged was the attempt to make a British version of the highly acclaimed U.S. comedy series *The Golden Girls*, under the title *Brighton Belles*, with Craig cast as Annie, the equivalent of Rose in the original. The scripts failed entirely to match the wit and vivacity of the U.S. original and the project was quickly abandoned.

—David Pickering

WENDY CRAIG. Born in Sacriston, County Durham, England, 20 June 1934. Attended Central School of Speech and Drama, London; Ipswich Repertory Theatre. Married: Jack Bentley; children: Alaster and Ross. Won first acting award at the age of three; popular star of domestic situation comedy series. Recipient: British Academy of Film and Television Arts Award, 1968; Variety Club TV Personality of the Year Awards, 1969 and 1973; *TV Times* Readers' Funniest Woman on TV, 1972–74; BBC Woman of the Year, 1984. Address: Richard Hatton, 29 Roehampton Gate, London SW15 5JR, England.

TELEVISION SERIES

1964	*Room at the Bottom*
1967–70	*Not in Front of the Children*
1971–74	*And Mother Makes Three*
1974–76	*And Mother Makes Five*
1978–82	*Butterflies*
1981–83	*Triangle*
1981–83	*Nanny*
1989	*Laura and Disorder* (also co-writer)
1993	*Brighton Belles*

FILMS

Room at the Top, 1959; *The Mind Benders*, 1963; *The Servant*, 1963; *The Nanny*, 1965; *Just Like a Woman*, 1966; *I'll Never Forget Whatshisname*, 1967; *Joseph Andrews*, 1977.

STAGE

The Secret Place, 1957; *Heart to Heart*, 1962; *Late Summer Affair*, 1962; *Room at the Top*.

CRAWFORD, HECTOR

Australian Producer and Media Executive

Hector Crawford was a Melbourne-based producer of radio and television programs. The most nationalist of Australian producers, his company was a family company not only in the sense of being dominated by the Crawford family, but also in the sense of being vertically organised so that every production was controlled from the top of the company. The company was also family oriented in terms of the values esteemed in many of the its programs: respect for authority, espousal of domestic values, celebration of Australian history and society. However, these were old-fashioned values and practices and they were found especially wanting in the 1980s when Crawford was to lose control, some years before his death, of the company he founded.

Hector Crawford was born in 1913 in Melbourne, where he acquired a musical training. While working as a clerk in the late 1930s, he began the *Music for the People* outdoor concerts which were broadcast by the *Herald* and *Weekly Times'* own radio station 3DB. In 1940 he became music and recording director of Broadcast Exchange of Australia's recording and radio production company, and in 1942 rose to the position of managing director. His sister, Dorothy Crawford, trained at the Melbourne Conservatorium and was a professional singer. She worked for the ABC in radio and drama productions before joining Broadcast Exchange in 1944 as drama producer. With the encouragement of 3DB, the two set up their own radio program production company, Hector Crawford Productions, in 1945.

Thanks to its special relationship with 3DB and sister stations in the Major Network, Crawford's was very successful in radio. In addition the market for local radio programs, which had developed considerably in wartime, continued to expand, and by 1950 the company was one of the largest in radio. The company's radio output specialised in music and drama series and features. Some of its important programs were *Melba*, *Melba Sings*, *The Blue Danube*, *John Turner's Family*, *D24*, and *No Holiday for Halliday*.

Within a week of going to air on television in late 1956, HSV Channel 7 (owned by the *Herald and Weekly Times* newspaper group), Crawford's was producing a quiz/game show, *Wedding Day*, for the station. However, between 1956 and 1960 HSV Channel 7 bought little except for some quiz shows and a modest sitcom series, *Take That*. In 1961, the company's fortunes improved, with HSV committing itself to the courtroom drama series *Consider Your Verdict*. Its modest success helped pave the way for Crawford's next major development. In 1964 the company sold the police series, *Homicide*, to HSV and the Seven Network. *Homicide* spawned two other Crawford police series, *Division 4* and *Matlock Police*. These, together with other company series such as *Ryan*, *Showcase* and *The Box*, made Crawford Productions a veritable "Hollywood on the Yarra". The company employed hundreds and had construction departments, sound stages and its own studios. Crawford's hiccupped briefly in 1975 with the cancellation of the three police series, but in late 1976, *The Sullivans* began on the Nine Network. It was the quintessential Crawford series, with good production values, solid entertaining drama which treated traditional institutions, most especially the Australian family in wartime, with great respect. The company was less successful with serials such as *Carson's Law*, *Skyways*, *Holiday Island* and *Good Vibrations*. However, Crawford's was much more successful with two other serials, *Cop Shop* and *The Flying Doctors*. In 1983 Crawford's made their first miniseries, the enormously successful *All the Rivers Run*. Other miniseries included *The Flying Doctors*, *Alice to Nowhere*, *My Brother Tom*, *Whose Baby?*, *All the Rivers Run II*, *This Man*, *This Woman* and *Jackaroo*. In addition, Crawford's made several films which had theatrical release. It also made two children's series, *The Henderson Kids* and *The Zoo Family*.

In 1974 Dorothy Crawford retired from the company because of ill health. Her son, Ian, then shared executive producer credits with Hector Crawford on all Crawford programs.

The larger companies in television drama packaging in Australia have weathered periods of financial difficulty not only because of the cash flow from past successes but also because of other sources of financial stability. In the case of Crawford's, it was the special relationship enjoyed with HSV Channel 7 and the Seven Network which bought a large number of programs from the company. The *Herald and Weekly Times* was also ready to help Crawford's with loans in times of need.

Hector Crawford
Photo courtesy of Crawfords Australia

In 1972, for example, Hector Crawford privately sold the company to the *Herald and Weekly Times*, only to buy it back a year later. Again, in 1985 Crawford sold 40% of shares to the group as well as a further 10% to Gordon and Gotch. This was the situation in early 1987 when Rupert Murdoch's News Ltd bought out the *Herald and Weekly Times* group and, already owning Gordon and Gotch, found itself owning half of Crawford Productions. With the special relationship with HSV Channel 7 at an end, in poor health after a throat operation, and deciding to capitalise on the extensive library, Hector Crawford sold the company to Ariadne, a property and tourist company in 1987. Hector Crawford continued as honorary chair and died early in 1991.

—Albert Moran

HECTOR CRAWFORD. Born in Melbourne, Australia, 14 August 1913. Studied at the Melbourne Conservatorium of Music. Married: Glenda Raymond, 1950, two children. Began career as a choral conductor at the Conservatorium; musical and recording director of radio broadcasting house, Broadcast Exchange of Australia, 1940, managing director, 1942; formed Hector Crawford Productions with older sister Dorothy, 1945; began producing musical radio programs such as *Music for the People*, *Opera for the People*, *The Melba Story*, *The Amazing Oscar Hammerstein*, *The Blue Danube*; produced dramatic radio shows *Sincerely Rita Marsden*, *My Imprisoned Heart*, *A Woman in Love*, *Inspector West*, and *Lone Star Lannigan*; entered Melbourne television with game-show productions, 1956; produced first one-hour drama series, *Consider Your Verdict*, 1961, followed by the immensely successful police series, *Homicide*, 1964; production expanded, at one stage having five one-hour drama series playing on all three of the Australian commercial television networks, 1974; sold controlling interests in Crawford Productions, 1985; retired in 1989. Member: Australian Film Commission, 1974; Australian

Film and Television School, 1972-76. Died in Melbourne, Australia, 11 March 1991.

TELEVISION SERIES (selection)

1961–64	*Consider Your Verdict*
1964–75	*Homicide*
1966–68	*Hunter*
1974–77	*The Box*
1976–82	*The Sullivans*

TELEVISION MINISERIES (selection)

| 1983 | *All the Rivers Run* |

RADIO

Music for the People; Opera for the People; The Melba Story; The Amazing Oscar Hammerstein; The Blue Danube; Sincerely Rita Marsden; My Imprisoned Heart; A Woman in Love; Inspector West; Lone Star Lannigan; Consider Your Verdict.

See also Australian Production Companies, *Homicide*

CRONKITE, WALTER

U.S. Broadcast Journalist

Walter Cronkite is the former *CBS Evening News* anchorman, whose commentary defined issues and events in America for almost two decades. Cronkite, whom a major poll once named the "most trusted figure" in American public life, often saw every nuance in his nightly newscasts scrutinized by politicians, intellectuals, and fellow journalists, looking for clues to the thinking of mainstream America. In contrast, Cronkite viewed himself as a working journalist, epitomized by his title of "managing editor," of the *CBS Evening News*. His credo, adopted from his days as a wire service reporter, was to get the story, "fast, accurate, and unbiased"; his trademark exit line was, "And that's the way it is."

After working at a public relations firm, for newspapers, and in small radio stations throughout the Midwest, in 1939 Cronkite joined United Press (UP) to cover World War II. There, as part of what some reporters fondly called the "Writing 69th," he went ashore on D-Day, parachuted with the 101st Airborne, flew bombing mission over Germany, covered the Nuremburg trials, and opened the UP's first post-war Moscow bureau.

Though he had earlier rejected an offer from Edward R. Murrow, Cronkite joined CBS in 1950. First at CBS' Washington affiliate and then over the national network, Cronkite paid his dues to the entertainment side of television, serving as host of the early CBS historical recreation series, *You Are There*. He even briefly co-hosted the *CBS Morning Show* with the puppet Charlemagne. In a more serious vein he narrated the CBS documentary series *The Twentieth Century*. Earlier, Cronkite had impressed many observers when he anchored CBS' coverage of the 1952 presidential nominating conventions.

In April 1962, Cronkite took over the anchorman's position from Douglas Edwards on the *CBS Evening News*. Less than a year later the program was expanded from fifteen to thirty minutes. Cronkite's first thirty-minute newscast included an exclusive interview with President John F. Kennedy. Barely two months later Cronkite was first on the air reporting Kennedy's assassination, and in one of the rare instances when his journalist objectivity deserted him, he shed tears.

Cronkite's rise at CBS was briefly interrupted in 1964: the network, disturbed by the ratings beating *CBS Evening News* was taking from NBC's Huntley and Brinkley, decided to replace him as anchor at the 1964 presidential nominating conventions with the team of Robert Trout and Roger Mudd. Publically accepting the change, but privately disturbed, Cronkite contemplated leaving CBS. However, over 11,000 letters protesting the change undoubtedly helped convince both Cronkite and CBS executives that he should stay on. In 1966, Cronkite briefly overtook the *Huntley-Brinkley Report* in the ratings, and in 1967 took the lead. From that time until his retirement *The CBS Evening News* was the ratings leader.

Initially, Cronkite was something of a "hawk" on the Vietnam War, although his program did broadcast contro-

Walter Cronkite
Photo courtesy of Walter Cronkite

versial segments, such as Morley Safer's famous "Zippo lighter" report. However, returning from Vietnam after the Tet offensive, Cronkite addressed his massive audience with a different perspective. "It seems now more certain than ever," he said, "that the bloody experience of Vietnam is a stalemate." He then urged the government to open negotiations with the North Vietnamese. Many observers, including presidential aide Bill Moyers speculated that this was a major factor contributing to President Lyndon B. Johnson's decision to offer to negotiate with the enemy and not to run for president in 1968.

A year later Cronkite was one of the foremost boosters of America's technological prowess, anchoring the flight of Apollo XI. Again his vaunted objectivity momentarily left him as he shouted, "Go, Baby, Go," when the mission rocketed into space. For some time Cronkite had seen the space story as one of the most important events of the future, and his coverage of the space shots was as long on information as it was on his famed endurance. In what critics referred to as "Walter to Walter coverage," Cronkite was on the air for 27 of the 30 hours that Apollo XI took to complete its mission.

By the same token, Cronkite never stinted on coverage of the Watergate Scandal and subsequent hearings. In 1972, following on the heels of the *Washington Post's* Watergate revelations, the *CBS Evening News* presented a twenty-two-minute, two-part overview of Watergate generally credited with keeping the issue alive and making it intelligible to most Americans.

Cronkite could also influence foreign diplomacy, as evidenced in a 1977 interview with Eygptian President Anwar Sadat, in which he asked Sadat if he would go to Jerusalem to confer with the Israelis. A day after Sadat agreed to such a visit, an invitation came from Israeli Prime Minister Menachem Begin. It was a step that would eventually pave the way for the Camp David accords and an Israeli-Eygptian Peace treaty.

Many criticized Cronkite for his refusal to take more risks in TV news coverage. Others felt that his credibility and prestige had greater impact because of his judicious display of those qualities. Similarly, Cronkite was critized because of his preference for short "breaking stories," many of them originating from CBS News' Washington bureau, rather than longer "Enterprisers," which might deal with long range and non-Washington stories. In addition, many felt that Conkite's demand for center stage—an average of six minutes out of the twenty-two minutes on an evening newscast focused on him—took time away from in-depth coverage of the news. Some referred to this time in the spotlight as "the magic."

In 1981, in accord with CBS policy, Cronkite retired. Since then, however, he has hardly been inactive. His New Year's Eve hosting of PBS's broadcast of the Vienna Philharmonic has become a New Year's Eve tradition. He has also hosted PBS documentaries on health, old age and poor children. In 1993 he signed a contract with the Discovery and Learning Channel to do thirty-six documentaries in three years.

Cronkite's legacy of separating reporting from advocacy has become the norm in television news. His name has become virtually synonymous with the position of news anchor worldwide—Swedish anchors are known as Kronkiters, but in Holland they are Cronkiters.

—Albert Auster

WALTER CRONKITE. Born in St. Joseph's, Missouri, U.S.A., 4 November 1916. Attended University of Texas, 1933–35. Married: Mary Elizabeth Maxwell, 1940; three children. Newswriter and editor, Scripps-Howard, also United Press, Houston, Texas; Kansas City, Missouri; Dallas, Austin, and El Paso, Texas; and New York City; United Press war correspondent, 1942–45, foreign correspondent, reopening bureaus in Amsterdam, Brussels; chief correspondent, Nuremberg war crimes trials, bureau manager, Moscow, 1946–48, manager and contributor, 1948–49, CBS-News correspondent, 1950–81, special correspondent, since 1981; managing editor, *CBS Evening News with Walter Cronkite*, 1962–81. Honorary degrees: American International College; Harvard University; LL.D., Rollins College, Bucknell University, Syracuse University; L.H.D., Ohio State University. Member: Academy of Television Arts and Sciences (president, national academy, New York chapter, 1959, Governor's Award, 1979); Association Radio News Analysts. Recipient: several Emmy Awards; Peabody Awards, 1962 and 1981; William A. White Award for journalistic merit, 1969; George Polk Journalism Award, 1971; Gold Medal, International Radio and Television Society, 1974; Alfred I. DuPont-Columbia University Award in Broadcast Journalism, 1978 and 1981; Presidential Medal of Freedom, 1981.

TELEVISION SERIES

1953–57	*You Are There*
1957–67	*The Twentieth Century*
1961–62	*Eyewitness to History*
1961–79	*CBS Reports*
1962–81	*The CBS Evening News with Walter Cronkite* (managing editor)
1967–70	*21st Century*
1980–82	*Universe* (host)
1991	*Dinosaur!*

TELEVISION SPECIALS (selection)

1975	*Vietnam: A War That Is Finished*
1975	*In Celebration of US*
1975	*The President in China*
1977	*Our Happiest Birthday*
1984	*Solzhenitsyn: 1984 Revisited*

PUBLICATIONS

The Challenges of Change. Washington, D.C.: Public Affairs Press, 1971.

Eye on the World. New York: Cowles, 1971.

Unger, Arthur. "'Uncle Walter' and the 'Information Crisis'" (interview). *Television Quarterly* (New York), Winter 1990.

"Covering Religion" (interview). *The Christian Century* (Chicago, Illinois), 14 December 1994.

Snow, Richard F. "He Was There" (interview). *American Heritage* (New York), December 1994.

FURTHER READING

Attanasio, Paul. "Anchors Away: Good Evening Dan, Tom and Peter. Now Buzz Off." *The New Republic* (Washington, D.C.), 23 April 1984.

Cronkite, Kathy. *On the Edge of the Spotlight: Celebrities' Children Speak Out About Their Lives.* New York: Morrow, 1981.

Rottenberg, Dan. "And That's the Way It Is." *American Journalism Review* (College Park, Maryland), May 1994.

See also Anchor; Kennedy, John F., Assassination; News (Network); Space Program and Television

CURTIN, JANE

U.S. Actor

Comic actor Jane Curtin is a veteran of two very successful television series. Her first two series coincided with and participated in the revival and redefinition of two familiar televisual forms: live comedy-variety shows and situation comedies. The former resurgence was initiated by NBC's *Saturday Night Live* (*SNL*) in 1975 when Curtin joined the troupe. The later rejuvenation developed with a number of new sitcoms in 1984, among them *Kate and Allie*, in which Curtin played Allie Lowell. Curtin's *Third Rock from the Sun* character continued some of qualities developed on these programs.

One of the original "Not-Ready-for-Prime-Time Players" on *SNL*, Curtin had the distinction of being the only cast member producer Lorne Michaels hired cold. Though like other cast members, she had worked in improvisational theater ("The Proposition"), Michaels had not met her nor worked with her, as he had with the rest of the cast. Less facile with physical comedy than Chevy Chase, less disposed to creating the broad characters of Gilda Radner, with a less elastic face than John Belushi, Curtin's cool, classic countenance made her a fitting choice for many "straight" parts. While Curtin would do a fair share of absurd characters (e.g. the nasal Mrs. Loopner, the mother in the Butts family, Prymaat Conehead, the mother in a family from another planet), more often than other women in the cast from 1975 to 1980 she played the "serious" roles (e.g. weekend anchor, Shana Alexander-type political combatant to Dan Akroyd's James Kilpatrick). Where Gilda Radner would outrageously parody journalist Barbara Walters (as Baba Wawa), Jane Curtin would do a more deadpan imitation of commentator Shana Alexander. Yet, square jawed and stoical, she would sometimes intentionally abandon this sober persona using the apparent break in her control to comic effect. This style, occasionally surfacing in *Third Rock*, is something of a trademark.

In an interview with James Brady years later Curtin was asked how she would rate her experience on *SNL*. She said on a scale of one to ten, it was a ten. Curtin was nominated for two Emmy Awards for her work on *SNL* before she left the show in 1980. She next appeared in a television series as a regular on a sitcom at a time when situation comedy was on the wane. In 1982 and 1983 only two sitcoms were getting ratings in the top 25: *Cheers* and *Newhart*. But in 1984 the phenomenally successful *The Cosby Show* and a number of other domestic sitcoms (with varied family forms) appeared, signaling a decade of domination by this television type. *Kate and Allie*, premiering in March 1984, was a part of this resurgence. This family consisted of two divorced women, Kate McArdle and Allie Lowell, who rented a flat together and were raising three children be-

Jane Curtin
Photo courtesy of Jane Curtin

tween them. Once again Curtin played the more conventional character: abandoned traditional wife Allie.

During the program the character Allie grew from a shy homebody to a woman returning to college and eventually running her own business through her domestic skills (cooking and organizing). Thus, Curtin was again playing a confident woman with an underlying vulnerability. She won two Emmy awards for her portrayal for the 1983–84 and the 1984–85 seasons. She stayed with the show until it ended in 1990.

Curtin appeared in a number of movies, both for the big screen and for television, during and after *Kate and Allie*, and tried another series that was not successful (*Working It Out*, 1990). It wasn't until January 1996 that she again "hit" with a program that drew on both a sitcom formula and the growing popularity of science-fiction TV programs (e.g. all the *Star Trek* descendants, *The X-Files*, etc.), *Third Rock from the Sun*. No doubt her role as the alien Prymaat Conehead in *SNL* and later in *The Coneheads* movie (1993) contributed to her hiring.

The premise of *Third Rock* is reminiscent of the Coneheads, as a group of aliens land on earth and live as a human family. The leader, played by John Lithgow, poses as a professor colleague of anthropologist Mary Allbright (Curtin). The interplay between the characters draws on much of Curtin's past style. Dr. Allbright is a conventional professional woman with a sober exterior who often breaks this pose to temporarily partake in the absurd behaviors of the aliens (e.g. breaking into showtunes in a diner, getting aroused by a slap in the face). In this program she is once again playing it straight but only part way.

—Ivy Glennon

JANE (THERESE) CURTIN. Born in Cambridge, Massachusetts, U.S.A., 6 September 1947. Elizabeth Seton Junior College, A.A. 1967; attended Northwestern University, 1967–68. Married: Patrick F. Lynch, 1975; one child: Tess. Began comedy career as company member of "The Proposition" comedy group, 1968–72; contributing writer and actor in off-Broadway production *Pretzels*, 1974–75; original cast member of *Saturday Night Live*, NBC, 1975–80; roles in several films, stage productions, and TV programs. Recipient: Emmy Awards 1983–84 and 1984–85; Address: Creative Artists Agency, 1888 Century Park East, Suite 1400, Los Angeles, California 90067, U.S.A.

TELEVISION SERIES

1975–80	*Saturday Night Live*
1978	*What Really Happened to the Class of '65?*
1984–90	*Kate and Allie*
1990	*Working It Out*
1996–	*Third Rock From the Sun*

MADE-FOR-TELEVISION MOVIES

1982	*Divorce Wars: A Love Story*
1987	*Suspicion*
1988	*Maybe Baby*
1990	*Common Ground*
1995	*Tad*

FILMS

Mr. Mike's Mondo Video, 1979; *Bob and Ray, Jane, Laraine and Gilda*, 1979; *How to Beat the High Cost of Living*, 1980; *O.C. and Stiggs*, 1985; *The Coneheads*, 1993.

STAGE

The Proposition (comedy group), 1968–72; *Pretzels*, 1974–75; *Candida*, 1981.

D

DAD'S ARMY

British Situation Comedy

The BBC comedy series *Dad's Army* was the creation of one of the most successful British television comedy writing and production teams, Jimmy Perry and David Croft. They created 81 half-hour episodes between 1968 and 1977 with audiences of 18.5 million in the early 1970s. The programme has developed a TV nostalgia popularity among its original audience as repeat transmissions (in 1989 for instance) and sales of home videocassettes testify. One of the key factors in the programme's success lay in its historical setting during the early years of World War II. *Dad's Army* features the comic ineptitude of a Home Guard platoon in Walmington-on-Sea, an imaginary seaside resort on the south coast of England. The Land Defence Volunteers were formed in 1940 as a reserve volunteer force comprising men who did not meet the standards of age and fitness required for regular military service. These units were soon officially

Dad's Army
Photo courtesy of the British Film Institute

re-named the Home Guard, but they also attracted the somewhat derisory nick-name of "Dad's Army".

Perry and Croft's scripts, based on vivid memories from the period, won them professional recognition with a screenwriting BAFTA Award in 1971 and their subsequent work secures them a central place within popular British television comedy. They went on to produce *It Ain't 'Alf 'Ot Mum!* (1976-81), set in a British Army entertainment corps posted in Burma during World War II, and *Hi-de-Hi* (1980-94), set in Maplins Holiday Camp in 1959. In their own way, these programmes have tapped into, and contributed to, television's myths about wartime Britain and the immediate post-war period of the 1950s. All three series feature ensemble casts of misfit characters brought together under a quasi-authoritarian order (a volunteer army, concert corps, or holiday camp staff) and whose weekly crises demand that the group pulls together against adversity.

The longevity and endearing appeal of *Dad's Army* in particular is explained in part by the way in which the series successfully constructs myths of British social unity and community spirit that were so sought after in the years following the revolutionary moment of the late 1960s. The revival of the series in the late 1980s pointed up the starker, more divided nature of contemporary British life, riven by class, racial and national identity tensions. *Dad's Army* depicts with humour, but obvious underlying affection, the "bulldog" spirit of Britain popularly taken to characterise public morale during the Blitz and its immediate aftermath (1940–41). Britain alone against the threat of Hitler's Nazi army occupying Europe is the subject of the programme's signature tune lyrics, "Who do you think you are kidding, Mr. Hitler, if you think old England's done", written by Perry and sung by war-time entertainer, Bud Flanagan in a clever recreation of a 1940s sound. The opening credit sequence depicts a map of Europe with advancing Nazi swastikas attempting to cross the English Channel. In its production style, *Dad's Army* exemplified the BBC's reputation for period detail and many episodes featured exterior sequences shot on rural locations in southeast England. This film footage was mixed with videotape-recorded interior scenes and a live studio audience provided laughter for the final broadcast version.

The humour of *Dad's Army* derives from a combination of ridiculous task or crisis situations, visual jokes and a gentle mockery of English class differentiation. Perry and Croft's skill was to script dialogue for a talented ensemble of character actors comprising the Walmington-on-Sea platoon, led by the pompous Captain Mainwearing (Arthur Lowe), the manager of the local bank. The other main characters included his chief clerk, Sergeant Wilson (John Le Mesurier), Frank Pike (Ian Lavender), the junior bank clerk, and Lance-Corporal Jones (Clive Dunn), the local butcher. The platoon's rank and file were made up of privates Frazer, the Scots undertaker (John Laurie), Godfrey (Arnold Ridley), a retired gentleman who lived with his two maiden sisters in a cottage, and Walker (James Beck),

a "spiv" who dealt in contraband goods. Mainwearing's main rival authority in Walmington is the chief air raid warden, Mr. Hodges (Bill Pertwee), a local greengrocer. They frequently battle over use of the church hall and office of the long-suffering camp Vicar (Frank Williams) and his toadying Verger (Edward Sinclair).

Perry and Croft's world in *Dad's Army* is largely male but women do feature, albeit in their absence or marginality. Underlying the appearance of the middle-class proprieties of marriage are dysfunctional relationships. Mainwearing's agoraphobic wife ("Elizabeth") never appeared in the series (except once as a lump in the top bunk of their Anson air-raid shelter). They obviously share a loveless marriage with her firmly in control over domestic arrangements. Similarly, Mrs. Pike (Janet Davies) is a young widower who entertains the debonair Sergeant Wilson, and although Frank refers to him as "Uncle Arthur" there is some suspicion that the lad is their illegitimate son. The amorous, larger than life Mrs. Fox (Pamela Cundell) gives her matronly attentions freely to the platoon's men and she eventually marries the elderly but eligible Corporal Jones.

Dad's Army is particularly significant in its comic treatment of English class tensions. Through narrative and character, Croft and Perry revisit a time when the war was being fought partly in the belief that the old social class divisions would give way to a more egalitarian post-war meritocracy. The chief manifestations of such tensions occur in exchanges between Captain Mainwearing and Sergeant Wilson. In a clever reversal of expectations, Croft made the captain a grammar school-educated, bespectacled and stout man whose social status has been achieved through hard work and merit. His superiority of rank, work status and self-important manner are nevertheless constantly frustrated by Wilson's upper-class pedigree, public-school education and nonchalant charm. Mainwearing's middle-class snobbery, brilliantly captured by Arthur Lowe, is also reflected in his attitudes toward the lower classes. A member of the managerial class, he looks down at uncouth tradesmen: "He's a green grocer with dirty finger nails," he says of his arch rival Hodges. Although *Dad's Army* is comic because it mocks such pretension, it is essentially a nostalgic look back to a social order that never existed in this form. The programme celebrates values such as "amateurism", "making do" and muddling through, values that in this presentation remain comic, but appear quaint to later generations of television viewers.

—Lance Pettitt

CAST

Capt. Mainwearing	Arthur Lowe
Sgt. Wilson	John Le Mesurier
Lance Cpl. Jones	Clive Dunn
Private Frazer	John Laurie
Private Walker	James Beck
Private Godfrey	Arnold Ridley
Private Pike	Ian Lavender

Chief Warden Hodges	. . . .	Bill Pertwee
Vicar	. . . .	Frank Williams
Verger	. . . .	Edward Sinclair
Mrs. Pike	. . . .	Janet Davies
Private Sponge	. . . .	Colin Bean
Private Cheeseman	. . . .	Talfryn Thomas
Colonel	. . . .	Robert Raglan
Mr. Blewitt	. . . .	Harold Bennett
Mrs. Fox	. . . .	Pamela Cundell

PRODUCER   David Croft

PROGRAMMING HISTORY   81 Half-hour episodes; 1 One-hour episode; 1 Insert

• BBC

July 1968–September 1968	6 Episodes
March 1969–April 1969	6 Episodes
September 1969–October 1969	7 Episodes
October 1969–December 1969	7 Episodes
September 1970–December 1970	13 Episodes
December 1970	Christmas Special
December 1971	Christmas Special
October 1972–December 1972	13 Episodes
October 1973–December 1973	7 Episodes
November 1974–December 1974	6 Episodes
September 1975–October 1975	6 Episodes
December 1975	Christmas Special
December 1976	Christmas Special
October 1977–November 1977	6 Episodes

FURTHER READING

Ableman, Paul. *The Defence of a Front Line English Village (ed. Arthur Wilson, MA)*. London: BBC Books, 1989.

Cook, Jim, editor. *TV Sitcom*. London: British Film Institute, 1982.

Perry, J., and David Croft. *Dad's Army* (five scripts). London: Hamish Hamilton, 1975.

Pertwee, Bill. *Dad's Army: The Making of a TV Legend*. London: David and Charles, 1989.

See also British Programming

DALLAS

U.S. Serial Melodrama

Dallas, the first of a genre to be named "prime-time soap" by television critics, established the features of serial plots involving feuding families and moral excess that would characterize all other programs of the type. Created by David Jacobs, *Dallas's* first five-episode pilot season aired in April 1978 on CBS, getting poor reviews, but later high ratings put it in the top ten by the end of its limited run. The central premise was a Romeo and Juliet conflict, set in contemporary Texas. Pamela Barnes and Bobby Ewing were the young lovers; their two families perpetuated the feud of their elders, Jock Ewing and Digger Barnes, over the rightful ownership of oil fields claimed by the Ewings.

In the pilot episodes and the twelve full seasons that would follow, the Ewing family remained the focus of *Dallas*. Indeed, the Ewing brothers, their wives, their offspring and all assorted relatives passing through would continue to live under one roof on Southfork, the family ranch. Bobby's older brother J.R., played with sly wit by Larry Hagman, would become a new kind of villain for television because of his centrality to the program and the depth both actor and writers gave to the character. Abusive to his alcoholic wife Sue Ellen, ruthless and underhanded with his nemesis Cliff Barnes and any other challenger to Ewing Oil, J.R. was nevertheless a loyal son to Miss Ellie and Jock, a devoted father to his son and heir, John Ross. Hagman's J.R. soon became the man viewers loved to hate.

For prime time in the late 1970s, *Dallas* was sensational, featuring numerous acts of adultery by both J.R. and Sue Ellen, the revelation of Jock's illegitimate son, Ray Krebs, who worked as a hired hand on Southfork, and the raunchy exploits of young Lucy, daughter of Gary, the third, largely

Dallas

absent, Ewing brother. It was the complicated stuff of daytime melodrama, done with big-budget glamour—high-fashion wardrobes, richly furnished home and office interiors, exteriors shot on location in the Dallas area.

During the 1978–79 season, writer-producer Leonard Katzman turned the prime-time drama into the first prime-time serial since *Peyton Place* when Sue Ellen Ewing found she was pregnant, her child's paternity uncertain. The generic formula was complete when that same season concluded with a cliffhanger: Sue Ellen was critically injured in a car accident and both her fate and the fate of her baby remained unresolved until September. Cliffhanger episodes became highly promoted Friday night rituals after the following season, which ended with a freeze-frame of villain-protagonist J.R. lying shot on the floor of his office, his prognosis and his assailant unknown. "Who Shot J.R.?" reverberated throughout popular culture that summer, culminating in an episode the following season which broke ratings records—76% of all American televisions in use tuned to *Dallas*. Even after 1985, when the program's ratings sagged, cliffhanger episodes in the spring and their resolutions in the fall would boost the aging serial back into the top ten.

In the midst of an ever-expanding cast of Ewings and Barnes, scheming mistresses, high-rolling oil men and white collar henchmen, the primary characters and relationships changed and evolved over the course of the serial. Bobby and Pam's marriage succumbed to J.R.'s plots to pull them apart, and both pursued other romances. After J.R. and Sue Ellen's marriage produced an heir, Sue Ellen stopped drinking and went on the offensive against J.R. Both Pam and Sue Ellen acquired careers. Ray Krebs rose from hired hand to independent rancher, always apart from the Ewing clan, but indispensable to it.

Like its daytime counterparts, *Dallas* adapted to the comings and goings of several of its star actors. When Jim Davis, who played Jock Ewing, died in 1981, his character was written out of the show, with Jock's plane disappearing somewhere over South America. The character was never recast, though several plotlines alluded to his possible reappearance, and his portrait continued to preside over key scenes in the offices of Ewing Oil. Barbara Bel Geddes, the beloved Miss Ellie, asked to be relieved from her contract for health reasons in 1984, and Donna Reed stepped into the role for one season, only to be removed when Bel Geddes was persuaded to return. During the 1985-86 season, Bobby Ewing was dead, at the request of actor Patrick Duffy, but the character returned when Duffy wanted back on the show. Bobby was resurrected when his death and all the rest of the previous season were redefined as Pam's dream. Linda Gray left the show in 1989, and her character, Sue Ellen, exited as an independent movie mogul whose final act of vengeance was to produce a painfully accurate film about J.R.

In the early 1980s, other serials joined the internationally successful *Dallas* on the prime-time schedule, each in some way defining itself in relation to the original. Among them, *Knots Landing* began as a spin-off of *Dallas*, featuring Gary Ewing and his wife Valene transplanted to a California suburb. ABC's *Dynasty* both copied the *Dallas* formula and stretched it to outrageous proportions. On the other hand, hour-long dramas, most notably *Hill Street Blues*, began grafting *Dallas*'s successful serial strategy onto other genres. Among the eighties generation of prime-time soaps, only *Knots Landing* outlasted *Dallas*, which concluded in May 1991. In the 1990s, the genre has been revamped in several serials on the Fox network. *Beverly Hills 90210*, *Melrose Place* and *Models, Inc.*—the last featuring *Dallas*'s Linda Gray—have pitched the genre to a younger generation of viewers.

—Sue Brower

CAST

John Ross (J.R.) Ewing, Jr.	Larry Hagman
Eleanor Southworth (Miss Ellie) Ewing (1978–1984, 1985–90)	Barbara Bel Geddes
Eleanor Southworth (Miss Ellie) Ewing (1984–85)	Donna Reed
John Ross (Jock) Ewing (1978–81)	Jim Davis
Bobby Ewing (1978–85, 1986–91)	Patrick Duffy
Pamela Barnes Ewing (1978–87)	Victoria Principal
Lucy Ewing Cooper (1978–85, 1988–90)	Charlene Tilton
Sue Ellen Ewing (1978–89)	Linda Gray
Ray Krebs (1978–88)	Steve Kanaly
Cliff Barnes	Ken Kercheval
Julie Grey (April 1978)	Tina Louise
Willard "Digger" Barnes (1978)	David Wayne
Willard "Digger" Barnes (1979–80)	Keenan Wynn
Gary Ewing (1978–79)	David Ackroyd
Gary Ewing (1979–81)	Ted Shackelford
Valene Ewing (1978–81)	Joan Van Ark
Liz Craig (1978–82)	Barbara Babcock
Willie Joe Garr (1978–79)	John Ashton
Jeb Amos (1978–79)	Sandy Ward
Kristin Shepard (1979–81)	Mary Crosby
Mrs. Patricia Shepard (1979, 1985)	Martha Scott
Dusty Farlow (1979–82, 1985)	Jared Martin
Alan Beam (1979–80)	Randolph Powell
Dr. Ellby (1979–81)	Jeff Cooper
Donna Culver Krebs (1979–87)	Susan Howard
Dave Culver (1979–82, 1986–87)	Tom Fuccello
Harve Smithfield	George O. Petrie
Vaughn Leland (1979–84)	Dennis Patrick
Connie (1979–81)	Jeanna Michaels
Louella (1979–81)	Megan Gallagher
Jordan Lee (1979–90)	Don Starr
Mitch Cooper (1979–82)	Leigh McCloskey
John Ross Ewing III (1980–83)	Tyler Banks
John Ross Ewing III (1983–91)	Omri Katz
Punk Anderson (1980–87)	Morgan Woodward
Mavis Anderson (1982–88)	Alice Hirson
Brady York (1980–81)	Ted Gehring

Alex Ward (1980–81) . . . . Joel Fabiani
Les Crowley (1980–81) . . . . Michael Bell
Marilee Stone (1980–87) . . . . Fern Fitzgerald
Afton Cooper (1981–84, 1989) . . . . . Audrey Landers
Arliss Cooper (1981) . . . . Anne Francis
Clint Ogden (1981) . . . . Monte Markham
Leslie Stewart (1981) . . . . Susan Flannery
Rebecca Wentworth (1981–83) . . . . Priscilla Pointer
Craig Stewart (1981) . . . . Craig Stevens
Jeremy Wendell (1981, 1984–88) . . . William Smithers
Clayton Farlow (1981–91) . . . . Howard Keel
Jeff Farraday (1981–82) . . . . Art Hindle
Katherine Wentworth (1981–84) . . . Morgan Brittany
Charles Eccles (1982) . . . . Ron Tomme
Bonnie Robertson (1982) . . . . Lindsay Bloom
Blair Sullivan (1982) . . . . Ray Wise
Holly Harwood (1982–84) . . . . Lois Chiles
Mickey Trotter (1982–83) . . . Timothy Patrick Murphy
Walt Driscoll (1982–83) . . . . Ben Piazza
Jarrett McLeish (1982–83) . . . . J. Patrick McNamara
Thornton McLeish (1982–83) . . . . . Kenneth Kimmins
Eugene Bullock (1982–83) . . . . E.J. Andre
Mark Graison (1983–84, 1985–86) . . . . . John Beck
Aunt Lil Trotter (1983–84) . . . . Kate Reid
Roy Ralston (1983) . . . . John Reilly
Serena Wald (1983–85, 1990) . . . Stephanie Blackmore
Peter Richards (1983–84) . . . . Christopher Atkins
Paul Morgan (1983–84, 1988) . . . . . Glenn Corbett
Jenna Wade (1983–88) . . . . Priscilla Presley
Charlie Wade (1983–88) . . . . Shalane McCall
Edgar Randolph (1983–84) . . . . . . Martin E. Brooks
Armando Sidoni (1983–84) . . . . Alberto Morin
Sly Lovegren (1983–91) . . . . Deborah Rennard
Betty (1984–85) . . . . Kathleen York
Eddie Cronin (1984–85) . . . . Fredric Lehne
Pete Adams (1984–85) . . . . Burke Byrnes
Dave Stratton (1984) . . . . Christopher Stone
Jessica Montfort (1984, 1990) . . . . Alexis Smith
Mandy Winger (1984–87) . . . . Deborah Shelton
Jamie Ewing Barnes (1984–86) . . . . Jenilee Harrison
Christopher Ewing (1984–91) . . . . . . Joshua Harris
Scotty Demarest (1985–86) . . . . Stephen Elliott
Jack Ewing (1985–87) . . . . Dack Rambo
Angelico Nero (1985–86) . . . . Barbara Carrera
Dr. Jerry Kenderson (1985–86) . . . . . . Barry Jenner
Nicholas (1985–86) . . . . George Chakiris
Grace (1985–86) . . . . Marete Van Kamp
Matt Cantrell (1986) . . . . Marc Singer

PRODUCERS   David Jacobs, Philip Capice, Leonard
Katzman

PROGRAMMING HISTORY   330 Episodes

• CBS

April 1978	Sunday 10:00-11:00
September 1978–October 1978	Saturday 10:00-11:00
October 1978–January 1979	Sunday 10:00-11:00
January 1979–November 1981	Friday 10:00-11:00
December 1981–May 1985	Friday 9:00-10:00
September 1985–May 1986	Friday 9:00-10:00
September 1986–May 1988	Friday 9:00-10:00
October 1988–March 1990	Friday 9:00 -10:00
March 1990–May 1990	Friday 10:00-11:00
November 1990–December 1990	Friday 10:00-11:00
January 1991–May 1991	Friday 9:00-10:00

FURTHER READING

Adams, John. "Setting as Chorus: An Iconology of Dallas."
    Critical Survey (Oxford), 1994.
Ang, Ien. *Watching Dallas: Soap Opera and the Melodramatic
    Imagination.* London and New York: Routledge, 1989.
Bonderoff, Jason. *The Official Dallas Trivia Quiz Book.* New
    York: New American Library, 1985.
Cassidy, Marsha F. "The Duke of Dallas: Interview with
    Leonard Katzman." *Journal of Popular Film and Televi-
    sion* (Bowling Green, Ohio), Spring 1988.
Coward, Rosalind. "Come Back Miss Ellie: On Character
    and Narrative in Soap Operas." *Critical Quarterly*
    (Manchester), Spring-Summer 1986.
Hirschfeld, Burt. *The Ewings of Dallas: A Novel.* New York:
    Bantam Books, 1980.
Kalter, Suzy. *The Complete Book of Dallas: Behind the Scenes
    of the World's Favorite TV Program.* New York: Abrams,
    1986.
Liebes, Tamar, and Elihu Katz. *The Export of Meaning:
    Cross-Cultural Readings of Dallas.* New York: Oxford
    University Press, 1990.
Mander, Mary S. "*Dallas*: The Mythology of Crime and the
    Moral Occult." *Journal of Popular Culture* (Bowling
    Green, Ohio), Fall 1983.
Masello, Robert. *The Dallas Family Album: Unforgettable
    Moments from the #1 TV Series.* New York: Bantam,
    1980.
Perlberg, Diane J., and Joelle Delbourgo, editors. *Quotations
    of J.R. Ewing.* New York: Bantam, 1980.
Silj, Alessandro, and Manuel Alvarado, editors. *East of Dal-
    las: The European Challenge to American Television.*
    London: British Film Institute, 1988.
White, Mimi. "Women, Memory and Serial Melodrama."
    Screen (Oxford), Winter 1994.

See also Hagman, Larry; Melodrama; Spelling, Aaron

DALY, TYNE

U.S. Actor

Tyne Daly, best known as half of the female cop team that formed *Cagney and Lacey*, won recognition for her role as the New York City detective who was also a wife and mother. With a background in the theater, Daly brought a cultivated artistry to the working-class role of Mary Beth Lacey. As written, the character was multi-faceted—a tough cop, a loving wife, a committed mother, a loyal friend. As played by Daly, Mary Beth was even more complex—innocent, compassionate and at times funny, but clear-eyed and confrontational in her dealings with both the "perps" and her best friend and partner, Christine Cagney (Sharon Gless). As Mary Beth, Daly created a female character for television who was smart though not college-educated, sexy without being glamorous. Mary Beth's marriage with Harvey Lacey (John Karlen) offered what Daly called "a love story" that marked a true departure from TV marriages—a lusty, devoted partnership.

It was Mary Beth's partnership with Christine, however, that drew the attention of most feminist critics for its twist on the countless pairs of male partners and buddies that have populated television. The professional and personal sides of Mary Beth and Christine's relationship often blurred; feelings inevitably got involved. Though seemingly the "softer" of the two, Mary Beth's more rational approach to her job served as ballast in the twosome's investigations.

In addition to the ongoing themes of marriage and women's relationships, Daly was given the opportunity to explore a number of other women's issues. In 1985, Mary Beth discovered a lump in her breast which proved to be cancerous. As a method actor, Daly "lived" with the illness during Mary Beth's diagnosis and treatment, which involved a lumpectomy and radiation rather than the disfiguring mastectomy. She told one reporter, "I realized that as long as there are women being led astray by the medical establishment, women getting hacked into pieces, it's important that I tell the story, and it's important that I face the music." The following season, Daly's pregnancy was written into the series. The episode in which Mary Beth gave birth to Alice aired on the same day that Daly gave birth to her daughter.

As the series came to a close, Daly commented, "I played the hell out of [Lacey]. I knew everything there was to know about her." Between 1982 and 1988, Daly's craft was recognized with four Emmys for best actress in a dramatic series.

Besides her work in *Cagney and Lacey*, Daly is best known for her performance as Mama Rose in Broadway's revival of *Gypsy*, for which she received the Tony Award as best actress in a musical. Daly also continues to work in television movies and series, choosing roles of social significance. She played the mother of a child with Down's syndrome in *Kids Like These* (1987), a homeless woman in *Face*

Tyne Daly
Photo courtesy of Tyne Daly

of a Stranger (1991), and a Quaker community leader in the series *Christy* (1994–95). She has also done more comic turns on *Wings* (which stars her brother, Tim Daly), and on Sharon Gless's series, *The Trials of Rosie O'Neill*, in which she played an "old friend" who had more in common in looks and manner with the brash Mama Rose than with shy, frumpy Mary Beth. Daly and Gless have also reprised their roles in several *Cagney and Lacey* made-for-television-movies, two-hour presentations in which the characters continue to develop, in which the memories of both characters and viewers are used to explore a friendship and professional relationship moving further into mid-life complexity.

—Sue Brower

TYNE DALY. Born in Madison, Wisconsin, U.S.A., 1947. Attended Brandeis University, Waltham, Massachusetts; American Music and Dramatic Academy. Married: Georg Stanford Brown (divorced); three daughters. Performed at American Shakespeare Festival; made television debut in *The Virginian;* appeared in film *The Enforcer,* 1976; starred in television series, *Cagney and Lacey,* 1982–88; appeared on Broadway in revivals of *Gypsy,* 1990 and 1991. Recipient: Emmy Awards, 1982, 1983, 1984, and 1988; Tony Award, 1990. Agent address: Blake Agency, 415 North Camden Drive, Beverly Hills, California 90210, U.S.A.

TELEVISION SERIES

1982–88	*Cagney and Lacey*
1994–95	*Christy*

MADE-FOR-TELEVISION MOVIES

1971	*In Search of America*
1971	*A Howling in the Woods*
1971	*Heat of Anger*
1973	*The Man Who Could Talk to Kids*
1974	*Larry*
1975	*The Entertainer*
1977	*Intimate Strangers*
1979	*Better Late Than Never*
1980	*The Women's Room*
1981	*A Matter of Life and Death*
1983	*Your Place or Mine*
1987	*Kids Like These*
1989	*Stuck with Each Other*
1990	*The Last to Go*
1991	*Face of a Stranger*
1992	*Columbo: A Bird In the Hand*
1994	*Cagney and Lacey: The Return*
1994	*The Forget-Me-Not Murders*
1995	*Cagney and Lacey: Together Again*
1995	*Cagney and Lacey: The View Through the Glass Ceiling*
1995	*Bye, Bye Birdie*

FILMS

John and Mary, 1969; *Angel Unchained*, 1970; *Play It as It Lays*, 1972; *The Adultress*, 1973; *The Enforcer*, 1976; *Telefon*, 1977; *Speedtrap*, 1978; *Zoot Suit*, 1982; *The Aviator*, 1985; *Movers and Shakers*, 1985.

STAGE

Gypsy; The Seagull; Call Me Madam; Come Back Little Sheba; Ashes; Black Angel; Gethsemane Springs; Three Sisters; Vanities; Skirmishes; The Rimers of Eldritch; Birthday Party; Old Times; The Butter and Egg Man; That Summer That Fall.

FURTHER READING

D'Acci, Julie. *Defining Women: Television and the Case of Cagney and Lacey.* Chapel Hill, North Carolina: University of North Carolina Press, 1994.

Gordon, Mary. "Sharon Gless and Tyne Daly." *Ms.* (New York), January 1987.

See also *Cagney and Lacey*

DANGER BAY

Canadian Family Adventure Series

A half-hour dramatic series co-produced by the Canadian Broadcasting Corporation (CBC) and the Disney Channel, *Danger Bay* was a family adventure series set in Canada's scenic west coast. It starred Donnelly Rhodes as Dr. Grant Roberts, a veterinarian and marine specialist at the Vancouver Aquarium who was also busy raising his children, Jonah and Nicole, played by Chris Crabb and Ocean Hellman.

The aquarium and nearby coastal waters off Vancouver provided the exotic backdrop for many of the show's adventures which often focused on the children but always involved the whole family. Plots usually presented some kind of peril or violence to the animals at the aquarium or surrounding area, and each week the strong and daring "Doc" Roberts would foil the greedy and selfish schemes of poachers, hunters, and developers who posed a threat to the animals and environment.

Danger Bay was fairly formulaic, filled with elements that were conventional to family series. It presented a strong father figure in Donnelly Rhodes, a motherly figure in Joyce, Dr. Robert's girlfriend, (played by Deborah Wakeham), and Jonah and Nicole with whom young viewers could identify. Moral and psychological tensions were also muted, reflecting the Disney producers' reluctance to deal with controversial issues such as sex, drugs, or alcohol, as did the other contemporary Canadian teenage drama series, *Degrassi Ju-nior High*. Instead, dramatic tension in *Danger Bay* usually involved a morality lesson related to subjects such as lying or cheating, and were always resolved with the help of patient fatherly advice. The series did, however, try to reflect a more sensitive attitude toward the environment, women (Joyce was a bush-pilot), and visible minorities but such issues very rarely drew any direct attention in the plots.

Danger Bay reflected the basic characteristics of wholesomeness and adventure. Its formulaic nature and rather innocent perspective led some Canadian critics to see it as an example of the "Disneyfication" of Canadian television drama and it has been sharply criticized for its timidity. Defenders of the series have argued that the show provided fast-paced action and fun for a young viewing audience. Nevertheless, as Canadian television drama historian Mary Jane Miller points out, it remains "a blend of action and fathering with lots of running, chasing, fixing, rescuing." *Danger Bay* ended its run on Canadian television after six seasons in the spring of 1990 at the same time that another Canadian television drama series, *Beachcombers*, ended after 19 seasons on the CBC.

—Manon Lamontagne

CAST

Dr. Grant Roberts	Donnelly Rhodes
Jonah Roberts	Chris Crabb

Nicole Roberts . . . . Ocean Hellman
Joyce . . . . Deborah Wakeham

PRODUCERS   Philip Saltzman, Mary Eilts

PROGRAMMING HISTORY   123 Episodes

• CBC

November 1984-February 1985	Mondays 8:30-9:00
November 1985-March 1986	Mondays 8:00-8:30
November 1986-March 1987	Wednesdays 7:30-8:00
November 1987-March 1990	Mondays 7:30-8:00

FURTHER READING

Miller, Mary Jane. *Turn Up the Contrast: CBC Drama Since 1952.* Vancouver: University of British Columbia Press, 1987.

Skene, Wayne. *Fade to Black: A Requiem for the CBC.* Toronto: Douglas and MacIntyre, 1993.

DANN, MICHAEL

U.S. Network Executive

Michael Dann was one of the most successful programming executives in U.S. network television during the 1950s and 1960s. He was known as a "master scheduler" and spent his most successful years at CBS working in tandem with CBS President James Aubrey. He began his television career shortly after World War II as a comedy writer and in 1948 joined NBC, where he stayed for the next ten years. Initially hired to work in publicity, he soon moved to the programming department and eventually served as head of NBC Entertainment under David Sarnoff. In 1958, he moved to CBS as vice president of programs in New York. In 1963 he was promoted to head of programming, and in 1966 he was appointed senior vice president of programs. During most of his tenure, CBS consistently ranked as the number one network in prime-time audience ratings.

Dann held the head programming position at CBS longer than anyone else (from 1963 to 1970), serving under five different CBS presidents. His success was attributable, in part, to an uncanny ability to gauge William Paley's probable reaction to most program ideas. Dann was often referred to as "the weathervane" for changing his opinions to match those of his bosses. In spite of this reputation Dann was not one to avoid controversy. Arthur Godfrey, a long-time audience favorite at CBS, had two prime-time programs ranked in the top 10; during the 1950s he did not get along with Dann and left CBS as a result. (The fact that Godfrey disappeared from public view suggests that Dann was probably correct in his assessment that Godfrey was "over the hill".)

Dann was also able to restore and establish good and long-lasting relationships with talent producers and advertisers—an area in which CBS had suffered. He felt that viewers preferred escapist television to realist television, and thought the half-hour situation comedy was the staple of any prime-time schedule. He also believed the network should renew any program with ratings high enough to produce a profit.

Another development during Dann's regime was a significant increase in the number of specials aired. While the staple of prime-time programming was, and remains, the weekly series, Dann believed that liberal use of special programming at strategic times would only enhance the network's ratings. One could argue that he was the innovator of what has come to be called "event television".

In 1966, he recognized that television (and CBS, in particular) faced a major crisis—the networks were running out of first-run theatrical movies. As a result, CBS bought the old Republic Pictures lot, turned it into the CBS Studio

Michael Dann
Photo courtesy of Broadcasting and Cable

Center, and went into feature film production. ABC and NBC soon followed suit.

Among the many successful programs introduced under Dann's leadership were *The Mary Tyler Moore Show*, *The Carol Burnett Show*, *Mission: Impossible*, *Mannix*, *Hawaii Five-0*, and *60 Minutes*. These program development and programming skills were put to the test in one particular instance. For years CBS had trouble competing in the very important 9:00-10:00 P.M. slot on Sunday evenings, despite a very strong lead-in program (*The Ed Sullivan Show*). NBC had *Bonanza*, the highly successful series, in that time period and CBS had failed with its previous counter-programming attempts (*Judy Garland Show*, *Garry Moore Show*, *Perry Mason*). Dann chose a new series for this slot, a series he believed would attract a younger audience, *The Smothers Brothers Comedy Hour*. The move proved quite successful. The Smothers Brothers' show became a hit, though not without its share of controversy. The most notable conflict arose over an episode involving folk singer Pete Seeger in 1967, who was scheduled to sing his anti-war song "Waist Deep in the Big Muddy". Dann wanted Seeger to delete one stanza of the song. When Seeger and the Smothers refused, Dann had the song deleted from the telecast. In February 1968, Seeger was again scheduled to appear. This time the song, in its entirety, aired.

Dann's conservative attitudes toward social and cultural standards appeared again when CBS decided to air *The Mary Tyler Moore Show*. Dann had the producers make one change—Mary could not be a divorced woman. He felt that premise too controversial and forced James L. Brooks and Allan Burns to rewrite the character as a woman who had recently broken off a long-term engagement.

Dann's power at CBS began to wane in the late 1960s, as did the ratings of some of the shows he had developed and scheduled. His new boss, Robert Wood, wanted innovation, not sameness. Dann was forced out when he opposed cancellation of hit "rural" series: *The Red Skelton Show*, *The Jackie Gleason Show*, *Beverly Hillbillies*, *Green Acres*, and *Hee Haw*. These shows were replaced by series such as *All in the Family*, deemed more socially relevant and, perhaps more importantly, more appealing to a younger age group whose greater spending power attracted advertisers. The public explanation for Dann's departure was the ever-available and undefined "health reasons." His successor was his protégé,

Fred Silverman, who would go on to head the programming departments of all three networks.

—Mitchell E. Shapiro

MICHAEL DANN. Born in Detroit, Michigan, U.S.A., 11 September 1921. Educated at the University of Michigan, B.A. in economics 1941. Married: 1) Joanne Himmell, 1949 (divorced, 1973), children: Jonathan, Patricia, and Priscilla; 2) Louise Cohen, 1973. Comedy writer, 1946–47; public relations staff, New Haven Rail Road, 1947–48; trade editor, NBC press department, 1948–49, coordinator of program package sales, 1949–50, supervisor, special telecasts, 1950–52, manager, television program department, 1952–54, director, program sales, 1954–56, vice president, television program sales, 1956–58; vice president, network programming, CBS, 1958–63, vice president, programs, CBS, 1963–66, senior vice president, 1966–70; vice president and assistant to president, Children's Television Workshop, 1970s; consultant, Warner Cable, planning programming for QUBE, 1974; developed concepts for Disney's Epcot Center; senior program advisor, ABC Video Enterprises, 1980; visiting lecturer in american studies and guest fellow, Yale University, 1973–78.

FURTHER READING

Barnouw, Erik. *A History of Broadcasting in the United States, Volume III: The Image Empire*. New York: Oxford University Press, 1970.

Marc, David, and Robert J. Thompson. *Prime Time, Prime Movers: From I Love Lucy to L.A. Law, America's Greatest TV Shows and the People Who Created Them*. Boston: Little, Brown, 1992.

Metz, Robert. *CBS: Reflections in a Bloodshot Eye*. Chicago: Playboy, 1975.

Paley, William S. *As It Happened: A Memoir*. Garden City, New York: Doubleday, 1979.

Shapiro, Mitchell E. *Television Network Prime-Time Programming, 1948-1988*. Jefferson, North Carolina: McFarland, 1989.

Slater, Robert. *This...Is CBS: A Chronicle of 60 Years*. Englewood Cliffs, New Jersey: Prentice Hall, 1988.

See also Columbia Broadcasting System; Paley, William S.; *Smothers Brothers Comedy Hour*

THE DANNY KAYE SHOW

U.S. Comedy/Variety Program

The *Danny Kaye Show*, which premiered on 25 September 1963, was designed as a showcase for the multi-talented entertainer who, before appearing on television, was already a veteran of the vaudeville circuit, the Broadway stage, film, radio, and nightclubs. The variety series was not Kaye's first foray into television: a 1957 *See It Now* program,

entitled *The Secret Life of Danny Kaye*, documented Kaye entertaining children around the world on behalf of UNICEF, an organization for which he worked for many years. In 1960, Kaye signed a $1.5 million contract for three annual special programs that would set the pattern for his later series. Although these specials were not critically successful, audience ratings (and two Emmy nominations for his second special with Lucille Ball) were sufficient for CBS to offer the entertainer his own weekly series. That same season, veteran performers Jerry Lewis and Judy Garland also premiered variety series, but faded quickly.

Unlike comedians such as Red Skelton or Bob Hope, whose series highlighted their monologues, Kaye's variety hour was similar in scope to Sid Caesar's *Your Show of Shows* and *Caesar's Hour*. Kaye's series was a mixture of sketches and special musical material that showcased his inimitable talents. The series attracted prominent guests who helped Kaye demonstrate his own versatility. He sang scat with Louis Armstrong and calypso with Harry Belafonte, danced with Gene Kelly, and performed in sketches with such stars as actor José Ferrer and comedian Dick Van Dyke.

Kaye's strength was his ability to work with a live studio audience. Most episodes included a "quiet" segment highlighting Kaye's ability to work one-on-one with his audience and provide a sense of intimacy. In this portion, Kaye would sit on a chair at the edge of the stage.

At times, he would tell a story that would highlight his talent for dialects or tongue-twisting dialogue. On other occasions he would engage in conversation with a child (Victoria Meyerick or, later, Laurie Ichino) or a group of children.

The series was produced by Perry Lafferty, who had previously produced variety series for Arthur Godfrey and Andy Williams. Writers for the series included Larry Gelbart (who later created *M*A*S*H*) and Mel Tolkin, both of whom had also written for *Caesar's Hour*. Although Kaye's supporting cast did not appear on a weekly basis, they included Harvey Korman, Gwen Verdon, Joyce Van Patten, the Earl Brown Singers, the Clinger Sisters, and the Tony Charmoli Dancers.

In its first season, *The Danny Kaye Show* garnered three Emmy Awards, including one for the show and one for its star. That same season, the series also received a George Foster Peabody Award as one of the best entertainment programs for the year. During the series' four-year run, it accumulated a total of six Emmy nominations.

Despite Kaye's enormous talents and popularity, the series failed to gain a wide audience and never achieved critical success. Considering Kaye's popularity among younger viewers, his late hour time slot (10:00-11:00 P.M.) was a major factor in his mediocre ratings. A lack of direction in the show's format and average material often resulted in childlike antics that some critics felt were inappropriate. In addition, competition from other network programs, such as NBC's *Wednesday Night at the Movies* and *I Spy*, contributed to the variety show's low ratings.

However, Kaye remained popular with his audience and legions of fans. In fact, the variety series was imported to the United Kingdom in 1964 for the premiere of the BBC-2 channel and ran there for three seasons.

After his show's cancellation in 1967, Kaye returned to television in a number of special programs, mostly aimed at

The Danny Kaye Show

younger viewers, including Hallmark Hall of Fame's *Peter Pan* (NBC, 1976) and *Pinocchio* (CBS, 1976). That same year, he hosted the Emmy Award-winning *Danny Kaye's Look at the Metropolitan Opera* (CBS, 1976).

His last television appearances were in the Emmy-nominated *Live from Lincoln Center: An Evening with Danny Kaye and the New York Philharmonic* (PBS, 1981) and the CBS docudrama, *Skokie* (CBS, 1981). For both these performances, Kaye was presented with another Peabody Award "for virtuoso performances and versatility as a superb clown and as a sensitive dramatic actor." Kaye died in 1987.

—Susan R. Gibberman

REGULAR PERFORMERS
Danny Kaye
Harvey Korman (1964–67)
Joyce Van Patten (1964–67)
Laurie Ichino (1964–65)
Victoria Meyerink (1964–67)

MUSIC
The Johnny Mann Singers (1963–64)
The Earl Brown Singers (1964–67)
The Tony Charmoli Dancers
Paul Weston and His Orchestra

PRODUCERS   Perry Lafferty, Robert Tamplin

PROGRAMMING HISTORY   96 Episodes

• CBS

September 1963–June 1967   Wednesday 10:00-11:00

FURTHER READING

Freedland, Michael. *The Secret Life of Danny Kaye.* New York: St. Martin's, 1985.

Gottfried, Martin. *Nobody's Fool: The Lives of Danny Kaye.* New York: Simon and Schuster, 1994.

Gould, Jack. "Danny Kaye Brightens Home Sets." *New York Times*, 26 September 1963.

Singer, Kurt Deutsch. *The Danny Kaye Story.* New York: Thomas Nelson, 1958.

"Soliloquy." *Newsweek* (New York), 6 November 1961.

"The Wednesday Question: Want to Watch Danny Kaye?" *Newsweek* (New York), 23 December 1963.

See also Kaye, Danny

DARK SHADOWS

U.S. Gothic Soap Opera

This enormously popular half-hour gothic soap opera aired on ABC-TV from 1966 until 1971, and showcased a panoply of supernatural characters including vampires, werewolves, warlocks, and witches. During its initial run, the series spawned two feature-length motion pictures, *House of Dark Shadows* (1970) and *Night of Dark Shadows* (1971), as well as thirty-two tie-in novels, comic books, records, Viewmasters, games, models, and trading cards. Fans of the show included both adults and children (it aired in a late afternoon time slot which allowed young people the opportunity to see it after school), and many of these fans began to organize clubs and produce fanzines not long after the show was canceled. These groups were directly instrumental in getting *Dark Shadows* re-run in syndication on local stations (often public broadcasting stations), throughout the 1970s and 1980s and in persuading series creator Dan Curtis to remake the show as a prime-time weekly drama on NBC-TV in 1991. Although the new show did not catch on with the public, the entire run of *Dark Shadows*, both the original series and the remake, are available on tape from MPI Home Video. Fans continue to hold yearly conventions, write their own *Dark Shadows* fanzines, collect memorabilia, and lobby the entertainment industry.

Set in Collinsport, Maine, the original series focused on the tangled lives and histories of the Collins family. Matriarch Elizabeth Collins Stoddard (well-known classical Hollywood movie star Joan Bennett) presided over the ancestral estate, Collinwood, along with her brother Roger Collins (Louis Edmonds). The show was in danger of being canceled after its first few months on the air until the character of Barnabas Collins, a 172-year-old vampire, was introduced. As played by Jonathan Frid, Barnabas was less a monster and more a tortured gothic hero, and he quickly became the show's most popular character. Governess Victoria Winters (Alexandra Moltke), waitress Maggie Evans (Kathryn Leigh Scott), and Elizabeth's daughter Carolyn (Nancy Barrett) became the first few women to fall sway to the vampire's charms. Dr. Julia Hoffman (Grayson Hall) attempted to cure him of his affliction, although she too subsequently fell in love with him. Barnabas was protected during the day by his manservant Willie Loomis (John Karlen), although Roger's son David (David Henesy) almost discovered his secret.

One of the series' most innovative developments was its use of time travel and parallel universes as narrative tropes which constantly reshuffled storylines and characters, enabling many of the show's most popular actors to play different types of characters within different settings. The

Dark Shadows
Photo courtesy of Dan Curtis Productions

first of these shifts occurred when governess Victoria Winters traveled back in time (via a seance) to the year 1795, so the series could explore the origins of Barnabas's vampirism. The witch Angelique (Lara Parker) was introduced during these episodes, as was the witch-hunting Reverend Trask (Jerry Lacy). After the 1795 sequence, Angelique returned to present-day Collinwood as Roger's new wife Cassandra; she continued to practice witchcraft under the direction of warlock Nicholas Blair (Humbert Allen Astredo). Soon other classic gothic narratives were pressed into service, and the 1968 episodes also featured a werewolf, a *Frankenstein*-type creation, and pair of ghosts a la *Turn of the Screw*.

Those ghosts proved to be the catalyst to another time shift, this time to 1897, wherein dashing playboy Quentin Collins (David Selby) was introduced. His dark good looks and brooding sensuality made him a hit with the fans, and his popularity soon began to rival that of Barnabas. The 1897 sequence marked the height of the show's popularity, and the writers created intricately interwoven stories about vampires, witches, gypsies, zombies, madwomen, and a magical Count Petofi (Thayer David). Quentin was turned into a werewolf only to have the curse controlled by a portrait, as in *The Picture of Dorian Gray*. When the show returned to the present time once again, it began working a storyline liberally cribbed from H. P. Lovecraft's "Cthulu" mythos. Through various time shifts and parallel universes, the show continued to rework gothic classics (including *Dr. Jekyll and Mr. Hyde*, *The Turn of the Screw*, *Rebecca*, *Wuthering Heights*, and *The Lottery*) until its demise in 1971. Ingenues came and went, including pre-*Charlie's Angels* Kate Jackson as Daphne Harridge, and Donna (*A Chorus Line*) McKechnie as Amanda Harris.

The popularity of *Dark Shadows* must be set against the counter-cultural movements of the late 1960s: interest in alternative religions, altered states of consciousness, and paranormal phenomena such as witchcraft. *Dark Shadows* regularly explored those areas through its sympathetic supernatural creatures, while most of the true villains of the piece turned out to be stern patriarchs and hypocritical preachers. (The show did come under attack from some fundamentalist Christian groups who dubbed the series "Satan's favorite TV show.") Monstrous characters as heroic or likable figures were appearing elsewhere on TV at this time, in shows such as *Bewitched*, *The Addams Family*, and *The Munsters*. Many fans of those shows (and *Dark Shadows*) apparently looked to these figures as playful counter-cultural icons, existing in a twilight world somewhere outside the patriarchal hegemony. Furthermore, since the show was shot live on tape and mistakes were rarely edited out, the series had a bargain-basement charm which appealed both to spectators who took its storylines seriously and to those who appreciated the spooky goings-on as camp. The range of acting styles also facilitated a camp appreciation, as did the frequently outlandish situations, costumes, and make up. In spite of these technical shortcomings, the gothic romance of the show appears to be one of its most enduring charms. Fan publications most regularly try to recapture the tragic romantic flavor of the show rather than its campiness, although some fans faulted the latter-day NBC remake for taking itself too seriously. Whatever their idiosyncratic reasons, *Dark Shadows* fans remain devoted to the property, and its characters remain popular icons in American culture.

—Harry M. Benshoff

CAST

Victoria Winters	Alexandra Moltke
David Collins	David Hennessy
Elizabeth Collins	Joan Bennett
Barnabas Collins	Jonathan Frid
Roger Collins	Louis Edmonds
Dr. Julia Hoffman	Grayson Hall
Maggie Evans	Kathryn Leigh Scott
Carolyn	Nancy Barrett
Quentin Collins	David Selby
Daphne Harridge	Kate Jackson
Angelique	Lara Parker
Nicholas Blair	Humbert Allen Astredo
Reverend Trask	Jerry Lacy
Count Petofi	Thayer David
Willie Loomis	John Karlen

PRODUCERS   Dan Curtis, Robert Costello

PROGRAMMING HISTORY

• **ABC**

June 1966–April 1971	Non-Primetime

CAST (primetime series)

Barnabas Collins	Ben Cross
Victoria Winters/Josette	Joanna Going
Elizabeth Collins Stoddard/Naomi	Jean Simmons
Roger Collins/Reverend Trask	Roy Thinnes
David Collins/Daniel (age 8)	Joseph Gordon-Levitt
Dr. Julia Hoffman/Natalie	Barbara Steele
Prof. Woodward/Joshua	Stefan Gierasch
Angelique	Lysette Anthony
Willie Loomis/Ben	Jim Fyfe
Mrs. Johnson/Abigail	Julianna McCarthy
Sheriff Patterson	Michael Cavanaugh
Joe Haskell/Peter	Ely Pouget
Sarah Collins	Veronica Lauren
Carolyn Stoddard	Barbara Blackburn

PRODUCER   Dan Curtis

PROGRAMMING HISTORY

• **NBC**

January 1991	Sunday 9:00-10:00
January 1991	Monday 9:00-10:00
January 1991	Friday 10:00-11:00

| January 1991-March 1991 | Friday 9:00-10:00 |
| March 1991 | Friday 10:00-11:00 |

FURTHER READING

Benshoff, Harry M. "Secrets, Closets, and Corridors Through Time: Negotiating Sexuality and Gender in *Dark Shadows* Fan Culture." In, Alexander, A., and C. Harris, editors. *Theorizing Fandom: Fans, Subcultures, and Identity*. Cresskill, New Jersey: Hampton Press, 1996.

Pierson, Jim. *Dark Shadows Resurrected*. Los Angeles and London: Pomegranate, 1992.
Scott, Kathryn Leigh, editor. *The Dark Shadows Companion*. Los Angeles and London: Pomegranate, 1990.
Scott, Kathryn Leigh. *My Scrapbook Memories of Dark Shadows*. Los Angeles and London: Pomegranate, 1986.

See also Soap Opera

DAVIES, ANDREW

British Writer

Andrew Davies is an incredibly prolific award winning writer and adapter. He began his career in 1960 writing radio plays, moving into television, stage plays, children's books, novels, and films. He combined writing with his work as a teacher, then university lecturer, until the age of 50. Both professions inform some of his writing, such as his highly autobiographical *Bavarian Night* (BBC *Play for Today)*, which deals with a parent-teacher association evening, and the hugely successful series *A Very Peculiar Practice,* about general practitioners on a university campus.

Davies has long been recognized as writing good roles for women. He created the character Steph Smith as a vehicle for his "early feminist plays" for radio. Steph was a knicker factory worker aspiring to the life of the sales representative. Davies' first play for television, *Who's Going to Take Me On?* (on *Wednesday Play*) also featured Steph.

The mainstay of his television work has been for the BBC. Initially he felt himself in danger of being regarded solely as a writer of BBC naturalistic material, and turned to non-naturalistic writing, such as *Fearless Frank Harris*, in the early 1970s. His other original television work includes *A Very Polish Practice*, a one-off sequel to his series, and the pilot for the London Weekend Television series, *Anna Lee.*

Davies is also well known for a great many adaptations and dramatisations which have won him a string of awards. Following dramatisations of R.F. Deiderfield, *To Serve Them all My Days*, and *Diana*, he has adapted a host of very high-profile dramas for the BBC. After the success of dramatisations of Michael Dobbs' *House of Cards* and its sequel, *To Play the King* (for which he was accused of a left-wing bias), he was commissioned for the much-heralded, expensive and extensive version of George Eliot's *Middlemarch*, the BBC's most costly drama serial to that date. *Middlemarch* was praised in the trade press as a fast-moving, faithful adaptation of the original.

Having suggested that adapting Jane Austen would be a thankless task, since so many viewers know her books word for word, Davies dramatised *Pride and Prejudice*. This BBC serial was another great popular and critical success, despite the fact that it was preceded by strong reactions from tabloid newspapers over the possibility it might feature nudity.

Davies enjoys adapting other authors' work, grateful for the existing plot in which to exercise his own humour and explore his preoccupations. There are also those originals he admires to the extent that he wishes solely to do them justice. In this category he cites *Anglo-Saxon Attitudes* and *The Old Devils*. He was involved in a very public struggle to get screen time for *Anglo-Saxon Attitudes*, attacking ITV's "flexipool" (or "indecision pool") in the process. It was then commissioned on the back of discussions regarding "quality."

As well as writing numerous children's books, Davies is also an award-winning writer of children's television. He wrote two original series of *Marmalade Atkins* for Thames TV, and dramatised *Alfonso Bonzo* as a six-part serial from his own children's novel. He has also written feature film screenplays, including *Circle of Friends* and an adaptation of his own book, *B. Monkey.*

—Guy Jowett

ANDREW (WYNFORD) DAVIES. Born in Rhiwbina, Cardiff, Wales, 20 September 1936. Attended Whitchurch Grammar School, Cardiff; University College, London, B.A. in English 1957. Married: Diana Huntley, 1960; children: one son and one daughter. Began career as teacher at St. Clement Danes Grammar School, London, 1958–61, and Woodberry Down Comprehensive School, London, 1961–63; lecturer, Coventry College of Education, 1963–71, and University of Warwick, Coventry, 1971–87. Wrote first play for radio, 1964; television and film writer; author of several stage plays and fiction aimed at both young and adult audiences. Recipient: *Guardian* Children's Fiction Award, 1979; *Boston Globe-Horn* Book Award, 1980; Broadcast Press Guild Awards, 1980, 1990; Pye Colour TV Award, 1981; Royal Television Society Award, 1987; British Academy of Film and Television Arts Awards, 1989, 1993; Writers Guild Awards, 1991, 1992; Primetime Emmy Award, 1991. Address: Lemon, Unna and Durbridge, 24 Pottery Lane, London W11 4LZ, England.

TELEVISION SERIES (selection)

1980	*To Serve Them all My Days*
1986–88	*A Very Peculiar Practice*
1989	*Mother Love*

1990	*House of Cards*
1993	*To Play the King*
1994	*Middlemarch*
1995	*Game On*
	(with Bernadette Davis)
1995	*Pride and Prejudice*

TELEVISION PLAYS (selection)

1967	*Who's Going to Take Me On?*
1970	*Is That Your Bod, Boy?*
1973	*No Good Unless It Hurts*
1974	*The Water Maiden*
1975	*Grace*
1975	*The Imp of the Perverse*
1976	*The Signalman*
1976	*A Martyr to the System*
1977	*Eleanor Marx*
1977	*Happy in War*
1977	*Velvet Glove*
1978	*Fearless Frank*
1978	*Renoir My Father*
1981	*Bavarian Night*
1983	*Heartattack Hotel*
1984	*Diana*
1985	*Pythons on the Mountain*
1987	*Inappropriate Behaviour*
1988	*Lucky Sunil*
1988	*Baby, I Love You*
1991	*Filipina Dreamers*
1992	*The Old Devils*
1992	*Anglo-Saxon Attitudes*
1992	*A Very Polish Practice*
1993	*Anna Lee*
1993	*Harnessing Peacocks*
1994	*A Few Short Journeys of the Heart*

FILM
Circle of Friends.

RADIO
The Hospitalization of Samuel Pellett, 1964; *Getting the Smell of It*, 1967; *A Day in Bed*, 1967; *Curse on Them, Astonish Me!*, 1970; *Steph and the Man of Some Distinction*, 1971; *The Innocent Eye*, 1971; *The Shortsighted Bear*, 1972; *Steph and the Simple Life*, 1972; *Steph and the Zero Structure Lifestyle*, 1976; *Accentuate the Positive*, 1980; *Campus Blues*, 1984.

STAGE
Can Anyone Smell the Gas?, 1972; *The Shortsighted Bear*, 1972; *Filthy Fryer and the Woman of Mature Years*, 1974; *Linda Polan: Can You Smell the Gas?*, *What Are Little Girls Made of?*, 1975; *Rohan and Julia*, 1975; *Randy Robinson's Unsuitable Relationship*, 1976; *Teacher's Gone Mad*, 1977; *Going Bust*, 1977; *Fearless Frank*, 1978; *Brainstorming with the Boys*, 1978; *Battery*, 1979; *Diary of a Desperate Woman*, 1979; *Rose*, 1980; *Prin*, 1990.

PUBLICATIONS (selection)
The Fantastic Feats of Doctor Boox. London: Collins, 1972.
Conrad's War. London, Blackie, 1978.
Marmalade and Rufus. London: Abelard-Schuman, 1979; New York: Crown, 1980.
Poonam's Pets, with Diana Davies. London: Methuen Children's, 1990. New York: Viking, 1990.
B. Monkey. London: Lime Tree, 1992.

FURTHER READING
"Pride and Prurience (Andrew Davies' Racy Adaptation of Jane Austen's Pride and Prejudice)." *The Economist* (London), 3 November 1990.
Rafferty, Frances. "Always One Page Ahead." *Times Educational Supplement* (London), 8 November 1991.

DAY, ROBIN

British Broadcast Journalist

Sir Robin Day is admired as one of the most formidable of political interviewers and commentators in British television and radio. An aspiring politician himself in the 1950s, he subsequently acquired a reputation for challenging questions and acerbic resistance to propagandist responses that made him the model for virtually all political interviewers who came after him.

As a student at Oxford, Day became president of the Oxford Union debating society and subsequently trained for the Bar before realizing that a career in the media was ideally suited to his talents. With athlete Chris Chataway, he was one of fledgling Independent Television New's (ITN) first two newscasters and created a considerable impact with his forceful personality and style of delivery, which was in marked contrast to the stuffier and more formal style of the BBC presenters. He

also developed his skills as a political interviewer for the small screen; in 1957, for instance, while working for ITN's *Roving Report* at a time when Britain and Egypt were still technically at war over the Suez Crisis, he scored a notable coup when he managed to secure an interview with Egypt's President Nasser.

After his own bid for parliament (as a candidate for the Liberals) failed in 1959, Day moved to the BBC as a reporter and presenter of *Panorama*, which under his leadership, carrying on from that of Richard Dimbleby, consolidated its reputation as the corporation's most influential political programme. Respected and indeed feared by politicians of all parties, Day became a national institution, instantly familiar with his breath-sucking speech, large black-rimmed spectacles and flamboyant spotted bow ties—and a favourite subject of impersonators.

Interviewees were rarely allowed to wriggle off the hook by the relentless Day, who showed scant respect for rank and title, and on several occasions guests were bludgeoned into making disclosures that would doubtless have otherwise remained unrevealed (though some viewers were appalled at Day's brusque persistence and called him rude and insensitive).

After 13 years with *Panorama*, Day hosted his own *Newsday* programme and also presented radio's *The World at One* for several years. In 1979, he was the first chair of the popular *Question Time* programme, based on radio's *Any Questions?*, in which prominent members of parliamentary and public life were invited to field questions on topical issues from a studio audience. Under Day's eagle eye the programme quickly established itself as the best of its kind and attracted a huge audience under both him and successive presenters. Since his departure from the programme, after some 10 years in the chair and by now a veteran of some 30 years' television experience and knighted in acknowledgment of his achievements, he has confined himself largely to occasional work for the satellite and regional television stations.

Some politicians have found Day's dogged—even belligerent—style of questioning too much to take and on several occasions notable figures have lost their temper. Defence Secretary John Nott was a particularly celebrated victim of the master-interviewer's attacks, snatching off his microphone and storming out of a television interview with Day at the time of the Falklands Crisis after taking offence at his questions.

—David Pickering

ROBIN DAY. Born in London, England, 23 October 1923. Attended Bembridge School; St. Edmund Hall, Oxford, B.A. with honors in jurisprudence 1951; Middle Temple, M.A.; Blackstone Entrance Scholar, 1951; Harmsworth Law School, 1952–53. Served in Royal Artillery, 1943–47. Married: Katherine Ainslie, 1965 (divorced, 1986); children: Alexander and Daniel. Called to the Bar, 1952; worked for British Information Services, Washington, 1953–54; freelance broadcaster, 1954; radio talks producer, BBC, 1955; newscaster and Parliamentary correspondent, Independent Television News, 1955–59; columnist, *News Chronicle*, 1959; worked on various ITV programs, 1955–59; ran unsuccessfully for Parliament, as a Liberal, 1959; hosted numerous BBC radio and television current affairs programs, including *Panorama, Newsday* and *Question Time*, from 1959; retired as regular presenter, 1989, but has since worked on satellite and regional television. LLD: University of Exeter, 1986; Keele University, 1988; University of Essex, 1988. Honorary Fellow, St. Edmund Hall, Oxford, 1989; Honorary Bencher, 1990. Member: Trustee, Oxford Literary and Debating Union; Phillmore Committee on Law of Contempt, 1971–74; Chair, Hansard Society, 1981–83. Knighted, 1981. Recipient: Guild of TV Producers' Merit Award, Personality of the Year, 1957; Richard

Robin Day
Photo courtesy of Robin Day

Dimbleby Award for factual television, 1974; Broadcast Press Guild Award, 1980; Royal Television Society Judges' Award, 1985.

TELEVISION SERIES

1955–59	*Independent Television News*
1955–59	*Tell the People*
1955–59	*Under Fire*
1957	*Roving Report*
1959–72	*Panorama* (presenter, 1967–72)
1976	*Newsday*
1979–89	*Question Time*
1992	*The Parliamentary Programme*
1992	*The Elder Statesmen*

RADIO

It's Your Line, 1970–76; *Election Call*, 1974, 1979, 1983, 1987; *The World at One*, 1979–87.

PUBLICATIONS (selection)

The Case for Televising Parliament. London: Hansard Society for Parliamentary Government, 1963.

Day by Day (autobiography). London: Kimber, 1975.

The Grand Inquisitor (autobiography). London: Pan, 1989.

...But with Respect (interviews). London: Weidenfeld and Nicholson, 1993.

FURTHER READING

Cox, Geoffrey. *Pioneering Television News: A First Hand Report on a Revolution in Journalism.* London: John Libby, 1995.

Milne, Alisdair. *DG: Memoirs of a British Broadcaster.* London: Hodder and Stoughton, 1988.

See also *Panorama*

THE DAY AFTER

U.S. Drama

The Day After, a dramatization of the effects of a hypothetical nuclear attack on the United States, was one of the biggest media events of the 1980s. Programmed by ABC on Sunday, 20 November 1983, *The Day After* was watched by an estimated half of the U.S. adult population, the largest audience for a made-for-TV movie to that time. The movie was broadcast after weeks of advance publicity, fueled by White House nervousness about its anti-nuclear "bias". ABC had distributed a half-million "viewer's guides" and discussion groups were organized around the country. A studio discussion, in which the U.S. Secretary of State took part, was conducted following the program. The advance publicity was unprecedented in scale. It centered on the slogan "*THE DAY AFTER*—Beyond Imagining. The starkly realistic drama of nuclear confrontation and its devastating effect on a group of average American citizens..."

The show was the brainchild of Brandon Stoddard, then president of ABC Motion Picture Division, who had been impressed by the theatrical film *The China Syndrome*. Directed by Nicholas Meyer, a feature film director, *The Day After* went on to be either broadcast or released as a theatrical feature in over 40 countries. In Britain, for example, an edited version was shown three weeks later, on the ITV commercial network, and accompanied by a Campaign for Nuclear Disarmament recruitment drive. It was critically dismissed as a typically tasteless American travesty of the major theme—in a country which had yet to transmit Peter Watkins' film on the same theme, *The War Game*.

Wherever it was shown, *The Day After* raised questions about genre, and about politically committed TV and its ideological effects. Was it drama-documentary, faction (how do you depict a catastrophe that has not yet happened?) or disaster movie? It could be seen as stretching the medium, in the lineage of *Roots* and *Holocaust*, manipulating a variety of prestige TV and film propaganda devices to raise itself above the ratings war and the attempt to address a notional universal audience about the twentieth century nightmare.

ABC defined the production both in terms of realism—for example, the special effects to do with the missiles and blast were backed up with rosters of scientific advisors—and of art, as a surrealist vision of the destruction of western civilization—as miniaturized in a mid-West town and a nuclear family (graphically represented in the movie poster). Network executives were particularly aware of the issue of taste and the impact of horror on sensitive viewers (they knew that Watkins' film had been deemed "too horrifying for the medium of television"), al-

though, contradictorily, the majority of the audience was supposed to be already inured to the depiction of suffering. The delicate issue of identification with victims and survivors was handled by setting the catastrophe in a real town with ICBM silos and by using a large cast of relatively unknown actors (though John Lithgow, playing a scientist, would become more famous) and a horde of extras, constellated around the venerable Jason Robards as a doctor. *Time* magazine opined that "much of the power came from the quasi-documentary idea that nuclear destruction had been visited upon the real town of Lawrence, Kansas, rather than upon some back lot of Warner Brothers." Scriptwriter Edward Hume decided to fudge the World War III scenario: "It's not about politics or politicians or military decision-makers. It is simply about you and me—doctors, farmers, teachers, students, brothers and kid sisters engaged in the usual love and labor of life in the month of September." (This populist

The Day After

dimension was reinforced when the mayor of Lawrence, Kansas, sent a telegram to Soviet leader Andropov.)

There is an American pastoralism at work in the depiction of prairie life. Director Nicholas Meyer (*Star Trek II*) was aware of the danger of lapsing into formulae, and wrote in a "production diary" for *TV Guide*: "The more *The Day After* resembles a film, the less effective it is likely to be. No TV stars. What we don't want is another Hollywood disaster movie with viewers waiting to see Shelley Winters succumb to radiation poisoning. To my surprise, ABC agrees. Their sole proviso: one star to help sell the film as a feature oversees. Fair enough." Production proceeded without the cooperation of the Defense Department, which had wanted the script to make it clear the Soviets started the war. Despite sequences of verite and occasional trappings of actuality, the plot develops in soap opera fashion, with two families about to be united by marriage. But it evolves to an image of a community that survives the nuclear family, centered on what is left of the local university and based on the model of a medieval monastery. Although November was sweeps month, there were to be no commercial breaks after the bomb fell. Even so, its critics assimilated the film to the category of made-for-TV treatment of sensational themes. Complained a *New York Times* editorial, "A hundred million Americans were summoned to be empathetically incinerated, and left on the true day after without a single idea to chew upon." Other critics found it too tame in its depiction of the effects of nuclear attack (abroad, this was sometimes attributed to American naivete about war)—a reproach anticipated in the final caption "The catastrophic events you have witnessed are, in all likelihood, less severe than the destruction that would actually occur in the event of a full nuclear strike against the United States". And some critics appreciated its aesthetic ambitions, which included a self-reflexive moment about inserting yourself into a Chinese landscape painting. Not since has the hybrid between entertainment and information, between a popular genre like disaster, and the address to the enlightened citizen, been as successfully attempted by a network in a single media event.

—Susan Emmanuel

CAST

Dr. Russell Oakes . . . . Jason Robards

Nancy Bauer . . . . JoBeth Williams

Stephen Klein . . . . Steve Guttenberg

Jim Dahlberg . . . . John Cullum

Joe Huxley . . . . John Lithgow

Eve Dahlberg . . . . Bibi Beach

Denise Dahlberg . . . . Lori Lethin

Alison Ransom . . . . Amy Madigan

Bruce Gallatin . . . . Jeff East

Helen Oakes . . . . Georgann Johnson

Airman McCoy . . . . William Allen Young

Dr. Sam Hachiya . . . . Calvin Jung

Dr. Austin . . . . Lin McCarthy

Reverend Walker . . . . Dennis Lipscomb

Dennis Hendry . . . . Clayton Day

Danny Dahlberg . . . . Doug Scott

Jolene Dahlberg . . . . Ellen Anthony

Marilyn Oakes . . . . Kyle Aletter

Cynthia . . . . Alston Ahearn

Professor . . . . William Allyn

Ellen Hendry . . . . Antonie Becker

Nurse . . . . Pamela Brown

Julian French . . . . Jonathan Estrin

Aldo . . . . Stephen Furst

Tom Cooper . . . . Arliss Howard

Dr. Wallenberg . . . . Rosanna Huffman

Cleo Mackey . . . . Barbara Iley

TV Host . . . . Madison Mason

Cody . . . . Bob Meister

Mack . . . . Vahan Moosekian

Dr. Landowska . . . . George Petrie

2nd Barber . . . . Glenn Robards

1st Barber . . . . Tom Spratley

Vinnie Conrad . . . . Stan Wilson

PRODUCERS   Robert Papazian, Stephanie Austin

PROGRAMMING HISTORY

• ABC

20 November 1983   8:00-10:35

FURTHER READING

Boyd-Bowman, Susan, "*The Day After*: Representations of the Nuclear Holocaust." *Screen* (London), July-October 1984.

DEATH ON THE ROCK

British Investigative Documentary

Death on the Rock was the title of a programme in the current affairs series *This Week*, made by Thames Television and broadcast on the ITV network on 28 April 1988. The programme investigated the incident, on Sunday, 6 March 1988, when three members of the IRA, sent to Gibraltar on an active service mission, were shot and killed by members of British special forces. The incident, and subsequently the programme about it, became controversial as a result of uncertainty and conflicting evidence about the manner in which the killing was carried out and the degree to which it was an "execution" with no attempted arrest. The programme interviewed witnesses who claimed to have heard no prior warning given by the SAS troops and to have seen the shooting as one carried out "in cold blood." Furthermore, the defence that the IRA team might, if allowed time, have had the capacity to trigger by remote control a car bomb in the main street, was also subject to criticism, including that from an army bomb disposal expert.

Claiming that its transmission prior to the official inquest was an impediment to justice, the then foreign secretary, Sir Geoffrey Howe, attempted to stop the programme being broadcast by writing to the chairman of the Independent Broadcasting Authority, Lord Thomson of Monifieth. Lord Thomson refused to prevent transmission noting that "the issues as we see them relate to free speech and free inquiry which underpin individual liberty in a democracy." Following transmission, there was widespread criticism of the programme's investigative stance in sections of the press (e.g. "Storm at SAS Telly Trial," *The Sun*; "Fury over SAS 'Trial by TV'," *Daily Mail*; "TV Slur on the SAS," *Daily Star*). Subsequently, a number of papers, notably *The Sunday Times* and *The Sun*, attempted to show not only that the programme's procedures of inquiry were faulty but that the character of some of its witnesses was dubious (in one case, this latter charge resulted in a successful libel action being brought).

Such was the debate which developed around the programme, intensified by one of its witnesses subsequently repudiating his testimony in it, that an independent inquiry was conducted at the behest of Thames Television. This inquiry was undertaken by Lord Windlesham, an ex-government minister with experience as a managing director in television, and Richard Rampton, a barrister specializing in defamation and media law. The inquiry's findings, which were published as a book in 1989, largely cleared the programme of any impropriety, although it noted a number of errors.

Any assessment of the *Death on the Rock* affair has to note a number of constituent factors. The hugely emotive and politically controversial issue of British military presence in Northern Ireland provides the backdrop. For much of the British public, the various bombing attacks of the IRA (many of them involving civilian casualties) seemed to give the incident in Gibraltar the character of a wartime event, whose legitimacy was unquestionable. At a more focused level, the Windlesham/Rampton report opened up, in unusual detail, on the narrative structure of current affairs exposition—its movement between interview and presenter commentary, its use of location material, its movements of evaluation. It also probed further back, into the way in which the programme was put together through the contacting of various witnesses and the investigations of researchers. This was set in the context of long-standing tension between the Conservative government and broadcasters, particularly investigative journalists, on the matter of "national interest" and on the "limits" which should be imposed (preferably self-imposed) on work which brought into question the activities of the state.

Death on the Rock
Photo courtesy of the British Film Institute

There is obviously little space here to look at the programme's form in any detail but a number of features in its opening suggest something of its character. The programme starts with a pre-title sequence which features two of its principal witnesses, Carmen Proetta and Stephen Bullock, in "soundbites" from the longer interviews. These go as follows:

(Witness 1) There was no exchange of words on either side, no warning, nothing said; no screams, nothing; just the shots.

(Witness 2) I should say they were from a distance of about four feet and that the firing was continuous; in other words, probably as fast as it's possible to fire.

After the titles, the programme is "launched" by the studio-based presenter (Jonathan Dimbleby):

The killing by the SAS of three IRA terrorists in Gibraltar provoked intense debate not only in Britain but throughout the world—and especially in the Republic of Ireland and the United States. There are perhaps those who wonder what the fuss is about, who ask "Does it really matter when or how they were killed?"; who say "They were terrorists, there's a war on; and we got to them before they got us." However in the eyes of the law and of the state it is not so simple...The question which goes to the heart of the issue, is this: did the SAS men have the law on their side when they shot dead (photo stills) Danny McCann, Sean Savage and Mairead Farrell who were unarmed at the time?
(photo of bodies and ambulance) Were the soldiers

acting in self-defence or were they operating what has become known as a "shoot to kill policy"—simply eliminating a group of known terrorists outside the due process of law, without arrest, trial or verdict?

Dimbleby concludes his introduction by promising the viewer something of "critical importance for those who wish to find out what really happened."

This use of a "shock" opener, followed by the framing of the report in terms which anticipate one kind of popular response but which set against this the need for questions to be asked, gives the programme a strong but measured start. Its conclusion is similarly balanced, anticipating at least some of the next morning's complaints by attempting to connect its own inquiries with the due process of the law:

That report by Julian Manyon was made, as you may have detected, without the co-operation of the British Government which says that it will make no comment until the inquest. As our film con-

tained much new evidence hitherto unavailable to the Coroner, we are sending the transcripts to his court in Gibraltar, where it's been made clear to us that all such evidence is welcomed.

Given the political debate it caused, there is little doubt that *Death on the Rock* is established as a marker in the long history of government-broadcaster relationships in Britain.

—John Corner

PROGRAMMING HISTORY

• ITV

28 April 1988

FURTHER READING

"A Child of Its Time." *The Economist* (London), 4 February 1989.

Windlesham, P., and R. Rampton. *The Windlesham/Rampton Report on 'Death on the Rock'.* London: Faber, 1989.

THE DEFENDERS

U.S. Legal Drama

The *Defenders* was American television's seminal legal drama, and perhaps the most socially-conscious series the medium has ever seen. The series boasted a direct lineage to the age of live television drama, but also possessed a concern for topical issues and a penchant for social comment that were singularly resonant with New Frontier liberalism. With its contemporary premise and its serious tone, *The Defenders* established the model for a spate of social-issue programs that followed in the early 1960s, marking a trend toward dramatic shows centered on non-violent, professional "heroes" (doctors, lawyers, teachers, politicians).

The series had its origins in a 1957 *Studio One* production entitled "The Defender," written by Reginald Rose, one of the most prominent writers from the age of live anthology dramas. Having collaborated with Rose on the original two-part "Defender" teleplay and other productions, veteran anthology producer Herbert Brodkin teamed again with the writer to oversee the series. Brodkin and Rose were able to attract a large number of anthology alumni as writers for the series, including Ernest Kinoy, David Shaw, Adrian Spies, and Alvin Boretz. Although Rose authored only eleven of *The Defenders'* 130 episodes, Brodkin, the cast, and the writing staff always acknowledged that Rose, as senior story editor, put his own indelible stamp on the show. *The Defenders'* creators went against the overwhelming tide of Hollywood-based programs, following the tradition of the live anthologies—and the more recent police drama *Naked City*—by mounting their show in New York. Although *The Defenders* was primarily a studio-bound operation, with minimal location shooting, its success proved to be a key

contributor to a small renaissance in New York-based production in the early 1960s.

The series concerned the cases of a father-and-son team of defense attorneys, Lawrence Preston (E.G. Marshall), the sharp veteran litigator, and his green and idealistic son Kenneth (Robert Reed). (Ralph Bellamy and William Shatner had originated the roles of "Walter and Kenneth Pearson" in the *Studio One* production.) During the show's four years on the air, Ken Preston became more seasoned in the courtroom, but for the most part character development took second place to explorations of the legal process and contemporary social issues.

As Rose pointed out a 1964 article, "the law is the *subject* of our programs: not crime, not mystery, not the courtroom for its own sake. We were never interested in producing a 'who-done-it' which simply happened to be resolved each week in a flashy courtroom battle of wits." Rose undoubtedly had in mind CBS' other celebrated defense attorney *Perry Mason* (1957-66) when he wrote these words. Although both were nominally "courtroom dramas" or "lawyer shows," *Perry Mason* was first and foremost a classical detective story whose climax played out in the courtroom, while *The Defenders* focused on the machinery of the law, the vagaries of the legal process, and system's capacity for justice. Although the Prestons took on their share of murder cases, their aim in such instances was to mount a sound defense or plead for mercy, not unmask the real killer on the witness stand.

Certainly *The Defenders* exploited the inherent drama of the courtroom, but it did so by mining the complexity of

The Defenders

the law, its moral and ethical implications, and its human dimensions. Rose and his writers found much compelling drama in probing the psychology of juries, the motives of clients, the biases of opposing counsel, the flaws of the system itself, and the fallibility of their own lawyer-heroes. The series frequently took a topical perspective on the American justice system, honing in on timely or controversial legal questions: capital punishment, "no-knock" search laws, custody rights of adoptive parents, the insanity defense, the "poisoned fruit doctrine" (admissibility of illegally obtained evidence), as well as immigration quotas and Cold War visa restrictions. *The Defenders* avoided simple stances on such cases, instead illuminating ambiguities and opposing perspectives, and stressing the uncertain and fleeting nature of justice before the law.

As Rose declared in *The Viewer* magazine, "We're *committed* to controversy." And indeed, the series often went beyond a strict focus on "the law" to probe the profound social issues that are often weighed in the courtroom. *The Defenders'* most controversial case was "The

Benefactor," in which the Prestons defend an abortionist—and in the process mount an unequivocal argument in favor of legalized abortion. Although the series regularly nettled some sponsors and affiliates, this 1962 installment marked a major crisis, with the series' three regular sponsors pulling their support from the episode. Another advertiser stepped in at the eleventh hour and sponsored the show, and the network reported that audience response to the program was 90% positive. As one CBS executive recalled to author Robert Metz, "Everybody survived, and that was the beginning of *The Defenders* dealing with issues that really mattered." While not all of the Prestons' cases were so politically-charged, the show took on current social concerns with some frequency. One of the series' most acclaimed stories, "Blacklist," offered a quietly powerful indictment of Hollywood blacklisting; in other episodes the Prestons defended a schoolteacher fired for being an atheist, an author accused of pornography, a conscientious objector, civil rights demonstrators, a physician charged in a mercy-killing, and neo-Nazis.

The Defenders tended to take an explicitly liberal stance on the issues it addressed, but it offered no easy answers, no happy endings. Unlike *Perry Mason*, courtroom victories were far from certain on *The Defenders*—as were morality and justice. "The law is man-made, and therefore imperfect," Larry tells his son near the end of "Blacklist." "We don't always have the answer. There *are* injustices in the world. And they're not always solved at the last minute by some brilliant point of law at a dramatic moment." With all their wisdom and virtue, the Prestons were fallible, constrained by the realities of the legal system, the skill of their opponents, the whims of juries, the decisions of the bench. Yet, if *The Defenders'* view of the law was resigned, it was also resilient, manifesting a dogged optimism, acknowledging the flaws of the system, but affirming its merits—that is, its ability to change and its potential for compassion. The Prestons wearily admitted that the system was not perfect, but they returned each week to embrace it because of its potential for justice—and because it's the only system we have (a point that has become almost a cliché on subsequent legal dramas like *L.A. Law* and *Law and Order*). It was this slender thread of optimism that enabled the defenders to continue their pursuit of justice, one case at a time.

As a serious courtroom drama, *The Defenders* series meshed well with network aims for prestige in the early sixties in the wake of the quiz show scandals and charges of creeping mediocrity in TV fare. The dramatic arena of the courtroom and the legal system allowed for suspense without violence, and the avoidance of formula plots characteristic of traditional crime and adventure drama. With consistently strong ratings and a spate of awards unmatched by any other series of its day, *The Defenders* proved that controversy and topicality were not necessarily uncommercial. The series was in the works well before FCC Chairman Newton Minow's 1961 "vast wasteland" speech, but there is little doubt that the new Minow-inspired regulatory atmosphere augured well for the rise of such programming. The show's success supported the development of a number of social-issue and political dramas in the following years, notably *Slattery's People* and *East Side, West Side*, and gave further impetus to a shift in network programming from action-adventure to character drama. But most significant of all, it grappled with larger ethical and political questions, pulling social problems and political debate to center stage, presenting a consistent, ongoing and sometimes critical examination of contemporary issues and social morality. In the episode entitled "The Star-Spangled Ghetto" (written by Rose) a judge takes the elder Preston to task for invoking the social roots of his clients' acts as part of his defense: "The courtroom is not the place to explore the questions of society." Lawrence Preston responds, "It is for me." So was the television courtroom, for Reginald Rose and the writers of *The Defenders*.

—Mark Alvey

CAST

Lawrence Preston . . . . E.G. Marshall

Kenneth Preston . . . . Robert Reed
Helen Donaldson (1961–1962) . . . . Polly Rowles
Joan Miller (1961–1962) . . . . Joan Hackett

PRODUCERS   Herbert Brodkin, Robert Maxwell, Kenneth Utt

PROGRAMMING HISTORY   132 Episodes

• CBS

September 1961–September 1963	Saturday 8:30-9:30
September 1963–November 1963	Saturday 9:00-10:00
November 1963–September 1964	Saturday 8:30-9:30
September 1964–September 1965	Thursday 10:00-11:00

FURTHER READING

"The Best of both Worlds." *Television* (New York), June 1962.

Bodger, Lowell A. "Shooting *The Defenders*." *American Cinematographer* (Hollywood, California), July 1963.

Crean, Robert. "On the (Left) Side of the Angels." *Today*, January, 1964.

Efron, Edith. "The Eternal Conflict Between Good and Evil." *TV Guide* (Radnor, Pennsylvania), July, 1962; reprint in Harris, Jay S., editor. *TV Guide: The First 25 Years*. New York: Simon and Schuster, 1978.

Gelman, Morris J. "New York, New York." *Television* (New York), December, 1962.

Metz, Robert. *CBS: Reflections in a Bloodshot Eye*. New York: Signet, 1975.

"$108,411 for an Hour's Work." *Television* (New York), September, 1961.

Oulahan, Richard, and William Lambert. "The Tyrant's Fall that Rocked the TV World." *Life* (New York), 10 September 1965.

Reginald Rose Collection, Wisconsin Center for Film and Theater Research.

Rose, Reginald. "Law, Drama, and Criticism." *Television Quarterly* (New York), Fall 1964.

"The Show that Dared to Be Controversial." *The Viewer*, May 1964.

Smith, Sally Bedell. *In all his Glory*. New York: Simon and Schuster, 1990.

Steinberg, Cobbett. *TV Facts*. New York: Facts on File, 1980.

Stempel, Tom. *Storytellers to the Nation*. New York: Continuum, 1992.

"Three Sponsors Withdraw from Program Dealing with Abortion; CBS to Show Drama as Scheduled." *New York Times* (New York), 9 April 1962.

Watson, Mary Ann. *The Expanding Vista: American Television in the Kennedy Years*. New York: Oxford University Press, 1990.

See also Bellamy, Ralph; Kinoy, Ernest; Rose, Reginald; *Studio One*

DEGRASSI (THE KIDS OF DEGRASSI STREET; DEGRASSI JUNIOR HIGH; DEGRASSI HIGH; DEGRASSI TALKS)

Canadian Drama Series

Over the decade of the 1980s, three *Degrassi* drama series appeared on the Canadian Broadcasting Corporation (CBC), Canada's public television network. The programs, all in half-hour format, began with *The Kids of Degrassi Street,* which was followed by *Degrassi Junior High,* then *Degrassi High.* Central *Degrassi* actors then reappeared in the CBC's 1991–92 season as roving interviewers and hosts of *Degrassi Talks,* a youth magazine program. This program focused on pertinent topics such as sex, work, and abuse, all examined from the perspectives of Canada's youth. This point of view was in keeping with the pre-credit program statement, "Real kids talking to real kids from the heart." The federal government's Health and Welfare Canada was a core sponsor of *Degrassi Talks,* suggesting official recognition and support of a distinct youth culture and an agenda of intentional socialization, using CBC television and the well-known *Degrassi* cast as teaching agents.

A two-hour television movie special, *School's Out!* (1992), completed the *Degrassi* coming-of-age cycle that had structured the three dramatic series and the magazine show. Programmed into a CBC Sunday evening slot, in early fall, *School's Out!* was scheduled to coincide with the beginning of the school year. In the movie, various *Degrassi* characters are confronted with the transitions that follow high school graduation—the anticipation of university, the dissolution of a high school romance, a tragic highway accident, rootlessness, work prospects, and, ultimately, a fall reunion at the wedding of a long-standing couple.

An outgrowth of the entire *Degrassi* project is *Liberty Street,* which features only one of the former actors, Pat Mastroianni, who plays a different character than previously, but with a similarly cocky persona. *Liberty Street* continues the *Degrassi* coming-of-age chronology, focusing on "twenty-something" characters struggling for independence in a downtown Toronto warehouse-apartment building that requires chronic upkeep and so affords dramatic situations that demand personal negotiations. Launched on the CBC as a series in the 1994–95 season, the characters were introduced in an earlier television movie special, *X-Rated,* a title that recalls writer Douglas Coupland's coinage for disenfranchised youth, popularised by his 1991 book *Generation X: Tales for an Accelerated Culture.* Linda Schuyler is credited as the creator and executive producer of *Liberty Street,* in association with the CBC.

The first three *Degrassi* series had also been created and produced by Schuyler and Kit Hood and their Playing With Time (PWT) Repertory Company, in association with CBC drama departments and the support of Telefilm Canada. Eventually, the series also drew support from associate producing entities such as WGBH-Boston, the U.S. Corporation for Public Broadcasting, and the Public Broadcasting Service (PBS).

The *Degrassi* series achieved international success and sales, and was programmed at various times on cable systems such as HBO, Showtime, Disney Channel, and the Public Broadcasting Service. But these international opportunities also confronted broadcasting and censorship standards which revealed cultural differences between Canada and the United States. A two-part *Degrassi High* episode concerning abortion, for example, was truncated by PBS for American audiences. This was not the case, however, with the CBC, which ran the complete version. PBS edited out a strong fetal icon from an open-ended narrative designed to confront television audiences with the moral and physical complexities facing teens who seek abortion. The editing decision raised public discussion in the arts and entertainment sections of major Canadian newspapers. In the short term, the Canadian media's coverage of PBS's action shored up the cultural attitude of the CBC. The corporation was willing to trust youth audiences, and their parents, to make their own judgments on alternatives, positive and negative, presented in the complete version of the episode.

Yan Moore, head writer of the *Degrassi* series, tailored the scripts with the vital participation of the repertory cast, young people drawn from schools in the Toronto area. The situations, topics, and dialogue were vetted in regular workshops involving the young actors. In the interest of constructing valid actions and responses for the characters, this type of earnest consultation ensured that the *Degrassi* series would remain youth centered, and that the dramas' durable realistic manner would avoid the plasticity common to television's generic sitcom families. Even as the actors grew within their roles over the first three series, and as new characters were added, a naturalistic acting style prevailed. If the acting at times appears untutored to some viewers, it remains closer to the look and speech of everyday youths than those of precocious kids and teens common to Hollywood film and television sitcoms.

From *The Kids of Degrassi Street* through *Degrassi High,* various schools serve as the essential narrative settings, though the dramatic situations mostly pivot on action that occurs outside the classroom: in the corridors, around lockers and yards, to and from school, at dances and other activities, in and around latch-key homes with parents usually absent or at the edges of the situations to be addressed by the youths themselves. These unofficial spaces outside the jurisdiction of authority figures serve as settings for the youth culture themes.

Even the backdrop for *Degrassi Talks* is a school bearing a "Degrassi High School" sign. From that location specific *Degrassi* actors introduce a week's topic. This sense of a familiar locale hearkens back to *The Kids of Degrassi Street,* filmed on Toronto's Degrassi Street in an innercity neighbourhood. In *Degrassi Talks,* the physical references to the school and to the

Degrassi Junior High
Photo courtesy of Janet Webb/Playing With Time, Inc.

actors who portray *Degrassi* characters carry forward the series' history. The actors appear to have graduated into role models of youth, with interspersed dramatic clips from past series serving as proof of their apprenticeship.

The evolutionary *Degrassi* series established high standards for representing youth on television, and influenced the development of other mature-youth series for public and private Canadian television—CBC-West's *Northwood* and CanWest-Global's *Madison,* for example. By integrating sensitive issues into the characters' narrative worlds, and by foregrounding and backgrounding various continuing characters as opposed to the convention of "principle" and

"secondary" figures, the *Degrassi* series developed depth and avoided topic-of-the-week formulas. Abortion, single parenthood, sex, death, racism, AIDS, feminism, gay issues: these became conditions the characters had to work through, largely on their own individual or shared terms, within the serialized narrative structures.

A generation of Canadian kids could be said to have grown up with the *Degrassi* series. The narrative themes held out implicit lessons for the targeted youth audiences—and for parental viewers. This teaching-learning ideology befitted the educational basis of the entire project as well as the cultural mandate of the CBC. With ethical lessons coded into the narratives, the characters were motivated to make mistakes, not merely choices, appropriate to them.

What makes the *Degrassi* project more than a mere projection of ethical lessons in episodic-series form, however, is the media-consciousness that invites viewers to ponder the dramatic futures of characters even when presented in genre-based television. The frequent use of freeze-frames at the ends of episodes suspends closure on dramatic topics and themes, in keeping with open-ended serialization. Over time, the maturity of the writing and the character development in the *Degrassi* series brought a rich dove-tailing of plots and sub-plots, often threaded with nondramatic cultural asides—youth gags, humour, and media allusions— that draw attention to the aesthetics of television construction and the need for informed viewership.

A useful example is "Black and White" (1988), a *Degrassi Junior High* episode focusing on the topic of interracial dating between a white female and a black male. Subtly, the female teen's parents reveal their main fear, miscegenation. The two teens come to make their own choices in a climate of parental overreaction (for their daughter's "own good") and arrive at a solution for their prom-night date. In subsequent episodes, the couple faces an ethical dilemma of their own making. The young man avoids revealing to his white girlfriend that he is attracted to another young woman, and has in fact been dating this black teen during the summer holiday. Jealousy follows deceit. The emotive complexity pushes viewers to recall the series' narrative past in order to contextualize the dilemma among the teens. And the story has thus become quite distinct from and far more complex than the original parental objections to interracial dating suggested.

The "Black and White" episode is structurally connected by a recurring photographic session conducted by two of the youngest boys in the school. One boy is blond and white, the other curly-haired and black. Both are "brains," who cajole older students into posing before their camera for the yearbook in postures reminiscent of "school daze" activities (holding a basketball, and the like). As photographers, the two boys constantly draw attention to looking, performing, and image-making, and bind us as television viewers to their collaborative function and humour. Following one commercial cluster, the narrative returns with an extreme close-up of the blonde boy as he dusts his camera's lens with a brush. His face, distorted in close up, indicates that he is cleaning the lens of the television camera, yet the effect of his direct gaze, as if penetrating the screen, engages us in the visual processes of his activity. His knowing grin adds a pleasurable dimension to his knowledge of creating a media-conscious effect. This very act of a youth constructing television imagery is at the heart of the *Degrassi* mandate to create television of narrative and cultural purpose—always from the perspectives of youth.

—Joan Nicks

CAST

Stephanie Kaye	Nicole Stoffman
Arthur	Duncan Waugh
Vula	Niki Kemeny
Joey Jeremiah	Pat Mastroianni
Wheels	Neil Hope
Yik	Siluck Saysansay
Spike	Amanda Spike
Shane	Bill Parrot
Caitlin	Stacie Mistysyn

PRODUCERS Kit Hood, Linda Schuyler

PROGRAMMING HISTORY

• CBC

THE KIDS OF DEGRASSI STREET
26 episodes

CAST

Griff	Neil Hope
Lisa	Stacie Mistysyn
Billy	Tyson Talbot
Karen	Anais Granofski
Rachel	Arlene Lot
Pete	John Ioannon
Benjy	Christopher Charlesworth

DEGRASSI JUNIOR HIGH

January 1987–March 1987	Sundays 5:00-5:30 (13 episodes)
January 1988–March 1988	Mondays 8:30-9:00 (13 episodes)
November 1988–March 1989	Mondays 8:30-9:00 (16 episodes)

DEGRASSI HIGH

November 1989–March 1990	Mondays 8:30-9:00 (15 episodes)
November 1990–March 1991	Mondays 8:30-9:00 (13 episodes)

FURTHER READING

Devins, Susan. "New Kids on the Block." *Cinema Canada* (Montreal, Quebec), April 1986.

Magder, Ted. "Making Canada in the 1990s: Film, Culture, and Industry." In, McRoberts, Kenneth, editor. *Beyond Quebec: Taking Stock of Canada*. Montreal: McGill Queen's University Press, 1995.

Miller, Mary Jane. "Will English Language Television Remain Distinctive? Probably." In, McRoberts, Kenneth, editor. *Beyond Quebec: Taking Stock of Canada*. Montreal: McGill Queen's University Press, 1995.

DEMOGRAPHICS

The term "demographics" is a colloquialism that derives from demography, "the study of the characteristics of human populations." Professional demographers, such as those who work at the United States Census Bureau, are concerned primarily with population size and density, birth and death rates, and in- and out-migration. But the practice of describing human groups according to distributions of sex, age, ethnicity, educational level, income, or other such has become a commonplace in many domains. These categories are called demographics.

In the television industry demographics are used in various ways, most of which can be characterized as either descriptive or analytical. First, demographics can be used to describe an audience. Such descriptive uses may be applied to an actual audience, as, for example: 54% female, 62% white, average age of 44. Or demographics may be used to describe a desired audience, as in "younger," or "higher income."

Second, demographics can be used to sort data about people for purposes of analysis. For example, data may be available from a study designed to assess people's evaluations of an evening newscast anchor. Researchers may be interested in the average evaluation across people, in the evaluations of specific subgroups of people, or in the differences between the evaluations of specific subgroups. For either of the latter two purposes one would divide the data according to the demographic categories of interest and calculate averages within those categories. It would then be possible to report the evaluations of women as distinct from those for men, those for higher and lower education groups, and so on.

Advertisers' interest in demographics arises from market research or advertising strategies that emphasize certain types of people as the target audience for their advertising. Commercial broadcasters, then, who earn their living by providing communication services to advertisers, are interested in demographics because the advertisers are. Because advertisers are more interested in some demographic categories than others, the commercial broadcasters have a financial interest in designing programming that appeals to people in those more desired demographic categories.

Independent of the specific advertising connection, demographic categories may also be used whenever generalizations are more important than precision. Individuals are sometimes interested in saying something more generally than precisely true. But for national television programmers, who must think in terms of audiences of several million people at a time, there is no other option. So their work is characterized by reliance on such generalizations as women like romance, men like action, young people won't watch unless we titillate them.

Uses of demographics to define and generalize about people is an instance of social category thinking. The rationale is that the available social categories, such as age, gender, ethnicity, and educational level, are associated with typical structures of opportunity and experience that in turn produce typical patterns of disposition, attitudes, interests, behaviors, and so on. The application of social category thinking often extends beyond that sensible rationale to include any instance where differences in a variable of interest can be associated with conveniently measured demographic differences. Age, for example, is easy to measure, amenable to being categorized, and associated with a great variety of differences in taste and activity. No one, of course, supposes that aging causes people to watch more television; but older adults do watch more than younger adults. The convenience of that knowledge outweighs the need for precision in the television industry.

—Eric Rothenbuhler

FURTHER READING

Becker, Lee B. "Racial Differences in Evaluation of the Mass Media." *Journalism Quarterly* (Urbana, Illinois), Spring, 1992.

Horovitz, Bruce. "A Case for Different Strokes; Black's TV Choices Differ from General Public, Ad Study Shows." *Los Angeles Times* (Los Angeles), 7 April 1992.

Lehmkuhl, D.C. "Seeing Beyond Demographics." *Marketing and Media Decisions* (New York), July 1983.

Mann, Judy. "Television Makes a Discovery (Orient Programs Toward Women)." *The Washington Post*, 17 November 1989.

Maxwell, Robert. "Videophiles and Other Americans." *American Demographics* (Ithaca, New York), July 1992.

Merriam, John E. "Clues in the Media." *American Demographics* (Ithaca, New York), February 1991.

Moshavi, Sharon D. "Study Shows Network's Demographic Strengths." *Broadcasting* (Washington, D.C.), 30 November 1992.

Roth, Morry. "See Zip Codes a New Key to Demographics." *Variety* (Los Angeles), 28 May 1990.

"TV and Cable Programming (U.S. Demographics)." *Television Digest* (Washington, D.C.), 21 June 1993.

See also Audience Research; Market; Programming

DENCH, JUDI

British Actor

One of the leading classical actors of her generation, Judi Dench is unique in having sustained a television career that, both in breadth and depth, more than matches her work for the stage. The three roles for which she received, in the same year, a clutch of best actress awards—a cancer ward sister in the single drama *Going Gently*, Ranyevskya in *The Cherry Orchard* and the gauche but capable Laura in the situation comedy *A Fine Romance*—epitomise the versatility of this distinctive and popular performer and the range of work with which she has been associated across a career spanning four decades and some thirty parts. She was made a Dame Commander of the British Empire in 1988.

Educated at a Quaker School, the spiritual discipline of which she has suggested deeply influenced her life and work, she trained at the Central School from 1954 to 1957. Her first television appearance, a small part in a live broadcast of the thriller *Family on Trial*, came within two years of her graduation and was followed soon after by the title roles in a six-part serialisation of Arnold Bennett's *Hilda Lessways* and a production by Stuart Burge of *Major Barbara*. She also played the part of a young tearaway in an early episode of *Z Cars* by John Hopkins, a character that became the basis of the disaffected daughter Terry, created for her by Hopkins in his ground-breaking family quartet *Talking to a Stranger* and for which she received the British Guild of Directors Award for Best Actress.

Dench has given notable performances in television presentations of Shakespeare. She played Katherine of France in the cycle of histories *An Age of Kings* in 1960, and at the end of the 1970s was in two screenings of Royal Shakespeare Company productions, as Adriana in *The Comedy of Errors* and opposite Ian McKellan in Trevor Nunn's landmark chamber production of *Macbeth*. In 1984 she appeared in John Barton's series of practical workshops for Channel 4, *Playing Shakespeare*. Her classical work for television includes a substantial number of period dramas and serialised novels, but it is in her commitment to a range of largely anti-heroic parts in contemporary television drama that she has most consistently won both popular and critical acclaim and where she has most effectively demonstrated her capacity for conveying what one critic called "transcendent ordinariness". In 1979 she played the real-life role of Hazel Wiles, the world-weary adoptive mother of a thalidomide child, in the BBC play *On Giant's Shoulders* and in 1981 she brought depth and complexity to the comparatively small role of Sister Scarli in *Going Gently*. In David Hare's *Saigon: Year of the Cat*, she played the reserved figure of Barbara Dean, an expatriate bank official caught up in a brief, passionate affair during the United States' final days in Vietnam—a performance described by Hare in his introduction to the published script as "silkenly sexy and intelligent, as only she can be."

Indeed, one of Dench's most instantly recognisable features is a vocal timbre so husky that an early commercial for which she had provided the voice-over had to be withdrawn because it was too suggestive. Other writers and directors have

Judi Dench
Photo courtesy of Judi Dench

remarked not only on her vocal technique but on the subtlety and insight of her approach to character. Her physical appearance—stocky, soft but strongly-featured (she was told at a film audition early in her career that she had everything wrong with her face)—might lend itself to comedy but she has never fallen into the trap of comfortable type-casting. Her performance as Bridget, the ill-treated divorcee returning to play havoc with her husband's marriage to a younger woman in the four-part serial *Behaving Badly*, trod a fine line between dowdy despair and spirited heroism. In the two long-running situation comedies, *A Fine Romance* (in which she played opposite her husband Michael Williams) and *As Time Goes By*, she brought to her characters the same quizzical intelligence that epitomizes her more serious work.

These two popular hits sealed her reputation as one of the few classical actors able to move with ease between the differing disciplines of stage and television acting and, as was proved by the unexpected West End success of the somber stage play *Pack of Lies* in 1983 (in which she and Williams also played opposite each), confirmed the often neglected synergy that exists between the two performance media. In 1991 she played the lead in the BBC's production of Rodney Ackland's rediscovered play *Absolute Hell*, later reprising the role at the National Theatre to great acclaim: and her performance in the National's staging of *A Little Night Music* in 1996 demonstrated a remarkable balance between the projection and scale required by the musical form and the finely tuned minutiae of emotional insight which has been the hallmark of her work for television.

—Jeremy Ridgman

JUDI DENCH. Born Judith Olivia Dench in York, England, 9 December 1934. Attended the Mount School, York; Central School of Speech Training and Dramatic Art, London. Married: Michael Williams, 1971; child: Tara. Stage debut, Old Vic Theatre, London, 1957; Broadway debut, 1958; actor, Old Vic Company, 1957–60; joined Royal Shakespeare Company, 1961; first television appearances, mid-1965; actor, dramas and situation comedies, from the early 1980s; debut as stage director, Renaissance Theatre Company, 1988. Officer of the Order of the British Empire, 1970; Dame Commander of the Order of the British Empire, 1988. Member: Royal Shakespeare Company (associate), from 1969; board of the Royal National Theatre, 1988–91. D. Litt: University of Warwick, Coventry, 1978; University of York, 1983; University of Birmingham, 1989, University of Loughborough, 1991; Open University, Milton Keynes, 1992. Recipient: Paladino d'Argentino Award, Venice Festival, 1961; *Variety* London Critics Award, 1966; Guild of Directors Award, 1966; *Plays and Players* Award, 1980; Society of West End Theatre Awards, 1980, 1983, 1987; *Evening Standard* Drama Awards, 1980, 1983, 1987; British Academy of Film and Television Arts Awards, 1965, 1981, 1985, 1987, 1988; *TV Times* Funniest Female on Television, 1981–82; American Cable Award, 1988. Address: Julian Belfrage Associates, 68 St James's Street, London SW1A 1LE, England.

TELEVISION SERIES

| 1981–84 | *A Fine Romance* |
| 1992– | *As Time Goes By* |

TELEVISION PLAYS

1959	*Family on Trial; Hilda Lessways*
1960	*An Age of Kings; Pink String and Sealing Wax*
1962	*Major Barbara*
1963	*The Funambulists*
1964	*Parade's End*
1966	*Talking to a Stranger; Days to Come*
1968	*On Approval*
1978	*The Comedy of Errors; Langrishe Go Down*
1979	*Macbeth; On Giant's Shoulders; A Village Wooing*
1980	*Love in a Cold Climate*
1981	*Going Gently; The Cherry Orchard*
1983	*Saigon: Year of the Cat*
1984	*Playing Shakespeare*
1985	*Mr. and Mrs. Edgehill; The Browning Version*
1986	*Ghosts*
1989	*Behaving Badly*
1990	*Can You Hear Me Thinking?*
1990	*The Torch*
1991	*Absolute Hell*

FILMS

The Third Secret, 1964; *A Study in Terror*, 1966; *He Who Rides a Tiger*, 1966; *Four in the Morning*, 1966; *A Midsummer Night's Dream*, 1968; *The Angelic Conversation*, (voice only), 1973; *Luther*, 1973; *The Third Secret*, 1978; *Nela* (voice only), 1980; *Dead Cert*, 1985; *Wetherby*, 1985; *A Room with a View*, 1985; *84 Charing Cross Road*, 1987; *A Handful of Dust*, 1987; *Henry V*, 1990; *Jack and Sarah*, 1994; *Hamlet*, 1995 *Goldeneye*, 1995.

STAGE (actor)

Hamlet, 1957; *Measure for Measure*, 1957; *A Midsummer Night's Dream*, 1957; *Twelfth Night*, 1958; *Henry V*, 1958; *The Double-Dealer*, 1959; *The Merry Wives of Windsor*, 1959; *As You Like It*, 1959; *The Importance of Being Earnest*, 1959; *Richard II*, 1960; *Romeo and Juliet*, 1960; *She Stoops to Conquer*, 1960; *A Midsummer Night's Dream*, 1960; *The Cherry Orchard*, 1961; *Measure for Measure*, 1962; *A Midsummer Night's Dream*, 1962; *A Penny for a Song*, 1962; *Macbeth*, 1963; *Twelfth Night*, 1963; *A Shot in the Dark*, 1963; *The Three Sisters*, 1964; *The Twelfth Hour*, 1964; *The Alchemist*, 1965; *Romeo and Jeannette*, 1965; *The Firescreen*, 1965; *Private Lives*, 1965; *The Country Wife*, 1966; *The Astrakhan Coat*, 1966; *St. Joan*, 1966; *The Promise*, 1966; *A Little Night Music*, 1966; *The Rules of the Game*, 1966; *Cabaret*, 1968; *A Winter's Tale*, 1969; *Women Beware Women*, 1969; *London Assurance*, 1970; *Major Barbara*, 1970; *The Merchant of Venice*, 1971; *The Duchess of Malfi*, 1971; *Toad of Toad Hall*, 1971; *Content to Whisper*, 1973; *The Wolf*, 1973; *The Good Companions*, 1974; *The Gay Lord Quex*, 1975; *Too True to Be Good*, 1975; *Much Ado About Nothing*, 1976; *The Comedy of Errors*, 1976; *King Lear*, 1976; *Pillars of the Community*, 1977; *The Way of the World*, 1978; *Cymbeline*, 1979; *Juno and the Paycock*, 1980; *Village Wooing*, 1981; *A Kind of Alaska*, 1982; *The Importance of Being Earnest*, 1982; *Pack of Lies*, 1983; *Mother Courage*, 1984; *Waste*, 1985; *Mr. and Mrs. Nobody*, 1987; *Antony and Cleopatra*, 1987; *Entertaining Strangers*, 1987; *Hamlet*, 1989; *The Cherry Orchard*, 1989; *The Sea*, 1991; *The Plough and the Stars*, 1991; *Coriolanus*, 1992; *The Gift of the Gorgon*, 1992; *The Seagull*, 1994; *Absolute Hell*, 1995.

STAGE (director)

Much Ado About Nothing, 1988; *Look Back in Anger*, 1989; *The Boys from Syracuse*, 1991; *Romeo and Juliet*, 1993.

FURTHER READING

Eyre, Richard. *Utopia and Other Places*. London: Vintage, 1994.

Jacobs, Gerald. *Judi Dench: A Great Deal of Laughter*. London: Weidenfeld and Nicholson, 1985.

Kaplan, Mike, editor. *Variety's Who's Who in Show Business*. New York: Bowker, 1989.

DEPOE, NORMAN

Canadian Broadcast Journalist

Norman DePoe was a pioneering figure in Canadian television news reporting, one of the heroic figures of front-line journalism. He was among the first of CBC-TV's high-profile television correspondents and helped to establish the traditions of television journalism in Canada. In the 1960s, he was a national institution, his gruff voice heard in almost every major news report on CBC-TV, when the public broadcaster dominated Canadian television news.

DePoe began his broadcasting career with CBC Radio in 1948, moved to the fledgling television service in 1956, joined the CBC-TV parliamentary bureau in 1959. He was named chief Ottawa correspondent in 1960. He became the first television reporter admitted to the Parliamentary press gallery and helped to provide legitimacy to the handful of broadcasters (five in 1959), whose attempts to gain admission to the gallery had been strenuously resisted by many newspaper writers. As media historian Allan Levine has put it in *Scrum Wars: The Prime Ministers and the Media*, "DePoe was the first television journalist who could compete on an intellectual level with the other stars of the gallery." He was well read and a skilful writer. Years after he had left the air in 1975, DePoe's hard-edged reporting style continued to set the standard for broadcast journalists. Politicians were quicker than print reporters to identify DePoe as a key player in the gallery and to foresee the dominance of television news in politics.

His physical features were assets on the screens of the 1960s, but in a way that would make him ill-suited to the glamorized television newsroom that came later. Raspy-voiced and rumpled, wrinkled and weary, DePoe cut an oddly romantic figure in the Bogart mold. He possessed a prodigious memory and a healthy disregard for those in power, whether they were in political offices, government bureaucracies or the management suites of the CBC. DePoe was famously contemptuous of producers and was not above criticizing them on air. For him political reporting was a solitary exercise and at times a splendid joust with those he covered. His contributions to national newscasts were much-envied models of economical incisiveness.

Even during his spell as the principal reporter on national affairs, DePoe was assigned to cover significant political stories in the United States and elsewhere in the world. An unabashed patriot, his comments about U.S. politics could be biting. The visibility afforded by foreign assignments only added to his reputation as an authoritative commentator on politics for the English-language television audience in Canada. For many Canadians in the late 1950s and 1960s, especially rural audiences served by few other national media, he was perhaps the most credible authority on political affairs in Ottawa and elsewhere. It is estimated that he gave some 5,000 television news reports, including coverage of 31 elections, several leadership conventions, and other major political events.

Norman DePoe
Photo courtesy of the National Archives of Canada

Although DePoe was widely revered, there was another side to his career. He led a romanticized life in journalism full of the kind of carousing bellicosity often stereotyped in American cinematic treatments of newswork. According to a successor in the Ottawa post, he was visibly inebriated during a live stand-up on at least one occasion, and the memoirs of contemporaries are replete with candid anecdotes or unmistakable hints about his rough-edged lifestyle. With respect to gossip about his drinking, he once remarked that "ninety percent of the stories are just not true." He fell out of favor with assignment editors in the early 1970s and in 1975 returned to radio news, finally retiring in 1976.

At the time of his death in 1980, DePoe was remembered by Knowlton Nash, another of the CBC's well-known correspondents and one-time head of CBC News, as "the most memorable reporter of our lifetime .... the most enjoyable, most charismatic, most effective electronic reporter Canada has ever seen, with a colorful, irrepressible style." He was regarded with wary respect by the political leaders of his standard of integrity, toughness and incisive reporting that has been hard to match.

—Frederick J. Fletcher and Robert Everett

NORMAN DEPOE. Born in Portland, Oregon, U.S.A., 4 May 1917. Educated at the University of British Columbia, 1934-38; University of Toronto, 1946-49. Married: 1) Madeline Myra, 1942, seven children; 2) Mary Elizabeth, 1974. Served as captain, the Royal Canadian Signal Corps, 1938–46. Reporter in CBC's overseas unit, war and post-war reports, 1939–52; joined CBC's News Department, 1948; news editor, *Graphic*, 1956; CBC television parliamentary correspondent, 1952–69; host, *The Public Eye*, 1965–69; interviewer, *Weekend*, 1969–72; host, *Newsmagazine* (later *CBC Newsmagazine*), 1973–75; retired from CBC, 1976. Died in 1980.

TELEVISION SERIES
1965–69   *The Public Eye*

1969–72   *Weekend*
1973–75   *Newsmagazine*

FURTHER READING

Levine, Allan. *Scrum Wars: The Prime Ministers and the Media.* Toronto: Dundurn, 1993.
Lynch, Charles. *A Funny Way to Run a Country: Further Memoirs of a Political Voyeur.* Edmonton, Canada: Hurtig, 1986.
Taras, David. *The Newsmakers: The Media's Influence on Canadian Politics.* Toronto: Nelson, 1990.
Troyer, Warner. *The Sound and the Fury: An Anecdotal History of Canadian Broadcasting.* Rexdale, Ontario: John Wiley, 1980.

DEREGULATION

When applied in the United States this general concept describes most American electronic media policy in the past two decades. Largely a bi-partisan effort, this fundamental shift in the Federal Communications Commission's (FCC) approach to radio and television regulation began in the mid-1970s as a search for relatively minor "regulatory underbrush" which could be cleared away for more efficient and cost-effective administration of the important rules that would remain. Congress largely went along with this trend, and initiated a few deregulatory moves of its own. The arrival of the Reagan Administration and FCC Chairman Mark Fowler in 1981 marked a further shift to a fundamental and ideologically-driven reappraisal of regulations long held central to national broadcasting policy. Ensuing years saw removal of many long-standing rules resulting in an overall reduction in FCC oversight of station and network operations. Congress grew increasingly wary of the pace of deregulation, however, and began to slow the FCC's deregulatory pace by the late 1980s.

Specific deregulatory moves—some by Congress, others by the FCC—included (a) extending television licenses to five years from three in 1981; (b) expanding the number of television stations any single entity could own from seven in 1981 to 12 in 1985—a situation under consideration for further change in 1995; (c) abolishing guidelines for minimal amounts of non-entertainment programming in 1985; (d) elimination of the Fairness Doctrine in 1987; (e) dropping, in 1985, FCC license guidelines for how much advertising could be carried; (f) leaving technical standards increasingly in the hands of licensees rather than FCC mandates; and (g) deregulation of television's competition (especially cable which went through several regulatory changes in the decade after 1983).

Deregulatory proponents do not perceive station licensees as "public trustees" of the public airwaves required to provide a wide variety of services to many different listening groups. Instead, broadcasting has been increasingly seen as just another business operating in a commercial marketplace which did not need its management decisions questioned by government overseers. Opponents argue that deregulation violates key parts of the Communications Act of 1934—especially the requirement to operate in the public interest—and allows broadcasters to seek profits with little public service programming required in return.

American deregulation has been widely emulated in other countries in spirit if not detail. Developed and developing countries have introduced local stations to supplement national services, begun to allow (if not encourage) competing media such as cable, satellite services, and videocassettes, and have sometimes loosened regulations on traditional radio and television. Advertising support along lines of the American model has become more widely accepted, especially as television's operating costs rise. But the American example of relying more on competition than regulation also threatens traditional public service broadcasting which must meet increasing competition for viewers by offering more commercially-appealing programs, usually entertainment—rather than culture-based.

—Christopher H. Sterling

FURTHER READING

Broadcast Deregulation. New York: Station Representatives Association, 1979.
Congressional Research Service. *Should the Federal Government Significantly Strengthen the Regulation of Mass Media Communication in the United States?* 96th Cong., 1st Session, House Document 96-167 (Washington, D.C.), 1979.
Fowler, Mark S., and Daniel L. Brenner. "A Marketplace Approach to Broadcast Regulation." *Texas Law Review* (Austin, Texas), February 1982.
Horwitz, Robert Britt. *The Irony of Regulatory Reform: The Deregulation of American Telecommunications.* New York: Oxford University Press, 1989.

Johnson, Leland L. *Toward Competition in Cable Television.* Cambridge, Massachusetts: MIT Press, 1994.

Krattenmaker, Thomas G., and Lucas A. Powe, Jr. *Regulating Broadcast Programming.* Cambridge, Massachusetts: MIT Press, 1995.

Le Duc, Don R. *Beyond Broadcasting: Patterns in Policy and Law.* White Plains, New York: Longman, 1987.

Powe, Lucas A., Jr. *American Broadcasting and the First Amendment.* Berkeley, California: University of California Press, 1987.

Tunstall, Jeremy. *Communications Deregulation: The Unleashing of America's Communications Industry.* Oxford: Basil Blackwell, 1986.

Weiss, Leonard W., and Michael W. Klass, editors. *Regulatory Reform: What Actually Happened.* Boston: Little, Brown, 1986.

See also Federal Communications Commission; License; United States: Cable

DESMOND'S

British Situation Comedy

Produced by Charlie Hanson and Humphrey Barclay, *Desmond's* was first broadcast on Channel Four in 1989 and finally came to an end in December 1995, a short time before its leading star, Norman Beaton, died. The half-hour weekly program has often been referred to as an "ethnic sitcom", in the sense that it featured a black family and their predominantly black friends. However, the series managed to reach a mainstream audience and thus appeal to viewers of all ages and cultures in Britain. It has also been popular in the Caribbean and in the United States, where it is broadcast on Black Entertainment Television.

Desmond's was also distinguished by its West Indian writer, Trix Worrell, previously an actor and graduate from the National Film and Television School in Britain. Although Worrell went on to direct *Desmond's*, the series was initially co-produced and directed by Charlie Hanson. Hanson had previously co-devised and produced *No Problem!*, Channel 4's first "black comedy" (1982–85). Many have argued that the *Desmond's* comic formula was more successful than previous "ethnic sitcoms". Although the series has often been compared to *The Cosby Show*, it can be seen as the first light entertainment programme to fully embrace the black community within a British context.

The series was based in Desmond's, a barber shop in Peckham. A core group of characters used the shop as a social meeting place. Norman Beaton played Desmond, a West Indian traditionalist, and Carmen Munroe played his loving and supportive wife, Shirley. Together they ran the southeast London barbershop, where their children and friends would often congregate. The couple's children were Gloria (Kim Walker), Sean (Justin Pickett) and Michael (Geff Francis). The dynamics and relationships between these various characters formed the basis of the comedy.

The setting of the programme was unique—a black sitcom based in the workplace. The series' antecedents, such as *No Problem!* and *The Fosters,* tended to focus on black family relationships within the family home. The cast of *Desmond's* were not passive characters in a stagnant setting, but socially mobile people in multiracial Britain. In this context the comedy introduced new types of protagonists such as Desmond, the

black entrepreneur, and his two sons, one an aspiring bank employee and the other a bright student. The characters in *Desmond's* were quite distinct types, neither caricatures nor stereotypes. Worrell was very keen to emphasise the differences within the African-Caribbean diaspora and so the audience was witness to racism and prejudice between, for example, Matthew (Gyearbuor Asante), the African eternal student and the West Indians characters. The series depicted a myriad of types, spanning across generations, lifestyles and politics, thus dispelling any notion of there being an essential black British subject. Indeed, generational, and other, differences among characters often triggered the hilarity.

Desmond's had its own unique method of team writing. To some extent, it became a training-ground for young, multicultural, creative talent. Many aspiring writers, producers, directors and production staff gained experience on the programme by learning how to create a long-running fresh situation comedy. Although the series lasted for five years on British television, those involved in the production often mentioned the pressures of producing what was generally perceived as a black comedy. Worrell and Hanson have both spoken of the expectations placed on them, simply because there were so few other black comedies on television. In the 1992 television documentary *Black and White in Colour*, Hanson commented that "Black situation comedy comes under the microscope far more than any other situation comedy on television." At the same time, the programme marked a progression in that most black British sitcoms have tended to focus on dysfunctional families and social problems. Carmen Munroe sees *Desmond's* as a landmark programme; in *Black and White in Colour* she noted that "we have successfully created a space for ourselves, where we can just be a real, honest, loving family, with problems like lots of people, and we can present that with some degree of truth and still not lose the comedy."

—Sarita Malik

CAST

Desmond	Norman Beaton
Shirley	Carmen Munroe

Desmond's
Photo courtesy of Channel Four

Gloria . . . . Kim Walker
Sean . . . . Justin Pickett
Michael . . . . Geff Francis
Matthew . . . . Gyearbuor Asante

PRODUCERS   Charlie Hanson, Humphrey Barclay

PROGRAMMING HISTORY

• Channel Four
1989–1995

See also Beaton, Norman; Munroe, Carmen

DETECTIVE PROGRAMS

Detective programs have been a permanent presence on American television; like their more numerous siblings, the police shows, their development enacts in miniature many aspects of the larger history of the medium as a whole. They began as live programs, recycling prose fiction, movies and radio shows, the earliest of them, such as *Man Against Crime* (1949–56, CBS, NBC, DuMont) and *Martin Kane, Private Eye* (1949–54, NBC), conceived and produced in New York City by advertising agencies. Erik Barnouw's history of American broadcasting discloses that the tobacco sponsors of *Man*

Against Crime prohibited fires and coughing from all scripts to avoid negative associations with their product; the book also describes the technical and narrative crudity of these early programs. The length of radio episodes could be gauged accurately by counting the words in the script, but the duration of live action on TV was unpredictable, varying treacherously from rehearsal to actual broadcast. To solve this problem, Barnouw writes, every episode of *Man Against Crime* ended with a search that the hero (played by Ralph Bellamy) could prolong or shorten depending on the time available.

Even the earliest detective shows can be subdivided into recognizable subgenres. *Man Against Crime* and *Martin Kane* are simple versions of the hard-boiled private eye, a figure invented in the 1920s in stories and novels by Dashiell Hammett and Raymond Chandler, and reincarnated in the movies of Humphrey Bogart and other tough-guy actors. Other 1950s series recycle detectives in the cerebral, puzzle-solving tradition of Arthur Conan Doyle, author of the Sherlock Holmes stories, and Agatha Christie. The character Holmes makes his first appearance on American television in 1954 in a syndicated filmed series that lasts only a single season. Ellery Queen, an American Sherlock Holmes type, first appearing in a cycle of popular novels beginning in 1929, appears on radio a decade later in a long-running weekly program, and on television in 1950 in a live series, *The Adventures of Ellery Queen* (1950–51, DuMont; 1951–52, ABC). This is the first of four series devoted to Ellery Queen, a mystery writer and amateur detective who is the direct inspiration for Angela Lansbury's long-running character in *Murder, She Wrote* (1984–96, CBS). The classic whodunit pleasures of Ellery Queen—as well as its relative indifference to social or psychological realism—are crystallized in its structure: Queen's adventures in all media usually conclude with a summary of the story's clues and a challenge to the reader or viewer to solve the mystery before Ellery himself supplies the answer in the epilogue.

A third subgenre of the detective story also makes an early appearance in the new medium. A hybrid of screwball comedy and mystery, this format usually centers on the adventures of a married or romantically entangled couple, amateurs in detection who are often distracted in the face of villainy and mortal danger by their own erotically-charged quarrels. Examples include: *Boston Blackie* (1951–53, syndicated), *Mr. and Mrs. North* (1952–53, CBS; 1954, NBC) and, a bit later, *The Thin Man* (1957–59, NBC). Each of these escapist half-comedies placed more emphasis on interpersonal badinage than on the realities of urban crime, although the social whirl of the modern city was often a background in all three series.

Like most television detectives of the 1950s, these protagonists had originated in older media. A durable embodiment of disreputable and elegant self-reliance, Blackie first appears in American magazine stories at the turn of the century, a jewel thief who moves easily in high society and has served time in prison but now prevents crime instead of committing it. Surreptitious and resilient, he turns up in silent films and reappears in sound movies and on radio in the 1940s. Still quick with a wisecrack, he is more respectable in his TV incarnation than his prototypes in the older media, according to several commentators, and aided by a girlfriend named Mary and a dog named Whitey, is said to have been remodeled in the image of the movie version of Nick Charles, hero of *The Thin Man*, who is also in partnership with a woman and a dog.

Mr. and Mrs. North has a similar mixed-media ancestry, originating in prose fiction in 1940 by a writing couple,

Richard and Frances Lockridge; in the next year *Mr. and Mrs. North* appears as a Broadway play, a Hollywood movie starring Gracie Allen as Mrs. North, and—most durably—in a weekly radio series that runs on CBS and later NBC until 1956, outlasting the TV series to which it gave rise. Gracie Allen's presence in this catalogue is a decisive clue to the stereotype of the lovably addled female on which *Mr. and Mrs. North* relies.

No such stereotype mars *The Thin Man*, but despite an energetic performance by Phyllis Kirk as Nora, the TV version is a mere derivative echo of its famous predecessors, Hammett's 1940 novel and, especially, the series of five MGM movies starring William Powell and Myrna Loy as Nick and Nora Charles (1934, 1936, 1939, 1941, 1944). The Kirk character hints at what comes across with charming serious authority in Myrna Loy's definitive Nora: unlike her imitators and competitors, this woman is no mere sidekick but her detective husband's true moral and intellectual equal—a rare female in this masculine genre.

Following the success of *I Love Lucy* (1951–61, CBS) and *Dragnet* (1952–59; revived, 1967–70, NBC), both filmed in Hollywood, production shifts to film and to the West Coast, and the economic structure of the new medium is stabilized: production companies sell programs to the networks, which peddle commercial slots to advertisers who have no direct creative control over programming. The standard format for crime shows changes from thirty minutes to an hour in the late 1950s and early 1960s, and crime series begin to exhibit a richer audio-visual texture, learning to exploit such defining features of television as its reduced visual field and the mandatory commercial interruptions.

Such an embrace of some of television's distinctive features surely helps to explain the success of the Raymond Burr *Perry Mason* (1957–66, CBS), one of the first TV series to achieve greater complexity—and popularity—than the books and radio episodes from which it derives. An American version of the whodunit, the program is a kind of primer on the uses and gratifications of genre formulas. Both a courtroom melodrama and a detective story, its appeal to viewers and its power as drama are grounded in TV-specific features. Its highly segmented narrative structure, for example, exploits the commercial interruptions, organizing the plot in predictable units that offer viewers the simultaneous pleasures of recognizable variations (different performers, settings, motives, etc.) within a familiar, orderly pattern. Every episode begins with a mini-drama, establishing a roster of plausible suspects for the murder in which it culminates. Every episode dramatizes the arrest and imprisonment of Perry's client, known to be innocent by the very fact that Perry has taken on the defense. The second half-hour of every episode is always a courtroom trial in which Perry's deductive genius and his brilliance in cross examination combine to force a confession from the real murderer. Every episode contains an explanatory epilogue, often at table in a restaurant or other convivial space signifying the restoration of normality and order, in which Perry discloses the chain

Honey West

Mickey Spillane's Mike Hammer

77 Sunset Strip

Kojak

of reasoning that led him to the truth. This intensification of the structural constraints inherent in the format of the weekly series strengthens or enables what must be called the mythic or ritual content of Perry Mason: an endlessly renewing drama of murder, justice perverted, justice redeemed.

The very title sequence of *Perry Mason* signals something of the way TV drama by the late 1950s had begun to develop an appropriately smalleaned audio-visual vocabulary: a confident, swooping camera glides through a courtroom to a close-up of the hero, its graceful dipping motion synchronized with the rhythms of Fred Steiner's dramatic theme music.

Similar audio-visual effects are intermittently present in two notable series created by Blake Edwards, *Richard Diamond, Private Detective* (1957–60, CBS, NBC) and *Peter Gunn* (1958–61, NBC, ABC), both of which center on wiseacre heroes whose sexual bravado is more important to their appeal than their brains or their marksmanship. *Richard Diamond*'s place in TV history is secured by two of its cast members: the protagonist was played by a young David Janssen, smooth-faced, unfurtive and just learning to mumble, in rehearsal for his memorable work in *The Fugitive* (1963–67, ABC), and *Harry O* (1974–76, ABC). The role of Diamond's throaty secretary belonged briefly in 1959 to Mary Tyler Moore, who received no billing in the credits, and, in keeping with the macho objectification of women common in detective mythology, was shown on camera only from the waist down.

Especially in its music, *Peter Gunn* was a more compelling program than *Richard Diamond*, though its plots were reductive and often as violent as those of *The Untouchables* (1959–63, ABC), notorious even in its own day for its surfeit of murder. Henry Mancini's original jazz variations—later collected in two best-selling albums—made an elegant, haunting undersong for the show's moody, film-noirish editing and camera work. Gunn himself, portrayed in a minimalist physical style by Craig Stevens, often repaired to a nightclub called "Mother's" where his girlfriend Edie Hunt (Lola Albright) sang jazz for a living.

Peter Gunn had a genuine individuality, but its half-hour episodes, photographed in black and white, must have seemed obsolete by the end of the decade. Hour-long series, shot in glossy, high-key color in exotic locales and filled with physical action became the standard during the 1960s. In a sense this trend was part of the industry project of finding ways to adapt action-adventure material to the exigencies of the small screen. Car chases and acrobatic action were not impossible on television, though such things could never be as riveting here as in the movies. But artful editing and clever camera placement—emphasizing action in depth that moved toward or away from the camera and avoided trajectories that ran across the screen into its confining borders—could create plausibly exciting effects. Glossy production values, then, often as an end in themselves, set the tone for most TV detectives of the 1960s.

One of the founding programs in this gloss and glamour mode was *77 Sunset Strip* (1958–64, ABC), produced by

Warner Brothers and created by Roy Huggins from his own 1946 novel. The theme music and lyrics for the show aimed for a tone of jivey, youthful "cool" and included the sound of snapping fingers. The show appealed strongly to younger viewers, primarily through the character of a jive-talking parking lot attendant called "Kookie" (Edd Byrnes), who was perpetually combing his luxuriant wavy hair and trying to persuade the detective heroes, played by Efrem Zimbalist, Jr., and Roger Smith, to let him work on their investigations. The series title named the agency's upscale Hollywood address, but many episodes required travel to exotic foreign locales where the camera could ogle wealth and pulchritude. Roger Smith wrote and directed the most memorable episode of the series, "The Silent Caper" (first telecast 3 June 1960), in which the hero learns about a mob kidnapping from newspaper headlines in the opening sequence and proceeds to rescue the distressed damsel in a series of heroic improvisations, the entire adventure unfolding without a single line of dialogue.

In this period of what might be called technical exploration, the private eye genre, like other forms of action-adventure, remains essentially plot-driven, and despite the fact that the protagonist returns each week for new adventures, every episode remains self-contained, void of any memory of prior episodes. Often effective visually but superficial in content, some of these programs even differentiated their heroes by strangely external and implausible attributes. *Cannon* (1971–76, CBS), played by William Conrad, was balding and fat, but his excessive weight and his fittingly cumbersome Lincoln Continental automobile did not noticeably inhibit his script-writers, who provided fisticuffs and races by foot and by vehicle sufficient to challenge an Olympic athlete or Grand Prix driver. Even more implausibly, James Franciscus's *Longstreet* (1971–72, ABC) was blind, and brought his seeing-eye dog and a special electronic cane to all investigations.

Mannix (1967–75, CBS) was perhaps the representative private eye of the era. Played by the rugged and athletic Mike Connors, Mannix was not physically challenged, but one might be tempted to doubt his brainpower, for he was quick to the punch and seemed to conduct most of his investigations by assault and battery.

Finally, in its third or "mature" stage—roughly corresponding to the mid-1970s and beyond—the private eye series combines the visual subtlety achieved over more than twenty-five years of such programming with a new complexity in content. The best detective shows develop a memory, the hero's prior adventures bear upon his current ones, and characters from earlier episodes or seasons reappear, adding complexity to themes and relationships. In the richest such programs character, not violent action, drives the story, and the subject matter itself engages reality more seriously and topically than the muscle-flexing violence of earlier shows had generally allowed.

Harry O (1974–76, ABC) and *The Rockford Files* (1974–80, NBC) are the primary examples of these principles of accretion and refinement. Equivalent instances among police shows are *Police Story* (1973–77, NBC), *Hill Street Blues* (1981–87, NBC), *NYPD Blue* (1993–), *Law and Order* (1990–) and *Homicide* (1993–). But a significant minority of other detective series beginning in the 1970s and after also achieve new levels of excellence and imaginative energy, combining memorable acting with elegant cinematography and often superior writing to become, at the least, provocative entertainment.

Such programs include *Columbo* (1971–77, NBC; continuing as an occasional TV-movie), technically a policeman but in spirit one of American television's wittiest variations on the mystery-puzzle format—the detective as triumphant (and dogged) rationalist as well as working-class avenger. *Tenafly* (1973–74, NBC) was a short-lived but thoughtful series centered on a black private eye, played by James McEachin, whose gentleness and husbandly decency undermine many media stereotypes. *Magnum, P.I.* (1980–88, CBS) starred Tom Selleck as an engaging and self-deprecating Vietnam veteran, living in the guest cottage on a picturesque estate in an even more picturesque Hawaii. Magnum's character deepened as the series continued, and some episodes explored the show's relation to its detective-story ancestry with modesty and wit. *Moonlighting* (1985–89, ABC) was a frequently brilliant, and abrasive postmodern variation on the *Thin Man* formula, with Bruce Willis and Cybill Shepherd, in fighting trim, trading insults and wise-cracking through the run of the series.

Harry O and *Rockford* remain the most compelling private detectives in television history. Both series are the work of writers, directors and producers with long experience in the crime genre and a specific history of collaboration with their stars. Janssen's creative ensemble included Howard Rodman, creator of the show and writer of the two pilot films that led to the series, producer-director Jerry Thorpe, directors Paul Wendkos, Richard Lang, Jerry London, and writers Michael Sloan, Robert C. Dennis, Stephen Kandel, and Robert Dozier. Garner's collaborators included his former agent-turned-executive producer Meta Rosenberg and such TV veterans as Roy Huggins, Stephen J. Cannell, David Chase, Juanita Bartlett, and Charles Floyd Johnson, some of whom had worked with him in movies and in his earliest jobs in television.

Anti-heroic in tone, both series draw creatively on their stars' previous work and also reflect something of the legacy of the anti-war movement and the broad social turmoil of the late 1960s and early 1970s. In a way both Harry and Rockford are adult drop-outs, living unpretentiously along the beaches of southern California. (Rockford's minimal domicile is actually a mobile home.) But both protagonists are a generation older than the youthful protesters of that era, and they project a wariness and skepticism that seem to originate not in naiveté or adolescent discontent but in part in the muddles, disillusionments, even the physical humiliations of middle age.

Janssen's Orwell especially is a figure of pain and diminished expectations, divorced and solitary, living on a disability pension from the San Diego police department. Fitting himself with rueful slowness into his broken-down toy of a sports car,

middle aged and sagging like its owner, or stiffly climbing the wooden steps of his rickety beach house, he seems a subversively modest hero, the fugitive grown older and wiser.

Less melancholy and wincing than Harry Orwell, Rockford is unpretentious and decent, equally post-heroic, probably the only TV detective to spend more time nursing his own injuries than inflicting them on others. Both Rockford and Orwell are great wheedlers, more likely to coddle or flatter information out of their sources than to threaten them. "Why should I answer you?" asks an officious bureaucrat in one episode of *Harry O.* Janssen's response is characteristic, a half-audible mumble, delayed for a moment as he settles on the edge of the bureaucrat's desk: "Because my feet hurt?"

Rockford is the richer, more various and more playful text, partly because it had the advantage of lasting six years, while *Harry O* was canceled abruptly after its second season despite reasonably strong ratings, possibly a casualty of the crescendo of complaints against media violence that developed in the mid-1970s. Like some police series, *Rockford* is something of a hybrid, combining elements of comedy and the daytime continuing serial with the private eye format. Though Rockford's adventures are self-contained, usually concluding within the confines of a single episode, his father "Rocky" (Noah Beery) and a wide circle of friends and professional colleagues are recurring characters, and the momentum of their lives as well as their unstable, shifting intimacy with Rockford himself deepen and complicate the program. The recurring women characters in *Rockford*—Jim's tough, competent lawyer Beth Davenport (Gretchen Corbett); the blind psychologist Megan Dougherty (Kathryn Harrold), a client who becomes Jim's lover; and Rita Capkovic (Rita Moreno), a resilient, loquacious prostitute who enlists Rockford's help in changing her life—exhibit qualities of intelligence, moral courage and independence rare in women characters in our popular culture and virtually non-existent in the molls and dolls of detective stories.

Valuable as a corrective to the still widespread notion that TV programs and especially crime shows are interchangeable and entirely ephemeral, the essentially internal history proposed here must be complicated and supplemented by other perspectives. Recent scholarship on popular culture would suggest that in the broadest sense, the TV detective show is part of a larger cultural project in which the conventions of genre function in part as enabling devices, their reassuring familiarity licensing an exploration of topics that might otherwise be too disturbing or threatening to acknowledge or discuss openly. Thus, all television programs, and particularly the prime-time genres, collectively sustain an open-ended, ongoing conversation about the nature of American culture, about our values and the norms of social life. Cop and private eye shows are fables of justice, heroism and deviancy, symbolically or imaginatively "policing" the unstable boundaries that define common ideas about crime, urban life, gender norms, the health or sickness of our institutions. The progression, that is, from *Dragnet* to *Hill Street Blues* discloses aspects of a social history of our society. But this is not a simple affirmation of such stories, nor of some comforting progress-myth. For our genre texts carry and rehearse and diffuse the lies, the prejudices and self-delusions of our society as well as its ideals. For example, *Harry O* and *Rockford* share the prime-time schedule with *Mannix* and *Charlie's Angels* (1976–81, ABC). Inevitably ambivalent, in conflict with themselves, genre stories reflect and embody cultural divisions.

A chief virtue, then, of television's most fundamental of all programs, the series, is precisely that it is continuing, theoretically endless. In this the TV series embodies a useful truth: that culture itself is a process, a shifting, unequal contention among traditional and emerging forces.

—David Thorburn

FURTHER READING

Barnouw, Erik. *The Image Empire*. New York: Oxford University Press, 1970.
Brooks, Tim, and Earle Marsh. *The Complete Directory to Prime Time Network TV Shows, 1946-Present*. New York: Ballantine, 1979; 3rd edition, 1985.

Gianakos, Larry James. *Television Drama Series Programming: A Comprehensive Chronicle, 1959–1975*. Metuchen, New Jersey: Scarecrow, 1978.
Kerr, Paul. "Watching the Detectives." *Primetime Magazine* (London), July 1981.
McNeil, Alex. *Total Television*. New York: Penguin, 1984.
Meyers, Richard. *TV Detectives*. San Diego, California: Barnes, 1981.
Norden, Martin F. "The Detective Show." In, Rose, Brian G., editor. *TV Genres: A Handbook and Reference Guide*. Westport, Connecticut: Greenwood, 1985.
Tibballs, Geoff. *The Boxtree Encyclopedia of TV Detectives*. London: Boxtree, 1992.
Thorburn, David. "Is TV Acting a Distinctive Art Form?" *The New York Times*, 14 August 1977.

See also Cannell, Steven J.; *Charlie's Angels*; Garner, James; Huggins, Roy; *Magnum, P.I.*; *Miss Marple*; *Moonlighting*; *Name of the Game*; *NBC Mystery Movie*; *Perry Mason*; *Peter Gunn*; *Rockford Files*; *Sherlock Holmes*; *Singing Detective*

DEVELOPMENT

The term "development" refers to the process in U.S. television program production (usually involving prime-time dramatic series) whereby a network pays an outside program supplier, or the program producer, to develop a potential series. This often involves an elaborate step deal, beginning with a verbal pitch of the series concept by the supplier. If the network is interested, it provides funds with which to develop story and script, and eventually the actual production of a pilot, or the originating episode of the series. The network may or may not to chose to air the pilot; if the pilot is run and performs satisfactorily, the network may decide to "pick up" the series for its regular schedule. The networks develop far more programs than they can possibly air, and thus program development clearly favors the networks despite the mutual dependency between buyers and suppliers. Indeed, program development well indicates the networks' long-standing control over TV programming, which they maintain today, even in the age of cable.

This was not the case in the early years of U.S. network television, when the industry relied primarily on the "radio model" of program development. As in network radio, TV programs were conceived and produced by advertising agencies on behalf of sponsors. The agencies also decided which network would air the program, and in many cases the actual time slot on the network schedule. The radio model proved untenable in the burgeoning TV industry, however, for three principal reasons: First, the increasing cost and complexity of TV series production made it difficult for sponsors to underwrite shows and for ad agencies to produce them. Second, the heavy emphasis on ratings and on scheduling meant that the ad agency's and sponsor's notion of an appropriate program and time slot might not (and often did not) jibe with the network's strategy for attracting and maintaining the largest possible audience during the crucial evening hours. And third, it was becoming ever more obvious that syndication (off-network reruns) would generate huge revenues for the companies which owned the programs and controlled their off-network afterlife. Thus, the networks gradually took control of programming and scheduling in the late 1950s, which had significant impact on TV program development.

Network control of programming was severely undercut in the early 1970s, however, which had a tremendous impact on the process—and the standardization—of program development. In the 1972-73 season, the networks' collective control of the television industry was challenged, primarily on antitrust grounds, by the Justice Department, the Federal Trade Commission, and the Federal Communications Commission (FCC). The most significant of these challenges in terms of programming (and development) were the FCC's so-called "fin-syn" regulations, which restricted the networks' right to finance and syndicate programs. As a direct result, program development quickly evolved from a haphazard, informal process to a standardized and heavily regulated set of procedures. With most prime-time dramatic series production now being farmed out, development became the primary focus of the industry—particularly the growing ranks of mid-management "development executives" at both the networks and the program suppliers.

Program development under fin-syn regulations was a rule-bound, pitch-to-pilot ritual. The pitch had to be verbal, since anything in writing required a contractual agreement. If the network-buyer was sufficiently interested in the pitch, then the supplier was contracted to develop the concept into a story treatment (synopsis), then into one or more scripts, and then into an actual series pilot. Depending on the supplier's track record and clout with the network, there might be guarantees with regard to airing the pilot or even picking up the series—a so-called "play or pay" deal. But for the most part, series development was a high-cost, high-risk venture, with the supplier sharing the risk because the costs for producing a pilot often exceeded what the network paid. And in most cases this investment was simply lost, since even successful TV producers could expect only about 10% of the series they developed to actually be picked up by a network.

Suppliers were more willing than ever to take the risks, of course, since fin-syn assured them the ownership and syndication rights to their series. The potential syndication payoff also increased dramatically in the late 1970s due to cable, which created a surge in the number of independent television stations and thus a wider market for off-network reruns. The emergence of cable networks and superstations in the 1980s further complicated program development by increasing the number of program buyers, and also by enhancing the off-network currency of even moderately successful series. Moreover, cable brought back the first-run syndicated dramatic series (most notably via *Star Trek: The Next Generation* in 1986), which had been phased out in the 1960s. These factors, along with the network penchant for "quick-yank" cancellation of weak series after only a few episodes, rendered development an even more crucial and pervasive aspect of the industry in the cable era. By the early 1990s, according to *Broadcasting* magazine, "70% to 80% of a network's costs are tagged to program development."

Program development persists in the mid-1990s, although a number of recent trends in the television and cable industries, and in the "entertainment industry" at large, may well affect the process. One trend has been the move by several studios (FOX, Warner Brothers, and Paramount) to create their own broadcast or cable networks, thereby serving not only as program suppliers but as buyers and distributors as well. A related trend involves the recent wave of mergers and acquisitions, as media conglomerates like Time Warner, Viacom-Paramount, and Disney-ABC move into every phase of production, distribution, and exhibition. Yet another related trend involves the deregulation of the television industry, most notably the 1995 scaling back of the FCC's fin-syn regulations. Now that the networks again can finance and syndicate their own programs, merging with suppliers is not only logical but inevitable.

As of mid-1996, however, the industry remains wedded to program development in much the same form as in the fin-syn era. In fact *Variety* reported that a record 42 series were picked up in 1995 by the four broadcast networks (ABC, CBS, NBC, and FOX), out of the 125 or so actually developed. And in 1996, a reported 145 series were in development for those four broadcast networks plus the Warner and Paramount cable networks—many, of course, by in-house production subsidiaries of the network's parent company, rather than by outside suppliers.

Program development persists for a number of reasons. First, development has been part of the industry's entrenched bureaucracy since the 1970s, and it will not be easily or readily dismantled. Second, although the networks clearly favor their in-house suppliers, the highly competitive nature of television programming necessarily will encourage the networks to look outside for fresh ideas or, even more likely, for top talent—especially proven writer-producers and established stars who wish to maintain a degree of independence. Finally and perhaps most importantly, the networks have grown accustomed to developing far more programs than they actually can purchase or schedule. This enables them to keep their options open, to test-market potential series, and to share the risks of development. Program suppliers continue to accommodate the networks, because the long-term syndication payoff is still much higher for a series which has aired on a major broadcast network. And thus program development remains a buyer's market and a routine industry practice even in the era of cable, deregulation, and media mergers, with the networks enjoying considerable industry power.

—Thomas Schatz

FURTHER READING

Anderson, Christopher. *Hollywood TV: The Studio System in the Fifties.* Austin: University of Texas Press, 1994.

Barnouw, Erik. *Tube of Plenty: The Evolution of American Television.* New York: Oxford University Press, 1975.

Cantor, Muriel G. *Prime-Time Television: Content and Control.* Beverly Hill, California: Sage, 1980.

Flint, Joe. "Networks Win, Hollywood Winces as Fin-syn Barriers Fall." *Broadcasting* (Washington, D.C.), 22 November 1993.

Freeman, Mike. "How Drama Boldly Goes First-Run." *Broadcasting* (Washington, D.C.), 17 February 1992.

Gitlin, Todd. *Inside Prime Time.* New York: Pantheon, 1983.

McClellan, Steve. "The TV Networks in Play." *Broadcasting* (Washington, D.C.) 11 November 1991.

Reel, A. Frank. *The Networks: How They Stole the Show.* New York: Scribner's, 1979.

Robins, J. Max. "TV Biz Sweats it Out in Development Hell." *Variety* (Los Angeles), 22-28 April 1996.

Robins, J. Max, and Brian Lowry. "Pilot Poker is now for High Rollers Only." *Variety* (Los Angeles), 4-10 April 1994.

DEVELOPMENT COMMUNICATION

Development communications are organized efforts to use communications processes and media to bring social and economic improvements, generally in developing countries. The field emerged in the late 1950s amid high hopes that radio and television could be put to use in the world's most disadvantaged countries to bring about dramatic progress. Early communications theorists like Wilbur Schramm and Daniel Lerner based their high expectations upon the apparent success of World War II propaganda, to which academia and Hollywood had contributed.

Also with World War II came dozens of new, very poor, countries, left by their former colonial overseers with little infrastructure, education, or political stability. It was widely accepted that mass media could bring education, essential skills, social unity, and a desire to "modernize." Walt Rostow theorized that societies progress through specific stages of development on their way to modernity, what he termed "the age of high mass consumption." Lerner suggested that exposure to Western media would create "empathy" for modern culture, and a desire to move from traditional to modern ways. Early development communications, especially that sponsored by the U.S. government, was also seen as a means of "winning hearts and minds" over to a capitalist way of life.

These early approaches made a number of erroneous assumptions, and have been largely forsaken in contemporary approaches to development. Obstacles to development were naively seen as rooted in developing countries, not as products of international relationships. Modernization was presumed to equate to Westernization, and to be a necessary prerequisite to meeting human needs. Development was seen as a top-down process, whereby centralized mass media could bring about widespread change. Producers of development media often failed to ask if the audience can receive the message (television penetration in developing countries is minimal and radio penetration in the early days of development communication was light), understand the message (a problem in countries with dozens of languages and dialects), act upon the message (with the necessary tools or other forms of structural support), and want to act upon the message. And because it was based upon a propaganda model, development communications efforts were often seen as propaganda and distrusted.

Projects embodying these philosophies have enjoyed little success. In the 1970s and 1980s, a new paradigm of development communication emerged which better recognized the process of deliberate underdevelopment as a function of colonialism, the great diversity of the cultures involved, the differences between elite versus popular goals for social change, the considerable political and ideological constraints to change, and the endless varieties of ways different cultures communicate.

But in some instances mass media technologies, including television, have been "magic multipliers" of development benefits. Educational television has been used effectively to supplement the work of teachers in classrooms in the teaching of literacy and other skills, but only in well designed programs which are integrated with other educational efforts. Consumer video equipment and VCRs have been used to supplement communications efforts in some small projects.

Some developing countries have demonstrated success in using satellite television to provide useful information to portions of their populations out of reach of terrestrial broadcasting. In 1975 and 1976, an experimental satellite communications project called SITE (Satellite Instructional Television Experiment) was used to bring informational television programs to rural India. Some changes in beliefs and behaviors did occur, but there is little indication that satellite television was the best means to that end. The project did lead to Indian development of its own satellite network. China has also embarked on an ambitious program of satellite use for development, claiming substantial success in rural education. When television has succeeded as an educational tool in developing countries, it is only when very specific viewing conditions are met. For example, programs are best viewed in small groups with a teacher to introduce them and to lead a discussion afterwards.

A variety of types of organizations work with local governments to develop communications projects. The United Nations provides multi-lateral aid to governments. Non-profit non-governmental organizations (NGO) conduct development projects worldwide using U.N., government, or private funding. And government agencies, such as the U.S. Agency for International Development (USAID) provide assistance to developing countries, but with political strings attached. There are three common types of development campaigns: Persuasion, changing what people do; Education, changing social values; and Informing, empowering people to change by increasing knowledge. This third approach is now perceived as the most useful. Instead of attempting to modernize people, contemporary efforts attempt to reduce inequality by targeting the poorest segments of society, involving people in their own development, giving them independence from central authority, and employing "small" and "appropriate" technologies. The emphasis has shifted from economic growth to meeting basic needs.

In this new view of development, communication becomes an important catalyst for change, but not its cause. Local folk media, for example, is employed to reduce media's bias toward literacy and provide information in a traditional, familiar form. Development journalism provides people with information on change in their society, and works at the local level to advocate change. Where mass media is now employed in developing societies, community newspapers and radio prove far more accessible and useful than television. The rapid spread of entertainment television in the developing world is proving to be more a disruption to traditional social structures than an agent of progress. One emerging genre of television does show promise for contributing to development. The *telenovela*, pioneered in Brazil, has demonstrated some success in disseminating "pro-social" messages. Such programs are now being evaluated in many countries for their effectiveness in contributing to population control, health education, and other development goals.

—Chris Paterson

FURTHER READING

Aggarwala, N. "What is Development News?" *Journal of Communication* (New York), 1979.

Agrawal, Binod. "Satellite Instructional Television: SITE in India." In, Gerbner, G. and M. Siefert, editors. *World Communications: A Handbook.* New York: Longman, 1984.

Arnove, R. F., editor. *Educational Television: A Policy Critique and Guide for Developing Countries.* New York: Praeger, 1976.

Boeren, Ad, and Kees Escamp, editors. *The Empowerment of Culture: Development Communication and Popular Media.* The Hague: Centre for the Study of Education in Developing Countries, 1992.

Hornik, Robert. *Development Communication: Information, Agriculture and Nutrition in the Third World.* New York: Longman, 1988.

Katz, E., and G. Wedell. *Broadcasting in the Third World.* Cambridge, Massachusetts: Harvard University Press, 1977.

Lee, Paul Siu-nam. "Mass Communication and National Development in China: Media Roles Reconsidered." *Journal of Communication* (New York), Summer 1994.

Lerner, D. *The Passing of Traditional Society: Modernizing the Middle East.* New York: Free Press, 1958.

MacBride, S. *Many Voices, One World.* Paris: UNESCO, 1980.

Mahan, Elizabeth. "Mass Media and Society in Twentieth-Century Mexico." *Journal of the West* (Manhattan, Kansas), October 1988.

McAnany, Emile G., editor. *Communications in the Rural Third World.* New York: Praeger, 1980.

Melkote, Srinivas. *Communication for Development in the Third World: Theory and Practice.* Thousand Oaks, California: Sage, 1991.

Rao, B. S. S. *Television for Rural Development.* New Delhi: Concept Publishing: 1992.

Rogers, Everett. "Inquiry in Development Communication." In, Asante, M., and W. Gudykunst, editors. *Handbook of International and Intercultural Communication.* Thousand Oaks, California: Sage, 1989.

Schramm, W. *Mass Media and National Development: The Role of Information in the Developing Countries.* Stanford, California: Stanford University Press, 1964.

See also Satellite

THE DICK VAN DYKE SHOW

U.S. Situation/Domestic Comedy

The *Dick Van Dyke Show*, which ran from 1961 to 1966 on the CBS network, ushered in the golden age of the situation comedy (even more than *I Love Lucy* or *The Honeymooners*) poised as it was on the threshold between the comedy-variety star vehicles of the 1950s (frequently still grounded in vaudeville) and the neorealist socio-comedies of the early 1970s (whose mainstay Mary Tyler Moore carried its pedigree). It was among the first network series to electively bring itself to closure, in the manner of *M*A*S*H, The Mary Tyler Moore Show,* or *Cheers,* and has proven one of the most resilient in syndication. And as social document, it managed to operate largely contemporaneously with the New Frontier and the thousand days of the Kennedy presidency.

The show was largely the autobiographical exegesis of Carl Reiner, whose previous tenure in workaday television had been with the legendary stable of writers surrounding *Your Show of Shows* and the Sid Caesar sketch vehicles of the mid-1950s. This same group went on to literally redefine American humor: on the Broadway stage (Neil Simon); the high and low roads of screen comedy (Woody Allen and Mel Brooks, respectively); and in television, both early and late (Larry Gelbart, *M*A*S*H*). But first and foremost was *Dick Van Dyke,* based loosely on Reiner's 1958 novel *Enter*

Laughing (he directed a tepid screen version in 1967), in which his Alan Brady is a thinly veiled Caesar—a comic monster, sporadically seen but ubiquitously felt.

Brady's writing staff comprises the college-educated Rob Petrie (the eponymous Dick Van Dyke), assigned to interject new blood into his team of more experienced subordinates, Buddy Sorrell (Morey Amsterdam) and Sally Rogers (Rose Marie), loosely patterned after *Show of Shows* writers Mel Brooks and Selma Diamond. This sense of autobiography even stretched to the Petries' New Rochelle address (Reiner's own, save for a single digit), as well as his immediate family (his son Rob Reiner in turn became the archetypal early-1970s post-adolescent as Michael Stivic on *All in the Family,* raising certain intriguing Freudian possibilities in the evolution of the sitcom). Rounding out the domestic American Century optimism is Rob's wife Laura (Mary Tyler Moore).

As author David Marc has noted, for all intents and purposes, the movies destroyed vaudeville once and for all, and as a form of penance, made it into a kind of "biblical era of modern mass culture." This impulse was inherited wholesale by television of the 1950s (a quick survey of *I Love Lucy* reruns should suffice), and in turn carried forward rather elegiacally in the many blackouts built into this show within a show. Van Dyke, a gifted physical performer, never missed an opportunity to reprise his mewling Stan Laurel, or engage in a bit of Catskills schtick (invariably veiled in nostalgia). Entire episodes were given over to aging radio scribes or vaudeville fixtures who had been brushed aside by the space-age wonder of broadcast TV. Even sidekicks Buddy and Sally, real-life vaudeville veterans often seemed little more than human repositories of the history of formalist comedy ("Baby Rose" Marie was a child singer on radio; Amsterdam, a cello prodigy whose act recalled Henny Youngman or Jack Benny, co-hosted the *Tonight Show* forerunner *Broadway Open House* in 1950, and—in a bit of New Frontier pre-science—wrote the paean to U.S. imperialism "Rum and Coca-Cola" for the Andrews Sisters).

Yet perhaps to counterbalance these misted reveries, the show just as often displayed an aggressive Kennedy-era sophistication and leisure-class awareness. Initially competing for the central role were Van Dyke and that other Brubeck hipster grounded squarely in Midwestern guilelessness, Johnny Carson (and if truth be known, another prominent casualty of afterhours blackout drinking). Meanwhile, all the hallmarks of the Kennedy zeitgeist are somewhere in attendance: Laura as the Jackie surrogate, attired in capris pants and designer tops; the Mafia, via the imposing Big Max Calvada (executive producer Sheldon Leonard); Marilyn Monroe, represented by the occasional *Alan Brady* guest starlet or lupine voluptuary; intelligence operatives who commandeer the Petries' suburban home on stakeout. Camelot references abound, with a Robert Frost-like poet, a Hugh Hefner surrogate, Reiner as a Jackson Pollack-modeled abstract painter, or Laura's praise for baby guru Dr. Spock.

Sophisticated film homages appear throughout: *Vertigo*'s "Portrait of Carlotta" becomes "the Empress Carlotta brooch"; *Citizen Kane*'s "Rosebud" turns up as son Richie's middle name. (According to confidante Peter Bogdanovich, Orson Welles reportedly took a break every afternoon to watch the show in reruns.) Civil rights are often squarely front and center as well, with Leonard claiming that one racially themed episode, "The Hospital," specifically allowed him to cast *I Spy* with Bill Cosby, in turn the medium's first superstar of color. Even Van Dyke's own little brother, Jerry Van Dyke, is afforded a brief nepotistic berth from which to triumph— in his case, over painful shyness, social ineptitude, and a somewhat pesky somnambulism, rather than innate ruthlessness and the reputation as White House hatchet man. And for purists, there's even a working conspiracy of sorts—the name "Calvada," scattered portentously throughout (Big Max "Calvada," "Drink Calvada" scrawled on a billboard, the name of their production company)—which is, in fact, a modified acronym for the show's partners: *CA*-rl Reiner, Sheldon *L*-eonard, Dick *VA*-n Dyke, and *DA*-nny Thomas.

But more than vague inspiration, the Kennedys provided direct participation as well. In 1960, Reiner wrote a pilot titled *Head of the Family*, virtually identical in every

The Dick Van Dyke Show

way, save for casting himself in the lead role. The package made its way to Rat Pack stalwart Peter Lawford, a burgeoning producer and brother-in-law of the future president. Family patriarch Joseph P. Kennedy, seeking to oversee family business during the campaign, read the pilot personally, and in turn volunteered production money. Although the pilot was unsuccessful, its recasting led directly to the later series.

The Dick Van Dyke Show ended in 1966 with a final episode surveying Rob's "novel"—a collection of favorite moments from the five-year run—which Alan Brady dutifully agrees to adapt as a TV series, thus reupping the autobiographical subtext one more level and providing Reiner the last laugh. This was perhaps in light of CBS' decision to enforce a full-color lineup the following season. As such, the series' cool, streamlined black and white mirrors perfectly the news images of the day, and functions as one of the few de facto time capsules on a finite and much-celebrated age.

—Paul Cullum

CAST

Rob Petrie	Dick Van Dyke
Laura Petrie	Mary Tyler Moore
Sally Rogers	Rose Marie
Maurice "Buddy" Sorrell	Morey Amsterdam
Ritchie Petrie	Larry Mathews
Melvin Cooley	Richard Deacon

Jerry Helper	Jerry Paris
Millie Helper	Ann Morgan Guilbert
Alan Brady	Carl Reiner
Stacey Petrie	Jerry Van Dyke

PRODUCERS   Carl Reiner, Sheldon Leonard, Ronald Jacobs

PROGRAMMING HISTORY   158 Episodes

• CBS

October 1961–December 1961	Tuesday 8:00-8:30
January 1962–September 1964	Wednesday 9:30-10:00
September 1964–September 1965	Wednesday 9:00-9:30
September 1965–September 1966	Wednesday 9:30-10:00

FURTHER READING

Butsch, Richard. "Class and Gender in Four Decades of Television Situation Comedy: plus ca change...." *Critical Studies in Mass Communication* (Annandale, Virginia), December 1992.

Hamamoto, Darrell Y. *Nervous Laughter: Television Situation Comedy and Liberal Democratic Ideology.* New York: Praeger, 1989.

Haralovich, Mary Beth. "Sitcoms and Suburbs: Positioning the 1950s Homemaker." *Quarterly Review of Film and Television* (Los Angeles, California), May 1989.

Javna, John. *The Best of TV Sitcoms: Burns and Allen to the Cosby Show, The Munsters to Mary Tyler Moore.* New York: Harmony, 1988.

Jones, Gerard. *Honey, I'm Home!: Sitcoms, Selling the American Dream.* New York: Grove Weidenfeld, 1992.

Leibman, Nina. *Living Room Lectures: The Fifties Family in Film and Television.* Austin: University of Texas Press, 1995.

Lipsitz, George. "The Meaning of Memory: Family, Class, and Ethnicity in Early Network Television." *Camera Obscura* (Berkeley, California), January 1988.

Marc, David. *Demographic Vistas: Television in American Culture.* Philadelphia: University of Pennsylvania Press, 1984.

———. *Comic Visions: Television Comedy and American Culture.* Boston, Massachusetts: Unwin-Hyman, 1989.

Rowe, Kathleen. *The Unruly Woman: Gender and the Genres of Laughter.* Austin: University of Texas Press, 1995.

Spigel, Lynn. *Make Room for TV: Television and the Family Ideal in Postwar America.* Chicago: University of Chicago Press, 1992.

Weissman, Ginny, and Coyne Sanders. *The Dick Van Dyke Show: Anatomy of a Classic.* New York: St. Martin's, 1983.

See also Comedy, Domestic Settings; Moore, Mary Tyler; Van Dyke, Dick

A DIFFERENT WORLD

U.S. Situation Comedy

A *Different World,* a spin-off of the top-rated *The Cosby Show,* enjoyed a successful run on NBC from 1987 to 1993. The half-hour, ensemble situation comedy was the first to immerse America in student life at an historically black college. Over the course of its run, the show was also credited with tackling social and political issues rarely explored in television fiction, and opening doors to the television industry for unprecedented numbers of young black actors, writers, producers and directors.

Set at Hillman College, a fictitious, historically black college in the South, the series began by focusing on the college experiences of sophomore Denise Huxtable (Lisa Bonet)—one of the four daughters featured on *The Cosby Show.* Denise's attempts to adjust to life away from her family's upper-middle-class nest, and her relationship with her roommates, typically fueled the plot of each episode. One of those roommates, Jaleesa Vinson (Dawnn Lewis), was a young divorcee who considered Denise to be somewhat of a spoiled snob. Another roommate, Maggie Lauten (Marisa Tomei), was one of the few white students on the mostly black campus; for her, as it was for much of the show's audience, Hillman was indeed "a different world." Other recurring characters were added throughout the

course of the first season: Whitley Gilbert (Jasmine Guy) was a rich Southern belle; Dwayne Wayne (Kadeem Hardison) was a fast-talking, but studious, New Yorker; Ron Johnson (Darryl Bell) was Dwayne's scheming sidekick; and Warren Oates (Sinbad) was the dorm director and gym teacher. Bonet and her character, Denise, left the show after the first season due to her real-life pregnancy.

Despite dismal initial reviews, *A Different World* capitalized from its Thursday at 8:30 P.M. time slot on NBC—between *The Cosby Show* and the ever-popular sitcom, *Cheers*—and finished second in the ratings its first season. The show and its creative staff were revamped for the second season, leading to third and fourth-place finishes for the 1988–89 and 1989–90 seasons, respectively. Among black viewers, however, the show consistently ranked first or second throughout most of its run.

As *The Hollywood Reporter* noted, the series was transformed "from a bland *Cosby* spin-off into a lively, socially responsible, ensemble situation comedy" only after Debbie Allen took over as producer-director following the first season. Allen, a prominent black dancer, choreographer and actress—and a graduate of historically black Howard University—drew from her college experiences in an effort to accurately reflect in the show the social and political life on black campuses. Moreover, Allen instituted a yearly spring trip to Atlanta where series writers visited two of the nation's leading black colleges, Morehouse and Spelman. During these visits, ideas for several of the episodes emerged from meetings with students and faculty. Symbolizing the show's transformation between the two seasons, perhaps, "the queen of soul," Aretha Franklin, was chosen to replace Phoebe Snow as vocalist for the title theme.

During Allen's tenure, casting changes also transformed the look and feel of the series. Several new characters were added, while certain characters from the first season were featured more prominently in order to add some spice. A cafeteria cook, Mr. Gaines (Lou Meyers), was added to give the series a flavor of southern culture. A hardworking, pre-medical student, Kim Reese (Charnele Brown), was also introduced as a foil for Whitley; she worked for Mr. Gaines in the cafeteria and eventually found herself caught in an on-again, off-again romantic relationship with Ron, one of the original characters. Similarly, Dwayne became entangled in a love-hate relationship with another original character, Whitley. The eventual marriage of Dwayne and Whitley became a major event in the storyline. Other new characters included Col. Taylor (Glynn Turman), the campus ROTC commander; Freddie Brooks (Cree Summer), an environmental activist with metaphysical leanings; Terrence Taylor (Cory Tyler), the son of Col. Taylor; and Lena James (Jada Pinkett), a feisty freshman from the Baltimore projects. Each new season, brought an incoming class of freshman and new featured characters. In short, following the departure of Bonet's character after the first season, the series became a true ensemble situation comedy.

A Different World is also notable for its attempts to explore a range of social and political issues rarely addressed on television—let alone in situation comedies. Featured characters regularly confronted such controversial topics as unplanned pregnancy, date rape, racial discrimination, AIDS, and the 1992 Los Angeles uprisings. Many observers also commended the series for extolling the virtues of higher education for African American youth at a time when many black communities were in crisis.

In the final analysis, *A Different World* might best be remembered for its cultural vibrancy, its commitment to show-casing black history, music, dance, fashion and attitude. This quality, no doubt, was due in large measure to the closeness of the series' creative staff to the material: the series featured a black woman as producer-director (Allen), another as headwriter (Susan Fales), and several other people of color (male and female) in key creative positions. Few series in the history of television can claim a comparable level of black representation in key decision-making positions.

—Darnell M. Hunt

A Different World

CAST

Denise Huxtable (1987–88) . . . . Lisa Bonet
Whitley Gilbert . . . . Jasmine Guy
Jaleesa Vinson . . . . Dawnn Lewis
Dwayne Wayne . . . . Kadeem Hardison
Ron Johnson . . . . Darryl Bell
Maggie Lauten (1987–88) . . . . Marisa Tomei
Millie (1987–88) . . . . Marie-Alise Recasner
Stevie Rallen (1987–88) . . . . Loretta Devine
J.T. Rallen (1987–88) . . . . Amir Williams
Gloria (1987–88) . . . . Bee-be Smith
Allison (1987–88) . . . . Kim Wayane
Walter Oakes (1987–91) . . . . Sinbad
Lettie Bostic (1988–89) . . . . Mary Alice
Col. Clayton Taylor (1988–93) . . . . . . Glynn Turman
Terrence Johann Taylor (1990–92) . . . . . Cory Tyler
Winifred "Freddie" Brooks (1988–93) . . . Cree Summer
Kim Reese (1988–93) . . . . Charnele Brown
Vernon Gaines (1988–93) . . . . Lou Myers
Ernest (1988–90) . . . . Reuben Grundy
Julian (1990–91) . . . . Dominio Hoffman
LenaJames (1991–93) . . . . Jada Pinkett
Charmaine Brown (1992–93) . . . . Karen Malina White
Gina Devereaux (1991–92) . . . . Ajai Sanders
Byron Douglas III (1992) . . . . Joe Morton
Shazza Zulu (1992) . . . . Gary Dourdon
Clint (1992–93) . . . . Michael Ralph

PRODUCERS   Marcy Carsey, Tom Werner, Anne Beatts, Thad Mumford, Debbie Allen, George Crosby, Lissa Levin

PROGRAMMING HISTORY   144 Episodes

• NBC

September 1987–June 1992	Thursday 8:30-9:00
July 1991–August 1991	Monday 8:30-9:00
July 1992–November 1992	Thursday 8:00-8:30
November 1992–January 1993	Thursday 8:30-9:00
May 1993–June 1993	Thursday 8:00-8:30
July 1993	Friday 8:00-8:30

FURTHER READING

Beller, Miles. "*A Different World.*" *The Hollywood Reporter* (Los Angeles), 21 September 1989.

Dates, Janette, and William Barlow, editors. *Split Image: African Americans in the Mass Media*. Washington, D.C.: Howard University Press, 1990.

"*A Different World.*" *Variety* (Los Angeles), 7 October 1987.

Gray, Herman. *Watching Race: Television and the Struggle for "Blackness."* Minneapolis: University of Minnesota Press, 1995.

Haithman, Diane. "Different Touch to *Different World.*" *Los Angeles Times*, 6 October 1988.

Honeycutt, Kirk. "Breaking Through the Walls: Tonight *A Different World* Broadcasts its 100th Episode on NBC. In Five Years It Has Grown from a Bland *Cosby* Spin-off into a Lively, Socially Responsible, Ensemble Situation Comedy." *The Hollywood Reporter* (Los Angeles), 17 October 1991.

Letofsky, Irv. "*A Different World.*" *The Hollywood Reporter* (Los Angeles), 24 September 1992.

MacDonald, J. Fred. *Blacks and White TV: Afro-Americans in Television Since 1948*. Chicago: Nelson-Hall, 1992.

McNeil, Alex. *Total Television*. New York: Penguin Books, 1991.

Vittes, Laurence. "*A Different World.*" *The Hollywood Reporter* (Los Angeles), 20 September 1990.

See also Carsey, Marcy; *Cosby Show*

DIGITAL TELEVISION

Digital television is the application of digital technology to television in the process of producing and transmitting television programming. Television was developed as an "analog" medium, but the replacement of analog technology with digital technology throughout the television production and transmission process promises to increase the capabilities of the medium.

The term "digital" refers to a type of electronic signal in which the information is stored in a sequence of binary numbers ("on" or "off", representing one and zero) rather than in a continuously varying signal (known as an analog signal). Almost all naturally occurring communication media, including sound and light waves, are analog signals. Because analog signals are composed of waves, they are extremely susceptible to interference, as the waves of external signals can interact with a specific signal, altering the shape of the wave. Digital signals are much less susceptible to interference because a slightly altered sequence of "on" and "off" signals can still be read as the original sequence of ones and zeroes.

The primary attributes of a digital signal are the sampling frequency and the bit rate. In order to convert an analog signal to a digital one, the signal must be "sampled" by measuring the height of the analog signal at discrete points in time. The "sampling frequency" is a measure of how many samples are taken to represent the analog wave. A higher sampling frequency indicates more samples, providing a more faithful reproduction of the analog signal. But doubling the sample rate means doubling the amount of data needed to represent the original analog signal. Bit rate refers to the number of different bits (zero/one values) used to represent each sample. A higher bit rate results in a greater number of values for the signal, and, hence, a higher resolution. (Each additional bit doubles the number of values for each signal, so that an eight-bit signal has twice the resolution of a seven-bit signal.) Most digital audio signals use eight or sixteen bits of information for each sample.

Digital signals have a number of advantages over analog signals. The primary advantage is that digital signals allow for perfect copies (and perfect copies of copies, etc.). Digital signals may also be manipulated by computers, allowing for elaborate modifications of digital video and audio signals. The primary drawbacks of digital signals are that it takes a great deal more space to store a digital signal than an analog one, and that extra equipment is needed to covert analog video and audio signals to digital signals, and later convert the digital signals back to analog.

Digital technology was first applied to television to create special video effects that were not possible using analog technology. The analog images were digitized, and mathematical algorithms processed the resulting data, allowing a picture to be blown up, shrunk, twisted, etc. The next innovation was the creation of digital video recorders, which stored television signals as a sequence of binary numbers. Digital video recording is extremely complicated because the sequence of numbers used to represent a single picture required much more storage space than the corresponding analog signal. However, copies of digital signals are exactly the same as the original, enabling higher-quality pictures during the editing process, especially when many signals have to be "layered" together to create a single picture or sequence.

The television production process is gradually moving from a system that interconnects a variety of digital sources with analog equipment to the use of an all-digital environment. Along the way, analog and digital tape formats will be replaced by new digital recording devices similar to computer disk drives, allowing random access to any portion of a recording.

Digital technology has also been applied to the process of transmitting television signals. The bandwidth necessary for high-definition television required development of a means of transmitting up to five times the video information of a traditional television signal in the same bandwidth. The solution was the application of digital compression technology. Digital compression is the process by which digital signals are simplified by removing redundancy. (For example, each of the thirty individual pictures used to create one second of video is quite similar to the previous picture. Instead of transmitting the entire picture again, some compression algorithms transmit only the parts of the picture that change from one picture to the next.) There are two general types of digital compression: "Lossless" compression, in which the decompressed signal is exactly the same as the uncompressed signal; and "lossy" compression, in which the decompressed signal contains less information (or less detail) than the original uncompressed signal.

The flexibility of digital signals has led many engineers to develop uses for digital broadcasting other than high-definition television. The use of digital compression will allow the transmission of at least four, and perhaps eight or more, standard-definition channels of programming in the same bandwidth required for a single analog channel. Furthermore, the fact that digital signals are less susceptible to interference will eventually allow more television stations on the air in a given market. (Interference problems with analog signals requires wide spacing of television stations on the same or adjacent channels, resulting in use of only a few channels in most cities to protect stations in nearby cities.)

One main problem with digital broadcasting is that it will require viewers to either buy new receivers or obtain adapters to convert digital signals to analog form for viewing on a traditional television receiver. Ultimately, the use of television by consumers should be revolutionized as they begin buying digital receivers and video recorders and enjoy the quality and flexibility provided by digital technology.

—August Grant

FURTHER READING

Alten, S. *Audio in Media.* Belmont, California: Wadsworth, 1981; 4th edition, 1994.

Chyt, H. S. "Digital Audio." In, Grant, August, editor. *Communication Technology Update.* Austin, Texas: Technology Futures, 1992; 5th edition, Newton, Massachusetts: Focal, 1996.

Straubhaar, Joseph, and Robert LaRose. *Communication Media in the Information Society.* Belmont, California: Wadsworth, 1996.

DILLER, BARRY

U.S. Media Executive

Barry Diller is an innovative television executive best known for organizing a fourth network at FOX Broadcasting to challenge the domination of American prime-time television by ABC, CBS, and NBC. Starting out in the mailroom of the William Morris Agency, Diller joined ABC's programming department in 1966 and was placed charge of negotiating broadcast rights to feature films from the major studios. As vice president in charge of feature films and program development in 1969, Diller inaugurated ABC's Movie of the Week, a regular series of ninety-minute films made exclusively for television. Premiering on 23 September 1969, the program became the most popular movie series in television history and helped ABC achieve parity with NBC and CBS in the ratings.

Made-for-television films (MFTs) had appeared intermittently on prime time since 1965, when NBC contracted with MCA for more than thirty World Premiere movies to be delivered over several years. But it was Diller who devised the formula that enabled MFTs to outstrip the ratings power of theatrical movies. Abandoning conventional narratives such as westerns and crime melodramas, Diller ordered social problem films that explored issues such as homosexuality (*That Certain Summer,* 1972), the Vietnam War (*The Ballad of Andy Crocker,* 1969), and drugs (*Go Ask Alice,* 1973). Capable of being quickly produced at a cost of around $350,000 each, docudramas, as they were called, probed current newspaper headlines and American popular culture for gripping topics targeted at young urban and adult audiences. By 1972, MFTs had become an established network programming practice.

In 1974 Diller was named chair of Paramount Pictures. He was hired by Charles Bluhdorn, head of Gulf and Western Industries, a sprawling conglomerate that had acquired Paramount in 1966. For ten years Diller oversaw a studio that produced hit television series that included *Laverne and Shirley* (1976–83), *Taxi* (1978–83), and *Cheers* (1982–93), and a string of motion picture, including *Saturday Night Fever* (1977), *Grease* (1978), *Raiders of the Lost Ark* (1981), *Terms of Endearment* (1983), and *Beverly Hills Cop* (1984).

Diller quit his job in 1984 over a dispute with Gulf and Western's new head, Martin S. Davis, and went to work for 20th Century-Fox. After the studio was acquired by Australian newspaper mogul Rupert Murdoch in 1985,

Diller embarked on a plan to launch a fourth television network to compete with the Big Three. The nucleus of the network consisted of Metromedia Television, a group of seven big-city television stations reaching 23% of the population, which Murdoch purchased from John Kluge in 1986 for $2 billion. Lining up an amalgam of local UHF and VHF stations, FOX Broadcasting started out cautiously in 1987 with only two nights of prime-time programming; by 1990 it had expanded its schedule to five nights. Diller had succeeded against all odds by developing low-cost "reality" programming such as *COPS* and *America's Most Wanted,* and alternative fare such as *In Living Color, Married...with Children,* and *The Simpsons,* aimed at the youth audience, from age 18 to 34.

In a move that surprised the industry, Diller quit 20th Century-Fox in 1992 and purchased a $25 million stake in QVC teleshopping network. As head of QVC, Diller launched a takeover bid for Paramount Communications (the new name of Gulf and Western after the conglomerate sold off its non-entertainment businesses) in 1993. The battle for Paramount was joined by Sumner Redstone's Viacom Inc., which submitted a winning bid of $9.6 billion in 1994. Foiled in his attempt to take over a major film studio, Diller resigned from QVC in 1995 and acquired Silver King Communications, a small group of UHF stations, in an attempt to create a hybrid cable TV network that would offer a full schedule of entertainment, sports, and news. To finance the venture, Diller had secured the backing of John Malone, president and CEO of Telecommunications Inc., the nation's largest cable operator. Although the outcome of the Silver King venture is unclear, Diller will likely remain a key player in the cable television industry for the indefinite future.

—Tino Balio

BARRY DILLER. Born in San Francisco, California, U.S.A., 2 February 1942. Assistant to vice president in charge of programming, ABC-TV, 1966; executive assistant to vice president in programming and director of feature films, ABC, 1968; vice president, feature films and program development, ABC, 1969; created TV movies of the week and miniseries as vice president, feature films, Circle Entertainment, division of ABC, 1971; vice president, prime-time TV, ABC, 1973; board chair and president, Paramount Pictures, 1974; president, Gulf and Western Entertainment and Communications Group (while retaining Paramount titles), 1983; resigned from Paramount and joined 20th Century-Fox as board chair and chief executive officer, 1984; chair and chief executive officer, Fox, Inc., 1985; named to board, News Corp. Ltd., June 1987; resigned from 20th Century-Fox, February 1992; chief executive officer, QVC Network, 1992–1995. Board of Directors: FCC Advisory Committee on Advanced TV Services; Museum TV and Radio; Academy of Arts and Sciences Foundation. Member: President's Export Council.

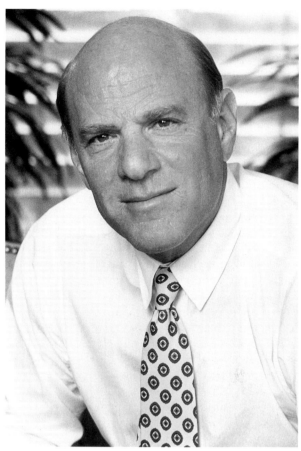

Barry Diller
Photo courtesy of Barry Diller

FURTHER READING

Auletta, Ken. "Barry Diller's Search for the Future: Annals of Communication." *The New Yorker* (New York), 22 February 1993.

———. "Network for Sale?" *The New Yorker* (New York), 25 July 1994.

"Barry Diller and Fox: Taking the High-risk Option" (interview). *Broadcasting* (Washington, D.C.), 1 January 1990.

Bart, Peter. "Dealing with Diller." *Variety* (Los Angeles, California), 2 March 1992.

Block, Alex Ben. *Outfoxed: Marvin Davis, Barry Diller, Rupert Murdoch, Joan Rivers and the Inside Story of America's Fourth Television Network.* New York: St. Martin's, 1990.

Corliss, Richard. "'The Barry and Larry Show': Barry Diller of QVC Corp. and Lawrence Tisch of CBS Plan Merger." *Time* (New York), 11 July 1994.

Freeman, Mike. "QVC's Diller: Redefining TV" (interview). *Broadcasting* (Washington, D.C.), 25 January 1993.

Goodell, Jeff. "Barry Diller" (interview). *Rolling Stone* (New York), 25 August 1994.

McClellan, Steve. "Diller Ponders Newfound Independents: Silver King Buy Puts Him Back in the Game." *Broadcasting and Cable* (Washington, D.C.), 4 September 1995.

Moshavi, Sharon D. "Diller's Next Moves: Cable Network, Putting Theatricals on PPV First." *Broadcasting* (Washington, D.C.), 25 November 1991.

Solomon, Jolie, and Charles Fleming. "Regarding Barry." *Newsweek* (New York), 25 July 1994.

"Vanity, Insanity and Fear (Time-Warner/Ted Turner and Barry Diller Attempt to Build Media Giants in Opposite Ways)." *The Economist* (London), 2 September 1995.

See also FOX Broadcasting Company; Movies on Television; Murdoch, Rupert

DIMBLEBY, RICHARD

British Broadcast Journalist

Richard Dimbleby was the personification of British television current affairs broadcasting in the 1950s and early 1960s and he set the standard for succeeding generations of presenters on the network, by whom he was recognized as the virtual founder of broadcast journalism. After working on the editorial staff of several newspapers, he joined the BBC as a radio news observer in 1936. When war broke out three years later, he became the BBC's first war correspondent, and, as such, within the constraints of often stifling official censorship, he brought the reality of warfare into homes throughout the length and breadth of Great Britain. Notably graphic broadcasts included despatches from the battlefield of Al-Alamein, from the beaches of Normandy during the D-Day landings, and a report sent back from a Royal Air Force bomber on a raid over Germany (in all he flew as an observer on some 20 missions). He was also the first radio reporter to reach the concentration camp at Belsen, from which he sent a moving account of what he saw, and he was the first to enter Berlin.

After the war, Dimbleby worked as a freelance broadcaster and made the switch to television, in time becoming the BBC's best-known commentator on current affairs and state events. Among the important state occasions he covered were the Coronation of Elizabeth II in 1953 and the funerals of John F. Kennedy and Sir Winston Churchill. The coronation broadcast was a particular personal triumph, establishing Dimbleby as the first choice commentator on all state events and, incidentally, promoting television sales by some 50%. Other milestones in his career included his participation in 1951 in the first Eurovision television relay and, in 1961, his appearance in the first live television broadcast from the Soviet Union.

In 1955 Dimbleby was selected as anchorman for the much-respected current affairs programme *Panorama*, and it is with this that his name is usually associated. Quizzing politicians of all colours with equal severity on behalf of the nation, he was praised by many as a defender of the public interest, and became almost synonymous with the BBC itself as a bastion of fairness and perspicuity in political debate. Under Dimbleby's direction, *Panorama* established itself as the current affairs programme *par excellence*, the weekly showing almost a political event itself, raising issues that Parliament hastened to deal with in order to show it was responsive to the electorate thus represented.

Viewers hung on the presenter's every word and besieged him with letters, begging him to use his evident influence to intervene personally in political issues of all kinds, from proposals for new roads to the Cuban missile crisis. One rare remark that did not go down so well was an infamous aside, "Jesus wept", which was unfortunately picked up by the microphone and prompted a stream of letters criticizing him for blasphemy.

Dimbleby did, though, also tackle lighter fare, and was much loved as chair of the radio programme *Twenty Questions* and as presenter of the homely *Down Your Way* series, in which he sought out prominent members of a given locality and passed the time of day with them. His standing with the British listening and viewing public was officially honoured in 1945, when he was made an Officer of the British Empire, and again in 1959, when he was promoted to Companion of the British Empire.

Dimbleby's premature death from cancer at the age of 52, shortly after broadcasting to 350 million people on the state funeral of Winston Churchill, was regretted by millions of viewers, and subsequently the annual Richard Dimbleby lectures were established in his memory. These were not his only legacy, however, for two of his sons, David and Jonathan, pursued similar careers in current affairs broadcasting and in their turn became two of the most familiar faces on British screens, earning reputations as fair but tough-minded interrogators of the political leaders of their generation. David Dimbleby emulated his father by, in 1974, becoming anchorman of *Panorama*, while Richard Dimbleby has occupied a similar role on such current affairs programmes as *This Week* and *First Tuesday*.

—David Pickering

RICHARD DIMBLEBY. Born in Richmond-upon-Thames, London, England, 25 May 1913. Attended Mill Hill School, London. Married: Dilys, 1937; children: Jonathan, David, Nicholas and Sally. Began career with the family newspaper, *The Richmond and Twickenham Times*, 1931; subsequently worked for the *Bournemouth Echo* and as news editor, for *Advertisers Weekly*, 1935–36; joined BBC Topical Talks department as one of the first radio news reporters, 1936; accompanied British Expeditionary Force to France as first BBC war correspondent, 1939; reported from front line in

Middle East, East Africa, the Western Desert and Greece, 1939–42; flew about 20 missions with Royal Air Force Bomber Command and was first reporter to enter Belsen concentration camp, 1945; after war became foremost commentator on state occasions, including coronation of Elizabeth II, 1953, and funeral of Winston Churchill, 1965; managing director, Dimbleby newspaper business, from 1954; presenter of BBC's *Panorama*, 1955–63. Officer of the Order of the British Empire, 1945; Commander of the Order of the British Empire, 1959. Died in London, England, 22 December 1965.

TELEVISION SERIES

1955–63   *Panorama*

RADIO
Twenty Questions; Down Your Way; Off the Record.

FURTHER READING

Dimbleby, Jonathan. *Richard Dimbleby: A Biography.* London: Hodder and Stoughton, 1975.
Miall, Leonard. *Inside the BBC: British Broadcasting Characters.* London: Weidenfeld and Nicholson, 1994.
Milne, Alasdair. *DG: Memoirs of a British Broadcaster.* London: Hodder and Stoughton, 1988.
Trethowan, Ian. *Split Screen.* London: H. Hamilton, 1984.

See also *Panorama*

THE DINAH SHORE SHOW(VARIOUS)

U.S. Music-Variety Show

A popular radio and television performer for over 40 years, Dinah Shore was known for the warmth of her personality and for her sincere, unaffected stage presence. Television favored her natural, relaxed style, and like Perry Como, to whom she was often compared, Shore was one of the medium's first popular singing stars. Even though by her own admission, Dinah Shore did not have a great voice, she put it to good advantage by enunciating lyrics clearly and singing the melody without distracting ornamentation. The result was the very definition of "easy listening."

By the time Shore first appeared on television, she was already well-known as a big band singer and radio performer. In 1952, she was chosen most popular female vocalist by a Gallup poll. She was also appearing in the best night clubs, making motion pictures, and selling approximately two million phonograph records per year. Miss Shore's subsequent two decades of television work merely enhanced her already remarkable career.

Dinah Shore first appeared on television in 1951 when she began a twice a week program over NBC. This fifteen-minute show was broadcast on Tuesday and Thursday evenings at 7:30 P.M. Jack Gould, *The New York Times* radio and television critic, enthused about the program: "Last week on her initial appearance, she was the picture of naturalness and conducted her show with a disarming combination of authority and humility."

The fifteen-minute program was produced by Alan Handley, who made a special effort to make the musical production numbers interesting. The imaginative backdrops he provided for Shore's songs were inspired by travel posters, *New Yorker* cartoons, history, literary classics, and Hollywood. Handley often checked department store window displays and went to the theater to get ideas for these numbers. On one occasion, he used a Georgia O'Keefe painting of a bleached cattle skull as a backdrop for a song

called "Cow Cow Boogie." On another occasion, he made a living Calder mobile out of his vocal quintet "The Notables" by suspending them from the ceiling of the studio.

In 1956, Shore began a one-hour program on NBC, *The Dinah Shore Chevy Show.* The program was extremely popular, and its theme song "See the USA in your

The Dinah Shore Chevy Show

Chevrolet . . . ," always ending with Shore's famous farewell kiss to the television audience, remain television icons. The high production values of her 15-minute program continued on the 60-minute show. The lineup usually contained two or three guests drawn from the worlds of music, sports, and movies. Shore was able to make almost any performer feel comfortable and could bring together such unlikely pairings as Frank Sinatra and baseball star Dizzy Dean.

The Dinah Shore Chevy Show was produced in Burbank, California, by Bob Banner, who also directed each episode. The choreographer was Tony Charmoli who occasionally danced on camera. Often the production numbers took advantage of special visual effects. For "76 Trombones," Banner used prisms mounted in front of the television cameras to turn 12 musicians into several dozen. The number was so popular that it was repeated on two subsequent occasions. For "Flim Flam Floo," Banner used the chromakey so that objects appeared and disappeared, and actors floated through the air without the aid of wires. In his review of the opening show of 1959, Jack Gould called the program "a spirited and tuneful affair." Shore, he wrote "sang with the warmth and infectious style that are so distinctly her own," and he judged that she "continues to be the best dressed woman in television."

Shore's musical variety program went off the air in May 1963. After that time, she appeared in a number of specials and later did a series of interview shows in the 1970's including *Dinah!, Dinah and Friends, Dinah and Her New Best Friends,* and *Dinah's Place.* Throughout her career, Shore remained one of the great ladies of the entertainment world.

—Henry B. Aldridge

THE DINAH SHORE SHOW

REGULAR PERFORMERS
Dinah Shore
The Notables, quintet (1951–55)
The Skylarks, quintet (1955–57)

MUSIC
Ticker Freeman, Piano
TheVic Schoen Orchestra (1951–54)

The Harry Zimmerman Orchestra (1954–57)

PRODUCER   Alan Handley

PROGRAMMING HISTORY

• NBC
November 1951–July 1957
Tuesday and Thursday 7:30-7:45

THE DINAH SHORE CHEVY SHOW

REGULAR PERFORMERS
Dinah Shore
The Skylarks, quintet (1956–57)
The Even Dozen (1961–62)

DANCERS
The Tony Charmoli Dancers (1957–62)
The Nick Castle Dancers (1962–63)

MUSIC
The Harry Zimmerman Orchestra (1957–61, 1962–63)
Frank DeVol and His Orchestral (1961–62)

PRODUCER   Bob Banner

PROGRAMMING HISTORY

• NBC

October 1956–June 1957	Friday 10:00-11:00
October 1957–June 1961	Sunday 9:00-10:00
October 1961–June 1962	Friday 9:30-10:30
December 1962–May 1963	Sunday 10:00-11:00

FURTHER READING
"Dinah Shore's TV Art." *Look* (New York), 15 December 1953.
Eells, G. "Dinah Shore." *Look* (New York), 6 December 1960.

See also Shore, Dinah

DINGO, ERNIE

Australian Actor

Ernie Dingo is an Aboriginal Australian actor who has had an extensive career in film and television. Best known to international audiences through his film roles as Charlie in *Crocodile Dundee II* and as the Australian detective who chases William Hurt around the globe in Wim Wenders' *Until the End of the World,* Dingo has also become a familiar and popular figure on Australian television.

Dingo's television career is particularly significant for the way it has broken new ground in the medium's presentation of cultural difference. Initially taking roles scripted specifically for an Aboriginal actor by white writers and directors, he has worked consistently to broaden expectations of what Aboriginality can include and to introduce and popularise an understanding of Aboriginal perspectives on Australian life.

Ernie Dingo grew up around the small Western Australian town of Mullewa, where the local Aboriginal people still speak the traditional Wudjadi language. He first moved into acting in Perth when a basketball team to which he belonged formed a dance and cultural performance group Middar. From there, he moved into stage roles in plays by Western Australian Aboriginal playwright Jack Davis, before gaining a role in the television miniseries *Cowra Breakout* (1985) by Kennedy Miller for the Channel Ten network. Dingo's background in traditional and contemporary Aboriginal culture have been important to his work in television because, as he points out, working as an Aboriginal actor frequently involves working also (usually informally) as a consultant, cultural mediator, co-writer and translator.

Dingo's first major screen roles were in film, in *Tudawali* (1985), *Fringe Dwellers* (1986) and *State of Shock* (1989), all of which had white script writers and directors but which dealt sympathetically with problems of racism and disadvantage encountered by Aboriginal people. All three were small release productions designed substantially for television adaptation and/or distribution. In 1988 he was awarded the Special Jury Prize at the Banff Television Festival for his powerful performance as one of Australia's first Aboriginal screen actors, Robert Tudawali, in *Tudawali.*

One of Dingo's main skills as an actor is an ability to engage audiences with an open, easy screen presence and use of humour, while also capturing serious moods dramatically and convincingly. It is perhaps this versatility, above all, which has made him highly effective as a cross-cultural communicator. Dingo's ability with lighter roles was first demonstrated by his performances in children's drama series, including *Clowning Around* (1992) and *A Waltz Through the Hills* (1990), for which he received an Australian Film Institute award for Best Actor in a Telefeature for his performance as an Aboriginal bushman, Frank Watson.

However, his first emergence as a popular figure of mainstream commercial television occurred with his inclusion in the comedy-variety program *Fast Forward.* He is particularly remembered for his comic take-off of prominent financial commentator Robert Gottliebsen, in which he imitated Gottliebsen's manner and appearance but translated his analysis of movements in share prices and exchange rates into colloquial Aboriginal English.

From *Fast Forward,* Dingo has moved on to roles in other popular programs such as *The Great Outdoors* and *Heartbreak High.* The latter two roles, as well as his role in *Fast Forward,* are significant because they are not clearly marked as specifically Aboriginal. In *The Great Outdoors,* Dingo appears alternately with other well-known Australian television personalities as a compere, or master of ceremonies, in light feature stories about leisure, travel and the environment. In *Heartbreak High,* he appears as Vic, a media studies teacher at multicultural Hartley High. Both roles have done much to normalise the appearance of Aboriginal people on Australian television and have provided an important counter to the often fraught treatment of Aboriginal issues in news and current affairs.

Dingo has also continued with serious dramatic roles with a major role as an Aboriginal police liaison officer, Vincent Burraga, in the Australian Broadcasting Corporation's highly acclaimed drama series *Heartland.* The series was in many ways groundbreaking, not only in its inclusion of Aboriginal people in script writing and production and frequent adoption of Aboriginal perspectives, but also for its naturalistic treatment of a cross-cultural romance between Vincent and white urbanite Elizabeth Ashton (Cate Blanchett). The series' ability to negotiate issues of cultural and political sensitivity was significantly dependent on Dingo's skills and magnetic screen presence.

Ernie Dingo has been acclaimed by some as one of Australia's finest contemporary actors. In addition, he has established a place as a major figure in extending mainstream awareness and understanding of Aboriginal Australia.

—Mark Gibson

ERNIE DINGO. Born in 1956. Began career as part of the Middar Aboriginal Dance Theatre, 1978; had various stage roles; in television, from 1985; appearances in episodes of *The Flying Doctors, Relative Merits, Rafferty's Rules, The Dirtwater Dynasty,* and *GP*; in film, from 1985; currently host of travel magazine television series, *The Great Outdoors.* Recipient: Banff Television Festival special prize; Australian Film Institute Award, 1990.

TELEVISION SERIES

1990	*Dolphin Cove*
1989–93	*Fast Forward*
1992	*Clowning Around*
1993	*The Great Outdoors*
1994	*Heartland*
1994–95	*Heartbreak High*

TELEVISION MINISERIES

1985	*Cowra Breakout*
1990	*A Waltz Through the Hills*

MADE-FOR-TELEVISION MOVIES

1986	*The Blue Lightning*

FILMS

Tudawali, 1985; *The Fringe Dwellers,* 1986; *Crocadile Dundee II,* 1988; *Cappuchino,* 1988; *State of Shock,* 1989; *Until the End of the World,* 1991; *Blackfellas,* 1993; *Mr. Electric,* 1993.

FURTHER READING

Lewis, Berwyn. "Comedian with a Sting." *Australia Now* (Canberra, Australia), 1993.
Coolwell, Wayne. *My Kind of People.* St Lucia: University of Queensland Press, 1993.
van Nunen, Linda. "The Games Ernie Plays." *Australian Magazine* (Sydney, Australia), January 1991.

See also *Heartbreak High*

DIRECT BROADCAST SATELLITE

Satellite Delivery Technology

Direct Broadcast Satellite (DBS) is a satellite-delivered program service meant for home reception. DBS programming is, in most respects, the same as that available to cable television subscribers. DBS subscribers, however, do not access their programs from terrestrial cable systems but rather directly from high powered telecommunications satellites stationed in geosynchronous orbit some 22,000 miles above the earth. Like cable systems, DBS program suppliers package a variety of program services or channels and market them to prospective DBS subscribers for a monthly fee.

The DBS business may be distinguished from the older Television Receive Only (TVRO) business in three important respects: technology, programming and cost. TVRO households (of which there are approximately four million in the United States) must purchase and install a satellite dish measuring between seven to ten feet in diameter and costing approximately $1,800. TVRO households receive about 75 channels of unscrambled programming but may also subscribe to a package of scrambled ("encrypted") program services for a monthly fee. TVRO programming is delivered via the three to six gigahertz (GHz) frequency range, known as the C-band, at a power of ten watts or less.

DBS dishes, on the other hand, measure 18 inches or less in diameter and cost approximately $700. DBS and TVRO program packages are similar, although DBS subscribers cannot receive the numerous unscrambled programming channels available to TVRO dish owners. DBS transmissions are delivered at the 11-to-15 GHz frequency range, known as the Ku-band, at a power that may exceed 120 watts. The higher power of the Ku-band allows a more directed satellite-to-receiver signal and, thus, requires a much smaller receiver dish than is required for C-band reception.

The origins of DBS date to 1975 when Home Box Office (HBO) first utilized a satellite to deliver its program service to local cable television systems. Numerous individuals, especially those living in rural areas beyond the reach of cable television, erected TVRO dishes on their property and accessed whatever programming they wanted as it flowed from satellites. Program suppliers soon objected to free receipt of their product by TVRO owners. As a result, HBO and similar services began scrambling their signals in 1985. TVRO owners thereafter were required to pay a subscription fee to receive such programming.

The first effort to create a true DBS service in the United States occurred in 1980 when the Satellite Television Corporation (STV) proposed such a service to the Federal Communications Commission (FCC). The FCC approved STC's proposal and invited other companies to propose DBS services. Of the 13 companies that responded to the FCC, proposals from eight of them—including such electronics industry giants as Western Union and RCA—eventually were approved. By the early 1990s, however, the high start-up cost of establishing a DBS service (estimated at more than a billion dollars) had forced many of the original DBS applicants either to delay or to abandon their projects altogether. What's more, DBS companies were uncertain that program suppliers that heretofore had provided programming exclusively to cable systems would extend their services to DBS. That matter was settled when the Cable Television Consumer Protection and Competition Act of 1992 prohibited cable program suppliers from refusing to sell their services to DBS operators.

FCC permission to launch DBS services included satellite transponder (or transmitter) assignment and DBS orbital slot assignment. Satellites providing a DBS service are allowed to occupy eight orbital slots positioned at 61.5, 101, 110, 119, 148, 157, 166, and 175 degrees west longitude.

A consortium of cable television system owners launched the first generation DBS service, called Primestar, in July 1991. Primestar utilized 45 watt transponders aboard GE American's Satcom K1 satellite to beam 67 program channels to some 70,000 households by 1995. Subscribers paid a monthly fee of $25-$35 for the Primestar service in addition to a $100-$200 installation fee for receiving hardware that Primestar continued to own.

A second generation DBS service became operational when the DBS-1 satellite went into orbit on 17 December 1993. The DBS-1, owned by Hughes Space and Communications Group, carried 32 transponders. Ten of the transponders were owned by United States Satellite Broadcasting (USSB), and the remaining transponders were owned by DirecTV. Although Primestar, DirecTV and USSB all transmitted via the Ku-band, the higher powered DBS-1 satellite allowed DirecTV and USSB subscribers to use a much smaller receiving dish.

DirecTV and USSB maintained a joint identity for marketing purposes and for selling the receiving system used for both DBS services. The receiving system was a package comprised of dish antenna, decoder unit, and remote control called the Digital Satellite System (DSS). The basic DSS unit retailed in 1995 for about $700 with installation costs ranging from $70 for a do-it-yourself kit to $200 for dealer assistance. By March 1995, over 400,000 of the systems had been sold.

DBS presents some major problems to subscribers. For instance, the receiving dish that requires a clear line-of-sight fix on the transmitting satellite may be blown out of alignment by heavy winds, thunderstorms will disrupt DBS signal reception, and DBS program services do not yet include local over-the-air television channels. However, DBS seems most appealing to persons who either are disenchanted with cable television or who live in areas that are not served by cable.

—Ronald Garay

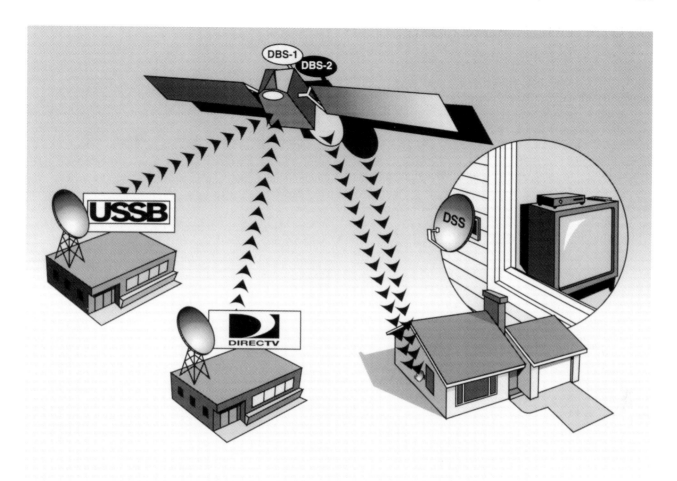

How DBS works: DBS programming is beamed from broadcast centers to DBS satellites. Digital programming is then beamed down from satellites to 18-inch satellite dish attached to side of a home. A set-top receiver picks up the programming signals from the dish and transmits them to viewers' televisions.
Illustration courtesy of DIRECTV

FURTHER READING

Grant, August E., and Kenton T. Wilkinson. *Communication Technology Update: 1993–1994.* Boston, Massachusetts: Focal, 1994.

Hudson, H.E. *Communication Satellites: Their Development and Impact.* New York: Free Press, 1990.

Mirabito, Michael M.A. *The New Communications Technology.* 2d edition, Boston, Massachusetts: Focal Press, 1994.

Rees, D.W.E. *Satellite Communications: The First Quarter Century of Service.* New York: Wiley, 1990.

Taylor, John P. *Direct-to-Home Satellite Broadcasting.* New York: Television/Radio Age, 1980.

See also Pay Cable; Pay-per-View Cable; Satellite; United States: Cable

DIRECTOR, TELEVISION

The television director, who sits atop the chain of command of the crew during the actual filming or taping of the show, is responsible for the visualization of the TV program, selecting the different camera angles and compositions that will used. Beyond this most general definition, however, the nature of the director's job, and the relative importance of the director's creative contribution to the finished product, varies greatly among different forms and genres of television.

One basic distinction in TV production exists between single-camera (film-style) and multi-camera work. In single-camera production each shot is staged individually, allowing precise camera positioning and lighting. Repeated "takes" are shot until the director is satisfied with the results. The action is filmed or taped out-of-sequence based on a logic of set-ups for camera and lighting. Actors must break their performance into non-continuous bits that still appear coherent when assembled later in the editing room. In this type of production, then, performance is adjusted to fit the visual scheme. Virtually all prime-time television dramas, programs generally one hour or longer, are produced in this manner. Common genres include action-adventure, crime, medical, courtroom, melodrama, and "prime-time soap opera." The television drama is the format in which the TV director has the most control and the most creative input—operating most like a feature film director. Yet, even here the director's role is more limited than a film director's. The series nature of television necessitates an exceptionally demanding production schedule and a rigid organization of labor, giving the director certain responsibilities, removing or restricting others.

In the production of films for theatrical exhibition directors frequently devise and initiate their own projects. Many film directors, such as Oliver Stone and Quentin Tarrantino, write their own screenplays. Even in cases where the director is hired after a producer has initiated a project, and a script has already been commissioned, the director has great leeway to interpret the material in her or his own way. In addition to controlling visual style, the director may also develop the themes, work with actors on characterizations, even participate in the rewriting of the script.

Television directors, however, work on a per-episode basis. Because of the highly compressed production schedule, any series will employ several different directors during a season. When the director arrives on the scene, the characterizations, themes and basic style of the show have already been established by previous episodes. In fact, such creative decisions were often made by the show's producer in the development of the series, and they remain the province of the producer during the run of the show. The director, then, takes an existing, basic aesthetic set-up and works out the details for the episode at hand. When film directors—Steven Speilberg, Michael Mann, David Lynch—work in television, they generally act as producers because from that position the more important creative choices are made.

Nevertheless, the direction of TV drama episodes still offers excellent opportunities for creative expression. A number of TV drama directors, including Spielberg, have gone on to become film directors. This was even more the case in the 1950s and 1960s when television served as a training ground for some of the most prominent directors to work in the American film industry. Arthur Penn, Sidney Lumet, Sam Peckinpah, Delbert Mann, Robert Altman and other directors moved from television to the big screen. More recently, some television directors, such as Thomas Carter, noted for directing outstanding pilots for *Miami Vice* and other shows, have become producers of their own television series. And in some cases prominent film directors—Lynch, Barry Levinson—have chosen to direct episodes in

the series they produce. In the spring of 1995 Quentin Tarrantino elected to direct the concluding episode of the first year of the NBC series *E.R.* because he found the show compelling.

In contrast to single-camera style, multi-camera television production requires that the visual scheme be adjusted around the performance. The on-camera talent deliver their performances in real-time, and the visualization is created by switching among a series of cameras trained on the unfolding event (and, in many cases, among several channels of electronically stored graphics). All "live" programs, including news and sports broadcasts, are produced this way. So, too, are talk, discussion and game shows which are shot "live-to-tape," then later broadcast with minimal editing. Directing in these genres offers less opportunity for creativity. Multi-camera style in itself introduces great technical limitations, but these are often less restricting than the constraints defined by the forms themselves—how much visual flair is desirable in a shot of Peter Jennings reading a report of the latest Mideast conflict? Usually, then, the visual elements in presentational "event" programs such as news, talk and sports generally follow a rigid pre-set pattern. This is a necessity given that the production needs to be created almost instantaneously, with little or no time to prepare for the specifics of the particular episode. (Indeed, much of the visual excitement in "live" events such as sports derives from technical features such as instant replay.)

Directing this type of production is more a craft than an art. Though it requires great skill, the demands are mostly technical. Directors of multi-camera television productions generally sit in a control room, viewing a bank of monitors on which the images from each camera and graphics source are displayed. They do not operate any studio controls—they must keep their eyes glued to the monitors. They should not even look away to check notes or a script, but must simply know how the program should unfold and be able to keep their mind ahead of the developing action. The director of an American football game must be ready for the cut to the downfield camera before the quarterback throws the pass, for example, or the talk show director should anticipate an outburst of audience response. And this intensity must be maintained for long periods, with commercials serving as brief breaks from the action. In some ways multi-camera direction is a verbal art form. The director literally "talks" the show into existence, calling out cues for edits, camera movements, effects and audio transitions, while different specialized crew persons, listening via headset, execute these commands.

During the 1950s, television drama specials and anthology series were shot in this multi-camera style, and often broadcast live. Directing in this context was especially challenging, requiring the dramatic skill of a stage director, the visual skills of a film director and the technical skills of a live TV director. These programs were often intimate psychological dramas. They called for relatively exacting visuals, which necessitated complicated camera and actor blocking schemes. For example, a primary camera and the lead actor had to be precisely positioned in order to get the required close-up without obstructing a second camera's view of the lead actress for the next shot. All these movements, of both cameras and actors, had to be executed perfectly in real time. It is easy to understand why, once the major film studios opened their facilities for TV productions, prime-time narrative shows quickly turned to film-style production. The producers were then able to establish considerably more control over the production process.

Daytime drama, soap opera in the United States, is a different story. Because multi-camera production can be completed much more quickly and is therefore much less expensive than film-style, soaps are still shot live-to-tape using multiple cameras. With little time for pre-production or rehearsal, the director must establish a visual sequence that can be executed essentially in real-time. Yet that visual design must also serve the dramatic needs of the show. This task is made somewhat easier by the formulaic nature of the genre, but the combination of technical and aesthetic challenges makes directing soap opera one of television's more difficult and under-appreciated tasks. This technique has been adopted for the production of prime time serials throughout Europe, for the *teleroman* in Quebec, and for *telenovelas* throughout Latin America.

The one other contemporary TV genre that employs multi-camera technique is the situation comedy. Until the 1960s and early 1970s most sitcoms were shot in single camera film-style, with the laugh track dubbed in later. Beginning with *All in the Family*, however, comedy producers adopted multi-camera production techniques. This enabled actors to perform complete scenes before a live audience, generating natural laughter. In some cases it also allowed the producer to schedule two performances of the same script, which enabled the selection of the "biggest" laughs for use in the soundtrack.

Sitcom production is actually a hybrid form, more likely to be shot with film cameras than video cameras. When this is the case, instead of cutting between cameras in real time with a switcher, all the cameras record the entire scene from different angles and edits are made in post-production, as in film-style work. Generally the shows are not performed from beginning to end in real time, but scene by scene, with breaks and retakes as needed. (The live audiences are apparently willing to laugh at the same joke more than once.) Still, this type of production is more a version of filmed theater than pure moving picture work, and a sitcom director operates more like a stage director. Sitcom visualization is usually very simple—lots of long shots to catch the physical nature of the comedy are intercut with a few close-up reaction shots. More extensive use of close-ups would be out of place since the actors usually employ broad gestures and strong vocal projection to communicate the performance to the back row of the live audience. The overall effect of this form is

the creation of a "proscenium style," as in the theatre. The camera serves as the surrogate audience and establishes a "fourth wall" which is rarely crossed.

In this production style, the director concentrates on working with the actors on timing and execution, and successful sitcom directors are known primarily for their ability to communicate with the stars of their shows. In many cases these directors work with a single show for its entire run, directing almost all the episodes. Jay Sandrich, for example, is noted for his work on *The Mary Tyler Moore Show* and *The Cosby Show,* and James Burrows is equally acclaimed for his direction of *Cheers.*

In many countries other than the United States the television director is afforded a role of greater prominence, much more akin to that of the film director. In most cases this situation holds because television productions have been limited to one or two episodes or to the miniseries. This role may change, however, as more and more television systems come to rely on regular schedules built around series production, with its attendant demand for tight production schedules and minimal pre-production opportunities. It is this industrial organization, itself the result of particular economic imperatives, that has defined the present role of the American television director, a role in which participation in the creative process is often secondary to that of the producer.

—David J. Tetzlaff

FURTHER READING

Aldridge, Henry B., and Lucy A. Liggett. *Audio/video Production: Theory and Practice.* Englewood Cliffs, New Jersey: Prentice Hall, 1990.

Armer, Alan A. *Directing Television and Film.* Belmont, California: Wadsworth, 1990.

Directors Guild of America. *Constitution and Bylaws.* Hollywood, California, 1991.

Green, Kathleen. "The Other Side of the Camera: Behind-the-scenes Jobs in Television and Motion Pictures." *Occupational Outlook Quarterly* (Washington, D.C.), Spring 1995.

Hickman, Harold R. *Television Directing.* New York: McGraw Hill, 1991.

Lewis, Colby. *The TV Director/Interpreter.* New York: Hastings House, 1968.

Kindem, Gorham. *The Live Television Generation of Hollywood Film Directors: Interviews with Seven Directors.* Jefferson, North Carolina: McFarland, 1994.

Randolph, Laura B. "Debbie Allen on Power, Pain, Passion and Prime Time." *Ebony* (Chicago), March 1991.

Ravage, John W. *Television: The Director's Viewpoint.* Boulder, Colorado: Westview, 1978.

Richards, Ron. *A Director's Method for Film and Television.* Boston, Massachusetts: Focal, 1992.

Schihl, Robert J. *Single Camera Video: From Concept to Edited Master.* Boston, Massachusetts: Focal, 1989.

————. *Talk Show and Entertainment Processes and Procedures.* Boston, Massachusetts: Focal, 1992

Shanks, Bob. *The Cool Fire.* New York: Vintage, 1977.

Taylor, Don. *Days of Vision: Working with David Mercer: Television Drama Then and Now.* London: Methuen, 1990.

Thomson, David. "Walkers in the World: Alan Clarke." *Film Comment* (New York), May-June 1993.

Wicking, Christopher, and Tise Vahimagi. *The American Vein: Directors and Directions in Television.* New York: Dutton, 1979.

See also Allen, Debbie; Almond, Paul; Cartier, Rudolph; Mann, Delbert; Producer in Television; Schaffner, Franklin

DISASTERS AND TELEVISION

One of television's most basic applications lies in its ability to portray the devastation of a disaster, whether nearby or far away, both as it occurs and in its aftermath. Natural and manmade disasters are ideal subjects and settings for television which continually seeks the dramatic, emotionally-charged, even the catastrophic to capture audience attention. In the process the medium sometimes serves a vital function, informing and instructing viewers in matters pertaining to safety and recovery.

Two main categories of disaster are routinely handled on television. The first, natural disasters, includes earthquakes, floods, hurricanes, blizzards and drought. Technological disasters, the second category, includes plane crashes, nuclear reactor failures, oil or chemical spills, and similar emergencies. Not included in these definitions are human conflicts/disasters such as riots and political coups, though the chaos and drama inherent in them is equally as intriguing to television. Indeed, at times, such events lead to a form of disaster coverage, as in the case of massive problems of disease and famine caused by the Rwandan civil wars. Generally, however, disasters of nature and technology encompass a wide range of catastrophes which have in common a certain unpredictability and ambiguity of blame. In other words, while human conflicts such as wars and riots are predicated on easily-identifiable antagonism, it is more difficult to assign blame or identify human fault for natural and technological disasters. They occur oftentimes with little or no warning, at least by most human calculations, and leave behind considerable damage, both human and structural. When such events occur, the public and the media are challenged to cope, left to try to make sense of a disaster in terms of its cause and its meaning. They are also challenged to learn from one disaster how best to communicate the next.

During the actual moments of a disaster television plays multiple roles. It is purveyor of information, storyteller, and sometimes agent of change. It can impart news of impending disaster, convey the effects of events that have taken place or are unfolding, and assign meaning. All of this is possible by virtue of the medium's technology and its cultural authority.

Actual disasters have been the topic of numerous TV genres, including made for TV movies, public service announcements for relief organizations such as the Red Cross, and entertainment-oriented musical relief efforts such as Live Aid and Band Aid. Yet while the range of television genres employed in framing disasters has broadened, by far most attention to disasters is still found in the news.

It has been argued that people are psychologically drawn to disaster news because it feeds an innate voyeuristic tendency. Whether or not that is the case, natural and technological disasters are newsworthy because they are out of the ordinary events, they wreak havoc and, particularly important in television, they are the stuff of interesting dramatic video footage. The way a disaster is reported on television depends on the characteristics of the disaster itself, but it also depends on characteristics of television news practice and television technology.

Television news is often a useful means of relaying information about stages of disasters as they develop. Natural disasters, such as hurricanes and tornadoes can be reason-

The aftermath of the Exxon Valdez disaster
Photo courtesy of AP/ World Wide Photos

ably predicted because of available sophisticated meteorological technology. Television may serve as a warning mechanism for residents of an area about to be hit by severe weather. However, even without the benefit of warning, television is capable of transmitting news of a disaster as it takes place and in its aftermath. Some natural events such as earthquakes are difficult to predict, and for technological disasters such as plane crashes and oil spills any form of prediction is virtually impossible. Resulting damage from these disasters, however, is completed within a relatively short amount of time. In the aftermaths of the 1989 Loma Prieta earthquake in California, the 1994 Los Angeles earthquake and the 1994 crash of the Delta Airlines shuttle outside Chicago, television news provided immediate, up-to-the-minute reports about the extent of damage and the clean-up and investigative efforts underway. The challenge for television news in such cases is to continuously provide information while trying to make sense of sudden chaos.

While earthquakes and plane crashes are relatively confined both in space and time, other disasters are more widespread and unfold over a much longer period. The Great Flood in the Midwest in 1993 developed throughout the summer and traveled south with the flowing rivers; the drought and famine in Somalia and Ethiopia were also widespread and were covered by television over a period of months or years. The challenge for television news in such ongoing disasters is to continually search for fresh angles from which to report, and new and interesting video to shoot. During the 1993 flood, network television news devoted evening news segments to its effects on farmers one evening, effects on small businesses another, and local and national relief efforts in yet another, all the while updating the audience on the progress of rising flood waters.

The role of television news in disasters is also spatially varied. In local settings or in the immediate area within which disaster has struck or is striking, television news is one of the primary means of disseminating information often vital to the physical and emotional health and safety of community residents. Television provides information about the risks they are under, where they can go for relief and who they should contact for specific needs. At times television becomes a conduit for personal messages. When severe weather conditions or the need for immediate access make television the only viable means of communication, individuals may use the medium to let others know they are safe or where they can be found.

In other situations distant disasters have a profound impact on one area. In such cases television is the fastest way to convey personal information to local residents. Shortly after the December 1988 crash of Pan Am flight 103 in Lockerbie, Scotland, local television newscasters in Syracuse, New York quickly obtained passenger lists to read over the evening news because many of the passengers were students at Syracuse University and most of their friends and relatives were unsuccessful in confirming passenger information with Pan Am. One of the greatest challenges to the local news-

room during periods of disaster is to coordinate efforts with local safety and law officials so that accurate and necessary information is conveyed to the public in an efficient manner. Local television news staffs also find that they must abandon typical daily routines in favor of quick action and greater flexibility in fulfilling tasks.

National television news plays a different role in reporting disaster. A national newscast crosses boundaries and shares disaster stories with a nationwide audience, evoking empathy, community, solidarity and sometimes national action. Hurricane Andrew, which struck the southeastern United States in 1993, the 1993 Midwest Flood and the January 1994 Los Angeles earthquake all developed as national disasters by virtue of the network television coverage they received. Network news reported daily on the damaging effects of these disasters. Network news anchors traveled to and reported from the disaster sites, helping to convey, even create, a sense of national significance. The effect of this type of coverage was a national outpouring of sympathy and grass-roots relief efforts. Daily footage of damage and homelessness brought on by the storm, flood and earthquake prompted residents from distant parts of the country to coordinate food and clothing drives to help their recently-victimized neighbors.

National disaster coverage can also lead to political action. TV coverage, particularly the pictures of damage to wildlife and the ecosystem, from the Exxon Valdez oil spill in Alaska's Prince William Sound in March 1989 brought the nation's attention to a technological disaster and invoked the outrage of environmental groups such as Greenpeace. The action of environmentalists in their clean-up efforts and their battles with Exxon became significant angles in the development of that disaster news story.

But television also has the power to divert audiences from these more complex questions of politics and responsibility. On 17 January 1994, for example, immediately after the Los Angeles earthquake, all of the national network news stations sent news teams to Los Angeles. Each shot scene after scene of the most devastating effects of this seismic tragedy, from broken water mains to exploding gas lines to dismantled freeway systems, and finally to the horrified, panicked and awe-struck faces of the earthquake victims. Larger issues, however, went unexplored. Working under the time constraints of broadcast news and emphasizing the pictorial chaos of disaster, television cannot or does not develop other aspects of disaster, including the governmental, policy and sometimes historic problems or implications.

Yet another type of political implication may emerge from news reports of distant international disasters, especially when they involve U.S. coverage of disaster in Third World nations. Critics have charged the U.S. press with geographic bias in covering disasters from the developing nations. Their argument, supported with detailed content analysis of news stories broadcast in the United States, points out that much of the reporting from these nations focuses on disasters and political upheaval. This practice is seen to create a distorted image of these nations, as chaos-ridden and prone to disaster, representations that support and perpetuate unequal power relations among dominant and developing nations.

Critics also argue that choices determining which disasters receive air time often depends on the connection that can be made with the United States. Those disasters in which Americans or American interests are harmed receive prominent coverage by the U.S. press, including television, while other disasters may be given minor coverage or be overlooked altogether. All these charges speak to television's ability to construct and assign meaning to the events it covers, including disasters.

In this context, then, television news does not merely convey information about disasters. It has the power to *define* disaster. Its penchant for striking visual content encourages newsgatherers to use the camera lens to frame numerous images of drama and chaos. As a result, television coverage of natural disasters is often framed in such a way as to convey hopelessness, presenting them as battles between powerless humans and powerful nature.

This power to create and assign meaning demonstrates television's central role in contemporary societies as is illustrated in the 1986 Chernobyl nuclear reactor disaster in the Soviet Union. One argument suggests that the accident would never have been international news had it not been for television, and goes on to claim that the Soviet government failed to adequately warn its citizens about the effects of the disaster by carefully choosing which images would be included in domestic television news coverage. It has been argued on the other hand, that United States news groups were also duped by outside agents when they accepted videotape of what they believed was actual footage from the site of the Chernobyl disaster, but turned out to be scenes shot somewhere in Italy. Such charges speak both to the power of television and the power of those who can control it to serve their own interests.

Besides framing disasters a certain way, assigning them a certain meaning, television also has the power to decide which disasters will be of significant interest to those outside the immediate area affected. Certain disasters receive national, even international, attention because they are given television air time. Earthquakes that affect a large number of people, both within the United States and abroad, receive far more coverage than earthquakes that have a similar Richter scale measure but don't wreak the same social havoc.

The importance of disasters as defined by television has even reached beyond news coverage and increasingly into entertainment television. Real-life disasters have become fodder for entertainment and persuasive television as the line between fact and fiction, news and entertainment, is increasingly blurred on TV of the mid to late 1980s and early 1990s. International relief efforts for famine victims in Africa, especially Ethiopia, included most notably the effort of producer Bob Geldof, who coordinated the 1985 Live Aid rock music fund-raiser which was transmitted internationally via satellite television. In this case television defined an international disaster by covering it as one in the news, then offered its own televised solution to the disaster by airing the Live Aid concert for relief. Real-life disasters are also the subject of made-for-TV movies. Sometimes called virtual disasters, these movies based on actual disasters became more common in the early 1990s. A movie such as *Triumph over Disaster: The Hurricane Andrew Story* is an example of television's efforts not only to capitalize on disaster for ratings points but also to define the order of reality.

Disasters can also sell. Images of disaster have been used in televised public service announcements for the Red Cross. News footage of recent hurricanes, floods and earthquakes were edited together into a 30-second spot urging Americans to contribute money to the Red Cross which has contributed relief to many disaster victims.

The power of television as a tool for information, for selling, and for defining reality can be witnessed throughout the coverage of natural and technological disasters. As television becomes more competitive in the late Twentieth Century, the drama guaranteed by disaster images practically ensures an audience across increasingly blurred genres.

—Katherine Fry

FURTHER READING

Adams, William C. "Whose Lives Count?: TV Coverage of Natural Disasters." *Journal of Communication* (New York), 1986.

Benthall, Jeremy. *Disasters, Relief and the Media.* London: I.B. Tauris, 1993.

Deppa, Joan. *The Media and Disasters: Pan Am 103.* New York: New York University Press, 1993.

Fensch, Thomas. *Associated Press Coverage of a Major Disaster: The Crash of Delta Flight 1141.* Hillsdale, New Jersey: L. Erlbaum, 1990.

Gaddy, Gary D., and Enoh Tanjong. "Earthquake Coverage by the Western Press." *Journal of Communication* (New York), 1986.

Kueneman, Rodney M., and Joseph E. Wright. "News Policies of Broadcast Stations for Civil Disturbances and Disasters." *Journalism Quarterly* (Urbana, Illinois), 1975.

Lasorsa, Dominic L., and Stephen D. Reese. "News Source Use in the Crash of 1987: A Study of Four National Media." *Journalism Quarterly* (Urbana, Illinois), 1990.

Lippert, Barbara. "Get Real: NBC's Week of Virtual Disasters Showed How TV Reality Is Collapsing Into Itself." *MediaWeek* (Brewster, New York), 1993.

Mellencamp, Patricia. "TV Time and Catastrophe, Or Beyond the Pleasure Principle of Television." In Mellencamp, Patricia, editor. *Logics of Television.* Bloomington, Indiana: Indiana University Press, and London: British Film Institute Publishing, 1990.

Newhagen, John E., and Marion Lewenstein. "Cultivation and Exposure to Television Following the 1989 Loma

Prieta Earthquake." *Mass Comm Review* (Philadelphia, Pennsylvania), 1992.

Nimmo, Dan, and James E. Combs. *Nightly Horrors: Crisis Coverage by Television Network News.* Knoxville, Tennessee: University of Tennessee Press, 1985.

Oberg, James E. *Uncovering Soviet Disasters: Uncovering the Limits of Glasnost.* New York: Random House, 1988.

Rubin, David M. "How the News Media Reported on Three Mile Island and Chernobyl." *Journal of Communication* (New York), 1987.

Singer, Eleanor, Phyllis Endreny, and Marc B. Glassman. "Media Coverage of Disasters: Effect of Geographic Location." *Journalism Quarterly* (Urbana, Illinois), 1991.

Singer, Eleanor. *Reporting on Risk: How the Mass Media Portray Accidents, Disease, Disaster and other Hazards.* New York: Russell Sage Foundation, 1993.

Smith, Conrad. *Media and Apocalypse: News Coverage of the Yellowstone Forest Fires, Exxon Valdez Oil Spill, and Loma Prieta Earthquake.* Westport, Connecticut: Greenwood, 1992.

Sood, Rahul, Geoffrey Stockdale, and Everett M. Rogers. "How the News Media Operate in Natural Disasters." *Journal of Communication* (New York), 1987.

Vincent, Richard C., Bryan K. Crow, and Dennis K. Davis. "When Technology Fails: The Drama of Airline Crashes in Network Television News." *Journalism Monographs* (Austin, Texas), November, 1989.

Waxman, Jerry J. "Local Broadcast Gatekeeping during Natural Disasters." *Journalism Quarterly* (Urbana, Illinois), 1973.

Wei, Ran. "Earthquake Prediction: Did the News Media Make a Difference?" *Mass Comm Review* (Philadelphia, Pennsylvania), 1993.

DISNEY, WALT

U.S. Animator/Producer/Media Executive

Walt Disney was a visionary filmmaker who brought his film library, his love of technology, and his business sense to American television in the mid-1950s. His ground-breaking television program, *Disneyland*, helped establish fledgling network ABC, pointed the way toward that network's increasing reliance on Hollywood-originated filmed programming, and provided much needed financing for Disney's pioneering theme park.

Since the late 1920s, Disney had been a public figure, Hollywood's best known independent studio head. He had first achieved success with animated short subjects starring the character with whom he is best associated, Mickey Mouse. In 1937, his studio had produced the first full-length animated motion picture, *Snow White and the Seven Dwarfs*. In the late 1940s, beginning with *Song of the South* (1946), the Disney studio had also branched out into live-action films, but it was primarily associated, then as now, with animation.

Unlike many other studios, Disney's had not prospered during World War II, when it had devoted much of its energies to producing films for the U.S. government. Indeed, the Disney studio had never made a great deal of money because of the time- and labor-intensive nature of animation work. After the war, Disney hoped to expand his enterprises. The key to this expansion, according to Christopher Anderson in *Hollywood TV* (1994), was diversification. Disney was ready to set his sights beyond the film industry.

Disney flirted with the new medium in the early 1950s, producing a one-hour special for NBC in 1950 and another in 1951. He discussed a possible series with both NBC and CBS, but only third-place network ABC was willing to give him what he wanted in exchange—funding for the amusement park he dreamed of opening in Anaheim, California. ABC executives were desperate to obtain programming that would enable them to compete with their more established

Walt Disney
Photo courtesy of the Walt Disney Company

rivals and were particularly interested in courting the growing family market in those baby-boom years.

Walt Disney and his brother Roy convinced the network to put up $500,000 toward the construction costs for the park, to be called (like the television program) Disneyland, and to guarantee its bank loans. In exchange, ABC would obtain 35% of the park and would receive profits from Disneyland concessions for ten years. Even more importantly to the network, Disney would deliver them a weekly, hour-long television program that would take advantage of his family-oriented film library.

The program *Disneyland* debuted on 27 October 1954, and quickly became ABC's first series to hit the top ten in ratings. A number of early episodes showed old Disney films or promoted new ones. (A documentary chronicling the filming of the upcoming *20,000 Leagues Under the Sea* added to the audience for that film and also earned Disney his first Emmy Award, for best documentary.)

The program's success was clinched in December 1954 with the introduction of the first of three episodes focusing on Davy Crockett. The day after the 15 December telecast of "Davy Crockett, Indian Fighter," Crockett mania swept through the country.

The "Davy Crockett" episodes established another new Disney tradition. Not only would Disney move his feature films to television; he would also reverse the process. Although ABC broadcast only in black and white, the Disney studio shot the "Davy Crockett" episodes in Technicolor. After telecasting each of the three hours twice during the winter and spring months of 1954 and 1955, the studio edited them into a film, which it released to theaters nationally and internationally in the summer of 1955. The film's high attendance increased the visibility of the *Disneyland* television program—and of all Disney's enterprises, including his new park.

When the park opened in July 1955, ABC aired a live special honoring America's new tourist mecca and its founder. Within a year, millions of viewers whose amusement appetites had been whetted by Disney's television program poured into Disneyland. In its first year, it grossed $10 million. Walt Disney and his company had shaped two new entertainment forms—and had made more money than ever before.

Disney himself served as the affable host of his program. In light of its success, his studio quickly generated other youth-oriented television shows for ABC. *The Mickey Mouse Club*, a daily daytime program featuring a likable group of youngsters known as the Mouseketeers, premiered a year after *Disneyland* and lasted for four seasons. *Zorro*, an adventure series about a masked, swashbuckling Spaniard in 19th-century California, ran from 1957 to 1959.

Disney continued to be best known, however, for the weekly program he hosted. In 1959, this show changed its name to *Walt Disney Presents*. In 1961, it moved to NBC and changed its name to *Walt Disney's Wonderful World of Color*. NBC's parent company, RCA, offered the Disney

studios an appealing sponsorship deal, hoping that Disney's colorful telefilms would help market color television receivers.

Disney was still the host of this version of the program at the time of his death in December 1966. His avuncular on-screen personality had endeared him to viewers of all ages. And his re-creation of American recreation through the dual marketing of the two Disneylands had forged new patterns in American cultural history, inextricably linking television to the film and amusement industries.

—Tinky "Dakota" Weisblat

WALT (WALTER) ELIAS DISNEY. Born in Chicago, Illinois, U.S.A., 5 December 1901. Attended McKinley High School, Chicago; Kansas City Art Institute, 1915. Married Lillian Bounds, 1925; children: Diane and Sharon. Served in France with Red Cross Ambulance Corps, 1918. Became commercial art apprentice to Ub Iwerks, 1919; joined Kansas City Film Advertising Company, producing, directing, and animating commercials for local businesses, 1920; incorporated Laugh-o-Gram Films, 1922; went bankrupt, 1923; moved to Hollywood and worked on several animated series, including *Alice in Cartoonland*, 1923; ended *Alice* series and began *Oswald the Lucky Rabbit* series, 1927; formed Walt Disney Productions, 1927; created *Steamboat Willie* (first cartoon to use synchronized sound and third to feature his creation Mickey Mouse), 1928; began distributing through Columbia, 1930; *Flowers and Trees* released through United Artists, first cartoon to use Technicolor and first to win Academy Award, 1932; began work on *Snow White and the Seven Dwarfs*, his first feature-length cartoon, 1934; Disney staff on strike, 1941; Disney developed several TV programs, 1951–60; formed Buena Vista Distribution Company for release of Disney and occasionally other films, 1954; hosted Disneyland TV series; opened Disneyland, Anaheim, California, 1955; premiered numerous *Walt Disney* television shows, including *The Mickey Mouse Club* and *Walt Disney's Wonderful World of Color*; Walt Disney World opened, Orlando, Florida, 1971. Recipient: Special Academy Award, 1932, 1941; Irving G. Thalberg Award, 1941; Best Director (for his work as a whole), Cannes Film Festival, 1953; two Emmy Awards. Died in Los Angeles, California, 15 December 1966.

TELEVISION SERIES

1954–58	*Disneyland*
1955–59	*The Mickey Mouse Club*
1958–61	*Walt Disney Presents*
1961–66	*Walt Disney's Wonderful World of Color*

FILMS (director, animator, and producer)
Newman Laugh-o-Grams series, 1920; *Cinderella; The Four Musicians of Bremen; Goldie Locks and the Three Bears; Jack and the Beanstalk; Little Red Riding Hood; Puss in Boots*, 1922; *Alice's Wonderland; Tommy Tucker's Tooth; Martha*, 1923; *Alice* series (12 episodes), 1924; *Alice* series (18

episodes), 1925; *Alice* series (9 episodes), 1926; *Alice* series (17 episodes), 1927; *Oswald the Lucky Rabbit* series (11 episodes), 1927; (15 episodes), 1928.

FILMS (as head of Walt Disney Productions; co-produced with Ub Iwerks)
Steamboat Willie, 1928; *Mickey Mouse* series (12 episodes), 1929; *Mickey Mouse* series (3 episodes), 1930; *Silly Symphonies* series, 1929; *Night*, 1930; *The Golden Touch*, 1935.

FILMS (as head of Walt Disney Productions)
Flowers and Trees, 1932; *Three Little Pigs*, 1933; *The Tortoise and the Hare*, 1934; *Snow White and the Seven Dwarfs*, 1937; *Ferdinand the Bull*, 1938; *Fantasia*, 1940; *Pinnochio*, 1940; *The Reluctant Dragon*, 1941; *Dumbo*, 1941; *Bambi*, 1942; *Victory Through Air Power*, 1943; *The Three Caballeros*, 1944; *Make Mine Music*, 1946; *Song of the South*, 1946; *Fun and Fancy Free*, 1947; *Melody Time*, 1948; *So Dear to My Heart*, 1948; *Ichabod and Mr. Toad*, 1949; *Cinderella*, 1950; *Alice in Wonderland*, 1951; *The Story of Robin Hood and His Merrie Men*, 1952; *Peter Pan*, 1953; *The Sword and the Rose*, 1953; *Rob Roy, the Highland Rogue*, 1953; *Toot, Whistle, Plunk and Broom*, 1953; *20,000 Leagues Under the Sea*, 1954; *The Littlest Outlaw*, 1954; *Lady and the Tramp*, 1955; *Davy Crockett and the River Pirates*, 1955; *The Great Locomotive Chase*, 1956; *Westward Ho the Wagons!*, 1956; *Johnny Tremain*, 1957; *Old Yeller*, 1957; *The Light in the Forest*, 1958; *Sleeping Beauty*, 1958; *Tonka*, 1958; *The Shaggy Dog*, 1959; *Darby O'Gil and the Little People*, 1959; *Third Man on the Mountain*, 1959; *Toby Tyler, or Ten Weeks With a Circus*, 1959; *Kidnapped*, 1960; *Pollyanna*, 196; *Ten Who Dared*, 1960; *Swiss Family Robinson*, 1960; *One Hundred and One Dalmatians*, 1960; *The Absent-Minded Professor*, 1960; *Moon Pilot*, 1961; *In Search of the Castaways*, 1961; *Nikki, Wild Dog of the North*, 1961; *The Parent Trap*, 1961; *Grayfriar's Bobby*, 1961; *Babes in Toyland*, 1961; *Son of Flubber*, 1962; *The Miracle of the White Stallions*, 1962; *Big Red*, 1962; *Bon Voyage*, 1962; *Almost Angels*, 1962; *The Legend of Lobo*, 1962; *Savage Sam*, 1963; *Summer Magic*, 1963; *The Incredible Journey*, 1963; *The Sword in the Stone*, 1963; *The Misadventures of Merlin Jones*, 1963; *The Three Lives of Thomasina*, 1963; *A Tiger Walks*, 1964; *The Moon-Spinners*, 1964; *Mary Poppins*, 1964; *Emil and the Detectives*, 1964; *Those Calloways*, 1964; *The Monkey's Uncle*, 1964; *That Darn Cat*, 1965; *The Ugly Dachshund*, 1966; *Lt. Robin Crusoe, U.S.N.*, 1966; *The Fighting Prince of Donegal*, 1966; *Follow Me, Boys!*, 1966; *Monkeys, Go Home!*, 1966; *The Adventures of Bullwhip Griffin*, 1966; *The Gnome-Mobile*, 1966; *The Jungle Book*, 1967.

FURTHER READING
Anderson, Christopher. *Hollywood TV: The Studio System in the Fifties.* Austin: University of Texas Press, 1994.
Bailey, Adrian. *Walt Disney's World of Fantasy.* New York: Everest House, 1982.
Eliot, Marc. *Walt Disney: Hollywood's Dark Prince: A Biography.* Secaucus, New Jersey: Carol, 1993.
Field, Robert Durant. *The Art of Walt Disney.* London: Collins, 1942.
Finch, Christopher. *The Art of Walt Disney: From Mickey Mouse to the Magic Kingdoms.* New York: H.N. Abrams, 1975.
———. *Walt Disney's America.* New York: Abbeville, 1978.
Heller, Scott. "Dissecting Disney." *The Chronicle of Higher Education* (Washington, D.C.), 16 February 1994.
Jackson, Kathy Merlock. *Walt Disney: A Bio-bibliography.* Westport, Connecticut: Greenwood, 1993.
Kurland, Gerald. *Walt Disney, The Master of Animation.* Charlotteville, New York: SamHar, 1971.
Maltin, Leonard. *The Disney Films.* New York: Crown, 1984.
Schickel, Richard. *The Disney Version: The Life, Times, Art, and Commerce of Walt Disney.* New York: Simon and Schuster, 1968.
Shows, Charles. *Walt: Backstage Adventures with Walt Disney.* La Jolla, California: Windsong, 1980.
Smoodin, Eric, editor. *Disney Discourse: Producing the Magic Kingdom.* New York: Routledge, 1994.
Thomas, Bob. *Walt Disney: An American Original.* New York: Simon and Schuster, 1976.
———. "Mickey and His Walter Ego." *Life* (New York), November 1988.

See also *Walt Disney* Programs

DISTANT SIGNAL

Cable Television Transmission Technology

The term "distant signal" refers to a television station transmission made available to one or more local cable systems by means other than off-air reception. Traditionally, distant signals have been imported via terrestrial microwave relays; today, however, communications satellites are also used for distant signal importation.

The earliest cable systems of the late 1940s and early 1950s, then known as CATV (Community Antenna Televi-sion), comprised little more than very tall community antennas connected by wire to homes within a given community. Under these conditions, retransmission of distant signals was limited to communities no more than approximately 100 miles from the nearest television stations. Consequently, many communities, particularly small communities in sparsely populated states of the western United States, were unable to benefit from community antennas.

By the mid 1950s, however, a number of these western towns had CATV systems served by microwave relays. The relays made it possible to retransmit broadcast signals over many hundreds of miles. The first such system, launched in 1953, brought a Denver signal to Casper, Wyoming. Within the next decade, microwave relays—many of which had been connected to form networks—covered a large portion of the West.

Eventually, microwave technology began to be used as more than simply a substitute for community antenna service. By the late 1950s, some cable operators were using microwave-carried signals to supplement signals received off the air. As improved technology brought about increased CATV channel capacity, operators began to seek extra programming options in order to make their service more attractive to potential subscribers. In the early 1960s, independent stations from large cities such as New York and Chicago became popular CATV channel options because of the amount of movies and local sports in their schedules.

Also, in the mid-to-late 1950s some operators began using microwave relays to bypass local or nearby signals entirely in order to provide their subscribers with more popular stations from distant cities. In most cases, the program quality of a local station serving only several thousand people could not be expected to equal that of a station serving millions, and with the technical capability to carry distant stations, CATV operators had little incentive to use the lower quality local programming. An outcry arose from the small-market broadcasters, who felt that CATV would draw viewers away. As local viewership decreased, they argued, so would advertising revenues. Hearings on this issue were held throughout the late 1950s by both Congress and the Federal Communications Commission (FCC), but no decisive regulatory action was taken to limit this type of CATV competition with broadcasters until a landmark 1963 court decison.

In this case, *Carter Mountain Transmission Corp. v. FCC*, a small Wyoming broadcast station challenged the FCC's licensing of a microwave company that intended to deliver distant signals to a CATV system in a community where the station's signal could be received off-air. The FCC ultimately denied the microwave license because the microwave outfit not only refused to guarantee the local station protection against program duplication on imported stations, but also refused to require the CATV to carry the local station's signal. The commission reasoned that, because microwave threatened to destroy a local broadcaster, it also threatened the loss of television service to a substantial rural population without access to CATV as well as to any other CATV non-subscribers. To grant the microwave company a license unconditionally would have been in direct conflict with the commission's policies favoring localism in broadcasting.

The *Carter Mountain* decision set in motion a series of FCC decisions on the status of CATV, culminating in its 1965 First Report and Order and the 1966 Second Report and Order. These two rulings recognized that CATV had become more than simply a retransmission medium for areas not served by broadcast television. It was beginning to enter broadcast markets, sometimes replacing local signals with distant signals. Even when local stations were offered in addition to distant stations in these markets, subscribers often would watch the distant rather than local stations. Thus the two rulings focused on setting guidelines for the carriage of local signals by CATV systems and on restricting the duplication of the local stations' programming by channels that carried imported distant stations. In addition, the 1966 rules temporarily limited growth of CATV in the nation's top 100 broadcast television markets, a provision strengthened by a 1968 FCC ruling which completely froze growth in the top 100 markets, pending further study of cable developments.

The 1972 Cable Television Report and Order, the next major FCC ruling regarding cable, also focused in large part on the importation of distant signals into broadcast markets. This extensive ruling contained one provision that affected the importation of distant independent stations and another that protected local stations' exclusive rights to syndicated programming. The latter, known as "syndicated exclusivity" or "syndex," became increasingly difficult to enforce as the number of cable program services increased, especially after satellites were introduced to the cable industry in the mid-seventies. Still, pressure from broadcasters continued to focus regulators' attention on the issue, and in 1990, an updated version of the syndex rules was enacted. Since then, cable operators have been obligated to black out any syndicated programming on distant signals that duplicates syndicated programs offered by local stations.

Distant signal importation has been important to the growth of the cable industry in that it has allowed cable operators some degree of selection in the types of broadcast signals they retransmit to their subscribers. The most popular distant signals used by modern cable systems are satellite-carried superstations such as WGN-Chicago, WOR-New York, and Ted Turner's WTBS, Atlanta.

—Megan Mullen

FURTHER READING

Gay, Verne. "Syndex Simplified." *Newsday* (Hempstead, New York), 31 December 1989.

LeDuc, Don R. *Cable Television and the FCC: A Crisis in Media Control.* Philadelphia: Temple University Press, 1973.

Seiden, Martin H. *Cable Television U.S.A.: An Analysis of Government Policy.* New York: Praeger, 1972.

See also Microwave; Must Carry Rules; Superstation; Translators; United States: Cable

DIXON OF DOCK GREEN

British Police Series

Beginning in 1955 and finally ending in 1976, *Dixon of Dock Green* was the longest running police series on British television. Although its homeliness would later become a benchmark to measure the "realism" of later police series, such as *Z Cars* and *The Bill,* it was an enormously popular series. *Dixon* should be seen as belonging to a time when police were generally held in higher esteem by the public than they have been subsequently. The series was principally set in a suburban police station in the East End of London and concerned uniformed police engaged with routine tasks and low-level crime. The ordinary, everyday nature of the people and the setting was further emphasised in early episodes of the series with the old, British music-hall song—"Maybe its because I'm a Londoner"—with its sentimental evocations of a cozy community, being used as the series theme song. Unlike later police series, *Dixon* focused less on crime and policing and more on the family-like nature of life in the station with Dixon, a warm, paternal and frequently moralising presence, as the central focus. Crime was little more than petty larceny. However, as the 1960s and the early 1970s brought ever more realistic police series from both sides of the Atlantic to the British public, *Dixon of Dock Green* would seem increasingly unreal, a rosy view of the police that seemed out of touch with the times. Yet the writer of the series maintained to the end of the program's time on air that the stories in the episodes were based on fact and that *Dixon* was an accurate reflection of what goes on in an ordinary police station.

Police Constable (PC) George Dixon was played by veteran actor Jack Warner. The figures of both Dixon and Warner were already well known to the British public when the series was launched. In 1949 in the Ealing film *The Blue Lamp,* Warner had first played the figure of Dixon. A warm, avuncular policeman, his death at the end of the film at the hands of a young thug (played by Dirk Bogarde) was memorably shocking and tragic. British playwright Ted Willis, who with Jan Read, had written the screenplay for *The Blue Lamp,* subsequently revived the figure of Dixon for a stage play and then wrote a series of six television plays about the policeman. Thus, the BBC took little chance in spinning-off the figure and the situation into a television series.

If Dixon was well-known to the public, the actor Jack Warner was even better known. Born in London in 1900, Warner had been a comedian in radio and in his early film career. Starting in the early 1940s he had broadened his range to include dramatic roles becoming a warmly human character actor in the process. But as well as playing in films with dramatic themes, such as *The Blue Lamp,* Warner continued to play in comedies such as the enormously successful Huggett family films made between 1948 and 1953.

In *Dixon of Dock Green,* Jack Warner as Dixon is a "bobby" on the beat—an ordinary, lowest-ranking policeman on foot patrol. With the inevitable heart of gold, Dixon

Dixon of Dock Green
Photo courtesy of BBC

was a widower raising an only daughter Mary (Billie Whitelaw in the early episodes, later replaced by Jeannette Hutchinson). Other regular characters included Sergeant Flint (Arthur Rigby), PC Andy Crawford (Peter Byrne), and Sergeant Grace Millard (Moira Mannon). From 1964 Dixon was a sergeant.

The series was the creation of writer Ted Willis, who not only wrote the series over its 20 years on British television but also had a controlling hand in the production. Longtime producer of the series was Douglas Moodie, whose other television credits include *The Inch Man* and *The Airbase. Dixon* was produced at the BBC's London television studios at Lime Green. The show began on the BBC in 1955 and ran until 1976. Altogether, some 439 episodes were made, at first running 30 minutes, and later 45 minutes. The early episodes were in black and white, while the later ones were in colour.

The BBC scheduled *Dixon* in the prime family time slot of 6:30 P.M. on Saturday night. At the time it started on air in 1955, the drama schedule of the BBC was mostly restricted to television plays so that *Dixon of Dock Green* had little trouble in building and maintaining a large and very loyal audience. In 1961, for example, the series was voted the second most popular program on British television, with an estimated audience of 13.85 million. Even in 1965 after three years of the gritty and grimy procedural police-work of *Z Cars*, the audience for *Dixon* still stood at 11.5 million. However as the 1960s wore on, ratings began to fall and this, together with health questions around Jack Warner, led the BBC to finally end the series in 1976.

—Albert Moran

CAST

George Dixon	Jack Warner
Andy Crawford	Peter Byrne
Mary Crawford	Billie Whitelaw/Jeanette Hutchinson
Sgt. Flint	Arthur Rigby
Insp. Cherry	Stanley Beard/Robert Crawdon
PC Lauderdale	Geoffrey Adams
Duffy Clayton	Harold Scott
Johnny Wills	Nicholas Donnelly
Tubb Barrell	Neil Wilson
Grace Milard	Moira Mannion
Jamie MacPherson	David Webster
Chris Freeman	Anne Ridler
Bob Penney	Anthony Parker
Alex Jones	Jan Miller
PC Jones	John Hughes
Kay Shaw/Lauderdale	Jacelyne Rhodes
Michael Bonnet	Paul Elliott
Jean Bell	Patricia Forde
Bob Cooper	Duncan Lamont
PC Swain	Robert Arnold
Liz Harris	Zeph Gladstone
Shirley Palmer	Anne Carroll
Betty Williams	Jean Dallas
PC Burton	Peter Thornton
DS Harvey	Geoffrey Kean
PC Roberts	Geoffrey Kenion
Insp. Carter	Peter Jeffrey
Ann Foster	Pamela Bucher
Brian Turner	Andrew Bradford
DC Pearson	Joe Dunlop
PC Newton	Michael Osborne
DC Webb	Derek Anders
Sgt. Brewer	Gregory de Polney
Alan Burton	Richard Heffer
Len Clayton	Ben Howard

PRODUCERS   Douglas Moodie, G.B. Lupino, Ronald Marsh, Philip Barker, Eric Fawcett, Robin Nash, Joe Waters

PROGRAMMING HISTORY   154 c. 30-minute episodes; 285 c. 45-minute episodes

• BBC

July 1955–August 1955	6 Episodes
June 1956–September 1956	13 Episodes
January 1957–March 1957	13 Episodes
September 1957–March 1958	28 Episodes
September 1958–March 1959	27 Episodes
September 1959–April 1960	30 Episodes
October 1960–April 1961	30 Episodes
September 1961–March 1962	27 Episodes
September 1962–March 1963	27 Episodes
October 1963–March 1964	26 Episodes
September 1964–March 1965	26 Episodes
October 1965–April 1966	31 Episodes
October 1966–December 1966	13 Episodes
September 1967–February 1968	20 Episodes
September 1968–December 1968	16 Episodes
September 1969–December 1969	16 Episodes
November 1970–March 1971	17 Episodes
November 1971–February 1972	12 Episodes
September 1972–December 1972	14 Episodes
December 1973–April 1974	16 Episodes
February 1975–May 1975	13 Episodes
March 1976–May 1976	8 Episodes

FURTHER READING

Cotes, Peter. "Obituary: Lord Willis." *The Independent* (London), 24 December 1992.

Scott, Richard. "Villainy by the Book." *The Times* (London), 12 November 1994.

West, Richard. "Sunday Comment: Bring Back the Friendly Bobby." *The Sunday Telegraph* (London), 13 June 1993.

See also British Programming

DOCTOR WHO

British Science-Fiction Programme

Doctor Who, the world's longest continuously-running television science fiction series, was made by the BBC between 1963 and 1989 (with repeats being shown in many countries thereafter, and negotiations with Steven Spielberg and others to make new programs, continuing into the mid-1990s). *Doctor Who*'s first episode screened in Britain on 23 November 1963, the day after the assassination of President Kennedy. Consequently this first episode of a low-budget series was swamped by "real life" television, and became a BBC institution quietly and by stealth, in the interstices of more epic television events. Similarly, in the first episode, the central character is a mysterious ('Doctor Who?') and stealthy figure in the contemporary world of 1963, not even being seen for the first eleven and a half minutes, and then appearing as an ominous and shadowy person who irresponsibly "kidnaps" his granddaughter's schoolteacher in his time machine (the Tardis). This mystery was the hallmark of the series for its first three years (when William Hartnell played the lead), as was the antihero quality of the Doctor (in the first story he has to be restrained from killing a wounded and unarmed primitive).

The Doctor was deliberately constructed as a character against stereotype: a "cranky old man," yet also as vulnerable as a child; an antihero playing against the more obvious "physical" hero of the schoolteacher Ian (played by the well-known lead actor in commercial television's *Ivanhoe* series). Its famous, haunting signature tune was composed at the new BBC Radiophonic Workshop, adding a futuristic dimension to a series which would never be high on production values. The program always attracted ambitious young directors, with (the later enormously successful) Verity Lambert as its first. The decision to continue with the series in 1966 when Hartnell had to leave the part, and to "regenerate" the Doctor on screen, allowed a succession of quirkily different personae to inhabit the Doctor. When it was decided in 1966 to reveal where the Doctor came from (the Time Lord world of Gallifrey), the mysteriousness of the Doctor could be carried on in a different way—via the strangely varied characterisation. Following Hartnell, the Doctor was played by the Chaplinesque "space hobo" Patrick Troughton; the dignified "establishment" figure of Jon Pertwee; the parodic visual mix of Bob Dylan and Oscar Wilde, Tom Baker; the vulnerable but "attractive to young women" Peter Davison; the aggressive and sometimes violent Colin Baker; and the gentle, whimsical Sylvester McCoy.

These shifts of personae were matched by shifts of generic style, as each era's producers looked for new formulae to attract new audiences. The mid-1970s, for example, under producer Philip Hinchcliffe, achieved a high point in audience ratings and was marked by a dramatic gothic-horror style. This led to a "TV violence" dispute with Mary Whitehouse's National Viewers and Listeners Association. The subsequent producer, Graham Williams, shifted the series to a more comic signature. This comedy became refined as generic parody in 1979, under script editor Douglas Adams (author of *Hitchhiker's Guide to the Galaxy*). *Doctor Who's* 17th season, which was both script edited by Adams and contained episodes written by him ("The Pirate Planet," "The City of Death") became notorious with the fans, who hated what they saw as the self-parody of *Doctor Who* as "*Fawlty Towers*" in space" (John Cleese appeared briefly in a brilliantly funny parody of art critics in "The City of Death").

Throughout *Doctor Who's* changes, however, the fans have remained critically loyal to the series. Fiercely aggressive to some producers and to some of the show's signatures, the fans' intelligent campaigns helped keep the program on the air in some of the more than 100 countries where it has screened; and in the United States, huge conventions of fans brought *Doctor Who* a new visibility in the 1980s. But the official fans have never amounted to more than a fraction of the audience. *Doctor Who* achieved the status of an institution as well as a cult.

Doctor Who

Doctor Who's status attracted high level, innovative writers; its formula to educate and entertain encouraged a range of storylines from space opera through parody to environmental and cultural comment. Its mix of current technology with relatively low budgets attracted ambitious young producers led to what one producer called a "cheap but cheerful" British show that fascinated audiences of every age group world-wide. But above all, its early, ambiguous construction opened the show to innovative, often bizarre, but always dedicated acting. With so many different characterisations and acting styles, the program, like the Doctor, was continuously "regenerating," and so stayed young.

—John Tulloch

CAST

The Doctor (first)	William Hartnell
The Doctor (second)	Patrick Troughton
The Doctor (third)	Jon Pertwee
The Doctor (fourth)	Tom Baker
The Doctor (fifth)	Peter Davison
The Doctor (sixth)	Colin Baker
The Doctor (seventh)	Sylvester McCoy
The Doctor (eighth)	Paul McGann
Susan Foreman	Carole Ann Ford
Barbara Wright	Jacqueline Hill
Ian Chesterton	William Russell
Vicki	Maureen O'Brien
Steven Taylor	Peter Purves

Katarina	Adrienne Hill	
Sara Kingdom	Jean Marsh	
Dodo Chaplet	Jackie Lane	
Polly Lopez	Anneke Wills	
Ben Jackson	Michael Craze	
Jamie McCrimmon	Frazer Hines	
Victoria Waterfield	Deborah Watling	
Zoe Heriot	Wendy Padbury	
Liz Shaw	Caroline John	
Jo Grant	Katy Manning	
Sarah-Jane Smith	Elizabeth Sladen	
Harry Sullivan	Ian Marter	
Leela	Louise Jameson	
Brigadier Lethbridge-Stewart	Nicholas Courtney	
K9	John Leeson	
Romana (first)	Mary Tamm	
Romana (second)	Lalla Ward	
Adric	Matthew Waterhouse	
Nyssa	Sarah Sutton	
Tegan Jovanka	Janet Fielding	
Turlough	Mark Strickson	
Perpugilliam Brown	Nicola Bryant	
Melanie Bush	Bonnie Langford	
Ace	Sophie Aldred	
Master (1971–73)	Roger Delgado	
Master (1981–89)	Anthony Ainley	

PRODUCERS Alex Beaton, Peter Bryant, Philip Hinchcliffe, Matthew Jacobs, Verity Lambert, Barry Letts, Innes Lloyd, John Nathan-Turner, Mervyn Pinfield, Derrick Sherwin, Peter Ware, John Wiles, Graham Williams II, Jo Wright

PROGRAMMING HISTORY

• BBC

679	c. 25-minute Episodes
15	c. 50-minute Episodes
1	90-minute 20th Anniversary Special Episode

November 1963–September 1964	42 Episodes
October 1964–July 1965	39 Episodes
September 1965–July 1966	45 Episodes
September 1966–July 1967	43 Episodes
September 1967–June 1968	40 Episodes
August 1968-June 1969	44 Episodes

January 1970-June 1970	25 Episodes
January 1971-June 1971	25 Episodes
January 1972-June 1972	26 Episodes
December 1972-June 1973	26 Episodes
December 1973-June 1974	26 Episodes
December 1974-May 1975	20 Episodes
August 1975-March 1976	26 Episodes
September 1976-April 1977	26 Episodes
September 1977-March 1978	26 Episodes
September 1978-February 1979	26 Episodes
September 1979-January 1980	20 Episodes
August 1980-March 1981	28 Episodes
January 1982-March 1982	26 Episodes
January 1983-March 1983	22 Episodes
25 November 1983 Anniversary Special	90-minute Episode
January 1984-March 1984	22 25-minute Episodes
	2 50-minute Episodes
January 1985-March 1985	13 50-minute Episodes
September 1986-December 1986	14 Episodes
September 1987-December 1987	14 Episodes
October 1988-January 1989	14 Episodes
September 1989-December 1989	14 Episodes

FURTHER READING

Bentham, Jeremy. *Doctor Who: The Early Years*. London: Allen, 1986.

Dicks, Terrance, and Malcolme Hulke. *The Making of Doctor Who*. London: Allen, 1980.

Haining, Peter. *Twenty Years of Doctor Who*. London: Allen, 1983.

———. *Doctor Who: 25 Glorious Years*. London: Allen, 1988.

Rickard, Graham. *A Day with a TV Producer*. Hove, England: Wayland, 1980.

Road, Alan. *Doctor Who—The Making of a Television Series*. London: Andre Deutsch, 1982.

Tulloch, John, and Manuel Alvarado. *Doctor Who: The Unfolding Text*. London: Macmillan, 1983.

Tulloch, John, and Henry Jenkins. *Science Fiction Audiences: Watching Doctor Who and Star Trek*. London: Routledge, 1995.

See also Lambert, Verity; Nation, Terry; Newman, Sidney; Pertwee, Jon; Sciencefiction Programs; Troughton, Patrick

DOCUDRAMA

The docudrama is a fact-based representation of real events. It may represent contemporary social issues—the "facts-torn-from-today's-headlines" approach—or it may deal with older historical events. U.S. television examples include *Brian's Song* (1971), the biography of Brian Piccolo who played football for the Chicago Bears but died young from cancer; *Roots* (1977), the history of a slave and his family; *Roe vs. Wade* (1989), the history of the Supreme Court decision legalizing abortion; *Everybody's Baby: The Rescue of Jessica McClure* (1989), the rescue of an eighteen-month-old baby from a well; and three versions of the Amy Fisher and Joey Buttafuoco affair (1993). The sources of the form derive from 19th- and 20th-century journalism, movies, and radio.

In most cases, a docudrama is produced in the manner of realist theater or film. Thus, events are portrayed by actors in front of an invisible "fourth wall"; shooting techniques obey the conventions of mainstream film or television (i.e. establishing shots with shot/reverse shots for dialogue, lighting constructed in a verisimilar manner, non-anachronistic mise-en-scene); no voice-over narrator comments on the actions once the events begin; and little or no documentary footage is interspersed. Unlike mainstream drama, however, the docudrama does make claims to provide a fairly accurate interpretation of real historical events. In other words, it is a nonfictional drama.

Thus, the docudrama is a mode of representation that, as its name reflects, combines categories usually perceived as separate: documentary and drama. This transgression, however, is not an actual one. Texts that claim to represent the real may be created out of various sorts of documents such as photographs, interviews, tape recordings of sounds, printed words, drawings, and narrators who attempt to explain what happened. Nonfictional texts may also use actors to reenact history. In all cases, the real is being represented and is thus never equal to the reality it represents. Some people point out that having any filmic recording of an event is a "text" with the same status as these other types of documents: film footage is necessarily taken from a particular angle and thus is an incomplete representation of an event.

The docudrama should be distinguished from fictional dramas which make use of reality as historical context but do not claim that the primary plot line is representing events that have actually occurred. An example of such a fictional use of history would be an episode in *Murphy Brown* in which Brown insists on questioning President Bush at a press conference and is then thrown out. The use of the real person Bush as backdrop to a fictional plot creates a "reality effect" for the fictional program but would not qualify the episode to be a docudrama.

Docudramas do not have to conform to the above aesthetic conventions. An early U.S. example of a series devoted to reenacting past events is *You Are There*. *You Are There* derived from the radio program *CBS Is There*, which ran from 1947 through 1950. On television it appeared from February 1953 through October 1957. *You Are There* violated the traditional taboo of avoiding anachronisms by having contemporary television reporters interview historical figures about the events in which they were supposed to have been participating, for example, during the conquest of Mexico.

The *You Are There* form for a docudrama, however, is very unusual. Most docudramas employ standard dramatic formulas from mainstream film and television and apply them wholesale to representing history. These conventions include a goal-oriented protagonist with clear motivations; a small number of central characters (two to three) with more stereotyping

Eleanor and Franklin: The White House Years

for secondary characters; causes that are generally ascribed to personal sources rather than structural ones (psychological traumas rather than institutional dynamics); a dramatic structure geared to the length of the program (a two-hour movie might have the normal "seven-act" structure of the made-for-television movie); and an intensification of emotional ploys.

The desire for emotional engagement by the viewers (a feature valuable for maintaining the audience through commercials) produces an inflection of the docudrama into several traditional genres. In particular, docudramas may appeal to effects of suspense, terror, or tears of happiness or sadness. These effects are generated by generic formulas such as those used in the detective, thriller, or horror genre. Although the outcome was known in advance, *Everybody's Baby* operates in the thriller mode: how will Baby Jessica be saved? Judicial dramas such as *Roe vs. Wade* or murder dramas such as *Murder in Mississippi* (the death of three civil rights workers) use suspense as a central affective device. Examples of terror are docudramas of murders or attempted murders by family members or loved ones, or of larger disasters such as the Chernobyl meltdown or plane crashes.

One of the most favored effects, however, is tears, produced through melodramatic structures. Some critics point out that docudramas tend to treat the "issue-of-the-week," and that such a concern for topical issues also produces an interest in social problems that might have melodramatic resolutions. Docudramas have treated incest, missing children, wife or child abuse, teenage suicide, alcoholism and drug addiction, adultery, AIDs-related deaths, eating disorders, and other "diseases-of-the week." The highly successful *Brian's Song*, which won five Emmys and a Peabody, is an excellent example of this subtype of docudrama. Its open sentimentality and use of male-buddy conventions along with the treatment of an interracial friendship uses the event of an early death by cancer to promote images of universal brotherhood. *The Burning Bed* (1984) or *The Karen Carpenter Story* (1989) wages war against pressures producing, respectively, domestic violence or anorexia nervosa.

Such implicitly or explicitly socially-conscious programs, however, raise the problem of interpretation. Indeed, docudramas, like other methods of representing reality, are subject to controversy regarding their offer of historical information through story-telling. Although historians now recognize how common it is to explain history through dramatic narratives, historians are still concerned about what effects particular types of dramatic narratives may have on viewers. Debates about docudramas (or related forms such as "reality TV") include several reservations.

One reservation is related to "dramatic license." In order to create a drama that adheres to the conventions of mainstream story-telling (particularly a sensible chain of events, a clear motivation for character behavior, and a moral resolution), writers may claim they need to exercise what they call dramatic license—the creation of materials not established as historical fact or even the violation of know facts. Such distortions include created dialogues among characters, expressions of internal thoughts, meetings of people that never happened, events reduced to two or three days that actually occurred over weeks, and so forth. Critics point out that it is the conventions of mainstream drama that compel such violations of history while writers of docudramas counter that they never truly distort the historical record. Critics reply that the dramatic mode chosen already distorts history which cannot always be conveniently pushed into a linear chain of events or explained by individual human agency.

Another reservation connected to the first is the concern that spectators may be unable to distinguish between known facts and speculation. This argument does not propose that viewers are not sufficiently critical, but that the docudrama may not adequately mark out distinctions between established facts and hypotheses, and, even if the docudrama does mark the differences, studies of human memory suggest that viewers may be unable to perceive the distinctions while viewing the program or remember the distinctions later.

A third reservation focuses on the tendency toward simplification. Critics point out that docudramas tend toward hagiography or demonization in order to compress the historical material into a brief drama. Additionally, complex social problems may be personalized so that complicated problems are "domesticated." Adding phone numbers to call to find help for a social problem may be good but may also suggest sufficient solutions to the social problem are already in place.

Outside the United States many of these problems have been addressed in different but related ways, and while the term docudrama is often used in a generic fashion, it may be applied to a range of forms. In the United Kingdom, for example, *Cathy Come Home* (1966), stands as one of the earliest and strongest explorations of the problem of homelessness. Created by writer Jeremy Sandford, producer Tony Garnett, and director Ken Loach, this program refuses the more conventional structures of dramatic narrative, inserting strong "documentary" style photography into the presentation and using "Cathy's" own voice as narrator-analyst for the harsh social situation in which she finds herself. Another voice, however, presents factual information in the form of statistics and other information related to the central topic of the piece. *Cathy Come Home* has been described as a "documentary-drama," a term that seeks to emphasise the serious and factual qualities of the show against the more conventional docudrama.

In Australia, versions of docudrama have often been used to explore social and national history. Productions such as *Anzacs, Gallipoli*, and *Cowra Outbreak* have focused on Australian participation in both World Wars and, in some views, are crucial texts in the construction of national identity.

In Canada, critics have applied the docudrama designation to a broader range of production styles, including works such as *The Valour and the Horror*, which combined documentary exploration with dramatized sequences. This program led to an ongoing controversy over the nature of the "real," and the "true." Because the presentation challenged received notions of Canadian involvement in World War II (notions themselves constructed from various experiences, memories, and records), the conflict took on an especially public nature. So, too, did arguments surrounding *The Boys of St. Vincent*, which dealt with child molestation in a church-run orphanage. The dramatization in this case was more complete, but clearly paralleled a case that was still in court at the time of production and airing.

What all these examples suggest is, on the one hand, that docudrama is a particularly useful form for television, whether for advertising profit, the exploration of social issues, the construction of identity and history, or some combination of these ends. On the other hand, the varied examples point to an ongoing aspect of television's status as a medium that both constructs narratives specifically defined as "fiction" and also purports to somehow record or report "reality." *You Are There* mixed "news," history, and fiction, categories often, and uncritically, considered distinct and separate. The mixture, the blurred boundaries among the conventions linked to these forms of expression and communication, and the public discussions caused by those blurrings and mixings, remain central to any full understanding of the practices and the roles of television in contemporary society.

—Janet Staiger

FURTHER READING

Caughie, John. "Progressive Television and Documentary Drama." In, Bennett, Tony, with others, editors. *Pop-*

ular Film and Television. London: British Film Institute, 1981.

Goodwin, Andrew, with others. *Drama-Documentary.* London: British Film Institute, 1983.

O'Connor, John E. *American History/American Television: Interpreting the Video Past.* New York: Ungar, 1983.

Rapping, Elaine. *The Movie of the Week: Private Stories, Public Events.* Minneapolis: University of Minnesota Press, 1992.

See also *Cathy Come Home; Power Without Glory; Six Wives of Henry VIII; Valour and the Horror*

DOCUMENTARY

The television documentary is an adaptable form of nonfiction programming that has served various functions throughout the medium's history: as a symbol of prestige for advertisers and networks, a focal point for national attention on complex issues, a record of the human experience and the natural world, and an instrument of artistic and social expression. Unlike other programming on American television, documentaries have typically been sustained for reasons other than high ratings and ad sales. Consequently, the health of the documentary form serves as an indicator of a network's commitment to news and as a barometer of social, political, and economic dynamics.

A documentary is defined as a nonfiction report that devotes its full time slot to one thesis or subject, usually under the guidance of a single producer. Part of the fascination with documentaries lies in their unique blend of writing, visual images, sound tracks, and the individual styles of their producers. In addition to their particular contribution to the television medium, however, documentaries are notable because they have intertwined with wrenching moments in history. These characteristics have inspired some to describe documentaries as among the finest moments on television and as a voice of reason, while others have criticized them as inflammatory.

TV documentaries, as explained by A. William Bluem in the classic *Documentary in American Television,* evolved from the late 1920s and 1930s works of photojournalists and film documentarists, like Roy Stryker, John Grierson, and Pare Lorentz. Bluem writes, "they wished that viewers might share the adventure and despair of other men's lives, and commiserate with the downtrodden and underprivileged." The rise of radio in World War II advanced the documentary idea, especially the distinguished works of CBS writer Norman Corwin and the reporting of Edward R. Murrow. In 1946, Murrow created the CBS documentary unit, which linked documentary journalism with the idea that broadcasters owed the public a news service in exchange for lucrative station licenses.

Technology has also been a force in the documentary's evolution. The editing of audiotape on the 1949 CBS re-

cord, *I Can Hear It Now,* facilitated the origin of the radio documentary. On NBC radio, the *Living* series (1949-51), used taped interviews and helped move the form away from dramatizations and toward actualities.

The genesis of the American TV documentary tradition is attributed to the CBS series *See It Now,* started in 1951 by the legendary team of Edward R. Murrow and Fred Friendly. *See It Now* set the model for future documentary series. Producers shot their own film rather than cannibalize other material, worked without a prepared script and allowed a story to emerge, avoided using actors, and produced unrehearsed interviews. This independence contributed to the credibility of *See It Now*'s voice, as did Murrow and Friendly's courage in confronting controversy.

The most notable of the *See It Now* programs include several reports on McCarthyism, an episode that illustrates the uneasy association that exists between controversial documentaries, politics, and industry economics. The Aluminum Company of America, Alcoa, sought to sponsor *See It Now,* which featured the esteemed Murrow, to improve its image following antimonopoly decisions by the courts.

As McCarthyism increasingly damaged innocent reputations, Murrow and Friendly used their series to expose the groundless attacks. "A Report on Senator Joseph R. McCarthy" in 1954 employed the Senator's own words to discredit his false claims. Such programs made CBS and Alcoa uneasy. Alcoa refused to publicize or pay for some of the productions. Changing market conditions forced the company to withdraw sponsorship at the end of the 1955 season, and the program lost its weekly time period.

In June 1955, CBS began airing *The $64,000 Question,* which greatly increased revenues for its time slot, as well as for adjacent periods. In a climate that included political pressure on the network and its sponsor, coupled with economic pressures that favored revenues over prestige, support for *See It Now* waned and the program was scaled back to occasional broadcasts that lasted until summer 1958.

Other notable series of the 1950s include television's first major project in the compilation tradition, *Victory at*

The Louvre: A Golden Prison

Sea (1952–53). Produced by Henry Solomon, this popular NBC series detailed World War II sea battles culled from 60 million feet of combat film footage. It was a paean to freedom and the overthrow of tyranny. Another popular series ran on CBS from 1957 to 1966. *The Twentieth Century* was a history class for millions of American TV viewers, produced throughout its entire run by Burton (Bud) Benjamin.

The absence of ABC as a major presence in the documentary field in the 1950s is a telling indicator of television history. ABC was the weak third network, lacking the resources, affiliate strength, and audience of its rivals. Since CBS and NBC dominated the airwaves, each could counterprogram the other's entertainment hits with documentaries. The more the industry tended toward monopoly, the better the climate for documentaries.

Documentaries soared in quality and quantity during the early 1960s, a result of multiple factors. In *The Expanding Vista: American Television in the Kennedy Years*, Mary Ann Watson articulates how the confluence of technology with social dynamics energized the television documentary movement. Pressure on the industry to restore network reputations following the quiz show scandals spurred the output of high-quality nonfiction programming.

The May 1961 "Vast Wasteland" speech by FCC chairman Newton N. Minow and the "raised eyebrow" of government further motivated the networks to accelerate their documentary efforts as a way of protecting broadcast station licenses and stalling FCC hints that the networks themselves should be licensed. President Kennedy was also an advocate of documentaries, which he felt were important in revealing the inner workings of democracy.

The availability of lightweight 16mm film equipment enabled producers to get closer to stories and record eyewitness observations through a technique known as *cinema verite*, or direct cinema. A significant development was the wireless synchronizing system, which facilitated untethered, synchronized sound-film recordings, pioneered by the Drew Associates.

Primary (1960) was a breakthrough documentary. Produced by Robert Drew and shot by Richard Leacock, the film featured the contest between Senators John Kennedy and Hubert Humphrey in the 1960 Wisconsin primary. For the first time, viewers of Time-Life's four television stations followed candidates through crowds and into hotel rooms, where they awaited polling results. Through the mobile-camera technique *Primary* achieved an intimacy technique never before seen, and established the basic electronic news

American Masters: Martha Graham: The Dancer Revealed

gathering shooting style. In *Crisis: Behind a Presidential Commitment*, Drew Associates producer Gregory Shuker took cameras into the Oval Office to observe presidential meetings over the crisis precipitated by Alabama Governor George Wallace, who physically blocked the entry of two African-American students to the University of Alabama. The program aired in October 1963 on ABC and triggered a storm of protest over the admission of cameras into the White House.

The peak for TV documentary production was the 1961–62 season—the three networks aired more than 250 hours of programming. Each network carried a prestige documentary series. *CBS Reports*, produced by Fred Friendly, premiered in 1959 and became a weekly documentary series in the 1961–62 season. *NBC White Paper*, produced by Irving Gitlin, first aired in November 1960 and immediately thrust itself into hotly contested issues,

like the U-2 spy mission and the Nashville lunch-counter sit-ins. The *White Paper* approach featured meticulous research and analysis.

At ABC the job of developing a documentary unit fell to John Secondari. Since sponsor Bell and Howell produced film cameras and projectors, the artistic quality of the filmed presentation was important and engendered an attention to aesthetics that carried over in later years on ABC News documentaries. The *Bell and Howell Close-Up!* series, which also aired productions by Drew Associates, like others of the period dealt with race relations, "Cast the First Stone" and "Walk in My Shows," and Cold War themes, "90 Miles to Communism" and "Behind the Wall."

Newton Minow also spurred network affiliates to increase documentary broadcasts. Clearances for *CBS Reports* jumped from 115 to 140 stations. The production of local documentaries surged, creating a favorable environment for

Against the Odds: The Artists of the Harlem Renaissance

Frontline: The Secret File on J. Edgar Hoover

independent producers. David Wolper, whose Wolper Productions enjoyed a growth spurt in 1961, said, "Maybe we should thank Newton Minow for a fine publicity job on our behalf." Wolper's unique contribution to syndicated TV documentaries includes "The Race for Space" (1958), and the series *Biography*, the *National Geographic Society Special*, and *The Undersea World of Jacques Cousteau*.

The favorable climate for TV documentaries in the Kennedy era also nurtured an international collaboration that began in late 1960. *Intertel* came into being when five groups of broadcasters in the four major English-speaking nations formed the International Television Federation. The participants were Associated Rediffusion, Ltd. of Great Britain, the Australian Broadcasting Commission, the Canadian Broadcasting Corporation, and in America, the National Educational Television and Radio Center and the Westinghouse Broadcasting Company. In the United States *Intertel* was piloted by NET's John F. White and Robert Hudson and by Westinghouse Group W executives Donald McGannon and Richard M. Pack. *Intertel* sought to foster compassion for the human problems of member nations— to teach countries how to live together as neighbors in a world community, which Bluem characterized as "the greatest service which the television documentary can extend."

In a speech reported in *Television Quarterly*, historian Erik Barnouw characterized the documentary as a "necessary kind of subversion" that "focuses on unwelcome facts, which

may be the very facts and ideas that the culture needs for its survival." Throughout the turbulent 1960s, documentaries regularly presented "unwelcome facts." ABC offered a weekly series beginning in 1964, called *ABC Scope*. As the Vietnam war escalated, the series became "Vietnam Report," from 1966-68. NBC aired *Vietnam Weekly Review*. CBS launched an ambitious seven-part documentary in 1968 called *Of Black America*.

The year 1968 also marked a change in the influence of network news and a drop in TV documentary production. Affiliate stations bristled over network reports on urban violence, the Vietnam War, and antiwar protests. The Nixon administration launched an assault on the media and encouraged station owners to complain about news coverage in exchange for deregulation. TV coverage of the Democratic National Convention triggered protests against network news.

During this social, political, and economic revolution, network management experimented with less-controversial programs. Each network introduced a newsmagazine to complement evening news and documentaries. Ray Carroll reports the newsmagazine became a substitute for documentaries in the late-1960s and throughout the 1970s, and the number of long-form reports dropped. *60 Minutes* on CBS premiered in 1968, and after a slow start for several years, achieved unparalleled success. NBC followed in 1969 with *First Tuesday*.

ABC's answer was *The Reasoner Report*, launched in 1973, the same year the network resurrected the *CloseUp!* documentary series. In the 1970s, ABC's entertainment programs began to attract large audiences. To establish itself as a full-fledged network, ABC strengthened its news division and added the prestige documentary series, *ABC CloseUp!*, produced by Av Westin, William Peters, Richard Richter, and Pam Hill. Under Hill's guidance, the *CloseUp!* unit excelled in documentary craft, featuring artfully rendered film, poetic language, and thoughtful music tracks.

The three-way competition for prime-time audiences reduced airtime for documentaries. However, ABC's re-entry into the documentary field forced competitors to extend their documentary commitment, a rivalry that carried into the Reagan years. Pressure continued to mount against documentaries, though, in the 1970s. In the most celebrated case, the 1971 CBS documentary *The Selling of the Pentagon* resulted in a Congressional investigation into charges of unethical journalism.

Network documentaries virtually disappeared during the Reagan years; in 1984 there were eleven. The FCC under Mark Fowler eliminated requirements for public-service programming. Competition from cable, independents, and videocassettes eroded network audiences. The Reagan administration advocated a society based on individualism; economics became paramount, while support for social programs declined.

Documentaries also suffered from controversies over the CBS programs *The Uncounted Enemy: A Vietnam Deception* and *People Like Us*, and from an increase in libel suits and deregulation, which offered financial incentives to broadcasters in lieu of public-service programming. In this environment, the network documentary, which was rooted in the Roosevelt era and frequently endorsed collective social programs, became an anachronism. The documentary's decline in the Reagan years is one indicator of the ebbing of the New Deal influence on American culture.

After the three network sales at mid-decade, the new owners required news divisions to earn a profit. The most successful experiment was the 1987 NBC Connie Chung life-style documentaries, *Scared Sexless* and *Life in the Fat Lane*. These programs demonstrated that a combination of celebrity anchor, popular subjects, and updated visual treatments could appeal to larger audiences. In time, as entertainment costs rose and ratings fell, these infotainment programs evolved into a stream of popular newsmagazines, which became cost-effective replacements for entertainment shows.

The documentary thrived on public television in the 1980s. PBS premiered *Frontline* in 1983, an acclaimed investigative series produced by David Fanning. The 13-hour *Vietnam: A Television History* also aired in 1983. In 1987, the network broadcast *Eyes on the Prize*. Produced by Henry Hampton, this moving series chronicles the story of the modern civil rights movement from the beginnings of the Montgomery bus boycott to the passage of the Civil

Rights Act of 1964. The success of *Eyes I* failed to translate into easier fund-raising for the second series, which was more controversial. Other PBS series include *P.O.V.*, *The American Experience*, and *NOVA*. In the 1980s, a shift in the political climate hindered government support for public television. Conservatives objected to what was perceived as a liberal bias in its programming. As on commercial television, the aura of controversy encumbers the documentary form on PBS.

Cable television has made a substantial commitment to noncontroversial documentaries since the mid-80s. The Arts and Entertainment Network, formed in 1984, features documentaries, as does The Discovery Channel, launched in 1985. To date none of the cable documentaries has attracted the viewership of their network counterparts, nor have they tackled sensitive issues on a regular basis.

This conforms to what has been a recurring relationship in the documentary experience and suggests another way in which the tone and frequency of documentaries reflect American culture: The greater the national emphasis on marketplace, the less likely it is for commercial documentaries to excel as craft or grapple with complex problems and suggest social action. The more the nation emphasizes public service, the greater the networks' commitment to documentary art and its ability to be a tool for social justice.

—Tom Mascaro

FURTHER READING

Barnouw, Erik. *Documentary*. New York: Oxford University Press, 1993.

Benjamin, Burton. *Fair Play : CBS, General Westmoreland, and How a Television Documentary Went Wrong*. New York: Harper and Row, 1988.

Bluem, A. William. *Documentary in American Television*. New York: Hastings House, 1965.

Brown, Les. "The FCC Proudly Presents the Vast Wasteland." *Channels of Communications* (New York), March/April 1983.

Carroll, Raymond Lee. *Factual Television in America: An Analysis of Network Television Documentary Programs, 1948–1975* (Ph.D. dissertation, University Wisconsin-Madison, 1978).

Curtin, Michael. "Packaging Reality: The Influence of Fictional Forms on the Early Development of Television Documentary." *Journalism Monographs* (Austin, Texas), February 1993.

———. *Redeeming the Wasteland: Television Documentary and Cold War Politics*. New Brunswick, New Jersey: Rutgers University Press, 1995.

Diamond, Edwin and Alan Mahony. "Once It Was 'Harvest of Shame'—Now We Get 'Scared Sexless'." *TV Guide* (Radnor, Pennsylvania) 27 August 1988.

Einstein, Daniel. *Special Edition: A Guide to Network Television Documentary Series and Special News Reports, 1955–1979*. Metuchen, New Jersey: Scarecrow Press, 1987.

Hammond, Charles Montgomery, Jr. *The Image Decade.* New York: Hastings House, 1981.

Jacob, Lewsi. *The Documentary Tradition.* New York: Hopkins and Blake, 1971.

Leab, Daniel, J. "See It Now: A Legend Reassessed" In, John E. O'Connor, editor, *American History/American Television, Interpreting the Video Past.* New York: Frederick Ungar Publishing, 1983.

Levin, Roy. *Documentary Explorations.* Garden City, NY: Anchor Press, 1971.

Mascaro, Tom. *Lowering the Voice of Reason: The Decline of Network Television Documentaries in the Reagan Years* (Ph.D. dissertation, Wayne State University, 1994).

NBC News. *The Invention of the Television Documentary : NBC News, 1950–1975.* New York: NBC. 1975.

Rosteck, Thomas. *"See It Now" Confronts McCarthyism: Television Documentary and the Politics of Representation.* Tucaloosa, Alabama : University of Alabama Press, 1994.

Swisher, Kara. "Discovery's Long, Hard Road," *Washington Post* (Washington, D.C.), 17 June 1991.

Unger, Arthur. "Frontline's David Fanning: Upholding the Documentary Tradition" (interview). *Television Quarterly* (New York), Summer 1991.

Watson, Mary Ann. *The Expanding Vista: American Television in the Kennedy Years.* New York: Oxford University Press, 1990.

———. "The Golden Age of the American Television Documentary," *Television Quarterly* (New York), 1988.

See also *Black and White in Color; Civilisation; Death on the Rock;* Drew, Robert; *Eyes on the Prize; Eyewitness to History; Fifth Estate; NBC Reports; NBC White Papers;* Secondari, John; *Selling of the Pentagon; Sylvania Waters; This Hour Has Seven Days; A Tour of the White House with Mrs. John F. Kennedy; The Uncounted Enemy; Valour and the Horror; Vietnam: A Television History; World in Action*

DOLAN, CHARLES F.

U.S. Media Executive

Charles F. Dolan is one of the least known but most powerful moguls in the modern cable television industry in the United States. In early 1995 his corporate creation, Cablevision Systems, Inc., ranked as the fifth largest operator in the United States, serving some 2.6 million subscribers in 19 states, about 1.5 million of them in the New York metropolitan area. "Chuck" Dolan's Cablevision Systems Corporation also owns and controls a number of noted cable television networks, headed by the popular and influential American Movie Classics. In 1995 *The New York Times* estimated Dolan's net worth at $175 million.

Headquartered in Long Island, New York, Dolan organized Cablevision Systems in 1973. He had started in the cable TV business a decade earlier with Sterling Television, an equipment supplier. During the 1960s Sterling acquired the franchise for Manhattan Island, and when Time, Inc., purchased Sterling, Dolan used the substantial proceeds to buy some Long Island systems that he turned into Cablevision Systems.

Dolan correctly figured the action for cable would move to the suburbs and turned the locus of Cablevision Systems to the millions of potential customers living in areas surrounding New York City, particularly in Long Island's close-in Nassau and Suffolk Counties. In time Dolan also acquired franchises controlling 190,000 customers in Fairfield, Connecticut, a quarter of a million more in Northern New Jersey, and 60,000 in West Chester County. He also purchased or built cable TV systems across the United States, in Arkansas and Illinois, in Maine and Michigan, in Missouri and Ohio.

In 1988 Dolan added NBC as a minority partner. General Electric had recently purchased NBC, and prior to that had helped Dolan finance the expansion of Cablevision Systems. Thereafter Dolan, with help from NBC,

Charles F. Dolan
Photo courtesy of Cablevision Systems Corporation

moved into cable network programming in a major way. He crafted American Movie Classics into the top classic movie channel on cable. Building through grass-roots marketing, American Movie Classics quietly became one of the fastest growing of cable networks as the 1990s opened. Soon *The New York Times* was lavishing praise on AMC (American Movie Classics): "It's more than nostalgia. It's a chance to see black-and-white films which may have slipped through the cracks. It's wall-to-wall movies with no commercials, no aggressive graphics, no pushy sound, no sensory MTV overload, no time frame. There's a sedate pace, a pseudo-PBS quality about AMC. It's the *Masterpiece Theater* of movies."

Sports programming has also done well for Dolan, but on a regional basis. Dolan's regional sports channels cablecast all forms of sports to the millions of subscribers, on his and other cable systems, in the New York City area. The New York Yankees and New York Mets baseball games are particularly successful. By 1994 Dolan had done so well he partnered with billion-dollar conglomerate ITT to purchase Madison Square Garden for $1 billion. Suddenly Cablevision Systems was the major player in sports marketing in the New York City area, owning the Knicks basketball team, the Rangers hockey team, the Madison Square Garden cable TV network, and the most famous venue for indoor sports in the United States. As of the mid-1990s, however, Dolan's other great experiments, 24-hour local news on cable TV and the Bravo arts channel, have not been this profitable.

Local around-the-clock news began in 1986 as News 12 Long Island. This niche service came about because of the long frustrating inability of New York City's over-the-air TV stations to serve Long Island. Viewers not only appreciated News 12's basic half-hour newswheel, but also its multi-part reports that ran for a half hour or more. Such programs would never be possible for telecast by a New York City television station under current economic constraints.

With prize-winning series on breast cancer, drug abuse, and Alzheimer's disease, News 12 Long Island established a brand image. During election campaigns, the channel regularly staged candidate debates, and local politicians loved having their faces presented there. But little money came in to pay for these features, and only after a decade did it seem that News 12 would finally make money.

The same difficult economic calculus affects the arts-oriented Bravo channel. It is popular with well-off consumers, but too few of these tune in on a regular basis. Bravo merely hangs on, cable casting only a half-day schedule.

Dolan's accomplishments have been considerable. Though not well known to the general public, he helped establish cable television as an economic, social, and cultural force in the United States during the final quarter of the 20th century. He represents the TV entrepreneur in the true sense of the word, comparable to more publicized figures who started NBC and CBS, David Sarnoff and William S. Paley.

Dolan continues to look to the future, seeking significant positions for his menu of cable programming networks and franchises on the "electronic superhighway." Like other cable entrepreneurs of the late 20th century, he has pledged 500 channels, movies on demand, and interactive video entertainment and information. As of the late 1990s those plans remain promises.

—Douglas Gomery

CHUCK F. DOLAN. Attended John Carroll University. Married: Helen, children: MariAnne, Theresa, Deborah, James, Patrick, Thomas. Served briefly in the U.S. Air Force at the end of World War II. Worked at a radio station during high school, writing radio scripts and commercials; operated sports newsreel business; joined Sterling Television, 1954; built first urban cable television system, in Manhattan, 1961; president, Sterling Manhattan Cable, 1961-72; creator, Home Box Office pay movie service, 1970; sold interests in Manhattan cable service and HBO to Time, Inc., 1973; created and served as chair and chief executive, Cablevision Systems, one of the country's largest cable installations, until 1995; developed first local all-news channel for cable; created Rainbow Program Enterprises, operator of regional and national cable networks, including American Movie Classics, Bravo and SportsChannel; elected chair of the National Academy of Television Arts and Sciences, 1996.

FURTHER READING

Burgi, Michael. "Cablevision's Bold Visionary." *Mediaweek* (Brewster, New York), 4 July 1994.
"Chuck Dolan of Cablevision on Making the Most of Cable's Head Start in the Wired Nation" (interview). *Broadcasting,* 31 October 1988.
Lieberman, David. "A Cable Mogul's Daring Dance on the High Wire." *Business Week* (New York), 5 June 1989.

DONAHUE, PHIL

U.S. Talk-Show Host

In recent years, the talk show has become the most profitable, prolific, and contested format on daytime television. The sensationalist nature of many of these shows has spawned much public debate over the potential for invasion of personal privacy and the exploitation of sensitive social issues. In this environment, Phil Donahue, who is widely credited with inventing the talk-show platform, appears quite tame. But in the late 1960s, when *The Phil Donahue Show* first aired on WLW-D in Dayton, Ohio, Donahue was considered a radical and scintillating addition to the daytime scene.

Working at the college station KYW as a production assistant, Donahue had his first opportunity to test his on-air abilities when the regular booth announcer failed to show up. He claims it was then that he became "hooked" on hearing the transmission of his own voice. The position he took after graduation, news director for a Michigan radio station, allowed him to try his hand at broadcast reporting and eventually led to work as a stringer for the *CBS Evening News* and an anchor position at WHIO-TV in Dayton in the late 1950s. There he first entered the talk-show arena with his radio show *Conversation Piece*, on which he interviewed civil rights activists (including Martin Luther King and Malcolm X) and war dissenters.

After leaving WHIO and a subsequent three-month stint as a salesman, the general manager of WLW-D convinced Donahue to host a call-in TV talk show. The show would combine the talk-radio format with television interview show. However, *The Phil Donahue Show* would start with two major disadvantages: a small budget and geographic isolation from the entertainment industries, preventing it from garnering star guests. In order to attract their audience, Donahue and his producers had to innovate—they focused on issues rather than fame.

The first guest on *The Phil Donahue Show* was Madalyn O'Hair, an atheist who felt that religion "breeds dependence" and who was ready to mount a campaign to ban prayer in public schools. During that same week in November 1967 the show featured footage of a woman giving birth, a phone-in vote on the morality of an anatomically correct male doll, and a funeral director extolling the workings of his craft. The bold nature of these topics was tempered by Donahue's appealing personality. He was one of the first male television personalities to exude characteristics of "the sensitive man" (traits and behaviors further popularized in the 1970s by actors such as Alan Alda), acquired through his interest in both humanism and feminism.

Donahue's affinity with the women's movement, his sincere style, and his focus on controversial topics attracted a large and predominately female audience. He told a *Los Angeles Times Reporter*, in 1992, that his show "got lucky because we discovered early on that the usual idea of women's programming was a narrow, sexist view. We found

Phil Donahue
Photo courtesy of Phil Donahue

that women were interested in a lot more than covered dishes and needlepoint. The determining factor [was], 'Will the woman in the fifth row be moved to stand up and say something?' And there's a lot that will get her to stand up." Donahue attempted to "move" his audience in a number of ways, but the most controversial approach involved educating women on matters of reproduction. Shows on abortion, birthing techniques, and a discussion with Masters and Johnson were all banned by certain local affiliates. According to Donahue's autobiography, WGN in Chicago refused to air a show on reverse vasectomy and tubal ligation because it was "too educational for women...and too bloody." Nevertheless, Donahue's proven success with such a lucrative target audience led to the accumulation of other major midwest markets as well as the show's eventual move to Chicago in 1974 and then to New York in 1985. By then the range of topics had broadened considerably, even to include live "space bridge" programs. Co-hosted with Soviet newscaster Vladimir Pozner, these events linked U.S. and Soviet citizens for live exchanges on issues common to both groups.

But by the 1980s, the increasing popularity of *Donahue* had led to a proliferation of local and nationally syndicated talk shows. As competition increased, the genre became racier, with less emphasis on issues and more on personal scandal. Donahue retained his niche in the market by dividing the show's focus, dabbling in both the political and the personal. He was able to provide interviews with political candidates, explorations of the AIDS epidemic, and revelations of the savings and loan crisis, alongside shows on safe-sex orgies, cross-dressing, and aging strippers.

In 1992, with 19 Emmy Awards under his belt, Donahue was celebrated by his fellow talk-show hosts on his 25th anniversary special as a mentor and kindly patriarch of the genre. Fellow talk show-host Maury Povich was quoted in *Broadcasting and Cable* as saying at the event "He's the granddaddy of us all and he birthed us all." Until 1996 Phil Donahue still broadcast out of New York, where he lives with his wife actress Marlo Thomas. Early in that year he announced it would be his last. Ratings for Donahue were declining and a number of major stations, including his New York affiliate, had chosen to drop the show from their schedules. In the spring of 1996 Donahue taped his final show, an event covered on major network newscasts, complete with warm sentiment, spraying champagne, and expected, yet undoubted, sincerity. The ending of this hugely successful run for a syndicated program no doubt presaged new career developments for Phil Donahue in television.

—Sue Murray

PHIL (PHILLIP) JOHN DONAHUE. Born in Cleveland, Ohio, U.S.A., 21 December 1935. Educated at the University of Notre Dame, B.B.A. 1957. Married: 1) Marge Cooney, 1958 (divorced, 1975); children: Michael, Kevin, Daniel, Jim, Maryrose; 2) actress Marlo Thomas, 1980. Began career as announcer, KYW-TV and AM, Cleveland, 1957; bank check sorter, Albuquerque, New Mexico; news director, WABJ radio, Adrian, Michigan; morning newscaster, WHIO-TV, where interviews with Jimmy Hoffa and Billy Sol Estes were picked up nationally; hosted *Conversation Piece*, phone-in talk show, 1963–67; debuted *The Phil Donahue Show*, Dayton, Ohio, 1967, syndicated two years later; relocated to Chicago, 1974–85; host, *Donahue*, 1974–96; relocated to New York City, 1985. Recipient: numerous Emmy Awards; Best Talk Show Host, 1988; Margaret Sanger Award, Planned Parenthood, 1987; Peabody Award, 1980. Address: Donahue Multimedia Entertainment, 30 Rockefeller Plaza, Suite 827, New York, New York, 10112, U.S.A.

TELEVISION

1969–74	*The Phil Donahue Show* (from Dayton, Ohio)
1974–85	*Donahue* (from Chicago)
1985–96	*Donahue* (from New York)

PUBLICATIONS

Donahue: My Own Story. New York: Simon and Schuster, 1980.

Haley, Kathy. "Talking with Phil" (interview). *Broadcasting* (Washington, D.C.), 2 November 1992.

The Human Animal. New York: Simon and Schuster, 1985.

Unger, Arthur. "I Cannot Be the BBC in an MTV World!" (interview). *Television Quarterly* (New York), Spring 1991.

FURTHER READING

Carbaugh, Donald A. *Talking American: Cultural Discourses on Donahue.* Norwood, New Jersey: Ablex Publishing, 1988.

Haley, Kathy. "From Dayton to the World: A History of the Donahue Show." *Broadcasting* (Washington, D.C.), 2 November 1992.

Heaton, Jeanne Albronda, and Nona Leigh Wilson. *Tuning in Trouble: Talk TV's Destructive Impact on Mental Health.* San Francisco, California: Jossey-Bass, 1995.

Kurtz, Howard. "Father of the Slide." *The New Republic* (Washington, D.C.), 12 February 1996.

McConnell, Frank. "What Hath Phil Wrought?" *Commonweal* (New York), 22 March 1996.

Mifflin, Laurie. "The Price of Being Earnest." *The New York Times*, 21 January 1996.

Priest, Patricia Joyner. *Public Intimacies: Talk Show Participants and Tell All TV.* Cresskill, New Jersey: Hampton, 1996.

See also *Phil Donahue Show*, Talk Shows

DOWNS, HUGH

U.S. Television Host

Hugh Downs, a venerable and extremely affable television host, is known for his intelligence, patience, and decency. The *Guinness Book of World Records* reports that Downs, among the most familiar figures in the history of the medium, has clocked more hours on television (10,347 through May 1994) than any other person in U.S. TV history.

Downs began his broadcasting career as a radio announcer at the age of 18 in Lima, Ohio, moving later to NBC Chicago as a staff announcer. In 1957 he became well known to American audiences as Jack Paar's sidekick on *The Tonight Show* and remained in that spot through 1962. In 1958 he began simultaneously hosting the original version of *Concentration*, helping to establish his niche of doing more serious and thought-provoking television even within the game show format.

He served as NBC's utility host for many of the network's 1950s and early 1960s news, information, and entertainment programs. He added *The Today Show* to his list of network assignments, replacing John Chancellor who had served for just 15 months as Dave Garroway's replacement on the original *Today Show*. Downs was the primary host of the *Today Show* for nine years.

Downs' reassuring, professional manner in the roles of announcer, sidekick, host, and anchor is unrivaled in U.S.

television. He has said that he tries to be the link between what goes on behind and in front of the camera and the audience at home, hoping that he serves as an "honest pipeline to the audience." He believes that television works best when a familiar presence is there to help guide viewers in and out of features and stories, however abbreviated that function may be. Since 1978 he has best demonstrated that commitment as the anchor or co-anchor of ABC's *20/20*. Downs came out of a very busy retirement to take the *20/20* position when a near-disastrous premier almost kept the show off the air.

His great affability and smooth manner have made it possible for him to get along well with whomever he has been paired, repeatedly taking the edge off some of the sharper moments with Jack Paar, who was well known for his outbursts, tantrums, and eccentricities. Ironically, Barbara Walters took the position across from Downs on *20/20* just after a major brouhaha developed when she was asked to leave her position as the first female network news co-anchor, paired unsuccessfully with Harry Reasoner. But with Downs the chemistry was right and the two have worked together successfully since 1984.

Intimates refer to Downs as one of the last "renaissance men." He is a proficient sailor and aviator—even though colorblind. He has composed, published, and had orchestral pieces performed, has hosted *Live from Lincoln Center* for PBS since 1990, and is exceptionally knowledgeable about science and health. One of his special interests is the U.S. space program. Another focuses on issues surrounding aging, and he has earned a post-graduate certificate in geriatric medicine while hosting *Over Easy* for the Public Broadcasting Service, the first successful television program in the United States about aging. Always modest, Downs shuns the "renaissance" label, preferring instead to call himself "a champion dilettante."

He is the author of eight books, including an autobiography, a collection of his science articles (on astronomy and the environment), an account of a sailing voyage across the Pacific, and five on the subjects of aging, health, and psychological maturity. Downs' public service commitments are also notable. He is currently the chair of the board of the United States Committee for UNICEF, chair of the Board of Governors of the National Space Society, and he serves as an elected member of the National Academy of Science, and a past-member of NASA's Advisory Council. He recently received an award from the American Psychiatric Association for his work on an ABC News special, *Depression, Beyond the Darkness*, and also received an Emmy for his work on *The Poisoning of America* about damage to the environment. He was named Broadcaster of the Year by the International Radio and Television Society in 1990. In 1995 he was honored with a special salute ceremony by the Museum of Broadcast Communications in Chicago.

—Robert Kubey

HUGH (MALCOLM) DOWNS. Born in Akron, Ohio, U.S.A., 14 February 1921. Attended Bluffton College, Ohio, 1938-39; Wayne State College, 1940–41; Columbia University, 1955-

Hugh Downs
Photo courtesy of Hugh Downs

56. Married: Ruth Shaheen, 1944; children: Hugh Raymond and Deirdre Lynn. Began career as staff announcer and program director, WLOK, Lima, Ohio, 1939–40; staff announcer, WWJ, Detroit, Michigan, 1940–42; staff announcer, NBC-Radio, Chicago, Illinois, 1943–54; in television, from 1949; chairman, board of directors, Raylin Productions, Inc, from 1960; special consultant to U.N. on refugee problems, 1961-64; science consultant to Westinghouse Laboratories and the Ford Foundation. Member: Actors' Equity Association; Screen Actors Guild, American Federation of Television and Radio Artists; National Space Institute; chair, U.S. Committee for UNICEF; Center for the Study of Democratic Institutions. Recipient: Emmy Award. Address: c/o *20/20*, American Broadcasting Corporation, 1330 Avenue of the Americas, New York City, New York 10019, U.S.A.

TELEVISION SERIES

1949	*Kukla, Fran, and Ollie* (announcer)	
1950	*Hawkins Falls*	
1951–55	*American Inventory*	
1951	*Your Luncheon Date* (announcer)	
1954–57	*The Home Show* (announcer)	
1956–57	*Sid Caesar's Hour* (announcer)	
1957–62	*The Jack Paar Show* (announcer)	
1958–68	*Concentration* (emcee)	

1962	*The Tonight Show* (announcer)
1962–72	*The Today Show* (host)
1972	*Not for Women Only* (host)
1974	*Variety* (host) (pilot only)
1977–83	*Over Easy*
1978–	*20/20* (host)
1985	*Growing Old in America* (host)

MADE-FOR-TELEVISION MOVIE

| 1976 | *Woman of the Year* |

TELEVISION SPECIALS

1975	*Broken Treaty at Battle Mountain: A Discussion* (moderator)
1986	*Liberty Weekend Preview* (reporter)
1986	*NBC's 60th Anniversary Celebration* (reporter)
1987	*Today at 35* (reporter)

FILMS

Nothing by Chance (documentary; executive producer and narrator), 1974; *Oh God! Book II*, 1980.

RADIO

WLOK, Lima, Ohio, 1939-40; WWJ, Detroit, Michigan, 1940-42; NBC Radio, Chicago, 1943–54.

PUBLICATIONS

A Shoal of Stars. Garden City, New York: Doubleday, 1967.
Rings Around Tomorrow. Garden City, New York: Doubleday, 1970.
Potential: The Way to Emotional Maturity. Garden City, New York: Doubleday, 1973.
Thirty Dirty Lies about Old Age. Niles, Illinois: Argus, 1979.
The Best Years Book: How to Plan for Fulfillment, Security, and Happiness in the Retirement Years. New York: Delacorte/Eleanor Fried, 1981.
On Camera: My Ten Thousand Hours on Television. New York: Putnam, 1986.
Fifty to Forever. Nashville, Tennessee: T.N. Publishers, 1994.
Perspectives. Atlanta, Georgia: Turner, 1995.

FURTHER READING

"Hugh Downs." *Ad Astra* (Washington, D.C.), July-August 1991.
"Hugh Downs: TV's Marathon Man." *Broadcasting* (Washington, D.C.), 5 February 1990.

See also Talk Shows; *Today Show; Tonight Show*

DRAGNET

U.S. Police Drama

From the distinctive four-note opening of its theme music to the raft of catch phrases it produced, no other television cop show has left such an indelible mark on American culture as *Dragnet*. It was the first successful television crime drama to be shot on film and one of the few prime time series to have returned to production after its initial run. In *Dragnet*, Jack Webb, who produced, directed, and starred in the program, created the benchmark by which subsequent police shows would be judged.

The origins of *Dragnet* can be traced to a semi-documentary film noir, *He Walked by Night* (1948), in which Webb had a small role. Webb created a radio series for NBC that had many similarities with the film. Not only did both employ the same L.A.P.D. technical advisor, they also made use of actual police cases, narration that provided information about the workings of the police department, and a generally low-key, documentary style. In the radio drama Webb starred as Sgt. Joe Friday and Barton Yarborogh played his partner. The success of the radio show led to a *Dragnet* television pilot, aired as an episode of *Chesterfield Sound Off Time* in 1951, and resulted in a permanent slot for the series on NBC Television's Thursday night schedule in early 1952. Yarborogh died suddenly after the pilot aired and was eventually replaced by Ben Alexander, who played Officer Frank Smith from 1953 to the end of the series in 1959.

Dragnet

Dragnet was an instant hit on television, maintaining a top 10 position in the ratings through 1956. The series was applauded for its realism—actually a collection of highly stylized conventions which made the show an easy target for parodists and further increased its cultural cachet. Episodes began with a prologue promising that "the story you are about to see is true; the names have been changed to protect the innocent," then faded in on a pan across the L.A. sprawl. Webb's mellifluous voice intoned, "This is the city. Los Angeles, California," and usually offered statistics about the city, its population, and institutions. Among the show's other "realistic" elements were constant references to dates, the time, and weather conditions. Producing the series on film permitted the use of stock shots of L.A.P.D. operations and location shooting in Los Angeles. This was a sharp contrast to the stage-bound "live" detective shows of the period. *Dragnet* emphasized authentic police jargon, the technical aspects of law enforcement, and the drudgery of such work. Rather than engaging in fist fights and gun play, Friday and his partner spent much screen time making phone calls, questioning witness, or following up on dead end leads. Scenes of the detectives simply waiting and engaging in mundane small talk were common. To save on costly rehearsal time Webb had actors read their lines off a TelePrompTer. The result was a clipped, terse style, that conveyed a documentary feel and became a trademark of subsequent series produced by Webb, including *Adam-12* and *Emergency*. *Dragnet* always concluded with an epilogue detailing the criminal's fate accompanied by a shot of the character shifting about uncomfortably before the camera.

Dragnet's stories, many written by James Moser, ran the gamut from traffic accidents to homicide. Other stories played on critical middle-class anxieties of the postwar period including juvenile delinquency, teenage drug use, and the distribution of "dirty" pictures in schools. Moral complexity was eschewed for a crime-doesn't-pay message sketched in stark black-and-white tones. Friday put up with little from lawbreakers, negligent parents, or young troublemakers. Program segments often concluded with the sergeant directing a tight-lipped homily to miscreants coupled with a musical "stinger" and an appreciative nod from his partner.

By 1954 *Dragnet* was watched by over half of America's television households. This success prompted Warner Brothers to finance and distribute a theatrical version of *Dragnet* (1954), signalling the rise of cross-promotion between film and television (Anderson, 1994). Further evidence of the show's popularity was found in the number of TV series that imitated its style, notably *The Lineup, M Squad,* and Moser's *Medic,* based on cases from the files of the Los Angeles County Medical Association. Conversely, other series like *77 Sunset Strip* and *Hawaiian Eye,* featuring younger, hipper detectives, were developed to provide an antidote to *Dragnet*'s dour approach to crime fighting. As *Dragnet* neared completion of its initial run in 1959 Friday

was promoted to lieutenant and Smith passed his sergeant's exam. Seven years later the show was revived by NBC as *Dragnet 1967.* Until it was cancelled in 1970, *Dragnet* was always followed by the year to distinguish the new series from its 1950s counterpart. In the new series Friday was once again a sergeant, now paired with Officer Bill Gannon (Harry Morgan). Though the style and format of the show remained the same, the intervening years and the rise of the counter culture had changed Friday from a crusading cop to a dyspeptic civil servant, alternately disgusted by the behavior of the younger generation and peeved at his partner's prattle about mundane topics. The program's conservatism was all the more apparent in the late 1960s as Friday's terse warnings of the fifties gave way to shrill lectures invoking god and country for the benefit of hippies, drug users, and protestors.

Webb's death in 1982 did not prevent another revival of *Dragnet* from appearing in syndication during the 1989-1990 season. Two younger characters filled in for Friday and his partner but the formula remained the same. This little-seen effort failed quickly in part because series such as *Hill Street Blues* and *COPS* had significantly altered the conventions of realistic police dramas. Those programs, and others like *NYPD Blue,* must be considered the true generic successors to the original *Dragnet.* As the archetypal television police drama *Dragnet* has remained a staple in reruns and continues to be an object of both parody and reverent homage.

—Eric Schaefer

CAST

Sgt. Joe Friday	Jack Webb
Sgt. Ben Romero (1951)	Barton Yarborough
Sgt. Ed Jacobs (1952)	Barney Phillips
Officer Frank Smith (1952)	Herb Ellis
Officer Frank Smith (1953–1959) . . .	Ben Alexander
Officer Bill Gannon (1967–1970) . . .	Harry Morgan

PRODUCER/CREATOR   Jack Webb

PROGRAMMING HISTORY

1952–1959	263 Episodes
1967–1970	100 Episodes

• NBC

January 1952–December 1955	Thursday 9:00-9:30
January 1956–September 1958	Thursday 8:30-9:00
September 1958–June 1959	Tuesday 7:30-8:00
July 1959–September 1959	Sunday 8:30-9:00
January 1967–September 1970	Thursday 9:30-10:00

FURTHER READING

Anderson, Christopher. *Hollywood/TV: The Studio System in the Fifties.* Austin: University of Texas Press, 1994.

"Detective Story." *Newsweek* (New York), 14 January 1952.

Hubler, Richard G. "Jack Webb: The Man Who Makes *Dragnet*." *Coronet* (New York), September 1953.

"Jack, Be Nimble!" *Time* (New York), 15 March 1954.

Luciano, Patrick, and Gary Coville. "Behind Badge 714: The Story of Jack Webb and *Dragnet* (Part One)." *Filmfax* (Evanston, Illinois), August-September 1993.

———. "Behind Badge 714: The Story of Jack Webb and *Dragnet* (Part Two)." *Filmfax* (Evanston, Illinois), October-November 1993.

Tregaskis, Richard. "The Cops' Favorite Make-Believe Cop." *Saturday Evening Post* (Philadelphia, Pennsylvania), 26 September 1953.

See also Police Programs; Webb, Jack

DRAMEDY

Dramedy is best understood as a television program genre which fuses elements of comedy and drama. According to Altman (1986), new genres emerge in one of two ways: "either a relatively stable set of semantic givens is developed through syntactic experimentation into a coherent and durable syntax, or an already existing syntax adopts a new set of semantic elements." Semantic elements are the generic "building blocks" out of which of program genres are constructed—those recurring elements such as stock characters, common traits, and technical features such as locations and typical shots. Syntax, or syntactic features, describes the ways these elements are related and combined. The recurring combination of semantic and syntactic elements creates a conventional type or category of program called a genre.

Arguably one of the clearest examples of the dramedy genre emerged in 1985 and 1986 when the Directors Guild of America nominated the hour-long television series *Moonlighting* for both Best Drama and Best Comedy, an unprecedented event in the organization's previous 50 years. *Moonlighting* combined the semantic elements or conventions of television drama (serious subject matter, complex and rounded central characters, multiple interior and exterior settings, use of textured lighting, single camera shooting on film) with the conventional syntactic features of television comedies (four-act narrative structure, repetition, witty repartee, verbal and musical self-reflexivity, hyperbole). Not all dramedies, however, were an hour long. For example, the half-hour series *Frank's Place* dealt with serious issues, had rounded and complex central characters, textured lighting, multiple settings, single camera shooting on film, no studio audience or laugh track, and a four-part nanrative structure. Given the economic organization of the American television schedule, in which "half-hour" is usually equated with "comedy," and "hour-long" with "drama," many dramedies were considered more comic than dramatic and vice versa.

Television, like most popular culture forms, is strongly generic; audiences come to television program viewing experiences with definite expectations about genre conventions; indeed, according to Warshow audiences welcome originality "only in the degree that intensifies the expected experience without fundamentally altering it." However, as a commercial enterprise, television piques audience members' interest and attracts viewers, at least in part by offering innovations on familiar genre forms. Thus, while dramedy may have taken the final step from invention to genre evoluton in the 1980s, several series during the 1970s occasionally experimented with individual "dramedic" episodes, including *M*A*S*H, Barney Miller,* and *Taxi.* After *Moonlighting* had garnered both popular success and critical acclaim, a number of television producers turned to dramedy's unique duality as a means of attracting audiences. Other television series which some critics have called dramedies include *The Days and Nights of Molly Dodd, Hooperman, The "Slap" Maxwell Story,* and *Northern Exposure.* However as the short runs of several of these series indicate, creating a highly rated dramedy is no easier than creating a popular series in another genre.

The Days and Nights of Molly Dodd

Critics, on the other hand, have quite uniformly praised television's dramedy series' sophistication and innovation. They argue that the appearance of dramedies, whose self reflexivity and intertextual references require a substantial degree of both popular and classic cultural literacy from viewers for full appreciation of their allusions and nuances, signifies a change in the relationships among television, audiences and society and indicates that television has "come of age" as an artistic medium.

—Leah R. Vande Berg

FURTHER READING

Alley, R. S. "Television Drama." In, Newcomb, H., editor. *Television: The Critical View*. New York: Oxford University Press, 1976; 2nd edition, 1979.

Altman, R. "A Semantic/Syntactic Approach to Film Genre." In, Grant, B. K., editor. *Film Genre Reader* Austin, Texas: University of Texas Press, 1986.

Cawelti, J. G. *Adventure, Mystery and Romance: Formula Stories as Art and Popular Culture*. Chicago: University of Chicago Press, 1976.

deLauretis, T. "A Semiotic Approach to Television as Ideological Apparatus." In, Newcomb, H., editor. *Television: The Critical View*. New York: Oxford University Press, 1976; 2nd edition, 1979.

Eaton, M. "Television Situation Comedy." In, Bennett, T., S. Boyd-Bowman, C. Mercer, and J. Wollacott, editors. *Popular Television and Film*. London: British Film Institute, 1981.

Horowitz, J. "Sweet Lunacy: The Madcap Behind *Moonlighting*." *New York Times Magazine* (New York), 30 March 1986.

Mintz, L. E. "Situation Comedy." In, Rose, B., editor. *TV Genres: A Handbook and Reference Guide*. Westport, Connecticut: Greenwood Press, 1985.

Newcomb, H. *TV: The Most Popular Art*. Garden City, New York: Anchor/Doubleday, 1974.

Newcomb, H. "Toward Television History: The Growth of Styles." *Journal of the University Film Association*. Carbondale, Illinois, 1978.

Vande Berg, L. R. "Dramedy: *Moonlighting* as an Emergent Generic Hybrid." *Communication Studies* (West Lafayette, Indiana), 1989.

Warshow, R. *The Immediate Experience*. Garden City: New York: Doubleday/Anchor, 1974.

Williams, J. P., "When You Care Enough to Watch the Very Best: The Mystique of *Moonlighting*." *Journal of Popular Film and Television* (Washington, D.C.), 1988.

See also *Frank's Place; Moonlighting; Northern Exposure; Wonder Years*

DREW, ROBERT

U.S. Documentary Film Producer

Robert Drew is a documentary producer, who, during the late 1950s and 1960s, pioneered a new documentary form for application in the network news departments. This form, which Drew dubbed "Candid Drama," also known as "Cinema Verite" or "Direct Cinema", did not, ultimately, reshape news programming, but it did provide the medium with a radically different way of covering historical and cultural events.

"Candid Drama," according to Drew, is a documentary filmmaking technique which reveals the "logic of drama" inherent in almost all human situations. In sharp contrast to typical television documentaries, which are simply "lectures with picture illustration," and for that reason usually are "dull," the candid drama documentary eschews extensive voice-over narration, formal interviews, on-air correspondents, or other kinds of staged and framed television formulae. Instead, through the slowly acquired photography and long, single takes—called real-time photography—of verite technique, the details and flavor of a scene become the important elements: the fatigue experienced by candidates on a campaign trail (*Primary*), the fervid concentration of a race car driver (*On the Pole*), capture our attention as much as the factual information about a campaign or the Indianapolis 500. According to Drew, the purpose of candid documentary is to engage the viewer's "senses as well as his

mind." Over a career that spans more than 30 years, Drew has produced over 100 films and videotapes, most of which employ the theory and methods of verite technique; and

Robert Drew
Photo courtesy of Drew Associates

unlike other practitioners of the form, he has also tried to procure a regular slot for verite on prime-time network programming.

Drew was first introduced to the power of documentary photography just after World War II, while demonstrating a new fighter plane for a *Life* magazine reporter and photography team (Drew had served as a fighter pilot during the war). Struck by the power of the resulting article, Drew, at the age of twenty-two, became a staff reporter for *Life*. In 1955 he accepted a Neiman fellowship at Harvard to formally pursue the problem of an alternative news theory in the medium of film. It was a time of rigorous talk, study and analysis, according to Drew, and upon his return to *Life*, he began making films as well as reporting. Some of these early experiments premiered on *The Ed Sullivan Show* and *The Jack Paar Show*. In 1960, Drew moved to Time's broadcast division, where, with the backing of Wes Tullen, vice president in charge of television operations, he obtained the funds for his first project and the means necessary to develop lightweight portable equipment. The engineering of the first small sync sound and picture camera unit, which he undertook with filmmaker Richard Leacock, has undoubtedly had an enormous impact on numerous documentarians working both for the major networks and independently. Sensitive and ephemeral moments could now be more easily captured than with the cumbersome camera, large camera crew and lighting system that had been used in news coverage to date.

Also at this time, Drew formed his company, Drew Associates, which enabled him to hire freelance cameramen and filmmakers, some of whom, such as D.A. Pennebaker, Richard Leacock and Albert Maysles, have since gone on to establish celebrated careers of their own. By March 1960, Drew was ready to select their first subject and settled on the Democratic presidential primary in Wisconsin, which pitted the young John Kennedy against Hubert Humphrey. For the last week of the campaign, three two-man crews tracked both Kennedy and Humphrey as they made their rounds of the hustings, photo sessions and the rare, private moments in between.

Primary, as this first film was named, still stands today as one of Drew Associate's best-known and celebrated works. It won the Flaherty Award for Best Documentary and the Blue Ribbon at the American Film Festival, while in Europe, according to Drew, "it was received as a kind of documentary second-coming." (The rough immediacy of the hand-held camera is said to have influenced Goddard's *Breathless*.) Kennedy, upon viewing *Primary*, liked it so much that he consented to Drew's request to make further candid films in his role as president. "What if I had been able to observe F.D.R. in the 24 hours before he declared war on Japan?" he said. And indeed, Drew Associates gained permission to film the president during a period of crisis. Called *Crisis: Behind a Presidential Commitment* (1963), this documentary chronicles the showdown between Alabama Governor George Wallace and the federal government over the integration of the University of Alabama. As in *Primary*,

domestic and personal details of the two main protagonists (Wallace and then-Attorney General Robert F. Kennedy) are intercut with the film's history-making moments—Wallace's initial refusal to back down and the government's decision to employ state troops. To Drew's great chagrin, however, the films were not broadcast over the networks. While regional outlets were found on occasion, the regular scheduling of these films, and the many others he produced, proved an elusive goal.

A joint Time, Inc.-ABC sponsorship allowed Drew Associates, however, to produce a series of films in 1960, for television, including a portrait of Indianapolis race driver, Eddie Sachs, *On the Pole*, and *Yanki No!*, about Latin American reaction to American foreign policy in the region. These two films prompted a Time, Inc.-ABC liaison to offer Drew a contract for a regular supply of candid documentary. In rapid-fire succession the company made about a half dozen more. They form a diverse list, including a profile of Nehru (which grew to a twenty-year documentary relationship with the Nehru "dynasty", with subsequent films on Indira Gandhi and her son, Rajiv). Yet the first season's series was to be the last produced under the arrangement; again, the regular scheduling of the films, which Drew had made the bedrock of his candid drama theory, did not materialize.

The reasons proffered for the ambivalence of the television industry include the political infighting that arose between Time and ABC and the growing difficulty of attracting a single sponsor for the projects; but perhaps the most compelling reason was the networks' unshakable preference for correspondent-hosted or narrated reporting. The predictable, and containable, effects of a regular news anchor has prevailed, with exceptions, over more poetic candid documentary. (Moments of verite reporting have nonetheless been produced in a few instances by the networks, Drew maintains, most notably the network coverage of American troops in Vietnam.) Once the first season of programming was complete, the three-way contractual relationship between Drew Associates, Time and ABC formally ended. The production company since then has managed to survive and produce prolifically on an independent contractual basis with a variety of sponsors, including ABC, PBS, the BBC, corporations, and governmental agencies, as well with its own Drew Associates funds, as an independent producer.

The resulting *oeuvre* consists of a wide variety of historical and high profile moments, intermingled with scenes of the ordinary in modern life. *Jane* (1962) shows us a young Jane Fonda at her Broadway debut. *A Man Who Dances* (1968), produced as part of series on the arts for Bell Telephone, about ballet dancer Edward Villella, won Drew an Emmy. Many have dealt with subjects the networks have hesitated to tackle in house; responding to a request by Xerox Corporation for a film "that the networks won't touch," Drew made *Storm Signal* (1966), a documentary on drug addiction; a three part series on gangs, produced for PBS' *Frontline* (1983–1984) delves into the world of gangs and an inner-city high school. A full ten years later, Drew

Associates completed *L.A. Champions*, also for PBS, about the basketball teams that play the streets of Southcentral Los Angeles, which, like Drew's first films, unobtrusively follows its main characters, and without a word of narration tells a stirring story.

—Susan Hamovitch

ROBERT LINCOLN DREW. Born in Toledo, Ohio, U.S.A., 15 February 1924. Served in U.S. Army Air Force, 1942. Reporter for *Life*, 1946, Detroit bureau chief, 1949, assistant picture editor, New York, 1950, Chicago correspondent, 1951; documentary filmmaker for film and television. Recipient: Nieman Fellowship from Harvard University, 1954; American Film Festival, Blue Ribbon Award, 1961 and 1978; Venice Film Festival, First Prize, 1964, 1965, and 1966; Council on International Non-Theatrical Events, Cine Golden Eagle, 1964, 1965, 1966, 1967, 1968, 1969 (twice), 1970, 1975, 1976, 1977 (twice), 1978, 1980, 1982, 1985, 1986, and 1991; International Cinema Exhibition, Bilboa, First Prize, 1967 and 1968; International Documentary Film Festival, First Prize, 1967; Emmy Award, 1969; Chicago Film Festival, Silver Hugo, 1978; Peabody Award, 1982; American Bar Association, Silver Gavel Award, 1983; International Film and TV Festival of New York, Gold Award, 1983; Education Writers Association, First Prize, 1985; DuPont-Columbia Award, Best Documentary, 1985–86.

DOCUMENTARY FILMS (selection)

Key Picture (Magazine X), 1954; *American Football*, 1957; *The B-52*, 1957; *Weightless (Zero Gravity)*, 1958; *Balloon Ascension*, 1958; *Bullfight*, 1959; *Yanki No!*, 1960; *Primary*, 1960; *On the Pole*, 1960; *X-Pilot*, 1961; *The Children Were Watching*, 1961; *Adventures on the New Frontier*, 1961; *Kenya (Part I: Land of the White Ghost; Part II: Land of the Black Ghost)*, 1961; *Eddie*, 1961; *David*, 1961; *Petey and Johnny*, 1961; *Mooney vs. Fowle*, 1961; *Blackie*, 1962; *Susan Starr*, 1962; *Nehru*, 1962; *The Road to Button Bay*, 1962; *The Aga Khan*, 1962; *The Chair*, 1962; *Jane (The Jane Fonda Story)*, 1962; *Crisis: Behind a Presidential Commitment*, 1963; *Faces of November*, 1964; *Mission to Malaya*, 1964; *Letters from Vietnam*, 1965; *In the Contest of the Queen*, 1965; *Assault on LeMans*, 1965; *The Big Guy*, 1965; *The Time of Our Lives*, 1965; *Men Encounter Mars*, 1965; *Storm Signal*, 1966; *Another Way*, 1966; *A Man's Dream: Festival of Two Worlds*, 1966; *International Jazz Festival*, 1966; *The New Met: Countdown to Curtain*, 1966; *On the Road with Duke Ellington*, 1967; *The Virtuoso Teacher*, 1967; *Carnival of the Menuhins*, 1967; *Edward Villella: A Man Who Dances*, 1968; *Jazz: The Intimate Art*, 1968; *Nelson Rockefeller*, 1968; *Another World, Another Me*, 1968; *Confrontation in Color*,

1968; *The Space Duet of Spider and Gumdrop*, 1969; *Songs of America*, 1969; *The Martian Investigators*, 1970; *The Sun Ship Game*, 1971; *Beyond the Limits*, 1972; *Late Start*, 1973; *Deal With Disaster*, 1973; *Saving the Birds*, 1973; *Helping the Blind*, 1973; *Junior Achievement*, 1973; *Teaching Reading*, 1973; *Children's Hospital*, 1973; *School Bus*, 1973; *State Legislature*, 1973; *Pittsburg, Kansas*, 1973; *Mississippi*, 1973; *Typewriter*, 1973; *Oceanography*, 1973; *Who's Out There? (Orson Wells and Carl Sagan)*, 1974; *Life in Outer Space*, 1973; *The Mind of Man*, 1973; *Saving Energy, It Begins at Home*, 1974; *Junk Cars*, 1974; *A Feat of Talent*, 1975; *The Tall Ships Are Coming*, 1975; *Christmas Birds*, 1975; *Ohio River*, 1975; *Conserving Energy*, 1975; *Apollo Soyez*, 1975; *Children Learn to Write by Dictating*, 1975; *World Food Crisis*, 1975; *Things Are Changing Around This School*, 1976; *Los Nietos, Urban League Training Center*, 1976; *Lodi Lady*, 1976; *Mr. Vernon Distar*, 1976; *Congressman Ruppe*, 1976; *What's In a Name?*, 1976; *Men of the Tall Ships*, 1976; *Six Americans on America: Chatham Massachusetts; Morristown, New Jersey; Savannah, Georgia; San Antonio, Texas; Freelandville, Indiana; San Francisco, California*, 1976; *Parade of the Tall Ships*, 1976; *Kathy's Dance*, 1977; *A Unique Fit—LTV Merger*, 1978; *Talent for America*, 1978; *Grasshopper Plague*, 1979; *Maine Winter*, 1979; *One Room Schoolhouse*, 1979; *Undersea at Seabrook*, 1979; *Images of Einstein*, 1979; *The Zapper*, 1979; *The Snowblower*, 1979; *Freeway Phobia*, 1980; *1980 Census*, 1980; *Durham Diets*, 1980; *Endorphins*, 1980; *Professor Rassias*, 1980; *Alcohol Car*, 1980; *Apex City*, 1980; *LTV '80*, 1980; *Spot Car*, 1980; *Blitz the Cities*, 1981; *Herself, Indira Gandhi*, 1982; *Fire Season* (also director), 1982; *784 Days That Changed America* (also writer), 1982; *Build the Fusion Power Machine*, 1984–85; *Being with John F. Kennedy*, 1984; *Frontline: Shootout on Imperial Highway*, 1984; *Warnings from Gangland* (also director), 1984-85; *Marshall High Fights Back* (also co-director), 1984–85; *The Transformation of Rajiv Gandhi*, 1985-86; *For Auction: An American Hero*, 1985–86; *OK Heart*, 1985–86; *Frontline: Your Flight is Cancelled*, 1987; *Messages from the Birds* (also photographer), 1987–88; *River of Hawks*, 1987–88; *Kennedy versus Wallace*, 1988–89; *London to Peking: The Great Motoring Challenge* (also photographer, writer), 1989–90; *Life and Death of a Dynasty* (also photographer), 1990–91; *L.A. Champions*, 1993.

FURTHER READING

O'Connell, P.J. *Robert Drew and the Development of Cinema Verite in America*. Carbondale: Southern Illinois University Press, 1992.

See also Documentary

DUBBING

Dubbing has two meanings in the process of television production. It is used to describe the replacement of one sound track (music, sound effects, dialogue, natural sound, etc.) by another. The technique is used in the production of both audio and audiovisual media. It is a post-production activity which allows considerable flexibility in "editing" the audio component of the visual. Dubbing includes activities such as the addition of music and sound effects to the original dialogue, the omission or replacement of unwanted or poorly recorded audio, or the re-recording of the entire dialogue, narration and music. Much like literary editing, dubbing allows considerable freedom to recreate the product. Synonymous terms include postsynchronizing, looping, re-recording, and electronic line replacement.

Dubbing is also one of the two major forms of "language transfer," i.e. translation of audiovisual works. Dubbing, in this sense, is the replacement of the dialogue and narration of the foreign or source language (SL) into the language of the viewing audience, the target language (TL).

Inherited from cinema, dubbing is extensively used for translating other-language television programs. Some countries and cultures prefer dubbing to subtitling and voice-over. In Europe, for example, the "dubbing countries" include Austria, France, Germany, Italy, Spain and Switzerland.

Dubbing, unlike subtitling, which involves a translation of speech into writing, is the oral translation of oral language. However, unlike "interpretation" in which the SL speaker and the TL interpreter are separate persons talking in their own distinct voices, dubbing requires the substitution of the voice of each character on the screen by the voice of one actor. It is, thus, a form of voice-over or revoicing. Dubbing is, however, distinguished from voice-over by its strict adherence to lip-synchronization. In order to seem "natural" or authentic, the performed translation must match, as closely as possible, the lip movements of the speaker on the screen. Moreover, there should be a strict, though easy to achieve, equivalence of extra-linguistic features of voice, especially gender and age. The matching of other markers of speech such as personality, class, and ethnicity is most difficult because these features are not universally available or comparable. Another requirement of successful dubbing is the compatibility of the dubber's voice with the facial and body expressions visible on the screen.

Lip synchronization is usually seen as the strongest constraint on accurate translation. The script editor modifies the "raw translation" of each utterance in order to match it with the lip movements of the person seen on the screen. Given the enormous differences between even closely related languages such as English and German, it is difficult to find TL words that match the SL lip movements; this is especially the case when speakers are shown in close-up. It has been argued, however, that a word by word or sentence by sentence translation is not needed, especially in entertainment genres such as soap operas. Lip synchronization can be better performed with a more pragmatic "plot-oriented translation." If translation aims at conveying the general tone of each scene rather than locating meaning in each sentence, there will be more freedom to find appropriate words for lip synchronization. Moreover, it is important to seek the equivalence of not only word and sentence meanings but also genres, text quality, character and cultural context. This approach is consistent with the claims of pragmatics, a new field of study which examines language use in social interaction. In either case, it would be more realistic to view dubbing, like other forms of language transfer, as an activity involving a recreation of the original text.

As the transnationalization of television and film increases the demand for language transfer, the controversy about the aesthetics, politics and economics of dubbing and subtitling continues in exporting and importing markets, and in multilingual countries where language transfer is a feature of indigenous audiovisual culture. The polarized views on dubbing/subtitling highlight the centrality and complexity of language in a medium which privileges its visuality. Audience sensitivity to language can even be seen in the considerable volume of intralanguage dubbing. The miniseries *Les filles de Caleb*, for example, produced in the French language of Quebec, was dubbed into the French standard for audiences in France. And Latin American producers and exporters of *telenovelas* have generally adopted a Mexican form of Spanish as their standard, following the lead of the earliest successful programs. Thus, dialect also acts as a barrier in the transnationalization of television within the same language community, and highlights the complex issues surrounding this apparently simple industrial process.

—Amir Hassanpour

FURTHER READING

Kilborn, Richard. "'Speak my Language': Current Attitudes to Television Subtitling and Dubbing." *Media, Culture Society* (London), 1993.

Luyken, Georg-Michael. *Overcoming Language Barriers in Television: Dubbing and Subtitling for the European Audience.* Manchester, England: European Institute for the Media, 1991.

Yvane, J. "The Treatment of Language in the Production of Dubbed Versions." *EBU Review* (Geneva, Switzerland), 1987.

See also Language and Television

DUMONT, ALLEN B.

U.S. Inventor/Media Executive

In 1931, Allen B. DuMont founded Allen B. DuMont Laboratories, Inc., in his garage with $1000—half of it borrowed. The company achieved its initial success as the primary U.S. manufacturer of cathode-ray tubes, which had become critical to the electronics industry. DuMont entered into television broadcasting—first experimentally, then as a commercial venture—in 1938. In fact, the only way to receive NBC-RCA's historic public broadcast of television outside their 1939 World's Fair pavilion was on sets made by DuMont Labs.

DuMont first became involved in broadcasting by building a radio transmitter and transmitter and receiver out of an oatmeal box while suffering from polio. In 1924, he received an electrical engeneering degree from Rensselaer Polytechnical Institute. After graduation, he joined the Westinghouse Lamp Company as an engineer at a time when 500 tubes a day were being produced. Later DuMont became supervisor and initiated technical improvements that increased production to 5,000 tubes per hour. In 1928, he worked closely with Dr. Lee DeForest on expanding radio, but left later to explore television.

DuMont achieved a number of firsts in commercial television practice, but with little success. He tried to expand his network too rapidly both in the number of affiliates and the number of hours of programming available to affiliates each week. Even as DuMont was developing into the first commercial television network, the other networks, most notably CBS and NBC, were preparing for the time when rapid network expansion was most feasible—experimenting with various program formats and talent borrowed from their radio networks, as well as encouraging their most prestigious and financially successful radio affiliates to apply for television licenses.

Prime-time programming was a major problem for DuMont. The network would not or could not pay for expensive shows that would deliver large audiences, thereby attracting powerful sponsors. When a quality show drew a large audience in spite of its budget, it was snatched by CBS or NBC. DuMont televised the occasional successful show, including *Cavalcade of Stars* (before Jackie Gleason left), *Captain Video*, and Bishop Fulton J. Sheen's *Life Is Worth Living*. The network never seemed to generate enough popular programming to keep it afloat, however—possibly because it lacked the backing of a radio network.

The NBC, CBS and ABC radio networks provided financial support for their television ventures while the fledgling industry was growing—creating what the FCC deemed "an ironic situation in which one communications medium financed the development of its competitor." DuMont's only outside financial assistance came from Paramount Studios between 1938 and 1941. The company created and sold class-B common stock exclusively to Paramount for one dollar per share and a promise to provide

Allen B. DuMont

film-quality programming that was never delivered. The sale was performed to off-set heavy investments in research, development, and equipment manufacture, but as a result, Allen DuMont relinquished half-interest in his company and Paramount gained a strong measure of "negative" control—with their board members able to veto motions and withhold payment of funds.

Although they ceased financially assisting DuMont in 1941, Paramount maintained a presence on DuMont's board of directors. The Federal Communications Commission (FCC) ruled in 1948 that DuMont and Paramount must combine the number of stations they owned under ownership rules, hurting DuMont's ability to secure exclusive network owned-and-operated programming outlets. One question that remains unanswered is the amount of control Paramount actually did have over the DuMont organization. In 1949 the number of Paramount-controlled DuMont board of directors positions was reduced from four to three, but the FCC decision on Paramount control was not reversed.

The FCC "freeze" from 1948 to 1952 hurt the DuMont Network because during a period when the company was financially capable of expansion due to profits from TV set sales, it could add few additional affiliates. DuMont did claim a large number of affiliates compared to the other networks, but many of these appear to have taken only a few shows per week from DuMont and relied primarily on an affiliation with CBS and NBC. Analysts have suggested that DuMont's lack of primary affiliates was a key factor in the network's demise.

One important factor contributing to the demise of the DuMont Network was Allen B. DuMont himself. Many people thought of him as a "bypassed pioneer" with no head for business. Major stockholders began to publicly question the soundness of his decisions, especially his desire to keep the TV network afloat despite major losses. In 1955, concerned holders of large blocks of DuMont stock began to wrest control from the company founder.

When the fiscally weakened DuMont corporation spun off its television broadcasting facilities in 1955, *Business Week* claimed that DuMont had been forced into television programming in order to provide a market for his TV receivers. No evidence has been found to support this claim, however. In markets where licenses for television stations were being granted during the postwar period, there were sufficient license applicants to provide audiences with programming to stimulate set sales. One reason DuMont television sales lagged behind other manufactures was that his sets were of higher quality, and consequently much more expensive. In fact, in 1951 DuMont cut back television set production by 60%—although profits from this division had been subsidizing the TV network—because other manufactures were undercutting DuMont's prices.

After the DuMont Television Network and its owned-and-operated stations were spun off into a new corporation, there remained only two major divisions of Allen B. DuMont Laboratories, Inc. In 1958 Emerson Electric Company purchased the DuMont consumer products manufacturing division. DuMont was no longer employed by his own company when the last division—oscillograph and cathode-ray tube manufacturing—was sold to Fairchild in 1960. DuMont was hired by Fairchild as group general manager of the A. B. DuMont Division of Fairchild Camera and Instrument Corporation until his death in 1965.

DuMont may have remained in television broadcasting despite fiscal losses in order to uphold the title once given him, "the father of commercial television."

His company pioneered many important elements necessary to the growth and evolution of the industry. DuMont engineers perfected the use of cathode-ray tubes as TV screens, developed the kinescope process, as well as the "magic eye" cathode-ray radio tuning indicator, and the first electronic viewfinder. DuMont was an intelligent and energetic engineer who took risks and profited financially from them—becoming history's first television millionaire. But when the big radio networks entered the field of television, DuMont was unable to compete with these financially powerful, considerably experienced broadcasters.

—Philip J. Auter

ALLEN B(ALCOM) DUMONT. Born in Brooklyn, New York, U.S.A., 29 January 1901. Educated at Rensselaer Polytechnic Institute, Troy, New York, B.S. in electrical engineering 1924. Married: Ethel; children: Allen B., Jr., and Yvonne. Began career with the Westinghouse Lamp Company; conducted TV experiments in his garage, 1920s; developed an inexpensive cathode-ray tube that would last for thousands of hours (unlike the popular German import CRT, which lasted only 25 to 30 hours), DeForest Radio Company, 1930; left to found his laboratory, 1931; incorporated DuMont Labs, 1935; sold a half-interest to Paramount Pictures Corporation to raise capital for broadcasting stations, 1938; DuMont Labs was first company to market home television receiver, 1939; granted experimental TV licenses in Passaic, New Jersey, and New York, 1942; DuMont TV Network separated from DuMont Labs, sold to the Metropolitan Broadcasting Company; Emerson Radio and Phonograph Corp. purchased DuMont's television, phonograph, and stereo producing division; remaining DuMont interests merged with the Fairchild Camera and Instrument Corp., 1960; named group general manager of DuMont divisions of Fairchild, 1960; named senior technical consultant, 1961. Honorary doctorates: Rensselaer and Brooklyn Polytechnic Institutes. Recipient: Marconi Memorial Medal for Achievement, 1945; American Television Society, 1943; several trophies for accuracy in navigation and calculations in power-boat racing. Died in Montclair, New Jersey, 16 November 1965.

FURTHER READING

Auter, Philip. J., and Douglas A. Boyd. "DuMont: The Original Fourth Television Network." *Journal of Popular Culture* (Bowling Green, Ohio), Winter, 1995.

Barnouw, Erik. *Tube of Plenty: The Evolution of American Television.* New York: Oxford University Press, 1990.

Bergreen, Laurence. *Look Now, Pay Later: The Rise and Fall of Network Broadcasting.* New York: Doubleday, 1980.

Bochin, Hal W. "The Rise and Fall of the DuMont Network." In, Lichty, Lawrence, and Malachi Topping, editors. *A Sourcebook on the History of Radio and Television.* New York: Hastings House, 1975.

Brooks, Tim, and Earle Marsh. *The Complete Directory to Prime Time Network TV Shows: 1946-Present.* New York: Ballantine, 1976; 3rd edition, 1985.

"The Five-Year Color War." *Television-Radio Age* (New York), 28 September 1987.

Hess, Gary. N. *An Historical Study of the Du Mont Television Network.* New York: Arno Press, 1979.

"Pioneer of TV DuMont Dies." *The Washington (D.C.) Post,* 16 November 1965.

Sterling, Christopher. H., and John M. Kittross. *Stay Tuned: A Concise History of American Broadcasting.* Belmont, California: Wadsworth, 1985; 2nd edition, 1990.

U.S. Federal Communications Commission. *Seventh Annual Report.* Washington, D.C.: Government Printing Office, 1941.

White, Timothy R. *Hollywood's Attempt to Appropriate Television: The Case of Paramount Pictures* (Ph.D. dissertation, University of Wisconsin-Madison, 1990).

See also Army-McCarthy Hearings; United States: Networks

DYER, GWYNNE

Canadian Journalist/Producer

Gwynne Dyer is a Canadian journalist, syndicated columnist and military analyst. He is best known for his documentary television series, *War*, which echoed the peace movement's growing concern over the threat of nuclear war in the early 1980s. Nominated for an Oscar in 1985, it was based on his own military experience and extensive study.

After serving in the naval reserves of Canada, the United States, and Britain, Dyer completed his doctoral studies in military history at King's College, University of London, in 1973. He lectured on military studies for the next four years before producing a seven-part radio series, *Seven Faces of Communism* for the CBC and ABC in 1978. This quickly led to other radio series, including *War*, in six parts, in 1981. Based on this series, he was invited by the National Film Board of Canada, the country's public film producer, to enlarge it into a seven-part film series in 1983. Upon release to critical acclaim, the series was broadcast in forty-five countries.

War was a reflection of Dyer's own growing concern about the proliferation of new technology, its impact on the changing nature of warfare and the growing threat of nuclear annihilation. Filmed in ten countries and with the participation of six national armies, it examined the nature, evolution and consequences of warfare. It featured interviews with top-level NATO and Warsaw Pact military leaders and strategist, many of whom spoke to the Western media for the first time. The series argued that in an era of total war, professional armies were no longer able to fulfill their traditional roles. The growth of nationalism, conscript armies and nuclear technology had brought the world perilously close to Armageddon. *War* offered the unique perspective of the soldier from the rigorous training of young U.S. marine recruits at the Parris Island Training Depot in South Carolina, to the field exercises conducted by NATO and Warsaw Pact countries in Europe. It presented military officers from both sides talking frankly about how nuclear technology had changed their profession and follows them as they vividly describe how any superpower conflict would inevitably lead to an all-out nuclear war. Dyer argued that the danger posed by the explosive mix of ideology and nuclear technology could only be mitigated by a total elimination of nuclear arsenals.

This award-winning series was soon followed by another production for the National Film Board of Canada in 1986, *The Defence of Canada*, an examination of Canada's military role on the international scene. Following similar arguments postulated in *War*, Dyer called for Canada to set an example by rethinking its position in NATO and NORAD. He maintained his ties in the Soviet Union and from 1988 to 1990 produced a six-part radio series *The Gorbachev Revolution*, which followed the thunderous changes occurring in Eastern Europe. He served as a military commentator in Canada during the Gulf War, and in 1994 his series *The Human Race* was

Gwynne Dyer

broadcast nationally on the CBC. It was a personal enquiry into the roots, nature and future of human politics and the threat posed by tribalism, nationalism and technology to the world's environment. He continues to publish his syndicated column on international affairs, which is published on over 300 papers in some 30 countries.

—Manon Lamontagne

GWYNNE DYER. Born in St. John's, Newfoundland, Canada, 17 April 1943. Educated at the Memorial University of Newfoundland, B.A. in history, 1963; Rice University, Houston, Texas, U.S.A., M.A. in military history 1966; King's College, University of London, Ph.D. in military and middle eastern history 1973. Served as reserve naval officer, Royal Canadian Naval Reserve, 1956-64, 1966-68; U.S. Naval Reserve, 1964–66; British Royal Navy Reserve, 1968–73. Lecturer in military history, Canadian Forces College in Toronto, Ontario; senior lecturer in war studies, Royal Military Academy, Sandhurst, England, 1973–77; producer of various radio and television special series, from 1978; syndicated columnist, international affairs from 1973.

Recipient: International Film Festival Awards; International Film Festival Awards, 1984; Best Writing Gemini for *The Space Between*, 1986.

TELEVISION DOCUMENTARY SERIES
1983   *War* (co-writer and host)
1986   *The Defence of Canada*
1994   *The Human Race* (host)

FILMS
The Space Between (co-writer/host), 1986; *Harder than It Looks*, 1987; *Escaping from History* (writer), 1994; *The Gods of Our Fathers* (writer), 1994; *The Tribal Mind* (writer), 1994; *The Bomb Under the World* (writer), 1994.

RADIO
Seven Faces of Communism, 1978; *Goodbye War*, 1979 (writer-narrator); *War*, 1981; *The Gorbachev Revolution*, 1988–90; *Millennium*, 1996.

FURTHER READING
"Dyer's Contrived Truth Doesn't Tackle the Real Consequences." *Vancouver* (Canada) *Sun*, 3 September 1994.
Dodds, Carolyn. "Too Close for Comfort." *Saturday Night* (Toronto), August 1988
"Recording a Global Culture." *Maclean's* (Toronto), 25 March, 1996.

See also Canadian Programming in English

DYKE, GREG
British Media Executive

Greg Dyke has been one of the most powerful leaders among the British independent television companies, having headed up TV-AM, Television South, and London Weekend Television. His 1995 departure from network television to become head of the television interests of the Pearson Group, and member of the board of the satellite-delivered television group British Sky Broadcasting (BSkyB), signalled the switch of his considerable influence from mainstream television to the new multi-channel systems. To outsiders, it suggested that the satellite companies were buying a man who understood competitive scheduling and who could help them to take audiences from both ITV and BBC.

Greg Dyke's success in the industry proved that it was no longer necessary for top British television people to come from Oxbridge and start their careers in the BBC. Unlike most BBC executives, Dyke had a varied career after leaving grammar school at age 16: he worked for various local papers, gained a politics degree at York University as a mature student, and became campaign organizer for Wandsworth Council of Community Relations.

His television career began when he joined *The London Program* in the 1970s, and rapidly rose to become producer of *Weekend World* and deputy editor of the *London Program*. In 1981 he was given command of his own creation, *The Six O'Clock Show*, an energetic magazine program fronted by Janet Street-Porter and Danny Baker. Dyke proved to his production teams that he was an inspirational manager and able administrator.

Dyke's greatest success was, almost single-handedly, to save TV-AM. The 1981 franchised breakfast company was heading for bankruptcy when Dyke was called in to bring back its audience. Dyke took the ailing breakfast show down-market, signalling this move with the introduction of bingo numbers, horoscopes, and a gormless puppet called

Roland Rat. The ratings rose from 200,000 to 1.8 million in 12 months, and the eventual gain was twentyfold. Observers waited to see if the Independent Broadcasting Authority would complain about these down-market tactics, but no breath of criticism was heard from the upmarket portals of their Knightsbridge headquarters. Better ratings were regarded as more important than cultural qualities.

Greg Dyke
Photo courtesy of the British Film Institute

Any program controller who could build ratings was much in demand. Dyke eventually resigned from TV-AM over budget cuts, and was quickly hired by Television South as director of programs, from where he returned to LWT as director of programs, and then chief executive. Perhaps his most significant promotion was to replace his good friend and former colleague John Birt on the ITV Program Controllers' group. When Dyke rose to become chair of that vital group, he effectively orchestrated the ITV companies' scheduling against the BBC.

Dyke's significance lies partly in the fact that a skilled manipulator of good ratings can also become a shrewd and successful company manager. LWT's chair Sir Christopher Bland, sent Dyke off to Harvard for a three month-management course. When he returned, Dyke showed that he was quite prepared to put business efficiency above his Labour Party principles, and over four years he made 690 staff redundant, with a lavish $45 million redundancy package. He claimed afterwards that to restructure completely a business for less than one year's profits was a good deal. One part of his changes involved transforming the South Bank Television Center into a profit center rather than a service organization. This move proved successful, and in 1995 no less than four different television organizations, the breakfast franchise GMGT, Carlton Television, Hatrick Productions and LWT itself all used the South Bank studios.

By 1993 Dyke was chief executive of London Weekend Television Holdings, chair of the ITV Association, and chair of ITV Sport. Under his command, LWT flourished as never before, with excellent programs like *Blind Date* and *Beadle's About*. But successful companies always risk the danger of being taken over unless they are protected by government regulation, as was the case for ITV companies. When the Conservatives abolished these restrictions in 1993, LWT was at risk. Granada swallowed LWT for $900 million in 1994 and Dyke resigned rather than work under Granada control. With $1.75 million dollars worth of share option, Dyke made a $12 million profit from the Granada bid.

Dyke is perhaps the outstanding ITV babyboomer: generous, perennially optimistic, and very widely experienced. His friends say he is motivated, streetwise and understands popular TV. His critics suggest that he is a lightweight, with a tendency to speak out quickly. Certainly his impact on ITV has been considerable. His move to Pearson and BSkyB illustrates clearly that the old ratings war between ITV and BBC is out of date; now terrestrial broadcasters will struggle together to protect their falling share of the market from the new mediums of cable and satellite programming.

—Andrew Quicke

GREGORY DYKE. Born 20 May 1947. Attended Hayes Grammar School; University of York, B.A. in politics. Two sons and two daughters. Had varied career, 1965–83, before being appointed editor in chief, TV-AM, 1983–84; director of programmes, TVS, 1984–87; director of programmes, 1987–91, deputy managing director, 1989–90, managing director and subsequently group chief executive, 1990–94, London Weekend Television; director, Channel Four Television, 1988–91; chair, ITV Council, 1991–94; director, BSkyB, since 1995; chair, Pearson Television, from 1995. Address: Pearson Television, Teddington Studios, Teddington Lock, Middlesex TW11 9NT, England.

See also British Production Companies; British Sky Broadcasting

DYNASTY

U.S. Serial Melodrama

Premiering as a three-hour movie on 12 January 1981, the prime-time soap opera *Dynasty* aired on ABC until 1989. *Dynasty* quickly worked its way into the top five rated programs, finishing fifth for the 1982-83 season and third for the 1983–84 season. It was the number one ranked program for the 1984–85 season, but rapidly began losing viewers. By its final season (1988–89), *Dynasty* finished tied for 57th place, and was unceremoniously dumped from ABC's roster leaving numerous dangling plotlines. These plotlines were tied up in a two-part, four-hour movie, *Dynasty: The Reunion*, which aired on ABC on 20 and 22 October 1991, some two years after the series' cancellation.

The soap opera focused primarily on the lives and loves of Blake Carrington (John Forsythe), a wealthy Denver oil tycoon, his wife Krystle (Linda Evans), ex-wife, Alexis (Joan Collins), daughter Fallon (Pamela Sue Martin, Emma Samms), sons Steven (Al Corley, Jack Coleman) and Adam (Gordon Thomson), as well as numerous extended family members and associates including Fallon's husband/ex-husband Jeff Colby (John James) and Krystle's niece and Steven's wife/ex-wife, Sammy Jo (Heather Locklear).

The program relied on both camp and excess for its appeal. Its characters and plotlines were sometimes absurd and broadly drawn, but it was the trappings of wealth, glamour, and fashion which drew viewers in some 70 countries to the program. With a weekly budget of $1.2 million ($10,000 of which went for clothing alone, including at least ten Nolan Miller creations per episode), *Dynasty* placed more emphasis on style than on plot.

The plotlines of this prime-time soap opera often resembled those of its daytime counterparts—kidnapped babies, amnesia, pregnancy, infidelity, and treachery. In fact, *Dynasty* made extensive use of one soap-opera staple—the return to life of characters presumed dead. Both Fallon and Steven Carrington were killed off only to return in later seasons played by different actors.

Just as often, however, *Dynasty*'s plots leaned toward the campy and absurd. One of the most talked about and ridiculed plots was the 1985 season-ending cliffhanger which saw the Carringtons gathered for a wedding in the country of Moldavia. Terrorists stormed the ceremony in a hail of machine-gun fire, but when the smoke cleared (at the start of the next season, of course), all of the primary characters were alive and basically unscathed.

While often criticized for its weak and at times absurd plots, *Dynasty* did provide juicy roles for women, notably Joan Collins' characterization of Alexis. Her character—scheming, conniving, and ruthless—was often referred to as a "superbitch," and was the quintessential "character you love to hate." Alexis was set in opposition to Krystle who was more of a "good girl"—sweet, loyal, and loving. One of the best-known scenes in *Dynasty* history was the 1983 "cat fight" between Alexis and Krystle in which they literally fought it out in a lily pond. Alexis met her match in the character of wealthy singer and nightclub owner, Dominique Devereaux (Diahann Carroll)—the first prominently-featured African-American character on a prime-time soap opera.

During its nearly nine-year run, *Dynasty* spawned the short-lived spin-off *Dynasty II: The Colbys* (1985-87) and gave rise to numerous licensed luxury products, including perfume, clothing, and bedding. Never before had television product licensing been so targeted to upscale adults.

When *Dynasty* left the air in 1989, it also marked the demise of the prime-time soap opera which had been a staple of television programming through the 1980s. Produced in part by Aaron Spelling, whose programs (e.g., *Charlie's Angels, The Love Boat, Beverly Hills, 90210*, and *Melrose Place*) have emphasized beauty, wealth, and glamour, *Dynasty* had proved the perfect metaphor for 1980s greed and excess. In declaring *Dynasty* the best prime-time soap of the decade, *TV Guide* asserted its "campy opulence gave it a superb, ironic quality—in other words, it was great trash."

—Sharon R.Mazzarella

CAST

Blake Carrington	John Forsythe
Krystle Jennings Carrington	Linda Evans
Alexis Carrington Colby	Joan Collins
Fallon Carrington Colby (1981–84) . .	Pamela Sue Martin
Fallon Carrington Colby (1985, 1987–89)	Emma Samms
Steven Carrington (1981–82)	Al Corley
Steven Carrington (1982–88)	Jack Coleman
Adam Carrington/Michael Torrance (1982–1989)	
. . . .	Gordon Thomson
Cecil Colby (1981–82)	Lloyd Bochner
Jeff Colby (1981–85, 1987–89)	John James
Claudia Blaisdel (1981–86)	Pamela Bellwood
Matthew Blaisdel (1981)	Bo Hopkins
Lindsay Blaisdel (1981)	Katy Kurtzman
Walter Lankershim (1981)	Dale Robertson
Jeannette	Virginia Hawkins

Dynasty

Joseph Anders (1981–83)	Lee Bergere
Kirby (1982–84)	Kathleen Beller
Andrew Laird (1981–84)	Peter Mark Richman
Sammy Jo Dean	Heather Locklear
Michael Culhane (1981, 1986–87) . .	Wayne Northrop
Dr. Nick Toscanni (1981–82)	James Farentino
Mark Jennings (1982–84)	Geoffrey Scott
Congressman Neal McEane (1982–84, 1987) .	Paul Burke
Chris Deegan (1983)	Grant Goodeve
Tracy Kendall (1983–84)	Deborah Adair
Farnsworth "Dex" Dexter (1983–89) . . .	Michael Nader
Peter de Vilbis (1983–84)	Helmut Berger
Amanda Carrington (1984–86) . . .	Catherine Oxenberg
Amanda Carrington (1986–87)	Karen Cellini
Dominique Deveraux (1984–87)	Diahann Carroll
Gerard (1984–89)	William Beckley
Gordon Wales (1984–88)	James Sutorius
Luke Fuller (1984–85)	William Campbell
Nicole Simpson (1984–85)	Susan Scannell
Charles (1984–85)	George DiCenzo
Daniel Reece (1984–85)	Rock Hudson
Lady Ashley Mitchell (1985)	Ali MacGraw
Danny Carrington (1985–88)	Jameson Sampley
Joel Abrigore (1985–86)	George Hamilton
Garrett Boydston (1985–86)	Ken Howard

PRODUCERS Richard and Ethel Shapiro, Aaron Spelling, E. Duke Vincent, Philip Parslow, Elaine Rich, Ed Ledding

PROGRAMMING HISTORY

• ABC

January 1981–April 1981	Monday 9:00-10:00
July 1981–September 1983	Wednesday 10:00-11:00
September 1983–May 1984	Wednesday 9:00-10:00
August 1984–May 1986	Wednesday 9:00-10:00
September 1986–May 1987	Wednesday 9:00-10:00
September 1987–March 1988	Wednesday 10:00-11:00
November 1988–May 1989	Wednesday 10:00-11:00

FURTHER READING

"The Best Prime-time Soaps." *TV Guide* (Radnor, Pennsylvania), 17 April 1993.

Dynasty: The Authorized Biography of the Carringtons, introduction by Esther Shapiro. Garden City, New York: Doubleday, 1984.

Feuer, Jane. "Reading *Dynasty*: Television and Reception Theory." *South Atlantic Quarterly* (Durham, North Carolina), Spring 1989.

Geraghty, Christine. *Women and Soap Opera: A Study of Prime Time Soaps.* Cambridge, England: Polity, 1991.

Gripsrud, Jostein. "The *Dynasty*-Event in Norway: The Role of Print Media." *Edda: Nordisk Tidsskrift for Litteraturforskning/Scandinavian Journal of Literary Research* (Dragvoll, Norway), 1989.

———. *The Dynasty Years: Hollywood Television and Critical Media Studies.* London and New York: Routledge, 1995.

———. "Toward a Flexible Methodology in Studying Media Meaning: *Dynasty* in Norway." *Critical Studies in Mass Communication* (Annandale, Virginia), 1990.

Schroder, Kim Christian. "The Playful Audience: The Continuity of the Popular Cultural Tradition in America." *The Dolphin: Publications of the English Department, University of Aarhus* (Aarhus, Denmark), 1989.

White, Mimi. "Women, Memory and Serial Melodrama." *Screen*, (Oxford, England), Winter 1994.

See also *Dallas*; Forsythe, John; Melodrama

E

AN EARLY FROST

U.S. Television Movie

An Early Frost, broadcast on 11 November 1985 on the NBC network, was the first American made-for-television movie and the second prime-time dramatic program to acknowledge the presence and spread of AIDS in the 1980s. Because the movie was about the potentially controversial topic of homosexuality and the impact of AIDS on the beleaguered community of gay men, much care went into the preproduction process. First, for more than a year, there was much interaction between writers Dan Lipman and Ron Cowen and NBC's Broadcast Standards and Practices department about the script. Such thorough development is highly unusual for most made-for-television movies. This interaction attempted to insure a delicate balance in the presentation of sensitive subject matter. In addition, NBC gathered a cast of actors—Aidan Quin, Genna Rowlands, Ben Gazzara, and Sylvia Sidney—who were most often associated with theatrically released films. The network also secured the service of Emmy-award winning director Jon Erman for the project. These choices, they hoped, would enhance the production's aura of quality and deflect any criticism about exploitation of the tragic pandemic.

Scriptwriters Lipman and Cowen consciously framed the narrative about AIDS in the generic conventions of the family melodrama. Strategically, this approach provided a familiar, less threatening environment in which to present information and issues surrounding gay men and the disease. At one level, the narrative of An Early Frost exposes the tenuous links which hold the middle-class Pierson family together. On the surface, life appears to be idyllic. Nick Pierson is the successful owner of a lumber yard. He and his wife Kate have reared two seemingly well-adjusted children in a suburban neighborhood. Son Michael is a rising young lawyer in Chicago. Daughter Susan has replicated her parents' lifestyle, married with one child and expecting a second.

Under the surface, however, several familial fissures exist. Nick's upwardly mobile class aspirations are stalled. Kate's creative talent as a concert pianist has been sublimated into the demands of being a wife and mother. Susan acquiesces to her own husband's demands, rather than follow her own desires. Unknown to the family, Michael, a closeted gay man, lives with his lover Peter. The fragile veneer of familial stability bursts apart when Michael learns he has AIDS,

exposing all the resentments which various family members have repressed.

The script also includes a parallel narrative thread exploring the conflicts in the gay relationship between Michael and Peter. Their relationship suffers from Michael's workaholic attitude towards his job. Conflict also grows out of Peter's openness about his gayness and Michael's inability to be open about his sexuality. The tension between the two is further exacerbated when Michael discovers that Peter has been unfaithful because of these conflicts.

When broadcast, An Early Frost drew a thirty-three share of the viewing audience, winning its time slot for the evening's ratings, and thus suggesting that the American public was ready to engage in a cultural discussion of the disease. Even so, the ratings success did not translate into economic profits for NBC. According to Perry Lafferty, the NBC vice president who commissioned the project, the

An Early Frost

network lost $500,000 in advertising revenues because clients were afraid to have their commercials shown during the broadcast. Apparently, advertisers believed the subject matter was too controversial because of its homosexual theme and too depressing because of the terminal nature of AIDS as a disease.

These concerns inhibited further production of other made-for-television scripts about AIDS until 1988. Ironically, the production quality of *An Early Frost* became a hallmark by which members of the broadcasting industry measured any subsequent development of movie scripts about AIDS. Arthur Allan Seidelman, director of an NBC afternoon school-break special about AIDS titled *An Enemy Among Us*, has stated, "there was some concern after *An Early Frost* was done that 'How many more things can you do about AIDS?'" Any new scripts had to live up to and move beyond the standard set by Cowen and Lipman's original made-for-television movie. Although providing the initial mainstream cultural space to examine AIDS, *An Early Frost*, also in some ways, hindered increased discussion of the disease in prime-time American broadcast programming precisely because it achieved its narrative and informational goals so well.

—Rodney A. Buxton

CAST

Nick Pierson	Ben Gazzara
Michael Pierson	Aidan Quin
Katherine Pierson	Gena Rowlands
Beatrice McKenna	Sylvia Sidney
Susan Maracek	Sydney Walsh
Bob Maracek	Bill Paxton
Victor DiMato	John Glover
Peter Hilton	D.W. Moffett
Dr. Redding	Terry O'Quinn
Christine	Cheryl Anderson

PRODUCER   Perry Lafferty

PROGRAMMING HISTORY

• NBC

11 November 1985

FURTHER READING

Buxton, Rodney. *Broadcast Formats, Fictional Narratives and Controversy: Network Television's Depiction of AIDS, 1983–1991* (Ph.D. Dissertation, University of Texas at Austin, 1992).

Farber, S. "A Decade into the AIDS Epidemic the TV Networks Are Still Nervous." *The New York Times*, 2 May 1991.

Russo, Vito. *The Celluloid Closet: Homosexuality in the Movies, Revised.* New York: Harper and Row, 1987.

Watney, Simon. *Policing Desire: Pornography, AIDS and the Media.* Minneapolis: University of Minnesota Press, 1987.

See also Sexual Orientation and Television

EAST SIDE/WEST SIDE

U.S. Drama

East Side/West Side, an hour-long dramatic series, first appeared on CBS in September 1963. Though it lasted only a single season, it is a significant program in television history because of the controversial subject matter it tackled each week and the casting of black actress Cicely Tyson in a recurring lead role as secretary Jane Foster.

During the Kennedy years, with an increased regulatory zeal emanating from the Federal Commmunications Commission, the networks attempted to de-emphasize the violence of action-adventure series. One result was an increase in character dramas. There was a trend toward programs based on liberal social themes in which the protagonists were professionals in service to society. As one producer of that era explained, "The guns of gangsters, policemen, and western lawmen were replaced by the stethoscope, the law book, and the psychiatrist's couch." This new breed of episodic TV hero struggled with occupational ethics and felt a disillusionment with values of the past.

Unlike action-adventure series in which heroes often settled their problems with a weapon, the troubles in New Frontier character dramas were not always resolved. Writers grappled with issues such as poverty, prejudice, drug addiction, abortion, and capital punishment, which do not lend themselves to tidy resolutions. Although the loose ends of a plot might be tied together by story's end, the world was not necessarily depicted as a better place at the conclusion of an episode.

East Side/West Side, produced by David Susskind and Daniel Melnick, was among the best of the genre and won instant acclaim. The program about a New York social worker appealed to sophisticates because, according to Lawrence Laurent of *The Washington Post*, it violated "every sacred tenet for television success." Typical TV heroes all had a similar look, said Laurent, "short straight noses, direct from a plastic surgeon, gleaming smiles courtesy of a dental laboratory." But Neil Brock, played by George C. Scott, observed Laurent, was "hooknosed and disheveled."

An exemplary episode of *East Side/West Side* entitled "Who Do You Kill?" aired on 4 November 1963. The story portrays how a black couple in their early twenties living in a Harlem tenement face the death of their infant daughter, who is bitten by a rat while in her crib. Diana Sands played the mother who works in a neighborhood bar to support the family. Her husband, played by James Earl Jones, is frustrated by unemployment and grows more bitter each day.

The week after the broadcast, Senator Jacob Javits, a liberal, pro-civil rights Republican, moved that two newspaper articles be entered into the *Congressional Record*: "A CBS Show Stars Two Negroes: Atlanta Blacks It Out," from the *New York Herald Tribune*, and from *The New York Times*, "TV: A Drama of Protest." Javits praised CBS for displaying courage in airing "Who Do You Kill?" and told his Senate colleagues he was distressed that not all Southern viewers had the opportunity to see the drama. The program, Javits said, "dealt honestly and sensitively with the vital problems of job discrimination, housing conditions and the terrible cancerous cleavage that can exist between the Negro and the white community." "Who Do You Kill?" he said, was "shocking in its revelations of what life can be like without hope."

The stark realism of the series was discomforting. Most viewers didn't know what to make of a hero who was often dazed by moral complexities. For CBS the series was a bust; one-third of the advertising time remained unsold and the program was not renewed. A few years later David Susskind reflected on the ratings problem of *East Side/West Side*: "A gloomy atmosphere for commercial messages, an integrated cast, and a smaller Southern station lineup, all of these things coming together spelled doom for the show. I'm sorry television wasn't mature enough to absorb it and like it and live with it."

—Mary Ann Watson

CAST

Neil Brock . . . . George C. Scott
Frieda Hechlinger . . . . Elizabeth Wilson
Jane Foster . . . . Cicely Tyson

PRODUCERS   David Susskind, Don Kranze, Arnold Perl, Larry Arrick

East Side/West Side

PROGRAMMING HISTORY   26 Episodes

• CBS

September 1963–September 1964   Monday 10:00-11:00

FURTHER READING

Watson, Mary Ann. *The Expanding Vista: American Television in the Kennedy Years.* New York: Oxford University Press, 1990.

See also Melodrama

EASTENDERS

British Soap Opera

*E*astEnders is one of Britain's most successful television soap operas. First shown on BBC1 in 1985, it enjoys regular half-hour prime-time viewing slots, originally twice and more recently three times a week, repeated in an omnibus edition at the weekend. Within eight months of its launch, it reached the number one spot in the ratings and has almost consistently remained amongst the top five programmes ever since (average viewing figures per episode are around 16 million). A brief dip in audience numbers in the summer of 1983 prompted a rescheduling masterstroke by the then BBC1 controller, Michael Grade, in order to avoid

the clash with ITV's more established soap, *Emmerdale Farm.* The brainchild of producer, Julia Smith, and script editor, Tony Holland, *EastEnders* is significant in terms of both the survival of the BBC and the history of British popular television drama.

In the increasingly competitive struggle with independent television for quality of programmes and appeal to mass audiences, the BBC claimed to have found in *EastEnders* the answer to both a shrinking audience and criticisms of declining standards. The programme is set in Walford, a fictitious borough of London's East End, and focuses on a number of predominantly working-class, often interrelated, families living in Albert Square. The East End of London was regarded as the ideal location for an alluring and long-running series as its historical significance in Britain renders it instantly recognisable, and as illustrative of modern urban Britain for possessing a mix of individuals who are, according to Smith and Holland, "multi-racial, larger-than-life characters". Much of the action takes place in and around the local pub, the Queen Vic, traditionally run by the Watts—originally villainous Den and his neurotic wife Angie, and later their estranged adoptive daughter, Sharon. The main characters are connected with the closely-knit Fowler/Beale clan, specifically Pauline and Arthur Fowler, their eldest children, Mark—a HIV-positive market trader, and Michelle—a strong-willed, single mother, together with cafe-owner Kathy Beale and the long-suffering Pat Butcher. Additional figures come and go, highlighting the belief that character turnover is essential if a contemporary quality is to be retained. At any one time, around eight families, all living or working in Albert Square, will feature centrally in one or other narrative.

EastEnders exhibits certain formal characteristics common to other successful British soap operas (most notably, its major competitor, Granada's *Coronation Street*), such as the working-class community setting and the prevalence of strong female characters. In addition, a culturally diverse cast strives to preserve the flavour of the East End, whilst a gender balance is allegedly maintained through the introduction of various "macho" male personalities. The expansion of minority representation signals a move away from the traditional soap opera format, providing more opportunities for audience identification with the characters and hence a wider appeal. Similarly, the programme has recently included more teenagers and successful young adults in a bid to capture the younger television audience. The programme's attraction, however, is also a product of a narrative structure unique to the genre. The soap opera has been described as an "open text", a term relating primarily to the simultaneous development and indeterminate nature of the storylines, and the variety of issue positions presented through the different characters. Such a structure invites viewer involvement in the personal relationships and family lives of the characters without fear of repercussions, through recognition of "realistic" situations or personal dilemmas rather than through identification with a central character. *EastEnders* is typical of the soap opera in this respect, maintaining at any one time two or more major and several minor intertwining narratives, with cliffhangers at the ends of episodes and (temporary) resolutions within the body of some episodes.

To fulfil its public service remit, the programme aims to both entertain and educate. The mystery surrounding the father of Michelle's baby and the emotionality of the AIDS-related death of Mark's girlfriend, Jill, illustrate how a dramatic representation of social issues in contemporary Britain successfully combines these elements. Throughout its ten-year history, issues such as drug addiction, abortion, AIDS, homosexuality, racial and domestic violence, stabbings and teenage pregnancy have

EastEnders
Photo courtesy of the British Film Institute

graced the programme's social and moral agenda. *EastEnders* strives to be realistic and relevant rather than issue-led, with the educational element professed as an incidental outcome of its commitment to realism. Such endeavours have been attacked, with criticisms of minority-group tokenism, depressive issue-mongering, and, paradoxically, lapses into Cockney stereotyping. However, over the last few years the number of "overly diagrammatic characters" such as "Colin the gay" (so described by Medhurst in *The Observer*) appears to have decreased, with new characters being introduced for their dramatic contribution rather than their sociological significance.

As with other British soaps, *EastEnders* differs from American soaps by its relentless emphasis on the mundane and nitty-gritty details of working-class life (no middle-class soap has yet succeeded for long in Britain) among ordinary-looking (rather than attractive) and relatively unsuccessful people. This potentially depressing mix is lightened by a dose of British humour and wit, by the dramatic intensity of the emotions and issues portrayed, and by the nostalgic gloss given to the portrayal of solidarity and warmth in a supposedly authentic community. In terms of the image of "ordinary life" conveyed by the programme, *EastEnders* is again typical of the soap opera for its ambivalences—showing strong women who are nonetheless tied to the home; a community which tries to pull together but a relatively disaffected youth; a romantic faith in love and marriage and yet a series of adulterous affairs and divorces. For its audience, *EastEnders* is highly pleasurable for its apparent realism, its honesty in addressing contentious issues, and for its cosy familiarity.

A regular feature of the weekly schedules, *EastEnders* has become a fundamental and prominent part of British television culture. Public and media interest extends beyond plot and character developments to the extra-curricular activities of cast members. While maintaining the essential soap opera characteristics, it distinguishes itself from the other major British soaps, appearing coarser, faster paced, and more dramatic than *Coronation Street* yet less controversial and more humourous than *Brookside*. In the words of Andy Medhurst of *The Observer*, "*EastEnders* remains the BBC's most important piece of fiction, a vital sign of its commitment to deliver quality and popularity in the same unmissable package". While in many ways typical of the genre, the obvious quality, cultural prominence and audience success of *EastEnders* has established the soap opera as a valued centre piece of early primetime broadcasting in Britain.

—Danielle Aron and Sonia Livingstone

CAST

Lou Beale	Anna Wing
Pauline Fowler	Wendy Richard
Arthur Fowler	Bill Treacher
Michelle Fowler	Susan Tully
Mark Fowler	David Scarboro
Pete Beale	Peter Dean
Kathy Beale	Gillian Taylforth
Ian Beale	Adam Woodyatt
Den Watts	Leslie Grantham
Angie Watts	Anita Dobson
Sharon Watts	Letitia Dean
Ethel Skinner	Gretchen Franklin
Dr. Legg	Leonard Fenton
Nick Cotton	John Altmn
Sue Osman	Sandy Ratcliff
Ali Osman	Najdet Salih
Saeed Jeffrey	Andrew Johnson
Naima Jeffrey	Shreela Ghesh
George Holloway	Tom Watt
Mary Smith	Linda Davidson
Tony Carpenter	Oscar James
Kelvin Carpenter	Paul Medford
Debbie Wilkins	Shirley Cheriton
Andy O'Brien	Ross Davidson
Dot Cotton	June Brown
Simon Wicks	Nick Berry
James Wilmott-Brown	William Boyd
Colin Russell	Michael Cashman
Pat Wicks/Butcher	Pam St Clements
Rod Norman	Christopher McHallem
Carmel Roberts	Judith Jacob
Barry Clark	Gary Hailes
Frank Butcher	Mike Reid
Cindy	Michelle Collins
Diane Butcher	Sophie Lawrence
Grant Mitchell	Ross Kemp
Phil Mitchell	Steve McFadden
Clyde Tavernier	Steven Woodcock
Mark Fowler	Todd Carty
Eddie Royle	Michael Melia
Rachel	Jacquetta May

PRODUCERS Julia Smith, Mike Gibbon, Corinne Hollingworth, Richard Bramall, Michael Ferguson, Pat Sandys, Helen Greaves, Leonard Lewis

PROGRAMMING HISTORY

• BBC

February 1985-Present

FURTHER READING

Buckingham, D. *Public Secrets: EastEnders and its Audience.* London: British Film Institute, 1987.

Frentz, S., editor. *Staying Tuned: Contemporary Soap Opera Criticism.* Ohio: Bowling Green State University Popular Press, 1992.

Geraghty, C. *Women in Soap Operas.* London: Polity Press, 1990.

Livingstone, S. M. *Making Sense of Television: The Psychology of Audience Interpretation.* Oxford: Pergamon, 1990.

———. "Why People Watch Soap Opera: An Analysis of the Explanations of British Viewers." *European Journal of Communication* (London), 1988.

See also British Programming; *Brookside, Coronation Street;* Soap Opera

EBERSOL, DICK

U.S. Media Executive

In his various executive positions Duncan Dickie Ebersol has contributed several innovations to the NBC television network. He shepherded *Saturday Night Live* onto the air, then returned as producer to "rescue" the show in the early 1980s. As president of NBC Sports, he pursued several inventive and sometimes risky programming packages such as the Olympics Triple-Cast and the Baseball Network. Throughout his career he has been recognized as one of television's more creative programmers.

Ebersol became hooked on television sports when he saw the debut of *ABC's Wide World of Sports* in 1963. Later, when that show was shooting in his area, he got errand jobs with the crew. By the winter of 1968 he was working as a research assistant for ABC's coverage of the Winter Olympics in Grenoble, France, and while finishing his studies at Yale, he worked full-time as a segment producer. In 1971, following graduation, he became an executive assistant and producer with Roone Arledge, vice president of ABC Sports and creator of *Wide World of Sports*.

NBC tried to hire Ebersol in 1974 by offering to name him president of their sports division, but at the age of 27, he decided he wasn't ready to compete against Arledge. Instead, he moved to NBC with a new title: director of Weekend Late Night Programming. At that time the programming slots following the Saturday and Sunday late news were a dead zone for all three networks. Affiliates made more money with old movies than with network offerings—in NBC's case, reruns of *The Tonight Show*. The network charged Ebersol with finding something, anything, to replace the Carson reruns.

Ebersol conceived of a comedy-variety revue aimed at young adults, an audience generally thought to be away from home—and television—on weekends. He assumed enough of them would stay home to watch a show featuring "underground" comedians like George Carlin and Richard Pryor, especially when supported with a repertory cast picked from new improv-based, television-savvy comedy groups such as Second City, the National Lampoon stage shows or the Groundlings. Ebersol also discovered Lorne Michaels, a former writer for *Rowan and Martin's Laugh-In,* who had produced specials for Lily Tomlin and Flip Wilson, and had been lobbying for just the kind of program Ebersol was thinking of.

As Michaels assembled the cast and writers, Ebersol ran interference for *Saturday Night Live* before nervous network management and affiliates. The pair spurned NBC's suggestions for safe hosts like Bob Hope and Joe Namath, and secured Pryor, Carlin and Tomlin for that role. As *Saturday Night Live* took off, NBC promoted Ebersol to vice president of Late-Night Programs, with an office in Burbank and responsibility over every late show that did not belong to Johnny Carson. Ebersol had become, at 28, the youngest vice president in NBC history.

By 1977, he had become head of NBC's comedy and variety programming. Unfortunately, this was a fallow time for comedy, especially for NBC. Ebersol has said that his only success in this period was hiring Brandon Tartikoff away from ABC to be his associate. After a confrontation with new programming director Fred Silverman, Ebersol quit his position at NBC, and Tartikoff replaced him. He went into independent production, taking over *The Midnight Special* and various sports programming. Shortly afterward, however, NBC asked him to rescue *Saturday Night Live (SNL).*

Lorne Michaels had left *SNL* after the 1979–80 season, and the original cast and writing staff left as well. Replacement producer Jean Doumanian's tenure proved a disaster: the show's daring, edgy satire went over the edge with sketches like "The Leather Weather Lady." NBC executives had seen enough with Doumanian's twelfth show, when cast member Charles Rocket absent-mindedly said "fuck" on the air. Doumanian was fired, and Ebersol agreed to produce the show if NBC would end *Midnight Special.*

Ebersol took *Saturday Night Live* off the air for a month of "retooling." Following this hiatus only one show was

Dick Ebersol
Photo courtesy of Dick Ebersol

broadcast before a writers' strike in early 1981 halted production until fall. Meanwhile, he fired all of the cast except rising stars Joe Piscopo and Eddie Murphy, and hired Christine Ebersole (no relation), Mary Gross, and Tim Kazurinsky. He also brought back the head writer from the first season, the brilliant but intimidating Michael O'Donoghue (who was fired by next January).

Critics considered Ebersol's *SNL* an improvement over the previous season, but the ratings were still lower than in the Doumanian era. The show's guest hosts devolved from hip comedians to NBC series players or stars of current movies to plug.

No Sleep Productions, Ebersol's production house, had brought *Friday Night Videos* to NBC in 1983, where Michael Jackson's groundbreaking "Thriller" video debuted. The next year, Ebersol took over *Friday Night Videos* full-time, and shared the reins on *Saturday Night Live* with Bob Tischler. For the 1984-85 season, the two shored up *SNL's* ratings with experienced comics like Billy Crystal, Harry Shearer, Christopher Guest and Martin Short. Afterward, Ebersol quit to spend more time at home, and Brandon Tartikoff, now his boss, hired Lorne Michaels as producer.

Ebersol continued to produce *Friday Night Videos* for NBC, while his wife, the actress Susan St. James, starred in CBS's *Kate and Allie* with Jane Curtin. In 1985, he produced *The Saturday Night Main Event*, a series of World Wrestling Federation matches, to rotate in *Saturday Night Live's* off weeks. In 1988, he produced the very late-night *Later with Bob Costas.*

Ebersol returned to NBC in April 1989 as president of NBC Sports. That July he was also named senior vice president of NBC News, a position that paralleled the situation of his mentor, Roone Arledge, at ABC. As the executive for the *Today Show,* Ebersol presided over Jane Pauley's removal from the anchor desk in favor of Deborah Norville. He took the heat for the resulting bad publicity, and was relieved of his *Today Show* duties.

Ebersol has enjoyed much greater success in sports programming. He helped NBC snare several Super Bowl contracts, then brought the National Basketball Association back to network television at the height of its popularity. NBC's coverage of the 1992 Olympic games in Barcelona received excellent ratings, but the network lost money, largely from its "Triple Cast" coverage offered on three pay-per-view cable channels. Corporate parent General Electric expressed its commitment to the Olympics, though, when they announced Ebersol would be executive producer of the 1996 Atlanta games.

Ebersol aided in the formation of the Baseball Network, an unusual joint venture between NBC, ABC and Major League Baseball. The league produced its own coverage of Friday or Saturday night games; ABC or NBC alternated scheduling *Baseball Night in America,* and affiliates chose games of local interest to carry. The Baseball Network opened after the 1994 All-Star Game, but was cut short by that year's players' strike. In 1995, as the delayed baseball season opened without a labor agreement and no guarantee against another strike, both networks pulled out of the venture.

In the past several years, Dick has often been named among the most influential people in sports by the *Sporting News.* His name had been bandied about to possibly become the next commissioner of baseball, but he preferred instead to sign a contract to continue as president of NBC Sports.

—Mark R. McDermott

DICK EBERSOL. Born in Torrington, Connecticut, U.S.A., 1947. Graduated from Yale University, New Haven, Connecticut, 1971. Married: Susan St. James, 1982; three children. Began broadcasting career as researcher, ABC Sports, 1967; segment producer, ABC Sports, 1969; executive assistant to Roone Arledge, ABC Sports, 1974; director, late-night weekend programming, NBC-TV, 1974; vice president, late-night weekend programming, NBC-TV, 1975; vice president, comedy, variety, and event programming, NBC-TV, 1977; independent producer, 1979; executive producer, *Saturday Night Live,* 1981; president, NBC Sports, since 1989; senior vice president, NBC News, since 1989. Address: NBC Sports, 30 Rockefeller Plaza, New York City, New York 10112, U.S.A.

TELEVISION SERIES (executive producer)

1981–85	*Saturday Night Live*
1983	*Friday Night Videos*
1985	*The Saturday Night Main Event*
1988	*Later with Bob Costas*

FURTHER READING

Clark, Kenneth R. "Reincarnated: In Susan Saint James' New Life, She's Betty Aster, Radio Star." *Chicago Tribune,* 1 June 1993.

Hill, Doug, and Jeff Weingard. *Saturday Night: A Backstage History of Saturday Night Live.* New York: Beech Tree, 1986.

Holtzman, Jerome. "On Baseball." *Chicago Tribune,* 13 June 1993.

"Live from New York—it's Dick Ebersol." *Broadcasting* (Washington, D.C.), 4 December 1989.

Mandese, Joe. "'There's a Lot Left for Me in Sports.'" *Advertising Age* (New York), 6 September 1993.

Niedetz, Steve. "On TV/Radio Sports." *Chicago Tribune,* 23 January 1995.

Shapiro, Mitchell E. *Television Network Prime-time Programming, 1948–1988.* Jefferson, North Carolina: McFarland, 1989.

See also Arledge, Roone; *Saturday Night Live;* Sports and Television

THE ED SULLIVAN SHOW

U.S. Variety Show

The Ed Sullivan Show was the definitive and longest running variety series in television history (1948–1971). Hosted by the eponymous awkward and fumbling former newspaperman, the show became a Sunday night institution on CBS. For twenty-three years the Sullivan show fulfilled the democratic mandate of the variety genre: to entertain all of the audience at least some of the time.

In the late 1940s, television executives strove to translate the principles of the vaudeville stage to the new medium, the amalgamation referred to as "vaudeo." As sports reporter, gossip columnist, and master of ceremonies of various war relief efforts, Ed Sullivan had been a fixture on the Broadway scene since the early 1930s. He had even hosted a short-lived radio series that introduced Jack Benny to a national audience in 1932. Although Sullivan had no performing ability (comedian Alan King quipped, "Ed does nothing, but he does it better that anyone else on television"), he understood showmanship and had a keen eye for emerging talent. CBS producer Worthington Miner hired him to host the network's inaugural variety effort *The Toast of the Town,* and, on 20 June 1948, Sullivan presented his premiere "really big shew," in the lingo of his many impersonators who quickly parodied his wooden stage presence and multitudinous malapropisms.

The initial telecast served as a basis for Sullivan's inimitable construction of a variety show. He balanced the headliner, generally an unassailable legend, this time Broadway's

Ed Sullivan with the Animals

Richard Rodgers and Oscar Hammerstein with the up-and-coming stars, Dean Martin and Jerry Lewis, fresh from the nightclubs in their television debut. He also liked to juxtapose the extreme ends of the entertainment spectrum: the classical, here pianist Eugene List and ballerina Kathryn Lee, with the novelty, a group of singing New York City fireman and six of the original June Taylor Dancers, called the "Toastettes." From the beginning, Sullivan served as executive editor of the show, deciding in rehearsal how many minutes each act would have during the live telecast in consultation with producer Marlo Lewis. In 1955, the title was changed to *The Ed Sullivan Show*.

Sullivan had a keen understanding of what various demographic segments of his audience desired to see. As an impresario for the highbrow, he debuted ballerina Margot Fonteyn in 1958 and later teamed her with Rudolf Nureyev in 1965; saluted Van Cliburn after his upset victory in the Tchaikovsky competition in Moscow; and welcomed many neighbors from the nearby Metropolitan Opera, including Roberta Peters, who appeared 41 times, and the rarely seen Maria Callas, who performed a fully staged scene from *Tosca*. As the cultural eyes and ears for middle America, he introduced movie and Broadway legends into the collective living room, including Pearl Bailey, who appeared 23 times; Richard Burton and Julie

Andrews in a scene from the 1961 *Camelot*; Sammy Davis, Jr., with the *Golden Boy* cast; former CBS stage manager Yul Brynner in *The King and I*; Henry Fonda reading Lincoln's Gettysburg Address; and the rising star Barbra Streisand singing "Color Him Gone" in her 1962 debut. Occasionally, he devoted an entire telecast to one theme or biography: "The Cole Porter Story," "The Walt Disney Story," "The MGM Story, and "A Night at Sophie Tucker's House."

What distinguished Sullivan from other variety hosts was the ability to capitalize on teenage obsession. His introduction of rock 'n' roll not only brought the adolescent subculture into the variety fold but also legitimized the music for the adult sensibility. Elvis Presley had appeared with Milton Berle and Tommy Dorsey, but Sullivan's deal with Presley's manager, Colonel Tom Parker, created national headlines. The sexual energy of Presley's first appearance on 9 September 1956 jolted the staid, Eisenhower conformism of Sullivan's audience. By his third and final appearance, Elvis was shot only from the waist up, but Sullivan learn how to capture a new audience for his show, the baby boom generation.

In 1964 Sullivan signed the Beatles for three landmark appearances. Their first slot on 9 February 1964 was at the height of Beatlemania, the beginning of a revolution in music, fashion, and attitude. Sullivan received the biggest ratings of his career, and, with a 60 share, one of the most watched programs in the history of television. Sullivan responded by welcoming icons of the 1960s counterculture into his arena, most notably the Rolling Stones, the Doors, Janis Joplin, and Marvin Gaye. One performer who never appeared was Bob Dylan, who walked off when CBS censors balked at his song "Talkin' John Birch Society Blues."

Although called "the great stone face" on screen, Sullivan was a man of intense passion off camera. He feuded with Walter Winchell, Jack Paar, and Frank Sinatra over his booking practices. He wrangled with conservative sponsors over his fondness for African American culture and openly embraced black performers throughout his career, including Bill "Bojangles" Robinson, Ethel Waters, Louis Armstrong, and Diana Ross. He also capitulated to the blacklisting pressures of *Red Channels* and denounced performers for pro-Communist sympathies.

Sullivan saw comedy as the glue that held his demographically diverse show together and allowed a nation to release social tension by laughing at itself. He was most comfortable around Borscht Belt comics as seen by the funnymen he most often enlisted: Alan King (37 times), Myron Cohen (47 times), and Jack Carter (49 times). When Sullivan's son-in-law, Bob Precht, took over as producer in 1960, there was a movement to modernize the show and introduce a new generation of comedians to the American audience, led by Mort Sahl, Woody Allen, Richard Pryor, and George Carlin. The comic act that appeared most on the Sullivan show was the Canadian team of Johnny Wayne and Frank Shuster (58 times); the parodic sketches of Wayne and Shuster assured Sullivan a sizable audience north of the border.

Sullivan was always on the lookout for novelty acts, especially for children. His interplay with the Italian mouse Topo Gigio revealed a sentimental side to Sullivan's character. He also was the first to introduce celebrities from the audience and often invited them on stage for a special performance. Forever the sports columnist, he was particularly enthralled by athletic heroes, and always had time on the show to discuss baseball with Mickey Mantle or Willie Mays and learn golf from Sam Snead or Ben Hogan.

The Ed Sullivan Show reflected an era of network television when a mass audience and, even, a national consensus seemed possible. Sullivan became talent scout and cultural commissar for the entire country, introducing more than 10,000 performers throughout his career. His show implicitly recognized that America should have an electronic exposure to all forms of entertainment, from juggling to opera. The Vietnam War, which fractured the country politically, also help to splinter the democratic assumptions of the variety show. By 1971, *The Ed Sullivan Show* was no longer a generational or demographic mediator and was canceled as the war raged on. Later in the decade, the audience did not require Sullivan's big tent of variety entertainment any longer; cable and the new technology promised immediate access to any programming desire. The Sullivan library was purchased by producer Andrew Solt in the 1980s and has served as the source of network specials and programming for cable services.

—Ron Simon

HOST
Ed Sullivan

MUSIC
Ray Bloch and His Orchestra

DANCE
The June Taylor Dancers

PRODUCERS   Ed Sullivan, Marlo Lewis, Bob Precht

PROGRAMMING HISTORY

• CBS

June 1948	Sunday 9:00-10:00
July 1948–August 1948	Sunday 9:30-10:30
August 1948–March 1949	Sunday 9:00-10:00
March 1949–June 1971	Sunday 8:00-9:00

FURTHER READING

Bowles, Jerry. *A Thousand Sundays: The Story of the Ed Sullivan Show.* New York: Putnam, 1980.
Harris, Michael David. *Always on Sundays—Ed Sullivan: An Inside View.* New York: Meredith, 1980.
Henderson, Amy. *On the Air: Pioneers of American Broadcasting.* Washington, D. C.: Smithsonian Institution Press, 1988.
Leonard, John. *A Really Big Show.* New York: Viking Studio Books, 1992.

See also Sullivan, Ed; Variety Programs

EDUCATIONAL TELEVISION

Broadcasting in the United States evolved as a commercial entity. Within this system efforts to use the medium for educational purposes always struggled to survive, nearly overwhelmed by the flood of entertainment programming designed to attract audiences to the commercials that educated them in another way—to become active consumers. Despite its clear potential and the aspirations of pioneer broadcasters, educational television has never realized its fullest potential as an instructional medium. Educational Television (ETV) in the United States refers primarily to programs which emphasize formal, classroom instruction and enrichment programming. In 1967, educational television was officially renamed "public television" and was to reflect new mandates of quality and diversity as specified by the Public Broadcasting Act. Public television incorporated "formal" (classroom) and "informal" (cultural, children's, lifelong learning) instructional programming into a collective alternative to commercial television. Despite commercial dominance, however, educational initiatives in American television continue to change with the introduction of new telecommunications technology. Cable and new media challenge and enhance the traditional definition of educational television in the United States.

Interest in educational television was expressed early. Educators envisioned television's potential as an instructional tool and sought recognition by Congress. The short-lived Hatfield-Wagner amendment proposed to reserve one-fourth of the broadcast spectrum for educational stations. But the Communications Act of 1934 became law without this specification, although the Federal Communications Commission (FCC) promised to conduct further inquiry into ETV.

The immediate post-war years created a deluge of requests for broadcast licenses. So overwhelmed, the FCC initiated a "television freeze" in 1948 (forbidding the issuance of new licenses) in order to re-organize the current system and to study the ultra-high frequency band (UHF). The period of the "TV Freeze" was an ideal opportunity to resurrect the debate over allotment of spectrum space for educational channels.

FCC commissioner Freida Hennock led the crusade. She understood that this would be the only opportunity to reserve spectrum space for educational television. When educators would be financially and technically prepared for television experiments, spectrum space might be unavailable. Hennock raised the consciousness of educators and citizens alike, and convinced some of them to form the first ad-hoc Joint Committee for Educational Television (JCET). Financial assistance from the Ford Foundation provided legal expertise, and enabled the JCET to successfully persuade the FCC to reserve channel space for noncommercial educational television stations. In 1953 the FCC allotted 242 channels for education. KUHT in Houston, Texas was the first noncommercial television licensee.

Although this was a major victory, the development of educational television was a slow process. The majority of educators did not have the financial or technical capabilities to operate a television station. Commercial broadcasters recognized their dilemma as a lucrative opportunity.

Commercial broadcasters lobbied against the reservation of channels for education. Although they claimed they were not opposed to ETV as a programming alternative, they were opposed to the "waste" of unused spectrum space by licensees who were financially unable to fill broadcasting time. Persuaded in part by the argument for economic efficiency, the FCC permitted the sale of numerous ETV stations to commercial broadcasters. Many universities, unable to realize their goals as educational broadcasters, profited instead from the from the sale of their unused frequencies to commercial counterparts.

From its inception, then, ETV was continually plagued with financial problems. As a noncommercial enterprise, ETV needed to rely on outside sources for funding. Federal funding created the potential for programming biases and the private foundations, such as the Ford Foundation, would not be able to sustain the growing weight of ETV forever. The 1962 Educational Television Facilities Act provided temporary relief. Thirty-two million federal dollars were granted for the creation of ETV stations only. Programming resources were still essential, however.

The establishment of the Carnegie Commission in 1965 was critical to the survival of ETV. For two years the commission researched and analyzed the future relationship between education and television. Some of their proposals included increasing the number of ETV stations, imposing an excise tax on all television sets sold, interconnection of stations for more efficient program exchange, and the creation of a "Corporation for Public Television." These mandates prompted Congress to enact the 1967 Public Broadcasting Act as an amendment to the Communications Act of 1934.

The evolution of ETV into "public television" forever changed the institution. The ETV curriculum of formal instruction was too narrow to entice sweeping federal recognition. As a result, ETV was endowed with a new name and a new image. The mandate of public television was diversity in programming and audience. Public television promised to educate the nation through formal instruction and enrichment programming emphasizing culture, arts, science, and public affairs. In addition, it would provide programming for "underserved" audiences (those ignored by commercial broadcasters) such as minorities and children. Ultimately, public television promised to be the democratization of the medium. Sadly, however, these public service imperatives could never flourish as originally intended in a historically commercial system.

Educational television provides programming which emphasizes formal instruction for children and adults. Literacy, mathematics, science, geography, foreign language and high school equivalency are a few examples of ETV's offerings. The most successful ETV initiatives in the United States are public television's children's programs. Staples such as *Sesame Street, 3-2-1 Contact, Mister Rogers' Neighborhood* and *The Reading Rainbow* teach children academic fundamentals as well as social skills.

Higher education initiatives in television, "distance learning," boasts an impressive but modest history. Distance learning programs, while significantly more intensive abroad, have been integral to realizing the American ETV "vision." Nontraditional instruction via "telecourse" is an alternative learning experience for adults who cannot, or do not choose, to attend a university.

Closed-circuit TV (CCTV) was used as early as the 1950s by universities to transmit classroom lectures to other locations on campus. The Pennsylvania State University CCTV project is an early example. In 1952 the Pennsylvania State CCTV system (sponsored by the Ford Foundation) was created to offer introductory college courses via television in order to eliminate overcrowded classrooms and faculty shortages. Although moderately successful in achieving these goals, overall the CCTV system proved unpopular with students because of the absence of student-teacher contact and the lackluster "look" of the programs, especially in comparison with the familiar alternative of commercial television. This experiment made clear a continuing reality; the appeal of an instructional program is often dependent upon its production quality.

The Chicago Television College was a more successful endeavor. Teacher training was another initiative undertaken by the Ford Foundation in the early days of educational television and in 1956, the Chicago Television College was created as a cost-effective way to accomplish this task. Approximately 400 students earned their Associate of Arts (A.A.) from the TV College. The majority of graduates were inmates from particular correctional facilities and home-bound physically challenged individuals.

The Public Broadcasting System (PBS) is a significant participant in distance learning. Its Adult Learning Service (ALS) distributes telecourses to universities nationwide which are broadcast by participating PBS stations. In conjunction with ALS is the Adult Learning Satellite Service (ALSS) which provides a more efficient delivery system of telecourses. Similarly, the Instructional Television Fixed Service (ITFS) transmits college courses to high school students via satellite and microwave relay. Workbooks and examinations often supplement the video "lessons." ITFS also transmits its signals to social service centers, correctional facilities and community colleges.

Formal instruction efforts by commercial broadcasters are historically scarce. A notable example, however, was the CBS/New York University collaboration entitled Sunrise Semester. For nearly three decades, a New York University university lecture would air at 6:00 A.M. for the edification of early risers.

Adult learners are only not the only beneficiaries of ETV's instructional programs. Preschool, elementary and secondary school students are all target audiences of ETV services. The National Instructional Television Satellite Schedule (NISS) is a primary distributor of such programming. *321 Contact* (science), *Futures* (math) and *American Past* (history) are just a few examples of NISS offerings. Enrichment programs such as these are used to enhance, not replace, traditional classroom instruction.

Sesame Street is the ETV staple of pre-school children internationally. Heralded for its ability to successfully combine education and entertainment, *Sesame Street* is an anomaly. No other broadcast or cable program has seriously rivaled its formula for success. (It is even used in Japan to teach high school students English.)

ETV is not unique to the home and classroom. More specialized uses have proliferated. For example, closed-cir-cuit television is frequently used by medical institutions as a more effective means to demonstrate surgical procedures to doctors and medical students and workplace programming is often used by corporations for training purposes or to teach safety procedures. Distance learning, classroom instruction and workplace programming represent part of the ETV mosaic, which is generally defined by programming which emphasizes formal and informal learning.

But educational television also includes "enrichment" programming emphasizing culture, the arts and public affairs as an alternative to commercial choices. Popular entertainment programs such as *Masterpiece Theater*, public affairs and news programs such as *Frontline* and *The MacNeil/Lehrer News Hour*, and nature programs such as *Nova* all attempt to meet the requirements of educational television as defined by broadcast law in the United States.

The expansion of the telecommunications environment has also yielded additional outlets for educational television. The surge of cable television has been the most significant challenge to ETV as it is defined and provided by public television. Public television has always justified its very existence in the United States in terms of its role as the sole provider of educational programming. However, the emergence of cable services such as Bravo, A and E, the Learning Channel, Discovery and Nickelodeon have challenged public television's position. These outlets provide viewers with the same quality programming as public television. Often, cable networks compete with public stations for the rights to the same programs, from the same program suppliers.

Advocates of public television will often justify its existence with two words—*Sesame Street.* Noncommercial programming, availability in all households and quality children's programming such as *Sesame Street* are the examples used by public broadcasters to warrant their claims to federal and viewer support. Cable television's contribution cannot be completely ignored, however.

Indeed, the vision of educational television is perhaps best exemplified by cable's public, educational and government (PEG) access channels. While not mandatory, most cable companies are willing to provide these channels as part of their franchise agreements. They point to the existence of PEG channels as examples of their philanthropy. PEG channels demonstrate a grassroots approach to television. Public access encourages individual program efforts, which often contribute to the enlightenment of the immediate community. Paper Tiger Television is one example of such video "activism."

Education provided on access channels offers much of the same formal instruction as public television. The Cable in the Classroom organization distributes programs created by various cable networks (e.g. A and E, CNN, TLC) for classroom use. The programs are commercial-free. Like public television, educational access offers formal instruction and distance learning. One of its most recognized services is the Mind Extension University which offers credit for college courses taken at home.

Government access channels supply viewers with the discussion of local and national policy debates. City council and school board meetings are presented here. For a national/international perspective, most cable systems offer C-SPAN and C-SPAN II in their basic service. PEG channels foster localism and serve the public interest. They are valid interpretations of broader concept of educational television.

Globally, educational television plays a more significant role than in the United States. Most international broadcasting systems developed as noncommercial public service organizations. Public service broadcasters, or state broadcasters, are supported almost exclusively by license fees—annual payments made by owners of television receivers. Because the community directly supports the broadcaster, there is a greater commitment by the broadcaster to meet their multitudinous programming needs. As a result, these systems more effectively exemplify the mandates of the American public television system—quality and diversity.

Sweeping deregulation, increased privatization and the introduction of cable television have posed new problems for the public service monoliths, however. The introduction and proliferation of commercially supported television casts doubt on the need for license fees. Public service broadcasters must find new ways to compete, to sustain their reputations as cultural assets. ETV and its relationship to higher education is most developed and more successful as a learning device in what has been called the Open University system. The lack of higher education opportunities in many countries has contributed to the validation of distance learning. Open universities are provided by public (service) broadcasters on every continent. The British Open University is the most notable example, existing as an archetype for similar programs worldwide. Created in 1969, the Open University confers college degrees to students enrolled in telecourses. Programs are supplemented by outside exams and work/textbooks. Degrees from the Open University are as valued as traditional college diplomas.

The University of Mid-America (UMA) was a failed attempt by public broadcasters in the United States to emulate the British system. In existence from 1974 to 1982, UMA attempted to provide traditional higher education through non-traditional methods. Funding problems coupled with a society unreceptive to the open university culture, hastened UMA's demise.

Educational television is similar throughout the industrialized world. The combination of formal classroom instruction and enrichment programming defines the genre. Educational television in the developing world also includes programming which directly effects the quality of life of its viewers. For example, in areas where television penetration is very low, audiences may gather at community centers to view programs on hygiene, literacy, child care and farming methods. In this respect, educational television provides the group with practical information to improve living standards. Such programming best exemplifies the global aims of educational television.

The promise of the electronic superhighway will fundamentally change educational television. Subtle nuances continue to emerge as a result of new technologies and the combination of old ones. Satellite technology has already provided a more effective delivery system for programming. Interactivity has revitalized instructional television in particular. Teleconferencing, for example, links classrooms globally. These services not only provide access to traditional learning but enhance the cultural literacy of students worldwide. The relationship between education and television in the changing telecommunications environment continues to evolve. As television becomes more "individualized," providing, for example, "menus" of lessons, applications, and experiments, educational television may become the programming of choice. The synergisms between the significant players (broad/cablecasters, telephone, hard/software companies, educators and government) will ultimately determine new outlets for educational television across the globe, but audiences—students and users—will reap the ultimate benefits.

—Sharon Zechowski

FURTHER READING

Adler, Richard, and Walter S. Baer. *Aspen Notebook: Cable and Continuing Education.* New York: Praeger, 1973.

Barnouw, Erik. *A History of Broadcasting in the United States. Vol. II—1933–1953, The Golden Web.* New York: Oxford University Press, 1968.

Carnegie Commission on Educational Television. *Public Television, a Program For Action: the Report and Recommendations of the Carnegie Commission on Educational Television.* New York: Harper and Row, 1967.

Fuller, Linda K. *Community Television in the United States: A Sourcebook on Public, Educational and Governmental Access.* Westport, Connecticut: Greenwood, 1994.

Gibson, George H. *Public Broadcasting: The Role of the Federal Government 1912–1976.* New York: Praeger, 1977.

Granger, Daniel. "Open Universities: Closing the Distances to Learning." *Change* (Washington, D.C.), July/August 1990.

Hawkridge, David, and John Robinson. *Organizing Educational Broadcasting.* Paris: UNESCO Press, 1982.

Head, Sydney W., and Christopher H. Sterling. *Broadcasting in America: A Survey of Electronic Media.* 6th edition, Boston, Massachusetts: Houghton Mifflin, 1990.

Howell, W.J. *World Broadcasting in the Age of Satellite: Comparative Systems, Policies and Issues in Mass Telecommunication.* Norwood, New Jersey: Ablex, 1986.

Hoynes, William. *Public Television for Sale: Media, the Market, and the Public Sphere.* Boulder, Colorado: Westview, 1994.

Kahn, Frank J., editor. *Documents of American Broadcasting.* Englewood Cliffs, New Jersey: Prentice-Hall, 1968; 3rd edition, 1978.

See also *Blue Peter*; Children and Television; Children's Television Workshop; National Education Television; Public Service Broadcasting; *Sesame Street*

EGYPT

Egypt began its television system, considered one of the most extensive and effective among all undeveloped countries of Asia and Africa, in 1960. Due to a well-financed radio service and film industry already in existence, Egypt, unlike other Arab countries, was able to start television production without importing engineering staff from abroad. Even with this beginning, however, the development of television has been complicated by many other social and cultural factors.

In the late 1950s, following the 1952 revolution, Egyptian President Gamel Abdul Nasser realized television's potential for helping to build Egypt into a new nation. Though the decision to start television service had been made earlier, the joint British-French-Israeli Suez invasion delayed work until late 1959. Egypt then signed a contract with Radio Corporation of America (RCA) to provide the country with a television network and the capacity to manufacture sets. After the RCA contract was signed, Egypt began construction of a radio and television center, completed in 1960, and the first television pictures appeared on 21 July 1960, using the 625-line European standard.

From the start, Egypt did everything on a grand scale. Thus, while most nations began their systems modestly with one channel, Egypt began with three. The entire system was initially totally subsidized by the government, receiving a direct grant every year. In 1969, however, an annual license fee of $15 per set was introduced and after 1979, revenue from advertising and from the sales of programs to other countries also helped in financing. At the present time, a surcharge, which goes to the broadcasting authority, is added to all electricity bills and provides additional funding for the system.

Egyptian television began its multi-channel operation under the control of the Ministry of Culture and National Guidance, an organization that figured prominently in the Nasser regime from the start. This ministry also used radio and television broadcasting for propaganda to support the ruling regime.

Television's role in the culture was heightened following the June 1967 war with Israel which resulted in an Egyptian defeat that was militarily, economically and psychologically devastating. Immediately after the war, there was a decrease in the amount of foreign programming shown. The third channel, over which much programming had been telecast, was eliminated, and the British and U.S. programs that constituted the bulk of imported programs were deemed unacceptable due to the break in diplomatic relations with those countries. Almost all forms of programming on television placed less emphasis on Egypt's military capability, tending instead, toward the nationalistic, the educational and the religious. Moving closer to the country's new military supplier, the former Soviet Union, television began showing films about Soviet and East European life. These programs were either provided free of charge or were inexpensive to purchase or lease.

The general technical quality of Egyptian television declined between 1967 and 1974 when there was less money for new equipment. Generally, however, the change in government after Nasser's death and Sadat's ascendancy to the presidency in 1970 did not appear to have much effect on television programming or the structure of the federation.

On 13 August 1970, radio, television and broadcast engineering were established as separate departments under the Ministry of Information. The new decree formally established the Egyptian Radio and Television Union (ERTU) and created four distinct sectors—radio, television, engineering and finance—each of which had a chairman who reported directly to the minister.

Following the October 1973 war, the Egyptian media took a very different approach to the national situation. Television programming, which took longer to produce and air than radio information, was somewhat more upbeat. As good news came in, it reflected confidence in an Egyptian recovery. After the Egyptian-Israeli engagement, Egyptian television shows dealt more often with the United Nations, the European countries, the United States and Israel. Agreements regarding military disengagements received a high priority for broadcast on the air. More than any other Egyptian mass medium, television was set to reflect the changing international political orientation of the country. Sadat's government gradually changed Egypt during the 1970s from a socialist orientation to one that was more hospitable to free enterprise and decidedly pro-West. After 1974, the door was formally opened to the West. Consequently, the number of Western programs on Egyptian television schedules increased.

The television organization decided during this time to continue the development of color. Though some believed color television was a luxury that Egypt could not afford, the favorable attitude among broadcasting officials prevailed. The French government had been successful in persuading Egypt to adopt the System Electronic Color Avec Memoire (SECAM) system and had installed its equipment in one of the Egyptian studios before the 1973 war. After the war, the decision was made to convert both production and transmission facilities to color, an action which improved the technical quality of Egyptian television by discarding the monochrome equipment that had been installed by RCA long before 1970. Older switchers and cameras, which were becoming difficult to repair or to purchase, were replaced. The new equipment was necessary for the production of programs to be sold to other countries that were also converting to color and after 1974 television revenues derived from advertising and from program sales to other Arab countries increased significantly. The Egyptian broadcasting authority changed from the SECAM system to PAL, however, in both studio and transmission in 1992.

Because of Egypt's peace treaty with Israel, many Arab countries joined the call by the more militant countries to isolate Egypt, remove it from the Arab League and boycott its exports. Many countries broke diplomatic relations with Egypt or reduced the size of diplomatic missions in Cairo. Countries that supported the boycott no longer purchased Egyptian television programs, stating that they did not need to buy directly from Egypt because so much quality material was available from Egyptian artists living outside the country. One response held that "the boycott organizers are interested in drawing the distinction between the Egyptian people and the Egyptian government." And indeed, many Egyptian producers moved to Europe to produce programs for sale to the Arab countries. However, Egyptian television program sales to the Arab world did not decrease as a result; they actually have increased.

During this period the Egyptian government was very seriously considering plans for a new satellite system. Technical staff personnel had already been sent to be trained in the United States. This undertaking, called the Space Center Project, was mainly designed for the distribution of television signals that would link the country through ground stations which would receive and rebroadcast programming to the villages. The proposal became active when the Egyptian president signed a document for the beginning of Nile Satellite in 1995, a satellite that not only covers the Egyptian state but also services the Arab world.

In addition to the two centralized television networks, a new strategy to decentralize the television broadcasting system was introduced in 1985. The policy was implemented by starting a third television channel which covers only the capital city. This was followed in 1988 by Channel 4 which covers the Suez Zone. Yet another channel was added in 1990 to cover Alexandria, and in 1994 Channel 6 was created to cover the Middle Delta. Most recently, in late 1994, Channel 7 was introduced in southern Egypt. In 1990 Egypt became the first Arab state to start an international television channel when the Egyptian Space Channel was introduced to the Arab world and later to Europe and the United States. Egypt was also the first to start a foreign national network, Nile TV, to serve expatriates in Egypt as well as to promote tourism in English and French languages.

In part as a result of these available channels, a television set has become a priority for any young couple getting married. Most prefer buying a television set to purchasing other important things for the house. Even a color set is considered a normal part of the household in middle-class families and the number of such sets has increased greatly since 1970. The price of television sets purchased in Egypt, however, reflects high import taxes, sometimes reaching 200%. This has led most Egyptians to buy their sets from abroad. Most Egyptian people working outside the country, especially in Saudi Arabia and the other Gulf states, return to Egypt with television sets because of the lower prices in the Gulf countries. Others acquire second-hand sets from individuals or dealers who sometimes help finance such transactions.

Egyptian shops do carry a variety of television receivers. These include foreign brands as well as sets assembled in Egypt, but the imported sets have a reputation of being more reliable. The government is attempting to reduce prices of locally made sets and in 1995 the number of television sets was estimated at 6,200,000.

Programming

From the beginning, Egyptian television has had a strong tie with Arabic culture. Historical, religious, geographical, political and linguistic bonds tied Egypt to the Arab countries. Egyptian television was influenced Arabic literature, religion, philosophy and music. The producers of the first programs, influenced to some extent by the example of contemporary programs from the East European countries and the Soviet Union, which were heavily cultural in content, quite naturally regarded Egyptian television programs as a proper vehicle for Arab literature and the arts. Egyptian television, then, performs the function of reinforcing and enhancing Arab culture, which is defined as a heritage in creative endeavor and thought. Its programs also raise the cultural level of the ordinary viewer by presenting refined items covering scientific, literary and artistic fields, as well as a great deal of Arab music and drama on traditional themes.

Television is an ideal medium for disseminating Egyptian culture because that culture is family-oriented and tends to center much of its education and entertainment around the home. Nevertheless, the content and style of television broadcasting available to these viewers has changed over time. The government still owns and operates the medium and sometimes uses it to convey political messages, but programming is now characterized by somewhat less politically motivated programming than was characteristic in the 1960s and 1970s. It contains more entertainment and popular culture and the Ministry of Information is trying to stress these aspects and reduce the amount of political content.

Entertainment programs such as the Egyptian soap operas and Egyptian music and songs are very popular. Foreign programs are also popular, especially those from Europe and the United States, which provides Egypt with many series, such as *The Bold and the Beautiful, Knots Landing, Love Boat*, and *Night Rider*. The famous American series, *Dallas,* however, was banned from television because officials thought it conveyed immoral messages to the public, especially to youth and children.

News is an important aspect of programming in Egypt because of the country's regional position and the fluctuating nature of political alignments in the Arabic-speaking area. As previously suggested, the 1960s, especially the events surrounding the 1967 war, was an era of crisis. Egyptian television penetrated the region. It was important for the government to maintain a strong news front to present its particular point of view. Newscasting in Egypt included a segment of official "commentary" when there was some special concern to be articulated. From these news broadcasts, as well as other programs, the policies of President Nasser were clear to the viewer, as were the identities of those who were considered the enemies of those policies.

Compared to the beginning of the 1960s there was a significant increase in the emphasis upon education at the beginning of the 1970s. It took almost the previous decade for the Ministry of Education to be convinced of the value of educational programs. Moreover, the educational programs were run first under the initiative of the broadcasters, who resisted turning any time over to the ministry. But enlightenment programs remain important in the schedule of Egyptian television and have increased measurably through the years.

Religion, of course, carries great weight in Egypt, an Islamic center. Readings from the Koran have always been broadcast on a regular basis by Egyptian television and religious commentaries or advice on proper moral and ethical behavior are featured. Coverage of the rituals of the Muslim Holy Day is presented as part of the attempt to maintain Islamic traditions and values. During the Muslim Holy Month of Ramadan, Egyptian television is exceptionally active in religious programming, exhorting the faithful and explicating the pertinence of Islamic history. In the period from 1980 to 1985 a close observer could notice an increase in religious programs.

Children's programming, which formerly was completely of foreign origin, has changed to suit the Egyptian culture. Almost all Egyptian programs for youth and women and programs dealing with art and literature have been given increased time on the television schedule.

The Current Broadcasting Industry

Egyptian information media have always been closely tied to politics. Television in Egypt is, typically, a monopoly under direct government supervision, operation and ownership. There are several reasons for this. First, the minimum cost of establishing a radio or television system is far greater than the minimum cost of establishing a newspaper, for example, and thus far beyond the capability of nearly all private persons in a developing country. Second, this high cost encourages the pooling of resources, or a monopoly. And because these media reach beyond borders and literacy barriers, the government has a much greater interest in controlling them or at least keeping them out of hostile hands. Anyone with a printing press has the technical capability of reaching the literate elite, and while this is seen by the government as a potential threat, it is not nearly as great a political liability as a monopoly radio station broadcasting to millions. Radio and television, which have the potential of instantaneously reaching every single person in the country and many outside it, are regarded by the Egyptian government as too important to be left to private interests. Third, radio and television are newer media, and the trend is toward greater authoritarian control over all media.

But catching up with new technology and the further development of television systems demands ever larger sums. Additional funds are even more necessary for producing high quality programs. Raising revenues for broadcasting thus will remain a major problem for Egypt, especially when the country is engaged in two huge broadcast projects, Nile Sat and the Television Production City. Each of these projects is projected to cost more than 1 billion Egyptian pounds (US$1=£.E.3.40).

The staff of the broadcasting industry represents a serious problem, especially in such a centralized television system. Currently, Egyptian television employs almost 14,000 people. Obviously, this large number of television workers is far above that required to produce programs and fill the broadcasting time and there are more workers than necessary for efficient operation of the two television channel services. The figure is especially excessive for a country with limited financial resources.

Along with advertising revenue and license fees (added monthly to the electricity bill), Egypt depends on sales of Egyptian programs to other countries as the main resource to finance television. Since the peace treaty with Israel, many Arab countries have boycotted Egypt's exports. Yet even in these circumstances Egypt received over $20 million from television program sales to other Arab countries from 1973 to 1978. Later, the creation of a program marketing company structured to give the impression of being independent from the government enabled some countries which wanted to buy Egyptian programs to do so without censure.

Even with such modifications and strategies the financing of radio and television broadcasting will continue to be a serious problem for the Egyptian government. Despite the realization of the importance of electronic media in the internal and external political process, funds to continue the dissemination of their services have become increasingly scarce, especially in view of the educational and health needs of the country. It is obvious, then, that Egypt must continue to struggle and to compromise to find funds needed to continue national broadcasting services.

—Hussein Y. Amin

FURTHER READING

Amin, Hussein Y. *An Egypt Based Model for the Use of Television in National Development* (Doctoral dissertation, Ohio State University, Columbus Ohio, 1986).

Amin, Hussein, and Douglas Boyd. "The Impact of Home Video Cassette Recorders on Egyptian Film and Television Consumption Patterns." *European Journal of Communication* (London), 1993.

Boyd, Douglas A. *Broadcasting in the Arab World*. Ames, Iowa: Iowa State University Press, 1993.

Head, Sydney. *Broadcasting in Africa*. Philadelphia, Pennsylvania: Temple University Press, 1975.

Rugh, William A. *The Arab Press*. New York: Syracuse University Press, 1987.

EISNER, MICHAEL

U.S. Media Executive

Michael Eisner joined the Disney Company in 1984 and helped re-craft it throughout the 1980s and 1990s. In the process he helped to make Disney into a television powerhouse, climaxing those efforts with a takeover of Capital Cities-ABC on the last day of July 1995. Through the final sixth of the twentieth century, the Disney Company, with its ever increasing profits, was held up as a quintessential American business success story. It produced popular culture fare embraced around the world—and did not sell out to the Japanese. Yet when Michael Eisner assumed leadership of the company, Disney was in trouble. It was Eisner and his staff who turned the ailing theme park company into a media powerhouse.

Eisner brought a rich base of executive experience to Disney. He had begun his career at the ABC television network and then moved to Paramount under former ABC boss, Barry Diller. The two men made Paramount the top Hollywood studio during the late 1970s and early 1980s. By 1978, just two years after Diller and Eisner arrived, Paramount had moved to the head of the major studio race. Led by *Grease, Saturday Night Fever*, and *Heaven Can Wait*, Paramount took in one-quarter of the Hollywood box office in that year.

When Eisner moved to Disney he moved immediately to revitalize the company. He hired Hollywood's new "Irving Thalberg," Jeffrey Katzenberg, then barely thirty, to make movies under two new "brand names": Touchstone Pictures and Hollywood Pictures. (Eisner and Katzenberg worked well together until 1994 when Katzenberg moved to Dream Works, Inc., with new partners Steven Spielberg and David Geffen.)

The new Disney turned out hit feature films including *Down and Out in Beverly Hills*, and *Ruthless People*. In 1987 when *Three Men and a Baby* pushed beyond $100 million in box-office take, it became the first Disney film ever to pass that vaunted mark. *Three Men and a Baby* represented a quintessential example of the new Disney, drawing its stars, Ted Danson and Tom Selleck, from the world of television.

From the base of solid theatrical film profits, Eisner then began to re-make Disney into a TV power. The studio quickly placed hits such as *Golden Girls* on prime-time schedules. By the early 1990s Disney's *Home Improvement* and *Ellen* consistently ranked in TV's prime-time top-ten. Disney also expanded into the TV syndication business. The company created a very successful syndicated program by hiring "film critics" Gene Siskel and Roger Ebert to "review" movies, including those produced by Disney.

But not all Disney moves into television prospered. Eisner revived Disney's family Sunday night TV show, with himself as host. But Eisner proved no "Uncle Walt" and he was forced to quietly cancel himself despite airing in a prized 7:00 P.M. Sunday time slot on ABC. Like many before and after him, Eisner could not compete successfully with CBS's *60 Minutes*.

Michael Eisner
Photo courtesy of Broadcasting and Cable

Nor did Disney's TV syndication efforts always mint gold. *Today's Business*, an early morning show which, although it aired initially in half the television markets in the United States, lasted but a few painful months in 1985. The Walt Disney Company pulled out, eating a $5 million loss.

Eisner had more success with cable TV as he expanded efforts to make the Disney Channel a pay cable TV power. Using a seemingly infinite set of cross promotional exploitation opportunities, the Disney Channel began to make money by 1990. By that year the channel could claim five million subscribers (of some sixty million possible cable households).

Eisner may have had the most early success in home video. He accomplished this in spades by packaging and proffering the "classics" of Disney animation in the expanding home video market. These video revenues provided an immediate boost to the corporate bottom line. In 1986 alone, home video revenues added more than $100 million of pure profit. In October 1987 when *Lady and the Tramp* was released on video, the Disney company had more than two million orders in hand before it ever shipped a copy. By the late 1980s *Bambi* and *Cinderella* were added to the list of the all time best sellers on video. Eisner placed *Bambi* and even *Fantasia* into "video sell through" so every family could buy and own a copy. *Aladdin* and *The Lion King* created even more profit and made the Disney operation Hollywood's leader in home video sales.

With all this, Eisner made the Disney balance sheets glow. From mid-1985 through late 1990 the company broke profit records for more than twenty straight quarters. Based on the good times of the 1980s operating margins and cash flow tripled. It was no wonder that in order to underscore their thriving new corporate colossus Eisner and company president Frank Wells changed the company name from Walt Disney Productions to the Walt Disney Company.

By 1991 the Walt Disney Company had become a true corporate power. Specifically, as 1991 began, it ranked in the top two hundred of all U.S. corporations in terms of sales and assets, an outstanding 43rd in terms of profits. In terms of its stock value Disney had grown into a $16 billion company, with mind boggling sales of $6 billion per annum, and profits approaching $1 billion per year. This was a media corporate giant, of a rank with Time Warner or Paramount, no marginal enterprise anymore.

It came as no surprise in July 1995 that Disney announced its most important move in television, the takeover of a broadcast television network. What was surprising, however, is that the network chosen by Disney was ABC, then the leading network, and its parent company Capital Cities. Additional surprise came from the quiet, unsuspected nature of the deal-making. As the story is reported, Eisner and Cap Cities President Thomas Murphy began their negotiations only days before the final deal was struck—and managed to keep it from reporters. For an announced $19 billion Disney had suddenly become one of the world's major media conglomerates. A few weeks later the surprise continued when Michael Ovitz, head of the Creative Artists Agency and often referred to as the most powerful man in Hollywood, became president of the new company.

For all his successes Michael Eisner was well rewarded. In 1990 surveys of the best paid corporate executives in the United States, Michael Eisner ranked in the top ten. From 1986 to 1990 he had been paid nearly $100 million for his efforts. The Disney Company hit a publicity apex in May, 1989 when it was revealed that Michael Eisner was the highest paid executive in the United States for 1988—at more than $40 million. Michael Eisner must be credited with creating in the Disney company one of the true media powerhouses of the end of the twentieth century.

—Douglas Gomery

MICHAEL EISNER. Born in Mt. Kisco, New York, U.S.A., 7 March 1942. Educated at Denison University, Granville, Ohio, B.A. 1964. Married: Jane Breckenridge; three sons. Began career in programming department of CBS; assistant to national programming director, ABC, 1966–68, manager specials and talent, director of program development, east coast, 1968–71, vice president, daytime programming, 1971–75, vice president, program planning and development, 1975–76, senior vice president, prime-time production and development, 1976; president and chief operating officer, Paramount Pictures Corp., 1976–84; chairman and chief executive oficer, Walt Disney Company, since 1984. Founding member of board, Points of Light Foundation, inspired by then President George Bush; past member of the board of trustees of Georgetown University. Board of trustees: Denison University and California Institute of the Arts; board member, American Hospital of Paris Foundation and Conservation International, and the University of California Los Angeles Executive Board for Medical Sciences. Address: Walt Disney Company, 500 South Buena Vista Street, Burbank, California 91521, U.S.A.

FURTHER READING

Auletta, Ken. "Awesome: Michael Eisner's Comeback ...." *The New Yorker* (New York), 14 August 1995.

———. "The Human Factor." *The New Yorker* (New York), 26 September 1994.

Boroughs, Don L. "Disney's All Smiles...." *U.S. News and World Report* (Washington, D.C.), 14 August 1995.

Flower, Joe. *Prince of the Magic Kingdom: Michael Eisner and the Re-Making of Disney.* New York: John Wiley, 1991.

Grover, Ron. *The Disney Touch: How a Daring Management Team Revived an Entertainment Empire.* Homewood, Illinois: Business One Irwin, 1991.

Huey, John. "Eisner Explains Everything." *Fortune* (Chicago, Illinois), 17 April 1995.

Jacobs, Rita D. "Modern Medici: Michael Eisner" (interview). *Graphis* (Zurich, Switzerland), September-October 1992.

"Meet the Boss" (excerpts from Charles Gibson's Television interview with Michael Eisner and Thomas Murphy). *Harper's Magazine* (New York), October 1995.

Schatz, Thomas. "Boss Men." *Film Comment* (New York), January-February 1990.

See also American Broadcasting Company; *Walt Disney Programs*

ELLERBEE, LINDA

U.S. Broadcast Journalist

Linda Ellerbee, respected and outspoken broadcast journalist, has functioned as a network news correspondent, anchor, writer, and producer. She is currently president of her own production company, Lucky Duck Productions. Gaining fame in the 1970s and 1980s for her stints as an NBC News Washington correspondent, *Weekend* co-anchor, reporter, and co-anchor of *NBC News Overnight*, Linda Ellerbee became a symbol for a different type of reporter: literate, funny, irreverent, and never condescending. Her personal style attracted a diverse and dedicated following of viewers for her stories, which covered everything from politics to pop culture. "And so it goes" is her trademark broadcast tag line and the title of her 1986 bestseller *"And So it Goes": Adventures in Television,* an amusing and candid look at the realities of the profession.

Ellerbee's career at NBC News climaxed with her appointment as co-anchor of an overnight news broadcast, *NBC News Overnight.* Though the program failed with audiences, Ellerbee and the concept were critical successes. The duPont Columbia awards cited *Overnight* as "possibly the best written and most intelligent news program ever." She left the network news business in 1986, after serving a stint as anchor for ABC News' short-lived *Our World.*

Her television production company, Lucky Duck Productions, has a reputation as a supplier of outstanding children's programming. Founded with partner Rolfe Tessem in 1987, the company has won three CableAces, two Peabodys, a duPont, and an Emmy. Each week Ellerbee writes and hosts *Nick News* and the quarterly *Nick News Special Editions,* the Nickelodeon news magazine for children and young people, both produced by Lucky Duck Productions. These shows have given Lucky Duck a reputation for introducing quality news journalism on a broad range of subjects to its audience. These series have been honored with a Peabody, Columbia-duPont Awards, the National Education Association, and the Parents Choice Awards. The Peabody citation given in 1991 notes the award was given for presenting news in a thoughtful and non-condescending manner for both children and adults. Other Lucky Duck projects for such clients as Nickelodeon, MTV, HBO, FOX, and Time-Life include several projects for young adults and documentary or news shows for all viewers.

In 1996 Ellerbee was again involved in expanding and experimenting with media forms. She began writing and hosting a monthly on-line public affairs interview program, *On the Record,* produced by Microsoft and Lucky Duck Productions, which combines print, television, and computer technology.

—Alison Alexander

LINDA ELLERBEE (Linda Jane Smith). Born in Bryan, Texas, U.S.A., 15 August 1944. Educated at Vanderbilt University, Nashville, Tennessee, 1962–64. Married: 1) Mac Smith,

Linda Ellerbee
Photo courtesy of Linda Ellerbee/Gittings/Skipworth, Inc.

1964 (divorced, 1966); 2) Van Veselka, 1968 (divorced, 1971), children: Vanessa and Joshua; 3) Tom Ellerbee, 1973 (divorced, 1974). Disc jockey, WSOM Chicago, 1964–65; program director, KSJO San Francisco, 1967–68; reporter, KJNO Juneau, Alaska, 1969–72; news writer, Associated Press, Dallas, 1972; television reporter, KHOU in Houston, Texas, 1972–73; general assignment reporter, WCBS-TV, New York City, 1973–76; reporter, Washington bureau of NBC News, 1976–78; co-anchor, network news magazine *Weekend,* 1978–79; correspondent, *NBC Nightly News,* 1979–82; co-anchor, *NBC News Overnight,* 198–84; co-anchor, *Summer Sunday,* 1984; reporter, *Today,* 1984–86; reporter, *Good Morning America,* 1986; anchor, ABC news show *Our World,* 1986–87; commentator, CNN, 1989; president, Lucky Duck Productions, since 1987; producer, writer, and host, *Nick News ,* since 1993; writer and founder, host, *On the Record,* on-line production with Microsoft, since 1996. Recipient: Peabody Award, 1991. Address: Lucky Duck Productions, 96 Morton Street, New York City, New York 10014, U.S.A..

TELEVISION SERIES

1978–79	*Weekend*
1979–82	*NBC Nightly News*
1982–84	*NBC News Overnight*

PUBLICATIONS

"And So It Goes": Adventures in Television. New York: Putnam's, 1986.

Move On: Adventures in the Real World. New York: Putnam's, 1991.

FURTHER READING

Lamb, Chris. "From TV Commentator to KFS Columnist." *Editor and Publisher* (New York), 27 October 1990.

"Linda Ellerbee: Telling Her Own Stories." *Broadcasting and Cable* (Washington, D.C.), 11 September 1995.

Orenstein, Peggy. "Women on the Verge of a Nervy Breakdown." *Mother Jones* (Boulder, Colorado), June 1989.

See also Children and Television

EMERSON, FAYE

U.S. Television Personality

Faye Emerson was one of the most visible individuals in the early days of U.S. television. A "television personality" (meaning talk-show host and more), her omnipresence during the infant days of TV made her one of the most famous faces in the nation and earned her the unofficial titles of "Television's First Lady" and "Mrs. Television."

Before television settled into stricter genre forms, when prime time was dominated by more presentational types of programming, "personalities" prospered. Variety shows abounded, as did low-cost, low-key talk shows which took advantage of TV's intimate nature. While the hosts of some of these shows were men—Ed Sullivan, Garry Moore, and Arthur Godfrey are among the better known "personalities"—the majority were female: Ilka Chase, Wendy Barrie, Arlene Francis, and others.

Faye Emerson had been a marginally successful film and stage actress before she embarked on her second career in television. A talent scout offered her a contract with Warner Brothers, when she was noticed in a local theater production, and she starred or co-starred in various "A" and "B" movies. Her career took an up-swing in 1944 when she married a second time, to Elliot Roosevelt, son of the president. The studio's publicity machine used this union to bring her greater fame and expanded Emerson's non-acting opportunities. As a "first daughter-in-law" she took part in presidential ceremonies and, with her husband, staged a successful trip to the Soviet Union in the late 1940s. She also acted on Broadway and on radio.

Emerson made her first television appearance of note in 1949 as a panelist, with her husband, on a game show. Her quick wit and breadth of knowledge—which upstaged her husband to such a degree she apologized on his behalf on air—made her something of a sensation. Later that year, actress Diana Barrymore was forced by illness to drop out of her soon-to-premiere local New York talk show. The producers phoned Emerson to take over and she accepted.

The Faye Emerson Show premiered in October 1949 and went national over CBS the following March. It quickly gained a following, snagging an average 22 rating. One month later, Emerson began a second talk show, this time on NBC. This made her one of the first people to have two shows simultaneously on two networks.

The late-night talk show of its day, Emerson frequently welcomed celebrity guests (actors, authors, other personalities). Sometimes the show was more free form. Sometimes it was simply Faye talking about her life and goings-on about town.

Faye Emerson

In retrospect, Emerson seemed a natural for early television, a medium which had to bridge the gap between the art of live drama and the appeal of wrestling. Emerson's combination of Hollywood good looks and social connections, along with her old-fashioned common sense and pleasant personality and friendly conversations about peoples, places and parties, made audiences want to welcome her into their homes. Adding to her appeal were her much talked about designer gowns featuring plunging necklines. It was believed this helped her attain much of her male viewership. (One wit would later say Faye Emerson put the "V" in TV.) The topic was such hot copy for a time that it inspired fashion/photo spreads in *Life* and other magazines. Finally, to move past it, Emerson brought it to a vote on her show. She asked viewers what she should wear. Ballots ran 95% in favor of Emerson's style staying as it was.

But Emerson was more than just window dressing. During the height of her fame she was a frequent substitute host for Edward R. Murrow on *Person to Person* and for Garry Moore on his show. She took part in so many game shows that a magazine once labeled her "TV's peripatetic panelist."

Emerson's omnipresence as a television performer should not be underemphasized. Before cable and satellites the average household was lucky to receive a handful of channels. Hosting various shows on various networks for much of the 1950s meant that even the most infrequent of audiences had to be aware of her as one of TV's first citizens. A viewing of Emerson's work today reveals a pleasant, largely unflappable but somewhat stiff talent. Still, she radiates glamour and remarkable camera presence.

In 1950, after divorcing Roosevelt, Emerson announced on her evening program her plans to marry musician Lyle C. "Skitch" Henderson. (It is believed she was the first person ever to make such an announcement on television.) In 1953, the two teamed for the show *Faye and Skitch*. Earlier in 1951, Emerson began hosting one of the medium's most expensive programs, *Faye Emerson's Wonderful Town*, in which she traveled the country and profiled different cities.

As the 1950s came to a close "TV personalities" found themselves with fewer opportunities. Some, like Arlene Francis, brilliantly reinvented themselves; others found themselves relegated to guest appearances before moving into retirement. Emerson was in this latter group. She continued to make TV appearances until 1963, when, rich and weary of show business, she sailed off for a year in Europe. Finding it to her liking, she seldom returned to the United States and died abroad in 1993.

Why Faye Emerson, "Mrs. Television," did not endure on the small screen while her masculine counterpart, "Mr. Television" Milton Berle, did can be ascribed to several factors. Perhaps most important was the fact that the TV personality never had a single marketable trait: neither comic nor singer, they were more like the good host or hostess at a private, intimate party. By the late 1950s, as talk shows left prime time, the party was over. TV production moved out of New York and left their kind of glamour behind.

Today, the lack of a clear lineage for the TV personality makes a full understanding of Emerson's appeal hard to grasp. Who today does exactly what Emerson did—Joan Rivers, Kathie Lee Gifford, the women of MTV? But as TV was beginning, it needed a friendly, unifying factor, a symbol to initiate audiences into its technology—and for millions of viewers that envoy was Faye Emerson.

—Cary O'Dell

FAYE EMERSON. Born in Elizabeth, Louisiana, U.S.A., 8 July 1917. Married: 2) Elliot Roosevelt, 1944; 3) Lyle C. "Skitch" Henderson, 1951. In films from 1930s; in television from 1949 as host, guest performer, panelist. Died in Majorca, Spain, 9 March 1993.

TELEVISION SERIES

1949–52	*With Faye*
1950	*The Faye Emerson Show*
1951–52	*Faye Emerson's Wonderful Town*
1953–54	*Faye and Skitch*

FILMS

Bad Men of Missouri, 1941; *Juke Girl*, 1942; *The Hard Way*, 1942; *Find the Blackmailer*, 1943; *Destination Tokyo*, 1943; *Air Force*, 1943; *The Mask of Dimitrios*, 1944; *Crime by Night*, 1944; *Danger Signal*, 1945; *Nobody Lives Forever*, 1946; *A Face in the Crowd*, 1957.

FURTHER READING

O'Dell, Cary. *Women Pioneers in Television*. Jefferson, North Carolina: McFarland, 1996.

E.N.G.

Canadian Drama

E.N.G., a Canadian television drama series set in the news studio of a local television station, ran successfully on the private CTV network for five seasons from 1989 to 1994. After a slow start, which almost led to its cancellation at the end of the first season, the series steadily gained in popularity as audiences responded to its blend of personal and public issues. It was sold to many countries and well-received when it appeared on the Lifetime cable network in the United States and on Channel 4 in Britain.

The letters in the title stand for "Electronic News Gathering" and were often seen on black-and-white images of news footage supposedly seen through the monitors of hand-held video cameras. Through its depiction of news gathering and studio production work, the series was able to respond to topical issues and comment on the role of the media in contemporary culture. The news stories were framed by the personal and professional relationships of the newsmakers, as the objectivity demanded of news reporting collided with the subjective feelings of the reporters or with commercial or political pressures.

The series began with the arrival of Mike Fennell (Art Hindle) to take over as news director, a position to which the executive producer, Ann Hildebrand (Sara Botsford) had expected to be promoted. As these two endeavored to establish a professional relationship, amid the various crises of the newsroom, Ann carried on a supposedly secret affair with Jake Antonelli (Mark Humphrey), an impetuous cameraman who often broke the rules and found himself in dangerous situations. In the course of the series, Mike and Ann became personally involved, and the final episodes left them trying to balance their careers and their relationship after the station's owners decided to adopt a "lifestyles" format.

The major significance of *E.N.G.* stems from its attempt to negotiate between the traditions of Canadian television and the formulas of the popular American programs that dominate CTV's schedule. In media coverage of the series, it was often compared with the CBC's *Street Legal*, which began two years earlier and which set its personal and professional entanglements in a Toronto law office. Both series were compared to such American hits as *L.A. Law* and *Hill Street Blues*, but both presented recognizably Canadian situations and settings. Since most original Canadian television drama has been produced by the CBC, a public corporation, the success of *E.N.G.* raised hopes that the private networks would offer more support to Canadian producers.

E.N.G. did have one foot in the Canadian tradition associated with the CBC and the National Film Board, a tradition of documentary realism and social responsibility, and it gave work to a number of veteran film and television directors. Yet the major project of the series was clearly to deliver the pleasures of "popular" television, using a formula which owed more to the melodramatic structures of the daytime soaps than to traditional Canadian suspicion of "crisis structures." When *E.N.G.* began, it used a fairly strict series format, each episode presenting a complete story with little cross-reference between episodes. The later seasons saw a movement toward a serial format as the personal lives of the characters assumed more importance.

But the basic formula remained the same throughout. A number of loosely-connected stories were interwoven, offering viewers a variety of characters and situations, and inviting them to make connections among the stories and to activate memories of other episodes in the series (and to make comparisons with other similar series). In "The Souls of Our Heroes" (March 1990), for example, the main story dealt with competing accounts of the events in Tiananmen Square, while Ann received an unexpected visit from a childhood friend and her two children and a producer attempted to enliven the Crime Catchers segment of the news with fictional re-enactments. "In the Blood"

E.N.G.
Photo courtesy of Alliance Communications

(January 1991) used the motif of "blood" to link its two main stories: an attempt to capture a day in the life of an AIDS victim and an investigation into an alleged miracle involving a bleeding statue of Jesus. In these episodes, and most others, the focus was on the implications of the way the news is reported: for the newsmakers themselves, for the people on whom they are reporting, and for the community that watches the final product.

Although *E.N.G.* was clearly indebted to similar American series, its ability to blend melodrama with a serious treatment of topical issues was not shared by *WIOU*, a short-lived series with a remarkably similar premise which appeared on CBS in the fall of 1990.

—Jim Leach

CAST

Mike Fennell . . . . Art Hindle
Ann Hildebrand . . . . Sara Botsford
Jake Antonelli . . . . Mark Humphrey

PRODUCER Robert Lantos

PROGRAMMING HISTORY

• CTV/Telefilm

1989–1994

See also Canadian Programming in English

ENGLISH, DIANE

U.S. Writer/ Producer

Diane English is in the enviable position of having several successful shows to her credit, a credit often shared with co-producer, and her husband, Joel Shukovsky. In addition to the programs—*Murphy Brown, Love and War* and the earlier *Foley Square* and *My Sister Sam*—their company also manages a lucrative eight-figure multiseries contract with CBS. The couple started their careers in public television (New York City's WNET) with English's adaptation of *The Lathe of Heaven*, and English went on to write nine TV movies before being offered the opportunity to "create-write-produce" the pilot for *Foley Square*, which, like her later shows, featured a strong female central character.

In a demanding profession, however, English's career has not been without controversy; *Murphy Brown* was attacked by Vice President Dan Quayle in the summer of 1992 when the main character on the series, a single professional woman played by Candice Bergen, decided not to terminate her unplanned pregnancy. Quayle's primary criticism was that the series mocked the importance of fathers by having a woman bear a child alone and call it "just another lifestyle choice." Quayle and English engaged in a heated and prolonged dispute through the media which made the series and English herself a household word. Some industry experts called the incident the single most important element contributing to the long-term ratings success of the show. For advertisers, in the following season, *Murphy Brown* was the most expensive show in television, with 30-second commercials on the show costing an average $310,000. Syndication sales were said to exceed $100 million. Because of her unusual combination of business and creative skills, English is often mentioned as "the only woman in television now capable of taking over the entertainment division at a major network."

—Cheryl Harris

DIANE ENGLISH. Born in Buffalo, New York, U.S.A., 1948. Graduated from Buffalo State College, 1970. Married: Joel Shukovsky. High-school English teacher, Buffalo, New York, 1970–71; WNET-TV, New York City, 1970s; columnist, *Vogue* magazine, New York City, 1977–80; in commercial television from 1985; creator, writer, producer, *Murphy Brown*, 1988–. Recipient: Writers Guild Award, 1990; Genie Award, American Women in Radio and Television, 1990; Commissioners' Award, National Commission on Working

Diane English and Joel Shukovsky
Photo courtesy of Shukovsky / English Entertainment

Women. Address: Shukovsky/English Productions, 4000 Warner Boulevard, Burbank, California, U.S.A.

TELEVISION SERIES

1985–86	*Foley Square*
1986–87	*My Sister Sam*
1988–	*Murphy Brown*
1992–95	*Love and War*

FURTHER READING

Alley, Robert S., and Irby B. Brown. *Murphy Brown: Anatomy of a Sitcom.* New York: Delta Books, 1990.
DeVries, Hibry. "Laughing off the Recession." *The New York Times*, 3 January 1993.

See also *Murphy Brown*

EQUAL TIME RULE

U.S. Broadcasting Regulatory Rule

The equal time rule is the closest thing in broadcast content regulation to the "golden rule." The equal time, or more accurately, the equal opportunity, provision of the Communications Act requires radio and television stations and cable systems which originate their own programming to treat legally qualified political candidates equally when it comes to selling or giving away air time. Simply put, a station which sells or gives one minute to Candidate A must sell or give the same amount of time with the same audience potential to all other candidates for the particular office. However, a candidate who can not afford time does not receive free time unless his or her opponent is also given free time. Thus, even with the equal time law, a well-funded campaign has a significant advantage in terms of broadcast exposure for the candidate.

The equal opportunity requirement dates back to the first major broadcasting law in the United States, the Radio Act of 1927. Legislators were concerned that without mandated equal opportunity for candidates, some broadcasters might try to manipulate elections. As one congressman put it, "American politics will be largely at the mercy of those who operate these stations." When the Radio Act was superseded by the Communications Act of 1934, the equal time provision became Section 315 of the new statute.

A major amendment to Section 315 came in 1959 following a controversial Federal Communications Commission (FCC) interpretation of the equal time provision. Lar Daly, who had run for a variety of public offices, sometimes campaigning dressed as Uncle Sam, was running for mayor of Chicago. Daly demanded free air time from Chicago television stations in response to the stations' news coverage of incumbent mayor Richard Daley. Although the air time given to Mayor Daley was not directly related to his re-election campaign, the FCC ruled that his appearance triggered the equal opportunity provision of Section 315. Broadcasters interpreted the FCC's decision as now requiring equal time for a candidate any time another candidate appeared on the air, even if the appearance was not linked to the election campaign.

Congress reacted quickly by creating four exemptions to the equal opportunity law. Stations who gave time to candidates on regularly scheduled newscasts, news interviews shows, documentaries (assuming the candidate wasn't the primary focus of the documentary), or on-the-spot news events would not have to offer equal time to other candidates for that office. In creating these exemptions, Congress stressed that the public interest would be served by allowing stations the freedom to cover the activities of candidates without worrying that any story about a candidate, no matter how tangentially related to his or her candidacy, would require equal time. The exemptions to Section 315 have also served the interests of incumbent candidates, since by virtue of their incumbency they often generate more news coverage then their challengers.

Since 1959, the FCC has provided a number of interpretations to Section 315's exemptions. Presidential press conferences have been labeled on-the-spot news, even if the president uses his remarks to bolster his campaign. Since the 1970s, debates have also been considered on-the-spot news events and therefore exempt from the equal time law. This has enabled stations or other parties arranging the debates to choose which candidates to include in a debate. Before this ruling by the FCC, Congress voted to suspend Section 315 during the 1960 presidential campaign to allow Richard Nixon and John Kennedy to engage in a series of debates without the participation of third party candidates. The FCC has also labeled shows such as *The Phil Donahue Show* and *Good Morning America* as news interview programs. However, appearances by candidates in shows which do not fit under the four exempt formats will trigger the equal opportunities provision, even if the appearance is irrelevant to the campaign. Therefore, during Ronald Reagan's political campaigns, if a station aired one of his films, it would have been required to offer equal time to Reagan's opponents.

Section 315 also prohibits a station from censoring what a candidate says when he or she appears on the air (unless it is in one of the exempt formats). Thus, a few years ago when a self-avowed segregationist was running for the governorship of Georgia, the FCC rejected citizen complaints over the candidate's use in his ads of derogatory language towards African Americans. More recently, the FCC has also rejected attempts to censor candidate ads depicting aborted fetuses. However, the FCC has permitted stations to channel such ads to times of day when children are less likely to be in the audience.

The equal opportunity law does not demand that a station afford a state or local candidate any air time. However, under the public interest standard of the Communications Act, the FCC has said that stations should make time available for candidates for major state and local offices. With regard to federal candidates, broadcast stations have much less discretion. A 1971 amendment to the Communications Act requires stations make a reasonable amount of time available to federal candidates. Once time is made available under this provision, the equal time requirements of Section 315 apply.

The 1971 amendments also addressed the rates which stations can charge candidates for air time. Before 1971, Congress only required that the rates charged candidates be comparable to those offered to commercial advertisers. Now, Section 315 commands that as the election approaches, stations must offer candidates the rate it offers its most favored advertiser. Thus, if a station gives a discount to a commercial sponsor because it buys a great deal of air time, the station must offer the same discount to any candidate regardless of how much time he or she purchases.

—Howard M. Kleiman

FURTHER READING

Donahue, Hugh Carter. *The Battle to Control Broadcast News: Who Owns the First Amendment?* Cambridge: Massachusetts Institute of Technology Press, 1989.

Rowan, Ford. *Broadcast Fairness: Doctrine, Practice, Prospects: A Reappraisal of the Fairness Doctrine and Equal Time Rule.* New York: Longman, 1984.

See also Deregulation; Federal Communications Commission; Political Processes and Television

THE ERNIE KOVACS SHOW (VARIOUS)

U.S. Comedy/Variety Program

In a few brief years in the 1950s there were actually a number of different Ernie Kovacs shows. The first, *Ernie in Kovaksland*, originated in Philadelphia, Pennsylvania, and appeared on NBC from July until August 1951. *The Ernie Kovacs Show* (first known as *Kovacs Unlimited*) was programmed on CBS from December 1952 to April 1953 opposite Milton Berle on NBC. Yet another *Ernie Kovacs Show* aired on NBC from December 1955 to September 1956. The existence of these separate shows is testament to both the success and failure of Ernie Kovacs. A brilliant and innovative entertainer, he was a failure as a popular program host; praised by critics, he was avoided by viewers.

Kovacs was one of the first entertainers to understand and utilize the television as a true "medium," capable of being conceived and applied in a variety of ways. He recognized the potential of live electronic visual technology and manipulated its peculiar qualities to become a master of the sight gag. Characters in pictures on the walls moved; sculptures undulated; pilots flew away without their planes. For one gag that lasted only a few seconds he spent $12,000: when a salesman (played by Kovacs) slapped the fender of a used car, the car fell though a platform. According to Kovacs, "Eighty percent of what I do is in the category of sight gags, no pantomime. I work on the incongruity of sight against sound."

Television was a new toy to Ernie Kovacs, a fascinating array of potential special effects. He created an invisible girlfriend who gradually disappeared as she undressed. He cut a girl in half with a hoola-hoop. As another young lady relaxed in a bath tub, a succession of characters climbed out through the soap bubbles. Ernie taped an orange juice can to a kaleidoscope, placed the can in front of a camera lens, turned a flashlight into the lens and created what might be the first psychedelic effect on TV. Kovacs loved the unusual, the unexpected. He tilted both the television camera and a table so that as a character seated at the table attempted to pour milk, the milk appeared to defy gravity and flow to the side.

Many of Kovacs' effects were remarkably simple. He used his face to illustrate the effects of the horizontal and vertical controls of a television set. As he adjusted the vertical, his face grew longer; as he adjusted the horizontal, it stretched side to side. To aid viewers who had black-and-white television sets, Kovacs labeled each piece of furniture on the set so viewers would know its color. As he opened a book, sound effects illustrated the plot. As he prepared to saw in half a woman inside a cabinet, two voices were heard from within.

Many of his characters were also simplistic. Percy Dovetonsils drank martinis and read poetry. The three apes of the Nairobi Trio never spoke: one played the keyboard, one directed the music, and the third hit the director with a set of drumsticks. Eugene, perhaps Kovacs' most memorable character, never spoke, but managed to sustain a thirty-minute program and win Kovacs an Emmy.

He did not neglect sound, but used it in its proper place, as a compliment to the visuals. He captured the sound of a bullet rolling inside a tuba. He used music to accompany the movements of office furniture: filing cabinets opened and closed, typewriter keys typed, telephone dials rotated, water bottles gurgled, all to the rhythm of music.

The influence of the Ernie Kovacs shows has been extensive. Dan Rowan, one of the hosts of *Rowan and Martin's Laugh-In*, said many of that show's ideas came from Ernie Kovacs. On *Saturday Night Live*, another show directly influenced by the earlier comic, sight gags were so much a staple that when Chevy Chase received an Emmy for his performance on SNL, he thanked Kovacs. And Kovacs' character "The Question Man," who supplied questions to answers submitted by the audience, reappeared as "Carnac" on *The Tonight Show Starring Johnny Carson*.

The Ernie Kovacs shows were products of the time when television was in its infancy and experimentation was acceptable. It is doubtful that Ernie Kovacs would find a place on television today. He was too zany, too unrestrained, too undisciplined. Perhaps Jack Gould of *The New York Times* said it best—for Ernie Kovacs, "the fun was in trying."

—Lindsy E. Pack

ERNIE IN KOVACSLAND

REGULAR PERFORMERS
Ernie Kovacs
The Tony DeSimone Trio
Edith Adams

PRODUCER   Ned Cramer

The Ernie Kovacs Show
Photo courtesy of Edie Adams

PROGRAMMING HISTORY

• NBC

July 1951–August 1951   Monday-Friday 7:00-7:15

THE ERNIE KOVACS SHOW (KOVACS UNLIMITED)

REGULAR PERFORMERS
Ernie Kovacs
Edie Adams
Ernie Hatrack
Trigger Lund

Andy McKay

PROGRAMMING HISTORY

• CBS

December 1952–April 1953   Tuesday 8:00-9:00

THE ERNIE KOVACS SHOW

REGULAR PERFORMERS
Ernie Kovacs
Edie Adams

Bill Wendell (1956)
Peter Hanley (1956)
Henry Lascoe (1956)
Al Kelly (1956)
Barbara Loden (1956)

PRODUCERS Barry Shear, Jack Hein, Perry Cross

PROGRAMMING HISTORY

• NBC

December 1955–September 1956   Monday 8:00-9:00

FURTHER READING

Gould, Jack. "The Humor of Ernie Kovacs." *The New York Times*, 21 January 1962.

"Kovacs Explains Wordless Shows." *The New York Times*, 21 December 1955.

Rico, Diana. *Kovacsland, a Biography of Ernie Kovacs.* San Diego, California: Harcourt Brace, 1990.

Whalley, David G. *Nothing in Moderation, a Biography of Ernie Kovacs.* New York: Drake, 1975.

See also Kovacs, Ernie

ETHICS AND TELEVISION

Television ethics are derived from early professional codes of broadcasting that began in the late 1920s and are grounded in problems and issues identified in early radio. For television these ethical systems came into their own and grew rapidly, in conjunction with the development of the new medium, during the 1960s. But they now no longer exist as they once did.

Like radio for a previous generation, television had the ability to penetrate the private home and its potential obtrusiveness was the subject of concern. It was, after all, a "guest" in the home and in that capacity it was able to serve the public interest—informing, instructing and enlightening. It also had the ability, recognized early on, for serving private interests driven by the desire for economic gain. The keen awareness of potential confrontation between service on the one hand, and the desire for laissez faire operation on the other, led to another set of possible conflicts—between self regulation and regulation by government. The broadcasting industry placed its faith and its interests in self regulation.

The industry created its own Code of Broadcasting which consisted of eight "rules." Four had to do with advertising and concern over "overcommercialization." The other rules dealt with general operations and responsible programming: no "fraudulent, deceptive or obscene" material. Many of these same ideas and even the language appeared again in the Television Code established in the early 1950s.

Early on, a vexing problem for the code, a potential problem in any ethical system, surfaced. It was the issue of penalty. As in any enforcement of self-regulated ethics, there was little room for harsh sanctions. The only penalty called for violators to be investigated and notified. Later the penalty was strengthened by adding notification among the broadcast community—the threat of ostracism among colleagues. When television came on the scene, radio had recently experienced rapid growth in its commercialization. And with that growth came continuing threats of further, more far reaching regulation from the Federal Communications Commission and the Federal Trade Commission. In an effort to keep the government regulators at bay, the broadcasters' "Code of Good Practice" became more definitive. One of the main elements focused on regulation of the amount of time that should be devoted to commercials.

The evolution of the code can be seen by examining the use of commercial time in the 1930s. While there could be some advertising (of a good-will nature) before 6:00 P.M., according to the code, "commercial announcements, as the term is generally understood, *should not* be broadcast between 7 and 11 p.m." That restriction then evolved to allow increased broadcasting of commercial messages, to 5 minutes, then 10, then 18 by 1970. When television assumed a dominant place in broadcasting, beginning in the early 1950s, the rules affecting commercial time evolved the same way, increasing the allowed time slowly over the years.

Although the National Association of Broadcasters (NAB) created a separate set of ethical guidelines for television, distinct from radio, the existing concerns were applied to the newer medium: time limits of advertising, types of products advertised, fraud, especially in advertising, and special sensitivity to programming and advertising directed to children. Other program themes, obviously taboo in their times, such as sexual suggestiveness and explicit violence, were also addressed.

At the same time each network installed its own staff for network Standards and Practices (S and P), to enforce their particular policies for advertising and programming. These were the offices and individuals often thought of as "network censors." Large corporations also created statements of policies concerning their professional ethics as related to broadcasting.

These network and company rules of self regulation were supplementary to the NAB's continuation of its two nationally visible codes, one for radio, one for television. But each of these was becoming unwieldy. A dozen or so pages of the Television Code of Good Practice contained a long list of programming prohibitions: hypnotism, occultism, and astrology, as well as obscene, profane or indecent material, and programs that ridiculed those with disabilities.

Still, the NAB Codes remained an important public relations device for the industry. At the apex of its use, NAB President Vince Wasilewski stated, "Our Codes are not peripheral activities. No activity of NAB is closer to the public."

As social mores changed and social and cultural climates became more permissive, so too did television programming. By the late 1970s and early 1980s, the code seemed hopelessly outdated, continually violated, unenforceable and generally ignored by the broadcasters.

In 1982, when advertisers were lined up for a limited amount of available time on the television networks, it appeared that the networks gave favor for its best time slots to the largest advertisers. Displeased, one of the smaller advertisers pointed out this practice to the Justice Department, claiming unfair competitive practices, a violation of anti-trust laws. The Justice Department took action against the National Association of Broadcasters, because, it said, the NAB Code, limiting the amount of available commercial time, was responsible for the network practice. The court agreed, and ordered the NAB to purge that part of the code. After some initial hesitancy, the NAB agreed.

For eight years, from 1982 to 1990, both radio and television had no code of professional ethics. During that period, research showed that although the networks and some large corporate broadcasters had their own codes, or standards and practices, there still seemed to be no universal guidance. One study, based on a national sample of broadcast managers, suggested that broadcasters preferred self regulation rather than government regulation. It also suggested some concern that without such self regulation, government regulation might increase.

In 1990, the NAB issued a new "Statement of Principles of Radio and Television Broadcasting," designed as a brief, general document intended to reflect the generally accepted standards of American broadcasting. The statement encouraged broadcasters to individually write their own specific policies. It also encouraged responsible and careful judgment in the selection of material for broadcast rather than forming a list of prohibition as was the case with the old code. Caution was advised in dealing with violence, drugs and substance abuse, and with sexually oriented materials, but there was also positive encouragement for responsible artistic freedom and responsibility in children's programming. The statement made it clear that these principles are advisory, rather than restrictive. Finally, the 1990 statement mentioned First Amendment rights and encouraged broad-

casters to align themselves with the audiences' expectations and the public interest.

The new philosophy concerning ethics in broadcasting reveals that:

- they are advisory rather than prohibitive;
- they should be centered in individual stations or corporations, rather than a national organization like NAB;
- since there is no provision for monitoring and enforcement on the national level, any concerns about ethics should come from individual stations and listeners/viewers;
- the decentralization of ethics may be indicative of a pluralistic society, where values and mores reflect distinct group perspectives, rather than a national standard.

Some observers bemoan the fact that there is no nationally visible standard—no way of measuring whether the language of a daring new television program is actually on the "cutting edge," or merely "bravado bunk." Yet, since the broadcast industry itself has been largely deregulated, the question remains whether this means there is now room for more self regulation, or whether self regulation itself should also be deregulated.

—Val E. Limburg

FURTHER READING

Alberto-Culver Co. v. National Association of Broadcasters. N1.83-2327 (D.C. filed 17 November1983), 12-13.

"Broadcasters Seek to Clean Up the Industry and Hope to Regulated Commercial Activities on the Air." *New York Times*, 7 April 1929.

Donaldson, Tom. "Ethical Dilemmas." *Electronic Media* (Chicago, Illinois), 29 March 1988.

Limburg, Val E. *Electronic Media Ethics.* Boston: Focal Press, 1994.

———. "The Decline of Broadcast Ethics: U.S. v. N.A.B." *Journal of Mass Media Ethics* (Provo, Utah), 1989.

National Association of Broadcasters. *Statement of Principles of Radio and Television Broadcasting* (directive to member stations). Washington, D.C.: NAB, 9 July 1990.

National Association of Broadcasters. *The Challenge of Self-Regulation.* Washington, D.C.: NAB, 1966.

"National Broadcasters Meet at Chicago and Adopt Code of Ethics." *New York Times*, 26 March 1929.

White, Llewellyn. *The American Radio.* Chicago: University of Chicago Press, 1947.

See also National Association of Broadcasters

ETHNICITY, RACISM AND TELEVISION See RACISM, ETHNICITY AND TELEVISION

EUROPEAN AUDIOVISUAL OBSERVATORY

The European Audiovisual Observatory is an information service network for the audiovisual profession. It was initiated by professional media practitioners in conjunction with governmental authorities to meet increasing information needs in the audiovisual sector. These groups expressed a common commitment towards improved flow and access to information, and towards more transparent information related to the television, cinema and video sectors of the media industries. The observatory was set up to provide reliable information services, and also to improve the infrastructure of information collection and dissemination in Europe.

The observatory was established in December 1992, and currently thirty-three European states and the European Commission are members. The observatory was created under the auspices of Audiovisual Eureka, and functions within the framework of the Council of Europe.

It is a unique European public service organisation that provides information services to the European television, cinema, video and new media industries. In particular, the observatory serves the information needs of the decision makers of production, broadcasting and distribution. Public administrators, consultants and lawyers, researchers and journalists needing information on the audiovisual sector are all target user groups of its services.

The Observatory provides market and economic, legal, and practical information relevant to audiovisual production and distribution. It is a focal point of audiovisual information, that puts information requesters in contact with the best information available. The observatory brings together the diversity of audiovisual information, guides information requesters to the best sources, and co-ordinates pan-European work towards more transparent information.

The observatory is a service organisation with several core-services. These services provide rapid response to daily information needs, as well as to long-term development needs for better data collection methods. The Information Service Desk handles individual requests for information. It is designed to answer questions quickly and accurately. It covers all three information areas of the observatory: market, legal and practical information.

The observatory prepares the following publications: an annual *Statistical Yearbook: Cinema, Television, Video and New Media in Europe;* a monthly journal, *IRIS – Legal Observations of the European Audiovisual Observatory;* and a quarterly journal on the information sources in the audiovisual sector, *Sequentia.*

The observatory also coordinates work towards transparent European data. It advises on questions relating to data collection and how to access information sources. It organises expert workshops seeking improved and more comparable European data in the audiovisual sector.

The information services of the observatory are based on its network of partners and correspondents. This co-operatively working network currently includes 150 information providers and literally covers greater Europe. It includes a large number of different information providers: public and private research and information organisations, universities, consultants, individual experts, ministries and administrations, and regional network-organisation in the media field. By centrally coordinating this multitude of sources, the observatory gives access to the most reliable and updated information on the European audiovisual industry.

Partners are information or research organisations that have an established track record of providing reliable information in the audiovisual field, either on the European or global level. Each partner has a specific responsibility or thematic area regarding information collection and provision. Partners will also help the observatory to perform its services. Partners also play an essential role in assisting the observatory in its work towards harmonisation of European audiovisual information.

Correspondent organisations are professional information organisations, and they complement and assist the observatory and its partners in collecting information from the member States. Correspondent organisations also advise on data collection, and on the accuracy and relevance of the information from their specific country. In each member state, there are different correspondents for legal, market and economic, and practical information.

European professional organisations are widely represented in the Advisory Committee of the observatory. Some of these organisations collect and maintain databases from their own areas of interest in the audiovisual sector. These organisations have also agreed to collaborate with the observatory in collecting and providing the most reliable data in their field of specialty.

—Ismo Silvo

FURTHER READING

IRIS 1996: Legal Developments in the Audiovisual Sector. European Audiovisual Observatory, Strasbourg, 1995.

1996 Statistical Yearbook: Cinema, Television, Video and New Media in Europe. European Audiovisual Observatory, Strasbourg, 1996.

EUROPEAN BROADCASTING UNION

The European Broadcasting Union (EBU), which is unrelated to the European Union, was formed 12 February 1950 by 23 broadcasting organizations from Europe and the Mediterranean rim at a conference in the Devonshire coastal resort of Torquay, England. The EBU now has active full members from forty-eight countries, associate members from thirty more countries, and four other approved participants. Members are radio and television companies, most of which are government-owned public service broadcasters or privately owned stations with public missions. Full active Members are based in countries from Algeria to the Vatican State, including almost all European countries. Associate members are not limited to those from European countries and the Mediterranean but include broadcasters from Canada, Japan, Mexico, Brazil, India and Hong Kong, as well as many others. Associate members from the United States include ABC, CBS, NBC, the Corporation for Public Broadcasting, and Turner Broadcasting.

The EBU is a nongovernmental international association, based in Geneva and governed by Swiss law and its own statutes. It is the successor to the first international association of broadcasters, the International Broadcasting Union (1925), which was also based in Geneva. Its principal aims are to promote cooperation between members and with broadcasting organizations throughout the world and to represent its members' interests in various fields, including legal, technical, and programming. The EBU is administered by a general assembly, which meets annually and elects an administrative council composed of fifteen active members. A president and two vice-presidents are chosen by the assembly from among the representatives of the members making up the council. Council membership is for four years, with re-election permitted. Because the EBU is based in Switzerland, the Swiss member, Société Suisse de Radiodiffusion et Télévision (SSR), has a permanent seat on the council. Four permanent committees, the Radio Programme Committee, the Television Programme Committee, the Legal Committee, and the Technical Committee, report to the council on the work of their working and *ad hoc* groups. Day-to-day operations are carried out by the Permanent Services staff, headed by the secretary-general.

One of the major activities of the EBU is the Eurovision scheme, consisting of program pooling and joint purchasing operations. Eurovision was the idea of Marcel Bezençon, once director of the SSR and president of the EBU. Eurovision was and is a television program clearing house which facilitates the exchange of programming between national networks throughout Europe. One of the early successes of the EBU was the relay on 2 June 1953, of the transmission of the coronation of Queen Elizabeth II to France, Belgium, the Netherlands, and Germany. The official birth of Eurovision as an international television network occurred 6 June

Courtesy of EBU

1954, when the famous Narcissus Festival from Montreaux, Switzerland, opened a series of live transmissions, the "Television Summer Season of 1954."

Eurovision brings news and program events to European viewers on a daily basis. It is a network comprised of a mixture of permanent satellite and terrestrial stations. Its programs are identified by a starburst logo and an excerpt of the introduction to *Te Deum*, a work of the 17th-century composer Marc-Antoine Charpentier.

The most important regular Eurovision activity is the daily news exchange, providing full members and associate members with much of their non-domestic and European news. Material is fed into the exchange by members and nonmember broadcasting unions which also take from the exchange. The news exchange began on a trial basis in 1958 and became regular in 1961. It has now been supplemented by a multilingual channel known as Euronews. Euronews is designed to provide Europeans with world and local news coverage from a European viewpoint. On 1 January 1993, the Euronews channel began broadcasting on 5 terrestrial circuits and 12 satellite circuits in English, French, German, Italian, and Spanish. Euronews is a postproduction channel, with none of its own reporters in the field. It has access to Eurovision material and news agencies for its content.

Another major Eurovision activity is its sports programming, including such events as the European Basketball Championships, European Athletics Cup, and European Swimming Championships. Eurovision operates a joint purchasing scheme for international sporting events. When members from two or more EBU countries are interested in a sporting event, they request coordination from the EBU, which either carries on negotiations itself or deputizes a member to do so on behalf of the EBU. Members may not carry out negotiations for national rights after joint negotiations have commenced, unless the joint negotiations fail. If the joint negotiations succeed, the rights are acquired on behalf of the interested members, who share the rights.

In 1989, the European Sports Network/Screensport Network, a commercial satellite channel, filed a complaint with the Commission of the European Communities alleging that the joint purchasing scheme for sporting events violated the competition (antitrust) law rules of the Treaty of Rome. After provissions were made for non-member access to the programming, the commission granted the EBU a five-year conditional exemption from the competition rules. However, in 1996, the Court of First Instance of the European Community nullified the decision; the joint purchasing scheme awaits further litigation

—Clifford A. Jones

FURTHER READING

Brack, Hans. *The Evolution of the EBU through its Statutes from 1950 to 1976.* Geneva, Switzerland: European Broadcasting Union, 1976.

Eugster, Ernest. *Television Programming Across National Boundaries: The EBU and OIRT Experiences.* Dedham, Massachusetts: Artech, 1983.

Type, Michael. "Facing the Future with Confidence: The EBU Celebrates 40 Years of Achievement." *EBU Review: Programmes, Administration, Law.* Geneva, Switzerland, 1990.

EUROPEAN COMMERCIAL BROADCASTING SATELLITE

ASTRA, the first independent European commercial satellite broadcasting system, commenced transmissions in early 1989. By the beginning of 1995, the ASTRA system had already achieved penetration of over 56 million households (approximately 150 million people) in twenty-two European countries. This is 35% of the 160 million TV households within the geographical target area and a 15% increase since the end of 1993.

The ASTRA system is owned and operated by Société Européen des Satellites (SES), a private company incorporated in Luxembourg and trading under a twenty-five year renewable franchise agreement with the Grand Duchy which retains a 20% interest. SES, founded in March 1985 and backed by private commercial interests all over Europe, has headquarters at the Château de Betzdorf in Luxembourg. From there it uplinks TV and radio signals to the orbiting satellite craft which comprise the system. The company's revenue is generated by leasing satellite transponders—effectively the equivalent of channel slots—to broadcasting organisations who pay annual rentals reputedly as high as £5 million per transponder. Despite global recession and widespread anxiety about the increasing fragmentation of the audio-visual audience, SES has found no shortage of potential customers, with transponder availability on each new satellite subject to heavy demand from broadcasters willing to gamble high investment and short-term unprofitability for healthier returns later.

ASTRA's first satellite, ASTRA 1A, was launched in December 1988 from the European Space Centre in Kourou, French Guiana, aboard an Ariane 4 rocket. It became operational in February 1989, 35,975 kilometres above the equator at its geostationary orbital position of 19.2 East. This was the first commercial European satellite specifically dedicated to television and radio transmission. The system was subsequently augmented by the launch of

ASTRA 1B in March 1991, while 1C followed in May 1993 and 1D in November 1994—all co-located at the same orbital position and with an active life-span of ten to twelve years. The sixty-four transponders of these four satellites provide over seventy separate analogue television services in either the PAL or D2Mac broadcast standards

Courtesy of ASTRA

as well as nearly forty radio channels approaching CD stereo quality. The "footprint," or geographical universe, of this satellite constellation extends from Iceland and Norway in the north to coastal Morocco, Sardinia and Belgrade, Yugoslavia in the south; from the Canary Islands in the west to Warsaw, Poland and Budapest, Hungary in the east, with some reception possible even as far east as Helsinki, Finland.

The available services are accessed via one of three methods of delivery, the most visible being individual direct-to-home dish antenna (DTH) which can be fixed or motorised and which, for successful reception in the footprint's central belt, can be as small as 60cm in diameter. Alternatively, in the case of viewers in multi-occupancy dwellings, reception is via communal satellite master antenna systems (SMATV). Many other viewers, including a large proportion in Germany, Holland and Belgium, receive signals relayed over cable networks.

A major factor in the early success of SES was Rupert Murdoch's 1988 decision to become ASTRA's first commercial client, taking four transponders initially on ASTRA 1A for his incipient Sky Television Service (subsequently British Sky Broadcasting), aimed principally at English speaking audiences in the UK and Western Europe. A considerable number of German broadcasting interests also migrated early to ASTRA and SES's evolving system was soon enabling diverse programme services in a wide variety of languages, ushering in a new era of themed private television and radio channels as alternatives to the general entertainment models commonly associated with terrestrial broadcasting. Of course, many of the ASTRA channels are transmitted in encrypted or scrambled form, available only to contracted subscribers possessing the necessary decoding device. Movies, sports, music, news, children, nostalgia and shopping channels are the most consistently popular.

ASTRA 1D inaugurated a significant new phase of technological development, for it is the first satellite in the system that can be operated in the BSS frequency band (Broadcast Satellite Services) reserved for future digital transmissions. Indeed, it already provides capacity for the first European digital test transmissions conducted in collaboration with appropriate hardware manufactures and programmers. In the late 1990s viewers can expect an increasing number of programme services to be made available simultaneously in both analogue and digital formats via the process of "dual illumination." SES, which plans to be a major influence in Europe's transition from the analogue to the digital age of TV and video, has signed firm contracts for the space launches of ASTRA satellites 1E, 1F and 1G in Summer 1995, the first half of 1996 and the first half of 1997 respectively. Each of these advanced satellites will be specially dedicated to digital transmissions and will significantly increase the potential capacity of the seven-satellite ASTRA system. They are expected to carry a total of 56 additional transponders, each capable, with the use of digital

compression, of transmitting up to 10 TV programmes simultaneously; they will also contribute to the introduction of HDTV. In November 1994 the profitable French subscription channel Canal Plus concluded a long-term agreement with SES covering six transponders for digital transmission of the channel's "programmes bouquet" to the different European language markets. Other digital partners, such as British Sky Broadcasting and the European pay-television group Nethold, are also participating in the evolving digital environment.

As many as eight ASTRA devices could theoretically be positioned at the same location before SES would need to find an alternative orbital slot for a second series of twenty-first century satellites. By then, the ASTRA system as a whole will be able to deliver literally hundreds of channels, programmes and services to homes all over Europe. But SES is unlikely to enjoy an indefinite monopoly. In April 1995, the European satellite agency EUTELSAT launched the first in a new series of "Hot Bird" high-technology broadcasting satellites which will compete for the same market. It remains to be seen whether sufficient consumer demand exists for two such major players in the European satellite transponder rental business.

—Tony Pearson

FURTHER READING

Alderman, Bruce. "Europe's TV Hopes Soar with Astra: Finally Launched DBS Bird's 16 Channels Promise a New Era for Commercial TV." *Variety* (Los Angeles), 14 December 1988.

"Astra, Euro Broadcast Satellite, Augurs New Era on Continent." *Variety* (Los Angeles), 8 February 1989.

Collins, Richard. *Satellite Television in Western Europe.* London: John Libbey, 1990.

Fox, Barry. "Astra Ups Its Options With Extra Satellites. *New Scientist* (London), 15 December 1990.

———. "Satellite Broadcasters Battle in the Sky." *New Scientist* (London), 22 October 1988.

Levine, Jonathan B. "This Satellite Company Runs Rings Around Rivals." *Business Week* (New York), 11 February 1991.

Margolis, Irv. "Europe's Satellite Picture: Cloudy or Bright?" *Television-Radio Age* (New York), 27 June 1988.

Marwick, Peat . *Satellite Personal Communications and Their Consequences for European Telecommunications, Trade, and Industry: Executive Summary: Report to the European Commission.* Brussels: European Commission, 1994.

Spellman, James D. "Private Satellites." *Europe* (Washington, D.C.), November 1993.

Television by Satellite and Cable. Strasbourg: Council of Europe, 1985.

Towards Europe-wide Systems and Services : Green Paper on a Common Approach in the Field of Satellite Communications in the European Community. Brussels: Commission of the European Communities, 1990.

EUROPEAN UNION: TELEVISION POLICY

The European Union (EU) is a unique form of international organization created by treaty but exhibiting characteristics of an embryonic federation. It is based on amendments to the European Coal and Steel Community (ECSC) Treaty of 1951 (Treaty of Paris), the European Economic Community (EEC) Treaty of 1957 (first Treaty of Rome), and the European Atomic Energy Community (EURATOM) Treaty of 1957. The name "European Union" derives from the Treaty on European Union (TEU) of 1992, better known as the Maastricht Treaty. For this purpose, the EU may be considered synonymous with the former terms EEC and EC (European Community). Since 1995, the EU included fifteen members: France, Germany, Italy, Belgium, the Netherlands, Luxembourg, the United Kingdom, Ireland, Greece, Spain, Portugal, Denmark, Austria, Sweden, and Finland.

Among the most important purposes of the original EEC Treaty were the creation of a Common Market and an increase in economic integration among the Member States. Economic integration was intended both to promote economic prosperity and aid in the prevention of further conflicts such as occurred in World War II. Television policy in the EU reflects the underlying purpose of promoting European integration and abolishing national barriers to the free movements of goods and services within the Common Market. By decision of the European Court of Justice in *Sacchi* (1974), a television signal is considered a provision of services under Articles 59 and 60 of the Treaty of Rome, and national barriers to cross-frontier broadcasting or the establishment of broadcasters from one Member State in another are intended to be abolished in most circumstances.

The EU's most important initiative in television policy is the establishment of a single EU market in television, the so-called "Television Without Frontiers" (TWF) Directive. A directive requires Member States to conform or harmonize their national legislation to standards or criteria laid down in the text of the directive. The TWF Directive, enacted by the Council of the EC in 1989, had the purposes of securing access for viewers and listeners in all Member States to broadcasting signals emanating from any other Member State and the harmonization of EU broadcast advertising standards. The European Parliament's Hahn Report on Radio and Television Broadcasting in the EC (1982) laid the groundwork for the formal TWF Directive a few years later. The Hahn Report advocated establishment of a unified European television channel and saw satellite television technology leading to a reorganization of the media in Europe and breaking down of the boundaries of national television networks.

The TWF Directive (1989) lays down minimum standards that, if met by any television program, allow it to freely circulate within the EU without restriction, provided that it complies with the legislation of the country of origin. The directive contains chapters devoted to promotion of television program production and distribution, protection of minors, television advertising and sponsorship, and right of reply. Advertising that promotes discrimination on grounds of race, sex, or nationality; is offensive to religious beliefs; or which encourages behavior prejudicial to health, safety, or the protection of the environment is prohibited or restricted. For example, advertising of alcoholic beverages is restricted, but advertising of tobacco products is totally prohibited. A right of reply is accorded to any person or organization whose legitimate interests have been damaged by an incorrect assertion of fact in a television program.

The TWF Directive also lays down two other policies which have an effect similar to the establishment of quotas on broadcasting in the EU. First, the directive requires member states to ensure "where practicable" and by "appropriate means" that broadcasters reserve for "European works" a majority of their transmission time, exclusive of news, sports events, games, advertising, and teletext services. This is intended to protect 50% or more of transmission time so defined from foreign (non-EU) competition. The second quota, designed to stimulate the production of European drama work, requires broadcasters to reserve 10% or more of their transmission time (as above) or alternatively, 10% of their programming budget, for European works created by producers who are "independent of broadcasters."

During the late 1980s and early 1990s, concern developed in Europe that a single market in television was an economic threat to national broadcasting markets and national media, as well as a threat to cultural and linguistic diversity in Europe. The threat is seen to derive from English language services and productions—originating from the United States, not England—in that only the United States is considered to have film and television industries organized on a scale large enough to take advantage of the single market. Indeed, one report indicates that the European market is largely dominated by United States productions in a proportion of 12:1. However, less than 50% of total transmission time on most European channels is accounted for by American programming.

Concern at the European level for the protection and aid of European programming has lead to audiovisual industry subsidy programs, such as the European Commission's MEDIA, MEDIA II, Action Plan for Advanced Television programs, and the Council of Europe's Eurimages fund. These are collectively intended to support and stimulate independent production and distribution networks for European works which are currently considered noncompetitive with U.S. programming imports.

European Union television policy thus simultaneously pursues the economic objective of creating a single market in broadcasting along with the fostering of cultural pluralism and protection of existing national and subnational broadcasting markets and institutions. The "Television Without Frontiers" approach, rooted in the fundamental purpose of the EU, has so far had more impact than other protectionist

policies. However, there are sharp differences between member states which could ultimately lead to less economic integration and more cultural and economic protectionism. In 1995, the TWF Directive was the subject of debate at the European Commission level concerning possible revision, but consideration of any amendments will be forthcoming.
—Clifford A. Jones

FURTHER READING

Cave, Martin. *Meeting Universal Service Obligations in a Competitive Telecommunications Sector.* Luxembourg: Office for Official Publications of the European Communities, 1994.
Collins, Richard. "Unity in Diversity? The European Single Market in Broadcasting and the Audiovisual, 1982–92." *Journal of Common Market Studies* (Oxford, England), 1994.
Commission of the European Communities. *Report by the Think-Tank on the Audiovisual Policy in the European Union.* Luxembourg: OOPEC, 1994.
European Parliament. "Report on Radio and Television Broadcasting in the European Community." Luxembourg: OOPEC, 1982.
Salvatore, Vicenzo. "Quotas on TV Programmes and EEC Law." *Common Market Law Review* (London), 1992.
Schwartz, Ivo E. "Broadcasting and the EEC Treaty." *European Law Review* (Andover, England), 1986.
Silj, Alessandro, with Manuel Alvarado. *East of Dallas: The European Challenge to American Television.* London: British Film Institute, 1988.
Wallace, Rebecca, and David Goldberg. "Television Broadcasting: The Community's Response." *Common Market Law Review* (London), 1989.

EUROVISION SONG CONTEST

International Music Program

The *Eurovision Song Contest* is a live, televised music competition that has received widespread ridicule since its debut in 1956. Certainly this has been true of the contest's reception in the United Kingdom, which informs the perspective from which this entry is written. Yet, as its longevity indicates, the program's importance within European television history is undeniable. While critics plead for the plug to be pulled on this annual celebration of pop mediocrity, the *Eurovision Song Contest (ESC)* continues unabated, extending its media reach (if not its musical scope) from year to year. The competition is truly massive in terms of its logistical and technical requirements, the audience figures and record sales it engenders, and the significance of the popular cultural moments it produces.

The *ESC* is the flagship of Eurovision light entertainment programming. Eurovision is the television network supervised by the European Broadcasting Union (EBU), and was established in the early 1950s to serve two functions: to share the costs of programming with international interest between the broadcasting services of member nations, and to promote cultural appreciation and identification throughout western Europe. At the time of the first Eurovision broadcast in 1954 there were less than five million television receivers in the whole continent (90% of these were in England). The network now stretches into northern Africa, the Middle East, and eastern Europe, with most transmissions conveyed via satellite to the receiving stations of member nations for terrestrial broadcast.

The overwhelming majority of Eurovision transmissions have fallen into the sports, news, and public affairs categories. In the 1950s, EBU officials, perceiving the need for the dissemination of popular cultural programming to offset the influence of the American media, decided to extend Italy's San Remo Song Festival into a pan-European occasion. This became the *ESC*, the first of which was held in Lugano, Switzerland, and was relayed to less than ten nations. Since that time the contest has developed into a spring ritual now viewed by 600 million people in 35 countries, including several in Asia and the Middle East (which don't even send representatives to the competition).

The *Eurovision Song Contest* is a long, live Saturday evening showcase of pop music talent that typically ranges from the indescribably bad, through the insufferably indifferent, to a few catchy little numbers. Contestants are chosen by their respective nations during earlier preliminary stages. The duly nominated acts, as cultural ambassadors for their country, then attend the big event and perform their tune. Conventionally, the host nation is determined by the winner of the previous year's contest. (e.g. Gigliola Cinquetti's triumph of 1964, "Non ho l'età," resulted in Radiotelevisione Italiana playing host in 1965.) The *ESC* is designed to be a grand affair, with expensive sets, full orchestra accompaniment, and a "special night out" atmosphere. Best behavior is expected from all concerned.

Following the performances, panels of judges from each nation call in their point allocations to the central auditorium where the contest is taking place, and a "high-tech" scoreboard tabulates the cumulative scores. As even the most ardent of critics will attest, this is a special moment for home viewers—one where elements particular to the *ESC* (technological accomplishment, anticipation induced by the live event, intercultural differences) combine for curious effect. Will your country's representatives beat the competition and incur the envy of other Europeans? Will the juries throw objectivity to the wind and vote according to national prejudice? Or will, as occurred to Norway's hapless Jahn

Eurovision Song Contest
Photo courtesy of EBU

Teigen on that unforgettable May night in 1978, a contestant endure the humiliating fate of receiving no points whatsoever?

Like its late-lamented Eurovision companion, *Jeux Sans Frontières*, the *ESC* pays homage to clean, amateur fun and the elevation of the unknown to the status of national hero. But unlike the excessively carnivalesque *JSF*, the *Eurovision Song Contest* attempts to avoid the very absurdity and mockery it unwittingly generates. For its first decade, the *ESC* was a wholesome, formal affair: the amorous ballads it featured helped to create a chasm between the competition's cultural mission and that of rock music that has never been bridged. In the late 1960s and early 1970s, youth orientation became a primary factor in determining victory. The 1968 winner, "La la la ..." from Spain's Massiel, inspired a succession of entries incorporating childish lyrics that avoided identifiable linguistic origins in order to garner wide jury appeal. A similar delve into formulism was initiated by the British Sandy Shaw the following year: "Puppet on a String" evoked a generically pan-European musical heritage with its oompah brass and circus ground melodies. In their triumphant international debut on the *ESC*, Abba opted for English and a continentally-recognizable historical event with "Waterloo" in 1974. The Swedish quartet's glam sensibilities and

subsequent commercial success multiplied the contest's kitsch quotient tenfold and launched a string of 2-girl/2-boy combos in its wake. Intimating its own concern over the increasingly imitative nature of the competition, the EBU stipulated various edicts that generated a spate of regional, folk-influenced entries in the late 1970s, all of which scored poorly with the judges. The 1980s witnessed the ascension of over-choreographed performance, and more explicit attempts to excite juries and viewers with soft, sanitized sex appeal. Efforts to resuscitate the *ESC* as a viable musical forum have resulted in recent efforts to modernize the look and style of the contest and to encourage a more professional approach to promotion through the participation of the corporate music industry.

In estimating the significance of the *Eurovision Song Contest*, perhaps less attention should be given to its bloated festivity or the derivative nature of the contenders' music. While its cultural merits are dubious, the event has become a television landmark. Its durability and notoriety have led the EBU to support the *Eurovision Competition for Young Musicians* and the *Eurovision Competition for Young Dancers* in order to further promote Eurocentric cultural understanding through televised stage performance.

—Matthew Murray

FURTHER READING

Barnes, Julian. "Pit Props." *New Statesman* (London), 6 April 1979.

Collins, Michael. "Eurotrash." *Punch* (London), 5 May 1989.

Dessau, Bruce. "Song Without End." *The Listener* (London), 28 April 1988.

Eugster, Ernest. *Television Programming Across National Boundaries: The EBU and OIRT Experience.* Dedham, Massachusetts: Artech House, 1983.

Kressley, Konrad M. "EUROVISION: Distributing Costs and Benefits in an International Broadcasting Union." *Journal of Broadcasting* (Washington, D.C.), Spring 1978.

See also Music on Television

EXPERIMENTAL VIDEO

Experimental video, video art, electronic art, alternative TV, community video, guerrilla television, computer art: these are a few of the labels that have been applied to a body of work that began to emerge in the United States. in the 1960s. Arguably, the most important of these labels is "experimental." The dominant goal of this video movement over the past 30 years has been change, achieved through the strategy of experimentation. The consistent target for this change has been television—commercially supported, network broadcast, mainstream television—whose success with mass audiences was the result of the repetition of proven formulas rather than aesthetic, ideological, or industrial innovation or experimentation. It is perhaps commercial television's ability to interpret the uncertain world within the context of familiar conventions that makes it an essential part of everyday life in America. And it is this body of familiar interpretations that became the challenge of experimental video artists.

In his book *Expanded Cinema* (1970), media visionary Gene Youngblood states "commercial entertainment works against art (experimentation), exploits the alienation and boredom of the public, by perpetuating a system of conditioned response to formulas." Youngblood's manifesto goes on to argue that any community requires experimentation in order to survive. He concludes, "The artist is always an anarchist, a revolutionary, a creator of new worlds imperceptibly gaining on reality."

One of the earliest of the video revolutionaries was Korean-born artist Nam June Paik. When he landed in the United States in 1964, Paik was already anxious to lead the experimental video revolution. One of his earliest works, *TV Magnet* (1965) challenged the viewing public to reexamine "television." Paik took a piece of furniture, the TV set, and changed its meaning by presenting it as sculpture. He demystified television by altering the magnetic polarity of the cathode-ray tube, demonstrating that the lines of light on the screen were clearly controlled by the large magnet sitting on top of the set rather than by some magical connection to the "real world." Most significantly, he changed the viewers' role as passive consumers to active creators by allowing them to interact with the piece by moving the magnet, thereby participating in the creation of the light patterns on the screen.

Paik is also credited with purchasing the first Sony Portapak, the first truly portable videotape recorder, in 1965. Usually, the Sony Portapak and not the altered TV set has been identified with the beginning of experimental video. For the first time, the low cost of the Portapak and its portability gave the experimental artists access to the means of producing television. Legend has it that Paik met a cargo boat in New York harbor, grabbed a Portapak, rode through the city in a cab shooting video and that night showed his street scenes, including the visit of Pope Paul VI, in Cafe a Go Go.

But Paik was not operating alone. In 1964, the same year Paik moved to the United States, Marshall McLuhan published *Understanding Media*. His declaration that "the medium is the message" became key passwords for Paik and a generation of experimental video makers who hoped to design and build a "Global Village" through alternative uses of telecommunications.

Many of these video artists followed the tradition of avant-garde filmmakers, seeking to define the unique properties of their medium. By the early 1970s, experimental video makers were trying to find ways to isolate the unique properties of video's electronic image. A profusion of technical devices began to appear, most notably among them, a variety of color synthesizers. Paik developed one synthesizer in collaboration with Shuya Abe. Concurrently, Stephen Beck, Peter Campus, Bill and Louise Etra, Stan VanderBeek, and Walter Wright built their own versions. These synthesizers allowed artists to work directly with the materials of the TV machine. They brought into the foreground TV's glowing surface composed of tiny points called pixels. By controlling voltages and frequencies, artists could change the color and intensity of the phosphorous pixels. In the process, they pushed the viewer away from the representational properties of TV and toward its powers of abstraction, to forms and patterns akin to those of modern painting.

None of the experimenters was more systematic in their pursuit of the unique properties and language of video than Steina and Woody Vasulka. The Vasulkas founded a studio-exhibition hall-meeting place, The Kitchen, in New York City as a locus of experimentation in video, dance, and music. As a teacher at the State University of New York at Buffalo, Woody Vasulka's established a video class that included the mathematics of television. Working first with the analog signal and then learning to digitize the electronic signal, Vasulka and his colleagues created a dialogue between the artist's imagination and the inner logic of the TV machine. Slowly an electronic vocabulary and grammar began to emerge and to shape to works such as *The Commission* (1983), in which electronic imaging codes are used to render the virtuosity of violinist Niccolo Paganini into visual narrative elements.

For many other video experimenters, however, the essence of the video revolution did not lie inside the machine, in its technical or formal qualities. These "video anarchists" responded instead to the Marxist call for the appropriation of the means of production. Their interpretation of McLuhan's famous phrase was that control of the medium determined the meaning of the message and so long as corporate American controlled the commercial TV, the message would be the same—"consume." The Sony Portapak gave these video makers a chance to produce. It did not matter that the Portapak produced low resolution black and white images, that the tape was almost impossible to edit, or that the equipment was sold by a large corporation. It was cheap, portable enough for one person to operate, and reproduced images instantly. It was finally a technology that gave the constitutional guarantee of "freedom of speech" a place on TV. The Federal Communications Commission (FCC) boosted the vision of a media democracy by requiring cable television companies to provide free public access channels in order to obtain franchises, and these access channels often provided the distribution and exhibition sites for experimental video makers.

Charismatic leaders such as George Stoney, who had worked in Canada's Challenge for Change program, rallied young video activists to the cause of media democracy. Throughout the 1970s public access centers, media centers, and video collectives sprung up across the country. Their names suggest their utopian intentions: Top Value TV (TVTV), People's Video Theater, the Alternate Media Center, Videofreex, Global Village, Video Free America, Portable Channel, Videopolis, and Paper Tiger. These groups and many others nurtured the movement. Global Village started a festival, The Kitchen hosted the First Women's Video Festival, and Paper Tiger organized a cable network of 400 sites linked via satellite. Deep Dish Television, as the network is called, still continues, airing controversial programs on such issues as censorship of the arts, The Gulf War, and AIDS.

As the United States moved into a more conservative social climate in the 1980s and 1990s, the idea of giving distribution access to the people has lost much of its influence on public policy. The FCC eliminated the public access requirements and the Telecommunications Act of 1996 leaves the notion of public access greatly weakened.

Nevertheless, neither the movement to explore the TV machine nor the movement to create more democratic media went unnoticed by the more mainstream forms of television. In fact, the United States system of public television, the Public Broadcasting Service, takes as part of its mission the provision of a site for alternate voices, innova-

tion, and the airing of controversy. These directives, it would seem, made PBS a natural forum for experimental video. Experience has proven otherwise.

In the early 1970s, WGBH producer, Fred Barzyk, created the New Television Workshop in Boston. Barzyk offered artists the use of non-broadcast quality half-inch video (the Portapak did not meet FCC blanking requirements) and then showed their work on *Artists' Showcase*. Other PBS venues followed, such as WNET's TV Laboratory in New York, KQED's Center for Experiments in Television in San Francisco, KTCA's *Alive from off Center* in Minneapolis, and the syndicated series, *P.O.V.* These programs flourished in the 1970s and early 1980s, yet most shut down because PBS station programmers across the country were always ambivalent about experimental media. They felt that their public trust required them to respond to ratings as did their counterparts in the commercial arena, and ratings for the experimental showcases were never large.

The commercial networks have made their own forays into the experimental movement. CBS, for example, explored the possibility of producing a show called *Subject to Change* with Videofreex. In the end, executives decided the show was "ahead of its time." NBC's *Today* show did hire Jon Alpert, co-director of the Downtown Community Television Center in New York City. Alpert's hand-held, personal, verité-style technique made him one of the few experimental artists who could move back and forth between the mainstream and alternate TV forums. He received both praise and criticism for doing so, as did others such as John Sanborn who made music videos for MTV and William Wegman who presented his famous dogs on David Letterman's programs. Michael Shamberg and the Raindance Corporation in their publication, *Guerrilla Television* (1971), had admonished "anyone who thinks that broadcast-TV is capable of reform just doesn't understand the media. A standard of success that demands 30 to 50 million people can only tend toward homogenization." The question for many experimenters, then, was whether Wegmen's dogs who had seemed so unique in half-inch black and white had been turned into "stupid pet tricks" by David Letterman.

As this example indicates, throughout the last three decades, the dilemma for experimental video artists has been to work with the substance of mass media without being swallowed by it. For many of them, working inside the networks has proven less satisfying than "making television strange" by placing it in new contexts such as museums, alternate spaces, and shopping malls.

Nam June Paik and his conceptual artists group Fluxus had led the way in the 1960s with their "de-collage" method that started with the removal of the TV set from its familial context in the home. Probably the most famous image of the experimental movement, however, is Ant Farm's *Media Burn* (1975). In this piece, a futuristic-looking Cadillac drives headlong through a burning pyramid of TV sets. Even viewers who missed the actual performance and have seen only a photograph of *Media Burn* could not miss Ant Farm's satirical stab at the power and influence of commercial television.

During the early years of the experimental video movements, the Everson Museum of Art, the Whitney Museum, the Museum of Modern Art, the Long Beach Museum of Art, and the Walker Art Center initiated video exhibition programs. Many of these works, often known as "video installations," were multi-channel. Gary Hill's *Inasmuch as It Is Always Already Taking Place* (1990) was a sixteen-channel installation with sixteen modified monitors recessed in a wall. The multi-channel capability allowed the artist to create new environments and contexts for the viewer. In their *Wraparound* (1982), Kit Fitzgerald and John Sanborn wanted to give the viewer the "everyday task of assimilating simultaneous information and eliminating the unwanted." In a measure of how far the artist intended to go to shake viewers out of their TV habit, Bill Viola placed a small TV set next to a pitcher and glass of water in what was depicted as a *Room for St. John of the Cross* (1983). Viola's ambition was to rediscover—in the context of the age of television—the experience of "love, ecstasy, passage through the dark night, and flying over city walls and mountains" that the 16th century mystic described in his poetry.

All of these works have taken the artists away from the low-cost and low-tech Portapak. Instead, they have embraced the advances, especially in 3/4-inch color video, computer editing, and mixing. Moreover, the budgets required for many of the installation works had put the artists back in contact with mainstream corporate America. El Paso Gas Company and the Polaroid Corporation, for instance, had contributed to the creation of Viola's *Room for St. John of the Cross*. No project symbolized more the ambition and frustrations of the experimental video artists learning to work with the commercial world than Dara Birnbaum's video wall constructed for the Rio Shopping Complex in Atlanta. A brilliantly conceived design related to Birnbaum's background in architecture and video, the wall, made up of 25 monitors, was a giant electronic bulletin board in the middle of the Rio mall's town square. The content of the monitors was triggered by the motion of the shoppers in the square and contained images that included news coming out of Atlanta-based CNN as well as reflections on the natural landscape that existed before the construction of the mall. The record of the contract negotiations involved in the creation of this project gives an indication of the struggle between a real estate developer and an artist to find a common language for their project. Beginning with the concept that the "art was a work for hire," the negotiations eventually reversed the point and concluded that the artist should retain the rights to the art and license it to the developer. In the end, developer Charles Ackerman told *Business Atlanta* magazine "this center will just smack you in the face with the idea that it is different. When you look at, you will think there is no limit to the imagination. Things don't have to be the way they always are."

By the 1980s and 1990s, experimental video attracted a whole new generation of artists. Many of the best of these were women, black, Hispanic, Asian, or gay. Most brought to their work a social or political agenda. Specifically, they challenged the white male power structure that dominated myth, history, society, the economy, the arts, and television. They questioned the whole narrative framework with its white male heroes conquering dark antagonists who threatened helpless females. Starting with the camera lens—which they described as an extension of the male gaze directed at the commodified woman—they deconstructed the whole apparatus of image making and image consuming.

Speaking for these artists, the narrator in Helen DeMichiel's *Consider Anything, Only Don't Cry* (1988), lays out their strategy:

> I rob the image bank compulsively. I cut up, rearrange, collage, montage, decompose, rearrange, subvert, recontextualize, deconstruct, reconstruct, debunk, rethink, recombine, sort out, untangle, and give back the pictures, the meanings, the sounds, the music, that are taken from us in every moment of our days and nights.

In DeMichiel's portrait of a woman trying to discover both her personal and culture identities, the intention was to produce a video quilt made up of images ranging from home movies to commercial ads. Indeed, the quilt, a favorite metaphor for the feminists' communal approach to art, produced in the viewer a perception of many pieces being stitched together rather the perception of monolithic unity derived from conventional narrative. The video quilt invited the viewer into the making of the work by patching in their own associations stimulated by the personal and public images rather than asking them to uncover the message of the author.

Joan Braderman in *Joan Does Dynasty* (1986), assumed the role of the viewer by skillfully layering a masked image of herself into scenes with *Dynasty* star, Joan Collins. Once "in" the scene, Braderman carried on her own commentary about Alexis's plot to wrest power from the Carrington patriarchy. Unlike Fluxus' appropriation of the TV set, Braderman did not want to leave the familiar grounds of popular television. She wanted in, but on her own terms—with her own lines, and her own images. In effect, she wanted to rearrange "television."

The challenge to the hegemony of white males spread rapidly in the 1980s and 1990s. Rea Tajiri and Janice Tanaka produced tapes to reclaim their memory and history that lay forgotten in the internment of Asian-Americans during World War II. In *Itam Hakin Hopit* (1984), Victor Masayesva used cutting-edge technology to celebrate the relevance of the Hopi's world view. Edin Velez, in his *Meta Mayan II* (1981), used slow motion to enhance the effect on the American audience of the return gaze of a Mayan Indian woman. In 1991, African-American artist, Philip Mallory Jones, launched his *First World Order Project*, designed to take advantage of the global "telecommunity" that had been created by technologies such as the satellite and the Internet. Jones's project focused on the knowledge and wisdom that rises out of the differences that exist in "others."

By the summer of 1989, the "differences" in "others" was too much for the establishment. Conservative political and cultural groups targeted the National Endowment for the Arts and its support of "morally reprehensible trash." The most famous examples were Robert Mapplethorpe's photos of brutal and extreme homosexual acts. The most infamous experimental film/video was *Tongues Untied* by African-American and gay artist, Marlon Riggs. Campaigns were mounted against this critically acclaimed work which was to air on the PBS series *P.O.V.* in the summer of 1991. In the end, 174 PBS stations refused to show the film. Marlon Riggs summed up the reaction of many in the experimental art field when he stated: "a society that shuts its eyes cannot grow or change or discover what's really decent in the world."

In *Expanded Cinema*, Gene Youngblood called for the "artist [to be] an anarchist, a revolutionary, a creator of new worlds imperceptibly gaining on reality." Experimental artists from Nam June Paik to Marlon Riggs responded. Scholars like Youngblood look upon the experimental movement as a protean force, constantly taking new shapes and revealing additional facets of life and humanity. Critics view it as a many-headed Hydra; each head when cut off is replaced by two others.

In 1984, Paik titled his live satellite broadcast between Paris, New York, and San Francisco, *Good Morning, Mr. Orwell.* The technology of big brother had arrived. Of course, the playful Paik's ambition was to demonstrate to Orwell how ridiculous technology was and how easily it could be humanized. In his book *Being Digital* (1995), Nicholas Negroponte supports Paik's optimism about human beings actively appropriating technology to achieve change:

> The effect of fax machines on Tiananmen Square is an ironic example, because newly popular and decentralized tools were invoked precisely when the government was trying to reassert its elite and centralized control. The Internet provides a world-wide channel of communication that flies in the face of any censorship and thrives especially in

places like Singapore, where freedom of the press is marginal and networking ubiquitous.

This is finally the proper context in which to judge the American experimental video movement. It is the desire to be free that has driven the experiments of American video artists and it is the possibility of liberating the full potential of all human beings that will lead them into experimental collaborations in the future.

—Ed Hugetz

FURTHER READING

Frohnmayer, John. *Leaving Town Alive: Confessions of an Arts Warrior.* New York: Houghton Mifflin, 1993.

Hall, Doug, and Sally Jo Fifer, editors. *Illuminating Video: An Essential Guide to Video Art.* New York: Aperture Foundation, 1990.

Hanhardt, John, editor. *Video Culture: A Critical Investigation.* New York: Visual Studies Workshop, 1986.

Heiferman, Marvin, Lisa Phillips, and John G. Hanhardt. *Image World: Art and Media Culture.* New York: Whitney Museum of American Art, 1989.

Huffman, Kathy Rae. *Video: A Retrospective.* California: Long Beach Museum of Art, 1984.

Huffman, Kathy Rae, and Dorine Mignot, editors. *The Arts for Television.* Los Angeles: Museum of Contemporary Art, and Amsterdam Stedelijk Museum, Amsterdam, 1987.

Judson, William D. *American Landscape Video: The Electronic Grove.* Pittsburgh, Pennsylvania: Carnegie Museum of Art, 1988.

London, Barbara. *Video Spaces: Eight Installations.* New York: Museum of Modern Art, 1995.

Negroponte, Nicholas. *Being Digital.* New York: Knopf, 1995.

Penny, Simon, editor. *Critical Issues in Electronic Media.* Albany: State University of New York Press, 1995.

Popper, Frank. *Art of the Electronic Age.* New York: Harry N. Abrams, 1993.

Zippay, Lori, editor. *Electronic Arts Intermix: Video.* New York: Electronic Arts Intermix, 1991.

See also Paik, Nam June

EYES ON THE PRIZE

U.S. Documentary Series

Eyes on the Prize, a critically acclaimed 14-part series dealing with the American Civil Rights Movement, was broadcast nationally by the Public Broadcasting Service. The first six programs, *Eyes on the Prize: America's Civil Rights Years* (1954–1965) was aired in January and February 1987. The eight-part sequel, *Eyes on the Prize II: America at the Racial Crossroads* (1965–1985) was broadcast in 1990.

Produced over the course of twelve years by Blackside, Inc., one of the oldest minority-owned film and television

production companies in the country, the series received over 23 awards, including two Emmys (for Outstanding Documentary and Outstanding Achievement in Writing), the duPont Columbia Award, the Edward R. Murrow Brotherhood Award for Best National Documentary, the International Documentary Association's Distinguished Documentary Award, Program of the Year and Outstanding News Information Program by the Television Critics Association, and the CINE Golden Eagle.

Eyes on the Prize
Photo courtesy of WTTW / Channel 11

In addition to its positive receptions from television critics and professionals, *Eyes on the Prize* was also lauded by historians and educators. Using archival footage and contemporary interviews with participants in the struggle for and against Civil Rights, the series presented the movement as multi-faceted. Watched by over 20 million viewers with each airing, it served as an important educational tool, reaching a generation of millions of Americans who have no direct experience with the historic events chronicled. Though the series included such landmark events as the Montgomery, Alabama bus boycott of 1955–56, the 1963 March on Washington, and the assassination of Dr. Martin Luther King, Jr., in 1968, it also documented the workings of the movement on a grass-roots level, presenting events and individuals often overlooked.

Eyes on the Prize I, narrated by Julian Bond, was launched by the episode entitled "Awakenings." It documents two events that helped focus the nation's attention on the oppression of African American citizens: the lynching of fourteen-year-old Emmett Till in 1955 and the Montgomery bus boycott, motivated by the arrest of Rosa Parks, who refused to relinquish her seat on a public bus to a white person. Parts two through six covered such topics as the key court case, *Brown v. the Board of Education*, the nationwide expansion of the movement, James Meredith's enrollment at the University of Mississippi, the Freedom Rides, and the passage of the Voting Rights Act.

Despite the critical and popular success of the first six episodes, executive producer Henry Hampton had a difficult time raising the six million dollars needed to fund the sequel. The reticence of both corporate and public granting organizations is attributed to the subject matter of *Eyes II*, issues which the United States has not yet resolved: the rise of the Black Panther Party, the Nation of Islam, the Black Consciousness Movement, the Vietnam War, busing, and Affirmative Action.

—Frances K. Gateward

FURTHER READING

Barol, Bill. "A Struggle for the Prize: Documenting the Last 20 Years of Civil Rights." *Newsweek* (New York), 22 August 1988.

"Eyes on Henry Hampton." *The New Yorker*, 23 January 1995.

Lord, Lewis J. "A Journey to Another Time and, to Many, Another World." *U.S. News and World Report* (Washington, D.C.), 9 March 1987.

Lyon, Danny. "Ain't Gonna Let Nobody Turn Me Round: Use and Misuse of the Southern Civil Rights Movement." *Aperture* (New York), Summer 1989.

See also Documentary; Racism, Ethnicity, and Television

EYEWITNESS TO HISTORY

U.S. News Program

CBS News conceived *Eyewitness to History* to cover U.S. presidential diplomacy and the Soviet Union during the last five months of 1959. Before the series settled into its Friday 10:30 to 11:00 P.M. period in September 1960, 16 of 28 programs were brought to the public before 8:30 P.M., with only two covering stories unrelated to President Eisenhower, Premier Khrushchev, President De Gaulle, and the summits in Paris. In September 1961 the series returned as *Eyewitness*, with the narrow, original focus gone, but the same need to cover late breaking national and international news. For four seasons *Eyewitness to History* stood as the center of growth at CBS News, and made a thirty-minute daily news program feasible in the eyes of network executives.

In the spring of 1963, *Eyewitness* was canceled after the news division was given permission for a thirty-minute nightly newscast. It was canceled not just to return time to the network schedule, but to shift Executive Producer Leslie Midgley and many of his producers to work on the *CBS Evening News*, assisting Don Hewitt, executive producer of the new program.

Midgley took pride in airing on Friday with stories that would appear in the national news magazines on Monday. The series pioneered construction of a program with combinations of live telecast, videotape, and film, and broke through many self-imposed limitations of news reporting. For the first time video cameras were shipped and used overseas, covering President Eisenhower. Unfortunately, the bulky nature of these cameras, difficult to move once optimally positioned, posed problems when crowds did not cooperate. In the United States video cameras were used extensively to cover Khrushchev's visit in 1959, but use of cameras in crowds again disrupted coverage on such historic programs as "Khrushchev on the Farm." The series also struggled with the early uses of two-inch videotape. The tape was fed to New York with specific time cues signaling when to start and stop. Unable at that time to edit two-inch tape electronically, film editors would actually cut two-inch tape, compiling the necessary sections. Initially, according to the producers, what made the series as historic as the events themselves was the use of a jet airplane to ship back tape and film of Eisenhower in Italy, India, Brazil, West Germany, England, Paris, Iran, Greece, Japan and Paris.

As the series pushed for coverage of events with multidimensional background stories, the production crew developed appropriate strategies. Editors cut negative film and projected it directly over the air by reversing the polarity in the control room. Certain stories aired only because the unit employed a two-projector system, switching between one projector, the studio camera, the other projector, and, sometimes, the video projector. Realizing the historical value of the two-inch tape, Midgley asked Sig Mickelson, CBS news president, to start a tape archive. He refused, preferring to reuse the tape—and part of the video record of significant historical, social, and cultural events was lost.

In the second season the series quickly gained a reputation for changing the announced topic, sometimes as late as Friday morning. Midgley began to send "field producers," a term that included unit members with other official titles, to different locations, sometimes holding open the possibility of any one of five stories. The series production relied heavily on news judgments of the field producers, who included Bernie Birnbaum, Russ Bensley, John Sharnick, Av Westin, and Philip Scheffler, individuals who would go on to major roles in the television news industry. Their decisions led to crucial alterations in plans and schedules. Twice, for example, in the second season, last minute developments growing out of tension over school integration in New Orleans were given precedence over already developing stories. Similarly, when the production unit was taping John F. Kennedy's announcement and introduction of Cabinet appointments on the day two jet airliners crashed over New York City, Midgley decided to cover the crash. The resulting journalism illustrated the production unit's expert response to such events—they were faster than units in news divisions in New York. Even late-breaking international stories received the unit's attention. They covered Yuri Gagarin orbiting the earth, causing cancellation of two shows on the Eichmann trial in Israel, and another on the events surrounding the Bay of Pigs and the return of prisoners. When anti-government factions seized the cruise ship *Santa Maria* off the coast of Brazil, Charles Kuralt was dispatched on another ship to intercept and film the incident, providing coverage for two weeks. If events surrounding a story halted, as they did during negotiations with the hijackers of *Santa Maria*, or if two events were simultaneously breaking, the series sometimes aired two fifteen-minute segments. After the second year, the CBS television network illustrated to potential advertisers the timeliness of the program by citing listings of the stories the series was preparing to cover.

Although the title changed, *Eyewitness* remained committed to covering presidential trips and diplomacy, keeping the production unit on tight deadlines according to the president's schedule. Certain shows, such as "Spring Arrives in Paris" and "The Big Ski Boom," were prepared over a two- or three-week period and were aired based on the happenstance of events unfolding and the logistics needed to cover the president. After the title change, coverage of diplomacy changed only slightly by placing the flow of events in something of a larger context, such as "Enroute to Vienna," and "The President in Mexico". But this shift was made possible by the developing expertise of the unit.

During the first year, *Eyewitness to History* highlighted corespondents Robert Pierpoint, Alexander Kendrik, Robert Trout, David Schoenbrun, Lou Cioffi, Ernest Leiser, and, especially Charles Collingwood, assigned to accompany the president. With Walter Cronkite as anchor in New York, two or three additional correspondents appeared in programs, from Washington D.C., and different parts of the world according to an event's implications. This structure remained constant throughout the series for coverage of presidential trips as well as for international incidents such as "The Showdown in Laos" and "India at War." Midgley utilized CBS reporters around the world, even those assigned to the *CBS Evening News*, setting the stage for the series' own cancellation, and the unit's re-assignment as a support mechanism for Walter Cronkite's thirty-minute broadcast.

Network politics at this time occasioned a period of instability with regard to the anchor seat. Charles Kuralt was named anchor for the second season of *Eyewitness to History*. Midgley and others inside CBS perceived Kuralt as following in the footsteps of Edward R. Murrow. But James Aubrey, president of CBS, disliked Kuralt's on camera appearance, and convinced Midgley to return Cronkite as anchor in January 1961. Cronkite's role as New York correspondent provided a scope of credibility absent from his other projects. When Cronkite went to the *CBS Evening News* on 16 April 1962, Charles Collingwood became anchor of *Eyewitness*.

At the series start, a critical dimension was added to the objective task of presenting news with Howard K. Smith's commentary on programs focused on diplomacy. In covering certain issues the distinct perspectives and arguments between producer and reporter became evident, as in the case of "Diem's War—Or Ours," and other reports on Vietnam.

Critics and the public were engaged by the urgency and depth *Eyewitness* brought to contemporary issues. Even when considering the new trend in jazz music, Bossa Nova, the producers presented a "critical look" at jazz. Even so the announcement of the program "Who Killed Marilyn Monroe?" brought such an outcry from Hollywood that Midgley changed it to "Marilyn Monroe, Why?"

For three years *Eyewitness to History* aggressively pursued such events as changes in the labor movement, government fiscal policy, the medical establishment and U.S. foreign relations. It was the training and proving ground for television journalists whose careers span most of the second half of the century they covered. And the series signaled CBS's turn to prominence in network television journalism.

—Richard Bartone

ANCHOR

Charles Kuralt	1960–1961
Walter Cronkite	1961–1962
Charles Collingwood	1962–1963

PROGRAMMING HISTORY

- CBS

August 1959–December 1959	Irregular Schedule of Specials
September	Friday 9:00-9:30
September 1960–June 1961	Friday 10:30-11:00
September 1961–August 1963	Friday 10:30-11:00

FURTHER READING

Adams, Val. "Exchange Visits Get TV Sponsor." *The New York Times,* 2 August 1959.

"Cronkite and Midgley: 'I Love Luce-id.'" *Variety* (Los Angeles), 3 January 1962.

Crosby, John. "The Journey." *New York Herald Tribune,* 23 December 1959.

Delatiner, Barbara. "CBS Had a Full Roster of Marilyn Experts." *Newsday* (Hempstead, New York), 13 August 1962.

Gates, Gary Paul. *Air Time: The Inside Story of CBS News.* New York: Harper and Row, 1978.

Guidry, Frederick. "Video Turns to Current History: *Eyewitness*—Foot Loose Scribe." *Christian Science Monitor* (Boston, Massachusetts), 5 October 1960.

Midgley, Leslie. *How Many Words Do You Want?* New York: Birch Lane, 1989.

"Midgley's 'Take 5, Use 1.'" *Variety* (Los Angeles), 5 April 1961.

Ranson, Jo. "*Eyewitness to History* to Get Shorter Title in Fall." *Radio TV Daily* (New York), 1 May 1961.

Schoenbrun, David. *On and Off the Air: An Informal History of CBS News.* New York: Dutton, 1989.

"The Speed Up in Television News Coverage." *Broadcasting* (Washington, D.C.), 2 January 1961.

"Stop the Cameras!" *TV Guide* (Radnor, Pennsylvania), 10 November 1962.

Van Horne, Harriet. "Disasters Test TV News." *New York Telegram,* 20 December 1960.

See also Documentary

F

FAIRNESS DOCTRINE

U.S. Broadcasting Policy

The policy of the United States Federal Communications Commission (FCC) that became known as the "Fairness Doctrine" is an attempt to ensure that all coverage of controversial issues by a broadcast station be balanced and fair. The FCC took the view, in 1949, that station licensees were "public trustees," and as such had an obligation to afford reasonable opportunity for discussion of contrasting points of view on controversial issues of public importance. The commission later held that stations were also obligated to actively seek out issues of importance to their community and air programming that addressed those issues. With the deregulation sweep of the Reagan Administration during the 1980s, the commission dissolved the fairness doctrine.

This doctrine grew out of concern that because of the large number of applications for radio station being submitted and the limited number of frequencies available, broadcasters should make sure they did not use their stations simply as advocates with a singular perspective. Rather, they must allow all points of view. That requirement was to be enforced by FCC mandate.

From the early 1940s, the FCC had established the "Mayflower Doctrine," which prohibited editorializing by stations. But that absolute ban softened somewhat by the end of the decade, allowing editorializing only if other points of view were aired, balancing that of the station's. During these years, the FCC had established *dicta* and case law guiding the operation of the doctrine.

In ensuing years the FCC ensured that the doctrine was operational by laying out rules defining such matters as personal attack and political editorializing (1967). In 1971 the commission set requirements for the stations to report, with their license renewal, efforts to seek out and address issues of concern to the community. This process became known as "Ascertainment of Community Needs," and was to be done systematically and by the station management.

The fairness doctrine ran parallel to Section 315 of the Communications Act of 1934 which required stations to offer "equal opportunity" to all legally qualified political candidates for any office if they had allowed any person running in that office to use the station. The attempt was to balance—to force an even handedness. Section 315 exempted news programs, interviews and documentaries. But the doctrine would include such efforts. Another major difference should be noted here: Section 315 was federal law, passed by Congress. The fairness doctrine was simply FCC policy.

The FCC fairness policy was given great credence by the 1969 U.S. Supreme Court case of *Red Lion Broadcasting Co., Inc. v. FCC*. In that case, a station in Pennsylvania, licensed by Red Lion Co., had aired a "Christian Crusade" program wherein an author, Fred J. Cook, was attacked. When Cook requested time to reply in keeping with the fairness doctrine, the station refused. Upon appeal to the FCC, the Commission declared that there was personal attack and the station had failed to meet its obligation. The station appealed and the case wended its way through the courts and eventually to the Supreme Court. The court ruled for the FCC, giving sanction to the fairness doctrine.

The doctrine, nevertheless, disturbed many journalists, who considered it a violation of First Amendment rights of free speech/free press which should allow reporters to make their own decisions about balancing stories. Fairness, in this view, should not be forced by the FCC. In order to avoid the requirement to go out and find contrasting viewpoints on every issue raised in a story, some journalists simply avoided any coverage of some controversial issues. This "chilling effect" was just the opposite of what the FCC intended.

By the 1980s, many things had changed. The "scarcity" argument which dictated the "public trustee" philosophy of the commission, was disappearing with the abundant number of channels available on cable TV. Without scarcity, or with many other voices in the marketplace of ideas, there were perhaps fewer compelling reasons to keep the fairness doctrine. This was also the era of deregulation when the FCC took on a different attitude about its many rules, seen as an unnecessary burden by most stations. The new chairman of the FCC, Mark Fowler, appointed by President Reagan, publicly avowed to kill the fairness doctrine.

By 1985, the FCC issued its *Fairness Report*, asserting that the doctrine was no longer having its intended effect, might actually have a "chilling effect" and might be in violation of the First Amendment. In a 1987 case, *Meredith Corp. v. FCC*, the courts declared that the doctrine was not mandated by Congress and the FCC did not have to continue to enforce it. The FCC dissolved the doctrine in August of that year.

However, before the commission's action, in the spring of 1987, both houses of Congress voted to put the fairness doctrine into law—a statutory fairness doctrine which the FCC would have to enforce, like it or not. But President Reagan, in keeping with his deregulatory efforts and his long-standing favor of keeping government out of the affairs of business, vetoed the legislation. There were insufficient votes to override the veto. Congressional efforts to make the doctrine into law surfaced again during the Bush administration. As before, the legislation was vetoed, this time by Bush.

The fairness doctrine remains just beneath the surface of concerns over broadcasting and cablecasting, and some members of congress continue to threaten to pass it into legislation. Currently, however, there is no required balance of controversial issues as mandated by the fairness doctrine. The public relies instead on the judgment of broadcast journalists and its own reasoning ability to sort out one-sided or distorted coverage of an issue. Indeed, experience over the past several years since the demise of the doctrine shows that broadcasters can and do provide substantial coverage of controversial issues of public importance in their communities, including contrasting viewpoints, through news, public affairs, public service, interactive and special programming.

—Val E. Limburg

FURTHER READING

Aufderheide, Patricia. "After the Fairness Doctrine: Controversial Broadcast Programming and the Public Interest." *Journal of Communication* (New York), Summer 1990.

Benjamin, Louise M. "Broadcast Campaign Precedents from the 1924 Presidential Election." *Journal of Broadcasting and Electronic Media* (Washington, D.C.), Fall 1987.

Brennan, Timothy A. "The Fairness Doctrine as Public Policy." *Journal of Broadcasting and Electronic Media* (Washington, D.C.), Fall 1989.

Broadcasters and the Fairness Doctrine: Hearing Before the Subcommittee on Telecommunications and Finance of the Committee. United States Congress. House Committee on Energy and Commerce. Subcommittee on Telecommunications and Finance. Washington, D.C. U.S. Congressional Documents, 1989.

Cronauer, Adrian. "The Fairness Doctrine: A Solution in Search of a Problem." *Federal Communications Law Journal* (Los Angeles), October 1994.

Donahue, Hugh Carter. "The Fairness Doctrine Is Shackling Broadcasting." *Technology Review* (Cambridge, Massachusetts), November-December 1986.

Hazlett, Thomas W. "The Fairness Doctrine and the First Amendment." *Public Interest* (New York), Summer 1989.

Krueger, Elizabeth. "Broadcasters' Understanding of Political Broadcast Regulation." *Journal of Broadcasting and Electronic Media* (Washington, D.C.), Summer 1991.

Rowan, Ford. *Broadcast Fairness: Doctrine, Practice, Prospects: A Reappraisal of the Fairness Doctrine and Equal Time Rule.* New York: Longmans, 1984.

Simmons, Steven J. *The Fairness Doctrine and the Media.* Berkeley: University of California Press, 1978.

Streeter, Thomas. "Beyond Freedom of Speech and the Public Interest: The Relevance of Critical Legal Studies to Communications Policy." *Journal of Communication* (New York), Spring 1990.

See also Deregulation; Federal Communications Commission; Political Processes and Television

FALK, PETER

U.S. Actor

Most notable for his role as television's preeminent detective Lt. Columbo, Peter Falk has developed a long and distinguished career in television and film. For his efforts, Falk has received numerous Emmy Awards for a detective role which has taken its place alongside other legendary literary sleuths. Since the late 1970s, Falk has continued to appear in feature films as well as reprise his Columbo character on television.

One of Falk's earliest roles was in *The Untouchables*, a series which launched a number of stars, including Robert Redford. Falk became a popular dramatic actor appearing in several anthology programs, including *Bob Hope Presents the Chrysler Theater* and *The DuPont Show of the Week*. He won his first of several Emmy awards in 1962 for his portrayal of Dimitri Fresco in *The Dick Powell Show's* presentation of the teleplay "The Price of Tomatoes."

In 1965, Falk landed the title role in the CBS series *The Trials of O'Brien*. A precursor to the Columbo character, O'Brien acted diligently in his professional duties yet slov-

enly in his personal life. The series lasted one season before cancellation. During the 1960s, Falk also appeared in a number of feature films, including *Murder, Inc.*, which garnered him an Oscar nomination.

The Columbo character, brainchild of veteran television producers Richard Levinson and William Link, came to Falk quite by accident. According to Mark Dawidziak, author of *The Columbo Phile*, Levinson and Link had experimented with the Columbo persona when they were writing for NBC's *Chevy Mystery Theater*. In that and subsequent versions, Columbo was always portrayed by an elderly gentleman. Thus, in 1968, when Levinson and Link approached Universal television with the idea for a TV movie based on their stage play "Prescription: Murder," the writers hoped to enlist Lee J. Cobb or Bing Crosby as Columbo. Peter Falk, a friend of Levinson and Link, had seen the script and was interested; when Cobb and Crosby refused, Falk won the part.

NBC was interested in turning the film into a series, but neither Falk nor Levinson and Link wanted to do weekly episodic television at the time. Three years later, when NBC promised to package *Columbo* in rotation with two other series in the *NBC Mystery Movie*, Falk and Levinson and Link agreed. The series enjoyed a successful run from 1971 to 1977; much of that success is due to Falk's brilliant portrayal of Columbo. According to Dawidziak, "Everything clicked—the disheveled appearance, the voice, the squint caused by his false right eye. It was all used to magnificent advantage in Falk's characterization."

In 1989, Falk reprised the Columbo role, this time for the *ABC Mystery Movie*; new *Columbo* episodes have been produced since. Between 1971 and 1990, Falk won four Emmy Awards for his role as Columbo. Since 1978, Falk has also appeared in such feature films as *The Cheap Detective* (1978), *The In-Laws* (1979), and *Roommates* (1994) and, as himself, in *Wings of Desire* (1987).

—Michael B. Kassel

PETER MICHAEL FALK. Born in New York City, New York, U.S.A., 16 September 1927. Graduated from Hamilton College, Clinton, New York; New School for Social Research, New York, B.A. 1951; Syracuse University, M.A. in public administration 1953. Married: 1) Alyce Mayo, 1960 (divorced, 1976); two daughters; 2) Shera Danese, 1976. Served 18 months as cook in merchant marine, 1945–46. Management analyst, Connecticut State Budget Bureau, 1953–55; began acting career with Mark Twain Maskers, Hartford, Connecticut; studied acting under Eva La Gallienne, White Barn Theater, Westport, Connecticut, 1955; moved to New York to pursue theatrical career, 1955; professional stage debut in Moliere's *Don Juan*, New York, 1956; studied acting with Jack Landau and Sanford Meisner, 1957; made film debut in *Wind Across the Everglades*, 1958; considered for Columbia contract, but rejected because of glass eye; formed Mayo Productions company in mid-1960s; created character of Lieutenant Columbo in made-for-television movie *Prescription: Murder*, 1968; starred in television series *Columbo*, 1971–77; directed several *Columbo* episodes. Recipient: Emmy Awards, 1962, 1972, 1975, 1976, and 1990.

TELEVISION SERIES

| 1965–66 | *The Trials of O'Brien* |
| 1971–77 | *Columbo* (also directed several episodes) |

MADE-FOR-TELEVISION MOVIES

1961	*Cry Vengeance*
1966	*Too Many Thieves*
1968	*Prescription: Murder*
1971	*Ransom for a Dead Man*
1976	*Griffin and Phoenix: A Love Story*
1989	*Columbo Goes to the Guillotine*
1990	*Columbo Goes to College*
1991	*Columbo: Grand Deception*
1991	*Caution: Murder Can Be Hazardous to Your Health*

Peter Falk

1992	*Columbo: A Bird in the Hand*
1992	*Columbo: No Time to Die*
1993	*Columbo: It's All in the Game*
1994	*Columbo: Butterfly in Shades of Grey*
1995	*Columbo: Strange Bedfellows*

TELEVISION SPECIALS

1961	*The Million Dollar Incident*
1966	*Brigadoon*
1971	*A Hatfull of Rain*
1986	*Clue: Movies, Murder and Mystery*

FILMS

Wind Across the Everglades, 1958; *Pretty Boy Floyd*, 1959; *The Bloody Broad*, 1959; *Murder, Inc.*, 1960; *The Purple Reef*, 1960; *Pocketful of Miracles*, 1961; *Pressure Point*, 1962; *The Balcony*, 1962; *It's a Mad, Mad, Mad, Mad World*, 1963; *Robin and the Seven Hoods*, 1964; *Italiana brava gente*, 1964; *The Great Race*, 1965; *Penelope*, 1966; *Luv*, 1967; *Lo sbarco di Anzio*, 1968; *Gli Intoccabili*, 1968; *Castle Keep*, 1969; *Rosolino paterno, soldato*, 1969; *Husbands*, 1970; *Step Out of Line*, 1970; *Machine Gun McCann*, 1970; *The Politics Film* (narrator), 1972; *A Woman Under the Influence*, 1974; *Mikey and Nicky*, 1976; *Murder by Death*, 1976; *Opening Night*, 1977; *The Cheap Detective*, 1978; *The Brink's Job*, 1978; *The In-Laws*, 1979; *The Great Muppet Caper*, 1981; *All the Marbles*, 1981; *Sanford Meisner: The Theater's Best Kept Secret*, 1984; *Big Trouble*, 1986; *Happy New Year*, 1987;

Duenos del silencio, 1987; *Wings of Desire*, 1987; *The Princess Bride*, 1987; *Rattornas Vinter*, 1988; *Vibes*, 1988; *Cookie*, 1989; *In the Spirit*, 1990; *Aunt Julia and the Scriptwriter*, 1990; *Tune in Tomorrow*, 1990; *My Dog Stupid*, 1991; *The Player*, 1992; *Roommates*, 1994.

STAGE

Don Juan, 1956; *The Changeling*, 1956; *The Iceman Cometh*, 1956; *St. Joan*, 1956; *Diary of a Scoundrel*, 1956; *Bonds of Interest*, 1956; *The Lady's Not for Burning*, 1957; *Purple Dust*, 1957; *Comic Strip*, 1958; *The Passion of Josef D*, 1964;

The Prisoner of Second Avenue, 1971; *Light Up the Sky*, 1987; *Glengarry Glen Ross*, 1985.

FURTHER READING

Dawidziak, Mark. *The Columbo Phile: A Casebook.* New York: Mysterious, 1989.
"Peter Falk." In, Shay, Don. *Conversations.* New York: Kaleidoscope, 1969.
"Interview." *Photoplay* (Chicago, Illinois), January 1979.

See also *Columbo*

FAMILY

U.S. Domestic Drama

Family, a weekly prime-time drama about a Southern California suburban family, ran from 1976 to 1980 on ABC. The show's pilot, which became the first episode of a six-part miniseries that aired in March 1976, was created by novelist and screenwriter Jay Presson Allen *(Forty Carats)*, directed by film director Mark Rydell *(On Golden Pond)*, and produced by film director Mike Nichols *(Who's Afraid of Virginia Woolf?, The Graduate)* as well as television moguls Aaron Spelling and Leonard Goldberg *(Charlie's Angels, Starsky and Hutch)*. The success of the miniseries—it recorded an astonishing 40 share in the ratings—led ABC to pick up *Family* as a regular series for their 1976–77 season. During its five seasons *Family* received fourteen Emmy Award nominations, three of them for Outstanding Drama Series. The show won four awards all in acting categories: Outstanding Lead Actress in a Drama Series (Sada Thompson in 1977), Outstanding Supporting Actress in a Drama Series (Kristy McNichol in 1976 and 1978) and Outstanding Supporting Actor in a Drama Series (Gary Frank in 1976).

Family's initial success came from the creative forces behind the project. These artists and producers, nevertheless, had to fight for three years (beginning 1973) before convincing ABC to give the series a chance. As Rowland Barber explains in "Three Strikes and They're On," during development ABC found the family portrayed in the series "at various critical times, (1) too well-educated and too well-dressed, (2) too true to life for Family Viewing Time and (9) simply 'too good for television'" (24). These attempts to dismiss the project were discarded once the miniseries proved to be a hit both with audiences and critics.

Family also became a success due to the renewed interest in dramatic shows during the mid-1970s (as witnessed by the huge success of the miniseries *Rich Man, Poor Man)*. In general, police/detective shows like *Police Woman, Charlie's Angels, S.W.A.T., Starsky and Hutch, Switch* and *Kojak* dominated the televisual panorama of the 1976-76 season. The appearance of non-violent, well-crafted and well-acted programs like *Family* constituted a refreshing alternative to the

predominant action-packed TV scene, which was readily embraced by TV audiences.

Family followed the saga of the Lawrences, a middle-class family from Pasadena, California. The clan consisted of the parents, Kate and Doug (played by Sada Thompson and the late James Broderick), and their three offspring: Nancy, divorcee, lawyer and mother of infant Timmy (originally played in the miniseries by Elaine Heilveil, Nancy was portrayed in the regular series by Meredith Baxter-Birney), Willie, a high-school drop-out who was nevertheless a talented and idealistic aspiring writer (played by Gary Frank), and free-spirited teenager Letitia, better known as "Buddy"

Family

(played by Kristy McNichol). During its 1978-79 season, a new regular character joined the series: Annie Cooper, an 11-year-old orphan girl whom the Lawrences decide to adopt (played by Quinn Cummings).

Throughout its five seasons, the series engaged a range of contemporary social issues within the parameters of its melodramatic structure. For example, the miniseries began with a pregnant Nancy discovering her husband Jeff (played by John Rubinstein) in bed with one of her girlfriends. This situation led to a divorce. Subsequently, the series explored, through the character of Nancy, issues related to the social position of a divorced, professional woman who was also a mother. On a couple of occasions, the show dealt with issues pertaining to homosexuality. In one episode, Willie's best friend came out of the closet, forcing Willie to reconsider his positions about both friendship and homosexuality. In another episode, Buddy had to face issues about bigotry when the school attempted to fire a teacher she admired who turned out to be a lesbian. On several occasions, the Lawrence matriarch found herself in difficult social, moral, and ethical positions that resulted from her situation as a middle-age woman. Once Kate faced the dilemma of possibly having to have an abortion when she discovered she was expecting a child at an age when risks and complications related to pregnancy are higher (she was over forty). In another episode, Kate had to confront her insecurities and fears when she decided to take a job outside the house. At one point in the series, Kate had to deal with the fact that she had breast cancer.

Not only did *Family* reclaim a place for hour-long (melo)dramatic series dealing with contemporary everyday topics during a time when action series ruled, but it also prepared the ground for the explosion of prime time soap operas such as *Dallas, Dynasty, Knots Landing,* and *Falcon Crest* that appeared during the late 1970s and 1980s.

—Gilberto M. Blasini

CAST

Kate Lawrence	Sada Thompson
Doug Lawrence	James Broderick
Nancy Lawrence Maitland (1976)	Elayne Heilveil
Nancy Lawrence Maitland (1976–1980)	Meredith Baxter-Birney
Willie Lawrence	Gary Frank
Letitia "Buddy" Lawrence	Kristy McNichol
Jeff Maitland	John Rubinstein
Mrs. Hanley (1976–1978)	Mary Grace Canfield
Salina Magee (1976–1977)	Season Hubley
Annie Cooper (1978–1980)	Quinn Cummings
Timmy Maitland (1978–1980)	Michael David Schackelford

PRODUCERS Aaron Spelling, Leonard Goldberg, Mike Nichols

PROGRAMMING HISTORY 94 Episodes

• ABC

March 1976–February 1978	Tuesday 10:00-11:00
May 1978	Tuesday 10:00-11:00
September 1978–March 1979	Thursday 10:00-11:00
March 1979–April 1979	Friday 8:00-9:00
May 1979	Thursday 10:00-11:00
December 1979–February 1980	Monday 10:00-11:00
March 1980	Monday 9:00-10:00
June 1980	Wednesday 8:00-9:00

FURTHER READING

Barbor, Rowland. "Three Strikes and They're On." *TV Guide* (Radnor, Pennsylvania), 21 January 1978.

See also Family on Television; Melodrama; Spelling, Aaron

FAMILY ON TELEVISION

The introduction of television after World War II coincided with a steep rise in mortgage rates, birth rates, and the growth of mass-produced suburbs. In this social climate, it is no wonder that television was conceived as, first and foremost, a family medium. Over the course of the 1950s, as debates raged in Congress over issues such as juvenile delinquency and the mass media's contribution to it, the three major television networks developed prime-time fare that would appeal to a general family audience. Many of these policy debates and network strategies are echoed in the more recent public controversies concerning television and family values, especially the famous *Murphy Brown* incident in which Vice President Dan Quayle used the name of this fictional unwed mother as an example of what is

wrong with America. As the case of Quayle demonstrates, the public often assumes that television fictional representations of the family have a strong impact on actual families in America. For this reason people have often also assumed that these fictional households ought to mirror not simply family life in general, but their own personal values regarding it. Throughout television history, then, the representation of the family has been a concern in Congress, among special interest groups and lobbyists, the general audience and, of course, the industry which has attempted to satisfy all of these parties in different ways and with different emphasis.

In the early 1950s, domestic life was represented with some degree of diversity. There were families who lived in suburbs, cities, and rural areas. There were nuclear families (such as that in *The Adventures of Ozzie and Harriet*) and childless couples (such as the Stevens of *I Married Joan* or Sapphire and Kingfish of *Amos 'n' Andy).* There was a variety of ethnic families in domestic comedies and family dramas (including the Norwegian family of *Mama* and the Jewish family of *The Goldbergs*). In addition anthology dramas such as *Marty* sometimes presented ethnic working-class families. At a time when many Americans were moving from cities to mass-produced suburbs these programs featured nostalgic versions of family and neighborhood bonding that played on sentimentality for the more "authentic" social relationships of the urban past. Ethnicity was typically popular so long as it was a portrayal of first generation European immigrants; black, Hispanic and Asian family life were almost never dealt with. When they were they were the butt of the joke such as the Cuban Ricky Ricardo with his Latin temper or the African American Beula with her job as the happy maid/mammy in a white household.

Meanwhile in 1950s documentaries and in fiction programming the family often served as the patriotic reason "why we fight" Communism—much as it served as a source of patriotism in the Norman Rockwell magazine covers of W.W.II. Action/adventure programs such as the syndicated series *I Led Three Lives*, contained numerous episodes in which Communists infiltrated families and threatened to pervert American youth. Paradoxically, however, the family also provided a reason why we fight the more extremist versions of anti-communism—especially that espoused by Senator Joe McCarthy. In 1952 Edward R. Murrow's *See It Now* presented "The Case of Milo Radulovich," about an Air Force pilot who was suspected for Communist sympathies. Murrow used interviews with Radulovich's sister and father to convince viewers that he was not a Communist but instead a true American with solid family values. From the outset then the family on television served both sentimental and political/ideological functions and these were often intertwined.

By the mid-1950s, as television production moved to Hollywood film studios and was also controlled by Hollywood independent production companies such as Desilu, the representation of family life became even more standardized in the domestic comedy. By 1960 all the ethnic domestic comedies and dramas disappeared and the suburban domestic comedy rose to prominence. Programs such as *The Donna Reed Show, Leave It to Beaver,* and *Father Knows Best* presented idealized versions of white middle-class families in suburban communities that mirrored the practices of ethnic and racial exclusion seen in America's suburbs more generally. Even while these programs captured the American imagination there was a penchant for social criticism registered in l950s science fiction/horror anthologies (such as *The Twilight Zone*'s "Monsters on Maple Street" that explored the paranoid social relationships and exclusionary tactics in America's suburban towns.) Within the domestic comedy form itself, the nuclear family was increasingly displaced by

An American Family
Photo courtesy of Thirteen/ WNET

a counter-programming trend that represented broken families and unconventional families. Coinciding with rising divorce rates of the 1960s numerous shows featured families led by a single father (including comedies such as *My Three Sons* and *Family Affair* and the Western *Bonanza*), while others featured single mothers (including comedies such as *Julia* and *Here's Lucy* and the western *The Big Valley*). In all these programs, censorship codes demanded that the single parent not be divorced; instead the missing parent was always explained through a death in the family. By 1967 the classic domestic comedies featuring nuclear families were all canceled, while these broken families, as well as a new trend of "fantastic families" in programs like *Bewitched* and *The Addams Family* accounted for the mainstay of the genre.

At the level of the news these fictional programs were met by the tragic break up of America's first family as the coverage of President John F. Kennedy's funeral haunted America's television screens. We might even speculate that the proliferation and popularity of broken families on television entertainment genres was in some sense a way our society responded to and aesthetically resolved the loss of our nation's father and the dream or nuclear family life that he and Jackie represented at the time. As the nation mourned, other program genres showed cause for more general sorrow. Despite the fact that domestic comedy families were well-to-do the 1960s also included depictions or America's underclass in hard-hitting socially relevant dramas such as the short-lived *East Side/West Side* that explored issues of child abuse and welfare in New York slums. Television also presented documentaries such as *Hunger in America* and *Harvest of Shame* that depicted underprivileged children, while other documentaries such as *Middletown* or *Salesmen* chronicled the everyday lives or typical Americans, demonstrating the impossibility of living up to the American family ideal. This trend toward social criticism was capped off in 1973 when PBS aired *An American Family* which chronicled the everyday life of Mr. and Mrs. William Loud and their suburban family by placing cameras in their home and surveying their day-to-day affairs. As the cameras watched, the Louds filed for divorce and their son came out as a homosexual. The discrepancies between these documentary/socially relevant depictions of American families and the more idealized images in the domestic comedy genre were now all too clear.

More generally the 1970s was a time of significant change as the portrayal of family life became more diverse, although never completely representative of all American lifestyles. Network documentaries continued to show the underside of the American Dream, while other genres took on the burden of social criticism as they attempted to reach a new demographic of young urban professionals, working women, and a rising black middle-class. Programs such as Norman Lear's *All in the Family, Maude,* and *The Jeffersons* flourished. *All in the Family* presented a working-class milieu and drew its comedy out of political differences among generations and genders in the household; *Maude* was the first program to feature a divorced heroine who, in one two part episode also had the first prime-time abortion. Other programs presented African America families ranging from shows like *The Jeffersons* who had, as the opening credits announced, finally got "a piece of the pie" to programs set in ghettos such as *Good Times.* Interracial families such as *Webster* depicted white parents bringing up black babies (although the reverse was never the case). In the mid-1970s through the present these new family formations have included programs featuring single moms (who were now often divorced or never married) such as *Kate and Allie, One Day at a Time,* and the more recent *Murphy Brown.* Drawing on previous working-girl/mother sitcoms like *Our Miss Brooks* or *Here's Lucy* the MTM studio precipitated a shift from literal biological families to a new concept of the family workplace. Here, in programs such as *The Mary Tyler Moore Show* co-workers were also co-dependents so that relationships were often ambiguously collegial and familial. Despite these innovations the 1970s and early 1980s still featured sentimental versions of family life including daytime soap operas, family dramas such as *Family* and *Eight Is Enough,* historical-family dramas such as *The Waltons, Little House on the Prairie,* and the popular comedy *The Brady Bunch.*

Over the course of the 1980s, the genre of prime-time soap opera served as television's answer to the Reagan era dream of consumer prosperity. Programs such as *Dallas* and *Dynasty* presented a world of high fashion, high finance, and for many, high camp sensibilities. Despite their idealized

upper-class settings these programs like daytime soaps or the 1960s *Peyton Place,* dealt with marital infidelity, incest, rape, alcoholism and a range of other issues that pictured the family as decidedly dysfunctional. Perhaps because these families were extremely wealthy, audiences could view their problems as a symptom of upper-crust decadence rather than a more general failure in American family life experienced by people of all social backgrounds. Wealth was also apparent in the enormously popular *Cosby Show,* which featured black professionals living an ideal family life. Unlike *Dallas* or *Dynasty,* however, which were widely appreciated for their escapist fantasies and/or "camp" exaggeration, *Cosby* was often taken to task for not being realistic enough.

In addition to prime-time soaps and family comedies, other programs of the 1980s and 1990s showcased dysfunctional families and/or families in crisis. Made-for-TV-movies such as *The Burning Bed* detailed the horrors of spousal abuse. In addition, during this period the television talk show has taken over the role of family therapist as programs such as *Geraldo, Oprah,* and *Jerry Springer* feature real-life family feuds with guests who confess to incest, spousal abuse, matricide, co-dependencies and a range of other family perversions. Unlike the daytime soap operas, these programs lack the sentiment of family melodrama and thus appear more akin to their contemporary cousin, the TV tabloid. These syndicated "tabloid" shows such as *COPS* or *America's Most Wanted* offer a range of family horrors as law enforcement agencies and vigilantes apprehend the outlaws of the nation.

They not only demonstrate how to catch a thief and other criminals, they also engage in didactic editorializing which either explicitly or implicitly suggests that crimes such as robbery, prostitution, or drug dealing are caused by dysfunctional family lives rather than by political, sexual, racial, and class inequities. Still, in other instances the family remains "wholesome," especially in the age of cable when the broadcast networks often try to win a family audience by presenting themselves as more clean cut than their cable competitors. (For example, in various seasons on different nights ABC and NBC have both fashioned lineups of family-oriented programs aimed at mothers and children.)

Over the course of the 1980s and through the present, innovation on old formats has also been a key strategy. Programs such as the popular sitcom *Family Ties* reversed the usual generational politics of comedy by making the parents more liberal than their conservative, money-obsessed son. In the latter 1980s the new FOX network largely ingratiated itself with the public by displaying a contempt for the "whitebread" standards of old network television. Programs such as *Married . . . with Children* parodied the middle-class suburban sitcom, while sitcoms such as *Living Single* and the prime-time soap, *Melrose Place* presented alternate youth-oriented lifestyles. ABC's *Roseanne* followed suit with its highly popular parody of family life that includes such unconventional sitcom topics as teenage sex, spousal abuse, and lesbian romance. By the mid-1990s ABC broadcast Roseanne's clone, *American Girl*, the first sitcom to feature the generational conflicts in a Korean family.

Parody and unconventional topicality were not the only solutions to innovation. If portrayals of contemporary happy families seemed somewhat disingenuous or at best cliché by the end of the 1980s television could still turn to nostalgia to create sentimental versions of family togetherness. For example, family dramas such as *The Wonder Years* and *Brooklyn Bridge* presented popular memories of baby boom America. Both nostalgia and parody are also the genius in the system of the cable network, Nickelodeon, which is owned by Viacom, the country's largest syndicator. Its prime-time line-up, which it calls "Nick at Nite," features Viacom-owned reruns of mostly family sitcoms from television's first three decades, and Nick advertises them through parodic slogans that make fun of the happy shiny people of old TV. Other cable networks have also premised themselves on the breakdown of nuclear family ideology and living arrangements by, for example, rethinking the conventional depictions of home life on broadcast genres. For instance, MTV's Generation X serialized programs under the general title, *The Real World*, chronicles the real life adventures of young people from different races and sexual orientations living together in a house provided by the network. Nevertheless, cable has also been extremely aware of ways to tap into the on-going national agenda for family values and has turned this into marketing values. Pat Robertson's Family Channel is an example of how the Christian right has used cable to rekindle the passion for a particular kind of family life, mostly associated with the middle-class family ideals of the 1950s and early 1960s. In this regard it is no surprise that the Family Channel includes reruns of *Father Knows Best*, but without the parodic campy wink of Nick at Nite's evening line-up.

Although television has consistently privileged the family as the "normal" and most fulfilling way to live one's life, its programs have often presented multiple and contradictory messages. At the same time that a sitcom featured June Cleaver wondering what suit to buy the Beaver, a documentary or news program showed the underside of family abuse or the severe poverty in which some families were forced to live. Because television draws on an enormous stable of representational traditions and creative personnel, and because the industry has attempted to appeal to large nationwide audiences the medium never presents one simple message. Instead it is in the relations among different programs and genres that we begin to get a view of the range of possibilities. Those possibilities have, of course, been limited by larger social ideologies such as the racism or homophobia which affects the quality and quantity of shows depicting nonwhite and non-heterosexual households. Despite these

on-going exclusions however it is evident that the family on television is as full of mixed messages and ambivalent emotions as it is in real life.

—Lynn Spigel

FURTHER READING

Boddy, William. *Fifties Television: The Industry and its Critics.* Urbana: University of Illinois Press, 1990.

Friedan, Betty. "Television and the Feminine Mystique." *TV Guide* (Radnor, Pennsylvania), 1 February and 8 February 1964.

Hammamoto, Darrell Y. *Nervous Laughter: Television Situation Comedy and Liberal Democratic Ideology.* New York: Praeger, 1989.

Haralovitch, Mary Beth. "Sitcoms and Suburbs: Positioning the 1950s Homemaker." *Quarterly Review of Film and Video* (Chur, Netherlands), May 1989.

Leibman, Nina. *Living Room Lectures: The Fifties Family in Film and Television.* Austin: University of Texas Press, 1995.

Lipsitz, George. "The Meaning of Memory: Family, Class, and Ethnicity in Early Network Television." *Camera Obscura* (Berkeley, California), January 1988.

Marc, David. *Comic Visions: Television Comedy and American Culture.* Boston, Massachusetts: Unwin Hyman, 1989.

———. *Demographic Vistas: Television in American Culture.* Philadelphia: University of Pennsylvania Press, 1984.

Meehan, Diana. *Ladies of the Evening: Women Characters of Prime-Time Television.* Metuchen, New Jersey: Scarecrow, 1983.

Mellencamp, Patricia. "Situation Comedy, Feminism, and Freud: Discourse of Gracie and Lucy." In Modleski, Tania, editor. *Studies in Entertainment: Critical Approaches to Mass Culture.* Bloomington: Indiana University Press, 1986.

Spigel, Lynn. *Make Room for TV: Television and the Family Ideal in Postwar America.* Illinois: University of Chicago Press, 1992.

Taylor, Ella. *Prime-time Families: Television Culture in Postwar America.* Berkeley: University of California Press, 1989.

See also *Adventures of Ozzie and Harriet; Amos 'n' Andy; Bewitched; Bonanza; Brady Bunch; Cosby Show; Dallas; Dynasty; Family Ties; Father Knows Best; Goldbergs; Good Times; I Love Lucy; Jeffersons; Julia; Kate and Allie; Leave It to Beaver; Married...With Children; Mary Tyler Moore Show; Maude; My Three Sons; Peyton Place; Roseanne; Waltons; Wonder Years*

THE FAMILY PLOUFFE/LA FAMILLE PLOUFFE

Canadian Serial Drama (Teleroman)

La famille Plouffe was created in 1953 in response to a lack of francophone television programming in Canada. Unlike its counterpart in English Canada which could pick up shows from American stations, the francophone division of the CBC, la Société Radio-Canada, was compelled to develop its own programs with very few resources. The early programs grew out of Quebec's strong tradition of radio drama, a tradition grounded in serial narratives. One such serial, Un homme et son péché, was heard by nearly 80% of the Quebec audience. It was only natural that such a formula would find its way to television. Teleromans, as these serials were called, were launched in the fall of 1953 with the debut of La famille Plouffe, which was broadcast live every Wednesday night. It was an instant hit and its phenomenal success prompted Radio-Canada to develop more shows of this genre which came to dominate the weekday primetime schedule.

The Family Plouffe/La famille Plouffe chronicled the daily life of a Quebec working-class family in the post-war era. It was an extended family which included: Théophile, the father, a former provincial cycling champion who had traded in his bicycle—and his youth—for work as a plumber; Joséphine, the naive and kind-hearted mother who doted on her adult children like a worried mother hen; Napoléon, the eldest, and protector of his siblings who mentored his younger brother Guillaume's dream of one day playing professional hockey; Ovide, the intellectual of the family whose education and love of art and music gave him an arrogant demeanour; and Cécile, the only daughter who, like many women in the post-war era, was faced with the choice between the traditional marriage, children, and security, and new aspirations of career independence.

Plots were generally cast in the form of quests whether for love, career advancement, security, or a sense of personal and national identity. These themes were woven with the daily problems and choices which confronted members of the family. Some commentators have argued that the Plouffes reflected the common experience of the "typical" French Canadian family and that viewers in Quebec could easily identify with the characters, their aspirations, the plots, and the settings. As nostalgic as this view may be, the Plouffes were still fictional. Moral ambiguities were almost always resolved to fit the conventional values of post-war Quebec. Women were expected to be homemakers, wives, and mothers. Those women who strayed from these norms, such as Rita Toulouse, were often depicted as wily and unpredictable. Men were expected to be good providers and strong patriarchs as symbolized by the fact that Théophile let his treasured bicycle fall into disrepair. It was only to be expected that Cécile would opt for marriage to Onésime Ménard and that Ovide would reconcile his elitist aspirations with his working-class environment.

A year following the successful premiere of the original series, CBC programmers decided to launch an English version. The version was essentially the same as its French counterpart, though modifications were made in the script to remove profane and vulgar language and any references to sex. The scripts were written by Roger Lemelin, the original and only French author, and the same cast of actors were used for the live broadcasts which were aired later in the week.

This decision was a unique experiment. Using the magic of television, all Canadians were able to follow the same story and though The Family Plouffe received good ratings in some smaller Canadian centers, the CBC's own internal surveys showed that the experiment to create a common Canadian cultural icon was a failure. In large cities where viewers had access to American stations, anglophone Canadians preferred to watch American programming. By the end of the 1958-59 season, the CBC had abandoned the practice of broadcasting language-versioned programming.

La famille Plouffe/The Family Plouffe was a unique "made-in-Canada" live drama. Nostalgic memories of its success prompted a return to the family kitchen in a television special Le crime d'Ovide Plouffe in 1982 which was also versioned and broadcast to anglophone Canadians. After more than two decades of separate programming, another attempt was made to broadcast a series to both English and French audiences in the late 1980s. The series Lance et compte/He Shoots, He Scores (1987–1988) was intended to appeal to Canadian common love of hockey, but like earlier experiments, ratings demonstrated that francophone and anglophone viewers wanted very different kinds of programs. The true legacy of La famille Plouffe was its influence in the development of the teleroman which was and has remained a uniquely "made-in-Quebec" television genre.

—Manon Lamontagne

CAST

Théophile Plouffe	Paul Guèvremont
Joséphine Plouffe	Amanda Alarie
Napoléon Plouffe	Emile Genest
Ovide Plouffe	Jean-Louis Roux, Marcel Houben
Guillaume Plouffe	Pierre Valcour
Cécile Plouffe	Denise Pelletier
Gédéon Plouffe	Doris Lussier
Démérise Plouffe	Nana de Varennes
Onéisme Ménard	Rolland Bédard
Rita Toulouse	Lise Roy, Janin Mignolet
Blanche Toulouse	Lucie Poitras
Jeanne Labrie	Thérèse Cadorette
Stan Labrie	Jean Duceppe
Révérend Père Alexandre	Guy Provost

Martine Plouffe . . . . Margot Campbell
Aimé Plouffe . . . . Jean Coutu
Flora Plouffe . . . . Ginette Letondal
Agathe Plouffe . . . . Clémence Desrochers
Rosaire Joyeux . . . . Camille Ducharme
Jacqueline Sévigny . . . . Amulette Garneau
Alain Richard . . . . Guy Godin
Hélène Giguère . . . . Françoise Graton
Alphonse Tremblay . . . . Ernest Guimond

DIRECTORS
Guy Beaulne
Jean Dumas
Jean-Paul Fugère (both versions)

PROGRAMMING HISTORY   194 episodes, live broadcast, black and white

• Société Radio-Canada/CBC
French Version
November 1953–May 1959   Wednesdays 8:30-9:00
English Version
November 1954–May 1955   Thursdays 8:00-8:30
November 1955–May 1956   Fridays 10:00-10:30
November 1956–May 1958   Fridays 8:30-9:00
November 1958–May 1959   Fridays 9:30-10:00

FURTHER READING

Raboy, Marc. *Missed Opportunities: The Story of Canada's Broadcasting Policy.* Montreal: McGill-Queen's University Press, 1990.
Rutherford, Paul. *When Television Was Young: Primetime Canada 1952–1967.* Toronto: University of Toronto Press, 1990.
Trofimenkoff, Susan. *The Dream of Nation.* Toronto: Gage, 1983.

FAMILY TIES

U.S. Domestic Comedy

Few shows better demonstrate the resonance between collectively-held fictional imagination and what cultural critic Raymond Williams called "the structure of feeling" of a historical moment than *Family Ties.* Airing on NBC from 1982 to 1989, this highly successful domestic comedy explored one of the intriguing cultural inversions characterizing the Reagan era: a conservative younger generation aspiring to wealth, business success, and traditional values serves as inheritor to the politically liberal, presumably activist, culturally experimental generation of adults who had experienced the 1960s. The result was a decade, paradoxical by America's usual post-World War II standards, in which youthful ambition and social renovation became equated with pronounced political conservatism. "When else could a boy with a briefcase become a national hero?" queried *Family Ties'* creator, Gary David Goldberg, during the show's final year.

The boy with the briefcase was Alex B. Keaton, a competitive and uncompromising, baby-faced conservative whose absurdly hard-nosed platitudes seemed the antithesis of his comfortable, middle-class, white, Midwestern upbringing. Yet Alex could also be endearingly (and youthfully) bumbling when tenderness or intimacy demanded departure from the social conventions so important to him. He could be riddled equally with self-doubt about his mettle for meeting the high standards he set for himself. During the course of the show, Alex aged from an unredoubtable high schooler running for student council president to a college student reconciled to his rejection by Princeton.

Alex's highly programmatic views of life led to continuous conflict with parents Steven and Elyse. Former war protestors and Peace Corps volunteers, these adults now found fulfillment raising their children and working, respectively, as a public television station manager and as an independent architect. If young Alex could be comically cynical, his parents could be relentlessly cheerful do-gooders

Family Ties

whose causes occasionally seemed chimerical. Yet (especially with Elyse) their liberalism could also emerge more authoritatively, particularly when it assumed the voice, not of ideological instruction, but of parental conscience and loving tolerance. And so *Family Ties* explored not just the cultural ironies of politically conservative youth, but the equally powerful paradox of liberal conscience. Here, that conscience was kept alive within the loving nuclear family, so constantly appropriated by conservatives as a manifestation of their own values.

Significantly, the show's timely focus on Alex and his contrasts with his parents was discovered rather than designed. *Family Ties'* creator was Gary David Goldberg, an ex-hippie whose three earlier network shows had each been canceled within weeks, leading him to promise that *Family Ties* would be his last attempt. He undertook the show as a basically autobiographical comedy which would explore the parents' adjustments to 1980s society and middle-aged family life. The original casting focused on Michael Gross and Meredith Baxter-Birney as the crucial Keatons. Once the show aired, however, network surveys quickly revealed that audiences were more attracted by the accomplished physical comedy, skillful characterization, and approachable looks of Michael J. Fox, the actor playing Alex. Audience reaction and Fox's considerable, unexpected authority in front of the camera prompted Goldberg and his collaborators to shift emphasis to the young man, a change so fundamental that Goldberg told Gross and Baxter-Birney that he would understand if they decided to quit. The crucial inter-generational dynamic of the show, then, emerged in a dialogue between viewers, who identified Alex as a compelling character, and writers, who were willing to reorient the show's themes of cultural succession around the youth. Goldberg's largely liberal writers usually depicted Alex's ideology ironically, through self-indicting punch lines. Many audiences, however, were laughing sympathetically, and Alex Keaton emerged as a model of the clean-cut, determined, yet human entrepreneur. *Family Ties* finished the 1983 and 1984 seasons as the second-highest rated show on television, and finished in the top 20 six of its seven years. President Ronald Reagan declared *Family Ties* his favorite program, and offered to make an appearance on the show (an offer pointedly ignored by the producers). FOX was able to launch a considerable career in feature films based on his popularity from the show.

Alex had three siblings. Justine Bateman played Mallory, the inarticulate younger sister who, unwilling to compete with the overachieving Alex, devotes herself to fashion and boyfriends, including the elder Keaton's nemesis, junkyard sculptor Nick (played by Scott Valentine). Tina Yothers played the younger daughter, Jennifer, an intelligent observer who could pronounce scathingly on either Alex or the parents' foibles. During the 1984 season, a baby boy joined the Keaton family, and was played by three separate children, as—by the next season—he quickly developed into a toddler.

Both *Family Ties'* creator and its production style are products of a specific set of events in Hollywood which, in the mid-1980s, granted promising writer-producers unusual opportunity and resources to pursue their creative interests. Goldberg's first jobs in television were as a writer and writer-producer for MTM Productions, the independent production company founded by Grant Tinker and Mary Tyler Moore. The company was initially devoted to the production of "quality" comedies, and known for the special respect it accorded writers. In the early 1980s, the booming syndication market and continued vertical integration prompted Hollywood to consider writers who could create new programs as important long-term investments. Paramount Studios raided MTM for its most promising talents, among them Goldberg. Like many of his cohorts, Goldberg was able to negotiate a production company of his own, partial ownership of his shows, and a commitment from Paramount to help fund his next project—all in exchange for Paramount's exclusive rights to distribute the resulting programs. Goldberg applied the methods of proscenium comedy production he had learned at MTM, developing *Family Ties* as a character-based situation comedy, sustained by imaginative dialogue, laudable acting, and carefully-considered scripts which sat at the focus of a highly collaborative weekly production routine. (*Inside Family Ties*, a PBS special produced in 1985, shows actors, the director, and writers each taking considerable license to alter the script; Goldberg mentions that he takes it for granted that 60% of a typical episode will be rewritten during the week.) Each episode was shot live before a studio audience, to retain the crucial excitement and unity of a stage play.

In *Family Ties'* third season, the program played an unprecedented role in the production industry's growing independence from the declining broadcast networks. Paramount guaranteed syndicators that it would provide them with a minimum of 95 episodes of *Family Ties*, though only 70 or so had been completed at the time. Anxious to capitalize on the booming syndication market, Paramount was, in effect, agreeing to produce the show even if NBC canceled it—a decision anticipating Paramount's later, successful distribution of *Star Trek: The Next Generation* exclusively through syndication.

—Michael Saenz

CAST

Elyse Keaton . . . . Meredith Baxter-Birney
Steve Keaton . . . . Michael Gross
Alex P. Keaton . . . . Michael J. Fox
Mallory Keaton . . . . Justine Bateman
Jennifer Keaton . . . . Tina Yothers
Andrew Keaton (1986–89) . . . . Brian Bonsall
Irwin "Skippy" Handelman . . . . Marc Price
Ellen Reed (1985–86) . . . . Tracy Pollan
Nick Moore (1985–89) . . . . Scott Valentine
Lauren Miller (1987–89) . . . . Courteney Cox

PRODUCERS Gary David Goldberg, Lloyd Garver, Michael Weinthorn

PROGRAMMING HISTORY   180 Episodes

• NBC

September 1982–March 1983   Wednesday 9:30-10:00

March 1983–August 1983	Monday 8:30-9:00
August 1983–December 1983	Wednesday 9:30-10:00
January 1984–August 1987	Thursday 8:30-9:00
August 1987–September 1987	Sunday 8:00-9:00
September 1987–September 1989	Sunday 8:00-8:30

See also Comedy, Domestic Settings; Family on Television

FAMILY VIEWING TIME

Prompted by widespread public criticism in 1974 the United States Congress exhorted the Federal Communications Commission (FCC) to take action regarding the perennial issues of alleged excesses of sex, crime, and violence in broadcast programming. Early in 1975 FCC chairman Richard E. Wiley reported to Senate and House Communications and Commerce Subcommittees recent steps taken by the FCC. They included discussions with corporate heads of television networks which resulted in four strategies for addressing the issues. The network heads adopted a self-declared "family viewing" hour in the first hour of network evening prime-time (8:00-9:00 P.M., Eastern time). Actions by the National Association of Broadcasters' Television Code review board expanded that "family hour" forward one hour into local station time (7:00-8:00 P.M.). The NAB also proposed "viewer advisories" related to program content that might disturb members of the audience, especially younger people. And the FCC made further efforts to define what it construed as "indecent" under the law, in a case involving Pacifica's WBAI(FM), New York.

Arthur R. Taylor, president of CBS Inc., had championed more acceptable early-evening programming but could only do so at CBS if competing networks followed suit. FCC chairman Wiley urged reluctant executives to adopt these actions. But to avoid inter-corporate collusion they felt the professional association (NAB) could best orchestrate the effort through its self-regulatory Industry Code of Practices. Enacting the code led to several results. Some early-evening shows with comedy and action deemed less suited for young viewers were displaced to later hours. West Coast producers, directors, and writers claimed the new structure infringed on their creative freedom and First Amendment rights. Later scheduling also led to lower audience ratings, partly from the stigma attached to some programs as inappropriate for viewing by families. Popular sitcom *All in the Family* suffered from the ruling; its producer Norman Lear protested against the policy and with celebrity colleagues and professional guilds mounted a lawsuit against it. Meanwhile some public-interest groups, including major religious organizations, objected to the policy for not going far enough; they claimed it sanitized only an hour or two of TV programming, leaving the rest of the 24-hour schedule open to "anything goes."

After extensive hearings U.S. district court judge Warren Ferguson ruled that, while the concept might have merit, the FCC had acted improperly in finessing the result by privately persuading the three network representatives to marshall the NAB's code provisions. Normal FCC procedure was to openly announce proposals for rule-making, then hold public hearings to develop a record from which federal rulings might be developed. Thus the Family Viewing policy was scuttled, apparently to the satisfaction of not only the creative community that produced programs but to most network personnel who had the complicated task of applying the principle to specific shows and time-slots, with direct impact on ratings and time-sales for commercial spots. Syndicators of off-network reruns also were relieved because the early-evening "fringe time" programmed by local stations had been brought into the ambit of the Code's provisions, limiting the kinds of shows aired then. But the reversal was frustrating to many members of Congress, to FCC chairman Wiley, and to CBS chief Arthur Taylor. Dubbed by many the "father of Family Viewing" Taylor had proclaimed the policy as the first step in twenty-five years to reduce the level of gratuitous TV violence and sex. John Schneider, president of the CBS/Broadcast Group, issued a statement after the court's decision: "The Court recognizes the right of an individual broadcaster to maintain programming standards, yet it denies this same right to broadcasters collectively, even though these standards are entirely voluntary. . . . To rule that broadcasters cannot, however openly and publicly, create a set of programming standards consonant with the demonstrated wishes of the American people leaves only two alternatives: no standards for the broadcasting community or standards imposed by government, which we believe would dangerously violate the spirit of the First Amendment. CBS's belief that family viewing is an exercise of broadcaster responsibility in the public interest is confirmed by its popular acceptance" reported by a major publication's two national polls.

The episode demonstrated the daunting task of guiding a complex mass entertainment medium in a pluralistic society with varied perspectives and values. Through the decades television came under increasing scrutiny for alleged permissiveness in drama and comedy programs. The theme of excessive "sex and violence" was sounded regularly in Congressional sessions from Senator Estes Kefauver in the 1950s to Senator Thomas

Dodd in the 1960s and Senator John Pastore in the 1970s. By 1975 House Communications Subcommittee chairman Torbert MacDonald, fearing the Family Viewing plan was no more than a public relations ploy, raised the perennial threat of licensing the source of national program service, the commercial networks. Meanwhile, the FCC sought to clarify the U.S. Code provision (Title 18, §1464) prohibiting obscene, indecent or profane language, to extend explicitly to visual depiction of such material.

The issue joined, of course, is the broadcaster's freedom to program a station or network without censorship by governmental prior restraining action (or by ex-post-facto penalty that constitutes implied restraint against subsequent actions). That freedom is closely coupled with the diverse public's right to have access to a wide range of programming that viewers freely choose to watch. The other side of that coin is the audience's right to freedom *from* what some consider offensive program content broadcast over a federally-licensed airwave frequency defined by Congress in 1927 and 1934 as a "natural public resource" owned by the public. The problem arises from the medium's pervasiveness (the Supreme Court's wording) which reaches into homes and beyond to portable receivers, readily available to young children often unable to be supervised around the clock by parents. FCC chairman Wiley explained to the Senate Commerce Committee in 1975: "we believe that the industry

reforms strike an appropriate balance between two conflicting objectives. On the one hand, it is necessary that the industry aid concerned parents in protecting their children from objectionable material; on the other hand, it is important that the medium have an opportunity to develop artistically and to present themes which are appropriate and of interest to an adult audience." The issue recurred, as deregulation of broadcast media in the 1980s and growing permissiveness of program content on proliferating cable channels was succeeded in the 1990s by widespread calls for "family values" in media. Senator Paul Simon engineered a waiver of anti-trust provisions enabling major networks and cable companies to collaborate on voluntary self-regulatory practices, to preclude threatened government enactments: "Son of Family Viewing?"

—James A. Brown

FURTHER READING

Cowan, Geoffrey. *See No Evil: The Backstage Battle over Sex and Violence on Television.* New York: Simon and Schuster, 1979.

Rowland, Willard D. *The Politics of TV Violence: Policy Uses of Communication Research.* Beverly Hills, California: Sage, 1983.

See also Censorship, Programming

FARNSWORTH, PHILO

U.S. Inventor

Philo Farnsworth, who has been called the forgotten father of television, won a prize offered by the *Science and Invention* magazine for developing a thief proof automobile ignition switch, at the age of thirteen. Most remarkable from his high-school experience was the diagram he drew for his chemistry teacher, Justin Tolman. This drawing proved to be the pattern for his later experiments in electronics and was instrumental in winning a patent interference case between Farnsworth and Radio Corporation of America (RCA). Farnsworth's work spanned the continent. His first laboratories were in his Hollywood home; later he and his family moved to San Francisco, Philadelphia, Fort Wayne, Indiana and Salt Lake City. Farnsworth's experimentation began in 1926 in San Francisco, where he established his first corporation, Farnsworth Television Incorporated, in 1929. And here the first crude television image was created from the Farnsworth system when a photograph of a young woman was transmitted in the San Francisco Green Street laboratory on 7 September 1927. The first patents for the Farnsworth television system were filed January 1927.

In 1931, Farnsworth moved to Philadelphia to establish a television department for Philco. By 1933 when Philco decided that television patent research was no longer a part

of its corporate vision, Farnsworth returned to his own labs. In 1938, he established the Farnsworth Television and Radio Corporation. This research and manufacturing company was later purchased by the International Telephone and Telegraph Company (IT and T). Farnsworth's work for

Philo Fransworth
Photo courtesy of Pem Farnsworth

IT and T included both television and nuclear fusion. In December 1938, Farnsworth moved to Salt Lake City to organize his last venture: Philo T. Farnsworth and Associates. Its purpose was to continue the work on fusion he started at IT and T.

According to the corporate prospectus for Farnsworth and Associates, the development of Farnsworth's ideas over the years resulted in "every television set sold utilizing at least six of his basic patents." Historian Leonard J. Arrington credits Farnsworth with 150 U.S. patents and "more than 100 foreign patents on various foreign inventions."

Farnsworth was an independent experimenter, a charismatic scientist, an idea person who was able to initiate ideas and convince investors. However, his primary focus was always in the laboratory. He was a workaholic and often left the business, investment and management responsibilities of his corporations to others as his experiments continued. He was often so immersed is his inventions that it was reported he would forget to eat. His health proved to be a challenge throughout his life. His wife Elma "Pem" Gardner-Farnsworth worked with him in the earliest labs as a technician and a bookkeeper. Fransworth himself said, "my wife and I started television." After he died it was his wife who worked to assure his recognition for his inventions and his consequent place in history. In many ways his work brings to an end the era of independent inventors. He was the recipient of numerous awards from scientific and honors societies, and the 1983 U.S. postal stamp commemorates the inventor. In 1981 a historical marker was placed on the San Francisco Green Street Building where the first Farnsworth television image was projected. In 1990 a statue was dedicated in Washington's Statuary Hall—the inscription reads *Philo Taylor Farnsworth: Inventor of Television.*

—Donald G. Godfrey

PHILO T(AYLOR) FARNSWORTH. Born in Beaver Creek, Utah, U.S.A., 19 August 1906. Educated at Rigby Idaho High School; attended Brigham Young University, 1923–25. Married Elma "Pem" Gardner, 1926, four children. Research director, Crocker Research Labs, 1926; founded Farnsworth Television Incorporated, 1929; organized television department for Philco, 1931–33; vice-president, founder, and director of research and engineering, Farnsworth Television and Radio Corporation, 1938; researcher in television and nuclear fusion, International Telephone and Telegraph Company, from 1949; president and director of research, Farnsworth Research Corporation, 1957; president and director, Philo T. Farnsworth and Associates, Inc., 1968. Honorary doctorates of science from the Indiana Institute of Technology, 1951; Brigham Young University, 1968. Member: American Physics Society. Named to the National Inventors Hall of Fame, 1968. Died in Salt Lake City, Utah, U.S.A.,11 March 1971.

FURTHER READING

Barnouw, Erik. *Tube of Plenty: The Evolution of American Television.* New York: Oxford University Press, 1975.

Everson, George. *The Story of Television: The Life of Philo T. Farnsworth.* New York: Norton, 1949.

Farnsworth, Elma G. *Distant Vision.* Salt Lake City, Utah: Pemberly Kent, 1989.

Farnsworth Papers. Arizona State University, Tempe, Arizona, and University of Utah Libraries, Salt Lake City, Utah.

Godfrey, Donald G., and Alf Pratte. "Elma 'Pem' Gardner Farnsworth: The Pioneering of Television." *Journalism History* (Northridge, California), Summer 1994.

Hofer, Stephen F. "Philo Farnsworth: Television's Pioneer." *Journal of Broadcasting* (Washington, D.C.), Spring 1979.

See also Television Technology

FATHER KNOWS BEST

U.S. Domestic Comedy

Father Knows Best, a family comedy of the 1950s, is perhaps more important for what it has come to represent than for what it actually was. In essence, the series was one of a number of middle-class family sitcoms, representing stereotypical family members. Today, many critics view it, at best, as high camp fun, and, at worst, as part of what critic David Marc once labeled the "Aryan melodramas" of the 1950s and 1960s.

The brainchild of the series' star Robert Young, who played insurance salesman Jim Anderson, and producer Eugene B. Rodney, *Father Knows Best* first debuted as a radio sitcom in 1949. In the audio version the title of the show ended with a question mark, suggesting that father's role as family leader and arbiter was dubious. The partner's

production company, Rodney-Young Enterprises, transplanted the series to television in 1954—without the questioning marker—where it ran until 1960, appearing at various times on each of the three networks.

Young and Rodney, friends since 1935, based the series on experiences each had with wives and children; thus, to them, the show represented "reality." Indeed, careful viewing of each of the series' 203 episodes reveals that the title was actually more figurative than literal. Despite the lack of an actual question mark, father didn't always know best. Jim Anderson could not only loose his temper, but occasionally be wrong. Although wife Margaret Anderson, played by Jane Wyatt, was stuck in the drudgery of domestic servitude, she was nobody's fool, often besting her husband and son, Bud (played by Billy Gray). Daughter Betty Anderson (Elinor Donahue)—known affectionately to her father as Princess—could also take the male Andersons to task, as could the precocious Kathy (Lauren Chapin), the baby of the family.

Like *Leave It to Beaver* creators Bob Mosher and Joe Connelly, Young and Rodney were candid about their attempts to provide moral lessons throughout the series. While none of the kids experienced the sort of social problems some of the real-life actors faced (Young was an alcoholic and the adult Chapin became a heroin addict), this was more the fault of television's then-myopic need for calm than Young and Rodney's desire to side-step the truth. The series certainly avoided the existence of the "Other America," as did most other American institutions.

Young won two Emmy Awards for his role, and Wyatt won three. A well-known film actor before his radio and television days, Young went on to later success in the long-running series *Marcus Welby, M.D.*, which may have been more appropriately called "Dr. Knows Best." After *Father Knows Best* moved into prime-time reruns in 1960, Donahue played Sheriff Andy Taylor's love interest, Miss Ellie, on *The Andy Griffith Show*. In 1977, NBC brought the Andersons back in two reunion specials, *Father Knows Best: The Father Knows Best Reunion* (May 1977) and *Father Knows Best: Home for the Holidays* (December 1977).

—Michael B. Kassel

Father Knows Best

CAST

Jim Anderson	Robert Young
Margaret Anderson	Jane Wyatt
Betty Anderson (Princess)	Elinor Donahue
James Anderson, Jr. (Bud)	Billy Gray
Kathy Anderson (Kitten)	Laurin Chapin
Miss Thomas	Sarah Selby
Ed Davis (1955–59)	Robert Foulk
Myrtle Davis (1955–59)	Vivi Jannis
Dotty Snow (1954–57)	Yvonne Lime
Kippy Watkins (1954–59)	Paul Wallace
Claude Messner (1954–59)	Jimmy Bates
Doyle Hobbs (1957–58)	Roger Smith
Ralph Little (1957–58)	Robert Chapman
April Adams (1957–58)	Sue George
Joyce Kendall (1958–59)	Jymme (Roberta) Shore

PRODUCERS Eugene Rodney, Robert Young

PROGRAMMING HISTORY 203 Episodes

• CBS

October 1954–March 1955	Sunday 10:00-10:30

• NBC

August 1955–September 1958	Wednesday 8:30-9:00

• CBS

September 1958–September 1960	Monday 8:30-9:00

FURTHER READING

Denis, Christopher Paul, and Michael Denis. *Favorite Families of TV*. New York: Citadel, 1992.

Leibman, Nina. *Living Room Lectures: The Fifties Family in Film and Television*. Austin: University of Texas Press, 1995.

Taylor, Ella. *Prime Time Families*. Berkeley: University of California Press, 1989.

See also Comedy, Domestic Settings; Family on Television; Young, Robert

FAWLTY TOWERS

British Situation Comedy

Considered to be one of the finest and funniest examples of British situation comedy, *Fawlty Towers* has become a critical and popular success throughout the world to the extent that all twelve of its episodes can stand as classics in their own right. The series succeeded in combining the fundamentals of British sitcom both with the traditions of British theatrical farce and with the kind of licensed craziness for which John Cleese had already gained an international reputation in *Monty Python's Flying Circus*. Comic writing of the highest quality, allied to painstaking attention to structure and detail, enabled *Fawlty Towers* to depict an extraordinarily zany world without departing from the crucial requirement of sitcom—the maintenance of a plausible and internally consistent setting.

Like so many sitcoms, the premise was simple, stable and rooted in everyday life (reputedly being based on the proprietor of a genuine Torquay hotel in which Cleese and the *Monty Python* team stayed whilst shooting location footage). Basil Fawlty (Cleese) and his wife Sybil (Prunella Scales) ran the down-at-heel seaside hotel of the title hampered by a lovingly-drawn cast of believable characters embellished in varying degrees from comic stereotype. Yet *Fawlty Towers* stood out from the commonplace through its intensity of pace and exceptional characterisation and performance, with the result that otherwise simple narratives were propelled, through the pandemonium generated by Basil and Sybil's prickly relationship, to absurd conclusions.

Cleese played Basil as a man whose uneasy charm and resigned awkwardness scarcely contained his inner turmoil. An inveterate snob, he was trapped between his dread of Sybil's wrath and his contempt for the most of the hotel's guests—the "riff-raff" whose petty demands seemed to interfere with its smooth running. In Sybil, Prunella Scales created a character which was the equal of Basil in plausible idiosyncrasy—more practical than him but entirely unsympathetic to his feelings, a gossiping, over-dressed put-down expert who could nevertheless be the soul of tact when dealing with guests.

Fawlty Towers turned on their relationship—an uneasy truce of withering looks and acidic banter born of her continual impatience at his incompetence and pomposity. For Basil, Sybil was "a rancorous coiffeured old sow", while she called him "an ageing brilliantined stick insect". With Basil capable of being pitched into wild panic or manic petulance at the slightest difficulty, the potential was always present for the most explosive disorder.

Powerless against Sybil, Basil vented his frustrations on Manuel (Andrew Sachs), the ever-hopeful Spanish waiter, whom he bullied relentlessly and with exaggerated cruelty. Manuel's few words of English and obsessive literalism ("I know nothing") drew on the comic stereotype of the "funny foreigner" but reversed it to make him the focus of audience sympathy, especially in later episodes. When the final show

Fawlty Towers

revealed Manuel's devotion to his pet hamster (actually a rat!), it was gratifying to find it named "Basil."

Connie Booth, co-writer of the series and Cleese's wife at the time, completed the principal characters as Polly, a beacon of relative calm in the unbalanced world of *Fawlty Towers*. As a student helping out in the hotel, her role was often to dispense sympathy, ameliorating the worst of Basil's excesses or Manuel's misunderstandings.

Such was Cleese's reputation, however, that even the smaller roles could be cast from the top-drawer of British comedy actors. Amongst these were Bernard Cribbins, Ken Campbell and, most notably of all, Joan Sanderson, whose performance as the irascible and deaf Mrs. Richards remains her most memorable in a long and successful career.

Beyond the tangled power relations of its principal characters, a large part of the comic appeal of *Fawlty Towers* lay in its combination of the familiar sitcom structure with escalating riffs of *Python*esque excess. The opening of each episode (with hackneyed theme, stock shots and inexplicably rearranged name-board) and the satisfying circularity of their plotting shared with the audience a "knowingness" about the norms of sitcom. Yet it was this haven of predictable composition which gave licence to otherwise grotesque or outlandish displays which challenged the bounds of acceptability in domestic comedy. Basil thrashing his stalled car with a tree-branch, concealing the corpse of a dead guest or breaking into Hitlerian goose-stepping before a party of Germans were incidents outside the traditional capacity of the form which could have been disastrous in lesser hands.

The British practice of making sitcoms in short series gave Cleese and Booth the luxury of painstaking attention to script and structure which was reflected in the show's consistent high quality. An interval of nearly four years separated the two series of *Fawlty Towers* and some episodes took four months and as many as ten drafts to complete. Perhaps as a result, the preoccupations of the series reflected those of the authors themselves. Basil's character was a study in the suppression of anger, a subject later explored in Cleese's popular psychology books. This, together with an acute concern with class, contributed to the peculiarly English flavour of the series and may have had its roots in his boyhood. A long-standing fascination with communication problems seems to have been the motivation for the creation of Manuel and is characteristic of much of the interaction in the show (as well as being the title of the episode involving Mrs. Richards).

Fawlty Towers has been shown repeatedly throughout the world. In the 1977–78 season alone it was sold to 45 stations in 17 countries, becoming the BBC's best-selling programme overseas for the year, although the treatment of Manuel caused great offence at the 1979 Montreux Light Entertainment Festival where *Fawlty Towers* was a notorious flop. More recently, however, it has successfully been dubbed into Spanish with Manuel refashioned as an Italian. In Britain, *Fawlty Towers* has almost attained the status of a national treasure and Basil's rages and many of his more outlandish outbursts ("He's from Barcelona", "Whatever you do, don't mention the war", "*My wife* will explain") have passed into common currency.

—Peter Goddard

CAST

Basil Fawlty	John Cleese
Sybil Fawlty	Prunella Scales
Manuel	Andrew Sachs
Polly	Connie Booth
Major Gowen	Ballard Berkeley
Miss Tibbs	Gilly Flower
Miss Gatsby	Renee Roberts

PRODUCERS   John Howard Davies, Douglas Argent

PROGRAMMING HISTORY   12 30-minute episodes

• BBC

19 September 1975–24 October 1975
19 February 1979–26 March 1979

FURTHER READING

Cleese, John, and Connie Booth. *The Complete Fawlty Towers*. London: Methuen, 1988.

Skynner, Robin A. C., and John Cleese. *Families and How to Survive Them*. London: Methuen, 1983.

Wilmut, Roger. *From Fringe to Flying Circus*. London: Methuen, 1980.

See also British Programming; Cleese, John; Scales, Prunella

THE FBI

U.S. Police Procedural

The *FBI*, appearing on ABC from 1965 to 1974, was the longest running series from the prolific offices of QM Productions, the production company guided by the powerful television producer, Quinn Martin. Long time Martin associate and former writer Philip Saltzman produced the series for QM with the endorsement and cooperation of the Federal Bureau of Investigation. As Newcomb and Alley report in *The Producer's Medium* (1983), Quinn Martin professed that he did not want to do the show, primarily because he saw himself and the Bureau in two different political and philosophical camps. But through a series of meetings with J. Edgar Hoover and other Bureau representatives, and at the urging of ABC and sponsor Ford Motor Company, Martin proceeded with the show.

The FBI marked the first time QM Productions chronicled the exploits of an actual federal law enforcement body and each episode was subject not only to general Bureau approval, but to the personal approval of director J. Edgar Hoover. Despite this oversight, Martin reported to Newcomb and Alley that the Bureau never gave him any difficulties regarding the stories produced for the show. The Bureau's only quibbles had to do with depicting the proper procedure an agent would follow in any given situation.

The FBI featured Inspector Lewis Erskine (Efrem Zimbalist, Jr.). For the first two seasons, Agent Jim Rhodes (Stephen Brooks) was Erskine's associate and boyfriend to his daughter, Barbara (Lynn Loring). Agent Tom Colby (William Reynolds) was Erskine's sidekick for the remainder of the series. All the principals answered to Agent Arthur Ward (Philip Abbot). Erskine was a man of little humor and a near obsessive devotion to his duties. Haunted by the memory of his wife, who had been killed in a job-related shoot-out, Erskine discouraged his daughter from becoming involved with an FBI agent, hoping to spare her the same pain. But his capacity for compassion ended there. This lack of breadth and depth sets Erskine apart from other protagonists in QM programs, but neither he nor his partners allowed themselves to become emotionally involved in their work which focused on a range of crimes, from bank robbery to kidnapping to the occasional Communist threat to overthrow the government.

Martin's attempts, with his team of writer/producers, to develop a multi-dimensional Lewis Erskine were met with resistance from the audience. Through letters to QM and ABC, viewers expressed their desire to see a more stoic presence in Erskine—one incapable of questioning his motives or consequences from his job. Erskine, Ward, Rhodes and Colby were asked to view themselves simply as the infantry in an endless battle against crime. The audience, apparently in need of heroes without flaws, called for and received its assurance in the form of these men from the Bureau. A female agent, Chris Daniels (Shelly Novack), appeared for the final season of the show.

The series drew critical scorn but was very successful for ABC, slipping into and out of the Top Twenty shows for the nine years of its run, and rising to the tenth position for the 1970–71 season. Shortly after the series left the air Martin produced two made-for-television films, *The FBI Versus Alvin Karpis* (1974), and *The FBI Versus the Ku Klux Klan* (1975).

In spite of the critics' attitude *The FBI* was Quinn Martin's most successful show. Media scholars point to the program as most emblematic of QM's approval and advocacy of strong law enforcement. The period from the late 1960s into the early 1970s was one of significant political and social turmoil. *The FBI* and other shows like it (*Hawaii 5-0, Mission: Impossible*) proposed an answer to the call for stability and order from a video constituency confused and shaken by domestic and international events seemingly beyond its control.

But despite this social context the series differed from other QM productions in its steady avoidance of contemporary issues of social controversy. *The FBI* never dealt substantively with civil rights or domestic surveillance or the moral ambiguities of campus unrest related to the Vietnam war. One departure from this pattern was sometimes found in the standard device which concluded many shows. Zimbalist would present to the audience pictures of some of the most wanted criminals in America and request assistance in capturing them. One of the more prominent names from this segment was James Earl Ray, assassin of Dr. Martin Luther King, Jr.

Within the dramatic narrative of *The FBI*, however, a resolute Erskine would pursue the counterfeiter or bank robber of the week bereft of any feelings or social analysis which might complicate the carrying out of his duties. For Martin, a weekly one-hour show was not the forum in which to address complex social issues. He did do so, however, in the made-for-television movies mentioned above.

The FBI occupies a unique position in the QM oeuvre. It is one of the most identifiable and recognizable of the QM Productions. It is also representative of the genre of law and order television which may have assisted viewers in imposing some sense of order on a world which was often confusing and frightening.

—John Cooper

The FBI

CAST

Inspector Lewis Erskine	Efrem Zimbalist, Jr.
Arthur Ward	Philip Abbott
Barbara Erskine (1965–66)	Lynn Loring
Special Agent Jim Rhodes (1965–67) . . .	Stephen Brooks
Special Agent Tom Colby (1967–73) .	William Reynolds
Agent Chris Daniels (1973–74)	Shelly Novack

PRODUCERS   Quinn Martin, Philip Saltzman, Charles Larson, Anthony Spinner

PROGRAMMING HISTORY   236 Episodes

• ABC

September 1965–September 1973	Sunday 8:00-9:00
September 1973–September 1974	Sunday 7:30-8:30

FURTHER READING

Martindale, David. *Television Detective Shows of the 1970s: Credits, Storylines, and Episode Guides for 109 Series.* Jefferson, North Carolina: McFarland, 1991.

Meyers, Richard. *TV Detectives.* San Diego: Barnes and London: Tantivy, 1981.

Newcomb, Horace, and Robert S. Alley. *The Producer's Medium: Conversations with Creators of American TV.* New York: Oxford University Press, 1983.

Powers, Richard Gid. *G-Men, Hoover's F.B.I. in American Popular Culture.* Carbondale: University of Southern Illinois Press, 1983.

See also Martin, Quinn; Police Programs

FCC See FEDERAL COMMUNICATIONS COMMISSION

FECAN, IVAN

Canadian Television Programming Executive

For years, Ivan Fecan was known to the Canadian broadcasting industry as TV's controversial "wunderkind." In 1985, when he was thirty-one years old, the Toronto native was recruited by the U.S. television network NBC as the new vice president of programming under then-programming chief Brandon Tartikoff. NBC and CBC had the Canadian comedy series *Second City TV* in common at that time and Fecan met with Tartikoff to discuss new program ideas. Impressed with the young man, Tartikoff, himself a young executive, offered Fecan the NBC job.

After two years at NBC, the head of English-language CBC, Denis Harvey, brought Fecan home as director of programming, where he began to institute program development, especially in comedy. He moved the award-winning young people's series, *Degrassi Junior High,* to Monday nights in prime time, where it flourished. He also hired a Canadian script doctor at CBS, Carla Singer, to work with the producer on *Street Legal,* the drama series about a group of Toronto lawyers. Although it started out with weak scripts and pedestrian directing, the series found its legs, became much more professional—some would say more "American"—and lasted eight years.

Fecan's rise to the highest levels of the industry can indeed be described as meteoric. Fecan began as a producer of the popular and respected three-hour radio magazine show, *Sunday Morning.* Moses Znaimer recognized his talent and took him away to be news director of Citytv, the hip new upstart local station. Two years later he became program director at CBC's Toronto station, CBLT. He updated that flagship station by bringing in electronic news gathering (ENG) equipment, two-way radios, and more reporters. Leaving news for the entertainment side of the business, Fecan spent sixteen months as head of CBC-TV's Variety Department. He is said to have renewed variety programming there by using more independent producing talent.

Fecan's goals were to make CBC programming break even, to attain an all-Canadian schedule, and to produce high-quality shows that audiences wanted to see. There are two schools of thought on his tenure as CBC's director of programming. One is that he brought polish and quality to the national network while boosting Canadian-pro-

duced shows; the second is that he turned the public broadcaster into a veritable clone of the American networks. What is not in dispute is that he shepherded some of the finest TV movies during his leadership, including *The Boys of St. Vincent, Conspiracy of Silence, Love and Hate, Glory Enough for All, Where the Spirit Lives, Life with Billy, Princes in Exile, Dieppe,* and *Liar, Liar.* In fact, *Love and Hate* (about the true story of a Saskatchewan politician who murdered his ex-wife) was the first Canadian movie of the week to be aired on a major U.S. network (NBC).

Ivan Fecan
Photo courtesy of Ivan Fecan

The series *Kids in the Hall, The Road to Avonlea, North of 60, Scales of Justice, 9B, Degrassi High, The Odyssey,* and *Northwood* came into existence because of Fecan. *Kids in the Hall* went on to become a hit on American television and *The Road to Avonlea* won awards all over the world and ran for seven years. In addition to *Kids in the Hall,* in the comedy arena, he launched *The Royal Canadian AirFarce, CODCO* and *This Hour Has 22 Minutes.*

Fecan made professional use of competitive scheduling and programming tools he had learned from Tartikoff and Grant Tinker at NBC. Negotiating that delicate balance between Canadian content and American revenues which has so often been a problem, he programmed American series in prime time to help bring in much needed money— *Kate and Allie, Hooperman, The Golden Girls,* and *The Wonder Years.* Some argued that *Street Legal* had become too Americanized, like *L.A. Law,* its counterpart, despite the obvious Toronto locations and the Canadian legal traditions and local issues. (The shows were developed and coincidentally went on air about the same time.) *Street Legal* also, however, began to draw more than a million viewers a week, a hit by Canadian standards, after two seasons of mediocrity.

A much more risky and dubious decision was to create *Prime Time News* at 9:00 P.M. to replace the Canadian tradition of *The National* and *The Journal* at 10:00 P.M. It turned out to be an unwise move and *The National* was soon returned.

Such shows as *Adrienne Clarkson Presents,* Harry Rasky's world-famous documentary specials, the documentary anthology *Witness,* and Patrick Watson's *The Struggle for Democracy* illustrate Fecan's commitment to Canadian production which is neither American-style nor draws large audiences. Canadian content grew from 78% to 91% under Fecan's direction and the amount of U.S. programming dropped. Although criticized for concentrating too much on the national network instead of on regional programming, Fecan strengthened the main network in a time when local stations were about to be cut or closed altogether by severe budget restraints not in his control. It has been claimed that CBC's audience share declined over his tenure, but in boom years for cable and pay, his work probably prevented much greater declines in ratings which all networks, even the three U.S. majors, suffered.

Fecan left CBC and joined Baton Broadcasting in January 1994 as senior group vice president and became executive vice president and chief operating officer in January 1995. Baton operates the commercial CTV, Canada's other national TV network.

—Janice Kaye

IVAN FECAN. Born in 1954. Educated at York University, Toronto, Canada, B.A. in fine arts. Producer, *Sunday Morning* radio show; news director, Citytv; program director, CBC, Toronto, head of network Variety department; moved to Hollywood as vice president of creative development, NBC, 1985; director of television programming, CBC, 1987; vice president, Baton Broadcasting, 1994, chief operating officer, 1995.

RADIO

Sunday Morning (producer).

FURTHER READING

"Baton Promotes Fecan to COO." *Financial Post Daily* (Toronto), 18 January 1995.
"Hefty Bonuses for Broadcasters." *Financial Post* (Toronto), 26-28 November 1994.
"Passing the Baton: Douglas Bassett Spearheads an Overhaul of Baton Broadcasting with Visionary Ivan Fecan." *Financial Post* (Toronto), 29 April-1 May 1995.

See also Canadian Programming in English; *Citytv; CODCO; Degrassi; Kids in the Hall; National; North of 60; Road to Avonlea; Royal Canadian Airfarce; Second City TV; Street Legal*

FEDERAL COMMUNICATIONS COMMISSION

U.S. Regulatory Commission

The United States Federal Communications Commission, created by an act of Congress on 19 June 1934, merged the administrative responsibilities for regulating broadcasting and wired communications under the rubric of one agency. Created during "The New Deal" with the blessings of President Franklin D. Roosevelt, the commission was given broad latitude to establish "a rapid, efficient, Nation-wide, and world-wide wire and radio communication service." On 11 July 1934 seven commissioners and 233 federal employees began the task of merging rules and procedures from the Federal Radio Commission, the Interstate Commerce Commission and the Postmaster General into one agency. The agency was organized into three divisions: Broadcast, Telegraph, and Telephone. Today, the agency employs approximately 1900 people and has extensive oversight responsibilities in new communications technologies such as satellite, microwave, and private radio communications.

The Act of 1934 and Organization of the FCC

The Federal Communications Commission (FCC) is an independent regulatory government agency. It derives its powers to regulate various segments of the communications industries through the Communications Act of 1934. Congress appropriates money to fund the agency and its activities, though recently the FCC raised revenues through an

Chair Reed E. Hundt

Commissioner Rochelle Chong

Commissioner Susan Ness

Commissioner James H. Quello

auction process for non-broadcast frequency spectrum. The Act enumerates the powers and responsibilities of the agency and its commissioners. Government radio stations are exempt from FCC jurisdiction. The Communications Act is divided into titles and sections which describe various powers and concerns of the Commission.

Title I describes the administration, formation, and powers of the Federal Communications Commission. The 1934 Act called for a commission consisting of seven members, reduced to five in 1983, appointed by the president and approved by Senate. The president designates one member to serve as chairman. The chairman sets the agenda for the agency and appoints bureau and department heads. Commissioners serve for a period of five years. The president cannot appoint more than three members of one political party to the commission. Title I empowers the commission to create divisions or bureaus responsible for various specific work assigned.

Title II concerns common carrier regulation. Common carriers are communication companies that provide facilities for transmission but do not originate messages, such as telephone and microwave providers. The act limits FCC regulation to interstate and international common carriers,

Title III of the act deals with broadcast station requirements. Many determinations regarding broadcasting regulations were made prior to 1934 by the Federal Radio Commission, and most provisions of the Radio Act of 1927 were subsumed into Title III of the 1934 Communications Act. Sections 303-307 define many of the powers given to the commission with respect to broadcasting. Other sections define limitations placed upon the commission. For example, section 326 within Title III prevents the commission from exercising censorship over broadcast stations. Provisions in the U.S. code also link to the Communications Act; for example, 18 U.S.C. 464 bars individuals from uttering obscene or indecent language over a broadcast station. And, section 315, the Equal Time Rule, requires broadcasters to afford equal opportunity to candidates seeking political office, and formally included provisions for rebuttal of controversial viewpoints under the contested Fairness Doctrine.

Titles IV and V deal with judicial review and enforcement of the act. Title VI describes miscellaneous provisions of the act including amendments to the act, and the emergency war powers of the president. Title VI extends FCC power to regulate cable television.

The 1934 Act has been considerably ammended since its passage. Many of the alterations have been in response to the numerous technical changes in communications that have taken place during the FCC's history, including the introduction of television, satellite and microwave communications, cable television, cellular telephone, and PCS (personal communications) services. As a result of these and other developments, new responsibilities have been added to the commission's charge. The Communications Satellite Act of 1962, for example, gave the FCC new authority for satellite regulation and the recent passage of the Cable Act

of 1992 required similar revisions to the 1934 Act. But the flexibility incorporated into the general provisions has allowed the agency to survived for sixty years. Though the FCC responsibilities have broadened to include supervision of these new technologies, it now shares regulatory power with other federal, executive and judicial agencies.

The FCC does have broad oversight over all broadcasting regulation. The FCC can license operators of various services and has recently used auctions as a means of determining who would be awarded licenses for personal communications services. The commission enforces various requirements for wire and wireless communication through the promulgation of rules and regulations. Major issues can come before the entire commission at monthly meetings; less important issues are "circulated" among commissioners for action. Individuals or parties of interest can challenge the legitimacy of the regulations without affecting the validity or constitutionality of the act itself. The language of the act is general enough to serve as a framework for the commission to promulgate new rules and regulations related to a wide variety of technologies and services. Though the agency has broad discretion to determine areas of interest and regulatory concern, the court, in *Quincy Cable TV, Inc. v. FCC,* reminded the FCC of its requirements to issue rules based on supportable facts and knowledge.

To more efficiently carry out all its tasks, the commission is divided into several branches and divisions. The Mass Media Bureau oversees licensing and regulation of broadcasting services. Common Carrier Bureau handles interstate communications service providers. The Cable Bureau oversees rates and competition provisions of the cable act of 1992. The Private Radio Bureau regulates microwave and land mobile services. Several offices within the FCC support the four bureaus. The Field Operations Bureau carries out enforcement, engineering and public outreach programs for the commission. The Office of Engineering and Technology provides engineering expertise and knowledge to the commission and tests equipment for compliance with FCC standards. The Office of Plans and Policy acts like the commission think tank.

The FCC and Broadcasting

Scholars differ on whether the FCC has used its powers to enforce provisions of the Communications Act wisely. Among the broad responsibilities placed with the FCC under section 303 are the power to classify stations and prescribe services, assign frequencies and power, approve equipment and mandate standards for levels of interference, make regulations for stations with network affiliations, prescribe qualifications for station owners and operators, levy fines and forfeitures, and issue cease and desist orders.

The most important powers granted to the commission are powers to license, short-license, withhold, fine, revoke or renew broadcast licenses and construction permits. These powers are based on the commission's own evaluation of whether the station has served in the public interest. Much of the debate over the FCC's wisdom, then, has focused on the determination of what constitutes fulfillment of a broadcast licensee's responsibilities under the "public interest, convenience and necessity" standard. Definitions and applications of this standard have varied considerably depending upon the composition of the commission and the mandates given by Congress. Though the FCC can wield the life-or-death sword of license revocation as a means of enforcing the standard, the commission has rarely used this power in its 60 year history.

Indeed, critics of the Federal Communications Commission argue that it has been too friendly and eager to serve the needs of large broadcast interests. Early FCC proceedings, for example, illustrate a pattern of favoring business over educational or community interests in license proceedings. But other scholars point to FCC actions against big broadcast interests by promulgating Duopoly, Prime-Time Access Rules (PTARs), and Syndication and Financial Interest Rules, all aimed at reducing the influence of large multiple license owners.

The commission has restated the public interest requirements numerous times over its sixty-year history. The Blue Book, The 1960 Programming Policy Statement, and Policy Statement Concerning Comparative Hearing were examples of FCC attempts to provide licensees with guidance as to what constituted adequate public service. Today, the FCC's reliance on "marketplace forces" to create competitive programming options for viewers and listeners reflects beliefs that economic competition is preferable to behavioral regulation in the broadcast industry.

Viewed over its sixty-year history, FCC decision making is generally seen as *ad hoc*. Frequent reversals of policymaking can be seen in commission decisions as the economic and technical conditions warranted changes in regulatory policy. Before the present era of deregulation, the FCC had promulgated extremely complex and detailed technical and operating rules and regulations for broadcasters, but it also gave licensees great latitude to determine what constituted service in the public interest based on local needs under its Ascertainment Policy. Once a station was licensed, the operator was required to monitor the technical, operational and programming aspects of the station. Files on all aspects of station operations had to be kept for several years. Today, under the general guidance of the "market," filing and renewal requirements for broadcasters are greatly reduced. However, when two or more applicants compete for the same license or when a Petition to Deny challenge is mounted, the commission makes a determination as to which of the competing applicants is best qualified to own and operate the broadcasting facility. Hearings follow strict procedures to ensure that the applicants' rights under the law are fully protected, and as a result the adjudicative process can be lengthy and cost applicants thousands of dollars in legal fees.

Reliance on "the marketplace rationale" began under Chairman Charles D. Ferris (1977-81), when the FCC em-

braced a new perspective on regulation and began licensing thousands of new stations in an effort to replace behavioral regulation with the forces of competition. Chairman Mark Fowler (1981-87) endorsed the marketplace model even more willingly than his predecessor. Yet, despite the flood of new stations, the Scarcity Rationale, based on limitations of the electromagnetic spectrum, remains a primary premise for government regulation over electronic media.

Broadcast licensees do not enjoy the same First Amendment rights as other forms of mass media. Critics charge that entry regulation—either through utilizing the concept of "natural monopoly" or severely limiting the number of potential licenses available—effectively uses the coercive power of government to restrict the number of parties who benefit from involvement in telecommunications. Breyer and Stewart note that, "Commissions operate in hostile environments, and their regulatory policies become conditional upon the acceptance of regulation by the regulated groups. In the long run, a commission is forced to come to terms with the regulated groups as a condition of survival." Critics say both the FRC and the FCC became victims of client politics as these two regulatory agencies were captured by the industries they were created to regulate.

Broadcast Regulation and FCC Policy Decisions

Throughout its history, a primary goal of the Federal Communications Commission has been to regulate the relationship between affiliated stations and broadcast networks, because the Communications Act does not grant specific powers to regulate networks. When the commission issued *Chain Broadcasting Regulations* the networks challenged the commission's authority to promulgate such rules, and sued in *National Broadcasting Co., Inc. et al. v. United States*. The Supreme Court upheld the constitutionality of the 1934 Act and the FCC's rules related to business alliances, noting the broad and elastic powers legislated by Congress. The FCC has used *The Network Case* as a precedent to ratify its broad discretionary powers in numerous other rulings.

On another front, at various times the commission has promulgated rules to promote diversity of ownership and opinion in markets and geographical areas. The Seven Station Rule limited the number of stations that could be owned by a single corporate entity. Multiple-Ownership and Cross-Ownership restrictions dealt with similar problems and monitored multiple ownership of media outlets—newspapers, radio stations, television stations—in regions and locations. Rules restricting multiple ownership of cable and broadcast television were also applied in specific situations. However, as more radio and television stations were licensed, restrictions limiting owners to few stations, a limitation originally meant to protect diversity of viewpoint in the local market, made less sense to the commission. In 1985, recognizing greater market competition, the commission relaxed ownership rules. In the years that followed, restrictions on Ascertainment, Limits on Commercials, Ownership, Anti-Trafficking, Duopoly and Syndication and Financial Interest Rules were also eased.

Still, it is the issue of First Amendment rights of broadcasters that has generated more public controversy in the sixty year history of the Communications Act of 1934 than any other aspect of communication law. Since the earliest days, the FRC and then the FCC insisted that because of "scarcity," a licensee must operate a broadcast station in the public trust rather than promote only his or her point of view. The constitutionality of the Fairness Doctrine and section 315 was upheld by the Court in *Red Lion Broadcasting v. FCC.* Broadcasters complained that the doctrine produced a "chilling effect" on speech and cited the possibility of fighting protracted legal battles in Fairness Doctrine challenges. Generally, though, the FCC determined station "fairness" based on the overall programming record of the licensee. The court reaffirmed the notion that licensees were not obligated to sell or give time to specific opposing groups to meet Fairness Doctrine requirements as long as the licensee met its public trustee obligations. But, as commissioners embraced deregulation, they began looking for ways to eliminate the Fairness Doctrine. In the *1985 Fairness Report,* the FCC concluded that scarcity was no longer a valid argument and the Fairness Doctrine inhibited broadcasters from airing more controversial material. Two cases gave the commission the power to eliminate the doctrine; in *TRAC v. FCC,* the court ruled that the doctrine was not codified as part of the 1959 Amendment to the Communications Act as previously assumed. Secondly, the FCC applied the Fairness Doctrine to a Syracuse television station after it ran editorials supporting the building of a nuclear power plant *(Meredith Corp. v. FCC, 809 F. 2d. 863 [1987]; Syracuse Peace Council 3 FCCR 2035 [1987]).* Meredith Corporation challenged the doctrine and cited the 1985 FCC report calling for the doctrine's repeal. The courts remanded the case back to the commission to determine whether the doctrine was constitutional and in the public interest. In 1987, the FCC repealed the doctrine, with the exception of the personal attack and political editorializing rules which still remain in effect.

Other First Amendment problems facing the commission include enforcing rules against indecent or obscene broadcasts (*FCC v. Pacifica*). After *Pacifica,* the FCC enforced a ruling preventing broadcasters from using the "seven dirty words" enumerated in comedian George Carlin's "Filthy Words" monologue on the air. However, "shock jocks" (radio disk jockeys who routinely test the boundaries of language use) and increasingly suggestive musical lyrics moved the FCC to take action against several licensees in 1987. In a formal Public Notice, the FCC restated a generic definition of indecency which was upheld by the U.S. Court of Appeals. Spurred by Congress, the commission stepped up efforts to limit the broadcast of indecent programming material, including the graphic depiction of aborted fetuses in political advertising. Various enforcement rules, including a "24 Hour Ban" and a "safe harbor" period from midnight to 6:00 A.M. have met with court challenges.

Other perennial areas of concern for the commission include television violence, the numbers of commercials broadcast in given time periods, the general banality of programming, and many issues related to children's television. Several FCC Chairmen and commissioners have been successful in using the "raised eyebrow" as an informal means of drawing attention to problems in industry practices. Calling television "a vast wasteland," a phrase adopted by many critics of television, Chairman Newton Minnow (1961–63) challenged broadcasters to raise programming standards. In 1974, under Richard Wiley (1972–77), the commission issued the Children's Television Programming and Advertising Practices policy statement starting a review of industry practices. And, Alfred Sikes (1989–92) called for "a commitment to the public trust" when he criticized television news coverage. Interest in children's television was further renewed in 1990 by the passage of the Children's Television Act which reinstated limits on the amount of commercial time broadcast during children's programming and requires the FCC to consider programming for children by individual stations at license renewal. The commission, under Chairman Reed Hundt (1993), has adopted a new Notice of Inquiry on compliance in this area. Congress has become increasingly interested in reducing the amount of violence on television. Industry representatives have issued a Statement of Principles concerning the depiction of violence in an effort to stave off FCC rulemaking.

Currently the FCC has many critics who feel that the agency is unnecessary and the Communications Act of 1934 outdated. Calls to move communication policymaking into the Executive Branch at the National Telecommunications and Information Administration (NTIA) or to reform the FCC have been heard from both industry and government leaders. Congress has grappled with FCC reform through the legislative process in its most recent sessions. Convergence of telephone and broadcasting technologies could make the separate service requirements under Titles II and III difficult to reform. Whether the commission will be substantially changed in the future is uncertain, but rapid changes in communications technology are placing new burdens on the commission's resources.

—Fritz J. Messere

FURTHER READING

Baughman, James L. *Television's Guardians: The FCC and the Politics of Programming, 1958–1967.* Knoxville, Tennessee: University of Tennessee Press, 1985.

Besen, Stanley, M., with others. *Misregulating Television: Network Dominance and the FCC.* Chicago: University of Chicago Press, 1984.

Breyer, Stephen G., and Richard B. Stewart, *Administrative Law and Regulatory Policy.* Boston: Little, Brown, 1979.

Cole, Barry, and Mal Oettinger, *Reluctant Regulators: The FCC and the Broadcast Audience.* Reading, Massachusetts: Addison-Wesley, 1978.

Communications Act of 1934, as amended; Communications Satellite Act of 1962, as amended; Pub.L. No. 416, 48 Stat. 562, § 1(Codified at 46 U.S.C.§ 151 [1992]).

Cowan, Geoffrey. *See No Evil: The Backstage Battle Over Sex and Violence on Television.* New York: Simon and Schuster, 1979.

Dizard, Wilson. *The Coming Information Age.* New York: Longman, 1982.

Engle, Eric. "FCC Regulation of Political Broadcasting: A Critical Legal Studies Perspective." *Communications and the Law* (New York), September 1992.

Federal Radio Commission, Annual Reports Numbers 1-7, 1927–33. Arno Press: New York, 1971.

Flannery, Gerald V. *Commissioners of the FCC, 1927–1994.* Lanham, Maryland : University Press of America, 1995.

Frohock, Fred M. *Public Policy: Scope and Logic.* Englewood Cliffs, New Jersey: Prentice-Hall, 1979.

Ginsburg, Douglas H., Michael H. Botein, and Mark D. Director. *Regulation of the Electronic Mass Media.* St. Paul, Minnesota: West Publishing, 1979; 2nd edition, 1991.

Greer, Douglas F. *Industrial Organization and Public Policy.* New York: MacMillan, 1980; 3rd edition, 1992.

Havick, John J., editor. *Communications Policy and the Political Process.* Westport, Connecticut: Greenwood, 1983.

Head, Sydney, Christopher Sterling, and Lemuel Schofield. *Broadcasting in America.* Boston: Houghton-Mifflin, 1956; 7th edition, 1994.

Hilliard, Robert L. *The Federal Communications Commission: A Primer.* Boston: Focal Press, 1991.

Horowitz, Robert Britt. *The Irony of Regulatory Reform.* New York: Oxford University Press, 1989.

Imhoff, Clement. "Clifford J. Durr and the Loyalty Question: 1942–1950." *Journal of American Culture* (Bowling Green, Ohio), Fall 1989.

Kahn, Frank J. editor. *Documents of American Broadcasting.* Englewood Cliffs, New Jersey: Prentice-Hall, 1969; 4th edition, 1984.

Kittross, John M., editor. *Documents in American Telecommunications Policy, vol. 1.* New York: Arno Press, 1977.

Krasnow, Erwin G., and Lawrence D. Longley. *The Politics of Broadcast Regulation.* 2d edition, New York: St. Martin's Press, 1978.

Lavey, Warren G. "Inconsistencies in Applications of Economics at the Federal Communications Commission." *Federal Communications Law Journal* (Los Angeles, California), August 1993.

Lowi, Theodore. *The End of Liberalism.* New York: W.W. Norton, 1969; 2nd edition, 1979.

McChensney, Robert W. *Telecommunications, Mass Media, and Democracy, The Battle for the Control of U.S. Broadcasting, 1928–1935.* New York: Oxford University Press, 1993.

McMillan, John. "Selling Spectrum Rights." *Journal of Economic Perspectives* (Nashville, Tennessee), Summer 1994.

National Association of Broadcasters. *Broadcast Regulation.* Washington, D.C.: NAB, 1995.

Paglin, Max D., editor. *A Legislative History of the Communications Act of 1934.* New York: Oxford University Press, 1989.

Radio Act of 1927, 44 Stat. 1162-66, 1168 (1927).

Ray, William B. *FCC: The Ups and Downs of Radio-TV Regulation.* Ames, Iowa: Iowa State University Press, 1990.

Rivera-Sanchez, Milagros. "Developing an Indecency Standard: The Federal Communications Commission and the Regulation of Offensive Speech, 1927–1964." *Journalism History* (Northridge, California), Spring 1994.

Smith, F. Leslie, Milan Meeske, and John W. Wright II. *Electronic Media and Government.* White Plains, New York: Longman, 1995.

Sterling, Christopher H., and John M. Kittross. *Stay Tuned.* Belmont, California: Wadsworth, 1978; 2nd edition, 1990.

Schwartman, Andrew J. "The FCC and the Fowler Years." *Television Quarterly* (New York), Fall 1990.

Special Issue on the Sixtieth Anniversary of the Communications Act of 1934. Federal Communications Law Journal (Los Angeles, California), December 1994.

U. S. Government, Office of Technology Assessment, Congress of the United States. *Critical Connections: Communication for the Future.* OTA-CIT-407, Washington, D.C.: U.S. Government Printing Office, 1990.

U.S. Department of Commerce. *NTIA Telecom 2000: Charting the Course for a New Century.* Washington, D. C.: U.S. Government Printing Office, 1988.

United States Federal Communications Commission. *Information Seeker's Guide: How to Find Information at the FCC.* Public Service Division, Office of Public Affairs, Federal Communications Commission (Washington, D.C.), 1994.

Veraldi, Lorna. "Gender Preferences." *Federal Communications Law Journal* (Los Angeles, California), April 1993.

Wilson, James Q. *American Government.* Lexington, Massachusetts: D.C. Heath,1986.

See also Allocation; Cable Television; Censorship; Children and Television; Deregulation; Equal Time Rule; Financial Interest and Syndication Rules; Hennock, Frieda B.; License; Hooks, Benjamin;Ownership; Political Processes and Television; Prime Time Access Rule; Public Interest, Convenience, and Necessity; Stations and Station Groups; Telcos; U.S. Policy: Communications Act of 1934;U.S. Policy: Telecommunications Act of 1996

FEDERAL TRADE COMMISSION

U.S. Regulatory Agency

In 1914, Congress passed the Federal Trade Commission Act (FTCA), thereby creating the Federal Trade Commission (FTC). The commission was given the mission of preventing "unfair methods of competition" (Pub. L. No. 203, 1914), and was designed to complement the antitrust laws. As such, the FTC originally was conceived as a protector of business and competition, with no direct responsibility to protect consumers.

In some of its first decisions, however, the commission found that the two interests were not mutually exclusive, since it was possible to steal business from a competitor by deceiving consumers. In fact, the FTC used this justification to protect consumers during its first 15 years of operation. But in 1931 the Supreme Court announced that the FTCA did not permit the commission to protect consumers, except where protection was a mere byproduct of protecting competitors (*FTC v. Raladam*, 283 U.S. 643). Consequently, in 1938, Congress amended the FTCA to enable the commission to protect both competitors and consumers, by adding power over "unfair or deceptive acts or practices" to the FTC's authority (Pub. L. No. 447).

Today, the FTC is the primary federal agency responsible for preventing citizens from being deceived, or otherwise injured, through advertising and other marketing practices. This responsibility applies to broadcast and print media, as well as any other means of communicating information from seller to buyer. In accord with its original mission, it also protects businesses from the unfair practices of competitors and, along with the Justice Department, enforces the antitrust laws. Each of these areas of commission jurisdiction touch the broadcast industry.

The FTC and the Antitrust Division of the Justice Department have an agreement to inform one another about their investigations and expected litigation, to avoid duplication of effort. The general mission for both is to preserve the competitive process, so that it functions in the most economically efficient manner possible and best serves the interest of the public.

The phrase "unfair methods of competition" is not defined in the FTCA, because it was designed to allow the FTC to adapt to an ever-changing marketplace. And courts have determined this power to be quite extensive. Consequently, the commission's oversight of competition generally involves enforcement of the Sherman and Clayton Acts, as well as the Robinson-Patman Act.

Thus, FTC antitrust actions can arise in cases of vertical restraints, entailing agreements between companies and their suppliers that might harm competition, and in cases of horizontal restraints, where direct competitors enter into a competition-limiting agreement. Those agreements can be subject to regulation whether their primary impact is on prices or on some non-price aspect of competition. This means that the FTC may intervene in situations intention-

ally designed to reduce competition, such as mergers and buy-outs, or in circumstances where competition may be unintentionally affected, as where a professional association adopts a "code of ethics" agreement.

During the 1970s, the FTC was perceived as being particularly aggressive at enforcing the antitrust laws. Some critics felt it also was somewhat inconsistent in its decisions. But under the Reagan Administration, in the early 1980s, the agency's regulatory philosophy changed. At President Reagan's direction, the agency experienced an infusion of "Chicago School" economists committed to deregulation and the belief that some of the Commission's previous actions were actually injurious to consumer welfare.

Since that time, while their involvement is less pronounced than during the Reagan era, those "Chicago School" economists have continued to influence FTC antitrust regulatory activity. The result has been less regulation of vertical restraints and price restrictions, and a greater focus on the benefits and *costs* to society in regulating horizontal restraints. Any contract or other agreement between competing businesses, even through a trade association, may be subject to FTC scrutiny. However, no regulation is likely unless the agency believes the harms to competition will outweigh the benefits.

With regard to television, the FTC's role in antitrust activity has focused on the flurry round of mergers and acquisitions taking place in the 1980s and 1990s. The commission paid close attention to the purchase of Capital Cities/ABC television network by the Disney company, and to the merger of Time-Warner and Turner Broadcasting Systems.

In the realm of advertising regulation the FTC has authority over both "deceptive" and "unfair" advertising and other marketing practices. For television, the commission's focus is on the content and presentation of commercials.

The "unfairness" power never was used extensively and, as a response to criticism that the power was too broad and subjective, it was somewhat limited by Congress between 1980 and 1994. But in 1994 Congress amended the FTCA to define "unfairness," and thereby circumscribe the commission's authority in that area.

The new definition of "unfairness" permits the commission to regulate marketing practices that (1) cause or are likely to cause substantial injury to consumers, (2) are not reasonably avoidable by consumers, and (3) are not outweighed by countervailing benefits to consumers or to competition. The implications of this definition are not yet known, but it is unlikely that the agency will make extensive use of its "unfairness" power in the near future.

By far, most regulation of advertising and marketing practices is based on the commission's "deceptiveness" power. As in the antitrust arena, advertising regulation experienced a shift in FTC philosophy during the Reagan presidency. The flow of "Chicago School" economists into the agency at that time led to a widespread perception that the FTC was engaged in less advertising regulation than it had been in earlier years. And in 1983, when the commission re-defined the term "deceptive" (*Cliffdale Associates*, 103 F.T.C. 110), many observers felt the new definition greatly diminished protection for consumers.

Under that new definition, the FTC will find a practice deceptive if (1) there is a representation, omission or practice that (2) is likely to mislead consumers acting reasonably under the circumstances, and (3) it is likely to affect the consumer's choice of, or conduct regarding, a product. The first requirement is obvious, and the FTC generally assumes that the last requirement is met. The second requirement, therefore, is the essence of this definition. The issue is not whether an advertising claim is "false." The issue is whether the claim is likely to lead consumers to develop a false belief.

The previous definition required only a "capacity or tendency" to mislead, rather than a "likelihood" and allowed protection of consumers who were not "acting reasonably." These changes were what bothered critics. But after a few years criticism virtually disappeared, and this definition continues to be FTC policy.

—Jef Richards

FURTHER READING

Ford, Gary T., and John E. Calfee. "Recent Developments in FTC Policy on Deception." *Journal of Marketing* (Chicago), July, 1986.

Kovacic, William E. "Public Choice and the Public Interest: Federal Trade Commission Antitrust Enforcement During the Reagan Administration." *The Antitrust Bulletin* (New York), Fall 1988.

Rosden, George Eric, and Peter Eric Rosden. *The Law of Advertising.* New York: Matthew Bender, 1996.

Shenefield, John H., and Irwin M. Stelzer. *The Antitrust Laws: A Primer.* Washington, D.C.: AEI Press, 1993.

Ward, Peter C. *Federal Trade Commission: Law Practice and Procedure.* New York: Law Journal Seminars-Press, 1988.

THE FIFTH ESTATE

Canadian Public Affairs Program

In an attempt to mirror the huge success of the U.S. program *60 Minutes,* the Canadian Broadcasting Corporation (CBC) in 1975 inaugurated its weekly public affairs program *The Fifth Estate.* Following the "four estates" of respectively, the clergy, nobility, the legislature, and print journalism, the "fifth estate" refers to the role of electronic broadcasting in society.

At the outset, the program's stated format and mandate was to be a weekly hour of innovative and inquisitive personal journalism. As such, the program adapted the American style of segmenting individual stories, introduced and narrated, and from time to time produced, by one of the program's hosts. Dubbed a magazine-type show, *The Fifth Estate* typically runs three such segments per show. Although based on American forms of public affairs programs, *The Fifth Estate* maintains a distinct link with Canada's tradition of documentary film-making. In particular, as a CBC-produced program whose mandate is to foster Canadian national identity, *The Fifth Estate*'s subject matters are drawn from all regions of the country. The program, therefore, also serves to educate Canadians about their own nation, its distinctive geography, cultures, languages and social problems.

The show is under the public affairs section of CBC programming, and its stories are framed within the language of contemporary news journalism. Not unlike the evening news or beat reporter, *The Fifth Estate* sees its role as a watchdog of government and public policy. And not surprisingly the program's hosts are usually drawn from the ranks of Canada's metropolitan daily newspapers. Similarly, hosts such as Hana Gartner have used the program as a stepping stone to prestigious anchor positions with the networks flagship newscast, *The National.*

The journalistic experience on *The Fifth Estate*'s staff has resulted in an aggressive and topical approach to public affairs in both Canada and abroad. From time to time this stance has raised the ire of individuals in question. In September 1993, for example, *The Fifth Estate* made front-page news when an entrepreneur unsuccessfully petitioned a Canadian court to place an injunction banning the broadcast of the prime-time program. At the international level *The Fifth Estate*'s documentary segment "To Sell a War",

The Fifth Estate
Photo courtesy of CBC

originally broadcast in December 1992, received widespread attention and acclaim for its detailing, in no uncertain terms, the Citizen's for a Free Kuwait misinformation campaign in the months leading up to the Gulf War. In 1993 "To Sell a War" was awarded the International Emmy for best Documentary.

—Greg Elmer

INTERVIEWER/HOSTS

Adrienne Clarkson, Eric Mailing, Ian Parker, Bob Johnstone, Peter Reilly, Warner Troyer, Hana Gartner, Bob McKeown, and others

PRODUCERS   Glenn Sarty, Ron Haggart, Robin Taylor

PROGRAMMING HISTORY

• CBC

September 1975– One Hour Weekly, Fall/Winter Season

FURTHER READING

Stewart, Sandy. *Here's Looking at Us: A Personal History of Television in Canada.* Toronto: CBC Enterprises, 1986.

See also Canadian Programming in English

FILM ON FOUR

British Film Series

The series *Film on Four* was announced on the opening night of Channel Four in November 1982, and helped to immediately draw attention to the distinctions between this and the three existing British television channels. Ostensibly, *Film on Four* occupies a curious position within British television. It was established by Jeremy Isaacs, Channel Four's first chief executive, following a European model, to encourage mainly new, independent filmmakers by offering funding for fictional, mainly feature length films. This was intended to lead to cinema distribution in many cases, where a film might gain a reputation before transmission on Channel Four. *Film on Four* is often considered to be particularly significant within film culture for providing vital financial support and for commissioning many films which have gained high regard. Indeed, Isaac's film investment policies made little economic sense in strictly television terms. He managed to secure around 8% of Channel Four's total programming funds and allocated it to fictional one-offs which would fill only 1% of air-time. However, it would be constrictive to overlook *Film on Four*'s integral position within television culture, particularly during the 1980s.

Traditionally the BBC had been the prime producers and supporters of television drama. However, in the period leading up to the early 1980s, it became increasingly difficult for the BBC to produce the single play for reasons involving changing production values, censorship and declining resources. The first head of *Film on Four*, David Rose, whose background was in BBC regional drama, commissioned a series of films which collectively represent a renaissance of highly contemporary drama. The films Rose promoted followed a writerly formula of neo-realism with socially displaced characters firmly positioned in a regional landscape. The resultant work, including Neil Jordan's *Angel* (1982) and Colin Gregg's *Remembrance* (1982), has been defined as being uncompromised by television's institutional modes of representation or by cinematic demands of impersonal spectacle.

Film on Four's only early success in the cinema was Peter Greenaway's *The Draughtsman's Contract* (1982), and, although the series had been established to encourage new ideas, in the early years the media argued that most of its products brought little that was innovative to television. Media support, credibility and international acclaim started to be gained three years on, primarily by Rose's investment in Wim Wender's art-house classic *Paris, Texas* (1984) and his funding of the surprise success, *My Beautiful Launderette* (Stephen Frears, 1984). Rose was awarded a special prize at Cannes (1987) for services to cinema and was heralded in Britain as the savior of the film industry. *Film on Four*'s successful output began to multiply with films such as *A Room with a View* (1985), *Hope and Glory* (1987), *Wish You Were Here* (1987) and *A World Apart* (1987), doing well at both the domestic and international box office. In addition to promoting new directors such as Stephen Frears and Chris Menges, *Film on Four* encouraged the work of established filmmakers including Peter Greenaway, Derek Jarman and Agnès Varda. After touring the festival circuit and cinema distribution the films were transmitted on television to respectable, although by no means outstanding, viewing figures—audiences averaged three million per film in 1990.

As only a minority of *Film on Four* products succeeded in returning any money to Channel Four, a general agreement was reached at the end of the 1980s that a large portion of the budget needed to be diverted to higher-rated, long-form drama. Rose was succeeded by David Aukin who continued to implement the recent policy of deliberate under-commissioning. With its much reduced budget, *Film on Four* could not keep up with massive inflation in production costs. Additionally, a sense of a general decrease in the quality of new projects and emerging talent surrounded the organization. Aukin showed less interest in promoting the film industry than in television itself, and aimed to concentrate on films a television audience would want to watch, rather than cinema award winners. For Aukin, it is almost

Film on Four: Shallow Grave
Photo courtesy of Channel Four

incidental that the best drama is produced on film because film remains the medium of choice for the greatest talent.

Whilst *Film on Four* necessarily cut its budget, the more financially secure BBC entered into a new phase of fiction making in the nineties. With the appointment of Mark Shivas, the BBC reformed its policies on feature length dramas in imitation of *Film on Four*. Its ambitions were in a higher budget area of filmmaking than Channel Four's, and consequently it accepted the risk of compromising artistic integrity for the demands of overseas financiers, in total contrast to Channel Four's puritanical policies. The BBC expounded its conviction towards the more mainstream, commercial category, and achieved theatrical successes with *Truly, Madly, Deeply* (1992) and *Enchanted April* (1991).

Channel Four continues with its film successes, principally *Four Weddings and a Funeral* (1994), and continues to offer less mainstream viewing with *Film on Four* and its related series *Film on Four International*—which buys domestic and foreign films post production—and *Short and Curlies*—a fifteen-minute slot presenting a short film, a type made only by Channel Four. *Film on Four* was original in that it promoted films with a socio-cultural importance, and allowed them to escape from the former confines of television drama as transient product. Whilst its main impact may have been to inject new life and creativity into British cinema in the 1980s, it is equally valid to claim that *Film on Four*, having been established so integrally to the channel's schedule, has more than anything else given Channel Four a unique identity, both in England and internationally.

—Nicola Foster

FURTHER READING

Saynor, James. "Writer's Television." *Sight and Sound* (London), November 1992.

See also British Programming; Channel Four

FINANCIAL INTEREST AND SYNDICATION RULES

U.S. Broadcasting Regulations

The Financial Interest and Syndication Rules (Fin-Sin Rules), or more precisely their elimination, may ultimately alter the television and film entertainment landscape as much as any event in the 1990s. The Federal Communications Commission (FCC) implemented the rules in 1970, attempting to increase programming diversity and limit the market control of the three broadcast television networks. The rules prohibited network participation in two related arenas: the financial interest of the television programs they aired beyond first-run exhibition, and the creation of in-house syndication arms, especially in the domestic market. Consent decrees executed by the Justice Department in 1977 solidified the rules, and limited the amount of prime-time programming the networks could produce themselves.

The rationales for Fin-Sin are numerous. The FCC was concerned that vertical integration (control of production, distribution and exhibition) unfairly increased the power of the networks. By taking away the long-term monetary rights to programs created by the networks, and severely restricting their participation in syndication, the FCC eliminated incentives for the networks to produce programs, thus separating production from distribution. Those in favor of Fin-Sin hoped that the rules would benefit independent television producers by giving them more autonomy from the networks (because financial interest would be solely in the hands of the production company), and allowing the producers to benefit from the lucrative syndication market. Proponents believed that by privileging independent producers in this way, the rules would cultivate more diverse and innovative television content. Another potential advantage of the rules was that independent television stations would benefit from the separation of the networks from syndication. If the networks owned the syndication rights to off-network programs, they might "warehouse" their programs, or steer popular reruns to network owned and operated stations and network affiliates to make those stations stronger in a particular market.

From the very beginning, however, the Fin-Sin Rules were controversial and contested. The networks felt that Fin-Sin was unfair and did not solve the intended problems. One anti-Fin-Sin argument noted that the expense of starting a national broadcast network—the financial barriers to entry—much more significantly explained the networks' control of television than their vertical integration. Others argued that the Fin-Sin Rules undermined the role of independent producers rather than enhanced them. Small independent producers, for example, often cannot afford to engage in the "deficit financing" required by the networks. Deficit financing involves receiving a below-cost payment from the networks during the first-run of a program. Large production organizations—like the Hollywood-tied Warner Television—are much more financially able than smaller companies to cope with the necessary short-term losses in

revenue, hoping to strike it rich in syndication. Critics of Fin-Sin therefore noted that Hollywood studios, rather than independents, grew stronger because of Fin-Sin, and that the smaller independents tended to produce conventional, but inexpensive, programs like talk shows and game shows rather than innovative programs.

In 1983, the FCC, swayed by these anti-Fin-Sin arguments and the general political climate favoring deregulation in many arenas, proposed eliminating most of the rules. However, a massive lobbying effort by Hollywood production organizations—efforts helped by a former Hollywood-actor President, Ronald Reagan—kept the rules in place.

In the early 1990s, however, other arguments were levied against Fin-Sin. When the rules were first implemented in the pre-cable, pre-FOX days of the 1970s, the networks' combined share of the television audience was around 90%. By the early 1990s, this share had dropped to roughly 65% because of the new forms of competition. Fin-Sin opponents also argued that the presence of vertical integration among other media companies—including organizations with television production arms like Time Warner—was unfair.

In 1991, then, the FCC relaxed the Fin-Sin Rules after an intense lobbying war pitting the major television producers (for Fin-Sin) against the major television distributors (against Fin-Sin). Appeals courts later relaxed the rules even further, in essence eliminating all traces of Fin-Sin by November 1995.

The elimination of the Fin-Sin Rules could ultimately have several long-term consequences for television. The first consequence is the merging of production organizations with distribution organizations. One example of this is increased in-house production by the big three networks. By 1992, for example, NBC was the single largest supplier of its own prime-time programming. Besides the distribution firms of television becoming more involved in production, production firms have gotten more involved in distribution. The creation of three new broadcast networks from 1986 to 1995 illustrates this. FOX Broadcasting, supported by its direct relationship with a Hollywood studio, is an early innovator here. In fact, the spark that led to the Fin-Sin elimination was FOX Broadcastings' 1990 request for Fin-Sin revisions. FOX, both a major producer and a mini network, wanted the transition to full network status to be unimpeded by Fin-Sin. Once the rules against the production-distribution merge were on their deathbed, Paramount and Warner Brothers soon joined FOX in forming studio-based television networks. The mid-1990s were likewise filled with rumors that a major studio, like Disney, might purchase one of the big three networks instead of starting one from scratch. And indeed, the rumors became fact when Disney purchased Cap Cities/ABC in 1995.

The future of independents—both independent producers and independent stations—may also be significantly affected by the demise of Fin-Sin. Independent producers worry that, at worst, the networks will no longer require their services and, at best, the nets will demand a share of syndication rights to programs and will privilege in-house productions with the best time slots. Independent stations worry that the networks will warehouse their best off-network programs, now that they will own the syndication rights. Some charged that the 1994 syndication of *The Simpsons*—sold to around 70 FOX affiliates—is a sign of the favoritism to come.

Finally, other critics note the dangers to programming diversity and advertising interference that may result from the deregulation. Now that the networks may benefit from syndication, for example, will they have an incentive to put on programs with high syndication potential, like situation comedies? Also, during the Fin-Sin era, prime-time network producers were at least superficially insulated from advertiser influence because of the separation of production from distribution. Advertisers paid the networks rather than the producers of TV content. Because the categories of production and distribution have collapsed together after Fin-Sin, advertisers may have more direct access to network production because they now write checks directly to organizations that produce as well as distribute.

Changes in the Financial Interest and Syndication Rules illustrate the significance of communication policy in affecting the daily menu of television choices available to the public. As much as alterations in technologies, techniques, and personalities, changes in the Fin-Sin Rules, and their possible disappearance, have an immediate, significant effect on the television industry and television audiences.

—Matthew P. McAllister

FURTHER READING

Auletta, Ken. *Three Blind Mice: How the TV Networks Lost Their Way.* New York: Random House, 1991.

Besen, Stanley M., with others. *Misregulating Television: Network Dominance and the FCC.* Chicago: University of Chicago Press, 1984.

Carter, Bill. "Networks Cleared to Syndicate Programs for 7-to-8 P.M. Slot; FCC Strikes Down a 25-year-old Access Rule." *New York Times,* 29 July 1995.

———. "Ruling Lets Networks Join Risk of Syndication." *New York Times,* 16 November 1993.

Covington, William G. "The Financial Interest and Syndication Rules in Retrospect: History and Analysis." *Communications and the Law* (New York), June 1994.

Creech, Kenneth. *Electronic Media Law and Regulation.* Boston, Massachusetts: Focal, 1993.

Ginsburg, Douglas H., *Regulation of the Electronic Mass Media: Law and Policy for Radio, Television, Cable, and the New Technologies.* St. Paul, Minnesota: West Publishing, 1991.

Jessell, Harry A. "Comments Box Fin-Syn Compass (FCC Receives Comment on New TV Syndication Rules). *Broadcasting* (Washington, D.C.), 25 June 1990.

———. "White House Sends Loud and Clear Fin-Syn Signal." *Broadcasting* (Washington, D.C.), 18 February 1991.

Kaplar, Richard T. *The Financial Interest and Syndication Rules: Prime Time for Repeal.* Washington, D.C.: The Media Institute, 1990.

"Opening on Capitol Hill: 'The Fin-Syn Story.'" *Broadcasting* (Washington, D.C.), 26 June 1989.

Stern, Christopher. "Faster End for Fin-Syn?" *Broadcasting and Cable* (Washington, D.C.), 10 April 1995.

United States Federal Communications Commission Network Inquiry Special Staff. New Television Networks: Entry, Jurisdiction, Ownership and Regulation. Washington, D.C.: U.S. Government Printing Office, 1980.

See also Deregulation; Federal Communications Commission; FOX Broadcasting Company; Programming; Reruns; Syndication

FIRESIDE THEATRE

U.S. Anthology Series

Fireside Theatre was the first successful filmed series on American network television. In an era when live television dominated network schedules, the series demonstrated that filmed programming could be successful and from the fall of 1949 to the spring of 1955, it was one of the ten most watched programs in the United States. Following *The Milton Berle Show* on Tuesday nights on NBC, *Fireside* was an anthology drama that presented a different half-hour story each week. In 1955, the series was changed to *Jane Wyman Presents the Fireside Theatre,* and though it soon became a distinctly different series under the title, *Jane Wyman Theater* (1955–58), the title usually refers to the entire run of the series.

For the first two years of network series television (1947 to 1949), all television shows were broadcast live from New York and many were anthology dramas, presenting weekly hour-long plays. *Kraft Television Theatre, Studio One,* and *Philco Television Playhouse* are outstanding examples of the form that dominated network schedules through the early 1950s. Videotape would not be available until 1956, and film was initially thought to be too expensive for weekly television production. For television critics working during the early years of the medium, the hour-long anthology dramas, with their adaptations of literary classics, serious dramas, and social relevance, represented the best of television. The worst was cheap, half-hour, Hollywood telefilms that did not, in their view, aspire to so-called serious drama or social relevance. *Fireside Theatre* fit this latter category.

The television series most often cited as the innovator in filmed programming is *I Love Lucy* (which was produced in Hollywood). However, when *I Love Lucy* premiered on CBS in 1951, *Fireside Theatre* had already been on the air for two years. To the show's sponsor and owner, Procter and Gamble, film offered several distinct advantages over live production. It made possible the creation of error-proof commercials. It allowed for closer control of content and costs. It created opportunities for added profits from syndication when programs were sold for repeated airing. And it enabled cost-effective distribution to the West Coast, not yet hooked into the coaxial cable network that linked East Coast and Midwest stations.

Producer, director, writer, and host Frank Wisbar is often considered the reason for *Fireside Theatre*'s success. Frank Wisbar Productions was the sole production company from 1951 to 1955 and for the show's first several seasons, Wisbar produced and directed most episodes, and even served as host in the 1952–53 season. To control costs, he wrote many episodes himself and used public domain and free-lance stories. Writers such as Rod Serling and Budd Schulberg saw their stories produced and then little-known and second-string movie actors such as Hugh O'Brian, Rita Moreno, and Jane Wyatt appeared on the series.

When *Fireside Theatre* premiered in April 1949, it began a three-month experimental period. Some of the 15-minute episodes were live and some were filmed. Genres were mixed, and included comedies, musicals, mysteries, and dramas. A half-hour format that presented two 15-minute filmed stories per episode was chosen for the 1949–50 season. These early episodes were often mysteries, reflecting Wisbar's background in horror and mystery movie making. (When these episodes were first shown in syndication they were called *Strange Adventure*.) Later seasons presented half-hour dramas, and while the stories continued to vary in genre (Westerns, comedies, melodramas, mysteries), family remained the central theme.

From 1953 to 1955 film actor Gene Raymond served as host and by the end of the 1954–55 season, as ratings declined, *Fireside Theatre* was completely overhauled—it became a different series. The title and theme music changed. But most significantly, film star Jane Wyman became host and producer. Wyman chose the scripts and acted in many of the episodes and her company, Lewman Productions, produced the series. It was now Wyman's show, which would remain on NBC until 1958.

Fireside Theatre established its place in the history of television by being the first successful filmed network series in the era of live broadcasting. It was also the first successful filmed anthology series in an era of prestigious live anthology

Fireside Theatre: Solitude

dramas. Scorned by critics, it was, for most of its seven seasons, a top-ten show on American television.

—Madelyn Ritrosky-Winslow

HOST
Frank Wisbar (1952–53)
Gene Raymond (1953–55)
Jane Wyman (1955–58)

PRODUCER   Frank Wisbar

PROGRAMMING HISTORY   268 Episodes

• NBC

April 1949–June 1957	Tuesday 9:00-9:30
September 1957–May 1958	Thursday 10:30-11:00

FURTHER READING
Lafferty, William. "'No Attempt at Artiness, Profundity, or Significance': *Fireside Theatre* and the Rise of Filmed Television Programming." *Cinema Journal* (Urbana, Illinois), 1987.

See also Anthology Drama; Wyman, Jane

FIRST PEOPLES' TELEVISION BROADCASTING IN CANADA

Canadian Programming Service

First Peoples of Canada have become internationally acknowledged as having the most advanced and fair Fourth World (indigenous peoples) broadcasting system, based on a 1991 legislated recognition of their collective communications and cultural rights as Peoples with a special status. In the Canadian context, "First Peoples" is an inclusive term referring to both the Inuit (known elsewhere as "Eskimos") and the Amerindian populations, the latter also known as First Nations. The language of the Inuit is Inuktitut. Aboriginal-initiated media in Northern Canada (North of the 55th parallel line) has had a relatively long history when compared with Fourth World/indigenous communities elsewhere. The stages through which this broadcasting history has evolved were initiated by First Peoples themselves as they struggled for their inclusion in the policy and practice decisions pertaining to broadcasting services to be received by their national communities. Partly as a result of the pioneering and persistent activities of First Peoples to make *their* programming an integral part of the Canadian media infrastructure, Canada has also come to be identified as a model of media resistance against the overwhelming forces of continental integration in North America.

It is difficult to talk about the introduction of television into the North without acknowledging its relationship to radio. This is because radio set a very special attitudinal context for the arrival of television. First Peoples expected that television would have local and regional indigenous input, as well as national, Southern-produced programming, as had been the case with radio. A brief overview of Northern radio is, therefore, foundational to understanding why First Peoples reacted the way they did to television.

Radio entered the North in the late 1920s, at the same time that airplanes began to develop easy access to the Arctic. By the early 1930s, trading posts, the Royal Canadian Mounted Police centres, and religious missions were equipped with high frequency radios to maintain contact with their headquarters in the South. Native peoples did not have direct access to these early radio services. In 1958, the Canadian Broadcasting Corporation's (CBC) Northern Service was established, taking over the infrastructure of shortwave transmitters established by the Canadian Armed Forces and the Department of Transport.

In 1960, the first Inuit-language broadcasts occurred and by 1972, 17% of the CBC shortwave service was in Inuktitut. Since the early 1970s, First Peoples have demanded access to radio in the North. All three levels of government have responded positively to native requests; seed money and core funding from provincial/territorial and federal government communications and cultural programs have assisted First Peoples in their radio development process. As a consequence, culturally-relevant, native-language radio programming has become an integral part of the Northern media infrastructure.

Radio is simple to learn, operate, and maintain; it is an important information tool and readily adaptable to local indigenous-language programming.

The Canadian federal government's public subsidisation of native-produced media began formally in 1974 with the development of its Native Communications Program (NCP). Between then and 1996, 117 First Peoples' community radio stations have become operational across Canada, including those below the Hamelin line (the line at latitude 55 that separates the North from the South). With the exception of the Inuit service in the Northwest Territories, whose CBC regional radio programming has always been and continues to be satisfactory and representative of their concerns, all other Northern regions have both a network of local radio stations and one publicly-subsidised regional service.

The Native Communications Program was terminated quite suddenly in 1990 by the Secretary of State, who stated that vertical budgetary cutbacks were the reason for its dissolution. Evidence of concrete program successes and public outcry did not result in the program's reinstatement. Funding for native local radio remains tenuous. In general, most Northern communities do not have a large enough advertising base to convert to private radio. They, therefore, depend on either public subsidy or some guaranteed way of maintaining stable funding. To date, most community radio stations operate radio bingos for their baseline fundraising strategy.

Regionally, both radio and television broadcasting evolved rapidly in response to the launching of the Anik satellite in 1972. In 1973, the North was hooked up to the South through radio and television services and for the first time, Inuit and First Nations were able to have access to the images, voices, and messages that United States and metropolitan-based Canadians produced with Southern audiences in mind. The parachuting in of Southern, culturally-irrelevant television programming into Northern communities by the CBC Northern Service acted as a catalyst for indigenous constituency groups to organize broadcasting services in their own languages (dialects), reflecting their own cultures, as they had achieved in radio. Almost immediately after its initial mystique dissipated, native peoples and their Southern supporters began to lobby for their own television programming and network services. They wanted participatory and language rights, as well as decision making responsibilities about programming and Southern service expansion. By the mid-1970s, First Peoples across the country had secured funding, established Native Communications Societies (NCS) to be the responsible administrative party for their communications activities, and begun operating local community television projects.

Beginning in 1976, in response to their clearly articulated demands, the federal government made large grants available for native organizations to be used for technical experiments with the Hermes (1976) and Anik B satellites (1978–81). In 1976, the Alberta Native Communications Society and Taqramiut Nipingat Incorporated (TNI) of Northern Quebec received money to do interactive audio experiments with the Hermes satellite. In 1978, funding was provided to Inuit Tapirisat (Brotherhood) of Canada (ITC) of the Northwest Territories and TNI to complete a more sophisticated interactive series of technical, community development, and educational experiments on the Anik B satellite. By 1981, after the establishment of five Northern television production studios, after two and a half years of staff training, and after six months of experimental access, it was unquestionably demonstrated that the organizations involved were capable of: (1) organizing complex satellite-based audio/video interactive experiments involving five communities; (2) managing five production centres and satellite uplink/downlink ground stations; (3) coordinating a large staff in different locations, as well as a budget of over a million dollars; (4) producing hundreds of hours of high quality program output; (5) documenting technical data related to satellite experimentation and viable uses of the satellite for Northern interactive communications; and, finally, (6) documenting the whole process as evidence of their credibility as a potential broadcasting licensee.

In 1981, based on the positive results of its Anik-B demonstration project called *Inukshuk,* the Inuit Broadcasting Corporation was licensed as a Northern television service by the Canadian Radio-television and Telecommunications Commission (CRTC), Canada's regulatory agency, to provide Inuktitut-language services to the Northwest Territories, Northern Quebec, and Labrador. In this same period, other Native Communications Societies across the North were at varying stages of radio and television development, also in preparation for the licensing process and all in support of the establishment of a legislated recognition of their media demands as a distinct constituency group within the Canadian state.

At this time, the federal government undertook a one-year consultation and planning process, the outcome of which was the Northern Broadcasting Policy (1983), and an accompanying program vehicle, the Northern Native Broadcast Access Program (NNBAP). These policy and funding decisions became the foundation for the eventual enshrinement of aboriginal broadcasting in the 1991 Broadcasting Act.

The Northern Broadcasting Policy set out the principle of "fair access" by native Northerners to the production and distribution of programming in their territories. It further established the principle of consultation with First Peoples before Southern-based decisions were to be made about Northern telecommunications services. By 1983, thirteen regional Native Communication Societies had been established to be the recipients of funding from the NNBAP. The NNBAP coordinators set up a program structure within the Department of the Secretary of State (Native Citizens Directorate) and were mandated to distribute $40.3 million over a four-year period. The money was to be used for the production of 20 hours of regional native radio and five hours of regional aboriginal television per week. Funding has eroded annually, but the program is still operational.

As the NNBAP implementation process proceeded, it became apparent that fair distribution of radio and television programming was a key problem because of the implicit assumption within the Northern Broadcasting Policy that this task would be taken care of by either CBC Northern Service or by CANCOM (Canadian Satellite Communications Inc.), a Northern program distributor. In both cases, negotiations between Native Communication Societies and broadcasters had become bogged down over prime time access hours and preemption of national programming.

In 1988, the federal government responded to persistent native lobbying by the National Aboriginal Communications Society (a lobby group representing the interests of the NCS groups) for more secure distribution services by laying out $10 million toward the establishment of a dedicated Northern satellite transponder (channel). By 1992, *Television Northern Canada* (TVNC) was on the air. Owned and programmed by 13 aboriginal broadcast groups, plus government and education organizations located in the North, it is a pan-Arctic satellite service that distributes 100 hours of programming to 94 Northern communities. It is considered to be a primary level of service in the North. In 1995, TVNC applied for permission from the CRTC to be placed on the list of eligible channels to be picked up by cable operators in the South. In November 1995, approval was granted, making it possible for TVNC to become available in a variety of Southern Canadian markets, should cable operators decide to make it part of their discretionary packages. It is already accessible on an off-air basis to those who own satellite dishes because its signal is not scrambled.

In December 1995, TVNC joined together with two Northern companies, Arctic Co-Operatives Limited and NorthwesTel, for the purposes of designing an information highway infrastructure that will meet the specific cross-cultural needs of Northerners.

Since 1992, First Peoples of Canada and consultants who have worked with them have become involved in international media development processes based on the assumption that sharing of communications experiences and resources among indigenous nations can only be beneficial. For example, initiatives encouraged by the United Nations, Canadian International Development Agency, and private organizations have included several media projects undertaken in Belize and Bolivia and television program exchanges have already taken place among Greenlandic, Alaskan, and Canadian Inuit, and aboriginal peoples from Australia.

Despite challenges for more secure, long-term funding and improved access, First Peoples of Canada have established themselves as pioneers in the development of cross-cultural television links across Canada's vast (sub)Arctic regions. Currently, they are extending their media knowledges outside of their Northern borders into the South and beyond. Technical advances in local, regional, and national telecommunications services, conjoined with the social and cultural goals of First Peoples' broadcasters, have demonstrated that it is possible to use media in a sensitive manner to express cultural heterogeneity, rather than homogeneity. To date, from the rudimentary evidence aggregated, it appears that First Peoples have refashioned television broadcasting. They have indigenized it—transformed it into a tool for inter-community and national development. They have utilized television programming as a vehicle of mediation into their own historically ruptured pasts and as a pathway into more globally-integrated futures.

—Lorna Roth

FURTHER READING

Canadian Radio-television Commission. Decision CRTC 91-826. *Television Northern Canada Incorporated.* Ottawa, Canada: CRTC, 28 October 1991.

———. *"Native Broadcasting Policy."* Public Notice CRTC 1990–1989. Ottawa, Canada. 20 September 1990.

———. *The 1980's—A Decade of Diversity: Broadcasting Satellites and Pay-TV. Report of the Committee on Extension of Service to Northern and Remote Communities.* Ottawa, Canada: Canadian Government Publishing House, 1980.

Government of Canada. *Broadcasting Act.* Ottawa, Canada, 4 June 1991.

———. *The Northern Broadcasting Policy.* News Release. 10 March 1983.

Koebberling, Ursel. *The Application of Communication Technologies in Canada's Inuit Communities* (Ph.D. dissertation, Simon Fraser University, 1988).

Mander, Gerry. *In the Absence of the Sacred: The Failure of Technology and the Survival of the Indian Nations.* San Francisco: Sierra Club Books, 1991.

Roth, Lorna. *Northern Voices and Mediating Structures: The Emergence and Development of First Peoples' Television Broadcasting in the Canadian North* (Ph.D. dissertation, Canada: Concordia University, 1994).

Roth, Lorna, and Gail Valaskakis. "Aboriginal Broadcasting in Canada: A Case Study in Democratization." In Raboy, Marc, and Peter A. Bruck, editors. *Communication for and Against Democracy.* Montreal: Black Rose Books, 1989.

Stiles, Mark, and William Litwack. *Native Broadcasting in the North of Canada.* Ottawa: Canadian Commission for UNESCO-Report 54, 1988.

Valaskakis, Gail. "Television and Cultural Integration: Implications for Native Communities in the Canadian North." In Lorimer, R., and D. Wilson, editors. *Communication Canada: Issues in Broadcasting and New Technologies.* Toronto: Kagan and Woo, 1988.

Wilson, Thomas C. *Ten Years of Satellite Television in the Eastern Arctic: Cultural Implications for the Diffusion of Educational Technology,* (Ph.D. dissertation, Concordia University, 1987).

See also Australian Programming (Aboriginal); Canadian Production Companies

FISHER, TERRY LOUISE

U.S. Writer/Producer

Terry Louise Fisher began her career not in television but as a lawyer in the Los Angeles district attorney's office. She later sidestepped into a specialty in entertainment law and in 1982 wrote for and produced the Emmy-award winning series *Cagney and Lacey.* Other shows followed: *Cutter to Houston* and *The Mississippi* for CBS, the television movie *This Girl for Hire* and *Your Place or Mine?* (all 1983). But she is best known for her work as co-creator (with Steven Bochco) and supervising producer of *L.A. Law* from 1986 to 1988. *L.A. Law,* which ended its run in 1994, was considered the quintessential example of 1980s "appointment television," perfectly capturing the greed, glitz, and power seeking of the decade, and capturing in the process of its narratives an audience intrigued by those very elements.

The power struggles among the show's law partners were echoed in Fisher's 1987 legal battle with Bochco, when a negotiation for Fisher to take over from Bochco as executive producer failed and he banned her from the set. Since then, Fisher has published two novels, has produced another

series and several made-for-television movies, and in 1995 was active in *Cagney and Lacey: The Return.* She also participated in a pilot for *Daughters of Eve,* the first international prime-time soap opera, to star Sophia Loren, financed by Proctor and Gamble.

—Cheryl Harris

TERRY LOUISE FISHER. Born in Chicago, Illinois, U.S.A., 1946. Entered law school at University of California, Los Angeles, 1968. Married and divorced. Worked as trial lawyer, Los Angeles District Attorney's Office; switched to entertainment law; worked on *Cagney and Lacey* series, 1982–85; supervising producer, *L.A. Law,* 1986–88; independent producer, made-for-television movies and television series, from 1988. Recipient: Emmy Awards, 1987 and 1988.

TELEVISION SERIES

1982–88   *Cagney and Lacey*
1983   *Cutter to Houston*

1983	*The Mississippi*
1986–94	*L.A. Law*
1987	*Hooperman* (co-writer)
1995	*Daughters of Eve* (pilot)

MADE-FOR-TELEVISION MOVIES

1983	*Your Place or Mine?*
1983	*This Girl for Hire*
1987	*Sister Margaret and the Saturday Night Ladies*
1990	*Blue Bayou*

| 1995 | *Cagney and Lacey: The Return* |

PUBLICATIONS

A Class Act (novel). New York: Warner, 1976.
Good Behavior (novel). New York: Warner, 1979.

FURTHER READING

Kort, Michele. "Terry Louise Fisher: How She Dreamed Up the Women of *L.A. Law*." *Ms.* magazine (New York), June 1987.

THE FLINTSTONES

U.S. Cartoon Comedy Series

The *Flintstones* was the first, and the longest running, animated situation comedy shown in prime-time television. Premiering on ABC on 30 September 1960, it gained high ratings in its first season, thus establishing animation as a viable prime time format. Produced by Hanna-Barbera (Bill Hanna and Joe Barbera), *The Flintstones* was patterned after Jackie Gleason's *The Honeymooners*. Designed as a program for the entire family, the program did not appear as "children's television" until its rebroadcast by NBC in 1967. Its popularity with teenagers in its 8:30 P.M. Friday time slot, however, presaged the late 1960s move to animation as the preeminent format for children's programming.

Fred and Wilma Flintstone and their best friends, Barney and Betty Rubble, lived in the prehistoric city of Bedrock but faced the problems of contemporary working-class life. After a day at the rock quarry, Fred and Barney arrived home in a vehicle with stone wheels and a fringe on top. Their lives revolved around their home, friends, and leisure activities: a world of drive-ins, bowling, and their "Water Buffalo" lodge. A baby dinosaur and a saber tooth tiger replaced the family dog and cat. In 1962 and 1963, Pebbles and Bamm Bamm appeared as the daughter and adopted son of the Flintstones and Rubbles respectively.

Aside from being the first animated series made for prime time, *The Flintstones* also broke new ground in that each episode contained only one story that lasted the full half hour. Until the 1960s, cartoons were generally only a few minutes long. Half-hour programs used three or four shorts (three- to four-minute cartoons) and a live "wrap-around," usually presented by a friendly "host," to complete the program. In another innovation, Hanna-Barbera produced *The Flintstones* using limited animation techniques. This assembly line method of creating drawings, combined with reduced and simplified body movement, made it possible to manufacture animation cells more cheaply. Because of the lowered cost and the appeal of animation to children, limited animation became the format of choice for children's television in the 1960s, a decade in which children's programming became almost entirely animated.

The Flintstones helped establish Hanna-Barbera Productions as a major Hollywood animation studio and by the late 1960s as the world's largest producer of animated entertainment films. *The Flintstones* also launched a multi-million dollar merchandising business with hundreds of toys and novelties placed on the market. Perhaps the most enduring product developed in this ancillary line was Flintstones vitamins, also used as a sponsor for the program. Citing the difficulties children might have in distinguishing cartoon characters from the products made in their likenesses, critics attacked the practice of advertising vitamins to children, and such ads were withdrawn in 1972. The Flintstones characters still appear in commercials for Pebbles' cereals, and other tie-ins include films (a major, live-action motion picture in 1994), traveling road shows, toys, and other children's products.

The Flintstones played on ABC in prime time through September 1966. The series was rebroadcast on Saturday mornings by NBC from January 1967 through September 1970. Various spin-offs and specials also appeared on the CBS or NBC Saturday morning lineup throughout most of the 1970s, and continue to reappear. *The Flintstones* is still available in syndication.

—Alison Alexander

CAST (Voices)

Fred Flintstone	Alan Reed
Wilma Flintstone	Jean Vander Pyl
Barney Rubble	Mel Blanc
Betty Rubble (1960–64)	Bea Benaderet
Betty Rubble (1964–66)	Gerry Johnson
Dino the Dinosaur	Mel Blanc
Pebbles (1963–66)	Jean Vander Pyl
Bamm Bamm (1963–66)	Don Messick

PRODUCERS   Bill Hanna, Joe Barbera

PROGRAMMING HISTORY

• ABC

September 1960–September 1963   Friday 8:30-9:00

The Flintstones

September 1963–December 1964   Thursday 7:30-8:00
December 1964–September 1966   Friday 7:30-8:00

FURTHER READING

Barnouw, Erik. *Tube of Plenty: The Evolution of American Television.* New York: Oxford University Press, 1975; revised edition, 1982.

Turow, Joseph. *Entertainment, Education and the Hard Sell: Three Decades of Network Children's Television.* New York: Praeger, 1981.

Woolery, George. *Children's Television: The First Thirty-Five Years, 1946–1981. Part 1: Animated Cartoon Series.* Metuchen, New Jersey: Scarecrow, 1983.

See also Cartoons; Children and Television; Hanna, William, and Joseph Barbera

THE FLIP WILSON SHOW

U.S. Comedy Variety Program

The *Flip Wilson Show* was the first successful network variety series with an African-American star. In its first two seasons, its Nielsen ratings placed it as America's second most-watched show. Flip Wilson based his storytelling humor on his background in black clubs, but adapted easily to a television audience. The show's format dispensed with much of the clutter of previous variety programs and focused on the star and his guests.

Clerow "Flip" Wilson had been working small venues for over a decade when Redd Foxx observed his act in 1965 and raved about him to Johnny Carson. As a result, Wilson made over 25 appearances on the *Tonight Show*, and in 1968, NBC signed him to a five-year development deal.

Wilson made guest appearances on shows such as *Rowan and Martin's Laugh-In* and the first episode of *Love, American Style*. On 22 September 1969, he appeared with 20 other up and coming comics in a Bob Hope special, which was followed by a *Flip Wilson Show* special, a pilot for the series to come. The special introduced many distinctive elements that would be part of the series, the most striking element the small round stage in the middle of the audience, from which Wilson told jokes and where guests sang and performed sketches with minimal sets.

For his opening monologue in that special, Wilson told a story about a minister's wife who tried to justify her new extravagant purchase by explaining how "the Devil made me buy this dress!" The wife's voice was the one subsequently used for all his female characters, whether a girlfriend or Queen Isabella ("Christopher Columbus going to *find* Ray Charles!"). Later in the special, he put a look to the voice in a sketch opposite guest Jonathan Winters. Winters played his swinging granny character, Maudie Frickert, as an airline passenger, and when Wilson donned a contemporary stewardess' outfit—loud print miniskirt and puffy cap—Geraldine Jones was born. The audience howled as Winters apparently met his match.

NBC was encouraged with the special to go forward with a regular series, and *The Flip Wilson Show* joined the fall lineup on 17 September 1970. Wilson appeared at the opening and explained that there was no big opening production number, because it would have cost $104,000. "So I thought I would show you what $104,000 looks like." Flashing a courier's case filled with bills before the camera and audience, he asked, "Now, wasn't that much better than watching a bunch of girls jumping around the stage?"

That monologue illustrated one of the chances Wilson and his producer, Bob Henry, took. They did away with the variety show's conventional chorus lines, singers and dancers, and allowed the star and his guests to carry the show. The creative gamble paid off as *The Flip Wilson Show* defeated all comers in its time slot and won two Emmy Awards in 1971: as Best Variety Show and for Best Writing in a Variety Show.

The show was also a landmark in the networks' fitful history of integrating its prime-time lineup. Nat "King" Cole had been the first African American to host a variety show, which NBC carried on a sustaining basis in 1956. Despite appearances by guests such as Frank Sinatra, Tony Bennett and Harry Belafonte, that program could neither attract sponsors, nor obstain sufficient clearances from affiliates. Cole left the air at the end of 1957. Later, NBC was more successful with Bill Cosby in *I Spy*, and Diahann Carroll as *Julia*. The week after *The Flip Wilson Show's* premiere, ABC debuted its first all-black situation comedy, an unsuccessful adaptation of Neil Simon's *Barefoot in the Park*.

During the run of his show Wilson created several other characters who flirted with controversy. There was the Rev.

The Flip Wilson Show

Leroy, of the Church of What's Happenin' Now, whose sermons were tinged with a hint of larceny; Freddy the Playboy: always, but unsuccessfully, on the make; and Sonny, the White House janitor, who knew more than the president about what was going on.

But Geraldine Jones was by far the most popular character on the series. Wilson wrote Geraldine's material himself and tried not to use her to demean black women. Though flirty and flashy, Geraldine was no "finger popping chippie." She was based partly on Butterfly McQueen's character in *Gone with the Wind*: unrefined but outspoken and honest ("What you see is what you get, honey!"). She expected respect and was devoted to her unseen boyfriend, "Killer." It also helped that Flip had the legs for the role, and did not burlesque Geraldine's build, though NBC Standards and Practices did ask him to reduce Geraldine's bust a little.

Another aspect of the show's appeal was its variety of guests. Like Ed Sullivan, Flip tried to appeal to as wide an audience as possible. The premiere saw James Brown, David Frost and the Sesame Street Muppets. A later show offered Roger Miller, the Temptations, Redd Foxx and Lily Tomlin, whom Freddy the Playboy tried to pick up. Roy Clark, Bobby Darin and Denise Nicholas joined Wilson for a "Butch Cassidy and the Suntan Kid" sketch.

The Flip Wilson Show turned out to be one of the last successful variety shows. CBS' 1972 offering, *The Waltons,* became a surprise hit, winning the same Thursday time slot. By the 1973–74 season, it was John-Boy and company who had the second most popular show of the season. NBC put Wilson's show to rest, airing its last episode on 24 June 1974.

—Mark R. McDermott

REGULAR PERFORMERS
Flip Wilson
The Jack Regas Dancers
The George Wyle Orchestra

PRODUCER Bob Henry

PROGRAMMING HISTORY

• NBC

September 1970–June 1971   Thursday 7:30-8:30
September 1971–June 1974   Thursday 8:00-9:00

FURTHER READING

Adir, Karin. *The Great Clowns of American Television.* Jefferson, North Carolina: McFarland, 1988.
Amory, Cleveland. "The Flip Wilson Show." *TV Guide* (Radnor, Pennsylvania), 10 October 1970.
"Flipping It." *Newsweek* (New York), 12 August 1968.
Franklin, Joe. *Joe Franklin's Encyclopedia of Comedians.* Secaucus, New Jersey: Citadel, 1979.
"I Don't Care if You Laugh." *Time* (New York), 19 October 1970.
O'Neil, Thomas. *The Emmys: Star Wars, Showdowns, and the Supreme Test of TV's Best.* New York: Penguin, 1992.
Pierce, Ronchitta. "All Flip Over Flip." *Ebony* (Chicago, Illinois), April 1968.
Robinson, Louie. "The Evolution of Geraldine." *Ebony* (Chicago, Illinois), December 1970.

See also Wilson, Flip; Variety Programs

FOR THE RECORD

Canadian Dramatic Anthology Series

For the Record was one of the most successful series ever produced and broadcast by the CBC. It used an anthology format, offering four to six new episodes each year linked only by the series title and a documentary-style approach to topical stories. Many episodes proved controversial, but the series was critically acclaimed for its thoughtful and intense treatment of difficult issues.

The idea for the series originated with John Hirsch, who was appointed head of television drama at the CBC in 1974. He felt that CBC drama should have the same urgency and relevance as the network's well-regarded current affairs programming and recruited Ralph Thomas as executive producer of a new series, which would become *For the Record*.

Although the producers and writers contributed a great deal to the success of the series, one of the key decisions taken by Thomas was to hire directors who had contributed to the growth of Canadian cinema in the 1960s and early 1970s. These filmmakers were part of Canada's "direct cinema" movement of low-budget feature films based on documentary techniques developed at the National Film Board. In the mid-1970s Canadian film moved toward the production of supposedly more commercial imitations of Hollywood style and, as a result, leading filmmakers, both anglophone and francophone, were pleased to find an outlet for their talents in a television series which stressed its difference from the U.S. network programs that dominated Canadian television screens.

The series officially got under way in 1977, but the basic approach was established in the previous season when five topical dramas were broadcast under the title *Camera '76*. These included "Kathy Karuks is a Grizzly Bear" (written by Thomas and directed by Peter Pearson), about the exploitation of a young long-distance swimmer, and "A Thousand Moons"

(directed by prolific Quebec filmmaker Gilles Carle), about an old metis woman who lives in a city but dreams of returning home to die. Six new programs were broadcast in the following season, when the series got its permanent name: two ("Ada" and "Dreamspeaker") were contributed by another Quebec director, Claude Jutra, while documentary filmmaker Allan King directed "Maria," about a young Italian-Canadian who attempts to unionize a garment factory. The most controversial production of the 1977 season was undoubtedly "The Tar Sands," written and directed by Pearson, which provoked a libel suit because of its depiction of recent dealings between the oil industry and politicians in Alberta.

By the end of the 1977 season the format and possibilities of the series had been firmly established; but these did not fit comfortably into existing categories of television programming. The episodes were presented as television dramas, but the location shooting made them seem more like films. After the legal problems with "The Tar Sands," the CBC disavowed the term "docudrama" which had been applied to the series and suggested instead "journalistic drama" or "contemporary, topical drama that is issue oriented."

Whatever the term, the series did allow for a range of approaches. Dramatized treatments of specific topical events (like "The Tar Sands") were rare, although viewers could often relate the fictional stories to similar stories recently in the news. More common were episodes (like "Maria") which dealt with an identifiable "social problem" in terms of its impact on characters seen as both individual and representative. While the "social problem" was a necessary ingredient, some episodes, notably those directed by Carle and Jutra, took on a poetic dimension with subjective fantasy sequences emerging from their social realism.

Some memorable episodes from later seasons dealt with rape ("A Matter of Choice," 1978), hockey violence ("Cementhead," 1979), separatism ("Don't Forget 'Je Me Souviens,'" 1979), television evangelism ("Blind Faith," 1982), farm bankruptcies ("Ready for Slaughter," 1983), gender discrimination ("Kate Morris, Vice President," 1984), and the beauty myth ("Slim Obsession," 1984).

The series was praised for its refusal to allow personal dramas to obscure the social implications of the issues. Whatever the outcome for the characters, the endings did not create the impression that the issues had been resolved, implying that solutions still needed to be sought in reality. Supporters of public broadcasting in Canada pointed to *For the Record* as an alternative to the formulas of commercial television, with its demand for clearly-defined conflicts and happy endings, and there was a widespread agreement that the series fulfilled the CBC's mandate to provide insight into Canadian society and culture. Its cancellation in 1985 could be seen as a response to commercial and political pressures on the CBC, although the public network has continued to broadcast similar realist dramas exploring topical issues.

—Jim Leach

PRODUCER   Ralph Thomas

PROGRAMMING HISTORY

• CBC

1976–1985

FURTHER READING

Collins, Richard. *Culture, Communication and National Identity: The Case of Canadian Television.* Toronto: University of Toronto Press, 1990

Feldman, Seth, editor. *Take Two.* Toronto: Irwin, 1984.

Gervais, Marc. "Lightyears Ahead: *For the Record.*" *Cinema Canada* (Montreal, Quebec), March 1977.

Henley, Gail. "On the Record: *For The Record'*s 10 Distinctive Years." *Cinema Canada* (Montreal, Quebec), April 1985.

Miller, Mary Jane. *Turn Up the Contrast: CBC Television Drama Since 1952.* Vancouver, Canada: University of British Columbia Press, 1987.

Morris, Peter. *The Film Companion.* Toronto: Irwin, 1984.

See also Canadian Programming in English

FORD, ANNA

British Broadcast Journalist

Anna Ford was independent television's first female newsreader and in time became one of the most popular and experienced of female news presenters in British television. Critics ascribed her early success as a newsreader primarily to her attractive looks, but she subsequently demonstrated even to her detractors that she was more than competent as a presenter and furthermore ready to brave controversy (something she was well used to even as a student, due to her committed Socialist views).

Before her recruitment as ITN's (Independent Television News) answer to the BBC's popular, though less vivacious, newsreader Angela Rippon in the late 1970s, Ford had already amassed some experience as a television presenter through her work as a reporter for *Reports Action, Man Alive* and other programmes. Reflecting her early training in education (she taught social studies to IRA internees in Belfast's Long Kesh prison, among others), she had also worked on broadcasts for the Open University and had then presented *Tomorrow's World* for a time before resigning because, she explained, she had no wish to become "a public figure." Ironically, this is exactly what she was shortly afterwards fated to become as a high-profile newsreader for *News at Ten*.

The most controversial stage in Ford's career opened in the early 1980s when she was one of the "Famous Five" celebrities behind the launching of the ill-starred TV-AM company, for which she presented the breakfast programme *Good Morning Britain*. When the new enterprise failed to

Anna Ford
Photo courtesy of Anna Ford

attract the required audiences, Ford (and Rippon) were unceremoniously sacked and it was speculated that her career in television was over. Ford's response to this was to pour a glass of wine on her former employer, M.P. Jonathan Aitken—an incident that hit the headlines and only confirmed Ford's reputation for belligerence.

Similarly controversial was Ford's widely reported refusal to wear flattering make-up on television to disguise the effects of aging, in protest, she said, of the "body fascism" of television bosses who insisted that female newscasters were only there to provide glamour. Critics of her stand attacked her for being aggressive and overtly feminist (they also expressed shock that she sometimes read the news while not wearing a bra), but many more admired her for her forthrightness. Those who had automatically written her off as "just a pretty face" were obliged to think again. It was a mark of her success in the argument that, some six years after the TV-AM debacle, Ford—now age 45—was readmitted to the fold as a newsreader for the BBC's prime-time *Six O'Clock News*. She has also continued to present occasional programmes on a wide range of educational and other issues.

—David Pickering

ANNA FORD. Born in Tewkesbury, Gloucestershire, England, 2 October 1943. Attended Wigton Grammar School, Cumbria; Manchester University. Married: 1) Alan Brittles in 1970 (divorced, 1976); 2) Mark Boxer, 1981 (died, 1988), children: Claire and Kate. Taught at Open University in Belfast for two years before joining Granada Television as researcher, 1974; moved to BBC, 1976; newscaster, ITN, 1978–82; also worked as researcher and presenter of school programmes; founder-member of TV-AM, 1982–83; newscaster, BBC, 1989. Recipient: TV Times Most Popular TV Personality (Female), 1978. Address: JGPM, 2 New Kings Road, London SW6 4SA, England.

TELEVISION SERIES

1974	*Reports Action*
1977	*Man Alive*
1977	*Tomorrow's World*
1978–81	*News at Ten*
1983	*Good Morning Britain*
1984	*Did You See...?*
1986	*Understanding Adolescents*
1987–89	*Network*
1987	*Understanding Families*
1987	*On Course*
1989–	*Six O'Clock News*

TELEVISION SPECIALS

1984	*West End Stage Awards*
1985	*Starting Infant School*
1985	*Communication*
1985	*Handicapped Children*
1985	*Children's Feelings*
1985	*Starting Secondary School*
1985	*Approaching Adolescence*
1985	*Warnings from the Future?*
1985	*Have We Lived Before?*
1986	*London Standard Film Awards*
1986	*Television on Trial*
1986	*Puberty*
1987	*Richard Burton Drama Award*
1987	*The Search for Realism*
1987	*The Struggle for Land*
1987	*The Price of Marriage*
1987	*Veiled Revolution*
1987	*ITV Schools: Thirty Years On*
1987	*Kimberley Carlile—Falling Through the Net*
1988	*Harold Pinter*
1988	*Wildscreen 88*
1988	*Fight to Survive?*
1988	*Network in Ireland*
1989	*British Academy Awards*
1989	*Mary Stott*
1992	*Edvard Munch: The Frieze of Life*
1992	*Family Planning Association*
1994	*Against All Odds*
1994	*Evening Standard British Film Awards 1993*
1994	*Understanding the Under-12s*

PUBLICATION

Men: A Documentary. London: Weidenfeld and Nicholson, 1984.

FORMAT SALES, INTERNATIONAL

In the process of international format sales the basic format of a programme is sold (or licensed) to a foreign production company to enable them to create a domestic version of the product. This practice, while more and more common, is hardly new.

In U.S. television's infancy it was common for successful radio shows to transfer to television (a practice incidentally that still takes place in the United Kingdom). The most popular of these early radio to TV transfers were game shows and human interest shows such as *This Is Your Life* which made its U.S. TV debut in 1952 and *Candid Camera* which was adapted from radio's *Candid Microphone* in 1948. This initiative demonstrated the durability and flexibility of certain formats and alerted programme creators to the feasibility of secondary usage of their creations. The rapid rise in popularity of television in the United States and the proliferation of networks to serve the public produced an ever increasing demand for programming so that, even by the early 1950s, a great number of formats had been tried and tested. The BBC Television service in Britain may have started three years before its U.S. counterpart but the U.S. service grew far more quickly (and didn't have a five year hiatus because of World War II, as did the BBC). The U.S. systems, consequently, were far more advanced in the areas of programme formats by the early 1950s when the BBC began to purchase successful formats from the United States. A year after *What's My Line?* debuted on CBS in 1950, the format rights were bought by Maurice Winnick for the BBC. The show proved as successful in the United Kingdom as in the United States. The original format for *What's My Line?* had been developed by former radio announcer Mark Goodson and former radio writer Bill Todman who had formed the Goodson-Todman Production Company in 1946. The Goodson-Todman company became the acknowledged masters of format development and created a slew of formats that were to sell successfully in many territories and be revived domestically on occasion, especially during the game show revival of the 1970s. (Other successful game show format holders include Chuck Barris and Merv Griffin.) Formats that sold in English speaking territories would often spawn shows with the same name as the original, hence *The Price Is Right* and *Beat the Clock* are titles as famous in the United Kingdom as in the United States. On other occasions the names of the new shows differ from the originals: in the United Kingdom, *The Match Game* is known as *Blankety Blank* and *Family Feud* is retitled *Family Fortune.*

With the United States' head start on format development expertise it was quite a while before the trend was reversed and the United States started buying formats in. The first game show the United Kingdom sold to the United States was *Whodunnit* in 1979 but in the 1960s another genre proved to be exportable: Comedy.

Given the huge potential financial rewards associated with a successful long-running situation comedy, U.S. producers were quick to exploit series formats that had been hits in the United Kingdom, rationalising that some of them would translate to an American audience. As early as the mid-1960s such experiments were undertaken. At that time film producer Joseph E. Levine decided to expand his empire (Embassy Pictures) to include network television and had the idea of acquiring the rights to produce an American version of the runaway U.K. hit sitcom *Steptoe and Son.* This was an ambitious move as *Steptoe and Son* was quite extreme, more hard hitting "kitchen-sink" drama than traditional sitcom. But Levine thought the hard edges could be softened enough to make the series palatable for the U.S. audience who, after all, had already demonstrated a willingness to identify with the working class by making *The Honeymooners* such a success in its time. Beefy film actor Aldo Ray was cast alongside Lee Tracey, but the pilot remained unsold. This remained the case until years later when Norman Lear would produce a successful U.S. version of the series, *Sanford and Son.* This adaptation came, however, after Lear had already changed the face of the U.S. sitcom genre with another U.K. format buy, *Till Death Us Do Part* which became the groundbreaking *All in the Family.*

Lear's success with these format changes gave rise to many similar deals. While many of the attempts at format copying have been failures, there have been notable successes. *Man About the House* (U.K.) spawned in the United States *Three's Company, Keep it in the Family* translated as *Too Close for Comfort,* etc. Certain companies (such as D. L. Taffner) specialise in format transfers, knowing enough about both markets to make astute decisions on whether a show would travel. Most successful British sitcoms are scrutinised carefully by U.S. producers and a huge percentage are optioned for a format change. Occasionally the trend occurs in reverse (the U.S. *Who's the Boss?* emerging in the United Kingdom as *The Upper Hand, The Golden Girls* becoming *The Brighton Belles*) but this is far rarer, almost certainly because most successful U.S. sitcoms appear in the United Kingdom in their original format. The United States' domination of the entertainment media results in local audiences being *au fait* with American society and culture and thus more willing and able to consume the original.

—Dick Fiddy

FURTHER READING

Hansen, Eric. "Sitcom Formats Fail to Please on Germany's RTL." *Variety* (Los Angeles), 29 March 1993.

Johnson, Debra. "Format Fever: The Risks and Rewards." *Broadcasting and Cable* (Washington, D.C.), 23 January 1995.

———. "King World International Has Licensed Format Rights to *Jeopardy!* to Poland's Telewizja Polska." *Broadcasting and Cable* (Washington, D.C.), 23 October 1995.

Tunstall, Jeremy. *The Media Are American: Anglo-American Media in the World.* London: Constable, 1977.

Wildman, Steven S., and Bruce M. Owen. *Video Economics.* Cambridge: Harvard University Press, 1992.

Williams, Michael. "U.S. Formats Boost Danish Pubcaster." *Variety* (Los Angeles), 27 April 1992.

See also *All in the Family;* Goodson, Mark, and Bill Todman; Lear, Norman; Quiz and Game Shows; *Sanford and Son; Steptoe and Son; Till Death Us Do Part*

THE FORSYTE SAGA

British Serial Drama

The Forsyte Saga, one of the most celebrated of British period drama series ever made, was first shown in 1967 and subsequently in many countries around the world, to universal acclaim. Based on the novels of John Galsworthy, the series was made in black and white and comprised twenty-six episodes covering the history of the aristocratic Forsyte family between the years 1879 and 1926 (actually rather longer than the period covered in the novels themselves).

The project was the brainchild of producer Donald Wilson, who first conceived the idea in 1955 and spent years planning the series and getting the necessary backing for it. The series finally got the go-ahead on the strength of the distinguished cast who were signed up for it. They included Kenneth More (Jolyon Forsyte), Eric Porter (Soames Forsyte), Nyree Dawn Porter (Irene Forsyte), Fay Compton (Ann Forsyte), Michael York ("Jolly" Forsyte) and newcomer Susan Hampshire (Fleur Forsyte). The plot revolved around the feuds and machinations of the Forsyte family and their London merchants' business (paving the way for such glossy soap operas of the 1980s as Dallas and Dynasty). Each episode culminated in a "cliffhanger" ending designed to

persuade viewers to tune in once again the following week. Among the most famous scenes was one in which the hapless Irene, unloved by her cold and possessive husband Soames, was brutally raped by him as their marriage fell apart. The scene was rendered even more convincing by bloodstains on Irene's dress (Eric Porter had inadvertently cut his hand on her brooch when tearing off her bodice).

The series enjoyed vast audiences, the first showing, on BBC2, attracting some six million viewers and the second showing, now on BBC1, attracting some 18 million. Publicans and vicars alike complained that they might just as well shut up shop on Sunday evenings as everyone stayed at home to see the next episode of the gripping saga. Similar success greeted the series in other parts of the world, including the United States, and The Forsyte Saga also earned the distinction of being the first BBC series to be sold to the Soviet Union. The worldwide audience was estimated as something in the region of 160 million.

The success of the series, which won a Royal Television Society Silver Medal and a BAFTA award for Best Drama, prompted the BBC to plough further resources into similar blockbusting "costume" dramas, a policy that in ensuing

The Forsyte Saga
Photo courtesy of BBC

years was to produce such results as *The Pallisers* (which was also produced by Donald Wilson) and *Upstairs, Downstairs*. In the United States it promoted the development of the miniseries in competition with the open-ended perpetual drama serial. The bosses of one U.S. television station, indeed, decided its viewers could not be expected to wait for the next episode and showed the entire series in one chunk, which lasted twenty-three hours and fifty minutes.

—David Pickering

CAST

Jolyon Forsyte	Kenneth More
Irene Forsyte	Nyree Dawn Porter
Soames Forsyte	Eric Porter
Old Jolyon	Joseph O'Connor
Fleur	Susan Hampshire
Jon	Martin Jarvis
Montague Dartie	Terence Alexander
Michael Mont	Nicholas Pennell
Winifred	Margaret Tyzack
"Jolly"	Michael York

PRODUCER   Donald Wilson

PROGRAMMING HISTORY   26 Episodes

• BBC2

January 1967–July 1967

See also Adaptations; Miniseries

FORSYTHE, JOHN

U.S. Actor

With his tanned, handsome mein, silver hair and urbane style, John Forsythe has been a recognizable television personality associated with suavity and upper-class elegance since the 1950s. He has made his mark chiefly in debonair paternal parts in several long-running television series. The actor's distinctive voice and precise diction have also served him well, particularly in parts where the actor was never seen on screen, as in the 1970s Aaron Spelling hit *Charlie's Angels,* in which Forsythe voiced the role of Charlie Townsend, the eponymous employer of a trio of female detectives.

Forsythe's first roles in fact permitted him to hone and showcase his vocal talents. After studying at the University of North Carolina, he began his career as a sports announcer for the Brooklyn Dodgers at Ebbets Field and then segued into acting in radio soap operas. Subsequent appearances on Broadway led to a motion picture contract with Warner Brothers and a Hollywood debut with Cary Grant in the film *Destination Tokyo.*

After World War II Forsythe went on to starring roles in a number of Broadway productions. While still in New York, he appeared in many of the live television shows based there, such as *Studio One, Kraft Television Theatre, Robert Montgomery Presents,* and *Schlitz Playhouse of Stars.* He subsequently moved to Los Angeles and took a starring role as a playboy Hollywood attorney responsible for raising his orphaned niece in the television series *Bachelor Father,* which was broadcast from 1957 to 1962. Forsythe was nominated for an Emmy for his first television role as a father figure, and he would be nominated again for his portrayal of the head of the Carrington clan in the hit show *Dynasty* in the 1980s.

ABC's answer to hit CBS show *Dallas, Dynasty* featured Forsythe in the role of patriarch Blake Carrington, head of a wealthy Denver family, plagued by a scheming ex-wife, a bisexual son, and other tribulations. The show, which ran

roughly in tandem with the Reagan era, was known for its opulent atmosphere, lavish sets and costumes and typical preoccupation with the problems of the wealthy ranging from murder and greed to lust and incest. The show, which hit its ratings peak in 1984–85, solidified Forsythe's "nice guy" image even in the role of a ruthless oil magnate,

John Forsythe

exploring plot lines focusing on his emotional reactions in opposition to Joan Collins' villainy, his son's sexuality, and his attempts to maintain the family. Blake Carrington even pitched his own line of cologne in advertisements featuring his love for his wife, who, in a commercial narrative extending from *Dynasty,* had the fragrance designed for him.

Forsythe won two Golden Globe Awards for Best Actor in a Dramatic Television Series for his work in *Dynasty.* Since the series ended in 1989, he has recreated his role as Blake Carrington in a reunion movie and appeared as the on-camera host for *I Witness Video.* He also starred in a 1992–93 series, a political satire sitcom called *The Powers that Be.*

—Diane M. Negra

JOHN FORSYTHE (John Lincoln Freund). Born in Penn's Grove, New Jersey, U.S.A., 29 January, 1918. Educated at the University of North Carolina and the New York Actor's Studio. Married: 1) Parker McCormick (divorced), child: Dall; 2) Julie Warren (died, 1994), children: Page and Brooke. Served in U.S. Army Air Corps. Public address announcer, Brooklyn Dodgers at Ebbets Field; appeared in radio soap operas; acted on stage, since early 1940s, actor in films, since 1944; actor on television, since 1947; host of Hollywood Park Feature Race, 1971–74. Member: United Nations Association; American National Theatre and Academy. Recipient: Golden Globe Awards, 1983, 1984. Address: 1560 Bellagio Road, Los Angeles, California 90049, U.S.A.

TELEVISION SERIES

1957–62	*Bachelor Father*
1965–66	*The John Forsythe Show*
1970–82	*World of Survival*
1971	*To Rome with Love*
1976–81	*Charlie's Angels* (voice)
1981–89	*Dynasty*
1992–93	*The Powers that Be*
1993–94	*I Witness Video*

MADE-FOR-TELEVISION MOVIES

1964	*See How They Run*
1968	*Shadow of the Land*
1971	*Murder Once Removed*
1973	*The Letters*
1973	*Lisa: Bright and Dark*
1974	*Cry Panic*
1974	*The Healers*
1974	*Terror on the 40th Floor*
1975	*The Deadly Tower*
1976	*Amelia Earhart*
1977	*Tail Gunner Joe*
1977	*Never Con a Killer*
1978	*Cruise Into Terror*
1978	*The Users*
1978	*With this Ring*
1980	*A Time for Miracles*
1981	*Sizzle*
1982	*The Mysterious Two*
1987	*On Fire*
1990	*Opposites Attract*
1991	*Dynasty: The Reunion*

FILMS

Destination Tokyo, 1944; *The Captive City,* 1952; *It Happens Every Thursday,* 1953; *The Glass Web,* 1952; *Escape from Fort Bravo,* 1953; *The Trouble with Harry,* 1956; *The Ambassador's Daughter,* 1956; *The Captive City,* 1962; *Kitten with a Whip,* 1964; *Madame X,* 1966; *In Cold Blood,* 1968; *Topaz,* 1969; *The Happy Ending,* 1970; *Goodbye and Amen,* 1977; *And Justice for All,* 1979; *Scrooged,* 1988; *Stan and George's New Life,* 1991.

STAGE

Dick Whittington and his Cat, 1939; *Vickie,* 1942; *Yankee Point,* 1942; *Winged Victory,* 1943; *Yellowjack,* 1945; *Woman Bites Dog,* 1946; *All My Sons,* 1947; *It Takes Two,* 1947; *Mister Roberts,* 1950; *The Teahouse of the August Moon,* 1953; *Detective Story,* 1955; *Weekend,* 1968; *The Caine Mutiny Court Martial,* 1971; *Sacrilege,* 1995.

See also *Charlie's Angels;* Comedy, Domestic Settings); *Dynasty*

FOUR CORNERS

Australian Current Affairs Program

Four Corners is Australia's longest running current affairs program, and is often referred to as the "flagship" of the government-funded Australian Broadcasting Corporation (ABC). *Four Corners* has gone to air continuously on the ABC since 1961 and has established itself not only as an institution of Australian television but more widely of Australian political life. The program has frequently initiated public debate on important issues as well as precipitated governmental or judicial inquiries and processes of political reform.

Four Corners was originally conceived as a program with a magazine format offering an informed commentary on the week's events. It filled a space on Australian television roughly comparable to the British Broadcasting Commission's *Panorama* (from which it often borrowed material in the 1960s) or the early current-affairs programming developed by Edward R. Murrow for the Columbia Broadcasting System in the United States. It was also notable for providing the first truly national orientation on news and current affairs in Australia, either on television or in print.

Stylistically, *Four Corners* has been an innovator in documentary strategies for Australian television and film. The program frequently presents itself as frankly personalised and argumentative. The narrator has generally appeared on-screen, a significant break with the off-screen "voice-of-God" narration which was the dominant convention in 1950s documentary. The involvement of the narrators-reporters with their subject, usually on locations, gives the program an immediacy and realism, while also opening up subjective points of view. As Albert Moran argues in "Constructing a Nation—Institutional Documentary Since 1945," these developments paralleled the emergence in the 1960s of direct cinema and cinéma verité as well as an increasing cultural pluralism reflected in documentary subject matter.

Since the mid-1970s, the program has developed the format of a 45-minute topical documentary introduced by a studio host, occasionally varied with studio debate. The most frequently cited examples are investigative reports which have had a direct impact on political institutions, such as a 1983 program "The Big League" which disclosed interference in court hearings of charges laid against prominent figures in the New South Wales Rugby League, or the 1988 program "The Moonlight State" which revealed corruption at high levels in the Queensland police force. However, the program has also been important for its "slice of life" portrayals of the everyday worlds of social relations, work, health and leisure, which have increased awareness of social and cultural diversity. It was very early to represent Australia as a multicultural society, with a report, for example, in 1961 on the German speaking community in South Australia.

Four Corners made an early reputation for testing the boundaries of expectations of television as a medium as well as of political acceptability. At a time when television current affairs genres were still unfamiliar, this sometimes involved little more than taking the camera outside the controlled space of the studio or the inclusion of unscripted material. A 1963 program on the Returned Servicemen's League (RSL), for example, stirred controversy for showing members of the organisation in casual dress drinking at a bar rather than exclusively in the context of formally structured studio debate. But controversy extended also to the kinds of political questions which were raised. The story on the RSL directly challenged the organisation on its claim to political neutrality. Another of the same period drew attention to the appalling living conditions and political disenfranchisement of Aboriginal people living on a reserve near Casino in rural New South Wales, an issue which had almost no public exposure at the time.

Four Corners has consistently been accused of political bias, particularly of a left-wing orientation, and for failing to abide by the ABC's charter which requires "balance" in the coverage of news and current affairs. The program is generally defended by its makers, ABC management, and supporters on the grounds that the importance of open public debate outweighs

Liz Jackson, host of Four Corners
Photo courtesy of the Australian Broadcasting Corporation

the damage that might be caused to interested parties and that, while the program may be argumentative, it is not unfair.

The program is also a frequent point of reference in debates over government funded broadcasting. *Four Corners* has never achieved high ratings by the standards of the commercial networks and is often contrasted in content and style to commercial rivals such as the Nine Network's *Sixty Minutes* which is able to claim much wider popular appeal. Despite increasing pressure on the ABC to become more commercially oriented, however, the program has continued to articulate values which are distinct from considerations of popularity—the importance of representing the positions and points of view of minorities, the necessity of forcing public institutions to accountability, and a place for television current affairs which performs an educative role. In doing so it is often taken as representative of the position and identity of publicly funded broadcasting as a whole.

—Mark Gibson

PRESENTERS/COMPERES/REPORTERS
Michael Charlton (1961)
Gerald Lyons (1962–63)
Frank Bennett (1964)
Robert Moore (1964)

John Penlington (1964)
Robert Moore (1965–67)
John Temple (1978)
Michael Willesee (1969–71)
David Flatman (1971–72)
Caroline Jones (1973–81)
Andrew Olle (1985–94)
Liz Jackson (1995)

PRODUCERS Bob Raymond (1961–62); Allan Ashbolt (1963); Gerald Lyons (1963); John Power (1964); Robert Moore (1965–67); Sam Lipski (1968); Allan Martin (1968–72); Tony Ferguson (1973); Peter Reid (1973–80); Paul Davies (1980–81); Paul Lyneham (1980–81); John Penlington (1980–81); John Temple (1980–81); Jonathon Holmes (1982–84); Peter Manning (1985–88); Ian Macintosh (1989–90); Marian Wilkinson (1991–92); Ian Carroll (1992–95); Harry Bardwell (1995); Paul Williams (1995); John Budd (1995–96)

FURTHER READING

King, Noel. "Current Affairs TV." *Australian Journal of Screen Theory* (Kensington, New South Wales), 1983.

Moran, Albert. "Constructing the Nation: Institutional Documentary Since 1945." In, Moran, Albert, and Tom O'Regan, editors. *The Australian Screen.* Melbourne: Penguin, 1989.

Pullan, Robert. *Four Corners—Twenty-Five Years.* Sydney: Australian Broadcasting Corporation, 1986.

See also Australian Programming

FOX BROADCASTING COMPANY

U.S. Network

The FOX television network was established, amidst shock, controversy, legal wrangling and uncertainty, in 1985. The historic significance of this event may be judged by six interrelated factors, the daring prime mover, Rupert Murdoch, the economic environment at the time, the complacency of the major television networks, disenchanted affiliate stations, the Federal Communications Commission (FCC), and the volatile nature of television programming.

Raised in Australia, Rupert Murdoch has been described by Merrill, Lee and Friedlander as "a free-market socialist with political leanings of a conservative nature." He is considered to be a "secretive, suspicious person," one who "alienates many people—especially government leaders." These assessments are not surprising given Murdoch's aggressive business methods and the powerful conglomeration of media holdings he has accumulated throughout the world.

Of the 150 newspapers and magazines he owns, about half the media markets are in Australia and one-third in Britain. In addition to his newspaper empire, he also owns television and cable systems in the United States and Europe. Among the many magazines he owns, *TV Guide,* with its circulation of 40 million, is of particular importance as far as TV is concerned.

In 1984, Murdoch purchased half ownership of 20th Century-Fox film corporation. The following year he acquired the remaining half of the corporation. These two purchases, totaling $575 million, gave him control over an extensive film library and rights to numerous television series (for example, *L.A. Law* and *M*A*S*H*).

Courtesy of FOX

With this enormous programming potential in hand, he was in a good position to form a television network, the FOX Broadcasting Company. In October 1985, Murdoch bought six independent, major market stations (WNEW-TV, New York; KTTV-TV, Los Angeles; WFLD-TV, Chicago; WTTG-TV, Washington, D.C.; KNBN-TV, Dallas; KRIV-TV, Houston). Later he acquired WFXT-TV in Boston. These stations enabled him to reach about 20% of all television households in the United States. For the first time since the 1960s the major networks were to experience a kind of aggressive competition that would threaten their very existence.

The founding of the FOX Broadcasting Company must be placed within a context of the general economic uncertainty and decline of network television. According to Sydney Head and Christopher Sterling, 1985 was the first year that network revenues fell slightly. By 1987, total revenues of ABC, CBS and NBC had dropped to $6.8 billion. For the first time ever, CBS recorded a net loss for the first quarter. As a result, all three networks adopted austerity measures, cutting budgets, laying off personnel and dumping affiliates.

To the big three, the competition of the FOX network could hardly have occurred at a worse time. FOX itself was not spared financial hardship. In 1988 the company lost $90 million and in 1989, $20 million. To hedge against increased profit erosion the three networks began to diversify their interests in cable television and shore up their owned and operated stations.

Economic uncertainty also affected network affiliate relationships. ABC, NBC and CBS tended to dominate the powerful and lucrative VHF stations throughout the United States, with the less profitable UHF stations being in the hands of independents. With the advent of the FOX network, a number of the VHF stations, previously affiliated with the major networks, jumped ship, providing a lucrative advantage to Murdoch. Some claim that Murdoch's exclusive National Football League contract was an added incentive to switch their allegiance. In one agreement with station group owner, New World, the FOX network gained twelve new stations which ended their affiliation with "Big Three" networks. Such "fickle behavior" on the part of affiliates sent shock waves through the established networks which had complacently relied upon their loyalty.

Opposition to Murdoch's aggressiveness did not go unchallenged by the networks. Americans have long been suspicious of the power and influence of foreign investors. For this reason, the navy strongly opposed British Marconi's monopoly of radio telephony in 1919, forcing the formation of RCA. Moreover, FCC licensing regulations specified that only U.S. citizens could own broadcasting stations. The FCC also regulated cross-ownership of media companies to avoid antitrust abuses.

In an attempt to thwart Rupert Murdoch's growing influence, the FCC, spurred on by NBC and the NAACP, investigated his citizenship and the ownership structure of the FOX network. Murdoch became a U.S. citizen in 1985, just prior to the founding of the FOX network. He also disclosed that FOX would assume virtually all economic risk for and reward of acquired stations. His disclosures were backed by sworn declarations of key FCC staffers and the independent legal counsel of Marvin Chirelstein of Columbia Law School.

Some reports claimed the disclosures were, in fact, deceptive. Murdoch's Australia-based News Corporation owned 24% of the FOX voting stock (just below the legal limit of 25%); the remaining 76% belonged to Barry Diller (20th Century-Fox) who was a U.S. citizen. In fact, News Corp. indirectly owned 99%, a reality which the FCC either ignored or failed to see. Still, in keeping with dereg-

ulation trends, and despite temporary congressional freezes, the FCC found in favor of Murdoch. This decision was a great victory for Murdoch and a major disappointment to the networks.

The new network strengthened its position with several strategies. By reducing the number of prime time hours offered each week and providing no morning shows or soap operas, FOX has given its affiliates much more freedom to schedule their own shows and commercial announcements. Rather than compete with the major networks using counter program strategies, FOX has tried to offer entertaining, low cost shows to its affiliates. Some programs in late night fringe (the Joan Rivers and Chevy Chase hosted talk shows) have not done well but others (such as *Married...with Children*, *21 Jump Street*, *The Tracy Ullman Show*, *Beverly Hills 90210* and *The Simpsons)* have been successful. The probable reason for these successes is that they target younger, trend-following viewers devoted to light entertainment. In addition, somewhat controversial program strategy, Murdoch has spent lavishly to obtain the rights to National Football League football, a major coup.

FOX's vertically integrated structure (a combination of 20th Century-Fox, FOX Network and Fox Stations) is also well suited to produce and distribute a large number of quality shows. The substantial collection of films in the vaults of 20th Century-Fox remain a rich resource, still to be developed.

—Richard Worringham

FURTHER READING

Fanning, Dierdre. "A Different Brand of Entertainment." *Forbes* (New York), 30 November 1987.

"Fox Gives Itself Three Years to Pass Big 3 Networks." *Television Digest* (New York), 26 June 1995.

Head, Sidney, and Christopher Sterling. *Broadcasting in America.* Boston: Houghton Mifflin, 1956; 7th edition, Princeton, New Jersey: Houghton Mifflin, 1990.

Larson, Eric. "Will Murdoch be Outfoxed?" *Time* (New York), 17 April 1995.

Merrill, John, John Lee, and Edward Friedlander. *Modern Mass Media.* New York: Harper and Row, 1990.

Robins, Max. "How Foreign is Fox?" *Variety* (Los Angeles), 5 December 1994.

Schmuckler, Eric. "NBC Challenges Fox Ownership." *MediaWeek* (Brewster, New York), 5 December 1994.

Smith, F. Leslie. *Perspectives on Radio and Television.* New York: Harper and Row, 1990.

Vivian, John. *The Media of Mass Communication.* Boston: Allyn and Bacon, 1993.

Wharton, Dennis. "Rupert Requests Relief." *Variety* (Los Angeles), 15 May 1995.

Zoglin, Richard. "Room for One More? The Fox Network Makes its Move Into Prime Time." *Time* (New York), 6 April 1987.

———. "Murdoch's Biggest Score." *Time* (New York), 6 June 1994.

FRANCE

In no other country in Europe have the audio-visual media been a greater stake in political struggle than in France, despite the fact that television, in particular, was very late in getting started and slow to develop. This lag may be attributed to both French anxiety about image-based culture, and to uncertainty about new technology. Within the public service tradition administered by a Jacobin state, television was tightly controlled and part of electoral spoils. Its informational and educational programmes achieved a high standard before deregulation in the 1980s, while popular programming languished in the shadow of American imports and the low cultural esteem in which they were held on the "audiovisual landscape". Television, unlike the cinema, was never considered part of the national culture, and so French program makers contributed little to the international circulation of programs, nor did intellectuals make much contribution to media theory.

French television's origins were not propitious. A few experiments in the 1930s culminated in the first regular programming in 1939, transmiited from the Eiffel Tower to a limited number of sets in Paris only. During the Occupation, the Germans used the medium to entertain their soldiers, thereby tainting the medium from the start. The post-war government revoked the Vichy law conceding broadcasting to the private sector, and the resulting state monopoly would remain unchallenged for four decades. In 1948, the then Secretary for Information, François Mitterrand, set a 819-line technical standard in deference to the electronic industry's ambitions, but the results were expensive sets and a service long confined to the Paris region. Heavy regulation and a centralized bureaucracy explain the slow development of a network compared with the United Kingdom or Germany. Studios were built in a suburb of Paris, and for many years the "Buttes-Chaumont" label connoted a heavily dramatic style, then scorned by the young *cinéphiles* in the sway of the *Nouvelle Vague*. Television was perceived as the refuge of classical academicism and the untalented; it was not until the 1980s that the pioneer "*réalisateurs de télévision*" began to receive their critical due. There were still only 3.5 million sets by 1963, but the figure was increasing dramatically each year of the "30 Glorieuses" in the Gaullist period, often stimulated by international broadcast events (*Eurovision* in 1954, *World Cup* football). The evening news at 20:00 became a national ritual, "*la grande messe*".

Under the Fifth Republic, television legislation mutated every four to five years on average, as governments pondered how best to govern what its intellectuals considered a monster in the living room, undermining literate culture and opening the way to commercial influences from abroad. But the government and the opposition distrusted TV—each believing it favored the other. Under the control of Ministers for Information, then for Culture, and occa-

sionally for Communication itself, there was no accountability, little audience research, and, scarcely any cultural legitimacy. Employees of state broadcasting had the status of civil servants, which made their right to free expression precarious. During the Algerian War, President Charles DeGaulle became the first head of state to use TV to justify his policy, but the government openly interfered with the news coverage of the conflict and many journalists quit or were dismissed. Legislation in 1959 transformed Radio-Télévision de France into a body (ORTF) with industrial and commercial objectives, but rejected both private TV and any protection against the threat of censorship.

A new breed of professionals came to the medium in the mid-1960s, when French television experienced something of a golden age under the ethos that the medium could make culture accessible to the people. The television diet leaned toward turgid studio productions of classic plays and novels (the spicy history serial *Les Rois Maudits* is remembered as refreshing in this context), and pedagogic series of "initiation" (*Lectures pour Tous, Le Camera Explore le Temps*). In the way of entertainment, there were variety shows, often associated with the popular crooner Guy Lux, and slapstick games shows like the French-originated *Jeux sans Frontières,* but little middlebrow fare, except for *Inspecteur Maigret* mysteries. A brief period of liberalization occurred after 1964 when a second channel (A2) was created, despite the fear of where competition might lead. (The new 615-line technical system was non-compatible with the rest of Europe, but was propagated to the Soviet bloc.) A third channel (FR3) was created in 1973 with a regional structure. An ORTF strike coincided with the events of May 1968, and 200 staff were fired. Less noticed that year was the first authorization of advertising, which would lead to a slowly creeping increase in the number of advertising minutes per hour, to the collection of ratings, and in turn to the break-up of ORTF and eventually what came to be called the "dictatorship of the Audimat".

In 1973, President Georges Pompidou was able to proclaim that television was the "voice of France" at home and abroad. It was the only country with three public service channels, none of which was autonomous from the government or in competition with each other for viewers. It was considered axiomatic that getting rid of the monopoly would lead to mediocrity. Neither the political left nor right was committed to freedom of communication, each for its own reasons. By 1974 there were 14 million sets receiving 7,400 program hours a year produced by 12,000 staff at ORTF. 1974 was the year the decision was finally taken to break up the "monster ORTF", whose functions were divided among seven autonomous bodies, but the government still drew the line on private broadcasting and maintained its right to appoint broadcast executives. In fact, the production wing would still get 90% of program commissions; there was very little independent production; and executives were still chosen for their political docility. Experimentation was hived off to INA, the Institut National de l'Audiovisuel, which also managed the archives and professional training. (Jean-Christophe Averty is usually singled out as the first producer to forge a specifically televisual style, one relying heavily on chromakey effects.) Programs remained much as before, and studio programs seemed even more boring and didactic. Imports from Britain (*The Forsyte Saga*) and the United States (*Roots, Holocaust*) merely raised the alarm among cultural elites about the public taste for serial fiction and about a marked decline in domestic quality programming. Television investment had become a major factor in film production.

President Giscard d'Estaing's government also launched France into telecommunications research and development in 1979, with a DBS satellite agreement with Germany, one of the first efforts to counter United States' and Japanese hegemony in this field. The D2MAC format, an intermediate step toward high definition, would prove an expensive mistake ten years later, another unfortunate consequence of the technocratic hold over the media.

Paradoxically, in the light of the Socialists' historical opposition to private ownership of the airwaves, it was under Socialist President François Mitterrand that deregulation finally occurred. In 1981 the Moinot Commission, charged with examining the state of affairs since the break-up of ORTF in 1974, found that decentralization and competition between the three channels were illusory and not promoting creative programming; serious programs were being pushed to the edges of the schedules, in favor of a high quotient of popular imports, a trend for which *Dallas* became the inflammatory label. A 1982 law abolished the state monopoly and "freed" communications: the prime channel, TF1, was sold outright and licenses for two more were granted, including the pay channel Canal Plus, which quickly became a major player in the audio-visual industries, spinning off its own feature film production company. Meanwhile, a belated attempt to cable the major cities got under way. Political controversy dogged the attribution of these private channels (Italian media mogul Silvio Berlusconi won one franchise) as well as the appointment of directors of the increasingly beleaguered state channels. The composition and powers of a relatively feeble regulatory agency changed with almost every government. The private TF1 quickly became the channel of reference, with almost half the general audience, while the revenues and audience share of France 2 and France 3 (as the state channels were re-named in 1994) gradually shrank.

At the international level, France had become the leading exponent of protectionist quotas for film and television, as well as of the view that the audiovisual market could be a way of creating—or defending—a common European cultural identity. France eschewed both cost-sharing initiatives with foreign partners and involvement in experiments in pan-European television, although she was increasingly worried about satellite penetration. Instead she chose the path

of Francophony with the TV5 satellite channel in partnership with French-speaking countries, and conducted a lobbying effort within the European parliament to endorse a European channel.

Surrounded by bitterness among socialist supporters that the government had surrendered the media to private interests, Culture Minister Jack Lang exploited both a lingering anti-Americanism and a revived Europeanism in order to launch a new public service channel with the habitual mission of exploiting new technologies and a cultural remit. *La Sept,* intially a wholly French channel lodged on the frequency of a bankrupt private channel, became ARTE when Germany became an equal partner in 1991.

The French view that cultural and political identity are necessarily linked predominated in European audiovisual policy; the debates on "world image battles" led to the European Community White Paper *Television without Frontiers,* which tackled the problem of English-language domination of the world image market by enjoining its member states to ensure, by all necessary means, that at least half the content of their television channels was of European origin. France's own quota was higher—60%—but the irony is that whatever its status as proponent of the European public cultural space, its *domestic* broadcasting policy has run in the direction of deregulation, to such an extent that the national regulatory body (Conseil Supérieur Audiovisuel) has been unable to enforce these quotas or to inhibit French investors from putting up money for English language films, ranging from *The Piano* to *Under Seige.* In fact, certain aspects of American production—like the use of multiple scriptwriters—are gradually being adopted in France. Nevertheless, the various governments under President François Mitterrand, even the conservative ones, have consistently proclaimed the importance of national and high cultural goals. France continued to argue for protectionism, as in the GATT discussions in 1993, when a lobby of intellectuals helped to secure the exclusion of film and TV from the treaty.

The state of French television in the mid-1990s is a mixed but unbalanced system, with the private TF1 and Canal Plus becoming major players in the international media market. The audiences for FR2 and FR3 shrink slightly each year, as the *redevance* (license fee) does not keep pace with rising program costs, and is widely flouted by viewers turning to the growing cable sector. The Franco-German cultural channel ARTE shares a wavelength with a daytime educational channel, which seems to perpetuate the same intellectual values that have always characterized French TV: didactic and avant-garde offerings, especially "authored" documentaries and "personal" films, made by the elites for the masses.

—Susan Emmanuel

FURTHER READING

Crane, Rhonda J. *The Politics of International Standards: France and the Color TV War.* Norwood, New Jersey: Ablex, 1979.

Emanuel, Susan. "Culture in Space: The European Cultural Channel." *Media, Culture and Society* (London), April 1992.

Mattelart, Armand, and Michèle Mattelart. *Re-Thinking Media Theory*. Minneapolis, Minnesota: University of Minnesota Press, 1991.

Miege, Bernard. "France: A Mixed System. Renovation of An Old Concept." *Media, Culture and Society* (London), January 1989.

Rigby, Brian. *Popular Culture in Modern France: A Study of Cultural Discourse*. London: Routledge, 1991.

See also Standards; Television Technology

FRANCIS, ARLENE

U.S. Talk-Show Host/Performer

Arlene Francis played a key role in television's first decades as performer, talk-show host, and guest star, appearing on many shows and proving herself to be one of the medium's most durable personalities. At the height of her popularity in the mid-1950s, she was rated the third most recognized woman in the United States.

Francis had a diverse and successful career on television, preceded by a versatile career as "femcee," actress, and radio performer. Her film career began in 1932 with *Murders on the Rue Morgue* and one can listen to her work as an actress on radio as early as 1936 on the Columbia Radio Workshop. During World War II she was the "femcee" of a radio show called *Blind Date*, a forerunner of *The Dating Game*, and she worked regularly as a featured actress on the Broadway stage before coming to television in the early 1950s. She appeared in a simulcast version of *Blind Date* from 1949 to 1952, and also on such shows as *By Popular Demand* and *Prize Performance*, but it was as a regular panelist on the popular quiz show, *What's My Line?*, that Francis became a household name on television. Known for her elegance and good humor, Francis would trade repartee each week with such figures as columnist Dorothy Kilgallen, publisher Bennet Cerf, and poet Louis Untermeyer.

Although *What's My Line?* was her bread-and-butter show over the next twenty-five years, versatility continued to mark Francis' career. In September 1950, shortly after she joined the panel of that word-and-wit show, she became the first "mistress" of ceremonies for NBC's *Saturday Night Revue: Your Show of Shows*, and she appeared frequently on other television shows in the 1950s, 1960s and 1970s.

Francis also made a major contribution to the history of television talk as host and managing editor of NBC's *Home* show. *Home* was the afternoon show teamed with *Today* and *Tonight*, in NBC President Sylvester "Pat" Weaver's trilogy of daily talk on NBC in the 1950s, each show anchored by a "communicator." Network executives knew that women represented a major part of the daytime audience and were key decision makers on consumer purchases. *Home* was NBC's attempt to capture that audience. To quote from the 1950s film, *On the Waterfront*, Francis "coulda been a contender." She was certainly one of the foremost talk-show hosts on television in the 1950s; if her show had continued into the 1960s, her national status as a talk-show host might have been assured. But *Home*, despite great popularity among its audience, was can-

celed after three-and-a-half years when Weaver was forced out of NBC by network founder David Sarnoff. Ultimately, Francis' career as a national talk-show host was a casualty of forces that were moving network television away from strong women hosts, serious topics, sustaining shows and public service, and toward immediate bottom line profits—the same forces that drove Edward R. Murrow from the air at CBS.

As host of *Home*, Francis established patterns of daytime talk that are still with us today. This daytime talk "magazine" of the air was designed to provide intelligent conversation and up-to-date information for a largely female audience, though men were in the audience as well. From 1954 to 1957, Francis was, along with Arthur Godfrey, Murrow, Dave Garroway, and Jack Paar, one of the founders of television talk. It was not until

Arlene Francis
Photo courtesy of Peter Gabel

Phil Donahue rose to national syndication prominence two decades later that another national talk-show host would make a similar appeal to women audiences. With more support from NBC management, or if Weaver had been able to continue as president, the *Home* show might have continued to build an audience and sustained itself into the 1960s. As it is, the story of Arlene Francis' role on *Home* reveals the limitations placed on women talk-show hosts in the male-dominated world of 1950s television.

The tensions placed on Francis' life as the managing editor and "boss" of her show are reflected in a 1957 *Mike Wallace Interview* on ABC. Wallace begins his interview with Francis by saying that a lot was being said and written about "career women" in America. "What," he asks her, "is it that happens to so many career women that makes them so brittle? That makes them almost a kind of third sex?" Francis replies: "Well, what happens to some of [the women] who have these qualities you've just spoken of, is that I suppose they feel a very competitive thing with men and they take on a masculine viewpoint and forget primarily that they are women.... Instead they become aggressive and opinionated. While men do it, it is part of the makeup of a man, and a man has always done it all his life. I do not think it is a woman's position to dominate." Yet when NBC came to Francis toward the end of Dave Garroway's long reign to ask her to co-host *Today* with Hugh Downs, she refused. Unresolved issues of power, issues that Barbara Walters was to struggle with and resolve in the 1960s and 1970s, limited Francis's options in the mid-1950s. By the end of her life Francis was considerably more reflective of her dilemma. In her autobiography, she writes that she had come to realize "how deeply my inability to express myself without becoming apprehensive about what 'they' might think had affected me. In short, my 'don't make waves' philosophy had inhibited my life to an incalculable extent.... I had forgotten that a few waves are necessary to keep the water from becoming stagnant."

In the later 1960s and 1970s, it was Francis' friend Walters, the person who did take the co-host position with Hugh Downs on the *Today* show, who became the preeminent national woman host of public affairs and news talk on television.

—Bernard M. Timberg

ARLENE FRANCIS. Born Arline Francis Kazanjian in Boston, Massachusetts, U.S.A., 20 October 1908. Attended Finch Finishing School and Theatre Guild School, New York City.

Married: 1) Neil Agnew, 1935 (divorced, 1945); 2) Martin Gabel, 1946; one child: Peter. Actress in film and radio from 1932; debuted on stage, 1936; took time off in World War II to sell war bonds; hosted and starred in television shows from 1949; regular panelist on *What's My Line?*, 1950–67; host and editor-in-chief, NBC-TV's daytime talk show *Home*, 1954–57.

TELEVISION SERIES

1949–55	*Soldier Parade*
1949–53	*Blind Date*
1950	*By Popular Demand*
1950	*Prize Performance*
1950	*Saturday Night Revue (Your Show of Shows)*
1950–67	*What's My Line?*
1953–55	*Talent Patrol*
1954–57	*Home*
1957–58	*The Arlene Francis Show*

FILMS

Murders in the Rue Morgue, 1932; *Stage Door Canteen*, 1943; *All My Sons*, 1948; *One Two Three*, 1961; *The Thrill of It All*, 1963; *Fedora*, 1979.

RADIO

45 Minutes From Hollywood; March of Time; Cavalcade of America; Portia Blake; Amanda of Honeymoon Hill; Mr. District Attorney; Betty and Bob; What's My Name?; Blind Date; It Happens Every Day; The Arlene Francis Show; Emphasis; Monitor; Luncheon at Sardis.

STAGE

One Good Year; The Women; Horse Eats Hat; Danton's Death; All That Glitters; Journey to Jerusalem; Doughgirls; The Overtons; The French Touch; Once More With Feeling; Tchin-Tchin; Beekman Place; Mrs. Daily; Late Love; Dinner at Eight; Kind Sir; Lion in Winter; Pal Joey; Who Killed Santa Claus?; Gigi; Social Security.

PUBLICATION

Arlene Francis: A Memoir, with Florence Rome. New York: Simon and Schuster, 1978.

See also Talk Shows; Weaver, Sylvester "Pat"

FRANK, REUVEN

U.S. Broadcast Journalist/Producer/Executive

In a career that parallels the rise and ebb of network television journalism, Reuven Frank helped shape the character of NBC News through his work as a writer and producer, a documentary and news magazine pioneer, news division president, and especially through his innovative coverage of national party conventions. In 1956, Reuven

Frank teamed Chet Huntley with David Brinkley to co-anchor the political conventions, a move that catapulted the two correspondents and NBC News to national fame.

Beginning with his first job at NBC in 1950, Reuven Frank realized he had an affinity for the process of film editing and an appreciation for the visual power of television, which became the signature of his career in TV news. The process of shaping film clips into coherent stories left an indelible impression on Frank. Competitor CBS News had built its strong reputation in radio, which emphasized words. *Camel News Caravan*, NBC's original 15-minute evening news program, on which Frank served as a writer, evolved from the newsreel tradition. An early partisan of television, Reuven Frank sought to exploit the medium's advantage over newspapers and radio to enable the audience to see things happen. "Pictures *are* the point of television reporting," he wrote.

This visual sense is clearly evident in the coverage of political conventions. Frank developed a method for orienting a team of four floor reporters—all but lost in a sea of convention delegates—toward live cameras. He established a communication center that simultaneously controlled news gathering, reporting, and distribution. The filter center, linked to the entire crew, advised the decision level when a report was ready for air. On cue from the decision level, the technical team would air the report. This tiered system of communication control became the industry standard.

The Huntley-Brinkley Report premiered in October 1956, with Reuven Frank as producer and lasted until Huntley's retirement in 1970, when the report was renamed *The NBC Nightly News*. Frank was the program's executive producer in 1963 when the report was expanded from fifteen to thirty minutes. In a memo to his staff Frank outlined NBC News policies for gathering, packaging, and presenting news reports. The guiding principle for developing NBC newscasts was based on Frank's belief that "the highest power of television journalism is not in the transmission of information but in the transmission of experience."

The early years of television provided Frank with opportunities to develop his ideas and to experiment with half-hour weekly series. In 1954 he introduced *Background*, which featured "history in the making" through specially shot films, expert commentary, and the newly designed process of electronic film editing. The documentary-style series went through several iterations, including *Outlook, Chet Huntley Reporting, Time Present...Chet Huntley Reporting*, and *Frank McGee Reports*.

A fierce advocate of free speech, Reuven Frank staunchly defended television's right and obligation to deliver unsettling news. He supported rival CBS in controversies over the documentaries *Harvest of Shame* (1960) and *The Selling of the Pentagon* (1971). He championed network coverage of the Civil Rights Movement, the Vietnam War, and the riot at the 1968 Democratic National Convention in Chicago. Frank also produced the acclaimed NBC documentary, *The Tunnel*, which depicts the escape of 59 East Germans beneath the newly constructed Berlin Wall in 1962. NBC aired the program over objections by the U.S. State Department, which delayed the broadcast because it came on the heels of the Cuban Missile Crisis. *The Tunnel* is the only documentary ever to win an Emmy Award as Program of the Year.

The Tunnel, as did other programs, exemplified one of Reuven Frank's lasting contributions to the content of NBC News reports, his attention to narrative structure and visual

Reuven Frank

images. In the 1963 operations memo to his staff, Frank wrote, "Every news story should, without sacrifice of probity or responsibility, display the attributes of fiction, of drama. It should have structure and conflict, problem and denouement, rising and falling action, a beginning, a middle, and an end. These are not only the essentials of drama; they are the essentials of narrative. We are in the business of narrative because we are in the business of communication."

Other of Frank's innovative series include *Weekend* and *NBC News Overnight*. *Weekend* was a 90-minute late night, youth-oriented newsmagazine introduced in 1974 that alternated with rock concerts and *Saturday Night Live*. *Weekend* evolved from *First Tuesday* (later called *Chronolog*), NBC's answer to *60 Minutes*. Later, in response to competition from the innovative all-news-network CNN's late-night news feeds, Frank developed *Overnight*, a program hosted by Lloyd Dobyns and Linda Ellerbee, and produced on a shoestring budget in a newsroom carved out of studio space. *Overnight* was a literate magazine show that affected a wry, thoughtful, and highly visual presentation of the news.

The title of Reuven Frank's memoir, *Out of Thin Air: The Brief Wonderful Life of Network News*, reflects his sense and appreciation of fortuitous timing. Frank credits former NBC president Robert Kintner for elevating the status of NBC News: "Those early years with Kintner emphasized news programs as never before, or since, on any network. There was money for reporters; there was money for documentaries; there was money for special programs. In his seven years as president, Kintner placed his stamp upon NBC as no one else in my four decades."

Reuven Frank left his mark on one of American television's premier news reporting services. After advancing through several roles and contributing to the development of a worldwide TV news network, Frank became president of NBC News in the tumultuous year of 1968. He held that position through the coverage of watershed events in the history of TV news, until 1973 when he returned to producing special projects for NBC News. In 1982, Frank was asked again to head the News Division, which he did until 1984. Robert E. Mulholland, then president of NBC, said of Frank's contributions, "Reuven wrote the book on how television covers the political process in America, has trained more top broadcast journalists than anyone alive, and simply embodies the very best professional traditions of NBC News."

—Tom Mascaro

REUVEN FRANK. Born in Montreal, Quebec, Canada, 7 December 1920. Educated at Harbord Collegiate Institute, Toronto, Canada; University College of the University of Toronto, 1937–40; City College of New York, B.S. in social science 1942; Graduate School of Journalism, Columbia University, M.S. 1947. Married: Bernice Kaplow, 1946; children: Peter Solomon and James Aaron. Served in the United States Army, 1943–46. Reporter, rewrite man, and night city editor, Newark *Evening News,* 1947–50; news writer, NBC News, 1950; news editor and chief writer, *Camel News Caravan,* 1951–54; supervised experiments in half-hour news forums such as *Background, Outlook,* and *Chet Huntley Reporting,* 1954 to early 1960s; executive vice president of NBC News, 1967–68, president, 1968–72, senior executive producer, and various other positions, 1972–82. Member: National Academy of Television Arts and Sciences; Writers Guild of America. Recipient: Sigma Delta Chi television newswriting award, 1955; several Emmy Awards; Yale University Poynter Fellow, 1970.

TELEVISION SERIES (selection)

1954–55	*Background* (managing editor)
1956–70	*The Huntley-Brinkley Report* (producer)
1958–63	*Chet Huntley Reporting* (producer)
1956–58	*Outlook* (producer)
1960	*Time Present...Edwin Newman Reporting* (producer)
1974–79	*Weekend* (producer)
1982–83	*NBC News Overnight*

TELEVISION SPECIALS (producer)

1953	*Meeting at the Summit*
1955	*The First Step into Space*
1956	*Antarctica: The Third World*
1958	*Kaleidoscope* ("The S-Bahn Stops at Freedom")
1958	*Kaleidoscope* ("The American Stranger")
1959	*Kaleidoscope* ("Our Man in the Mediterranean")
1959	*Kaleidoscope* ("The Big Ear")
1959	*Back to School*
1959	*Too Late for Reason*
1960	*World Wide '60* ("Freedom is Sweet and Bitter")
1960	*World Wide '60* ("The Requiem For Mary Jo")
1960	*World Wide '60* ("Where is Abel, Your Brother? ")
1961	*Our Man in Hong Kong*
1961	*Berlin: Where the West Begins*
1961	*The Great Plane Robbery*
1962	*Our Man in Vienna*
1962	*The Land*
1962	*Clear and Present Danger*
1962	*The Tunnel*
1962	*After Two Years: A Conversation with the President*
1963	*The Trouble with Water...Is People*
1963	*A Country Called Europe*
1965	*The Big Ear*
1966	*Daughters of Orange*
1973	*If That's a Gnome, This Must Be Zurich*

PUBLICATIONS

"Dialogue: Reuven Frank and Don Hewitt." *Television Quarterly* (New York), November 1962.

Out of Thin Air: The Brief Wonderful Life of Network News. New York: Simon and Schuster, 1991.

"Let's Put on a Convention." *Media Studies Journal* (New York), Winter 1995.

FURTHER READING

Bluem, A. William. *Documentary in American Television.* New York: Hastings House, 1965.

Einstein, Daniel. *Special Edition: A Guide to Network Television Documentary Series and Special News Reports, 1955–1979.* Metuchen, New Jersey: Scarecrow, 1987.

Matusow, Barbara. *The Evening Stars.* New York: Houghton Mifflin, 1983.

Watson, Mary Ann. *The Expanding Vista: American Television in the Kennedy Years.* New York: Oxford University Press, 1990.

FRANKENHEIMER, JOHN

U.S. Director

John Frankenheimer is sometimes likened to a "wunderkind in the tradition of Orson Welles" because he directed numerous quality television dramas while still in his twenties. He is also one of a handful of directors who established their reputation in high-quality, high-budget television dramas and later moved on to motion pictures.

As with other television directors of the 1950s, Frankenheimer began his training in the theater, first with the Williams Theater Group at Williams College and then as a member of the stock company and director at Highfield Playhouse in Falmouth, Massachusetts. He later moved to Washington, D.C., where he acted in an American Theater Wing production. While in Washington, he both acted in and directed radio productions and began working at WTOP-TV.

After a stint with the U.S. Air Force, during which he directed two documentaries, Frankenheimer began his television career as an assistant director at CBS. He worked on weather and news shows, and moved on to *Lamp unto My Feet*, *The Garry Moore Show*, and Edward R. Murrow's *Person to Person*. As his career advanced, Frankenheimer directed dramatizations on *See It Now* and *You Are There* (working under director Sydney Lumet). He also directed episodes of the comedy series *Mama* (based on John Van Druten's play *I Remember Mama*), but it was his directorial efforts on television anthologies where Frankenheimer made his mark.

Frankenheimer began directing episodes of the suspense anthology series *Danger* in the early 1950s. Producer Martin Manulis hired Frankenheimer as a co-director on the critically acclaimed *Climax!*, an hour-long drama series which was originally aired live. When Manulis moved on to CBS' *Playhouse 90* in 1954, he brought Frankenheimer with him. Over the next few years, Frankenheimer directed 140 live television dramas on such anthologies as *Studio One* (CBS), *Playhouse 90*, *The DuPont Show of the Month* (CBS), *Ford Startime* (NBC), *Sunday Showcase* (NBC), and *Kraft Television Theatre* (NBC). He directed such productions as *The Days of Wine and Roses*, *The Browning Version* (which featured the television debut of Sir John Gielgud), and *The Turn of the Screw* (which featured Ingrid Bergman's television debut).

Frankenheimer's production of Ernest Hemingway's *For Whom the Bell Tolls* (*Playhouse 90*) was one of the first dramas to be presented in two parts (12 and 19 March 1959) and, at $400,000, was the most expensive production at that time. Unlike most of his other productions, *For Whom the Bell Tolls* was taped for presentation because the actors were involved in other theatrical productions in New York. The production's intensive five-week rehearsal and ten-day shooting schedule had to be organized around the actors' other theatrical appearances.

Most directors of live television came from a similar theatrical background and, as such, used a static camera and

John Frankenheimer

blocked productions in a manner similar to a live stage play. A firm believer that a production is the sole creative statement of its director, Frankenheimer was one of the first directors of the "golden age" to utilize a variety of camera angles and movement, fast-paced editing, and close-ups to focus the audience's attention (some critics have labeled his technique as gimmicky or contrived). Frankenheimer's most famous use of the camera appears in his 1962 film *The Manchurian Candidate*, in which one shot is slightly out of focus. Ironically, the shot, which has been widely acclaimed as artistically brilliant was, according to the director, an accident and merely the best take for actor Frank Sinatra.

Frankenheimer went on to make other memorable films, such as *The Birdman of Alcatraz* (which he had, at one time, wanted to do as a live *Playhouse 90* production in 1955), *Seven Days in May*, *Grand Prix*, *The Fixer*, and *The Iceman Cometh*. Personal problems and a decline in the number of quality scripts offered him forced Frankenheimer into an absence from the industry. Returning to television in the 1990s, Frankenheimer directed the original HBO production *Against the Wall* about the 1971 Attica Prison riot. Always drawn to intimate stories and psychological portraits, in this production Frankenheimer explores the relationship between the officer taken as hostage and the inmate leader of the uprising.

Frankenheimer has received six Emmy nominations for his directorial work on television, including: *Portrait in Celluloid* (1955, *Climax*, CBS), *Forbidden Area* (1956, *Playhouse 90*, CBS), *The Comedian* (1957, *Playhouse 90*), *A Town Has Turned to Dust* (1958, *Playhouse 90*), and *The Turn of the Screw* (1959, *Ford Startime*, NBC).

—Susan R. Gibberman

JOHN (MICHAEL) FRANKENHEIMER. Born in Malba, New York, U.S.A., 19 February 1930. Williams College, B.A. 1951. Married: 1) Carolyn Miller, 1954 (divorced); two daughters; 2) Evans Evans, 1964. Served in Film Squadron, U.S. Air Force, 1951-53. Began career as actor, 1950-51; assistant director, later director, CBS-TV, New York, from 1953; director, *Playhouse 90* television series, Hollywood, 1954-59; directed first feature film, *The Young Stranger*, 1957; formed John Frankenheimer Productions, 1963. Recipient: Christopher Award, 1954; Grand Prize for Best Film Director, 1955; Critics Award, 1956-59; Brotherhood Award, 1959; Acapulco Film Festival Award, 1962. Address: c/o John Frankenheimer Productions, 2800 Olympic Boulevard., Suite 201, Santa Monica, California, 90404, U.S.A.

TELEVISION SERIES (selection)

1948–58	*Studio One*
1950–55	*Danger*
1953–57	*You Are There*
1954–58	*Climax*
1954–59	*Playhouse 90*

MINISERIES

1996	*Andersonville*

MADE-FOR-TELEVISION MOVIES

1982	*The Rainmaker*
1994	*Against the Wall*
1994	*The Burning Season*

FILMS (selection)

The Young Stranger, 1957; *The Young Savages*, 1961; *The Manchurian Candidate*, (also co-produced), 1962; *All Fall Down*, 1962; *Birdman of Alcatraz*, 1962; *Seven Days in May*, 1963; *The Train*, 1964; *Grand Prix*, 1966; *Seconds*, 1966; *The Extraordinary Seaman*, 1968; *The Fixer*, 1968; *The Gypsy Moths*, 1969; *I Walk the Line*, 1970; *The Horsemen*, 1970; *L'Impossible Objet (Impossible Object)*, 1973; *The Iceman Cometh*, 1973; *99 44/100 Dead*, 1974; *French Connection II*, 1975; *Black Sunday* (also bit role as TV controller), 1976; *Prophecy*, 1979; *The Challenge*, 1982; *The Holcroft Covenant*, 1985; *52 Pick Up*, 1986; *Across the River and Into the Trees*, 1987; *Dead Bang*, 1989; *The Fourth War*, 1989.

PUBLICATIONS

"Seven Ways with *Seven Days in May*." *Films and Filming* (London), June 1964.

"Criticism as Creation." *Saturday Review* (New York), 26 December 1964.

Au Werter, Russell. "Interview." *Action* (Los Angeles), May-June 1970.

Gross, L., and R. Avrech. "Interview." *Millimeter* (New York), August 1971.

"Filming *The Iceman Cometh*." *Action* (Los Angeles), January/February 1974.

Applebaum, R. "Interview." *Films and Filming* (London), October-November, 1979.

Broeske, P. "Interview." *Films in Review* (New York), February 1983.

"Interview." *Films and Filming* (London), February 1985.

FURTHER READING

"Backstage at *Playhouse 90*." *Time* (New York), 2 December 1957.

Casty, Alan. "Realism and Beyond: The Films of John Frankenheimer." *Film Heritage* (New York), Winter 1966–67.

Combs, Richard. "A Matter of Conviction." *Sight and Sound* (London), 1979.

Cook, B. "The War Between the Writers and the Directors: Part II: The Directors." *American Film* (Washington, D.C.), June 1979.

_____. "Directors of the Decade: John Frankenheimer." *Films and Filming* (London), February 1984.

"Dialogue on Film: John Frankenheimer." *American Film* (Washington, D.C.), March 1989.

Drew, B. "John Frankenheimer: His Fall and Rise." *American Film* (Washington, D.C.), March 1977.

Filmer, Paul. "Three Frankenheimer Films: A Sociological Approach." *Screen* (London), July-August 1969.

Higham, Charles. "Frankenheimer." *Sight and Sound* (London), Spring 1968.

Madsen, Axel. "*99 and 44/100 Dead*." *Sight and Sound* (London), Winter 1973–74.

Mayersberg, Paul. "John Frankenheimer." *Movie* (London), December 1962.

Pratley, Gerald. *The Cinema of John Frankenheimer*. London: A. Zwemmer, and New York: A.S. Barnes, 1969.

Scheinfeld, Michael. "The Manchurian Candidate." *Films in Review* (New York), 1988.

Thomas, John. "John Frankenheimer, the Smile on the Face of the Tiger." *Film Quarterly* (Berkeley), Winter 1965–66.

Weinraub, Bernard. "Back to Hollywood's Bottom Rung, and Climbing." *The New York Times*, 24 March 1994.

See also Anthology Drama; Golden Age of Television; *Playhouse 90*; *Studio One*

FRANK'S PLACE

U.S. Dramedy

Frank's Place, an exceptionally innovative half-hour television program sometimes referred to as a "dramedy," aired on CBS during the 1987–88 television season. The program won extensive critical praise for the ways in which it used conventions of situation comedy to explore serious subject matter. As *Rolling Stone* writer Mark Christensen commented, "rarely has a prime-time show attempted to capture so accurately a particular American subculture—in this case that of blue-collar blacks in Louisiana."

In 1987 *Frank's Place* won the Television Critics Association's award for outstanding comedy series. One 1988 episode, "The Bridge," won Emmy Awards for best writing in a comedy series (writer and co-executive producer, Hugh Wilson) and outstanding guest performance in a comedy series (Beah Richards). Tim Reid, star and co-executive producer, received an NAACP Image Award. In spite of its critical success, however, the show did not do well in the ratings and was not renewed by CBS.

Frank's Place was developed by Wilson and Reid from a suggestion by CBS executive Kim LeMasters. Wilson, an alumnus of the heyday of MTM Productions, had previously produced *WKRP in Cincinnati*, a sitcom favorite in which Reid played super-cool disc jockey, Venus Flytrap. The premise for their new show centered on Frank Parrish (played by Reid), an African-American college professor from Boston who inherits a New Orleans restaurant from his estranged father. Wilson, who had directed for film as well as television, decided against using the standard situation comedy production style—videotaping with three-cameras in front of a live audience. He opted instead for film-style production, single camera with no laugh track. Thus, from the beginning, *Frank's Place* looked and sounded different. Changed, too, were the broad physical humor and snappy one-liners that characterize most situation comedies. These were replaced with a more subtle, often poignant humor as Frank encountered situations his formal education had not prepared him for. He's the innocent lost in a bewildering world, a rich and complex culture that appears both alien and increasingly attractive to him. And he is surrounded by a surrogate family who wish him well but know he must ultimately learn from his mistakes.

The ensemble cast included Hanna Griffin (played by Daphne Maxwell Reid), a mortician who became a romantic interest for Frank, and Bubba Weisberger (Robert Harper), a white Jewish lawyer from an old southern family. The restaurant staff included Miss Marie (Frances E. Williams), the matriarch of the group; Anna-May (Francesca P. Roberts), the head waitress; Big Arthur (Tony Burton), the accomplished chef who rules the kitchen; Shorty La Roux (Don Yesso), the white assistant chef; Tiger Shepin (Charles Lampkin), the fatherly bartender; Cool Charles (William Thomas Jr.), his helper. Reverend Deal (Lincoln Kilpatrick),

Frank's Place

a smooth-talking preacher in constant search of a church or a con-man's opportunity, was another regular.

Frank's journey into the world of the southern working-class African-American begins when he visits Chez Louisiane, the creole restaurant he inherited and plans to sell. The elderly waitress Miss Marie puts a voodoo spell on him to ensure that he will continue to run the restaurant in his father's place. After Frank returns to Boston, his plumbing erupts, telephones fail him, the laundry loses all his clothes, his girlfriend leaves him, and his office burns. Convinced he has no choice, he returns to New Orleans, to the matter-of-fact welcome of the staff, the reappearance of his father's cat, and the continuing struggle to turn the restaurant into a profitable venture.

Story lines in many episodes provide comic and pointed comments on the values and attitudes of the dominant culture. In one story, college recruiters bombard young basketball star Calvin with virtually identical speeches about family and tradition and campus life. Calvin's naive expectations of becoming a professional athlete contrast with Frank's concern about academic opportunities. In another episode, the chairman of a major corporation stops in for a late night dinner. Commenting on efforts to oust him, he eloquently condemns speculators who use junk bonds to buy companies they know nothing about and with which they create no real value or service. The plot takes an ironic turn when he realizes his partners may have made mistakes in plotting the takeover and he enthusiastically schemes to thwart them.

Class and racial issues emerge in many story lines. On Frank's first night back in New Orleans, he wonders why there are so few people in the restaurant. Tiger explains with a simple observation: their clientele are working people who eat at home during the week—and white folks are afraid to come into the neighborhood at night. In a later episode Frank is flattered when he is invited to join a club of African-American professionals. Not until Anna-May pulls out a brown paper bag and contrasts it with Frank's darker skin does he understand that those who extended the invitation meant to use him to challenge to the light-skin bias of the club members.

Throughout the series tidy resolutions are missing. A group of musicians from East Africa, in the United States on a cultural tour, stop at Frank's Place. One of them, who longs to play the jazz that's forbidden at home, decides to defect. Frank refuses to help him and he is rebuffed by jazz musicians. But in the closing scene, as he sits listening in a club, he gets an inviting nod to join the musicians when they break. The final frame freezes on a close-up of his face as he rises, suspended forever between worlds. In another episode, a bum moves into a large box in the alley and annoys customers by singing and begging in front of the restaurant. Nothing persuades him to leave until one evening Frank tries unsuccessfully to get him to talk about who he is, where he's from, the reasons for his choices. When Frank steps outside the next morning, he's gone. A final image, as Frank dusts off the hat left on the sidewalk, resonates with a recognition of kinship and loss. Visual sequences in many episodes suggest the loneliness of Frank's search for father, for self, for his place in this community.

Various explanations have been offered for the decision to cancel *Frank's Place* after one season. In spite of a strong beginning, the show's ratings continued to drop. Viewers who expected the usual situation comedy formula were puzzled by the show's style. Frequent changes in scheduling made it difficult for viewers to find the show. CBS, struggling to improve its standing in the ratings, was not willing to give the show more time in a regular time slot to build an audience. The large ensemble and the film-style techniques made the show expensive to produce. In the end, it was undoubtedly a combination of reasons that brought the series to an end.

Frank's Place, however, deserves a continuing place in programming history. As Tim Reid told *New York Times* reporter Perry Garfinkel, it did present blacks not as stereotypes but as "a diverse group of hard-working people."

Hugh Wilson attributed this accuracy to the racially mixed group of writers, directors, cast and crew. Authenticity was heightened by the careful researching of details. Individual stories were allowed to determine the style of each episode. Some were comic, some serious, some poignant. All of them, however, were grounded in a compelling sense of place and a respect for those who inhabit Chez Louisiane and its corner of New Orleans.

—Lucy A. Liggett

EXECUTIVE PRODUCERS   Hugh Wilson, Tim Reid

CAST

Frank Parish	Tim Reid
Sy "Bubba" Weisburger	Robert Harper
Hannah Griffin	Daphne Maxwell Reid
Anna-May	Francesca P. Roberts
Miss Marie	Frances E Williams
Mrs. Bertha Griffin-Lamour	Virginia Capers
Big Arthur	Tony Burton
Tiger Shepin	Charles Lampkin
Reverend Deal	Lincoln Kilpatrick
Cool Charles	William Thomas, Jr.
Shorty La Roux	Dan Yesso

PRODUCERS   Hugh Wilson, Tim Reid, Max Tash

PROGRAMMING HISTORY

• CBS

September 1987–November 1987	Monday 8:00-8:30
December 1987–February 1988	Monday 8:30-9:00
February 1988–March 1988	Monday 9:30-10:00
March 1988	Tuesday 8:00-8:30
July 1988-October 1988	Saturday 8:30-9:00

FURTHER READING

Christensen, Mark. "Just Folks." *Rolling Stone* (New York), 10 March 1988.

Collier, Aldore. "Hollywood's Hottest Couple." *Ebony* (Chicago), January 1988.

Garfinkel, Perry. "*Frank's Place*: The Restaurant as Life's Stage." *The New York Times*, 17 February 1988.

Gray, Herman. *Watching Race: Television and the Struggle for "Blackness."* Minneapolis: University of Minnesota Press, 1995.

Hill, Michael E. "Frank's Place Serving Rich Television with No Calories." *Washington Post TV Week*, 16 December 1987.

"Host." *People Weekly* (New York), 25 April 1988.

Newcomb, Horace. "The Sense of Place in *Frank's Place*." In, Thompson, Robert J., and Gary Burns, editors. *Making Television: Authorship and the Production Process*. New York, Praeger, 1990.

O'Connor, John J. "Two New Series in Previews." *The New York Times*, 15 September 1987.

Reeves, Jimmie L., and Campbell, Richard. "Misplacing *Frank's Place*: Do You Know What it Means to Miss New Orleans?" *Television Quarterly* (New York), 1989.

Rense, Rip. "Tim's Place: The Executive Suite." *TV Guide* (Radnor, Pennsylvania) 16-22 April 1988.

Spotnitz, Frank. "Tim Reid." *American Film* (Washington, D.C.), October 1990.

Thompson, R. J., and Burns, G. "Authorship and the Production Process." *Millimeter* (New York), March 1988.

White, Mimi. "What's the Difference? *Frank's Place* in Television." *Wide Angle* (Athens, Ohio), July-October 1991.

See also Comedy, Workplace; Dramedy; Racisim, Ethnicity, and Television; Reid, Tim

FREDERICK, PAULINE

U.S. Broadcast Journalist

Pauline Frederick's pioneering broadcast career covered nearly 40 years and began at a time when broadcasting was virtually closed to women. During these decades, she was the primary correspondent covering the United Nations for the National Broadcasting Company (NBC) and was the first broadcast newswoman to receive the coveted Peabody Award for excellence in broadcasting.

Frederick began her career as a teenager, covering society news for the *Harrisburg Telegraph*. She turned down a full-time position there in favor of studying political science at American University in Washington, D.C. Later she received her master's degree in international law, and at the suggestion of a history professor, combined her interests in journalism and international affairs by interviewing diplomats' wives. She broke into broadcasting in 1939 when NBC's director of women's programs, Margaret Cuthbert, asked her to interview the wife of the Czechoslovakian minister shortly after Germany overran that country.

Her interviews continued until America joined World War II. She then worked a variety of jobs for NBC, including script writing and research. After touring Africa and Asia with other journalists—over the protests of her male boss at NBC who thought the trip too difficult for a woman—she quit her job with NBC and began covering the Nuremberg trials for ABC radio, the North American Newspaper Alliance, and the Western Newspaper Alliance.

Denied a permanent job because she was female, she worked as a stringer for ABC, covering "women's stories." Her break came when she was assigned to cover a foreign ministers' conference in an emergency: her male boss had two stories to cover and only one male reporter. In a few months, the United Nations became her regular beat, and in 1948, ABC hired her permanently to cover international affairs and politics. In 1953, NBC hired her to cover the United Nations.

Over the next two decades she covered political conventions, the Korean War, Mideast conflicts, the Cuban missile crisis, the Cold War and the Vietnam War. After retiring from NBC, she worked for National Public Radio as a commentator on international affairs. Frederick received many honors, including election to the presidency of the United Nations Correspondents Association, named to Sigma Delta Chi's Hall of Fame in 1975, 23 honorary doctorate degrees in journalism, law, and the humanities.

Of her life, Frederick once said, "I think the kind of career I've had, something would have had to be sacrificed. Because when I have been busy at the United Nations during crises, it has meant working day and night. You can't very well take care of a home when you do something like that, or children." Through her work she advanced the position of women in broadcast news and became an important role model for newswomen everywhere.

—Louise Benjamin

PAULINE FREDERICK. Born in Gallitzin, Pennsylvania, U.S.A., 13 February 1908. Educated at American University in Washington, D.C., B.A. in political science, M.A. in international law.

Pauline Frederick

Married: Charles Robbin, 1969. Feature writer for newspapers and magazines, from late-1930s; radio interviewer, NBC, 1938–45; war correspondent, North American Newspaper Alliance, 1945–46, political reporter, ABC, 1946–53; reporter and interviewer, NBC, 1953–74; foreign affairs commentator, National Public Radio, 1974–90. Recipient: Peabody Award, 1954; Paul White Award from the Radio-Television News Directors Association, 1980; Alfred I. duPont Awards' Commentator Award. Died in Lake Forest, Illinois, 9 May 1990.

TELEVISION

1946–53   ABC News (reporter)
1953–74   NBC News (reporter)

RADIO

NBC (reporter) 1938–45; National Public Radio (commentator), 1974–90.

PUBLICATION

Ten First Ladies of the World. New York: Meredith, 1967.

FURTHER READING

Foremost Women in Communications. New York: Foremost Americans Publications Corporation, 1970.

Gelfman, Judith. *Women in Television News.* New York: Columbia University Press, 1976.

Hosley, David, and Gayle Yamada. *Hard News: Women in Broadcast Journalism.* New York: Greenwood, 1987.

Nobile, Philip. "TV News and the Older Woman." *New York Times,* 10 August 1981.

Talese, Gay. "Perils of Pauline." *Saturday Evening Post* (Philadelphia, Pennsylvania), 26 January 1963.

FREED, FRED

U.S. Documentary Producer

Fred Freed was a leading practitioner of prime-time documentary during the genre's heyday of the 1960s. Working on the network flagship series, *NBC White Paper,* he produced close to forty major documentaries, which earned him seven Emmy and three Peabody awards. Describing himself as an "old-fashioned liberal," Freed believed that documentary could stimulate change by providing audiences with detailed information about pressing social issues. Yet Freed was also a prominent member of a generation of documentary producers who courted mass audiences with narrative techniques that would later spread to network news reporting and television magazine programs.

Freed began his media career after a stint in the Navy during World War II. Starting out as a magazine editor, he moved to radio and ultimately to network television in 1956. One year later, he joined CBS as a documentary producer working under Irving Gitlin, the head of creative projects in the news and public affairs division. During the late 1950s, CBS News was well endowed with talented personnel and the competition for network airtime was extremely fierce. The CBS evening schedule almost exclusively featured entertainment fare with the exception of irregularly scheduled broadcasts of *See It Now,* produced by Edward R. Murrow and Fred Friendly. The cancellation of this series in 1958 generated intense dissatisfaction among the news and public affairs staff, many of them frustrated with the marginal time periods devoted to information fare. Partly in response to internal dissension, CBS management in 1959 announced the inauguration of a new prime-time documentary series, *CBS Reports.* Gitlin and his colleagues were disappointed to learn, however, that Friendly had been tapped for the slot of executive producer. Shortly thereafter Gitlin, Freed, and

producer Albert Wasserman were wooed away by NBC president Robert Kintner, who promised them a prestigious prime-time series of their own.

Fred Freed

Beginning in 1960, *NBC White Paper* was a central component of the peacock network's efforts to dislodge CBS from its top billing in broadcast news. A former journalist, Kintner was a vigorous supporter of the news division, believing it both good citizenship and good business. Over the next several years, NBC News grew rapidly and its documentary efforts earned widespread acclaim from critics and opinion leaders. Under Gitlin's leadership, Freed and Wasserman produced numerous programs focusing on significant foreign policy issues, then a key concern of the Kennedy administration and Federal Communications Commision (FCC) chair Newton Minow. Programs on the U-2 debacle, the Berlin crisis, and political unrest in Latin America received prominent attention. Yet all three documentarists were also determined to use narrative techniques in an effort to make such issues accessible to a broad audience. At the time, Freed commented, "In a world so interesting we always manage to find ways of making things dull. This business of blaming audiences for not watching our documentaries is ridiculous."

With this credo in mind, Freed produced documentaries about "The Death of Stalin" and "The Rise of Khrushchev" that featured tightly structured storylines with well-developed characters. Similarly, his analyses of the Bay of Pigs invasion and the Cuban Missile Crisis were built around dramatic moments in which historical figures struggled against Promethean odds. Freed's increasingly creative use of audio and visual elements is conveyed in a tightly edited opening sequence of the latter documentary as a nuclear missile ominously emerges from its silo accompanied by the piercing sound of a military alarm claxon. Much like a feature film, the editing of the visual imagery dramatically sets the terms for the story that followed.

Freed and his documentary colleagues also experimented during the early 1960s with camera framing techniques that would later become standard conventions of television news. For example, Freed would have his camera operator zoom in for tight close-ups during particularly emotional moments of an interview. This was a significant break from the standard head-and-shoulders portrait shots then used on nightly news and Sunday talk shows. It was intended to engage viewers on both an affective and intellectual level.

Despite these dramatic techniques, network documentaries only occasionally generated ratings that were comparable with entertainment fare. By the middle of the decade, all three networks trimmed back their commitment to the genre for a variety of reasons and producers Wasserman and Gitlin moved on to other opportunities. Yet Freed remained with *White Paper* and continued to play a leading role with the series into the 1970s. He made major documentaries about the urban crisis, gun control, and environmental issues. He also produced numerous instant specials on breaking news events as well as three super-documentaries, which featured an entire evening of prime-time devoted to a single issue. This concept, which was distinctive to NBC, originated in 1963 with a program on civil rights. It was followed in 1965 by Freed's twenty-year survey of American foreign policy and in 1966 by his program on organized crime. In

1973 he produced NBC's last super-documentary, an evening devoted to "The Energy Crisis." One year later, in the midst of a busy schedule of documentary production, Freed succumbed to a heart attack at the age of 53. His passing also marked the demise of *NBC White Paper,* for the network mounted only three more installments before the end of the decade. Although *White Paper* very occasionally returns to prime time, it lacks the autonomy, prestige, and resources that were characteristic of the series during the Freed era.

—Michael Curtin

FRED FREED. Born 25 August 1920. Began career as magazine editor and writer; in broadcasting from 1949; managing editor, NBC-TV, for the daytime program *Home,* 1955; documentary producer, CBS-TV, late 1950s; producer, NBC's *Today Show,* 1961; exclusively in documentary production later. Recipient: three Peabody Awards; two duPont-Columbia Awards; seven Emmy Awards. Died in March 1974.

TELEVISION SPECIALS (selection)

1961	*NBC White Paper: Krushchev and Berlin*
1962	*NBC White Paper: Red China*
1962	*The Chosen Child: A Study in Adoption*
1962	*Dupont Show of the Week: Fire Rescue*
1963	*Dupont Show of the Week: Comedian Backstage*
1963	*Dupont Show of the Week: Miss America: Behind the Scenes*
1963	*NBC White Paper: The Death of Stalin: Profile on Communism*
1963	*NBC White Paper: The Rise of Krushchev: Profile on Communism*
1964	*Dupont Show of the Week: The Patient in Room 601*
1964	*NBC White Paper: Cuba: Bay of Pigs*
1964	*NBC White Paper: Cuba: The Missile Crisis*
1965	*NBC White Paper: Decision to Drop the Bomb*
1965	*American White Paper: United States Foreign Policy*
1965	*NBC White Paper: Oswald and the Law: A Study of Criminal Justice*
1966	*NBC White Paper: Countdown to Zero*
1966	*American White Paper: Organized Crime in America*
1967	*The JFK Conspiracy: The Case of Jim Garrison*
1968	*NBC White Paper: The Ordeal of the American City: Cities Have No Limits*
1968	*NBC White Paper: The Ordeal of the American City: The People are the City*
1969	*NBC White Paper: The Ordeal of the American City: Confrontation*
1969	*Who Killed Lake Eerie?*
1969	*Pueblo: A Question of Intelligence*
1970	*NBC White Paper: Pollution Is a Matter of Choice*
1971	*NBC White Paper: Vietnam Hindsight: How It Began*

1971   *NBC White Paper: Vietnam Hindsight:*
        The Death of Diem
1973   *NBC Reports: And Now the War Is Over...*
        The American Military in the 1970s
1973   *NBC Reports: Murder in America*
1973   *NBC Reports: But Is this Progress?*
1974   *NBC White Paper: The Energy Crisis:*
        American Solutions

FURTHER READING

Bluem, A. William. *Documentary in American Television.* New York: Hastings House, 1965.

Curtin, Michael. *Redeeming the Wasteland.* New Brunswick, New Jersey: Rutgers University Press, 1995.

Einstein, Daniel. *Special Edition: A Guide to Network Television Documentary Series and Special News Reports, 1955–1979.* Metuchen, New Jersey: Scarecrow, 1987.

Hammond, Charles M. *The Image Decade.* New York: Hastings House, 1981.

Yellin, David. *Special; Fred Freed and the Television Documentary.* New York: Macmillan, 1973.

See also *NBC White Paper*

"FREEZE" OF 1948

On 30 September 1948 the Federal Communications Commissions (FCC) of the United States announced a "freeze" on the granting of new television licenses (those already authorized were allowed to begin or continue operations). The Commission had already granted over 100 licenses and was inundated with hundreds of additional applications. Unable to resolve several important interference, allocation and other technical questions because of this rush, the FCC believed that the freeze would allow it to hold hearings and study the issues, leading to something of a "master blueprint" for television in the United States. This "time out" was originally intended to last only six months, but the outbreak of the Korean War as well as the difficult nature of some of the issues under study, extended the freeze to four years. During this time, there were 108 VHF television stations on the air and over 700 new applications on hold. Only 24 cities had two or more stations; many had only one. Most smaller and even some major cities, Denver, Colorado and Austin, Texas, for example, had none at all.

Ultimately, five major, not unrelated, issues became the focus of deliberations: 1) the designation of a standard for color television; 2) the reservation of channel space for educational, noncommercial television; 3) the reduction of channel interference; 4) the establishment of a national channel allocation map or scheme; and, 5) the opening up of additional spectrum space.

With the 14 April 1952 issuance of the commission's *6th Report and Order,* the freeze was finally lifted. This document presented to an anxious broadcast industry and impatient viewers the resolutions to the five questions.

The decision on color came down to a choice between an existing but technologically unsophisticated CBS mechanical system which was incompatible with existent television receivers (i.e., "color" signals could not be received on black and white television sets) and an all-electronic system proposed by RCA which was compatible but still in development. The commission approved the CBS system but it was never implemented because the television set manufacturing industry refused to build what it considered to be inferior receivers. The FCC rescinded its approval of the CBS system in 1950 and, in 1953, accepted the RCA system as the standard.

The reservation of channel space for noncommercial, educational television was spearheaded by FCC Commissioner Frieda B. Hennock. When the channel reservation issue was raised for radio during the deliberation leading up to the Communications Act of 1934, the industry view prevailed. Broadcasting was considered too valuable a resource to entrust to educators or others who had no profit motive to spur the development of the medium. Exactly zero spectrum space was set aside for noncommercial (AM) radio. Hennock and others were unwilling to let history repeat in the age of television. Against heavy and strident industry objection (*Broadcasting* magazine said such a set-aside was "illogical, if not illegal"), they prevailed. Two hundred and forty-two channels were authorized for educational, noncommercial television, although no means of financial support was identified. The commission acquiesced because it reasoned that if the educators succeeded, it would be viewed as prescient; if the educators failed, at least the commission had given them an opportunity. Additionally, Hennock and her forces were a nuisance: the noncommercial channel issue was helping keep the freeze alive and there were powerful industry and viewer forces awaiting its end.

Channel interference was easily solved through the implementation of strict rules of separation for stations broadcasting on the same channel. Stations on the same channel had to be separated by at least 190 miles (some geographic areas, the Gulf and Northeast regions, for example, had somewhat different standards). A few stations had to change channels to meet the requirements.

Channel allocation took the form of city-by-city assignment of one or more channels based on the general criterion of fair geographic apportionment of channels to the various states and to the country as a whole. The "assignment table" that was produced gave some cities, New York and Los Angeles, for example, many stations. Smaller locales were allocated smaller numbers of outlets.

The question of opening up additional spectrum space for more television stations was actually the question of how much of the UHF band should be utilized. Eventually, the entire 70 channel UHF band was authorized. Therefore, the television channels then available to American broadcasters and their viewers were the existing VHF channels of 2 through 13 and the new UHF channels of 14 through 83.

—Kimberly B. Massey

FURTHER READING

Barnouw, E. *A History of Broadcasting in the United States, Volume II: The Golden Web.* New York: Oxford University Press, 1970.

———. *A History of Broadcasting in the United States, Volume III: The Image Empire.* New York: Oxford University Press, 1970.

———. *Tube of Plenty: The Evolution of American Television.* New York: Oxford University Press, 1975.

Bergreen, Laurence. *Look Now, Pay Later: The Rise of Network Broadcasting.* Garden City, New York: Doubleday, 1980.

The First 50 Years of Broadcasting: The Running Story of the Fifty Estate, edited by Editors of *Broadcasting Magazine.* Washington, D.C.: Broadcasting Publications, 1982.

Kahn, F.J. *Documents of American Broadcasting.* New York: Appleton-Century-Crofts, 1968.

Sterling, C.H., and J.M. Kittross. *Stay Tuned: A Concise History of American Broadcasting.* Belmont, California: Wadsworth, 1990.

See also Allocation; Color Television; Federal Communications Commission; Hennock, Frieda B.; License; Educational Television

FRENCH, DAWN

British Actor

Dawn French is one half of Britain's top female comedy duo, French and Saunders, as well as a highly successful writer, comedian and actress in her own right. She and partner Jennifer Saunders have become an outstanding double act whilst also following successful solo careers.

French's television debut was an auspicious one, as a member of a group of "alternative" comedians known as the Comic Strip, on the opening night of Britain's fourth TV channel, Channel Four, in 1982. "Five Go Mad in Dorset," a spoof of author Enid Blyton's popular children's adventure books, clearly showed that French was a comic actress to watch. The following two years saw two series of *The Comic Strip Presents* in which French played everything from housewives to hippies.

In 1985 French approached the kind of comedy which she and Saunders would eventually make very much their own. *Girls on Top,* a sitcom about four bizarre young women sharing a flat in London, gave French as co-star and co-writer a chance to develop further the type of character she so loves to play. Amanda was an overgrown teenager, sexually inexperienced and aware of the sexual powers of woman, yet so "right-on" that she is somehow unable to do other than caricature them. A second series followed in 1986, as did appearances with Saunders on Channel Four's cult late-night comedy show *Saturday Live,* but in 1987 French and Saunders moved as a double act to the BBC for their own co-written series, *French and Saunders.* This was broadcast on BBC2, the nurturing ground for so much of Britain's new generation of comic talent. This first series took the form of a cheap and badly rehearsed variety show, hosted by the two women. Saunders was the rather grumpy, irritable half of the partnership, with French portraying a bouncy, enthusiastic, schoolgirlish character. This format was dropped for the second series, and instead the programmes were a mixture of sketches and spoofs.

With an uncanny ability to pick up on the foibles and fears of childhood, and particularly teenage girlhood, French always played the fervent, excitable girl, generally leading the more sullen and awkward Saunders into mis-

Dawn French (upper) with Jennifer Saunders
Photo courtesy of the British Film Institute

chief, whether it be discussing the schoolboys they fancy, or playing games in the school playground. This ability to draw on universal but commonplace memories of what now seem petty and trivial matters of girlhood and turn them into fresh and original comedy is one of the things which has set French and her partner above virtually all other female performers except, perhaps, Victoria Wood. Further series of *French and Saunders* have seen their transfer from BBC2 to the more popular BBC1. While their inventiveness has increased, there has been no diminution in their ability to latch on to the way women behave with each other. In particular they have become skilled at extraordinarily clever film spoofs, with French playing Julie Andrews in *The Sound of Music* one week and Hannibal Lecter in *Silence of the Lambs* the next.

French's first solo starring role came in 1991 with *Murder Most Horrid*, a series of six comic dramas with a common theme of violent death, in which she played a different role every week. The series was commissioned for French and enabled her to play everything from a Brazilian aupair in "The Girl from Ipanema" to a naive policewoman in "The Case of the Missing". A second series of *Murder Most Horrid* in 1994 was even more ambitious, with roles ranging from an old woman whose family are trying to murder her to a woman who disguises herself as a man in order to become a doctor.

If there had been any doubt about French's acting ability, this had been dispelled the previous year, 1993, in the BBC Screen One drama *Tender Loving Care*. In this work, French played a night nurse in the geriatric ward of a hospital. There she helps many of her charges "on their way" with her own brand of tender loving care, believing that by killing them she is doing them a service. It was a beautifully understated and restrained performance.

After the General Synod of the Church of England voted to permit women to become priests, one *French and Saunders* sketch concerned French's receipt of a vicar's outfit after having received permission to become the first female comedy vicar, complete with buck teeth and dandruff. This soon proved prophetic when French was cast as the Reverend Geraldine Granger, "a babe with a bob and a magnificent bosom," in Richard Curtis's *The Vicar of Dibley*. French's portrayal of a female vicar sent to a small, old-fashioned, country parish is possibly her most popular to date. The public quickly took this series to their hearts, and French shone even amidst an ensemble cast of very experienced character actors.

French's influence can probably be felt in other areas of British comedy too. She is married to Britain's top black comedian, Lenny Henry, and is often quoted as having influenced him during the early stage of their relationship to

abandon his then somewhat self-deprecating humour, in order to explore what it is like to be a black Briton today.

French and Saunders currently have an exclusive contract with the BBC which gives them scope for expanding beyond the confines of their double act. Their first project, *Dusty*, a documentary about Dusty Springfield, was not entirely successful, but there can be no doubt that whether it is as part of a double act or as a solo actress, Dawn French can be assured of a place at the heart of British television for a considerable number of years.

—Pamela Logan

DAWN FRENCH. Born in Holyhead, Wales, 1957. Attended St. Dunstan's Abbey, Plymouth; Central School of Speech and Drama, London. Married: Lenny Henry, 1984; child: Billie. Met Jennifer Saunders at Central School of Speech and Drama and formed alternative comedy partnership with her, appearing at the Comic Strip club, London, from 1980; participated with Saunders in the Channel Four *Comic Strip Presents* films and then in own long-running *French and Saunders* series; has also acted in West End theatre. Address: Peters, Fraser and Dunlop, The Chambers, Chelsea Harbour, Lots Road, London SW10 0XF, England.

TELEVISION SERIES

1982–92	*The Comic Strip Presents* ("Five Go Mad in Dorset", "Five Go Mad on Mescalin", "Slags", "Summer School", "Private Enterprise", "Consuela", "Mr Jolly Lives Next Door", "The Bad News Tour", "South Atlantic Raiders", "GLC", "Oxford", "Spaghetti Hoops", "Le Kiss", "The Strike")
1985	*Happy Families*
1985–86	*Girls on Top* (also co-writer)
1987–	*French and Saunders*
1991; 1994–	*Murder Most Horrid*
1993	*Tender Loving Care*
1994	*The Vicar of Dibley*

FILM

The Supergrass, 1985.

STAGE (selection)

When I Was a Girl I Used to Scream and Shout; An Evening with French and Saunders; The Secret Policeman's Biggest Ball; Silly Cow.

PUBLICATION

A Feast of French and Saunders. London: Mandarin, 1992.

See also Saunders, Jennifer

FRIENDLY, FRED W.

U.S. Broadcast Journalist and Media Commentator

Fred W. Friendly, a pioneering CBS News producer and distinguished media scholar, has enjoyed a sixty-year career as remarkable for its longevity as for its accomplishments. As the technically creative and dramatically inspired producer for CBS correspondent Edward R. Murrow, Friendly helped enliven and popularize television news documentary in the decade after World War II, when television news was still in its infancy. After resigning from CBS as its News Division president in 1966, Friendly found a second career as an author and as creator of a series of moderated seminars on media and society.

Friendly got his start in broadcasting during the Great Depression with a staff position at a small radio station in Providence, Rhode Island. It was as a successful radio producer that Friendly was teamed with Murrow in the late 1940s to create a series of documentary albums entitled *I Can Hear It Now.* When Murrow made the jump to television reporting, he brought Friendly with him as his principal documentary producer. Armed with a flair for the dramatic and his experience as a technical innovator in radio, Friendly set out to do for television what he had already done for radio documentaries. The result, in 1952, was the debut of the highly-acclaimed *See It Now*, a weekly series hosted by Murrow that broke new ground with its intrepid probing into subjects of serious socio-political significance and its stunning visual style. The successful combination of Friendly's energy and Murrow's stature hit its professional peak in 1954, with their decision to broadcast a documentary attack on Senator Joseph McCarthy that helped change the tide of popular opinion against the anti-communist demagogue.

In his later years at CBS, Friendly was given broader responsibility to create a variety of news programs, including the landmark hourly documentary series, *CBS Reports,* and a political forum that would later be known as *Face the Nation.* As president of CBS News in the mid-1960s, Friendly struggled to keep his news division independent of profit-conscious and entertainment-oriented corporate decision-making at CBS Inc., which he considered a threat to the autonomy and integrity of his news operations. In March of 1966, Friendly argued vociferously to management that CBS had a journalistic obligation to carry extensive live coverage of the first Senate hearings to question American involvement in Vietnam. When the network opted instead to air reruns of *I Love Lucy,* Friendly resigned from CBS in protest.

Friendly, in his post-CBS years, turned his interests to writing and teaching about media and law. In a span of twenty years, Friendly authored several books that traced the history of people involved in landmark Supreme Court cases, including *Minnesota Rag, The Good Guys, The Bad Guys and the First Amendment,* and *The Constitution: That Delicate Balance.* At the Ford Foundation in the mid-1970s

Fred W. Friendly
Photo courtesy of Fred W. Friendly

and, later, as the Edward R. Murrow Professor of Broadcast Journalism at Columbia University, Friendly collaborated with some of the country's leading lawyers, journalists and politicians to create a series of roundtable debates on media and society. Now known as *The Fred Friendly Seminars,* broadcasts of these programs have become a fixture of the Public Broadcasting Service.

—Michael Epstein

FRED W. FRIENDLY. Born Ferdinand Friendly Wachenheimer in New York City, New York, U.S.A., 1915. Educated at Cheshire Academy and Nichols Junior College. Married: Ruth W. Mark; two sons, one daughter (from previous marriage), and three stepsons. Served in U.S. Army, Information and Education Section, 1941–45. Broadcast producer, journalist for WEAN radio, Providence, Rhode Island, 1937–41; wrote, produced, and narrated radio series *Footprints in the Sands of Time,* 1938, later, at NBC, *Who Said That,* quiz based on quotations of famous people;

collaborated with Edward R. Murrow in presenting oral history of 1932–45 (recorded by Columbia Records under title *I Can Hear It Now*); *I Can Hear It Now: The Sixties* with Walter Cronkite; editor and correspondent in India, Burma, and China for CBI Roundup, 1941–45; co-producer, CBS radio series *Hear It Now*, 1951, and CBS TV series *See It Now*, 1952–55; past executive producer, with Edward R. Murrow, CBS TV show *CBS Reports*, 1959–60; president, CBS News, New York, 1964–66; Edward R. Murrow professor emeritus broadcast journalist Columbia University Graduate School of Journalism, and director, Seminars on Media and Society, since 1966; adviser on communications, Ford Foundation, 1966–80; director, Michele Clark Program for minority journalists, Columbia University, 1968–75; member, Mayor's Task Force on CATV and Telecommunications, New York City, 1968; distinguished visiting professor, Bryn Mawr College, 1981; visiting professor, Yale University, 1984; commissioner, Charter Revision Committee for City of New York, 1986–90; Montgomery fellow, Dartmouth College, 1986. Honorary degrees: Grinnell College, University of Rhode Island; New School for Social Research; Brown University; Carnegie-Mellon University; Columbia College, Chicago; Columbia University; Duquesne University; New York Law School; University of Southern Utah; College of Wooster, Ohio; University of Utah. Member: American Association of University Professors; Association for Education in Journalism. Military awards: Decorated Legion of Merit and four battle stars; Soldier's Medal for heroism. Recipient: 35 major awards for *See It Now*, including Overseas Press Club, Page One Award, New York Newspaper Guild, and National Headliners Club Award, 1954; 40 major awards for *CBS Reports*; 10 Peabody Awards for TV production; numerous awards from journalism schools; DeWitt Carter Reddick Award, 1980.

TELEVISION SERIES

1952–55   *See It Now*
1958–59   *Small World*
1959–60   *CBS Reports*
1980–   *Media and Society Seminars*

1986   *Managing Our Miracles: Healthcare in America* (moderator)
1989   *Ethics in America*

RADIO

Producer, reporter, correspondent: WEAN, Providence, Rhode Island, 1937-41; NBC Radio, 1932-45; CBS Radio, 1951.

PUBLICATIONS

See It Now, edited with Edward R. Murrow. New York: Simon and Schuster, 1955.
Due to Circumstances Beyond Our Control. New York: Random House, 1967.
The Good Guys, The Bad Guys, and The First Amendment. New York: Random House, 1975.
Minnesota Rag, with Martha J.H. Elliott. New York: Random House, 1981.
The Constitution: That Delicate Balance. New York: Random House, 1984.

FURTHER READING

"Bar Association Honors Fred Friendly (American Bar Association Lifetime Achievement Gavel Award)." *The New York Times*, 12 August 1992.
Boyer, Peter J. *Who Killed CBS?: The Undoing of America's Number One News Network.* New York: Random House, 1988.
Gates, Gary Paul. *Air Time: The Inside Story of CBS News.* New York: Harper and Row, 1978.
Kendrick, Alexander. *Prime Time: The Life of Edward R. Murrow.* Boston: Little, Brown, 1969
Klages, Karen. "Ethics on TV." *ABA Journal* (Chicago), January 1989.
Schoenbrun, David. *On and Off the Air: An Informal History of CBS News.* New York: Dutton, 1989.
Sperber, A. M. *Murrow, His Life and Times.* New York: Freundlich, 1986.

See also Army-McCarthy Hearings; Columbia Broadcasting System; Murrow, Edward R.; *Person to Person*; *See it Now*

FRONT PAGE CHALLENGE

Canadian Panel Quiz/Public Affairs Program

Front Page Challenge, television's longest continuously running panel show, was one of the most familiar landmarks on the Canadian broadcasting landscape. During much of its 38-season run on the Canadian Broadcasting Corporation (CBC), from 1957 to 1995, it was among Canadian television's most popular programs, regularly drawing average audiences of one to two million in the small Canadian market; towards the end, viewership dropped, numbering about 500,000 in the show's final season. A book was published in 1982 to mark the show's 25th anniversary.

Front Page Challenge was first born as a summer fill-in show; at the time, it was one of many quiz shows on the air, a genre popular because of the low production costs involved, and *Front Page Challenge* was in fact named after an American quiz favourite of the time, called *The $64,000 Challenge*. A half-hour program, *Front Page Challenge* featured four panelists, usually well-known journalists, who

Front Page Challenge
Photo courtesy of CBC

would ask yes-or-no questions in an attempt to correctly identify a mystery challenger connected to a front-page news item, as well as the news item itself. After the panelists had guessed correctly—or been stumped—they would proceed to interview the challenger.

Equal parts quiz show and current affairs panel, *Front Page Challenge*'s hybridization of televisual genres drew in not only audience members attracted by the entertainment value of the quiz show format, but also viewers who were curious about who the week's mystery challengers would be and eager to hear them interviewed by *Front Page Challenge*'s panel of crack journalists. Long before current affairs programs or all-news channels like CNN or *CBC Newsworld* began to offer similar fare, *Front Page Challenge* provided Canadians with a humane look at the newsmakers they read about in their morning papers. Over the years, some of the show's guests included figures as diverse as Indira Gandhi—saying she would never go into politics—Eleanor Roosevelt, hockey player Gordie Howe, Tony Bennett, and Errol Flynn, along with Mary Pickford, a Canadian and one of cinema's first stars. Walter Cronkite even announced his new job as CBS anchor on the program.

As a television program noted for its attention to the newspaper, *Front Page Challenge* panelists were almost exclusively eminent Canadian newspaper workers. For most of the show's run, well-known reporter Gordon Sinclair and journalist-writer Pierre Berton joined actress Toby Robins to form the panel, with a guest panelist making a fourth, and Fred Davis hosting the show. Broadcaster Betty Kennedy replaced Robins in 1961, and upon Gordon Sinclair's death in 1984, he was replaced by author and columnist Alan Fotheringham. Another prominent reporter, Jack Webster, was added as a permanent fourth panelist in 1990.

That *Front Page Challenge* pointed not to the everyday world, but to other points within the media universe—the television program's very name evokes the newspaper—is significant as more than a sign of the times, however. By building a show in which competence in recalling newspaper headlines is the most important attribute, *Front Page Challenge* helped reinforce the social importance attached to what is reported in the media. The show's use of the newspaper as a frame of reference for significant events had the effect of perpetuating the idea that news happens in the real world, and that the media simply reflect these goings-on. As much research has shown, though, what we read in the newspaper is as much the result of the institutionalized conditions of newspaper reporting as it is of what goes on "out there"—the news is constructed by the media. *Front Page Challenge,* then, was an early example of the proliferation of television programs which recycle media content as news—*Entertainment Tonight* is perhaps the best-known example—and demonstrates how this type of programming tends, among other things, to contribute to the "aura" of media, in which the media world comes to stand in for the lived world.

As the product of the quiz show genre popular in the 1950s and 1960s, *Front Page Challenge* stood both within and outside of that television format, and thus provides a unique vantage point from which to look at the quiz or game show. Whereas the game show is characterized by its catapulting unknown, everyday individuals from the private sphere into the public sphere of television—providing home viewers with an easy locus of identification—*Front Page Challenge* featured only well-known public figures or newsmakers. Indeed, the only way an ordinary viewer might hope to participate in the program, other than becoming involved in a news event, was by successfully writing to *Front Page Challenge* and suggesting a front-page story to be used. Unlike other game or quiz shows, there was little competition—the panel worked together as a team—and almost no prizes to be won. Even the home viewers themselves were positioned in an unorthodox way on *Front Page Challenge:* whereas in other game shows the viewer plays along with the contestants, often shouting out the answer in her or his living room before it emerges from the television speaker, the *Front Page Challenge* viewer was able to actually see the mystery challenger, who stood behind the panelists, hidden from their eyes, but in full view of the camera.

Eliminating the elements of the quiz show genre seen as crass or vulgar helped to provide *Front Page Challenge* with an air of legitimacy and respectability that the straight quiz show did not enjoy; the show's evocation of the newspaper's seriousness, its panelists, and its location on the state broadcasting network marked it as a "quality" television program. This controlled distance from what was seen as "American mass culture" helped distance it considerably from the quiz-show scandals which plagued American broadcasting in the 1960s—including *The $64,000 Challenge.*

When *Front Page Challenge* was taken off the air in 1995, a move emblematic of major restructuring at the CBC, it signalled the end of an era in Canadian television broadcasting. The program's mixing of quiz show and public affairs, its lending of journalistic credence to the game show genre, and the interest with which audiences tuned in to hear and watch newsmakers of the day exemplified television's ability to convey the humane qualities and attributes of those who were in the news.

—Bram Abramson

HOSTS

Win Berron, Fred Davis

PANELISTS

Toby Robbins, Alex Barris, Gordon Sinclair, Betty Kennedy, Pierre Berton, Alan Fotheringham, Jack Webster

MODERATORS

Win Barron, Alex Barris, Fred Davis

PRODUCERS Harvey Hart, James Guthro, Andrew Crossan, Don Brown, and others

PROGRAMMING HISTORY

• CBC

1957–1995   Weekly Half Hour

FURTHER READING

Barris, Alex. *Front Page Challenge: The 25th Anniversary.* Toronto: Canadian Broadcasting Corporation, 1981.

Gould, Terry. "Front Page Challenged." *Saturday Night* (Toronto), July/August 1995.

Grossberg, Larry. "The In-difference of Television." *Screen* (London), 1987.

Knelman, Martin. "The Eternal Challenge." *Saturday Night* (Toronto), March 1992.

McLuhan, H. Marshall. *Understanding Media.* New York: McGraw Hill, 1964.

Stam, Robert. "Television News and Its Spectator." In, E. Ann Kaplan, editor. *Regarding Television.* Frederick, Maryland: American Film Institute, 1983.

Tuchman, Gaye. *Making News: A Study in the Construction of Reality.* New York: Free Press/MacMillan, 1978.

Valpy, Michael. "No more *Front Page Challenge.* No more Canada?" *The Globe and Mail* (Toronto), 15 April 1995.

See also Berton, Pierre; Canadian Programming in English

FROST, DAVID
British Broadcast Journalist/Producer

David Frost is an outstanding television presenter, political interviewer and producer, who is successful on both sides of the Atlantic. The awards recognizing his achievements in television include two Golden Roses from the Montreux international festival (for *Frost Over England*), as well as two Emmy awards (for *The David Frost Show*) in the United States. His long career was honored by knighthood in 1993.

Frost was one of the first generation of university graduates who bypassed Fleet Street and went straight into television. While at Cambridge, he showed his satirical talent in the *Footlights Revue* and edited the university newspaper, *Granta*. In 1961 he moved to London to work for ITV during the day and perform in cabarets at night. His nightclub performance drew the attention of BBC producer Ned Sherrin, who invited him to host *That Was the Week That Was*, often called *TW3*. In the "satire boom" of the early 1960s the irreverent, topical and politically oriented *TW3* introduced satire to television in Britain. Among others topics, the program poked fun at the Royal family, the church, high politics, and the respectable tenets of British life. *TW3* brought the divisions of British society to the surface, and the ensuing controversy made the BBC discontinue it. From 1964 to 1965 Frost co-hosted the next, milder satirical program *Not So Much a Programme, More a Way of Life*. At its most successful, this program bore significant resemblance to *TW3* and reached the same end.

The success of *TW3* made Frost a transatlantic commuter after NBC had bought the rights and put on the American version (1964-65) with executive producer Leland Hayward. The shorter, less political and outspoken program never had the same impact as its British counterpart, but made Frost's name in the United States, nevertheless.

Back in Britain, BBC's new show *The Frost Report* (1966–67) focused on one topic per program and tackled social and contemporary issues as opposed to the political and topical focus of *TW3* and *Not So Much....* Drawing on the talents of John Cleese, Ronnie Barker and Ronnie Corbett, the program brought humor to the topics of education, voting and the like. The working environment provided for the development of a new humorous trend in Britain, and five of the comedians went on to form *Monty Python's Flying Circus*.

From 1966 to 1968 *The Frost Programme* at ITV showed the beginning of the transition from the comedian to the serious interviewer. Frost pioneered such TV techniques as directly involving the audience in the discussions and blending comedy sketches with current affairs. From this time on Frost's mixture of politics with entertainment would draw mixed responses from critics. At this time his "ad-lib interviewing" style, as he calls it, was characterized by rather remorseless fire on well-chosen subjects, and led to his label as the "tough inquisitor".

David Frost
Photo courtesy of David Paradine Television, Inc.

From anchorman to executive producer Frost filled many different roles in the television business. In 1966 he founded David Paradine Ltd., and as an entrepreneur he put a consortium together to acquire the ITV franchise for London Weekend Television in 1967. LWT's programming did not live up to its franchise undertaking in the long run and was criticized in Britain for emphasizing entertainment to the detriment of substantial programming.

On the strength of his British chat shows Group W (the U.S. Westinghouse Corporation television stations) selected Frost to anchor an interview daily from 1969 to 1972. Frost kept his London shows and fronted *The David Frost Show* in the United States. He used more one-to-one interviews than before and managed to mix friendly conversation with confrontation. Throughout these endeavors Frost's instinct for television, his handling of the audience, and his ability to put guests at ease and make them accessible justify the label "The Television Man," given him years earlier by the BBC's Donald Baverstock.

Frost's television personality status, niceness, and ability to market himself well enabled him to attract prominent interviewees. He has interviewed every British prime minister since Harold Wilson as well as leading politicians and celebrities from a number of different countries. His specials *The Next President* (1968, 1988, 1992) has become a regular on American television featuring interviews with presidential candidates in the run-up for the presidency. The most famous of the big interviews characterizing Frost's recent focus is *The Nixon Interviews* (1977). This interview is the only televised assessment Richard Nixon gave about his conduct as president, including the Watergate affair. The interviews were syndicated on a barter basis and were subsequently seen in over 70 countries.

When interviewing leading public figures Frost retains his persistence, but he has refined his style into an apparently soft interrogative method where the strength of a question is judged more by the range of possible responses. Unlike his entertainment-oriented shows, which were often followed by rows over questions of bias, the big interviews are usually judged as fair and balanced.

On the way to fame as a serious political interviewer Frost had a new chance to combine politics and satire. As executive producer he helped to launch *Spitting Image* in 1984. This show, a scathing satire, picked up on already existing perceptions of politicians and highlighted them in puppet caricatures. When Margaret Thatcher was portrayed as a bald man who ate babies and lived next door to Hitler, the life-size puppets were thought to be as dangerous for politicians as *TW3* was. As a result, before the 1987 elections the program was not even broadcast. In another transAtlantic parallel, this popular program also made it into the United States. In 1986 NBC carried *Spitting Image: Down and Out in the White House*, hosted by David Frost, and in 1987 *The Ronnie and Nancy Show* special appeared on the screens.

In 1982 Frost successfully bid for a commercial breakfast television franchise, TV-am, and became director of the new venture. Despite the five famous flagship presenters, TV-am as a whole faced the same criticism as London Weekend Television. Its leisurely approach to hard news, especially during the Gulf War, was thought to cost it the franchise in 1991.

After losing TV-am, Frost signed a contract with the U.S. Public Broadcasting Service in 1990 to produce *Talking with David Frost*, a monthly interview program. In the program Frost interviewed Yitzhak Rabin, General Norman Schwarzkopf, and Ted Turner, as well as numerous other famous and infamous personalities. At times he has been criticized for an interviewing style thought to be too sympathetic towards his influential guests.

Frost's business ventures also include filmmaking, where he acts as executive producer. The satirical *The Rise and Rise of Michael Rimmer* (1970), featuring Peter Cook taking over the prime ministership, and *The Search for Josef Mengele* (1985) documentary indicate the variety of films he has produced. As a writer, Frost draws on his commuter observations. Apart from other writings, he published his autobiography in 1993.

In Britain Frost has often been criticized for his showbiz leanings, his mannerisms and his apparent ability to use the fame bestowed by television to further his career in a number of different fields. Nevertheless, his flair for television and his ability to produce high-quality current affairs and interview programs are widely recognized. His excellent political interviews show how television is able to provide insights into political decisions and contribute to the historical record. Throughout his long career, Frost has always been ready to experiment with something new. His personal contributions to satire and political programs as well as his business ventures make him a prominent figure of broadcasting.

—Rita Zajacz

DAVID (PARADINE) FROST. Born in Tenderden, Kent, England, 7 April 1939. Attended Gillingham Grammar School; Wellington Grammar School; Gonville and Caius College, Cambridge M.A. Married: 1) Lynne Frederick, 1981 (divorced, 1982); 2) Carina Fitzalan-Howard, 1983; children: Miles, Wilfred and George. Served as presenter of Rediffusion specials, 1961; established name as host of *That Was the Week That Was*, 1962–63; later gained reputation as an aggressive interviewer on *The Frost Programme* and other shows; co-founder, London Weekend Television; chair, David Paradine Group of Companies, since 1966; served on British/U.S. Bicentennial Liaison Committee, 1973–76, and has hosted shows on both sides of the Atlantic; interviewed Richard Nixon for television, 1977; director, TV-am, since 1981, helped launch TV-am commercial breakfast television company, 1982. LLD, Emerson College, Boston, Massachusetts. President, Lord's Taverners, 1985, 1986. Order of the British Empire, 1970; knighted, 1993. Recipient: Golden Rose of Montreux (twice); Royal Television Society Silver Medal, 1967; Richard Dimbleby Award, 1967; Emmy Awards, 1970, 1971; Guild of Television Producers Award, 1971; TV Personality of the Year, 1971; Religious Heritage of America Award, 1971; Albert Einstein Award, 1971. Address: David Paradine Ltd, 5 St. Mary Abbots Place, London W8 6LS, England.

TELEVISION SERIES

1961	*This Week*
1961	*Let's Twist on the Riviera*
1962–63	*That Was the Week That Was*
1963	*A Degree of Frost*
1964–65	*Not So Much a Programme, More a Way of Life*
1966–67	*The Frost Report*
1966–67	*David Frost's Night out in London*
1966–68	*The Frost Programme*
1968–70	*Frost on Friday*
1969–72	*The David Frost Show*
1971–73	*The David Frost Revue*
1973	*A Degree of Frost*
1973	*Frost's Weekly*
1974	*Frost on Thursday*

1975–76	We British
1976	Forty Years of Television
1977	The Frost Programme
1977–78	A Prime Minister on Prime Ministers
1977–78	The Crossroads of Civilization
1978	Headliners with David Frost
1979–82	David Frost's Global Village
1981–86	David Frost Presents the International Guinness Book of World Records
1981–92	Frost on Sunday
1982	Good Morning Britain
1986–88	The Guinness Book of Records Hall of Fame
1987–88	The Next President with David Frost
1987–88	Entertainment Tonight
1987–93	Through the Keyhole
1989	The President and Mrs. Bush Talking with David Frost
1991–	Talking with David Frost
1993–	The Frost Programme
1993–	Breakfast with Frost

TELEVISION (producer)

1967	At Last the 1948 Show
1967–70	No—That's Me Over Here!
1968	The Ronnie Barker Playhouse,

MADE-FOR-TELEVISION MOVIES

1975	James A. Michener's Dynasty
1978	The Ordeal of Patty Hearst

TELEVISION SPECIALS (selection)

1966	David Frost at the Phonograph
1967	Frost over England
1968	Robert Kennedy, The Man
1970	Frost over America
1972–77	Frost over Australia
1973–74	Frost over New Zealand
1973	That Was the Year That Was
1975	The Unspeakable Crime
1975	Abortion—Merciful or Murder?
1975	The Beatles—Once upon a Time in America
1975	David Frost Presents the Best
1976	The Sir Harold Wilson Interviews
1977	The Nixon Interviews
1978	Are We Really Going to Be Rich?
1979	A Gift of Song—Music For Unicef Concert
1979	The Bee Gees Special
1979	The Kissinger Interviews
1980	The Shah Speaks
1980	The American Movie Awards
1980	The 25th Anniversary of ITV
1980	The Begin Interview
1980	Elvis—He Touched Their Lives
1981	The BAFTA Awards
1981	Show Business
1981	This Is Your Life: 30th Anniversary Special

1981	The Royal Wedding
1981	Onward Christian Soldiers
1982	The American Movie Awards
1982	A Night of Knights: A Royal Gala
1982	Rubinstein at 95
1982	Pierre Elliott Trudeau
1982	The End of the Year Show
1982–83	Frost over Canada
1983	David Frost Live by Satellite from London
1983	The End of the Year Show
1984	David Frost Presents Ultra Quiz
1985	That Was the Year That Was
1985	The Search for Josef Mengele
1985–86	Twenty Years on
1986	Spitting Image: Down and Out in the White House
1987	The Ronnie and Nancy Show
1987	The Spitting Image Movie Awards
1987–88	The Spectacular World of Guinness Records
1988	ABC Presents a Royal Gala
1991	The Nobel Debate

FILMS (producer)

The Rise and Rise of Michael Rimmer, 1970; Charley One-Eye, 1972; Leadbelly, 1974; The Slipper and the Rose, 1975; The Remarkable Mrs. Sanger, 1979.

RADIO

David Frost at the Phonograph, 1966, 1972; Pull the Other One, 1987, 1988, 1990.

STAGE

An Evening with David Frost, 1966.

PUBLICATIONS

That Was the Week That Was. London: Allen, 1963.

How to Live Under Labour—Or at least Have as much a Chance as Anybody Else. London: Heinemann, 1964.

To England with Love. London: Hodder and Stoughton; 1967.

The Presidential Debate. New York: Stein and Day, 1968.

The Americans. New York: Stein and Day, 1970.

Whitlam and Frost. London: Sundial, 1970.

I Gave Them a Sword: Behind the Scenes of the Nixon Interviews. New York: Morrow, 1978.

I Could Have Kicked Myself, with Michael Deakin. London: Futura, 1982.

Who Wants to Be a Millionaire?, with Michael Deakin. London: Deutsch, 1983.

David Frost's Book of the World's Worst Decisions, with Michael Deakin. New York: Crown, 1983.

David Frost's Book of Millionaires, Multimillionaires, and Really Rich People, with Michael Deakin. New York: Crown, 1984.

The Mid-Atlantic Companion, with Michael Shea. London: Weidenfeld and Nicholson, 1986.

The Rich Tide, with Michael Shea. London: Collins, 1986.

David Frost: An Autobiography (Part One: From Congrega-tions to Audiences). London: Harper Collins, 1993.

FURTHER READING

Briggs, Asa. *The History of Broadcasting in the United Kingdom. Volume V: Competition.* London: Oxford University Press, 1995.

Frischauer, Willi. *Will You Welcome Now.... David Frost.* London: Michael Joseph, 1971.

Tinker, Jack. *The Television Barons.* London: Quartet, 1980.

See also British Programming; *Spitting Image*; *That Was the Week That Was*

FRUM, BARBARA

Canadian Broadcast Journalist

Barbara Frum was one of Canada's most respected and influential woman journalists. She began her career in journalism as a freelance writer and commentator for various CBC radio programs. She quickly branched out into the print media, writing various columns for national newspapers such as the *Globe and Mail, The Toronto Star* and a television column for the *Saturday Night* magazine. In 1967, she made a brief foray into television as a co-host for an information program *The Way It Is* , but it was in radio that she first gained notoriety.

In the fall of 1971, she took on the co-hosting duties of *As It Happens*, a new innovative newsmagazine show on CBC radio which followed the 6:00 P.M. news. At a time when the national broadcaster was struggling to develop programs that would keep its listeners beyond the supper-hour newscast, the show's young producer, Mark Starowicz, proposed a format based largely on newsmaker interviews that would provide an in-depth examination of the stories behind the headlines. Through the use of long-distance telephone and radio, listeners were connected to world events. In this format, Frum shone. She quickly gained the reputation as a tough, incisive and well-informed inter-viewer. For ten years, she interviewed numerous world lead-ers, national politicians and other newsmakers as well as those affected by the news. She was respected as one of Canada's foremost woman journalists. She was honoured with numerous awards during her tenure, most notably the National Press Club of Canada Award for Outstanding Contribution to Canadian Journalism in 1975; Woman of the Year in literature, arts and education category of the Canadian Press in 1976; and the Order of Canada in l979.

In the 1980s CBC television decided to move its national newscast, *The National*, from its traditional 11:00 P.M. timeslot to 10:00 P.M. The news division of CBC television had long been considering such a move, hoping to capture a larger audience since studies had shown that a large number of viewers retired to bed prior to 11:00 P.M. Realizing that it was a huge gamble, CBC executives appointed Starowicz, the producer of *As It Happens*, to translate his radio success to the newsmagazine program, *The Journal*. He, in turn, looked to Frum, who had been instrumental in the success of *As It Happens*. After months of preparation, the new current affairs program, *The Jour-*

nal, was launched on 11 January 1982. In the weeks that followed it became the most-watched and highly respected newsmagazine show in Canada.

It featured many innovations and made use of the latest electronic news gathering technology. Features, such as field reports and short documentaries, public forums and debates, as well as a series of reports on business, sports, arts and entertainment, and science news were interwoven with the interview portion of the program. The show featured two female hosts. Barbara Frum was joined by Mary Lou Finley in the hosting duties and a higher profile was assigned to women reporters and journalists than on most other stations.

The show relied heavily on Frum's skill as an inter-viewer. The interview portion of *The Journal* accounted for

Barbara Frum
Photo courtesy of the National Archives of Canada

60% of the program. She remained the dominant and permanent presence on a show which saw many new co-hosts. All of Canada was deeply saddened by the news of her sudden death on 26 March 1992 from complications of chronic leukemia. Tributes poured in from colleagues, co-workers and the public at large. Months following her passing, the CBC announced that it would move its newscast and newsmagazine program, *The National* and *The Journal*, from 10:00 P.M. to 9:00 P.M. Once again, executives argued that studies showed that aging babyboomers were retiring to bed at an earlier time. This move proved to be less successful than the first endeavour and two years later the CBC was forced to reverse itself after ratings had fallen off by half. Amid these changes and reversals *The Journal* was transformed into the present *Primetime News. As It Happens* continues its run, having celebrated its 25th year on the air.

—Manon Lamontagne

BARBARA FRUM. Born in Niagara Falls, New York, U.S.A., 8 September 1937. Married: Murray, 1957, children: David, Linda, Matthew. Educated at University of Toronto, Canada, B.A. in history 1959. Began career as radio commentator and writer of reviews and magazine articles; worked briefly in television, 1961; current affairs interviewer in radio, CBC, 1971–82; co-host, *The Journal*, television news magazine, 1982–92. Recipient: four ACTRA Awards; National Press Club of Canada Award, 1975; Order of Canada, 1979. Died in Toronto, Canada, 26 March 1992.

TELEVISION

| 1967 | *The Way It Is* |
| 1981–92 | *The Journal* (host-interviewer) |

RADIO

Weekend (interviewer-contributor), 1969-72; *As It Happens* (associate), 1971–82; *Barbara Frum* (host), 1974–75; *Quarterly Report* (co-host), 1977–82.

FURTHER READING

"CBC Pays Tribute to Barbara Frum." *Globe and Mail* (Toronto), 22 June 1993.

"Friends Gather to Bid Colleague Goodbye." *Globe and Mail* (Toronto), 6 April 1992.

Levine, Allan. *Scrum Wars: The Prime Ministers and the Media.* Toronto: Dundurn Press, 1993.

Stewart, Sandy. *Here's Looking at Us: A Personal History of Television in Canada.* Toronto: CBC Enterprises, 1986.

Taras, David. *The Newsmakers: The Media's Influence on Canadian Politics.* Toronto: Nelson, 1990.

See also Canadian Programming in English; *National/The Journal*; Starowicz, Mark

THE FUGITIVE

U.S. Adventure/Melodrama

Popularly known as the longest chase sequence in television history, *The Fugitive* ran through 118 episodes before a climactic two-part episode brought this highly regarded series to a close—with all the fundamental story strands concluded. The wrap-up ending was a rather rare and unusual decision on behalf of the producers as well as something of a television "first". Premiering on ABC on Tuesday 17 September 1963, *The Fugitive* went on to present some of the most fascinating human condition dramas of that decade, all told in a tight, self-contained semi-documentary style. By its second season the program was number 5 in the ratings (27.9) and later received an Emmy Award for Outstanding Dramatic Series of 1965. For its fourth and final season the program was produced in color, having enjoyed three years of suitably film noir-like black and white photography, ending on a high note that drew the highest TV audience rating (72 percent) up to that time.

Based on a six-page format, inspired by Victor Hugo's *Les Miserables*, by writer-producer (and *Maverick* and *77 Sunset Strip* creator) Roy Huggins, ABC brought in executive producer Quinn Martin to supervise the project. He in turn brought on board line producer Alan Armer (who went on to oversee 90 episodes) and hired David Janssen to play the title character. While Huggins' original outline saw the wrongly-convicted character behave like an oddball, since society was treating him like one anyway, Martin's concept of the character was something less bizarre: a put-upon but basically decent person. At first, however, ABC executives worried that perhaps viewers would feel the only honourable thing for Kimble to do would be to turn himself in. Martin's production expertise, evidenced in the footage they viewed, changed their minds. In the pilot episode, "Fear in a Desert City", the audience was introduced to the story of Dr. Richard Kimble, arriving home in the fictional town of Stafford, Indiana, to witness a One-Armed Man running from his house, leaving behind his murdered wife. In the same episode "blind justice" saw fit to charge Kimble himself with the murder and sentence him to the death house. This narrative was assured immediately of viewer sympathy and interest. That the train enroute to the prison where Kimble was to be executed was accidentally derailed, rendering his captor Lt. Philip Gerard unconscious and thus allowing Kimble to escape, propelled the hero into a "willed irresponsibility without a concomitant sense of guilt", as Roy Huggins put it. In other words, the (mid-1960s) TV viewer felt perfectly at ease with this particular "outlaw" because what was happening was not his fault.

Not unlike the western hero, which U.S. television had embraced since the 1950s and with which it still had something of an infatuation, Kimble had the appeal of the rootless wanderer whose commitments to jobs, women or society were temporary, yet who at the same time deserved our sympathy as something of a tragic figure. The series' and the introspective character's success lay largely with the appeal of actor David Janssen's intensity in the part (Janssen's first television hit had been as the lead in the slick *Richard Diamond, Private Detective* series of the late 1950s). The drama of the stories came not so much from the transient occupations of the fleeing hero, such as sail mender in Hank Searls' "Never Wave Good-bye" or dog handler in Harry Kronman's "Bloodline", but from the dilemma of the Kimble character himself, something Janssen was able to convey with an almost nervous charm.

The other principal members of the cast were Canadian actor Barry Morse as the relentless Javert-like Lt. Gerard, who only appeared in about one out of four stories but who seemed always ominously present, Jacqueline Scott as Kimble's sister Donna Taft, Diane Brewster as Kimble's wife Helen, in occasional flashbacks, and the burly Bill Raisch as the elusive One-Armed Man Fred Johnson. Raisch, who had lost his right arm during World War II but nevertheless went on to become a stand-in for Burt Lancaster, may have been the show's "MacGuffin", the prime motivation for Kimble to stay one step ahead of the law, but his character was rarely seen on screen; during the first two years of production Raisch worked on the program only four days.

Using the general format of an anthology show, but with continuing characters (in the manner of the contemporary Herbert Leonard series *Naked City* and *Route 66*), the producers, writers and directors were given license to deal with characters, settings and stories not usually associated with what was in essence a simple man-on-the-run theme. Under various nondescript aliases (but most frequently as "Jim"), Kimble traversed the United States in pursuit of the One-Armed Man and along the way became involved with ordinary people who were usually at an emotional cross-roads in their lives. The opportunities for some magnificent guest performances as well as interesting locations were immense (in the early years of production the crew spent six days on each episode with about three of them on location): Sandy Dennis in Alain Caillou and Harry Kronman's "The Other Side of the Mountain" (West Virginia), Jack Klugman in Peter Germano and Kronman's "Terror at High Point" (Salt Lake City, Utah), Eileen Heckart in Al C. Ward's "Angels Travel on Lonely Roads", parts one and two (Revenna, Nevada and Sacramento, California), Jack Weston in Robert Pirosh's "Fatso" (Louisville, Kentucky). The series also featured a number of different directors, including Ida Lupino, Laslo Benedek, Walter Grauman, Robert Butler, Richard Donner, Mark Rydell, Gerd Oswald, and Joseph Sargent; Barry Morse even got an opportunity to direct an episode.

The Fugitive

Then in 1967—Tuesday, 29 August—the running stopped. It was actor William Conrad's final *Fugitive* narration after four years of keeping viewers tuned in to Kimble's circumstances and thoughts. By the fourth year of production Janssen was physically and nervously exhausted. When ABC, which had grossed an estimated $30,000,000 on the series, suggested a fifth year Janssen declined the offer and Quinn Martin, in a move quite unorthodox to series television, decided to bring Kimble's story to a conclusion. The definitive two-part episode, "The Judgment", written by George Eckstein and Michael Zagor, and directed by Don Medford, saw Kimble track the One-Armed Man to an amusement park in Santa Monica where in a climactic fight, with Kimble about to be killed, the real murderer is shot down by Gerard. The final episode pulled a Nielsen score of 45.9. Now, with Kimble exonerated, both he and Gerard were now free to pursue their own paths. Janssen, too, continued his own career; after *The Fugitive* he starred in *O'Hara, U.S. Treasury* (1971–72) and *Harry O* (1974–76).

While other series with similar themes followed (*Run for Your Life*, the comedy *Run, Buddy, Run*), it is to *The Fugitive*'s credit that it remains one of the more fondly remembered of the 1960s drama series. Harrison Ford starred as an energetic Kimble in Warner Brothers' successful 1993 feature remake, *The Fugitive*, with Tommy Lee Jones as Gerard.

—Tise Vahimagi

CAST

Dr. Richard Kimble	David Janssen
Lieutenant Philip Gerard	Barry Morse
Donna Taft	Jacqueline Scott
Fred Johnson, the One-Armed Man	Bill Raisch

PRODUCERS   Quinn Martin, Wilton Schiller

PROGRAMMING HISTORY   120 Episodes

• ABC

September 1963–August 1967   Tuesday 10:00-11:00

FURTHER READING

Cooper, John. *The Fugitive: A Compete Episode Guide.* Ann Arbor, Michigan: Popular Culture, 1994.

Dern, Marian. "Ever Want to Run Away from it All?" *TV Guide* (Radnor, Pennsylvania), 22 February 1964.

Harding, H. "Rumors about the Final Episode." *TV Guide* (Radnor, Pennsylvania), 27 February 1965.

Marc, David, and Robert J. Thompson. *Prime Time, Prime Movers.* Boston: Little, Brown, 1993.

Robertson, Ed. *The Fugitive Recaptured.* Los Angeles: Pomegranate, 1993.

See also Jannsen, David; Martin, Quinn

FURNESS, BETTY

U.S. Actor/Media Personality/Consumer Reporter

Betty Furness—whose first regular television appearances were in 1945 and whose last were in 1992—enjoyed one of the most diverse, remarkable careers in U.S. television, both as commercial spokeswoman and, later, as a pioneering consumer reporter.

Born Elizabeth Mary Furness in New York City in 1916, Furness was raised in upper class fashion by a Park Avenue family. Her first job was in 1930 when, at the age of fourteen, she began modeling for the Powers agency. Her pert and pretty looks, and her educated speaking voice, soon gained the attention of Hollywood. She was signed by RKO movie studios in 1932 and moved, with her mother, to California. While taking her senior year of school on the studio lot, Furness starred in her first film. She would go on to act in over thirty films, the majority of them forgettable. After seeking greater fulfillment in stage roles on the west coast and after the birth of her daughter and the failure of her first marriage, Furness, with her daughter, journeyed to New York hoping to land theater parts. A self-described "out of work actress," Furness found herself able and willing to break into the very infant medium of television.

For a few months in the spring of 1945, Furness endured blistering heat, from the lights needed to illuminate the set, and other primitive technologies to host DuMont's "Fashions Coming and Becoming." By 1948, she was in front of the television cameras again as an actress for an episode of *Studio One,* an anthology program sponsored by Westinghouse appliances. In that era of live television, many commercials were also done live, frequently performed to the side of the main set. Furness was unimpressed with the actor hired to perform the commercial and offered to take a stab at it. Company executives were impressed and offered her the $150 a week job pitching their products. Following her philosophy of never turning down a job, Furness signed on.

With TV still apparently innocent, audiences had not yet grown jaded by TV commercials and the people who appeared in them. Furness's blend of soft sell and common sense was soon moving the merchandise. Her delivery was always smooth and memorized (she refused cue cards), her

Betty Furness
Photo courtesy of Westinghouse Electric Corporation

tone pleasant and direct, and her look pretty, approachable. In little time the company had signed her to be their sole pitchwoman. And soon the pitchwoman was selling out stores and receiving, on average, one thousand pieces of fan mail a week.

Furness's place in the popular culture cannon was assured after her work for Westinghouse at the 1952 national political conventions. Westinghouse was the convention's sole sponsor and, as their spokesperson, Furness was in every ad. By conventions' end she had logged more air time than any speaker of either party and made her tag line "You can be SURE if it's Westinghouse" into a national catch phrase. From January to July 1953, Furness hosted *Meet Betty Furness,* a lively, informative daily talk show—sponsored by Westinghouse—on NBC. Later she acted as hostess on the Westinghouse sponsored *Best of Broadway* and made regular appearances on *What's My Line?* and *I've Got a Secret.*

Furness's affiliation with Westinghouse ended (by mutual agreement) in 1960. Though financially well-off, Furness wanted to keep working. She attempted to obtain jobs at the networks as an interviewer but found the going rough. As Mike Wallace and Hugh Downs had experienced, Furness was facing the challenge of putting her commercialized past behind her. While waiting to break in again in TV, Furness worked in radio and for Democratic political causes. She also entered the last of her three marriages when she married news producer Leslie Midgely in 1967.

It was while preparing for her wedding that Furness got a call from President Johnson. Familiar with her work on behalf of Democrats, and impressed with her work ethic, Johnson offered her the job of Special Assistant for Consumer Affairs. Furness, again following her job philosophy, took the position and with it transformed herself from actor-spokeswoman into political figure. She later recalled it as the best decision of her life.

Still in the public mind as the "Westinghouse lady," consumer groups voiced criticism at her appointment. But Furness threw herself into learning consumer issues, testifying before congress, and traveling the country. Within the year she had silenced her critics and won over such forces as Ralph Nader and the influential consumer affairs magazine, *Consumer Reports.* Furness held her White House position until the end of the Johnson administration in 1969. Later she headed the consumer affairs departments of both New York City and New York state. Then she reentered broadcasting for the second act of her television career. She was signed by WNBC in New York specifically to cover consumer issues, the first full time assignment of its kind. Furness found herself now—at age 58—pioneering a new type of TV journalism.

Over the next eighteen years, Furness took a hard line against consumer fraud and business abuse. Her reports criticized Macy's department store, Sears, and Lane Bryant among other businesses. She was also the first to report on the Cabbage Patch Doll craze and on the defective Audi automobile. In 1977, her local show *Buyline: Betty Furness* won the Peabody.

Earlier in 1976, Furness filled in as co-host on *Today* between the tenures of Barbara Walters and Jane Pauley. From that time on she contributed regular consumerism pieces to the program. Furness made her last TV appearances in 1992. Since battling cancer in 1990, Furness had abbreviated her work week to four days. NBC used that reason to oust her, and she was given notice in March in one of the most blatant examples of ageism in media history. Though both *Today* and WNBC aired tributes to her during her last week, Furness did not keep her frustration out of the press. Nor did she hide her desire to keep working. But a reemergence of cancer prevented it and she passed away in April of 1994.

It is hard to place Betty Furness's career in a historical context because it was so eccentrically one of a kind. Of the legions who pitched products from the 1950s and 1960s, hers remains the only name still very much a part of popular history. In her movement from political insider to TV commentator she laid the groundwork for Diane Sawyer and Mary Matalin. And in her work as a consumer advocate she predates John Stossel and others who have since adopted that as their beat.

In assessing the career of Betty Furness one stumbles upon a feminist retelling of the Cinderella story: a smart, savvy woman who turned her back on TV make believe and soft sell to embrace hard news and tough issues. That one individual's life encompasses such width and depth speaks well not only for the far-reaching talents of one woman but also for the progression of women's roles in the latter half of the twentieth century and for the dynamic development of television and its ability to record them both.

—Cary O'Dell

BETTY FURNESS. Born in New York City, New York, U.S.A., January 1916. Attended Brearly School, New York City, 1925–29; Bennett School, Millbrook, New York, 1929–32. Married: 1) John Waldo Green, 1937 (divorced, 1943); daughter, Barbara Sturtevant; 2) Hugh B. Ernst Jr., 1945 (died, 1950); 3) Leslie Midgley, 1967. Began career as teenage model, John Robert Powers agency; movie picture actor, 1932–39; appeared in stage plays, including *Doughgirls,* 1937–60; appeared on CBS radio, *Ask Betty Furness,* 1961–67; columnist, *McCall Magazine,* 1969–70; special consumer affairs assistant to U.S. president, 1967–69; worked for Common Cause, 1971–75; joined WNBC-TV as consumer reporter, 1974, and weekly contributor to *Today,* 1976. Honorary degrees: L.L.D., Iowa Wesleyan College, 1968, Pratt Institute, 1978, Marymount College, 1983; D.C.L., Pace University, Marymount College Manhattan, 1976. Died in New York, 2 April 1994.

TELEVISION

1950-51	*Penthouse Party*
1951	*Byline*
1953	*Meet Betty Furness*
1954–55	*The Best of Broadway* (host, spokesperson)
1976–92	*Today Show*

FILMS (selection)

Professional Sweetheart, 1933; *Emergency Call,* 1933; *Lucky Devils,* 1933; *Beggars in Ermine,* 1934; *Keeper of the Bees,* 1935; *Magnificent Obsession,* 1935; *Swing Time,* 1936; *The President's Mystery,* 1936; *North of Shanghai,* 1939.

RADIO

Dimensions, 1962; *Ask Betty Furness,* 1962.

STAGE (selection)

Doughgirls.

FURTHER READING

O'Dell, Cary. *Women Pioneers in Television.* Jefferson, North Carolina: McFarland, 1996.

See also *Today Show*